W9-ABC-139

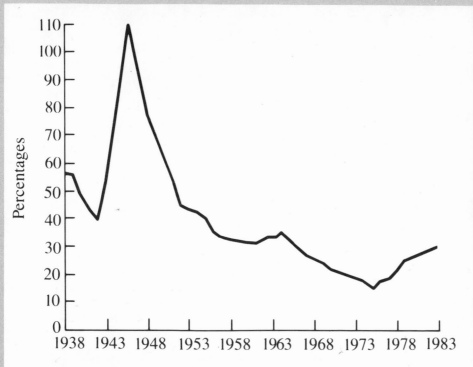

(i) Net government debt as a percentage of GNP

... payments on it have not **risen in proportion to the GNP since the end of World War II.** Two significant ratios are plotted here on a ratio scale. The national debt, after rising sharply through World War II, was a declining fraction of GNP until 1975, after which there has been a continual rise. Interest payments reached 2.9 percent of GNP in 1948, but for the last 25 years they have remained at under 3.0 percent. Clearly the picture of a spendthrift government adding recklessly to the burden of the national debt is overstated.

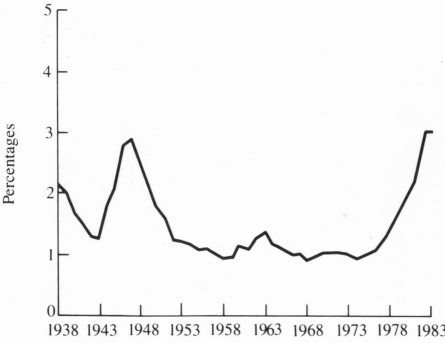

(ii) Net interest on government debt as a percentage of GNP

Source: Public Accounts, Department of Finance.

ECONOMICS
FIFTH EDITION

Richard G. Lipsey
QUEEN'S UNIVERSITY

Douglas D. Purvis
QUEEN'S UNIVERSITY

Peter O. Steiner
THE UNIVERSITY OF MICHIGAN

HARPER & ROW, PUBLISHERS, New York
Cambridge, Philadelphia, San Francisco,
London, Mexico City, São Paulo, Singapore, Sydney

1817

Sponsoring Editor: John W. Greenman
Development Editor: Mary Lou Mosher
Project Editor: Nora Helfgott
Text Design: Helen Iranyi
Cover Photo: Saquen a L'Anse, St. Jean, Quebec,
    Courtesy of Gscheidle, Image Bank
Text Art: J&R Art Services, Inc., and Vantage Art,
    Inc.
Production: Kewal K. Sharma
Compositor: Ruttle, Shaw & Wetherill, Inc.
Printer and Binder: Kingsport Press

Economics, Fifth Edition

Library of Congress Cataloging in Publication Data

Lipsey, Richard G., 1928–
    Economics.

    Rev. ed. of: Economics/Richard G. Lipsey . . .
[et al.]. 4th ed. © 1982.
    Includes index.
    1. Economics.   I. Purvis, Douglas D.   II. Steiner,
Peter Otto, 1922–   . III. Economics.   IV. Title.
HB171.5.E334 1985   330   84–25257
ISBN   0-06-044077-5

85 86 87 88 9 8 7 6 5 4 3 2 1

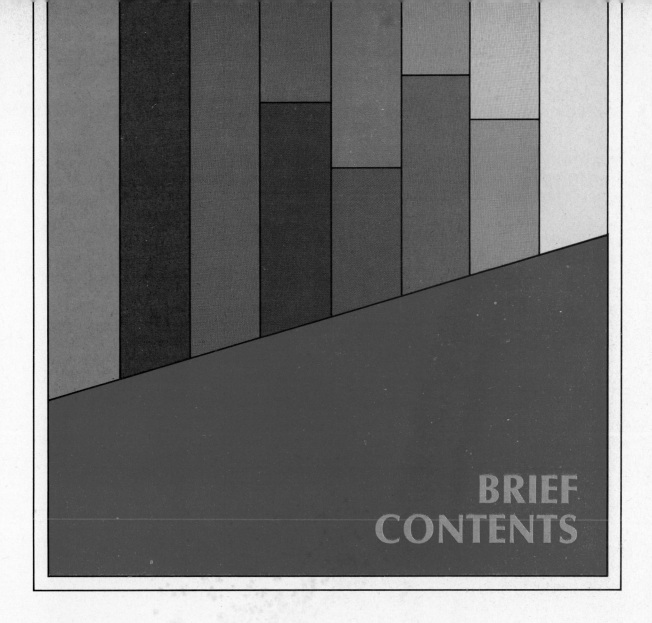

BRIEF CONTENTS

MACROECONOMICS

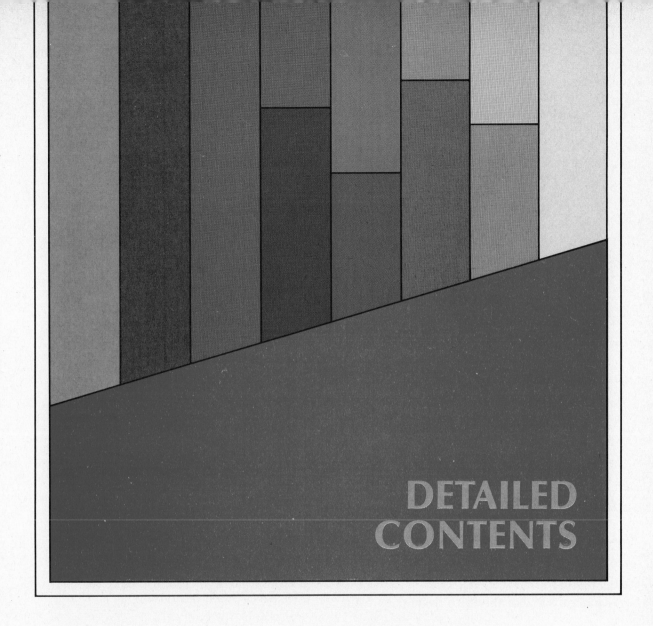

DETAILED CONTENTS

PREFACE

Our basic motivation in writing *Economics* always has been, and in this fifth edition still is, to provide a book that reflects the enormous changes in economics over the last 40 years. Economics is always changing, but in the last few decades there has been a change of such importance that we do ourselves and our students a great disservice if we neglect it. During this period economics has moved very rapidly toward becoming a science. We apply the term *science* neither to praise nor to castigate

economics, but to describe its movement toward the characteristic that distinguishes any science: the systematic confrontation of theory with observation.

The quotation from Lord William Beveridge on page xxx of this book is our text—in the preacher's sense of that word. Beveridge was scolding the profession in 1937, but things since then have clearly changed for the better. Today economists are pushing back the frontiers of ignorance about the economic environment in order both to understand it and to control it. But new problems and new phenomena continually challenge our existing knowledge. Economists are therefore continually concerned with the relations among theory, institutions, and facts and must regard every theory as subject to empirical challenge.

A second major theme of this book concerns the relations between economic theory and economic policy. Four decades of systematic observations have improved our knowledge of how things are related to one another quantitatively, and this knowledge has greatly increased the economist's power to say sensible and relevant things about public policy. This is not to deny that there are still great areas where economists' knowledge is painfully sparse, as the current debates about how to cope with the twin problems of unemployment and inflation, and on the appropriate mix of monetary and fiscal policy, remind us.

The third major feature of the book relates to the way we view modern students. We have tried in several different ways to be as honest with them as is possible within the confines of an introductory textbook. No subject worth studying is always easy, and we have not glossed over hard points just because they are hard. We have tried to follow Einstein's advice: Make things as simple as possible, but not simpler. We do not approve of slipping particularly hard bits of analysis past students without letting them see what is happening and what has been assumed, nor do we approve of teaching them things they will have to unlearn if they go on in economics (a practice sometimes justified on the grounds that it is important to get to the big issues quickly).

Effective criticism of existing ideas is the springboard to progress in science, and we believe that an introduction to economics should also introduce students to methods for testing, criticizing, and evaluating the present state of the subject. We do not accept the notion that if you suggest the possibility of criticism to students, they will make hasty and confused criticisms. Students will always make criticisms and evaluations of their courses, and their criticisms are much more likely to be

informed and relevant if they are given both practice and instruction in how to go about challenging in an effective, constructive manner what they have been taught rather than reverting to mere dogmatic assertion of error or irrelevance.

MAJOR REVISIONS IN THIS EDITION

This revision is the most comprehensive we have undertaken since the second edition. Users of previous editions will want to check the details of the new table of contents carefully. The most basic change is the revision of the presentation of macroeconomic theory and policy, as described in detail below. But other major changes have been made throughout the book. We believe our treatment is now more up-to-date, more relevant to contemporary issues, and easier for students. Only time—and your letters—will tell us if we are right.

Changes in Microeconomics

Major changes have been introduced, but roughly the same chapter structure remains. These changes include the following:

1. *Micro 100 pages shorter.* We have cut over 100 pages from the micro half of the book. We have done this by reducing the number of examples, second-order qualifications, and other "fringe material." We believe that the new treatment has gained much in tightness while losing none of its essential material.
2. *What everyone should know about distribution but didn't have time to learn.* Our surveys show that many instructors, hard pressed for time, omit the entire distribution section. We feel that this is a shame since some of the ideas found in this section, such as the distinction between economic rents and transfer earnings, are fundamental to all of economics. To remedy this situation, we have written a wholly new introductory chapter to this section that contains the minimum that we think every student should know. We urge instructors who do not cover

the more detailed material that follows to assign this one chapter, Chapter 17.

3. *International economics restructured.* All of the micro material on the international economy is now gathered together towards the end of the micro half of the book. Chapter 21, "The Gains from Trade," gives more emphasis to gains made possible from exploiting returns to scale. Chapter 22 includes a discussion of the apparent failure of the most recent meeting of the GATT, and of the sources of growing worldwide pressure for increased protectionism.

4. *Micro underpinnings of macro economics.* We have provided some *micro*economic theoretical underpinnings for the *macro*economic controversy about how firms and markets respond to fluctuations in aggregate demand and whether or not labor markets clear. Issues of price flexibility (Chapter 14) and the existence of involuntary unemployment (Chapter 19) are newly discussed.

5. *Changing world conditions allowed for.* We have addressed sharply changing world conditions that require substantial rewriting to update the discussion, for example, of OPEC (Chapter 16) and agriculture (Chapter 6).

Beyond this, as with every revision, there are new topics or new approaches to exposition that have been suggested to us or that simply seem timely to introduce. We have expanded the discussion of efficiency and inefficiency, and the case for and against relying on the free market to allocate resources and distribute income. This change affects, and we think improves, our whole treatment of microeconomics, but especially Chapters 12, 13, and 24. We have eliminated the fourth edition's Chapter 10 ("Demand Theory in Action"), which many of you told us you did not have time to cover, but retained some of its empirical findings on demand elasticities to enliven the previously theoretical Chapter 5. We have reorganized the demand (household choice) material so as to make it easier to choose *either* marginal utility *or* indifference curve approaches. Among the new material are discussions of the likelihood of destructive com-

petition, predatory practices, moral hazard, and principal-agent issues.

Changes in Macroeconomics

Virtually every chapter in macroeconomics has been extensively revised. In addition, there is one new chapter (Chapter 30), as well as important structural changes. The basic approach taken in the fourth edition has been retained, but with considerable changes. Specifically, the treatment of the *AS* curve has been totally rethought. All the other "core" macro chapters have been thoroughly revised to incorporate fully the *AD/AS* approach.

In more detail, the most important changes are:

1. *A new treatment of aggregate supply.* The new Chapter 30 treats in detail the factors influencing the slope of the *AS* curve and the forces that cause the *AS* curve to shift. The distinction, important for most of the remaining chapters, between the short-run aggregate supply curves (*SRAS*) and long-run aggregate supply curves (*LRAS*) is met and carefully explained.

The numerous *AS* curves look complex at first, but in our experience they are wholly teachable. We feel that the effort is worth making because we are alarmed at the number of textbooks that carry out the bulk of their analysis with a single, stable *AS* curve. This simplifies teaching, but it risks serious confusion. The alert student, faced with a fixed *AS* curve and an *AD* curve that can be shifted by policy, will wonder why anyone would hesitate to pay the price of a once-and-for-all increase in the price level in order to obtain a permanent increase in output and employment. And who would hesitate, faced with such a trade-off?! Economists complained a decade ago at the false trade-off between *inflation* and employment implied by a stable Phillips curve. The stable *AS* curve is one derivative more naive. Surely no one wants to raise a generation of students who see a false trade-off between the *price level* and employment. Yet this is what is encouraged by carrying a stable *AS* curve through several chapters and only dropping it late in the course. To avoid such serious confusions, we introduce the shifting, short-run *AS* curve and the vertical, long-run *AS* curve at the outset.

2. *An expanded introduction.* The revised Chapter 26 not only describes the key macro variables but also discusses how and why these variables matter in economic welfare and economic policy.

3. *Revised treatment of current policy issues.* Part Ten now includes separate chapters on inflation (Chapter 36) and unemployment (Chapter 37). Inflation is discussed in terms of the *AD/AS* model; the Phillips curve discussion appears in an appendix. Economic growth is included in this part (Chapter 38), reflecting our belief that issues of growth and productivity are again at the forefront of economic debate.

4. *A reorganized treatment of monetary economics.* The treatment of money has been reorganized. Chapters 35 and 37 from the fourth edition have been shortened and combined into one chapter, Chapter 33, that contains detailed discussions of recent deregulation of the banking system and the changing definitions of key monetary aggregates. Chapter 34 treats the role of money in macroeconomics and develops in detail the monetary adjustment mechanism underlying the slope of the *AD* curve. Chapter 35 on monetary policy now includes a discussion of the targets and instruments framework, and of the recent monetary policy focus on controlling monetary aggregates and disinflation.

5. *Full use of AD-AS analysis throughout.* All of the core macro chapters have been revised thoroughly to incorporate fully the *AD-AS* approach. The same has been done to the theoretical sections of Chapters 31 through 34. (In addition, Chapter 32 also contains a new section on the economics of budget deficits.)

6. *Three approaches for the price of one.* Chapter 27 now offers *three* approaches to accounting for national income—the output, expenditure, and income approaches—to give both a more complete and a clearer discussion than was possible using only two approaches. This material has

been completely rewritten both to improve its teachability and to present the theory in a manner more consistent with conventions used in preparing the National Income Accounts.

7. *Revisions to macro international material.* While open-economy issues are even more thoroughly integrated into the core theory chapters than ever, there is a new section, Part Eleven, which pulls together the major international material. Chapter 39 presents the core discussion of international monetary arrangements. It has been rewritten to focus on recent experience with flexible exchange rates. The discussion of the collapse of the gold standard and the Bretton Woods system has been relegated to the appendix. Chapter 41 is a much-revised discussion of macro economic policy in an open economy.

8. *A controversial ending.* The last chapter, "Macroeconomic Controversies," is completely new and includes a discussion of the issues which divide "conservatives" and "interventionists" and a presentation of the central ideas in the debate surrounding rational expectations and the new classical economics.

TEACHING AIDS

Tag lines and captions for figures and tables. The boldface tag line below or next to the figure or table indicates succinctly the central conclusion intended by the illustration; the lightface caption provides information needed to reach that conclusion. Titles, tag lines, and captions are, with the figure or table, a self-contained set, and many students find them a useful device for reviewing.

Boxes. The material in "boxes" contains examples or materials that are relevant extensions of the text narrative but need not be read in sequence. The boxes are all optional. *Some* contain further theoretical material that some instructors like to cover while others like to omit. Others contain illustrations and applications of the points covered in the text. The basic principle is that the material is all optional although much of it is, we hope, interesting. The boxes, now numbered for easy reference, give instructors flexibility in expanding or contracting the coverage of specific chapters.

End-of-chapter material. Each chapter contains a Summary, a list of Topics for Review, and a set of Discussion Questions. The questions are particularly useful for class discussion or for "quiz sections." They are answered in the Instructor's Manual.

Mathematical notes. Mathematical notes to the body of the text are collected in a self-contained section at the end of the book. Since mathematical notation and derivation is not required to understand the principles of economics, but is helpful in more advanced work, this seems to us to be a sensible arrangement. It provides clues to the uses of mathematics for the increasing numbers of students who come to beginning economics with some background in math, without encumbering the text with notes that may appear formidable to those who find mathematics arcane or frightening. Students with a mathematical background have many times told us they find the notes helpful.

Glossary. The glossary covers widely used definitions of economic terms. Because some users treat micro- and macroeconomics in that order, and others in reverse order, words in the glossary are printed in boldface type when they are first mentioned in *either half* of the text.

Endpapers. Inside the front cover are two figures; one represents the relative importance of the national debt, and the other represents federal revenues and expenditures, 1967–1983. Inside the back cover is a list of the most commonly used abbreviations in the text and a set of useful data from the Canadian economy.

Supplements

Our book is accompanied by a workbook, *Study Guide and Problems,* prepared by Professors Douglas Auld and Kenneth Grant. This workbook has been thoroughly revised with the assistance of Professor Fredric Menz. The workbook is designed to be used either in the classroom or by the students working on their own.

An *Instructor's Manual,* prepared by us, and a *Test Bank,* prepared by Delbert Ogden, are available to instructors adopting the book. The Test Bank is also available in a computerized form; contact the publisher for details.

USING THE BOOK

This textbook reflects to some extent the way its authors would teach their own courses. Needs of students differ; some want to have material that goes beyond the average class level, but others have gaps in their backgrounds. To accommodate the former, we have included more material than we would assign to every student. Also, because there are many different kinds of first-year economics courses in colleges and universities, we have included more material than normally would be included in any single course. Requests and suggestions from users of previous editions have prompted us to include some additional alternative material.

Although teachers can best design their own courses, it may be helpful if we indicate certain views of our own as to how this book *might* be adapted to different courses.

Sequence

Because the choice of order between macro and micro is partly a personal one, it cannot be decided solely by objective criteria. We believe that in the 1980s there are good reasons for preferring the micro-macro order. Whereas in the immediate post-World War II years, the major emphasis was on the development of both the theory and the policy implications of Keynesian economics, the thrust over the last 20 years has been to examine the micro underpinnings of macro functions and to erect macroeconomics on a firmer base of micro behavioral relations. Virtually every current macro controversy to which one wishes to draw a student's attention turns on some micro underpinning. For "micro-firsters" this poses no problem. For "macro-firsters" it is often hard to explain what is at issue.

For those who prefer the macro-micro order and who wish to reverse the order of our book, we have attempted to make reversibility virtually painless. The overview chapter that ends Part One has been built up to provide an improved base on which to build either the microeconomics of Part Two or the macroeconomics of Part Eight. Chapter 4 should be assigned after Chapter 3, even in macro-first courses. Where further microeconomic concepts are required—as in the macro investment chapter—we have added brief sections to make the treatment self-contained, while providing review material for those who have been through the microeconomic section.

One-Term Courses

Thorough coverage of the bulk of the book supposes a two-term course in economics. A number of first courses in economics are only one term (or equivalent) in length and our book can be easily adapted to such courses. Suggestions for use of this book for such courses are given on pages xxvii–xxviii. We recognize that for any one-term course a choice must be made among emphases. Most one-term survey courses necessarily give some coverage to theory and to policy, to micro- and to macro-economics, but the relative weights vary. Instructors will wish to choose the topics to be included or excluded and to vary the order to suit their own preferences.

ACKNOWLEDGMENTS

The starting point for this book was *Economics*, Seventh Edition, by Richard G. Lipsey, Peter O. Steiner, and Douglas D. Purvis. It would be impossible to acknowledge here all the teachers, colleagues, and students who contributed to that book. Hundreds of users have written to us with specific suggested improvements, and much of the credit for the fact that the book does become more and more teachable belongs to them. We can no longer list them individually but we thank them all most sincerely.

Colin Tener and John Karikari provided excellent research assistance. We also express thanks to Paul Arrya, St. Mary's University; James Cairns, Royal Military College; Frank Lewis, Queen's University; John Graham, Dalhousie University; and Colin Jones, University of Victoria, for detailed comments and suggestions for revision of particular chapters. A few individuals provided reviews of the fourth edition that were most helpful in preparing the present edition. These are Torben Andersen, Red Deer College; Avi J. Cohen, York University; Beverly A. Cook, University of New Brunswick; Don Dawson, McMaster University; Michael J. Hare, University of Toronto; and V. C. Olshevski, University of Winnipeg. In addition, the micro chapters of the revision were read by Judith Alexander, Simon Fraser University; Ted English, Carleton University; and Malcolm Rutherford, University of Victoria. The macro chapters were seen by Norman E. Cameron, St. John's College, University of Manitoba; S. Glenn Clarke, The University of Lethbridge; and Robert Comeau, Dalhousie University. Douglas Auld and Kenneth Grant, who prepared the study guide, have contributed to this edition as well.

Special thanks is due to Patricia Casey-Purvis and Ellen McKay for careful and efficient handling of the manuscript at all stages.

Richard G. Lipsey
Douglas D. Purvis
Peter O. Steiner

SUGGESTED OUTLINE FOR A ONE-TERM COURSE[1]

Basic core chapters for courses covering both micro and macro

INTRODUCTION

1 The Economic Problem
2 Economics As a Social Science
3 An Overview of the Economy

MICROECONOMICS

4 Demand, Supply, and Price
5 Elasticity of Demand and Supply
9 The Role of the Firm
10 Production and Cost in the Short Run

[1] A one-term course can cover about 20 to 22 full chapters. The core consists of about 18 chapters. Selections from other chapters, as listed below or according to the instructor's own preferences, can produce courses with various emphases.

11 Production Cost in the Long and Very Long Run
12 Pricing in Competitive Markets
13 Pricing in Monopoly Markets
17 Factor Pricing
21 The Gains from Trade
24 Benefits and Costs of Government Intervention

MACROECONOMICS

26 Inflation, Unemployment, and Growth: An Introduction to Macroeconomics
27 Measuring National Income
28 National Income and Aggregate Demand
29 Changes in National Income I: The Role of Aggregate Demand
30 Changes in National Income II: The Role of Aggregate Supply
32 Fiscal Policy
33 The Nature of Money and Monetary Institutions
34 The Role of Money in Macroeconomics

Chapters that can be added to give different emphases to different courses[2]

MICROECONOMICS

*7   Supply and Demand in Action
15   Theories of Imperfect Competition
*16 Monopoly Versus Competition
18   Factor Demand and Supply

[2] Chapters shown with an * are particularly appropriate for courses with a heavy policy orientation. Chapters not listed here or in the core seem to us to be of lower priority in a one-term course, but they are not necessarily too difficult.

*19 The Labor Market
22   Barriers to Free Trade
*25 Microeconomic Policy II: Public Finance and Public Expenditure

MACROECONOMICS

35   Monetary Policy
36   Inflation
37   Employment and Unemployment
38   Economic Growth
*41 Macroeconomic Policy in an Open Economy
42   Macroeconomic Controversies

TO THE STUDENT

A good course in economics will give you some real insight into how an economy functions and into some of the policy issues that are currently the subject of serious debate. Like all rewarding subjects, economics will not be mastered without effort. A book on economics must be worked at. It cannot be read like a novel.

Each student must develop an individual technique for studying, but the following suggestions may prove helpful. It is usually a good idea to read a chapter quickly in order to get the general run of the argument. At this first reading you may want to skip the "boxes" and any footnotes. Then, after reading the topics for review and the discussion questions, reread the chapter more slowly, making sure that you understand each step of the argument. With respect to the figures and tables, be sure you understand how the conclusions stated in the brief tag lines below each table or figure have been reached. You should be prepared to spend time on difficult sections; occasionally, you may spend an hour on only a few pages. Paper and a pencil are indispensable equipment in your reading. It is best to follow a difficult argument by building your own diagram while the argument unfolds rather than by relying on the finished diagram as it appears in the book. It is often helpful to invent numerical examples to illustrate general propositions. The end-of-chapter questions require you to apply what you have studied. We advise you to outline answers to some of the questions. In short, you should seek to understand economics, not to memorize it.

After you have read each part in detail, reread it quickly from beginning to end. It is often difficult to understand why certain things are done when they are viewed as isolated points, but when you reread a whole part, much that did not seem relevant or entirely comprehensible will fall into place in the analysis.

We call your attention to the glossary at the end of the book. Any time you run into a concept that seems vaguely familiar but is not clear to you, check the glossary. The chances are that it will be there, and its definition will remind you of what you once understood. If you are still in doubt, check the index entry to find where the concept is discussed more fully. Incidentally, the glossary, along with the captions under figures and tables and the end-of-chapter summaries, may prove very helpful when reviewing for examinations.

The bracketed colored numbers in the text itself refer to a series of over 50 mathematical notes that are found starting on page M-1. For those of you who like mathematics or prefer mathematical argument to verbal or geometric exposition, these may prove useful. Others may ignore them.

We hope that you will find the book rewarding and stimulating. Students who used earlier editions made some of the most helpful suggestions for revision, and we hope you will carry on the tradition. If you are moved to write to us, please do.

EINSTEIN STARTED FROM FACTS

The Morley-Michelson measurements of light, the movements of the planet Mercury, the unexplained aberrancies of the moon from its predicted place. Einstein went back to facts or told others where they should go to confirm or to reject his theory—by observation of stellar positions during a total eclipse. . . .

. . . It is not necessary, of course, for the verification of a new theory to be done personally by its propounder. Theoretical reasoning from facts is as essential a part of economic science as of other sciences, and in a wise division of labour there is room, in economics, as elsewhere, for the theoretician pure and simple, for one who leaves the technical business of verification to those who have acquired a special technique of observation. No one demanded of Einstein that he should visit the South Seas in person, and look through a telescope; but he told others what he expected them to see, if they looked, and he was prepared to stand or fall by the result. It is the duty of the propounder of every new theory, if he has not himself the equipment for observation, to indicate where verification of his theory is to be sought in facts—what may be expected to happen or to have happened if his theory is true, what will not happen if it is false.

[Now consider by way of contrast the behaviour of the participants in a current controversy in economics.] . . . None of them takes the point that the truth or falsehood of . . . [a] theory cannot be established except by appeal to facts; none of them tests it by facts himself. The distinguishing mark of economic science, as illustrated by this debate, is that it is a science in which verification of generalisations by reference to facts is neglected as irrelevant.

. . . I do not see how . . . [members of the public who survey the controversy] can avoid the conclusion that economics is not a science concerned with phenomena, but a survival of medieval logic, and that economists are persons who earn their livings by taking in one another's definitions for mangling. . . .

I know that in speaking thus I make enemies. I challenge a tradition of a hundred years of political economy, in which facts have been treated, not as controls of theory, but as illustrations. I shall be told that in the Social Sciences verification can never be clean enough to be decisive. I may be told that, in these sciences, observation has been tried and has failed, has led to shapeless accumulations of facts which themselves lead nowhere. I do not believe for a moment that this charge of barrenness of past enquiries can be sustained; to make it is to ignore many achievements of the past and to decry much solid work that is being done at this School and elsewhere. But if the charge of barrenness of realistic economics in the past were justified completely, that would not be a reason for giving up observation and verification. It would only be a reason for making our observations more exact and more numerous. If, in the Social Sciences, we cannot yet run or fly, we ought to be content to walk, or to creep on all fours as infants. . . . For economic and political theorising not based on facts and not controlled by facts assuredly does lead nowhere. . . .

There can be no science of society till the facts about society are available. Till 130 years ago we had no census, no knowledge even of the numbers and growth of the people; till fifteen years ago we had no comprehensive records about unemployment even in this country, and other countries are still where we were a generation or more ago; social statistics of every kind—about trade, wages, consumption—are everywhere in their infancy. . . .

From Copernicus to Newton is 150 years. Today, 150 years from the *Wealth of Nations*, we have not found, and should not expect to find, the Newton of economics. If we have traveled as far as Tycho Brahe we may be content. Tycho was both a theorist and an observer. As a theorist, he believed to his last day in the year 1601 that the planets went round the sun and that the sun and the stars went round the earth as the fixed centre of the universe. As an observer, he made with infinite patience and integrity thousands of records of the stars and planets; upon these records Kepler, in due course, based his laws and brought the truth to light. If we will take Tycho Brahe for our example, we may find encouragement also. It matters little how wrong we are with our theories, if we are honest and careful with our observations.

Extracts from Lord William Beveridge's farewell address as Director of the London School of Economics, June 24, 1937. Published in *POLITICA*, September 1937.

PART ONE
THE NATURE
OF ECONOMICS

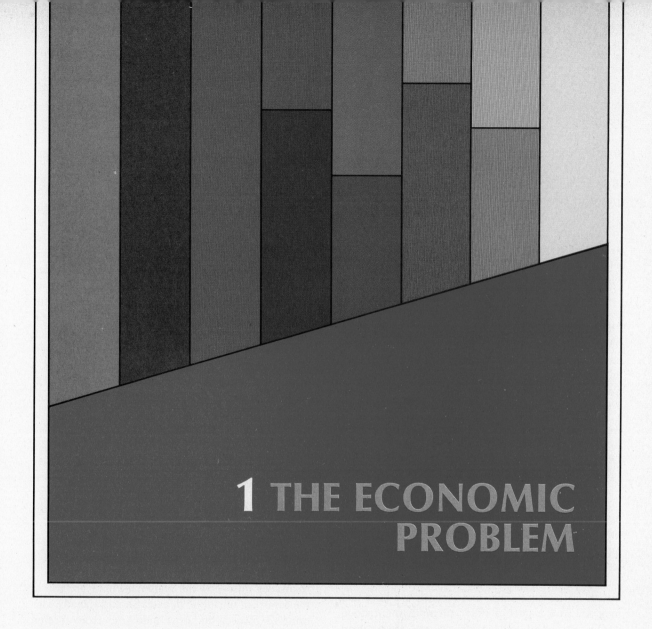

1 THE ECONOMIC PROBLEM

Many of the world's most pressing problems are economic. The dominant problem of the 1930s was the massive unemployment of workers and resources known as the Great Depression. The wartime economy of the 1940s solved that problem but created new ones, especially that of how to reallocate scarce resources quickly between military and civilian needs. By the 1950s inflation was becoming a major problem in many countries. It is still with us. Much attention in the latter half of the 1960s was directed at a slowdown in the pace of economic growth. The central problems of the 1970s were the rising cost of energy—oil prices increased tenfold over the decade—and the emergence of the disturbing combination of rising unemployment *and* rising inflation called *stagflation*. High unemployment, particularly among young workers and among workers in the traditional "smokestack industries," is a major problem of the 1980s. Problems change over the decades, yet there are always problems.

Of course, not all the world's problems are primarily economic. Political, biological, social, cultural, and philosophic issues often predominate. But no matter how "noneconomic" a particular problem may seem, it will almost always have a significant economic dimension.

The crises that lead to wars often have economic roots. Nations fight for oil and rice and land to live on, although the rhetoric of their leaders evokes God, glory, and the fatherland.

The current rate of world population growth is 2.2 persons a second, or about 70 million per year; the economic consequences are steady pressures on the available resources and land. Unless the human race can find ways to increase its food supply as fast as its numbers, increasing millions face starvation.

CURRENT ECONOMIC PROBLEMS

Unemployment and Inflation

Virtually every minister of finance in recent history has included in his budget speeches a statement establishing full employment and stable prices as twin goals of economic policy. Reasonable as that may sound, the fact is that we have seldom had both full employment and completely stable prices at the same time, and recently we have had neither. At the start of 1984, unemployment stood at 11 percent of the labor force and prices were rising at an annual rate of nearly 5 percent.

Are zero unemployment and zero inflation reasonable *long-run* goals? What is an "acceptable" level of unemployment? Can we be sure that we will never again experience the trauma of the 1930s, when up to a quarter of all those who sought work were unable to find it? What is an "acceptable" amount of inflation? Why do prices in some countries rise 30 percent or 40 percent a year, while in others they rise at a rate of 2 percent or 3 percent? Why did inflation accelerate dramatically over most of the world in the early 1970s? Can a country control unemployment and inflation?

International Trade and Protection

The issue of free trade versus protectionism has been prominent throughout Canada's history because of the crucial role of external trade in the nation's economic development. According to the widely accepted "staples theory," early Canadian economic growth was based on the exploitation of relative advantage in products with a large natural resource content. The thesis, initially propounded by Professor Harold Innes of the University of Toronto, says that prosperity depended on the strength of export markets for a succession of staples—fish, fur, timber, and wheat—each of which dominated a particular period of Canadian history.

After Confederation, the protective tariff as a means of fostering domestic manufacturing was adopted as a major element in Sir John A. MacDonald's National Policy, which emerged in the 1870s. The tariff and the transcontinental railway completed in 1885 were the key elements in a program of economic nationalism that sought to reduce the country's dependence on unstable export markets for raw materials and to promote an east-west flow of trade that would consolidate the political union of the provinces.

Although a century of industrialization has greatly reduced the proportion of the labor force directly engaged in working with raw materials, the issues raised by the National Policy are still at the forefront of public debate. Should Canada continue to protect domestic industries from foreign competition? What would be the consequences of free trade? Would our industries survive and prosper? Would new ones emerge? Or would we resort to being "hewers of wood and drawers of water"?

Productivity and Growth

Canadians pride themselves on having one of the highest standards of living in the world and a rapid rate of growth in their output of goods and services. During the 1970s the annual rate of growth of total output averaged 4.2 percent, down from the 5.2 percent average of the 1960s. And while the 1960s saw one of the longest periods of *sustained* growth in the nation's history, growth since the 1970s has been sporadic. There was a relatively severe slowdown in 1974–1975 and again in 1981–1982.

Growth in output per person *employed*, often called *productivity*, slowed dramatically during the seventies. While productivity grew at an average annual rate of 2.7 percent between 1947 and 1973, during the last half of the seventies it averaged less than 1 percent annually. Since productivity growth accounts for much of the growth in total output produced in the economy, this slowdown is a matter of major significance.

What causes such a loss of momentum in the economy? Is it the uncertain state of today's economy? Is it the burden of high taxes on both individuals and business? Is it the heavy drain imposed on the economy by the government's increasing regulation of business to provide cleaner, safer working conditions, bigger unemployment benefits, and more generous pensions and medical care?

Can we find ways to reverse the slowdown in our nation's economic growth? Do we *want* another century of rapid growth and industrialization? Without the automobile, the airplane, and electricity, ours would be a different and less comfortable world. But because of them, air pollution has become not only a major inconvenience, but may also be dangerously warming the earth's atmosphere. Is large-scale pollution the inevitable companion of economic growth? If it is, how much growth do we really want? If it is not, how can we achieve growth with less pollution?

Government and the Individual

Poverty is a dominant problem in the world. It is still a major problem in Canada, even though the average Canadian continues to be among the richest individuals in the world. How can poverty survive in the midst of relative plenty? Who are the poor, and what makes them so? Can poverty ever be eliminated in Canada? Is a more equal distribution of income a desirable or attainable national goal?

Do governmental policies improve or impair the lot of those who are poor?

Do we, as John Kenneth Galbraith charges, allocate too little to government expenditure for such valuable things as health and education while growing sated on frivolous, privately produced goods such as electric can openers? Or, as charged by Milton Friedman, do we instead invite the government to do badly many things that private groups could do well? Do we, as some "supply-side" economists charge, create *dis*incentives to productive labor by imposing high tax rates to pay for all those governmental expenditures while providing a "welfare net" that saps people's initiative even as it protects them from economic hardship?

Government Deficits and the National Debt

Almost everyone running for public office these days calls for a major reduction in government deficits, but no minister of finance seems able to achieve it. In 1983 the federal government had the biggest deficit in Canadian history. Does it really matter? Do these deficits cause inflation? The national debt in 1983 was over $100 billion. Does such a number threaten national bankruptcy, or is it well within reasonable bounds? Since politicians apparently cannot balance the federal budget on their own, should we compel them to do so by law?

Energy

Energy is vital to an industrial economy. Over the last 200 years, North America's output has grown and with it our demand for the earth's limited fossil fuels.

Throughout most of our history, the increase in energy consumption caused no serious problems because new supplies were discovered as rapidly as old ones were exhausted. In the 1970s a dramatic change occurred. The world price of oil rose sharply, and prices of other sources of energy followed suit. By 1976 Canada became a net importer of oil and natural gas. For a while in the late 1970s and early 1980s, talk of an energy crisis was common; many talked of the need to restore Canada's "energy self-sufficiency."

Are we cured of our addiction to petroleum, or is the present easing of the energy crisis only apparent, due more to temporarily improved supplies than to our learning to live with less? Are the world's supplies of oil and gas adequate to meet its demands for energy? Can nuclear or solar energy render oil and gas as unnecessary as oil and gas rendered whale oil? What is the appropriate rate at which to deplete our petroleum reserves? Should the government ration energy, or will the free market effectively prevent an energy disaster?

WHAT IS ECONOMICS?

We have listed a few of today's important issues on which economic analysis is designed to shed light. One way to define the scope of economics is to say that it is the social science that deals with such problems. Fifty years ago such all-embracing definitions were popular. Perhaps the best known was Alfred Marshall's: "Economics is a study of mankind in the ordinary business of life." A more penetrating definition might be the following:

The problems of economics concern the use of scarce resources to satisfy unlimited human wants.

Scarcity is inevitable and is central to economic problems. What are society's resources? Why is scarcity inevitable? What are the consequences of scarcity?

Resources and Commodities

A society's resources consist of the free gifts of nature—such as land, forests, and minerals—and human resources, both mental and physical, and all sorts of manufactured aids to further production, such as tools, machinery, and buildings. Economists call such resources **factors of production**[1] because they are used to produce those things that people desire. The things produced are

[1] The definitions of the terms in boldface type are gathered together in the Glossary at the end of the book.

called **commodities.** Commodities may be divided into goods and services. **Goods** are tangible (e.g., cars or shoes), and **services** are intangible (e.g., haircuts or education). Notice the implication of positive value contained in the terms *goods* and *services*. (Compare the terms *bads* and *disservices*.)

Goods and services are the means by which people seek to satisfy some of their wants. The act of making goods and services is called **production,** and the act of using them to satisfy wants is called **consumption.** Goods are valued for the services they provide. An automobile, for example, helps to satisfy its owner's desires for transportation, mobility, and possibly status.

Scarcity

For the preponderance of the world's 4 billion human beings, *scarcity* is real and ever-present. In relation to desires (for more and better food, clothing, housing, schooling, vacations, entertainment, and so on), existing resources are woefully inadequate; there are enough to produce only a small fraction of the goods and services that are wanted.

Is not Canada rich enough that scarcity is nearly banished? After all, we have been characterized as the affluent society. Whatever affluence may mean, it does not end the problem of scarcity. Most households that earn $50,000 a year (a princely amount by worldwide standards) have no trouble spending it on things that seem useful to them. Yet it would take more than twice the present output of the Canadian economy to produce enough to allow all Canadian households to consume that amount.

Choice

Because resources are scarce, all societies face the problem of deciding what to produce and how to divide it among their members. Societies differ in who makes the choices and how they are made, but the need to choose is common to all.

Just as scarcity implies the need for choice, so choice implies the existence of cost.

Opportunity Cost

A decision to have more of one thing requires a decision to have less of something else. It is this fact that makes the first decision costly. We look first at a trivial example and then at one which vitally affects all of us; both examples involve precisely the same fundamental principles.

Consider the choice that must be made by a small boy who has 10 cents to spend and who is determined to spend it all on candy. For him there are only two kinds of candy in the world: gumdrops, which sell for 1 cent each, and chocolates, which sell for 2 cents. The boy would like to buy 10 gumdrops and 10 chocolates, but he knows (or will soon discover) that this is not possible. (In technical language, it is not an *attainable combination*, given his scarce resources.) There are, however, several attainable combinations that he might buy; 8 gumdrops and 1 chocolate, 4 gumdrops and 3 chocolates, 2 gumdrops and 1 chocolate, and so on. Some of these combinations leave him with money unspent, and he is not interested in them. Only six combinations (as shown in Figure 1-1) are both attainable and use all his money.

After careful thought, the boy has almost decided to buy 6 gumdrops and 2 chocolates, but at the last moment he decides that he simply must have 3 chocolates. What will it cost him to get this extra chocolate? One answer is 2 gumdrops. To get the extra chocolate he must sacrifice 2 gumdrops, as is shown in Figure 1-1. Economists would describe the 2 gumdrops as the opportunity cost of the third chocolate.

Another answer is that the cost of the third chocolate is 2 cents, but given the boy's budget and his intentions, this answer is less revealing than the first one. Where the real choice is between more of this and more of that, the cost of "this" is fruitfully looked at as what you cannot have of "that." The idea of opportunity cost is one of the central insights of economics.

Every time one is forced by scarcity to make a choice, one is incurring opportunity costs. These costs are measured in terms of foregone alternatives.

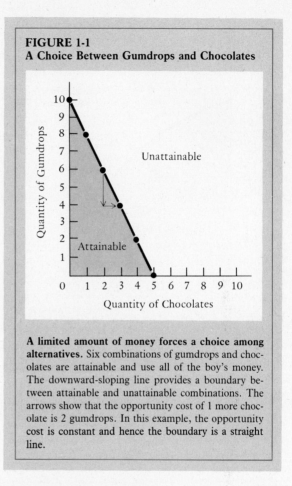

FIGURE 1-1
A Choice Between Gumdrops and Chocolates

A limited amount of money forces a choice among alternatives. Six combinations of gumdrops and chocolates are attainable and use all of the boy's money. The downward-sloping line provides a boundary between attainable and unattainable combinations. The arrows show that the opportunity cost of 1 more chocolate is 2 gumdrops. In this example, the opportunity cost is constant and hence the boundary is a straight line.

Production Possibilities

Although the previous example concerned a minor consumption decision, the essential nature of the decision is the same whatever the choice being made. Consider, for example, the important social choice between military and nonmilitary goods—between swords and plowshares. Such a choice is similar to the one facing the boy deciding what candies to buy with his dime. It is not possible to produce an unlimited quantity of both arms and civilian goods. If resources are fully employed and the government wishes to produce more arms, then less of all other goods must be produced, thereby reducing the quantity of goods available to satisfy

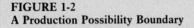

FIGURE 1-2
A Production Possibility Boundary

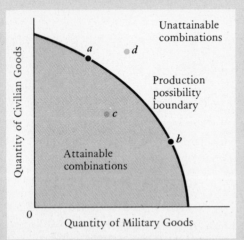

The downward-sloping boundary shows the combinations that are just attainable when all of the society's resources are efficiently employed. The quantity of military goods produced is measured along the horizontal axis, the quantity of civilian goods along the vertical axis. Thus any point on the diagram indicates some amount of each kind of good produced. The production possibility boundary separates the attainable combinations of goods such as *a*, *b*, and *c* from unattainable combinations such as *d*. It slopes downward because resources are scarce: More of one good can be produced only if resources are freed by producing less of the other goods. Points *a* and *b* represent efficient use of the society's resources. Point *c* represents either inefficient use of resources or failure to use all the available resources.

civilian wants. The opportunity cost of more arms is foregone civilian goods.

The choice is illustrated in Figure 1-2. Because resources are limited, some combinations—those that would require more than the total available supply of resources for their production—cannot be obtained. The downward-sloping curve on the graph divides the combinations that can be obtained from those that cannot be obtained. Points to the right of this curve cannot be obtained be-

cause there are not enough resources; points to the left can be obtained without using all the available resources; and points on the curve can just be obtained if all the available resources are used. The curve is called the **production possibility boundary.** It slopes downward because, when all resources are being used, having more of one kind of good requires having less of the other kind.

A production possibility boundary illustrates three concepts: scarcity, choice, and opportunity cost. Scarcity is implied by the unattainable combinations above the boundary; choice, by the need to choose among the attainable points; opportunity cost, by the downward slope of the boundary.

The shape of the production possibility boundary in Figure 1-2 implies that more and more civilian goods must be given up to achieve equal successive increases in military goods. This shape, referred to as *concave* to the origin, indicates that the opportunity cost grows larger and larger as we increase the amount of arms produced. (Drawn as a straight line, as in Figure 1-1, the curve implies that the opportunity cost of one good in terms of the other stays constant, no matter how much of it is produced.) As we shall see, there are reasons to believe that the case of rising opportunity cost applies to many important choices.[2]

Types of Economic Problems

Modern economies involve thousands of complex production and consumption activities. Although the complexity is important, many basic decisions that must be made are not very different from those made in a primitive economy in which people work with few tools and barter with their neighbors. Nor do capitalist, socialist, and Communist economies differ in their need to solve the same basic problems, though they do differ, of course, in how they

[2] The importance of scarcity, choice, and opportunity cost has led some people to define economics as the problem of allocating scarce resources among alternative and competing ends. The issues emphasized by this definition are very important. But, as will be seen in the next section, there are other, equally important, issues in economics that are omitted by this definition.

solve them. Most problems studied by economists can be grouped under four main headings.

1. What Is Produced and How?

These questions concern the allocation of scarce resources among alternative uses, called **resource allocation.** The combination of goods actually chosen from all the attainable combinations determines the allocation of resources among the nation's industries. Because resources are scarce, it is desirable that they be used efficiently. Hence it matters which of the available methods of production is used to produce each of the goods that is to be produced.

2. What Is Consumed and by Whom?

How does the production of commodities translate into consumption? What role does international trade play in this? Economists want to understand what determines the distribution of a nation's total output among its population. Who gets a lot? Who gets a little? Why?

Microeconomics. These first two questions fall within **microeconomics,** which concerns the allocation of resources and the distribution of income as they are affected by the workings of the price system and government policies.

3. What Causes Unemployment and Inflation? Are They Related?

When the economy is in a recession, unemployed workers would like to have jobs, the factories in which they could work are available, the managers and owners would like to be able to operate the factories, raw materials are available in abundance, and the goods that could be produced by these resources are needed by individuals in the community. But for some reason, resources remain unemployed. This forces the economy *inside* its production possibility boundary, at a point such as *c* in Figure 1-2.

The world's economies have often experienced bouts of prolonged and rapid changes in price levels. In recent decades, the course of prices has almost always been upward. The seventies saw a period of accelerating inflation in North America and in most of the world.

Inflation slowed in the first half of the 1980s, while unemployment soared. Were these two events related? Why do governments worry that short-run reductions in either unemployment or inflation will be at the cost of increasing the other?

4. What Causes Changes in Productive Capacity?

The capacity to produce commodities to satisfy human wants grows rapidly in some countries and slowly in others, and in yet other countries it actually declines. Growth in productive capacity can be represented by a pushing outward of the production possibility boundary, as shown in Figure 1-3. If the economy's capacity to produce goods and services is growing, combinations that are unattainable today will become attainable tomorrow. Growth makes it possible to have more of all goods.

Macroeconomics. Questions 3 and 4 fall within **macroeconomics,** the study of the determination of economic aggregates such as total output, total employment, the price level, and the rate of economic growth.

ALTERNATIVE ECONOMIC SYSTEMS

In this book, the four basic questions outlined above will be examined in the context of a market economy in which private firms and households interact in markets with some assistance and interference from the government. We study this kind of economy for several reasons. First, this is the kind of economy *we* live in. Second, it is the economic environment in which the serious study of economics was born and has grown.

Today, however, a third of the world's population lives in the Soviet Union and China, countries that reject our kind of economic system. They utilize centrally planned answers to the questions listed above. At least another third of the world's

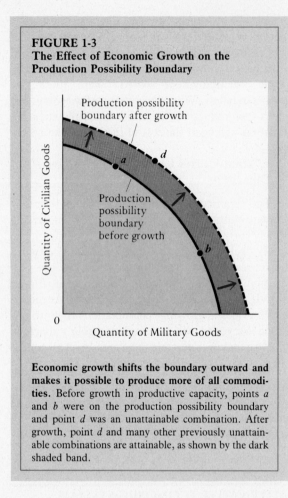

FIGURE 1-3
The Effect of Economic Growth on the Production Possibility Boundary

Production possibility boundary after growth

Production possibility boundary before growth

Quantity of Civilian Goods

Quantity of Military Goods

Economic growth shifts the boundary outward and makes it possible to produce more of all commodities. Before growth in productive capacity, points *a* and *b* were on the production possibility boundary and point *d* was an unattainable combination. After growth, point *d* and many other previously unattainable combinations are attainable, as shown by the dark shaded band.

population lives in countries whose economies have not yet developed to the point where the model of either the *free-market* or the *planned* economy fits them closely; many are "uncommitted" economically as well as politically.

Insofar as economics describes the ways in which people respond to incentives and mobilize scarce means to given ends, the same economic principles are applicable under a variety of different institutional, political, and social arrangements.

All economies face scarcity, and all must decide how to allocate scarce resources and distribute goods and services; all may face problems of inflation, unemployment, balance-of-payments deficits, and unsatisfactory rates of growth.

Because all economies face many common problems, economic analysis can contribute valuable insights even where familiar institutions are modified or absent.

Differences Among Economies

It is common to speak of only two economic systems, capitalism and socialism. But this is at best a simplification and at worst a confusion. There are dozens of economic systems in existence today, not just two. Just as there are many differences among Canada, the United States, the United Kingdom, Germany, Sweden, Japan, France, Greece, and Brazil, so are there differences among the institutions of the Soviet Union, China, Poland, Bulgaria, Cuba, Czechoslovakia, and Yugoslavia. Countries are dissimilar in many respects: in who owns resources, in who makes decisions, in the role of government planning, in the nature of the incentives offered to people, and in the way the economy grows.

Which dissimilarities are important? Differences of opinion about the answer to this question may lead to important disparities in evaluation. Canadians may view their economy as being the reason for their high standard of living and see in their well-stocked stores proof of the superiority of free enterprise capitalism. Russians may look at their economy and see its absence of urban unemployment and comprehensive welfare services as proof of its superiority to the North American economy. Sweden's slum-free public housing, nationalized medicine, and high productivity in privately owned industry lead many Swedes to regard their "mixed" economy as very satisfying.

Ownership of Resources

Who owns a nation's farms and factories, its coal mines and forests? Who owns its railways, its streams and golf courses? Who owns its houses and hotels?

One characteristic of the system called capitalism is that the basic raw materials, the productive assets of the society, and the final goods are predominantly privately owned. By this standard Canada is predominantly a capitalistic economy. Although most productive assets in Canada are privately held, public ownership (including publicly owned business enterprises, called Crown Corporations) extends beyond the usual basic services such as schools, the Post Office, and local transport systems to include most electric power supplies, health insurance, the Canadian Broadcasting Corporation, Canadian National Railways, and Air Canada.

In contrast, in a socialistic society the ownership of productive assets is public. Today there are no completely socialistic societies. Although the Soviets officially designate their economy as socialistic, there are three sectors—agriculture, retail trade, and housing—in which some private ownership exists. If the USSR is not a pure socialist economy, it is sufficiently near the public ownership end of the spectrum to distinguish it from Canada and the United States near the private ownership end.

Other countries fall between them on the spectrum. Great Britain has six times in this century elected Labour governments that have been officially committed to socialism to the point of nationalizing key industries: railroads, steel, coal, gas, electricity, atomic power, postal services, telephone, telegraph, airlines, and some trucking. Although many key British industries are publicly owned, many of those that produce goods and services for household consumption and capital goods for firms are privately owned and controlled. Furthermore, a major thrust for privatization—returning publicly owned firms to private ownership—has been underway since 1980. Ownership patterns are genuinely variable rather then of an either/or variety. Figure 1-4 shows the division of fixed investment between public and private sectors in 11 countries.

With respect to the ownership of resources—and virtually every other dimension of an economy—three basic points are worth remembering:

1. Every real economy is "mixed" rather than pure.
2. Among countries the mixture differs in ways that are appreciable and significant.
3. Over time, the mixture changes.

The Decision Process (Coordinating Principles)

A distinction is sometimes made between two kinds of systems: a *market system*, in which decisions are made impersonally and in a decentralized

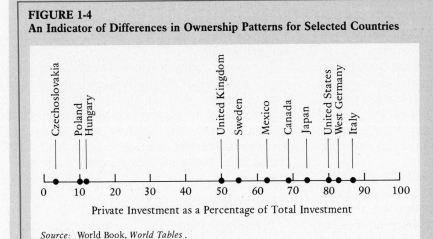

FIGURE 1-4
An Indicator of Differences in Ownership Patterns for Selected Countries

Private Investment as a Percentage of Total Investment

Source: World Book, *World Tables* .

Actual economies never rely solely on private or solely on public investment. These estimates are based on the percentage of gross fixed investment accounted for by the private sector. Such investment provides additions to the stock of productive capital. Private capital investment plays a role even in Communist countries; public capital is a significant part of investment in all countries.

TABLE 1–1 COMPARATIVE ECONOMIC SYSTEMS: OWNERSHIP AND DECISION PATTERNS

Decision pattern	Ownership pattern	
	Predominantly private	Predominantly public
Substantially decentralized with use of market	United States	Yugoslavia
Predominantly centralized with use of command principle	Nazi Germany	USSR

Each of these combinations of private and public ownership and centralized and decentralized control has occurred in practice. This table is a simplification that highlights differences among economic systems. It would be an interesting exercise to use a grid that gives several, rather than just two, gradations for each variable and then attempt to place current and past economies in the appropriate cells.

way by the interaction of individuals in markets, and a *command system,* in which centralized decision makers decide what is to be done and issue appropriate commands to achieve the desired results.

Again, no country offers an example of either system working alone. But it is true that some economies—those of Canada, the United States, France, and Yugoslavia, for example—rely much more heavily on market decisions than do the economies of East Germany, the Soviet Union, and Cuba. Yet even in Canada the command principle does operate: minimum wages, and quotas on some agricultural outputs and clothing imports are obvious examples. More subtle examples concern public expenditures and taxes that in effect transfer command of some resources from private individuals to public officials.

In the planned economies of the Soviet bloc, where plans and targets, quotas and directives are important aspects of the decision-making system, there is substantial command at work. But markets are used too. At the retail level, for example, people can spend their incomes with substantial discretion on a wide variety of goods.

Table 1-1, though it suppresses many subtle distinctions, focuses on important tendencies in certain twentieth century economies by a simple classification according to ownership and decision patterns. The table suggests at once that Communist countries such as the USSR and Yugoslavia differ significantly from one another as well as from Canada.

Much economic behavior depends more on the decision pattern than on the ownership pattern. Thus in the United Kingdom, while many key industries are publicly owned, their control is vested in semi-autonomous boards over which Parliament exerts very little control. By and large, the boards try to make their enterprises profitable, and to the extent that they succeed, their behavior will be similar to that of profit-seeking, privately owned firms. In predicting their market behavior, economic theorists need not concern themselves with the legal distinction between public and private ownership any more than they need concern themselves with the distinction between corporations and partnerships.

In contrast, firms in Hitler's Germany were under a high degree of state control, even though they were privately owned. An attempt to predict their behavior using the assumption that the owners are seeking profits would not have been successful, because the central decision makers were concerned with goals quite different from profit maximization.

Incentive Systems

Psychologists know that people (and most other living creatures) respond to reward and punishment. Incentives may be of two kinds—the carrot or the stick—and of almost infinite variety. Direct monetary rewards, in the form of wages or profits or bribes, are well understood. Indirect monetary rewards, such as special housing, vacations, or subsidized education, are not always as readily identified, but they can be effective. Nonmonetary "carrots" include praise, medals, certificates, and applause. Prison terms, public ridicule, and other penalties are used to punish aberrant behavior in all societies; in some societies coercion and fear provide even stronger motivation.

Comparative Systems: A Summary

Perhaps the most important empirical observation about different economies is that a wide variety of economic systems seem able to coexist and to be successful.

No economic system seems to do everything better than any major competing system; indeed, each has its strengths and weaknesses. To talk of "better" and "worse" in this context may itself be misleading: Different economic systems imply different choices between current and future consumption, between individual or collective choices, between degrees of freedom or coercion, between stability and growth.

The economic institutions of a society reflect in part its values, but they also reflect habits and traditions, experiments and inertia. These institutions change with time in given countries and vary at a given time among countries. In the variety of experience, economists hope to find many clues as to which instruments best achieve which ends.

In the contemporary experience, it looks as if the *command principle* may make the management of certain macro problems much easier than in a market system, but it also appears that the command principle is much less well suited than the market to handling micro allocations. Although a command system can achieve great sacrifices in the interests of growth, the evidence suggests no simple conclusion, for many countries with very different economic systems have achieved rapid growth. It is clear that markets are less personal than bureaucrats, and this makes them more acceptable to many people because they are less arbitrary and less subject to autocratic abuse.

Ends and Means

Many, perhaps most, people in Western societies value the *means* of the free market and democratic processes even more highly than they value the *ends* of high and rising living standards. Most North Americans distrust the agglomeration of central power and the erosion of democratic institutions that accompany a high degree of socialism. Many believe there is no need to choose between means and ends because they feel the free market and democracy produce better results than do alternative systems in terms of both means and ends.

How many Canadians would decide to go over to Russian-style socialism, even if it could be *proved* that it would produce higher material living standards than the free-market system? In the 1930s it was believed that Fascist dictatorships were more efficient than democracies. Mussolini, it was said, "made the Italian trains run on time." It is debatable that the belief was correct, but most people accepted it. Yet few Canadians advocated that Canada become a Fascist dictatorship.

In many less-developed countries, ordinary people often put more importance on the ends, higher living standards, than on the means of achieving them. They may regard a change of means per se as unimportant. The choice between a centralized and a decentralized economy may seem to be simply one of which group will exploit them—government officials or powerful monopoly interests. If a highly planned socialistic economy offers them a good chance of a 4 percent growth rate, while a democratically oriented market society offers 2 percent, they may well choose the planned society. To warn them that in so choosing they may throw away their freedom is likely to evoke the reply: What has freedom meant to us in the past but the freedom to be hungry and exploited?

Economic and Political Objectives in Market Economies

Decisions on interrelated issues of policy are made by many different bodies. Federal and provincial parliaments pass laws, the courts interpret laws, the governments decide which laws to enforce with vigor and which to soft-pedal, the Department of Finance and the Bank of Canada influence monetary factors, and a host of other agencies and semi-autonomous bodies determine actions in respect to different aspects of policy goals. Because of the multiplicity of decision makers, it would be truly amazing if fully consistent behavior resulted. The majority of Canadians believe that there are advantages to this separation of responsibilities, but one of its consequences is that inconsistent decisions will be made.

Another problem arises from the fact that in a democracy legislators and political officials have as important goals their own and their leader's reelection. This means, for example, that any measure that imposes large costs and few benefits obvious to the electorate over the next few years is unlikely to find favor, no matter how large the long-term benefits are. There is a strong bias toward myopia in an elective system. Although much of this bias stems from shortsightedness and selfishness, some of it reflects genuine uncertainty about the future. The further into the future the economist calculates, the wider the margin of possible error. It is not surprising that politicians who must worry about the next election often tend to worry less about the long-term effect of their actions. "After all," they may argue, "who can tell what will happen 20 years hence?"

These problems of political decision making are what George Bernard Shaw had in mind when he said the only strong argument in favor of democracy is that all its alternatives are even worse.

SUMMARY

1. Economic problems are among the important concerns of every generation. A common feature of such problems is that they concern the use of limited resources to satisfy virtually unlimited human wants.

2. Scarcity is a fundamental problem faced by all economies. Not enough resources are available to produce all the goods and services people would like to consume. Scarcity makes it necessary to choose. All societies must have a mechanism for deciding what commodities will be produced and in what quantities.

3. The concept of opportunity cost emphasizes the problem of scarcity and choice by measuring the cost of obtaining a unit of one commodity in terms of the number of units of other commodities that could have been obtained instead.

4. Four basic questions faced by all economies are these: What commodities are being produced and how? What commodities are being consumed and by whom? What causes unemployment and inflation, and are they related? What causes productive capacity to change?

5. Not all economies resolve these questions in the same ways or equally satisfactorily. Economists study how these questions are answered in various societies and the consequences of using one method rather than another to provide answers.

6. Actual economies can differ from one another in a great variety of ways, and such capsule characterizations as "capitalism," "socialism," and "communism" represent simplifications of complex matters.

7. Among the important dimensions in which economies can differ from one another are (a) the pattern of ownership of goods and resources; (b) the nature of the decision process used, with a particularly important distinction concerning "command" versus "market" decision mechanisms; (c) the nature of the incentive systems used; and (d) the relative concern about ends and means.

8. It is necessary to distinguish between certain ends that are being sought and the means by which they will be achieved. Economics does not allow a

"scientific" choice between alternative ends: It does not tell which of competing goals should be adopted. Economic analysis can help to determine whether a particular measure contributes to stated goals and at what cost.

TOPICS FOR REVIEW

Scarcity and the need for choice
Choice and opportunity cost
Production possibility boundary
Resource allocation
Unemployed resources
Growth in productive capacity
Alternative economic systems
Ends and means

DISCUSSION QUESTIONS

1. What does each of the following quotations tell you about the policy conflicts perceived by the person making the statement and about how he or she has resolved them?
   a. "We've got so many people out of work, and we've got so much unused industrial capacity, that I think if we carefully target employment opportunities around the country, we can decrease unemployment substantially before we start becoming equally concerned about inflation."
   b. Russell Baker, commenting on the decision of Nantucket Island residents to approve a Holiday Inn to cater to oil drillers: "Economics compels us all to turn things into slums. Although it will be too bad, it will be absolutely justifiable. An economic necessity. Another step down the ladder to paradise."
   c. "Considering our limited energy resources and the growing demand for electricity, Canada really has no choice but to use all of its possible domestic energy sources, including nuclear energy. Despite possible en-

vironmental and safety hazards, nuclear power is a necessity."
   d. The king of Saudi Arabia: "Increasing oil production in order to lower oil prices would be the most damaging thing that could happen to humanity. Experts say that if oil consumption continues to increase as it has, oil reserves will dry up by the end of this century."
2. What is the difference between scarcity and poverty? If everyone in the world had enough to eat, could we say that food was no longer scarce?
3. Consider the right to free speech in political campaigns. Suppose that the Flat Earth Society, the Rhinoceros Party, and the Conservative party all demand equal time on network television in a federal election. What economic questions are involved? Can there be freedom of speech without free access to the scarce resources needed to make one's speech heard?
4. Evidence accumulates that the use of chemical fertilizers, which increases agricultural production greatly, causes damage to water quality. Show the choice involved between more food and cleaner water in using such fertilizers. Use a production possibility curve with agricultural output on the vertical axis and water quality on the horizontal axis. In what ways does this production possibility curve reflect scarcity, choice, and opportunity cost? How would an improved fertilizer that increased agricultural output without further worsening water quality affect the curve? Suppose a pollution-free fertilizer were developed; would this mean there would no longer be any opportunity cost in using it?
5. Explain why the government cannot avoid making policy decisions on wage and price controls, the size of tariffs, public support of separate schools, and the external value of the Canadian dollar. Was there a policy about wages before any minimum-wage laws were passed?
6. "What the world of economics needs is an end to ideology and *isms*. If there is a best system of economic organization, it will prove its superiority in its superior ability to solve economic problems." Do you agree with this statement? Would you expect that if the world survives for another hundred years, a single form of economic system would be found superior to all others? Why or why not?

2 ECONOMICS AS A SOCIAL SCIENCE

Economics is generally regarded as a social science. What exactly does it mean to be scientific? Can economics ever hope to be "scientific" in its study of those aspects of human behavior with which it is concerned? The first step in answering these questions is to be able to distinguish between positive and normative statements. The ability to make this distinction has been one of the reasons for the success of science in the last 300 years.

The Distinction Between Positive and Normative

The success of modern science rests partly on the ability of scientists to separate their views on *what does happen* from their views on *what they would like to happen*. For example, until the nineteenth century Christians, Jews, and Muslims believed that the earth was only a few thousand years old.

About 200 years ago, evidence that some existing rocks were millions or even billions of years old began to accumulate. Most people found this hard to accpt: it forced them to rethink their religious beliefs. Many wanted to the evidence to be wrong; they wanted rocks to be only a few thousands years old. Nevertheless, on the evidence accumulated until today virtually everyone accepts that the earth is neither thousands, nor millions, but 4 or 5 billion years old. This advance in our knowledge came because the question "How old are observable rocks?" could be separated from the feelings of scientists (many of them devoutly religious) about the age they would have liked the rocks to be. Distinguishing what *is* from what we would *like* the facts to show depends on recognizing the difference between positive and normative statements.

Positive statements concern what is, was, or will be. **Normative statements** concern what one believes ought to be.

Positive statements, assertions, or theories may be simple or complex, but they are basically about matters of fact.

Disagreements over positive statements are appropriately settled by an appeal to the facts.

Normative statements, because they concern what ought to be, are inextricably bound up with philosophical, cultural, and religious systems. A normative statement is one that makes, or is based on, a value judgment—a judgment about what is good and what is bad.

Disagreements over normative statements cannot be settled merely by an appeal to facts.

Some related issues about disagreement among economists are taken up in Box 2-1.

The Distinction Illustrated

The statement "It is impossible to break up atoms" is a postive statement that can quite definitely be (and of course has been) refuted by empirical observations, while the statement "Scientists ought not to break up atoms" is a normative statement that involves ethical judgments. The questions "What government policies will reduce unemployment?" and "What policies will prevent inflation?" are positive ones, while the question "Ought we to be more concerned about unemployment than about inflation?" is a normative one. The statement "A government deficit will reduce unemployment but cause an increase in prices" is a very simple hypothesis in positive economics, a hypothesis that can be tested by an appeal to empirical observation, whie the statement "Because unemployment ought to matter more than inflation, a government deficit is sound policy" is a normative hypothesis that cannot be settled solely by an appeal to observation.

The Importance of the Distinction

If we think something ought to be done, we can deduce other things that, if we wish to be consistent, ought to be done; but we can deduce nothing about what is done (i.e., is true). Similarly, if we know that two things are true, we can deduce other things that must be true, but we can deduce nothing about what is desirable (i.e., *ought* to be).

It is logically impossible to deduce normative statements from only positive statements or positive statements from only normative ones.

As an example of the importance of this distinction in the social sciences, consider the question "Has the payment of generous unemployment benefits increased the amount of unemployment?" This positive question can be turned into a testable hypothesis by asserting something like: "The higher the benefits paid to the unemployed, the higher will be the total amount of unemployment." If we are not careful, however, our attitudes and value judgments may get in the way of our study of this hypothesis. Some people are opposed to the welfare state and believe in an individualist, self-help ethic. They may hope that the hypothesis will be found correct because its truth could then be used as an argument against welfare measures in general. Others feel that the welfare state is a good thing, reducing misery and contributing to human

BOX 2–1 WHY ECONOMISTS DISAGREE

If you listen to a discussion among economists on "As It Happens" or "Sunday Morning" or if you read about their debates in the daily press or weekly magazines, you will find economists constantly disagreeing among themselves. Indeed, it is often said that, if you ask any two economists for their opinion on any matter, you would get at least three answers. One very widespread reason for rejecting economists' advice is that they never completely agree on any issue. Why do economists constantly disagree, and what should we make of this fact?

In a recent column in *Newsweek*, Charles Wolf, Jr., suggests four reasons for the disagreement among economists: (1) Different economists use different benchmarks: Inflation is *down* compared with last year but *up* compared with the 1950s. (2) Economists fail to make it clear to their listeners whether they are talking about the short run or long run: tax cuts will stimulate consumption in the short run and investment in the long run. (3) Economists fail to acknowledge the full extent of their ignorance. (4) Different economists have different values, and these normative views play a large part in their public discussions.

There is surely some truth in each of these assessments. But there is a fifth and even more important reason: the public's *demand for disagreement*. For example, suppose that all economists in fact agree to the proposition that unions are not a major cause of inflation. This view would be unpalatable to some individuals. Those who are hostile to unions, for instance, would like to blame inflation on them and would be looking for an intellectual champion. Fame and fortune would await the economist who espoused their cause, and a champion would soon be found.

This fact assures that there will not be unanimity among economists on any issue over which the public or policy makers are split. This forces anyone wanting to know the profession's opinion on a given issue to form a judgment by first determining what proportion of the profession supports it and how much weight to give to a particular view.

Disagreement does exist but can also be exaggerated. Media coverage is a major source of exaggeration. When the media cover an issue, they naturally wish to give both sides of it. Normally, the public will hear one or two economists for each side of a debate, regardless of whether the profession is divided right down the middle or is nearly unanimous in its support of one side. Thus the public will not know that in one case a reporter could have chosen from dozens of economists to present each side while in the second case the reporter had to spend three days trying to locate someone willing to take a particular side because nearly all economists contacted thought it was wrong. On many issues, the profession overwhelmingly supports one side. In their desire to show both sides of the case, however, the media present the public with the appearance of a profession equally split over all matters.

Thus, anyone seeking to discredit economists' advice by showing that they disagree will have no trouble supporting his or her case. But those who wish to know if there is a majority view or even a strong consensus will find one on a surprisingly large number of issues. Of course, there are also genuine disagreements among economists on many issues, especially those that involve recent and incompletely understood events, and there will always be controversies at the frontiers of current research. But there is no evidence to suggest that disagreements among economists are more common now than in the past.

dignity. They may hope that the hypothesis is wrong because they do not want welfare measures to produce results of which people disapprove.

In spite of different value judgments and social attitudes, however, evidence is accumulating on this particular hypothesis. As a result, we have much more knowledge than we had ten years ago of why, where, and by how much (if at all) unemployment benefits increase unemployment. This evidence could never have been accumulated or accepted if investigators had not been able to distinguish their feelings on how they wanted the answer to turn out from their assessment of evidence on how people actually behaved.

Positive statements such as the one just considered assert things about the world. If it is possible for a statement to be proved wrong by empirical evidence, we call it a *testable statement*. Many positive statements are testable, and disagreements over them are appropriately handled by an appeal to the facts.

In contrast to positive statements, which are often testable, normative statements are never testable. Disagreements over such normative statements as "It is wrong to steal" or "It is immoral to have sexual relations out of wedlock" cannot be settled by an appeal to empirical observations. Thus, for a rational consideration of normative questions, different techniques are needed from those used for a rational consideration of positive questions. Because of this, it is convenient to separate normative and positive inquiries. We do this not because we think the former are less important than the latter, but merely because they must be handled in different ways.

The distinction between positive and normative allows us to keep our views on how we would like the world to work separate from our views on how the world actually does work. We may be interested in both. It can only obscure the truth, however, if we let our views on what we would like to be bias our investigations of what actually is. It is for this reason that the separation of the positive from the normative is one of the foundation stones of science and that scientific inquiry, as it is normally understood, is usually confined to positive questions.

Limits on the Distinction

While the distinction between positive and normative is useful, it is not the be-all and end-all of scientific analysis for several reasons.

The classification is not exhaustive. The classifications *positive* and *normative* do not cover all statements that can be made. For example, there is the important class of *analytic statements*. The truth or falsehood of these statements depends only on the rules of logic. Thus the sentence "*If* all humans are immortal *and if* you are a human, *then* you are immortal" is a true analytic statement. It tells us that *if* two things are true, *then* a third thing must be true. The truth of this *statement* is not dependent on whether or not its individual parts are in fact true. Indeed the sentence "All humans are immortal" is a positive statement which has been decisively refuted. Yet no amount of empirical evidence on the mortality of humans can upset the truth of the "if-then" sentence quoted above. Analytic statements—which proceed by logical analysis—play an important role in scientific work and form the basis for much of our ability to theorize.

Not all positive statements are testable. A positive statement asserts something about the universe. It may be empirically true or false in the sense that what it asserts may or may not be true of the universe. If it is true, it adds to our knowledge of what can and cannot happen. Many positive statements are refutable: if they are wrong this can be ascertained (within a margin for error of observation) by checking them against data. For example, the positive statement that the earth is less than 5,000 years old was tested and refuted by a mass of evidence accumulated in the nineteenth century.

The statement "Angels exist and frequently visit the earth in visible form" is, however, also a positive statement. It asserts something about the universe. But we could never refute this statement with evidence because, no matter how hard we searched, believers could argue that we did not look in the right places or in the right way, or that angels do not reveal themselves to nonbelievers, or any one of a host of other alibis. Thus statements that could conceivably be refuted by evidence if they are wrong are a subclass of positive statements; other positive statements are irrefutable.

The distinction is not unerringly applied. Because the positive-normative distinction helps the advancement of knowledge, it does not follow that all scientists automatically and unerringly apply it. Scientists are human beings. Many have strongly held values, and they may let their value judgments get in the way of their assessment of evidence. Nonetheless, the desire to separate *what is* from *what we would like to be* is a guiding light, an ideal, of science. The ability to do so, albeit imperfectly, is attested to by the acceptance, first by scientists and then by the general public, of many ideas that were initially extremely unpalatable—ideas such as the extreme age of the earth and the theory of evolution.

Positive and Normative Statements in Economics

Economics, like other sciences, is concerned with questions, statements, and hypotheses that could conceivably be shown to be wrong by actual observations of the world. It is not necessary to show them to be either consistent or inconsistent with the facts tomorrow or the next day; it is only necessary to be able to imagine evidence that could show them to be wrong. Other questions, including normative ones, cannot be settled by a mere appeal to empirical observation. Of course, this does not mean that they are unimportant. Such questions as "Should we subsidize higher education?" and "Should we send food to Afghanistan?" must be decided by means other than a simple appeal to facts. In democracies such questions are often settled by voting.

This does not mean that economists or anyone else need confine their discussions to testable statements. Economists can usefully discuss value judgments as long as they do not confuse such judgments with evaluations of testable statements.

Indeed the pursuit of what appears to be a nor-

mative statement will often turn up positive hypotheses on which the *ought* conclusion depends. For example, there are probably very few people who believe that government control of industry is in itself good or bad. Their advocacy or opposition is based on beliefs that can be stated as positive rather than normative hypotheses. For example: "Government control reduces efficiency, changes the distribution of income, and leads to an increase of state control in other spheres." A careful study of this subject would reveal enough positive economic questions to keep a research team of economists occupied for many years.

The Scientific Approach

Very roughly, the scientific approach, or the scientific method as it is sometimes called, consists of relating questions to evidence. When presented with a controversial issue, scientists will ask what the evidence is. They may then take a stand on the issue, with more or less conviction depending on the weight of the evidence. If there is little or no evidence, scientists will say that at present it is impossible to take a stand. They will then set about searching for relevant evidence. If they find that the issue is framed in terms that make it impossible to gather evidence for or against it, they will then usually try to recast the question so that it can be answered by an appeal to the evidence.

In some fields, the scientist, having reframed the question, is able to generate observations that will provide evidence for or against the hypothesis. Experimental sciences such as chemistry and some branches of psychology have an advantage because it is possible for them to obtain relevant evidence through controlled laboratory experiments. Other sciences such as astronomy and economics cannot do this. They must wait for natural events to produce observations that may be used as evidence in testing their theories.

The ease or difficulty with which one can collect evidence does not determine whether a subject is scientific or nonscientific.

How scientific inquiry proceeds and the ease with which it can be pursued do, however, differ substantially between fields in which laboratory experiment is possible and those in which it is not. Here we shall consider general problems more or less common to all sciences.

Is Human Behavior Predictable?

Is it possible to conduct a scientific study in the field of human behavior? It is sometimes argued that the answer is no because natural sciences deal with inanimate matter that is subject to natural "laws" while the social sciences deal with human beings who have free will and therefore cannot be made the subject of natural laws.

Natural Versus Social Sciences

The notion that natural and social sciences differ fundamentally in their ability to predict ignores the contributions of biology and other life sciences that deal successfully with animate matter. When this point is granted, it may be argued that the life sciences deal with simple living material, while only the social sciences deal with human beings, who are the ultimate in complexity and who alone possess free will. Many social observers, while accepting the success of the natural and the life sciences, hold that there cannot be a successful social science. Stated carefully, this view implies that inanimate and nonhuman animate matter will show stable responses to certain stimuli, while humans will not. For example, if you put a match to a dry piece of paper, the paper will burn, whereas if you subject human beings to torture, some will break down and do what you want them to do and others will not. Even more confusing, the same individual may react differently to torture at different times.

Does human behavior show sufficiently stable responses to factors influencing it to be predictable within an acceptable margin of error? This is a positive question that can be settled only by an appeal to evidence and not by *a priori* speculation. (*A priori* may be defined as the use of knowledge

that is prior to actual experience.) The question itself might concern either the behavior of groups or that of isolated individuals.

Group Behavior Versus Individual Behavior

It is a matter of simple observation that when a group of individuals is considered, they do not behave capriciously but instead display stable responses to various forces that act on them. The warmer the weather, for example, the more people visit the beach and the higher the sales of ice cream and Coca-Cola. It may be hard to say if or when one individual will buy an ice cream cone or a Coke, but a stable response pattern from a large group of individuals can be seen.

There are many situations in which group behavior can be predicted accurately without certain knowledge of individual behavior. No social scientist can predict, for example, when an apparently healthy individual is going to die, but death rates for large groups are stable enough to make life insurance a profitable business. This would not be so if group behavior were capricious. Although social scientists cannot predict what particular individuals will be killed in auto accidents in the next holiday weekend, they can come very close to knowing the total number who will die. The more objectively measurable data they have (for example, the state of the weather on the days in question and the trend in gasoline prices), the more closely they will be able to predict total deaths.

The difference between predicting individual and group behavior is illustrated by the fact that economists can predict with fair accuracy what households as a group will do when their take-home pay is increased. Some individuals may do surprising and unpredictable things, but the total response of all households to a permanent change in tax rates that leaves more money in their hands is predictable within quite a narrow margin of error. This stability in the response of households' spending to a change in their available income is the basis of economists' ability to predict successfully the outcome of major revisions in the tax laws.

This does not mean that people never change their minds or that future events can be foretold by a casual study of the past. The stability discussed here is a stable response to causal factors (e.g., next time it gets warm, ice cream sales will rise) and not merely inertia (e.g., ice cream sales will go on rising in the future because they have risen in the past).

The "Law" of Large Numbers

Successfully predicting the behavior of large groups is made possible by the statistical "law" of large numbers. Broadly speaking, this law asserts that random movements of many individual items tend to offset one another. This law is based on one of the most beautiful constants of behavior in the whole of science, natural and social, and yet it can be derived from the fact that human beings make errors! The law is based on the so-called *normal curve of error*.

What is implied by this law? Ask any one person to measure the length of a room and it will be almost impossible to predict in advance what sort of error of measurement will be made. Dozens of things will affect the accuracy of the measurement and, furthermore, the person may make one error today and quite a different one tomorrow. But ask a thousand people to measure the length of the same room, and we can predict within a very small margin just how this *group* will make its errors. We can assert with confidence that more people will make small errors than will make large errors, that the larger the error the fewer will be the number making it, that roughly the same number of people will overstate as will understate the distance, and that the average error of all individuals will be zero.

If a common cause should act on each member of the group, it is possible to predict the average behavior of the group even though any one member may act in a surprising fashion. If, for example, each of the thousand individuals is given a tape measure that understates "actual" distances, it can be expected that, on the average, the group will understate the length of the room. It is, of course, quite possible that one member, who had in the

past been consistently undermeasuring distance because of psychological depression, will now overmeasure the distance because the state of his health has changed. But some other event may happen to another individual that will turn her from an overmeasurer into an undermeasurer. Individuals may act strangely for inexplicable reasons. But the group's behavior, when the inaccurate tape is substituted for the accurate one, will be predictable precisely because the odd things that one individual does will tend to cancel out the odd things some other individual does.

Irregularities in individual behavior tend to cancel one another out, and the regularities tend to show up in repeated observations.

The Nature of Scientific Theories

Some regularity between two or more things is observed, and we ask why this should be so. A *theory* attempts to explain why.

Once we have a theory, we are able to predict as yet unobserved events. For example, national income theory predicts that an increase in the government's budget deficit will reduce the unemployment rate. The simple theory of market behavior predicts that, under specified conditions, the introduction of a tax on a commodity will be accompanied by an increase in the price of the commodity but that the price increase will be less than the amount of the tax.

Theories are used in explaining observed phenomena. A successful theory enables us to predict the consequences of various occurrences.

Any explanation whatsoever of how given observations are linked together is a theoretical construction. Theories are used to impose order on these observations, to explain how what is seen is linked together. Without theories there would be only a shapeless mass of meaningless observations.

The choice is not between theory and observation but between better or worse theories to explain observations.

What Is a Theory and How Is It Tested?

A theory consists of (1) a set of definitions that clearly define the *variables* to be used, (2) a set of *assumptions* that outline the conditions under which the theory is to apply, (3) one or more *hypotheses* about the relationships between the variables, and (4) *predictions* that are deduced from the assumptions of the theory and can be tested against actual empirical observations.

Variables

Theories are concerned with how various things, called variables, are related to one another. A **variable** is something that can take on different possible values. Variables are the basic elements of theories, and each one needs to be carefully defined.

Price is an example of an important economic variable. The price of a commodity is the amount of money that must be given up to purchase one unit of that commodity. To define a price we must first define the commodity to which it attaches. Such a commodity might be one dozen grade A large eggs. We could then inquire into the price of such eggs sold in, say, supermarkets in Red Deer, Alberta. This would define the variable. The particular values taken on by the variable might be $.98 on July 1, 1984, $1.02 on July 8, 1984, and $.99 on July 15, 1984.

There are many distinctions between kinds of variables; two of the most important are discussed below.

Endogenous and exogenous variables. **Endogenous variables** are those that are explained within a theory. **Exogenous variables** are those that influence the endogenous variables but are themselves determined by considerations outside of the theory.

For example, consider the theory that the price of apples in Victoria on a particular day is a function of several things, one of which was the weather in the Okanagan Valley during the previous apple-growing season. We can safely assume that the state of the weather is not determined by economic con-ditions. The price of apples in this case is an endogenous variable—something determined within the framework of the theory. The state of the weather in the Okanagan is an exogenous variable; changes in it influence prices because they affect the output of apples, but the weather is uninfluenced by these prices.

Other words are sometimes used for the same distinction. One frequently used pair is *induced* for endogenous and *autonomous* for exogenous.

Stock and flow variables. A flow variable has a time dimension; it is so much per unit of time. The quantity of grade A large eggs purchased in Halifax is a flow variable. No useful information is conveyed if we are told that purchases were 2,000 dozen eggs unless we are also told the period of time over which these purchases occurred. Two thousand dozen per hour would indicate an active market in eggs, while 2,000 dozen per week would indicate a sluggish market.

A stock variable has no time dimension; it is just so much. Thus, if the egg marketing board has 2 million dozen eggs in warehouses around the country, that quantity is a stock. All those eggs are there at one time. The stock variable is just a number, not a rate of flow of so much *per day* or *per month.*

Economic theories use both flow variables and stock variables, and it takes a little practice to keep them straight. The amount of income earned is a flow; there is so much per year or per month or per hour. The amount of a household's expenditure is also a flow—so much spent per week or per month. The amount of money in a bank account or a miser's hoard (earned, perhaps, in the past, but unspent) is a stock—just so many thousands of dollars. The key test is always whether a time dimension is required to give the variable meaning.

Assumptions

Assumptions are essential to theorizing. Students are often concerned about the justification of assumptions, particularly if they seem unrealistic. Usually it is not appropriate to criticize the simplifying assumptions of a theory only on the grounds that they are unrealistic. All theory is an abstraction from reality. If it were not, it would merely duplicate the world and would add nothing to our understanding of it. A good theory abstracts in a useful way; a poor theory does not.

An assumption may mean many different things. When you encounter an assumption in economic theory, ask yourself whether it is being used to convey the idea that (1) the world actually behaves as assumed, (2) the factor under consideration is irrelevant to the theory, (3) the theory only holds when the condition specified in the assumption actually holds, or (4) a convenient fiction is being introduced to simplify some quite complex piece of behavior. An assumption that meets any one of these criteria may be useful.

For example, suppose an economic theory starts out: "Assume that there is no government." Surely, says the reader, this assumption is totally unrealistic, and I cannot therefore take seriously anything that comes out of the theory. Clearly this assumption is not justified under category 1 above. But this assumption may merely be the economist's way of saying that, whatever the government does, even whether it exists, *is irrelevant for the purposes of this particular theory.* Now, put this way, the statement becomes an empirical assertion. The only way to test it is to see if the predictions that follow from the theory do or do not fit the facts that the theory is trying to explain. If they do, then the theorist was correct in the assumption that the government could be ignored for the particular purposes at hand. In this case the criticism that the theory is unrealistic because there really is a government is completely beside the point.

Alternatively, the assumption may be used to indicate that the theory is meant to hold only in the absence of government, either because the presence of government will upset the theory (category 3 above) or because the government presence will have an effect so complex that we cannot be sure the theory will still be true (category 4).

Hypotheses

Relations among variables. The critical step in theorizing is formulating hypotheses. A hypoth-

esis is a statement about how two or more variables are related to each other. For example, it is a basic hypothesis of economics that the quantity produced of any commodity depends, among other things, upon its price. Thus, according to an economic hypothesis, two variables, the price of eggs and the quantity of eggs produced, are related.

Functional relations.[1] A **function,** or a functional relation, is a formal expression of a relation among variables.

The particular hypothesis that the quantity of eggs produced is related to the price of eggs is an example of a functional relation in economics. In its most general form, it merely says that quantity produced is related to price. A more specific hypothesis may be that as the price of eggs falls, the quantity produced will also fall. In other words, in this hypothesis price and quantity vary *positively* with each other. In the case of many hypotheses of this kind, economists can be even more specific about the nature of the functional relation. On the basis of detailed factual studies, economists often have a pretty good idea of by *how much* quantity produced will change as a result of specified changes in price—that is, they can predict magnitude as well as direction.

Predictions

A scientific prediction is not the same thing as a prophecy.

A scientific prediction is a conditional statement that takes the form: *If* you do this, *then* such and such will follow.

If hydrogen and oxygen are mixed under specified conditions, *then* water will be the result. *If* the government has a large budget deficit, *then* the unemployment rate will fall. It is most important to realize that this prediction is very different from the statement: "I prophesy that in two years' time there will be a large decrease in unemployment because the government will decide to have a large

[1] The appendixes for each chapter appear starting on page A-1. The appendix to this chapter (page A-3) gives a more detailed discussion of functional relations and the use of graphs in economics.

BOX 2–2 CAN HYPOTHESES BE PROVED OR REFUTED?

Most hypotheses in economics are universal statements. They say that whenever certain specified conditions are fulfilled, cause X will always produce effect Y. Such universal hypotheses cannot be proved correct with 100 percent certainty. No matter how many observations are collected that agree with the hypothesis, there is always some chance that a long series of untypical observations has been made or that there have been systematic errors of observation. After all, the mass of well-documented evidence accumulated several centuries ago on the existence of the power of witches is no longer accepted, even though it fully satisfied most contemporary observers. The existence of observational errors—even on a vast scale—has been shown to be possible, although (one fervently hopes) it is not very frequent. Observations that disagree with the theory may begin to accumulate, and after some time a theory that looked certain may begin to look rather shaky.

By the same token a universal hypothesis can never be proved false with 100 percent certainty. Even when current observations consistently conflict with the theory, it is still possible that a large number of untypical cases or systematic errors of observation has been selected. For instance, evidence was once gathered "disprov-

ing" the hypothesis that high income taxes tend to discourage work. More recent research suggests that economists may have been wrong to reject the theory that high taxes tend to discourage work. As a result of measurement errors and bad experimental design, the conflicting evidence may not have been as decisive as was once thought.

There is no absolute certainty in any knowledge. No doubt some of the things we now think true will eventually turn out to be false, and some of the things we currently think false will eventually turn out to be true. Yet while we can never be certain, we can assess the balance of evidence.

Some hypotheses are so unlikely to be true, given current evidence, that for all practical purposes we may regard them as false. Other hypotheses are so unlikely to be false, given current evidence, that for all practical purposes we may regard them as true.

This kind of practical decision must always be regarded as tentative. Every once in a while we will find that we have to change our mind: Something that looked right will begin to look doubtful, or something that looked wrong will begin to look possible.

budget deficit." The government's decision to have a budget deficit or surplus in two years' time will be the outcome of many emotions, objective circumstances, chance occurrences, and so on, few of which can be predicted by the economist. If the economist's prophecy about the level of unemployment turns out to be wrong because in two years' time the government does not have a large deficit, then all that has been learned is that the economist is not a good guesser about the behavior of the government. However, *if* the government does have a large deficit (in two years' time or at any other time) and *then* the rate of unemployment does

not decrease, a conditional scientific prediction has been contradicted.

Testing Theories

A theory is tested by confronting its predictions with evidence. It is necessary to discover if certain events are followed by the consequences predicted by the theory. For example, is an increase in the government's budget deficit followed by a decrease in unemployment? Box 2-2 gives a more detailed discussion of testing economic theories.

Generally, theories tend to be abandoned when

FIGURE 2-1
The Interaction of Deduction and Measurement in Theorizing

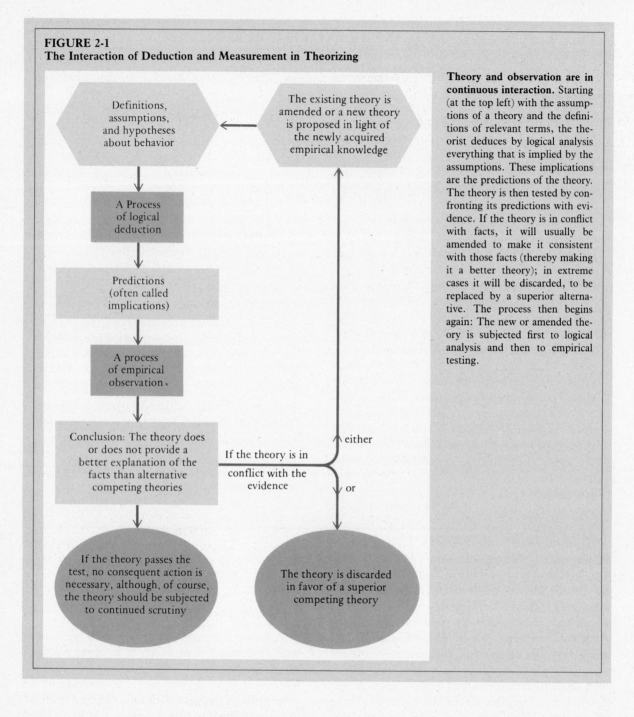

Theory and observation are in continuous interaction. Starting (at the top left) with the assumptions of a theory and the definitions of relevant terms, the theorist deduces by logical analysis everything that is implied by the assumptions. These implications are the predictions of the theory. The theory is then tested by confronting its predictions with evidence. If the theory is in conflict with facts, it will usually be amended to make it consistent with those facts (thereby making it a better theory); in extreme cases it will be discarded, to be replaced by a superior alternative. The process then begins again: The new or amended theory is subjected first to logical analysis and then to empirical testing.

they are no longer useful. And theories cease to be useful when they cannot predict the consequences of actions in which one is interested better than the next best alternative. When a theory consistently fails to predict better than the available alternatives, it is either modified or replaced. Figure 2-1 summarizes the discussion of theories.

Economics As a Developing Science

Economics is like other sciences in at least two respects. First, there are many observations of the world for which there are, at the moment, no fully satisfactory theoretical explanations. Second, there are many predictions that no one has yet satisfactorily tested. Serious students of economics must not expect to find a set of answers to all their questions as they progress in their study. Very often they must expect to encounter nothing more than a set of problems that provides an agenda for further research. Even when they do find answers to problems, they should accept these answers as tentative and ask even of the most time-honored theory, "What observations would be in conflict with this theory?"

Economics is still a young science. On the one hand, economists know a good deal about the behavior of the economy. On the other hand, many problems are almost untouched. Students who decide to specialize in economics may find themselves, only a few years from now, formulating a theory to account for some of the problems mentioned in this book; or they may end up making a set of observations that will upset some venerable theory described in these pages.

A final word of warning: Having counseled a constructive disrespect for the authority of accepted theory, it is necessary to warn against adopting an approach that is too cavalier. No respect attaches to the person who says, "This theory is for the birds; it is *obviously* wrong." This is too cheap. To criticize a theory effectively on empirical grounds, one must demonstrate, by a careful set of observations, that some aspect of the theory is contradicted by the facts. This is a task worth attempting, but it is seldom easily accomplished.

SUMMARY

1. It is possible, and fruitful, to distinguish between positive and normative statements. Positive statements concern what is, was, or will be, while normative statements concern what ought to be. Disagreements over positive statements are appropriately settled by an appeal to the facts.

2. The success of scientific inquiry depends on separating positive questions about the way the world works from normative questions about how one would like the world to work, then formulating positive questions precisely enough so that they can be settled by an appeal to evidence and by finding means of gathering the necessary evidence.

3. Some people feel that although natural phenomena can be subject to scientific inquiry and "laws" of behavior, human phenomena cannot. The evidence, however, is otherwise. Social scientists have observed many stable human behavior patterns. These form the basis for successful predictions of how people will behave under certain conditions.

4. The fact that people sometimes act strangely, even capriciously, does not destroy the possibility of a scientific study of group behavior. Indeed, the odd and inexplicable things that one person does will tend to cancel out the odd and inexplicable things that another person does.

5. Theories are designed to give meaning and coherence to observed sequences of events. Theories thus pervade all attempts to explain events. A theory consists of a set of definitions of the variables to be employed, a set of assumptions about how things behave. Any theory has certain logical implications that must be true if the theory is true. These are the theory's predictions.

6. A theory provides predictions of the type "*if* one event occurs, *then* another event will also occur." An important method of testing theories is to confront their predictions with evidence. The progress of any science lies in finding better explanations of events than are now available. Thus, in any developing science, one must expect to discard present theories and replace them with demonstrably superior alternatives. Such a process improves the quality of the explanations.

7. The important concept of a functional relation is discussed in more detail in the appendix to this chapter, which begins on page A-3.

TOPICS FOR REVIEW

Positive and normative statements
Testable statements
The law of large numbers, and the predictability of human behavior
The roles of variables, assumptions, and predictions in theorizing
Endogenous and exogenous variables
Stock and flow variables
Functional relations
The scientific approach
Prediction versus prophecy

DISCUSSION QUESTIONS

1. A baby doesn't ''know'' of the theory of gravity, yet in walking and eating the child soon learns to use its principles. Distinguish between behavior and causation of behavior. Does a business executive or a farmer have to understand economic theory to behave in a pattern consistent with economic theory?
2. ''If human behavior were completely capricious and unpredictable, life insurance could not be a profitable business.''

Explain. Can you think of any businesses that do *not* depend on predictable human behavior?
3. Write five statements about inflation. (It does not matter whether the statements are correct, but you should confine yourself to those you think might be correct.) Classify each statement as positive or normative. If your list contains only one type of statement, try to add a sixth statement of the other type. Check the validity of your positive statements as well as you can against the data given in this text (see *Inflation* in the index). If you are not yet satisfied of their validity, outline how you would go about completing the test of your statements.
4. Each of the following unrealistic assumptions is sometimes made. See if you can visualize situations in which each of them might be useful.
    a. The earth is a plane.
    b. There are no differences between men and women.
    c. There is no tomorrow.
    d. People are wholly selfish.
5. ''The following theory of wage determination proceeds on the assumption that labor unions do not exist.'' Of what use can such a theory be in Canada today?
6. What may first appear to be untestable statements can often be reworded so that they can be tested by an appeal to evidence. How might you do that with respect to each of the following assertions?
    a. The Canadian economic system is the best in the world.
    b. The provision of free medical care for more and more people will inevitably end in socialized medicine for all, and socialized medicine will destroy our standards of medical practice by destroying the doctor's incentive to do his or her job well.
    c. Robotics ought to be outlawed, because it will destroy the future of the working classes.
    d. Inflation is ruining the standard of living of the Canadian worker and destroying the integrity of the family.

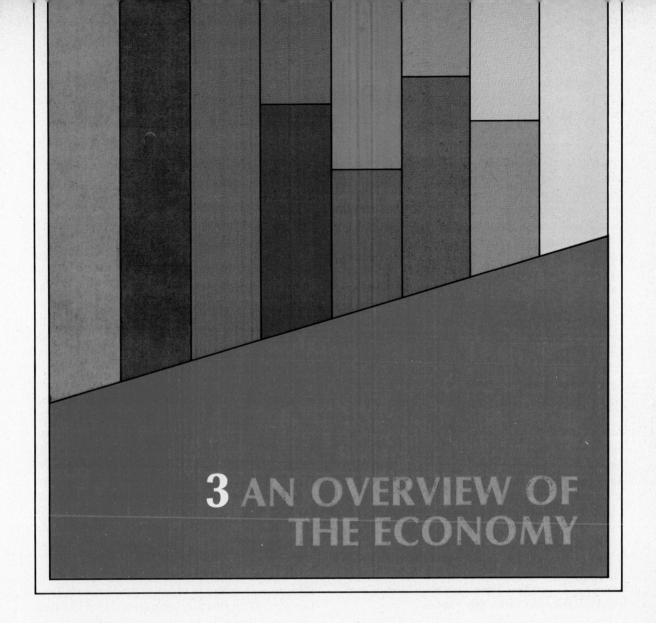

3 AN OVERVIEW OF THE ECONOMY

The Evolution of Market Economies

Until about 10,000 years ago, virtually all human societies were based on food gathering. Ten thousand years represents little more than an instant in the millions of years in which humanoid creatures have been on earth. Settlement began with the original agricultural revolution, when human beings first found it possible to stay in one place and survive. Gradually abandoning their nomadic life of hunting and food gathering, people settled down to tend crops that they had learned to plant and animals that they had learned to domesticate. Since that time all societies have faced the problem of choice under conditions of scarcity.

Surplus, Specialization, and Trade

Along with permanent settlement, the agricultural revolution brought surplus production. Farmers could produce substantially more than they needed for survival. The agricultural surplus allowed the creation of new occupations and thus new economic and social classes such as artisans, soldiers, priests, and government officials. Freed from having to grow their own food, these new classes turned their talents to performing specialized services and producing goods other than food. They also produced more than they themselves needed, so they traded the excess to obtain whatever other goods they required.

The allocation of different jobs to different people is called **specialization of labor.** Specialization has proven extraordinarily efficient compared with self-sufficiency for at least two reasons. First, individual talents and abilities differ, and specialization allows each person to do the job he or she can do relatively best, while leaving everything else to be done by others. People not only do their own thing; they do their own best thing. Second, a person who concentrates on one activity becomes better at it than could a jack-of-all-trades.

The exchange of goods and services in early societies commonly took place by simple mutual agreement among neighbors. In the course of time, however, trading became centered in particular gathering places called markets. Today we use the term **market economy** to refer to a society in which people specialize in productive activities and meet most of their material wants through exchanges voluntarily agreed upon by the contracting parties.

Specialization must be accompanied by trade. People who produce only one thing must trade most of it to obtain all the other things they require.

The earliest market economies depended on **barter,** the trading of goods directly for other goods. But barter can be very costly in terms of time spent searching out satisfactory exchanges. When money evolved, it made trade easier. Money eliminates the inconvenience of barter by allowing the two sides of the transaction to be separated. If a farmer has wheat and wants a hammer, he does not have to search for an individual who has a hammer and wants wheat. He merely has to find someone who wants wheat. The farmer takes money in exchange, then finds another person who wishes to trade a hammer and swaps the money for the hammer.

By eliminating the need for barter, money greatly facilitates trade and specialization.

The Division of Labor

Market transactions in early economies mainly involved consumption goods. Producers specialized in making a commodity and then traded it for the other products they needed. The labor services required to make the product would usually be provided by the makers themselves, by apprentices learning to be craftsmen, or by slaves. Over the last several hundred years, many technical advances in methods of production have made it efficient to organize agriculture and industry on a large scale. These technical developments have made use of what is called the **division of labor,** which is a further step in the specialization of labor. This term refers to specialization within the production process of a particular commodity. The labor involved is divided into a series of repetitive tasks, and each individual does a single task that may be just one of hundreds of tasks necessary to produce the commodity. Today it is possible for an individual to work on a production line without knowing what commodity emerges at the end of that line!

To gain the advantages of the division of labor, it became necessary to organize production in large factories. With this development workers lost their status as craftsmen and became members of the working class, wholly dependent on their ability to sell their labor to factory owners and lacking a plot of land to fall back on for subsistence in times of need. The day of small craftsmen who made and sold their own goods was over. Today's typical workers do not earn their incomes by selling commodities they personally have produced; rather they sell their labor services to firms and receive money wages in return. They have increasingly become cogs in a machine they do not fully understand or control. Adam Smith, the eighteenth cen-

BOX 3–1 THE DIVISION OF LABOR

Adam Smith began *The Wealth of Nations* with a long study of the division of labor. Among other things, he had this to say.

The greatest improvements in the productive powers of labour . . . have been the effects of the division of labour.

To take an example . . . the trade of the pinmaker; a workman not educated to this business (which the division of labour has rendered a distinct trade), nor acquainted with the use of the machinery employed in it could scarce, perhaps, with his utmost industry, make one pin in a day, and certainly could not make twenty. But in the way in which this business is now carried on . . . it is divided into a number of branches. . . . One man draws out the wire, another straightens it, a third cuts it, a fourth points it, a fifth grinds it at the top for receiving the head; to make the head requires two or three distinct operations; to put it on, is a peculiar business, to whiten the pins is another; it is even a trade by itself to put them into the paper; and the important business of making a pin is, in this manner, divided into about eighteen distinct operations, which, in some manufactories, are all performed by distinct hands, though in others the same man will sometimes perform two or three of them.

Smith observes that even in small factories, where the division of labor is exploited only in part, output is as high as 4,800 pins per person per day!

Later Smith discusses the general importance of the division of labor and the forces that limit its application.

Each animal is still obliged to support and defend itself, separately and independently, and derives no sort of advantage from that variety of talents with which nature has distinguished its fellows. Among men, on the contrary, the most dissimilar geniuses are of use to one another; the different products of their respective talents, by the general disposition to truck, barter, and exchange, being brought, as it were, into a common stock, where every man may purchase whatever part of the produce of other men's talents he has occasion for.

As it is the power of exchanging that gives occasion to the division of labour, so the extent of this division must always be limited by the extent of that power, or, in other words, by the extent of the market. When the market is very small, no person can have any encouragement to dedicate himself entirely to one employment for want [i.e., lack] of the power to exchange all that surplus part of the produce of his own labour, which is over and above his own consumption, for such parts of the produce of other men's labour as he has occasion for.

Smith notes that there is no point in specializing to produce a large quantity of pins, or anything else, unless there are enough persons making other commodities to provide a market for all the pins that are produced. Thus, the larger the market, the greater the scope for the division of labor and the higher the resulting opportunities for efficient production.

tury Scottish political economist, was the first to develop the idea of the division of labor, as discussed in Box 3-1.

Markets and the Allocation of Resources

The term **resource allocation** refers to the way in which the available factors of production are distributed among the various uses to which they might be put. There are not enough resources to produce all the goods and services that could be consumed. It is therefore necessary to allocate the available resources among their various possible uses and in so doing to choose what to produce and what not to produce. In a market economy, millions of consumers decide what commodities to buy and in what quantities; a vast number of firms produce these commodities and buy the factor services that are needed to make them; and millions of factor owners decide to whom they will sell these services. These individual decisions collectively determine the economy's allocation of resources.

In a market economy, the allocation of resources is the outcome of countless independent decisions made by consumers and producers, all acting through the medium of markets.

Our main objective in this chapter is to provide an overview of this market mechanism.

THE DECISION MAKERS

Economics is about the behavior of people. Much that we observe in the world and that economists assume in their theories can be traced back to decisions made by individuals. There are millions of individuals in most economies. To make a systematic study of their behavior more manageable, we categorize them into three important groups: households, firms, and the government (central authorities).[1] These groups are economic theory's cast of characters, and the market is the stage on which their play is enacted.

Households

A **household** is defined as all the people who live under one roof and who make, or are subject to others making for them, joint financial decisions. The members of households are often referred to as consumers. Economic theory gives households a number of attributes.

First, economists assume that each household makes consistent decisions, as though it consisted of a single individual. Thus economists ignore many interesting problems of how the household reaches its decisions. Family conflicts and the moral and legal problems concerning parental control over minors are dealt with by other social sciences.[2] These problems are avoided in economics by the assumption that the household is the basic decision-making atom of consumption behavior.

Second, economists assume that each household is attempting to achieve the goal of maximizing its *satisfaction* or *well-being* or *utility,* as the concept is variously called. The household tries to do this within the limitations of its available resources.

Third, economists assume that households are the ultimate owners of factors of production. They sell the services of these factors to firms and receive their incomes in return.

Firms

A **firm** is defined as the unit that employs factors of production to produce commodities that it sells to other firms, to households, or to government. For obvious reasons a firm is often called a *producer.* Economic theory gives firms several attributes.

First, economists assume that each firm makes consistent decisions, as though it were a single individual. Thus economics ignores the internal problems of how particular decisions are reached. In doing this, economists assume that the firm's internal organization is irrelevant to its decisions. This allows them to treat the firm as the atom of behavior on the production or supply side of commodity markets, just as the household is treated as the atom of behavior on the consumption or demand side.

Second, economists assume that most firms make their decisions with a single goal in mind: to make as much profit as possible. This goal of *profit maximization* is analogous to the household's goal of utility maximization.

Third, economists assume that firms, in their

---

[1] Although in basic economic theory we can get away with three sets of decision makers, it is worth noting that there are others. Probably the most important are such nonprofit organizations as private universities and hospitals, charities such as the Canadian Cancer Society, and funding organizations such as the Donner Foundation. These bodies are responsible for allocating some of the economy's resources.

[2] In academic work, as elsewhere, a division of labor is useful. However, it is important to remember that when economists speak of *the* consumer or *the* individual, they are in fact referring to the group of individuals composing the household. Thus, for example, the commonly heard phrase *consumer sovereignty* really means *household sovereignty.*

role as producers, are the principal users of the services of factors of production. In markets where factor services are bought and sold, the roles of firms and households are thus reversed from what they are in commodity markets: In factor markets firms do the buying and households do the selling.

Government (Central Authorities)

The term **government** is used in economics in a very broad sense to include all public officials, agencies, government bodies, and other organizations belonging to or under the direct control of governments. Provincial and municipal governments, as well as the federal government, are included. In Canada the term *government* also includes the prime minister, the cabinet, the Bank of Canada, the city council, commissions and regulatory bodies, the legislature, and the police force, among others. Sometimes this broad concept of government is referred to by the more descriptive term **central authorities.** It is not important to draw up a comprehensive list, but one should have in mind a general idea of the organizations that have legal and political power to exert control over individual decision makers and over markets.

It is *not* a basic assumption of economics that the government always acts in a consistent fashion or as though it were a single individual. Two important reasons for this may be mentioned here. First, the mayor of Saint John, an Alberta legislator, and a member of Parliament from Quebec represent different constituencies, and therefore they may express different and conflicting views and objectives.

Second, individual public servants, whether elected or appointed, have personal objectives (such as staying in office, achieving higher office, power, prestige, and personal aggrandizement) as well as public service objectives. Although the balance of importance given to the two types of objectives will vary among persons and among types of office, both will almost always have some importance. It would be a rare MP, for example, who would vote against a measure that slightly reduced the "public good" if this vote almost guaranteed

his defeat at the next election. ("After all," he could reason, "if I am defeated, I won't be around to vote against *really* bad measures.")

MARKETS AND ECONOMIES

We have seen that households, firms, and the government are the main actors in the economic drama. Their action takes place in markets.

Markets

The word *market* originally designated a place where goods were traded. The St. Lawrence Market in Toronto is a famous modern example of markets in the everyday sense, and most cities have produce markets. Much early economic theory attempted to explain price behavior in just such markets. Why, for example, can you sometimes obtain bargains at the end of the day and at other times get what you want only at prices that appear exorbitant relative to prices quoted only a few hours before?

As theories of market behavior were developed, they were extended to cover commodities such as wheat. Wheat produced anywhere in the world can be purchased almost anywhere else in the world, and the price of a given grade of wheat tends to be nearly uniform the world over. When we talk about the wheat market, the concept of a market has been extended well beyond the idea of a single place to which the producer, the storekeeper, and the homemaker go to sell and buy.

Economists distinguish two broad types of markets: **product markets,** in which firms sell their outputs of goods and services, and **factor markets,** in which households sell the services of the factors of production they control.

Economies

An **economy** is rather loosely defined as a set of interrelated production and consumption activities. It may refer to activity in a region of one country (*the economy of the Maritimes*), in a country (*the Canadian economy*), or in a group of countries (*the economy of Western Europe*). In any economy the allocation of resources is determined by the production, sales, and purchase decisions made by firms, households, and the government.

A **free-market economy** is an economy in which the decisions of individual households and firms (as distinct from the government) exert the major influence over the allocation of resources.[3]

The opposite of a free-market economy is a **command economy,** in which the major decisions about the allocation of resources are made by the government and in which firms and households produce and consume only as they are ordered.

The terms *free-market* and *command economy* are used to describe tendencies that are apparent, even though no real economies rely solely on either free markets or commands. Thus in practice all economies are **mixed economies** in the sense that some decisions are made by firms and households and some by the government.

Sectors of an Economy

The parts of an economy are usually referred to as **sectors** of that economy. For example, the agricultural sector is the part of the economy that produces agricultural commodities.

Market and Nonmarket Sectors

Producers make commodities. Consumers use them. Commodities may pass from one group to the other in two ways: they may be sold by producers and bought by consumers through markets, or they may be given away.

When commodities are bought and sold, producers must cover their costs with the revenue they obtain from selling the product. We call this *marketed production,* and we refer to this part of the country's activity as belonging to the **market sector.**

When the product is given away, the costs of production must be covered from some source other than sales revenue. We call this *nonmarketed production,* and we refer to this part of the country's activity as belonging to the **nonmarket sector.** In the case of private charities, the money required to pay for factor services may be raised from the public by voluntary contributions. In the case of production by the government—which accounts for the bulk of nonmarketed production—the money is provided from government revenue, which in turn comes mainly from taxes.

Whenever a government enterprise *sells* its output, its production is in the market sector. But much state output is in the nonmarket sector by the very nature of the product provided. For example, one could hardly expect the criminal to pay the judge for providing the service of criminal justice. Other products are in the nonmarket sector because governments have decided that there are advantages to removing them from the market sector. This is the case, for example, with education. Public policy places it in the nonmarket sector even though much of it could be provided by the market sector.

The Private and Public Sectors

An alternative division of a country's productive activity is between private and public sectors. The **private sector** refers to all production that is in private hands and the **public sector** refers to all production that is in public hands. The distinction between the two sectors depends on the legal distinction of ownership. In the private sector, the organization that does the producing is owned by households or other firms; in the public sector, it is owned by the state. The public sector includes all production of goods and services by the government plus all production by government-operated industries that is sold to consumers through ordinary markets.

[3] Free-market economies are sometimes called *capitalist economies;* in fact, the term *capitalist* often is used as a synonym for *free market.* In Marxist literature, *capitalist* refers to the private ownership of the factor of production, called *capital.* But it is possible to be capitalist in Marx's sense of the word and yet have overwhelming public intervention into markets. Thus, *capitalist* (private ownership of capital) does not mean the same as *free* (uncontrolled) *market.* For most purposes of modern economies, it is who controls the markets rather than who owns the capital that is the important matter.

The distinction between market and nonmarket sectors is economic: it depends on whether or not the costs of producing commodities are recovered by selling them to users. The distinction between the private and public sectors is legal: it depends on whether the producing organizations are privately or publicly owned.

MICROECONOMICS AND MACROECONOMICS

An Overview of Microeconomics

Early economists observed the market economy with wonder. They saw that most commodities were made by a large number of independent producers and yet in approximately the quantities that people wanted to purchase them. Natural disasters aside, there were neither vast surpluses nor severe shortages of products. They also saw that in spite of the ever-changing requirements in terms of geographical, industrial, and occupational patterns, most laborers were able to sell their services to employers most of the time.

How does the market produce this order in the absence of conscious coordination by the government? It is one thing to have the same good produced year in and year out when people's wants and incomes do not change; it is quite another thing to have production adjusting continually to changing wants, incomes, and techniques of production. Yet this relatively smooth adjustment is accomplished by the market—albeit with occasional, and sometimes serious, interruptions.

The great discovery of eighteenth century economists was that the price system is a social control mechanism.

Adam Smith, in his classic *The Wealth of Nations*, published in 1776, spoke of the price system as "the invisible hand." It allows decision making to be decentralized under the control of millions of individual producers and consumers but nonetheless to be coordinated. Two examples may help to illustrate how this coordination occurs.

A Change in Demand

For the first example, assume that households wish to purchase more of some commodity than previously. To see the market's reaction to such a change, imagine a situation in which farmers find it equally profitable to produce either of two crops, carrots or brussels sprouts, and so are willing to produce some of both commodities, thereby satisfying the demands of households who wish to consume both. Now imagine that consumers develop a greatly increased desire for brussels sprouts and a diminished desire for carrots. This change might have occurred because of the discovery of hitherto unsuspected nutritive or curative powers of brussels sprouts.

When consumers buy more brussels sprouts and fewer carrots, a shortage of brussels sprouts and a glut of carrots develop. To unload their surplus stocks of carrots, merchants reduce the price of carrots—in the belief that it is better to sell them at a reduced price than not to sell them at all. Sellers of brussels sprouts, however, find that they are unable to satisfy all their customers' demands for that product. Sprouts have become scarce, so merchants charge more for them. As the price rises, fewer people are willing and able to purchase sprouts. Thus making them more expensive limits the demand for them to the available supply.

Farmers see a rise in the price of brussels sprouts and a fall in the price of carrots. Brussels sprout production has become more profitable than in the past: The costs of producing sprouts remain unchanged at the same time that their market price has risen. Similarly, carrot production will be less profitable than in the past because costs are unchanged but the price has fallen. Attracted by high profits in brussels sprouts and deterred by low profits or potential losses in carrots, farmers expand the production of sprouts and curtail carrot production. Thus the change in consumers' tastes, working through the price system, causes a reallocation of resources—land and labor—out of carrot production and into brussels sprout production.

As the production of carrots declines, the glut of carrots on the market diminishes and their price begins to rise. On the other hand, the expansion in brussels sprout production reduces the shortage and the price begins to fall. These price movements will continue until it no longer pays farmers to contract carrot production and to expand brussels sprout production. When the dust settles, the price of sprouts is higher than it was originally but lower than it was when the shortage sent the price soaring before output could be adjusted; and the price of carrots is lower than it was originally but higher than when the initial glut sent the price tumbling before output could be adjusted.

The reaction of the market to a change in demand leads to a transfer of resources. Carrot producers reduce their production; they will therefore be laying off workers and generally demanding fewer factors of production. Brussels sprout producers expand production; they will therefore be hiring workers and generally increasing their demand for factors of production.

Labor can probably switch from carrot to sprout production without much difficulty. Certain types of land, however, may be better suited for growing one crop than the other. When farmers increase their sprout production, their demands for those factors especially suited to sprout growing also increase—and this creates a shortage of these resources and a consequent rise in their prices. Meanwhile, with carrot production falling, the demand for land and other factors of production especially suited to carrot growing is reduced. A surplus results, and the prices of these factors are forced down.

Thus factors particularly suited to sprout production will earn more and will obtain a higher share of total national income than before. Factors particularly suited to carrot production, however, will earn less and will obtain a smaller share of the total national income than before.

Changes of this kind will be studied more fully later; the important thing to notice now is how a change in demand initiated by a change in consumers' tastes causes a reallocation of resources in the direction required to cater to the new set of tastes.

A Change in Supply

For a second example, consider a change originating with producers. Begin as before by imagining a situation in which farmers find it equally

profitable to produce either sprouts or carrots and in which consumers are willing to buy, at prevailing prices, the quantities of these two commodities that are being produced. Now imagine that, at existing prices, farmers become more willing to produce sprouts than in the past and less willing to produce carrots. This shift might be caused, for example, by a change in the costs of producing the two goods—a rise in carrot costs and a fall in sprout costs that would raise the profitability of sprout production and lower that of carrot production.

What will happen now? For a short time, nothing at all; the existing supply of sprouts and carrots on the market is the result of decisions made by farmers at some time in the past. But farmers now begin to plant fewer carrots and more sprouts, and soon the quantities on the market begin to change. The quantity of sprouts available for sale rises, and the quantity of carrots falls. A shortage of carrots and a glut of sprouts results. The price of carrots consequently rises, and the price of sprouts falls. This provides the incentive for two types of adjustments. First, households will buy fewer carrots and more sprouts. Second, farmers will move back into carrot production and out of sprouts.

This example began with a situation in which there was a shortage of carrots that caused the price of carrots to rise. The rise in the price of carrots removed the shortage in two ways: It reduced the quantity of carrots demanded and it increased the quantity offered for sale (in response to the rise in the profitability of carrot production). Remember that there was also a surplus of brussels sprouts that caused the price to fall. The fall in price removed the surplus in two ways: It encouraged consumers to buy more of this commodity and it reduced the quantity of sprouts produced and offered for sale (in response to a fall in the profitability of sprout production).

These examples illustrate a general point:

The price system is a mechanism that coordinates individual, decentralized decisions.

The existence of such a control mechanism is beyond dispute. How well it works in comparison with alternative coordinating systems has been in serious dispute for over a hundred years. It remains today a major unsettled social question.

Microeconomics and Macroeconomics Compared

Microeconomics and macroeconomics differ in the questions each asks and in the level of aggregation each uses.

Microeconomics deals with the determination of prices and quantities in individual markets and with the relations among these markets. Thus it looks at the details of the market economy. It asks, for example, how much labor is employed in the fast food industry and why that amount is increasing. It asks about the determinants of the output of brussels sprouts, pocket calculators, automobiles, and Mother's Pizzas. It asks, too, about the prices of these things—why some prices go up and others down. Economists interested in microeconomics analyze how prices and outputs respond to exogenous shocks caused by events in other markets or government policy. They ask, for example, how a new innovation, a government subsidy, or a drought will affect the price and output of beet sugar and the employment of farm workers.

In contrast, macroeconomists focus their attention on much broader aggregates. They look at such things as the total number of people employed and unemployed, at the average level of prices and how it changes over time, at national output, and at aggregate consumption. Macroeconomics ask what determines these aggregates and how they respond to changing conditions. Whereas microeconomics looks at demand and supply with regard to particular commodities, macroeconomics looks at *aggregate* demand and *aggregate* supply.

An Overview of Macroeconomics

We can group together all the buyers of the nation's output and call their total desired purchases **aggregate demand**. We can also group together all the producers of the nation's output and call their total desired sales **aggregate supply**. Explaining the magnitude of these and why they change are among the major problems of macroeconomics. The consequences of such changes can be serious.

Major changes in aggregate demand are called *demand shocks*, while major changes in aggregate supply are called *supply shocks*. When these shocks occur there will be important changes in the broad averages and aggregates, including total output, total employment, and the average levels of prices and wages, that are the concern of macroeconomics. Government actions sometimes are the *cause* of demand or supply shocks. At other times they are reactions to such shocks and are used in an attempt to cushion or change the effects of such shocks.

The Circular Flow of Income

One way to gain insight into aggregate demand and aggregate supply is to view the economy as a giant set of flows. A major part of aggregate demand arises from the purchases of consumption commodities by the nation's households. These purchases generate income for the firms that produce and sell commodities for consumption. A major part of aggregate supply arises from the production and sale of consumption goods by the nation's firms. This production generates income for all the factors that are employed in making these goods.

The black portion of Figure 3-1 focuses on firms and households, and on two sets of markets—factor markets and product markets—through which their decisions are coordinated. Consider households first. The members of households want commodities to keep them fed, clothed, housed, entertained, healthy, and secure. They also want commodities to educate, edify, beautify, stupefy, and otherwise amuse them. Households have resources with which to attempt to satisfy these wants. But not all their wants can be satisfied with the resources available. Households are forced, therefore, to make choices as to what goods and services to buy in product markets that offer them myriad ways to spend their incomes.

Now consider firms. They must choose among the products they might produce and sell, among the ways of producing them, and among the var-

FIGURE 3-1
The Circular Flow of Expenditures and Income

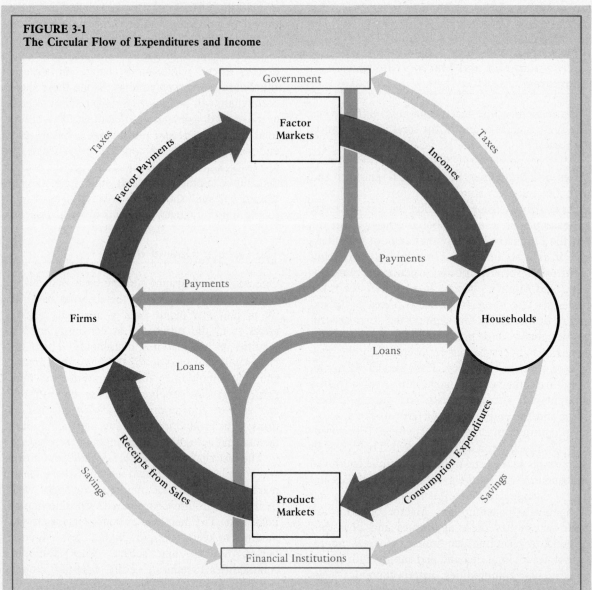

The interaction of firms and households in product and factor markets generates a flow of expenditure and income. These flows are also influenced by other institutions such as governments and the financial system. Factor services are sold by households through factor markets, which leads to a flow of income from firms to households. Commodities are sold by firms through product markets, which leads to a flow of receipts from households to firms. If these primary flows, shown by the dark gray shaded arrows, were the only flows, the circular flow would be a closed system. But other institutions, such as governments and financial institutions, play roles. For example, governments may inject funds in the form of government payments to households and firms, and banks may inject funds in the form of loans to households and firms for investment expenditures. Such *injections* are illustrated by the dark color arrows. Similarly, governments may withdraw funds in the form of taxes, and financial institutions may do so by accepting funds that households and firms wish to save. Such *withdrawals* are illustrated by the light color arrows.

ious quantities (and qualities) they can supply. Firms must also buy factors of production. Payments by firms to factor owners provide the owners of the factors with incomes. The recipients of these incomes are households whose members want commodities to keep them fed, clothed, housed, entertained. We have now come full circle!

The action of this drama involves firms and households inextricably bound up with one another. Payments flow from households to firms through product markets and back to households again through factor markets.

If the economy consisted only of households and firms, if households spent *all* the income they received on buying goods and services produced by firms, and if firms distributed *all* their receipts to households either by purchasing factor services or by distributing profits to owners, then the circular flow would be very simple indeed. All household receipts would be passed on to firms, and all firm receipts would be passed back to households. The circular flow would be a completely closed system; aggregate demand and aggregate supply would consist only of consumption goods; and macroeconomics would involve little more than measuring the flows of production of and expenditure on consumption goods.

The circular flow is not, however, a completely closed system. First, households do not spend all their income. Some of the income is saved. These savings pass through financial markets and into the hands of firms and governments who borrow the funds and spend them. Some of household income goes to governments as income taxes and so is not available to be spent by households. These two *leakages* from the circular flow are shown by the light-colored arrows flowing out of the households in Figure 3-1. As a result, total household demand for consumption goods and services falls short of total household income.

The second reason why the circular flow is not a closed system is that there are elements of aggregate demand that do not arise from household spending and hence elements of aggregate supply that are not produced for the purpose of meeting household demand. The two main additional elements are investment and government expenditure.[4] A major element of aggregate demand stems from firms who borrow in order to purchase such investment goods as plant and equipment. A further major component of aggregate demand comes from governments—Federal, Provincial, and Municipal. They add to total expenditure on the nation's output by requiring the production of a whole range of goods and services from national defense through the provision of justice to the building of roads and schools. These two major additions to the circular flow of income are shown by the dark-colored arrows flowing into the firms in Figure 3-1. The production of government and investment goods produces incomes for households in the same way as the production of consumption goods.

When any of these elements of aggregate demand changes, aggregate output and total income earned by households are likely to change as a result. Thus, studying the determinants of total consumption, investment, and government spending is crucial to understanding the causes of changes both in the nation's total output and in the employment generated by the production of that output.

The Next Step

Soon you will be going on to study either micro- or macroeconomics. Whichever branch of the subject you study first, it is important to remember that micro- and macroeconomics are complementary, not competing, theories and that both are needed for a full understanding of the functioning of a moden economy.

SUMMARY

1. This chapter provides an overview of the workings of the market economy. Modern economies

[4] Additional elements related to international trade are discussed later.

are based on the specialization and division of labor, which necessitate the exchange of goods and services. Exchange takes place in markets and is facilitated by the use of money. Much of economics is devoted to a study of how markets work to coordinate millions of individual, decentralized decisions.

2. In economic theory, three kinds of decision makers—households, firms, and government—interact in markets. Households are assumed to maximize their satisfaction (to the best of their ability) and firms to maximize their profits, but government may have multiple objectives.

3. A free-market economy is one in which the allocation of resources is determined by the production, sales, and purchasing decisions made by firms and households acting in response to such market signals as prices and profits.

4. Subdivisions of an economy are called sectors. Economies are commonly divided into market and nonmarket sectors and into public and private sectors. These divisions cut across each other; the first is based on the economic distinction of how costs are covered, and the second is based on a legal distinction of ownership.

5. It is common to distinguish microeconomics and macroeconomics. Microeconomics deals with the determination of prices and quantities in individual markets and the relations among those markets. In a general way it is concerned with the price system, which provides a set of signals that reflects changes in demand and supply and to which producers and consumers can react in an individual but nonetheless coordinated manner.

6. The microeconomic interactions between households and firms through markets may be illustrated in a circular flow diagram that traces money flows between households and firms. These flows are the starting point for studying the circular flows of aggregate income that are key elements of macroeconomics.

7. A key difference between micro- and macroeconomics is in the level of aggregation to which

attention is directed. Microeconomics looks at prices and quantities in individual markets and how they respond to various shocks that impinge on those markets. Macroeconomics looks at broader aggregates such as aggregate consumption, employment and unemployment, and the rate of change of the price level.

8. The circular flow of income focuses on the "circle" running from household purchases of consumption goods which generate income for firms whose payments to factors then flow back to the households as income. This circular flow is not a simple closed system because not all income received by households is spent for the output of firms and some receipts of firms are not paid out to households. Also, some payments to firms do not result from the spending of households and some payments to households do not result from the spending of firms. The flows of expenditure in the economy determine total output, total income, and total employment.

9. The questions asked in micro- and macroeconomics may differ, but they are complementary parts of economic theory. They study different aspects of a single economic system, and both are needed for an understanding of the whole.

TOPICS FOR REVIEW

Specialization and the division of labor
Economic decision makers
Markets and market economies
Market and nonmarket sectors
The private and public sectors
The price system as a social control mechanism
The relation between microeconomics and macroeconomics
The circular flow of income

DISCUSSION QUESTIONS

1. Suggest some examples of specialization and division of labor among people you know.
2. There is a greater variety of specialists and specialty stores

in large cities than in small cities having populations with the same average income. Explain this in economic terms.

3. Define the household of which you are a member. Consider your household's income last year. What proportion of it came from the sale of factor services to firms? Identify the other sources of income. Approximately what proportion of the expenditures by your household became income for firms?

4. "It is not from the benevolence of the butcher, the brewer, or the baker that we expect our dinner, but from their regard to their self-interest. We address ourselves, not to their humanity, but to their self-love, and never talk to them of our necessities, but of their advantages, not to their humanity, but to their self-love, and never talk to them out of our necessities, but of their advantages." Do you agree with this quotation from *The Wealth of Nations?* How are "their self-love" and "our dinner" related to the price system? What are assumed to be the motives of firms and of households?

5. Trace the effect of a sharp change in consumer demand away from cigarettes and toward chewing gum as a result of continuing reports linking smoking with lung cancer and heart disease. Can producers of cigarettes do anything to prevent their loss of profits?

6. Make a list of decision makers in the economy today that do not fit into the categories of firm, household, and government. Are you sure that the concept of a firm will not stretch sufficiently to cover some of the items on your list?

7. Consider a major baby boom such as occurred following World War II. Trace out some significant microeconomic and macroeconomic effects of such a boom.

8. Which, if any, of the arrows in Figure 3-1 do each of the following affect in the first instance?
   a. Households increase their consumption expenditures by reducing saving.
   b. The government lowers income-tax rates.
   c. In view of a recession, firms decide to postpone production of some new products.
   d. Consumers like the 1987 model North American cars and borrow money from the banking system to buy them in record numbers.
   e. The E.T. fad dies out as consumers shift their expenditures to other items.

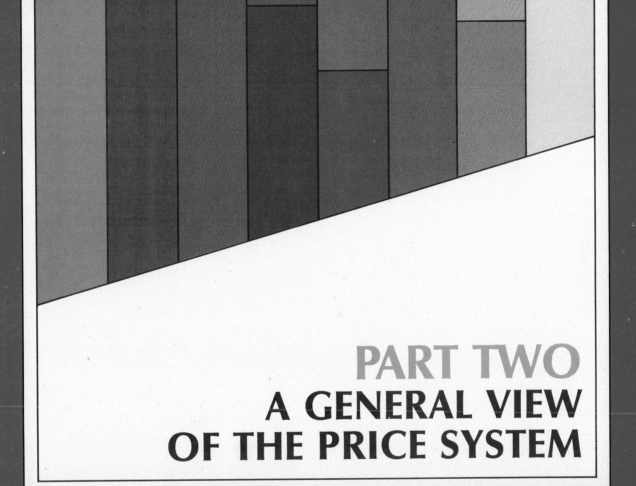

PART TWO
A GENERAL VIEW
OF THE PRICE SYSTEM

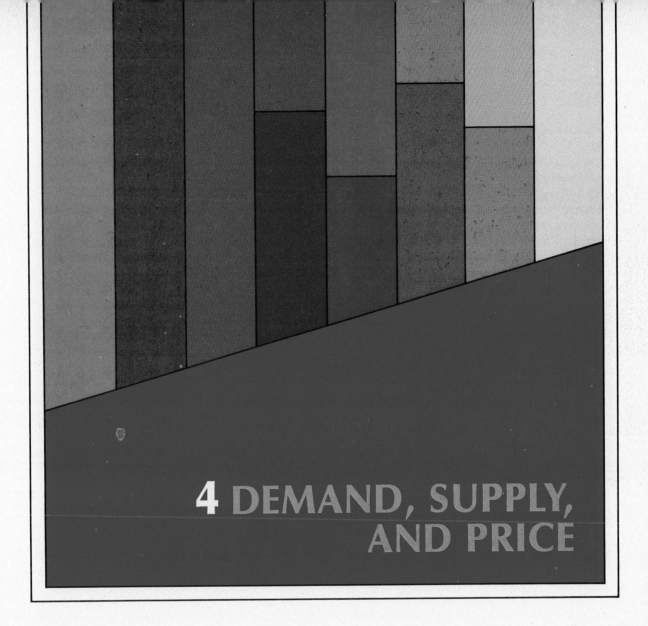

4 DEMAND, SUPPLY, AND PRICE

Some people believe that economics begins and ends with the "law" of supply and demand. It is, of course, too much to hope for "economics in one lesson." (An unkind critic of a book with that title remarked that the author needed a second lesson.) Still, the so-called laws of supply and demand are an important beginning in the attempt to answer vital questions about the market system.

A first step is to understand what determines the demands for commodities and the supplies of them. Then we can see how supply and demand operate together to determine price and how the price system as a whole allows the economy to reallocate resources in response to changes in demand and in supply. Supply and demand prove to be helpful concepts in discussing both the price system's successes and its failures. They also can be used to discuss the consequences of particular forms of government intervention such as price controls, minimum-wage laws, and sales taxes.

DEMAND

The Canadian consumer spent about $229 million on goods and services in 1983. What was it spent on, and why? Table 4-1 shows the composition of this expenditure and how it has changed over nearly 30 years. Economists ask many questions about the pattern of consumer expenditure: Why is it what it is at any moment of time? Why does it change in the way it does? Why did the fraction of total consumer expenditure for food decline from more than one-fourth in 1930 to less than one-sixth by 1983? Why did Canadian consumers allocate only 6 percent of total expenditure to automobiles in 1930 and over 10 percent in the 1970s? Why do Canadians now heat their homes with electricity, oil, and natural gas when 30 years ago they used coal? How have they reacted to the large changes in fuel prices that occurred in the late 1970s and early 1980s? Why do people who build houses in Norway and the American West rarely use brick, while it is commonly used in England and eastern North America? Why have the maid and the washerwoman been increasingly replaced by the vacuum cleaner and the washing machine?

TABLE 4–1 COMPOSITION OF PERSONAL CONSUMPTION EXPENDITURES, 1951 AND 1982 (Percentages)

	1951	1982
Durable goods	9.2	16.2
Automobile and parts	5.4	6.2
Furniture and household equipment	2.8	3.8
Other	1.0	6.1
Semidurable goods	16.0	13.5
Clothing and footwear	9.1	8.7
Other	6.9	4.8
Nondurable goods	34.7	27.9
Food	27.1	18.3
Electricity, gas, and other fuels	3.0	2.9
Gasoline, oil and grease	2.0	2.5
Other	2.6	4.2
Services	40.1	42.5
Housing and household services	13.6	16.8
Health services	2.6	1.8
Other	23.9	23.9

Source: Statistics Canada, 13–531, 13–20; Department of Finance, *Economic Review.*

The declining relative importance of food and clothing and the rising importance of gasoline and oil and services of all kinds stand out.

Quantity Demanded

The total amount of a commodity that all households wish to purchase is called the **quantity demanded** of that commodity.[1] It is important to notice three things about this concept. First, quantity demanded is a *desired* quantity. It is how much households are willing to purchase, given the price of the commodity, other prices, their incomes, tastes, and so on. This may be a different amount than households actually succeed in purchasing. If sufficient quantities are not available, the amount households wish to purchase may exceed the amount they actually do purchase. To distinguish

these two concepts, the term *quantity demanded* is used to refer to desired purchases, and phrases such as **quantity actually bought** or **quantity exchanged** are used to refer to actual purchases.

Second, *desired* does not refer to idle dreams, but to effective demands—that is, to the amounts people are willing to *buy* given the price they must pay for the commodity.

Third, quantity demanded refers to a continuous *flow* of purchases. It must therefore be expressed as so much per period of time: 1 million oranges *per day*, 7 million *per week*, or 365 million *per year*. If you were told, for example, that the quantity of new television sets demanded (at current prices) in Canada was 100,000, this would mean nothing until you were also told the period of time involved. One hundred thousand television sets demanded *per day* would be an enormous rate

[1] In this chapter we concentrate on the demand of *all* households for commodities. Of course, what all households do is only the sum of what each individual household does, and in Chapters 7 and 8 we shall study the behavior of individual households in greater detail.

of demand; 100,000 *per year* would be a very small rate. (The important distinction between stocks and flows is discussed on page 23.)

What Determines Quantity Demanded?

How much of some commodity will all households be willing to buy per month? This amount is influenced by the following important variables. [1][2]

1. The commodity's own price
2. The prices of related commodities
3. Average household income
4. Tastes
5. The distribution of income among households
6. The size of the population

We cannot understand the separate influence of each variable if we start by trying to consider what happens when everything changes at once. Instead, we can consider the influence of the variables one at a time. To do this, we hold all but one of them constant. Then we let that one selected variable vary and study how it affects quantity demanded. We can do the same for each of the other variables in turn, and in this way we can come to understand the importance of each.[3] Once this is done, we can aggregate the separate influences of two or more variables to discover what would happen if several things changed at the same time—as they often do in practice.

Holding all other influencing variables constant is often described by the words "other things being equal" or by the equivalent Latin phrase, *ceteris paribus*. When economists speak of the influence of the price of wheat on the quantity of wheat

demanded *other things being equal*, they refer to what a change in the price of wheat would do to the quantity demanded if all other factors that influence the demand for wheat did not change.

Demand and Price

We are interested in developing a theory of how commodities are priced. Thus we are necessarily interested in the influence on quantity demanded of each commodity's own price. We begin by holding all other influences constant and asking: How do we expect the quantity of a commodity demanded to vary as its own price varies?

A basic economic hypothesis is that the lower the price of a commodity, the larger the quantity that will be demanded, other things being equal.

Why might this be so? Commodities are used to satisfy desires and needs, and there is almost always more than one commodity that will satisfy any given desire or need. Such commodities compete with one another for the purchasers' attention. Hunger may be satisfied by meat or vegetables, a desire for green vegetables by broccoli or spinach. The need to keep warm at night may be satisfied by several woollen blankets or one electric blanket, or for that matter by a sheet and a lot of oil burned in the furnace. The desire for a vacation may be satisfied by a trip to the seashore or to the mountains, the need to get there by different airlines, a bus, a car, even a train. And so it goes: Name any general desire or need, and there will be at least two and often dozens of different commodities that will satisfy it.

Now consider what happens if we hold income, tastes, population, and the prices of all other commodities constant and vary only the price of one commodity. As that price goes up, the commodity becomes an increasingly expensive way to satisfy a want. Some households will stop buying it altogether; others will buy smaller amounts; still others may continue to buy the same quantity. Because many households will switch wholly or partially to other commodities to satisfy the same want, it follows that less will be bought of any commodity

---

[2] Notes giving mathematical demonstrations of the concepts presented in the text are designated by colored reference numbers. These notes can be found beginning on page M-1.

[3] A relation in which many variables—in this case average income, population, tastes, and many prices—influence a single variable—in this case quantity demanded—is called a *multivariate* relation. The technique of studying the effect of each of the influencing variables one at a time, while holding the other variables constant, is common in mathematics. Indeed, it is such a common procedure that there is a mathematical concept, the partial derivative, explicitly designed to accomplish this task.

whose price has risen. As meat becomes more expensive, for example, households may switch to some extent to meat substitutes; they may also forego meat at some meals and eat less meat at others.

Alternatively, a fall in a commodity's price makes it a cheaper method of satisfying a want. Purchasers as a whole will buy more of it. Consequently, they will buy less of similar commodities whose prices have not fallen and which as a result have become expensive *relative to* the commodity in question. As pocket calculators have fallen in price over the last 20 years, more and more of them have been purchased. When a bumper tomato harvest drives prices down, shoppers switch to tomatoes and cut their purchases of many other vegetables that now look relatively more expensive.

The Demand Schedule and the Demand Curve

How can the relationship between quantity demanded and price be portrayed? One method is to use a **demand schedule.** This is a numerical tabulation showing the quantity that is demanded at selected prices.

Table 4-2 is a hypothetical demand schedule for carrots. It lists the quantity of carrots that would be demanded at various prices on the assumption that average household income is fixed at $20,000 (and that tastes and all other prices do not change).

A second method of showing the relation between quantity demanded and price is to draw a graph. The six price-quantity combinations shown in Table 4-2 are plotted on the graph shown in Figure 4-1, which has price on the vertical axis and quantity on the horizontal axis. The smooth curve drawn through these points is called a **demand curve.** It shows the quantity that purchasers would like to buy at each price. The curve slopes down-

TABLE 4–2 A DEMAND SCHEDULE FOR CARROTS

	Price per ton p	Quantity demanded when average household income is $20,000 per year (thousands of tons per month) D
U	$ 20	110.0
V	40	90.0
W	60	77.5
X	80	67.5
Y	100	62.5
Z	120	60.0

The table shows the quantity of carrots that would be demanded at various prices, *other things equal.* For example, row W indicates that if the price of carrots were $60 per ton, consumers would desire to purchase 77,500 tons of carrots per month, given the values of the other variables that affect quantity demanded (such as average household income).

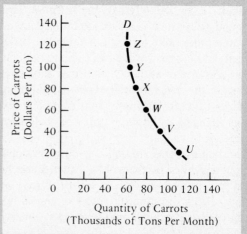

FIGURE 4-1
A Demand Curve for Carrots

This demand curve relates quantity of carrots demanded to their price; its downward slope indicates that quantity demanded increases as price falls. The six points correspond to the price-quantity combinations shown in Table 4-2. Each row in the table defines a point on the demand curve. The smooth curve drawn through all of the points and labeled *D* is the demand curve.

ward to the right, which indicates that the quantity demanded increases as the price falls.

Each point on the demand curve indicates a single price-quantity combination. The demand curve as a whole shows more.

The demand curve represents the relation between quantity demanded and price, other things being equal.

When economists speak of the conditions of demand in a particular market as being given or known, they are referring not just to the particular quantity being demanded at the moment (i.e., not just to one point on the demand curve), but to the entire demand curve—to the functional relation whereby desired purchases are related to all the possible alternative prices of the commodity.

Thus the term **demand** refers to the entire relation between price and quantity (as shown, for example, by the schedule in Table 4-2 or the curve in Figure 4-1). In contrast, a single point on a demand schedule or curve is the *quantity demanded* at that point (for example, at point *W* in Figure 4-1, 77,500 tons of carrots a month are demanded at a price of $60 a ton).

Shifts in the Demand Curve

The demand schedule is constructed, and the demand curve plotted, on the assumption of *ceteris paribus*. But what if other things change, as surely they must? What, for example, if households find themselves with more income? If they spend their extra income, they will buy additional quantities of commodities *even though prices are unchanged*.

But if households increase their purchases of any one commodity whose price has not changed, the purchases cannot be represented on the original demand curve. They must be represented on a new demand curve, which is to the right of the old curve. Thus the rise in household income has shifted the demand curve to the right. This illustrates the operation of an important general rule.

A demand curve is drawn on the assumption that everything except the commodity's own price is held constant. A change in any of the variables previously held constant will shift the demand curve to a new position.

A demand curve can shift in many ways; two of them are particularly important. If more is bought at *each* price, the demand curve shifts right so that each price corresponds to a higher quantity than it did before. If less is bought at *each* price, the demand curve shifts left so that each price corresponds to a lower quantity than it did before.

The influence of changes in variables other than price may now be studied by determining how changes in each variable shift the demand curve. Any change will shift the demand curve to the right if it increases the amount people wish to buy, other things remaining equal, and to the left if it decreases the amount households wish to buy, other things remaining equal.

Average household income. If the income of the average household increases, households can be expected to purchase more of most commodities even though commodity prices remain the same.[4] Considering all households, we expect that no matter what price we pick, more of any commodity will be demanded than was previously demanded at the same price. This shift is illustrated in Table 4-3 and Figure 4-2.

A rise in average household income shifts the demand curve for most commodities to the right. This indicates that more will be demanded at each possible price.

Other prices. We saw that the downward slope of a commodity's demand curve occurs because the lower its price, the cheaper the commodity is, relative to other commodities that can satisfy the same needs or desires. Those other commodities are called **substitutes.** Another way to accomplish the same change is for the price of the substitute commodity to rise. For example, carrots can become cheap relative to cabbage either by lowering the price of carrots or by raising the price of cabbage. Either change will tend to increase the quantity of carrots households are prepared to buy.

---

[4] Such commodities are called *normal goods*. For commodities called *inferior goods*, the amount purchased falls as income rises. These concepts are defined and discussed in Chapter 5.

TABLE 4–3 TWO ALTERNATIVE DEMAND SCHEDULES FOR CARROTS

Price per ton p	Quantity demanded when average household income is $20,000 per year (thousands of tons per month) D_0		Quantity demanded when average income is $24,000 per year (thousands of tons per month) D_1	
$ 20	110.0	(U)	140.0	(U')
40	90.0	(V)	116.0	(V')
60	77.5	(W)	100.8	(W')
80	67.5	(X)	87.5	(X')
100	62.5	(Y)	81.3	(Y')
120	60.0	(Z)	78.0	(Z')

An increase in average income increases the quantity demanded at each price. When average income rises from $20,000 to $24,000 per year, quantity demanded at a price of $60 per ton rises from 77,500 tons per month to 100,800 tons per month. A similar rise occurs at every other price. Thus the demand schedule relating columns p and D_0 is replaced by one relating columns p and D_1. The graphical representations of these two functions are labeled D_0 and D_1 in Figure 4-2.

A rise in the price of a substitute for a commodity shifts the demand curve for the commodity to the right; more will be purchased at each price.

For example, a rise in the price of a substitute for carrots could shift the demand curve for carrots from D_0 to D_1 in Figure 4-2.

Consider the class of commodities that are called **complements.** These are commodities that tend to be used jointly with each other. Cars and gasoline are complements; so are golf clubs and golf balls, electric stoves and electricity, an airplane trip to Banff and lift tickets on the mountain. Since complements tend to be consumed together, a fall in the price of either will increase the demand for both.

A fall in the price of a complementary commodity will shift a commodity's demand curve to the right; more will be purchased at each price.

For example, a fall in the price of airplane trips to Banff will lead to a rise in the demand for lift

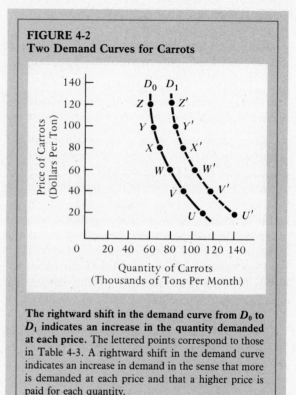

FIGURE 4-2
Two Demand Curves for Carrots

The rightward shift in the demand curve from D_0 to D_1 indicates an increase in the quantity demanded at each price. The lettered points correspond to those in Table 4-3. A rightward shift in the demand curve indicates an increase in demand in the sense that more is demanded at each price and that a higher price is paid for each quantity.

tickets at Banff even though their price is unchanged.

Tastes. Tastes have a large effect on people's desired purchases. A change in tastes may be long lasting, such as the shift from fountain pens to ballpoint pens or from slide rules to pocket calculators. Or it may be a short-lived fad such as hula hoops or Billy Beer. In either case a change in tastes in favor of a commodity shifts the demand curve to the right. More will be bought at each price.

Distribution of income. If a constant total of income is redistributed among the population, demands may change. If, for example, the government increases the deductions that may be taken for children on income tax returns and compensates by raising basic tax rates, income will be transferred from childless persons to heads of large families. Demand for commodities more heavily bought by the childless will decline, while demand for commodities bought by those with large families will increase.

A change in the distribution of income will shift to the right the demand curves for commodities bought most by those gaining income, and it will shift to the left the demand curves for commodities bought most by people losing income.

Population. Population growth does not by itself create new demand. The additional people must have purchasing power before demand is changed. Extra people of working age, however, usually mean extra output, and if they produce, they will earn income. When this happens, the demand for all the commodities purchased by the new income earners will rise. Thus it is usually (although not always) true that:

A rise in population will shift the demand curves for commodities to the right, indicating that more will be bought at each price.

These shifts are summarized in Figure 4-3.

Movements Along the Demand Curve Versus Shifts of the Whole Curve

Suppose you read in today's newspaper that the rising price of housing has caused a declining demand as people have found ways of economizing on their use of housing. Then tomorrow you read that the rising price of housing has been caused by a rising demand for housing. The two statements appear to contradict each other. The first associates a rising price with a declining demand, the second associates a rising price with a rising demand. How can both statements be true? The answer is that they refer to different things. The first describes a movement along a demand curve in response to a change in price; the second describes a shift in the whole demand curve. Using the words *declining demand* and *rising demand* in each case can only cause confusion.

Consider first the statement that less is being bought because it has become more expensive. This refers to a movement along a given demand

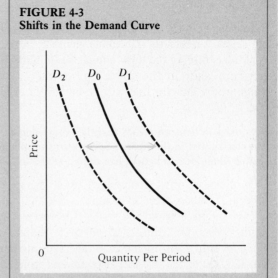

**FIGURE 4-3
Shifts in the Demand Curve**

A shift in the demand curve from D_0 to D_1 indicates an increase in demand; a shift from D_0 to D_2 indicates a decrease in demand. An increase in demand means that more is demanded at each price. Such a rightward shift can be caused by a rise in income, a rise in the price of a substitute, a fall in the price of a complement, a change in tastes that favors the commodity, an increase in population, or a redistribution of income toward groups who favor the commodity.

A decrease in demand means that less is demanded at each price. Such a leftward shift can be caused by a fall in income, a fall in the price of a substitute, a rise in the price of a complement, a change in tastes that disfavors the commodity, a decrease in population, or a redistribution of income away from groups who favor the commodity.

curve, and reflects a change between two specific quantities being bought, one before the price rose and one afterward. Any one point on a demand curve represents a specific amount being bought at a specified price. It represents, therefore, a particular quantity demanded. A movement along a demand curve is referred to as a change in the quantity demanded. [2]

A movement down a demand curve is called an *increase* (or a *rise*) in the quantity demanded; a movement up the demand curve is called a *decrease* (or a fall) in the quantity demanded.

Now consider the shift in demand. We have seen that *demand* refers to the whole demand curve. Economists reserve the term **change in demand** to describe a shift in the whole curve—that is, a change in the amount that will be bought at *every* price.

An *increase in demand* means that the whole demand curve has shifted to the right; a *fall in demand* means that the whole demand curve has shifted to the left.

To illustrate this terminology, look again at Table 4-3. When average income is $20,000, an increase in price from $60 to $80 decreases the *quantity demanded* from 77.5 to 67.5 thousand tons a month. An increase in average income from $20,000 to $24,000 increases *demand* from D_0 to D_1.

SUPPLY

Canada's private sector produced goods and services worth nearly $360 billion in 1983. A broad classification of *what* was produced is given in Table 4-4. Economists have as many questions to ask about production and its changing composition as they do about consumption. The percentages shown in Table 4-4 reflect some of the changes in 26 years. Even more dramatic changes are visible in more detailed data.

For example, through the 1960s and early 1970s the chemical, petroleum, and electrical products industries all grew in relative importance. In the mid-seventies, export-oriented industries such as forest products, primary metals, and transportation equipment all suffered declines. And at the end of the decade, investment-oriented industries such as machinery, electrical products, and metal fabricating were growing rapidly.

Economists want to know why. Why did the aluminum industry grow faster than the steel industry? Why, even within a single industry, did some firms prosper and grow, others hold their

TABLE 4-4 DOMESTIC PRODUCT BY INDUSTRY OF ORIGIN, SELECTED YEARS (Percentage Distribution)

Industry group[a]	1961	1971	1981
	Percentage distribution		
Agriculture, forestry, fishing, and trapping	6.6	4.6	3.6
Mining, quarrying, and oil wells	4.7	4.1	2.9
Manufacturing	26.8	24.6	23.2
Construction	6.3	7.6	6.6
Transportation, storage, and communication	10.8	9.8	11.5
Utilities	3.0	2.9	3.5
Wholesale and retail trade	13.8	12.5	13.4
Finance, insurance, and real estate	13.0	12.8	14.2
Other services	15.0	21.1	21.1
Total	100.0	100.0	100.0

Source: Statistics Canada, 11–003, 13–201.
[a] Excluding government and government enterprises.

Since 1961 agriculture, mining, and manufacturing have all declined in relative importance, while utilities, finance, and services have gained. Construction, transportation, and trade show considerable fluctuation with no evident trend.

own, and still others decline and fail? Why and how do firms and industries come into being? All these questions and many others are aspects of a single question: *What determines the quantities of commodities that will be produced and offered for sale?*

Full discussion of these questions of supply will come later (in Part Four). For now it is enough to develop the basic relation between the price of a commodity and the quantity that will be produced and offered for sale by firms, and to understand what forces lead to shifts in this relationship.

Quantity Supplied

The amount of a commodity that firms wish to sell is the **quantity supplied** of that commodity. This is the amount that firms are willing to offer for sale; it is not necessarily the amount they succeed in selling. The term **quantity actually sold** or **quantity exchanged** indicates what they actually succeed in selling. Quantity supplied is a flow; it is so much per unit of time.

Notice that while we use different terms (quantity demanded and quantity supplied) to distinguish desired purchases from desired sales, we use the same term, *quantity exchanged*, to describe actual purchases and actual sales. This reflects an important fact: Although households may desire to purchase an amount that differs from what sellers desire to sell, they cannot succeed in buying what someone else does not sell. A purchase and a sale are merely two sides of the same transaction. Looked at from the buyer's side, there is a purchase; looked at from the seller's side, there is a sale.

Since desired purchases do not have to equal desired sales, different terms are needed to describe the two separate amounts. But because the quantity actually purchased must be the same amount as the quantity actually sold, both can be described by a single term, *quantity exchanged*.

What Determines Quantity Supplied?

How much of a commodity will firms be willing to produce and offer for sale? The following are the most important variables that influence quantity supplied. [3]

1. The commodity's own price
2. The prices of other commodities
3. The costs of inputs
4. The goals of the firm
5. The state of technology

The situation is the same here as it is on the demand side. The list of influencing variables is long, and we will not get far if we try to discover what happens when they all change at the same time. So again we use the very convenient *other things equal* technique to study the influence of the variables one at a time.

Supply and Price

Since we want to develop a theory of how commodities get priced, we are necessarily interested in the influence on quantity supplied of a commodity's own price. We start by holding all other influences constant and asking: How do we expect the quantity of a commodity supplied to vary with its own price?

A basic economic hypothesis is that for many commodities the higher their prices, the larger the quantity that will be supplied, other things being equal.

Why might this be so? It is because the profits that can be earned from producing a commodity are almost certain to increase if the price of that commodity rises while the costs of factors used to produce it remain unchanged. Furthermore, if the prices of other commodities remain unchanged, the profits that can be earned by producing them will be unchanged, and as a result there will be a rise in *relative* profitability of producing the commodity whose price has risen. This will make firms, which are in business to earn profits, wish to produce more of the commodity whose price has risen and less of other commodities.

Notice, however, the qualifying word *many* in the hypothesis stated above. It is used because, as we shall see in Part Four, there are exceptions to this rule. Although the rule states the usual case, a rise in price (*other things equal*) is not always necessary to call forth an increase in quantity in the case of all commodities.

The Supply Schedule
and the Supply Curve

The general relationship just discussed can be illustrated by a supply schedule that shows the quantities that producers would wish to sell at alternative prices of the commodity. A **supply schedule** is analogous to a demand schedule: The former shows what producers would be willing to sell, while the latter shows what households would be willing to buy at alternative prices of the commod-

TABLE 4–5 A SUPPLY SCHEDULE FOR CARROTS

	Price per ton p	Quantity supplied (thousands of tons per month) S
u	$ 20	5.0
v	40	46.0
w	60	77.5
x	80	100.0
y	100	115.0
z	120	122.5

The table shows the quantities that producers wish to sell at various prices, *other things equal*. For example, row y indicates that if the price were $100 per ton, producers would wish to sell 115,000 tons of carrots per month.

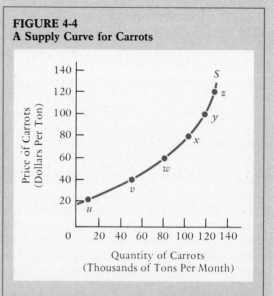

FIGURE 4-4
A Supply Curve for Carrots

This supply curve relates quantity of carrots supplied to their price; its upward slope indicates that quantity supplied increases as price increases. The six points correspond to the price-quantity combinations shown in Table 4-5. Each row in the table defines a point on the supply curve. The smooth curve drawn through all of the points and labeled S is the supply curve.

ity. Table 4-5 presents a hypothetical supply schedule for carrots.

A **supply curve,** the graphic representation of the supply schedule, is illustrated in Figure 4-4. Once again, while each point on the supply curve represents a specific price-quantity combination, the whole curve shows more.

The supply curve represents the relation between quantity supplied and price, other things being equal.

When economists speak of the conditions of supply as being given or known, they refer not just to the particular quantity being supplied at the moment (that is, not to just a particular point on the supply curve) but to the entire supply curve, to the complete functional relation by which desired sales are related to all possible prices of the commodity.

Supply refers to the entire relation between supply and price. A single point on the supply curve refers to the *quantity supplied* at that price.

Shifts in the Supply Curve

A shift in the supply curve means that at each price a quantity different from the previous quantity will be supplied. An increase in the quantity supplied at each price is shown in Table 4-6 and graphed in Figure 4-5. This change appears as a rightward shift in the supply curve. In contrast, a decrease in the quantity supplied at each price would appear as a leftward shift. A shift in the supply curve must be the result of a change in one of the factors that influence the quantity supplied other than the commodity's own price. The major possible causes of such shifts are summarized in the caption of Figure 4-6 and are considered briefly below.

For supply, as for demand, there is an important general rule.

A change in any of the variables (other than the commodity's own price) that affect the amount of a commodity that firms are willing to produce and sell will shift the whole supply curve for that commodity.

TABLE 4–6 TWO ALTERNATIVE SUPPLY SCHEDULES FOR CARROTS

Price per ton p	Quantity supplied before cost-saving innovation (thousands of tons per month) S_0		Quantity supplied after the innovation (thousands of tons per month) S_1	
$ 20	5.0	(u)	28.0	(u')
40	46.0	(v)	76.0	(v')
60	77.5	(w)	102.0	(w')
80	100.0	(x)	120.0	(x')
100	115.0	(y)	132.0	(y')
120	122.5	(z)	140.0	(z')

A cost-saving innovation increases the quantity supplied at each price. As a result of the cost-saving innovation, quantity supplied at $100 per ton rises from 115,000 to 132,000 tons per month. A similar rise occurs at every price. Thus, the supply schedule relating p and S_0 is replaced by one relating p and S_1.

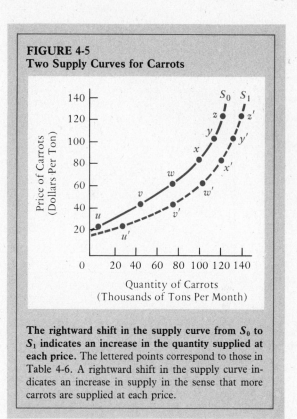

FIGURE 4-5
Two Supply Curves for Carrots

The rightward shift in the supply curve from S_0 to S_1 indicates an increase in the quantity supplied at each price. The lettered points correspond to those in Table 4-6. A rightward shift in the supply curve indicates an increase in supply in the sense that more carrots are supplied at each price.

Other prices. Commodities may be substitutes or complements in production as well as in consumption. Land that grows wheat can also grow corn, or it can be used to raise hogs. Suppose the price of corn falls, and as a result corn is less profitable to produce. Some farmers will shift from corn to wheat production. Thus a fall in the price of corn may shift the supply curve of wheat to the right, indicating that at each price of wheat more will be supplied than before.

Since commodities are alternative outputs for producers, a fall in the price of one commodity may shift the supply curve of another to the right.

Prices of factors of production. Other things being equal, the higher the price of any input used to make a commodity, the less will be the profit from making it. We expect, therefore, that the higher the price of the inputs, the lower will be the amount supplied at any given price of the product.

A rise in the costs of inputs shifts the supply curve to the left, indicating that less will be supplied at any given price.

Technology. At any time, what is produced and how it is produced depends on what is known. Over time knowledge changes; so do the quantities of individual commodities supplied. The enormous increase in production per worker that has been going on in industrial societies for about 200 years is largely due to improved methods of production. Yet the Industrial Revolution is more than a historical event; it is a present reality. Discoveries in chemistry have led to lower costs of production of well-established products, such as paints, and to a large variety of new products made of plastics and synthetic fibers. The invention of transistors and silicon chips has revolutionized production in television, high-fidelity equipment, computers, and guidance-control systems.

Any technological change that decreases production costs will increase the profits that can be

FIGURE 4-6
Shifts in the Supply Curve

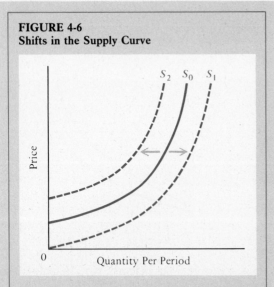

A shift in the supply curve from S_0 to S_1 indicates an increase in supply; a shift from S_0 to S_2 indicates a decrease in supply. An increase in supply means that more is supplied at each price. Such a rightward shift can be caused by certain changes in producers' goals, improvements in technology, decreases in the prices of other commodities, or decreases in the prices of factors of production that are important in producing the commodity.

A decrease in supply means that less is supplied at each price. Such a leftward shift can be caused by certain changes in producers' goals, increases in the prices of other commodities, or increases in the prices of factors of production that are important in producing the commodity.

earned at any given price of the commodity. Since increased profitability tends to lead to increased production, this change will shift the supply curve to the right, indicating an increased willingness to produce the commodity and to offer it for sale at each possible price.

Movements Along the Supply Curve Versus Shifts of the Whole Curve

As with demand, it is important to distinguish movements along supply curves from shifts of the whole curve. The term **change in supply** is re-

served for a shift of the whole supply curve. This means a change in the quantity supplied at each price of the commodity. A movement along the supply curve indicates a *change in the quantity supplied* in response to a change in the price of the commodity. Thus an *increase in supply* means that the whole supply curve has shifted to the right; an *increase in the quantity supplied* means a movement upward to the right along a given supply curve.

THE DETERMINATION OF PRICE BY DEMAND AND SUPPLY

So far demand and supply have been considered separately. The next question is this: How do the two forces interact to determine price in a competitive market? Table 4-7 brings together the demand and supply schedules from Tables 4-2 and 4-5. The quantities of carrots demanded and supplied at each price may now be compared.

There is only one price, $60 a ton, at which the quantity of carrots demanded equals the quantity supplied. At prices of less than $60 a ton there is a shortage of carrots because the quantity demanded exceeds the quantity supplied. This is often called a situation of **excess demand.** At prices greater than $60 a ton, there is a surplus of carrots because the quantity supplied exceeds the quantity demanded. This is called a situation of **excess supply.**

To discuss the determination of market price, suppose first that the price is $100 a ton. At this price, 115,000 tons would be offered for sale, but only 62,500 tons would be demanded. There would be an excess supply of 52,500 tons a month. We assume that sellers will then cut their prices to get rid of this surplus and that purchasers, observing the stock of unsold carrots, will offer less for what they are prepared to buy.

The tendency for buyers to offer, and sellers to ask for, lower prices when there is excess supply implies a downward pressure on price.

Next consider the price of $20 a ton. At this price, there is excess demand. The 5,000 tons pro-

TABLE 4–7 DEMAND AND SUPPLY SCHEDULES FOR CARROTS AND EQUILIBRIUM PRICE

(1) Price per ton p	(2) Quantity demanded (thousands of tons per month) D	(3) Quantity supplied (thousands of tons per month) S	(4) Excess demand (+) Excess supply (−) (thousands of tons per month) D − S
$ 20	110.0	5.0	+ 105.0
40	90.0	46.0	+ 44.0
60	77.5	77.5	0.0
80	67.5	100.0	− 32.5
100	62.5	115.0	− 52.5
120	60.0	122.5	− 62.5

Equilibrium occurs where quantity demanded equals quantity supplied—where there is neither excess demand nor excess supply. These schedules are those of Tables 4-2 and 4-5. The equilibrium price is $60. For lower prices, there is excess demand; for higher prices there is excess supply.

duced each month are snapped up very quickly, and 105,000 tons of desired purchases cannot be made. Rivalry between would-be purchasers may lead to their offering more than the prevailing price to outbid other purchasers. Also, perceiving that they could have sold their available supplies many times over, sellers may begin to ask a higher price for the quantities that they do have to sell.

The tendency for buyers to offer, and sellers to ask for, higher prices when there is excess demand implies an upward pressure on price.

Finally, consider a price of $60. At this price, producers wish to sell 77,500 tons a month and purchasers wish to buy that quantity. There is neither a shortage nor a surplus of carrots. There are no unsatisfied buyers to bid the price up, nor are there unsatisfied sellers to force the price down. Once the price of $60 has been reached, therefore, there will be no tendency for it to change.

An equilibrium implies a state of rest, or balance, between opposing forces. The **equilibrium price** is the one toward which the actual market price will tend. It will persist once established, unless it is disturbed by some change in market conditions.

The price at which the quantity demanded equals the quantity supplied is called the equilibrium price.

Any other price is called a **disequilibrium price:** quantity demanded does not equal quantity supplied, and price will be changing. A market that exhibits excess demand or excess supply is said to be in a state of **disequilibrium.**

When the market is in equilibrium, quantity demanded equals quantity supplied. Anything that must be true if equilibrium is to be obtained is called an **equilibrium condition.** In the competitive market, the equality of quantity demanded and quantity supplied is an equilibrium condition. [4]

This same story is told in graphic terms in Figure 4-7. The price of $60 is the equilibrium price because at that price there is neither excess supply nor excess demand. All other prices are disequilibrium prices, and if they occur, the market will not be in a state of rest. At prices below the equilibrium, there will be shortages and rising prices; at prices above the equilibrium, there will be surpluses and falling prices.

The quantities demanded and supplied at any price can be read off the two curves, while the magnitude of the shortage or surplus is shown by the horizontal distance between the curves at each

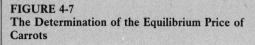

FIGURE 4-7
The Determination of the Equilibrium Price of Carrots

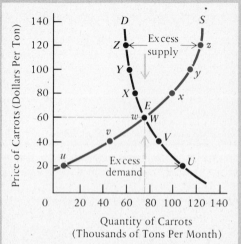

The equilibrium price corresponds to the intersection of the demand and supply curves. Point E indicates the equilibrium. At a price of $60, quantity demanded equals quantity supplied. At prices above the equilibrium, there is excess supply and downward pressure on price. At prices below equilibrium, there is excess demand and upward pressure on price.

price. The figure makes it clear that the equilibrium price occurs where the demand and supply curves intersect. Below that price there will be a shortage and hence an upward pressure on the existing price. Above it there will be a surplus and hence a downward pressure on price. These pressures are represented by the vertical arrows.

The "Laws" of Supply and Demand

Changes in any of the variables other than price that influence quantity demanded or supplied will cause a shift in either the supply curve or the demand curve (or both). There are four possible shifts: (1) a rise in demand (a rightward shift in the demand curve); (2) a fall in demand (a leftward shift in the demand curve); (3) a rise in supply (a rightward shift in the supply curve); and (4) a fall in supply (a leftward shift in the supply curve).

To analyze the effects of any of these shifts we use the method known as **comparative statics.**[5] We start from a position of equilibrium and then introduce the change to be studied. The new equilibrium position is determined and *compared* with the original one. The differences between the two positions of equilibrium must result from changes in the data that were introduced—for everything else has been held constant.

The four shifts give rise to effects that embody the four so-called laws of supply and demand. Each of the four laws describes what happens when an initial position of equilibrium is disturbed by an exogenous event that shifts one of the curves and destroys the equilibrium at the original price and quantity. The shift then causes adjustments (or endogenous changes) that establish a new position of equilibrium.[6]

Figure 4-8, which illustrates the four laws of supply and demand, generalizes our specific discussion about carrots. Previously, we had given the axes specific labels, but from here on we will simplify. Because it is intended to apply to any commodity, the horizontal axis is simply labeled *Quantity.* This should be understood to mean quantity per period in whatever units output is described. *Price* should be understood to mean the price measured as dollars per unit of quantity for the same commodity. The laws of supply and demand are:

1. A rise in demand causes an increase in both the equilibrium price and the equilibrium quantity exchanged.
2. A fall in demand causes a decrease in both the equilibrium price and the equilibrium quantity exchanged.
3. A rise in supply causes a decrease in the equilibrium

[5] The term *statics* is used because we are not concerned about the actual path by which the market goes from the first equilibrium position to the second. Analysis of that path would be described as dynamic analysis.
[6] The detailed argument in each case follows that of pages 56–57 and Figure 4-7 as to what happens when supply does not equal demand. Be sure you understand the market *behavior* that gives rise to each of the four "laws" summarized here.

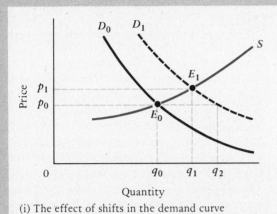

(i) The effect of shifts in the demand curve

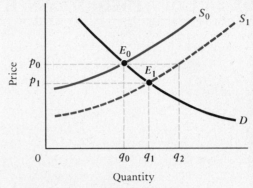

(ii) The effect of shifts in the supply curve

The effects on equilibrium price and quantity of shifts in either supply or demand are called the laws of supply and demand.

A rise in demand. In (i) if demand rises from D_0 to D_1, excess demand of q_0q_2 develops at price p_0. Price and quantity both rise to their new equilibrium values at p_1 and q_1.

A fall in demand. In (i) if demand falls from D_1 to D_0, an excess supply develops at p_1. Price and quantity both fall to their new equilibrium values at p_0 and q_0.

A rise in supply. In (ii) if supply rises from S_0 to S_1, an excess supply of q_0q_2 develops at p_0. Price falls and quantity rises to their new equilibrium values at p_1 and q_1.

A fall in supply. In (ii) if supply falls from S_1 to S_0, an excess demand develops at p_1. Price rises and quantity falls to their new equilibrium values at p_0 and q_0.

price and an increase in the equilibrium quantity exchanged.

4. A fall in supply causes an increase in the equilibrium price and a decrease in the equilibrium quantity exchanged.

In this chapter we have studied many forces that can cause demand or supply curves to shift. These were summarized in Figures 4-3 and 4-6. By combining this analysis with the four "laws" of supply and demand, we can link many real-world events that cause demand or supply curves to shift with changes in market prices and quantities.

The theory of the determination of price by demand and supply is beautiful in its simplicity. Yet, as we shall see, it is powerful in its wide range of applications.[7] Box 4-1 discusses another aspect of these laws.

---

[7] The laws of supply and demand apply in competitive markets where a supply curve exists and slopes upward. As we shall see later, not all markets satisfy these conditions.

The Laws of Demand and Supply in an Open Economy

So far in this chapter we have discussed the determination of price in a single domestic market. But what about all those goods that are traded internationally? A brief look at these may be a useful exercise at this point.

To start we need to define a few terms. An economy that engages in international trade is called an **open economy.** One that does not is called a **closed economy,** and a situation with no international trade is called **autarky.** In this section we examine the simple case of a **small open economy (SOE),** which is an economy whose exports and imports are small enough in relation to the total volume of world trade that changes in the quantities it imports or exports do not influence the prices of goods established in world markets. For many countries and commodities, this is an empirically applicable assumption.

BOX 4–1 LAWS, PREDICTIONS, HYPOTHESES

In what sense can the four propositions developed for supply and demand be called laws? They are not like acts passed by Parliament, interpreted by courts, and enforced by the police; they cannot be repealed if people do not like them. Nor are they like the laws of Moses, revealed to man by the voice of God. Are they natural laws similar to Newton's law of gravity? In labeling them *laws*, economists clearly had in mind Newton's laws as analogies.

The term *law* is used in science to describe a theory that has stood up to substantial testing. A law of this kind has not been proved to be true for all times and all circumstances, nor is it regarded as immutable. As observations accumulate, laws may often be modified or the range of phenomena to which they apply may be restricted or redefined. Einstein's theory of relativity, for one example, forced such amendments and restrictions on Newton's laws.

The "laws" of supply and demand have stood up well to many empirical tests, but no one believes they explain all market behavior. Indeed, the range of markets over which they seem to meet the test of providing accurate predic-

tions is now much smaller than it was 80 years ago. It is possible—though most economists think it unlikely—that at some future time they would no longer apply to any real markets. They are thus laws in the sense that they predict certain behavior in certain situations and the predicted behavior occurs sufficiently often to lead people to continue to have confidence in the predictions of the theory. They are not laws—any more than are the laws of natural science—that are beyond being challenged by present or future observations that may cast their predictions in doubt. Nor is it heresy to question their applicability to any particular situation.

Laws, then, are hypotheses that have led to predictions that seem to account for observed behavior. They are theories that—in some circumstances at least—have survived attempts to refute them. It is possible, in economics as in the natural sciences, to be impressed both with the "laws" we do have and with their limitations: to be impressed, that is, both with the power of what we know and with the magnitude of what we have yet to understand.

We also divide all goods into two types. **Nontradables** are goods and services that are produced and sold domestically and do not enter into international trade. Their prices are set on domestic markets by domestic supply and demand. **Tradables** are goods and services that enter into international trade. For a small open economy, the prices of tradables, whether the economy imports or exports them, are given, since they are set on international markets.

Nontraded Goods

Equilibrium is where the quantity demanded by domestic purchasers is equal to the quantity sup-

plied by domestic producers. In effect, the pricing of nontraded goods is what we have discussed so far in this chapter. Price of nontradables is set by the forces of domestic demand and domestic supply.

Traded Goods

Traded goods prices are set on international markets, while domestic demand and supply determine the quantities that are consumed, produced, and traded at that price.

Exports. Domestic demand and supply would establish a domestic price in the absence of world trade. If, however, the given world price exceeds that domestic price, the good will be exported. Since the small open economy's exports are an insignificant fraction of total world production and consumption of the commodity, the world price will dominate, and the excess of domestic quantity supplied over domestic quantity demanded at that price will be exported. This is analyzed in detail in Figure 4-9.

Notice that trade raises the price of the exported good above its autarky level. Notice also that the equilibrium is no longer where domestic quantity demanded equals domestic quantity supplied; instead, the equilibrium price is the given world price, and the excess of domestic quantity supplied over domestic quantity demanded is exported.

Imports. If the world price is less than the autarky price, the good will be imported, as shown

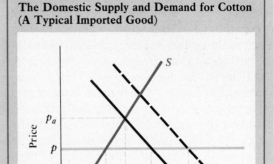

FIGURE 4-10
The Domestic Supply and Demand for Cotton (A Typical Imported Good)

Imports are determined by the excess domestic demand for a tradable good at the world price. D and S are the domestic demand and supply schedules. In autarky, at price p_a quantity q_a would be produced and consumed domestically. If the world price of cotton, p, is less than the autarky price, p_a, the country will import cotton. At the world price p, quantity supplied will be q_2, domestic consumption will be q_1, and q_2q_1 will be imported. A rise in domestic demand to D' increases the quantity imported to q_2q_1'.

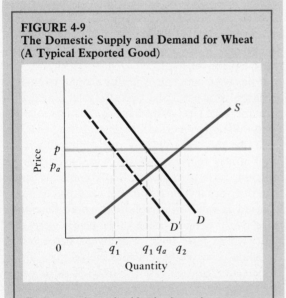

FIGURE 4-9
The Domestic Supply and Demand for Wheat (A Typical Exported Good)

Exports are determined by the domestic excess supply of a tradable good at the world price. D and S are the domestic demand and supply schedules. In autarky, the domestic price would be p_a, and quantity q_a would be produced and consumed domestically. If the world price of wheat, p, exceeds the autarky price, p_a, the country will export wheat. At the world price p, quantity supplied will be q_2, domestic consumption will be q_1, and q_1q_2 will be exported. A fall in domestic demand to D' increases the quantity exported to $q_1'q_2$.

in Figure 4-10. Notice that trade lowers the price of the imported good below its autarky level. Notice also that the equilibrium is once again not where domestic quantity demanded equals domestic quantity supplied; price is given by the world price, and the excess of domestic quantity demanded over domestic quantity supplied is met by imports.

For an open economy, equilibrium in markets for traded goods is consistent with domestic demand for those goods being different from domestic supply. If at the world price quantity demanded domestically exceeds quantity supplied domestically, the good will be imported; if quantity supplied domestically exceeds quantity demanded domestically, the good will be exported.

Effects of Changes in Domestic Supply and Demand

Suppose that domestic residents experience a change in tastes. At the same prices, and values of other variables that influence quantity demanded, they decide to consume less of the exported good and more of the imported good. This decision is illustrated in Figure 4-9, where the demand for the exported good shifts to the left, and in Figure 4-10, where the demand for imported goods shifts to the right. At the prevailing world prices, these shifts lead to an increase in the quantity of exports and also to an increase in the quantity of imports.

The effects of a change in domestic supply can also be studied. For example, an increase in domestic wages would increase the cost of producing both the imported and the exported good. This would reduce the quantity that would be supplied domestically at each price; that is, the supply curves shift upward. The reader can verify that *ceteris paribus* this would lead to an increase in the quantity of imports and a decrease in the quantity of exports.

In a small open economy, other things being equal, shifts in domestic supply and demand lead to changes in quantities imported and exported rather than to changes in prices.

Since the economy we are studying is assumed to be small relative to the whole world, these changes in domestic demand or supply do not have a noticeable effect on world prices. The result of shifts in domestic demand or supply is a change in the *quantities* of imports and exports. The assumption that world prices are constant means that, in effect, the domestic economy can buy or sell any quantities of tradable goods it wants on world markets.

The Theory of Price in an Inflationary World

Up to now we have developed the theory of the prices of individual commodities under the assumption that all other prices remained constant. Does this mean that the theory is inapplicable to an inflationary world when virtually all prices are rising? Fortunately the answer is no.

The key lies in what are called *relative prices*. We have mentioned several times that what matters for demand and supply is the price of the commodity in question relative to the prices of other commodities. This is called its **relative price**.

In an inflationary world we are often interested in the price of a given commodity as it relates to the average price of all other commodities. If, during a period when the general price level rose by 40 percent, the price of oranges rose by 60 percent, then the price of oranges rose relative to the price level as a whole. Oranges became *relatively* expensive. However, if oranges had risen in price by only 30 percent when the general price level rose by 40 percent, then the relative price of oranges would have fallen. Although the money price of oranges rose substantially, oranges became *relatively* cheap.

In Lewis Carroll's famous story *Through the Looking Glass*, Alice finds a country where you have to run in order to stay still. So it is with inflation. A commodity's price must rise as fast as the general level of prices rises just to keep its relative price constant.

It has been convenient in this chapter to analyze a change in a particular price in the context of a constant price level. The analysis is easily extended to an inflationary period by remembering that any force that raises the price of one commodity when other prices remain constant will, given general inflation, raise the price of that commodity faster than the price level is rising. For example, a change in tastes in favor of carrots that would raise their price by 20 percent when other prices were constant, would raise their price by 32 percent if at the same time the general price level goes up by 10 percent.[8] In each case the price of carrots rises 20 percent *relative to the average of all prices*.

In price theory, whenever we talk of a change in the price of one commodity we mean a change relative to other prices.

If the price level is constant, this change requires only that the money price of the commodity in

----

[8] Let the price level be 100 in the first case and 110 in the second. Let the price of carrots be 120 in the first case and x in the second. To preserve the same relative price rise we need x such that $120/100 = x/110$, which makes $x = 1.32$.

question should rise. If the price level is itself rising, this change requires that the money price of the commodity in question should rise faster than the price level.

SUMMARY

1. The amount of a commodity that households wish to purchase is called the *quantity demanded*. It is a flow expressed as so much per period of time. It is determined by the commodity's own price, the prices of related commodities, average household income, tastes, the distribution of income among households, and the size of the population.

2. Quantity demanded is assumed to increase as the price of the commodity falls, other things being equal. The relationship between quantity demanded and price is represented graphically by a demand curve that shows how much will be demanded at each market price. A movement along a demand curve indicates a change in the quantity demanded in response to a change in the price of the commodity.

3. A shift in a demand curve represents a change in the quantity demanded at each price and is referred to as a *change in demand*. The demand curve shifts to the right (an increase in demand) if average income rises, if the price of a substitute rises, if the price of a complement falls, if population rises, or if there is a change in tastes in favor of the product. The opposite changes shift the demand curve to the left (a decrease in demand).

4. The amount of a commodity that firms wish to sell is called the *quantity supplied*. It is a flow expressed as so much per period of time. It depends on the commodity's own price, the prices of other commodities, the costs of factors of production, and the state of technology.

5. Quantity supplied is assumed to increase as the price of the commodity increases, other things being equal. The relationship between quantity supplied and price is represented graphically by a supply curve that shows how much will be supplied

at each market price. A movement along a supply curve indicates a change in the quantity supplied in response to a change in price.

6. A shift in the supply curve indicates a change in the quantity supplied at each price and is referred to as a *change in supply*. The supply curve shifts to the right (an increase in supply) if the prices of other commodities fall, if the costs of producing the commodity fall, or if, for any reason, producers become more willing to produce the commodity. The opposite changes shift the supply curve to the left (a decrease in supply).

7. The equilibrium price is the one at which the quantity demanded equals the quantity supplied. At any price below the equilibrium there will be excess demand, while at any price above the equilibrium there will be excess supply. Graphically, equilibrium occurs where demand and supply curves intersect.

8. Price is assumed to rise when there is a shortage and to fall when there is a surplus. Thus the actual market price will be pushed toward the equilibrium price, and when it is reached, there will be neither shortage nor surplus and price will not change until either the supply curve or the demand curve shifts.

9. Using the method of comparative statics, the effects of a shift in either demand or supply can be determined. A rise in demand raises both equilibrium price and quantity; a fall in demand lowers both. A rise in supply raises equilibrium quantity but lowers equilibrium price; a fall in supply lowers equilibrium quantity but raises equilibrium price. These are the so-called laws of supply and demand.

10. In a small open economy, the prices of traded goods are set in international markets. Domestic demand and supply then determine the quantities of exports and imports.

11. Price theory is most simply developed in the context of a constant price level. Price changes discussed in the theory are changes *relative to* the average level of all prices. In an inflationary period, a rise in the relative price of one commodity means that its price rises by more than the price level; a fall in its relative price means that its price rises by less than the price level.

TOPICS FOR REVIEW

Quantity demanded and quantity exchanged
Demand schedules and demand curves
Quantity supplied and quantity exchanged
Supply schedules and supply curves
Movements along a curve and shifts in the curve
Changes in quantity demanded and changes in demand
Changes in quantity supplied and changes in supply
Equilibrium, equilibrium price, and disequilibrium
Comparative static analysis
The "laws" of supply and demand
Imports and exports
Relative price

DISCUSSION QUESTIONS

1. What shifts in demand or supply curves would produce the following results? (Assume that only one of the two curves has shifted.)
   a. The price of pocket calculators has fallen over the last few years and the quantity exchanged has risen greatly.
   b. As the Canadian standard of living rose over the past three decades, both the prices and the consumption of prime cuts of beef rose steadily.
   c. A leading department store is offering $1.20 for 100 pennies.
   d. Summer sublets in Kingston, Ontario, are at rents of 50 percent or less of the regular rental.
   e. Because the "preppy look" is in, the sale of jeans has declined.
   f. Federal safety and antipollution regulations decrease the sales of North American car manufacturers.
   g. "Gourmet food market grows as affluent shoppers indulge."
2. Recently the U.S. Department of Agriculture predicted bumper crops of corn and wheat. But its chief economist, Don Paarlberg, warned consumers not to expect prices to decrease since the costs of production were rising and foreign demand for American crops was increasing. "The classic pattern of supply and demand won't work this time," Mr. Paarlberg said. Discuss his observation.

3. Explain each of the following in terms of changes in supply and demand.
   a. DuPont increased the price of synthetic fibers, although it acknowledged demand was weak.
   b. "Master Charge has replaced sugar-daddy," a Beverly Hills furrier said, explaining the rise in sales of mink coats.
   c. The Edsel was a lemon when produced in 1958–1960, but it is now a best-seller among cars of its vintage.
   d. Some of the first $10 Canadian Olympic coins were imperfectly stamped. Dealers are paying as much as $750 for these flawed pieces.
4. What would be the effect on the equilibrium price and quantity of marijuana if its sale were legalized?
5. The relative price of a color television set has dropped drastically over time. Would you explain this falling price in terms of demand or supply changes? What factors are likely to have caused the demand or supply shifts that did occur?
6. Classify the effect of each of the following as (a) a decrease in the demand for fish, (b) a decrease in the quantity of fish demanded, or (c) other. Illustrate each diagrammatically.
   a. The government of Iceland bars fishermen of other nations from its waters.
   b. People buy less fish because of a rise in fish prices.
   c. The Roman Catholic Church relaxes its ban on eating meat on Fridays.
   d. The price of beef falls and as a result households buy more beef and less fish.
   e. In the interests of training marine personnel for national defense, the government decides to subsidize the fishing industry.
   f. It is discovered that eating fish is better for one's health than eating meat.
7. "The effect of price changes often eludes analysis. For example, two of the food groups that have shown absolute decreases in consumption per capita—flour and potatoes— have also shown decreases in price relative to the prices of all goods. Consumption of meat per capita has been rising in the face of an increase in relative prices." Do the changes elude your analysis? How would you reword this statement to make clear what you think did happen?
8. Predict the effect on price of at least one commodity of each of the following:
   a. Winter snowfall is at record high in Alberta, but drought continues in Eastern Township ski areas.
   b. A recession decreases employment in Oshawa automobile factories.
   c. The French grape harvest is the smallest in 20 years.

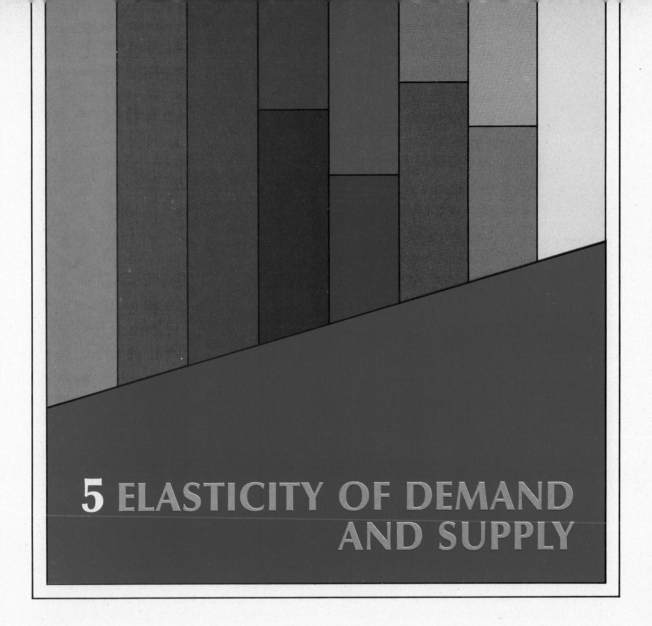

5 ELASTICITY OF DEMAND AND SUPPLY

The laws of supply and demand predict the *direction* of changes in price and quantity in response to various shifts in demand and supply. But very often it is not enough to know merely whether quantity rises or falls in response to a change in price; it is also important to know by how much.

When flood damage led to major destruction of the onion crop, onion prices rose generally. In one city, they rose 42 percent in one week. Not surprisingly, consumption fell. In this case, the press reported that many consumers stopped using onions altogether and substituted onion salt, sauerkraut, cabbage, and other products. Other consumers still bought onions but in reduced quantities. Overall consumption was down sharply. Were aggregate dollar sales of onions (price *times* quantity) higher or lower? A government concerned with the effect of a bad crop on farm income will not be satisfied with being told that food prices will rise and quantities consumed will fall; it will

FIGURE 5-1
The Effect of the Shape of the Demand Curve

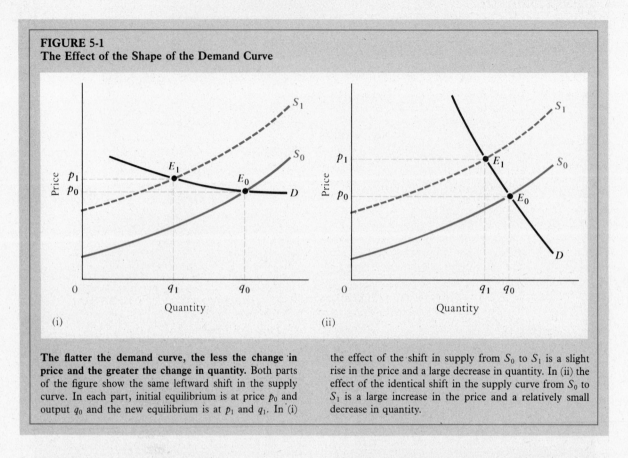

(i)   (ii)

The flatter the demand curve, the less the change in price and the greater the change in quantity. Both parts of the figure show the same leftward shift in the supply curve. In each part, initial equilibrium is at price p_0 and output q_0 and the new equilibrium is at p_1 and q_1. In (i) the effect of the shift in supply from S_0 to S_1 is a slight rise in the price and a large decrease in quantity. In (ii) the effect of the identical shift in the supply curve from S_0 to S_1 is a large increase in the price and a relatively small decrease in quantity.

need to know by approximately how much they will change if it is to assess the effects on farmers.

Measuring and describing the extent of the responsiveness of quantities to changes in prices and other variables is often essential if we are to understand the significance of these changes. This is what the concept of elasticity seeks to do.

PRICE ELASTICITY OF DEMAND

Suppose there is a fall in a farm crop—that is, a leftward shift in the supply curve. The two parts of Figure 5-1 show the same leftward shift. Because the demand curves are different, the effects on equilibrium price and quantity are different.

A shift in supply can have very different effects, depending on the shape of the demand curve.

The difference may have great policy significance. Consider what would happen if the government persuaded farmers to produce more of a certain crop. (It might, for example, pay a subsidy to farmers for growing this crop.) If the government is successful, then at every possible price of the product there will be an increase in the quantity farmers would be willing to produce. Thus the whole supply curve of the product would shift to the right. This may be visualized in both parts of Figure 5-1 by assuming that the supply curve shifts from S_1 to S_0.

Figure 5-1(i) illustrates a case in which the quantity consumers demand is very sensitive to price changes. The extra production brings down price, but because the quantity demanded is very responsive, only a small change in price is necessary to restore equilibrium. The effect of the government's policy, therefore, is to achieve a large increase in the production and sales of this commodity and only a small decrease in price.

Figure 5-1(ii) shows a case in which the quantity demanded is quite unresponsive to price changes. As before, the increase in supply at the original price causes a surplus that brings the price down. But this time the quantity demanded by consumers does not increase very much in response to the fall in price. Thus the price continues to drop until, discouraged by lower and lower prices, farmers reduce the quantity supplied very nearly to the level attained before they received the increased incentive to produce. The effect of the government's policy is to bring about a large fall in the price and only a small increase in the quantity produced and sold.

In the cases shown in Figure 5-1, it can be seen that the government's policy has exactly the same effectiveness as far as farmers' willingness to supply the commodity is concerned (the supply curve shifts are identical). But the effects on the equilibrium price and quantity are very different because of the different degrees to which the quantity demanded by consumers responds to price changes. If the purpose of the policy is to increase the quantity of this commodity produced and consumed, then the policy will be a great success when the demand curve is similar to the one shown in Figure 5-1(i), but it will be a failure when the demand curve is similar to the one shown in Figure 5-1(ii). If, however, the main purpose of the policy is to achieve a large reduction in the price of the commodity, the policy will be a failure when demand is as shown in (i) but it will be a great success when demand is as shown in (ii).

Price Elasticity: A Measure of the Responsiveness of Demand

We have seen that the responsiveness of the quantity demanded to changes in price is important. In Figure 5-1 a measure of demand responsiveness can be obtained by comparing the steepness of the two demand curves because they were both drawn on the same scale. Thus, for any given price change, the quantity changes more on the flatter curve than it does on the steeper one. However, it can be very misleading to inspect a *single* curve and to conclude from its general appearance something about the degree of responsiveness of quantity demanded to price changes. You can make a curve appear as steep or as flat as you like by changing the scales. For example, a curve that looks steep when the horizontal scale is 1 cm = 100 units will look much flatter when the horizontal scale is 1 cm = 1 unit if the same vertical scale is used in each case.

Instead of gaining a vague general impression from the shape of demand curves, one could note the actual change in quantity demanded in response to a certain price change. But it would still be impossible to compare degrees of responsiveness for different commodities.

Assume that we have the information shown in Table 5-1. Should we conclude that the demand for radios is not as responsive to price changes as the demand for beef? After all, price cuts of $.20 cause quite a large increase in the quantity of beef demanded but only a small increase in radios.

There are two problems here. First, a reduction of price of $.20 will be a large price cut for a low-priced commodity and an insignificant price cut for a high-priced commodity. The price reductions listed in Table 5-1 represent very different fractions of the total prices. It is usually more revealing to know the percentage change in the prices of the various commodities. Second, by an analogous argument, knowing the quantity by which demand

TABLE 5–1 PRICE REDUCTIONS AND CORRESPONDING INCREASES IN QUANTITY DEMANDED

Commodity	Reduction in price	Increase in quantity demanded
Beef	$.20 per pound	7,500 pounds
Men's shirts	.20 per shirt	5,000 shirts
Radios	.20 per radio	100 radios

TABLE 5–2 PRICE AND QUANTITY INFORMATION UNDERLYING DATA OF TABLE 5–1

Commodity	Unit	Original price	New price	Average price	Original quantity	New quantity	Average quantity
Beef	per pound	$ 1.70	$ 1.50	$ 1.60	116,250	123,750	120,000
Men's shirts	per shirt	8.10	7.90	8.00	197,500	202,500	200,000
Radios	per radio	40.10	39.90	40.00	9,950	10,050	10,000

These data provide the appropriate context of the data given in Table 5–1. The table relates the $.20 per unit price reduction of each commodity to the actual prices and quantities demanded.

changes is not very revealing unless the level of demand is also known. An increase of 7,500 pounds is quite a significant reaction of demand if the quantity formerly bought was 15,000 pounds, but it is only a drop in the bucket if the quantity formerly demanded was 10 million pounds.

Table 5-2 shows the original and new levels of price and quantity. Changes in price and quantity expressed as percentages of the average prices and quantities are shown in the first two columns of Table 5-3.[1] **Elasticity of demand,** the measure of responsiveness of quantity demanded to price changes, is symbolized by the Greek letter eta, η. It is defined as: [5]

$$\eta = \frac{\text{percentage change in quantity demanded}}{\text{percentage change in price}}$$

This measure is frequently called **demand elasticity** or, when it is necessary to distinguish this measure of elasticity from other related concepts, *price elasticity of demand* since the variable causing the change in quantity demanded is the commodity's own price.

[1] The use of averages is designed to avoid the ambiguity caused by the fact that, for example, the $.20 change in the price of beef is a different percentage of the original price, $1.70, than it is of the new price, $1.50 (11.8 percent versus 13.3 percent). We want the elasticity of demand between any two points (A and B) to be independent of whether we move from A to B or from B to A; as a result, using either "original" prices and quantities or "new" prices and quantities would be less satisfactory than using averages. In this illustration, $.20 is unambiguously 12.5 percent of $1.60 and applies to a price increase from $1.50 to $1.70, as well as to the decrease discussed in the text. Further discussion is found in the appendix to this chapter, which begins on page A-14.

Interpreting Numerical Elasticities

Because demand curves slope downward, an *increase* in price is associated with a *decrease* in quantity demanded and vice versa. Since the percentage changes in price and quantity have opposite signs, demand elasticity is a negative number. We shall follow the usual practice of ignoring the negative sign and speak of the measure as a positive number, as we have done in the illustrative calculations of elasticity in Table 5-3. Thus, the more responsive the quantity demanded, for example, radios relative to beef, the greater the elasticity of demand and the higher the measure: 2.0 compared to 0.5.

The numerical value of elasticity can vary from zero to infinity. Elasticity is zero when quantity

TABLE 5–3 THE CALCULATION OF DEMAND ELASTICITIES

Commodity	(1) Percentage decrease in price	(2) Percentage increase in quantity	(3) Elasticity of demand (2) ÷ (1)
Beef	12.5	6.25	0.5
Men's shirts	2.5	2.5	1.0
Radios	0.5	1.0	2.0

Elasticity is the percentage change in quantity divided by the percentage change in price. The percentage changes are based on average prices and quantities shown in Table 5–2. For example, the $.20 per pound decrease in the price of beef is 12.5 percent of $1.60. A $.20 change in the price of radios is only 0.5 percent of the average price per radio of $40.

demanded does not respond at all to a price change. As long as the percentage change in quantity is less than the percentage change in price, the elasticity of demand has a value of less than one. When the two percentage changes are equal to each other, elasticity is equal to one. When the percentage change in quantity exceeds the percentage change in price, the value for the elasticity of demand is greater than one.

When the percentage change in quantity is less than the percentage change in price (elasticity less than one), the demand is said to be **inelastic.** When the percentage change in quantity is greater than the percentage change in price (elasticity greater than one), the demand is said to be **elastic.** This terminology is important, and you should become familiar with it. It is summarized in the first half of Box 5-1.

A demand curve need not—and usually does not—have the same elasticity over every part of the curve. Figure 5-2 shows that a downward-sloping, straight-line demand curve does not have a constant elasticity. A straight line has constant elasticity only when it is vertical or when it is horizontal. Figure 5-3 illustrates three special demand curves with constant elasticities.

Price Elasticity and Changes in Total Expenditure

The total amount spent by purchasers is also the total revenue of the sellers. How does total revenue received by sellers of a commodity react when the price of a product is changed? The simplest example will show that it may rise or fall in response to a decrease in price. Suppose 100 units of a commodity are being sold at a unit price of $1. The price is then cut to $.90. If the quantity sold rises to 110, the total revenue of the sellers falls from $100 to $99; but if quantity sold rises to 120, total revenue rises from $100 to $108.

What happens to total revenue depends on the price elasticity of demand. If elasticity is less than unity (that is, less than one), the percentage change in price will exceed the percentage change in quantity. The price change will then dominate so that

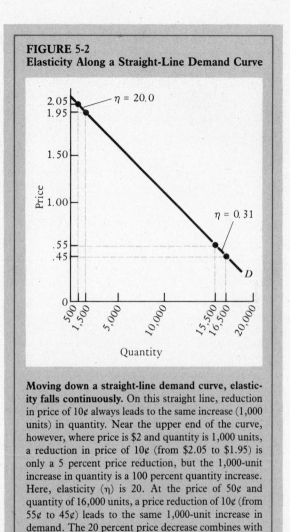

FIGURE 5-2
Elasticity Along a Straight-Line Demand Curve

Moving down a straight-line demand curve, elasticity falls continuously. On this straight line, reduction in price of 10¢ always leads to the same increase (1,000 units) in quantity. Near the upper end of the curve, however, where price is $2 and quantity is 1,000 units, a reduction in price of 10¢ (from $2.05 to $1.95) is only a 5 percent price reduction, but the 1,000-unit increase in quantity is a 100 percent quantity increase. Here, elasticity (η) is 20. At the price of 50¢ and quantity of 16,000 units, a price reduction of 10¢ (from 55¢ to 45¢) leads to the same 1,000-unit increase in demand. The 20 percent price decrease combines with the 6.25 percent quantity increase to give an elasticity of 0.31.

total revenue will change in the same direction as the price changes. If, however, elasticity exceeds unity, the percentage change in quantity will exceed the percentage change in price. The quantity change will then dominate so that total revenue will change in the same direction as quantity changes (that is, in the opposite direction to the change in price).

Notice what happened to total revenue when the

BOX 5–1 TERMINOLOGY OF ELASTICITY

Terminology	Symbol	Numerical measure of elasticity	Verbal description
A. Price elasticity of demand [supply]	$\eta[\eta_S]$		
Perfectly or completely inelastic		Zero	Quantity demanded [supplied] does not change as price changes
Inelastic		Greater than zero, but less than one	Quantity demanded [supplied] changes by a smaller percentage than does price
Unit elasticity		One	Quantity demanded [supplied] changes by exactly the same percentage as does price
Elastic		Greater than one, but less than infinity	Quantity demanded [supplied] changes by a larger percentage than does price
Perfectly, completely, or infinitely elastic		Infinity	Purchasers [sellers] are prepared to buy [sell] all they can at some price and none at all at an even slightly higher [lower] price
B. Income elasticity of demand	η_Y		
Inferior good		Negative	Quantity demanded decreases as income increases
Normal good		Positive	Quantity demanded increases as income increases:
Income-inelastic		Greater than zero, less than one	less than in proportion to income increase
Income-elastic		Greater than one	more than in proportion to income increase
C. Cross-elasticity of demand	η_X		
Substitute		Positive	Price increase of a substitute leads to an increase in quantity demanded of this good (and less of the substitute)
Complement		Negative	Price increase of a complement leads to a decrease in quantity demanded of this good (as well as less of the complement)

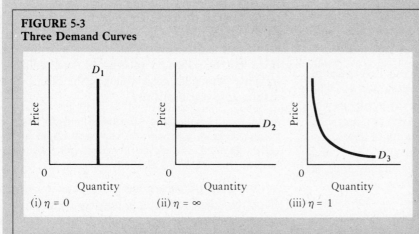

FIGURE 5-3
Three Demand Curves

(i) $\eta = 0$ (ii) $\eta = \infty$ (iii) $\eta = 1$

Each of these demand curves has constant elasticity. D_1 has *zero elasticity:* The quantity demanded does not change at all when price changes. D_2 has *infinite elasticity:* A small price increase decreases quantity demanded from an indefinitely large amount to zero. D_3 has *unit elasticity:* A given percentage increase in price brings an equal percentage decrease in quantity demanded at all points on the curve.

prices of radios, shirts, and beef fell in our example. (The calculations are shown in Table 5-4.) In the case of beef, the demand is inelastic and a cut in price lowered the sellers' revenue; in the case of radios, the demand is elastic and a cut in price raised revenue. The borderline case is men's shirts; here the elasticity is unity and the cut in price leaves revenue unchanged.

These examples illustrate more general relationships:

1. If demand is elastic, a fall in price increases total revenue and a rise in price reduces it.

2. If demand is inelastic, a fall in price reduces total revenue and a rise in price increases it.
3. If elasticity of demand is unity, a rise or a fall in price leaves total revenue unaffected. [6]

Consider two real examples. When a bumper potato crop in North America sent prices down 50 percent, quantity sold increased only 15 percent and potato farmers found their revenues falling sharply. Demand was clearly inelastic. When, some years ago, Salt Lake's transit authority cut its bus fares from $.25 to $.15 for the average journey, the volume of passenger traffic increased from 4.4 million to 14 million journeys within two years

TABLE 5–4 THE CHANGES IN TOTAL REVENUE (TOTAL EXPENDITURE) FOR THE EXAMPLE OF TABLE 5–2

Commodity	Price × quantity (original prices and quantities)	Price × quantity (new prices and quantities)	Change in revenue (expenditure)	Elasticity of demand from Table 5–3
Beef	$ 197,625	$ 185,625	− $12,000	0.5
Men's shirts	1,599,750	1,599,750	0	1.0
Radios	398,995	400,995	+ 2,000	2.0

Whether revenue increases or decreases in response to a price cut depends on whether demand is elastic or inelastic. The $197,625 figure is the product of the original price of beef ($1.70) and the original quantity (116,250 pounds). The $185,625 is the product of the new price ($1.50) and quantity (123,750), and so on.

and revenues rose sharply. Demand was clearly elastic.

What Determines Elasticity of Demand?

Table 5-5 shows some measured elasticities of demand. Evidently they can vary considerably. The main determinant of elasticity is the availability of substitutes. Some commodities, such as margarine, cabbage, lamb, and Fords, have quite close substitutes—butter, other green vegetables, beef, and similar makes of cars. A change in the price of these commodities, *the prices of the substitutes remaining constant,* can be expected to cause much substitution. A fall in price leads consumers to buy more of the commodity and less of the substitutes, and a rise in price leads consumers to buy less of

the commodity and more of the substitutes. Other, more broadly defined commodities, such as all foods, all clothing, cigarettes, and gasoline, have few if any satisfactory substitutes. A rise in their price can be expected to cause a smaller fall in quantity demanded than would be the case if close substitutes were available.

A commodity with close substitutes tends to have an elastic demand, one with no close substitutes an inelastic demand. The closer the substitutes for a commodity, the greater the elasticity of demand.

Closeness of substitutes—and thus measured elasticity—depends both on how the commodity is defined and on the time period. This is explored in following sections.

Definition of the commodity. For food taken as a whole, demand is inelastic over a large price range. It does not follow, however, that any one food, such as white bread or beef, is a necessity in the same sense. Therefore individual foods can have quite elastic demands and they frequently do.

Durable goods provide a similar example. Durables as a whole are less elastic than individual kinds of durable goods. For example, when the price of television sets rises, many households may replace their lawnmower or their vacuum cleaner instead of buying that extra television set. Thus, while their purchases of television sets fall, their total purchases of durables do not.

Because most specific manufactured goods have close substitutes, studies show they tend to have price-elastic demand. Millinery, for example, has been estimated to have an elasticity of 3.0. In contrast, clothing in general tends to be inelastic.

Any one of a group of related products will tend to have an elastic demand, even though the demand for the group as a whole may be inelastic.

Long-run and short-run elasticity of demand. Because it takes time to develop satisfactory substitutes, a demand that is inelastic in the short run may prove elastic when enough time has passed. For example, before the first OPEC price shocks

---

TABLE 5–5 ESTIMATED PRICE ELASTICITIES OF DEMAND (Selected Commodities)[a]

Inelastic demand (less than unity)	
Apples (Canada)	0.1
Sugar	0.3
Public transportation	0.4
All foods	0.4
Gasoline	0.6
All clothing	0.6
Butter (Canada)	0.8
Consumer durables	0.8
Demand of approximately unit elasticity[b]	
Beef	
Beer	
Marijuana	
Elastic demand (greater than unity)	
Furniture	1.2
Electricity	1.3
Domestic lamb and mutton (U.K.)	1.5
Automobiles	2.1
Millinery	3.0

[a] For the United States except where noted.
[b] Greater than 0.9 and less than 1.1

The wide range of price elasticities is illustrated by these selected measures. These elasticities, from various studies, are representative of literally hundreds of existing estimates. Explanations of some of the differences are discussed in the text.

FIGURE 5-4
Short- and Long-Run Demand Curves

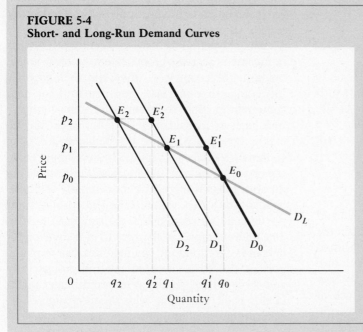

The long-run demand curve is more elastic than the short-run curves. D_L is a long-run demand curve. Suppose consumers are fully adjusted to price p_0. Equilibrium is then at E_0, with quantity demanded q_0. Now suppose price rises to p_1. In the short run, consumers will react along the short-run demand curve D_0 and reduce consumption to q_1'. Once time has permitted the full range of adjustments to price p_1, however, a new equilibrium at E_1 will be reached with quantity q_1, leading to a new short-run demand curve D_1. A further rise in price to p_2 would lead first to a short-run equilibrium at E_2' but eventually to a new long-run equilibrium at E_2. The screened long-run demand curve is more elastic than the short-run curves.

of the mid-1970s, the demand for gasoline was thought to be highly inelastic because of the absence of satisfactory substitutes. But the very large price increases over the 1970s have led to the development of smaller, more fuel-efficient cars and to less driving. The most recent estimates of elasticity of demand for gasoline have risen from around 0.6 to around unity. Given another decade in which to develop substitutes, gasoline demand may prove to be elastic.

The degree of response to a price change, and thus the measured price elasticity of demand, will tend to be greater the longer the time span considered.

Because the elasticity of demand for a commodity changes over time as consumers adjust their habits and substitutes are developed, the demand curve also changes; hence a distinction can be made between short-run and long-run demand curves.

A *short-run demand curve* shows the response of

quantity demanded to a change in price for a given structure of the durable goods that use the commodity and for the existing sets of substitute commodities. A different short-run demand curve will exist for each such structure.

The *long-run demand curve* shows the response of quantity demanded to a change in price after enough time has passed to assure that all adjustments to the changed price have occurred. For example, a change in price of, say, electricity may not have its major effect until the stock of appliances and machines that use electricity has been adjusted. This adjustment may take a long time.

The relation between long-run and short-run demand curves is shown in Figure 5-4. The principal conclusion, already suggested in the discussion of elasticity, is:

The long-run demand curve for a commodity will tend to be substantially more elastic than any of the short-run demand curves.

The importance of this distinction will be evident in the chapters that follow.

OTHER DEMAND ELASTICITIES

Demand depends on other factors besides its own price, and measures of the responsiveness of demand to these other factors can be defined. Two of the most important of these other factors are income and prices of other goods.

The Concept of Income Elasticity

One of the most important determinants of demand is the income of the potential customers. When the Food and Agricultural Organization of the United Nations (the FAO) wants to estimate the future demand for some crop, it needs to know by how much world income will grow and how much of that additional income will be spent on the particular foodstuff. For example, as a nation gets richer, its consumption patterns change, with relatively more being spent on meat and relatively less on staples such as rice and potatoes.

The responsiveness of demand to changes in income is termed **income elasticity of demand** and may be symbolized η_y.

$$\eta_y = \frac{\text{percentage change in quantity demanded}}{\text{percentage change in income}}$$

For most goods, increases in income lead to increases in demand and income elasticity will be positive. These are called **normal goods**. Goods for which consumption decreases in response to a rise in income have negative income elasticities and are called **inferior goods**.

The income elasticity of normal goods may be less than unity (inelastic) or greater than unity (elastic), depending on whether (say) a 10 percent increase in income leads to less than or more than a 10 percent increase in the quantity demanded.[2]

The reaction of demand to changes in income is

[2] It is common to use the terms *income-elastic* and *income-inelastic* to refer to income elasticities of greater or less than unity. See Box 5-1.

extremely important. We know that in most Western economies economic growth has caused the level of income to double every 20 to 30 years over a sustained period of at least a century. This rise in income is shared to some extent by most households in the country. As they find their incomes increasing, they increase their demands for most commodities. But the demands for some commodities such as food and basic clothing will not increase very much, while the demands for other commodities increase rapidly. In developing countries such as Ireland and Mexico, the demand for durable goods is increasing most rapidly as household incomes rise, while in the United States it is the demand for services that is rising most rapidly. The uneven impact of the growth of income on the demands for different commodities has very important effects on the economy and groups in it, and these will be studied at several different points in this book, beginning with the discussion of agriculture in Chapter 6.

The Determinants of Income Elasticity

The variations in income elasticities shown in Table 5-6 suggest that the more basic or staple a commodity, the lower its income elasticity. Food as a whole has an income elasticity of 0.2, consumer durables of 1.8. In Canada pork and such starchy roots as potatoes are inferior goods; their quantity consumed falls as income rises.

Does the distinction between luxuries and necessities explain differences in income elasticities? The table suggests that it does. The case of meals eaten away from home is one example; such meals are almost always more expensive, calorie for calorie, than meals prepared at home. It would thus be expected that at lower ranges of income restaurant meals would be regarded as an expensive luxury, but the demand for them would expand substantially as households became richer. This is in fact what happens.

Does this mean that the market demand for the foodstuffs that appear on restaurant menus will also have high income elasticities? Generally the answer is no; when a household eats out rather than pre-

TABLE 5–6 ESTIMATED INCOME ELASTICITIES OF DEMAND (Selected Commodities)[a]

Inferior goods (negative income elasticities)	
Milk	−0.3
Starchy roots	−0.2
Inelastic normal goods (0.0 to 1.0)	
Coffee (U.S)	0.0
Wine (France)	0.1
Vegetables	0.2
All food (U.S.)	0.2
Poultry	0.3
Beef and veal	0.4
Housing (U.S.)	0.6
Cigarettes (U.S.)	0.8
Elastic normal goods (greater than 1.0)	
Gasoline (U.S.)	1.1
Cream (U.K.)	1.7
Wine	1.8
Consumer durables (U.K.)	1.8
Poultry (Ceylon)	2.0
Restaurant meals (U.K.)	2.4

[a] For Canada except where noted.

Income elasticities vary widely across commodities and sometimes across countries. The basic source of food estimates by country is the FAO, but many individual studies have been made. Explanations of some of the differences are discussed in the text.

paring meals at home, the main change is not in what is eaten but in who prepares it. The additional expenditure on "food" goes mainly to pay cooks and waiters and to yield a return on the restaurateur's capital. Thus, when a household expands its expenditure on restaurant food by 2.4 percent in response to a 1 percent rise in its income, most of the extra expenditure on "food" goes to workers in service industries; little, if any, finds its way into the pockets of farmers. Here is a striking example of the general tendency for households to spend a higher proportion of their incomes on services as their incomes rise.

The more basic an item in the consumption pattern of households, the lower its income elasticity.

So far we have focused on differences in income elasticities among commodities. However, income elasticities for a single commodity also vary with the level of a household's income. When incomes are very low, households may eat virtually no meat and consume lots of starchy foods such as bread and potatoes; at higher levels, they may eat the cheaper cuts of meat and more green vegetables along with their bread and potatoes; at yet higher levels they are likely to eat more (and more expensive) meat, to substitute frozen for canned vegetables, and to eat a greater variety of foods.

What is true of individuals is also true of countries. Studies show that for different countries at comparable stages of economic development, income elasticities are similiar. But the countries of the world are at various stages of economic development and so have widely different income elasticities for the same products. Notice in Table 5-6 the different income elasticity of poultry in Canada, where it is a standard item of consumption, and in Sri Lanka, where it is a luxury.

Graphic Representation

Increases in income shift an ordinary demand curve to the right for a normal good and to the left for an inferior good. Figure 5-5 shows a different kind of graph, an **income-consumption curve** that resembles the ordinary demand curve in one respect: It shows the relation of quantity demanded to *one* variable, other things held constant. The variable, however, is not price but household income. (An increase in the price of the commodity, incomes remaining constant, would shift the curves shown in Figure 5-5 downward.)

The figure shows three different patterns of income elasticity. Goods that consumers regard as necessities will have high income elasticities at low levels of income but show low income elasticities beyond some level. The obvious reason is that as incomes rise it becomes possible for households to devote a smaller proportion of their income to meeting basic needs and a larger proportion to buying things they have always wanted but could not afford. Some of these necessities may even become inferior goods. So-called luxury goods will not tend to be purchased at low levels of income

FIGURE 5-5
Income-Consumption Curves of Different Commodities

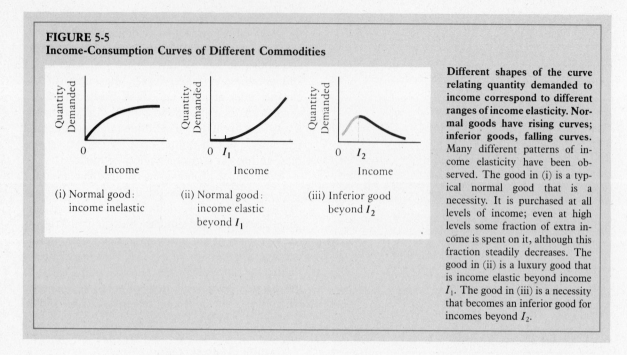

(i) Normal good:
    income inelastic

(ii) Normal good:
     income elastic
     beyond I_1

(iii) Inferior good
      beyond I_2

Different shapes of the curve relating quantity demanded to income correspond to different ranges of income elasticity. Normal goods have rising curves; inferior goods, falling curves. Many different patterns of income elasticity have been observed. The good in (i) is a typical normal good that is a necessity. It is purchased at all levels of income; even at high levels some fraction of extra income is spent on it, although this fraction steadily decreases. The good in (ii) is a luxury good that is income elastic beyond income I_1. The good in (iii) is a necessity that becomes an inferior good for incomes beyond I_2.

but will have high income elasticities once incomes rise enough to permit households to sample the better things of life available to them.[3]

Cross-Elasticity of Demand

The responsiveness of demand to changes in the prices of other commodities is called **cross-elasticity of demand**. It is denoted η_x and defined as

$$\eta_x = \frac{\text{percentage change in quantity demanded of one good, } X}{\text{percentage change in price of another good, } Y}$$

[3] In Figure 5-5, in contrast to the ordinary demand curve, quantity demanded is on the vertical axis. This follows the usual practice of putting the to-be-explained variable (called the *dependent variable*) on the vertical axis and the explanatory variable (called the *independent variable*) on the horizontal axis. It is the ordinary demand curve that has the axes "backward." This practice dates to Alfred Marshall's *Principles of Economics* (1890), the classic that is one of the foundation stones of modern price theory. [7] For better or worse, Marshall's scheme is now used by everybody—although mathematicians never fail to wonder at this further example of the odd ways of economists.

Cross-elasticity can vary from minus infinity to plus infinity. Complementary commodities will have negative cross-elasticities. Cars and gasoline, for example, are complements. A large rise in the price of gasoline will lead (as it has in Canada) to a decline in the demand for cars as some people decide to do without a car and others decide not to buy a second (or third) car. Substitute commodities have positive cross-elasticities. Cars and public transport are substitutes. A large rise in the price of cars (relative to public transport) would lead to a rise in the demand for public transport as some people shifted from cars to public transport.

Measures of cross-elasticity sometimes prove helpful in defining whether producers of similar products are in competition with each other. Glass bottles and tin cans have a high cross elasticity of demand. The producer of bottles is thus in competition with the producer of cans. If the bottle company raises its price, it will lose substantial sales to the can producer. Men's shoes and women's shoes have a low cross elasticity. Thus a producer of men's shoes is not in close competition with a producer of women's shoes. If the former raises its price, it will not lose many sales to the latter. This kind of knowledge has been extremely important in antitrust cases where the issue was whether a firm in one industry was or was not in active competition with firms in another industry. Indeed, many of the most interesting studies of cross-elasticity have been made during combines investigations to determine whether specific products are substitutes. Whether cellophane and Saran Wrap, or aluminum cable and copper cable, are or are not substitutes may determine questions of monopoly under the law. The positive or negative sign and the size of cross-elasticities tell us whether or not goods are substitutes.

The terminology of elasticity is important. It is summarized in Box 5-1, which deserves careful study.

SUPPLY ELASTICITY

The concept of elasticity can be applied to supply as well as to demand. Just as elasticity of demand measures the response of quantity demanded to changes in any of the forces that influence it, so elasticity of supply measures the response of quantity supplied to changes in any of the forces that influence it. We will focus on the commodity's own price as a factor influencing supply.

Elasticity of supply measures the responsiveness of the quantity supplied to a change in the commodity's own price. It is denoted η_s and defined as

$$\eta_s = \frac{\text{percentage change in quantity supplied}}{\text{percentage change in price}}$$

The supply curves considered in this chapter all have positive slopes: An increase in price causes an increase in quantity sold. Such supply curves all have positive elasticities.

There are important special cases. If the supply curve is vertical—the quantity supplied does not change as price changes—elasticity of supply is zero. This would be the case, for example, if sup-

pliers produced a given quantity and dumped it on the market for whatever it would bring. A horizontal supply curve has an infinitely high elasticity of supply: A small drop in price would reduce the quantity producers are willing to supply from an indefinitely large amount to zero. Between these two extremes elasticity of supply will vary with the shape of the supply curve.[4]

What Determines Elasticity of Supply?

Supply elasticities are very important for many problems in economics. We shall discuss them only briefly here for two reasons. First, much of the treatment of demand elasticity carries over to supply elasticity and does not need repeating. For example, the ease of substitution can vary in production as well as in consumption. If the price of a commodity rises, how much more can be produced profitably? This depends in part on whether it is easy to shift from the production of other commodities to the one whose price has risen. If agricultural land and labor can be readily shifted from one crop to another, the supply of any one crop will be more elastic than if they cannot. Here also, as with demand, length of time for response is critical. It may be difficult to change quantities supplied in response to a price increase in a matter of weeks or months but easy to do so over a period of years. For example, new oil fields can be discovered, wells drilled, and pipelines built over a period of years, but not in a few months. Thus elasticity of oil supply is much greater over five years than over one year.

The second reason for brevity of treatment is that supply elasticity depends to a great extent on how costs behave as output is varied, an issue that will be treated at length in Part Three. If costs of production rise rapidly as output rises, then the stimulus to expand production in response to a price rise will be choked off by increases in costs.

[4] Steepness, which is related to absolute rather than percentage changes, is *not* always a reliable guide. As is shown in the appendix to this chapter, any upward-sloping straight line passing through the origin has an elasticity of +1.0 over its entire range.

In this case supply will tend to be rather inelastic. If, however, costs rise only slowly as production increases, a rise in price that raises profits will elicit a large increase in quantity supplied before the rise in costs puts a halt to the expansion in output. In this case supply will tend to be rather elastic.

SUMMARY

1. Elasticity of demand (also called *price elasticity*) is a measure of the extent to which the quantity demanded of a commodity responds to a change in its price. We define it as the percentage change in quantity divided by the percentage change in price that brought it about. Elasticity is defined to be a positive number that varies from zero to infinity.

2. When the numerical measure of elasticity is less than 1, demand is *inelastic*. This means that the percentage change in quantity is less than the percentage change in price that brought it about. When the numerical measure exceeds unity, demand is *elastic*. This means that the percentage change in quantity is greater than the percentage change in price that brought it about.

3. Elasticity and the total revenue of sellers are related in this way: If elasticity is less than unity, a fall in price lowers total revenue; if elasticity is greater than unity, a fall in price raises total revenue; and if elasticity is unity, total revenue does not change as price changes.

4. The main determinant of the price elasticity of demand is the availability of substitutes for the commodity. The more and better the substitutes, the higher the elasticity. The price elasticity of a commodity group tends to be higher the more narrowly it is defined and the more adequate are its substitutes. Any one of a group of close substitutes will tend to have an elastic demand even though the group as a whole has a highly inelastic demand.

5. Elasticity of demand tends to be greater the longer the time over which adjustment occurs. Items that have few substitutes in the short run may develop ample substitutes when consumers and producers have time to adapt.

6. Income elasticity is the percentage change in quantity demanded divided by the percentage change in income that brought it about. It tends to be lower the more basic, or staple, is the commodity. Thus luxuries tend to have higher income elasticities than necessities. The income elasticity of demand for a commodity will usually change as income varies. For example, a commodity that has a high income elasticity at a low income (because increases in income bring it within reach of the typical household) may have a low or negative income elasticity at higher incomes (because with further rises in incomes it can be replaced by a superior substitute).

7. Cross-elasticity is the percentage change in quantity demanded divided by the percentage change in the price of some other commodity that brought it about. It is used to define commodities that are substitutes for one another (positive cross-elasticity) and commodities that complement one another (negative cross-elasticity).

8. Elasticity of supply is an important concept in economics. It measures the ratio of the percentage change in the quantity supplied of a commodity to the percentage change in its price. It is the analogue on the supply side to the elasticity of demand.

9. An appendix to this chapter, for students with some mathematics training, extends the analysis.

TOPICS FOR REVIEW

Elasticity of demand
Significance of elastic and inelastic demands
The relation between demand elasticity and total expenditure
Income elasticity of demand
income-elastic and income-inelastic
Normal goods and inferior goods
Short-run and long-run demand curves
Cross-elasticity of demand
Substitutes and complements
Elasticity of supply

DISCUSSION QUESTIONS

1. From the following quotations what (if anything) can you conclude about elasticity of demand?
   a. "Good weather resulted in record wheat harvests and sent wheat prices tumbling. For many wheat farmers the result has been calamitous."
   b. "Ridership always went up when bus fares came down, but the increased patronage never was enough to prevent a decrease in overall revenue."
   c. "When the British Columbia Telephone Company started charging for directory assistance calls, the number of [such] calls dropped 80 percent."
   d. "The 30 percent increase in postal rates has led us [The Narrangansett Electric Co.] to have 60 percent of our bills hand delivered instead of mailed."
   e. "Coffee to me is an essential—you've gotta have it no matter what the price."

2. What would you predict about the relative price elasticity of demand of (a) food, (b) meat, (c) beef, (d) chuck roast, (e) Safeway chuck roast? What would you predict about their relative income elasticities?

3. "Avocados have a very limited market, not greatly affected by price until the price falls to less than $.12 a pound. Then they are much demanded by manufacturers of dog food." Interpret this statement in terms of price elasticity.

4. "Home computers have proved the big surprise of the 1980s in sales appeal. But per capita sales are much lower in Puerto Rico than Canada, lower in Newfoundland than in Ontario. Manufacturers are puzzled by the big differences." Can you offer an explanation in terms of elasticity?

5. What elasticity measure or measures would be useful in answering the following questions?
   a. Will cheaper transport into the central city help keep downtown shopping centers profitable?
   b. Will raising the bulk-rate postage rate increase or decrease the postal deficit?
   c. Are producers of toothpaste and mouthwash in competition with each other?
   d. What effect will falling gasoline prices have on the sale of cars that use diesel fuel?
   e. Why do rising interest rates hurt the sales of houses and of art that is purchased as an investment?

6. Interpret the following statements in terms of the relevant elasticity concept:
   a. "As fuel for tractors has gotten more expensive, many farmers have shifted from plowing their fields to no-till farming. No-till acreage increased from 30 million acres in 1972 to 95 million acres in 1982."
   b. "Fertilizer makers brace for dismal year as farm slump is projected."
   c. "When farmers are hurting, small towns feel the pain."

7. It has been observed recently that obesity is a more frequent medical problem for the relatively poor than for the middle-income classes. Can you use the theory of demand to shed light on this observation?

8. Suggest commodities that you think might have the following patterns of elasticity of demand.
   a. High income elasticity, high price elasticity
   b. High income elasticity, low price elasticity
   c. Low income elasticity, low price elasticity
   d. Low income elasticity, high price elasticity

9. Look at Table 5-5. Can you suggest why gasoline is inelastic but electricity is elastic? Why is furniture more elastic than all consumer goods taken together?

10. Look at Table 5-6. Can you suggest why gasoline is more income elastic than cigarettes or housing? Or why coffee is less income elastic than beef?

6 SUPPLY AND DEMAND IN ACTION: PRICE CONTROLS AND AGRICULTURE

The method of comparative statics has immediate application to many real-world problems. The method, you will recall, is to start from a position of equilibrium in the market and then introduce the change to be studied—for example, a shift to the left of the supply curve. Then we determine the new equilibrium position and compare it with the original one. The differences between the two positions of equilibrium (higher price, lower quantities actually exchanged) can be attributed to the change introduced for that is the only change that has been allowed to occur.

In this chapter we apply supply and demand analysis to situations in which the government has set either minimum or maximum prices. We then examine two case studies in some detail: rent controls and the problem of agriculture.

CONTROLLED PRICES

In a free market, price tends to move toward its equilibrium value, where the quantities demanded and supplied are equal. Some government price

controls are designed to hold the market price below equilibrium. In so doing they cause quantity
demanded to exceed quantity supplied at the controlled price, creating shortages. Other government
policies are designed to hold prices above equilibrium. In so doing they cause quantity supplied to
exceed quantity demanded at the controlled price,
creating surpluses.

Quantity Exchanged at Disequilibrium Prices

What happens when price controls are used to hold
price at some disequilibrium value? What determines the quantity actually traded on the market?
The key to this question is the simple fact that any
voluntary market transaction requires both a willing buyer and a willing seller. This means that if
quantity demanded is less than quantity supplied,
the demand will determine the amount actually
exchanged, while the rest of the quantity supplied
will remain in the hands of the unsuccessful sellers.
On the other hand, if quantity demanded exceeds
quantity supplied, the supply will determine the
amount actually traded, while the rest of the quantity demanded will represent desired purchases of
unsuccessful buyers.

**At any disequilibrium price, quantity exchanged is de-
termined by the *lesser* of quantity demanded or quantity supplied.**

This is shown graphically in Figure 6-1. Quantity exchanged at any price is determined by the
curve *on the left* at that price—that is, the demand
curve above, and the supply curve below, the equilibrium price.

Floor Prices

The government sometimes establishes a minimum
or **floor price** for a good or service. Minimum
wages for labor and guaranteed prices for certain
agricultural commodities are well-known examples. If the floor price is set at or below the equilibrium price, it will have no effect because equilibrium will still be attainable and will not be

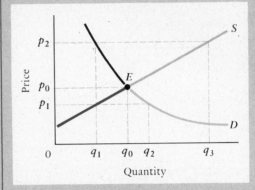

**FIGURE 6-1
The Determination of Quantity Exchanged in
Disequilibrium**

In disequilibrium, quantity exchanged is determined
by the *lesser* of quantity demanded or quantity
supplied. At p_0 the market is in equilibrium, with
quantity demanded equal to quantity supplied at q_0.
For prices below p_0, such as p_1, the quantity exchanged
will be determined by the supply curve. For example,
the quantity q_1 will be exchanged at the disequilibrium
price p_1 in spite of the excess demand of q_1q_2. For
prices above p_0, such as p_2, the quantity exchanged
will be given by the demand curve. For example, the
quantity exchanged will be only q_1 at the price p_2 in
spite of the excess supply of q_1q_3. Thus the darker
portions of the S and D curves show the whole set of
actual quantities exchanged at different prices.

inconsistent with the floor price set by law. If,
however, the floor price is above the equilibrium
price, it is said to be binding or "effective." We
shall deal with situations in which it is binding.

Sometimes floor prices are simply rules that
make it illegal to sell the commodity below the
prescribed price. That is the case with the minimum wage, which is examined in some detail in
Chapter 19. Sometimes the government establishes
floor prices by announcing that it will guarantee a
certain price, if necessary by buying the product
itself at that price. Such guarantees are a feature
of much of agricultural policy, which is examined
in detail later in this chapter.

No matter what the mechanism, the key result
of floor prices is always the same, as is illustrated
in Figure 6-2.

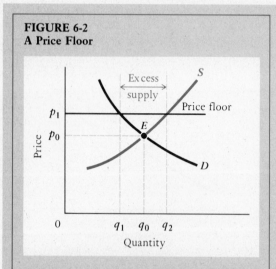

**FIGURE 6-2
A Price Floor**

If a price floor is above the equilibrium price, quantity supplied will exceed quantity demanded. The free-market equilibrium is at E, with price p_0 and quantity q_0. If the government makes it illegal for the price to fall below p_1, it has established an effective price floor. Quantity supplied will exceed quantity demanded by q_1q_2. If the government does nothing, this excess supply will be in private hands and will either go to waste or accumulate in inventories. If the government buys the excess supply, sellers will get rid of the full quantity they wish to produce, q_2, but the government will have the quantity q_1q_2 to store or dispose of.

Effective floor prices cause excess supply. Either an unsold surplus will exist or someone must step in and buy the excess production.

The consequences of excess supply will of course differ from commodity to commodity. If the commodity is labor which is subject to a minimum wage, excess supply translates into people without jobs. If the commodity is wheat, and more is produced than can be sold, the surplus wheat must accumulate in grain elevators or government warehouses. These consequences may or may not be "worth it" in terms of the other goals achieved. But the consequences are inevitable whenever the floor price is set above the market clearing equilibrium price, and nothing further is done.

Why might the government wish to incur these consequences? The answer lies in the fact that those who actually succeed in selling their commodities at the floor price are better off than if they had to accept the lower equilibrium price. Workers and farmers are among those who have persuaded the government to help them raise the prices of what they sell by establishing minimum prices.

Ceiling Prices

It is common in wartime, and increasingly frequent in peacetime, for the government to fix the *maximum prices* at which certain goods and services may be sold. Price controls on oil, natural gas, and rental housing have been common features of the Canadian scene for some or all of the time since World War II.

Although frequently referred to as fixed or "frozen" prices, most price controls actually specify the highest permissible price, often called the **ceiling price**, that producers may legally charge. Once again, we shall confine our attention to situations in which the ceiling price is binding—that is, below the free-market equilibrium price. The key result is shown in Figure 6-3.

Effective ceiling prices cause excess demand, and the quantity exchanged will fall below its equilibrium amount.

In inflationary situations, price controls often take the form of "freezing" prices at current free-market levels. At the moment of imposition the price control is not effective, but as inflation occurs the free-market price rises, and thus the controlled price becomes an effective ceiling price.

Allocating a Commodity in Short Supply

What happens to the excess demand caused by effective ceiling prices? The free market eliminates excess demand by allowing price to rise, thereby allocating the available supply among would-be purchasers. Since this does not happen under price ceilings, some other method of allocation must be

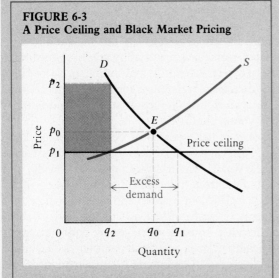

FIGURE 6-3
A Price Ceiling and Black Market Pricing

A ceiling price below the equilibrium price causes excess demand and invites a black market. Equilibrium price is at p_0. If a price ceiling is set at p_1, the quantity demanded will rise to q_1 and the quantity supplied will fall to q_2. Quantity actually exchanged will be q_2. Although excess demand is q_2q_1, price may not legally rise to restore equilibrium. If all the available supply of q_2 were sold on a black market, price to consumers would rise to p_2, with black marketeers earning receipts shown by the shaded areas. The dark shaded area shows the profit of those who buy at the ceiling price and sell at the black market price.

adopted. Experience shows that certain alternatives are likely.

If stores sell their available supplies on a first-come, first-served basis, people will rush to those stores that are said to have stocks of any commodity in short supply. In many Eastern European and African countries where prices of "essentials" are subject to effective price ceilings, the word—even the rumor—that a shop is selling supplies of a scarce commodity can cause a local stampede. Buyers often spend hours in line waiting to get into the shop, and supplies are usually exhausted long before all can be served. This is why standing in lines is a way of life in so many command economies today.

A different system develops if storekeepers individually decide who will get the scarce commodities. Goods may be kept "under the counter" and sold only to regular customers. This happened in 1978, during the American gasoline shortage. Some gas station operators sold only to regular customers. When sellers decide to whom they will (and will not) sell scarce supplies, allocation is by **sellers' preferences**.

If the government dislikes the distribution that results from sellers' preferences, it can do at least two things. First, it can pass laws requiring suppliers to sell on a first-come, first-served basis. To the extent that this legislation is effective, it leads to allocation according to willingness to stand in line. These laws are not easily enforceable, and there is little doubt that some available supplies are sold to favored customers according to sellers' preferences.

Second and more drastic, the government can ration the commodity. To do so, it prints only enough coupons to match the available supplies and then distributes the coupons to purchasers, who will need both money and ration coupons to buy the commodity. The coupons may be distributed equally among the population or on the basis of age, family status, occupation, or any other criterion.

Rationing substitutes the government's preferences for the seller's preferences in allocating a price-controlled commodity.

Black Markets

Ceiling prices, with or without rationing, usually give rise to black markets. In a **black market** goods are sold (illegally) at prices above the legal maximum price. Most products have many retailers, and although it may be easy to police the producers, it is often impossible to control effectively the price at which retailers sell to the general public.

Suppose the government can control producers but not retailers. Production remains at the level consistent with the maximum permitted price because the producers receive the controlled price for their product. At the retail level, however, the opportunity for a black market arises because purchasers are willing to pay more than the ceiling price for the limited amounts of the commodity that are available.

The potential for a black market always exists whenever binding ceiling prices are imposed because a profit can be made by buying at the controlled price and selling at the black market price.

Figure 6-3 illustrates the case in which all the available supply is sold on a black market. This case is extreme because there are honest people in every society and because governments ordinarily have considerable power to enforce their price laws. Thus some, but not all, of a price-controlled commodity is sold on the black market.

Does the existence of a black market mean that the goals sought by imposing ceiling prices have been thwarted? This question can be answered only when we know what the government hopes to achieve with its ceiling price. Governments might be interested mainly in (1) restricting production (perhaps to release resources for war production), (2) keeping prices down, or (3) satisfying notions of equity in the consumption of a commodity that is temporarily unusually scarce. When ceiling prices are accompanied by a black market, the first objective, but not the second and third, is achieved. The second objective is frustrated to the extent that goods find their way onto the black market. If equity is the goal, effective ceiling prices on manufacturers plus an extensive black market at the retail level may produce the worst possible results. There will be less to go around than if there were no controls, and the available quantities will tend to go to those with the most money or the least social conscience.

RENT CONTROLS: A CASE STUDY OF CEILING PRICE CONTROL

A widespread, growing use of ceiling prices in North America today relates to the rental of houses and apartments for private occupancy. Rent controls have been used the world over, with similar consequences: the creation of severe housing shortages, private allocation systems, and black markets. For example, to make up the difference between the controlled rent and the free-market rent, the landlord may charge the new tenant a grossly inflated sum for a few shabby sticks of furniture. Alternatively, landlords may ration in accordance with their own preferences for tenants and discriminate against such groups as students and families with young children.

Controls have existed in New York City, London, Paris, and many other large cities at least since World War II. Controls are newer in Canada, and most date from the anti-inflation policies introduced in 1975. In Sweden and Britain, where rent controls on unfurnished apartments have existed for decades, housing shortages are endemic except in neighborhoods where population is declining. Whole areas of London are full of abandoned, rotting houses that would have lasted for centuries but that, at controlled rentals, did not even pay the owner the cost of upkeep. When British controls were extended to furnished apartments in 1973, the supply of such accommodations dried up, at least until loopholes were found in the law. When rent controls were initiated in Rome in 1978, a housing shortage developed virtually overnight. This kind of induced shortage led University of Chicago Professors George Stigler and Milton Friedman to point to the conflict between "ceilings" and "roofs."

Rent controls are just a special case of ceiling prices. Controls are usually imposed to freeze rents at their current level at a time when equilibrium rents are rising either because demand is shifting rightward (due to forces such as rising population and income) or because supply is shifting leftward (due to forces such as rising costs). Soon rents are being held below the free-market equilibrium level and excess demand appears. Figure 6-3 can be applied to rent controls. The following predictions about rent controls are simply applications to housing of results that apply to any commodity subject to binding ceiling prices.

1. There will be a housing shortage in the sense that quantity demanded will exceed quantity supplied.

2. The actual quantity of accommodation will be less than if free-market rents had been charged.

3. The shortage will lead to alternative allocation schemes. Landlords may allocate by sellers' preferences, or the government may intervene. In the housing market, government intervention usually takes the form of security-of-tenure laws, which protect the tenant from eviction and thus give existing tenants priority over potential new tenants.

4. Black markets will appear. Landlords may require large lump-sum entrance fees from new tenants. In general, the larger the housing shortage, the bigger the sum required. In the absence of security-of-tenure laws, landlords may force tenants out when their leases expire, and they may even try to evict them to extract a large entrance fee from new tenants.

Special Aspects of the Housing Market

Housing has unusual attributes that make the analysis of rent controls somewhat special. The most important is the nature of the commodity itself. So far in this book we have mainly considered markets for commodities that are consumed soon after they are produced. But housing is an example of a **durable good,** a good that yields its services only gradually over an extended period of time. Once built, an apartment can last for decades or even centuries, yielding its valuable services continuously over that time.

Thus the supply of rental accommodation depends on the *stock* of rental housing available, and in any year it is composed mainly of buildings built in prior years. The stock is added to by conversions of housing from other uses and construction of new buildings, and it is diminished by conversions to other uses and demolition or abandonment of existing buildings whose economic life is over. The stock usually changes slowly from year to year.

These considerations mean we can draw more than one supply curve for rental accommodation, depending on how much time is allowed for reactions to occur to any given level of rents. We shall distinguish just two such curves. The *long-run sup-ply curve* relates rents to the quantity of rental accommodation that will be supplied after sufficient time has passed for all adjustments to be made. The *short-run supply curve* relates rents to quantity supplied when only a short time—say, a few months—is allowed for adjustments to be made in response to a change in rents. We shall assume that in the short run very few new conversions and very little new construction can occur. As we saw in Chapter 5, elasticity of supply is likely to be greater in the long run than in the short run.

The Long-Run Supply Curve

Among the many suppliers of rental accommodations are large investment companies and individuals with modest savings invested in one or two small apartments. There is a large potential source of supply, for it is relatively easy to build a new apartment or to convert an existing house and offer its units for rent. If the expected return from investing in new apartments rises significantly above the return on comparable other investments, there will be a flow of investment funds into the building of new apartments. However, if the return from apartments falls significantly below that obtainable on comparable investments, funds will go elsewhere. The construction of new apartments will fall off and possibly stop altogether. Old apartments will not be replaced as they wear out, so the quantity available will fall drastically. Therefore:

The long-run supply curve of apartments is highly elastic.

The Short-Run Supply Curve

Now consider the supply response over a few months. What if rents rise? Even though it immediately becomes profitable to invest in new apartments, it may well take years for land to be obtained, plans drawn up, and construction completed. Thus a long time may pass between the decision to create more apartments and the occupancy by tenants of the new apartments built in response to market signals. Of course, some existing housing can be more quickly converted to rental uses, but in many cases even this will take more than a few months.

What if rents fall? New construction will fall off, which will surely decrease the supply at some time in the future. It will, however, pay the owners of existing apartments with no attractive alternative use of their rental units to rent them for whatever they will earn, providing that the rentals at least cover current out-of-pocket costs such as taxes and heating. Some rental housing can be abandoned or converted to other uses, but, again, this will not usually happen very quickly. Thus:

The short-run supply curve tends to be quite inelastic at the level of the quantity currently supplied.

The longer the time horizon, the less inelastic it will be. For the very short run, however, it is likely to be almost completely inelastic.

Supply Response to Changes in Rents

If rents rise due to a housing shortage, what will the supply response be? In the short run, the quantity will remain more or less the same because the short-run supply curve is inelastic. For a while existing landlords will make **windfall profits,** profits that bear no relation to current or historical costs. Yet these profits are the spur to the long-run allocation of resources. New construction and conversions will begin, and after a year or two new rental units will begin to come onto the market. The quantity will continue to expand until a new point on the long-run supply curve has been attained. At that point all windfall profits have been eliminated.

If rents decrease, the quantity supplied will also remain more or less unchanged because of the inelastic short-run supply curve. Landlords who were breaking even will now suffer windfall losses. As the profitability of supplying rental accommodations falls, new construction will be curtailed. But it will take time before the stock of rental housing shrinks to its new point on the long-run supply curve. Only then will it again pay to maintain the stock of rental housing.

Short-run windfall profits or losses provide the signals that bring about long-run supply adjustments in a free market.

Because houses are durable, they will not quickly disappear. But owners of rental properties can speed the shrinkage in various ways. Some apartments can be converted into cooperatives or condominiums. Other apartments occupy land with valuable alternative uses. If rents fall far enough, it will pay to demolish those apartments and use the land for something else. (Of course, it requires a substantial and long-lasting fall in rents before demolition costs are worth incurring.)

Many existing apartment buildings and other rental accommodations have no real alternative uses and will continue to serve as apartments until they are abandoned as useless. Yet the useful life of an apartment depends on how well it is maintained. In general, the less spent on maintenance and repairs, the shorter the structure's effective life. The lower the rents, the less will it pay landlords to spend on upkeep, and thus the faster the apartment will "wear out."

If rental revenues fall below the minimum costs of operation (which include taxes and heating), the owner may simply abandon the apartment. Although this may sound extreme, it has happened repeatedly. When it happens, a stock of housing that might have lasted decades or even centuries is dissipated within a few years.

The special features of the housing market lead to an important additional prediction about rent controls.

Because the long-run supply curve of rental housing is highly elastic, rent controls that hold rents below their free-market levels for an extended period will inevitably lead to a large reduction in the quantity of rental housing available.

This prediction is illustrated in Figure 6-4.

The Demand for Rental Housing

There are many reasons to expect the demand for apartments and other forms of rental housing to be

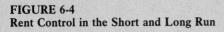

FIGURE 6-4
Rent Control in the Short and Long Run

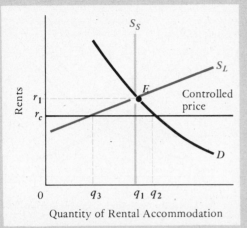

Quantity of Rental Accommodation

Rent control causes housing shortages that worsen as time passes. The controlled rent, r_c, is below the equilibrium rent r_1. The short-run supply of housing is shown by the inelastic curve S_S. Thus quantity supplied remains at q_1 in the short run, and the housing shortage is q_1q_2. Over time the quantity supplied shrinks, as shown by the long-run supply curve S_L. In long-run equilibrium there are only q_3 units of rental accommodation, far fewer than when controls were instituted. Since the long-run supply is quite elastic, the housing shortage of q_3q_2 that occurs after supply has fully adjusted ends up being much larger than the initial shortage of q_1q_2.

move out of parental homes as quickly as they might otherwise do).

Such occurrences contribute to a highly elastic demand for rental housing: Increases in rents will sharply decrease the quantity demanded.

Rent controls prevent such increases in rents from occurring. Thus, even while the supply of rental housing is shrinking for the reasons discussed above, the signal to economize on rental accommodation is *not* given through rising rentals. The housing shortage grows as the stock of rental accommodation shrinks while nothing decreases the quantity demanded.

Why Rent Controls Fail

Long-Run Increases in Demand

Consider long-term increases in the demand for rental accommodation. For example, in-migration may be increasing the population rapidly, creating severe local housing shortages and forcing up rents. Such increases in rentals give the signal that apartments are very profitable investments. A consequent building boom will lead to increases in the quantity supplied, and it will continue as long as windfall profits can be earned.

If rent controls are imposed in the face of such long-term increases in demand, they will prevent short-run windfalls, but they will also prevent the needed long-run construction boom from occurring. Thus controls will convert a temporary shortage into a permanent one. This is illustrated in Figure 6-5.

Inflation in Housing Costs

Rent controls also fail when they are introduced to protect tenants from rent increases in an inflationary world. Inflation raises both the costs of construction of new housing and the costs of operating and maintaining existing housing. As we saw in Chapter 4, a rise in costs shifts the supply curve upward and to the left. Fixed rent controls in an economy that is experiencing a steady infla-

quite elastic. As the relative price of rental accommodation in an area rises, each of the following will occur:

1. Some people will stop renting and buy instead.
2. Some will move to where rental housing is cheaper.
3. Some will economize on the amount of housing they consume by renting smaller, cheaper accommodations (or renting out to others a room or two in their present accommodations).
4. Some will double up and others will not "undouble" (for example, young adults will not

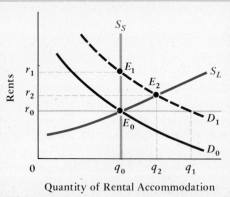

FIGURE 6-5
Rent Controls and Increasing Demand

Quantity of Rental Accommodation

Rent controls prevent a temporary skyrocketing of rents when demand rises, but also prevent the long-term supply adjustment to demand increases. Demand is initially D_0 with available rental accommodation of q_0 and rents r_0. An increase in demand would temporarily raise rents to r_1 given the stock of rental accommodation q_0, fixed in the short run. Free-market rents would fall over time to r_2 as the quantity of accommodation rose along S_L from q_0 to q_2. Controlling rents at r_0 would prevent the windfall profits associated with the temporary rise in rents to r_2, but would also prevent the adjustment of the supply of accommodation, and thus give rise to a permanent housing shortage of $q_0 q_1$.

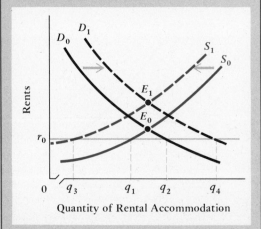

FIGURE 6-6
An Ever-growing Housing Shortage

Quantity of Rental Accommodation

In a growing, inflation-prone economy, rent control will cause the housing shortage to worsen year by year. In a growing economy the demand curve is continually shifting rightward as more people with higher real incomes demand more housing. In an inflationary economy the supply curve is continually shifting leftward because construction, maintenance, and operating costs are rising. Such shifts, when combined with rent control, cause the housing shortage to grow over time. For example, when the curves are D_0 and S_0, rent control at r_0 is accompanied by a housing shortage of $q_1 q_2$. When the curves have shifted to D_1 and S_1, however, the same controlled rent causes an overall housing shortage of $q_3 q_4$.

tion will produce a housing shortage that grows over time. If inflation is combined with growth in demand, the growth in the housing shortage becomes very large (see Figure 6-6).

Of course the housing shortage does not need to grow if the controlled rent is allowed to rise as fast as the equilibrium rent. But the usual *purpose* of controls is to hold rents down in the face of rapid increases in costs and demand. As a result, controlled rents have been allowed to rise over the years much less fast than the rate of inflation. Thus the housing shortage in fact grows over the years, although not as fast as it would if controlled rents were *never* changed.

The Alternatives to Rent Controls

Most rent controls in Canada today are meant to protect lower-income tenants not only against profiteering by landlords in the face of severe local shortages, but also against the steadily rising cost of housing. It is often argued that construction costs are now too high to erect buildings that offer apartments at rents ordinary people can afford. Suppose this to be true. How could this problem be handled?

One possibility is to control rents below the cost

of new building, with the inevitable consequence of a housing shortage that grows as the stock of rental accommodation wears out and is not replaced.

An alternative is for government to fill the gap between total demand and private supply with subsidized public housing. This would be financed at the taxpayers' expense (since the high costs of housing must be paid by someone).

A third possibility is to let rents rise on the free market sufficiently to cover costs. If "ordinary people" (and others) really decide they cannot afford these apartments and will not rent them, then the building of apartments will cease. It is more likely, however, in light of past consumer behavior, that agonizing choices will be made to spend a higher proportion of total income on housing and/or to economize on housing.

The costs of providing additional housing cannot be voted out of existence; they can only be transferred from one set of persons to another.

In Canada, some modifications to rent control programs have been introduced to deal with some of the issues raised in this chapter. For example, in Vancouver controls do not apply to apartments renting for more than a stated limit, and in Ontario they do not apply to new buildings. Although both policies still involve the transfer of costs and benefits from one group to another and both still lead to some of the problems with rent controls outlined before, they both attempt to avoid the costs associated with the induced reduction of supply associated with a comprehensive rent control policy.

Several European countries have been through the whole process of imposing rent controls to protect tenants and ending up with excess demand and an increasingly expensive program of subsidized public housing. In the face of other public needs, they are now trying to give more scope to private markets for housing, but policies of rent controls are always politically popular. Only time will tell how far the United States is to travel the same path. Economics cannot tell society which hard choice to make, but it can show what the choices

are. The greatest danger is that the long-run costs will be neglected in making the choice.

In the light of the overwhelming evidence about the problems rent controls have created, one might justifiably ask where the pressure for rent controls comes from. This is taken up in Box 6-1.

THE PROBLEMS OF AGRICULTURE

The "farm problem" has plagued most nations in the non-Communist world. Left to operate on its own, the price system produces two characteristic problems in agriculture. First, prices fluctuate widely from year to year, causing much uncertainty about farm income. Second, there is a long-run tendency for farm incomes to be depressed below urban incomes in spite of both extremely rapid rises in agricultural productivity and a long-term shift of labor from the farms.

This latter movement has been dramatic. In 1900 over 40 percent of the Canadian labor force worked in agriculture; by 1930 it was down to 29 percent; and today it has fallen to 5 percent. Other things being equal, this shift should reduce the supply of agricultural products and raise, not lower, farm prices and incomes.

To deal with the farm problem, governments have tried a variety of techniques including price supports, crop insurance, transportation and storage subsidies, and marketing boards. But each of these "solutions" seems to bring problems of its own, often more serious than the original problem they were meant to solve.

Long-Term Trends

Perhaps surprisingly, it has been steady growth of productivity that has caused many of agriculture's long-term problems. Pressure has come from both the demand and the supply sides of agricultural markets.

Demand. In this century output per worker in Canada has increased at an average annual rate of

BOX 6–1 THE CLAMOR FOR RENT CONTROL

In the face of the predicted and observed consequences, why does rent control persist and even grow? The answer is largely that the primary victims of rent control do not identify themselves as such, while the primary beneficiaries do.

Whatever the overall effects of rent control, existing tenants who can stay in their present locations will benefit from it. Existing tenants know that rent controls hold down the cost of housing. (The only risk to them comes if landlords allow their apartment buildings to deteriorate.) Thus existing tenants constitute an important political constituency for rent controls.

If the beneficiaries of rent control are existing tenants, who are the victims? The housing shortage hurts those who will want rental housing that will not be there in the future. The elderly couple who fight to keep rent control on the apartment they occupy are behaving wholly in their own best interest. But they are making life more difficult for the next generation of aged couples, many of whom will not find housing of the same quality if rent controls are kept. The welfare family protected today will have a hard time finding housing if it moves when the opportunity for a job arises or when its present apartment house is abandoned. Minority groups generally will find that their members are hurt in the long run by the steadily shrinking quantity and quality of available rental housing.

Why do so many people favor rent controls when control-induced shortages will make it more difficult for them to find a suitable apartment? The answer, when it is not an ideological dislike of landlords, seems to be that they do not recognize the link between the lower rents they will pay—if they are lucky enough to find a rent controlled apartment where they want it—

and the *decreased chance* of finding such an apartment. If they knew that rent control was the reason they had to wait so long and search so hard to find accommodation, they might prefer to pay the free-market rent. But they do not know this—and once "in," they will be protected by rent controls.

Thus the call for rent control comes both from existing tenants, who gain at the expense of those who do not have secured leases in rental housing, and from potential tenants, who underestimate the adverse effects on *them* of the control-induced housing shortage. In contrast, the *articulate* opposition is the much smaller group of landlords. The silent victims, who are the future unsuccessful searchers for rental units, may never realize the causal link between rent controls and the housing shortage from which they suffer.

That many individuals are either selfish or myopic in calling for rent control is understandable. That their leaders and public representatives do not appreciate and weigh the long-term consequences is less comprehensible except in very political terms. Economic theory predicts and worldwide experience confirms that rent controls create shortages, that shortages do not benefit the population as a whole, that the real costs of providing housing do not diminish when controls are imposed, and that when the private market does not provide housing, either tenants will bear the cost by doubling up or doing without or public taxes will have to be raised to provide public housing. Perhaps the politicians who need to be elected to obtain the power to choose must judge next month's election (and hence today's constituency) to be more important than the adverse long-run effects.

almost 2 percent. Such increases in production lead to increases in the income of the population. How do households wish to consume their extra income? The relevant measure is income elasticity of demand, which shows the effect of increases in income on the demands for various goods. Income elasticities vary considerably among goods. At the levels of income existing in Canada and other advanced industrial nations, most foodstuffs have low income elasticities because most people are already well fed. When these people get extra income, they tend to spend much of it on consumer durables, and on such services as entertainment and travel. Thus, as incomes grow, the demand for agricultural goods tends to increase relatively slowly (if population remains stable).

If productivity were expanding uniformly among industries, the demands for goods with low income elasticities would be expanding more slowly than output. In such industries excess supplies would develop, prices and profits would be depressed, and resources would be induced to move elsewhere. Exactly the reverse would happen for industries producing goods with high income elasticities. Demands would expand faster than supplies, prices and profits would tend to rise, and resources would move into the industries producing these goods.

Supply. The above shows what would happen if there were an equal rate of growth of productivity in all industries. In fact, growth in agricultural productivity has been well *above* the average for the economy. Encouraged by government-financed research, by subsidies, and by a government-assured demand for farm output at a stable price, agricultural productivity has increased enormously in this century. Since 1947, for example, Canadian farm output per agricultural worker has grown at the rate of about 5 percent per year, nearly twice the rate of growth of total output per worker. These productivity increases shift the supply curves of agricultural goods rapidly to the right, indicating a greatly increased ability and willingness to produce at each price.

Resource reallocation. We have seen that demand has been increasing only slowly while supply has been increasing rapidly. If resources had not been reallocated out of farming, there would have been enormous increases in output that could hardly have been sold within Canada or exported at any price.

Reallocations of resources in a free-market economy take place under the incentives of low prices, low wages, and depressed incomes in the declining sector, and high prices, wages, and incomes in the expanding sector. But incentives of this kind prove painful—indeed pain is the spur—to those who live and work on farms, especially when resources move slowly in response to depressed incomes. It is one thing for the farmer's son or daughter to move to the city; it may be quite another for the farmer and the farmer's parents, who are set in their ways. Because farmers are people—and voters—governments tend to respond to their cries for help in overcoming the depressed conditions in agriculture that free markets often produce.

Notice that the same problem exists for any industry where growth in demand is low while productivity growth is high. Similar problems are beginning to affect such durable consumer goods industries as automobiles and refrigerators.

Short-Term Fluctuations

Why is short-term volatility of prices typical of most agricultural markets?

Farm crops are subject to variations in output because of many forces completely beyond the farmer's control. Some variation is simply a matter of season, but pests, floods, and lack of rain can drastically reduce farm output, and exceptionally favorable conditions can cause production greatly to exceed expectations. By now you should not be surprised to hear that such unplanned fluctuations in output cause fluctuations in farm prices. Not only does price theory predict this obvious consequence, it also predicts other, less obvious ones that help us to understand some of the farmer's problems.

FIGURE 6-7
The Effect on Price of Unplanned Variations in Output Depends on Elasticity of Demand

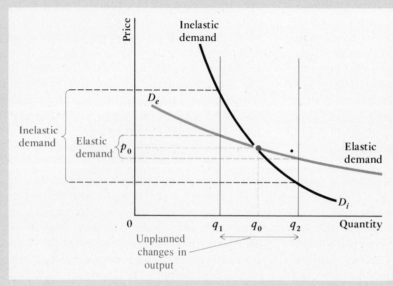

An unplanned fluctuation in output of a given size leads to a much sharper fluctuation in price if the demand curve is inelastic than if it is elastic. Suppose that the expected price is p_0 and the planned output is q_0 The two curves D_i and D_e are *alternative* demand curves. If actual production always equaled planned production, the equilibrium price and quantity would be p_0 and q_0 with either demand curve. Unplanned variations in output, however, cause quantity to fluctuate year by year between q_1 (a bad harvest) and q_2 (a good harvest). When demand is inelastic (shown by the heavy curve), prices will show large fluctuations. When demand is elastic (shown by the screened curve), price fluctuations will be much smaller.

The basic behavior is illustrated in Figure 6-7. Variations in farm output cause prices to fluctuate in the opposite direction to crop sizes. A bumper crop sends prices down; a small crop sends them up. The price changes will be larger, the less elastic the demand curve.

Because farm products often have inelastic demands, price fluctuations tend to be large in response to unplanned changes in production.

What are the effects on the receipts of farmers? If the commodity in question has an elasticity of demand greater than unity, increases in the quantity supplied will raise farmers' receipts. If the demand is inelastic, farmers' receipts will rise when price rises and fall when price falls.

Wherever demands are inelastic, good harvests will bring reductions in total farm receipts and bad harvests will bring increases.

Because many farm products have inelastic demands, farm receipts often vary inversely with crop size. When nature is bountiful and produces a bumper crop, farmers' receipts dwindle; when nature is moderately unkind and output falls unexpectedly, receipts rise. The interests of the farmer and the consumer are exactly opposed in such cases. This conflict was dramatically illustrated in 1977 and 1978 when worldwide grain failures sent grain prices skyrocketing and farm incomes up— and triggered the largest rise in consumer food prices in 25 years. In 1982 and 1983 fair weather and bumper crops brought relief in the supermarkets but led to lower incomes to farmers.

Cyclical Fluctuations in Prices and Incomes

As the tide of national and international prosperity ebbs and flows, demand curves for all commodities rise and fall. The effects on prices and outputs depend on the elasticity of *supply*. Industrial products typically have rather elastic supply curves, so shifts in demand cause fairly large changes in outputs but only small changes in prices. Agricultural commodities as a whole often have rather inelastic supplies because acreage and labor devoted to agricultural uses are not quickly transferred to nonagricultural uses when demand falls and then returned to agriculture quickly when demand rises.

Given an inelastic supply curve for agricultural products as a whole, farm prices, farm receipts, and farm income will be very sensitive to demand shifts, as Figure 6-8(i) illustrates. A sharp drop in demand (a leftward shift of the demand curve) will cause hardship among those whose income depends on farm crops.

However, in comparing the position of agriculture with that of industry, it is incomes received—not prices—that matter. The results in Figure 6-8(ii) are primarily due to a decline in quantity sold rather than a decline in price, but that does not make it less painful.[1]

---

[1] Farm income is not simply farm profits, for the wages paid to farm labor are also incomes attributable to farming. Similarly, the incomes earned in industry include the wages and salaries of workers as well as the profits of business people. When output drops greatly, as in Figure 6-8(ii), many businesses will lay off workers, and so on. This reduces incomes earned from industrial production.

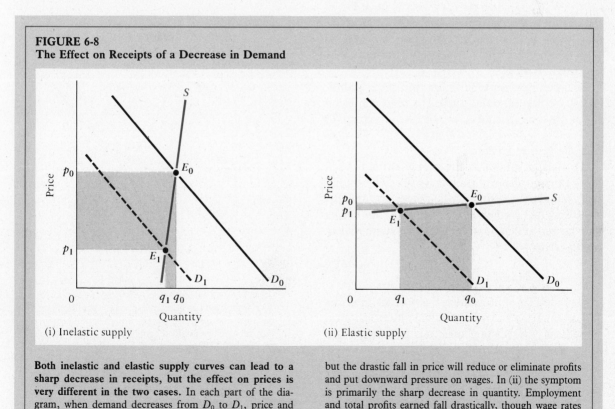

FIGURE 6-8
The Effect on Receipts of a Decrease in Demand

(i) Inelastic supply

(ii) Elastic supply

Both inelastic and elastic supply curves can lead to a sharp decrease in receipts, but the effect on prices is very different in the two cases. In each part of the diagram, when demand decreases from D_0 to D_1, price and quantity decrease to p_1 and q_1 and total receipts decline by the shaded area. In (i) the symptom is mainly the sharp decrease in price. Output and employment remain high, but the drastic fall in price will reduce or eliminate profits and put downward pressure on wages. In (ii) the symptom is primarily the sharp decrease in quantity. Employment and total profits earned fall drastically, though wage rates and profit margins on what is produced may remain close to their former level.

In addition to changes in domestic demand, the Canadian agricultural sector has to contend with cycles in economic conditions in other countries, because about one-third of farm production is exported.

Agricultural Stabilization and Support Plans

Governments throughout the world intervene in agricultural markets in attempts to deal with the problems just studied. They try to stabilize agricultural prices and incomes in the face of short-term and uncontrollable fluctuations in supply and cyclical fluctuations in demand. They also seek to support agricultural prices and incomes at levels sufficient to guarantee farmers what is regarded as reasonable or decent living standards. In so doing they often weaken the incentive for resources to leave farming, and thus, if there is a long-run problem, make it worse.

Because income stabilization and price stabilization are not the same, there has been confusion about what is intended in schemes designed to achieve "orderly agricultural marketing." We shall consider several schemes.

To start, assume that the supply curve in each case refers to planned (or average) production per year, but actual production fluctuates around that level. In a free market, as we have seen, this causes both prices and farm receipts to fluctuate widely from year to year.

The Ever-Normal Granary

One method of preventing fluctuations in prices and gross receipts is for individual farmers to form a producers' association that tries to stabilize—to keep "ever normal"—the supply *actually coming onto the market* in spite of variations in production. It does this by storing a crop in years of above-average production and selling out of its storage elevators in years of below-average production.

Since one farmer's production is an insignificant part of total production, there is no point in an individual farmer's holding some production off the market in an effort to prevent a fall in price in a year of bumper crops. But if all farmers get together and agree to vary the supply coming onto the market, then collectively they can have an effect on price. The appropriate policy is illustrated in Figure 6-9.

Since revenues accrue to the producers when the goods are actually sold on the market, total revenues can be stabilized by keeping sales constant at the equilibrium output even though production varies. This can be accomplished by adding to or subtracting from inventories the excesses or shortages of production.

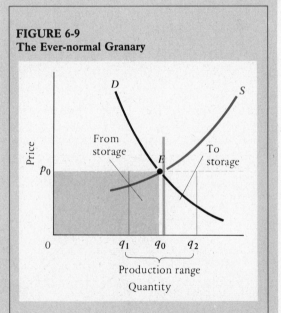

FIGURE 6-9
The Ever-normal Granary

The ever-normal granary scheme stabilizes the quantity sold by farmers even though actual production varies. The planned supply curve is S; p_0 and q_0 are the equilibrium price and quantity, respectively. Actual production varies between q_1 and q_2. When production is q_2 the producers' association sells q_0 and stores q_0q_2. When production is q_1 it still sells q_0, supplementing the current production by selling q_1q_0 from its stored crops. Producers' revenue is stabilized at $p_0 \times q_0$ (the shaded area) every year.

The fully successful ever-normal granary stabilizes both prices and revenues of producers.

The costs of this plan are those of providing storage and of organizing and administering the program. A potential danger is that in order to get higher prices the producers' association will sell on average less than is produced and will find itself with ever-increasing stockpiles of the crop.

Government Price Supports at the Equilibrium Price

Because there are many difficulties in organizing and administering private stabilization schemes such as the ever-normal granary, why cannot the government do the same thing more efficiently?

Suppose the government, instead of the producers' association, enters the market, buying and adding to its own stocks when there is a surplus and selling—thereby reducing its stocks—when there is a shortage. If it had enough grain elevators and warehouses, and if its support prices were set at a realistic level, the government could stabilize prices indefinitely. But, as Figure 6-10 illustrates, it would not succeed in stabilizing farmers' revenues and incomes, for farmers would find their revenues high with a bumper crop and low with a poor crop.

Government price supports at the equilibrium price would not stabilize revenues. They would, however, reverse the pattern of revenue fluctuation.

In effect, the government policy imposes a demand curve that is perfectly elastic at the support price. This stabilizes price, but it does not stabilize receipts to producers.

Revenue Stabilization by Government Purchases and Sales

Obviously there must be a government buying and selling policy that will stabilize farmers' receipts. What are its characteristics? As has been seen, too much price stability causes receipts to vary directly with production and too little price stability causes receipts to vary inversely with pro-

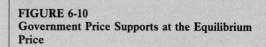

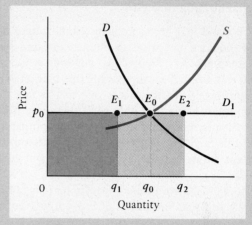

FIGURE 6-10
Government Price Supports at the Equilibrium Price

Government price supports at the equilibrium price stabilize prices (not quantities sold by farmers) and do not accumulate surpluses but cause revenues to vary directly with production. Actual production varies around the equilibrium level of q_0. When production is q_2 the government buys q_0q_2 and stores it. When production is q_1 the government sells q_1q_0 from storage. The quantity sold to the public is always q_0, and this stabilizes price at p_0. The government policy converts the demand curve facing farmers to D_1. If q_0 is average production, there is no trend toward the accumulation of storage crops.

Farmers' revenue varies from $p_0 \times q_1$ (the darker shaded area) when production is q_1, to $p_0 \times q_2$ (the entire shaded area) when production is q_2.

duction. It appears that the government should aim at some intermediate degree of price stability. If the government allows prices to vary in inverse proportion to variations in production, then receipts will be stabilized. A 10 percent rise in production should be met by a 10 percent fall in price, and a 10 percent fall in production by a 10 percent rise in price.

To stabilize farmer's receipts, the government must make the demand curve facing the farmers one of unit elasticity. It must buy in periods of high output and sell in periods of low output, but only enough to let prices change in inverse proportion to farmers' output.

Problems with Agricultural Stabilization Schemes

To avoid long-term problems, stabilization policies should allow prices to fluctuate around their free-market levels. In practice, however, prices are often stabilized *above* the average free-market equilibrium levels. Partly this is due to the fact that stabilization is not the only goal; there is a desire to assure farmers a standard of living comparable with that of city dwellers. This involves attempting to *raise* farm incomes in addition to stabilizing them.

Here too the government buys in periods of high output and sells in periods of low output, but on average it buys much more than it sells, so that unsold surpluses accumulate. This is illustrated in Figure 6-11.

While prices are often stabilized above their equilibrium level, subsidies to keep food prices paid by the consumer below the equilibrium price are also common. Some of the problems associated with these policies are taken up in Box 6-2.

Problems with Agricultural Policies: A Recap

Box 6-3 discusses some general lessons concerning market and nonmarket means of allocating resources. In this section we review some specific issues that arise in the context of agriculture.

Accumulating Surpluses

A key difficulty of plans that seek to raise farm income by raising prices above free-market levels is the tendency to accumulate surpluses. Eventually, if agricultural surpluses persist, the stored crops will have to be destroyed, dumped on the market for what they will bring, or otherwise disposed of at a fraction of their cost. If the crops are thrown on the market and allowed to depress the price, then the original purposes for which the crops were purchased—price stabilization and rais-

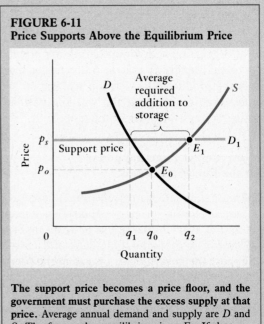

FIGURE 6-11
Price Supports Above the Equilibrium Price

The support price becomes a price floor, and the government must purchase the excess supply at that price. Average annual demand and supply are D and S. The free-market equilibrium is at E_0. If the government will buy any quantity at p_s, the demand curve becomes the light black curve D_1 and equilibrium shifts to E_1. The average addition to storage is the quantity q_1q_2. The government purchases add to farmers' receipts and to government expenditures.

ing of farm incomes—are defeated. If the crops are destroyed or allowed to rot, the efforts of a large quantity of the country's scarce factors of production (the land, labor, and capital that went into producing the stored goods) will have been wasted.

Destroying crops is a vexing moral problem when millions are starving, but if the stored crops are not to depress the price, they must be kept off the market. Giving crops away to those who would not otherwise buy them is sometimes attempted, but it is hard to achieve. Selling grain at cut-rate prices for conversion to gasohol has recently been proposed.

Any of these "solutions" will mean that the agricultural support program will show a deficit, for goods will have been purchased that cannot be sold except at a large loss. This deficit means that tax-

BOX 6–2 THE POLITICAL ECONOMY OF FOOD SUBSIDIES

Many governments in diverse parts of the world have adopted policies to hold food prices below their costs of production. These policies typically involve price controls in retail markets and subsidies to producers. Low food prices are understandably popular with ordinary people, particularly in poorer countries where food takes up a large percentage of total household expenditure.

The governments' motivations are not always clear. To some extent they may be motivated by a genuine but misguided feeling that holding food prices low is the best way to raise the welfare of ordinary citizens. To some extent, however, governments may be making the short-term political calculation that low food prices are the way to court popular support. Whatever the motives involved, the long-term consequences are usually disastrous, not only for the economy, but also for the body politic.

When the state holds food prices below their costs of production, which include what farmers must be paid for producing the food, the difference must be made up by a state-financed subsidy. The revenue to pay the subsidy must come from one of two sources. First, it may come from the public, either in the form of tax revenue or (unlikely in poor countries) government borrowing. Second, it may come from government creation of new money. In this case the result is inflation because the state pays its subsidy by giving out new purchasing power that has no counterpart in the form of new production available to be purchased.*

Most countries, including communist ones, have suffered some inflation over the last two decades. As inflation proceeds the temptation is to hold the rate of increase in food prices below the rate of inflation. As a result, the price of

food typically rises at a rate below the overall rate of inflation. This increases the amount of the state's food subsidy as the gap between costs of production and selling prices is widened. Furthermore, as food becomes relatively cheaper and cheaper—since food prices are not rising as fast as other prices—people are induced to buy more food than they would if the prices covered the full costs of production. This also increases the total subsidy that the state must pay.

These forces cause the total subsidy bill to grow continuously until the state's finances cannot support it. At this point a food crisis arises, and the state has no choice but to raise the price of food. Having postponed the decision until the last possible moment, the price increases that will make any real dent in the total subsidy bill are dramatic. Typically, prices will be raised from 50 to 100 percent.

This is the real shock to consumers. They could have adjusted, although with pain, to prices that rose, say, 7 percent every year, and so raised food prices by just over 100 percent over 10 years. But to be faced with stable prices for 10 years and then see a sudden doubling of prices can be traumatic. In these circumstances food riots commonly break out, and existing governments—whether dictatorial or democratic—are sometimes toppled.

Governments in the Eastern bloc (most notably Poland), Africa (including Ghana and Nigeria), and Asia (including Burma and China) have found themselves in such predicaments. Economic analysis helps us understand their problems by showing what happens when real costs are ignored by state planners. The next time you read of a food riot accompanying some sudden government-legislated increase in food prices, congratulate yourself that you probably understand more economics than the policymakers involved. You might also wish that you could share your knowledge with them.

* The details of how the state creates new money and how new money creates inflation are discussed in Part Nine.

BOX 6–3 FOUR GENERAL LESSONS ABOUT RESOURCE ALLOCATION

We have examined several examples of government intervention in markets that might have been left unregulated. Our discussion suggests four widely applicable lessons.

1. Costs May Be Shifted, But They Cannot Be Avoided

Production, whether in response to free-market signals or to government controls, uses resources; thus it involves costs to society. If it takes 5 percent of the nation's resources to provide housing at some stated average standard, those resources will not be available to produce other commodities. For society there is no such thing as free housing. The average standard of living depends on the amounts of resources available to the economy and the efficiency with which these resources are used. *It follows that costs are real* and are incurred no matter who provides the goods. Rent controls, housing subsidies, or public provision of housing can change the share of the costs of housing paid by particular individuals or groups—lowering the share for some, raising the share for others—but they cannot make the costs go away.

Different ways of *distributing* the costs may also affect the total amount of resources used, and thus the costs incurred. Controls that keep prices and profits of some commodity below free-market levels will lead to increased quantities demanded and decreased quantities supplied. Unless government steps in to provide additional supplies, fewer resources will be al-

located to producing the commodity. If government chooses to supply all the demand at the controlled prices, more resources will be allocated to it, which means fewer resources will be devoted to other kinds of goods and services. The opportunity cost of more housing is less of something else.

2. Free-Market Prices and Profits Encourage Economical Use of Resources

Prices and profits in a market economy provide signals to both demanders and suppliers. Prices that are high and rising (relative to other prices) provide an incentive to purchasers to economize on the commodity. They may choose to satisfy the want in question with substitutes whose prices have not risen so much (because they are less costly to provide) or to satisfy less of that want by shifting expenditure to the satisfaction of other wants. There is substantial scope for such economizing reactions even for commodities as "necessary" as housing: *some* housing is necessary, but a particular quantity is not.

On the supply side, rising prices tend to produce rising profits. High profits attract further resources into production. Short-term windfall profits that bear no relation to current costs repeatedly occur in market economies; they cause resources to move into those industries with profits until profits fall to levels that can be earned elsewhere in the economy.

Falling prices and falling profits provide the opposite motivations. Purchasers are inclined to buy more; sellers are inclined to produce less

payers generally will be paying farmers for producing goods that no one in the nation is willing to purchase at prices that come near covering costs.

When support schemes begin to produce ever-larger surpluses, the next step is often to try to

limit each farmer's production. Quotas may be assigned to individual farmers and penalties imposed for exceeding them. Or bonuses may be paid for leaving the land idle and for plowing crops under. Such measures waste resources, because the de-

and to move resources out of the industry and into more profitable undertakings.

3. Controls Inhibit the Allocative Mechanism

Some controls prevent prices from rising (in response, say, to an increase in demand). If the price is held down, the signal is never given to consumers to economize on a commodity that is in short supply. On the supply side, when prices and profits are prevented from rising (on the grounds, for example, that no more than a "fair" return should be earned at all times), the profit signals that would attract new resources into the industry are never given. The shortage continues, and the movements of demand and supply that would resolve it are not set in motion.

In the opposite case, where there is excess supply, an appropriate response would be some increase in quantity purchased and some decrease in production accompanied by a shift of resources to production of other, more valued commodities. Falling prices and profits would motivate such shifts. When prices are prevented from falling in the face of temporary surpluses (on the grounds, for example, that producers of an essential product must have a fair return guaranteed to them), the signals that would increase purchases or push resources out of an industry are never given.

4. Controls Require Alternative Allocative Mechanisms

If the price system with its profit incentives is not used to allocate resources, alternative methods will necessarily appear. Temporary fluctuations in demand and supply will give rise to severe shortages and surpluses. During times of shortages, allocation will be by sellers' preferences unless the state imposes rationing. During periods of surplus, there will be unsold supplies or illegal price cutting unless the state buys and stores the surpluses. Long-run changes in demand and costs will not induce resource reallocations through private decisions. As a result, the state will be put under strong pressure to step in. It will have to force or order resources out of industries where prices are held too high—as it has tried to do in agriculture. The state will also have to force or order resources into industries where prices are held too low—as it can do, for example, by providing public housing.

Whenever a specific alternative scheme of allocation is imposed, it is costly in a number of additional ways. First, the allocation itself usually requires the use of resources for administering and enforcing the rules. Second, the use of the state's power takes the mixed economy one step further away from the free enterprise economy and toward a command economy. Third, the freedom of some individuals to act in what they consider their own best interest is limited. Sometimes the benefits of the policies will justify the costs, sometimes they will not. Justified or not, the costs are always present and are often large.

sired output could be produced with fewer resources and the remaining resources used to produce other goods. All they dispense with is the visible symbol of trouble, the accumulating surpluses.

Frustrating the Resource Reallocation Mechanism

A second difficulty arises because of the long-term need to reallocate resources out of agriculture.

In a free-market society, the mechanism for a continued reallocation of resources out of low income elasticity industries and into high income elasticity ones is a continued depressing tendency of prices and incomes in contracting industries, and a continued buoyant tendency of prices and incomes in expanding industries.

Stabilization schemes that guarantee a "reasonable" income to farmers provide no incentives for resources to transfer out of the agricultural sector. Unless some other means is found to persuade resources to transfer, a larger and larger proportion of the resources in agriculture will become redundant, since increases in productivity will be raising quantity supplied faster than income growth is raising quantity demanded. If, however, the government does not intervene at all, leaving the price mechanism to accomplish the resource reallocation, it will be faced with the problem of a more or less permanently depressed sector of the community.

Agricultural Policy in Canada

Marketing Boards and the Use of Quotas

The primary method by which agricultural stabilization is attempted in Canada is through the operation of marketing boards. Sales through them account for about half of all farm cash receipts. Most marketing boards were established under provincial legislation, but their ability to control markets was initially constrained by lack of cooperation among them. The federal government has attempted to coordinate provincial activities through the Agricultural Products Marketing Act of 1972. One of the first boards to be established under this act was the Canadian Egg Marketing Agency, which in its initial stages was a classic case of price supports leading to accumulation of surpluses. The Canadian Dairy Commission initially created similar conditions in the market for skim milk powder.

Typically the method used to stave off surplus production is to establish quotas that limit the output of each individual producer. To the extent that the total quota allocation is less than the free-market equilibrium quantity, the marketing board can

maintain the price above the equilibrium level without generating surpluses and provide holders of quotas with profits in excess of those they would earn in a free market (see Figure 6-12). If the right to produce conferred by a quota is transferable either by itself or jointly with the farm to which it is attached, it will have a market price. For example, it had been estimated in the mid 1970s that the right to produce broiler chickens in Ontario commanded a price in the neighborhood of $5 per bird. A farmer wishing to enter the industry at what was said to be a minimum efficient family farm level (50,000 birds) had to pay something like $250,000 for the right to produce, over and above the cost of buildings, equipment, and land.

The high value placed on quotas is an indicator of the success of marketing boards in raising the incomes of farmers. On the other hand, it suggests that consumers are providing a very substantial

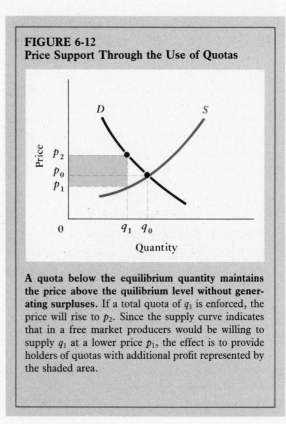

FIGURE 6-12
Price Support Through the Use of Quotas

A quota below the equilibrium quantity maintains the price above the quilibrium level without generating surpluses. If a total quota of q_1 is enforced, the price will rise to p_2. Since the supply curve indicates that in a free market producers would be willing to supply q_1 at a lower price p_1, the effect is to provide holders of quotas with additional profit represented by the shaded area.

subsidy. On the basis of data on quota values, Professors Grubel and Schwindt have estimated that the operation of the British Columbia Milk Board in 1975 cost consumers in that province about $12 million per year, or about $48 on the average for a family of four.[2]

Besides being costly to consumers, it is not clear that quotas distribute income in favor of the farmers most in need. In particular, new producers who wish to enter the industry must purchase quotas from existing holders, so the benefit of the extra profits accrues entirely to those who received the initial allocation and thereby reaped a windfall gain.

The Marketing of Wheat

Basically there are two types of government marketing boards. The first seeks to influence prices. To influence prices, a significant part of total supply must be controlled. This type of marketing board can, as we have seen, adopt either of two major strategies. It can leave supply uncontrolled and accept the long-term average price but try to iron out short-term fluctuations in price due to temporary shifts in demand or supply. Alternatively, it can seek to restrict supply, thereby keeping prices above their competitive levels and earning "monopoly profits" for producers at the expense of consumers. Many Canadian marketing boards, including the majority of provincial boards, are the latter type.

The second type of marketing board accepts prices as set on world markets and merely acts as a selling agency for producers. The benefits such boards offer to producers need not be at the cost of consumers. Some Canadian market boards are this type, such as the Canadian Wheat Board.

The origins of government involvement in the marketing of Canadian wheat can be traced back to the early 1900s, when disparities in bargaining power emerged between western farmers and grain buyers. The growers' associations protested that unfair practices and control of prices were carried

out by the companies controlling the elevators to which the farmers delivered their grain. The government's response was limited; except for the World War I period, government intervention before 1930 was confined to regulation of marketing procedures such as grading, inspection, and provision of railway facilities, and provincial government participation in and subsidization of cooperative elevator companies. Heavy involvement by the government of Canada in the marketing of wheat arose out of the disruptions of the Great Depression. Pressures to establish a national marketing board had built up during the 1920s, when the growers' vulnerability to the vagaries of the international wheat situation became the dominant concern, the proportion of output exported having grown to more than 70 percent.

Under the Canadian Wheat Board Act of 1935, each year the government estimates the average price at which it expects the wheat crop to be sold. Seventy-five percent of that price is then paid to each farmer on delivery of his wheat. After the board sells the wheat, any proceeds in excess of the initial payments are distributed to the producers in proportion to the amount of wheat supplied by each. Should the sales revenue be less than the initial payments, the loss is absorbed by the government. But such a disastrous mistake—final price less than 75 percent of estimated price—rarely occurs, so the board's activities are largely self-financing.

The goals of the Wheat Board are not to influence world prices. Instead, by paying farmers 75 percent of the estimated average selling price over the year, the board provides farmers with a secure cash flow early in the selling period. The board also serves to secure farmers' incomes against intra-year fluctuations in wheat prices. It does this by pooling all its receipts and paying them out to farmers according to the amount of wheat delivered by each farmer but irrespective of the date within the year of that delivery. So the farmer is relieved of worry about what the spot price of wheat may be on the day that he makes his delivery. These functions of the board appear to be in farmers' interests. Most farmers like the annual averaging

[2] H. W. Grubel and R. W. Schwindt, *The Real Cost of the B.C. Milk Board* (Vancouver, B.C.: Fraser Institute, 1977.)

of receipts, most find the information provided by an early estimate of this year's price useful, and most find the early cash flow of 75 percent of the estimated selling price provided on delivery valuable.

Stocks. The board still has to decide whether to sell all of this year's crop or to carry some over as stocks until next year. During the 1960s it had to contend with fluctuations in yield per acre (from 17.9 to 27.9 bushels) and in annual export demand (between 277 and 585 million bushels). Large contracts with the USSR and China accounted for a substantial portion of the strong demand experienced in the mid-1960s. The carryover of wheat in storage grew steadily from 400 million bushels to over a billion, a level substantially higher than necessary to provide a buffer stock.

In an attempt to reduce the level of accumulated stocks, the government resorted at the end of the 1960s to an acreage reduction scheme under which compensation payments were made to farmers who reduced their acreage below 1969 levels. A substantial reduction in seeded acreage and production was induced, but ironically this was accomplished just as world markets were about to make a dramatic about-face. Exports returned to the high levels experienced in the mid sixties (again much of the increase was accounted for by sales to the USSR), and by the end of 1972–1973 stocks had fallen to the lowest level since 1952.

Carryover stocks remained low until the 1976–1977 crop year, when the prairie crop reached a record level of 840 million bushels. At the same time production increased in the United States and the Soviet Union, and the international market was once again flooded with wheat. Predictably, prices sagged; they fell below $3 a bushel, compared with the peak level of $6 in late 1974. This depressed market was costly to Canadian taxpayers because the federal government is committed to maintaining farm incomes. (Under the Western Grain Stabilization Plan, established in 1975, participating farmers are guaranteed that their net cash receipts will not fall below the average of the preceding five years.)

Over the four crop years ending in mid 1980, exports recovered steadily if not sensationally. Despite bumper crops of more than 700 million bushels in both 1977–1978 and 1978–1979 (due to record yields in both years of over 28 bushels per acre), stocks were historically low in August 1980. However, the world grain market was disrupted by the United States embargo on exports to the Soviet Union following the latter's incursion into Afghanistan. Carryover stocks remained fairly steady in the early 1980s as increased supply due to bumper crops in 1982–1983 were matched by strong export demand.

Prospects for Canadian Farm Policy

Until five or ten years ago, most economists would have agreed that despite substantial government intervention—or perhaps because of it—the agricultural sector was still a major trouble spot in the economy, and farm policy an expensive but predictable failure.

Yet few would have urged the government to cease its intervention altogether. For to leave to the price mechanism the task of reallocating resources out of farming would mean facing the prospect of a more or less permanently depressed sector of the community. It is doubtful that any Canadian political party would be willing to accept the social and political consequences of leaving this sector to fend for itself.

The 1970s were prosperous years for agriculture, with growing world population and income and significant enough crop failures abroad to create a serious food shortage. Yet intervention in the agrucultural sector—widely agreed to be expensive and wasteful and to impede long-run adjustments—*increased* during the decade. The worldwide recession that began in 1980 brought severe problems in the farm sector, including a record number of farm bankruptcies. Not surprisingly, this led to revived demands by farmers for increased protection and subsidization. Despite the initial assessment of past policies, there seems little basis to expect any major changes in the next few years. Marketing boards will survive and grow and prices will continue to be supported above equilibrium levels, leading to either increasing carryover stocks or subsidies for not growing crops.

Prospects for World Agriculture

Throughout the 1950s and 1960s the agricultural sectors of Western European and North American economies showed behavior confirming the predictions developed above. Subsidies and price supports led to overproduction and ever-growing surpluses that strained government warehouses everywhere to overflowing. Then, however, came a very significant change. Throughout the 1970s, the demands for many of the agricultural products produced by advanced Western countries soared. A few of the most important reasons may be mentioned.

First, the world population explosion has reached dramatic proportions, adding in a matter of decades thousands of millions of new mouths to feed. Second, agricultural production, particularly of grains, has been disappointingly low in the USSR and other countries of the Eastern bloc. A major cause has been a failure of their system of collectivized agriculture to produce anything like the rate of growth of output that the farmers of Western countries have achieved. As a result, the 1970s and 1980s have seen massive sales of Western output to Eastern countries. Third, although the income elasticities of demand for many foodstuffs are low in advanced Western countries, they remain quite high for meat in general and for beef in particular.

For these and other reasons, the chronic excess supply and rising stocks of unsold output that characterized Western agriculture in the 1950s and 1960s are much abated. The United States, the leading supplier of food exports for the rest of the world, had stopped its payments to farmers for keeping land out of production, and has brought nearly all of its idle crop land back into production. For that nation, then, three decades of agricultural surpluses, which grew to seemingly unmanageable proportions, have given way to several years of excess demand.

The rising world demand has certainly helped European agriculture but it has not yet allowed it to exist in its present form without major subsidies. The subsidization program at a high level of income not only inhibits the transfer of resources out of agriculture (as analyzed above), it also protects high-cost, small-scale farming which, since the abandonment of American farm supports, has given way in the United States to lower-cost, large-scale farming. As a result, the EEC common agricultural policy still involves very large transfers of income from urban taxpayers to subsidized farmers. Because the United Kingdom is the most urbanized of the EEC countries, the intersectoral transfers become in its case an international transfer. British taxpayers pay large sums to subsidize farmers in continental Europe. This source of serious EEC conflict in the 1980s was easily predicted by price theory well before the United Kingdom entered the Common Market.

Whether its predictions are gloomy or cheerful, welcome or unwelcome, it is clear that the theory of price in competitive markets is a remarkable tool for explaining much of what we see in the world around us and for predicting in advance the effects of many changes, whether natural or policy induced.

SUMMARY

1. The elementary theory of supply, demand, and price provides powerful tools for analyzing and understanding some real-world problems and policies. This chapter and the next one illustrates a few of them.

2. Effective floor prices cause surpluses. Either the potential seller is left with quantities that cannot be sold, or the government must step in and buy the surplus. Effective ceiling prices cause shortages and provide a strong incentive for black marketeers to buy at the controlled price and sell at the higher free-market price.

3. Rent controls are a persistent and spreading form of price ceiling. The major consequence of effective rent control is a shortage of rental accommodation that gets worse due to a slow but inexorable decline in the quantity and quality of rental housing.

4. Agriculture commodities are subject to wide fluctuations in market prices, which cause fluctuations in producers' incomes. This is because of year-to-year unplanned fluctuations in supplies combined with inelastic demand, and because of cyclical fluctuations in demand combined with inelastic supplies. Where demand is inelastic, large crops tend to be associated with low total receipts and small crops with high total receipts.

5. Fluctuations in farm income can be reduced by a producers' association that stores unsold crops when output is high and sells from inventories when output is low, or by appropriate government purchases and sales in the open market.

6. Price stabilization schemes historically tend to involve stabilization above average free-market equilibrium levels. The result is a buildup of surpluses. To avoid these surpluses, marketing boards in Canada have established quotas that limit the output of individual producers.

7. The long-term problems of agriculture arise from a high rate of productivity growth on the supply side and a low income elasticity on the demand side. This means that, unless many resources are being transferred out of agriculture, quantity supplied will increase faster than quantity demanded year after year. If existing prices are maintained, and if farmers are guaranteed a market for all their output at these prices, the yearly farm surplus will tend to increase.

8. All wheat produced in Canada is marketed through the Canadian Wheat Board. Wide fluctuations in yields and export demand have hampered its efforts to stabilize the income of growers. Carryover stocks grew rapidly during the 1960s, but were reduced to historically low levels in the mid 1970s as a result of an upturn in world demand. In the late 1970s, record yields and bumper crops led to some increase in carryover stocks, but growth in exports was also rapid, so that at the end of the decade stocks were still historically low.

9. The early 1970s witnessed a worldwide food shortage and a boom in agriculture. Whether this promises an end to long-term farm problems depends on whether our farm products will remain competitive in world markets at prices that the world's growing population will pay. The late 1970s brought both bumper crops domestically and buoyant world demand.

TOPICS FOR REVIEW

Comparative statics
Ceiling prices and price floors
Black markets
Allocative function of windfall profits
The effect of controls on allocation
Alternative allocative mechanisms
Price supports at and above the level of free-market equilibrium
Price stabilization versus income stabilization
Income elasticity and long-term resource reallocation

DISCUSSION QUESTIONS

1. "When a controlled item is vital to everyone, it is easier to start controlling the price than to stop controlling it. Such controls are popular with consumers, regardless of their uneconomic consequences. In this respect oil price controls resemble rent controls." Explain why it may be uneconomic to have such controls, why they may be popular, and why, if they are popular, the government might nevertheless choose to decontrol prices.

2. "Since the demand for these exceeds the supply, applications should be made well in advance." This is from a university catalog's description of married students' quarters. Comment on the allocative system being used by the university authorities.

3. Medical and hospital care in Britain is provided free to individuals by the National Health Service, with the costs paid by taxation. Some British doctors complain that patients want "too much" medical care; patients complain that they have to wait "too long" in doctors' offices for the care they get and months or years for needed operations. Use the theory of supply and demand to discuss

these complaints. Would you expect a private (pay) medical market to grow up alongside the National Health Service? Would you expect the government to welcome or discourage such a second service?

4. Predict the consequences of extending the legal minimum wage to the services of children, including those for mowing lawns and babysitting.

5. Consider a law school that has 1,000 qualified applicants for 200 places in the first-year class. It is debating a number of alternative admission criteria: (a) a lottery, (b) date of initial application, (c) grades, (d) recommendations from alumni, (e) place of residence of applicant. An economist on the faculty determines that if the tuition level were doubled, the excess demand would disappear. Argue for (or against) using the tuition rate to replace each of the other suggested criteria.

6. It is sometimes asserted that the rising costs of construction are putting housing out of the reach of ordinary citizens. Determine who bears the cost when rentals are kept down by

   a. Rent controls
   b. A subsidy to tenants equal to some fraction of their rent payments
   c. Low-cost public housing

7. In England rents are set by public bodies instructed to fix fair rents without regard for local conditions of demand and supply. What might this mean? Analyze some of the effects of this policy on the workings of local housing markets.

8. After the 1980 provincial election in Ontario, in which the Progressive Conservatives won a majority, there was considerable speculation that rent controls would be abandoned. Gordon Walker, the minister responsible for housing policy, announced that while some relaxation of controls might be considered for rural areas with high vacancy rates, controls would remain in places where they are needed, such as metropolitan Toronto, with its low vacancy rate. What is meant by the phrase "where they are needed"? Analyze the effects of this type of selective rent control policy.

   In 1983 Nova Scotia decided to keep rent controls and B.C. to drop them. Predict the vacancy rate in 1988.

9. In 1974 the Kenya Meat Commission (KMC) decided it was undemocratic to allow meat prices to be out of the reach of the ordinary citizen. It decided to freeze meat prices. Six months later, in a press interview, the managing commissioner of the KMC made each of the following statements.

   a. "The price of almost everything in Kenya has gone up, but we have not increased the price of meat. The price of meat in this country is still the lowest in the world."
   b. "Cattle are scarce in the country, but I do not know why."
   c. "People are eating too much beef, and unless they diversify their eating habits and eat other foodstuffs the shortage of beef will continue."

   Do the facts allegedly make sense, given KMC's policy?

10. What would be the effects of a university policy that dictated equal pay to every university teacher of given age whatever his or her ability and field of study?

PART THREE
**CONSUMPTION,
PRODUCTION,
AND COST**

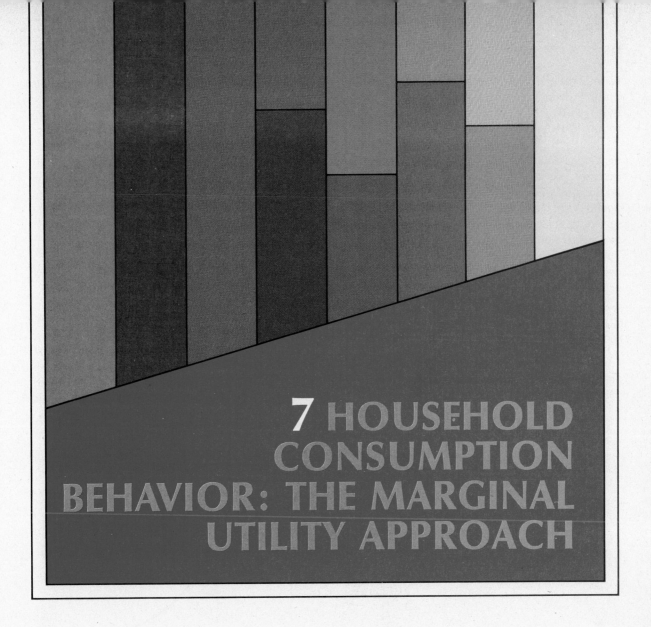

7 HOUSEHOLD CONSUMPTION BEHAVIOR: THE MARGINAL UTILITY APPROACH

In Part Two we saw that demand is an important part of the explanation of market prices, and that the shape of demand curves has a great influence on the way in which markets behave. But why do market demand curves have the shape they do? To deal with this question, we need to go behind market curves to study the individual household behavior on which they depend.

Market Demand Curves and Household Demand Curves

Market demand curves tell how much is demanded by all purchasers. For example, in Figure 4-1 (see page 48), the market demand for carrots was 90,000 tons when the price was $40 per ton. This 90,000 tons is the sum of the quantities demanded by millions of different households. It may be made up of 4 pounds for the McDaniels, 7 pounds for the Tremblays, 1.5 pounds for the Wilsons, and so on. The demand curve for carrots also tells us that when the price rises to $60, aggregate quantity demanded falls to 77,500 tons per month. This quantity too can be traced back to individual households. The McDaniels might buy only 3 pounds, the Tremblays 6.5 pounds, and the Wilsons none at all. Notice that we have now described two points not only on the market demand curve, but on the demand curves of each of these households.

Aggregate behavior is merely the sum of the behavior of individual households. The market demand is the horizontal sum of the demand curves of the individual households.

It is the *horizontal* sum because we wish to add quantities demanded at a given price, and quantities are measured in the horizontal direction on a

conventional demand curve graph. This process is illustrated in Figure 7-1.

The question why market demand curves have the shape they do becomes the question why do individual demand curves have the shape they do. Economists have long sought to understand individual household behavior. In this chapter and the next we explore two approaches. Each comes up with the same basic answers, but each offers somewhat different insights.

MARGINAL UTILITY THEORY

Early economists, struggling with the problem of what determines the relative prices of commodities, encountered what they came to call the **paradox of value:** Necessary commodities such as water have prices that are low compared with the prices of luxury commodities such as diamonds. Water is

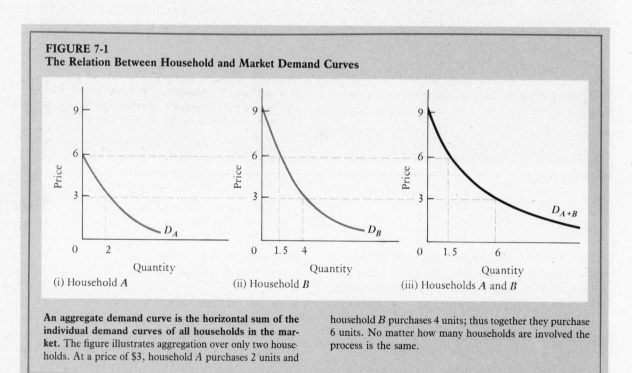

FIGURE 7-1
The Relation Between Household and Market Demand Curves

(i) Household *A*

(ii) Household *B*

(iii) Households *A* and *B*

An aggregate demand curve is the horizontal sum of the individual demand curves of all households in the market. The figure illustrates aggregation over only two households. At a price of $3, household *A* purchases 2 units and household *B* purchases 4 units; thus together they purchase 6 units. No matter how many households are involved the process is the same.

necessary to our existence, while diamonds are friv-olous and could disappear from the face of the earth tomorrow without causing any real upset. Does it not seem odd then, these economists argued, that water is so cheap, and diamonds are so expensive? It took a long time to resolve this apparent paradox, so it is not surprising that even today the confusion persists and clouds many current policy discus-sions. The key to solving this problem lies in the important distinction between marginal and total utility.

Marginal and Total Utility

The satisfaction someone receives from consuming commodities is called his or her **utility**. **Total util-ity** refers to the total satisfaction from consuming some commodity. **Marginal utility** refers to the change in satisfaction resulting from consuming a little more or a little less of the commodity.

Thus, for example, the total utility of consuming 10 units of any commodity is the total satisfaction those 10 units provide. The marginal utility of the tenth unit consumed is the satisfaction added by the consumption of that unit—or, in other words, the difference in total utility between consuming 9 units and consuming 10 units.[1]

The significance of this distinction can be seen by considering two questions: (1) If you had to give up consuming one of the following commodities completely, which would you choose: water or the movies? (2) If you had to choose between one of the following, which would you pick: increasing your water consumption by 35 gallons a month (the amount required for an average bath) or attending one more movie a month?

In (1) you are comparing the value you place on your total consumption of water with the value you place on all your attendance at the movies. You are comparing the *total utility* of your water consump-

tion with the *total utility* of your movie attendance. There is little doubt that everyone would answer (1) in the same way, revealing that the total utility derived from consuming water exceeds the total utility derived from attending the movies.

In (2) you are comparing the value you place on a small addition to your water consumption with the value you place on a small addition to your movie attendances. You are comparing your *mar-ginal utility* of water with your *marginal utility* of movies.

In responding to (2), some might select the extra movie; others might select the extra water. Fur-thermore, their choice would depend on whether it was made at a time when water was plentiful (marginal utility of a little more water, *low*), or when water was scarce, so that they might put quite a high value on obtaining a little more water (mar-ginal utility of a little more water, *high*).

The Hypothesis of Diminishing Marginal Utility

The basic hypothesis of utility theory, called the *law of diminishing marginal utility,* is:

The utility any household derives from successive units of a particular commodity will diminish as total con-sumption of the commodity increases, the consumption of all other commodities being held constant.

Consider further the case of water. Some mini-mum quantity is essential to sustain life, and a person would, if necessary, give up all his or her income to obtain that quantity of water. Thus, the marginal utility of that much water is extremely high. More than this bare minimum will be drunk, but the marginal utility of successive glasses of water drunk over a period will decline steadily.

Evidence for this hypothesis will be considered later, but you can convince yourself that it is at least reasonable by asking yourself a few questions. How much money would induce you to cut your consumption of water by one glass per week? The answer is, very little. How much would induce you to cut it by a second glass? By a third glass? To only one glass consumed per week? The answer to

---

[1] Here and elsewhere in elementary economics it is common to use interchangeably two concepts that mathematicians distin-guish. Technically, *incremental* utility is measured over a discrete interval, such as from 9 to 10, while marginal utility is a rate of change measured over an infinitesimal interval. But common usage applies the word *marginal* when the last unit is involved, even if a one-unit change is not infinitesimal. [8]

the last question is, quite a bit. The fewer glasses you are consuming already, the higher the marginal utility of one more or one less glass of water.

But water has many uses other than for drinking. A fairly high marginal utility will be attached to some minimum quantity for bathing, but much more than this minimum will only be used for more frequent baths and for having a water level in the tub higher than is absolutely necessary. The last weekly gallon used for bathing is likely to have a low marginal utility. Again, some small quantity of water is necessary for tooth brushing, but many people leave the water running while they brush. They can hardly pretend that the water going down the drain between wetting and rinsing the brush has a high utility. When all the extravagant uses of water by the modern consumer are considered, it is certain that the marginal utility of the last, say, 30 percent of all units consumed is very low, even though the total utility of *all* the units consumed is extremely high.

Utility Schedules and Graphs

The schedule in Table 7-1 is hypothetical. It merely illustrates the assumptions that have been made about utility. The table shows that total utility rises as the number of movies attended each month rises. Everything else being equal, the more movies the household attends each month, the more satisfaction it gets—at least over the range shown in the table. But the marginal utility of each additional movie per month is less than that of the previous one (even though each movie adds something to the household's satisfaction). The marginal utility schedule declines as quantity consumed rises. [9] The same data are shown graphically in the two parts of Figure 7-2.

Maximizing Utility

A basic assumption of the economic theory of household behavior is that households try to make themselves as well off as they possibly can in the circumstances in which they find themselves. The members of a household seek to maximize their

TABLE 7-1 TOTAL AND MARGINAL UTILITY SCHEDULES

Number of movies attended (per month)	Total utility	Marginal utility
0	0	
1	30	30
2	50	20
3	65	15
4	75	10
5	83	8
6	89	6
7	93	4
8	96	3
9	98	2
10	99	1

Total utility rises but marginal utility declines as this household's consumption increases. The marginal utility of 20, shown as the second entry in the last column, arises because total utility increased from 30 to 50—a difference of 20—with attendance at the second movie. To indicate that the marginal utility is associated with the change from one rate of movie attendances to another, the figures are recorded between the rows. When plotting marginal utility on a graph, it is plotted at the midpoint of the interval over which it is computed.

total utility. Sometimes this assumption is taken to mean that households are narrowly selfish and have no charitable motives. Not so; if, for example, the household derives utility from giving its money away to others, this can be incorporated into the analysis. The marginal utility it gets from a dollar given away can be compared with the marginal utility it gets from a dollar spent on itself. The assumption of utility maximization is sometimes criticized as being obviously unrealistic. Such criticisms are discussed and assessed in Box 7-1.

The Equilibrium of a Household

How can a household adjust its expenditure so as to maximize the total utility of its members? Should it go to the point at which the marginal utility of each commodity is the same—that is, the

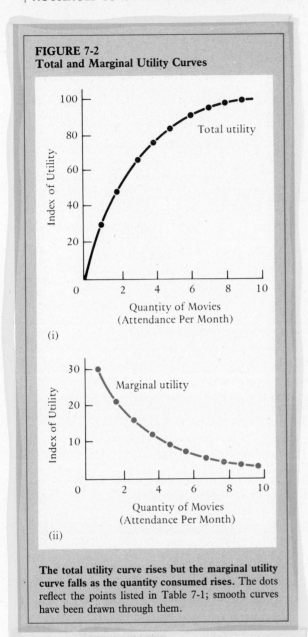

FIGURE 7-2
Total and Marginal Utility Curves

(i)

(ii)

The total utility curve rises but the marginal utility curve falls as the quantity consumed rises. The dots reflect the points listed in Table 7-1; smooth curves have been drawn through them.

for a unit of another, the first commodity would represent a poor use of its money if the marginal utility of each were equal. The household would be spending $3 to get satisfaction it could have acquired for only $1.

The household maximizing its utility will allocate its expenditure among commodities so that the utility of the last dollar spent on each is equal.

Imagine that the household is in a position in which the utility of the last dollar spent on carrots yields three times the utility of the last dollar spent on brussels sprouts. In this case, total utility can be increased by switching a dollar of expenditure from sprouts to carrots and gaining the difference between the utilities of a dollar spent on each.

The utility-maximizing household will continue to switch its expenditure from sprouts to carrots as long as a dollar spent on carrots yields more utility than a dollar spent on sprouts. But this switching reduces the quantity of sprouts consumed and, given the law of diminishing marginal utility, raises the marginal utility of sprouts; at the same time, it increases the quantity of carrots consumed and thereby lowers the marginal utility of carrots.

Eventually, the marginal utilities will have changed enough so that the utility of a dollar spent on carrots is just equal to the utility of a dollar spent on sprouts. At this point there is nothing to be gained by a further switch of expenditure from sprouts to carrots. If the household persisted in reallocating its expenditure, it would further reduce the marginal utility of carrots (by consuming more of them) and raise the marginal utility of sprouts (by consuming less of them). Total utility would then be lower because the utility of a dollar spent on sprouts would now exceed the utility of a dollar spent on carrots.

Let us now leave carrots and sprouts and deal with commodities in general. Denote the marginal utility of the last unit of X by MU_x and its price by p_x. Let MU_y and p_y refer to a second commodity. The marginal utility per dollar of X will be MU_x/p_x. For example, if the last unit adds 30 units to utility and costs $2, then its marginal utility per dollar is $30/2 = 15$.

point at which it would value equally the last unit of each commodity consumed? This would make sense only if each commodity had the same price per unit. But if a household must spend $3 to buy an additional unit of one commodity and only $1

BOX 7–1 DOES DEMAND THEORY REQUIRE HOUSEHOLDS TO BE PERFECTLY RATIONAL?

It is tempting to dismiss utility maximization theory out of hand with the objection that it is unrealistic. After all, most of us know people who occasionally buy strawberries in spite of, or even because of, a rise in their price, or who spend a week's pay on a binge or a frivolous purchase that they afterward regret.

To judge such an observation, it is helpful to distinguish three possible uses of demand theory. The first use is to study the aggregate behavior of all households—as illustrated, for example, by the market demand curve for a product. The second use is to make statements about an individual household's probable actions. The third use is to make statements about what each household will certainly do.

The criticisms cited above apply only to the third use of demand theory. The observations referred to refute only the prediction that *all* households *always* behave as assumed by the theory. To predict the existence of a relatively stable downward-sloping market demand curve (the first use), or to predict what an individual household will probably do (the second use), we do *not* require that *all* households behave as is assumed by the theory all of the time. Consider two illustrations.

First, some households may always behave in a manner not assumed by the theory. Households whose members are mental defectives or have serious emotional disturbances are obvious possibilities. The inconsistent or erratic behavior of such households will not cause market demand curves to depart from their downward slope, provided these households account for a minority of total purchasers of any product. Their erratic behavior will be swamped by the normal behavior of the majority of households.

Second, an occasional irrationality or inconsistency on the part of every household will not upset the downward slope of the market demand curve so long as these isolated inconsistencies do not occur at the same time in all households. As long as such inconsistencies are unrelated across households, occurring now in one and now in another, their effect will be offset by the normal behavior of the majority of households.

The downward slope of the demand curve requires only that at any moment of time most households are behaving as assumed by the theory. This is compatible with inconsistent behavior on the part of some households all of the time and on the part of all households some of the time.

The condition required for a household to maximize its utility is, for any pair of commodities,

$$\frac{MU_x}{p_x} = \frac{MU_y}{p_y} \qquad [1]$$

This says that the household will allocate its expenditure so that the utility gained from the last dollar spent on each commodity is equal.

This is the fundamental equation of the utility theory of demand. Each household demands each good (for example, movie attendance) up to the

point at which the marginal utility per dollar spent on it is the same as the marginal utility of a dollar spent on another good (for example, water). When this condition is met, the household cannot shift a dollar of expenditure from one commodity to another and increase its utility.

An Alternative Interpretation of Household Equilibrium

If we rearrange the terms in Equation [1] we can gain additional insight into household behavior.

$$\frac{MU_x}{MU_y} = \frac{p_x}{p_y} \qquad [2]$$

If the two sides of Equation [2] are not equal, the household can increase its total satisfaction by rearranging its purchases. Assume, for example, that the price of a unit of X is twice the price of a unit of Y, $(p_x/p_y = 2)$, while the marginal utility of a unit of X is three times that of a unit of Y, $(MU_x/MU_y = 3)$. It will now pay the household to buy more X and less Y. If, for example, it reduces its purchases of Y by two units, it will free enough purchasing power to buy a unit of X. Since one new unit of X bought yields 1.5 times the satisfaction of two units of Y foregone, this switch is worth making. What about a further switch of X for Y? As the household buys more X and less Y, the marginal utility of X will fall and the marginal utility of Y will rise. The household will go on rearranging its purchases—reducing Y consumption and increasing X consumption—until, in this example, the marginal utility of X is only twice that of Y. At this point there is no further room to increase total satisfaction by rearranging purchases between the two commodities.

Now consider what the household is doing. It is faced with a set of prices that it cannot change. The household responds to these prices, and maximizes its satisfaction, by adjusting the things it can change—the quantities of the various goods it purchases—until Equation [2] is satisfied for all pairs of commodities.

This sort of equation—one side representing the choices the outside world gives decision makers and the other side representing the effect of those choices on their welfare—recurs in economics. It reflects the equilibrium position reached when decision makers have made the best adjustment they can to the external forces that limit their choices.

Each household faces the same set of market prices. When all households are fully adjusted to these prices, each and every household will have identical ratios of its marginal utilities for each pair of goods. Of course a rich household may consume more of each commodity than will a poor household. The rich and the poor households (and every

other household) will, however, adjust their *relative* purchases of each commodity so that the relative marginal utilities are the same for each household. Thus, if the price of X is twice the price of Y, each household will purchase X and Y to the point at which the household's marginal utility of X is twice its marginal utility of Y.

The Derivation of the Household's Demand Curve

To derive the household's demand curve for a commodity, it is only necessary to ask what happens when there is a change in the price of that commodity. To do this for candy, take Equation [2] and let X stand for candy and Y for all other commodities.

What will happen if, with all other prices constant, the price of candy rises? The household that started from a position of equilibrium will now find itself in a position in which[2]

$$\frac{MU \text{ of candy}}{MU \text{ of } Y} < \frac{\text{price of candy}}{\text{price of } Y} \qquad [3]$$

To restore equilibrium, it must buy less candy, thereby raising its marginal utility until once again Equation [2] is satisfied (where X is candy).[3] The common sense of this is that the marginal utility of candy *per dollar* falls when its price rises. The household began with the utility of the last dollar spent on candy equal to the utility of the last dollar spent on all other goods, but the rise in candy prices changes this. The household buys less candy (and more of other goods) until the marginal utility

---

[2] The inequality sign ($<$) always points to the smaller of two magnitudes. When the price of candy rises, the right-hand side of Equation [2] increases. Until the household adjusts its consumption patterns, the left-hand side will stay the same. Thus Equation [2] is replaced by Inequality [3].

[3] For most consumers, candy absorbs only a small proportion of total expenditure. If in response to a change in its price, expenditure on candy changes by $5 per month, this represents a large change in candy consumption but only a negligible change in the consumption of other commodities. Hence, in the text we proceed by assuming that the marginal utilities of other commodities do not change when the price and consumption of candy changes.

of candy rises enough to make the utility of a dollar spent on candy the same as it was originally.

This analysis leads to the basic prediction of demand theory.

A rise in the price of a commodity (with income and the prices of all other commodities held constant) will lead to a decrease in the quantity of the commodity demanded by each household.

If this is what each household does, it is also what all households taken together do. Thus the theory predicts a downward-sloping market demand curve.

USING MARGINAL UTILITY THEORY

Consumers' Surplus

Assume that you would be willing to pay as much as $100 a month for the amount of a commodity you consume rather than do without it. Further, assume that you actually buy the commodity for $60 instead of $100. What a bargain! You have paid $40 less than the top figure you were willing to pay. Yet this sort of bargain is not rare; it occurs every day in any economy where prices do the rationing. Indeed it is so common that the $40 "saved" in this example has a name: *consumers' surplus*. A precise definition will come later; in the meantime, let us see how this surplus arises.

Consumers' surplus is a direct consequence of diminishing marginal utility. To illustrate the connection, suppose we have collected the information shown in Table 7-2 on the basis of an interview with Mrs. Schwartz. Our first question is this: If you were getting no milk at all, how much would you be willing to pay for one glass per week? With no hesitation, she replies, $3. We then ask: If you had already consumed that one glass, how much would you pay for a second glass per week? After a bit of thought she answers, $1.50. Adding one glass per week with each question, we discover that she would be willing to pay $1 to get a third glass per week and $.80, $.60, $.50, $.40, $.30, $.25, and $.20 for successive glasses from the fourth to the tenth glasses per week. The information shows

TABLE 7–2 CONSUMERS' SURPLUS ON MILK CONSUMPTION BY ONE CONSUMER

(1) Glasses of milk consumed per week	(2) Amount the consumer would pay to get this glass	(3) Consumers' surplus if milk costs $.30 per glass
First	$3.00	$2.70
Second	1.50	1.20
Third	1.00	0.70
Fourth	0.80	0.50
Fifth	0.60	0.30
Sixth	0.50	0.20
Seventh	0.40	0.10
Eighth	0.30	0.00
Ninth	0.25	—
Tenth	0.20	—

Consumers' surplus on each unit consumed is the difference between the market price and the maximum price the consumer would pay to obtain that unit. The table shows the value that a single consumer, Mrs. Schwartz, puts on successive glasses of milk consumed each week. Because marginal utility declines, she would pay successively smaller amounts for each additional unit consumed. As long as she would be willing to pay more than the market price for any unit, she will buy that unit and obtain a consumers' surplus on it. The marginal unit is the one valued just at the market price and on which no consumers' surplus is earned.

that she puts progressively lower valuations on each additional glass of milk, and this illustrates the general concept of diminishing marginal utility.

But Mrs. Schwartz does not have to pay a different price for each glass of milk she consumes each week. Instead she finds that she can buy all the milk she wants at the prevailing market price. Suppose the price is $.30. She will buy eight glasses per week (one each weekday and two on Sunday) because she values the eighth glass just at the market price while valuing all earlier glasses at higher amounts. Because she values the first glass at $3 but gets it for $.30, she makes a "profit" of $2.70 on that glass. Between her $1.50 valuation of the second glass and what she has to pay for it she clears a "profit" of $1.20. She clears $.70 on the third glass, and so on. These "profit" amounts are called her consumers' surpluses on each glass. They are shown in column 3 of the table; the total surplus is $5.70 per week.

While other consumers would put different numerical values into Table 7-2, diminishing marginal utility implies that the figures in column 2 would be declining for each consumer. Since a consumer will go on buying further units until the value he or she places on the last unit equals the market price, it follows that there will be a consumers' surplus on every unit consumed except the last one.

In general, **consumers' surplus** is the difference between the total value consumers place on all the units consumed of some commodity and the payment they must make to purchase that amount of the commodity. The total value placed by each consumer on the total consumption of some commodity can be estimated in at least two ways: The valuation that the consumer places on each successive unit may be summed; or the consumer may be asked how much he or she would pay to consume the amount in question if the alternative were to have none of the commodity.[4]

The data in columns 1 and 2 of Table 7-2 give Mrs. Schwartz's demand curve for milk. It is her demand curve because she will go on buying glasses of milk as long as she values each glass at least as much as the market price she must pay for it. When the market price is $3 per glass, she will buy only one glass; when it is $1.50, she will buy two glasses—and so on. The total valuation is the area below her demand curve, and consumers' surplus is that part of the area that lies above the price line. This is shown in Figure 7-3. Figure 7-4 shows that the same relation holds for the smooth market demand curve that indicates the total amount all consumers would buy at each price.

[4] This is only an approximation, but it is good enough for our purposes. More advanced theory shows that the calculations presented here ignore an "income effect." As a result, they slightly overestimate consumers' surplus. Although it is sometimes necessary to correct for this bias, no amount of refinement upsets the general result that we establish here: When consumers can buy all units they require at a single market price, they pay for the quantity consumed much less than they would be willing to pay if faced with the choice between that amount and nothing.

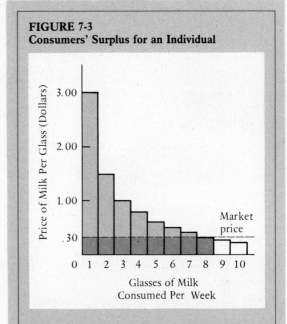

FIGURE 7-3
Consumers' Surplus for an Individual

Consumers' surplus is the sum of the extra valuations placed on each unit over and above the market price paid for each. This figure is based on the data in Table 7-2. Mrs. Schwartz will pay the dark shaded area for the eight glasses of milk she will consume per week when the market price is 30¢ a glass. The total value she places on these eight glasses is the entire shaded area. Hence her consumers' surplus is the light shaded area.

The Paradox of Value Revisited

We saw at the beginning of this chapter that early economists found it paradoxical that the market often valued necessary commodities such as water much lower than it valued such luxuries as diamonds. They distinguished a commodity's *value in use* (its total utility) and its *value in exchange* (its total market value, that is, price *times* quantity).[5] It seemed reasonable to them that commodities

[5] The total utilities of two commodities cannot be simply related to their relative market *prices*, since the latter can be made anything we want by choosing the units appropriately. For example, one barrel of diamonds is expensive relative to one barrel of water, but a one-carat diamond is cheap relative to one reservoir full of water.

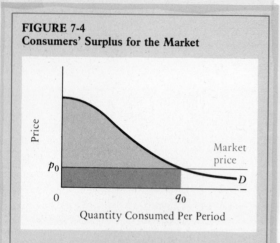

FIGURE 7-4
Consumers' Surplus for the Market

Total consumers' surplus is the area under the demand curve and above the price line. The demand curve shows the amount consumers would pay for each unit of the commodity if they had to buy their units one at a time. The area under the demand curve shows the total valuation consumers place on all units consumed. For example, the total value that consumers place on q_0 units is the entire shaded area under the demand curve up to q_0. At a market price of p_0 the amount paid for q_0 units is the dark shaded area. Hence consumers' surplus is the light shaded area.

with high use values should have high market values. A precise statement of what they expected is this: For any two commodities, the ratio of their values in exchange should conform to the ratio of their values in use. In the case of water and diamonds, this led to the *incorrect* prediction that

$$\frac{p \times q \text{ of diamonds}}{p \times q \text{ of water}} = \frac{\text{total utility of diamonds}}{\text{total utility of water}} \quad [4]$$

The paradox of value was resolved when later economists showed that Equation [4] was inconsistent with the assumption that households maximize utility. The reason is that utility-maximizing behavior relates *marginal* utilities to prices (as shown in Equation [2]), not total utilities to total values purchased (as hypothesized in Equation [4]).

Thus, for example, the fact that air is free means that people will use it until its marginal utility is zero. However, its zero value in exchange does not

preclude its having a high value in use (total utility). To understand the case of water and diamonds, remember that water is cheap because there is enough of it that people consume it to the point at which its *marginal* utility is very low; they are not prepared to pay a high price to obtain a little more of it. Diamonds are expensive because they are scarce (the owners of diamond mines keep diamonds scarce by limiting output), and those who buy them have to stop at a point where marginal utility is still high; they are prepared to pay a high price for an additional diamond.

Elasticity of Demand: Necessities and Luxuries

It is common to distinguish necessities and luxuries on the basis of total utilities. In this usage, *luxuries* have low total utilities—they can be dispensed with altogether if circumstances require—while *necessities* are essential to life—they have high total utilities because certain minimum quantities of them are essential.

A frequent error arises when people try to use these commonsense notions of luxuries and necessities to predict demand elasticities. They argue that since luxuries can easily be given up, they will have highly elastic demands: when their prices rise, households can stop purchasing them. On the other hand, necessities ought to have almost completely inelastic demands because when prices rise, households have no choice but to continue to buy them. But elasticity of demand depends on marginal utilities, not total utilities.

Demand theory leads to the prediction that when the price of a commodity—say, eggs—rises, the household will reduce its purchase of eggs enough to increase its *marginal* utility to the point where the marginal utility per dollar spent on eggs is the same as for other commodities whose prices did not rise. But will the reduction in quantity required to raise the marginal utility be a little or a lot? This depends on the shape of the marginal utility curve in the range that is relevant. If the marginal utility curve is flat, a large change in quantity is required and demand will be elastic. If the curve is steep, a small change will suffice and demand will be inelastic. Figure 7-5 presents two possible responses to a doubling in price. It leads to these important conclusions:

The response of quantity demanded to a change in price (i.e., the elasticity of demand) depends on the marginal utility over the relevant range and has no necessary relation to the total utility of the good.

Free Goods, Scarce Goods, and Freely Provided Goods

A **free good** is one for which the quantity supplied exceeds the quantity demanded at a price of zero. Such goods will therefore not command positive prices in a free-market system. Since a household's total utility can always be increased by its consuming more of any good having positive marginal utility, it follows that free goods will be consumed up to the point at which their marginal utilities are zero. At some times in some places, air, water, salt, sand, and wild fruit have been free goods. Note that a good may be free at one time or place but not at another.

A **scarce good** is one for which the quantity demanded exceeds the quantity supplied at a price of zero. Such goods will therefore command positive prices in a free-market system. Most goods are scarce goods. If all such goods had zero prices, the total amount that people would want to consume would greatly exceed the amount that could be produced by all the economy's resources.

Sometimes a scarce good is freely provided to consumers by the government. Whatever the merits of a particular free distribution, the economic consequences are clear. Households will treat it as free to them and consume to the point of zero marginal utility. This point is illustrated in Figure 7-6. Since every unit consumed requires resources to produce, the government in this situation is using scarce resources to produce a good that has a low marginal utility. If some resources were withdrawn from the production of this commodity, total utility would fall very little. Those resources could then be used for producing other goods with a high marginal utility, thus raising total utility.

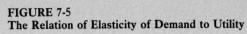

FIGURE 7-5
The Relation of Elasticity of Demand to Utility

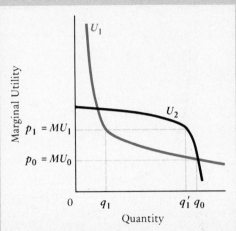

Elasticity of demand is determined by marginal utilities in the relevant range, not total utilities. Consider two different marginal utility curves for a commodity, U_1 and U_2. Suppose price is p_0. Given either utility curve the household consumes the quantity q_0, where the last unit consumed has a marginal utility of MU_0. When the price doubles to p_1, the household must cut its consumption. The marginal utility required to achieve a new equilibrium doubles to MU_1. If the black line U_2 is the household's marginal utility curve, consumption only falls to q_1' and the household will have a very inelastic demand curve for the product. If, however, the colored line U_1 is the household's marginal utility curve, consumption falls to q_1 and the household will have a very elastic demand curve. Although the shape of the marginal utility curve in the relevant range is thus important, its shape outside of this range is irrelevant. But total utility depends upon the whole area under the curve. Depending on what happens between 0 and q_1, the colored curve can show more or less total utility. Thus total utility has no influence on the household's behavior when it seeks to raise marginal utility from MU_0 to MU_1.

"Just" Prices

People often have strong views about the prices charged for certain commodities. These are often an emotional reaction to the total utilities of goods rather than to their marginal utilities. We often

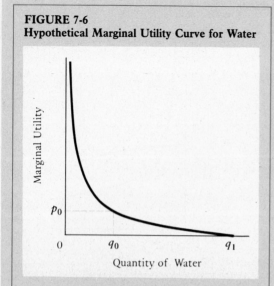

FIGURE 7-6
Hypothetical Marginal Utility Curve for Water

The imposition of a modest price may greatly reduce the quantity of water consumed without causing a large total sacrifice in the utility derived from water consumption. Suppose water is a scarce commodity, not a free good. If water is priced at p_0, consumers will consume q_0 units per month. Lowering the price to zero would increase the consumption to q_1. Much of the water that a household would consume at a zero price has a very low marginal utility.

hear an argument such as this: Water is a necessity of life to rich and poor; it is wrong, therefore, to make people pay for so necessary a commodity. The government, so goes the argument, should freely provide such goods.

The relevant question when deciding between a zero price and a modest price for water is not "Is water so necessary that we do not want to deprive anyone of *all* of it?" but rather "Are the marginal uses of water so important that we are willing to use scarce resources to provide the necessary quantities?" Clearly, the two questions can be given different answers.

Evidence about the consumption of water at various prices suggests that the marginal utility curve for water is shaped like the curve in Figure 7-6. The difference between providing water free and

charging a modest price for it may mean a great deal in the quantity of water consumed. The additional water is costly to provide, and its provision requires scarce resources that could have been used to produce other things. If the utility of the commodities foregone is higher than the utility of the extra water consumed, then people are worse off as a result of receiving water free. A charge for water would release resources from water production to produce goods that yield a higher utility.

Similar considerations apply to food, medical services, and a host of other commodities that are necessities of life but also have numerous low utility uses which will be encouraged if the commodity is scarce but is provided very cheaply or for free.

Box 7-2 provides a very different example of the distinction between marginal and total utility.

Used Car Prices: The Problem of "Lemons"

It is common for people to regard the huge loss of value of a new car in the first year as a sign that consumers are overly style conscious and will always pay a big premium for the latest in anything. Professor George Akerlof of the University of California suggests a different explanation based upon the proposition that the utility expected to be received from a one-year-old car purchased on the used car market will be lower than that of the average one-year-old car. Consider his theory.

Any particular model year of automobiles will include a certain proportion of "lemons"—cars that have one or more serious defects. Purchasers of new cars of a certain year and model take a chance on their car's turning out to be a lemon. Those who are unlucky and get a lemon are more likely to resell their car then those who are lucky and get a quality car. Hence in the used car market there will be a disproportionately large number of lemons for sale. Similarly, not all cars are driven in the same manner. Those that are driven long distances or under bad conditions are much more likely to be traded in or sold used than those that are driven on good roads and in moderate amounts.

BOX 7–2 WHAT DO ATTITUDE SURVEYS MEASURE?

Consider a type of survey that is popular both in the daily newspapers and in sociology and political science. These surveys take the form of asking such questions as:

Do you like the Liberals more than the Progressive Conservatives?

In deciding to live in area A rather than area B, what factors influenced your choice? List the following in order of importance: neighbors, schools, closeness to swimming area, price and quality of housing available, play areas for children, general amenities.

In choosing a university, what factors were important to you? List in order of importance: environment, academic excellence, residential facilities, parents' opinion, school opinion, athletic facilities, tuition.

You should be able to add other examples to this list (which was drawn from real cases). *All of the above survey questions, and most of those you might add, attempt to measure total rather than marginal utilities.* The total value being asked about includes the consumers' surplus. There is of course nothing illegal or immoral about this. People are free to measure anything that interests them, and in some cases knowledge of total utilities may be useful. But in many cases, actual behavior will be determined by marginal utilities, and anyone who attempts to predict such behavior from a (correct) knowledge of total utilities will be hopelessly in error.

Where the behavior being predicted involves an either-or decision, such as a vote for the Liberal or the Conservative candidate, total utility attached to each choice will indeed be what matters because the voters are choosing one or the other. But where the decision is marginal, between a little more and a little less, total utility is not what will determine behavior.

A recent newspaper poll in a large city showed that two-thirds of the city's voters rated its excellent school system as one of its important assets. Yet in a subsequent election the voters turned down a school bond issue. Is this irrational behavior, as the newspaper editorials charged? Does it show a biased sample in the poll? It demonstrates neither. The poll measured the people's assessment of the total utility derived from the school system (high), while the bond issue vote depended on the people's assessment of the marginal utility of a little more money spent on the school system (low). There is nothing contradictory in anyone's feeling that the total utility of the city's fine school system is very large but that the city has other needs that have a higher marginal utility than further money spent on school construction.

A recent survey showed—paradoxically, it claimed—that many Americans are getting more pleasure from their families just at the time that they are electing to have smaller families. There is nothing paradoxical about a shift in tastes that increases the marginal utility of the first two or three children and reduces the marginal utility of each further child. Nor is there any paradox in a parent's getting a high total utility from the total time spent with the children but assigning a low marginal utility to the prospect of spending additional time with them each evening.

Thus buyers of used cars are right to be suspicious of why the car is for sale, while salespeople are quick to invent reasons ("It was owned by a little old lady who only drove it on Sundays"). Because it is very difficult to identify a lemon, or a badly used car, before buying it, the purchaser will be prepared to buy a used car only at a price low enough to offset the increased probability that it is of poor quality.

These are wholly sensible consumer responses

to uncertainty and may explain why one-year-old cars typically sell for a discount much larger than can be explained by the physical depreciation that occurs in one year in the average car of that model. The large discount reflects the lower utility the purchaser can expect from a used car because of the higher probability that it will be a lemon.

SUMMARY

1. Market demand curves reflect the aggregate of the consumption behavior of the millions of households in the economy.

2. Marginal utility theory distinguishes between the total utility gained from the consumption of all units of some commodity and the marginal utility resulting from the consumption of one more unit of the commodity.

3. The basic assumption made in utility theory is that the utility the household derives from the consumption of successive units of a commodity per period of time will diminish as the consumption of that commodity increases.

4. Households maximize utility and thus reach equilibrium when the utility derived from the last dollar spent on each commodity is equal. Another way of putting this is that the marginal utilities derived from the last unit of each commodity consumed will be proportional to their prices.

5. Consumers' surplus arises because a household can purchase every unit of a commodity at a price equal to the value it places on the last unit purchased. Diminishing marginal utility implies that the household places a higher value on all other units purchased and hence that all but the last unit purchased will yield a consumers' surplus.

6. It is vital to distinguish between total and marginal utilities because choices concerning a bit more and a bit less cannot be predicted from a knowledge of total utilities. The paradox of value involved a confusion between total and marginal utilities.

TOPICS FOR REVIEW

Market demand and individual household demand curves
Total utility and marginal utility
The hypothesis of diminishing marginal utility
Conditions for maximizing utility
The interpretation of $MU_x/MU_y = p_x/p_y$
Consumers' surplus
The paradox of value

DISCUSSION QUESTIONS

1. Why is market demand the *horizontal* sum of individual demand curves? Is the vertical sum different? What would a vertical sum of individual demand curves show? Can you imagine any use of vertical summation of demand curves?

2. Which of the choices implied below involve a consideration of marginal utilities and which total utilities?
   a. The provincial legislature debates whether 17-year-olds should be given the vote.
   b. A diet calls for precisely 1,200 calories per day.
   c. My doctor says I must give up smoking and drinking or else accept an increased chance of heart attack.
   d. When Armand Hammer decided to buy the Rembrandt painting *Juno* for a record $3.25 million, he called it the "crown jewel of my collection."
   e. I enjoyed my golf game today, but I was so tired that I decided to stop at the seventeenth hole.

3. Explain the transactions described in the following quotations in terms of the utility of the commodity. Interpret "worthless" and "priceless" as used here.
   a. "Bob Koppang has made a business of selling jars of shredded U.S. currency. The money is worthless, and yet he's sold 53,000 jars already and has orders for 40,000 more—at $5 a jar. Each jar contains about $10,000 in shredded bills."
   b. "Leonardo da Vinci's priceless painting *Genevra de' Benci* was sold to the National Gallery of Art for $5 million."

4. The *New York Times* called it the great liver crisis. Chopped liver is a delicacy on the table, particularly the kosher table, but in the late 1970s it was a glut on the market. Prices had sunk to a 20-year low as supplies had risen to an all-time high due to a very high cattle slaughter. What do the following quotations from the *Times'* story tell you about the marginal and total utility of liver?
   a. "Grade A-1 liver is being used for cats and dogs instead

of people. It's unheard of, it's a waste," says the manager of Kosher King Meat Products. "Even Israel is drowning in chopped liver."

b. "They're falling all over their feet to sell to me," said the president of Mrs. Weinberg's Kosher Chopped Liver Co., which uses 3,500 pounds of liver daily. "I've been offered prices so low I can't believe them."

c. "The nature of people being what they are, even though they like a good bargain, they're not going to eat something that doesn't agree with their taste."

5. "A survey shows that most people prefer butter to margarine." What exactly might this mean? Supposing it to be true, can you acccount for the facts that many people buy some of both butter and margarine each month and that in total more pounds of margarine are sold than pounds of butter?

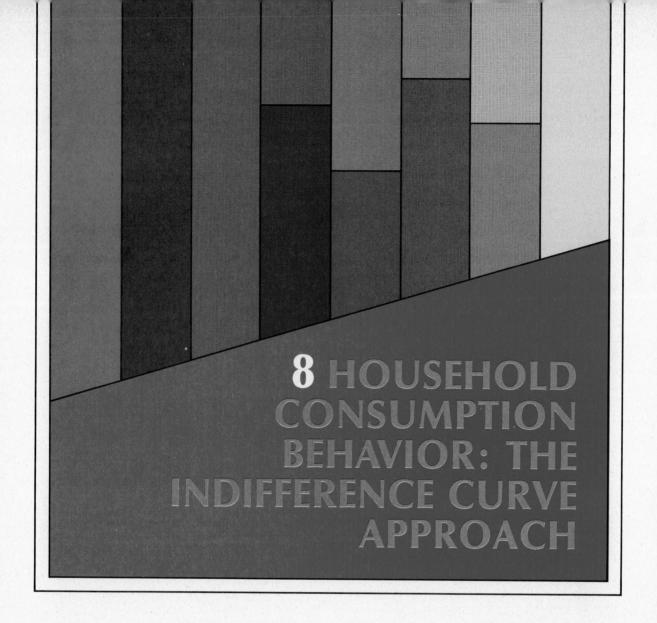

8 HOUSEHOLD CONSUMPTION BEHAVIOR: THE INDIFFERENCE CURVE APPROACH

The marginal utility approach to household behavior discussed in Chapter 7 came first historically. It is still valued because of the great insights that the concept of marginal utility opened up. With the publication in 1939 of Sir John R. Hicks' classic *Value and Capital*, an alternative approach often called indifference curve analysis became popular in English-language economics.[1] This is not a com-

---

[1] Hicks, whose career has been spent mainly at Oxford, was the first British recipient of the Nobel prize in economics for the contributions to economics that he made in *Value and Capital* and elsewhere. He did not invent indifference curve analysis; he took over, popularized, and extended the use of a concept developed by the great Italian economist Vilfredo Par-

eto in the first decade of this century. As is so often true in science, it is not the discoverer or the inventor but the one who makes the timely and insightful application who has the major impact. Thus it was Hicks, not Pareto, who led to the almost universal use of indifference analysis by economists in the 1940s and 1950s.

peting theory but a slightly different way of looking at choices by households. Its major innovation was to dispense with the notion of a *measurable* concept of utility that is required by marginal utility theory.

THE BUDGET LINE

Consider a household faced with the choice between only two goods, food (*F*) and clothing (*C*). (Simplifying by considering only choices between two goods reveals all the essential points we are interested in.) Suppose that the household has a certain money income, say $120 a week, and that the prices for food and clothing are fixed at the outset at $4 a unit for food and $2 a unit for clothing. For the purpose of our example, suppose that the household does not save; its only choice is in deciding how much of its $120 to spend on food and how much to spend on clothing.

The household's choices are shown by the line *ab* in Figure 8-1, which shows the combinations of food and clothing that it can buy. It could spend all its income on clothing and obtain 60*C* and no *F* per week. It could also go to the other extreme and purchase only food, buying 30*F* and no *C*. Or it could go to an intermediate position and consume some of both goods; for example, it could spend $40 to buy 10*F* and the remaining $80 to buy 40*C*.

The household's **budget line** indicates all the combinations available to the household if it spends all its income. (It is also sometimes called an *isocost line* since all points on it represent bundles of goods with the same total cost of purchase.)

Among the important properties of the budget line are the following. (You should check enough examples against Figure 8-1 to satisfy yourself that they are true.)

1. Points on the budget line represent bundles of commodities that exactly use up the household's income. (Try the point 20*C* and 20*F*.)
2. Points between the budget line and the origin represent bundles of commodities that use up less than the household's income. (Try the point 20*C* and 10*F*.)

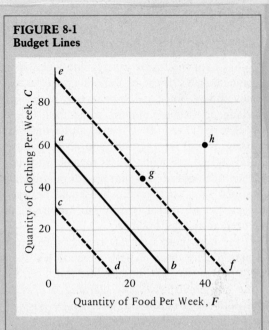

**FIGURE 8-1
Budget Lines**

The budget line shows the quantities of goods available to a household given its money income and the prices of the goods it buys. Any point indicates a combination (or *bundle*) of so much food and so much clothing. Point *h*, for example, indicates 60 units of clothing and 40 units of food per week. With an income of $120 a week and prices of $4 for food and $2 for clothing, the household's budget line is *ab*. This line shows all the combinations of *F* and *C* available to a household spending that income at those prices. Neither combination *g* nor *h* is attainable.

An increase in money income from $120 to $180, with money prices of *F* and *C* constant, shifts the budget line outward to the parallel line *ef*. At this level of income, combination *g* is attainable. A decrease in money income to $60 shifts the budget line to *cd*.

3. Points above the budget line represent combinations of commodities costing more to purchase than the household's present income. (Try the point 30*C* and 40*F*.)

The budget line shows all combinations of commodities that are available to the household given its money income and the prices of the goods it purchases, if it spends all its income on them.

Shifts in the Budget Line

Changes in Money Income

What happens to the budget line when money income changes? If the household's money income is halved from $120 to $60 per week, prices being unchanged, then the amount of goods it can buy will also be halved. If it spends all its income on clothing, it will now get $30C$ and no F (point c in Figure 8-1; if it spends all its income on food, it will get $15F$ and no C (point d). All possible combinations now open to the household appear on budget line cd, which is closer to the origin than the original budget line.

If the household's income rises to $180, it will be able to buy more of both commodities than it could previously. The budget line shifts outward. If the household buys only clothing, it can have $90C$; if it buys only food, it can have $45F$; if it divides its income equally between the two goods, it can have $45C$ and $22.5F$.

Variations in the household's money income, with prices constant, shift the budget line parallel to itself.

Proportional Changes in Prices of Both Goods

Changing both prices in the same proportion shifts the budget line parallel to itself in the same way that a money income change shifted it. Doubling both prices with money income constant halves the amount of goods that can be purchased and thus has exactly the same effect on the household's budget line as halving money income with money prices constant. In both cases the household's original budget line is shifted inward. Similarly, a reduction of both prices causes the budget line to shift outward in exactly the same manner that an increase in money income does.

Proportional changes in the prices of both goods, with money income constant, shift the budget line parallel to itself.

It is now apparent that it is possible to have exactly offsetting changes in prices and money incomes. Such a situation leaves the real choices available to the household unchanged.

A change in money income and a *proportional* change of the same amount in all money prices leaves the position of the budget line unchanged.

Changes in Relative Prices

The price of a commodity usually refers to the amount of money that must be spent to acquire one unit of the commodity. This is called the **absolute price** or **money price**. A relative price is the ratio of two absolute prices. The statement "the price of F is $4" refers to an absolute price; "the price of F is twice the price of C" refers to a relative price.

A change in a relative price can be accomplished by changing both of the absolute prices in different proportions or by holding one price constant and changing the other. It is useful for our purposes to do the latter. The effects of such a change are shown in Figure 8-2. The basic conclusion that emerges is this:

A change in relative prices changes the slope of the budget line.

The economic significance of the slope of the budget line for food and clothing (which we have just seen to be related to the relative prices of the two commodities) is that it reflects the opportunity cost of food in terms of clothing. To increase food consumption with expenditure constant, one must move along the budget line, consuming less clothing. Again suppose the price of food (p_F) is $4 and the price of clothing (p_C) is $2. With income fixed, it is necessary to forego the purchase of two units of clothing to acquire one unit extra of food. The opportunity cost of food in terms of clothing is thus two units of clothing. But it can also be stated as p_F/p_C, which is the relative price.

Notice that this relative price ($p_F = 2p_C$) is consistent with an infinite number of absolute prices. If $p_F = 40 and $p_C = 20, it still takes the sacrifice of two units of clothing to acquire one unit of food. This shows that it is relative, not absolute, prices that determine opportunity cost. The general conclusion is that the opportunity cost of F in terms of C is measured by the slope of the budget line or (the equivalent) by the relative price ratio. [10]

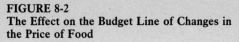

FIGURE 8-2
The Effect on the Budget Line of Changes in the Price of Food

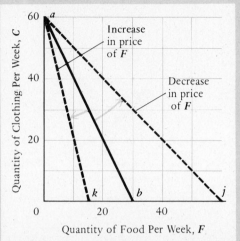

A change in the price of one commodity changes relative prices and thus changes the slope of the budget line. The original budget line *ab* arose from a money income of $120, with units of *C* priced at $2 and units of *F* at $4. A fall in the price of *F* to $2 doubles the quantity of *F* obtainable for any given quantity of *C* purchased and pivots the budget line outward to *aj*. A rise in the price of *F* to $8 reduces the quantity of *F* obtainable and pivots the budget line inward to *ak*.

Real and Money Income

A household's **money income** is its income measured in money units, so many dollars and cents per week or per year. A household's **real income** is the purchasing power of its money income—that is, the quantity of goods and services that can be purchased with its money income.

If money prices remain constant, any change in money income will cause a corresponding change in real income. If the household's money income rises by 10 percent (say from $10,000 to $11,000), the household can if it wishes buy 10 percent more of all commodities—its real income has also risen by 10 percent.

If prices change, however, real and money in-comes will not change in the same proportion—indeed, they can easily change in opposite directions. Consider a situation in which all money prices rise by 10 percent. If money income rises by any amount less than 10 percent, real income falls. If money income also rises by 10 percent, real income will be unchanged. Only if money income rises by more than 10 percent will real income also rise.

Changes in real income are shown graphically by shifts in the budget line. When the budget line in Figure 8-1 shifts outward, away from the origin, real income rises. When the line shifts inward, toward the origin, real income falls. The household's ability to purchase goods and services is measured by real income, not by money income.

INDIFFERENCE CURVE ANALYSIS

What the household does is determined by both what it can do and what it would like to do. The budget line shows what it *can do*. What it *wants to do* is determined by its tastes.

An Indifference Curve

We start by taking an imaginary household and giving it some quantity of each of the two goods, say 18 units of clothing and 10 units of food. (A consumption pattern for a household that contains quantities of two or more distinct goods is called a *bundle* or a *combination* of goods.) Now offer the household an alternative bundle of goods, say 13 units of clothing and 15 units of food. This alternative has 5 fewer units of clothing and 5 more units of food than the first one. Whether the household prefers this bundle depends on the relative valuation that it places on 5 more units of food and 5 fewer units of clothing. If it values the extra food more than the foregone clothing, it will prefer the new bundle to the original one. If it values the food less than the clothing, it will prefer the original bundle. If the household places the same value on the extra food as on the foregone clothing, it is said to be *indifferent* between the two bundles.

Assume that after much trial and error a number

of bundles that the household is indifferent between have been identified—each bundle gives the household equal satisfaction. These are shown in Table 8-1.

There will of course be combinations of the two commodities other than those enumerated in the table that will give the same level of satisfaction to the household. All these combinations are shown in Figure 8-3 by the smooth curve that passes through the points plotted from the table. This curve is an indifference curve. In general, an **indifference curve** shows all combinations of goods that yield the same satisfaction to the household. A household is *indifferent* between the combinations indicated by any two points on one indifference curve.

Any points above and to the right of the curve show combinations of food and clothing that the household would prefer to combinations indicated by points on the curve. Consider, for example, the combination of 20 food and 18 clothing, which is represented by point *g* in the figure. Although it may not be obvious that this bundle must be preferred to bundle *a* (which has more clothing but less food), it is obvious that it will be preferred to bundle *c* because there is both less clothing and less food represented at *c* than at *g*. Inspection of the graph shows that *any* point above the curve will be obviously superior to *some* points on the curve in the sense that it will contain both more food and more clothing than those points on the

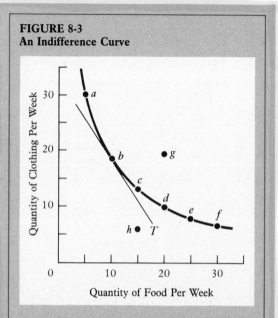

FIGURE 8-3
An Indifference Curve

This indifference curve shows combinations of food and clothing that yield equal satisfaction and among which the household is indifferent. Points *a* to *f* are plotted from Table 8-1. The smooth curve through them is an indifference curve; each combination on it gives equal satisfaction to the household. Point *g* above the line is a preferred combination to any point on the line; point *h* below the line is an inferior combination to any point on the line. The slope of the line *T* gives the marginal rate of substitution at point *b*. Moving down the curve from *b* to *f*, the slope flattens, showing that the more food and the less clothing the household has, the less willing it will be to sacrifice further clothing to get more food.

TABLE 8-1 ALTERNATIVE BUNDLES GIVING A HOUSEHOLD EQUAL SATISFACTION

Bundle	Clothing	Food
a	30	5
b	18	10
c	13	15
d	10	20
e	8	25
f	7	30

These bundles all lie on a single indifference curve. Since all of these bundles of food and clothing give equal satisfaction, the household is "indifferent" among them.

curve. But since all points on the curve are equal in the household's eyes, the point above the curve must be superior to *all* points on the curve. By a similar argument, points below and to the left of the curve represent bundles that are inferior to bundles represented by points on the curve.

The Marginal Rate of Substitution

How much clothing would the household be prepared to give up to get one more unit of food? The answer to this question measures what is called the marginal rate of substitution of clothing for food. The **marginal rate of substitution (MRS)** is the amount of one commodity a consumer would be prepared to give up to get one more unit of another commodity. The first basic assumption of indifference theory is that the algebraic value of the MRS is always negative. This means that to gain a positive change in its consumption of one commodity, the household is prepared to incur a negative change in its consumption of a second.

Graphically the negative marginal rate of substitution is shown by the downward slope of all indifference curves. (See, for example, the curve in Figure 8-3.)

The Hypothesis of Diminishing Marginal Rate of Substitution

The second basic assumption of indifference theory is that the marginal rate of substitution between any two commodities depends on the amounts of the commodities currently being consumed by the household. Consider a case in which the household has a lot of clothing and only a little food: Common sense suggests that the household might be willing to give up quite a bit of its plentiful clothing to get one unit more of scarce food. Now consider a case in which the household has only a little clothing and a lot of food: Common sense suggests that the household would be willing to give up only a little of its scarce clothing to get one more unit of already plentiful food.

This example illustrates the hypothesis of the **diminishing marginal rate of substitution.** The less of one commodity, A, and the more of a second commodity, B, the household has already, the smaller will be the amount of A it will be willing to give up to get one further unit of B.

The hypothesis says that the marginal rate of substitution changes systematically as the amounts of two commodities presently consumed vary. The more A and the less B the household currently has, the less B will it be willing to give up to get a further unit of A. The graphic expression of this is that the slope of any indifference curve becomes flatter as the household moves downward to the right along the curve. [11] In Figure 8-3 a movement downward to the right means that less clothing and more food is being consumed. The decreas-

TABLE 8–2 THE MARGINAL RATE OF SUBSTITUTION BETWEEN CLOTHING AND FOOD

Movement	(1) Change in clothing	(2) Change in food	(3) Marginal rate of substitution (1) ÷ (2)
From a to b	−12	5	−2.4
From b to c	− 5	5	−1.0
From c to d	− 3	5	− .6
From d to e	− 2	5	− .4
From e to f	− 1	5	− .2

The marginal rate of substitution of clothing for food declines as the quantity of food increases. This table is based on Table 8-1. When the household moves from a to b, it gives up 12 units of clothing and gains 5 units of food; it remains at the same level of overall satisfaction. The household at point a was prepared to sacrifice 12 clothing for 5 food (i.e., $^{12}/_5$ = 2.4 units of clothing per unit of food obtained). When the household moves from b to c, it sacrifices 5 clothing units for 5 food units (a rate of substitution of 1 unit of clothing for each unit of food).

ing steepness of the curve means that less and less clothing need be sacrificed to get one further unit of food.

The hypothesis is illustrated in Table 8-2, which is based on the example of food and clothing in Table 8-1. The last column of the table shows the rate at which the household is prepared to sacrifice units of clothing per unit of food obtained. At first the household will sacrifice 2.4 units of clothing to get 1 unit more of food, but as its consumption of clothing diminishes and that of food increases, the household becomes less and less willing to sacrifice further clothing for more food.[2]

---

[2] Movements between widely separated points on the indifference curve have been examined. In terms of a very small movement from any of the points on the curve, the rate at which the household will give up clothing to get food is shown by the slope of the tangent to the curve at that point. The slope of the line T, which is a tangent to the curve at point b in Figure 8-3, may thus be thought of as the slope of the curve at that precise point. It tells us the rate at which the household will sacrifice clothing per unit of food obtained when it is currently consuming 18 clothing and 10 food (the coordinates of point b).

The Indifference Map

So far we have constructed only a single indifference curve. However, starting at any other point in Figure 8-3, such as g, there will be other combinations that will yield equal satisfaction to the household. If the points indicating all these combinations are connected, they will form another indifference curve. This exercise can be repeated as many times as we wish, and as many indifference curves as we wish can be generated. The farther any indifference curve is from the origin, the higher will be the level of satisfaction given by any of the combinations of goods indicated by points on the curve.

A set of indifference curves is called an **indifference map**, an example of which is shown in Figure 8-4. It specifies the household's tastes by showing its rate of substitution between the two commodities for every level of current consumption of these commodities. When economists say that a household's tastes are *given*, they do not mean that the household's current consumption pattern is given; rather, they mean that the household's entire indifference map is given.

The Equilibrium of the Household

Indifference maps describe the preferences of households. Budget lines describe the possibilities open to the household. To predict what households will actually do, both sets of information must be put together. This is done in Figure 8-5. The household's budget line is shown in the figure by the straight line, while its tastes are shown by its indifference map (a few of whose curves are shown in the figure). Any point on the budget line is attainable. But which point will actually be chosen by the household?

Since the household wishes to maximize its satisfactions, it wishes to reach its highest attainable indifference curve. Inspection of the figure shows that if the household purchases any bundle on its budget line at a point cut by an indifference curve, a higher indifference curve can be reached. Only when the bundle purchased is such that the indifference curve is tangent to the budget line is

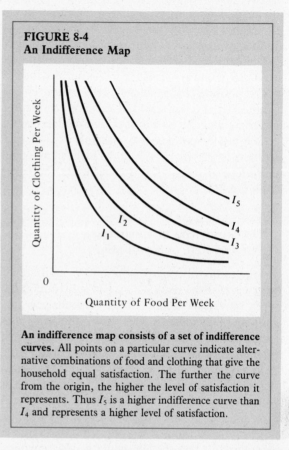

**FIGURE 8-4
An Indifference Map**

Quantity of Clothing Per Week

I_5

I_2

I_1

I_4

I_3

0

Quantity of Food Per Week

An indifference map consists of a set of indifference curves. All points on a particular curve indicate alternative combinations of food and clothing that give the household equal satisfaction. The further the curve from the origin, the higher the level of satisfaction it represents. Thus I_5 is a higher indifference curve than I_4 and represents a higher level of satisfaction.

it impossible for the household to alter its purchases and reach a higher curve.

The household's satisfaction is maximized at the point where an indifference curve is tangent to the budget line.

At such a tangency position, the slope of the indifference curve (the household's marginal rate of substitution of the goods) is the same as the slope of the budget line (the relative prices of the goods in the market).

The common sense of this result is that if the household values goods at a different rate than the market does, there is room for profitable exchange. The household can give up some of the good it values relatively less than the market and take in return some of the good it values relatively higher than the market does. When the household is pre-

FIGURE 8-5
The Equilibrium of a Household

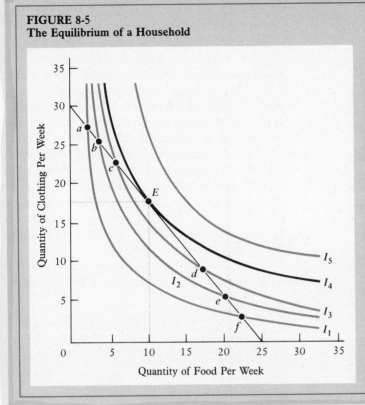

Equilibrium occurs at E, where an indifference curve is tangent to the budget line. The household has an income of $750 a week and faces prices of $25 a unit for clothing and $30 a unit for food. A combination of C and F indicated by point a is attainable, but by moving along the budget line higher indifference curves can be reached. The same is true at b and c. At E, however, where an indifference curve is tangent to the budget line, it is impossible to reach a higher curve by moving along the budget line. If the household did alter its consumption bundle by moving from E to c or d, for example, it would move to the lower indifference curve I_3 and thus to a lower level of satisfaction.

pared to swap goods at the same rate as they can be traded on the market, there is no further opportunity for it to raise its satisfaction by substituting one commodity for the other.

The household is presented with market prices that it cannot itself change. It adjusts to these prices by choosing a bundle of goods such that, at the margin, its own subjective evaluation of the goods conforms with the evaluations given by market prices.

The Reaction of the Household to a Change in Income

We have seen that a change in income leads to parallel shifts of the budget line—inward toward the origin when income falls and outward away from the origin when income rises. For each level of income there will be an equilibrium position at

which an indifference curve is tangent to the relevant budget line. Each such equilibrium position means that the household is doing as well as it possibly can for that level of income. If we move the budget line through all possible levels of income, and if we join up all the points of equilibrium, we will trace out what is called an **income-consumption line**, an example of which is shown in Figure 8-6. This line shows how consumption bundles change as income changes, with relative prices held constant.

The Reaction of a Household to a Change in Price

We already know that a change in the relative price of the two goods changes the slope of the budget line. Given a price of clothing, for each possible price of food there is an equilibrium con-

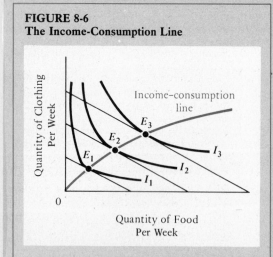

FIGURE 8-6
The Income-Consumption Line

The income-consumption line shows how the household's purchases react to a change in income with relative prices held constant. Increases in income shift the budget line out parallel to itself, moving the equilibrium from E_1 to E_2 to E_3. By joining up all the points of equilibrium, an income-consumption line is traced out.

sumption position for the household. Connecting these positions traces out a **price-consumption line,** as is shown in Figure 8-7. Notice that as the relative price of food and clothing changes, the relative quantities of food and clothing purchased also change. In particular, as the price of food falls, the household buys more food.[3]

Derivation of Demand Curves

If food and clothing were the only two commodities purchased by households, we could derive a demand curve for food from the price-consumption line of Figure 8-7. On an indifference map, that line represents how the quantity of food demanded varied as the price of food changed, with the price of clothing unchanged. To use indifference theory

[3] There is a rarely encountered but theoretically possible exception to this rule, a Giffen good, which is described in the last part of this chapter.

to derive the kind of demand curve introduced in Chapter 4, however, it is necessary to depart from the world of two commodities that we have used so far in this chapter.

What happens to the household's demand for some commodity, say carrots, as the price of that commodity changes, *all other prices being held constant?* In Figure 8-8 a new type of indifference map is plotted in which the quantity of carrots is represented on the horizontal axis and the value of all other goods consumed is represented on the vertical axis. We have in effect used "everything but carrots" as the second commodity. The indifference curves give the rate at which the household is prepared to swap carrots for money (which allows it to buy all other goods) at each level of consumption of carrots and of other goods.

Given the money price of carrots and the household's income, a budget line can be obtained show-

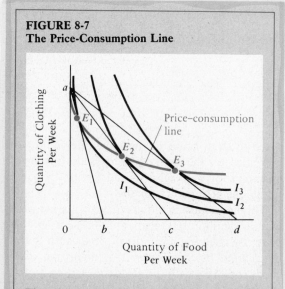

FIGURE 8-7
The Price-Consumption Line

The price-consumption line shows how the household's purchases react to a change in one price with money income and other prices held constant. Decreases in the price of food (with money income and the price of clothing constant) pivot the budget line from ab to ac to ad. The equilibrium position moves from E_1 to E_2 to E_3. By joining up all the points of equilibrium, a price-consumption line is traced out.

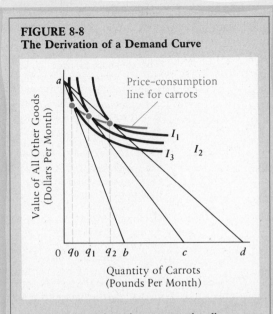

FIGURE 8-8
The Derivation of a Demand Curve

Value of All Other Goods (Dollars Per Month)

Price-consumption line for carrots

I_1

I_3 I_2

0 q_0 q_1 q_2 b c d

Quantity of Carrots
(Pounds Per Month)

Every point on the price-consumption line corresponds to both a price of the commodity and a quantity of the commodity demanded; this is the information required for a demand curve. The household has a of income; if it buys no carrots, it can consume a worth of all other goods. For each price of carrots there is a single budget line. As the price of carrots falls, the budget line pivots from ab to ac to ad, and the quantity of carrots demanded rises from q_0 to q_1 to q_2. This leads to a downward-sloping demand curve for carrots.

ing all those combinations of carrots and other goods that the household can consume for its given level of money income and the given price of carrots. Now assume a change in the money price of carrots. By joining the points of equilibrium, we can trace a price-consumption line between carrots and all other commodities in the same way that such a line was traced for food and clothing in Figure 8-7.

Figure 8-8 is similar to Figure 8-7, but notice two differences. First, the axes are labeled differently, and second, the price-consumption line in Figure 8-8 is crowded into the upper part of the diagram, indicating that whatever the price of carrots, the household does not spend a large part of

its income on them. Every point on the price-consumption line corresponds to one price and one quantity of carrots demanded. In the figure, the quantity of carrots consumed increases as their price falls. These pairs of price-quantity values can be transferred to a new figure, whose axes represent price of carrots and quantity of carrots, and used to plot a downward-sloping demand curve.

The Slope of the Demand Curve[4]

The price-consumption line in Figure 8-8 slopes down to the right as price decreases, indicating that the quantity of carrots demanded increases. But, as a little experimentation will show you, one can draw indifference curves in such a way that, in response to a decrease in price, the quantity demanded remains unchanged—that is, the demand would be perfectly inelastic. It is even possible that in response to a decrease in price, less is actually consumed rather than more. This possibility, which means that a commodity might have an upward-sloping demand curve, has been discussed at length in demand theory. A good with such a demand curve is called a **Giffen good,** after the Victorian economist who is thought to have observed such a case. The conditions that would bring this situation about are not often found in the real world, but we can deepen our understanding of the economic theory of demand by seeing what they are.

Income and Substitution Effects

A fall in the price of a commodity can lead a household to increase purchases of it for two different reasons. First, because its relative price has fallen, people will tend to substitute the commodity for other, more expensive goods, even if the household's total purchasing power remains unchanged. This is called the **substitution effect.** Second, a fall in the price of one commodity with all other prices constant has the effect of a rise in income by making it possible for the household to have more of all goods. This is a second incentive to

[4] The remainder of this chapter may be omitted without loss of continuity.

FIGURE 8-9
The Income Effect and the Substitution Effect in Indifference Theory

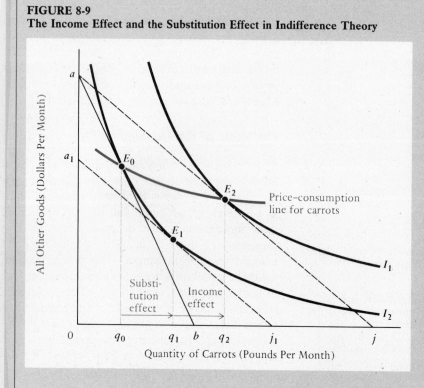

The substitution effect is defined by sliding the budget line around a fixed indifference curve; the income effect is defined by a parallel shift of the budget line. The original budget line is at ab and a fall in the price of carrots takes it to aj. The original equilibrium is at E_0 with q_0 of carrots consumed and the final equilibrium is at E_2 with q_2 of carrots consumed. To remove the income effect, imagine reducing the household's income until it is just able to attain its original indifference curve by shifting the line aj to a parallel line nearer the origin until it just touches the indifference curve that passes through E_0. The intermediate point E_1 divides the quantity change into a substitution effect q_0q_1 and an income effect q_1q_2. It can also be defined by sliding the original budget line ab around the indifference curve until its slope reflects the new relative prices.

increase quantity consumed and is called the **income effect** of a price change.

We illustrate these two effects graphically in Figure 8-9, which is similar to Figure 8-8 but examined under a magnifying glass. Points E_0 and E_2 are on the price-consumption line for carrots. The increase in quantity of carrots demanded is the result of both a substitution and an income effect. Figure 8-9 separates the two effects. We can think of this separation as occurring in the following way. The substitution effect is defined by sliding the budget line around a fixed indifference curve until it is tangent at the slope that represents the lower price. This leads to a move from point E_0 to an imaginary equilibrium point such as E_1. The income effect is then defined by a parallel shift of the budget line that is required to move from E_1 to the actual new equilibrium point, E_2. The move from

E_1 to E_2 is as if the household's income is increased with no change in price from an initial position of E_1.

In Figure 8-9 income and substitution effects are in the same direction, both tending to increase quantity demanded when price falls. Is this necessarily the case? The answer is no. While it follows from the convex shape of indifference curves that the substitution effect is always in the same direction, income effects can be in either direction. The direction depends on the distinction we drew earlier between normal and inferior goods.

The Slope of the Demand Curve for a Normal Good

For a normal good, an increase in real income due to a decrease in the price of the commodity

FIGURE 8-10
Income and Substitution Effects for Inferior Goods

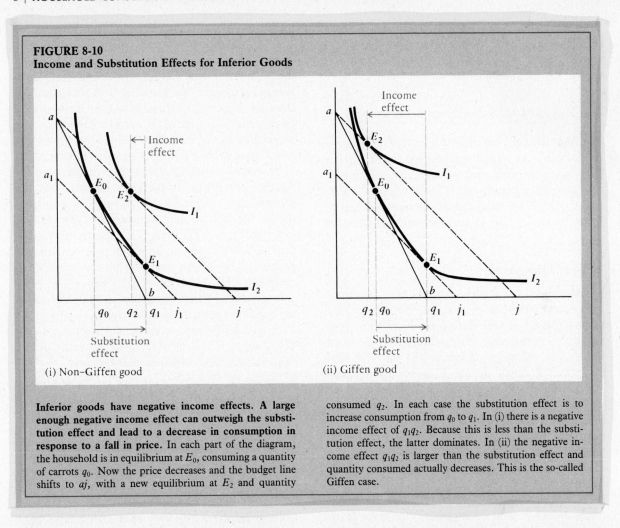

(i) Non–Giffen good

(ii) Giffen good

Inferior goods have negative income effects. A large enough negative income effect can outweigh the substitution effect and lead to a decrease in consumption in response to a fall in price. In each part of the diagram, the household is in equilibrium at E_0, consuming a quantity of carrots q_0. Now the price decreases and the budget line shifts to aj, with a new equilibrium at E_2 and quantity consumed q_2. In each case the substitution effect is to increase consumption from q_0 to q_1. In (i) there is a negative income effect of q_1q_2. Because this is less than the substitution effect, the latter dominates. In (ii) the negative income effect q_1q_2 is larger than the substitution effect and quantity consumed actually decreases. This is the so-called Giffen case.

leads to its increased consumption, reinforcing the substitution effect. Because quantity demanded increases, the demand curve slopes downward.

The Slope of the Demand Curve for an Inferior Good

Figure 8-10 shows indifference curves for an inferior good. The income effect is negative in each part of the diagram. This follows from the nature of an inferior good: as income rises, less of the good is consumed. In each case the substitution effect serves to increase the quantity demanded as price decreases and is offset to some degree by the negative income effect. The final result depends upon the relative strengths of the two effects. In 8-10(i) the negative income effect only partially offsets the substitution effect and thus quantity demanded increases as a result of the price decrease, though not as much as for a normal good. This is the typical pattern for inferior goods, and it too leads to downward-sloping demand curves, often relatively inelastic ones.

In 8-10(ii) the negative income effect actually outweighs the substitution effect and thus leads to an upward-sloping demand curve. This is the Giffen case. For this to happen the good must be inferior. But that is not enough; the change in price must have a negative income effect *strong enough* to offset the substitution effect. A combination of circumstances that makes this possible is not often expected, and therefore an upward-sloping market demand curve is at most an infrequent exception to the rule that demand curves slope downward.

The Shape of Market Demand Curves

The **law of demand** asserts that the price of a product and the quantity demanded in the market vary inversely with each other. Criticisms of the law have taken various forms, focusing on the Giffen good and on the good whose demand is perfectly inelastic. Let us consider each of these in turn.

The Giffen Good

Great interest was attached to Giffen's apparent refutation of the law of demand. He is supposed to have observed that during the nineteenth century a rise in the price of imported wheat led to an increase in the price of bread, but that the consumption of bread by the British working class increased.

While there is some doubt that what Giffen asserted really occurred, it is certainly possible. Suppose that bread is the diet staple of a great many people and that its price rises sharply. This may be expected to compel larger expenditures on bread, further impoverishing many households to the point where they are forced to substitute bread (even though it is more expensive) for more luxurious forms of nourishment. While possible, the fact is that such cases are all but unknown in the real world.

Perfectly Inelastic Demand Curves

Even if demand curves do not slope *upward to the right* as the previous cases have suggested, the substantial insight provided by the law of demand would be diminished if there were many important commodities for which changes in price had virtually no effect on quantity demanded.

It is surprising how often the assumption of a vertical demand curve is implicit. A common response of urban bus or subway systems to financial difficulties is to propose a percentage fare increase equal to the percentage their deficit is of their revenues. Even professors are not immune: At a meeting of the American Association of University Professors, a motion was introduced "to raise annual dues by 20 percent, in order to raise revenues by 20 percent"—in spite of the empirical evidence that a previous increase in dues had led (as the theory would predict) to a significant drop in membership.

It was once widely argued that the demand for gasoline was virtually perfectly inelastic—on the ground that people who had paid thousands of dollars for cars would never balk at a few pennies extra for gas. The events of recent years have proven how wrong that argument was: Higher gas prices led to smaller cars, to more car pools, to more economical driving speeds, and to less pleasure driving. Falling gas prices in the early 1980s have led to a reversal of these trends.

As we have seen, a mass of accumulated evidence suggests that most demand curves do in fact slope downward to an appreciable degree.

For practical purposes, the hypothesis of the downward-sloping demand curve can be regarded as conforming with the evidence.

SUMMARY

1. Indifference curves and indifference theory provide an alternative way of studying household consumption behavior. The basic constructs of indifference curve analysis are the budget line and the indifference map.

2. The budget line shows all combinations of commodities that are available to the household given its money income and the prices of the goods it purchases.

3. Variations in the household's money income shift the budget line parallel to itself. Changes in relative prices change the slope of the budget line.

4. While the budget line describes what the household *can* purchase, indifference curves describe the household's tastes and, therefore, refer

to what it would *like* to do. A single indifference curve joins combinations of commodities that give the household equal satisfaction and among which it is therefore indifferent. An indifference map is a set of indifference curves.

5. The basic hypothesis about tastes is that of a diminishing marginal rate of substitution. This hypothesis states that the less of one good and the more of another the household has, the less willing it will be to give up some of the first good to get a further unit of the second. Graphically, this means indifference curves are downward-sloping and convex to the origin.

6. The household achieves an equilibrium that maximizes its satisfactions given its budget line at the point at which an indifference curve is tangent to its budget line.

7. The income-consumption line shows how quantity consumed changes as income changes with relative prices constant.

8. The price-consumption line shows how quantity consumed changes as relative prices change. When prices change, the household will consume relatively more of the commodity whose relative price falls and relatively less of the commodity whose relative price rises. The price-consumption line between one commodity and all other commodities contains the same information as an ordinary demand curve. Transferring the price-quantity pairs to a diagram whose axes represent price and quantity leads to a conventional demand curve.

9. The effect of a change in price of one commodity, all other prices and money income constant, changes not only relative prices but also real incomes. A price decrease can affect consumption both through the substitution effect and the income effect.

10. Demand curves for normal goods slope downward because both income and substitution effects work in the same direction, a decrease in price leading to increased consumption.

11. For an inferior good, a decrease in price leads to more consumption via the substitution effect and

less consumption via the income effect. In the extreme case of a Giffen good, the negative income effect actually more than offsets the substitution effect, and the consumption of the commodity could decrease as a result of a price decrease. This is a theoretical possibility without much empirical revelance.

12. The so-called law of demand leads to the prediction that the market demand curve for a commodity will slope downward and to the right except in very special circumstances. A great deal of empirical evidence supports the law of demand.

TOPICS FOR REVIEW

The budget line
Real income and money income
Indifference curves and indifference maps
The marginal rate of substitution
The tangency of the budget line and an indifference curve
The price-consumption and income-consumption lines
Income effect and substitution effect
Inferior goods and Giffen goods
The law of demand

DISCUSSION QUESTIONS

1. Is a household relatively better off if its money income is decreased by 10 percent or if the prices of all the goods it buys are increased by 10 percent? Does it matter in answering this question whether the household spends all its income?

2. Some people do not care about the difference between two similar products. To see what effect this would have on their behavior, draw a typical indifference curve of a man who values white and whole wheat bread identically. Show his consumption equilibrium position when the price of white bread is held constant at $1.00 a loaf while that of whole wheat changes from $.80 to $1.00 to $1.20. How does this behavior differ from that of a household that likes both kinds of bread but has a diminishing marginal rate of substitution between white and whole wheat bread?

3. Between 1978 and 1983 the after-tax money incomes of Canadian households rose by 78.8 percent while the CPI rose by 58.6 percent. What happened to real incomes?

4. When no-frills houses came on the market, they were regarded as a response to high prices. But they have captured
more of the market than expected. Some builders estimate
they may ultimately constitute 80 percent of all houses sold.
Suggest alternative explanations of this unexpected success.
A leading builder says, "It's just like people driving smaller
cars and drinking beer instead of Scotch." Is it also like
students wearing running shoes instead of sneakers, or today's parents having fewer children than their parents did?
Which of these things represent changes in taste, and which
represent responses to changes in prices or incomes? If you
don't know, what economic data would be useful in answering the question?

5. A reliable newspaper reports that synthetic motor oil is
gaining in sales despite its high price relative to natural oil.
What can account for a synthetic oil's selling at $4.95 a
liter when the best conventional oils were readily available
at about $1.50?

6. Answer question 5 on page 123 (in Chapter 7), using indifference curve analysis.

9 THE ROLE OF THE FIRM

Ask almost anyone you know to name 10 North American business firms. The odds are overwhelming that the lists will include some of these firms: General Motors Corporation, U.S. Steel, General Electric, Bell Canada, Dow Chemical, the T. D. Bank, Dome Petroleum, DuPont, Canadian Pacific, Canadaire, Air Canada, London Life, the CBC, and CBS. Drive around Gananoque, Ontario, and note at random 10 firms that come into view. They will probably include Dominion super-

market, Harding's Drugstore, a PetroCan service station, Donevan's Hardware, the Modern Cafe, and the Bank of Montreal. Drive through Manitoba or Saskatchewan and look around you: Every farm is a business firm as well as a home.

Firms develop and survive because they are efficient institutions for organizing resources to produce goods and services and for organizing their sale and distribution. While General Motors, Haabs, and the Manitoba farm are all *firms*, what do they have in common? It is not hard to count ways in which they are different. But insight can also be gained in treating them all under a single heading. This is what economic theory does. Economists usually assume that the firm's behavior can be understood in terms of a common motivation. Whether the firm is Ma and Pa's Bar and Grill or the Ford Motor Company and whether a particular decision is made by the board of directors, the third vice-president in charge of advertising, or the owner-manager is regarded as irrelevant to predicting what decisions are made.

Before studying how the firm is treated in economic theory, we shall examine more closely the firm in North America today, to see from what we are abstracting. Criticisms that the theory neglects differences among firms will be considered in Chapter 16.

THE ORGANIZATION OF PRODUCTION

Proprietorships, Partnerships, and Corporations

There are three major forms of business organization: the single proprietorship, the partnership, and the corporation. In the **single proprietorship,** a single owner makes all decisions and is personally responsible for everything done by the business. In the **partnership,** there are two or more joint owners. Either may make binding decisions, and each partner is personally responsible for everything done by the business. In the **corporation,** the firm legally is an entity on its own. The owners (the stockholders) are not each personally responsible for everything that is done by the business. Owners elect a board of directors who hire managers to run the firm under the board's supervision.

In most sectors of the Canadian economy the corporation is the dominant form of organization. In 1982, 71 percent of the establishments in the manufacturing industries were those of incorporated companies. Moreover, the average size of cor-

porate establishments was much larger; their share of employees was 92 percent and their share of the value of shipments was 95 percent. Only in agriculture and in services (e.g., medicine, law, barbering, accounting) is the corporation relatively unimportant, and even here its share of the business is steadily rising.

The Proprietorship and the Partnership: Advantages and Disadvantages

The major advantage of the single proprietorship is that the owner can readily maintain full control over the firm. The owner is the boss. The disadvantages are, first, that the size of the firm is limited by the capital the owner can personally raise and, second, that the owner is personally responsible in law for all debts of the firm.

The ordinary (or general) partnership overcomes to some extent the first disadvantage of the proprietorship but not the second. Ten partners may be able to finance a much bigger enterprise than could one owner, but they are still subject to unlimited liability. Each partner is fully liable for all the debts of the firm.

Obviously, people with substantial personal assets will be unwilling to enter a partnership unless they have complete trust in the other partners and a full knowledge of all the obligations of the firm. As a direct consequence of unlimited liability, it is difficult to raise money through a partnership from persons who wish to invest but not be active in the business. Investors may be willing to put up $1,000 but unwilling to jeopardize their entire fortune; if, however, a person joins a partnership in order to do the former, he or she may also do the latter.

The **limited partnership** avoids some of these difficulties. General partners continue to have unlimited liability, but there will also be limited partners. The limited partner's liability is restricted to the amount he or she has invested in the firm. Such partners do not participate in the management of the firm or engage in agreements on behalf of the partnership. In effect, the limited partnership permits some division of the functions of decision making, provision of capital, and risk taking.

In most respects, this division of responsibility

is more effectively achieved through the corporation. But there are certain professions in which general partnership is traditional. These include law, medicine, and (until recently) brokerage. Partnerships survive in these fields partly because each depends heavily on a relationship of trust with its clients, and the partners' unlimited liability for one another's actions is thought to enhance public confidence in the firm.

The Corporation: Advantages and Disadvantages

The corporation is regarded in law as an entity separate from the individuals who own it. It can enter into contracts, it can sue and be sued, it can own property, it can contract debts, and it can generally incur obligations that are the legal obligations of the corporation *but not of its owners*. The right of the corporation to be sued may not seem to be an advantage but it is, because it makes it possible for others to enter into enforceable contracts with the corporation.

Although some corporations are very small or are owned by just a few stockholders who also manage the business, the most important type of corporation is one that sells shares to the general public. The company raises the funds it needs for the business by the sale of stock, and the shareholders become the company's owners. They are entitled to share in corporate profits. When paid out, profits are called **dividends. Undistributed profits** also belong to the owners, but they are usually reinvested in the firm's operations. If the corporation is liquidated, shareholders split up any assets that remain after all debts are paid.

Diffuse ownership of corporate shares implies that the owners cannot all be managers. Stockholders, who are entitled to one vote for each share they own, elect a board of directors. The board defines general policy and hires senior managers who are supposed to translate this general policy into detailed decisions.

Should the company go bankrupt, the personal liability of any one shareholder is limited to whatever money that shareholder has actually invested in the firm. This is called **limited liability.**

From a shareholder's viewpoint, the most important aspect of the corporation is limited liability.

The corporation's advantage is that it can raise capital from a large number of individuals, each of whom shares in the firm's profits but has no liability for corporate action beyond risking the amount invested. Thus, investors know their exact maximum risk and may simply collect dividends without needing to know anything about policy or operation of the firm they own collectively. Because shares are easily transferred from one person to another, a corporation has a continuity of life unaffected by frequent changes in owners.

From the individual owner's point of view, there are disadvantages in investing in a corporation. First, the owner may have little to say about the management of the firm. For example, if those who hold a majority of the shares decide that the corporation should not pay dividends, an individual investor cannot compel the payment of "his" or "her" share of the earnings. Second, the income of the corporation is taxed twice. The corporation is today taxed on its income at a rate of nearly 50 percent before dividends are paid. Dividends are paid out of the after-tax income. Then individual stockholders are also taxed on any dividends paid to them. This "double taxation" of corporate income is viewed by some as unfair and discriminatory; others see it as the price to be paid for the advantage of incorporation. Judging from the continuing importance of the corporation in Canada, despite a corporate tax rate that has long been around 50 percent, the price has not been prohibitive.

The Rise of the Modern Corporation

The corporate form of organization is employed today wherever large enterprises are found. The principal reason is that it has decisive advantages over any other form in raising the vast sums of capital required for major enterprises. Historically, the limited liability company developed whenever large accumulations of capital in a single firm were required. The corporate form has spread even to the service industries and agriculture, as firms in these industries grew in size.

The direct predecessor of the modern corporation was the English chartered company of the sixteenth century. The Muscovy Company, granted a charter in 1555, the East India Company, first chartered in 1600, and the Hudson's Bay Company, chartered in 1609 and still going strong in Canada 375 years later, are famous early examples of joint-stock ventures with limited liability. Their special needs for many investors to finance a ship that would not return with its cargo for years—if it returned at all—made this *exceptional* form of organization seem desirable.

In the next three centuries, the trading company's needs (e.g., large capital requirements and the need to diversify risk) were seen to exist in other fields, and charters were granted in the fields of insurance, banking, and turnpikes and canals. The Industrial Revolution, which made the large firm efficient, extended the needs for large amounts of capital committed over long periods of time to many more fields. During the nineteenth century, the demand for a general rather than a special privilege of incorporation became strong. General laws permitting incorporation with limited liability, *as a matter of right rather than special grant of privilege,* became common in England and North America during the late nineteenth century.

Today incorporation is relatively routine, although it is subject to a variety of provincial laws. Moderate fees are charged for the privilege of incorporation, and a company can choose to incorporate either federally or under the regulations of one of the provinces.

Government and Production

In most Western countries, including Canada, it is necessary to add two other ways of organizing production—public corporations and the provision of goods and services by various levels of government without *direct* charge to the consumer.

Crown corporations are owned by the government but are operated by a more or less independent, government-appointed board. The Canada Post Office, Petrocan, Quebec Hydro, and B.C. Hydro are all important crown corporations, and

there are many more. In 1979 there were 344 federal and 197 provincial crown corporations operating in Canada. Crown corporations are organized and function in a manner similar to private corporations, with one major difference. In the face of operating losses, they can draw on the government for support via subsidies, operating grants, and loan guarantees.

Government provision of goods and services is also an increasingly important form of production. Important examples found in all countries include agencies providing defense, public transportation, and education services. In many other countries health services are also provided free, or at a subsidized rate, through the government sector.

The Financing of Firms

The money a firm raises for carrying on its business is sometimes called its **money capital** as distinct from its **real capital**, the physical assets that constitute plant, equipment, and inventories. Money capital may be broken down into **equity capital**, provided by the owners, and **debt**, which consists of the funds borrowed from persons who are not owners of the firm.

The use of the term "capital" to refer to both an amount of money and a quantity of goods can be confusing, but it is usually clear from the context which is being referred to. The two uses are not independent, for much of the money capital raised by a firm will be used to purchase the capital goods the firm requires for production.

There are two basic methods by which a firm raises capital: equity financing and debt financing.

Equity Financing

The owners of the firm are its **stockholders**—those who have put up money to purchase shares in the firm. They make their money available to the firm and risk losing it in return for a share of any profits the firm makes.

Stockholders usually carry voting rights and have only a residual claim on profits. After all other claims have been met, the remaining profits, if any, belong to the stockholders. There is no legal limit to the profits that may be earned by the company and therefore no limit to potential dividends that may be paid out to common stockholders. Firms are not obliged by law to pay out any fixed portion of profits as dividends, and in fact practices among corporations vary enormously. Firms sometimes pay out a large fraction and hold back only enough to meet contingencies; at other times they pay small or no dividends in order to reinvest retained funds in the enterprise.

As this suggests, there are two ways for the firm to raise equity. One is to issue and sell new shares. Another is to reinvest, or plow back, some or all of its own profits, thus increasing the stake existing shareholders have in the firm.

Reinvestment has become an extremely important source of funds in modern times: In Canada, over $14 billion per year is obtained for investment in this fashion. The shareholder who does not wish his or her profits to be reinvested can do very little about it except to sell the stock and invest in a company with a policy of paying out a larger fraction of its dividends.

Debt Financing

Firms can also raise money by issuing debt, either by selling bonds or by borrowing from banks and other financial institutions. Debtholders are creditors, not owners, of the firm. They have loaned money to the firm in return for a promise to pay a stated sum of money each year by way of interest on the loan and, of course, a promise to repay the loan at a stated time in the future (say 10, 20, or 30 years hence). This promise to pay is a legal obligation on the firm's part whether or not profits have been made. If these payments cannot be met, the debtholders can force the firm into bankruptcy. Should this happen, the debtholders have a prior claim on the firm's assets. Only when the debtholders and all other creditors have been repaid in full can the stockholders attempt to recover anything for themselves.

Much of the firm's short-term and some of its long-term monetary needs are met through bank loans. This is true of giant corporations as well as of small businesses. Banks, however, limit the amounts they are willing to lend companies, typically to specified fractions of the companies' total financial needs.

Many small businesses that are not well established cannot sell stocks to the public, nor can they raise all the funds they require from banks. Several government agencies, such as the Federal Business Development Bank, have been established to help such firms get access to funds at "reasonable" rates.

A major disadvantage to the corporation of raising capital through issuing debt is that interest payments must be met whether or not there are profits. Many a firm that would have survived a temporary crisis had all its capital been equity financed has been forced into bankruptcy because it could not meet its contractual obligations to pay interest to its debtholders.

The Firm in Economic Theory

IBM and Alice's Restaurant certainly make decisions in different ways. Indeed, within a single large corporation decisions are made by different groups of people. For example, someone at IBM decided to introduce a small computer in 1981. Someone else decided to call it the IBM personal computer and market it for home use. Someone else decided how and where to produce it. Someone else decided its price. Someone else decided how best to promote its sales. The common aspect of these decisions is that all were in pursuit of the same goal—the manufacture and sale of successful computers and related products to earn profits for IBM.

Economic theory assumes that the same principles underlie each decision made within a firm and that the decision is uninfluenced by who makes it. The assumption that all firms are the same is further discussed in Box 9-1.

Motivation: Profit Maximization

It is assumed that the firm makes decisions in such a way that its profits will be as large as possible. In other words, the firm is assumed to *max-*

BOX 9-1 DIFFERENT KINDS OF FIRMS

In economic theory the firm is defined as the unit that makes decisions with respect to the production and sale of commodities. This single definition covers a variety of business organizations from the single proprietorship to the corporation, and a variety of business sizes from the inventor operating in his garage and financed by whatever he can extract from a reluctant bank manager to vast undertakings with tens of thousands of shareholders and creditors. We know that in large firms, decisions are actually made by many different individuals. We can nonetheless regard the firm as a single consistent decision-making unit because of the assumption that all decisions are made to achieve the common goal of maximizing the firm's profits.

Whether a decision is made by a small independent proprietor, a plant manager, or a board of directors, that person or group is the firm for the purpose of that decision. This is a truly heroic assumption; it amounts to saying that for purposes of predicting those aspects of their behavior that interest us, we can treat a farm, a corner grocery, a department store, a small law

partnership, General Motors, and a giant multinational corporation, all under the umbrella of a single theory of the behavior of the firm. If this turns out to be even partially correct, it will prove enormously valuable in revealing some unity of behavior where to the casual observer there is only bewildering diversity.

You should not be surprised, therefore, if at first encounter the theory appears rather abstract and out of touch with reality. To generalize over such a wide variety of behavior, the theory must ignore many features with which we are most familiar and which distinguish the farmer from the grocer and each of them from the Exxon Corporation. Any theory that generalizes over a wide variety of apparently diverse behavior necessarily has this characteristic because it ignores those factors that are most obvious to us and that create in our minds the appearance of diversity. If it were not possible to do this, it would be necessary to have dozens of different theories, one for each type of firm. The task of learning economics would then be much more complex than it now is!

imize its profits. The concept of profits requires careful definition, which will be given later in this chapter. For now we may treat profits in the everyday sense of the difference between the value of the firm's sales and the costs to the firm of producing what is sold.

The assumption of profit maximization provides a principle by which a firm's decisions can be predicted.

Economists predict the firm's behavior by studying the effect that making each possible choice would have on profits. They then predict that from these alternatives the firm will select the one that produces the largest profits.

At this point you may well ask if it is sensible to build a theory on such a simple assumption

about the motives of business people. Of course some business people are inspired by motives other than an overwhelming desire to make money. Cases in which they use their positions to seek political influence or pursue charitable objectives are not difficult to document.

This theory does not say, however, that profit is the *only* factor that influences business people. It says only that profits are so important that a theory which assumes profit maximization to be the sole motive will produce predictions that are substantially correct.[1]

---

[1] A major exception to this is crown corporations, which typically are not profit-maximizing organizations. Other theories, usually relating to political and bureaucratic behavior, have evolved to explain the behavior of crown corporations.

Why is this assumption made? First, it is necessary to make *some* assumption about what motivates decision makers if the theory is to predict how they will act. Second, a great many of the predictions of theories based on this assumption have been confirmed by observation. Third, no alternative assumption has yet been shown to yield more accurate predictions. However, the assumption has been criticized, and alternatives have been suggested (see Chapter 16).

Inputs and Factors of Production

Firms make profits by producing and selling commodities. Production is roughly like a sausage machine. Certain elements, such as raw materials and the services of capital and labor, are fed in at one end, and a product emerges at the other. The materials and factor services used in the production process are called **inputs,** and the products that emerge are called **outputs.**

Literally hundreds of inputs enter into the output of a specific good. Among the inputs entering into automobile production are, to name only a few, sheet steel, rubber, spark plugs, electricity, machinists, cost accountants, fork-lift operators, managers, and painters. These inputs can be grouped into four broad classes: (1) those that are inputs to the automobile manufacturer but outputs to some other manufacturer, such as spark plugs, electricity, and sheet steel; (2) those that are provided directly by nature, such as land; (3) those that are provided directly by households, such as labor; and (4) those that are provided by the machines used for manufacturing automobiles.

The first class of inputs is made up of goods produced by other firms. These products appear as inputs only because the stages of production are divided among different firms so that, at any one stage, a firm is using goods produced by other firms as inputs. If these products are traced back to their sources, all production can be accounted for by the services of only three kinds of inputs, which are called *factors of production.* All the gifts of nature, such as land and raw materials, the economist calls **land.** All physical and mental efforts provided by people are called **labor** services. All machines and other production equipment are called **capital,** and defined as man-made aids to further production.

Extensive use of capital—the services of machines and other capital goods—is one distinguishing feature of modern as opposed to primitive production. Instead of making consumer goods directly with only the aid of simple natural tools, productive effort goes into the manufacture of tools, machines, and other goods that are desired not in themselves but as aids to making further goods. The use of capital goods renders the production processes *roundabout.*

Economic Efficiency

In general, there is more than one way to produce a given product. It is possible to produce agricultural commodities by farming a small quantity of land, combining a great deal of labor and capital with each acre of land, as is done in Belgium. It is also possible to produce the same commodities by farming a great deal of land, using only a small amount of labor and capital per acre of land, as is done in Australia. Indeed, if this were not the case there would be no need for firms to face the decision of how to produce.

Faced with alternative production processes, how does the firm decide which is best? One meaning of *best* is the process that uses the fewest inputs for producing a given output—that is, the one that is technically most efficient. Another meaning for best is the process that *costs* the least for producing a given output, the one that is economically most efficient. **Technological efficiency** measures use of inputs in physical terms; **economic efficiency** measures use in terms of costs.[2] An example distinguishing the concepts is shown in Box 9-2.

The economically most efficient method is the one that costs the least. Economic efficiency depends on factor prices *and* on technological efficiency.

_____

[2] Efficiency plays an important role in economic discussions. We shall discuss it at greater length in Chapter 12.

BOX 9–2 TECHNOLOGICAL VERSUS ECONOMIC EFFICIENCY: AN EXAMPLE

Suppose, given the state of technology, there are only four known ways to produce 100 widgets per month:

	Quantity of inputs received	
	Capital	Labor
Method A	6	200
Method B	10	250
Method C	10	150
Method D	40	50

Method B is technologically inefficient because it uses more of both inputs than does method A. Among the other three methods, method A uses the least capital, but it is the most labor-using.* Method D conserves labor but uses much more capital. Method C is intermediate between them. (If you consider method D technologically most efficient because it uses only 90 units of all resources, think again.)

---

* There is yet a third concept of efficiency, "engineering efficiency," in which least use of a particular factor is involved. When engineers speak of the efficiency of an engine, they may mean how much of the fuel it turns into power.

Methods A, C, and D are all technologically efficient because no one of them uses more of both resources than either of the others.

Which one is the least costly—that is, is economically efficient? We cannot tell without knowing the costs of capital and of labor. Economic efficiency depends on factor prices. Consider the three cases shown in the table below. As we move from case I to II to III, a unit of labor becomes increasingly expensive *relative to* a unit of capital.

Method A is economically efficient when labor is cheap relative to capital. Method C becomes efficient when labor gets somewhat more expensive relative to capital. Finally, when labor gets very expensive relative to capital, method D, which uses least labor per unit of capital, becomes economically efficient.

To test your understanding, answer these questions:

1. Can a technologically *inefficient* method ever be economically efficient?
2. Is there a set of factor prices for which *both* method C and method D will be economically efficient?

	Factor prices per unit		Total cost of factors		
	Capital	Labor	Method A	Method C	Method D
Case I	$50	$3	$ 900	$950	$2,150
Case II	20	5	1,120	950	1,050
Case III	15	5	1,090	900	850

COST AND PROFIT TO THE FIRM

The Meaning and Measurement of Cost

Economic efficiency is defined in terms of cost. But what is cost? **Cost,** to the producing firm, is the *value* of inputs used in producing its output.

Notice the use of the word *value* in the definition. A given output produced by a given technique, say 6,000 cars produced each week by the Ford Motor Company with its present production methods, will have a given set of inputs associated with it—so many working hours of various types of laborers, supervisors, managers, and technicians, so many tons of steel, glass, and aluminum, so much electric light and other services, and so many hours of the time of various machines. The cost of each must be calculated in money terms. The sum of these separate costs is then the total cost to the Ford Motor Company of producing 6,000 cars per week.

Assigning Costs

An economist may be interested in a firm's behavior for several reasons: (1) to *describe* actual behavior of a firm, (2) to *predict* how the firm's behavior will respond to specified changes in the conditions it faces, (3) to *help* the firm make the best decisions it can in achieving its goals, and (4) to *evaluate* how well firms use scarce resources.

The same measure of cost need not be correct for all these purposes. For example, if the firm is misinformed about the value of some resource, it will behave according to that misinformation. In describing or predicting the firm's behavior, economists should use the information the firm actually uses, even if the economist knows it is incorrect. But in helping the firm to achieve its goals, economists should substitute the correct information.

Economists use a well-established definition of costs in solving problems of the kind cited in items 3 and 4 of the above list. If business people use the same definition and have the same information, the economist's definition will be appropriate for problems of types 1 and 2 as well. This will be assumed for the moment.

Opportunity Cost

Although the details of economic costing vary, they are governed by a common principle that is sometimes called *user cost* but is more commonly called *opportunity cost*.

The cost of using something in a particular venture is the benefit foregone (or opportunity lost) by not using it in its best alternative use.

An old Chinese merchants' proverb says: "Where there is no gain, the loss is obvious." The sense of this proverb is that the merchant who shows no gain has wasted time—time that could

have been used in some other venture. The merchant has neglected the opportunity cost of his time. Box 9-3 considers opportunity cost more generally.

The Measurement of Opportunity Cost by the Firm

To measure opportunity cost, the firm must assign to each factor of production that it has used a monetary value equal to what it has sacrificed to use the factor. Applying this principle to specific cases, however, reveals some tough problems.

Purchased and Hired Factors

Assigning costs is a straightforward process when inputs purchased in one period are used up in the same period and where the price the firm pays is determined by forces outside the firm. Many raw material and intermediate-product purchases fall into this category. If the firm pays $110 per ton for coal delivered to its factory, it has sacrificed its claims to whatever else $110 can buy, and thus the purchase price is a reasonable measure of the opportunity cost to it of using one ton of coal.

For hired factors of production, where the rental price is the full price, the situation is identical. Borrowed money is paid for by **interest**. An **interest rate** is the percentage charged for the use of funds, so that the interest payment, equal to the interest rate times the amount borrowed, is the money price paid to use the funds for one year. Interest payments measure the opportunity cost of borrowed funds. Most labor services are hired and the cost includes the wages paid. It also includes the employer's contribution to pension funds, to unemployment and disability insurance, and to other fringe benefits.

Imputed Costs

Cost must also be assessed for factors of production that the firm uses but neither purchases nor hires for current use. Since no payment is made to anyone outside the firm, these costs are not so

BOX 9–3 OPPORTUNITY COST MORE GENERALLY

Opportunity cost plays a vital role in economic analysis, but it is also a fundamental principle that applies to a wide range of situations. It is one of the great insights of economics. Consider some examples:

■ George Bernard Shaw, on reaching his 90th birthday, was asked how he liked being 90. He is reputed to have said, "It's fine, when you consider the alternative."

■ Llewelyn Formed likes to hear both Peter Truman and Knowlton Nash. If he finally settles on Truman, what is the opportunity cost of this decision?

■ Link Heartthrob, a 31-year-old bachelor, is thinking about marrying at last. But, although he thinks Miss Piggy is a lovely girl, he figures that if he marries her, he will give up the chance of wedded bliss with another girl he may meet next year. So he decides to wait a while. What other information do you need to determine the opportunity cost of the decision?

■ Serge Ginn, M.D., complains that now that he is earning large fees he can no longer afford to take the time for a vacation trip to Europe. In what way does it make sense to say that the opportunity cost of his vacation depends upon his fees?

■ Retired American General William Russ, who is married to a very wealthy woman, has decided to contribute $5,000 to a political candidate he likes very much. His lawyer points out to him that since he is in the 50 percent tax bracket, and since political contributions are not deductible from his income, the real cost of his contribution is the same as giving an extra $10,000 to his favorite charity, the Gen. Russ Foundation. Is the opportunity cost of the political contribution $5,000 or $10,000?

obvious. They are called **imputed costs.** If the most profitable lines of production are to be discovered, the opportunity cost of these factors should be reckoned at values that reflect what the firm might earn from the factors if it shifted them to their next best use. The following examples all involve imputed costs.

Using the firm's own money. Consider a firm that uses $100,000 of its own money that it could instead have loaned out at 10 percent per year.

Thus, $10,000 (at least) should be deducted from the firm's revenue as the cost of funds used in production. If, to continue the example, the firm makes only $6,000 over all other costs, then one should say not that the firm made a profit of $6,000 by producing but that it lost $4,000. For if it had closed down completely and merely loaned out its money to someone else, it could have earned $10,000.

Costs of durable assets. The costs of using assets owned by the firm, such as buildings, equipment, and machinery, consist of the cost of the money tied up in them and a charge, called **depreciation,** for the loss in value of the asset because of its use in production. Depreciation includes both the loss in value due to physical wear and tear and that due to obsolescence. The economic cost of owning an asset for a year is the loss in value of the asset during the year.

Accountants use several conventional methods of depreciation based on the price originally paid for the asset. One of the most common is *straight-line depreciation,* in which the same amount of historical cost is deducted in every year of useful life of the asset. While historical costs are often useful approximations, they may in some cases differ seriously from the depreciation required by the opportunity cost principle. Consider two examples of the possible error involved.

Assets that may be resold. A woman buys a $600 set of downhill skis that she intends to use for six years. She may think that, using straight-line depreciation, this will cost her $100 per year. But if after one year the value of her skis on the used market is $400, it has cost her $200 to use the skis during the first year. Why should she charge herself $200 depreciation during the first year? After all, *she* does not intend to sell the skis for six years. The answer is that one of the purchaser's alternatives was to buy a one-year-old pair of skis and use them for five years. Indeed, that is the very position she is in after the first year. Whether she likes it or not, she has paid $200 for the use of the skis during the first year of their life. If the market had valued her skis at $550 after one year (instead of $400), the depreciation would have been only $50.

Sunk costs. In the previous example, an active used-asset market was considered. At the other extreme, consider an asset that has no alternative use. This is sometimes described as the case of "sunk" costs. Assume that a firm has a set of machines it purchased some time ago for $100,000. These machines should last 10 years and the firm's accountant calculates the depreciation costs of these machines by the straight-line method at $10,000 per year. Assume also that the machines can be used to make one product and nothing else. Suppose too that they are installed in the firm's plant, they cannot be leased to any other firm, and their scrap value is negligible. In other words, the machines have no value except to this firm in its current operation. Assume that if the machines are used to produce this product, the cost of all other factors utilized will amount to $25,000, while the goods produced can be sold for $29,000.

Now, if the accountant's depreciation "costs" of running the machines are added in, the total cost of operation comes to $35,000; with revenues at $29,000, this makes an annual loss of $6,000 per year. It appears that the goods should not be made!

The fallacy in this argument lies in adding in a charge based on the sunk cost of the machines as one of the costs of current operation. The machines have no alternative uses whatsoever. *Clearly their opportunity cost is zero.* The total costs of producing this line of goods is thus only $25,000 per year (assuming all other costs have been correctly assessed), and the line of production shows an annual profit of $4,000, not a loss of $6,000.

To see why the second calculation leads to the correct decision, notice that if the firm decides this line of production is unprofitable and does not continue it, it will have no money to pay out and no revenue received on this account. If the firm takes the economist's advice and pursues the line of production, it will pay out $25,000 and receive $29,000, thus making it $4,000 per year richer than if it had not done so. Clearly, production is worth undertaking. The amount the firm happened to have paid out for the machines in the past has no bearing whatever on deciding the correct use of the machines once they are installed on the premises.

Because they involve neither current nor future costs, sunk costs should have no influence on deciding what is currently the most profitable thing to do.

This "bygones are bygones" principle extends well beyond economics and is often ignored in poker, in war, and perhaps in love. Because you have invested heavily in a poker hand, a battle, or a courtship does not mean you should stick with it if the prospects of winning become very small. At every moment of decision, you should be concerned with how benefits from this time forward compare with current and future costs.

Risk taking. One difficult problem in imputing costs concerns the evaluation of the service of risk taking. Business enterprise is often a risky affair. The risk is borne by the owners of the firm who, if the enterprise fails, may lose the money they have invested in the firm. The owners will not take these risks unless they receive a remuneration in return. They expect a return that exceeds what they could have obtained by investing their money in a virtually riskless manner, say, by buying a government bond.

Risk taking is a service that must be provided if the firm is to carry on production, and it must be paid for by the firm. If a firm does not yield a return sufficient to compensate for the risks involved, the firm will not be able to persuade people to contribute money to it in return for a part ownership in the firm.

Suppose, in investing $100,000 in a class of risky ventures, a businesswoman expects that most of the ventures will be successful but some will fail. In fact, she expects about $10,000 worth to be a total loss. (She does not know which specific projects will be the losers, of course.) Suppose further that she requires a 20 percent return on her total investment. To earn a $20,000 profit and recover the $10,000 expected loss, she needs to earn a $30,000 profit on the $90,000 of successful investment. This is a rate of return of 33⅓ percent. She charges 20 percent for the use of the capital, plus 13⅓ percent for the risk she takes.

Patents, trademarks, and other special advantages. Suppose a firm owns a valuable patent or a highly desirable location, or produces a popular brand-name product such as Coca-Cola, Chevrolet, or Marlboro. Each of these involves an opportunity cost to the firm in production (even if it was acquired free) because if the firm does not choose to use the special advantage itself, it could sell or lease it to others. Typically, the value of these advantages will differ from their historical cost. Indeed, typically several alternative uses will be open to the owner. The opportunity cost in any one is the value foregone in the *best* alternative use.

Profits: Their Meaning and Significance

Profits, although often defined loosely in everyday usage, may be given a series of more precise definitions. **Economic profits** on goods sold are the difference between revenues received from the sale and the opportunity cost of the resources used to make them. (If costs are greater than revenues, such "negative profits" are called *losses*.)

This definition includes in costs (and thus excludes from profits) the imputed returns to capital and to risk taking. This use of the words "profit" and "loss" gives specialized definitions to words that are in everyday use. They are, therefore, a potential source of confusion to the student who runs into other uses of the same words. Table 9-1 may help clarify the definitions.

Some economists, while following substantially

TABLE 9–1 THE CALCULATION OF ECONOMIC PROFITS: AN EXAMPLE

Gross revenue from sales	$1,000
Less: direct cost of goods sold (materials, labor, electricity, etc.)	650
"Gross profits" (or "contributions to overhead")	350
Less: indirect costs (depreciation, overhead, management salaries, interest on debt, etc.)	140
"Net profits" before income taxes	210
Less: imputed charges for own capital used and for risk taking $\Big\} =$ "normal profits"	100
Economic profits before income taxes	110
Less: income taxes payable	100
Economic profits after income taxes	$ 10

The main difference between "economic profits" and the usual everyday definition of profits is the subtraction of imputed charges for use of capital owned by the firm and for risk taking. Income tax is levied on whatever definition of profits the taxing authorities choose, usually closely related to "net profits."

the same definitions, label as **normal profits** the imputed returns to capital and risk taking just necessary to prevent the owners from withdrawing from the industry. These normal profits are, of course, what has been defined as the opportunity costs of risk taking and capital. Whatever they are called, they are costs that have to be covered if the firm is to stay in operation in the long run.

Other Definitions of Profits

Business firms define profits as the excess of revenues over the costs with which accountants provide them. We explore in the appendix to this chapter some of the differences between accountants' and economists' views of business transactions. Some of these differences affect the meaning of profits. Accountants do not include as costs charges for risk taking and use of owners' own capital, and thus these items are recorded by businesses as part of their profits. When a businessman says he *needs* profits to stay in business, he is making sense within his definition, for his "profits" must be large enough to pay for those factors of production that he uses but that the accounting profession does not include as costs.

The economist would express the same notion by saying that the business needs to cover *all* its costs, including those not employed in accounting conventions. If the firm is covering all its opportunity costs, then it could not do better by using its resources in any other line of activity than the one currently being followed.

A situation in which revenues equal costs (economic profits of zero) is a satisfactory one—because all factors, hidden as well as visible, are being rewarded at least as well as in their *best* alternative uses.

With zero economic profits then, you can do no better, although you might do worse. To reverse the Chinese proverb cited earlier, "Where there is no loss compared to the best alternative use of every factor, the gain is obvious."

The income tax authorities have yet another definition of profits, which is implicit in the thousands of rules as to what may and may not be included as a deduction from revenue in arriving at taxable income. In some cases, the taxing authorities allow more for cost than the accountant recommends; in other cases, they allow less.

Profits and Resource Allocation

When resources are valued by the opportunity cost principle, their costs show how much these resources would earn if used in their best alternative uses. If there is an industry in which all firms' revenues exceed opportunity costs, all the firms in the industry will be earning profits. Thus, the owners of factors of production will want to move resources into this industry because the earnings potentially available to them are greater there than in alternative uses of the resources. If in some other industry firms are incurring losses, some or all of this industry's resources are more highly valued in other uses, and owners of the resources will want to move them to those other uses.

Economic profits and losses play a crucial signaling role in the workings of a free-market system.

Profits in an industry are the signal that resources can profitably be moved into the industry. Losses are the signal that the resources can profitably be moved elsewhere. Only if there are zero economic profits is there no incentive for resources to move into or out of an industry.

SUMMARY

1. The firm is the economic unit that produces and sells commodities. The economist's definition of the firm abstracts from real-life differences in size and form of organization of firms.

2. The single proprietorship, the partnership, and the corporation are the major forms of business organization in Canada today. The corporation is the most common business wherever large-scale production is required. The corporation is recognized as a legal entity; its owners, or shareholders, have a liability that is limited to the amount of money they have actually invested in the organization. Corporate ownership is readily transferred by sale of shares in securities markets.

3. Economic theory assumes that the same principles underlie each decision made within the firm and that the actual decision is uninfluenced by who makes it. The key behavioral assumption is that the firm seeks to maximize its profit.

4. Because a commodity can be produced in more than one way, the firm must decide *how* to produce. Efficiency measures are based on the relative amount of inputs necessary to produce a given output. Technological efficiency evaluates units of input in physical terms. Economic efficiency evaluates them in terms of costs.

5. The opportunity cost of using a resource is the value of that resource in its best alternative use. If the opportunity cost of using a resource in one way is less than or equal to the benefit from a particular use of resource, there is no superior way of using it.

6. Measuring opportunity cost to the firm requires some difficult imputations in cases involving resources not purchased or hired for current use. Among these imputed costs are those for use of owners' money, depreciation, risk taking, and any special advantages that the firm may possess.

7. A firm maximizing profits, defined as the difference between revenue and opportunity cost, is making the best allocation of the resources under its control, according to the firm's evaluation of its alternatives.

8. Profits and losses provide important signals concerning the reallocation of resources. Profits earned in an industry provide a signal that more resources can profitably move into the industry. Losses show that some resources have more profitable uses elsewhere and serve as a signal for them to move out of that industry.

9. The appendix to this chapter introduces balance sheets and profit and loss statements and uses them to discuss some of the differences between the concept of profits used by accountants and that used by economists.

TOPICS FOR REVIEW

The firm in theory and in the economy
The role of profit maximization
Single proprietorship, partnership, and corporation
Advantages of the corporation
Inputs and factors of production
Economic efficiency
Opportunity costs
Economic and other definitions of profits
Profits and resource allocation

DISCUSSION QUESTIONS

1. Can the economic theory of the firm be of any help in analyzing the productive decisions of such nonprofit organizations as governments, churches, and colleges? What, if any, role does the notion of opportunity cost play for them?

2. In *The Engineers and the Price System*, Thorstein Veblen argued that businessmen who made decisions about financing, pricing, and the like were largely superfluous to the operation of a business. In his view, knowledge of the technology would be sufficient to ensure efficient operation of firms. Discuss Veblen's contention.

3. "There is no such thing as a free lunch." Can anything be costless? Gas stations have traditionally provided free services, including windshield cleaning, air pumps for tire inflation, and road maps. Now, many sell road maps and have discontinued free services. Indeed, self-service stations are becoming increasingly popular with motorists who like the lower gas prices of those stations. Under what conditions will profit-maximizing behavior lead to the coexistence of full-service and self-service gas stations? What would determine the proportions in which each occurred?

4. What is the opportunity cost of
   a. A politician's being fined $10,000 and sent to prison for one year
   b. Lending $500 to a friend
   c. Not permitting a $116-million electric power dam to be built because it would destroy the snail darter, a rare 3-inch-long fish found only in that particular river
   d. Towing icebergs to Saudi Arabia to provide drinking water at the cost of $.50 per cubic meter

5. Is straight-line depreciation an appropriate method of assessing the annual cost to the typical Canadian household of using a passenger automobile? Some firms that use trucks allocate the cost on a per-mile basis. Why might this method be more nearly appropriate for trucks than for automobiles owned by households?

6. Having bought a used car from Smiling Sam for $900, you drive it two days and it stops. You now find that it requires an extra $500 before it will run. Assuming that the car is not worth $1,400 fixed, should you make the repairs?

7. "To meet the 1981 standard of 3.4 grams of carbon monoxide per mile driven, General Motors has calculated that it will cost $100 million and prolong 200 lives by one year each, thus costing $500,000 per year of extra life. Human lives are precious, which is why it is so sad to note another use of that money. It has been estimated that the installation of special cardiac-care units in ambulances could prevent premature deaths each year at an average cost of only $200 for each year of extra life."

Assume the facts in this quotation are correct. If the money spent on carbon monoxide control would have been spent on cardiac care units instead, what is the opportunity cost of the carbon monoxide requirement? If the money would not have been so spent but simply reduced automobile companies' costs, what is the opportunity cost? In either case, do the facts tell us whether the regulation of carbon monoxide to the 3.4 gram level is desirable or undesirable?

8. Which concept of profits is implied in the following quotations:
   a. "Profits are necessary if firms are to stay in business."
   b. "Profits are signals for firms to expand production and investment."
   c. "Increased depreciation lowers profits and thus benefits the company's owners."

10 PRODUCTION AND COST IN THE SHORT RUN

Of the four North American automobile manufacturers, General Motors is year-in and year-out more profitable than Ford, and Ford more profitable than Chrysler and American Motors. The prices charged for comparable models are approximately the same, but the profits *per automobile* are very different. A good part of the reason lies in the very different levels of output. General Motors has about a 60 percent share of the four companies' aggregate sales, Ford a 25 percent share, Chrysler a 12 percent share, and American Motors Corporation only about a 3 percent share. American Motors with dollar sales of nearly $3 billion may not sound like a small company, but for the automobile industry it is because the costs of making and selling cars decline sharply with increases in the volume of cars produced.

Thus the smaller companies are at a big disadvantage relative to GM even if they are as imaginative in design, management, and salesmanship.

Over the past 40 years several once-profitable smaller producers, among them Packard, Crosley, Studebaker, and Kaiser-Frazer, were unable to increase their volume and found that costs had become greater than revenues. They left the industry after suffering heavy losses. This experience illustrates one important aspect of the theory of cost of production: Cost of production per unit may be very different for different levels of output.

A different aspect of the theory of costs relates to factor prices. When rising feed prices reached the point at which the cost of feeding chickens as they grow exceeded the price of fully grown chickens, farmers killed off their stocks and chicken production fell drastically. Similarly, during a period when price controls were in effect, meat packers were squeezed between the legal maximum price at which they could sell and the rising cost of the livestock they bought. Some of them suspended production.

In the previous chapter we defined costs of production. In this chapter we see how and why costs vary with the level of production and with changes in factor prices.

CHOICES OPEN TO THE FIRM

Consider a firm producing a single product in a number of different plants. If its rate of sales has fallen off, should production be reduced correspondingly? Or should production be held at the old rate and the unsold amounts stored up against an anticipated future rise in sales? If production is to be reduced, should a single plant be closed or should some plants be put on short time? Such decisions concern how best to use *existing* plant and equipment. They involve time periods too short to build new plants or to install more equipment.

Rather different decisions must be made when managers do long-range planning. Should the firm adopt a highly automated process that will greatly reduce its wage bill, even though it must borrow large sums of money to buy the equipment? Should it continue to build new plants that use the same techniques it is now using? Or should it spend money on research and development (R&D) to try to discover new methods of production? These matters concern what a firm should do when it is changing or replacing its plant and equipment. Such decisions may take a long time to put into effect.

Time Horizons for Decision Making

To reduce to manageable proportions the decisions firms are constantly making, economists organize the decisions into three theoretical groups: (1) How best to employ existing plant and equipment (the *short run*). (2) What new plant and equipment and production processes to select, given the framework of known technical possibilities (the *long run*). (3) What to do about encouraging the invention of new techniques (the *very long run*).

The Short Run

Short-run decisions are those made when the quantity of some inputs cannot be varied. The firm cannot change the quantity of some inputs, called **fixed factors,** that it has on hand, and it is committed to make any money payments that are associated with these fixed factors.[1] Inputs that can be varied in the short run are called **variable factors.** The fixed factor is usually an element of capital (such as plant and equipment), but it could be land, the services of management, or even the supply of skilled labor.

The short run does not correspond to a definite number of months or years. In some industries, it may extend over many years; in others, it may be only a matter of months or weeks. Furthermore, it may last a different period of time when an industry is expanding than when it is contracting.

---

[1] Sometimes it is physically impossible to increase the quantity of a fixed factor in a short time. For instance, there is no way to build a hydroelectric dam or a nuclear power plant in a few months. Other times it might be physically possible, but prohibitively expensive, to increase the quantity. For example, a suit-manufacturing firm could conceivably rent a building, buy and install new sewing machines, and hire a trained labor force in a few days if money were no consideration. Economists regard prohibitive cost along with physical impossibility as a source of fixed factors.

In the electric power industry, for example, it takes three or more years to acquire and install a steam-turbine generator. An unforeseen increase in demand will involve a long period during which the extra demand must be met as best it can with the existing capital equipment. In contrast, a machine shop can acquire new equipment or sell existing equipment in a very few weeks, so the short run is correspondingly short. An increase in demand will have to be met with the existing stock of capital for only a brief time, after which it will be possible to adjust the stock of equipment to the level made desirable by the higher demand.

The Long Run

Long-run decisions are those made when all inputs may be varied but the basic technology of production is unchanged. Again, the long run does not correspond to a specific period of time.

The special importance of the long run in production theory is that it corresponds to the situation facing the firm when it is planning to go into business, to expand the scale of its operations, to branch out into new products or new areas, or to modernize, replace, or reorganize its method of production.

The firm's planning decisions characteristically are made with freedom to choose from a variety of given production processes, each of which uses factor inputs in different proportions.

The Very Long Run

Unlike the short and long run, the **very long run** concerns the opportunities arising from changing technology. Technological changes lead to new and improved products and production techniques. Some of these technological advances arise from within the firm as part of its own research and development efforts. For example, much of the innovation in cameras and films has been due to the efforts of the Kodak and Polaroid companies. Firms in certain other industries may merely adopt technological changes developed elsewhere. For example, the transistor and the electronic chip have revolutionized dozens of industries that had noth-

ing to do with developing them in the first place. The firm must regularly decide how much to spend in its efforts to change its technology either by developing new techniques or adapting techniques developed by others.

Connecting the Runs: The Production Function

The various "runs" are simply different aspects of the same basic problem: getting output from inputs efficiently. They differ in terms of what the firm is able to change.

The relation between inputs into the production process and the quantity of output obtained is called the **production function**. A simplified production function in which there are only two inputs, labor and capital, will be considered here, but the conclusions apply equally when there are many inputs. The variation of output and cost under the assumption that one of the two inputs is fixed is examined in this chapter. (Capital is taken to be the fixed factor and labor the variable one.) The long-run situation in which both inputs can be varied is covered in the next chapter.

SHORT-RUN CHOICES

Total, Average, and Marginal Products

Assume that a firm starts with a fixed amount of capital (say four units) and contemplates applying various amounts of labor to it. Table 10-1 shows three different ways of looking at how output varies with the quantity of the variable factor. As a first step, some terms need to be defined.

1. **Total product** (*TP*) means the total amount produced during a given period of time by all the inputs employed. If the inputs of all but one factor are held constant, total product will change as more or less of the variable factor is used. This variation is shown in columns 1 and 2 of Table 10-1, which gives a total product schedule. Figure 10-1(i) shows such a schedule graphically. (The shape of the curve will be discussed shortly.)

TABLE 10–1 THE VARIATION OF OUTPUT WITH CAPITAL FIXED AND LABOR VARIABLE

(1) Quantity of labor (L)	(2) Total product (TP)	(3) Average product (AP)	(4) Marginal product (MP)
0	0	—	
			15
1	15	15.0	
			19
2	34	17.0	
			14
3	48	16.0	
			12
4	60	15.0	
			2
5	62	12.4	

The relation of output to changes in the quantity of labor can be looked at in three different ways. Capital is assumed to be fixed at four units. As the quantity of labor increases, the rate of output (the total product) increases. Average product increases at first and then declines. The same is true of marginal product.

Marginal product is shown between the lines because it refers to the *change* in output from one level of labor input to another. When graphing the schedule, *MP*s of this kind should be plotted at the midpoint of the interval. Thus, graphically, the marginal product of 12 would be plotted to correspond to quantity of labor of 3.5.

2. **Average product (AP)** is merely the total product per unit of the variable factor, labor. The number of units of labor will be denoted by *L*.

$$AP = TP/L$$

It is shown in column 3 of Table 10-1. Notice that as more of the variable factor is used, average product first rises and then falls. The level of output where average product reaches a maximum (34 units in the example) is called the **point of diminishing average productivity.**

3. **Marginal product (MP)**, sometimes called **incremental product,** is the change in total product resulting from the use of 1 unit more of the variable factor. [12]

$$MP = \Delta TP/\Delta L$$

Computed values of marginal product are shown in column 4 of Table 10-1.[2] The figures in this column are placed between the other lines of the

[2] ΔL is read "a change in the quantity of labor."

table to stress that the concept refers to the *change* in output caused by the *change* in quantity of the variable factor. For example, the increase in labor from 3 to 4 units ($\Delta L = 1$) raises output by 12 from 48 to 60 ($\Delta TP = 12$). Thus the *MP* equals 12, and it is recorded between 3 and 4 units of labor. Note that the *MP* in the example rises and then falls. The level of output at which marginal product reaches a maximum is called the **point of diminishing marginal productivity.**

Figure 10-1(ii) plots average product and marginal product curves. Although three different schedules are shown in Table 10-1 and three different curves are shown in Figure 10-1, they are all aspects of the same single relationship that is described by the production function. As we vary the quantity of labor, with capital fixed, output changes. Sometimes it is interesting to look at the total output, sometimes at the average output, and sometimes at the marginal change.

Finally, bear in mind that the schedules of Table 10-1 and the curves of Figure 10-1 all assume a specified quantity of the fixed factor. If the quantity of capital had been, say, 6 or 10 instead of the 4 units that were assumed, there would be a different set of total product, average product, and marginal product curves. The reason for this is that if any specified amount of labor has more capital to work with, it can produce more output—that is, its total product will be greater.

The Shape of the Marginal and Average Product Curves

The Law of Diminishing Returns

The variations in output that result from applying more or less of a variable factor to a given quantity of a fixed factor are the subject of a famous economic hypothesis. Usually it is called the **law of diminishing returns.**

The hypothesis states that if increasing amounts of a variable factor are applied to a given amount of a fixed factor, eventually a situation will be reached in which each additional unit of the variable factor adds less to total product than did the previous unit.

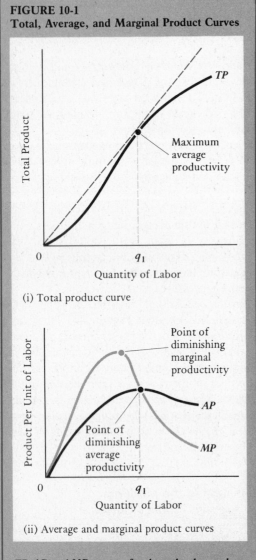

FIGURE 10-1
Total, Average, and Marginal Product Curves

Total Product

TP

Maximum
average
productivity

0   q_1

Quantity of Labor

(i) Total product curve

Product Per Unit of Labor

Point of
diminishing
marginal
productivity

AP

Point of
diminishing
average
productivity

MP

0   q_1

Quantity of Labor

(ii) Average and marginal product curves

TP, AP, and *MP* **curves often have the shapes shown here.** (i) The total product curve shows the total product steadily rising, first at an increasing rate, then at a decreasing rate. This causes both the average and the marginal product curves in (ii) to rise at first and then decline. The point of maximum average product (also called the point of diminishing average productivity) is q_1 where *TP* is tangent to the ray from the origin. At this point $MP = AP$.

The common sense of diminishing marginal product is that the fixed factor limits the amount of additional output that can be realized by adding more of the variable factor. The hypothesis of diminishing returns predicts only that sooner or later the *MP* curve will decline. It is conceivable that marginal returns might diminish from the outset, so that the first unit of labor contributes most to total production and each successive unit contributes less than the previous unit. (This is the case in what is known as the Cobb-Douglas production function.)

It is also possible for the marginal product to rise at first and decline later. Thus, what is called the law of diminishing marginal returns might more accurately be described as the law of *eventually* diminishing marginal returns. The reason for such a rise and decline is clear when it is seen in the context of the organization of production.

Consider the use of a variable number of workers in a manufacturing operation. If there is only one worker, that worker must do all the tasks, shifting from one to another and becoming competent in each. As a second, third, and subsequent workers are added, it is often possible to break the tasks into a large number of separate jobs, with each laborer specializing in one job and becoming expert at it. This process is called the *division of labor.* If additional workers permit more and more efficient divisions of labor, marginal product will rise. This may go on for some time, but (according to the hypothesis of diminishing returns) the scope for such economies must eventually disappear and sooner or later the marginal products of additional workers must decline. When this happens, each additional worker will increase total output by less than the previous worker increased it. This sort of case is the one that is illustrated in Figure 10-1, where marginal product rises at first and then declines.

Eventually, marginal product may reach zero and become negative. It is not hard to see why this occurs, when you consider the extreme case where there are so many workers in a limited space that additional workers simply get in the way.

The hypothesis is usually described in terms of

BOX 10–1 DIMINISHING RETURNS

The law of diminishing returns applies in a wide range of circumstances. Here are three examples.

■ When Southern California Edison was required to modify its Mojave power plant to reduce the amount of fly ash emitted into the atmosphere, it discovered that a series of filters applied to the smokestacks could do the job. A single filter eliminated half the discharge. Five filters in series reduced the fly ash discharge to the 3 percent allowed by law. When a state senator proposed a new standard that would permit no more than 1 percent fly ash emission, the company brought in experts who testified that such a requirement would require at least 15 filters per stack and would triple the cost.

■ B.C.'s Campbell River, a noted sport fishing river, has become the center of a thriving, well-promoted tourist trade. As the fishing pressure has increased, the total number of fish caught has steadily increased, but the number of fish per person fishing has decreased and the average hours fished for each fish caught has increased.

■ Gallup, Roper, and all other pollsters, as well as all students of statistics, know that you can use a sample to estimate characteristics of a very large population. Even a relatively small sample can provide a useful estimate—at a tiny fraction of the cost of a complete enumeration of the population. However, sample estimates are subject to *sampling error*. If, for example, 38 percent of a sample approves of a certain policy, the percentage of the population that approves of it is likely to be close to 38 percent, but it might well be anywhere from 36 to 40 percent.

The theory of statistics shows that the size of the expected sampling error can always be reduced by increasing the sample size. The 4 percent interval (in the example above) could be cut in half—to 2 percent—by *quadrupling* the sample size. That is, if the original sample had been 400, a new sample of 1,600 would halve the expected error. To reduce the interval to 1 percent, the new sample would have to be quadrupled again—to 6,400. In other words, there are diminishing marginal returns to sample size.

diminishing marginal returns, but it can equally well be stated in terms of diminishing average returns. The law of diminishing *average* returns states that if increasing quantities of a variable factor are applied to a given quantity of fixed factors, the average product of the variable factor will eventually decrease. [13]

The Significance of the Law of Diminishing Returns

Empirical confirmation of both diminishing marginal and diminishing average returns occurs frequently. Some examples are illustrated in Box 10-1. One might wish that it were not so. There would then be no reason to fear that the world population explosion will bring with it a food crisis. If the marginal product of additional workers applied to a fixed quantity of land were constant, world food production could be expanded in proportion to the population merely by keeping a constant fraction of the population on farms. But with fixed techniques, diminishing returns dictate an inexorable decline in the marginal product of each additional laborer because an expanding population has a fixed world supply of agricultural land.

Thus, unless there is a continual improvement in the techniques of production, continuous population growth will bring with it, according to the hypothesis of diminishing returns, declining average living standards and eventually widespread famine. This was the gloomy prediction of the nineteenth century English economist Thomas Malthus. As a result of this widely publicized prediction, economics became known in the nineteenth century as the dismal science. Indeed, the prediction was fulfilled in many countries of the third world. It was not fulfilled, however, in the advanced countries because improvements in the techniques of production were much more rapid than Malthus had foreseen. (This is discussed in more detail in Box 11-1 on page 177.)

The Relation Between Marginal and Average Curves

Notice that in Figure 10-1(ii) the *MP* curve cuts the *AP* curve at the latter's maximum point. Although the relation between marginal and average curves is a mathematical one and not a matter of economics, it is important to understand how these curves are related. [14]

The average product curve slopes upward as long as the marginal product curve is above it; it makes no difference whether the marginal curve is itself sloping upward or downward. The common sense of this relation is that if an additional worker is to raise the average product of all workers, his or her output must be greater than the average output of all other workers. It is immaterial whether the new worker's contribution to output is greater or less than the contribution of the worker hired immediately before; all that matters is that his or her contribution to output exceeds the average output of *all* workers hired previously. (The relation between marginal and average measures is further illustrated in Box 10-2.)

Short-Run Variations in Cost

We now shift our attention from the firm's production function to its costs. We consider firms that are not in a position to influence the prices of the inputs they employ. These firms must pay the going market price for all inputs.[3] Given these prices and the physical returns summarized by the product curves, the costs of different levels of output can be calculated.

Cost Concepts Defined

The following brief definitions of several cost concepts are closely related to the product concepts just introduced.

1. **Total cost** (*TC*) means the total cost of producing any given level of output. Total cost is divided into two parts, total fixed costs (*TFC*) and total variable costs (*TVC*). **Fixed costs** are those that do not vary with output; they will be the same if output is 1 unit or 1 million units. These costs are also referred to as *overhead costs* or *unavoidable costs*. All costs that vary directly with output, rising as more is produced and falling as less is produced, are called **variable costs.** In the example of Table 10-1, since labor was the variable factor of production, the wage bill is a variable cost. Variable costs are often referred to as *direct costs* or *avoidable costs*.

2. **Average total cost** (*ATC*), also called **average cost** (*AC*), is the total cost of producing any given output divided by that output. *ATC* may be divided into **average fixed costs** (*AFC*) and **average variable costs** (*AVC*) in the same way that total costs were.

Although average *variable* costs may rise or fall as production is increased (depending on whether output rises more rapidly or more slowly than total variable costs), it is clear that average fixed costs decline continuously as output increases. A doubling of output always leads to a halving of fixed costs per unit of output. This is a process popularly known as *spreading one's overhead*.

3. **Marginal cost** (*MC*), sometimes called **incremental cost,** is the increase in total cost resulting from raising the rate of production by one unit. Because fixed costs do not vary with output, marginal fixed costs are always zero. Therefore marginal costs are necessarily marginal variable costs,

---

[3] The important problems that arise when the firm is in a position to influence the prices it pays for its factors of production are considered in Chapter 19.

BOX 10–2 GARY CARTER'S BATTING STATISTICS

The relationship between the concepts of marginal and average measures is very general. An illuminating example comes from the *Baseball Encyclopedia*. The table shows the average batting percentage—number of hits (output) divided by number of official at bats (input)—of Montreal Expos star catcher Gary Carter during the first six years of his National League baseball career. For each year column 1 gives his lifetime batting percentage as of the start of that year's baseball season. Column 2 gives his batting percentage during that year. Column 3 gives his lifetime batting percentage at the end of the season. This, of course, is also the entry in column 1 for the next year.

An interesting relationship exists among these columns: *Whenever his performance during a season is better than his lifetime average at the start of the season, his lifetime average rises*. This occurred (trivially) in his first season, 1974; in 1977, when he had a good year batting .284, thus raising his lifetime average from .256 to .266; and again in 1979. *Whenever his performance during a season is worse than his lifetime average at the start of the season, his lifetime average falls*. This occurred in 1975, the second

season in the table but really his official rookie season, when he (understandably) was unable to match his auspicious performance in his infrequent at bats in 1974. It also occurred in 1976 and 1978, when he had a below-average year and as a result saw his lifetime average fall.

This illustrates an important relationship between marginal (in this case, current year) and average (in this case, lifetime) measures.

If the average is to rise, all that matters is that the marginal is above the average; if the average is to fall, all that matters is that the marginal is below the average.

Year	Old average (Lifetime batting percentage at start of season)	Marginal (Batting percentage during the season)	New average (Lifetime batting percentage at end of season)
1974	.000	.407	.407
1975	.407	.270	.279
1976	.279	.219	.256
1977	.256	.284	.266
1978	.266	.255	.263
1979	.263	.283	.267

and a change in fixed costs will leave marginal costs unaffected. For example, the marginal cost of producing a few more potatoes by farming a given amount of land more intensively is the same, whatever the rent paid for the land. [15]

Short-Run Cost Curves

Take the production relationships in Table 10-1. Assume that the price of labor is $10 per unit and the price of capital is $25 per unit. The cost schedules for these values are shown in Table 10-2.[4]

---

[4] If you do not see where any of the numbers come from, review Table 10-1 and the definitions of cost just given.

Figure 10-2 plots cost curves that are similar in shape to those arising from the data in Table 10-2. Notice that the marginal cost curve cuts the *ATC* and *AVC* curves at their lowest points. This is another example of the relation (discussed above) between a marginal and an average curve. The *ATC* curve, for example, slopes downward as long as the marginal cost curve is below it; it makes no difference whether the marginal cost curve is itself sloping upward or downward.

Short-run average variable cost. In Figure 10-2 the average variable cost curve reaches a minimum and then rises. With fixed factor prices, when average product per worker is a maximum,

TABLE 10–2 THE VARIATION OF COSTS WITH CAPITAL FIXED AND LABOR VARIABLE

(1) Labor (L)	(2) Output (q)	Total cost ($)			Marginal cost ($ per unit) (6) (MC)	Average cost ($ per unit)		
		(3) Fixed (TFC)	(4) Variable (TVC)	(5) Total (TC)		(7) Fixed (AFC)	(8) Variable (AVC)	(9) Total (ATC)
0	0	100	0	100		—	—	—
					0.67			
1	15	100	10	110		6.67	0.67	7.33
					0.53			
2	34	100	20	120		2.94	0.59	3.53
					0.71			
3	48	100	30	130		2.08	0.62	2.71
					0.83			
4	60	100	40	140		1.67	0.67	2.33
					5.00			
5	62	100	50	150		1.61	0.81	2.42

The relation of cost to level of output can be looked at in several different ways. These cost curves are computed from the product curves of Table 10-1, given the price of capital of $25 per unit and the price of labor of $10 per unit. Marginal cost (in column 6) is shown between the lines of total cost because it refers to the *change* in cost divided by the *change* in output that brought it about. For example, the *MC* of $.71 is the $10 increase in total cost (from $120 to $130) divided by the 14-unit increase in output (from 34 to 48). For graphical purposes, marginal costs should be plotted midway in the interval over which they are computed. The *MC* of $.71 would be plotted at output 41.

average variable cost is a minimum. [16] The common sense of this proposition is that each additional worker adds the same amount to cost but a different amount to output, and when output per worker is rising, the cost per unit of output must be falling—and vice versa.

The hypothesis of eventually diminishing average productivity implies eventually increasing average variable costs.

Short-run average total cost curve. Short-run *ATC* curves are often drawn U-shaped. This reflects the assumptions that (1) average productivity is increasing when output is low but (2) at some level of output average productivity begins to fall fast enough to cause average variable costs to increase faster than average fixed costs fall. When this happens, *ATC* increases.

Marginal cost curves. In Figure 10-2 the marginal cost curve is shown as a declining curve that reaches a minimum and then rises. This is the mirror image of the usual shape of the marginal product curve. The reason is clear. With a fixed price per unit of the variable factor, if extra units of the variable factor produce increasing quantities

of output (marginal *product* rising), the cost per unit of extra output must be falling (marginal *cost* falling). If marginal product is falling, marginal cost will be rising. Thus, the hypothesis of eventually diminishing marginal product implies eventually increasing marginal cost. [17]

The Definition of Capacity

The output that corresponds to the minimum short-run average total cost is often called by economists and business people the **capacity** of the firm. Capacity in this sense is not an upper limit on what can be produced. Instead it is the largest output that can be produced without encountering rising average costs per unit. In Figure 10-2(ii) capacity output is q_c units, but higher outputs can be achieved, provided the firm is willing to accept the higher per unit costs that accompany output "above capacity." A firm producing with **excess capacity** is producing at an output smaller than the point of minimum average total cost.

The technical definition gives the word *capacity* a meaning different from that in everyday speech, but the concept proves useful, and in any case it is widely used in economic and business discussions.

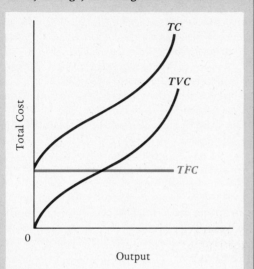

FIGURE 10-2
Total, Average, and Marginal Cost Curves

(i) Total cost curves

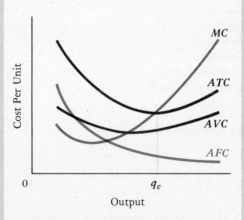

(ii) Marginal and average cost curves

TC, AC, and *MC* **curves often have the shapes shown here.** (i) Total fixed cost does not vary with output. Total variable cost and the total of all costs ($TC = TVC + TFC$) rise with output, first at a decreasing rate, then at an increasing rate. The total cost curves in (i) give rise to the average and marginal curves in (ii). *AFC* declines as output increases. *AVC* and *ATC* fall and then rise as output increases. *MC* does the same, intersecting *ATC* and *AVC* at their minimum points. Capacity output is q_c, the minimum point on the *ATC* curve.

A Family of Short-Run Cost Curves

A short-run cost curve shows how costs vary with output for a given quantity of the fixed factor—say, a given size of plant.

There is a different short-run cost curve for each given quantity of the fixed factor.

A small plant for manufacturing nuts and bolts will have its own short-run cost curve. A medium-size plant and a very large plant will each have its own short-run cost curve. If a firm expands and replaces its small plant with a medium-size plant, it will move from one short-run cost curve to another. This change from one plant size to another is a long-run change. How short-run cost curves of plants of different size are related to each other is studied in the next chapter.

SUMMARY

1. The firm's production decisions can be classified into three groups: (a) how best to employ existing plant and equipment (the short run); (b) what new plant and equipment and production processes to select, given the framework of known technical possibilities (the long run); and (c) what to do about encouraging, or merely adapting to, the invention of new techniques (the very long run).

2. The short run involves decisions in which one or more factors of production are fixed. The long run involves decisions in which all factors are variable but in which technology is given. In the very long run, technology can change.

3. The production function describes the ways in which different inputs may be combined to produce different quantities of output. Short-run and long-run situations can be interpreted as implying different kinds of constraints on the production function. In the short run, the firm is constrained to use no more than a given quantity of some fixed factor; in the long run, it is constrained only by the available techniques of production.

4. The theory of short-run behavior depends on

the productivity of variable factors when combined with fixed factors. The concepts of total, average, and marginal product represent alternative ways of looking at the relation between output and the quantity of the variable factor of production.

5. The law of diminishing returns asserts that if increasing quantities of a variable factor are combined with a given quantity of fixed factors, the marginal and the average product of the variable factor will eventually decrease. This hypothesis leads directly to implications of rising marginal and average costs.

6. Given physical productivity schedules and the costs per unit of factors, it is a simple matter of arithmetic to develop the whole family of short-run cost curves.

7. Short-run average total cost curves are drawn as U-shaped to reflect the expectation that average productivity increases for small outputs but eventually declines sufficiently rapidly to offset advantages of spreading overheads. The output at the minimum point of a short-run average total cost curve is called the plant's capacity.

8. There is a whole family of short-run cost curves, one for each quantity of the fixed factor.

TOPICS FOR REVIEW

Short run, long run, and very long run
Marginal and average productivity
The law of diminishing returns
The relation between marginal and average curves
The relation between productivity and cost
Marginal cost and average cost
Capacity and excess capacity

DISCUSSION QUESTIONS

1. Is the short run the same number of months for increasing output as for decreasing it? Must the short run in industry

A be the same length for all firms in the industry? Under what circumstances might the short run actually involve a longer time span than even the very long run?

2. How would the following factors increase or reduce the relative importance of short-run decisions for management?
   a. A guaranteed annual employment contract of at least 48 40-hour weeks of work for all employees
   b. A major economic depression during which there is substantial unemployment of labor and in which equipment is being used at well below capacity levels of production
   c. A speeding up of delivery dates for new easy-to-install equipment

3. Indicate whether each of the following conforms to the hypothesis of diminishing returns; and if so, whether it refers to marginal or average returns, or both.
   a. "The bigger they are, the harder they fall."
   b. As more and more of the population receive smallpox vaccinations, the reductions in the smallpox disease rate for each additional 100,000 vaccinations become smaller.
   c. For the seventh year in a row, the average depth of drilling required to hit oil increased.
   d. Five workers produce twice as much today as 10 workers did 40 years ago.

4. Consider the education of a human being as a process of production. Regard years of schooling as one variable factor of production. What are the other factors? What factors are fixed? At what point would you expect diminishing productivity to set in? For an Einstein, would it set in during his lifetime?

5. Suppose that each of the following news items is correct. Discuss each in terms of its effects on average total cost.
   a. The Ontario Ministry of Education reports that the increasing level of education of our youth has led both to higher productivity and to increases in wages.
   b. During the winter of 1977 many factories were forced by fuel shortages to reduce production and to operate at levels of production far below capacity.
   c. For the third year in a row, the Post Office's production exceeded its capacity.
   d. NASA reports that the space program has led to development of electronic devices that have brought innovations to many industries.

6. "Because overhead costs are fixed, increasing production lowers costs. Thus small business is sure to be inefficient. This is a dilemma of modern society, which values both smallness *and* efficiency." Discuss.

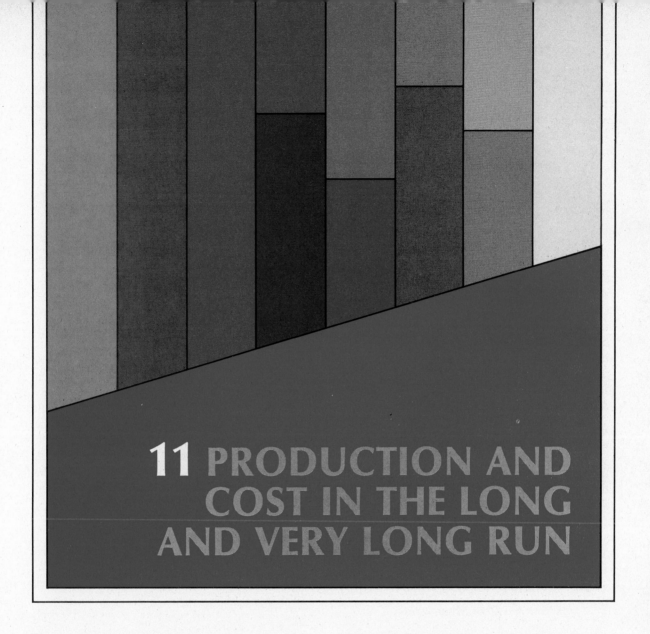

11 PRODUCTION AND COST IN THE LONG AND VERY LONG RUN

In the short run, with only one factor variable, there is only one way to produce a given output: by adjusting the input of the variable factor until the desired level of output is achieved. Thus, in the short run, the firm must make a decision about its output, but once it has decided on a rate of output there is only one technically possible way of achieving it. In the long run, all factors are variable. If a firm decides on some rate of output, it has an additional decision to make: By which of the many technically possible methods will the output be produced? Should the firm adopt a technique that uses a great deal of capital and only a small amount of labor, or should it adopt one that uses less capital but more labor?

THE LONG RUN: NO FIXED FACTORS

When all factors can be varied it is necessary for the firm to choose among the many alternative methods of production available to it. The long run is concerned with firms' choosing plant and equipment in order to earn maximum profits.

Long-run planning decisions are important. A firm deciding on a new steel mill and the machinery to go into it can choose among many alternatives. But once installed, that equipment is fixed for a long time. If the firm makes a wrong choice now, its survival may be threatened; if it estimates shrewdly, it may reward both owners and foresighted managers with large profits and bonuses.

Long-run decisions are difficult because the firm must anticipate what methods of production will be efficient not only today but in the years ahead, when costs of labor and raw materials may have changed. The decisions are difficult too because the firm must estimate how much output it will want to produce. Is the industry of which it is a part growing or declining? Will new products emerge to render its buggy whips less useful than an extrapolation of past sales suggests?

Profit Maximization in the Long Run

Any firm that is trying to maximize its profits should in the long run select the method that produces its long run output at the lowest possible cost. This implication of the hypothesis of profit maximization is called **cost minimization**. From the alternatives open to it, the firm chooses the least costly ways of achieving any specific output.

Conditions for Cost Minimization

What can a firm do in the long run to make its costs as low as possible? The firm does not have the least costly method of production if it is possible to substitute one factor for another so as to keep its output constant while reducing its total cost.

The firm's choice of factor mix. This idea can be stated more formally: The firm should substitute one factor (for example, capital) for another factor (for example, labor) as long as the marginal product of the one factor *per dollar expended on it* is greater than the marginal product of the other

factor *per dollar expended on it*. The firm cannot have minimized its costs as long as these two magnitudes are unequal. Using K to represent capital, L labor, and p the price of a unit of the factor, the necessary condition of cost minimization may be stated:

$$\frac{MP_K}{p_K} = \frac{MP_L}{p_L} \tag{1}$$

This equation is analogous to the condition for the utility-maximizing household, given on page 114, in which the household equated the marginal utility per dollar of two goods.

To see why this equation needs to be satisfied if costs of production are to be minimized, suppose that the left-hand side of Equation [1] is equal to 10, showing that the last dollar spent on capital produced 10 units of output, while the right-hand side is equal to 4, showing that the last dollar spent on labor added only 4 units to output. In such a case, the firm, by using $2.50 less of labor, would reduce output by 10 units. But it could regain that lost output by spending $1 more on capital.[1] Making such a substitution of capital for labor would leave output unchanged and reduce cost by $1.50. Thus the original position was not the cost-minimizing one.

Whenever the two sides of Equation [1] are not equal, there are factor substitutions that will reduce costs.

By rearranging terms in Equation [1] we can look at the cost-minimizing condition a bit differently.

$$\frac{MP_K}{MP_L} = \frac{p_K}{p_L} \tag{2}$$

The ratio of the marginal products on the left-hand side compares the contribution to output of the last unit of capital and the last unit of labor. If the ratio is 4, this means one unit more of capital will add 4 times as much to output as one unit more of labor. The right-hand side compares the cost of one unit more of capital to the cost of one unit

---

[1] The argument in the previous two sentences assumes that the marginal products do not change when expenditure is changed by a few dollars.

more of labor. Suppose the right-hand side is 2. Capital, although twice as expensive, is 4 times as productive. It will pay the firm to switch to a method of production that uses more capital and less labor. If, however, the right-hand side is any number more than 4, it will pay to substitute labor for capital.

How much should inputs be changed? We have seen that when the ratio MP_K/MP_L is 4 while the ratio P_K/P_L prices is 2, the firm will substitute capital for labor. But how far does the firm go in making this substitution? There is a limit because as the firm uses more capital, its marginal product falls, while as it uses less labor, the marginal product of labor rises. Thus the ratio MP_K/MP_L falls. When it reaches 2, the firm need substitute no further. The ratio of the marginal products is equal to the ratio of the prices.[2]

This formulation shows how the firm can adjust the elements over which it has control (the quantities of factors used, and thus the marginal products of the factors) to the prices or opportunity costs of the factors given by the market. A precisely analogous adjustment process is involved when households adjust their consumption of goods to the market prices of those goods (see page 115).

The long-run equilibrium of the firm. The firm will have the long run equilibrium factor ratio when there is no room for cost-reducing substitutions. Looking at Equation [1], we see that

The firm is in long-run equilibrium with respect to factor proportions when the marginal product per dollar spent on each factor is the same or equivalently when the ratio of the marginal products of factors is equal to the ratio of their prices.

The Principle of Substitution

Suppose that a firm is producing where the cost-minimizing conditions shown in Equations [1] or [2] are met but that the cost of labor increases while the cost of capital remains unchanged. The least-cost method of producing any output will now use less labor and more capital than was required to produce the same output before the factor prices changed. This is because P_K/P_L in Equation [2] falls and to restore the equality, more capital and less labor must be used, lowering MP_K and raising MP_L until MP_K/MP_L falls by the same amount as P_K/P_L.

The prediction called the **principle of substitution** follows from the assumption that firms minimize their costs.

Methods of production will change if the relative prices of factors change. Relatively more of the cheaper factor and less of the more expensive one will be used.

The principle of substitution plays a central role in the allocation of resources in a market economy since it shows how firms will respond to changes in relative factor prices. Such changes are caused by the changing relative scarcity of factors to the economy as a whole. The individual firm is thus motivated to use less of factors that have become scarcer to the economy.

The principle of substitution may be readily illustrated. As construction workers' wages have risen sharply relative to the wages of factory labor and the cost of machinery, many home builders have shifted from on-site construction to panelization. Panelization is a method of building standardized modules so that the wiring, plumbing, insulation, and painting are done at the factory. The bulk of the work is performed by machinery and by assembly line workers, whose wages are only half those of on-site construction workers.

Consider another example. One country has a great deal of land and a small population. Here the price of land will be low while, because labor is in short supply, the wage rate will be high. Producers of agricultural goods will tend to make lavish use of the cheap land while economizing on expensive labor; thus a production process will be adopted that utilizes a low ratio of labor to land. Suppose a second country is small in area and has a large population. Here the demand for land will be high relative to its supply, and land will be relatively expensive while labor will be relatively cheap. Firms producing agricultural goods will tend to

---

[2] In the optional section of this chapter dealing with isoquants (see pages 170–175), this process is given a graphic analysis similar to that given household behavior in Chapter 8.

FIGURE 11-1
A Long-Run Average Cost Curve

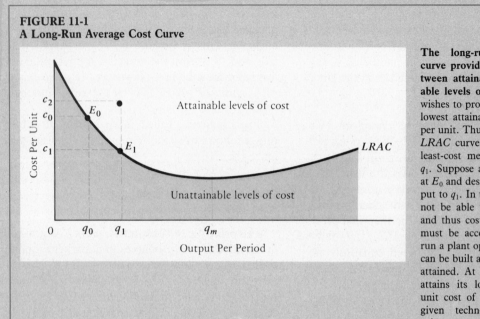

The long-run average cost curve provides a boundary between attainable and unattainable levels of cost. If the firm wishes to produce output q_0, the lowest attainable cost level is c_0 per unit. Thus point E_0 is on the $LRAC$ curve. E_1 represents the least-cost method of producing q_1. Suppose a firm is producing at E_0 and desires to increase output to q_1. In the short run it will not be able to vary all factors, and thus costs above c_1, say c_2, must be accepted. In the long run a plant optimal for output q_1 can be built and cost of c_1 can be attained. At output q_m the firm attains its lowest possible per unit cost of production for the given technology and factor prices.

economize on land by using a great deal of labor per unit of land; thus, a productive process will be adopted that uses a high ratio of labor to land.

Once again we see the price system operating as an automatic control system. No single firm needs to be aware of nationwide factor surpluses and scarcities. They are, however, reflected by market prices. So individual firms that never look beyond their own private profit are led to economize on factors that are scarce to the nation as a whole. Thus, the price system leads profit-maximizing firms to take account of the nation's relative factor scarcities when deciding which of the possible methods of production to adopt.

Cost Curves in the Long Run

There is a best (least-cost) method of producing each level of output when all factors are free to be varied. In general, this method will not be the same for different levels of output. If factor prices are given, a minimum cost can be found for each possible level of output and, if this minimum achiev-

able cost is expressed as an amount per unit of output, we can obtain the long-run average cost of producing each level of output. When this information is plotted on a graph, the result is called a **long-run average cost curve (*LRAC*)**. Figure 11-1 shows such a curve.

This long-run average cost curve is determined by the technology of the industry (which is assumed to be fixed) and by the prices of the factors of production. It is a "boundary" in the sense that points below the curve are unattainable, points above the curve are attainable, and points on the curve are also attainable if sufficient time elapses for all inputs to be adjusted.

The *LRAC* curve divides the cost levels that are attainable with known technology and given factor prices from those that are unattainable.

The Shape of the Long-Run Average Cost Curve

The long-run average cost curve shown in Figure 11-1 falls at first and then rises. This curve is often described as U-shaped, although "saucer-shaped" might be more accurate.

Decreasing costs. Over the range of output from zero to q_m the firm has falling long-run average costs. An expansion of output results in a reduction of long-run average costs. Since the prices of factors are assumed to be constant, the reason for the decline in long-run average costs must be that output increases faster than inputs as the scale of the firm's production expands. Over this range of output the firm is often said to enjoy long-run **increasing returns.**[3]

Increasing returns may arise as a result of increased opportunities for specialization of tasks made possible by the division of labor. Adam Smith's classic discussion of this important point is given in Box 3-1 on page 31. Increasing returns may also arise because of substitution of one input for another. Even the most casual observation of the differences in production technique used in large-size and small-size plants shows the differences in factor proportions.

For example, assembly line techniques, body-stamping machinery, and multiple-boring engine-block machines in automobile production are economically efficient only when individual operations are repeated thousands of times. Using elaborate harvesting equipment (which combines many individual tasks that would otherwise be done by hand and by tractor) provides the least-cost method of production on a big farm but not on a few acres.

Typically, as the level of planned output increases, capital is substituted for labor and complex machines for simpler machines. Robotics is a contemporary example. Electronic devices can handle huge volumes of operations very quickly, but unless the level of production requires very large numbers of operations, it does not make sense to use robotics or other forms of automation.

Increasing costs. Over the range of outputs greater than q_m the firm encounters rising costs. An expansion in production, even after sufficient time has elapsed for all adjustments to be made, will be accompanied by a rise in average costs per unit of output. If costs per unit of input are constant, this rise in costs must be the result of an expansion in output less than in proportion to the expansion in inputs. Such a firm is said to suffer long-run **decreasing returns.**[4] Decreasing returns imply that the firm suffers some diseconomy of scale. As its scale of operations increases, diseconomies, say of management, are encountered that increase its per unit costs of production.

Constant returns. In Figure 11-1 the firm's long-run average costs fall to output q_m and rise thereafter. Another possibility should be noted: The firm's *LRAC* curve might have a flat portion over a range of output around q_m. With such a flat portion, the firm would be encountering constant costs over the relevant range of output. This would mean that the firm's average costs per unit of output do not change as its output changed. Since factor prices are assumed to be fixed, this must mean that the firm's output is increasing exactly as fast as its inputs are increasing. Such a firm is said to be encountering **constant returns.**

The Relation Between Long-Run and Short-Run Costs

The various short-run cost curves mentioned at the conclusion of Chapter 10 and the long-run curve studied in this chapter are all derived from the same production function. Each assumes given prices for all factor inputs. In the long run, all factors can be varied; in the short run, some must remain fixed. The long-run average cost curve (*LRAC*) shows the lowest cost of producing any output when all factors are variable. The short-run average cost curve (*SRAC*) shows the lowest cost of producing any output when one or more factors is not free to vary.

---

[3] Economists shift back and forth between speaking in physical terms (i.e., increasing *returns* to production) and cost terms (i.e., decreasing *costs* of production). Thus, the same firm may be spoken of as having decreasing costs or enjoying increasing returns.

[4] Long-run decreasing returns differ from the short-run diminishing returns that we encountered earlier. In the short run, at least one factor is fixed and the law of diminishing returns ensures that returns to the variable factor will eventually diminish. In the long run, all factors are variable and it is possible that physically diminishing returns would never be encountered—at least as long as it was genuinely possible to increase inputs of all factors.

The short-run cost curve cannot fall below the long-run curve because the *LRAC* curve represents the *lowest* attainable costs for every output. It might be the same curve if precisely the same-size plant was the best for any level of output. But that is not likely. The usual situation is that as the level of output is increased, a larger plant is required to achieve the lowest attainable costs. This is shown in Figure 11-2.

We saw at the end of Chapter 10 that a *SRAC* curve such as that in Figure 11-2 is one of many such curves. Each curve shows how costs vary as output is varied from a base output, holding some factors fixed at the quantities most appropriate to the base output (see Figure 11-3). The long-run curve is sometimes called an **envelope curve** because it encloses the whole family of short-run curves. Each short-run cost curve is tangent to

(touches) the long-run curve at the level of output for which the quantity of the fixed factor is optimal and lies above it for all other levels of output.

Shifts in Cost Curves

The cost curves derived so far show how cost varies with output, given constant factor prices and fixed technology. Changes in either technological knowledge or factor prices will cause the entire family of short-run and long-run cost curves to shift. Loss of existing technological knowledge is rare, so technological change normally works in only one direction, to shift cost curves downward. Improved ways of making existing commodities will mean that lower-cost methods of production become available. (Technological change is discussed in the last section of this chapter.)

Factor price changes can exert an influence in either direction. If a firm has to pay more for any factor that it uses, the cost of producing each level of output will rise; if the firm has to pay less, costs will fall.

A rise in factor prices shifts the family of short-run and long-run cost curves upward. A fall in factor prices or a technological advance shifts the entire family of cost curves downward.

Although factor prices usually change gradually, they sometimes rise suddenly and drastically. This was the case in the 1970s. One reason was the sharp general inflation that beset the North American economy; a second reason was the sudden and dramatic increase in energy prices that was triggered by the rise in the price of oil following the emergence of OPEC as an effective cartel.

ISOQUANTS: AN ALTERNATIVE ANALYSIS OF THE FIRM'S INPUT DECISIONS[5]

The production function gives the relation between the factor inputs that the firm uses and the output

---

FIGURE 11-2
Long-Run and Short-Run Average Cost Curves

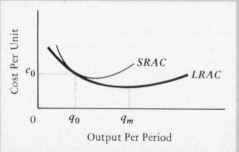

The short-run average cost curve is tangent to the long-run curve at the output for which the quantity of the fixed factors is optimal. If output is varied around q_0 units with plant and equipment fixed at the optimal level for producing q_0, costs will follow the short-run cost curve. Whereas *SRAC* and *LRAC* are at the same level for output q_0 where the fixed plant is optimal for that level, for all other outputs there is too little or too much of the fixed factor and *SRAC* lies above *LRAC*. If some output other than q_0 is to be sustained, costs can be reduced to the level of the long-run curve when sufficient time has elapsed to adjust the fixed factors.

---

[5] The material in this section (pages 170–176) can be omitted without loss of continuity.

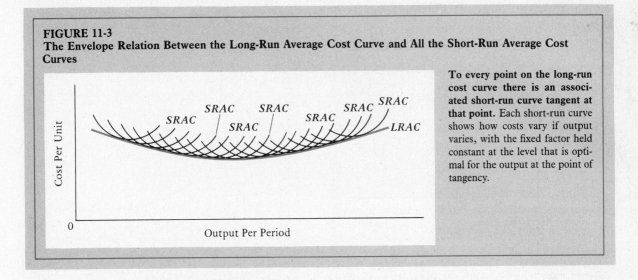

FIGURE 11-3
The Envelope Relation Between the Long-Run Average Cost Curve and All the Short-Run Average Cost Curves

To every point on the long-run cost curve there is an associated short-run curve tangent at that point. Each short-run curve shows how costs vary if output varies, with the fixed factor held constant at the level that is optimal for the output at the point of tangency.

that it obtains. In the long run, the firm can choose among many different combinations of inputs that will yield it the same output. The production function and the choices open to the firm can be given a graphical representation using the concept of an isoquant.

A Single Isoquant

Table 11-1 illustrates by hypothetical example those combinations of two inputs (labor and capital) that will each serve to produce a given quantity of output. The data from Table 11-1 are plotted in Figure 11-4. A smooth curve is drawn through the points to indicate that there are additional ways, not listed in the table, of producing six units.

This curve is called an **isoquant.** It shows the whole set of technologically efficient possibilities for producing a given level of output—six units in this example. This is an example of graphing a three-variable function in two dimensions. It is analogous to the contour line on a map that shows all points of equal altitude and to an indifference curve that shows all combinations of commodities that yield an equal utility.

As we move from one point on an isoquant to another, we are *substituting one factor for another*

while holding output constant. If we move from point *b* to point *c*, we are substituting one unit of labor for three units of capital. The **marginal rate of substitution (MRS)** measures the rate at which one factor is substituted for another with output held constant. Graphically, the marginal rate of substitution is measured by the slope of the isoquant at a particular point. Table 11-1 shows the calculation of some rates of substitution between various points of the isoquant.

The marginal rate of substitution is related to the marginal products of the factors of production. To see how, consider an example. Assume that at the present level of inputs of labor and capital the marginal product of a unit of labor is two units of output while the marginal product of capital is one unit of output. This means if the firm reduces its use of capital and increases its use of labor to keep output constant, then it needs to add only one-half unit of labor for one unit of capital given up. Hence the marginal rate of substitution, the change in capital divided by the change in labor, is -2. If, at another point on the isoquant with more labor and less capital, the marginal products are two for capital and one for labor, the firm will have to add two units of labor for every unit of capital it gives up. Now the marginal rate of substitution is equal to $-\frac{1}{2}$. The above illustration shows that the re-

TABLE 11–1 ALTERNATIVE METHODS OF PRODUCING SIX UNITS OF OUTPUT: POINTS ON AN ISOQUANT

Method	K	L	ΔK	ΔL	Rate of substitution $\Delta K/\Delta L$
a.	18	2			
b.	12	3	−6	1	−6.0
c.	9	4	−3	1	−3.0
d.	6	6	−3	2	−1.5
e.	4	9	−2	3	−0.67
f.	3	12	−1	3	−0.33
g.	2	18	−1	6	−0.17

An isoquant describes the firm's alternative methods for producing a given output. The table lists some of the methods indicated by a production function as being available to produce six units of output. The first combination uses a great deal of capital (K) and very little labor (L). As we move down the table, labor is substituted for capital in such a way as to keep output constant. Finally, at the bottom, most of the capital has been replaced by labor. The rate of substitution between the two factors is calculated in the last three columns of the table. Note that as we move down the table, the absolute value of the rate of substitution declines.

quired changes in factor inputs, and therefore the marginal rate of substitution, depends on the ratio of the marginal products of the factors of production. [18] Using MP_L and MP_K to denote the marginal products of labor and capital respectively, we state the proposition in symbols:

$$MRS = \frac{\Delta K}{\Delta L} = -\frac{MP_L}{MP_K}$$

To illustrate look again at the example given in the previous paragraph. The first MRS of -2 can be obtained either by dividing ΔK by ΔL, which is $-1/(\frac{1}{2})$, or by dividing MP_L by MP_K and adding a minus sign, which is $-(\frac{2}{1})$.

Isoquants satisfy two important conditions: They are downward-sloping and they are convex viewed from the origin. What is the economic meaning of each of these conditions?

The downward slope indicates that each factor input has a positive marginal product. If the input of one factor is reduced and that of the other is held constant, output will be reduced. Thus, if one

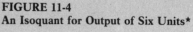

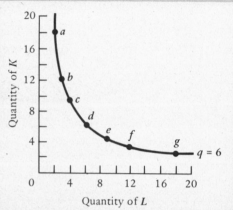

Isoquants are downward-sloping and convex. The downward slope reflects the requirement of technological efficiency. A method that uses more of one factor must use less of the other factor if it is to be technologically efficient. The convex shape of the isoquant reflects a diminishing marginal rate of substitution. Starting from point *a*, which uses relatively little labor and much capital, and moving to point *b*, 1 additional unit of labor can substitute for 6 units of capital (while holding production constant). But from *b* to *c*, 1 unit of labor substitutes for only 3 units of capital. The geometrical expression of this is that moving along the isoquant to the right, the slope of the isoquant becomes flatter.

★The lettered points are plotted from the data in Table 11-1.

input is decreased, production can only be held constant if the other factor input is increased. The marginal rate of substitution has a negative value: Increases in one factor must be balanced by decreases in the other factor if output is to be held constant.

To understand convexity, consider what happens as the firm moves along the isoquant of Figure 11-4 downward and to the right. Labor is being added and capital reduced to keep output constant. If labor is added in increments of exactly one unit, how much capital may be dispensed with each time? The key to the answer is that both factors are assumed to be subject to the law of diminishing returns. Thus the gain in output associated with each additional unit of labor added is *diminishing* while the loss of output associated with each additional unit of capital foregone is *increasing*. It therefore takes ever-smaller reductions in capital to compensate for equal increases in labor. This implies that the isoquant is convex viewed from the origin.

An Isoquant Map

The isoquant of Figure 11-1 referred to six units of output. There is another isoquant for seven units, another for 7,000 units, and a different one for every rate of output. Each isoquant refers to a specific output and connects alternative combinations of factors that are technologically efficient methods of achieving that output. If we plot a representative set of these isoquants on a single graph, we get an **isoquant map** like that in Figure 11-5. The higher the level of output along a particular isoquant, the further away from the origin it will be.

Isoquants and Cost Minimization

Finding the efficient way of producing any output requires finding the least-cost factor combination. To find this combination when both factors are variable, factor prices need to be known. Suppose, to continue the example, that capital is priced at $4 per unit and labor at $1. In Chapter 7 a budget line was used to show the alternative combinations of goods a household could buy; here an **isocost line** is used to show alternative combinations of factors a firm can buy for a given outlay. Four different isocost lines appear in Figure 11-6. The

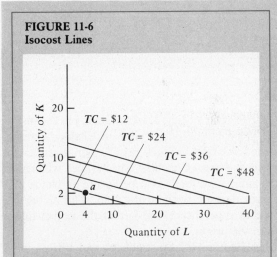

FIGURE 11-6
Isocost Lines

Each isocost line shows alternative factor combinations that can be purchased for a given outlay. The graph shows the four isocost lines that result when labor costs $1 a unit and capital $4 a unit and expenditure is held constant at $12, $24, $36, and $48 respectively. The line labeled $TC = $12 represents all combinations of the two factors that the firm could buy for $12. Point a represents 2 units of K and 4 units of L.

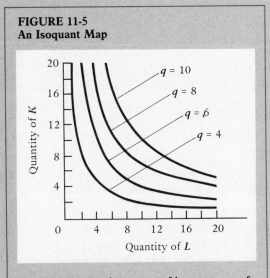

FIGURE 11-5
An Isoquant Map

An isoquant map shows a set of isoquants, one for each level of output. The figure shows four isoquants drawn from the production function and corresponding to 4, 6, 8, and 10 units of production.

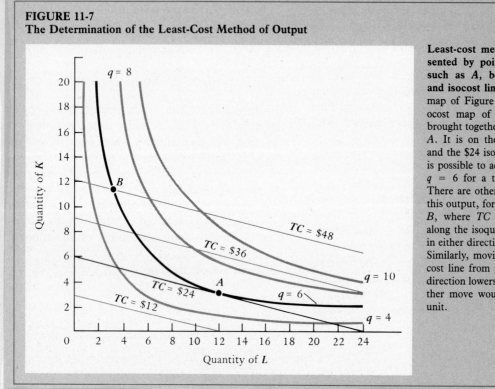

FIGURE 11-7
The Determination of the Least-Cost Method of Output

Least-cost methods are represented by points of tangency, such as *A*, between isoquant and isocost lines. The isoquant map of Figure 11-5 and the isocost map of Figure 11-6 are brought together. Consider point *A*. It is on the 6-unit isoquant and the $24 isocost line. Thus it is possible to achieve the output $q = 6$ for a total cost of $24. There are other ways to achieve this output, for example at point *B*, where $TC = 48. Moving along the isoquant from point *A* in either direction increases cost. Similarly, moving along the isocost line from point *A* in either direction lowers output. Thus either move would raise cost per unit.

slope of each reflects *relative* factor prices, just as the slope of the budget line in Chapter 7 represented relative product prices. For given factor prices a series of parallel isocost lines will reflect the alternative levels of expenditure on factor purchases that are open to the firm. The higher the level of expenditure, the farther the isocost line is from the origin.

In Figure 11-7 the isoquant and isocost maps are brought together. The economically most efficient method of production must be a point on an isoquant that just touches (i.e., is tangent to) an isocost line. If the isoquant cuts the isocost line, it is possible to move along the isoquant and reach a lower level of cost. Only at a point of tangency is a movement in either direction along the isoquant a movement to a higher cost level. The lowest

attainable cost of producing six units is $24. This cost level can be achieved only by operating at *A*, the point where the $24 isocost line is tangent to the six-unit isoquant. The lowest average cost of producing six units is thus $24/6 = $4 per unit of output.

The least-cost position is given graphically by the tangency point between the isoquant and the isocost lines.

Notice that point *A* in Figure 11-7 indicates not only the lowest level of cost for six units of output, but also the highest level of output for $24 of cost. Thus, we find the same solution if we set out *either* to minimize the cost of producing six units of output *or* to maximize the output that can be obtained for $24. One problem is said to be the "dual" of the other.

FIGURE 11-8
The Effects of a Change in Factor Prices on Costs and Factor Proportions

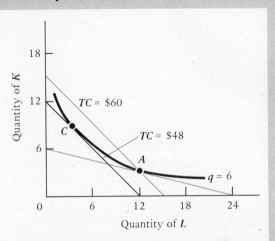

(i) The effect on the isocost line of an increase in the price of labor.

(ii) Substitution of capital for labor resulting from an increase in the price of labor.

An increase in the price of labor pivots the isocost line inward and thus increases the cost of producing any output. It also changes the slope of the isocost line and thus changes the least-cost method of producing. (i) The rise in price of *L* from $1 to $4 a unit (with price of *K* constant at $4) pivots the *TC* line inward. Any output previously produced for $24 will cost more at the new prices if it used any amount of labor. The new cost of producing *A* rises from $24 to $60. (ii) The steeper isocost line is tangent to the isoquant at *C*, not *A*. Costs at *C* are $48, higher than they were before the price increase but not as high as they would be if the factor substitution had not occurred.

The slope of the isocost line is given by the ratio of the prices of the two factors of production. The slope of the isoquant is given by the ratio of their marginal products. When the firm reaches its least-cost position, it has equated the price ratio (which is given to it by the market prices) with the ratio of the marginal products (which it can adjust by varying the proportions in which it hires the factors). In symbols,

$$\frac{MP_L}{MP_K} = \frac{p_L}{p_K}$$

This is equivalent to Equation [2] on page 166. We have now derived this result by use of the isoquant analysis of the firm's decisions. [19]

Isoquants and the Principle of Substitution

Suppose that with technology unchanged—that is, with the isoquant map fixed—the price of one factor changes. Suppose that with the price of capital unchanged at $4 per unit, the price of labor rises from $1 to $4 per unit. Originally, the efficient factor combination for producing 6 units was 12 units of labor and 3 units of capital. It cost $24. To produce that same output in the same way would now cost $60 at the new factor prices. Figure 11-8 shows why that is not efficient: The slope of the isocost line has changed, which makes it efficient to substitute the now relatively cheaper capital for the relatively more expensive labor.

This illustrates the principle of substitution:

Changes in relative factor prices will cause a partial replacement of factors that have become relatively more expensive by factors that have become relatively cheaper.

Of course, substitution of capital for labor cannot fully offset the effects of a rise in cost of labor, as Figure 11-8(i) shows. Consider the output attainable for $24. In the figure, there are two isocost lines representing $24 of outlay—at the old and new price of labor. The new isocost line for $24 lies everywhere inside the old one (except where no labor is used). The isocost line must therefore be tangent to a lower isoquant. This means that if production is to be held constant, higher costs must be accepted—but because of substitution it is not necessary to accept costs as high as would accompany an unchanged factor proportion. In the example, six units can be produced for $48 rather than the $60 that would have been required if no change in factor proportions had been made.

This leads to the predictions that

A rise in the price of one factor with all other factor prices constant will (1) shift upward the cost curves of commodities that use that factor and (2) lead to a substitution of factors that are now relatively cheaper for the factor whose price has risen.

Both these predictions were stated earlier in the chapter; now they have been derived formally using the isoquant technique.

THE VERY LONG RUN

In the long run the nation's producers do the best they can to produce known products with the techniques and the resources currently available. The best they can do is to be on, rather than above, their long-run cost curves. *In the very long run, the techniques and resources that are available change.* These changes cause shifts in long-run cost curves. These, along with the development of new prod-

ucts, are major sources of economic growth, the long-run rise in output that accounts for rising living standards.

Let us consider in more detail each of these three changes. All are related to technology, broadly defined.

New Techniques

First is the change in the techniques available for producing existing products. Over an average lifetime in the twentieth century, such changes have been dramatic. About the same amount of coal is produced today as 50 years ago, but the number of coal miners is less than one-tenth of what it was then. Seventy years ago roads and railways were built by gangs of workers using buckets, spades, and draft horses. Today bulldozers, steam shovels, giant trucks, and other specialized equipment have banished the workhorse from construction sites and to a great extent have displaced the pick-and-shovel worker.

Quality of Labor

Second, improvements in such intangibles as health and education raise the quality of labor services. Today's managers and workers are healthier and better educated than their grandparents. Even unskilled workers today tend to be literate and competent in arithmetic, and their managers are apt to be trained in modern scientific methods of business control and computer science.

New Goods

Third is the change in available goods and services. Television, polio vaccine, nylon, calculator watches, and personal computers did not exist two generations ago. Other products are so changed that the only connection they have with the "same" commodity produced in the past is the name. A 1984 Ford automobile is very different from a 1931 Ford. Modern jets are revolutionary compared with the DC-3, which itself barely resembled Lindbergh's *Spirit of St. Louis.* In our discussion of long-run demand curves in Chapter 5, we looked

BOX 11–1 THE ROLE OF PRODUCTIVITY GROWTH

We saw in Chapter 10 that economics used to be known as the dismal science because some of its predictions were dismal. Malthus and other classical economists predicted that in the long run the pressure of more and more people on the world's limited resources would cause a decline in output per person. Human history would see more and more people living less and less well, with the surplus population that could not be supported dying off from hunger and disease.

This prediction has proven wrong for the industrial countries for two main reasons. First, the population has not expanded as rapidly as foreseen by early economists writing before birth control techniques were widely known. Second, techniques of production have expanded so rapidly during the last 150 years that our ability to squeeze more out of limited resources has expanded faster than the population.

To measure the extent of technological change, economists utilize the notion of *productivity*, defined as a measure of output per unit of resource input. This concept highlights society's ability to get more and better output from the basic resources of the economy. One widely used measure of productivity is output *per hour* of labor.* The rate of increase in productivity provides a measure of the progress caused by technical change.

Growth in productivity permits increases in output per person and thus contributes to rising standards of living.

Our great-grandparents would have regarded today's standard of living in most industrialized countries as unattainable. An apparently modest rate of increase in productivity of 2 percent per year leads to a doubling of output per hour of labor every 35 years. Productivity in Canada increased at a rate greater than this in every decade from 1900 to 1970.

In other countries the growth rate has been even higher. Since World War II productivity in Germany has increased at 5 percent per year, doubling output every 14 years, and in Japan it has increased at more than 9 percent per year— a rate that doubles output per hour of labor approximately every 8 years! In many countries, including Canada, productivity growth at a stable rate came to be taken for granted as an automatic source of ever-increasing living standards.

Then, abruptly, after 1965 productivity increases dropped sharply below their historic trends. This drop happened worldwide to some degree but was particularly acute in the United States and Canada. Indeed, from 1976 to 1980 North American nonagricultural productivity did not increase at all. If this should prove to be permanent, the consequences will be severe. Lower productivity growth combined with a stable level of employment leads to a lower rate of increase of real output. Combined with declining employment, it may actually contribute to declining output per person. Declining productivity growth means that living standards rise more slowly or actually decline.

It remains to be seen whether this decline signified a new trend or was largely the result of short-term cyclical factors. The recovery following the recession of 1981–1982 witnessed a remarkable productivity boom which may or may not put us back on the track of rapid trend productivity growth.

* It is the measure we shall use. Other possible measures include output *per worker* and output *per person*.

at just such technological changes in response to rising relative prices when we spoke of the development of smaller, more fuel-efficient cars in the wake of rising gasoline prices. Similarly, much of the move to substitute capital for labor in North American industry in response to rising wage rates has taken the form of developing new labor-saving methods of production.

The importance of very long run forces in influencing living standards is further discussed in Box 11-1. The significance of the very long run to our discussion in this chapter is that very long run changes are often endogenous responses to economic signals. Consider the effect of a very large rise in the price of some major fuel source due to its increasing scarcity. Long ago the example would have been wood, later it would have been coal, and now it is petroleum. In the short run, costs of products that use this fuel source rise. The cost increases will be largest for those firms that make extensive use of the fuel in question. In the long run, substitution will occur. Known techniques that are economical in their use of this fuel will be substituted in place of techniques that make lavish use of the fuel. This will tend to reduce costs, and the reduction will be most for these products that are most able to substitute away from the high-cost fuel. In the very long run, new techniques that use alternative fuels will be invented. The industries that are most successful in developing these new techniques will enjoy the greatest cost reduction.

Of course, technological change sometimes stems from the work of scientists in research institutions far removed from economic incentives. In this case, the shift can be regarded as exogenous to the economic system. Often, however, it occurs in response to growing scarcity and rising price of some important input or changed conditions that create an opportunity for some new product. In these cases the technological change is endogenous to the economic system.

The message is important:

The response of the economic system to some major shifts in input prices takes place first within the context of fixed factors such as existing plant and equipment (the short run), then in the context of changes in all factors but constrained by existing technology (the long run), and then within the context of changing technology (the very long run).

The long-term ability of the economy to adapt to change is enormous, but such adaptations may be spread over a long time and will not be fully visible until important very long run adaptations have occurred.

SUMMARY

1. There are no fixed factors in the long run. The profit-maximizing firm chooses, from the alternatives open to it, the least costly way of achieving any specific output. A long-run cost curve represents the boundary between attainable and unattainable levels of cost for the given technology.

2. The principle of substitution says that efficient production will substitute cheaper factors for more expensive ones. If the relative prices of factors change, more of cheaper factors and less of costlier ones will be used.

3. The shape of the long-run cost curve depends on the relationship of inputs to outputs as the whole scale of a firm's operations changes. Increasing, constant, and decreasing returns lead to decreasing, constant, and increasing long-run average costs.

4. The long-run and short-run cost curves are related. Every "long-run" cost corresponds to *some* quantity of each factor and is thus on some short-run cost curve. The short-run cost curve shows how costs vary when that particular quantity of a fixed factor is used to produce outputs greater than or less than those for which it is optimal.

5. Cost curves shift upward or downward in response to changes in the prices of factors or the introduction of changed technology. Increases in factor prices shift the cost curves upward. Decreases in factor prices or technological advances that make it possible to produce the same amount of output with lower quantities of all inputs shift cost curves downward.

6. An isoquant shows all of the combinations of factors that can be used to produce a given amount of output. The slope of the isoquant is the marginal rate of substitution between the two factors of production, and it is equal to the ratio of their marginal products.

7. An isoquant is downward-sloping because both factors have positive marginal products. If one is diminished, the other must be increased if output is to be held constant. The isoquant is convex viewed from the origin because both factors have diminishing marginal productivity.

8. An isoquant map is a series of isoquants, each of which gives the combinations of two factors that will produce a given level of output.

9. The firm will be minimizing its costs of producing a given level of output if it produces where an isoquant is tangent to an isocost line. This implies that the ratio of the marginal products of the factors is equal to the ratio of their prices.

10. Over extended periods, the most important influence on costs of production and the standard of living has been the increases in output made possible by new technology and reflected in increasing productivity. These considerations involve the so-called very long run.

11. Although some technological changes are exogenous to the economic system, many are endogenous responses to changing factor prices and scarcities.

TOPICS FOR REVIEW

The implication of cost minimization
The interpretation of $MP_K/MP_L = p_K/p_L$ and of $MP_K/P_K = MP_L/P_L$
The principle of substitution
Increasing, decreasing, and constant returns

The envelope curve
A single isoquant and an isoquant map
The marginal rate of substitution
The tangency of an isoquant and an isocost line
Sources of changes in technology

DISCUSSION QUESTIONS

1. Why does the profit-maximizing firm choose the least costly way of producing any given output? Might a non-profit-maximizing organization such as a university or a church or a government intentionally choose a method of production other than the least costly one? Might an ordinary business corporation do so intentionally?

2. In Dacca, Bangladesh, where gasoline costs $3 a gallon and labor is typically paid less than 20¢ an hour, Abdul Khan pedals a bicycle-ricksha (pedicab) for his living. It's exhausting work that is coming under increasing attack by those who feel it is an inhumane practice. "We really want to get rid of them and move to motorized taxis, but I'm afraid it will take a long, long time," says the Bangladesh information officer. Ricksha drivers earn $2 a day, which is more than a skilled worker gets in Dacca. Explain the use of pedicabs in Dacca but not in New York or Tokyo. Comment on the information officer's statement.

3. Use the principle of substitution to predict the effect of each of the following:
   a. During the 1960s, salaries of professors rose much more rapidly than those of teaching assistants. During the 1970s, salaries of teaching assistants rose more than those of professors.
   b. The cost of land in big cities increases more than the cost of high-rise construction.
   c. Gold leaf is produced by pounding gold with a hammer. The thinner it is, the more valuable. The price of gold is set on a world market, but the price of labor varies among countries.
   d. OPEC keeps oil prices increasing faster than prices of most other raw materials.

4. In 1979 a federal official urged firms to make necessary "long-run adjustments to the energy shortage by reducing energy input per unit of output." How exactly might this be done? Is this use of *long-run* the economists' use of that concept?

5. Israel, a small country, imports the "insides" of its automobiles but manufactures the bodies. If this makes eco-

nomic sense, what does it tell us about cost conditions of automobile manufacture?

6. Name five important modern products that were not available when you were in grade school. Make a list of major products that you think have increased their sales at least tenfold in the last 30 years. Consider to what extent the growth in each series may reflect product or process innovation.

7. Comment on the following quotations: "OPEC can hold the entire world up for ransom since oil is essential to the working of the modern economy"—an economic journalist writing in 1977. "It was extremely lucky for the world that methods of using coal to smelt iron ore were developed just when the supplies of wood needed for the existing charcoal method of smelting were nearing exhaustion"—an economic historian writing in 1980. "Home heating is subject to many fads and fashions such as the outburst of interest in solar heating in the 1970s and a significant reduction of such interest in the 1980s"—a social commentator writing in 1984.

PART FOUR
MARKETS AND PRICING

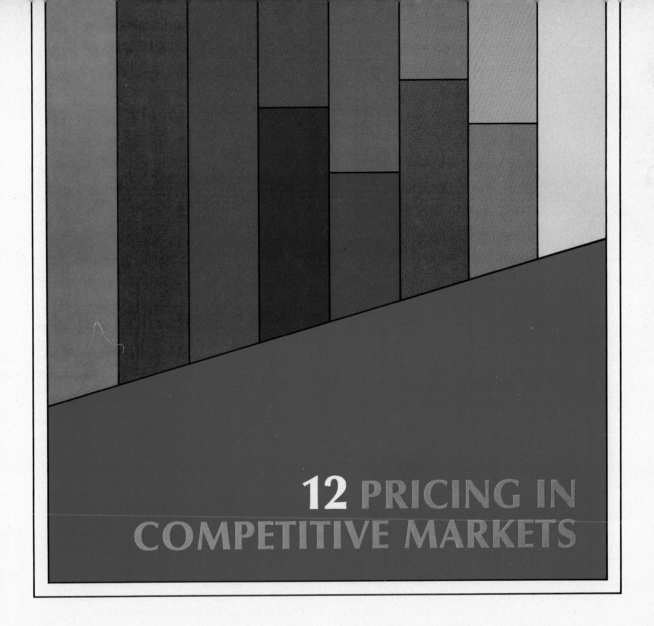

12 PRICING IN COMPETITIVE MARKETS

MARKET STRUCTURE AND FIRM BEHAVIOR

Is Goodyear in competition with Goodrich? Does Eatons compete with Simpsons? Is the farmer from Brandon, Manitoba, in competition with a wheat farmer from Biggar, Saskatchewan? In the ordinary meaning of the noun *competition* and the verb *compete*, the answers to the first two questions are plainly yes, and the answer to the third question is probably no.

Goodyear and Goodrich both advertise extensively to persuade tire buyers to buy *their* product. Everyone knows that Eatons and Simpsons watch each other closely and that keen comparison shoppers check their respective prices and qualities. But nothing the Manitoba farmer can do will affect either the sales or the profits of the Saskatchewan farmer.

Competitive Behavior and Competitive Market Structure

To sort out the question of who is competing with whom and in what sense, it is useful to distinguish between the behavior of individual firms and the type of market in which the firms operate. The concept of competitive behavior is quite distinct from the concept of competitive market structure.

In everyday use, competitive behavior refers to the degree to which individual firms actively compete with one another. Economists, however, often use the term to describe the behavior of firms operating in a *competitive market structure*. The degree of *competitiveness of the market structure* refers to the extent to which individual firms *lack* power to influence the price or other terms on which their products are sold.

Goodrich and Goodyear certainly engage in competitive behavior in the everyday sense of the term. It is also true that both individually and together they have some power over the market. Either firm could raise its prices and still continue to sell tires; each has the power to decide—within limits set by buyers' tastes and the prices of competing tires—what price consumers will pay for its product.

The Manitoba and the Saskatchewan wheat farmers do not engage in active competitive behavior with each other, in the everyday use of the term. They operate, however, in a market over which they have no power; neither has significant power to change the market price for its wheat by altering its behavior. They operate in a competitive market.

At one extreme of market structures, economists use a theory in which no single firm has any market power. There are so many firms that each must accept the price set by the forces of market demand and supply. In this theory of the *perfectly competitive market structure* there is no need for individual firms to behave competitively with respect to one another, since none has any power over the market. One firm's ability to sell its product does not depend on the behavior of any other firm. The distinction between interfirm competitive *behavior* and the competitive *structure* of the market in which the firm operates is the key to understanding the

otherwise puzzling statement that a firm in a perfectly competitive industry does not behave competitively in the everyday use of that term.

The theory of the perfectly competitive market structure applies directly to a number of real-world markets. It also provides a benchmark for comparison with other market structures in which there are so few firms that each has some market power.

The Significance of Market Structure

From the point of view of a buyer, the **market** consists of those firms from which it can buy a well-defined product; from the point of view of a firm, the market consists of those buyers to whom it can sell a well-defined product. A group of firms that sells a well-defined product, or closely related set of products, is said to constitute an **industry**. The market demand curve is the demand curve for an industry's product.[1]

Although market demand curves and cost curves of individual firms are the basic elements of the theory of product pricing, they are not themselves sufficient to provide a theory of price. Consider a firm that produces a specific product for sale in a particular market and competes for customers with other firms in the same industry. If it knows the demand curve it faces, it knows the price it could charge for each level of sales and thus knows its potential revenues. If it also knows its costs, the firm can readily calculate the profits that would be associated with any rate of output and can choose the rate that maximizes its profits.

But what if the firm only knows *its* costs and the *market* demand curve for its products? Because it does not know its *own* demand curve, it does not know what its own sales would be at any price it might charge. To know how its own demand would change as its own price is changed, it needs to know how other firms will respond. If it reduces its price by 10 percent, will other sellers also reduce

---

[1] An industry typically sells many different products and sells in many markets. For our elementary treatment, we shall focus attention on the single-product firm and the market in which that product is sold.

their prices? If so, by how much? Obviously, this will have an effect on the firm's sales and thus on its revenues and profits.

The relation of a firm's demand curve to the market demand curve also depends on such variables as the number of sellers in the market and the similarity of their products. For example, if there are only two large firms in an industry, each may be expected to meet most price cuts that the other makes; but if there are 5,000 small firms, a price cut by one may go unmatched. If two firms are producing identical products, they may be expected to behave differently with respect to each other than if they were producing similar but not identical products.

Market structure is defined as those characteristics of market organization that affect firms' behavior and performance. The number of sellers and the nature of the product are the most significant dimensions of market structure. There are others as well, such as the ease of entering the industry, the nature and size of the purchasers of the firm's products, and the firm's ability to influence demand by advertising. To reduce these aspects to manageable proportions, economists have focused on a few theoretical market structures that they believe represent a high proportion of the cases actually encountered in market societies. In this chapter and the next two, we shall look at four market structures: perfect competition, monopoly, monopolistic competition, and oligopoly.

Before considering any of these market structures, it is useful to deal with the rules of behavior common to all firms that seek to maximize profits.

Profit-Maximizing Behavior[2]

Marginal Revenue

A firm interested in maximizing its profits must look to its costs and its revenues. In Chapter 10 we defined *marginal cost* as the addition to the firm's

[2] Formal proofs of the propositions discussed in the text are given in the Mathematical Notes.

total cost caused by increasing the rate of production by one unit. It is now helpful to define a parallel revenue concept. **Marginal revenue** is the addition to the firm's total revenue caused by an increase in the rate of sales by one unit. So marginal revenue shows what the firm gains on the revenue side by selling a bit more (and what revenue it loses by selling a bit less).

Rule 1. The firm always has the option of producing nothing. If it exercises this option, it will have an operating loss equal to its fixed costs. If it decides to produce, it will add the variable cost of production to its fixed costs, and the receipts from the sale of its product to its revenue. Therefore, if there is some level of output for which revenue exceeds variable cost, it will pay the firm to produce; if, however, revenue is less than variable cost at every level of output, the firm will actually lose more by producing than by not producing.

A firm should not produce at all if the total revenue from selling its product does not equal or exceed the total variable cost of producing it. [20]

Rule 2. If a firm decides that, according to rule 1, production is worth undertaking, it must decide how much to produce. Common sense dictates that on a unit-by-unit basis, if any unit of production adds more to revenue than it does to cost, that unit will increase profits; if it adds more to cost than to revenue, it will decrease profits. If the firm is in a position where a further unit of production will increase profits, it should expand output. From this it follows that the only time it should leave its output unaltered is when the last unit produced adds the same amount to costs as it does to revenue.[3]

Assuming that it pays the firm to produce at all, it should produce where marginal revenue equals marginal cost. [21]

These rules apply to all profit-maximizing firms whatever the market structure in which they op-

[3] There is also a third rule that is needed to distinguish between profit-*maximizing* and profit-*minimizing* positions: The marginal cost curve should cut the marginal revenue curve from below. This rule is important in more advanced theorizing. [22]

erate. The rules refer to each firm's cost and own revenues. Before we can apply the rules we need to consider particular market structures in order to relate the demand curve for an industry's product and the demand curves—and thus the revenue curves—facing individual firms.

THE ELEMENTS OF THE THEORY OF PERFECT COMPETITION

The Assumptions of Perfect Competition

The theory of **perfect competition** is built on two critical assumptions, one about the behavior of the individual firm and one about the nature of the industry in which it operates.

The *firm* is assumed to be a **price taker;** that is, the firm is assumed to act as though it can alter its rate of production and sales within any feasible range without such action having a significant effect on the price of the product it sells. Thus, the firm must passively accept whatever price happens to be ruling on the market.

The *industry* is assumed to be characterized by **freedom of entry and exit;** that is, any new firm is free to set up production if it so wishes, and any existing firm is free to cease production and leave the industry. Existing firms cannot bar the entry of new firms, and there are no legal prohibitions on entry or exit.

The ultimate test of the theory based on these assumptions will be the usefulness of its predictions, but because students are often bothered by the first assumption, it is worth examining whether it is in any way reasonable. To do this, we contrast the demands for the products of an automobile manufacturer and a wheat farmer.

An automobile manufacturer. General Motors is aware that it has market power. If it substantially increases its prices, sales will fall off; if it lowers prices substantially, it will sell more of its products. If GM decides on a large increase in production that is not a response to a known or anticipated rise in demand, it will have to reduce prices in order to sell the extra output. The automobile man-

ufacturing firm is *not* a price taker. The quantity that it is able to sell will depend on the price it charges, but it does not have to accept passively whatever price is set by the market. In other words, the firm manufacturing automobiles is faced with a downward-sloping demand curve for its product. It may select any price-quantity combination consistent with that demand curve.

A wheat farmer. In contrast, an individual firm producing wheat is just one of a very large number of firms all growing the same product; one firm's contribution to the total production of wheat will be a tiny drop in an extremely large bucket. Ordinarily, the firm will assume that it has no effect on price and will think of its own demand curve as being horizontal. Of course, the firm can have *some* effect on price, but a straightforward calculation will show that the effect is small enough that the firm can justifiably neglect it.

The market elasticity of demand for wheat is approximately 0.25. This means that if the quantity of wheat supplied in the world increased by 1 percent, the price would have to fall by 4 percent to induce the world's wheat buyers to purchase the whole crop. Even huge farms produce a very small fraction of the total crop. In a recent year an extremely large Canadian wheat farm produced about 50,000 tons, only about 1/4,000 of total world production of 200 million tons. Suppose a large wheat farm increased its production by 20,000 tons, say from 40,000 to 60,000 tons. This would be a big percentage increase in its own production but an increase of only 1/100 of 1 percent in world production. Table 12-1 shows that this increase would lead to a decrease in the world price of 4/100 of 1 percent (4¢ in $100) and give the firm an elasticity of demand of 1,000! This is a very high elasticity of demand; the farm would have to increase its output 1,000 percent to bring about a 1 percent decrease in the price of wheat. Because the firm's output cannot be varied this much, it is not surprising that the firm regards the price of wheat to be unaffected by any change in output that it could conceivably make.

It is only a slight simplification to say that the firm is unable to influence the world price of wheat and that it is able to sell all that it can produce at

TABLE 12–1 THE CALCULATION OF A FIRM'S ELASTICITY OF DEMAND (η_F) FROM MARKET ELASTICITY OF DEMAND (η_M)

Given
$\eta_M = 0.25$
World output = 200 million tons
Firm's output increases from 40,000 to 60,000 tons, a 40% increase over the average quantity of 50,000 tons

Step 1. Find the percentage change in world price:

$$\eta_M = -\frac{\text{percentage change in world output}}{\text{percentage change in world price}} = 0.25$$

$$\text{Percentage change in world price} = -\frac{\text{percentage change in world output}}{\eta_M}$$

$$= -\frac{1/100 \text{ of } 1\%}{0.25}$$

$$= -4/100 \text{ of } 1\%$$

Step 2. Compute the firm's elasticity of demand:

$$\eta_F = -\frac{\text{percentage change in firm's output}}{\text{percentage change in world price}}$$

$$= -\frac{+40\%}{-4/100 \text{ of } 1\%} = +1,000$$

Because even a large change in output to the firm is a minute change in world wheat production, the effect on world price is very small. Thus the firm's elasticity of demand is high. This table relies on the concept of elasticity of demand developed in Chapter 5. Step 1 shows that a 40 percent increase in the firm's output leads to only a tiny decrease in the world's price. Thus, as step 2 shows, the firm's elasticity of demand is very high: 1,000.

The arithmetic is not important, but understanding why the wheat farm will be a price taker in these circumstances is vital.

the going world price. In other words, the firm is faced with a perfectly elastic demand curve for its product—it is a price taker.

The difference between General Motors and the wheat farmer is one of degree of market power. The wheat firm, as an insignificant part of the whole market, has no power to influence the world price of wheat. But the automobile firm does have power to influence the price of automobiles because its own production represents a significant part of the total supply of automobiles.

Demand and Revenue for the Perfectly Competitive Firm

The demand curve facing a single firm in perfect competition is horizontal because variations in its production over the range that we need to consider for all practical purposes will have a negligible ef-

fect on price. Of course, if the single firm increased its production by a vast amount, a thousandfold say, this might well cause a significant increase in supply and the firm would be unable to sell all it produced at the going price. The horizontal (perfectly elastic) demand curve does not mean that the firm could actually sell an infinite amount at the going price; rather, the variations in production *that it will normally be practicable for the firm to make* will leave price virtually unaffected. Figure 12-1 contrasts the demand curve for a competitive industry and for a single firm in that industry.

Total, Average, and Marginal Revenue

The notions of total, average, and marginal revenue are the demand counterparts of the notions of total, average, and marginal cost that we considered in Chapter 10. We focus now on the receipts to a seller from the sale of a product.

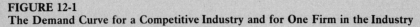

FIGURE 12-1
The Demand Curve for a Competitive Industry and for One Firm in the Industry

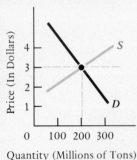

Quantity (Millions of Tons)

(i) Industry demand curve

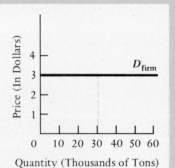

Quantity (Thousands of Tons)

(ii) Competitive firm's
       demand curve

The industry's demand curve is downward-sloping; the firm's demand curve is virtually horizontal. Notice the difference in the quantities shown on the horizontal scale in each part of the figure. The competitive industry is assumed to be operating at a level where price is equal to $3, producing approximately 200 million tons. The firm takes the market price as given to it and considers producing up to 60 thousand tons. The firm's demand curve in (ii) appears horizontal because of the change in the quantity scale compared to (i). The firm's output variation has only a tiny effect on industry output. If one plotted the industry demand curve from 199,970 thousand tons to 200,030 thousand tons on the scale used in (ii), the D curve would appear virtually horizontal.

Total revenue (*TR*) is the total amount received by the seller. If *q* units are sold at *p* dollars each, $TR = p \cdot q$. (The dot between *p* and *q* is a "times" sign, frequently used instead of $p \times q$, to avoid confusion with variables labeled *x*.)

Average revenue (*AR*) is the amount of revenue *per unit* sold: This is the price of the product.

*Marginal revenue (*MR*),* sometimes called incremental revenue, has already been defined. It is the change in total revenue resulting from an increase in the firm's rate of sales by one unit. [23]

Calculations of these revenue concepts for a price-taking firm are illustrated in Table 12-2. The table shows that as long as the firm's output does not affect the price of the product it sells, both average and marginal revenue will be equal to price at all levels of output. Thus, graphically (as is shown in Figure 12-2), average revenue and marginal revenue are both horizontal lines at the level of market price. Since the firm can sell any quantity it wishes at this price, the same horizontal line is also the *firm's* demand curve.

If the market price is unaffected by variations in the firm's output, then the firm's demand curve, the average revenue curve, and the marginal revenue curve coincide in the same horizontal line.

Total revenue, of course, does vary with output;

since price is constant, it follows that total revenue rises in direct proportion to output.

SHORT-RUN EQUILIBRIUM: FIRM AND INDUSTRY

The Firm's Equilibrium Output

In perfect competition the firm is a price taker and can adjust to varying market conditions only by

TABLE 12–2 REVENUE CONCEPTS FOR A PRICE-TAKING FIRM

Price p	Quantity q	$TR = p \cdot q$	$AR = TR/q$	$MR = \Delta TR/\Delta q$
$3.00	10	$30.00	$3.00	
3.00	11	33.00	3.00	$3.00
3.00	12	36.00	3.00	3.00
3.00	13	39.00	3.00	3.00

When price is fixed, $AR = MR = p$. Marginal revenue is shown between the lines because it represents the change in total revenue (e.g., from $33 to $36) in reponse to a change in quantity (from 11 to 12 units),

$$MR = \frac{36 - 33}{12 - 11} = \$3 \text{ per unit}$$

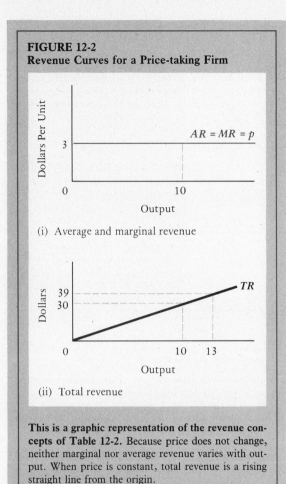

FIGURE 12-2
Revenue Curves for a Price-taking Firm

(i) Average and marginal revenue

(ii) Total revenue

This is a graphic representation of the revenue concepts of Table 12-2. Because price does not change, neither marginal nor average revenue varies with output. When price is constant, total revenue is a rising straight line from the origin.

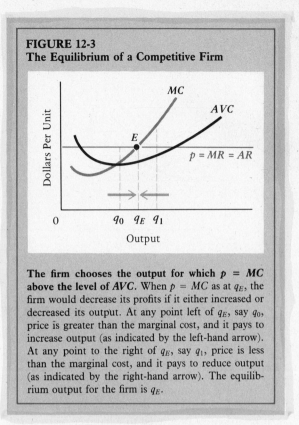

FIGURE 12-3
The Equilibrium of a Competitive Firm

The firm chooses the output for which $p = MC$ above the level of AVC. When $p = MC$ as at q_E, the firm would decrease its profits if it either increased or decreased its output. At any point left of q_E, say q_0, price is greater than the marginal cost, and it pays to increase output (as indicated by the left-hand arrow). At any point to the right of q_E, say q_1, price is less than the marginal cost, and it pays to reduce output (as indicated by the right-hand arrow). The equilibrium output for the firm is q_E.

changing the quantity it produces. In the short run it has fixed factors, and the only way to vary its output is by using more or less of those factors that it can vary. Thus, the firm's short-run cost curves are relevant to its output decision.

We saw earlier that any profit-maximizing firm will seek to produce at the level of output at which marginal cost equals marginal revenue. In the immediately preceding section we saw that a perfectly competitive firm's demand and marginal revenue curves coincide in the same horizontal line whose height represents the price of the product.

For a perfectly competitive firm, marginal revenue equals price.

It follows immediately that a perfectly competitive firm will equate its marginal cost of production to the market price of its product (as long as price exceeds average variable cost).

The market determines the price at which the firm sells its product. The firm picks the quantity of output that maximizes its profits. This is the output for which $p = MC$. When the firm is maximizing profits, it has no incentive to change its output. Therefore, unless prices or costs change, the firm will continue producing this output because it is doing as well as it can do, given the situation. The firm is said to be in **short-run equilibrium,** which is illustrated in Figure 12-3.

The perfectly competitive firm is a quantity adjuster. It pursues its goal of profit maximization by increasing or decreasing quantity until it equates its short-run marginal cost with the prevailing price of its product—a price that is given to it by the market.

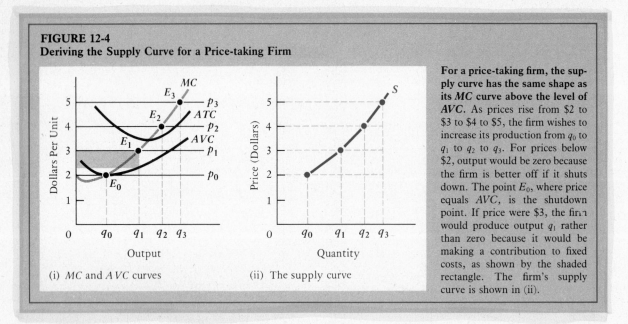

FIGURE 12-4
Deriving the Supply Curve for a Price-taking Firm

(i) *MC* and *AVC* curves

(ii) The supply curve

For a price-taking firm, the supply curve has the same shape as its *MC* curve above the level of *AVC*. As prices rise from \$2 to \$3 to \$4 to \$5, the firm wishes to increase its production from q_0 to q_1 to q_2 to q_3. For prices below \$2, output would be zero because the firm is better off if it shuts down. The point E_0, where price equals *AVC*, is the shutdown point. If price were \$3, the firm would produce output q_1 rather than zero because it would be making a contribution to fixed costs, as shown by the shaded rectangle. The firm's supply curve is shown in (ii).

The market price to which the perfectly competitive firm responds is itself set by the forces of demand and supply. The individual firm, by adjusting quantity produced to whatever price is ruling on the market, helps to determine market supply. The link between the behavior of the firm and the behavior of the competitive market is provided by the market supply curve.

Short-Run Supply Curves

The Supply Curve of One Firm

Figure 12-4(i) shows a firm's marginal cost curve with four alternative levels of price. Each such price line is the firm's demand curve *if* the market price is at that level. The firm's marginal cost curve gives the marginal cost corresponding to each level of output. We require a supply curve that shows the quantity the firm will supply at every price. For prices below *AVC*, the firm will supply zero units (rule 1). For prices above *AVC*, the firm will equate price and marginal cost (rule 2 modified by

the proposition that $MR = p$ in perfect competition). From this it follows that

In perfect competition the firm's supply curve is identical to its marginal cost curve above *AVC*.

The Supply Curve of an Industry

Figure 12-5 illustrates the derivation of an industry supply curve for an example of only two firms. The general result is that

In perfect competition the industry supply curve is the horizontal sum of the marginal cost curves (above the level of average variable cost) of all firms in the industry.

The reason for this is that each firm's marginal cost curve tells us how much that firm will supply at each given market price, and the industry supply curve is the sum of what each firm will supply. This supply curve, based on the short-run marginal cost curves of the firms in the industry, is the industry's **short-run supply curve.**

In Part Two we used short-run industry supply curves as an important part of our analysis. We

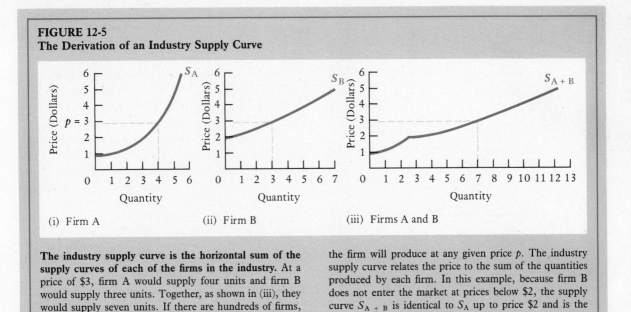

FIGURE 12-5
The Derivation of an Industry Supply Curve

(i) Firm A (ii) Firm B (iii) Firms A and B

The industry supply curve is the horizontal sum of the supply curves of each of the firms in the industry. At a price of $3, firm A would supply four units and firm B would supply three units. Together, as shown in (iii), they would supply seven units. If there are hundreds of firms, the process is the same: Each firm's supply curve (which is derived in the manner shown in Figure 12-4) shows what the firm will produce at any given price p. The industry supply curve relates the price to the sum of the quantities produced by each firm. In this example, because firm B does not enter the market at prices below $2, the supply curve $S_{A + B}$ is identical to S_A up to price $2 and is the sum of $S_A + S_B$ above $2.

have now derived these short-run curves for competitive industries and shown how they are related to the behavior of individual profit-maximizing firms.

Producers' Surplus

In Chapter 7 we defined the concept of consumers' surplus in connection with a downward-sloping demand curve. (See Figure 7-4 and the discussion in the text accompanying it.) There is a corresponding concept called producers' surplus which occurs in connection with an upward-sloping short-run supply curve. **Producers' surplus** is the difference between the amount producers are paid for all units sold of a commodity and the aggregate minimum amount they would have required to produce each successive unit. The supply curve shows the price required to produce each unit of output. As Figure 12-6 illustrates, in a competitive market with a rising supply curve all units except the last one produced earn for the firm a price greater than

the amount required to produce them in the short run. The sum of these excesses of price over supply price constitutes the producers' surplus; graphically, it is the area above the supply curve and between the market price line. This shows the amount by which total revenues received exceed total *variable* cost. It is available to meet depreciation and other fixed costs and to provide a return to invested capital.

The Determination of Short-Run Equilibrium Price

The industry short-run supply curve and demand curve together determine the market price. (This happens in the manner analyzed in Chapter 4.) Although no one firm can influence market price significantly, the collective actions of all firms in the industry (as shown by the industry supply curve) and the collective actions of households (as shown by the industry demand curve) together de-

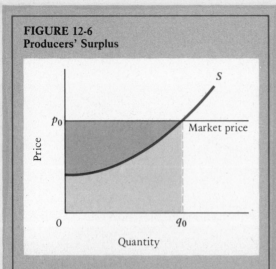

FIGURE 12-6
Producers' Surplus

Total producers' surplus is the area above the supply curve and under the price line. The short-run supply curve shows the amount producers would have to be paid to produce each unit of output. The area under the supply curve (the light shaded area) shows the minimum amount—their total variable costs—they would require if forced to sell their units one by one. If the market price is p_0 and q_0 is sold, producers receive the price p_0 for all units; graphically this is shown by both the light and dark shaded areas. The dark shaded area is the producers' surplus and represents the excess of revenue over variable costs received by producers.

termine market price at the point where the demand and supply curves intersect.

At the equilibrium market price, each firm is producing and selling a quantity for which its marginal cost equals the market price. No firm is motivated to change its output in the short run. Since total quantity demanded equals total quantity supplied, there is no reason for market price to change in the short run; the market and all the firms in the industry are in short-run equilibrium.

Short-Run Profitability of the Firm

Although we know that when the industry is in short-run equilibrium the competitive firm is max-

imizing its profits, we do not know *how large* these profits are. It is one thing to know that a firm is doing as well as it can in particular circumstances; it is another to know how well it is doing.

Figure 12-7 shows three possible positions for a firm in short-run equilibrium. In all cases, the firm is maximizing its profits by producing where $p = MC$, but in (i) the firm is making losses, in (ii) it is just covering all costs, and in (iii) it is making profits in excess of all costs. In (i) it might be better to say that the firm is minimizing its losses rather than maximizing its profits, but both statements mean the same thing. The firm is doing as well as it can, given its costs and prices.

LONG-RUN EQUILIBRIUM

While Figure 12-7 shows three possible short-run equilibrium positions for the profit-maximizing firm in perfect competition, not all of them are possible equilibrium positions in the long run.

The Effect of Entry and Exit

The key to long-run equilibrium under perfect competition is entry and exit. We have seen that when firms are in *short-run* equilibrium, they may be making profits or losses or just breaking even. Since costs include the opportunity cost of capital, firms that are just breaking even are doing as well as they could if they invested their capital elsewhere. Thus there will be no incentive for existing firms to leave the industry; neither will there be an incentive for new firms to enter the industry, for capital can earn the same return elsewhere in the economy. If, however, existing firms are earning profits in excess of the opportunity cost of capital, new capital will enter the industry to share in these profits. If existing firms are making losses, capital will leave the industry because a better return can be obtained elsewhere in the economy. Let us consider the process in a little more detail.

If all firms in the competitive industry are in the position of the firm in Figure 12-7(iii), new firms

FIGURE 12-7
Alternative Short-Run Equilibrium Positions of a Competitive Firm

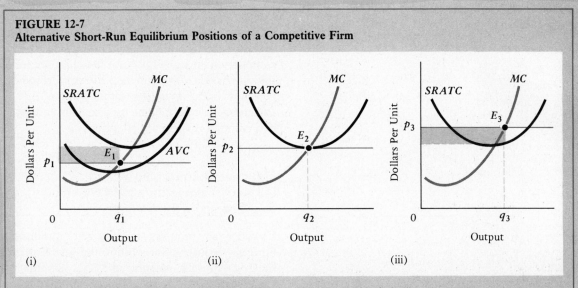

When it is in short-run equilibrium, a competitive firm may be suffering losses, breaking even, or making profits. The diagrams show a firm with given costs faced with three alternative prices p_1, p_2, and p_3. In each part of the diagram, E is the point at which $MC = MR$ = price. Since in all three cases price exceeds AVC, the firm is in short-run equilibrium.

In (i) price is p_1 and the firm is suffering losses, shown by the color shaded area, because price is below average total cost. Since price exceeds average variable cost, it pays the firm to keep producing, but it does *not* pay it to replace its capital equipment as the capital wears out.

In (ii) price is p_2 and the firm is just covering its total costs. It does pay the firm to replace its capital as it wears out since it is covering full opportunity cost of its capital.

In (iii) price is p_3 and the firm is earning profits, shown by the gray shaded area, in excess of all its costs.

will enter the industry, attracted by the profitability of existing firms. Suppose that in response to high profits for 100 existing firms, 20 new firms enter. The market supply curve that formerly added up the outputs of 100 firms now must add up the outputs of 120 firms. At any price, more will be supplied because there are more producers.

This shift in the short-run supply curve, with an unchanged market demand curve, means that the previous equilibrium price will no longer prevail. The shift in supply will lower the equilibrium price, and both new and old firms will have to adjust their output to this new price. This is illustrated in Figure 12-8. New firms will continue to enter and price will continue to fall until all firms in the industry are just covering their total costs. Firms will then be in the position of the firm in

Figure 12-7(ii), which is called a *zero-profit equilibrium.*

Profits in a competitive industry are a signal for the entry of new capital; the industry will expand, forcing price down until the profits fall to zero.

If the firms in the industry are in the position of the firm in Figure 12-7(i), they are suffering losses. They are covering their variable costs, but the return on their capital is less than the opportunity cost of this capital; the firms are not covering their total costs. This is a signal for the exit of firms. As plant and equipment are discarded, they will not be replaced. As a result, the industry's short-run supply curve shifts left and market price rises. Firms will continue to exit and price will continue to rise until the remaining firms can cover

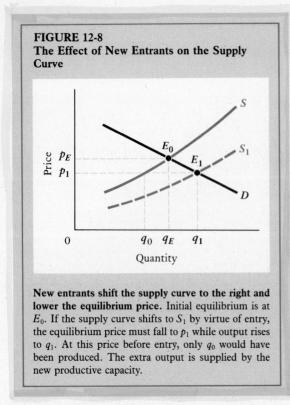

FIGURE 12-8
The Effect of New Entrants on the Supply Curve

New entrants shift the supply curve to the right and lower the equilibrium price. Initial equilibrium is at E_0. If the supply curve shifts to S_1 by virtue of entry, the equilibrium price must fall to p_1 while output rises to q_1. At this price before entry, only q_0 would have been produced. The extra output is supplied by the new productive capacity.

their total costs—that is, until they are all in the zero-profit equilibrium illustrated in Figure 12-7(ii). Exit then ceases.

Losses in a competitive industry are a signal for the exit of capital; the industry will contract, driving price up until the remaining firms are covering their total costs.

In all of this we see profits serving their function of allocating resources among the industries of the economy.

Cost in Long-Run Equilibrium

An industry is nothing more than a collection of firms; for an industry to be in long-run equilibrium, each firm must be in long-run equilibrium. It follows that when a perfectly competitive industry is in long-run equilibrium, all firms in the in-

dustry will be selling at a price equal to minimum average total cost—that is, they must be in zero-profit equilibrium, as in Figure 12-7(ii). This result plays an important role in the appeal of perfect competition to economists, as we shall see. (Further discussion of costs in long-run equilibrium will be found in the appendix to this chapter.)

The theory can now be used to help understand two commonly observed situations.

The Long-Run Response of a Perfectly Competitive Industry to a Change in Technology

Consider an industry in long-run equilibrium. Since the industry is in equilibrium, each firm must be in zero-profit equilibrium. Now assume that some technological development lowers the cost curves of newly built plants. Since price is just equal to the average total cost for the old plants, new plants will now be able to earn profits, and more of them will now be built. But this expansion in capacity shifts the short-run supply curve to the right and drives price down.

The expansion in capacity and the fall in price will continue until price is equal to the *SRATC* of the *new* plants. At this price, old plants will not be covering their long-run costs. As long as price exceeds their average variable cost, however, such plants will continue in production. As the outmoded plants wear out, they will gradually disappear. Eventually a new long-run equilibrium will be established in which all plants use the new technology.

What happens in a competitive industry in which technological change occurs not as a single isolated event, but more or less continuously? Plants built in any one year will tend to have lower costs than plants built in any previous year.[4] This

---

[4] This statement refers to real resource costs, which tend to fall due to technological change. Of course, in times of general inflation, *money* costs of plants may well be rising. In the comparisons made here, we are assuming that costs have been adjusted for changes in the general price level.

FIGURE 12-9
Plants of Different Vintages in an Industry with Continuing Technical Progress

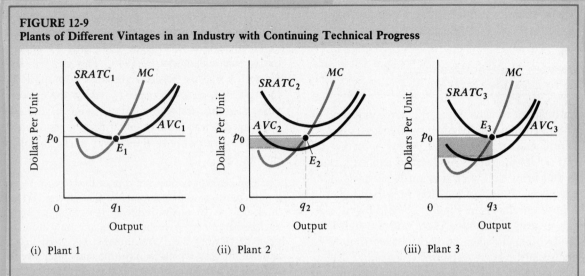

(i) Plant 1   (ii) Plant 2   (iii) Plant 3

Entry of progressively lower-cost firms forces price down, but older plants with higher costs remain in the industry as long as price covers average variable cost. Plant 3 is the newest plant with the lowest costs. Long-run equilibrium price will be determined by the average total costs of plants of this type since entry will continue as long as the owners of the newest plants expect to earn profits from them. Plant 1 is the oldest plant in operation; it is just covering its AVC, and if the price falls any further it will be closed down. Plant 2 is a plant of intermediate age. It is covering its variable costs and earning some contribution toward its fixed costs. In (ii) and (iii), the shaded area shows the excess of revenues over variable costs.

is a common occurrence; it is illustrated in Figure 12-9.

Industries subject to continuous technological change have a number of interesting characteristics. One is that plants of different ages and different levels of efficiency will exist side by side. Critics who observe the continued use of older, less efficient plants and urge that "something be done to eliminate these wasteful practices" miss the point of economic efficiency.

If the plant is already there, the plant can be profitably operated as long as it can do anything more than cover its variable costs. As long as a plant can produce goods that are valued by consumers at an amount above the value of the resources currently used up for their production (variable costs), the value of society's total output is increased by using that plant to produce goods.

A second characteristic of such an industry is that price will be governed by *the minimum ATC of the most efficient plants.* Entry will continue until plants of the latest vintage are just expected to earn normal profits over their lifetimes. The benefits of the new technology are passed on to consumers because all units of the commodity, whether produced by new or old plants, are sold at a price that is related solely to the *ATC* of the new plants. Owners of older plants find their returns over variable costs falling steadily as more and more efficient plants drive the price of the product down.

A third characteristic is that old plants will be discarded (or "mothballed") when the price falls below their *AVC*. This may occur well before the plants are physically worn out. In industries with continuous technical progress, capital is usually discarded because it is *economically obsolete,* not because it has physically worn out. Old capital is obsolete when its average variable cost exceeds the average total cost of new capital.

Industries That Are Declining Due to a Steady Decrease in Demand

What happens when a competitive industry in long-run equilibrium begins to suffer losses due to a permanent and continuing decrease in the demand for its products? As demand declines, price falls and firms that were previously covering *ATC* are not now able to do so. They find themselves in the position shown in Figure 12-7(i). Firms earn losses instead of breaking even, and the signal for exit of capital is given. But exit takes time. The economically correct response to a steadily declining demand is to not replace old equipment and to continue to operate with existing equipment as long as variable costs of production can be covered.

Gradually, equipment will break down and not be repaired or replaced. The capacity of the industry will shrink, slowly at first. If demand keeps declining, capacity must keep shrinking.

Declining industries typically present a sorry sight to the observer. Revenues are below long-run total costs, and as a result new equipment is not brought in to replace old equipment as it wears out. The average age of equipment in use thus rises steadily. The untrained observer seeing the industry's very real plight is likely to blame it on the antiquated equipment in use.

The antiquated equipment in a declining industry is the effect rather than the cause of the industry's decline.

It would not usually make sense for firms to modernize in the face of steadily falling demand even when new, improved equipment is available. To do so would increase the industry's capacity and its output, thereby making its overall plight still worse. Price would fall even more rapidly, adding further to the losses of existing firms.

A striking example of the confusion of cause and effect in a declining industry occurred during the debate over the nationalization of the coal industry in Great Britain in the period between the two world wars. The view that public control was needed to save the industry from the dead hand of third-rate, unenterprising private owners was commonly held and was undoubtedly a factor leading to its nationalization in 1946. The late Sir Roy Harrod, a leading British economist from the 1920s to the 1960s, shocked many by taking the opposite view, arguing that the rundown state of the coal industry in some parts of Great Britain represented the correct response of the owners to the signals of the market.

Economic efficiency does not consist in always introducing the most up-to-date equipment that an engineer can think of. . . . In not introducing new equipment, the managements may have been wise, not only from the point of view of their own interest, but from that of national interest, which requires the most profitable application of available capital . . . it is right that as much should be extracted from the inferior mines as can be done by old-fashioned methods [i.e., with equipment already installed], and that they should gradually go out of action.[5]

The general point that Professor Harrod makes is extremely important. Capital resources are scarce; to install new plant and equipment in a genuinely declining industry is to use scarce resources where they will not lead to the largest possible increases in the value of output. It is in the public and the private interest that what appear to be antiquated methods be employed in declining industries.

Problems with policies to prop up declining industries are further discussed in Box 12-1.

THE APPEAL OF PERFECT COMPETITION

The theory of perfect competition shows that profit-maximizing price-taking firms, responding to prices set by the impersonal forces of supply and demand, will be motivated to provide all commodities for which total revenues are equal to or greater

[5] Roy Harrod, *The British Economy* (New York: McGraw-Hill, 1963), page 54.

than total costs. They will be motivated to produce every unit for which price is greater than marginal cost, and they will thus expand production up to the point where price equals marginal cost. The entry and exit of firms will, in long-run equilibrium, push prices to the level of minimum average total costs—that is, to the lowest level attainable for the given technology and factor prices.

Consider an economy in which every industry operates as a perfectly competitive industry. For the nineteenth century liberal economists, such a world was more than a theoretical model, it was a most attractive ideal. One of them, Bascom, glowingly characterized such an economic system as "more provocative of virtue than virtue herself." The appeal of a competitive economy has both noneconomic and economic aspects.

The Noneconomic Appeal of Competition

In a perfectly competitive economy, there are many firms and many households. Each is a price taker, responding as it sees fit, freely and without coercion, to signals sent to it by the market. For one who believes in the freedom of individuals to make decisions and who distrusts all power groups, the perfectly competitive model is almost too good to be true. No single firm and no single consumer has any power over the market. Individual consumers and producers are quantity adjusters who respond to market signals.

Yet the impersonal force of the market produces an appropriate response to all changes. If tastes change, for example, prices will change, and the allocation of resources will change in the appropriate direction. Throughout the entire process, no one will have any power over anyone else. Dozens of firms will react to the same price changes, and if one firm refuses to react, there will be countless other profit-maximizing firms eager to make the appropriate changes.

Because the market mechanism works, it is not necessary for the government to intervene. Market reactions, not public policies, will eliminate short-

ages or surpluses. There is no need for government regulatory agencies or bureaucrats to make arbitrary decisions about who may produce what, how to produce it, or how much it is permissible to charge for the product. If there are no government officials to make such decisions, there will be no one to bribe to make one decision rather than another.

In the impersonal decision-making world of perfect competition, neither private firms nor public officials wield economic power. The market mechanisms, like an invisible hand, determines the allocation of resources among competing uses.

It is a noble model: no one has power over anyone, and yet the system behaves in a systematic and purposeful way. Many will feel that it is a pity that it corresponds so imperfectly to economic reality as we know it today. Not surprisingly, some people still cling tenaciously to the belief that the perfectly competitive model describes the world in which we live; so many problems would disappear if only it did.

The Economic Appeal of Perfect Competition: Efficiency

The Concept of Inefficiency

Resources are scarce relative to the wants of society's members, so it is desirable not to waste them. When labor is unemployed and factories lie idle (as occurs in serious recessions), their potential current output is lost. If these resources could be reemployed, total output would be increased and hence everyone could be made better off.

But full employment of resources by itself is not enough to prevent the waste of resources. Even when resources are being fully used, they may be used inefficiently. Let us look at three possible sources of inefficiency in resource use.

1. If firms do not use the least costly method of producing their chosen outputs, they will waste resources. For example, in a firm that achieves its monthly production of 30,000 pairs of shoes at a resource cost of $400,000 when it could be done at

BOX 12–1 GOVERNMENT SUPPORT OF THREATENED FIRMS

Troubled industrial giants pose serious concerns for policymakers. Whether it be the Chrysler Corporation, Massey Ferguson, or a large textile firm, the threatened bankruptcy of such a company often calls forth a government policy to support that company. Bankruptcy means that the firm has not been able to meet its financial obligations, and its creditors—both its suppliers and those who have lent it money—foreclose. In considering potential government support, it is useful to distinguish three different cases.

Firms That Can Cover Variable Costs

What is often forgotten is that real capital equipment does not crumble away just because a firm goes bankrupt. A company may get into financial difficulties for many reasons. It may have been mismanaged, or the demand for its product may have declined. It may be able to cover its variable costs, but be unable to meet its debt obligations. As long as the real capital can cover its variable costs of operation, someone will find its operation profitable.

If such a firm goes bankrupt, its shareholders—and possibly also its creditors—will suffer the initial losses. The firm, however, will be reorganized. Its capital will continue to operate, and it will continue to employ workers. Some cutbacks and firings may be involved in making the firm once again viable. As long as it can earn anything above its variable costs, the firm's creditors can operate it and regain some of what the firm owes them.

When the government steps in to save such a firm from bankruptcy, it is common for policymakers to say they are doing this to save jobs. The government is really saving the investments of the owners and creditors of the firm, not the jobs of the work force.

Firms That Cannot Cover Variable Costs

Sometimes firms that go bankrupt find they are no longer able to cover even their variable costs of production. They will then go out of business, and all their employees will lose their jobs.

As growth proceeds, the pattern of demands and costs shifts; some industries decline and others expand. So we can always expect to find declining industries, and in them firms that are closing their doors and creating unemployment. However, we can also expect to find expanding industries, and in them growing firms that are seeking to expand their employment.

When the government steps in and supports the declining industries, the consequences can be serious. The nation's scarce resources are wasted when they are used to produce goods that consumers value less than the cost of the variable inputs that make up those goods.

To prop up declining industries is to reduce

a cost of only $350,000, resources are being used inefficiently. If the lower cost method were used, $50,000 worth of other commodities could be produced each month by transferring the resources saved to their best alternative use.

2. If some firms are too large and others too small, each will not be producing at the lowest point on its long-run average cost curve. Thus any given level of the industry's production will use more resources than is necessary.

3. If too much of one product and too little of another is produced, resources are also being used inefficiently. To take an extreme example, say that so many shoes were produced that their *marginal* utility was zero, while the marginal utility of coats remained high at the current level of output. Since

the growth rate by preventing the factors of production—labor and capital—from moving to sectors that are growing. To attempt to freeze a particular industrial pattern in a changing world is to impose heavy and growing costs on the economy and in the end to attempt an impossible task.

Regional Policy

The third major reason for supporting industries that are unable to stand on their own relates to regional policy. Industries are sometimes subsidized because policymakers believe that living standards in these areas would otherwise be too low. In effect this represents a transfer of income in the form of a subsidy from wealthier areas to poorer areas. Although this may appeal to many of us in the interests of justice, the subsidizing of inefficient industries nevertheless represents an inefficient way to effect the income transfer. The payment of direct transfers where the recipients may then spend the money as they wish is usually a more efficient method. However, this is often less popular because it creates a direct gift rather than a chance to be employed (even though the employment is not efficient from the nation's point of view).

It is quite possible for a well-to-do major part of the country to subsidize a less well-to-do smaller part of the country (small in terms of population and resources)—as, for example, when the rest of Canada subsidizes industries in the Maritimes. Whether or not this is efficient, the policy will not "break the bank." But if a major part of the country's industry, such as the industrial sector of Quebec and Ontario, were to be subsidized in the same way, the burden would quickly become intolerable.

Experience shows that propping up declining industries in the end succeeds not in saving them, but only in delaying their demise—at large national costs. And when the government finally withdraws its support, the decline is much more abrupt and hence more difficult to adjust to than it would have been had the industry been allowed to decline gradually under the market force of steadily declining demand.

One can only hope that governments recognize that the decay of certain industries and the collapse of certain firms is an inevitable part of growth. The appropriate response is to provide welfare and retraining schemes that cushion the blow of change, moderating the effects on the incomes of those who lose their jobs and making it easier for them to retrain and transfer to expanding sectors of the economy. Appropriate intervention intended to increase mobility and reduce the social and personal costs of mobility is a viable long-run policy. To try to freeze the existing structure by shoring up the inevitably declining industry is not.

---

no one places any value on the last pair of shoes produced, while someone does place a high value on an additional coat, no one will be made worse off by reducing the output of shoes, yet someone will be made better off by using the resources to increase the production of coats.

These examples suggest that we must refine our ideas of the waste of resources beyond the simple notion of ensuring that all resources are used. Economists define rather precisely what is meant by efficiency and inefficiency in resource use.

Resources are said to be used *inefficiently* when it would be *possible* by using them differently to make at least one household better off without making any household worse off. Conversely, resources are said to be used *efficiently* when it is impossible by using them differently to make any one household better off without making at least one other household worse off.

Efficiency in the use of resources is often called **Pareto-efficiency** or **Pareto-optimality** in honor of the great Italian economist Vilfredo Pareto (1848–1923), who pioneered in the study of efficiency.

So much for the meaning of efficiency; now how do we achieve it? The three sources of inefficiency numbered above suggest important conditions that must be fulfilled if economic efficiency is to be attained.

Productive Efficiency

The first condition of economic efficiency is that output must be produced at the lowest possible cost of production. This condition is defined as **productive efficiency.** It implies, first, that every firm be on its long-run average cost curve. If this condition is not met, there is (by definition) a less costly way for that firm to produce at that given output level. It further implies that industry output is produced as cheaply as possible. If one firm is producing "too little" output—that is, producing along the downward-sloping part of its *LRAC* curve—and another firm is producing "too much" output—that is, producing more than is required to achieve the minimum level of average total cost—then industry costs can be decreased by having the first firm produce more and the second firm produce less. If in equilibrium all firms are producing at the minimum points of their long-run average cost curves, both implications of productive efficiency have been met. As we saw above, a perfectly competitive industry in long-run equilibrium meets these conditions.

A competitive industry in long-run equilibrium satisfies the condition of productive efficiency. The product is produced as cheaply as possible.

Allocative Efficiency

Productive efficiency avoids the first two sources of inefficiency mentioned above. The third source concerns the appropriate mix of products. Resources must be allocated among the various goods, and they are not being used efficiently when they are being used to produce products that no one wants. **Allocative efficiency** obtains when it is impossible to change the allocation of resources in such a way as to make someone better off without making someone else worse off.

What is the right mix? How many shoes and how many coats should be produced for allocative efficiency? The answer is that (under certain conditions that we shall specify later) the allocation of resources to any one commodity is efficient when its price is equal to its marginal cost of production, that is, $p = MC$.

This rather subtle condition has been one of the most influential ideas in the whole of economics. To understand it, we need to remind ourselves of two points established earlier: First, the price of any commodity indicates the value that each household places on the last unit of the commodity that it consumes (per period); second, marginal cost indicates the value that the resources used to produce the marginal unit of output would have in their best alternative uses.

The first proposition follows directly from marginal utility theory (see page 110). A household will go on increasing its rate of consumption of a commodity until the *marginal* valuation that it puts on the commodity is equal to its price. The household gets a consumers' surplus on all units but the marginal unit because it values them more than the price it has to pay. On the marginal unit, however, it only "breaks even" because the valuation placed on it is just equal to its price.

The second proposition follows from the nature of opportunity cost (see pages 147–148). The marginal cost of producing some commodity is the opportunity cost of the resources used. Opportunity cost reflects the value of the resources in their best alternative uses.

To see how these propositions fit together, assume that shoes sell for $30 a pair but have a marginal production cost of $40. If one less pair of shoes were produced, the value that households place on the pair of shoes not produced would be $30. But by the meaning of opportunity cost, the resources that would have been used to produce that pair of shoes could instead produce other goods (say a coat) valued at $40. If society can give up something its members value at $30 and get in return something its members value at $40, the original allocation of resources is inefficient. Someone can be made better off, and no one need be worse off.

This is easy to see when the same household gives up the shoes and gets the coat. But it follows even when different households are involved, for the gaining household could compensate the losing household and still come out ahead.

Assume next that shoe production is cut back until the price of a pair of shoes rises from $30 to $35 while its marginal cost falls from $40 to $35. The efficiency condition is now fulfilled in shoe production because $p = MC = \$35$. Now if one less pair of shoes were produced, $35 worth of shoes would be sacrificed while at most $35 worth of other commodities could be produced with the freed resources.

In this situation the allocation of resources to shoe production is efficient because it is not possible to change it and make someone better off without making someone else worse off. If one household were to sacrifice the pair of shoes, it would give up goods worth $35 and would then have to get all of the new production of the alternative commodity produced just to break even. It cannot gain without making another household worse off. The same argument can be repeated for every commodity, and it leads to this conclusion:

The allocation of resources is efficient when each commodity's price equals its marginal cost.

Allocative efficiency is thus satisfied when $p = MC$ in all industries. This is given a graphic interpretation in Box 12-2. Since in perfect competition, $p = MC$ in equilibrium:

Universal perfect competition fulfills the condition for allocative efficiency by ensuring that price equals marginal cost in every industry.

Some Words of Warning About the Efficiency of Perfect Competition

An economy that consisted of perfectly competitive industries would in equilibrium achieve allocative and productive efficiency. This is because the forces of competition push equilibrium price to the level where $p = MC = ATC$.

Before jumping to the conclusion that perfect competition is the best of all possible worlds and that government policy ought to do everything possible to achieve it, we must consider certain qualifications. Four will be mentioned here, to be developed in later chapters.

Costs may be higher under perfect competition than under alternative market structures. In a competitive industry, production occurs at the lowest level of cost attainable by the competitive firm. But it is possible, for example, that firms in a perfectly competitive industry may not innovate as rapidly as firms in another industry structure, and thus the cost of producing the competitive output will not be as low as it might be.

This matter is discussed more fully in Chapters 13, 14, and 16.

Perfect competition may not pertain simultaneously everywhere in the economy. Our argument about allocative efficiency rested on $p = MC$ everywhere in the economy. But there are many industries in which price does not and cannot equal marginal cost. (The reasons will be explored in Chapter 15.) In these circumstances there is no general presumption of what the effect will be of prices equaling marginal costs *somewhere* in the economy. Thus, if price does not equal marginal cost in industry A, the fact that $p = MC$ in industry B may not lead to allocative efficiency.

This proposition illustrates what is known as the "theory of the second best": We may know how to identify the best of all possible worlds (from the limited point of view of the optimum we are discussing), but we may have a harder task when attempting to rank two situations in the very imperfect world in which we live.

Private costs may be poor measures of society's costs. Producing a good up to the point at which the price just equals the *firm's* marginal cost is efficient from society's point of view only if the firm's private costs reflect the opportunity costs to

BOX 12–2 A GRAPHIC INTERPRETATION OF ALLOCATIVE EFFICIENCY

Consider a competitive industry where forces of demand and supply establish a competitive price. Because the industry supply curve represents the sum of the marginal cost curves of the firms in the industry, the market clearing price is one at which $p = MC$. In the figure, such a price is shown as p^*, and the corresponding output is q^*. For every unit produced up to this output, the value consumers would be willing to pay (as shown by the demand curve) is greater than the opportunity cost of the resources used to produce it (as shown by the $S = MC$ curve).

Consider the gray shaded areas. The light gray shaded area between the demand curve and the price line is what we have defined as the *consumers' surplus* associated with output q^* (see pages 116–117). The dark gray shaded area above the supply curve and below the price line is the *producers' surplus* associated with the output q^*.

Allocative efficiency is achieved when the *sum* of the surpluses is maximized. This occurs at the output q^*, where $p = MC$. For any output less than q^*, such as q_1, a slight increase in output toward q^* would lead to an addition to both consumers' and producers' surplus. This is because at the level of output q_1 consumers' valuation of the commodity (shown by the de-

mand curve) exceeds the opportunity cost of producing it (shown by the supply curve).

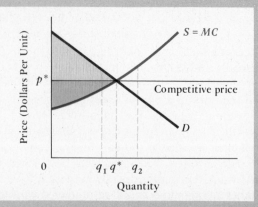

For any output greater than q^*, such as q_2, this is not the case. For every unit beyond q^*, the demand curve (what consumers would pay) is below the supply curve (what producers must be paid). Extra units beyond q^* would subtract from both producers' and consumers' surpluses.

Producers' plus consumers' surplus is maximized *only* at output q^*, which is thus the only output that is allocatively efficient. If some invisible authority wanted producers to "maximize the sum of producers' and consumers' surplus," it would instruct producers to produce every unit up to q^*. The perfectly competitive market price, p^*, provides exactly that signal!

society of using the resources elsewhere. As we shall see in Chapter 24, this is often not the case because of what are called *externalities*. For example, if the competitive firm uses resources it does not pay for (such as the clean air around its factories), it may produce too much output and too much pollution to be efficient. It does so because *its* own marginal costs fail to include the value that members of society place on some of the resources (clean air) the firm uses up.

Efficiency is not the only goal. A competitive economy distributes output as well as produces it. A freely functioning competitive economy might produce a distribution of income consisting of one millionaire and 999 paupers. Such an economy may be more efficient than an economy with 1,000 persons of roughly equal income. Before one can speak of a competitive economy as being "virtuous," one must consider goals other than efficiency. This matter is discussed further in Chapter 24.

SUMMARY

1. Market behavior is concerned with whether and how individual firms compete against one another; market structure is concerned with the type of market firms operate in. Market structure affects the degree of power that individual firms have to influence such market variables as the price of the product. Under the market structure known as perfect competition, individual firms are price takers. Therefore they do not have any incentive to indulge in competitive behavior against other producers in the same industry.

2. A profit-maximizing firm will produce at a level of output where (a) price is at least as great as average variable cost, and (b) marginal cost equals marginal revenue.

3. The two critical assumptions of the theory of perfect competition are that firms are price takers and that the industry displays freedom of entry and exit. A firm that is a price taker will adjust to different market conditions by varying its output.

4. The perfectly competitive firm's short-run supply curve is identical to its MC curve above AVC. The perfectly competitive industry's short-run supply curve is the horizontal sum of its firms' supply curves (i.e., the horizontal sum of the firms' marginal cost curves).

5. When perfectly competitive firms are producing in short-run equilibrium, they must be covering their variable costs. But they may be making losses (price less than average total cost), making profits (price greater than average total cost), or just breaking even (price equal to average total cost).

6. In the long run, profits or losses will lead to the entry or exit of capital from the industry. Entry or exit will push a competitive industry to a long-run zero-profit equilibrium and move production to the level consistent with minimum average total cost. Long-run equilibrium is discussed at greater length in the appendix to this chapter starting on page A-25.

7. The long-run response of a growing, perfectly competitive industry to steadily changing technology is the gradual replacement of less efficient plants and machines by more efficient ones. Older machines will be utilized as long as price exceeds AVC; only when price falls below AVC will they be discarded and replaced by more modern ones. The long-run response of a declining industry will be to continue to satisfy demand from its existing machinery as long as price exceeds AVC. Despite the appearance of being antiquated, this is the correct response to steadily falling demand.

8. The great appeal of perfect competition as a means of organizing production has both noneconomic and economic elements. The noneconomic appeal lies in the decentralized decision making of myriad firms and households. No individual exercises power over the market. At the same time, it is not necessary for the government to intervene to determine resource allocation and prices.

9. The economic appeal of perfect competition arises from the fact that, under certain conditions, it exhibits both productive and allocative efficiency. Productive efficiency is achieved because the same forces that lead to long-run equilibrium lead to production at the lowest attainable cost. Allocative efficiency is achieved because in competitive equilibrium, price equals marginal cost for every product and hence no shift of resources can increase the satisfaction of any household without decreasing it for some other household.

10. The efficiency of perfect competition should be understood yet interpreted with caution. Four qualifications to its being ''ideal'' are: (a) costs may be higher under perfect competition than under alternative market structures; (b) perfect competition will not exist simultaneously everywhere in the economy; (c) private costs may be poor measures of society's costs; (d) efficiency is not the only goal of the members of society.

TOPICS FOR REVIEW

Competitive behavior and competitive market structure
Behavioral rules for the profit-maximizing firm
Price taking and a horizontal demand curve

Average revenue, marginal revenue, and price under perfect competition

The relation of the industry supply curve to firms' marginal cost curves

Producers' surplus

Role of entry and exit in achieving equilibrium

Short-run and long-run equilibrium of firms and industries

Productive and allocative efficiency

Pareto-optimality (and Pareto-efficiency)

DISCUSSION QUESTIONS

1. Consider the suppliers of the following commodities. What are the elements of market structure that you might want to invoke to account for differences in their market behavior? Could any of these be characterized as perfectly competitive industries?
   a. Television broadcasting
   b. Automobiles
   c. Sand and gravel
   d. Medical services
   e. Mortgage loans
   f. Retail fruits and vegetables
   g. Soybeans

2. Which of the following observed facts about an industry are inconsistent with its being a perfectly competitive industry?
   a. Different firms use different methods of production.
   b. There is extensive advertising of the industry's product by a trade association.
   c. Individual firms devote 5 percent of sales receipts to advertising their own product brand.
   d. There are 24 firms in the industry.
   e. The largest firm in the industry makes 40 percent of the sales and the next largest firm makes 20 percent, but the products are identical and there are 61 other firms.
   f. All firms made large profits in 1980.

3. In which of the following sectors of the Canadian economy might you expect to find competitive behavior? In which might you expect to find industries that were classified as operating under perfectly competitive market structures?
   a. Manufacturing
   b. Agriculture
   c. Transportation and public utilities
   d. Wholesale and retail trade
   e. Criminal activity

4. In the 1930s the U.S. coal industry was characterized by easy entry and price taking. Because of large fixed costs in mine shafts and fixed equipment, however, exit was slow. With declining demand, many firms were barely covering their variable costs but not their total costs. As a result of a series of mine accidents, the federal government began to enforce mine safety standards, which forced most firms to invest in new capital if they were to remain in production. What predictions would competitive theory make about market behavior and the quantity of coal produced? Would coal miners approve or disapprove of the new enforcement program?

5. Suppose entry into an industry is not artificially restricted but takes time because of the need to build plants, acquire know-how, and establish a marketing organization. Can such an industry be characterized as perfectly competitive? Does ease of entry imply ease of exit, and vice versa?

6. What, if anything, does each one of the following tell you about ease of entry or exit in an industry?
   a. Profits have been very high for two decades.
   b. No new firms have entered the industry for 20 years.
   c. The average age of the firms in a 40-year-old industry is less than seven years.
   d. Most existing firms are using obsolete equipment alongside newer, more modern equipment.
   e. Profits are low or negative; many firms are still producing, but from steadily aging equipment.

7. In the 1970s grain prices in North America rose substantially relative to other agricultural products. Explain how each of the following may have contributed to this result; then consider how a perfectly competitive grain industry might be expected to react in the long run.
   a. Crop failures caused by unusually bad weather around the world in several years
   b. Rising demand for beef and chickens because of rising population and rising per capita income
   c. Great scarcities in fishmeal, a substitute for grain in animal diets, because of a mysterious decline in the anchovy harvest off Peru
   d. Increased Soviet purchases of grain on the world market

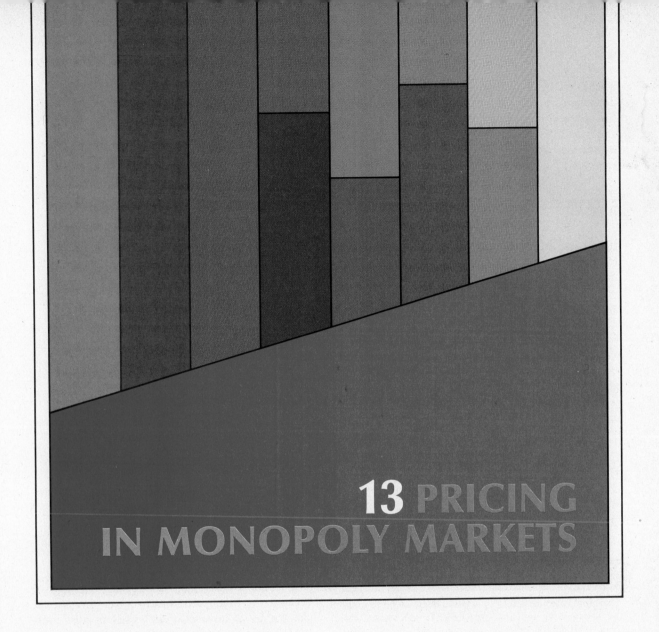

13 PRICING IN MONOPOLY MARKETS

Is Bell Canada a monopoly? How about IBM, U.S. Steel, the National Football League, or the Coca-Cola Company? Just as the word *competition* has both an everyday meaning and a more specialized technical one, so too does *monopoly*. The word *monopoly* comes from the Greek words *monos polein*, which mean "alone to sell." It is convenient for now to think of **monopoly** as the situation in which the output of an entire industry is controlled by a single seller. This seller will be called the monop-olist. Later in this chapter we will define monopoly in a less restrictive way.

Because the monopolistic firm is the only pro-ducer of a particular product, its demand curve is identical with the demand curve for that product. The market demand curve, which shows the ag-gregate quantity that buyers will purchase at every price, also shows the quantity that the monopolist will be able to sell at any price it sets.

The importance of this is that the monopolist,

unlike the firm in perfect competition, faces a downward-sloping demand curve. The monopoly firm knows that it faces a trade-off between price and quantity: Sales can be increased only if price is reduced, while price can be increased if sales are reduced.

A SINGLE-PRICE MONOPOLIST

In the first part of this chapter we confine ourselves to a monopoly that charges a single price for all units of the product that are sold.

The Monopolist's Revenue Curves

Given the market demand curve, the monopolist's average revenue and marginal revenue curves can be readily deduced. When the seller charges a single price for all units sold, average revenue per unit is identical with price. Thus, the market demand curve is also the average revenue curve for the

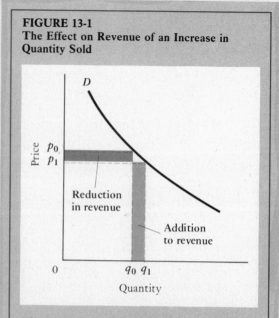

FIGURE 13-1
The Effect on Revenue of an Increase in Quantity Sold

For a downward-sloping demand curve, marginal revenue is less than price. A reduction of price from p_0 to p_1 increases sales by one unit from q_0 to q_1 units. The revenue from the extra unit sold (i.e., its price) is shown as the lighter shaded area. But to sell this unit, it is necessary to reduce the price on each of the q_0 units previously sold. The loss in revenue is shown as the darker shaded area. Marginal revenue of the extra unit is equal to the *difference* between the two areas.

TABLE 13–1 THE RELATION OF AVERAGE REVENUE AND MARGINAL REVENUE: A NUMERICAL ILLUSTRATION

Price $p = AR$	Quantity q	$TR = p \times q$	$MR = \Delta TR/\Delta q$
$9.10	9	$81.90	
9.00	10	90.00	$8.10
8.90	11	97.90	7.90

Marginal revenue is less than price because price must be lowered to sell an extra unit. A monopolist can choose either the price or the quantity to be sold. But choosing one determines the other. In this example, to increase sales from 10 to 11 units, it is necessary to reduce the price on all units sold from $9 to $8.90. The extra unit sold brings in $8.90, but the firm sacrifices $.10 on each of the 10 units that it could have sold at $9 had it not wanted to increase sales. The net addition to revenue is the $8.90 minus $.10 times 10 units, or $1, making $7.90 altogether. Thus the marginal revenue resulting from the increase in sales by 1 unit is $7.90, which is less than the price at which the units are sold.

Marginal revenue is shown displaced by half a line to emphasize that it represents the effect on revenue of the *change* in output.

monopolist. But marginal revenue is less than price because the monopolist has to lower the price it charges on *all* units in order to sell an *extra* unit. [24] This is an important difference from the case of perfect competition; it is explored numerically in Table 13-1 and graphically in Figure 13-1.

Figure 13-2 illustrates the average and marginal revenue curves for a monopolist, based on a straight-line demand curve.[1]

In Chapter 5 (pages 69–71) we discussed the

---

[1] It is helpful (for sketching revenue curves, etc.) to remember that if the demand curve is a downward-sloping straight line, the *MR* curve also slopes downward and is twice as steep. Its price intercept (where $q = 0$) is the same as that of the demand curve, and it cuts the quantity axis (where $p = 0$) at just half the output that the demand curve does. [25]

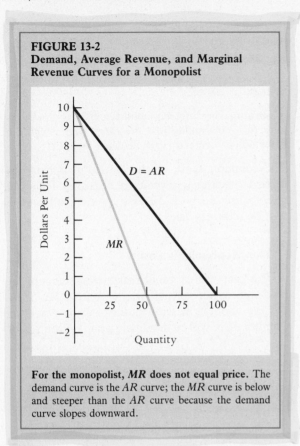

FIGURE 13-2
Demand, Average Revenue, and Marginal Revenue Curves for a Monopolist

For the monopolist, *MR* does not equal price. The demand curve is the *AR* curve; the *MR* curve is below and steeper than the *AR* curve because the demand curve slopes downward.

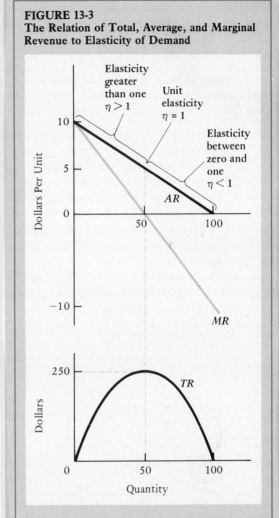

FIGURE 13-3
The Relation of Total, Average, and Marginal Revenue to Elasticity of Demand

When *TR* is rising, *MR* is greater than zero and elasticity is greater than unity. In this example, for outputs from 0 to 50, marginal revenue is positive, elasticity is greater than unity, and total revenue is rising. For outputs from 50 to 100, marginal revenue is negative, elasticity is less than unity, and total revenue is falling.

relation between elasticity of demand and total revenue. Figure 13-3 summarizes this earlier discussion and extends it to cover marginal revenue. When the demand curve is elastic, total revenue rises as quantity rises (therefore marginal revenue must be positive). When the demand curve is inelastic, total revenue falls as quantity rises (therefore marginal revenue must be negative).

The Monopolist's Equilibrium

To describe the profit-maximizing position of a monopolist, we need only bring together information about the monopolist's revenues and its costs and apply the rules developed in Chapter 12 (page 185). Note that since the technological conditions restricting the monopolist's ability to produce are the same as for a competitive firm, the short-run cost curves are the same in both cases. The key difference lies in the demand conditions. The competitive firm is faced with a perfectly elastic demand curve. This not only fixes its price, but also implies that price equals marginal revenue. The monopoly firm faces a downward-sloping demand curve. Hence, its actions influence price. This causes the firm's marginal revenue to differ from price; as we have seen, MR is less than price.

> The monopolist produces an output such that marginal revenue equals marginal cost. The price corresponding to that output is given by its demand curve.

This profit-maximizing position is shown in each part of Figure 13-4.

Note for future reference a key respect in which this monopolistic equilibrium differs from that of a firm in perfect competition. While a competitive firm produces at an output where $p = MC$, the monopolistic firm produces at an output where p is greater than MC. Later we shall return to discuss some implications of this.

Our earlier discussion of the relation between elasticity and revenue has one interesting implica-tion for monopoly behavior. Since marginal cost is always greater than zero, the profit-maximizing monopoly (which produces where MR equals MC) will produce where MR is positive; that is, where demand is elastic.

> A profit-maximizing monopolist will never push its sales of a commodity into the range over which the commodity's demand curve becomes inelastic.

The common sense of this is that if demand is inelastic, marginal revenue is negative. Thus the monopolist can both increase revenue and reduce cost by reducing sales.

The Monopolist's Profits

The fact that a profit-maximizing monopolist produces at an output where $MR = MC$ says nothing about how large profits will be—or even whether there will be monopoly profits. Profits may

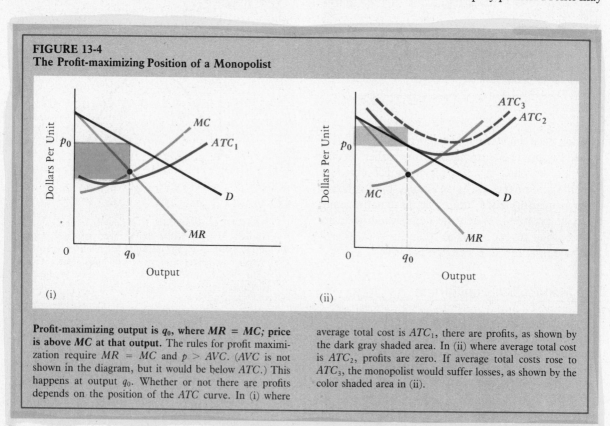

FIGURE 13-4
The Profit-maximizing Position of a Monopolist

Profit-maximizing output is q_0, where $MR = MC$; price is above MC at that output. The rules for profit maximi-zation require $MR = MC$ and $p > AVC$. (AVC is not shown in the diagram, but it would be below ATC.) This happens at output q_0. Whether or not there are profits depends on the position of the ATC curve. In (i) where

average total cost is ATC_1, there are profits, as shown by the dark gray shaded area. In (ii) where average total cost is ATC_2, profits are zero. If average total costs rose to ATC_3, the monopolist would suffer losses, as shown by the color shaded area in (ii).

exist, as shown in Figure 13-4(i), and indeed they may persist for a long time because as long as the firm retains its monopoly, entry of new firms does not push price down to the level of average total cost.

But, as Figure 13-4(ii) shows, the profit-maximizing monopolist may break even or suffer losses. Nothing guarantees that a monopolist will make profits, and if it cannot eliminate its losses, the firm will eventually fail.

A Monopolist's Supply Curve?

In describing the monopolist's profit-maximizing behavior, we did not introduce the concept of a supply curve, as we did in the discussion of perfect competition. A supply curve relates the quantity supplied to the price offered. In perfect competition, the industry short-run supply curve is known as soon as the marginal cost curves of the individual firms are known. This is because the profit-maximizing firms equate marginal cost to price. Given marginal costs, it is possible to know how much will be produced at each price.

In monopoly there is no unique relation between market price and quantity supplied.

Like all profit-maximizing firms, a monopolistic firm equates marginal cost with marginal revenue; but, unlike firms in perfect competition, for the monopolist marginal revenue does not equal price. Because the monopolist does *not* equate marginal cost to price, it is possible for different demand conditions to give rise to the same output but to differing prices.[2]

Equilibrium of the Firm and Industry

When a monopolist is the only producer in an industry, there is no need for separate theories of the firm and the industry, as is necessary with perfect competition. The monopolist *is* the industry. Thus the profit-maximizing position of the firm shown in Figure 13-4 is the short-run equilibrium of the industry.

In a monopolized industry, as in a perfectly competitive one, profits provide an incentive for new firms to enter. If such entry occurs, the equilibrium position will change and the firm will no longer be a monopolist. This is illustrated by the example in Box 13-1.

Barriers to entry are impediments to the entry of new firms into an industry.

If monopoly is to persist in the long run, there must be barriers to the entry of other firms into an industry.

Barriers may come about in many ways. Patent laws, for instance, may create and perpetuate monopolies by conferring on the patent holder the sole right to produce a particular commodity. A firm may be granted a charter or a franchise that prohibits competition by law. Monopolies may also arise because of economies of scale. The established firm that is able to produce at a lower cost than any new, small competitor may well retain a monopoly through a cost advantage.

A monopoly may also be perpetuated by force or by threat. Potential competitors can be intimidated by threats ranging from sabotage to a price war in which the established monopoly has sufficient financial resources to ensure victory.

It is the barriers to entry in one form or another that allow a monopolist to earn profits that persist in the long run. In perfect competition, an equilibrium in which firms earn profits can occur in the short run, but cannot last longer than it takes for entry to force prices down to the level of average total cost. Because of barriers to entry, the short-run profitable equilibrium of a monopolist can continue indefinitely.

The Inefficiency of Monopoly

In Chapter 12 we saw that (subject to certain qualifications) perfect competition produces efficient results. By leading firms to produce at levels of

---

[2] In order to know the amount produced at any given price, it is necessary to know something about the shape and position of the marginal revenue curve in addition to knowing the marginal cost curve. This means that there is not a supply curve independent of the demand curve for the monopolist's product.

BOX 13–1 THE PRICE OF HAIRCUTS AND THE PROFITS OF BARBERS

Assume that there are many barber shops and freedom of entry into barbering: anyone who qualifies can set up as a barber. Assume that the going price for haircuts is $10 and that at this price all barbers believe their income is too low. The barbers hold a meeting and decide to form a trade association. They agree on the following points: First, all barbers in the city must join the association and abide by its rules; second, any new barbers who meet certain professional qualifications will be required to join the association before they are allowed to practice their trade; third, the association will recommend a price for haircuts that no barber shall undercut.

The barbers intend to raise the price of haircuts in order to raise their incomes. You are called in as a consulting economist to advise them of the probable success of their plan. Suppose you are persuaded that the organization does have the requisite strength to enforce a price rise to, say, $14. What are your predictions about the consequences?

You now need to distinguish between the short-run and the long-run effects of an increase in the price of haircuts. In the short run the number of barbers is fixed. Thus, in the short run the answer depends only on the elasticity of the demand for haircuts.

If the demand elasticity is less than 1, total expenditure on haircuts will rise and so will the incomes of barbers; if demand elasticity exceeds 1, the barbers' revenues will fall. Thus you need some empirical knowledge about the elasticity of demand for haircuts.

Suppose on the basis of the best available evidence you estimate the elasticity of demand over the relevant price range to be 0.45. You then predict that barbers will be successful in raising incomes in the short run. A 40 percent rise in price will be met by an 18 percent fall in business, so the total revenue of the typical barber will rise by about 15 percent.*

* Let p and q be the price and quantity before the price increase. Total revenue after the increase is $TR = (1.40p)(.82q) = 1.148pq$.

---

output at which $p = MC$ and $p = ATC$, it satisfies conditions of both productive and allocative efficiency. It also leads to production at the minimum point on the ATC curve, the lowest attainable cost of production.

Productive Efficiency

The output of a monopolized industry will in general be different from that of a competitive industry. A monopolist, just like any other firm, will wish to produce its profit-maximizing output at the lowest cost *for that output*. Thus it will be motivated to achieve productive efficiency for that output. Since there is only one firm, the issue of allocating that output among firms does not arise.

Allocative Inefficiency

While productively efficient, the monopolist will produce the "wrong" output from the standpoint of efficiency. As we have seen, the monopolist chooses an output at which the price charged is greater than marginal cost. This violates the conditions for allocative efficiency (discussed on page 200). When price equals marginal cost, consumers pay for the last unit purchased an amount just equal to the opportunity cost of producing that unit. But at a monopoly price and output, price is greater than marginal cost. Thus consumers pay for the last unit an amount that exceeds the opportunity cost of producing it.

Consumers would be prepared to buy additional

Now what about the long run? If barbers were just covering costs before the price change, they will now be earning profits. Barbering will become an attractive trade relative to others requiring equal skill and training, and there will be a flow of barbers into the industry. As the number of barbers rises, the same amount of business must be shared among more and more barbers, so the typical barber will find business—and thus profits—decreasing. Profits may also be squeezed from another direction. With fewer customers coming their way, barbers may compete against one another for the limited number of customers. The association does not allow them to compete through price cuts, but they can compete in service. They may spruce up their shops, offer their customers expensive magazines to read, and so forth. This kind of competition will raise operating costs.

These changes will continue until barbers are just covering their opportunity costs, at which time the attraction for new entrants will vanish. The industry will settle down in a new long-run equilibrium in which individual barbers make incomes only as large as they did before the price rise. There will be more barbers than there were in the original situation, but each barber will be working for a smaller fraction of the day and will be idle for a larger fraction (the industry will have excess capacity). Barbers may prefer this situation; they will have more leisure. Customers may or may not prefer it: They will have shorter waits even at peak periods, and they will get to read a wide choice of magazines, but they will pay more for haircuts.

But you were hired to report to the barbers with respect to the effect on their incomes, not the effect on their leisure. The report that you finally present will thus say: "You will succeed in the short run (because you face a demand curve that is inelastic), but your plan is bound to be self-defeating in the long run unless you are able to prevent the entry of new barbers."

units for an amount greater than the cost of producing these units. Recall that opportunity cost is the market value consumers would receive if the resources were used in their best alternative use. Some consumers could be made better off, and none worse off, by shifting extra resources into production of the monopolized commodity, thus increasing production of the product. This is illustrated graphically in Box 13-2.

The monopoly output is not allocatively efficient.

The Inefficiency of Monopoly: A Warning

Just as the conclusion that perfect competition is efficient was subject to some words of warning (see pages 201–202), so too is the conclusion about the inefficiency of monopoly. The detailed comparison of monopoly and competition we defer to Chapter 16, but a preview is in order. Much of the case against monopoly depends on the monopoly's having the same costs as a competitive industry, yet producing allocatively inefficient quantities. This assumption has been called into question in the very long run. For example, if monopolists engage in more innovation than would firms in a competitive industry, the cost curves of the industry may shift downward enough to create productive efficiencies in the very long run that will more than offset any allocative inefficiency. (The important question of the influence of market structure on innovation is discussed in Chapter 16.)

BOX 13–2 THE ALLOCATIVE INEFFICIENCY OF MONOPOLY ILLUSTRATED

In Box 12-2 on page 202, we gave a graphic interpretation of allocative efficiency. That analysis can be extended here.

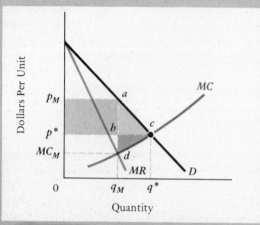

Allocative efficiency occurs at that level of output where price equals marginal cost. In the figure below, this occurs when output is q^* and price is p^*. The monopolist, however, produces only q_M, where marginal revenue equals marginal cost. As a result monopoly price p_M, is greater than marginal cost. The monopolist gains (at the expense of consumers) by raising price and restricting output. *But the monopolist's gain is smaller than consumers' losses.*

First consider the effect on the producer of charging a price, p_M, higher than p^*. On the first q_M units sold, there is a big increase in the producer's profits, shown by the color shaded rectangle (p^*p_Mab). To be sure, the producer loses some profits on the sales from q_M to q^*. These lost profits are shown by the dark gray shaded area (*bcd*). The net gain to the producer is the colored rectangle *minus* the dark gray shaded triangle.

Now consider consumers. Their loss of consumers' surplus is the colored rectangle *plus* the light gray shaded triangle *abc*. The colored rectangle is a pure redistribution from consumers to the monopolist. It reflects extra payments by consumers on the first q_M units. Such a redistribution does not affect allocative efficiency.

But the two shaded areas are losses to one group that are not gains to the other group. They are the deadweight losses.

The monopolist, by restricting output and raising price above the competitive level, gains a larger share of a smaller "pie." The deadweight loss arises because of the decrease in the size of the pie caused by not producing units that consumers value above the opportunity cost of production.

THE NATURE AND EXTENT OF MONOPOLY POWER

The *theory* of monopoly just developed assumes that the monopolist is unconcerned about competition. It is, however, difficult to imagine a firm without *any* competition. Every product has some substitutes for the services it provides. Some products have fairly close substitutes, and even a single seller producing such a product will have close rivals. Other products may have no existing close substitute, but new products may be developed

that will compete with it. For these reasons it is useful to recognize monopoly power as a variable that can be relatively slight or nearly complete, rather than as an attribute which either does or does not exist.

Monopoly power exists to the extent that a firm is insulated from loss of customers to other sellers.

Any producer facing a downward-sloping demand curve could choose the price-quantity combination (where $MR = MC$) that appears to maximize its profits. *But this price might not turn out to be the long-run profit-maximizing price* because the choice of a particular price-quantity combination may itself lead to changes in the behavior of other firms that in turn *shift* the original firm's demand curve.

Consider an example. The Coca-Cola Company is the sole producer of Coca-Cola and faces a downward-sloping demand curve. But suppose the demand curve for Coke shows that if the price is cut by 20 percent *and* if all other soft drink suppliers keep their prices at their present levels, sales of Coke will increase by 50 percent. Why does it not do so? The answer is that if it did, other soft drink prices would not remain unchanged—and the company knows this.

If other soft drink producers cut their prices in response, Coca-Cola's sales would not increase as much as its demand curve predicts based on the assumption of no changes in other's prices. Sales might increase by (say) only 10 percent. The company's profits would then decrease rather than increase.

The larger the *shifts* in a demand curve that are induced by a firm's changing its price, the less is that firm's monopoly power. Such shifts have two main sources. The first (as in the Coca-Cola example) is the price reactions of existing producers of substitute products. The second is the entry of new firms that succeed in capturing part of the sales that the monopolist included in "its" demand curve. Such shifts in the demand curve, from either cause, limit the market power of the firm and reduce its profits.

Since no firm is perfectly insulated from all competition for all time, total monopoly power does not exist. Monopoly power is a variable.

Measuring Monopoly Power

Measuring monopoly power is not easy. Ideally, prices, outputs, and profits of firms in any industry should be compared with what they would be if all firms were under unified (monopoly) control and were fully insulated from entry. But such a hypothetical comparison does not lend itself to measurement.

In practice, two alternative summary statistics are widely used to measure monopoly power: concentration ratios and profits.

Concentration Ratios

The **concentration ratio** shows the fraction of total market sales controlled by the largest group of sellers. Common types of concentration ratios cite the share of total market sales made by the largest four or eight firms. How well concentration ratios measure effective monopoly power is a matter of debate among economists.

A first problem is to define the market with reasonable accuracy. For one example, concentration ratios in national cement sales are low, but they understate the market power of cement companies because heavy transportation costs divide the cement *industry* into a series of regional *markets*, in each of which there are relatively few firms.

A second problem is the interpretation of concentration ratios. Clearly, market share is one measure of the *potential* power to control supply and set price. The inclusion in concentration ratios of the market shares of several firms rests on the possibility that large firms will, in one way or another, adopt a common price–output policy that is no different from the policy they would adopt if they were in fact under unified management. Such behavior is commonly referred to as **collusion.**

Such collusive behavior may occur with or without an actual agreement to collude. If no agreement actually occurs, lawyers speak of **conscious parallel action** and economists of **tacit collusion** when referring to the noncollusive parallel behavior that results. Concentration ratios measure the *actual* exercise of monopoly power only if collusion—whether overt or tacit—occurs.

High concentration ratios may be necessary for the exercise of monopoly power, but they are not sufficient. They tend to show the potential for monopoly power, but not necessarily the actuality.

Profits as a Measure of Monopoly Power

Many economists, following the lead of Professor Joe S. Bain, use profit rates as a measure of monopoly power. By *high profits*, these economists mean returns sufficiently in excess of all opportunity costs that potential new entrants desire to enter the industry. Persistently high profits, so goes the logic, are indirect evidence that neither rivalry among sellers nor entry of new firms prevents existing firms from pricing as if they were monopolists.

Using profits in this way requires care because, as we have seen (page 150), profits as reported in firms' income statements are not pure profits over opportunity cost. In particular, allowance must be made for differences in risk and in required payments for the use of owners' capital.

While neither concentration ratios nor profit rates are ideal measures of the degree of market power that a firm, or group of firms, actually exercises, both are of value and are widely used. In fact, concentration ratios and high profit rates are themselves correlated. Because of this, alternative classifications of markets and industries, according to their monopoly power measured in these two ways, do not differ much from one another. In spite of the difficult problems of measuring monopoly power, the theory of monopoly is widely used by economists and policymakers.

A MULTIPRICE MONOPOLIST

So far in this chapter we have assumed that the monopolist charges the same price for every unit of product no matter to whom, or where, it sells it. But other situations are possible.

Raw milk is often sold at one price when it is to go into fluid milk but at a lower price when it is to be used to make ice cream or cheese. Doctors in some countries charge for their services according to the incomes of their patients. Movie theaters may have lower admission prices for children than for adults. Railroads charge different rates per ton mile for different products. Electric companies sell electricity more cheaply for industrial than for home use. State universities charge out-of-state students higher tuition than residents. Japanese steel companies sell steel more cheaply in the United States than in Japan.

Price discrimination occurs when a producer sells different units of a specific commodity to buyers at two or more different prices, for reasons not associated with differences in cost. Not all price differences represent price discrimination. Quantity discounts, differences between wholesale and retail prices, and prices that vary with the time of day or the season of the year are not generally considered price discrimination because the same physical product sold at a different time or place or in different quantities may have different costs.

If an electric power company has unused capacity at certain times of day, it may be cheaper to provide service at those hours than at peak demand hours. If the price differences reflect cost differences, they are nondiscriminatory. However, when price differences rest merely on different buyers' valuations of the same product, they are discriminatory. It does not cost a movie theater operator less to fill a seat with a child than an adult, but it may pay to let the children in at a discriminatory low price if few of them would attend at the full adult fare.

Why should a firm want to sell some units of output at a price well below the price it gets for other units? Why, in other words, does it practice price discrimination?

Why Price Discrimination Pays

Persistent price discrimination comes about either because different buyers may be willing to pay different amounts for the same commodity or because one buyer may be willing to pay different amounts for different units of the same commodity. (You should now review the discussion of consumers' surplus on pages 116–118.) The basic point about price discrimination is that in either of these circumstances sellers may be able to capture some of the consumers' surplus that would otherwise go to buyers.

Discrimination Among Units Sold to One Buyer

Look back to Table 7-2 on page 116, which showed the consumer's surplus received by one consumer if she bought eight glasses of milk at a single price. If the firm could sell her each glass separately, it could capture this consumer's surplus. In the example, it would sell the first unit for $3, the second for $1.50, the third for $1, and so on until the eighth was sold for $.30. The firm would get total revenues of $8.10 rather than the $2.40 received by selling at the single price. In this example, the firm has been able to discriminate perfectly and extract every bit of the consumer's surplus.

Of course, such perfect price discrimination may not be possible. But suppose the firm could charge two different prices, one for the first four units sold, and one for the next four sold. If it sold the first four for $.80 and the next four for $.30, it would receive $4.40—less than if it could discriminate perfectly, but more than it would receive from sale at any single price.

Discrimination Among Buyers

Think of the demand curve in a market containing individual buyers, each of whom has indicated the price he or she is prepared to pay for a single unit. Suppose for simplicity that there are only four buyers, the first of whom is prepared to pay any price up to $4, the second $3, the third $2, and the fourth $1. Suppose the product has a marginal cost of production of $1 per unit for all units. If the seller is limited to a single price, it will maximize its profits by charging $3, sell two units, and earn profits of $4. If the seller can discriminate between units, it could charge the first buyer $4, and the second $3—thus increasing profits from the first two units to $5. Moreover, it could also sell the third unit for $2, and the fourth unit for $1. Its revenues and its profits would increase.

Price Discrimination More Generally

Demand curves slope downward because different units are valued differently, either by one individual owing to diminishing marginal utility or by different individuals. That fact, combined with a single price, gives rise to consumers' surplus.

The ability to charge multiple prices gives a seller the opportunity to capture some (or, in the extreme, all) of the consumers' surplus.

In general, the more prices that can be charged, the greater the seller's ability to increase its revenue at the expense of consumers. This is illustrated in Figure 13-5.

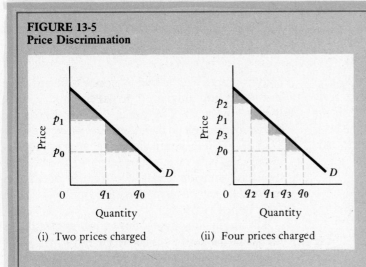

FIGURE 13-5
Price Discrimination

(i) Two prices charged
(ii) Four prices charged

Multiple prices permit a seller to capture buyers' consumers' surplus. Suppose in either diagram that if a single price were charged, it would be the price p_0. Quantity q_0 would be sold, and consumers' surplus would be the entire area above p_0 and below the demand curve. In (i) two prices are charged: p_1 for the first q_1 units and p_0 for other units. Consumers' surplus is reduced to the two shaded areas and the seller's revenue increased accordingly. In (ii) four prices are charged: p_2 for the first q_2 units, p_1 for the units between q_2 and q_1, and so on. Producers' revenues are increased and consumers' surplus further reduced to the shaded areas. At the extreme, if a different price could be charged for each unit, producers could extract every bit of the consumers' surplus, and the price discrimination would be perfect.

BOX 13–3 PRICE DISCRIMINATION GRAPHICALLY ANALYZED

A monopolist who can discriminate between markets will allocate output between them so that marginal revenues in each will be equal. Total output will be such that marginal cost equals overall marginal revenue.

Consider a monopoly firm which sells a single product in two distinct markets, A and B. Customers in one market cannot buy in the other because the two markets are completely insulated from each other. The demand and marginal revenue curves for each market are shown in (i) and (ii) of the figure.

Allocation of a Given Total Output

How will a profit-maximizing monopolist behave in each market? To begin, imagine the firm deciding how best to allocate *any* given output, q^*, between the two markets. Because output is fixed (arbitrarily at q^*), there is nothing the firm can do about costs. The best thing to do therefore is to maximize the total revenue that is received from selling q^* in the two markets. *To do this, the firm will allocate sales between the markets until the marginal revenues of the last unit sold in each are the same.*

Consider what would happen if this strategy were not followed. If the marginal revenue of the last unit sold in market A exceeded the marginal revenue of the last unit sold in market B, the firm could keep overall output constant at q^* but reallocate a unit of sales from market B to market A, thereby gaining a net addition in revenue equal to the difference between the marginal revenues in the two markets. It therefore pays the firm to reallocate a given total output between markets whenever marginal revenues are not equal in the two markets.

Choosing Total Output

The determination of profit-maximizing output and prices is shown in the figure. The firm's marginal cost varies with its total output, as shown in (iii). Thus we cannot just put the *MC* curve onto the diagram for each market, for the marginal cost of producing another unit for sale in market A will depend on how much is being produced for sale in market B, and vice versa. To determine what overall production should be, we need to know overall *marginal revenue*. To find this, we merely sum the separate quan-

It follows, for any given output, that if a seller is able to price discriminate, it can increase revenues received (and thus also its profits) from the sale of those units. [26] But price discrimination is not always possible, even if there are no legal barriers to its use.

When Is Price Discrimination Possible?

Discrimination among units of output sold to the same buyer requires that the seller be able to keep track of the units a buyer consumes each period. Thus the tenth unit purchased by a given buyer in

a given month can be sold at a price different from that of the fifth unit *only* if the seller can keep track of who buys what. This can be done by the electric company through its meter readings or by the magazine publishing firm's distinguishing between renewals and new subscriptions. It may also be done by establishments giving a certificate or coupon providing, for example, a reduced price car wash for a return visit.

Discrimination among buyers is only possible if the goods cannot be resold by the buyer who faces the low price to the buyer who faces the high price. However much the local butcher might like to charge the banker's wife twice as much for ham-

tities in each market that correspond to each particular marginal revenue. The appropriateness of this procedure follows from the argu-

(divided into q_A units in market A and q_B in market B). This is shown in the figure by the MR curve in (iii).

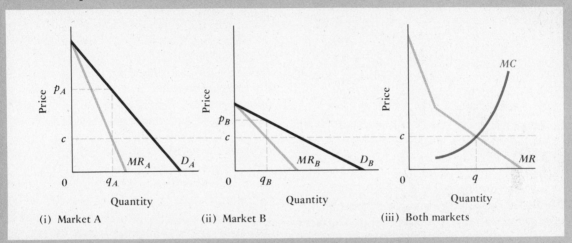

(i) Market A   (ii) Market B   (iii) Both markets

ment that at any value of total production, sales will be allocated to equate marginal revenues in the two markets. If, for example, the tenth unit sold in market A and the fifteenth unit sold in market B each have a marginal revenue of $c in their separate markets, then the marginal revenue of $c corresponds to overall sales of q units

Profit-maximizing total output is at q in (iii), where MR and MC intersect. Because marginal revenue is c in each market, market outputs are q_A and q_B respectively. Although marginal revenue is equal in the two markets, the prices P_A and P_B (read off the demand curves) are not.

burger as he charges the taxi driver, he cannot succeed in doing so. Madame Banker can always shop for meat in the supermarket, where her husband's occupation is not known. Even if the butcher and the supermarket agreed to charge her twice as much, she could hire the taxi driver to shop for her. The surgeon, however, may succeed in discriminating (if all reputable surgeons will do the same) because it will not do the banker's wife much good to hire the taxi driver to have her operations for her.

Price discrimination is possible only if the seller can distinguish individual units bought by a single buyer or separate buyers into classes such that resale among classes is impossible.

Ability to prevent resale tends to be associated with the character of the product or the ability to classify buyers into readily identifiable groups. Services are less easily resold than goods; goods that require installation by the manufacturer (e.g., heavy equipment) are less easily resold than movable goods such as household appliances. An interesting example of nonresalability occurs in the case of plate glass. Small pieces sell much more cheaply per square foot than bigger pieces, but the person who needs glass for a 6′ × 10′ picture window

BOX 13–4 IS PRICE DISCRIMINATION BAD?

The consequences of price discrimination differ from case to case. No matter what an individual's values are, he or she is almost bound to evaluate individual cases differently.

Secret rebates. A very large oil-refining firm agrees to ship its product to market on a given railroad, provided that the railroad gives the firm a secret rebate on the transportation cost and does not give a similar concession to rival refiners. The railroad agrees and is thereby charging discriminatory prices. This rebate gives the large oil company a cost advantage that it uses to drive its rivals out of business or to force them into a merger on dictated terms. (John D. Rockefeller was accused of using such tactics in the early years of the Standard Oil Company.)

Use of product. When the Aluminum Company of America had a virtual monopoly on the production of aluminum ingots, it sold both the raw ingots and aluminum cable made from the ingots. At one time ALCOA sold cable at a price 20 percent *below* its price for ingots. (Of course, the cable price was above ALCOA's cost of producing cable.) It did so because users of cable could substitute copper cable, but many users of ingot had no substitute for aluminum. In return for its "bargain price" for cable, ALCOA made the purchasers of cable agree to use it only for transmission purposes. (Without such an agreement, any demander of aluminum might have bought cable and melted it down.)

Covering costs. A product that many people want to purchase has a demand and cost structure such that there is no single price at which a producing firm can cover total costs. However, if the firm is allowed to charge discriminatory prices, it will be willing to produce the product and it may make a profit. This is illustrated in the figure.

Because *ATC* is everywhere higher than the demand curve, no single price would lead to

---

cannot use four pieces of 3′ × 5′ glass. Transportation costs, tariff barriers, and import quotas separate classes of buyers geographically and may make discrimination possible.

It is, of course, not enough to be able to separate buyers or units into separate classes. The seller must be able to control the supply to each group. This is what makes price discrimination an aspect of the theory of monopoly.[3] A graphic illustration of price discrimination is given in Box 13-3.

[3] For price discrimination to be profitable, the different groups must have different degrees of willingness to pay. The hypothesis of diminishing marginal utility (see page 111) would lead to the prediction that different valuations are placed by an individual on different units, and differences in income and tastes would lead to the prediction that different subgroups will have different elasticities of demand for a given commodity. Thus, the potential for profitable price discrimination is usually present.

Positive Aspects of Price Discrimination

The positive consequences of price discrimination are summarized in two propositions.

1. For any given level of output, the most profitable system of discriminatory prices will provide higher total revenue to the firm than the profit-maximizing single price.

This proposition was illustrated graphically in Figure 13-5. All it requires is a downward-sloping demand curve. To see that this is reasonable, remember that a monopolist with the power to discriminate *could* produce exactly the same quantity as a single-price monopolist and charge everyone the same price. Therefore, it need never get *less*

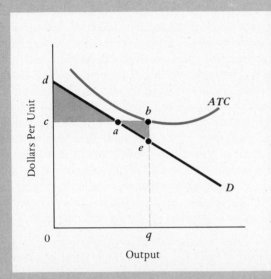

revenues equal to costs. A price-discriminating monopolist may be able to cover cost. The total cost of output q is the area $0cbq$. The maximum revenue attainable at any output by perfect discrimination is the area under the demand curve.

For output q that area, shown as gray shaded, exceeds total cost since the gray shaded triangle cda is greater than the color shaded triangle abe.

Equitable fares. For many years, British railways were not allowed to discriminate among passengers in different regions. To prevent discrimination, a fixed fare per passenger mile was specified and charged on all lines, whatever their passenger traffic and whatever the elasticity of demand for the services of the particular line. In the interests of economy, branch lines that could not cover costs closed down. Some lines stopped operating even though their users preferred rail transport to any alternatives and the strength of their preference was such that they would have willingly paid a price sufficient for the line to yield a profit. But the lines were closed because it was thought inequitable to discriminate against the passengers on these lines.

revenue, and it can do better if it can raise the price on even one unit sold.

2. **Output under price discrimination will generally be larger than under single-price monopoly.**

Remember that a monopolistic firm which must charge a single price produces less than the perfectly competitive industry because it is aware that by producing and selling more, it drives down the price against itself. Price discrimination allows it to avoid this disincentive. To the extent that the firm can sell its output in separate blocks, it can sell another block without spoiling the market for the block already being sold. In the case of *perfect* price discrimination, where every unit of output is sold at a different price, the profit-maximizing firm will produce every unit for which the price charged can be greater than or equal to its marginal cost.

It will, therefore, produce the same output as the firm in perfect competition.

Normative Aspects of Price Discrimination

The predicted combination of higher average revenue and higher output does not in itself have any *normative* significance. It will typically lead to a different distribution of income and a different level of output than when the seller is limited to a single price. The ability of the discriminating monopolist to capture some of the consumers' surplus will seem undesirable to consumers but not to the monopolist. How outsiders view the transfer may depend on who gains and who loses. For instance, when railroads discriminated against small farmers, the results aroused public anger; when doctors in private practice discriminate by giving low-priced service to poor patients, it is taken to be necessary since the poor would not be able to afford medical care if doctors charged all their patients the same fees.

Price discrimination, we have seen, tends to lead to larger output than is produced by a single-price monopoly. Thus price discrimination tends to *decrease* the allocative inefficiency of monopoly. Indeed, under perfect price discrimination the monopolist produces up to the point where price equals marginal cost and thus achieves allocative efficiency.

The fact that price discrimination may actually improve efficiency may seem paradoxical, for price discrimination has a bad reputation among economists and lawyers. To many people *discrimination* has odious connotations. Laws make certain kinds of price discrimination illegal. But was discrimination by airlines in giving senior citizens lower standby fares really bad? Some further examples are explored in Box 13-4.

There are two quite separate questions involved in evaluating a particular example of price discrimination. First is whether it increases the available *sum* of producers' and consumers' surplus. This is the question of allocative efficiency. Second is who gets whatever surplus is available. This is a question of distribution. Economists can identify both kinds of effects, and the desirability of each can be debated. Whether an individual judges price discrimination as "evil" depends on the details of the particular example as well as on personal value judgments. Very often it is the income redistribution caused by price discrimination that accounts for the strong emotional reactions to price discrimination.

Systematic and Unsystematic Discrimination

The discussion so far has been concerned with systematic and persistent price discrimination. Systematic price discrimination most often consists of classifying buyers according to age, location, industry, or the use they intend to make of the product, and then charging different prices for the different "classes" of buyers. It may also take other forms, such as charging more for the first unit bought than for subsequent units, or vice versa.

Another sort of price discrimination is common. Any firm that occasionally gives a favorite customer a few cents off, or shaves its price to land a new account, is also engaged in price discrimination. If these practices are used irregularly, they are called *unsystematic discrimination*. Such discrimination is not really part of the price structure, and we have ignored it here. This does not mean that it is unimportant; on the contrary, unsystematic price discrimination plays a major role in the dynamic process by which prices change in response to changing conditions of supply and demand.

The causes and consequences of systematic price discrimination are very different from those of unsystematic price discrimination.

The law, however, is generally unable to distinguish between the two kinds of price discrimination and so hits at both. Legislation, motivated solely by a desire to attack systematic discrimination, may have unforeseen and possibly undesired effects on unsystematic discrimination. Because unsystematic price discrimination is important for the working of competition, prohibiting it may aid the maintenance of monopoly power.

SUMMARY

1. In the basic theory of monopoly an entire industry is supplied by a single firm that sets a single price for its product.

2. The monopolist's own demand curve is identical with the market demand curve for the product. The market demand curve is the monopolist's average revenue curve. The monopoly firm's marginal revenue is always less than its average revenue.

3. When the monopolist is maximizing profits, marginal revenue is positive, and thus elasticity of demand is greater than unity. The amount of profits a monopolist earns may be large, small, zero, or negative in the short run, depending on the relation of demand and cost.

4. For monopoly profits to persist in the long run, profits must not be negative and there must be effective barriers to entry.

5. Monopolists restrict output below the competitive level and hence do not achieve the allocative efficiency associated with perfect competition. That is, the monopolist does not produce the output that maximizes the sum of consumers' and producers' surplus.

6. Monopoly power is limited by the presence of substitute products, by the development of new products, and by the possibility of entry of new firms. It exists to the extent that a firm is insulated from loss of customers to other sellers. In practice, the degree of monopoly power may best be thought of as a variable. Two widely used measures of the degree of monopoly power are concentration ratios and the size of profits.

7. Price discrimination occurs when different units of the same commodity are sold for different prices, for reasons not associated with differences in costs. A successful price discriminator captures some of the consumers' surplus that would exist at a single price.

8. Successful price discrimination requires ability to control the supply of the product offered to particular buyers and to prevent the resale of the commodity from one buyer to another.

9. For any given level of output, the best system of discriminatory prices will provide higher total revenue to the firm than the best single price. Under price discrimination output is larger than under a single-price monopoly; as a result, the allocative inefficiency of a price-discriminating monopoly is less than that of a single-price monopoly.

10. Price discrimination also affects the distribution of income. Purchasers get less, while the firm gets more of the consumers' surplus than under single-price monopoly.

TOPICS FOR REVIEW

The relationship of price and *MR* for a monopolist
Allocative inefficiency of monopoly
Measures of monopoly power
Price discrimination
Conditions that make price discrimination both possible and
  profitable

DISCUSSION QUESTIONS

1. Suppose that only one professor teaches economics at your school. Would you say this professor is a monopolist who can exact any "price" from students in the form of readings assigned, tests given, and material covered? Suppose that two additional professors are hired; has the original professor's monopoly power been decreased?

2. Imagine a monopoly firm with fixed costs but no variable or marginal costs—for example, a firm owning a spring of water that produces indefinitely, once certain pipes are installed, in an area where no other source of water is available. What would be the firm's profit-maximizing price? What elasticity of demand would you expect at that price? Would this seem to be an appropriate pricing policy if the water monopoly were municipally owned? Suppose now that entry becomes easy because of the discovery of many additional springs. What price behavior would you expect to occur? What price equilibrium would be predicted?

3. Each of the following has some "monopoly power": Xerox Corporation, Pepsi-Cola Company, Gulf Oil, OPEC, Bell Canada, and the Post Office. In each case, what do you think is the basis of the monopoly power? How might you decide which of the organizations listed has the greatest degree of monopoly power?

4. Which of these industries—licorice candy, copper wire, outboard motors, coal, local newspapers—would you most like to monopolize? Why? Does your answer depend on several factors or just one or two? Which would you as a consumer least like to have monopolized by someone else? If your answers are different in the two cases, explain why.

5. A movie exhibitor, Aristotle Murphy, owns movie theaters in two Nova Scotia towns of roughly the same size, 50 miles apart. In Monopolia he owns the only chain of theaters; in Competitia there is no theater chain, and he is but one of a number of independent operators. Would you expect movie prices to be higher in Monopolia than in Competitia in the short run? In the long run? If differences

occurred in his prices, would Mr. Murphy be discriminating in price?

6. Airline rates to Europe are higher in summer than in winter. Canadian railroads charge lower fares during the week than on weekends. Electricity companies charge consumers lower rates, the more electricity they use. Are these all examples of price discrimination? What additional information would you like to have before answering?

7. Discuss whether each of the following represents price discrimination. In your view, which are the most socially harmful?

a. Standby fares on airlines that are less than full fare

b. Standby fares available only to bona fide students under 22 years of age

c. First class fares that are 50 percent greater than tourist fares, recognizing that two first class seats use the space of three tourist seats

d. Negotiated discounts from list price, where sales personnel are authorized to bargain hard and get as much in each transaction as the traffic will bear

e. Higher tuition for out-of-province university students

f. Higher tuition for law students than for history students

14 INDUSTRIAL ORGANIZATION AND THEORIES OF IMPERFECT COMPETITION

Texaco, Shell, and Imperial Oil are three of the "major" oil companies. They are not, singly or collectively, monopolists, nor are they firms in perfect competition. Yet they are typical of many real firms in our economy. Do the two basic theories of pricing behavior we have studied—perfect competition and monopoly—have any relevance to their behavior?

The two essential features of perfect competition are first, firms so numerous that none has any power to influence price (firms are price takers) and second, freedom of entry and exit. The two essential features of monopoly are blockaded entry and a demand curve that is essentially the same for the firm as for the industry. Do the theories of perfect competition and monopoly provide a sufficient basis for understanding real market behavior? Sixty years ago, most economists would have said yes; today most would say no. Many economists believe that although the models of monopoly and perfect competition are clearly useful, there is a need for other models as well. This chapter suggests some of them.

STRUCTURE OF THE CANADIAN ECONOMY

Our first task is to look at the facts. How competitive or monopolistic are Canadian industries?

Two Groupings of Canadian Industries

It is relatively easy to divide much of Canadian industry into two broad groups, those with a large number of relatively small firms and those with a few relatively large firms.

Sectors with Many Small Firms

Between 40 and 50 percent of the economy's national product is produced by industries made up of a large number of small firms. This includes most agricultural production, most services (travel agents, lawyers, plumbers, television technicians, etc.), most retail trade (stores, gas stations, etc.), most wholesale trade, most construction, and industries whose major business is exchange (real estate agents, stockbrokers, etc.).

The competitive model, with the addition of government intervention where necessary, does quite well in describing many of these industries. This is obviously so where the business of the industry is exchange rather than production. Foreign exchange markets and stock exchanges are notable examples. Agriculture also fits fairly well in most ways; the individual farmer is clearly a price taker, entry into farming is easy, and exit is possible though not in fact very rapid.

Some other industries, however, do not seem to be described by the perfectly competitive model even though they contain many firms. In the retail trades and services, for example, most firms have some influence over prices. The local grocery, supermarket, discount house, and department store not only consider weekend specials and periodic

sales important to business success, they spend a good deal of money advertising them. Moreover, each store in these industries has a unique location that may give it some local monopoly power over nearby customers. In wholesaling, the sales representative is regarded as a key figure—which would not be true if the firm could sell all it wished at a given market price. We are, as Professor R. L. Bishop has observed, "a race of eager sellers and coy buyers, with purchasing agents getting the Christmas presents from the salesmen rather than the other way around."

The first group of industries therefore contains some that are clearly described by the model of perfect competition and many others that are not.

Sectors with a Few Large Firms

About 50 percent of the national product is produced by industries dominated by a few large firms. The names of these firms are part of the average citizen's vocabulary. In this category fall most transportation firms (e.g., Canadian Pacific Airlines and Voyageur Colonial Coach Lines), communications (CTV, Southam Newspapers, Bell Canada), public utilities and crown corporations (Ontario Hydro and the Canadian Post Office), and much of the manufacturing sector.

A casual look at manufacturing can be misleading unless one distinguishes between products and firms. In some manufacturing industries there are many differentiated products produced by only a few firms. In soaps and detergents, for example, a vast variety of products is produced by a mere two firms, Lever Brothers and Procter & Gamble. Similar circumstances exist in chemicals, breakfast foods, cigarettes, and numerous other industries where many more or less competing products are in each case produced by a very few firms. Clearly these industries are not perfectly competitive. Yet neither do they appear to be monopolies, for the few firms typically compete energetically against one another.

Cases of single-firm monopolies outside the regulated industries are few. They include the Eddy Match Company, which was virtually the sole producer of wooden matches in Canada between 1927 and 1940, and Canada Cement Limited, which produced nearly all the output of cement until the 1950s. At the time of the Royal Commission on Price Spreads (1935), Canadian Industries Limited produced all ammunition and explosives, the Consolidated Mining and Smelting Company produced over 90 percent of lead and over 70 percent of zinc, while 70 percent of the nickel used in Canada was refined by the International Nickel Company.

Many of the large companies no longer hold such dominant positions in their respective markets. Imperial Oil Company refined approximately 80 percent of all gasoline sold in Canada in 1921, but the company's percentage of total output had fallen to 55 percent by 1932 and to 38 percent in 1968. In the mid-1930s approximately 70 percent of tobacco output was accounted for by the Imperial Tobacco Company; by 1968 the company's sales represented only 42 percent of industry output.

The most striking cases of monopoly in today's economy are in transportation and public utilities. All railway rates in Canada are regulated by the Railway Transport Committee of the Canadian Transport Commission. Telephone rates of the two federally chartered companies, Bell Canada and British Columbia Telephone, are also subject to the regulation of the Canadian Transport Commission, and the rates of companies operating in the Atlantic and Prairie provinces fall under provincial regulation.

Even here, however, the monopoly sometimes exists only because of government regulation. For example, if a legal monopoly were not enforced by the government, postal and parcel delivery services would be fiercely competitive. In other cases a monopoly that seems quite unassailable will not persist over the decades. Technological breakthroughs have already been made that will make voice communication a competitive industry in the foreseeable future. The days of the monopoly of the telephone company are clearly numbered.

Monopoly and perfect competition do not *describe* much of the Canadian economy. Many industries with numerous firms depart from some of the conditions of perfect competition; most industries with no more than a few firms depart from the conditions of monopoly.

Patterns of Concentration in Manufacturing

Table 14-1 shows four-firm concentration ratios in selected Canadian manufacturing industries. Many of these industries approximate neither pure competition nor single-firm monopoly.

The concentration ratios alone provide limited information about the state of competitive rivalry, though they have long been used as an index of

TABLE 14–1 CONCENTRATION RATIOS IN SELECTED MANUFACTURING INDUSTRIES, 1980

Industry	Four-firm concentration ratio (percent)
Breweries	99
Motor vehicles	93.7
Cane and beef sugar procedures	92.0[a,b]
Aluminum rolling, casting, etc.	88.1
Cement	84.4
Iron and steel mills	77.9
Radio and television sets	77.1[a]
Distilleries	74.9
Agricultural implements	61.9
Petroleum refining	61.7
Soft drinks	48.2
Motor vehicle parts	44.6
Dairy products	37.0
Bakeries	33.5
Sporting goods	31.8
Pulp and paper mills	30.9
Pharmaceuticals and medicines	27.1
Shoes	25.5[a]
Men's clothing	20.6
Women's clothing	6.4

Source: Statistics Canada, 31–402.
[a] Figure given is for 1978; figure for 1980 is secret.
[b] Six-firm concentration ratio is 100.0.

Concentration varies greatly among manufacturing industries. The concentration ratios show the share of the industry's shipments accounted for by the four largest firms.

TABLE 14–2 COMPARISON OF LEVEL OF CONCENTRATION IN CANADA AND THE UNITED STATES

Number of companies required to account for 80% of shipments	CANADA (1965)		Percentage of total value of shipments	UNITED STATES (1963)		Percentage of total value of shipments
	Industries			Industries		
	Number	Percentage of total		Number	Percentage of total	
Up to 4	24	20.7	32.5	3	2.6	13.6
Over 4 to 8	22	19.0	8.2	7	6.0	4.2
Over 8 to 20	23	19.8	16.5	16	13.8	18.5
Over 20 to 50	20	17.2	15.5	31	26.7	15.8
Over 50	27	23.3	27.3	59	50.9	47.9
Total	116	100.0	100.0	116	100.0	100.0

Source: Department of Consumer and Corporate Affairs, *Concentration in the Manufacturing Industries of Canada,* 1971.

Canadian manufacturing is more highly concentrated than U.S. manufacturing. For example, about 40 percent of shipments in Canada are made by industries in which eight or fewer firms account for 80 percent of total industry shipments. The corresponding figure for the United States is less than 18 percent of shipments.

monopoly power. There is often intense rivalry in such concentrated industries as distilling, brewing, cigarette producing, and automobile manufacturing. Moreover, concentration ratios computed on a national basis neglect the regional nature of many markets. The cement industry would not appear to be a monopoly, since four firms account for 84 percent of industry output. It has been estimated, however, that 90 percent of cement is shipped less than 60 miles; therefore there may be substantial regional monopoly power within the industry.

In other industries the concentration ratios may overstate the degree of monopoly power. The fact that four firms account for 88 percent of aluminum rolling and casting may be misleading because aluminum competes with many other metals that are substitutes in a number of uses. Similarly, the high concentration in automobiles overstates the degree of monopoly power in that industry, for it does not take into account the effect of import competition from the Volkswagens, Datsuns, and Toyotas that are now so familiar on Canadian streets.

Canada and the United States

It is of some interest to compare the concentration in manufacturing industries in Canada with that in the United States. In some respects the Canadian economy differs materially from the U.S. economy. The population in Canada is slightly more than 10 percent of the U.S. population, while

TABLE 14–3 DISTRIBUTION OF INDUSTRIES BY FOUR-FIRM CONCENTRATION RATIO, 1980

Top four-firm concentration quartiles (percent)	Industries		Percentage of total value added
	Number	Percentage of total	
75–100	29	17.6	17.3
50–74	48	28.7	24.0
25–49	64	38.3	37.7
Up to 24	26	15.4	21.0
Total	167	100.0	100.0

The importance, both in numbers and in value added, of the intermediate categories indicates the inappropriateness of classifying many industries as either perfectly competitive or pure monopolies. This table, derived from the same source as Table 14-1, classifies manufacturing industries according to the market share of the four largest firms.

GNP is slightly less than 10 percent of the U.S. total. Foreign trade is of greater importance in the Canadian economy than in the American.

Although similarities in standard of living, consumption patterns, and education in the two countries have caused many similarities in industrial structure, the Canadian manufacturing sector is substantially more concentrated than the American.

A study published by the Department of Consumer and Corporate Affairs in 1971 yielded 116 industries or groups of industries for which meaningful comparisons between the United States and Canada could be made. The data obtained, given in Table 14-2, indicate the relatively higher concentration in Canadian manufacturing. Recent studies indicate that this basic relationship has continued to hold.[1]

Table 14-3 shows that in just under one-half of manufacturing industries, the four largest firms control more than 50 percent of the value of shipments. Such industries are not monopolies because there are several firms in the industry, and these firms engage in rivalrous behavior. Residents even of small towns will find more than one drugstore, garage, barber, and dress shop competing for their patronage. Similarly, manufacturers of computers, television sets, and chemicals belong to industries in which there are several close domestic rivals (and often foreign competitors). But neither are these firms in perfectly competitive markets. Often there are only a few major rival firms in an industry, but even when there are many, *they are not price takers.*

Virtually all consumers' goods are differentiated commodities. Any one firm will typically have several lines of a product that differ more or less from each other and from competing lines produced by other firms. There is no market setting a single price for razor blades, or television sets, that equates overall demand to overall supply. Instead, it is in the nature of such products that *sellers must*

state a price at which they are willing to sell. (Of course, a certain amount of "haggling" is possible, particularly at the retail level, but this is usually within well-defined limits set by the price initially quoted by the seller.)

Rivalrous behavior among firms that are not price takers immediately takes us out of the domain of either perfect competition or monopoly. We thus require additional market structures if we wish to explain the behavior.

The inadequacy of the perfect competition and monopoly models in dealing with much of Canadian industry has led to intense study of two further kinds of market structure, called *monopolistic competition* and *oligopoly*. Before turning to a detailed discussion of these two market structures, we note an important common feature.

The Importance of Administered Prices

In perfect competition, firms face a market price that they are unable to influence, and they adjust their quantities to that price. In perfect competition, firms are price takers and quantity adjusters. Changes in market conditions facing firms are signaled by changes in the market prices they face.

In all other market structures, firms face downward-sloping demand curves and thus know that they have a choice of price for their product. Since firms have some control over their prices, they must decide on a price to quote. In such circumstances, we say that the firm administers its price. The term **administered prices** refers to prices that are set by the decisions of individual firms rather than by impersonal market forces.

When a firm sets its price, the amount it sells is determined by its demand curve. Changes in market conditions change the amount that can be sold at its administered price. The changed conditions may or may not lead the firm to change the price that it charges.

With market structures other than perfect competition, firms set their prices and then let demand determine their sales. Changes in market conditions are signaled to the firm by changes in the quantity it can sell at its administered price.

---

[1] Professor Richard Caves of Harvard University recently led a team of researchers that studied competition in Canada. Their report, published in 1980, concluded that the relation between concentration ratios in 85 matched Canadian and U.S. industries is quite close, with the mean concentration ratio in Canada somewhat higher.

IMPERFECT COMPETITION AMONG THE MANY

Before the 1930s economists mainly studied the two polar market structures of perfect competition and monopoly. Then in the 1930s dissatisfaction with these two extremes caused a shift of emphasis to other theories of market structure. Because they emphasized competitive *behavior* while also emphasizing the absence of the conditions of perfect competition, these market forms were called *imperfect competition*. One of them was embodied in a wholly new theory; the other had been studied for over a century. We consider first the wholly new theory which outlined a market structure called **monopolistic competition.** The theory was developed in two classic books, one by the British economist Joan Robinson, the other by the American economist Edward Chamberlin.

The market envisaged in the new theory was similar to perfect competition in that there were many firms with freedom of entry and exit. But it differed in one important respect: Each firm had some power over price because each sold a product that was differentiated significantly from those of its competitors. One firm's soap might be similar to another firm's soap, but it differed in chemical composition, color, smell, softness, brand name, and a host of other characteristics that mattered to customers. This is the phenomenon of **product differentiation.** It implies that each firm has a certain degree of local monopoly power over its own product. This is the "monopolistic" part of the theory. The monopoly power is severely restricted, however, by the presence of similar products sold by many competing firms and by free entry and exit. This is the "competition" part of the theory.

From a theoretical point of view, the major difference between monopolistic and perfect competition lies in the assumptions of homogeneous and differentiated products. Firms in perfect competition sell a **homogeneous product,** which from a practical point of view means a product similar enough across the industry so that no one firm has any power over price. Firms in monopolistic competition sell a **differentiated product,** which from a practical point of view means a group of commodities similar enough to be called a product but dissimilar enough that the producer of each has some power over its own price.[2]

The Excess Capacity Theorem

There are two major characteristics of monopolistic competition. First, each firm is not a price taker. Instead, each firm faces a downward-sloping demand curve. But the curve is rather elastic because similar products sold by other firms provide many close substitutes. The downward slope of the demand curve provides the potential for monopoly profits in the short run.

Second, freedom of entry and exit forces profits to zero in the long run. If profits are being earned by existing firms in the industry, new firms will enter. Their entry will mean that the demand for the product must be shared among more brands. Thus the demand curve for any one firm's brand will shift left. Entry continues until profits fall to zero. Thus average revenue must equal average cost at some level of output but exceed it at none. Together these requirements imply that when a monopolistically competitive industry is in long-run equilibrium, its firms will be producing where their demand curves are tangent to (i.e., just touching at one point) their average total cost curves.

Two curves that are tangent at a point have the same slope at that point. If a downward-sloping demand curve is to be tangent to the average total cost curve, the latter must also be downward-sloping at the point of tangency. In such a situation, each firm is producing an output less than the one for which its *ATC* reaches its minimum point.

The zero-profit equilibrium of a monopolistically competitive firm occurs at an output less than the one at which average total cost is a minimum.

---

[2] The discussion here refers to large-group monopolistic competition, which occupied economists for several decades after Chamberlin's and Robinson's writings. Small-group monopolistic competition is discussed in the section on oligopoly.

This prediction is known as the **excess capacity theorem**. It is an implication of the assumptions of downward-sloping demand curves and free entry. To recapitulate: Free entry pushes firms to the point at which the demand curve is tangent to the average total cost curve. The demand curve slopes downward because buyers are supposed to think in such terms as, "I *prefer* Del Monte peaches"; "I *trust* Mr. Green, even if he is a little more expensive"; and "Isn't that the brand Joe DiMaggio uses?" But if the demand curve slopes downward, it must be tangent to the average total cost in its declining portion. This prediction is illustrated in Figure 14-1.

The excess capacity theorem aroused passionate

debate. It suggests that industries selling differentiated products are inefficient because they have excess capacity in long-run equilibrium and thus have a higher level of production costs than necessary. The modern conclusion, however, is that the "excess capacity" of monopolistic competition does not necessarily indicate inefficiency.

Monopolistic competition produces a wider range of products but less cheaply than perfect competition.

With differentiated products there is a choice available to consumers among several brands. Clearly, people have different tastes; some prefer one differentiated product and some prefer another. For example, each brand of breakfast food or video game has its devotees. This creates a trade-off—from the point of view of consumer welfare—between producing more products to better satisfy diverse tastes and producing any given set of products at the lowest possible cost.

Under these conditions how can consumers' satisfactions be maximized? This is *not* done by increasing production of one or two brands of a product until each is produced at its least-cost point. Instead, the number of differentiated products must be increased until the gain from adding one more equals the loss from having to produce each existing product at a higher cost (because less of each is produced). For this reason, among others, the charge that monopolistic competition would lead to a waste of resources is no longer accepted as necessarily, or even probably, true.

The Relevance of Monopolistic Competition

Perhaps the major blow the theories of Robinson and Chamberlin suffered was the slow realization that monopolistically competitive industries were rarely, if ever, found in reality. At first this claim may sound surprising because there are many industries in which many slightly differentiated products compete for the buyers' attention. The catch, however, is that in most such cases the industries have only a few firms, each of which sells a large number of products.

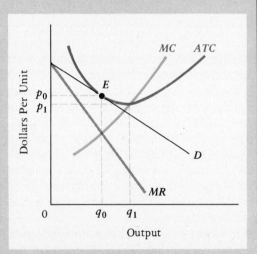

FIGURE 14-1
The Long-Run Equilibrium of a Firm in Monopolistic Competition

A monopolistically competitive firm in equilibrium has zero profits and excess capacity. Equilibrium is at point E where $MC = MR$ and where the demand curve is tangent to ATC. This results from free entry of firms with closely similar products. Price is p_0 and quantity q_0. Price is greater and quantity is less than the purely competitive equilibrium price and quantity (p_1 and q_1). At equilibrium, the monopolistically competitive firm has excess capacity of q_0q_1.

Consider the soap and detergent industry. Among the well-known brands currently on sale in Canada are Cheer, Dash, Duz, Gain, Oxydol, Tide, Dreft, Ivory Snow, Ivory Liquid, Joy, Cascade, Camay, Lava, Safeguard, Zest, Mr. Clean, Top Job, Spic and Span, Comet, and Samson. Surely this is impressive differentiation among a large number of products. This list of products might appear to provide a perfect example of monopolistic competition. But *every one* of the products named above is manufactured by a single company, Procter & Gamble, which, with Lever Brothers, dominates sales of soaps, cleansers, and detergents in North America. Clearly, such industries are not the large-group case envisaged by the framers of the theory of monopolistic competition.

Today, product differentiation occurs mainly where a small group rather than a large group of firms compete with each other.[3]

The Lasting Contribution of Monopolistic Competition

Looking back, we see that the original theory of monopolistic competition contributed at least two important things to the development of economics. In the 1920s and 1930s, perfect competition was under attack for the lack of realism of its assumptions. The theory of monopolistic competition recognized the facts of product differentiation, the ability of firms to influence prices, and the presence of advertising. The incorporation of these factors into a new theory encouraged economists to consider the question of their effects on the operation of the price system.

The Modern Theory of Monopolistic Competition

Today it is the small-group case of rather than the large-group case of monopolistic competition

that seems relevant. In the last half of the 1970s there was a great outburst of theorizing about all aspects of product differentiation.[4]

This modern theory is the direct descendant of the earlier theories of monopolistic competition. The focus remains on product differentiation and on industrial structures thought to describe the nature of the modern economy. The new theory is consistent with the famous propositions of Chamberlin and Robinson that it pays firms to differentiate their products, to advertise heavily, and to engage in other forms of nonprice competition. These are characteristics to be found in the world but not in perfect competition. Most of the modern theory of product differentiation relates to industries with a small number of firms. This is the theory of oligopoly.

IMPERFECT COMPETITION AMONG THE FEW

Manufacturing industries are often characterized by small groups of firms rather than large groups. **Oligopoly** is a market structure in which there are relatively few firms that have enough market power that they may not be regarded as price takers (as in perfect competition) but are subject to enough rivalry that they cannot consider the market demand curve as their own. In most of these cases entry is neither perfectly easy nor wholly blockaded. In many industries, a small number of firms—between three and a dozen—tend to dominate the industry, and newcomers find it hard to establish themselves.

While the North American automobile industry is a somewhat extreme example of this, its experience is revealing. Today three large firms and one much smaller firm constitute the industry. At least one of them is struggling to survive. No one has successfully entered the industry in the more than

---

[3] At first sight retailing may appear to be closer to the conditions of monopolistic competition than is manufacturing. Certainly every city has a very large number of retailers selling any one commodity. The problem is that they are differentiated from each other mainly by their geographical location, each firm having only a few competing close neighbors.

[4] It is one of those regrettable facts of life that the theory that studies market structures where a *small* number of firms compete to sell a large number of differentiated products has also taken the name *monopolistic competition*. The term now refers to any industry in which more than one firm sells differentiated products.

50 years since the Dodge brothers split with Ford and started making their own cars. Henry Kaiser attempted to enter in 1946. His Kaiser-Frazer came on the market, but despite the postwar boom in car sales the company suffered staggering losses and quietly withdrew in 1953. Recently, foreign automobile firms have been setting up plants in North America. These are not new entrants into the world's automobile industry, however, but merely new plants being set up by old established firms.

The cigarette industry with only eight firms in the entire industry is similar to automobiles. What makes the automobile industry unusual is the absence of a "competitive fringe."

In contrast, there are 192 petroleum refiners in the United States, but the 142 smallest firms together account for only 6 percent of value of output. There are 121 tire and tube manufacturing companies, of which the 100 smallest supply in aggregate less than 3 percent of the market. Oligopoly is not inconsistent with a large number of small sellers when the "big few" dominate the decision making in the industry.

Typically in oligopolistic industries, prices are administered and products differentiated, and the intensity and nature of rivalrous behavior varies greatly from industry to industry and from one period of time to another. This variety has invited extensive theoretical speculation and empirical study. Two important facts have been established and their significance debated. First, in oligopolistic industries, short-run cost curves are very flat rather than U-shaped. Second, oligopolistic prices change relatively infrequently; they are sometimes said to be "sticky."

Short-Run Costs in Oligopoly

Saucer-shaped Average Variable and Marginal Cost Curves

Ever since economists began measuring manufacturing firms' costs, they have reported very flat variable short-run cost curves. By now, the evidence is overwhelming that in manufacturing, and

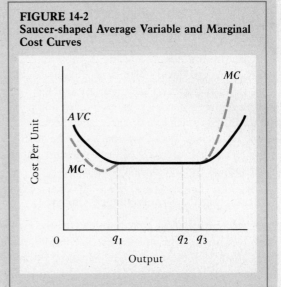

FIGURE 14-2
Saucer-shaped Average Variable and Marginal Cost Curves

When *AVC* is horizontal, marginal costs coincide with average variable costs and are likewise constant per unit of output. It is possible to design a plant that achieves roughly constant variable and marginal costs over a large range of output. Such a curve is shown here. While average variable costs decrease for outputs up to q_1 and increase beyond q_3, they are constant over the large range q_1 to q_3. The level of output q_2 is normal capacity output, which is the average output the firm hopes to achieve. This is less than the level of output at which either *AVC* or *ATC* is a minimum. With this cost curve, the firm can vary production over the whole interval from q_1 to q_3 and have constant marginal costs per unit.

in some other industries, cost curves are shaped like the curve shown in Figure 14-2, with a long, flat, middle portion and sharply rising sections at each end. (This "saucer" shape is to be compared with the traditional U-shaped cost curve shown in Figure 10-2 on page 163.) For such a cost curve, there is a large range of output over which average variable costs are constant. Over that range marginal costs are equal to average variable costs, and they too are constant per unit of output. [27]

Given a flat-bottomed cost curve, the nature of capacity output as we previously defined it becomes very much less useful because there is a wide range of output for which average cost is approximately minimized. It is now useful to distinguish between capacity output (as defined on page 162) where *ATC* is a minimum and normal capacity output, a somewhat lower level (such as q_2 in Figure 14-2) that the firm hopes to maintain on average.[5] The margin between normal capacity output and capacity output is available to meet unexpected, seasonal, or cyclical peaks in demand. The firm expects to use it in periods of peak demand but not in periods of average or slack demand.

Explaining the Saucer-shaped Curves

Why are many cost curves saucer-shaped rather than U-shaped? The answer is that firms design plants that yield this result. They do so on purpose, so that they can accommodate the inevitable seasonal and cyclical swings in demand for their products. As Professor George Stigler (the 1982 Nobel Laureate in Economics) was the first to point out, a firm faced with the two possible *AVC* curves, such as those shown in Figure 14-3, might well prefer to build a plant that results in the flat-bottomed one if it anticipates widely fluctuating demand. On average, the saucer-shaped curve leads to lower costs, even though at normal capacity output, the U-shaped cost curve dips below it.

How does it happen that the firm has a choice of the shape of its short-run average cost curve? Consider again the law of diminishing returns first encountered on page 157. The U-shaped short-run cost curve arises when a variable amount of one factor, say labor, is applied to a fixed amount of a second factor, say capital. Thus, as output is varied, factor proportions are necessarily varied. The argument for a U-shaped curve rests on first ap-

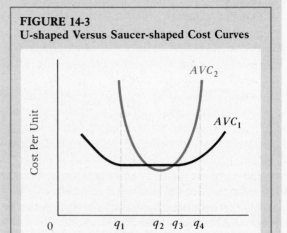

FIGURE 14-3
U-shaped Versus Saucer-shaped Cost Curves

A firm anticipating fluctuating output may choose a plant with a flat-bottomed cost curve. AVC_1 and AVC_2 are alternatives based on how a plant is designed and built. While the colored AVC_2 curve achieves lower unit costs than does the black AVC_1 if output is very close to q_2, it is much less adaptable to either higher or lower outputs. If the firm could count on producing q_2 every period, it would prefer the plant yielding AVC_2. But if it anticipated outputs ranging from q_1 to q_4, it might well prefer AVC_1.

plying too low a ratio of the variable factor to the fixed factor and then applying too high a ratio. As production is increased, starting from a very low level, more of the variable factor is used and a more efficient combination with the fixed factor achieved. Once the optimal combination is achieved, further units of the variable factor lead to too high a ratio and rising average variable costs. Only one quantity of labor leads to the precisely optimal factor proportions. This argument assumes that all the fixed factor must be used all of the time; in other words, that the fixed factor is *indivisible*.

While a plant can be built that way, it may also be built so that the fixed factor is in fact *divisible*. Even though the firm's plant and equipment may be fixed in the short run, so that no more is avail-

---

[5] There are really three different levels of capacity output that are sometimes talked about. In terms of Figure 14-2, there is first the level, q_2, which we call *normal capacity output*. Second, there is the higher level, q_3, where marginal and average *variable* costs turn sharply upward. Third, there is the still higher output (not shown) where *ATC* is minimum. Since average fixed costs decline steadily, average total cost is declining over the whole horizontal range of the flat *AVC* curve. All of this is confusing. Business almost always uses the concept of normal capacity. You can usually tell what economists mean from the context.

able, it may well be possible to utilize less than all the fixed capital.

Consider as a simple example a "factory" that consists of 10 sewing machines in a shed, each with a productive capacity of 20 units per day when operated for 1 shift by 1 operator. If 200 units per day are required, then all 10 machines are operated on a normal shift. If demand falls to 180, then 1 operator can be laid off. But there is no need to have the 9 remaining operators dashing about trying to work 10 machines. Clearly, 1 machine can be "laid off" as well, and the ratio of *employed* labor to *employed* machines held constant. Production can go from 20 to 40 to 60 all the way to 200 without any change in factor proportions of factors in use. In this case we would expect the factory to have constant marginal costs from 20 to 200 units and only then to encounter rising costs, as production must be expanded by overtime and other means of combining more labor with the maximum supply of 10 machines.

In such a case, the fixed factor is divisible. Since some of it can be left unemployed, there is no need to depart from the most efficient ratio of labor used to capital used as production is decreased. Thus, average variable costs can be constant over a large range, up to the point at which all the fixed factor is used.

The possibility of designing plants in which physical capital is divisible, combined with the advantage of doing so in an economy in which demand for a firm's product varies greatly from period to period, can account for the observed empirical fact of saucer-shaped plant cost curves.

A similar situation occurs when a firm has many plants. For example, a plywood manufacturer with 10 or more plants chooses to cut its output by temporarily closing one or more plants while operating the rest at normal capacity output. In this case too, the firm's short-run variable costs tend to be constant over a wide range of output.

Sticky Prices

One of the most striking contrasts between perfectly competitive and oligopolistic markets con-

cerns the behavior of prices. In perfect competition prices change continually in response to changes in demand and supply. Oligopolistic prices change less frequently. Manufacturers of radios, automobiles, television sets, and men's suits do not change their prices with anything like the frequency that prices change in markets for basic materials or stocks and bonds. If you price a man's suit or a woman's skirt today in your local store, chances are that the price will be the same when you return to the store tomorrow. Of course, prices do change, but in oligopolistic industries prices usually change by significant amounts at discrete intervals in time.

The basic empirical finding is as follows:

Oligopolistic firms do not alter their prices every time demand shifts. Instead, they fix prices and let quantity sold do the adjusting in the short term.

This phenomenon is often referred to as the *stickiness* of oligopolistic prices. Before considering possible explanations of why prices may be sticky, it is important to recognize that they do change.

When Oligopolistic Prices Do Change

Oligopolistic prices ordinarily change when there are major changes in costs of production. Rises in raw material prices or wage rates are passed on fairly quickly by rises in product prices.[6] Also, major reductions in costs, as when a new product such as the home computer is being developed, are usually followed by steady and major reductions in prices. This is because of the rivalry among oligopolistic firms: If one firm fails to cut price when costs fall, another firm will do so, seeking thereby to increase its market share.

Major unexpected shifts in demand also typically lead to price adjustments in oligopolistic prices. If an industry finds itself faced with an

---

[6] Oligopolistic pricing may, however, convert more or less continuous changes in input prices into discrete changes in output prices. Say that inflation is steadily raising the prices of industrial raw materials as determined in perfectly competitive markets. Firms find it expensive to change list prices every day or every week. They will therefore make discrete jumps in their output prices every few months, first getting output prices ahead of input prices, then slowly falling behind until a further adjustment of output prices is necessary.

apparently permanent and unexpected downward shift in demand, it will often cut its prices in an attempt to retain its market until longer-term adjustments can be made. For example, the North American car industry was faced with declining demand in the early 1980s due to its lag in developing small, fuel-efficient cars that were competitive with Japanese imports. It offered big rebates that slashed prices to levels that could not be maintained in the long run.

When Prices Are Sticky

The rigidity of oligopolistic prices lies not in the situations considered above. Instead, it lies mainly in *predictable* cyclical and seasonal shifts in demand. The ebb and flow of business activity is well known to firms, even if its precise course cannot be predicted in advance. Oligopolistic firms hold their prices fairly constant in the face of normal fluctuations in demand. These fluctuations thus cause output to vary while prices stay relatively stable.

Explaining Sticky Prices

Numerous theories have been offered to explain the stickiness of oligopolistic prices. An early interpretation stems from the pioneering work of two Oxford economists, Robert Hall and Charles Hitch. Their view was that businesspeople were conventional creatures of habit who were clearly not profit maximizers. They calculated their full costs at normal capacity and then added a conventional markup to determine price. They sold whatever they could at that price. Thus, demand fluctuations caused quantity rather than price fluctuations. This view of the conventional markup successfully explained the observed oligopolistic price stickiness but did not explain the observed fact that markups varied from time to time. We shall look at it more closely in Chapter 16. A second early explanation, much embraced a generation ago but now largely abandoned, is the so-called theory of the kinked demand curve, described in Box 14-1.

Most economists today believe that two forces

account for the stickiness of oligopolistic prices. First, flat short-run average cost curves are frequently found for oligopolistic firms. Second, there are high costs of changing administered prices—including the costs of printing new list prices for the many products of a typical multiproduct firm, the costs of notifying all customers, the accounting and billing difficulty of keeping track of frequently changing prices, and the loss of customer and retailer loyalty due to the uncertainty caused by frequent changes in prices.

The theory spelled out. This explanation of sticky prices is illustrated in Figure 14-4 on page 237. Firms make their decisions in stages. They estimate their *normal demand curve,* which is the average of what they can expect to sell at each price over booms and slumps. Having built a plant consistent with this demand and the expected fluctuations in output, they then pick as their "normal price" the profit-maximizing price for their normal demand curve. Short-run fluctuations in demand are met by holding price constant and varying output. This avoids all the costs involved in repeated change in prices.

The behavior just described is profit-maximizing behavior. Because the cost of changing prices is high, often the best thing a firm can do is to set the price that maximizes profits for average demand and then adjust output rather than price as demand varies over the cycle.

Implications of the theory. The behavior described has a number of other important implications.

1. As long as output remains within a range where the average cost curve is flat, the price charged tends to be a relatively fixed markup over cost. Thus the notion of a normal price is consistent with "normal markups" of the sort that led Hall and Hitch to their theory of sticky prices.
2. Cyclical fluctuations in demand are met by quantity adjustments rather than price adjustments.
3. Cost changes in either an upward or a downward direction are passed on through price

BOX 14–1 THE KINKED DEMAND CURVE

An explanation of oligopolistic price stickiness was developed in the 1930s by the economist Paul Sweezy. This theory predicts price stickiness in the face of significant shifts both in demand and in costs.

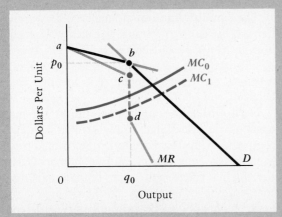

Professor Sweezy's explanation was based on a novel demand curve for the oligopolist firm. Each oligopolist conjectures that its rivals will match any price decreases it makes but will not follow it in any price increases. If the firm raises its price and no one follows, it will lose market share and its sales will fall off rapidly; its demand curve will be very flat. If the firm lowers its price and everyone follows, it will not gain

market share and its sales will expand only in proportion to the expansion in the industry's sales. The demand curve for price cuts will thus be steeper than the demand curve for price increases. The resulting **kinked demand curve** is shown in the figure.

The black curve abD is the firm's perception of its own demand curve. The corresponding marginal revenue curve is the discontinuous curve $acdMR$. [28] A shift in marginal cost from MC_0 to MC_1 changes neither the price nor the output that maximizes profits.

With the kinked demand curve there is an interval over which the firm's profit-maximizing price will be unchanged despite changing economic conditions. This theory predicts that prices will be inflexible in response to changes in costs anywhere in the interval from c to d.

This ingenious theory survives in many textbooks to this day. It has, however, almost no supporting evidence. Its two main deficiencies are first, while it predicts a tendency for a price, once set, to be maintained, it says nothing about what price is set initially. Second, it predicts price stickiness not only in the case of fluctuating demand, but also in the face of sharp shifts in costs. This latter prediction is repeatedly contradicted by empirical evidence.

changes (although possibly with a lag because oligopolistic firms find it costly to make continuous price changes).

4. Oligopolistic firms receive signals from the economy just as do perfectly competitive firms. But the form the signals take is different. While market changes are signaled to perfect competitors by a price change, oligopolies receive their signals about changes in market conditions from a change in their volume of sales.

The second and the third implications are especially important when we study some current

controversies in macroeconomics. We shall return to them in Chapter 42.

Longer-Run Theories of Oligopoly Behavior

The discussion above concentrated on the short-run pricing decisions of oligopolistic firms. We now consider how these prices are set, and this raises the most critical aspect of oligopoly: Firms know they have identifiable rivals whose behavior they cannot afford to neglect. If Simpsons watches Eatons, so too does Eatons watch Simpsons.

An oligopolistic firm's price and output decisions depend on how it *thinks* its competitors will react to its moves, and the outcome of its policy depends on how they *do* in fact react. Under these circumstances there is no simple set of rules for the equilibrium either of the firm or of the small group of firms that constitutes the industry. Neither is there a set of simple predictions about how the firms will react, either individually or collectively, to changes in such things as taxes, costs, and market demand.[7]

In the face of this complexity, economists have sometimes proposed simplifying models, and sometimes turned to empirical findings to suggest generalizations. We shall look at examples of each.

Cournot-Nash Equilibrium

A pathbreaking attack on the oligopoly problem occurred as long ago as 1838 in the work of the French economist A. A. Cournot. He dealt with the special case of an industry containing only two firms, called a **duopoly.** The two firms sold an identical product. Cournot assumed that each firm chose its profit-maximizing output on the assumption that the other firm would hold its own output constant. He then showed that if each firm in turn adjusted to the last move made by its competitor (on the assumption that the competitor would make no further move), a stable equilibrium would be reached in which the market was divided between the two firms in a definite way. Each firm would charge the same price as the other, and that price would be higher than the perfectly competitive price but lower than the price a monopolist would charge. This finding established oligopoly

as a truly intermediate case between perfect competition and monopoly.

Firms in the situation analyzed by Cournot will raise price and lower output when costs rise, and they will usually raise price and raise output when demand increases. Thus changes in price and quantity are in the same direction as under perfect competition, though the magnitude of the changes will be different.

The equilibrium Cournot analyzed has survived in modern theorizing. It is now called a **Nash equilibrium** or a **Cournot-Nash equilibrium.** It is the equilibrium that results when each firm makes its decisions on the assumption that all other firms' behavior will be unchanged.

Nash equilibria can be determined for many oligopolistic situations. Their properties can be compared with the equilibria that would result from perfect competition and from monopoly (usually, higher prices and lower output than under competition; lower prices and higher output than under monopoly). The price-quantity differences can also be studied when equilibrium changes under the impact of shifts in input costs or demand for the industry's output.

To many economists the Cournot-Nash assumption that each firm takes its rival's behavior as given seems simply wrong in a great many small-group situations. The Ford Motor Company knows (or quickly learns) that if it slashes the prices of some of its cars, GM, Chrysler, and American Motors will react by adjusting their prices on comparable cars. Similar considerations apply when General Mills considers changing the advertising for one of its breakfast cereals or Lever Brothers the prices of its soaps.

Thus not only must an oligopolistic firm be concerned with how *buyers* of its products will react to changes it makes, it must anticipate how each of a few identified rival *sellers* will react.

---

[7] It is often said that, under these circumstances, price and output are *indeterminate.* Such a statement is misleading since the price and output do, of course, get determined somehow. What is meant, however, is that, under oligopoly, price and output are not uniquely determined by the same factors as in large-group cases. In small-group cases an additional set of factors—competitors' real and imagined reactions to each other's behavior—contributes to the determination of price and output.

Conjectural Variations

Some economists dealing with oligopoly broadened the Cournot approach by assuming that each

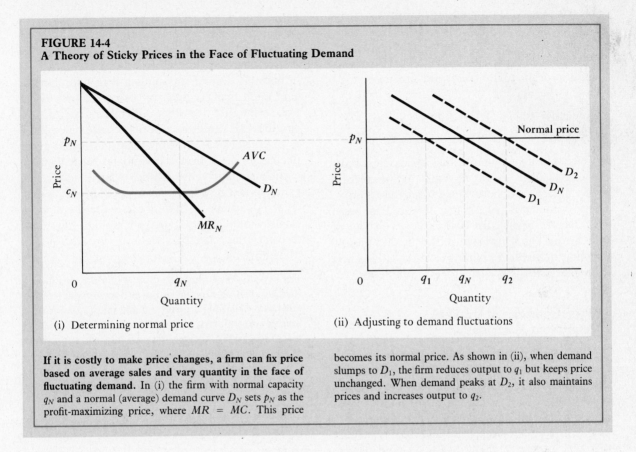

FIGURE 14-4
A Theory of Sticky Prices in the Face of Fluctuating Demand

(i) Determining normal price

(ii) Adjusting to demand fluctuations

If it is costly to make price changes, a firm can fix price based on average sales and vary quantity in the face of fluctuating demand. In (i) the firm with normal capacity q_N and a normal (average) demand curve D_N sets p_N as the profit-maximizing price, where $MR = MC$. This price becomes its normal price. As shown in (ii), when demand slumps to D_1, the firm reduces output to q_1 but keeps price unchanged. When demand peaks at D_2, it also maintains prices and increases output to q_2.

firm recognized its interdependence with its rivals and made its decisions subject to what are called *conjectural variations*. A firm making a price decision conjectures what variations its choice would induce its rivals to make in their prices and takes those variations into account in its decisions.

One problem with this approach is that a wide range of conjectural variations is possible. For example, firm A might assume that whatever price it sets, its rivals will set the same price. Or it might assume that its rivals will undercut any price it charges. Equilibrium can be shown to exist for many conjectural variations. Unfortunately, there is almost no end to the possible patterns of conjectural variation or the range of outcomes that is possible. Unless one knows that one set of conjec-

tural variations is the way firms "really think," one cannot predict actual behavior.

Additional Problems for Industries Producing Differentiated Products

All the difficulties mentioned above arise even for oligopolists selling a homogeneous product. Another set of oligopoly problems arises when firms sell differentiated products. For example, one brand of cigarettes sold by the American Tobacco Company differs not only from all other brands sold by that company, but from all brands sold by competing companies. With differentiated products, each product is distinct from every other product, and firms can use quality changes, advertising, and multiple products as competitive weapons. This added complexity means that (so far as pure theory is concerned) almost anything is possible under conditions of oligopoly. This is not very helpful in dealing with real-world situations.

Empirically Based Approaches to Oligopolistic Behavior

Because the oligopoly problem is so complex, some economists have sought to build a theory from observations of the behavior of oligopolistic firms. These economists believe that we need to begin with detailed knowledge of the actual behavior of such firms. The knowledge is then used to narrow the range of theoretically possible cases by selecting those that actually occur.

The Hypothesis of Qualified Joint Profit Maximization

While explicit collusion is illegal in Canada, why cannot a small group of firms that recognize their interdependence simply act in a common manner? If all firms behave as though they were branches of a single firm, they can achieve the ends of a monopolist by adopting price and output policies that will maximize their *collective* (joint) *profits.* Every firm is interested, however, in *its own* profits, not the industry's profits, and it may pay one firm to depart from the joint profit-maximizing position if, by so doing, it can increase its share of the profits.

The hypothesis of qualified joint profit maximization thus rests on the notion that a firm in an oligopolistic industry responds to *two* sets of influences.

Any oligopolistic firm wants to cooperate with its rivals to maximize their joint profits; it also wants to receive as large a share of the profits as possible.

Consider the conflicting pressures on an oligopolistic firm when it chooses its price. First, if firms in a group recognize that they are interdependent and face a downward-sloping industry demand curve, they will recognize that their joint profits depend on the price each of them charges. This pulls each firm to cooperate with its rivals in charging the same price that a single firm would charge if it monopolized the industry.

Second, despite this pull, a firm may hope to gain more than its rivals by being the first to cut price. But if it does this, other firms may follow and the total profits earned in the industry will fall as prices are pushed below their joint profit-maximizing level. A firm that initiates such a price-cutting strategy must balance what it expects to gain by securing a larger *share* of the profits against what it expects to lose because there will be a smaller total of profits to go around. Box 14-2 discusses the related problem of why cartels tend to be unstable.

The hypothesis of qualified joint profit maximization is that the relative strength of the two tendencies (toward and away from joint profit maximization) varies from industry to industry in a systematic way that may be associated with observable characteristics of firms, markets, and products.

Let us consider some examples.

Some Specific Hypotheses About Oligopolistic Behavior

1. The tendency toward joint maximization is greater for small numbers of sellers than for larger numbers. Here the argument concerns both ability and motivation. When there are few firms, they will know that one of them cannot gain sales without inducing retaliation by its rivals. Also, a few firms can tacitly coordinate their policies with less difficulty than can many firms.

2. The tendency toward joint maximization is greater for producers of very similar products than for producers of sharply differentiated products. The argument here is that the more nearly identical the products of sellers, the closer will be the direct rivalry for customers and the less the ability of one firm to gain a lasting advantage over its rivals. Such sellers will tend to prefer joint efforts to achieve a larger pie to individual attempts to increase their individual shares.

3. The tendency toward joint maximization is greater in a growing than in a contracting market. The argument here is that when demand is growing, firms can utilize their capacity fully without resorting to attempts to "steal" their rivals' customers. In contrast, when firms have excess capacity, they are tempted to give price concessions to attract customers. But when their rivals retaliate, price cuts become general.

4. The tendency toward joint maximization is greater when the industry contains a dominant firm rather than a set of more or less equal competitors. A dominant firm may become a **price leader,** which is a firm that sets the industry's price while all other firms fall into line. If a dominant firm knows that it really is a price leader, it can set the monopoly price, confident that all other firms will follow it. Even if a dominant firm is not automatically a price leader, other firms may look to it for judgment about market conditions, and its decisions become a tentative focus for quasi-agreement.

5. Tacit price fixing to maximize joint profits will cause nonprice competition that will take the industry away from its joint maximizing position. The argument here is that when firms seek to suppress their basic rivalry by avoiding price competition, rivalry will break out in other forms. Firms may seek to increase their market shares through extra advertising, quality changes, the establishment of new products, bonuses, giveaways, and a host of similar schemes which leave their list prices unchanged.

6. The tendency toward joint profit maximizing is greater, the greater are the barriers to entry of new firms. The high profits of existing firms will attract new entrants, who will drive down price and reduce profits. The greater the barriers to entry, the less this will occur. Thus the greater the entry barriers, the closer the profits of existing firms can be to their joint maximizing level. Such barriers to entry may be natural or created by the firm. Perhaps the most important empirical observation about actual oligopoly behavior is the critical importance of what Professor Joe S. Bain called the *condition of entry.* It is worth a closer look.

Barriers to Entry

Suppose firms in an oligopolistic industry succeed in raising prices above long-run average total costs so that economic profits are earned. Why do these profits not cause further firms to enter the industry? Why does entry not continue until the extra output forces price down to the level where only the opportunity cost of capital is being earned (i.e., economic profits are zero)?

The answer lies in *barriers to entry,* which are anything that puts new firms that wish to enter an industry at a significant competitive disadvantage relative to established firms. Barriers are of three sorts: natural barriers, barriers created by existing firms, and barriers created by government policy. We discuss the first two in this chapter.

Natural Barriers

Natural barriers to entry may result from an interaction between market size—as shown by the market demand curve—and economies of scale—as shown by the firm's long-run average total cost curve (*LRATC*).

One type of natural barrier depends on the shape of the *LRATC* curve and in particular on what is called **minimum efficient scale (MES).** This term refers to the smallest size firm that can reap all the available economies of large scale.

Suppose the technology of an industry is such that the typical firm's *MES* is 10,000 units a week at an *ATC* of $10 per unit and that at a price of $10 the total quantity demanded is 30,000 units per week. Clearly there is room for no more than three plants of efficient size—and hence three firms at most will serve this market. Even if these firms tacitly agree to reduce output to 9,000 units each and raise price, there is not room for an additional firm.

Natural barriers to entry occur when the output at which *MES* is achieved is large relative to total demand. Under these circumstances a small number of existing

BOX 14–2 PROBLEMS IN ATTEMPTS TO COLLUDE

Sellers of goods and services often seek collective action to raise what they consider excessively low prices. Cocoa producers in west Africa, wheat producers in the United States and Canada, the Organization of Petroleum Exporting Countries (OPEC), coffee growers in Brazil, taxi drivers in many cities, and labor unions throughout the world have all sought to obtain, through collective action, some of the benefits of departing from perfectly competitive situations. Basically they have sought to form organizations to regulate the price and output of the goods or services they supply.

The motive behind this drive for monopoly power is easy to understand. The equilibrium position of a perfectly competitive industry is one in which a restriction of output and a consequent increase in price will always increase the profits of all producers.

This is particularly obvious when (as is so often the case with agricultural goods) the demand for the product is inelastic at the equilibrium price; then marginal revenue is negative. Because marginal cost is positive, since it surely costs something to produce every extra unit, a reduction in output will not only raise the total revenues of producers, it will also reduce total costs.

It is equally true that the industry's profits can be increased, even if demand is elastic at the competitive equilibrium price. At such an equilibrium, each firm is producing where marginal cost equals price. Because the market demand curve slopes downward, the industry's marginal revenue is less than price—and thus less than marginal cost. Therefore, in competitive equilibrium, the last unit sold necessarily contributes more to the industry's costs than to its revenue.

In a perfectly competitive industry, profits will increase if the producers enter into an effective agreement to restrict output.

The big "if" is the ability to form and maintain an *effective* agreement. A **cartel** is an organization of producers designed to eliminate competition among its members, usually by restricting output. OPEC is the best-known cartel of modern times, and for a time it was the most effective. An unusual set of circumstances led to OPEC's success. The more usual experience is for cartels to break down.

Cheating: The Instability of Cartels

A cartel attempts to reduce the output of a commodity by getting each producing firm to agree to restrict its output. While there is an incentive under perfect competition for all producers to enter into such an agreement, there is also an incentive for each producer to violate it.

firms may earn profits without inducing a further firm to enter the market.

A second type of natural cost barrier occurs when there are **absolute cost advantages.** This means that existing firms have average cost curves significantly lower over their entire range than those of potential new entrants. Among possible sources of such an advantage are control of crucial patents or resources, knowledge that comes only from "learning by doing" in the industry, and established credit ratings that permit advantageous purchasing and borrowing. Each of these may be regarded as only a temporary disadvantage by new

To see how this would happen, consider a producers' cooperative that raises prices by cutting production. Suppose that every firm except one restricts its output. That one firm will be doubly well off in that it can sell its original output at the new, higher price received by all other firms that have restricted their production. But the same is true for *each* firm.

A co-op organized mainly to restrict output is subject to competing pressures, illustrated in the figure. Each of the firms is better off if the co-op is formed and is effective; but each firm is even better off if every other firm plays ball while only it does not. Yet if everyone cheats (or stays out of the co-op), everyone will be worse off.

Cartels tend to be unstable because of the incentives for individual producers to violate output quotas.

The history of schemes to raise farm incomes by limiting crops bears ample testimony to the accuracy of this prediction. Crop restriction agreements often break down, and prices fall, as individuals exceed their quotas. The great bitterness and occasional violence that is sometimes exhibited by members of crop restriction plans against nonmembers and members who cheat is readily understandable.

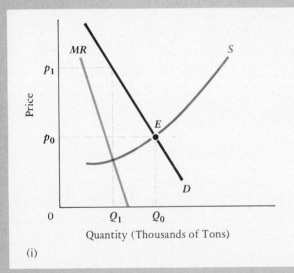

(i)

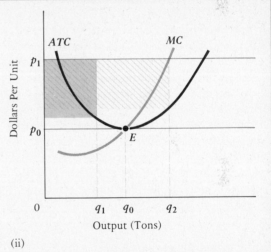

(ii)

firms, which, given time, might develop their own know-how, patents, and satisfactory credit ratings.

This kind of barrier, however, makes it possible for existing firms to charge a price such that although existing firms earn profits, new entrants may face losses for some time after entry. This price is known as a **limit price.** The early losses, which persist until the new firms' *ATC*s fall to the level of the going price, can make entry seem sufficiently unprofitable—in spite of the expectation of later profits—to prevent entry.

Some interesting implications for policies to deal with international trade in an *open* economy like Canada's are discussed in Box 14-3.

BOX 14–3 MES, INDUSTRY RATIONALIZATION, AND THE EASTMAN-STYKOLT HYPOTHESIS

Declining costs can lead to a minimum scale at which production is efficient. For many industries this *MES* exceeds the total domestic market for the product. Importing the commodity from larger foreign countries would then be cheaper than producing it domestically, and competitive forces would lead to the elimination of the domestic industry.

Professors Harry Eastman and Stephen Stykolt of the University of Toronto and other economists have argued that many Canadian industries are in this situation and that without tariffs and other forms of protection from foreign competition, the domestic industries might disappear. The protection so afforded allows domestic production in these industries to be profitable even at a scale well below the industry's *MES*.

In the view of many economists, by propping up such industries and hence preventing resources from moving to more productive uses, this policy has resulted in a costly and inefficient industrial structure. Such protection has also, it is contended, led to the extensive foreign ownership of Canadian industry, for many of the protected industries are dominated by foreign-

owned multinational corporations that build branch plants in Canada as a way of circumventing the trade barriers that make it unprofitable to export to Canada directly.

What would happen if the barriers to trade were removed? Would these corporations then serve the Canadian market more efficiently from their lower-cost U.S. plants? To answer this question, we must examine further the sources of the economies of scale.

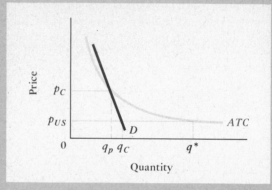

In many industries scale economies arise from the ability to sustain long production runs. With a small market, there is then a trade-off between efficient scale and product diversity. For exam-

Firm-Created Barriers to Entry

If natural entry barriers do not exist, oligopolistic firms can earn long-run economic profits only if they can create barriers that prevent their profits from attracting new entrants into the industry. Some are plainly illegal, such as hiring thugs to "persuade" potential rivals to stay away. This method is not uncommon in industries controlled by criminals. Others are more genteel—and if they are illegal it is under antitrust laws, not as ordinary crimes. Consider two.

Predatory pricing. A firm that is considering

entry will not do so if faced with certain losses after entry. One way existing firms can create such a situation is to cut prices to—or below—cost whenever entry occurs and keep them there until the entrant goes bankrupt. The existing firms sacrifice profits while doing so, but they send a discouraging message to future as well as present potential rivals.

There is much controversy concerning predatory pricing. Some economists argue that pricing policies that appear to be predatory can be explained by other motives and that existing firms only hurt themselves when they engage in such practices instead of reaching an accommodation

ple, the Canadian pulp and paper industry, if it were to produce solely for the domestic market, would operate inefficiently because of the costs of having to change production runs frequently in order to produce paper of different weights, grades, colors, and widths. One possible response to moving to freer trade would be for the domestic industry to specialize in only a few particular products lines, thereby lengthening production runs and reaping the economies of scale. However, most domestic production would then be exported; diversity in domestic consumption would have to be provided by imports.

This specialization in narrow product lines and the resultant *intraindustry* trade is often called *rationalization* of the domestic industry.* Such a process provides the domestic economy with the twin benefits of efficient scale in production and diversity in consumption. This is illustrated in the figure.

The figure shows the *ATC* and domestic de-

* Intraindustry trade occurs when a country simultaneously exports and imports goods produced in the same industry. For example, Canada engages in intraindustry trade in automobiles.

mand curves *for a particular product line. MES* is reached at an output level of q^*, far in excess of the domestic demand q_C at the price corresponding to *ATC* for the efficient scale of output. Protection of the domestic industry allows the Canadian price p_C to exceed the foreign price p_{US} and leads to output and consumption of q_p. Free trade causes prices to fall to p_{US}, domestic demand rises to q_C, and domestic output rises to the efficient level, q^*. The difference between domestic production and consumption, q^*q_C, is exported. For other product lines, the removal of protection barriers also causes prices to fall and domestic demand to grow, but the demand is satisfied by imports. Hence the advantages of efficiency in production and diversity in consumption are realized.

Such rationalization is possible through explicit international agreement. Is it possible without such agreement? One example of such an agreement is the Automotive Products Trade Act (the "Auto Pact") passed in Canada in 1965. An assessment of the Auto Pact and a discussion of the contrasting case of industries where rationalization occurs without explicit agreement appear in the twin boxes on pages 373 and 375.

with new entrants. Others argue that predatory pricing seems to have been observed and that it is in the long-run interests of existing firms to punish new entrants even when it is costly to do so in the short run.

Advertising. The heavy levels of advertising in differentiated oligopolistic industries may be partly motivated by a desire to erect entry barriers. Suppose there are few scale economies so that a new firm can reach minimum costs at an output that is low relative to total industry output. Thus there are only weak natural barriers to entry. (This is the

case, for example, in the cigarette and soap industries.) Existing firms can create entry barriers by imposing fixed costs on new entrants. These fixed costs raise the *MES* of all firms, including new entrants.

Where there is much effective brand-image advertising, a new firm will have to spend a great deal on advertising its product in order to bring it to the public's attention. If the firm's sales are small, advertising costs *per unit sold* will be very large. Only when sales are large, so that the advertising costs can be spread over a large number of units, will costs per unit be brought down to a level low enough that they will not confer a significant competitive disadvantage on the new firm.

Figure 14-5 illustrates how heavy advertising can shift the cost curves of a firm with a low *MES* to make it one with a high *MES*. In essence, what happens is that a scale advantage of advertising is added to a low *MES* of production, with the result that the overall *MES* is raised. Thus a new entrant who must both produce and advertise finds itself at a substantial cost disadvantage relative to its established rivals.

A firm with no natural entry barriers may be able to create them by use of nonprice competition. Advertising, of course, does things other than create barriers to entry. Among them, it may perform the useful function of informing buyers about their alternatives, thereby making markets work more smoothly. Indeed, a new firm may find that advertising is essential, even when existing firms do not advertise at all, simply to call attention to its entry into an industry where it is unknown.

Oligopoly and Resource Allocation

Firms in oligopolistic markets (as well as monopolies) administer their prices. The market signaling system works slightly differently when prices are determined by the market than when they are administered. Changes in the market conditions for both inputs and outputs are signaled to the perfectly competitive firm by changes in the *prices* of its inputs and its outputs. Changes in the market conditions for inputs are signaled to the oligopolist by changes in the prices of its inputs. Changes in the market conditions for the oligopolist's product are typically signaled, however, by a change in sales at the administered price.

The oligopolist that administers its price gets a signal when the demand for its product changes, the signal taking the form of a variation in its sales.

Rises in costs of inputs will shift cost curves upward, and oligopolistic firms will be led—if the shift is not reversed—to raise price and lower output. Rises in demand will cause the sales of oligopolistic firms to rise. Firms will then respond by

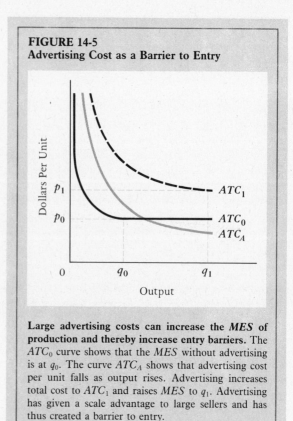

FIGURE 14-5
Advertising Cost as a Barrier to Entry

Large advertising costs can increase the *MES* of production and thereby increase entry barriers. The ATC_0 curve shows that the *MES* without advertising is at q_0. The curve ATC_A shows that advertising cost per unit falls as output rises. Advertising increases total cost to ATC_1 and raises *MES* to q_1. Advertising has given a scale advantage to large sellers and has thus created a barrier to entry.

increasing output, thereby increasing the quantities of society's resources that are allocated to producing that commodity.

The market system reallocates resources in response to changes in demand and costs in roughly the same way under oligopoly as it does under perfect competition.

Although the market system allocates resources under oligopoly in a manner that is qualitatively similar to what happens under perfect competition, the actual allocation is not likely to be the same. Generally, oligopolistic industries will earn profits and will charge prices that exceed marginal cost (because the firms face downward-sloping demand curves and will equate marginal cost to marginal revenue, not to price). In this respect oligopoly is similar to monopoly.

There is a wide range of oligopolistic behavior.

Some oligopolies succeed in coming close to the sort of joint profit maximization that would characterize monopoly. Others compete so intensely among themselves that they approximate competitive prices and outputs. The allocative consequences vary accordingly.

Oligopoly is an important market structure in today's economy because there are many industries where the *MES* is simply too large to support large-group competition. Oligopoly will not, in general, achieve the optimal allocative efficiency of perfect competition. Rivalrous oligopoly, however, may produce more satisfactory results than monopoly. The defense of oligopoly as a market form is that it may be the best of the available alternatives where the *MES* is large. The challenge to public policy is to keep oligopolists competing. Public policies that have this objective are discussed in Chapter 15.

SUMMARY

1. A review of the structure of the Canadian economy shows that while there are both large-firm and small-firm sectors, most of the industries involved do not conform to the models of either perfect competition or monopoly.

2. In market structures other than perfect competition, firms tend to administer prices and accept the quantities they can sell at those prices. Changes in market conditions are signaled not by the prices they face, but by the quantities they can sell.

3. Monopolistic competition is a market structure in which firms sell a differentiated product. Large-group monopolistic competition does not apply to a significant number of industries in today's world. Differentiated products abound, but generally they are produced in industries that contain a small number of firms, each one of which sells many such products. This is small-group oligopoly.

4. Oligopoly is a market structure in which (a) the firms in an industry are sufficiently few so that they recognize they are interdependent; (b) anything that one firm does will probably lead to a reaction by rival sellers; (c) typically, entry is neither perfectly free nor entirely blockaded.

5. A key empirical finding about oligopolistic industries is that short-run cost curves tend to be very flat over a substantial range of output. A second important empirical finding is the relative stickiness of oligopoly prices in response to seasonal and cyclical fluctuations in output. This stickiness results from a combination of the flat short-run cost curves and the costs involved in changing administered prices frequently. Oligopolistic firms find it profitable to accept output fluctuations while keeping prices fixed, as demand fluctuates cyclically around longer-term normal levels.

6. The outcome of oligopolistic situations in the long run depends on the strategies adopted by the various rivals. Therefore, there are many possible patterns of behavior to understand, explain, and predict. A very general hypothesis of qualified joint profit maximization says that firms are motivated by two sets of opposing forces, one set moving them toward joint profit maximization and the other moving them away from it. The six specific hypotheses given in the text illustrate how observable variables may influence the two sets of opposing forces.

7. Oligopolies persist because of barriers to entry, which may be natural or created. Natural barriers include large minimum efficient scales and absolute cost advantages. Advertising is an illustration of a firm-created barrier.

8. Under oligopoly the price system works to reallocate resources in response to changes in demand and costs in qualitatively the same way as it does under perfect competition. Oligopoly may not be as efficient as perfect competition, but it is responsive to major changes in economic conditions.

TOPICS FOR REVIEW

Concentration ratios
Administered prices
Product differentiation

Saucer-shaped short-run average costs
Sticky prices
Barriers to entry
Minimum efficient scale

DISCUSSION QUESTIONS

1. Does the consumer benefit from lower prices, by higher quality, by more product variety, by advertising? If trade-offs are necessary (more of one means less of another), how would you evaluate their relative importance with respect to the following products?
   a. Vitamin pills
   b. Beer
   c. Cement
   d. Bath soap
   e. Women's dresses
   f. Television programs
   g. Prescription drugs
2. White sidewall tires cost about $1 per tire more to manu-facture than black sidewall tires, and they lower somewhat the durability of tires. At the retail level the extra cost of a white sidewall tire is at least $5 per tire. Yet 70 percent of all passenger car tires manufactured in the North America in 1983 were the white sidewalls. What, if anything, do these facts tell you about the market structure of the man-ufacture, distribution, or marketing of automobile tires? If white sidewalls are found to be somewhat more likely to suffer blowouts, should their use be prohibited by law?
3. It is sometimes said that there are more drugstores and gasoline stations than are needed. In what sense might that be correct? Does the consumer gain anything from this plethora of retail outlets? How would you determine the optimal number of movie theaters or gasoline stations in a city of 100,000 people?
4. Are any of the following industries monopolistically com-petitive? Explain your answer.

   a. Textbook publishing (Fact: There are over 50 elementary economics textbooks in use somewhere in North Amer-ica this year.)
   b. College education
   c. Cigarette manufacture
   d. Restaurant operation
   e. Automobile retailing
5. It has been estimated that if automobile companies did not change models for 10 years, the cost of production would be reduced by approximately 30 percent. In view of this fact, why are there annual model changes? Which, if any, of the reasons you have suggested depend on the industry's being oligopolistic? Should frequent model changes be for-bidden by law?
6. Compare and contrast the effects on the automobile and the wheat industries of each of the following.
   a. The effect of a large rise in demand on quantity sold
   b. The effect of a large rise in costs on price
   c. The effect on price of a temporary cut in supplies coming to market due to a three-month rail strike
   d. The effect on price and quantity sold of a rush of cheap foreign imports
   e. The effects of a large rise in the price of one of the industry's important imports
   In light of your answers, discuss general ways in which oligopolistic industries fulfill the same general functions as do perfectly competitive industries.
7. It is illegal in Canada for competitors to fix prices by agree-ment, yet conspiracies have been discovered and punished. Why should firms take the risk of collusion when it is perfectly legal for each to simply charge the price that maximizes the joint profits of the group? What factors might you hypothesize that would make collusion more (or less) likely?
8. Many people in advertising have thought that economists, with their emphasis on efficiency in the allocation of re-sources, have not been duly appreciative of the role of advertising in influencing consumer preferences. What roles does economic analysis give to advertising? Which are regarded as improving resource allocation and which as worsening it?

15 MONOPOLY VERSUS COMPETITION

Monopoly has long been regarded with suspicion. In *The Wealth of Nations* (1776), Adam Smith—the founder of modern economics—developed a ringing attack on monopolies and monopolists. Since then, most economists have criticized monopoly and advocated freer competition. In Chapters 12 and 13 we saw that perfect competition has appealing features and that it is efficient in ways that monopoly is not.

Is a preference for competition and a distrust of monopoly justified? Can competition be too intense for the public good? This chapter carries further the comparison of monopoly and competition in terms of their predicted effects, then looks at the principal policies for dealing with monopoly and competition in Canada.

Throughout the discussion we speak of *monopoly* in the sense of monopoly power, not merely of the single firm. Similarly we speak of *competition* to refer to competitive behavior, which goes beyond the market structure of perfect competition.

COMPARISONS BETWEEN MONOPOLY AND COMPETITION

A number of interesting questions can be asked concerning the differences between industries showing monopolistic and those showing competitive behavior. For example, we may ask whether a change in market structure affects the level of cost, or whether monopoly provides greater incentives to innovate, or what conditions are most conducive to destructive competition. We shall examine each of these, but first we shall look at the essence of the "case against monopoly."

The Monopolization of a Competitive Industry with No Change in Costs

The case against monopoly is to a great extent based on the following prediction:

If a perfectly competitive industry should be monopolized, and if the cost curves of all productive units are unaffected by this change, the price will rise and the quantity produced will fall.

Assume that a competitive industry is monopolized as the result of a single firm's buying out all the individual producers and operating each one as an independent plant. Further assume that cost curves are not affected by this change.

When the industry is monopolized, it becomes profitable to drive price up. As long as neither market demand nor costs change, it will always pay the monopolist who charges a single price to restrict output below, and to raise price above, their perfectly competitive levels (see Figure 15-1).

The consequences of this change in equilibrium price and quantity were presented in Chapters 12 and 13: (1) At competitive but not monopolistic equilibrium, the level of average cost is necessarily the lowest attainable, given the technology of the society; and (2) at competitive but not monopolistic

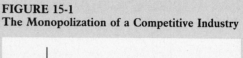

FIGURE 15-1
The Monopolization of a Competitive Industry

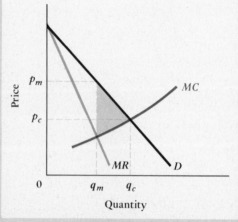

When a competitive industry is monopolized, output falls and price rises and a deadweight loss occurs. The competitive industry's supply curve and the monopolist's marginal cost curve are identical. The industry faces demand curve D. A competitive industry would produce q_c at price p_c. The monopolist reduces output to q_m because units between q_m and q_c add more to its cost than to its revenue. The shaded area shows that consumers were willing to pay more for each unit of lost output than its marginal cost of production. This deadweight loss of monopolization is a source of allocative inefficiency. It is the sum of the consumers' and producers' surpluses lost by reducing output from q_c to q_m.

equilibrium, $p = MC$, and thus allocative efficiency is achieved.

Under these circumstances, monopolization of a competitive industry introduces allocative inefficiency, and it may lead to productive inefficiency. Notwithstanding, the question of monopoly *versus* competition continues to be hotly debated because most economists are now aware that costs are not unaffected by market structure.

The Effect of Market Structure on Cost

What if costs are affected when an industry is monopolized or when a large number of small firms is replaced by a small number of large firms? If any savings occur from combining numerous competing groups into a single integrated operation, the costs of producing any given level of output will be lower than they were previously. If cost reductions are large enough, output will be increased and price will be lowered as a result of the replacement of a perfectly competitive industry by one or more firms with monopoly power. This may occur in two very different ways.

Advantages of Large Scale

The cost advantage of having 1 railroad between two points rather than 50 railroads (or 1 water company in a city, or 1 telephone system in a country) is obvious. In such situations, it would be inefficient to have a large number of firms each producing a small output at a high cost per unit. If such a situation existed, any firm that grew bigger than its rivals would soon find itself in a position to cut price below its rivals' costs and monopolize the industry. This situation is called **natural monopoly.** It exists where the size of the market allows at most one firm of efficient size.

Natural monopoly is just the extreme version of the more common situation where advantages of scale make perfect competition wholly unattainable because there is room for only a small number of firms of efficient size.

Today the effective choice is usually not between monopoly and perfect competition but between more or less oligopoly.

Whenever there are long-run advantages of large-scale production, of marketing and distribution, of learning by doing, or of innovation or invention, the minimum efficient scale (*MES*) of firms will tend to be large.

When *MES* is large, it is likely that productive efficiency will be improved, rather than worsened, by a shift from perfect competition to a more concentrated market structure.

Advantages of Scope

Even if there are no advantages of large-scale *plants*, large *firms* may be able to achieve econo-mies, and thus lower costs, by multiproduct production and associated large-scale distribution, national advertising, and large-scale purchasing. Such economies have been described as **economies of scope** rather than of scale.

Economies of scope cause the cost curves of large, integrated firms to be lower than the cost curves of many small firms producing the same output. In such a case the few large firms will be more productively efficient than the many small firms. But since they will have market power they will not be allocatively efficient: Given their costs, they will produce too little. How they compare with perfect competition depends on the size of the cost savings they can effect. If the cost savings are large enough, output may be larger and price lower than under perfect competition. Then, as illustrated in Figure 15-2, consumers benefit from the monopolization of the industry in spite of the emergence of some monopoly profits. The reason is that cost savings are large enough so that both producers and consumers can gain.

Natural and Unnatural Monopolies

In industries with either scale or scope economies, large-group market structures will give way to small-group structures. Since large firms have a competitive advantage over small firms, the average size of firms in the industry will grow while the number of firms shrinks until the cost advantages are fully exploited. At this point there may be a few large firms remaining (oligopoly) or just one (monopoly).

Monopolies can also grow up as a result of one firm taking over its rivals even when there is no cost advantage to size. In this case, however, the monopoly position cannot be exploited unless entry barriers are created. Otherwise, any attempt to raise the price to earn monopoly profits will cause new small firms to enter. Since there are no cost advantages to size, any price that allows the large firm to make profits also allows the new small firm to enter.

In such industries small-group market structures and pure profits persist only if artificial barriers to entry can be achieved.

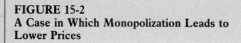

**FIGURE 15-2
A Case in Which Monopolization Leads to
Lower Prices**

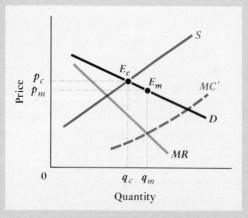

If monopolization lowers costs sufficiently, it may
lead to greater output and lower price than competition. D and S are the demand and supply curves of
a competitive industry that is in equilibrium at E_c with
p_c and q_c. If costs are unaffected by monopolization,
S will become the monopolist's marginal cost curve
and the monopolist will restrict output and raise price.
However, if the monopolization reduces costs to MC',
the equilibrium will be at E_m, with p_m less than p_c and
q_m greater than q_c.

Market Structure and
Innovation: The Very Long Run

The classical case against monopoly concerns the
allocation of resources within the context of a fixed
technology. We are now going to consider the very
long run, where the production function is changing due to the discovery of lower-cost methods of
producing old products and the introduction of
new and improved products. We shall ask if market
organization affects the rate of innovation.

*The incentive to introduce cost-saving inno-
vations.* Both the monopolist and the perfect competitor have a profit incentive to introduce cost-

reducing innovations. A monopoly can always increase its profits if it can reduce its costs. We saw
in Chapter 13 (page 208) that a cost reduction will
cause the monopoly to produce more, to sell at a
lower price, and thus to increase its profits. Furthermore, since it is able to prevent the entry of
new firms into the industry, these additional profits
will persist into the long run. Thus, from the standpoint of maximizing profits, a monopoly has both
a short- and a long-run incentive to reduce its costs.

The firm in perfect competition or in monopolistic competition has the same incentive in the
short run, but not in the long run. In the short
run, a reduction in costs will allow a firm that was
just covering costs to earn profits. In the long run,
other firms will be attracted into the industry by
these profits. Existing firms will copy the cost-
saving innovation, and new firms will enter the
industry using the new techniques. This will go on
until the profits of the innovator have been eliminated.

The effectiveness of profits as an incentive to
reduce costs for a firm in competition will thus
depend on the magnitude of the extra profits and
on how long they persist. If, for example, it only
takes a few months for existing firms and new
entrants to copy and install the new invention, then
the original innovating firm will earn profits for
only a few months. These may not be sufficient to
compensate for the risks and the costs of developing the innovation. In such cases, the incentive to
innovate will be absent from a competitive industry. On the other hand, if it takes several years for
other firms to copy and install the cost-saving innovation, then the profits earned over these years
by the innovating firm may be more than sufficient
to compensate for all costs and risks. In this case,
the incentive to innovate is present in a competitive
industry.

Monopolies have both a short- and long-run incentive
to innovate; competitive firms have only a short-run
incentive.

Funds for research and development. So far
we have considered the profit incentive to introduce new innovations. Another consideration is the

availability of the resources needed to finance research to invent new methods and new products. It is often held that the large profits available to monopolistic firms provide a ready fund out of which research and development will be financed. The typical perfectly competitive firm, according to this argument, is earning only enough money to cover all its costs, and it will have few funds to spare for research and development. Supporters of this view can point to much illustrative evidence. They note, for example, that few of the innovations that have vastly raised agricultural productivity over the last century were developed by the typical competitive farming unit; rather, they were developed by a few oligopolistic or monopolistic manufacturers of farm equipment and by researchers in universities and in government-financed research institutions.

Penalties for not innovating. A further argument is that competitive firms *must* innovate or they will lose out to their competitors, while although monopolists have an incentive to innovate, they do not need to do so because they are insulated from potential competitors by their barriers to entry. There is lack of agreement on the importance of this argument. Opponents would argue, first, that it is wrong to think a monopolist or oligopolist is shielded from all competition. It is always possible that some new firm will be able to break into the market by developing some new, similar, but superior product that evades existing patents and other barriers to entry. Furthermore, the larger the monopoly profits of the existing firm(s), the larger the incentive for new firms to break into the market. Thus, it is argued, all monopoly and oligopolistic firms are in potential competition with possible new entrants, and the firm that sits back and does not innovate will not long remain profitable.

The second argument opponents would advance is that the penalty for not innovating is not always high in perfect competition. If innovations are hard to copy, then there *is* a strong incentive for a competitive firm to innovate and a big penalty for firms that do not innovate, because a long time will be

needed before other firms can copy and catch up with the innovator. On the other hand, if innovations are easy to copy, there is a smaller incentive for the competitive firm to innovate and a smaller penalty for the firm that fails to innovate, since it is easy for it to copy and catch up with the innovator. The discussion may be summarized as follows:

All firms have an incentive to innovate, since they can increase their profits with a successful innovation. The greater the barriers to entry and the harder it is for other firms already in the industry to copy the innovation, the longer will the profits of innovating persist, and thus the larger will be the incentive to innovate. In competitive industries without barriers to entry, there will be little incentive to make innovations that are very easily copied, since both the profits of innovating and the losses from not innovating ahead of other firms will be very short-lived.

Schumpeter's defense of oligopoly and monopoly. The greatest opponent of the classical position on monopoly was the distinguished Austrian (and later American) economist, Joseph A. Schumpeter. Schumpeter's theory relies on many of the forces just discussed. His basic argument has two main parts. The first is that innovations that lower costs of production—by increasing output per head and creating economic growth—have a much larger effect on living standards than any "misallocation" of resources causing too much production of one kind of commodity and too little of another at any one time. The second part is based on his theory that innovation is functionally related to market forms in such a way that there is likely to be much more innovation under monopoly and oligopoly than under monopolistic and perfect competition. Let us look at each of these points in turn.

According to the classical case, monopoly results in a misallocation of resources, with too few resources devoted to producing goods in the monopolistic sector and too many in the competitive sector. Schumpeter believed that the losses due to this misallocation were small relative to the gains and losses due to variations in the rate of economic growth. Modern measures made since Schumpeter wrote have tended to support him in this contention. It appears very unlikely that the losses due to monopolistic and oligopolistic misallocations have amounted to more than 2 or 3 percent of a country's national income.[1] But the national income of most countries was for many years growing at that rate each year, and a growth rate of 3 percent per year doubles material living standards in under 25 years.

The second part of Schumpeter's argument is that monopolistic and oligopolistic market forms are more conducive to growth than perfect competition. He claimed that only the incentive of profits leads people to take the great risks of innovation, and that monopoly power is much more important than competition in providing the climate in which innovation occurs. The large short-run profits of the monopolist provide the incentive for others to try to usurp some of these for themselves. If a frontal attack on the monopolist's barriers to entry is not possible, then the barriers will be circumvented by such dodges as the development of similar products against which the monopolist will not have entry protection. Schumpeter called the replacing of one monopoly by another through the invention of new products or new production techniques the *process of creative destruction*. An example of this process is discussed in Box 15-1.

Since, in Schumpeter's theory, monopoly and oligopoly are more conducive to growth-creating innovations than is perfect competition, it follows that the "worse" the allocation of resources at any moment in time (i.e., the greater the amount of monopolization), the more rapid the rate of innovation and the resulting long-run rise in living standards. This important hypothesis cannot be handled with normal long-run theory, because long-run theory *assumes* constant technology.

Schumpeter put part of his argument in the following words:

What we have got to accept is that it [monopoly and oligopoly] has come to be the most powerful engine of progress and in particular of the long-run expansion of total output not only in spite of, but to a considerable extent through, this strategy [of creating monopolies] which looks so restrictive when viewed in the individual case and from the individual point of time. In this respect, perfect competition is not only impossible but inferior, and has no title to being set up as a model of ideal efficiency. It is hence a mistake to base the theory of government regulation of industry on the principle that big business should be made to work as the respective industry would work in perfect competition.[2]

Schumpeter's theory leads to the policy conclusion that attempting to break up monopolies and oligopolies and trying to make the economy behave as if it were perfectly competitive is undesirable, since it will reduce rather than raise the rate of growth of living standards.

Consider an example. Let there be two countries, each with a national income of 100 that is growing at 3 percent per year. Country A breaks up its monopolies and thereby achieves an immediate rise of national income to 105 but a fall in its growth rate to 2 percent. Country B lives with its monopolies and continues to have a 3 percent growth rate. The arithmetic of growth then tells us that country B will catch up with country A in 5 years' time, and in 50 years' time country B will have an income of just over 1.5 times that of country A. Clearly, given these figures, the long-term *losses* caused by breaking up A's monopolies are very large indeed.

The effect of alternative market forms on the process of innovation and economic growth is an extremely important question. Unfortunately, it is one on which existing theory and empirical studies shed all too little light.

Patents and the Incentive to Innovate

Economists who believe that competitive market structures best serve consumers by assuring them low prices, but who worry about the possible lack of incentives to innovate under competition, believe that other institutions, such as the patent laws, can provide the necessary incentives.

Patent laws confer a temporary monopoly on the use of an invention. The intent of the patent laws

---

[1] In one of the most famous of these studies, Professor Harberger of the University of Chicago puts the figure at about one-tenth of 1 percent of the U.S. national income!

[2] *Capitalism, Socialism, and Democracy,* 3rd ed. (New York: Harper & Row, 1950), page 106.

BOX 15–1 EROSION OF A MONOPOLY

The very great power of the incentive to share in a monopoly profit, whether created by a successful cartel or in some other way, can be illustrated by the case of ball-point pens, where a monopoly was created by product innovation.

In 1945, Milton Reynolds developed a new type of pen that wrote with a ball bearing rather than a conventional nib. He formed the Reynolds International Pen Company, capitalized at $26,000, and began production on October 6, 1945.

The Reynolds pen was introduced with a good deal of fanfare by Gimbels, which guaranteed that the pen would write for two years without refilling. The price was set at $12.50 (the maximum price allowed by the wartime Office of Price Administration). Gimbels sold 10,000 pens on October 29, 1945, the first day they were on sale. In the early stages of production, the cost of production was estimated to be around $.80 per pen.

The Reynolds International Pen Company quickly expanded production. By early 1946 it employed more than 800 people in its factory and was producing 30,000 pens per day. By March 1946 it had $3 million in the bank.

Macy's, Gimbels' traditional rival, introduced an imported ball-point pen from South America. Its price was $19.98 (production costs unknown).

The heavy sales quickly elicited a response from other pen manufacturers. Eversharp introduced its first model in April, priced at $15. In July 1946 *Fortune* magazine reported that Sheaffer was planning to put out a pen at $15, and Eversharp announced its plan to produce a "retractable" model priced at $25. Reynolds introduced a new model but kept the price at $12.50. Costs were estimated at $.60 per pen.

The first signs of trouble emerged. The Ball Point Pen Company of Hollywood put a $9.95 model on the market, and a manufacturer named David Kahn announced plans to introduce a pen selling for less than $3. *Fortune* reported fears of an impending price war in view of the growing number of manufacturers and the low cost of production. In October, Reynolds introduced a new model, priced at $3.85, that cost about $.30 to produce.

By Christmas 1946 approximately 100 manufacturers were in production, some of them selling pens for as little as $2.98. By February 1947 Gimbels was selling a ball-point pen made by the Continental Pen Company for $.98. Reynolds introduced a new model priced to sell at $1.69, but Gimbels sold it for $.88 in a price war with Macy's. Reynolds felt betrayed by Gimbels. Reynolds introduced a new model listed at $.98. By this time, ball-point pens had become economy rather than luxury items, but they were still highly profitable.

In mid 1948 ball-point pens were selling for as little as $.39 and costing about $.10 to produce. In 1951 prices of $.25 were common. Within six years the power of the monopoly was gone forever. Ever since then the market has been saturated with a wide variety of models and prices of pens ranging from $.19 up. Their manufacture is only ordinarily profitable.

is to lengthen the short-run period during which whoever controls the invention can earn supernormal profits as a reward for inventing it. Once the patent expires—and sometimes even before, as we saw in the case of ball-point pens, Box 15-1—other firms can copy the invention and, if there are no other barriers to entry, production will expand until profits fall to normal. There is little doubt that without patent laws, many inventions would be copied sooner and the original innovators would not earn as much extra revenue to compensate them for the costs and risks of development. Thus patents do increase the rewards to invention. Just how much actual extra invention occurs is a subject of substantial debate.

Because patented items *can* be imitated, the real advantage of patents to the competitive firm should not be exaggerated. Some have argued that patents may be of even greater advantage to a monopolistic than to a competitive firm. A monopolist, so goes the argument, has the resources to develop, patent, and "keep on the shelf" processes that might enable a potential competitor to challenge its position.

The Incentive to Engage in Destructive Competition

Competition, when it works well, leads to prices at the level of minimum attainable long-run average total costs. Firms generate revenues just sufficient to maintain their capital stock and to replace it as it wears out. As we saw in Chapter 12, in the short run with overall excess capacity, firms may find it profitable to operate with prices below *LRAC* as long as price exceeds average *variable* cost. This provides a signal for resources to leave the industry, and when they have done so, an equilibrium is achieved, with the remaining firms covering average total costs.

Circumstances can arise, however, that cause a chronic *long-run* tendency for firms to engage in excessive competition and result in prices that do not recover total costs in the long run. Such a situation is often described as *destructive competition,* or sometimes as *cutthroat competition.*

Destructive competition requires that long-lived capital investments play a big part in the total cost picture. For example, airlines, coal mining companies, and steamship lines often find that their average total costs are primarily fixed costs arising from large initial capital investments. In any short-run period, depreciation costs can be ignored (under the bygones are bygones principle). Over the life of the equipment, however, unless sufficient funds are earned to replace capital as it wears out, the industry will surely shrink. In such circum-

stances, *too much* competition could conceivably occur. It would cause severe difficulties for an industry that could survive under less competitive conditions.

To see how this can happen, consider a simplified example in which marginal costs are zero and all costs are for the purchase of fixed capital equipment. The capital costs $100,000 and lasts 10 years. At full capacity output, the firm's capital can produce 10,000 units of output per year. The firm must earn $10,000 a year—an average of $1 per unit for 10,000 units—if it is to cover its capital costs. A single-firm monopolist (we assume) finds that it pays to sell its capacity output of 10,000 units for $3 per unit. It does so, and earns profits of $20,000 over full (capital) cost. Attracted by the high profits, a second and third firm enter, each with a plant costing $100,000 and a capacity of 10,000 units of output per year. They offer to sell at $3, and each captures one-third of the market.

Although each firm covers its costs by selling 3,333 units per year at the $3 price, all three firms now find they have excess capacity, for they are sharing the original monopolist's market. Since marginal costs are zero, one of them reasons, "Why not cut prices a bit and sell all my potential output?" He cuts price to $2.90 and at first greatly increases his sales. His rivals, however, lose customers and they retaliate. Price falls to $2.50, then to $2. Each firm gains some sales, since market quantity demanded increases, but each firm still has excess capacity. A price war develops and does not stop until price has been driven down to the price at which each seller is at full capacity. Say that price is $.40. Each of the sellers is doing better than shutting down, since revenue of $.40 a unit for 10,000 units ($4,000) exceeds the nonexistent variable costs. But none of the firms is earning enough to cover its full costs over the lifetime of its plant.

If this situation continues, after 10 years each will have earned only $40,000, not enough to cover the capital costs of $100,000 every 10 years. Eventually, two of the three firms will leave the industry. The survivor can then replace its plant, charge the monopoly price of $3 a unit, and earn profits if no one else enters. But this will invite entry, and we are back at the beginning again.[3]

The example just discussed is extreme in that it assumed the variable costs were zero. But there are many industries in which variable costs, which must be covered by current operations, are small relative to total costs, which must be covered in the long run. Airlines are perhaps a prime example. Once an airline owns a fleet of planes, extra passengers can be carried at very low marginal cost. Even flying extra flights with the same number of planes (although it requires extra gasoline, pilots, and others) is far less costly than adding planes to the fleet. The gap between total costs and variable costs combines with excess capacity to create conditions in which sellers are tempted on the one hand to collude and on the other to engage in price cutting to fill their planes.

Filling stations provide another example. The variable costs of selling an extra liter of gasoline are small relative to the fixed costs that must be met in these industries. Frequent price wars illustrate the instability of price competition in this industry.

In such industries, successful collusion will lead to prices above the competitive level; uncontrolled price competition may lead to a chronic tendency for prices well below the competitive level. Policymakers face a dilemma. A monopolist would restrict output and raise price above the long-run competitive level. But replacing monopoly with unbridled competition might not work. Myopic, short-run competitive behavior would drive price down to variable cost and lead to a situation in which no firm could stay in the industry long. The industry then would suffer from chronic destructive competition. This view of destructive competition, especially in oligopolistic industries with more than three or four firms, was prevalent in the 1930s, when excess capacity was the general rule. It led to some direct legislative attempts to exempt price stabilization activities from antitrust control and to many regulatory agencies' changing their behavior, as we shall see.

Later generations of economists have been more skeptical about the occurrence of destructive competition. They do not deny occasional price wars but believe that such situations tend to self-correct fairly rapidly. However, many businesspeople and regulators are not persuaded by the economists' arguments. Whether conditions for chronic destructive competition occur frequently is an extremely important unresolved empirical question. Those who believe that they do support government regulation to limit competition or advocate a tolerant attitude toward price-stabilizing activities. Those who believe that firms need no such protection (on the ground that they can learn to avoid destructive competition) tend to advocate leaving the market alone except to implement antitrust activities that discourage collusion or price fixing. Much of the current debate about regulation and deregulation turns on this issue.

PUBLIC POLICY TOWARD MONOPOLY

The evaluation of government policies to deal with monopolies reflects the distinction between artificial and natural monopoly.

The theory of monopoly leads to three principal predictions. (1) Where monopoly power exists in an industry, it will lead to a restriction of the flow of resources into the industry and thus to the employment of fewer resources than would be used under competitive conditions. (2) Consequently firms with monopoly power will be able to charge higher prices and will be able to earn profits in excess of opportunity costs. (3) Their owners will command a larger share of the national income than they would under conditions of competition.

Combines Laws and Natural Monopolies

The belief that competition produces ideal results and monopoly worse results underlies the present-day **combines laws**, which prohibit the operation of monopolies, attempts to monopolize, and conspiracies in restraint of trade.

---

[3] The example is based on the model of the nineteenth century French mathematician Joseph Bertrand.

The first Canadian policies with respect to anticompetitive practices were proposed in the late nineteenth century, an era when economists believed not only that perfect competition produced ideal results, but also that perfect competition was the feasible alternative to monopoly. Although modern economists are no longer so confident about the feasibility of perfect competition and the evils of monopoly power, competition (and the laws that promote it) is still regarded as playing a key role in the successful working of the market economy. The laws originally adopted in 1889 and 1890 have been changed, but their basic pro-competition stance still prevails in current legislation.

It is also true that throughout the history of Canadian policy, legislation has been directed chiefly at the misuse and abuse of power by large associations and only rarely at combinations per se. In introducing legislation proposed in 1910, Mackenzie King, then minister of labour, stated during a debate in the House of Commons that "this measure seeks to afford the means of conserving to the public some of the benefits which arise from large organizations of capital. . . ."

This apparent acceptance of the need for large firms in the business sector has been explained in terms of the *staples theory* of economic growth (see page 367). This theory held that much of Canada's real growth was tied to a succession of export staples such as fur, wheat, lumber, and base metals. The exploitation of these resources required not only large amounts of private capital in a country where capital was scarce, but also substantial "social overhead" capital in the form of an extensive east-west transportation network. In addition, uncertainty was created by the wide price fluctuations to which these products were subject. The result was a reliance on firms with substantial monopoly power and considerable direct government support.

The Nature of Competition Policy

The concern with monopoly power and control of particular product markets, whether by merger or by internal growth of the firm, is only one aspect of competition policy. Other activities such as some forms of price discrimination, collusive agreements concerning prices to be charged or market shares, and resale price maintenance (control by a manufacturer of the price at which a retailer sells a product) are also of concern because it is believed that they limit actual or potential competition.

In practice, it becomes difficult to determine just when an offense has been committed and whether there is a real threat to competition. Ideally the law should reflect economic analysis, but this is difficult given the problem of drafting a statute that will cover all future situations and the uncertainty concerning what interpretation the courts will place on its provisions. Further, economists are frequently not in agreement on the likely consequences of various forms of behavior of firms in imperfectly competitive markets.

Canadian Competition Policy Before 1975

Government policy with respect to trusts and industrial combinations in Canada dates from 1888, when a Select Committee of the House of Commons initiated an investigation into alleged combinations in trade. Initial legislation, enacted in 1889, made it an offense to combine or agree to lessen competition unduly or to restrain trade. The Combines Investigation Act of 1910, created powers for the minister of labour to appoint a board of three commissioners to carry out a full inquiry and publish a report of its finding. In framing this legislation, the Canadian government was influenced by what was regarded as the unhappy experience of the United States with its Sherman Antitrust Act (1890). There was no inclination to copy the "trustbusting" activities that involved the American antitrust division of the Department of Justice in a large number of prosecutions during the period 1904–1911, when the courts adopted a strict interpretation of the Sherman Antitrust Act.[4]

---

[4] This period of vigorous prosecution ended with the enunciation by the Supreme Court of the "rule of reason." In forcing Standard Oil Company and American Tobacco Company to divest themselves of a large share of their holdings of other companies, the Court stated that only *unreasonable* combinations in restraint of trade merited conviction under the Sherman Antitrust Act.

Instead, early Canadian legislation relied strongly on the publicity attached to an investigation as a deterrent to restrictive trade practices.

The Combines Investigation Act of 1923 provided punishment for past participation in the formation or operation of a combine. In 1935 the legislation was amended to prohibit discriminatory pricing that substantially lessened competition or eliminated a competitor, and in 1951 resale price maintenance was added to the list of proscribed practices. With these amendments, the legislation prohibited three broad classes of activity: (1) combinations such as price-fixing agreements that unduly lessen competition, (2) mergers or monopolies that may operate to the detriment of the public interest, and (3) unfair trade practices (after 1960).

A large number of cases of unfair trade practices were successfully pursued, but—compared to the U.S. enforcement experience—there was a striking paucity of merger cases. During the 60 years following the first legislation in 1910, only two full-scale cases came before the courts. Both defendants, Canadian Breweries, Limited, and B. C. Sugar Refining Company, were acquitted by the trial courts and neither decision was appealed. One plea of guilty was entered to a merger charge in 1970, and in 1973 the crown obtained an order, without a full trial, prohibiting a merger. In 1974, K. C. Irving, Limited, was convicted, but this judgment was reversed on appeal.

The reason most often cited for the lack of combines enforcement in Canada was the inability of criminal legislation to cope with complex economic issues. Under criminal law, the government must prove beyond a reasonable doubt that the accused has committed the offense. In the United States, most antitrust cases are civil cases in which a lesser standard of proof is required to obtain a conviction. In American merger cases litigated since 1950, for example, when a substantial share of the market has been controlled, the courts have generally found that the merger restricts competition and is therefore illegal.

There is also some doubt whether the penalties imposed for violations in Canada were effective. The most common penalty, the criminal fine, which on only one occasion exceeded $25,000 for a single company, may not have deterred contraventions of the act.

Canadian courts have also appeared less willing than American courts to assess economic evidence. Mr. Justice Hope in *R. v. Container Materials, Ltd.* (1940) expressed this reluctance with the caveat "Our Lady of the Common Law is not a professed economist," and Mr. Justice Spence in *R. v. Howard Smith Paper Mills* (1959) reemphasized the courts' difficulty:

Surely the determination of whether or not an agreement to lessen competition was "undue" by a survey of one industry's profits against profits of industry generally, and a survey of the movement of the prices in that one industry against the movement of prices generally, would put the Court to the essentially non-judicial task of judging between conflicting political theories. It would entail the Court's being required to conjecture—and by a Court it would be nothing more than mere conjecture, since a Court is not trained to act as an arbitrator of economics—whether better or worse results would have occurred to the public if free and untrammelled competition had been permitted to run its course.

The New Competition Policy

A major review of Canadian legislation was begun in 1966 by the Economic Council of Canada. Its recommendations, published in a report in 1969, together with those of a committee of experts appointed by the Department of Consumer and Corporate Affairs, formed the basis of proposed amendments to the Combines Investigation Act. The amendments were subsequently presented to Parliament in two stages.

The Stage I amendments were proclaimed on January 1, 1976. They included provisions for extending the Combines Investigation Act to service industries, for allowing civil actions to be brought for damages resulting from contraventions of the act, and for strengthening legislation against misleading advertising. One significant feature of the Stage I amendments is that they give the Restrictive Trade Practices Commission (RTPC) the power to order suppliers to cease certain practices. Customers were protected by prohibiting suppliers from refusing to supply, providing exclusive dealerships, restricting the way the good is sold, or requiring tied sales. As a result, the way in which many goods are retailed has changed considerably.

The sections of the amendments that deal with *misleading advertising* are extensive. Although the commission cannot act directly in such cases, the Department of Consumer and Corporate Affairs has shown itself to be quite willing to prosecute on the advice of the commission. Claims about product quality must now be based on adequate tests. Advertising a product at a bargain price when the supplier does not or cannot supply the product in reasonable quantities, and supplying a product at a price higher than the advertised price, except when the advertised price is erroneous and is immediately corrected, are explicitly prohibited.

The Stage II amendments deal with the issues of conspiracies and of mergers and monopolization. Initially this stage proposed the transfer of certain practices from criminal to civil law and recommended the appointment of a Competition Board to replace the courts in the examination of trade practices, but more recent amendments abandoned the Competition Board in favor of a larger role for the civil courts. The Stage II amendments had not been passed by the spring of 1984.

Current Issues

The current situation seems very unsatisfactory for two reasons. Recent decisions made by the courts have emasculated the existing legislation, and the government has failed to successfully introduce new legislation.

Problems with existing legislation arise in the context of both mergers and conspiracy charges. The courts have proved willing to find fault in merger cases only when there is evidence that a monopoly has been created, and then only when the evidence also shows that real "detriment" arises. Detriment is typically interpreted as predatory behavior that causes injury to a potential competitor. Convictions on conspiracy charges appear, if anything, even harder to obtain. Draft legislation has been put forward, but none has yet been passed into law. There are, of course, substantial difficulties in preparing legislation to deal with these issues—as evidenced, for example, by the American experience with legislation designed to penalize predatory behavior but which itself has been used to restrict competition.

The flurry of activity surrounding the new competition policy and much government rhetoric about "increasing competitive forces and reducing structural rigidities" have given these issues a very high profile in the public debate, but they so far have resulted in very little real change.

Regulation of Natural Monopoly

Natural monopoly arises because of economies of scale (as was discussed on page 249). Policymakers have not wanted to compel the maintenance of several smaller, less efficient producers when a single firm would be much more efficient; neither have they wanted to give a monopolist the opportunity to restrict output, raise price, and appropriate as profits the gains made available by virtue of large-scale production.

The public utility concept grew out of the recognition by economists that when there are major economies of large-scale production, protection of the public interest by competition is impractical, if not impossible.

One possible response to this dilemma is for government to assume ownership of the single firm and instruct (or delegate to) the managers of the *nationalized* industry how much to produce and what price to charge. Many countries have done precisely that with telephone and railroad services, among others. In Canada this solution has been followed, for example, with Canadian National Railways, the CBC, and provincial electric power companies.

Public utility regulation gives to appropriate public authorities (usually specially constituted regulatory commissions such as the Canadian Transport Commission) control over the price and quantity of service provided by a natural monopoly, with the object of achieving the efficiency of a single seller without the output restriction of the monopolist.

In return for giving a company a franchise or license to be the sole producer, the public utility regulators reserve the right to regulate its behavior.

Regulation of this kind has been prevalent for almost a century. In Canada, railway rates have been regulated since the passage of the Railway Act of 1888, and public utility regulation has since spread to other forms of transportation—airlines, trucking, pipelines—and to the standard utilities—telephone, electricity, water, and gas.

Although regulatory commissions were first created to deal with natural monopoly problems, most regulatory activity is no longer of that kind. Many other commissions have been set up. They are often referred to as the "alphabet agencies" because of the common use of their initials as shorthand names and the broad spectrum of activities they attempt to regulate. Provincial bodies such as the Ontario Securities Commission (OSC) and the Quebec Securities Commission (QSC) are concerned mainly with consumer protection. The federal National Energy Board (NEB) regulates the interprovincial transmission of oil and natural gas and must approve exports of electricity, oil, and natural gas. Many activities of the Canadian Radio and Television Commission (CRTC) and the Canadian Transport Commission (CTC) concern the orderly use of airways and skyways—the prevention of chaotic competition. We limit our discussion in this chapter to natural monopoly regulation; some discussion of other regulatory activities will be found in Chapter 24.

Regulated Prices

The dilemma of natural monopoly is illustrated in Figure 15-3. To achieve low costs, a single large producer is necessary, but an unregulated profit-maximizing monopoly would restrict output, raise price, and fail to provide the large volume of output at a low price that the technology makes possible.

What price should a regulatory commission permit? It might wish to set price equal to marginal cost (the way it would be in perfect competition), but such a price and quantity would surely lead to losses, for marginal cost is necessarily below aver-

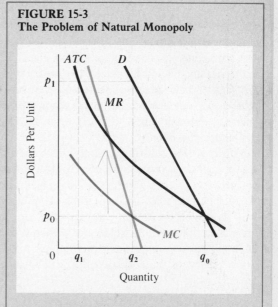

FIGURE 15-3
The Problem of Natural Monopoly

Cost conditions in a situation of natural monopoly are such that a single firm is needed to achieve the economies of scale, but a monopolist finds it profitable to restrict output to maximize profits. Because ATC declines sharply, efficiency is served by having a single firm. Clearly, one firm producing at q_0 would be more efficient than several firms each producing q_1 at a cost of p_1 per unit. But an unregulated monopoly would restrict output to q_2 and charge price p_1, thereby depriving consumers of the advantages of large-scale production.

age cost when average cost is falling. This is illustrated in Figure 15-4. Such a pricing scheme would require a continuing subsidy of the resulting losses.

As an alternative, regulation has often aimed at setting prices high enough to permit firms to cover all their costs yet low enough to achieve the large sales required to reap the scale economies that characterize natural monopoly situations. If a regulatory commission knew exactly what the demand curve and the cost curves looked like, it could simply pick the intersection of the demand curve and the average total cost curve. This is called *average cost pricing*. It is important to note that average cost pricing will not, in general, lead to allocative efficiency even if achieved exactly. This is also shown in Figure 15-4.

In attempting to implement average cost pricing, regulatory commissions have tended to judge prices according to the level of profits they produce. Generally, having set prices, regulatory agencies permit price increases when profits fall below "fair" levels and require price reductions when profits exceed such levels. This is referred to as *rate-of-return regulation*.

While it is true that if the appropriate price is charged, economic profits will be zero, the reverse is not necessarily true. Profits can be zero because of inefficient operation or misleading accounting, as well as pricing at the lowest attainable level of average cost. Thus commissions that rely on profits as their guide to pricing must monitor a number of other aspects of the regulated firm's behavior.

Problems for Regulations

Definition of costs. If a company is to be allowed to charge a price determined as "cost plus a fair profit" (as the regulators say), and if that price is below the profit-maximizing one, it is clearly in the firm's interest to exaggerate reported costs. One major activity of regulatory commissions has been to define rules of allowable costing. Cost supervision is an important activity of public utility regulation for another reason as well. Without it, managers of the regulated industries might have little incentive to be efficient and might simply let costs drift upward.

The rate base. Average total cost includes an appropriate rate of return on the capital invested in the business. Suppose it is agreed that a firm should be allowed to earn a rate of return of 11 percent on its capital. The **rate of return** is defined as the ratio of net revenue to invested capital. What is the value of the capital to which 11 percent is to be applied? The allowable amount is called the **rate base.** There has been no more controversial area than this in public utility regulation. Should the original cost or the reproduction cost of the firm's assets be used?

It does not make much difference unless prices

are changing, but in the inflationary situation of recent decades, reproduction cost is uniformly higher than original costs and thus leads to higher bases, higher permitted profits, and higher rates to users. If the major concern is to generate earnings to buy replacement equipment, reproduction cost is appropriate. If the major concern is to generate profits to compensate past capital investments, original cost may be appropriate. Regulatory commissions (and the courts) have vacillated on this issue.[5]

A fair return. The permitted rate of return that is implicit in the theory of public utility regulation is the opportunity cost of the owners' capital, with allowances for risk. Regulatory commissions have paid some attention to overall earnings rates in the economy, and the level of permitted earnings has changed slightly over time. But fairness and tradition have played a much larger role than considerations of opportunity cost, and regulatory commissions have been slow to adjust permitted rates of return to changing market conditions.

For decades, permitted rates of return of 6 to 9 percent were employed. But when market interest rates soared to double-digit figures during the late 1970s, the traditional levels were not sufficient to induce new investment. Yet regulatory commissions have been reluctant to permit the large increases in prices that would result from sharp increases in the permitted rate of return.

Curtailment of service. While regulatory commissions regulate prices with an eye on profits, they do not guarantee profits. Because profits are not guaranteed, a regulated utility in a declining in-

---

[5] The precise nature of regulatory rules is important because the rules affect the incentives of those regulated. Economists Harvey Averch and Leland Johnson have shown that a regulated utility has a lesser incentive to resist high capital costs than an unregulated one and that in some circumstances it pays the unregulated utility to buy relatively unproductive equipment. This is true because if profits depend on the rate base, it often pays the firm to increase its rate base. Thus the notion of "necessary and prudent investments" enters into regulatory rules. This tendency for one regulation to lead to a need for yet further regulation has been called the *tar-baby effect*, after a fictional creature made of tar who overcame an attacker by enmeshing it.

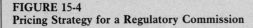

FIGURE 15-4
Pricing Strategy for a Regulatory Commission

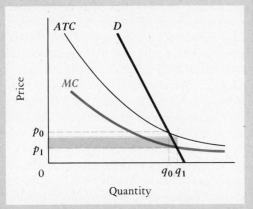

Average cost pricing is the goal of regulatory commissions, which seek the lowest prices possible without losses for natural monopolies. Although perfect competition leads to production where price equals marginal costs, here the price cannot be set at p_1, where demand equals marginal cost, because the firm would necessarily suffer losses (the shaded area). Price p_0 covers all costs (including the opportunity cost of capital). The corresponding output q_0 achieves some but not all of the cost advantages of large-scale output.

its profits and is shirking its public service responsibility, or whether it is truly in trouble.

A short-term, long-term trade-off? Economists who accept both the force of the argument that monopolistic firms can earn large exploitive profits in the short term *and* Schumpeter's argument about the very long run face a policy dilemma. In the short term, firms that gain monopoly power may earn very large profits at the expense of consumers. In the long term, however, attempts to control these monopolies may inhibit the creative destruction process that makes us all better off through productivity growth.

For these economists the policy world is not a simple place, and policies that achieve desired goals over one time span must be constantly scrutinized to see if they are producing undesired results over other time spans.

What Does Regulation Protect?

While the main thrust of antitrust policy and the original purpose of the regulatory commissions was the protection of *competition*, a parallel and for a time growing aspect of public policy in these areas was a shift to protection of *competitors* against the rigors of competition.

Perhaps the easiest way to understand this protectionist theme within antimonopoly policy is to notice that the distributive aspects of monopoly have been at least as important to public policymakers as the allocative inefficiencies that so concern economists. In the industrial sectors of the economy, corporate managers and stockholders typically earn average income. Thus the higher salaries and higher dividends of corporate monopoly tend to lead to a more unequal distribution of income. Monopoly power, when exercised by those who are relatively poor rather than relatively rich, has frequently been supported rather than opposed by the government. For example, the efforts of farmers to increase farm income have not only been approved but actively promoted by public policies of crop restriction, price supports, and exemption of marketing boards from combines laws. Labor unions are also exempt from combines prosecu-

dustry may have a serious problem. If it is failing to make profits equal to the permitted rate, it may apply for permission to increase its prices, but if its demand is elastic, a rise in rates will lead to a reduction in revenues and may reduce profits.

Often public transportation companies faced with low profits apply for permission to cut back on service on their low profit routes to concentrate on their more profitable routes. The regulators may want the regulated company to "cross-subsidize" the less popular routes with profits from the more popular routes; at the same time, they do not want to force the company into bankruptcy. Thus, each time a curtailment of service is proposed, regulators must make the difficult determination of whether the company is merely trying to increase

tions, and the efforts of unions to achieve some degree of monopoly power over the supply of labor were also supported actively by those public policies that encouraged the growth of unions.

Many aspects of these protectionist views survive in legal opinions that are still valid today. To many economists, they fail to distinguish between acts that injure competition (such as price fixing) and acts that injure competitors (such as cutting prices below the level of an inefficient firm's costs).

Evaluating Regulation

The moral of the public utility experience is that what looks like a simple and straightforward theory of regulating natural monopoly turns out in practice to be highly complex. In large part this is because regulated companies adapt their behavior to the rules that are imposed on them—and thus begins a chain of adaptation and change by regulators and regulated that produces a complex and cumbersome apparatus. Moreover, the need for due process in decisions that affect property rights has made procedures and decisions legalistic and resource-using.

Regulation brings both costs and benefits. Today's great debate is, "Do the benefits justify the costs?" The debate is its most heated with respect to environmental and safety regulatory activities, but it extends to public utility regulation as well. The costs of regulation include more than the costs of running regulatory commissions and the costs imposed on the courts by seemingly endless appeals. Regulatory costs are also imposed on businesses that must strive to comply with paperwork.

Professor Richard Posner of the University of Chicago estimated that milk price regulation added about 10 percent to milk prices in the United States. The president's Council of Economic Advisers estimated that regulation accounted for a rise of about one point per year in the cost of living. Murray Weidenbaum of Washington University and Willard Butcher of Chase Manhattan Bank put the cost of regulation even higher: as much as $100 billion per year. Whether these estimates are realistic is debated. And there are, of course, benefits.

Ralph Nader and others counter the Weidenbaum "costs" with equally impressive (and equally controversial) dollar estimates of "benefits."

The alleged benefits and costs are difficult—if not impossible—to measure with any precision. Much of the debate is ideological, notwithstanding its expression in terms of dollar estimates of benefits and costs. Is keeping the cost to consumers of electricity artificially low a benefit or a cost? It surely benefits some consumers, yet it just as surely involves some resource misallocation. Are the accidents avoided by industrial safety standards worth the extra expenditures they require? Victims of such accidents may answer differently than those who pay more for the products. These questions are not readily answered on a scientific basis.

Some, including Professor George Stigler of the University of Chicago, believe the evidence shows that the levels of prices, quantities, and profits are about the same under public utility regulation as they would have been without it; they even go so far as to suggest that unregulated monopoly would have performed better.

There seems in 1984 to be a remarkable consensus that such regulation has failed to live up to the expectations held for it. Perhaps the most widely held view is that regulation, even when effective at first, becomes too rigid and unresponsive to change and as a result fails to recognize and to permit such competition as is possible. Given changing technology, yesterday's natural monopoly of a single railroad may become but one mode of transportation in a competitive transportation industry. Wire telephone communications are no longer unique, given radio and satellites. Even the Post Office is not the only way to send written messages and parcels from one place to another. Thus, the scope of natural monopoly regulation keeps changing. But regulators tend to cling to, and in some cases are legally committed to, rules and assumptions that may no longer fit the world they are regulating.

As to the fear of catastrophic, destructive competition, it has faded greatly since its heyday in the 1930s. If belief in destructive competition survives today, it is mostly in the fear of *foreign* competition with traditional North American industries. Indeed, the view is widespread that the regulation of North American industries is an important barrier to their competition in what are increasingly world markets.

Changes in regulation in some form or another seem likely to continue over the next decade in response to this growing consensus. Some favor rapid deregulation and reliance on market forces. Others believe that the deficiencies lie in the structure of regulation and that changing the way regulation is carried out will improve matters. Still others think that the failures of regulation require nationalization or new legislation defining a novel approach to what regulators should do.

Which of many proposed directions for regulatory reform will be followed is unclear at this stage. In the United States deregulation of airlines has been accomplished, that of motor carriers is underway, and Congress has decreased the regulatory authority of the ICC and the FTC. The breakup of AT&T as a result of the 1982 settlement of its long-standing antitrust case will pave the way for much less regulation of its activities, and it is now free to compete in areas where it was previously excluded.

There is no similar trend toward deregulation currently apparent in Canada, though the revisions to the Bank Act passed in 1980 did lift some restrictions with respect to the operations of foreign banks within Canada. However, the present regulatory commissions are not without political support and are generally staunchly defended *by the regulated industries themselves*.

Will the experience with deregulation quickly resolve the key factual questions about whether the free market works better than regulation? The answer is probably no. One cannot quickly undo the effects of decades of regulation and move to a long-run unregulated equilibrium. Industries such as the airlines developed under regulation and made long-term investments on the expectation that regulatory rules would continue in effect. After 30 or 40 years of regulation, all the decision makers in the industry were geared toward a regulatory rather than a free-market environment. When, suddenly, the environment changed, all sorts of transitional

problems occurred, as was to be expected, and these may take years to work themselves out.

The American experience with airline deregulation suggests why it is difficult to evaluate results. Starting in 1978, the Civil Aeronautics Board (CAB) removed regulations on airline rate making and on protecting individual airline routes. The initial responses seemed almost miraculous: tumbling air fares, supersaver discounts, increased air service on popular routes, increased passenger travel, and a boom in the industry. But a year later fares were *up* 25 to 40 percent over the regulated levels; some of the major carriers were having severe financial troubles—one of them, Braniff, went bankrupt—service to certain locations had been curtailed; and the euphoria of a year earlier was gone. Some new carriers have established themselves, others have not. Fares between certain cities are much lower than they would have been, others are higher.

But it will be years before enough experience exists to permit a definitive evaluation of the benefits and costs of airline deregulation. Without hard evidence, one can find assertions on each side. To the president of United Airlines, the answer was that while fares had risen, they had risen much less than would have been the case with regulation—that is, deregulation was a success. To the senior vice-president of American Airlines, deregulation was raising costs and thus prices by encouraging excess capacity on most routes. In his view, deregulation was an expensive failure.

SUMMARY

1. The usual criticism of monopoly is based on the proposition that if costs, demand, and products are unchanged, the monopolization of a previously competitive industry will lead to a rise in price and a decline in output. In such circumstances, monopoly will lead to allocative inefficiency and may lead to productive inefficiency.

2. Levels of cost are not independent of market structures. If there are advantages of large scale in production, distribution, marketing, or purchasing, the minimum efficient size of the firm may be too large to be compatible with conditions of perfect competition. In such cases a shift from competition to a more concentrated market structure—oligopoly or monopoly—may lead to lower costs and increased efficiency. Because costs are not independent of market structure, the case in favor of competition and against concentration of market power is weakened. Most economists believe that substantial competition is compatible with efficient operation of industry and that it is desirable to foster at least that amount of competition.

3. A major issue in the evaluation of different market structures concerns the incentive provided for invention and innovation. Joseph Schumpeter believed that the incentive to innovate was so much greater under monopoly that it was to be preferred to perfect competition. While few modern economists go that far, the empirical evidence suggests that technological change and innovation can to a measurable extent be traced to the efforts of large firms in oligopolistic industries.

4. Another issue in the evaluation of market structures concerns the possibility of chronic excessive competition, in which industries characterized by heavy fixed investments will, if unregulated, be led into price wars that threaten the survival of an industry that could survive under less competitive conditions. While this possibility surely exists, many economists are highly skeptical about whether it is sufficiently likely to warrant all the protectionism it has spawned.

5. The policy implications of the classical view of monopoly and competition led policy in two directions: public utility regulation to deal with natural monopoly and competition policy to deal with other kinds of monopoly.

6. Historically, Canada has not pursued an aggressive competition policy, particularly in comparison with the United States. Early legislation relied strongly on public disclosure rather than penalties as a deterrent to illegal practices. The new Competition Act promises stricter enforcement through the use of civil review procedures rather than criminal prosecution.

7. The original philosophy of public utility regulation was to grant a monopoly where necessary to achieve the advantages of large-scale production but to prevent the monopolist from restricting output and raising price. The most common regulatory approach has been to regulate prices. This is done by watching profits: allowing price increases only if necessary to permit the regulated utility to earn a fair return on its capital and requiring price decreases if profits rise above the approved level.

8. Implementation of this straightforward theory encounters difficulties because any set of rules becomes a set of signals that induces patterns of response from those regulated. Natural utility regulation appears to most observers not to have been an unqualified success. To some, this is because the regulators have not made much difference. To others, it is because regulators have tended to shift their focus from protection of consumers to protection of the firms being regulated.

9. Protection of firms *from* competition has been a parallel theme with protection *of* competition itself from the earliest days of antitrust and public utility regulation. During the Great Depression, it emerged as a dominant theme, and some believe that it has permanently transformed the regulatory environment.

10. The entire regulatory apparatus has come under close scrutiny in recent years. In the United States major bills have been passed deregulating airlines and motor carriers. In Canada there has not been as strong a trend toward deregulation. How far the deregulation movement will go is sure to be a major political issue of the rest of the 1980s.

TOPICS FOR REVIEW

Effects of monopolizing a competitive industry
Competition and allocative efficiency
The effect of market structure on costs
Destructive competition

Competition policy
Natural monopoly
Difficulties of public utility regulation
Protection of competition versus protection of competitors
Deregulation

DISCUSSION QUESTIONS

1. "I think there are some people, in and out of government, who get a little confused and associate bigness with badness. Success alone is now evidence enough to warrant intensive scrutiny by the government to determine how the success can be remedied—as if it were some sort of disease. The age of Orwell's doublethink, prophesied for 1984, has come early. For now, to win is to lose. The real losers are the consumers. They lose the advantages of free competition; new and better products, lower prices and wider choices." Comment on these views of a leading GM executive.

2. Economists Armen Alchian and Reuben Kessel have advanced the hypothesis that monopolists choose to satisfy more of their nonmonetary aims than do perfect competitors. Consider three aims:
   a. Exercising the prejudices of the monopolists against certain racial minorities
   b. Enjoying a good life with big expense accounts
   c. Promoting their political philosophies by advertising and broadcasting

   What theoretical arguments could support the Alchian-Kessel hypothesis? Would the same arguments apply to oligopolists?

3. Evaluate the wisdom of having the Department of Consumer and Corporate Affairs use profits as a measure of monopoly power in deciding whether to prosecute a case. Would such a rule be expected to affect the behavior of firms with high profits? In what ways might any changes be socially beneficial and in what ways socially costly?

4. Price-fixing agreements are (with some specific exemptions) violations of the combines policy. Consider the effects of the following. In what way, if at all, should they be viewed as being similar to price-fixing agreements?
   a. A manufacturer "recommending" minimum prices to its dealers
   b. Manufacturers publishing product price lists that are changed only every three months
   c. A trade association that publishes "average industry total costs of production" every month

5. Under what circumstances should some aspect of market structure or market conduct be treated as *illegal* per se—that is, without considering the effect in the particular case?

6. It is often asserted that when a regulatory agency such as a public utilities commission is established, it will ultimately become controlled by the people it was intended to regulate. This argument raises the question of who regulates the regulators. Can you identify why this might happen? How might the integrity of regulatory boards be protected?

7. "In a competitive market the least-cost production techniques are revealed by entry and exit, while in public utility regulation they are revealed by commission rate hearings. It is easier to fool the commission than the market. Therefore, wherever possible, competition should be permitted." Discuss.

16 WHO RUNS THE FIRM AND FOR WHAT ENDS?

Does the continuing success of the Canadian economy depend on the initiative of healthy, independent, private firms? Does it depend instead on increased public scrutiny and control of the behavior of these firms? Does it require subsidization or protection of our firms from foreign competition? Is the economy's apparent failure to perform as well in the past decade as it did in previous decades due to a failure of private firms? Or is it perhaps due to increasing government interference with their activities?

What light does the theory we have studied so far shed on these important questions? In standard economic theory firms are users of factors of production and producers of commodities. They face cost and demand curves that are largely determined by forces beyond their control. They seek to maximize their profits by keeping their costs as low as possible and producing to satisfy consumers' demands. They care only about profits, and their decisions are uninfluenced by their internal structure. Thus they contribute to our high living standards by producing, as cheaply as possible, goods that satisfy consumers' demands.

The successful firm is the one that best satisfies consumers' demands, while the firm that consistently does not do this will eventually fail. The ultimate source of all profits is consumers' desires. (Even monopoly profits depend on consumers' willingness to buy the product the monopolist controls.) The need for firms to respond to consumers' desires is an important part of any argument for the free enterprise system. If firms did not so respond, there would be little justification in allowing them to exert major influences on the allocation of the country's resources.

An important body of criticism disputes this standard theory of the firm. It says instead that firms have the power to control market conditions. They manipulate demand by advertising, and they are not under heavy competitive pressure to produce efficiently by holding costs down. Firms, the critics continue, do not even seek to maximize profits. Instead they seek other goals that are determined by their internal structure, and these goals often cause them to behave in ways that are socially undesirable.

If true, such criticisms would support the view that firms hinder rather than advance consumer welfare and that they need to be forced by government to act in the social interest. In this chapter we will study some of these criticisms. We begin with those that strike at the very core of standard microeconomic theory.

DO FIRMS CONTROL THE MARKET?

The Galbraith Hypothesis

John Kenneth Galbraith and consumer advocate Ralph Nader argue that it is *not* consumers' wants that create the market signals that in turn provide the profit opportunities that motivate business behavior. Instead, large corporations have the power to create and manipulate demand. Firms must plan and invest for an uncertain future, and the profitability of the enormous investments they make is threatened by the unpredictability of events. Firms try to make the future less unpredictable by actively manipulating market demand and by co-opting government agencies that are supposed to control their activities.

Manipulation of demand. The most important unpredictable events that may jeopardize corporate investments are unexpected shifts in market demand curves. To guard against unexpected declines in demand, corporations spend vast amounts on advertising that allows them to sell what they want to produce rather than what consumers want to buy. At the same time, corporations decide not to produce some products that consumers would like to buy. This reduces the risks inherent in investing in wholly new and untried products and avoids the possibility that successful new products might spoil the market for an existing product.

According to this hypothesis, we consumers are the victims of the corporations; we are pushed around at their whim, persuaded to buy things we do not really want, and denied products we would like to have. In short, we are brainwashed ciphers with artificially created wants, and we have no real autonomy with respect to our own consumption.

Corruption of public authorities. A second threat to the long-range plans and investments of corporations comes from uncontrollable and often unpredictable changes in the nature of government interference with the freedom of the corporation. This political threat is met by co-opting or corrupting the members of legislatures who pass laws affecting corporations, and the government agencies that are supposed to be regulating them. Corporation managers, according to the theory, indirectly subvert public institutions, from universities to regulatory agencies.

Government, instead of regulating business and protecting the public interest, has become the servant of the corporation. It supplies the corporate sector with such essential inputs as educated, trained, healthy, socially secure workers. Government also serves the giant corporation through policies concerning tariffs, import quotas, tax rules, subsidies, and research and development. These policies protect the industrial establishment from competitive pressures and reinforce its dominance and profitability.

Corruption of our value system. The managers of modern firms have great power. The corporations they manage earn large profits that can be reinvested to further the achievement of the values of the ruling group; a group that Galbraith calls the *technostructure*. The values of this "ruling class" emphasize industrial production, rapid growth, and materialistic aspirations at the expense of the better things of life (such as cultural and aesthetic values) and the quality of the environment.

More important, the industrial managers join with the military in a military-industrial complex that utilizes, trains, and elevates the technicians to positions of power and prestige not only in industry but in the armed services, in the defense establishment, and in the highest positions of government. In so doing, the corporations and their managers threaten to dominate if not subvert our foreign as well as our domestic policies.

The new industrial state. The foregoing is an outline of what Galbraith calls the *New Industrial State*.[1] If Galbraith's thesis were substantially correct, we would have to make major revisions in our ideas of how free-market economies work.

According to Galbraith's New Industrial State, the largest corporations (1) largely control market demand rather than being controlled by it, (2) co-opt government processes instead of being constrained by them, and (3) utilize their substantial discretionary power against the interests of society.

The Evidence for the Hypothesis

Many facts lend superficial support to Galbraith's hypothesis. The corporate giants are well known

to all of us. Leading the *Financial Post*'s list of the top 200 Canadian industrial companies is General Motors of Canada, with annual sales in excess of $5 billion. Other companies with sales above $2 billion include Imperial Oil, Canadian Pacific, Bell Canada, Massey-Ferguson, Alcan, and International Nickel. If power comes with size, a "few" people—perhaps two or three hundred strategically placed executives of the country's leading corporations—have great power over economic affairs. Moreover, this corporate elite forms in many ways a close-knit group with common values and a (small "c") conservative point of view.[2] They exercise political influence through lobbying, contributions to political parties, and direct participation in the process of governing.

It is also true, as the hypothesis predicts, that the great corporations, along with many smaller firms, spend vast amounts on advertising. These expenditures are obviously designed to influence consumers' demand, and there is little doubt that if firms such as Lever Brothers, Gulf Oil, Molson's, and GM cut their advertising, they would lose sales to their competitors.

Similarly, it is true that much of the pollution of our environment is associated with industries that consist of well-known large firms. If automobiles, steel, oil, industrial chemicals, detergents, and paper are the primary sources of our pollution, surely Ford, Stelco, Dow Chemical, Texaco, Procter & Gamble, and Abitibi Paper are significantly to blame.

Doubts About the Hypothesis

Sensitivity to Market Pressures

Even the largest, most powerful industries are not immune to market pressures. Ford's Edsel was a classic example of the market's rejecting a product. The penetration of small foreign cars into the North American market forced the automobile industry into first the compact car and then the still

---

[1] These views did not originate with the publication in 1967 of Galbraith's book by that title nor with the formation of "Nader's Raiders." Much earlier James Burnham wrote *The Managerial Revolution* and Robert Brady sounded an alarm in *Business as a System of Power*. Thorstein Veblen had predicted the technocratic takeover of society in *The Engineers and the Price System* in 1921, and Karl Marx predicted the subversion of the government bureaucrat by the businessman more than a century ago.

[2] See Peter C. Newman, *The Canadian Establishment*, vol. 1 (Toronto: McClelland and Stewart, 1975).

cheaper subcompacts. In spite of this, massive losses were suffered by North American automobile manufacturers as consumers turned in very large numbers to foreign cars whose low costs and high gas mileages they preferred even in the face of heavy advertising of North American cars. In similar fashion, changing patterns of demand have produced constant changes in the list of leading companies.

Turnover in the list of leading companies is continuous and revealing. In the United States, only two, U.S. Steel and Exxon (Standard Oil of New Jersey), were in the top 10 both in 1910 and in 1982. Today's giants include automobile, oil, airline, computer, and electric power companies—for the obvious reason that demand for these products is strong.

Are these demand shifts explained by the corporate manipulation of consumers' tastes through advertising, or by more basic changes? Advertising has two major aspects: It seeks to inform consumers about the available products, and it seeks to influence consumers by altering their demands. The first aspect, informative advertising, plays an important part in the efficient operation of any free-market system; the second aspect is one through which firms seek to control the market rather than to be controlled by it.

Clearly, advertising does influence consumers' demand. If GM were to stop advertising, it would surely lose sales to Ford, Chrysler, and foreign imports, but it is hard to believe that the automotive society was conjured up by the advertising industry. When you are persuaded to fly CP air, your real alternative is hardly a covered wagon, a bicycle, or even a Pacific Coachlines bus; more likely you are foregoing Air Canada or Pacific Western Airlines.

Careful promotion can influence the success of one rock group over another, but could it sell the waltz to today's teenager? Taste making through advertising unquestionably plays a role in shaping demand, but so too do basic human attitudes, psychological needs, and technological opportunities.

Certainly advertising shifts demands among very similar products. It is hard to believe, however, that the national economy or the average person's system of values would be fundamentally changed if there were available one more or one less make of automobile or television set or brand of shoes. A look at those products that have brought basic changes to the economy—and perhaps to our value systems—suggests that these products succeeded *because consumers wanted them,* not because advertising campaigns brainwashed people into buying them. Consider a few major examples.

The automobile transformed North American society and is in demand everywhere, even in Communist countries where only informative advertising exists. The Hollywood movie had an enormous influence in shaping our world and in changing some of our values; it was—and still is—eagerly attended throughout the world, whether or not it is accompanied by advertising. The jet airplane has shrunk the world: It has allowed major league sports to expand beyond the northeastern and midwestern cities that could be reached by an overnight bus or rail journey; it has made the international conference a commonplace; and it has made European, Hawaiian, and Caribbean vacations a reality for many.

For better or worse, the birth control pill has revolutionized many aspects of behavior in spite of the fact that it has never been advertised in the mass media. Television has changed the activities of children (and adults) in fundamental ways. Among others, it has created national rather than regional markets in dozens of commodities.

The new products that have significantly influenced the allocation of resources and social attitudes, such as those mentioned above, have succeeded because consumers wanted them; most of those that failed did so because they were not wanted—at least not at prices that would cover their costs of production. Box 16-1 deals with a case study of a giant firm which found out the hard way just how little control it could exert over the market.

The evidence suggests that the allocation of resources owes more to the tastes and values of consumers than it does to corporate advertising and related activities.

BOX 16–1 THE MARKET CONTROLS THE FIRM: THE A&P STORY

The Great Atlantic and Pacific Tea Company (A&P), was the world's first grocery chain store. In 1859, A&P opened 100 stores in New York City, and their large-scale purchasing and low-price policies led the company and the concept to prosper. By 1912 A&P was running a national chain of economy stores in the United States whose central policy was described as "cash and carry, no deliveries, no credit, no advertising, no telephone."

Although widely copied—Kroger's was formed in 1887 and Safeway in 1915, among many others—A&P was dominant, with over 50 percent of the chain food sales all through the 1920s and into the 1930s. The firm was so dominant in the 1930s that American antitrust authorities tried to restrain it, and legislation was introduced to limit its ability to compete so effectively.

Did A&P control the market? Many in and out of the company believed that it did, but events were to show that it did not. Its first big mistake occurred in the early 1930s, when it made the decision to neglect an innovation in

marketing—the supermarket. Supermarkets consisted of several departments (meat, produce, and baked goods as well as dry groceries) under one roof and relied on self-service. A&P was a *grocery* chain and used clerks. Scale efficiencies and lower labor costs enabled the supermarkets to operate much more economically than traditional clerk-operated chain grocery stores.

"King Kullen the Price Wrecker" opened the first supermarket in 1930 and, aided by the depression, was extremely successful. Supermarkets spread rapidly. A&P believed that supermarkets were a passing fad, and it refused to go along. Part of this was its feeling of loyalty to its clerks, who would have had a difficult time finding new jobs during the depression.

But A&P's policy, whatever the motivation, meant higher labor costs and higher prices than its supermarket competitors. In 1937 John Hartford, the company president, belatedly and reluctantly decided that A&P should enter the supermarket business seriously. By then, A&P had lost more than half its market share.

Who Controls the Government?

Is government subservient to big business? Lobbying is a legal, large-scale activity employed by many groups. Big business has its influence, but so do farmers, labor unions, and small business.

Cases of corrupt behavior have been documented at all levels of government. It does not follow, however, that government is subservient to the corporations and that decision making by the former is *dominated* by the wishes of the latter.

In the United States, government contracts bolster the aerospace industry, yet Lockheed's deep financial trouble in the 1970s came in part as a result of government decisions. Tobacco companies have seen government agencies first publicize the hazards of their principal product and then restrict their advertising. Airlines finally lost their

decades-long battle to prevent the introduction of the cheap transatlantic air fares, and in the United States have now lost virtually all regulatory bolstering of fare structures and limitation of competition on routes.

These examples show that while business often succeeds in attempts to protect its commercial interests through political activity, it does so within limits. Where the truth lies between the extremes of "no influence" and "no limits" is a subject of current research. Yet it does seem safe to say that, first, corporations have a lot of political influence and, second, there are some serious constraints on the ability of corporations to exert political influence over all levels of government.

The controversy over policy alternatives is important. Much of the credit for the dialogue belongs to Galbraith and Nader. Important policy

Though A&P never regained the 50 percent market share it had in the early 1930s, its profit levels and rates rebounded as the depression ended and A&P supermarkets were opened. By the early 1950s, it had secured roughly 33 percent of the chain grocery market. Although less dominant than in its heyday, it was still the leading chain.

The second crisis of A&P's existence was the opening in the 1950s and 1960s of suburban shopping malls. A&P resisted this trend because traditional company policy had been against signing long-term leases for store locations. Long-term leases were, however, necessary to secure stores in suburban malls. Company policy clashed with market necessity, and the latter won. By the time A&P realized its mistake, the prime locations had been taken by the company's competitors.

A&P had believed that it was big and powerful enough to continue attracting customers without moving to giant stores in high-rent suburban shopping malls. In later years, as gasoline costs rose and large numbers of women entered the work force, the demand for one-stop shopping grew. When other stores increased brand coverage and started stocking nonfood items, A&P's shelves in its smaller stores were already full. Between 1953 and 1971, A&P's gross sales stayed roughly constant at between $5 and $6 billion—but its market share slid from 30 to 12 percent. By 1972 it was losing money, and over the decade of the 1970s its losses continued. Late in the 1970s, the question was not whether A&P was too powerful, but rather whether it would even survive.

As the 1980s began, A&P was once again rebuilding—by closing many of its too-small, badly located stores and by employing new marketing techniques copied from its competitors. Today it has less than 10 percent of a market it once dominated and is fighting to survive. It is too early to tell if it will make it.

Does the firm control the market? A&P thought so, and found out that it was wrong.

---

issues are at stake—whether and how to change the behavior of corporation. The same issues arise whether corporations are primarily responding to market signals or are impervious to them. If the public does not approve the results of corporate behavior, it will want to control the behavior.

DO FIRMS MAXIMIZE PROFITS?

Most critics of the theory of the firm accept what Galbraith denies—that industries face market demand curves which firms can influence only slightly. The criticism is that because firms are controlled by people other than their stockholders, firms seek to maximize something other than profits.

In major areas of the business world, the days of the single proprietor who is both owner and manager of a company are gone forever. Diversification of ownership is a major characteristic of the modern corporation. Does it matter? Traditional profit-maximizing theory answers no. The three hypotheses considered next suggest that the answer is yes.

The Hypothesis of Minority Control

It is quite possible for the owners of a minority of the stock to control a majority of the shares that are voted and thus to exercise effective control over the decisions of the corporation.

This possibility arises because not all shares are actually voted. Each share of common stock has one vote in a corporation. Shares must be voted at the annual meeting of stockholders, either in person or by assigning a **proxy** to someone attending. Any individual or group controlling 51 percent of the stock clearly controls a majority of the votes.

But suppose one group owns 30 percent of the stock, with the remaining 70 percent distributed so widely that few of the dispersed group even bother to vote; in this event, 30 percent may be the overwhelming majority of the shares *actually voted*. In general, a very small fraction (sometimes as little as 5 percent) of the shares may exercise dominant influence at meetings of stockholders.

The hypothesis of minority control is that a well-organized minority often controls the destiny of the corporation against the wishes of the majority.

Dispersed ownership and minority control are well established in the corporate sector. But the hypothesis requires more than that a minority control the voting shares; it requires that stockholders be able to exert a significant influence on the firm's behavior *and* that the controlling minority have interests and motives different from the holders of the majority of the firm's stock. If all stockholders are mainly interested in having the firm maximize its profits, then it does not matter, as far as market behavior is concerned, which set of stockholders actually influences the firm's policy.

There is no accepted evidence to show that controlling groups of stockholders generally seek objectives different from those sought by the holders of the majority of the firm's stock. Of course, disagreements between stockholder groups sometimes arise. A colorful phenomenon in corporation history is the **proxy fight,** in which competing factions of stockholders (or management) attempt to collect the voting rights of the dispersed and generally disinterested stockholders.

The Hypothesis of Intercorporate Control Groups

If each member of a small group holds directorships in several companies, the group can control the board of directors of many different companies without being so obvious as to have the identical set of persons on each and every board. By controlling the boards of directors, this group can exert effective and relatively discreet control over the companies themselves.

The hypothesis of intercorporate control groups says that otherwise independent companies are subject to common control through interlocking directorates.

The factual basis of this hypothesis is that many individuals are directors of many companies. According to Peter Newman, there are significant interlocking connections among about a quarter of the corporate directors in Canada. In particular he documents the links between the chartered banks and their corporate clients provided by individuals who serve on the boards of both.

For the hypothesis of intercorporate control groups to have implications for behavior requires that boards of directors control the policies of corporations in ways that would not be approved by managers or by stockholders. Notice that this requirement places the hypothesis in conflict with the next one to be given, for one cannot hold simultaneously that managers make the effective decisions, ignoring the interests of shareholders and directors, and that directors make the effective decisions, ignoring the interests of managers and shareholders.

There is much evidence about interlocks, but there is no substantial evidence that the common directors exert any significant influence altering the firm's behavior from what it would be if no such interlocking existed. Why, then, do they occur? There may be good reasons, even if such directors do not systematically alter firm behavior. Some individuals are wanted by many corporations for their expertise and the prestige their names convey.

The Hypothesis of the Separation of Ownership from Control

A different consequence of diversified ownership was suggested in the 1930s by A. A. Berle and Gardiner Means. They hypothesized that, because of diversified ownership and the difficulty of assembling stockholders or gathering proxies, the managers rather than the stockholders or the directors exercise effective control over the corporation.

The hypothesis of the separation of ownership from control is that managerial control occurs and leads to different behavior than would stockholder control.

In the modern corporation, the stockholders elect directors, who appoint managers. Directors are supposed to represent stockholders' interests and to determine broad policies that the managers will carry out. In order to conduct the complicated business of running a large firm, a full-time professional management group must be given broad powers of decision. Although managerial decisions can be reviewed from time to time, they cannot be supervised in detail. In fact the links are typically weak enough that top management often does truly control the corporation over long periods of time.

As long as directors have confidence in the managerial group, they accept and ratify their proposals, and stockholders elect and re-elect directors who are proposed to them. If the managerial group behaves badly, it may later be removed and replaced—but this is a disruptive and drastic action, and it is infrequently employed.

Within wide limits, then, effective control of the corporation's activities resides with the managers. Although the managers are legally employed by the stockholders, they remain largely unaffected by them. Indeed, the management group characteristically asks for, and typically gets, the proxies of enough stockholders to elect directors who will reappoint it—and thus it stays in office.

The hypothesis of the separation of ownership from control requires not only that the managers be able to exert effective control over business decisions, but that they wish to act differently from the way the stockholders and directors wish to act. One such view is found in the sales maximization theory.

Sales maximization. This theory begins with the separation of management and ownership. In the giant corporation, the managers need to make some minimum level of profits to keep the share-

holders satisfied; after that they are free to seek growth unhampered by profit considerations. This is a sensible policy on the part of management, the argument runs, because salary, power, and prestige all rise with the size of a firm as much as with its profits. Generally the manager of a large, normally profitable corporation will earn a salary considerably higher than that earned by the manager of a small but highly profitable corporation.

The sales maximization hypothesis says that managers of firms seek to maximize their sales revenue, subject to a profit constraint.

Sales maximization subject to a profit constraint leads to the prediction that firms will sacrifice some profits by setting price below, and output above, their profit-maximizing levels. See Figure 16-1.

DO FIRMS MAXIMIZE ANYTHING? NON-MAXIMIZING THEORIES OF THE FIRM

Many students of large and complex organizations have been critical of economic theory for regarding modern corporations as "simple profit-maximizing computers." They believe that firms are profit-oriented in the sense that, other things being equal, they prefer more profits to less. They do not believe, however, that firms are profit-maximizers.

Maximization has two aspects. A firm is a *local maximizer* if it maximizes profits that can be earned with its present range of commodities and its present markets. A firm is a *global maximizer* if it surveys and chooses from all possible courses of action, which will include new products, new markets, and radically new sales and production techniques. It is fairly easy to gather evidence showing that most firms are not global maximizers; it is more difficult to do the same for local maximization.

Non-Maximization Due to Ignorance

One group of critics says that profit-maximizing theory is inadequate because firms, however hard

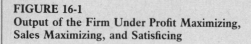

FIGURE 16-1
Output of the Firm Under Profit Maximizing,
Sales Maximizing, and Satisficing

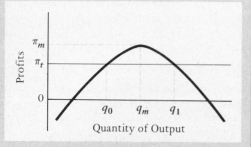

The "best" level of output depends on the motivation of the firm. The dark black curve shows the level of profits associated with each level of output. A profit-maximizing firm produces output q_m. A sales-maximizing firm, with a minimum profit constraint of π_t produces the output q_1. A satisficing firm, with a target level of profits of π_t is willing to produce any output between q_0 and q_1. Thus satisficing allows a range of outputs on either side of the profit-maximizing level while sales maximizing results in a higher output than does profit maximizing.

people cannot be employing concepts of which they are unaware.

This observation, assuming it to be correct, does refute the theory that firms make decisions by calculating marginal values and consciously equating them. But it does not refute the theory that firms maximize profits. The mathematical concepts of marginal cost and marginal revenue (these are just the *first derivatives* of the total cost and total revenue functions by another name) are used by economic theorists to discover what will happen as long as, by one means or another—be it guess, hunch, clairvoyance, luck, or good judgment—the firms do approximately succeed in maximizing their profits. The constructs of the theory of the firm are logical tools used to discover the consequences of certain behavior. They are not meant to be descriptions of *how* firms reach their decisions. If firms are maximizing their profits, then the tools of economic theory allow us to predict how they will react to certain changes (e.g., the introduction of a tax), and this prediction is independent of the thought process by which firms actually reach their decisions.

they may try, cannot reach decisions in the way the theory predicts. This criticism has several aspects, some crude and some quite sophisticated.

Business People Do Not Understand Marginal Concepts

One of the crudest criticisms is based on the observation that business people do not calculate in the manner assumed by the theory. Sometimes business people are interviewed and it is discovered (apparently to the surprise of the interviewer) that they have never heard of the concepts of marginal cost and marginal revenue. It is then argued that: (1) the theory assumes business people equate marginal cost to marginal revenue; (2) empirical observations show that business people have not heard of marginal cost and marginal revenue; (3) therefore the theory is refuted, because business

Business Calculations Are Cruder Than Assumed by Profit-Maximizing Theory

A similar argument stems from the observation that firms do not calculate down to single units with such a fine degree of accuracy as is assumed in profit-maximizing theory. In the verbal presentation of the theory of the firm, it is usually stated that firms will increase production until the cost of producing the very last unit is just equal to the revenue gained from its sale. This is merely a verbal statement of the mathematical conditions for the maximization of the profit function. The observation that firms do not calculate down to single units is not of itself relevant as a test of the theory. The marginal analysis allows us to predict how firms will respond to certain changes in the data; if they are maximizing their profits they will be observed to respond in this way, even though they calculate in a much cruder fashion than mathematicians do.

Firms Have Inadequate Information

More sophisticated critics point out that the information available to decision makers is simply not adequate to permit them to reach the decisions economists predict they will reach. This argument generally takes one of three forms: that firms are the victims of their accountants, and base their decisions on accounting concepts, which differ from economic ones; that the natural lag between accumulating and processing data is such that important decisions must be made on fragmentary and partially out-of-date information; or that firms cannot afford to acquire as much information as economists assume them to have.

Non-Maximization by Choice

Alternatives to profit maximization are usually based on observations of actual firms. The observations and the theories all have in common the implication that firms *choose* not to be profit maximizers.

Full-Cost Pricing

Most manufacturing firms are price setters: they must quote a price for their products rather than accept a price set on some impersonal competitive market. Simple profit-maximizing theory predicts that these firms will change their prices in response to every change in demand and costs that they experience. Yet students of large firms have long alleged that this much price flexibility is not observed. In the short run, prices of manufactured goods do not appear to vary in response to every shift in the firm's demand. Instead, they appear to change rather sluggishly.

This short-run behavior is consistent with the hypothesis of **full-cost pricing**, which was originally advanced in the 1930s by Robert Hall, a British economist, and Charles Hitch, an American, following a series of detailed case studies of actual pricing decisions made in Oxford. Case studies in the intervening decades have continued to reveal the widespread use of full-cost pricing procedures.

The full-cost pricer, instead of equating marginal revenue with marginal cost, sets price equal to average cost (at normal-capacity output) plus a conventional markup.

The firm changes its prices when its average costs change substantially (as a result of such events as a new union contract or a sharp change in the prices of key raw materials), and it may occasionally change its markup. However, its short-run pricing behavior is rather conventional and is not characterized even by local profit maximization.

Modern supporters of profit-maximizing theory accept the full-cost evidence but argue that it reveals only the administrative procedure by which prices are set from day to day. They hold that management makes frequent changes in markups in an attempt to maximize profits. Thus they believe that, while firms may be full-cost pricers from day to day, they are profit maximizers with respect to their average experience over, say, a year.

Modern critics of profit-maximizing theory accept the evidence that full-cost prices are sometimes changed in the profit-maximizing direction. They hold, however, that the prevalence of conventional full-cost practices shows that prices are typically not at their profit-maximizing level. They also hold that the prevalence of full-cost pricing shows that firms are creatures of custom that make fairly small, profit-oriented changes at fairly infrequent intervals.

We have seen in Chapter 14 that the short-term stickiness of oligopolistic prices can be accounted for under profit-maximizing theory by the fact that it is costly for a multiproduct firm to change its list prices. The possible conflict between full-cost and profit-maximizing theory then concerns only the setting of the markup that relates prices to costs. If markups are conventional and only rarely revised, then there is a conflict. If, however, the markup is the profit-maximizing one for normal capacity output, then full-cost pricing can be consistent with profit maximization where it is costly to change prices.

Organization Theory

According to profit-maximizing theory, firms constantly scan available alternatives and choose the most profitable ones. A common criticism of this theory is that behavior is influenced seriously by the organizational structure of the firm. **Organization theory** argues that in big firms decisions are made after much discussion by groups and committees and that the structure of the process affects the substance of the decisions.

The central prediction of organization theory is that different decisions will result from different kinds of organizations, even when all else is unchanged.

One proposition that follows from this theory is that large and diffuse organizations find it necessary to develop standard operating procedures to help them in making decisions. These decision rules arise as compromises among competing points of view and, once adopted, are changed only reluctantly. An important prediction following from this hypothesis is that the compromises will persist for long periods of time despite changes in conditions affecting the firm. Even if a particular compromise were the profit-maximizing strategy in the first place, it would not remain so when conditions changed. Thus profits will not usually be maximized.

Another prediction is that decision by compromise will lead firms to adopt conservative policies that avoid large risks. Smaller firms not faced with necessity of compromising competing views will take bigger risks than larger firms.

Organization theorists have suggested an alternative to profit-maximization that they call **satisficing.** Satisficing theory was first suggested by Professor Herbert Simon of Carnegie-Mellon University, who in 1978 was awarded the Nobel Prize in economics for his work on firm behavior. Speaking of his theory, he wrote: "We must expect the firm's goals to be not maximizing profits but attaining a certain level or rate of profit, holding a certain share of the market or a certain level of sales."

According to the satisficing hypothesis, firms will strive to achieve certain target levels of profits, but having achieved them, they will not strive to improve their profit position further. This means that the firm could produce any one of a range of outputs that yield at least the target level of profits rather than the unique output that maximizes profits. This too is illustrated in Figure 16-1.

Satisficing theory predicts not a unique equilibrium output but a range of possible outputs that includes the profit-maximizing output somewhere within it and the sales-maximizing output at the upper limit.

Evolutionary Theories

The modern evolutionary theories advanced by such economists as Richard Nelson and Sidney Winter of Yale University build on the earlier theories of full-cost pricing and satisficing. Nelson and Winter argue that firms do not—indeed, could not—behave as profit-maximizing theory predicts. They accept that firms desire profits and even strive for profits; what they deny is that firms maximize profits globally or even locally.

Evolutionary theorists have gathered much evidence to show that tradition seems to be paramount in firms' planning. The basic effort at the early stages of planning is directed, they argue, toward the problem of performing reasonably well in established markets and maintaining established market shares. They quote evidence to show that suggestions, made by planners in preliminary planning documents, to do something entirely new in some areas, even on a 10-year horizon, are usually weeded out in the reviewing process. They believe that most firms spend very little effort on *planning* to enter entirely new markets, and still less on direct efforts to leave or even reduce their share in long-established markets.

These attitudes were illustrated by one firm which, although faced with obviously changing circumstances, reported that "We have been producing on the basis of these raw materials for more than 50 years with success, and we have made it a policy to continue to do so."

The evolutionary theory of the firm draws many analogies with the biological theory of evolution. Here are two of the most important.

The genes. In biological theory, behavior patterns are transmitted over time by genes. Rules of behavior fulfill the same function in the evolutionary theory of the firm. In Sidney Winter's words: "That a great deal of firm decision behaviour is routinized . . . is a 'stylized fact' about the realities of firm decision process. Routinized . . . decision procedures . . . cover decision situations from pricing practices in retail stores to such 'strategic' decisions as advertising or R and D effort, or the question of whether or not to invest abroad." Winter talks of firms "remembering by doing" according to repetitive routines. He adds that government policymakers tend to have unrealistic expectations about firms' flexibility and responsiveness to changes in market incentives. These expectations arise from the maximizing model, whose fatal flaw, Winter alleges, is to underestimate the importance and difficulty "of the task of merely continuing the routine performance, i.e., of preventing undesired deviations."

The mutations. In the theory of biological evolution, mutations are the vehicle of change. In the evolutionary theory of the firm, this role is played by innovations. Some innovations are similar to those discussed in Chapter 13, the introduction of new products and new production techniques. However, a further important class of innovations in evolutionary theory is the introduction of new rules of behavior. Sometimes innovations are thrust on the firm; at other times the firm consciously plans for and creates innovations.

According to maximizing theory, innovations are the result of incentives—the "carrot" of new profit opportunities. In evolutionary theory, the firm is much more of a satisficer, and it usually innovates only under the incentive of the "stick" either of unacceptably low profits or some form of external prodding. Firms change routines when

they get into trouble, not when they see a chance to improve an already satisfactory performance. For example, in the growing markets of the 1960s many firms continued all sorts of wasteful practices that they shed fairly easily when their profits were threatened in the more difficult economic climate of the 1970s.

The Significance of Non-Maximizing Theories

An impressive array of evidence can be gathered in apparent support of various non-maximizing theories. What would be the implications if they were accepted as being better theories of the behavior of the economy than profit maximization?

If non-maximizing theories are correct, the economic system does not perform with the delicate precision that follows from profit maximization. But the system described by evolutionary theory *does* function. Firms sell more when demand goes up and less when it goes down. They also alter their prices and their input mixes when hit with the "stick" of sufficiently large changes in input prices.

Evolutionary theory does not upset the broad case for the price system: that it produces a coordinated response from decentralized decision makers to changes in tastes and costs.

But profit-oriented non-maximizing firms will also exhibit a great deal of inertia. They will not respond quickly and precisely to small changes in market signals from either the private sector or government policy. Neither are they likely to make radical changes in their behavior even when the profit incentives to do so are large. This casts doubt over the efficacy of government policies that make relatively small changes in incentives, hoping that firms will respond to these as profit maximizers.

Non-maximizing models imply sensitivity of the price system to large but not to small changes in signals caused by changes in demand, costs, or public policy.

Profits, however, are unmistakably a potent force in the life—and death—of firms. The resilience of profit-maximizing theory and its ability to predict how the economy will react to some major changes (such as the recent dramatic increases in energy prices) suggests that firms are at least strongly motivated by the pursuit of profits and that, other things being equal, they prefer more profits to less profits.

If profit-maximizing theory should eventually give way to some more organizationally dominated theory, the new theory will still be a profit-oriented theory. The search for profits and the avoidance of losses drive the economy even when firms do not turn out to be continual profit maximizers.

How Far Can Corporations Depart from Profit-Maximizing Behavior?

Many of the criticisms of modern microeconomic theory assume that firms seek to do things other than maximize their profits. If the present management elects not to maximize its profits, this implies that some other management could make more money by operating the firm. A major restraint on existing managements is the threat of a stockholder revolt or a takeover bid.

A management that fails to come close to achieving the profit potential of the assets it controls becomes a natural target for acquisition. The management of the acquiring firm makes a **tender offer** (or **takeover bid,** as it is sometimes called) to the stockholders of the target firm, offering them what amounts to a premium for their shares, a premium it can pay because it expects to increase the firm's profits. Managers who wish to avoid takeover bids cannot let the profits of their firm slip far from the profit-maximizing level—because their unrealized profits provide the incentives for takeovers.

Some, though by no means all, of the so-called conglomerate firms have specialized in this kind of takeover. In the last two decades the example par excellence of this has been International Telephone and Telegraph, which acquired (among other companies) Avis Car Rental, Continental Baking, Sheraton Hotels, Canteen Food Service, and Hartford Life Insurance. In each case it substantially increased the operating profits of the acquired company after the takeover.

The pressure of the threat of takeovers severely limits the discretion of corporate management to pursue goals other than profit maximization.

SUMMARY

1. A sweeping attack on the traditional theory of the behavior of the firm is made by Galbraith, along with Nader and others. He argues that large corporations manipulate markets, tastes, and governments instead of responding to market and governmental pressures. While there is evidence about the influence of large corporations, there is also much evidence of market influence on corporate behavior.

2. In recent years, serious concern has developed over whether corporations should represent the interests of their owners and managers or whether they should be responsible to a broader public interest. Consumerists argue for the latter point of view; others prefer to rely on markets and government control to protect the public interest.

3. The widespread ownership of the modern corporation leads to the question: Who really controls the modern corporation? Attempts to answer this question have led to alternative theories that firms maximize something other than profits. Three important hypotheses have been advanced.

a. A minority group of stockholders often controls the corporation against the wishes of the majority. The fact of minority control is widely accepted, but there is little evidence to suggest that the minority usually coerce the majority.

b. A small group of people effectively controls a large section of the economy through the mechanism of interlocking directorates. This hypothesis is not widely accepted (although interlocking directorships do exist).

c. Because of the widespread ownership of the corporation, stockholders cannot exert effective control over the managers; thus the latter have the real control of the organization and operate it for their advantage rather than that of the stockholders. This hypothesis has some serious, but by no means universal, support.

4. These and other hypotheses suggest that firms may seek to maximize something other than profits. One alternative is Baumol's hypothesis of sales maximization: Firms seek to be as large as possible (judged by sales revenue), subject to the constraint that they achieve a minimum rate of profit.

5. An alternative set of hypotheses denies that firms maximize profits in either the local or the global sense of maximization.

a. Organization theorists see firms as insensitive to short-term fluctuations in market signals. Their reason lies in the decision-making structure of large organizations, which must rely on routines and rules of thumb rather than on fresh calculations of profitabilities as each new situation presents itself.

b. The full-cost hypothesis states that firms determine price by adding a customary—and infrequently changed—markup to full costs. This also makes their pricing behavior relatively insensitive to short-term fluctuations in demand.

c. Evolutionary theorists build on full-cost and organizational theories. They see the firm as a profit-oriented entity in a world of imperfect information, making small, profit-oriented changes from its present situation but being more resistant to large, "structural" changes. Resources are still reallocated by evolutionary firms as demand and costs shift, but usually more in response to the "stick" of threatened losses than the "carrot" of possible extra profits.

6. Under both maximizing and non-maximizing theories, profits are an important driving force in the economy, and changes in demand and costs cause changes in profits, which cause firms to reallocate resources. The speed and precision, but not the general direction of the reallocations, are what is different between maximizing and non-maximizing theories.

TOPICS FOR REVIEW

The New Industrial State
The long-run sensitivity of firms to market pressures
Consumerism
Alternate maximizing theories
Ownership, management, and control of corporate decisions
Sales maximization
Non-maximizing theories
Full-cost pricing
Satisficing
Evolutionary theories

DISCUSSION QUESTIONS

1. In 1976 the automobile manufacturers introduced their 1977 models. GM and American Motors (AMC) put major emphasis on smaller, more economical cars, and Ford and Chrysler stayed with their 1976 model sizes. Read the following news headlines (which appear in chronological order) and then discuss the light they shed on the hypothesis that firms control the market.

   a. "GM's 1977 Line Runs Ahead of the Pack. The Big Question: Do People Want Small Cars?"
   b. "Ford, Chrysler, Beam; AMC in Trouble on Sales."
   c. "GM's Fuel-Saving Chevette: Right Car at the Wrong Time."
   d. "Price Cuts and Rebates Lift Sales of Small AMC and GM Cars."
   e. "GM Confirms Plans to Drop the Subcompact Vega."

   What do these further events reveal about the same hypothesis?:

   f. "In 1979 auto firms sold all the small cars they could produce. But they were left with sizable unsold inventories of large cars, and as a result they are preparing to alter their production mix in favor of small cars."
   g. "By 1981, all North American car makers were in trouble, as Japanese imports grew to over 25 percent of the North American market."

2. "Because automobile companies were interested only in profits, they would not produce the safer, less polluting, but more expensive cars that the public really wanted. Legislation was necessary, therefore, to force producers to meet consumer needs." Discuss.

3. Assume that each of the following assertions is factually correct. Taken together, what would they tell you about the prediction that big business is increasing its control of the Canadian economy?

   a. The share of total manufacturing assets owned by the 200 largest corporations has been rising steadily for the last 25 years.
   b. The number of new firms begun every year has grown steadily for the last 25 years.
   c. The share of manufacturing in total production has been decreasing for 40 years.

d. Profits as a percent of national income are no higher now than half a century ago.

4. "Our economy, like an engine, must have fuel to operate. And the fuel our economy runs on is profit. Profits keep it going—and growing. But there is strong evidence that the economy's fuel supply is running low. Profits of U.S. corporations today are about 5 percent on sales—less than the 1965 rate.

"We Americans have become accustomed to a quality of life that can survive only through profits. For profits not only create jobs and goods, they furnish essential tax revenues. Federal, state, and local taxes finance the countless programs that our citizens demand—from paving the roads on which we drive to building our country's defense forces . . . to helping millions of Americans who need some form of assistance."

Comment on this excerpt from an Allied Chemical Corporation advertisement.

5. "The business of the businessman is to run his business so as to make profits. If he does so, he will serve the public interest better than if he tries to decide what is good for society. He is neither elected nor appointed to that task." Discuss.

6. "Our list prices are really set by our accounting department: they add a fixed markup to their best estimates of fully accounted cost and send these to the operating divisions. Managers of these divisions may not change those prices without permission of the Board of Directors, which is seldom given. Operating divisions may, however, provide special discounts if necessary to stay competitive." Does this testimony by the president of a leading manufacturing company support the full-cost pricing hypothesis?

7. The leading automobile tire manufacturers (Goodyear, Firestone, etc.) sell original equipment (OE) tires to automobile manufacturers at a price below the average total cost of all the tires they make and sell. This happens year after year. Is this consistent with profit-maximizing behavior in the short run? In the long run? If it is not consistent, what does it show? Do OE tires compete with replacement tires?

PART FIVE

THE DISTRIBUTION OF INCOME

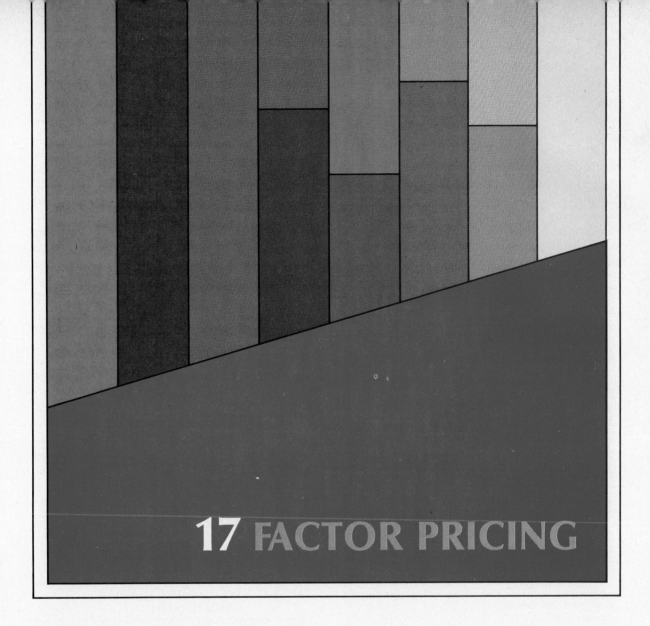

17 FACTOR PRICING

Are the poor getting poorer and the rich richer, as Karl Marx thought they would? Are the rich becoming relatively poorer and the poor relatively richer, as Alfred Marshall hoped they would? Is the distribution of income affected by social changes such as the increased participation of women in the labor force, or by changes in public policy toward poverty? Should we reject the view held by Italian economist Vilfredo Pareto that inequality of income is a social constant determined by forces that are possibly beyond human understanding and probably beyond human influence?

The founders of classical economics, Adam Smith and David Ricardo, were concerned with the distribution of income among what were then the three great social classes: workers, capitalists, and landowners. To deal with this question, they defined three factors of production: labor, capital, and land. The return to each of these factors was the income of each of the three classes in society.

Smith and Ricardo were interested in what determined the income of each group relative to the total national income, and in how a nation's economic growth affected this income distribution. Their theories predicted that as society progressed, landlords would become relatively better off and capitalists would become relatively worse off. Karl Marx provided different answers to the same questions: He concluded that as growth occurred, capitalists would become better off at the expense of workers (at least until the whole capitalist system collapsed).

These and similar nineteenth century debates focused on the distribution of total income among the major factors of production, now called the **functional distribution of income**. Table 17-1 shows data for the functional distribution of income in Canada in 1982.

Although functional distribution categories (wages, rent, profits) pervade current statistics, much of the attention of non-Marxist economists has shifted to another way of looking at differences in incomes. Around the beginning of the present century, Pareto studied what is now called the **size distribution of income**, the distribution of income among different households without reference to the social class to which they belonged. He discovered that inequality in income distribution was great in all countries and, more surprisingly, that the degree of inequality was quite similar from one country to another. Tables 17-2 and 17-3 show that in Canada in 1983 there was substantial inequality in the distribution of income.

Inequality in the distribution of income is shown graphically in Figure 17-1. This curve of income distribution, called a **Lorenz curve**, shows how much of total income is accounted for by given proportions of the nation's families. (The farther the curve bends away from the diagonal, the more unequal is the distribution of income.) In 1981 the bottom 20 percent of all Canadian families received only 6.6 percent of all income earned. The present size distribution of income is virtually unchanged from what it was 20 years ago.

There are good reasons why much of the attention of modern economists is devoted to the size, rather than the functional, distribution of income. After all, some capitalists (such as the owners of small retail stores) are in the lower part of the income scale, while some wage earners (such as skilled athletes) are at the upper end of the income scale. Moreover, if someone is poor, it matters little whether that person is a landowner or a worker.

TABLE 17–1 FUNCTIONAL DISTRIBUTION OF NATIONAL INCOME IN CANADA, 1982

Type of income	Billions of dollars	Percentage of total
Employee compensation	208.0	76.7
Corporate profits	21.1	7.9
Proprietors' income, including rent	13.0	4.8
Interest	28.9	10.6
Total	27.10	100.0

Source: Statistics Canada, 13–001.

Total income is classified here according to the nature of the factor service that earned the income. While these data show that employee compensation is about 77 percent of national income, they do not show that workers and their families receive only that fraction of national income. Many households will have income in more than one category listed in the table.

TABLE 17–2 INCOME OF CANADIAN FAMILIES, 1981

Income class	Percentage of families
Less than $5,000	2.6
$5,000–6,999	2.5
$7,000–9,999	5.4
$10,000–11,999	4.7
$12,000–14,999	5.8
$15,000–24,999	23.0
$25,000–44,999	39.8
$45,000 or more	16.2

Source: Statistics Canada, 13–208.

The median family income was about $29,000 in 1981.

TABLE 17–3 INEQUALITY IN FAMILY INCOME DISTRIBUTION, 1981

Family income rank	Percentage share of aggregate income
Lowest fifth	6.6
Second fifth	15.6
Middle fifth	23.7
Fourth fifth	21.2
Highest fifth	32.9
	100.0

Source: Statistics Canada, 13-208.

While far from showing overall equality, income distribution is relatively equal for the middle 80 percent of the distribution. If the income distribution were perfectly equal, each fifth of the families would receive 20 percent of aggregate income.

Today those who study inequality focus on influences such as race, sex, age, education, occupation, and region of residence.

We shall look closely at the poverty problem in Chapter 20. In order to understand this and other problems concerning the distribution of income, we must first study how the income of households is determined and what forces cause it to change.

It is tempting to give superficial explanations of differences in income with remarks like "People earn according to their ability." But incomes are distributed much more unequally than any *measured* index of ability, be it IQ, physical strength, or typing skill. In what sense is Tom Watson five times as able a golfer as Curtis Strange? His average score is only 1 percent better, yet he earns five times as much. If answers couched in terms of worth and ability are easily refuted, so are answers such as "It's all a matter of luck," or "It's just the system."

THE THEORY OF DISTRIBUTION

How does economic theory explain the distribution of income more satisfactorily than the superficial explanations just considered?

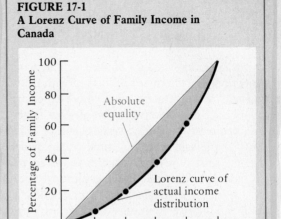

**FIGURE 17-1
A Lorenz Curve of Family Income in Canada**

The size of the shaded area between the Lorenz curve and the diagonal is a measure of the inequality of income distribution. If there were complete income equality, the bottom 20 percent of income receivers would receive 20 percent of the income, and so forth, and the Lorenz curve would be the diagonal line. Because the lower 20 percent receive only 5 percent of the income, the actual curve lies below the diagonal. The lower curve shows actual Canadian data. The extent to which it bends away from the straight line indicates the amount of inequality in the distribution of income.

The income earned by any factor has, in a purely arithmetical sense, two components: the quantity of the income-earning service that is provided and the price per unit paid for it. For example, the amount a worker earns in wages depends on the number of hours worked and the hourly wage received.

The traditional or neo-classical theory of distribution says that a factor's income is determined in the same way that price and quantity of any other commodity are determined. According to this view, distribution theory involves little that is new. It merely requires that we understand the particular

considerations that influence the demand and supply of a factor of production.

Factor Income and Factor Prices

As with the market theory studied in Chapter 4,
the theory of distribution is concerned with *relative*
magnitudes. One factor becomes "more expensive"
when its price rises relative to that of other factors.
In an inflationary world most prices will be rising,
but not at the same rate. So some factors will be
becoming relatively more expensive, some relatively cheaper. We shall use the phrase "rise in
price" to mean a rise in relative price, and the
phrase "fall in price" to mean a fall in relative price
(see pages 62–63 for fuller discussion).

In this chapter we consider competitive markets.
Microeconomic theory states that the competitive
market price of any commodity or factor is determined by demand and supply. The competitive
market determination of the equilibium price and
quantity, and thus the money income of a factor of
production, is illustrated in Figure 17-2. Look
again at Figure 4-8, page 59, to see why this analysis is familiar.

According to the neo-classical theory of distribution,
the problem of distribution is just a special case of the
problem of the pricing of any good or service.

The theory of factor prices is absolutely general. If
one is concerned with labor, one should interpret
factor prices to mean wages; if one is dealing with
land, factor prices should be interpreted to mean
land rents, and so on.

Factor Price Differentials

If all units of labor were identical and if all benefits
were monetary, then the price of labor would be
the same in all uses.[1] Workers would tend to move
from low-priced occupations to high-priced ones.
The quantity of labor supplied would diminish in
occupations in which wages were low, and the resulting shortage would tend to force those wages

[1] Similar remarks apply to all other factors of production.

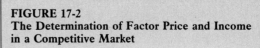
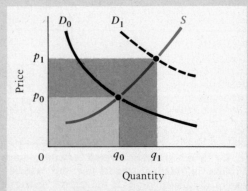

FIGURE 17-2
**The Determination of Factor Price and Income
in a Competitive Market**

Demand and supply for factors determine prices and
quantities of factors in competitive factor markets.
With demand and supply curves D_0 and S, the price
of the factor will be p_0 and the quantity employed q_0.
The total income earned by the factor is the lighter
shaded area. A shift in demand from D_0 to D_1 raises
equilibrium price and quantity to p_1 and q_1. The income earned by the factor rises by the darker shaded
area.

up; the quantity of labor supplied would increase
in occupations in which wages were high, and the
resulting surplus would force wages down. The
movement would continue until there were no further incentives to change occupations—that is, until wages were equalized in all cases. In fact, however, wage differentials commonly occur. These
differentials may be divided into two distinct types.

Dynamic Differentials

Some factor-price differentials reflect a temporary state of disequilibrium. These are self-elimi-
nating and are called **dynamic differentials**, or **disequilibrium differentials**. They are brought about
by circumstances such as the growth of one industry and the decline of another. Such differentials
themselves lead to reallocations of factors, and

these reallocations will in turn act to eliminate the differentials.

Consider the effect on factor prices of a rise in the demand for air transport and a decline in the demand for railroading. There will be an increase in airlines' demand for factors and a decrease in the railroad industry's demand for factors. Relative factor prices will go up in the airline industry and down in railroading.[2] The differential in factor prices will itself foster a net movement of factors from the railroad industry to the airline industry, and this movement will cause the dynamic price differentials to lessen and eventually disappear. How long this process takes will depend on how easily factors move from one industry to the other—that is, on the extent of factor mobility.

Equilibrium Differentials

Some factor price differentials may persist in equilibrium without generating forces that eliminate them. These **equilibrium differentials** are related to intrinsic differences in the factors themselves, to differences in the cost of acquiring skills, and to different nonmonetary advantages of different factor employments.

Intrinsic differences. If various units of a factor have different characteristics, the price paid may differ among these units. Intelligent and manually dextrous workers may earn more than less intelligent and less dextrous workers. Highly fertile land will earn more than poor land. These differences will persist even in long-run equilibrium.

Acquired differences. Equilibrium differences are also caused by acquired differences in factors. If the fertility of land can be increased by expensive methods, then that land must command a higher price than lower-fertility land. If it did not, landlords would not incur the costs of improving fertility. The same holds true for labor. It is costly to acquire most skills. An architect and a mechanic

must both train for some time to acquire the necessary skills. Unless the earnings of architects and mechanics remain sufficiently above what can be earned in less skilled occupations, people will not incur the cost of training for these occupations.

Nonmonetary advantages. Whenever working conditions differ among various uses for a single factor, that factor will earn different equilibrium amounts in its various uses. The difference between a faller's and a bucker's wages in the logging industry is only partly a matter of skill; the rest is a compensation for the higher risk of falling trees compared to cutting them up on the ground. If their wages were the same, there would be an excess supply of buckers and a shortage of fallers.

The same set of forces accounts for equilibrium differences in regional earnings of otherwise identical factors. Welders and carpenters earn more in Whitehorse and Inuvvick than they do in Peterborough or Sherbrooke. Without the higher pay in unattractive locations, people would not be willing to work there. Similarly, if enough people prefer living in the beautiful Maritime Provinces to living in Ontario industrial towns, equilibrium wages in comparable occupations will be lower in the Maritimes than in Ontario.

Differentials and Factor Mobility

The distinction between dynamic and equilibrium differentials is closely linked to factor mobility.

Dynamic differentials lead to, and are eroded by, factor movements; equilibrium differentials are related to differences and advantages that cannot be eliminated by factor mobility.

Dynamic differentials tend to disappear over time: equilibrium differentials persist indefinitely.

Equal Net Advantage

The removal of dynamic differentials and the persistence of equilibrium ones lead to a generalization called the *hypothesis of equal net advantage.* This hypothesis follows from the presumption that owners of factors will choose that use of their fac-

---

[2] Railroad workers do not necessarily need to retrain for the airline industries. The chain of substitution may be more complex than that, or it may take the form of exit from railroads through retirement and expansion in airlines as young workers start off in that industry.

BOX 17–1 COULD PER CAPITA INCOMES AND UNEMPLOYMENT RATES BE EQUALIZED ACROSS CANADIAN PROVINCES?

The answer to the question posed in the title is almost certainly no—at least when we consider the kinds of policy tools likely to be available to any foreseeable Canadian government.

This answer comes form a simple application of the hypothesis of *equal net advantage*. As long as provinces differ in their nonmonetary attractiveness, there will be equilibrium differences in their per capita incomes and/or unemployment rates. Why is this so?

Consider low levels of income. Low incomes may be the result of strong natural economic forces that will not yield to such simple-minded policy measures as raising local demand. For example, suppose that province A—despite strong physical, climatic, and social attractions—has a set of natural endowments that will not produce as high an income per person employed as province B. Deficiencies in economic opportunities in a particular province might arise for many reasons: Inadequate resource base, technological backwardness, slow growth in demand for one region's products, and rapid natural growth of the labor force are just a few.

Suppose that because of migration costs, cultural and language differences, climatic advantages, or other local amenities, many people choose to live in province A even though they earn lower incomes there. Markets can adjust to such regional differences in two basic ways.

If wages and prices are flexible, real wages and incomes will fall in province A for those kinds of workers who are in excess supply. The falling real wages will give the province an advantage in new lines of production. Real wages will continue to fall until everyone who is willing to stay at the lower wage has a job and those who are not have migrated. In long-run equilibrium, province A is a low-wage, low-income province, but it has no special unemployment problem. Those who do not value its amenities as much as they value the higher incomes to be earned in province B, or who are subject to lower migration costs, will have left. What the price system does is to equalize net advantages. It does not equalize economic advantage, because the noneconomic advantages of living in province A exceed those of living in province B.

The second possibility arises because we do not have these flexibilities in wages today. Min-

tors that produces the greatest net advantage to themselves, where net advantage includes both monetary and nonmonetary rewards. The **hypothesis of equal net advantage** states that in eroding dynamic differentials, factor mobility tends to equalize the net advantage earned by factors in different locations and occupations.

This hypothesis plays the same role in the theory of distribution as the assumption that firms seek to maximize profits plays in the theory of production. It leads to the prediction that the units of each kind of factor of production will be allocated among various uses in such a way that their owners could not receive a higher net return in any other use.

Nonmonetary advantages have a big role to play in explaining differences in levels of pay in different occupations and jobs. But since they are quite stable over time, they do not diminish the importance of monetary advantages. Variations in monetary advantages tend to lead to changes in *net* advantage, and thus they play a big role in reallocating resources.

A change in the relative rate of pay of a factor between two uses will tend to change the net advantages of the uses. It will lead to a shift of some units of that factor to the use whose rate of pay has increased.

This implies a rising supply curve for a factor

imum wage laws, national unions, and nation-wide pay scales for the federal civil service put substantial restraints on possible interprovincial wage differentials. People who prefer province A remain there, yet wages do not fall to create a wage incentive to move to B. Instead, unemployment rates in A rise until (1) the extra uncertainty of finding a job and (2) the lower lifetime income expectations because of bouts of unemployment just balance both the nonpecuniary advantages that A enjoys over B and the costs of moving from A to B. In the long run, those who are willing to stay in spite of the higher unemployment remain, and the others leave.

In these circumstances, increasing local demand, even where that is possible, will lower the rate of out-migration but *not* the unemployment rate. This is because in the long run A's unemployment rate must remain sufficiently high relative to B's to balance the relative amenity and migration-cost advantages that province A enjoys over B.

In these circumstances trade restrictions, such as "employ local labor only" laws and labor market policies such as employment subsidies, will not reduce unemployment though they will increase employment. As new jobs are created, the rate of out-migration slows so that the rate of unemployment is unchanged. Unless the province's policies are sufficient to create jobs for everyone entering its labor force, all that will happen when more jobs are created is that fewer people will migrate. The local supply rises as fast as the local demand for labor, and the unemployment rate is left unchanged.

The foregoing argument does not imply that nothing can be done for regions that have lower incomes or higher unemployment rates. There are many reasons why we might wish to make income transfers to poorer regions. However, it is important to realize that if the differential is an equilibrium phenomenon, no amount of policy intervention will remove it. If the policies continue to be strengthened as long as these differentials in unemployment persist, expenditures will rise and rise and rise, and the ultimate goal of equalization will continue to prove elusive.

in any particular use. When the price of a factor rises in that use, more will be supplied to that use. This factor supply curve (like all supply curves) can *shift* in response to changes in other variables. For example, one thing that can shift it is a change in size of nonmonetary benefits.

Policy Issues

Trade unions, governments, and other bodies often have explicit policies about earnings differentials. The success of such policies depends to a great extent on the kind of differential that is being attacked. Success may follow an attack on a dynamic differential that would otherwise be slow to adjust. Only a short time ago large differentials opened up between earnings in Alberta and those in central and eastern Canada. These were disequilibrium differentials associated with an economic boom in Alberta. Any policies that sped up the movement of labor to Alberta would have hastened the time when the earnings differential between the two regions was narrowed.

But now consider a case where two areas have persistent differences in their nonmonetary attractions. Say, for example, that province A has a much better climate than province B. Equilibrium wages for comparable jobs will be lower in A than in B.

BOX 17-2 ORIGINS OF THE CONCEPT OF ECONOMIC RENT

In the early nineteenth century there was public debate about the price of wheat in England. The high price was causing great hardship because bread was a primary source of food for the working class. Some argued that wheat had a high price because landlords were charging very high rents to tenant farmers. In order to meet these land rents, the prices that farmers charged for their wheat also had to be raised to a high level. In short, it was argued that the price of wheat was high because the rents of agricultural land were high. Those who held this view advocated restricting the rents landlords were able to charge.

David Ricardo argued that the situation was exactly the reverse. The price of wheat was high, he said, because there was a shortage caused by the Napoleonic wars. Because wheat had a high price, it was profitable to produce it and there was keen competition among farmers to obtain land on which to grow wheat. This competition in turn forced up the rents of wheat land. If the price of wheat were to fall so that wheat growing became less profitable, then the demand for land would fall and the price paid for the use of land (i.e., its rent) would also fall. Ricardo advocated removing the tariff so that imported wheat could come into the country, thereby increasing the supply and bringing down both the price of wheat and the price of the land on which it was grown.

Stated formally, the essentials of Ricardo's argument were these: Land was regarded as having only one use, the growing of wheat. The supply of land was fixed. Nothing had to be paid to prevent land from transferring to a use other than growing wheat because it had no

other use. No self-respecting landowner would leave land idle as long as he could obtain some return, no matter how small, by renting it out. Therefore, all the payment to land—that is, rent—was a surplus over and above what was necessary to keep it in its present use. Given a fixed supply of land, the price depended on the demand for land, which depended upon the demand for wheat. Rent, the term for the payment for the use of land, thus became the term for a surplus payment to a factor over and above what was necessary to keep it in its present use.

Later, two facts were realized. First, land itself often had alternative uses, and from the point of view of any one use, part of the payment made to land would necessarily have to be paid to keep it in its present use. Second, factors of production other than land also often earn a surplus over and above what is necessary to keep them in their present use. Television stars and great athletes, for example, are in short and fairly fixed supply, and their potential earnings in other occupations are often quite moderate. But because there is a huge demand for their services as television stars or athletes, they may receive payments greatly in excess of what is needed to keep them from transferring to other occupations.

Thus it appears that all factors of production are pretty much the same; part of the payment made to them is a payment necessary to keep them from transferring to other uses, and part is a surplus over and above what is necessary to keep them in their present use. This surplus is now called *economic rent*, whether the factor is land or labor or a piece of capital equipment.

The differential will be such as to equal the net advantages of living in A rather than B. The higher wage in B will just compensate for its lower attractions. If public policy now enforces equal wages in the two provinces, a disequilibrium will be created. People will move from province A to province B until some other disadvantages are created in B to offset the climatic advantage. This might be overcrowding or higher unemployment.

If earnings differentials are prevented from changing to equalize net advantages, then factors will continue to be reallocated until some other differences arise to equalize the net advantage among alternative uses.

Since Confederation, an important national policy has been to reduce regional income disparities in Canada. To the extent that different regional per capita incomes are equilibrium reflections of different nonmonetary advantages, the attempt will not succeed. This matter is explored further in Box 17-1.

TRANSFER EARNINGS AND ECONOMIC RENT

We now come to one of the most important distinctions in all of economics, that between transfer earnings and economic rent. The amount that a factor must earn in its present use to prevent it from transferring to another use is called its **transfer earnings**. Any excess it earns over this amount is called its **economic rent**. The distinction is critical in predicting the effects of changes in earnings on the movement of factors.

The concept of economic rent, a surplus over transfer earnings, is analogous to the notion of economic profit as a surplus over opportunity cost. The terminology is confusing because rent also means the price paid to hire land. How the same term came to be used for these two different concepts is explored in Box 17-2.

The Division of Factor Earnings

In most cases the actual earnings of a factor of production will be a composite of transfer earnings

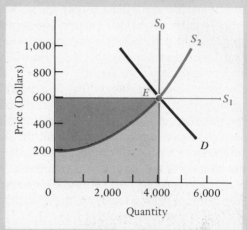

FIGURE 17-3
The Division of Factor Payments Between Economic Rent and Transfer Earnings

The division of total factor payments between economic rent and transfer earnings depends on the shape of the supply curve. A single demand curve is shown with three different supply curves. In each case the competitive equilibrium price is $600, and 4,000 units of the factor are hired. The total payment ($2.4 million) is represented by the entire shaded area.

When the supply curve is vertical (the line S_0), the whole payment is economic rent because a decrease in price would not lead any unit of the factor to move elsewhere.

When the supply curve is horizontal (the line S_1), the whole payment is transfer earnings because even a small decrease in price offered would lead all units of the factor to move elsewhere.

When the supply curve rises to the right (the curve S_2), part of the payment is rent and part is transfer earnings. As shown by the height of the supply curve, at a price of $600 the 4,000th unit of the factor is just receiving transfer earnings, but the 2,000th unit (for example) is earning well above its transfer earnings. The aggregate of economic rents is shown by the dark shaded area, and the aggregate of transfer earnings by the light shaded area.

and economic rent. It is possible, however, to imagine cases in which earnings are either all transfer earnings or all economic rent. The possibilities are illustrated in Figure 17-3. When the supply curve is perfectly inelastic (vertical), the whole of the payment is an economic rent: Even if the price were to fall to nearly zero, this would not lead suppliers to decrease the quantity supplied. The price actually paid allocates the fixed supply to those employers most willing to pay for it. When the supply curve is perfectly elastic (horizontal), the whole of the price paid is a transfer earning: If the purchaser does not pay this price, it will not obtain any quantity of the factor.

The more usual situation is that of a smoothly rising supply curve. In this case a rise in the price serves the allocative function of attracting more units of the factor into employment, but the same rise in the factor's price provides an extra economic rent to all units of the factor already employed. We know it is an economic rent because the owners of these units were willing to supply them at a lower price. This is a general result:

If a factor becomes scarce in any of its uses, its price will rise. This will serve the allocative function of attracting additional units, but it will also give an economic rent to all units of the factor already in that employment, whose transfer earnings were already being covered.

Kinds of Transfers

How much of a given payment to a factor is economic rent and how much is transfer earnings depends on what sort of transfer we are considering. Consider first the transfer of a factor from one firm to another within a single industry. The supply of the factor to one firm is highly elastic, since factors can easily move among firms in the same industry. Thus almost all the factor's earnings will be transfer earnings. If the firm in question did not pay the factor the going price, then the factor would move to another firm in the same industry.

Second, consider the transfer of a factor from one industry to another. Mobility among industries will be less than mobility among firms in one industry. Thus the supply curve of a factor to one industry will be less elastic than the supply curve to one firm. From the point of view of the industry, part of the payment is transfer earnings and part economic rent. The moral is that we cannot point

to a given factor and assert that, of its income of $8,000, say $6,000 is transfer earnings and $2,000 rent, for it all depends on what transfer we are considering.

Labor

Some labor is always able to move from job to job, and something must be paid to keep a given unit of labor in its present use. This amount is transfer earnings. How much has to be paid to keep labor in its present use depends on what the use is.

Consider first the movement among firms in one industry. Assume, for example, that carpenters receive $24 for working a normal eight-hour day. Then a single small construction firm will have to pay $24 per day or it will not obtain the services of any carpenter. To that one firm, the whole $24 is a transfer payment; if it were not paid, carpenters would not remain with that firm.

Second, consider movement among industries. Consider, for example, what would happen if as a result of a decline in demand for buildings, all construction firms reduced the wages offered to carpenters. Now carpenters could not move to other construction firms to get more money. If they did not like the wages offered, they would have to move to another industry. If the best they could do elsewhere was $18 per day, they would not begin to leave the construction industry until wages in that industry fell below $18. In this case the transfer earnings of carpenters in construction would be $18. When they were receiving $24 (presumably because there was heavy demand for their services), the additional $6 was an economic rent from the point of view of the construction industry.

Third, consider movement among occupations. Assume that there is a decline in the demand for carpenters in all industries. The only thing to do, if one does not like the wages, is to move to another occupation. If no one was induced to do this until the wage fell to $15, then $15 would be the transfer earnings for carpenters in general. The wage of $15 has to be paid to persuade people to be carpenters.

Some very highly specialized types of labor are

in inelastic supply. Some singers and actors, for example, have a special style and talent that cannot be duplicated, whatever the training. The earnings such persons receive are mostly economic rents: They enjoy their occupations and would pursue them for very much less than the high remuneration they actually receive. Their high reward occurs because they are in *very scarce supply relative to the demand for their services*. When this demand rises, their earnings rise permanently; when the demand falls, their earnings fall permanently.

Capital

If a piece of capital equipment has several uses, then the analysis of the last section can be repeated. Much equipment, however, has only one use. In this case, any income that is received from its operation is rent. Assume, for example, that when some machine was installed it was expected to earn $5,000 per year in excess of all its operating costs. If the demand for the product now falls off so that the machine can earn only $2,000, it will still pay to keep it in operation rather than to scrap it. Indeed, it will pay to do so as long as it yields any return at all over its operating costs.[3] Thus, all the return earned by the installed machine is economic rent because it would still have been allocated to its present use—it has no other—as long as it yielded even $1 above its operating costs. Thus, *once the machine has been installed*, any net income it earns is rent.

The machine will, however, wear out eventually, and it will not be replaced unless it is expected to earn a return over its lifetime sufficient to make it a good investment for its owner. Thus, over the long run, some of the revenue earned by the machine is transfer earnings; if the revenue is not earned, a machine will not continue to be allocated to that use in the long run.

In this case just considered, whether a payment made to a factor is economic rent or a transfer earnings depends on the time span under consid-

eration. In the short run all the income of a machine with only one use is a rent, while in the long run some (possibly all) of it is transfer earnings. Factor payments that are economic rent in the short run and transfer earnings in the long run are called **quasi-rents**.

Land

The formal analysis for land is identical to that given in the case of labor. How much of the payment made to a given piece of land is a transfer payment depends on the nature of the transfer.

Consider first the case of an individual wheat farmer. He must pay the going price of land in order to prevent the land from being transferred to the use of other wheat farmers. From his point of view, therefore, the whole of the payment he makes is transfer earnings to land.

Second, consider a particular agricultural industry that uses land. In order to secure land for, say, wheat production, it will be necessary to offer at least as much as the land could earn when put to other uses. From the point of view of the wheat industry, that part of the payment made for land which is equal to what it could earn in its next most remunerative use is transfer earning. If that much is not paid, the land will be transferred to the alternative use. If, however, land particularly suitable for wheat growing is scarce relative to the demand for it, then the actual payment for the use of this land may be above the transfer earnings; any additional payment is an economic rent.

Next consider movement between agricultural and urban uses. Land is very mobile between agricultural uses because its location is usually of little importance. In the case of urban uses, however, location of the land is critical. From this point of view, land is of course completely immobile. If there is a shortage of land in central Toronto, such land as is available will command a high price; but no matter what the price paid, the land in rural areas will not move into central Toronto. The very high payments made to urban land are economic rents. The land is scarce relative to demand for it, and it commands a price very much above what it

---

[3] This is just another way of stating the proposition given in Chapter 12, page 185, that it pays a firm to continue in operation in that short run as long as it can cover its variable costs of production.

BOX 17–3 TAXES, WELFARE, AND THE SUPPLY OF LABOR

Many people believe that today's high income taxes tend to reduce the supply of labor by lowering the incentive for people to work. They protest that it is not worth their while to work because of the crushing tax burdens they have to shoulder. Yet such objective evidence as exists suggests that high taxes do not always reduce the supply of effort. To the extent that they do, the aggregate effect may be small.

There is a good theoretical basis for a small aggregate effect. A tax cut sets up two opposing forces, and the final effect on the amount of work done by people depends on the relative strengths of each. An example will suggest why this is so.

Consider Barry Bluecollar, who has a job on an assembly line. He typically takes 5 hours a week off and so works only 35 hours, with a take home pay of $8.50 an hour or $297.60 per week. Now suppose there is a tax cut so that his take-home pay rises to $10 an hour. He might elect to work a little more, since every hour he works now nets him $10 instead of $8.50. Say his average weekly hours rise to 37. He will then raise his take-home pay by $72.50 to $370. Economists call the tendency to work more because the reward for an hour's work has risen the *substitution effect*.

However, Bluecollar might elect to work a little less, since with the rise in hourly take-home pay, he can have more income *and* get more leisure. Suppose he elects to take off an extra 3 hours a week. His take-home pay is now $320 a week (32 hours at $10 compared to the $297.50 before the tax cut). Now he has 3 more hours of leisure a week *and* $22.50 more income. Economists call the tendency to work less because it is possible to have more income and more leisure the *income effect*.

If the substitution effect dominates, people respond to a tax cut by working more. If the income effect dominates, they work less. Either result is theoretically possible. So a tax cut may raise or lower the amount of work people want to do. A good deal of research has shown that while some people may work fewer hours in response to rising taxes, others feel poorer and thus work more to maintain their after-tax incomes. The most recent research suggests at most a small net disincentive up to a level of marginal tax rates of 50 percent, such as exist today in Canada.

Work-Related Welfare Schemes

Throughout the world, many welfare payments depend on the household not working. Sometimes the welfare payments are reduced a dollar

---

could earn in agricultural uses. The payment it receives is thus well in excess of what is necessary to prevent it from transferring from urban back to agricultural uses.[4]

[4] From the point of view of one particular type of urban use, however, high rents are transfer earnings. Movie theaters, for example, account for but a small portion of the total demand for land in central Toronto; if there were no cinemas at all, rentals of land would be about what they are now. Thus the cinema industry faces a perfectly elastic supply of land in central Toronto, and the whole of the price that it pays for its land is a transfer payment which must be paid to keep the land from transferring to other urban uses. Thus the old examination

Some Policy Implications

Increasing the Supply of a Factor

Consider the effect of wage increases on the quantity of labor supplied. For example, if the

question, "Is it correct to say that the price of cinema seats is high in central Toronto because the price of land is high?" should be answered in the affirmative, not in the negative, as examiners often seemed to expect. The view that the prices of *all* goods and services in central Toronto are high because rents are high can, however, be denied.

for every dollar of income the household earns. In even more extreme cases, the payments cease altogether if the household earns any income. In either case, these payments produce a severe disincentive to work, and we can hardly be surprised if households respond rationally to these market signals.

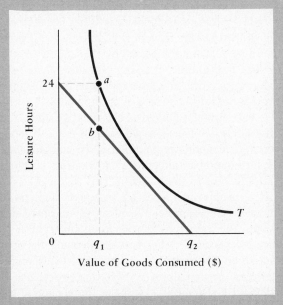

The figure illustrates a case in which welfare payments are reduced a dollar for every dollar

of income earned. If the household is totally unemployed, it can achieve point a on the figure: It has 24 hours of leisure to consume and q_1 of goods, where q_1 is its welfare receipts. The wage rate in the market presents the household with a trade-off between leisure and goods indicated, in the absence of welfare payments, by the slope of the budget line from 24 to q_2. But if the household begins at a and starts to work, it loses a dollar of welfare for every dollar of income it earns. It thus moves down the vertical line a to b, giving up leisure and gaining no net increase in income.

Only after b, when welfare payments are zero, will the household gain at the margin for working more. The household's budget line thus starts at a, falls vertically to b, and then follows the "normal" budget line to q_2.* This type of system provides a severe disincentive to work. Any household whose indifference curve through the welfare point a lies everywhere above the budget line (such as the curve T on the figure) will rationally decide not to work even though it would work if it could add its wages to its welfare earnings.

* You can draw for yourself diagrams to show the disincentives of intermediate cases where each dollar of income causes some reduction of some amount less than a dollar in welfare payments.

government wants more physicists, it could subsidize physicists' salaries. As we have seen, such a policy may well have an effect on supply. It may influence schoolchildren uncertain about their career choice to become physicists. But it will also mean that a great deal of money will have to be spent on extra payments to people who are already physicists. These payments will be economic rents, since existing physicists have demonstrated that they are prepared to be physicists at their old salaries.

An alternative policy, which may produce more

physicists per dollar spent, is to subsidize scholarships and fellowships for students who will train to become physicists. The policy tends to operate at the margin on persons just deciding whether to enter the occupation. It avoids the payment of additional rents to persons already in the occupation. Graphically, it is shown by a rightward shift in the supply curve because there will now be *more* persons in the occupation at each price of the factor.

If the supply curve is highly inelastic, an increase in the quantity supplied may be achieved more easily and at less cost by shifting the supply curve to the right rather than by moving along it.

Another policy issue related to factor supplies is taken up in Box 17-3.

Urban Land Values and Land Taxes

The high payments made to urban land are largely economic rents. The land is scarce relative to the demand for it, and it commands a price very much above what it could earn in agricultural uses. The payment it receives is thus well in excess of what is necessary to prevent it from transferring from urban back to agricultural uses. A society with rising population and rising per capita real income tends also to have steadily rising urban land prices. This fact has created a special interest in taxes on land values.

Who ultimately pays such taxes? If the same tax rate is applied to land in all uses, the relative profitability of different uses will be unaffected, and thus a landlord will not be tempted to change the allocation of his land. Land will not be forced out of use, because land that is very unprofitable will have a low market value and so pay little tax. Thus there will be no change in the supply of goods that are produced with the aid of land, and, since there is no change in supply, there can be no change in their prices. Farmers will be willing to pay exactly as much as they would have offered previously for the use of land. Because the prices of agricultural goods and the prices paid by tenants for land will be unchanged, the whole of the tax will be borne by the landlord. The incomes earned by landlords will fall by the full amount of the tax, and land values will fall correspondingly (because land is now a less attractive investment than it was previously).

The Single-Tax Movement

Taxation of land values has had enormous appeal in the past. The peak occurred about 100 years ago, when the "single-tax movement," led by American economist Henry George, commanded great popularity. George's book, *Progress and Poverty*, is—as books on economic issues go—an all-

time best-seller. It pointed out that the fixed supply of land, combined with a rapidly rising demand for it, allowed the owners of land to gain from the natural progress of society without contributing anything. Along with many others, George was incensed at this "unearned increment." He calculated that most of government expenditure could be financed by a single tax that did nothing more than remove the landlords' unearned increment.

Two problems arise with any attempt to tax economic rent. First, the theoretical statement refers to *economic rent*, not to the payment actually made by tenants to landlords. What is called rent in the world is partly an economic rent and partly a return on capital invested by the landowner. The policy implications of taxing rent depend on being able in practice to identify *economic rent*. At best, this is difficult; at worst, it is impossible.

The second problem is a normative one. If, in the interests of justice, we want to treat all recipients of economic rent similarly, we will encounter insurmountable difficulties. Increasing economic rent accrues to the owners of any factor that is in fixed supply and faces an increased demand. If there is, for example, a fixed supply of opera singers in the country, they gain economic rent as the society becomes richer and the demand for opera increases, without there being any corresponding increase in the supply of singers. No one has yet devised a scheme that will tax the economic rent but not the transfer earnings of such divergent factors as land, patents, football players, and High Court judges.

When George died, he left the huge royalties from his book to finance schools of "economic science" that were to propagate his theories and policy recommendations. These schools are maintained throughout the world even today. The appeal of a single tax has, however, receded. This is partly because of the difficulties mentioned above and partly because, with the great increase in the size of government, even an effective tax on economic rent would finance only a tiny portion of government expenditures. But the hostility toward unearned increments of landowners still survives in various forms of tax in many modern countries.

SUMMARY

1. The functional distribution of income refers to the shares of total national income going to each of the major factors of production. It focuses on sources of income. The size distribution of income refers to the shares of total national income going to various groups of households. It focuses only on the recipient of income, not its source.

2. The income of a factor of production is composed of two elements: (a) the price paid per unit of the factor and (b) the quantity of the factor used. The determination of factor prices and quantities is an application of the same price theory used to determine product prices and quantities.

3. In competitive factor markets, prices are determined by demand and supply, but factor price differentials occur. Dynamic differentials in the earnings of different units of factors of production serve as signals of a disequilibrium and induce factor movements that eventually remove the differentials. Equilibrium differentials reflect differences among units of factors as well as nonmonetary benefits of different jobs; they can persist indefinitely.

4. The hypothesis of equal net advantages is a theory of the allocation of the total supply of factors to particular uses. Owners of factors will choose the use that produces the greatest net advantage, allowing for monetary and nonmonetary advantages of a particular employement. In so doing, they will cause all dynamic factor price differentials to be eliminated.

5. Transfer earnings are what must be paid to a factor to prevent it from transferring to another use. Economic rent is the difference between a factor's transfer earnings and its actual earnings. Whenever the supply curve is upward-sloping, part of the factor's earnings is transfer earnings and part is rent.

6. Temporary rents to factors (often called quasi-rents) emerge in response to changes in patterns of demand. They play an important role in signaling

factors to relocate and hence in leading to an efficient allocation of resources.

7. The existence of rents in a factor's price has a potentially important policy implication: If supply is inelastic, raising the factor's price may be a relatively expensive way to induce increases in the quantity of the factor supplied.

TOPICS FOR REVIEW

Functional and size distribution of income
Dynamic and equilibrium differentials
Factor mobility
Equal net advantage
Transfer earnings and economic rent

DISCUSSION QUESTIONS

1. Other things being equal, how would you expect each of the following to affect the size distribution of after-tax income? Do any of them lead to clear predictions about the functional distribution of income?
   a. An increase in unemployment
   b. Rapid population growth in an already crowded city
   c. An increase in food prices relative to other prices
   d. An increase in social insurance benefits and taxes
2. Consider the effects on the overall level of income inequality in Canada of each of the following.
   a. Labor force participation of women increases sharply because many women shift from work in the home to full-time paid jobs.
   b. Increasing use by Western Ontario tobacco producers of foreign workers who are in Canada illegally.
   c. Increasing numbers of minority group members studying law and medicine.
3. Distinguish between economic rent and transfer earnings in each of the following payments for factor services.
   a. The $200 per month a landlord receives for the use of an apartment leased to students.
   b. The salary of the prime minister.
   c. The $500,000 annual salary of Wayne Gretzky.
   d. The salary of a window cleaner who says "It's dangerous, dirty work, but it beats driving a truck."
4. Which of the following are dynamic and which equilibrium differentials in factor prices?

a. The differences in earnings of football coaches and wrestling coaches
b. A "bonus for signing on" offered by a construction company seeking carpenters in a tight labor market
c. Differences in monthly rental charged for three-bedroom houses in different parts of the same metropolitan area

5. Equal pay for equal work is a commonly held goal. What would be the consequences of legislation enforcing equal pay for unequal work?

6. A common current slogan is "equal pay for work of equal value." Assume that legislation is passed to this effect and that the court interprets work of equal value to be work performed by people with equivalent educational backgrounds. Discuss some of the consequences of this policy.

7. Rent controls often succeed in reducing rents paid by tenants in the short run but at the cost of a growing housing shortage in the long run. What does this tell us about the nature of the earnings of landlords in the short and the long run? (Consider the categories of rent and transfer earnings.)

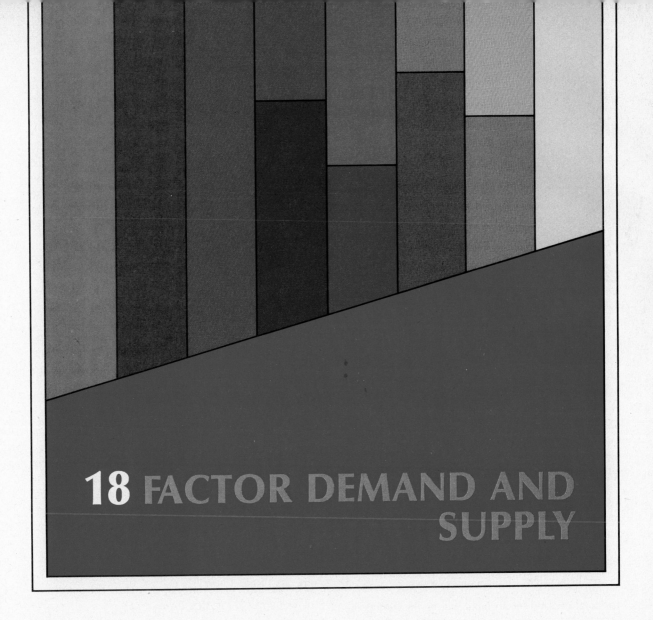

18 FACTOR DEMAND AND SUPPLY

Why are the demands for some factors inelastic and for other factors elastic? Why are some factors supplied inelastically so that heavy demand for them creates large economic rents, while the supplies of other factors are highly elastic so that most of their earnings are transfer payments? Why do the demand and supply curves for some factors shift a lot, while the curves for other factors remain relatively stable? To deal with these and many other related subjects, we need to inquire further into the determinants of the demand for and supply of factors of production.

In the previous chapter we discussed the functional distribution of income in terms of the three factors of production distinguished by the classical economists: land, labor, and capital. In this chapter we focus on these factors as inputs into firms' production processes. Firms also use as inputs products produced by other firms—steel, glue, and electricity are examples. However, if we look back to the production of these inputs, we discover that they are made using land, labor, and capital, and other produced inputs. If we trace back far enough, we can net out all those inputs that are the outputs of other firms, and so focus on basic inputs of the economy—the three factors of production already identified. Hence in this chapter we talk of inputs and factors interchangeably. While this is accurate for the economy as a whole, any particular firm will use as inputs products produced by other firms as well as land, labor, and capital.

THE DEMAND FOR INPUTS

Firms require inputs not for their own sake, but in order to produce the goods and services they sell. The demand for any input, therefore, depends on the existence of a demand for the goods it helps produce; it is described as a **derived demand**.

The demand for computer programmers and technicians is growing as we use more and more electronic computers. The demand for carpenters and building materials rises or falls with the amount of house building. Anything that increases the demand for new housing—population growth, lower interest rates on mortgages, and so on—will increase the demand for the inputs required to build houses.

Typically one input will be used in making many commodities. Steel is used in dozens of industries, as are the services of carpenters.

The total demand for an input will be the sum of the derived demands for it in every activity in which it is used.

Marginal Productivity Theory

Because demand for factors is a derived demand, its properties can be derived from the conditions for firms seeking to maximize profits, which were discussed in Chapter 10. All profit-maximizing firms, whether they are selling under conditions of perfect competition, monopolistic competition, oligopoly, or monopoly, produce to the point at which

marginal cost equals marginal revenue. Similarly, all profit-maximizing firms will hire units of the variable factor up to the point at which the last unit of any variable factor employed adds as much to revenue as it does to cost. Thus it is a simple implication of profit maximization that firms hire units of a variable factor up to the point where the marginal cost of the factor (i.e., the addition to the total cost resulting from the employment of one more unit) equals the marginal revenue produced by the factor.

Because we use the term *marginal revenue* to denote the change in revenue resulting when the rate of product sales is increased by one unit, we shall use another term, **marginal revenue product (MRP)**, to refer to the change in revenue caused by the sale of the product contributed by *an additional unit of the variable factors*. [29] We may now state more concisely the equilibrium condition stated above:

| The marginal cost of the variable factor | = | The marginal revenue product of that factor | [1] |

If the firm is unable to influence the price of the variable factor by buying more or less of it (i.e., if the firm is a price taker when *buying factors*), then the marginal cost of the factor is merely its price. The cost, for example, of adding an extra laborer to the firm's work force is the wage that must be paid. In these circumstances firms adjust the quantity of the variable factor they hire at the established market price, and we may state the condition of Equation [1] in this form:

$$w = MRP \qquad [2]$$

where w is the price of a unit of the factor.

A profit-maximizing firm that is a price taker in factor markets hires a factor up to the point at which its price equals the marginal revenue product.

We saw in Chapter 10 that marginal product falls as more workers are employed. (This is due to the law of diminishing returns; see page 157.) Because of this, firms that are equating the price of a factor to its *MRP* will buy more of the factor if its price falls. They increase their use of the factor until its *MRP* is driven down to the value of its new lower price.[1]

The proposition that in equilibrium factors will be paid the value of their respective marginal products is often called the **marginal productivity theory of distribution**. This is nothing more than an implication of profit maximization. Over the years, however, the theory has been the subject of many emotional attacks and defenses, and without doubt has often been seriously misunderstood. Some of these issues are taken up further in Box 18-1.

The Slope of the Demand Curve

What happens to quantity demanded when a factor's price rises?

One effect works through the link between a factor's price and the price of the good or service it helps to produce. Consider, for example, a rise in the wages of carpenters, which increases the cost of producing houses. The rise in cost shifts the supply curve of houses upward. This leads to a rise in the price of houses and to a decrease in the number of houses sold. If fewer houses can be sold, fewer will be built and smaller quantities of factors will be needed. Thus there will be a decrease in the quantity demanded of carpenters used to produce houses.

A second effect relates to substitution among factors: When the price of one factor goes up, other, relatively cheaper, factors will be substituted. For example, if carpenters' wages rise relative to those of factory workers, some prefabricated door and window frames made by factory workers will be used in place of on-the-job carpentry. This is simply the principle of substitution in operation.

Demand curves for factors slope downward because of (1) the effect of factor price changes on the prices of the commodities the factor makes and (2) the substitution of relatively cheaper for relatively more expensive factors.

The elasticity of demand for a factor measures the degree of response of the quantity of the factor that is demanded to a change in its price. The three major forces that determine the elasticity of a factor's demand curve are often called *the principles of derived demand*.

The demand for the final commodity. Other things being equal, elasticity of demand for a factor will be larger the more elastic is the demand for the commodity that the factor helps to make. If an increase in the price of the commodity causes a large fall in the quantity demanded (i.e., the demand for the commodity is very elastic), there will be a large decrease in the quantity of factors needed to produce it in response to a rise in the factor's price. But if the increase in the price of the commodity causes only a small fall in its quantity demanded (i.e., the demand for the commodity is inelastic), there will be only a small decrease in the quantity of the factors now required in response to a rise in their price.

Ease of substitution. Obviously, the greater the ease with which one factor can be substituted for another in response to changes in relative factor prices, the greater is the elasticity of demand for those factors. The ease of substitution depends on the substitutes available and technical conditions of production. Even in the short run it is possible to vary factor proportions in surprising ways. For example, in automobile manufacture and in building construction, glass and steel can be substituted for each other simply by varying the dimensions of the windows. Grain in the form of gasohol can substitute for oil as automobile fuel, and so on.

Nor are such direct (if dramatic) short-run substitutions the end of the story. In the long run a factory that has a particular technique embodied in its equipment (and thus cannot easily vary factor proportions in the short run) can be replaced. Plant and equipment are continually being replaced, and more or less capital-intensive methods can be adopted in new plants in response to changes in factor prices. Similarly, engines that use less gasoline per mile will be developed if the price of gasoline remains high.

The importance of the factor. The elasticity of

---

[1] The way in which marginal productivity theory can be used to derive a firm's demand curve for a factor is discussed in the appendix to this chapter, starting on page A-32.

BOX 18–1 THE MARGINAL PRODUCTIVITY THEORY OF DISTRIBUTION

The result that factors will, in equilibrium, earn the value of their marginal products is often called the *marginal productivity theory of distribution*. This is an important yet frequently misunderstood proposition. It means that all units of a factor will be paid a price equal to that factor's marginal revenue product. It applies to all factors in long-run equilibrium because all factors are variable in the long run.

This theory is nothing more than an implication of profit maximization: Any firm that is maximizing its profits must hire each variable factor up to the point where the last unit hired adds just as much to costs (the price of one factor) as it does to revenue (the *MRP*). Nonetheless, misconceptions about the theory exist. Indeed, in certain quarters *marginal productivity theory* is a dirty word, for it seems to say that each factor, including labor, is paid exactly the value of what it produces. The theory has been criticized on the grounds that it is inhumane and that it falsely implies that the market leads to factor prices that, however low they might be, are "just." Both criticisms rest on misconceptions of what the theory says and implies.

Inhumanity?

Marginal productivity theory does not take into account the differences between human services and other services. Some think the theory inhumane because it treats human labor as it treats a ton of coal or a wagonload of fertilizer.

The marginal productivity theory is only a theory of the *demand* for a factor. It predicts only what profit-maximizing employers would like to buy. It predicts that desired purchases of a factor depend on the price of the factor, the technical conditions of production, and the demand for the product produced using the factor. *Supply* conditions undoubtedly differ between human and nonhuman factors, but these differences are accommodated within the theory of distribution, as we shall see. No evidence has been gathered to indicate that it is necessary to have separate theories of the demand for human and nonhuman factors of production.

Justice?

In a world of perfectly competitive factor markets, the theory predicts that in equilibrium all factors receive payment equal to the values of their marginal products. Some eminent economists in the past spoke as if this led to a just distribution because factors were rewarded according to the value of their own contributions to the national product. "From each according to his ability; to each according to his own contribution" might have been the slogan for this group. Many critics of the low levels of wages which then prevailed reacted passionately to a theory that was claimed to justify them.

According to the marginal productivity theory, however, each worker does not receive the value of what he or she personally contributes to production. The worker receives instead the value of what one more worker would add to production if that worker were taken on while all other factors were held constant. If 1 million similar workers are employed, then each of the 1 million will receive a wage equal to the extra product that would have been contributed by the millionth laborer if he or she had been hired while capital and all other factors remained unchanged. Whether such a distribution of the national product is or is not "just" may be debated. The marginal productivity theory does not say, however, that each unit of a factor receives as income the value of its own contribution to production. Indeed, where many factors cooperate in production, it is generally impossible to divide total production into the amounts contributed by each unit of each factor of production.

It is possible both to hold that marginal productivity tends to determine how people get paid and to believe that government policies which change the distribution of income are desirable. Many economists hold both positions.

demand for a factor is greater the larger is the fraction of total costs that are payments to the factor.[2] Suppose that wages are 50 percent of the costs of producing a good, while raw materials account for 15 percent. A 10 percent rise in the price of labor raises the cost of producing the commodity by 5 percent (10 percent of 50 percent), but a 10 percent rise in the price of raw materials raises the cost of the commodity by only 1.5 percent (10 percent of 15 percent). The larger the increase in cost, the larger the increase in the commodity's price—and hence the larger the decrease in the quantity demanded of the commodity and the factors used to make it.

Some Efficiency Implications

We have seen that individual profit-maximizing employers will hire any factor up to the point where the last unit hired adds as much to costs as it does to revenue. This means that factors tend to get used where they add most to production. If factors were not priced according to their scarcity, there would be no criteria by which to allocate them among uses. This is not just idle speculation. In the early years of the Communist experiment in Russia, interest—which is the price paid for the use of capital—was banned for ideological reasons. This led to very inefficient resource allocation. Some of the issues involved in this case are discussed in Box 18-2.

THE SUPPLY OF FACTORS

Two important economic questions concern the supplies of factors: First, to what extent do eco-

nomic forces determine the total supply of a factor to the whole economy? Second, to what extent do such forces determine the supply available to a particular industry that wants to purchase only a part of the total supply?

The Total Supply of Factors

It might seem plausible to assume that the total supplies of factors available to the economy are fixed and not subject to economic influences. After all, there is an absolute maximum to the world's land area; there is an upper limit to the number of workers; there is only so much sand and gravel, coal, oil, copper, and iron ore in the earth. In none of these cases, however, are we near the upper limits. The *effective* supplies of land, labor, and natural resources are thus not fixed in any meaningful sense. What, then, causes variations in the supply of a factor of production available to the *whole economy*?

The Total Supply of Labor

The total supply of labor means the total number of hours of work that the population is willing to supply. This quantity is often called the **supply of effort.** It has many obvious determinants such as the rewards for working, the age at which people enter the labor force and retire from it, and the length of the conventional work week. It also has many less obvious ones. For one example, social trends such as the women's liberation movement can cause major changes in labor force participation. For another, the whole pattern of tax rates, unemployment insurance, and welfare payments affects the relative advantages of working and not working.

The evidence is overwhelming that these things affect working. What is debated, however, is how large their impact is. As was discussed more fully in Box 17-3, the evidence shows some, but relatively small, adverse effects of taxes on the supply of effort. Sometimes, however, welfare schemes have exerted a severe disincentive to work. While most people prefer work to "sponging off the government," they can hardly be blamed for respond-

[2] This is necessarily true when there is only one variable factor of production. When there are many variable factors, we must also consider the ease of substitution. For example, copper tubing may be a small part of building costs, but if aluminum tubing is nearly a perfect substitute, the demand for copper tubing may be quite elastic. In contrast, the demand for tubing of some kind may be quite inelastic. The text statement is another example of something that is correct, *other things being equal:* For a given degree of substitutability among factors, the demand for any factor will be more elastic the larger the proportion of total costs that are payments to that factor.

BOX 18–2 CAPITAL, CAPITALISTS, AND CAPITALISM

Capital goods are man-made aids to further production. Their two most essential characteristics are first, that they are produced inputs into further production rather than things found in nature, and second, that they tend to be durable, lasting for many periods of production. Because their production uses scarce resources, they have an opportunity cost.

A capitalist is simply one who owns capital goods. The roles played by the capitalist in different economic philosophies often have ideological overtones. For example, to many Marxists the capitalist is a villain; to many liberals the capitalist is a necessary evil; while to many conservatives the capitalist is the hero who steers the economy through the risky channels that lead to ever-higher living standards. Ideology aside, if there is capital, someone must own it. Capital may be predominantly in private hands (in which case the economy is sometimes described as capitalistic), or it may be entirely owned by the state, in which case the economy will be described as socialistic or communistic. In virtually all economies, some capital is owned privately and some publicly.

No matter who owns the capital goods, they are indispensable in the productive process. A primitive society in which there are no capital goods—no spear, no lever, no stone for grinding grain, no jug for carrying water—has never occurred in recorded human history.

Capital goods, like other valuable products, are scarce in the sense that most producers would like to have more of them than they would have if the price were zero. Any economic system interested in maximizing production will want to allocate scarce capital to its most productive uses. One effective way of doing this is to assign a price to capital that is meant to reflect its opportunity cost and to allow firms to use more capital only if the capital earns enough to cover this price. Actually charging producers for use of capital serves such important functions that it is hard to eliminate the charge without serious consequences.

Early Communist rulers thought differently. Payments for use of capital were officially barred during the years following the Russian Revolution of 1917 on the ground that a communistic society should purge itself of this reminder of capitalism. But prices are such an efficient allocative device that today all Communist states use them for allocating scarce capital among competing uses. Furthermore, their planners give a good deal of attention to setting the correct price for capital.

If capital is privately owned and a price charged for its use, the payments go to the capitalists and become their incomes. In Communist countries capital is owned by the state, and payments for its use go to the state. The desirability of private versus public ownership of the means of production (the term often used in Socialist and Communist literature to describe capital) is still debated hotly.

ing rationally to an incentive system that severely penalizes any work done by welfare recipients.

The Total Supply of Arable Land

If the term *land* is used to refer to the total area of dry land, then the total supply of land in a country will be almost completely fixed. It was nineteenth century practice (following Ricardo) to define land as the *original and inexhaustible powers of the soil*. But dust bowls were a phenomenon unknown to Ricardo, who also did not know that the deserts of North Africa were once fertile plains. Clearly the supply of fertile land is not fixed; considerable care and effort is required to sustain the productive power of land. If the return to land is low, its fertility may be destroyed within a short time. Moreover, scarcity and high prices may make it worthwhile to increase the supply of arable land by irrigation and other forms of reclamation.

The Total Supply of Natural Resources

People worry—sometimes when it is too late—about exhausting natural resources. The great iron ore deposits of the Mesabi Range were exhausted in 1965, and America's known supplies of oil and gas had shrunk by 1982 to less than an 11-year supply.[3]

The problem of actual exhaustion of natural resources does not arise as often as one might think. There is frequently a large undiscovered or unexploited quantity of a given resource or of an adequate substitute. The exhaustion of high-grade iron ore reserves in the United States did not end steel production—partly as a result of the discovery of ways to use low-grade iron ores once thought worthless and partly because new supplies in Labrador and the Caribbean have been developed.

Emerging shortages lead to their own corrections. As long as oil remains sufficiently valuable, it will pay to find more of it. As oil becomes scarce, its price will rise. A sufficient increase in the price of oil would make it economically worthwhile to process the vast quantities of previously unexploited shale oil.

Ultimately, of course, there is an upper limit, and resources can be exhausted; worse, they can be contaminated or otherwise despoiled so as to render them useless before they have been consumed.

The Total Supply of Capital

Capital is a man-made factor of production, and its supply is in no sense fixed. The supply of capital in a country consists of the stock of existing ma-

chines, plant, equipment, and so on. The stock is diminished by the amount that wears out each year and is increased by the production of new capital goods. On balance, the trend has been for the capital stock to grow over the decades.

The Supply of Factors to Particular Uses

Most factors have many uses; a given piece of land can be used to grow any one of several crops, or it can be subdivided for a housing development. A computer programmer in Southern Ontario can work in a variety of automobile plants, or in a dozen other industries, or even in the physics laboratories at the University of Toronto. A lathe can be used to make many different products and requires no adaptation when it is turned from one use to another. Plainly it is easier for any one user to acquire more of a scarce factor of production than it is for all users to do so simultaneously. One use or user can bid resources away from another use or user, even though the total supply is fixed.

The total supply must be allocated among all the different uses to which it can possibly be put. This allocation is explained by the hypothesis of equal net advantage, which we studied in Chapter 17. If the factor's owners are concerned with making as much money as they can, they will move their factor to that use at which it earns the most money. Because owners of factors take things other than money into account—such as risk, convenience, and a good climate—both monetary and nonmonetary rewards are important in influencing factor movements.

Factor Mobility

When considering the supply of a factor to a particular use, the most important concept is *factor mobility*, a concept we also encountered in Chapter 17. A factor that shifts easily between uses in response to small changes in incentives is said to be highly mobile, and it will be in very elastic supply in any one of its uses because small increases in the price offered will attract many units of the factor

---

[3] It should not be inferred that supplies of oil and gas will be exhausted by 1993. The known supply was reported to be at most 20 years in every year from 1920 to 1950; in other words, each year as much was discovered as was used. What is new in recent years is that discovery has lagged behind production, and thus the number of years of known supply has been shrinking.

from other uses. A factor that does not shift easily from one use to another, even in response to large changes in remuneration, is said to be highly immobile. It will be in inelastic supply in any one of its uses because even a large increase in the price offered will attract only a small inflow from other uses.

Mobility of land. Land, which is physically the least mobile of factors, is one of the most mobile in an economic sense. Consider agricultural land. Within a year at most, one crop can be harvested and a totally different crop planted. A farm on the outskirts of a growing city can be sold for subdivision and development on short notice.

Once land is built on, as urban land usually is, its mobility is much reduced. A site on which a hotel has been built can be converted into an office building site, but it takes a large differential in the value of land use to make such a conversion worthwhile because the hotel must be torn down.

Although land is highly mobile among alternative uses, it is completely immobile as far as location is concerned. This locational immobility has important consequences, including high prices for desirable locations and the tendency to build tall buildings that economize on the use of land where it is very scarce, as in the centers of large cities.

Mobility of capital. While some kinds of capital equipment—lathes, trucks, and computers, for example—can be readily shifted among uses, many others are comparatively unshiftable. A great deal of machinery is utterly specific: Once built, it must be used for the purpose for which it was designed, or else not used at all. (It is the immobility of much fixed capital equipment that makes the exit of firms from declining industries a slow and difficult process.)

In the long run, capital is highly mobile. When capital goods wear out, firms might simply replace them with identical goods. But the firm has many other options: it may buy a newly designed machine to produce the same goods; it may buy machines to produce totally different goods, or it may spend its resources in other ways. Such decisions lead to changes in the long-run allocation of a country's stock of capital among various uses.

Labor mobility. Labor is unique as a factor of production in that the supply of the service requires the physical presence of the owner of the source of the service. Absentee landlords can obtain income from land located in remote parts of the world while continuing to live in the place of their choice. Investment can be shifted from iron mines in northern Ontario to mines in Labrador while the owners of the capital commute between New York and the French Riviera. But when a worker employed by a firm in Moose Jaw decides to supply labor service to a firm in Lethbridge, the worker must physically travel to Lethbridge. This has an important consequence.

Because of the need for physical presence, nonmonetary considerations are much more important in the allocation of labor than in the allocation of other factors of production.

People may be satisfied with or frustrated by the kind of work they do, where they do it, those they do it with, and the social status of their occupations. Since these considerations influence their decisions about what they will do with their labor services, they will not move every time they can earn a higher wage.

Nevertheless, according to the hypothesis of equal net advantage, occupational and job movement will occur when there are changes in the wage structure. The mobility that does occur depends on many forces. For example, it is not difficult for a secretary to shift from one company to another or to take a job in Kamloops instead of in Prince George, but it can be difficult for a secretary to become an editor or a fashion model in a short period of time. There are three considerations here: ability, training, and inclination. Lack of any one will stratify some people and make certain kinds of mobility difficult for them.

An important key to labor mobility is time. The longer the time interval, the easier it is to change occupations.

Some barriers may seem insurmountable for a person once his or her training has been completed. It may be impossible for a farmer to become a surgeon or a truck driver to become a professional athlete, even if the relative wage rates change greatly. But the children of farmers, doctors, lawyers, and athletes, when they are deciding how much education or training to obtain, are not nearly as limited in their choices as their parents, who have completed their education and are settled in their occupations.

Thus the labor force as a whole is more mobile than individual members of it. At one end of the age distribution people enter the labor force from school; at the other end they leave it via retirement or death. The turnover due to these causes is about 3 or 4 percent per year. Over a period of 20 years, a totally different occupational distribution could appear merely by redirecting new entrants to jobs other than the ones left vacant by workers leaving the labor force, without a single individual ever changing jobs. The role of education in adapting people to available jobs is very great. In a society in which education is provided to all, it is possible to achieve large increases in supply of any desired labor skill within a decade or so.

THE RELEVANCE OF DISTRIBUTION THEORY

Factor pricing, and hence the distribution of income, is a by-product of the market allocation system. This allocation helps to determine both the quantities of the various goods and services that are produced and the methods by which they are produced.

Does the theory of distribution satisfactorily explain the allocation process in our economy? For the answer to be yes, it is necessary to give affirmative answers to two more basic questions. First, do market conditions of demand and supply play important roles in determining factor earnings? Second, do factors move in response to changes in factor earnings?

Some would answer no to each question. They argue that prices of products and factors bear little relation to market conditions because prices and wages are administered by oligopolies and giant unions. Such administered prices and wages are sticky downward and tend to rise annually at a bit more than the general rate of inflation. Products

with above-average price increases are produced by firms with above-average market power, and the more powerful unions get the biggest wage increases. Entry barriers in industry and mobility barriers for factors of production, that argument continues, prevent significant movements of resources in response to product and factor price differentials that exist or develop. Thus, they argue, the theory of distribution we have studied is irrelevant to the real world.

In the following sections of this chapter, we examine whether market forces do in fact play the roles predicted by the theories of competition and monopoly in determining factor prices and the allocation of resources.

Do Market Conditions Determine Factor Earnings?

Factors Other Than Labor

Most nonhuman factors are sold on competitive markets. The theory predicts that changes in the earnings of these factors will be associated with changes in market conditions. Overwhelmingly the evidence supports this prediction, as shown by the examples that follow.

The prices of plywood, tin, rubber, cotton, and hundreds of other materials fluctuate daily in response to changes in their demand and supply. The responses of factor markets to the many shortages that seemed to characterize the North American economy in the 1970s provide dramatic confirmation. When the price of agricultural commodities shot up following a grain shortage, farm income soared. When oil became scarce, prices rose and oil producers and owners of oil properties found their profits and incomes rising rapidly. Not only did the relative prices of oil products rise, so did the relative prices of commodities, such as chemical fertilizers and air travel, that make use of petroleum products. When oil become abundant in the early 1980s, these trends were reversed.

Land in the heart of growing cities provides another example. Such land is clearly fixed in supply, and values rise steadily in response to increasing demand for it.[4] Very high land values even make it worthwhile to destroy durable buildings in order to convert the land to more productive uses. Many historic buildings in our cities have been pulled down, to be replaced by high-rise office buildings. The skyscraper is a monument to the high value of urban land. In many smaller cities the change from shopping downtown to shopping in outlying shopping centers has lessened the demand for land downtown and influenced relative land prices. The increase in the price of land on the periphery of every growing city is a visible example of the workings of the market.

Similar results occur in markets that are far from being perfectly competitive. In 1979 the price of power in virtually all forms rose sharply in response to the extra energy shortage caused by the change in government in Iran. Oligopolists producing key metals such as zinc, molybdenum, steel, and aluminum have not hesitated to increase prices as their costs of production rose or when demand outran their production. Further examples can be found in almost every issue of the *Financial Post* and the *Wall Street Journal*, but the point should now be clear:

The prices and earnings of nonhuman factors are successfully predicted by market theories of factor pricing.

Labor

When we apply the theory to labor, we encounter two important sets of complications. First, labor being the human factor of production, nonmonetary considerations loom large in its incentive patterns, and thus market fluctuations may have less effect. Second, the competitive and noncompetitive elements of labor markets occur in different proportions from market to market. These complications make it harder to answer the question: Do market conditions determine factor earnings? Monopolistic elements and nonmonetary rewards, both difficult to measure, must be carefully specified if the theory that labor earnings respond to market forces is to be confirmed. Nevertheless, there is a mass of evidence to support the theory.

[4] A friend is fond of saying, "Nobody buys land any more; its price is much too high because everybody wants it."

Market fluctuations in demand and supply. Do earnings respond to normal fluctuations of demand and supply as the theory predicts? The evidence shows that they often do. The competitive theory predicts that a decline in the demand for a product will cause a decline in the derived demand for the factors that make the product and thus a decline in their owners' incomes. A rise in the demand for a product will have the opposite effect. Cases come easily to mind.

With the advent of the automobile, many skilled carriage makers saw the demand for their services decline rapidly. Earnings fell, and many older workers found that they had been earning substantial economic rents for their scarce but highly specific skills. They suffered large income cuts when they moved to other industries. Workers who acquired skills wanted in the newly expanding automotive industry found the demands for their services and their incomes rising rapidly

More recently there has been a large increase in the earnings of premier professional athletes. In part this has been caused by rising demand due to expansion in the number of professional teams. In part it has resulted from increased revenues to the teams and leagues from televising sports, which has increased the marginal revenue product of the athletes. And in part it has been the result of athletes' acquiring the right to offer their services to more than one employer, thereby reducing the ability of employers to hold down wages by acting as monopsonists.

One group that has been suffering the chill winds of the consequences of factor price determination on competitive markets is college graduates. During the 1970s the earnings of college graduates fell relative to other workers as employment opportunities dropped sharply, especially for new graduates. The downturn is explained by slackening demand due to changes in industrial structure (e.g., substituting sophisticated computers for college-trained persons) and continued growth of supply.

Wage changes induced by market conditions have little to do with abstract notions of justice or merit. If you have some literary talent, why can you make a lot of money writing copy for an advertising agency but very little money writing poems? It is not because an economic dictator or group of philosophers has decided that advertising is more valuable than poetry. It is because in the Canadian economy there is a large demand for advertising and only a tiny demand for poetry.

Effects of monopoly elements in labor markets. A strong union—one able to bargain effectively and to restrict entry of labor into the field—can cause wages to rise well above the competitive level. Highly skilled plasterers, plumbers, and electricians have all managed to restrict entry into their trades and as a result maintain wages well above their transfer earnings. Many similar cases have been documented. Unions can and do succeed in raising wages and incomes when they operate in small sections of the whole economy. The high earnings attract others to enter the occupation or industry, and the privileged position can be maintained only if entry can be effectively restricted.

Not only can monopoly elements raise incomes above their competitive levels, they can also prevent wages from falling in response to decreases in demand. Of course, if the demand disappears more or less overnight, there is nothing any union can do to maintain incomes. But the story may be different when, as is more usually the case, demand shrinks slowly but steadily.

Consider coal mining in the years just after World War II. From 1945 to 1965 the production of coal declined as oil, gas, and electricity were steadily substituted for it. The coal that was produced was used largely by electric utilities, and it was mined by ever more capital-using and labor-saving techniques. Both these forces led employment to shrink steadily.

What would competitive theory predict about wages? Coal mining was plainly a declining labor market from 1945 until 1965. Competitive theory would predict relatively low wages and low incomes, followed by exit of the most mobile coal miners under this forceful disincentive, and hard times for those who decide to stick it out. Precisely this happened in Canada. Average wages, which in 1945 had been 36 percent above those in manufacturing, fell steadily until in 1965 they were 8 per-

cent below those in manufacturing. Employment declined to 35 percent of its previous level, and those who remained in coal mining saw their relative incomes fall.

In the United States, however, this was *not* the pattern. Faced with a similar decline in production, relative wages actually rose in coal mining, from 18 percent above manufacturing in 1945 to 34 percent above it in 1965. Employment did fall—indeed by 1965 employment was only 30 percent of the 1945 level. But those who kept jobs did relatively well.

What happened was that a powerful union, the United Mine Workers, prevented wages from falling. By raising wages despite falling demand, the union actually accelerated the decline in employment. Economic theory suggests that lower wages *or* declining employment opportunities (or both) will serve to decrease labor earnings and trigger movements of factors out of the industry. The lower employment that accompanied the "high wage" policy of the United Mine Workers Union discouraged the young from waiting for jobs in the industry. As workers left the industry because of retirement, ill health, or death, they were not replaced.

Since 1965 the demand for coal miners has rebounded as the demand for coal to produce electricity has surged. As a result, in both the United States and Canada—as theory predicts—employment rose sharply *and* wages in coal mining shot up relative to those of all industry. Consequently labor earnings in coal mining rose sharply.

All these examples support the general proposition:

Earnings of labor respond to significant changes in market conditions.

Do Factors Move in Response to Changes in Earnings?

The theory of factor supply says that factors will move among uses, industries, and places, taking both monetary and nonmonetary rewards into account. They will move in such a way as to equalize the net advantages to the owners of factors. Because there are impediments to the mobility of factors, there may be lags in the response of factors to changes in relative prices, but in due course adjustments will occur. We now ask: Does the world behave in the way theory predicts?

Factors Other Than Labor

The most casual observation reveals that the allocative system works pretty much as described by the theory with respect to land, materials, and capital goods.

Land is transferred from one crop to another in response to changes in the relative profitabilities of the crops. Land on the edge of town is transferred from rural to urban uses as soon as it can earn substantially more as a building site than as a corn-

field. Materials and capital goods move from use to use in response to changes in relative earnings in those uses.

This is hardly surprising. Nonmonetary benefits do not loom large for factors other than labor, and the theories of both competition and monopoly predict that quantities supplied will respond to increases in earnings generated by increased demand.

In the case of nonhuman factors, there is strong evidence that factors move in response to earnings differentials.

Labor

Labor mobility can occur in many dimensions. Labor can move among occupations, industries,

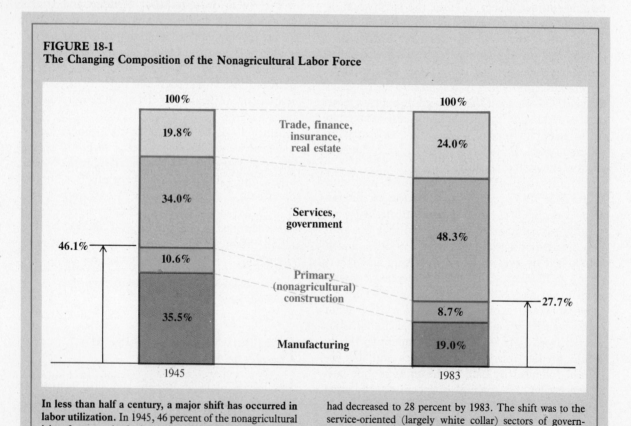

FIGURE 18-1
The Changing Composition of the Nonagricultural Labor Force

	1945	1983
Trade, finance, insurance, real estate	19.8%	24.0%
Services, government	34.0%	48.3%
Primary (nonagricultural) construction	10.6%	8.7%
Manufacturing	35.5%	19.0%

46.1% ← (bracket for bottom two 1945 blocks)
27.7% ← (bracket for bottom two 1983 blocks)

In less than half a century, a major shift has occurred in labor utilization. In 1945, 46 percent of the nonagricultural labor force was in the heavy industrial (largely blue collar) sectors. As shown by the bottom two blocks, this figure had decreased to 28 percent by 1983. The shift was to the service-oriented (largely white collar) sectors of government, trade, finance, and other services.

BOX 18-3 DEINDUSTRIALIZATION: FROM BIG STEEL TO BIG MAC

The growth of employment in services and retail trade over the last three decades has been dramatic. Employment in these two sectors has risen three times faster than total employment and sixteen times faster than employment in the goods-producing sector, with the growth concentrated in three areas: eating and drinking places, health services, and business services. In the United States, today's *total* employment in manufacturing of durable goods (under 11 million persons) is less than the *increase* in employment in services over the last two decades.

The nature of employment has changed as a result of the changing composition of output. There is more part-time work and more contact with the public. The role of women in the work force has increased, and women are concentrated in the sectors of greatest expansion in job opportunities. In many industrial areas where men have been laid off by the steel mills and auto factories, their wives and daughters have found jobs in restaurants and offices while the men search in vain. The fact that in these areas many women are working while many men are not reflects an important change in the North American economy—and in North American society—over the last decade.

Does it matter to the economy if one kind of worker (e.g., service workers) increasingly replaces another kind (e.g., heavy industrial workers)? It is a change that worries many labor leaders and industrialists. Service jobs usually pay less than jobs in manufacturing, particularly in such basic manufacturing industries as steel and automobiles. A typical steel worker earns $9 to $10 per hour, a McDonald's kitchen worker less than $4 per hour. Because of this differential, service jobs generally make a smaller contribution to national income than do manufacturing jobs.

Looking at traditional service industries, many observers wondered if the service sector could generate the high levels of growth that were generated by the manufacturing sector. Surely, they argued, the opportunities for substituting labor for capital are much less in producing hamburgers than automobiles. Today observers are not so sure. After all, McDonald's made a major breakthrough by eliminating much of the labor found in traditional restaurants. More important, perhaps, many of the new service industries based on applications of the silicon chip seem to have unlimited scope for raising labor productivity by giving each employee more and more capital with which to work.

So one of today's great unsettled questions is: Can the service-oriented society have a really favorable growth performance? Current observers are much less inclined to give a pessimistic answer than were observers of even a decade ago.

---

skill categories, and regions. These categories are not exclusive; to change occupation from a farm laborer to a steelworker, for example, a person will also have to change industries and probably towns.

Response to changes in demand. Figure 18-1 illustrates one dimension of labor mobility. The shifts among sectors that have occurred in the postwar period indicate the substantial adaptability of the labor force to changing patterns of demand for the outputs of various sectors. The process of deindustrialization evident in this figure is discussed further in Box 18-3.

A second dimension of labor mobility is reflected in recent provincial migration patterns. The Prairies were large net recipients of migrants in the early decades of the century, a fact largely associated with the western movements brought on by the wheat boom. The following decades saw a net outflow from the Prairies, though Alberta was a net recipient in the 1970s, primarily because of the boom in resource-based industries. The Maritimes experienced continued net out-migration until the 1970s, and except for the 1950s so has Quebec. The basic picture is one of Canada's having a very mobile population.

From decade to decade, labor is highly mobile in response to changes in demand.

Related issues of regional economic policy were taken up in Chapter 17; see especially Box 17-1.

Barrriers to labor mobility. There are, of course, barriers to labor mobility. Unions, pension funds, and other institutions can and do inhibit labor mobility substantially. By influencing supplies of labor in various markets, they exert considerable influence on labor earnings. It is easier to move from one occupation to another within one industry when there is a single industrial union than it is when each occupation in the industry is organized in its own craft union. It is easier to move between two industries in the same occupation when both are organized by craft unions than it is when each has its own industrial union.

Provincial governments have erected major barriers to mobility in the form of occupational licensing, differential training requirements, and the like.

Labor mobility: Summary. The theories of competitive and monopolistic factor markets go a long way in explaining what we see and in predicting many of the consequences of changes in market conditions on labor mobility and the consequences of barriers to mobility on the welfare of those trapped by immobility.

Of course not all behavior is neatly explained by the theory. For example, despite the recent decline in academic salaries and job opportunities, many more students today persist in getting Ph.D.s in fields such as history and English than can reasonably expect to find jobs that will require or utilize their training. Economists can speculate about such behavior—for example, by saying that for many students, graduate education is a consumption good as well as an investment in human capital, or that the nonmonetary advantages of an academic

position are large enough to be worth the gamble of finding a job. But such hypotheses go beyond elementary economics. At this stage we have to be satisfied with a theory that explains much, but not all, behavior.

SUMMARY

1. The demand for any factor is *derived* from the demand for commodities the factor is used to make. Factor demand curves slope downward because a change in a factor's price will affect the cost of production (and thus product price, quantity produced, and the need for factors) and because of the ability to substitute cheaper for more expensive factors.

2. A profit-maximizing firm will hire units of any variable factor until the last unit hired adds as much to costs as it does to revenue. If factors are bought in a competitive market, the addition to cost will be the price of a unit of a factor. From this comes the important condition that in competitive equilibrium, the price of a factor will equal its marginal revenue product. This is the marginal productivity theory of distribution.

3. The elasticity of factor demand will tend to be greater (a) the greater is the elasticity of demand of the products it makes, (b) the greater is the proportion of the total cost of production accounted for by the factor, and (c) the easier it is to substitute one factor for another.

4. The marginal productivity theory of factor demands has the important implication that factors will be allocated efficiently among competing uses.

5. The total supplies of most factors are variable over time and respond to some degree to economic influences. The most important influences are not the same for labor, arable land, natural resources, and capital.

6. Factor mobility (shiftability in use) influences the supply of factors to particular uses. Land is mobile between uses but cannot change its geographical location. Capital equipment is durable, but firms regularly replace discarded or worn-out machinery with totally different machines and so change the composition of the nation's capital stock gradually but steadily. Labor mobility is greatly affected by nonmonetary considerations. The longer the period of time allowed to elapse, the more mobile is the labor force.

7. Market conditions exercise a powerful influence on factor earnings. This is most evident for non-human factors such as raw materials and land. For labor, the influence of nonmonetary factors is greater because the owners of labor must accompany their labor services to work. Nevertheless, market forces exert powerful influences on earnings of labor.

8. There is much evidence of the movement of factors in response to changes in earnings. Factor mobility is typically greater for nonhuman factors than it is for labor. Even where impediments to mobility exist, factors (including labor) tend to move in response to persistent differences in earnings or employment opportunities.

TOPICS FOR REVIEW

Derived demand for factors
Marginal revenue product
Elasticity of factor demand
Total supply of a factor
Supply of a factor to a particular use
Factor mobility

DISCUSSION QUESTIONS

1. The demands listed below have been increasing rapidly in recent years. What derived demands would you predict have risen very sharply? Where will the extra factors of production demanded be drawn from?
   a. The demand for electric power
   b. The demand for medical services
   c. The demand for international and interregional travel
2. Can the following factor prices be explained by the marginal productivity theory of distribution?

a. The actor James Garner is paid $25,000 for appearing in a ten-second commercial. The model who appears in the ad with him is paid $250.
b. First prizes in a recent tennis tournament were: men's singles, $40,000; women's singles, $30,000; men's doubles, $15,000; women's doubles, $6,000; mixed doubles, $4,800.
c. The same jockey is paid 50 percent more money for winning a ¾ mile race with a $150,000 first prize than a 1½ mile race with a $100,000 prize—on the same horse.
d. The manager of the Toronto Blue Jays is paid *not* to manage in the third year of a three-year contract.

3. Consider the large-scale substitution of jumbo jets, each with a seating capacity of about 350, for jets with a seating capacity of about 125. What kinds of labor service would you predict to have experienced an increase in demand, and what kinds a decrease? Under what conditions would airplane pilots (as a group) be made better off economically by virtue of the switch?

4. Participation in the work force in Canada as a percentage of the population aged 14 and over has risen only slightly in the last ten years, but its composition has changed substantially. For example:
   a. Almost all men between 25 and 45 years of age continue to participate in the work force.
   b. The percentage of women aged 25 and over has risen sharply.
   c. The percentage of men over 65 has dropped.
   Hypothesize about social and economic changes that might explain these conditions. How do they relate to the theory of distribution?

5. A recent study showed that after taking full account of differences in education, age, hours worked per week, weeks worked per year, etc., professionally trained people earned approximately 15 percent less if they worked in universities than if they worked in government service. Can this be accounted for by the theory of distribution?

6. To what extent do the same principles help to explain the following:
   a. Why horse owner Robert Sangster paid $8.25 million for an untested yearling son of Northern Dancer
   b. Why baseball magnate George Steinbrenner signed a 10-year contract with outfielder Dave Winfield that amounts to about $22 million
   Are there important differences between the market for horses and for baseball players?

7. Discuss the implications of the federal government changing its policy of paying all its secretaries according to the same salary scale, regardless of location, to one that adapted the salary scale to local market conditions.

19 THE LABOR MARKET

Why do workers in the meat-packing industry get the same pay for the same work, no matter where they work in Canada? Why do carpenters get different wages in different locations? Why do railroad employees, who work in a declining industry, get higher rates of pay than equally skilled workers in many expanding industries? How does a worker in a plant employing 5,000 people "ask for a raise"? How does a worker let her employer know that she would be glad to trade so many cents per hour in wages for a better medical insurance scheme? Why do strikes occur?

The competitive theory of factor price determination tells us a lot about factor prices, factor movements, and the distribution of income. Indeed, for the pricing of many nonhuman factors, there is little need to modify the competitive model. Much of what is observed about labor markets is also consistent with the theory. But not all of it is.

Labor is in many ways the exceptional factor of production. The owners of capital or land need not be present when their services are rendered; indeed, the owners need not even live close to where these factors are employed. In contrast, the owner of labor must be present when labor services are delivered. As a result, nonmonetary factors such as location and working conditions are likely to be more important in the labor market than in markets for other factors of production. Considerations other than material advantage enter the relationship between employer and employee, for it is a relationship between people who look for loyalty, fairness, appreciation, and justice along with paychecks and productivity.

Labor unions, employers' associations, and collective bargaining are features of the labor market. These institutions are important because they influence wages and working conditions. They also affect the levels of employment and unemployment in many industries. Discrimination, also a feature of labor markets, is discussed in Box 19-1.

Because of these features, labor markets are characteristically imperfectly competitive, and sometimes monopolistic. The theory of factor price determination must therefore be extended somewhat before it can be applied to the full range of problems concerning the determination of wages.

THEORETICAL MODELS OF WAGE DETERMINATION[1]

In a labor market, firms are the buyers and workers are the sellers. Noncompetitive elements can enter on either or both sides of the market and influence the outcome of the wage bargain.

Two extreme but relevant cases are, first, where there are so many employers that no one of them can influence the wage rate by varying its own demand for labor and, second, where there is a

[1] Remember that, unless otherwise specified, we are dealing with real wages—that is, wages relative to the price level.

single purchaser of labor. In the former case, labor is said to be purchased under competitive conditions; in the latter case, under monopsonistic conditions. **Monopsony** means a single buyer; it is the equivalent, on the purchasing side, of a monopoly (a single seller). What is the effect of introducing a union into each of these extreme situations?

A Union in a Competitive Labor Market

Where there are many employers and many unorganized workers there is a competitive factor market of the kind discussed in the previous chapter. Under competitive conditions the wage rate and level of employment are set by supply and demand. This is shown in Figure 19-1 on page 318.

Suppose a union enters such a market and sets a wage for the industry above the competitive level. By so doing it is establishing a minimum wage below which no one will work. This changes the supply curve of labor. The industry can hire as many units of labor as are prepared to work at the union wage, but no one at a lower wage. Thus the industry (and each firm) faces a supply curve that is horizontal at the level of the union wage up to a quantity of labor willing to work at that wage. This too is shown in Figure 19-1. The intersection of this new supply curve and the demand curve establishes a wage rate and level of employment that differ from the competitive equilibrium.

The major effects of a union's setting a wage above the competitive level are (1) to raise the wage rates of those who remain employed; (2) to lower the actual amount of employment in the industry; and (3) to create a group of workers who would like to obtain jobs in the industry but cannot.

The resulting unemployment presents a problem for the union. A conflict of interest has been created between employed and unemployed union members. Pressure to cut the wage rate may develop among the unemployed, but the union must resist this pressure if the higher wage is to be maintained.

BOX 19–1 FEMALE–MALE DIFFERENTIALS IN LABOR MARKETS

Discrimination reduces a group's ability to get and keep jobs, as well as the wages earned in those jobs. Evidence from the United States suggests that discrimination against blacks results in higher unemployment rates for black workers than for white workers. But the problems of women in the labor force result more from lower wages than from unemployment.

Adult women in the last three decades increased their labor force participation from 30 percent in 1961 to almost 50 percent by 1980. (This is still short of the 80 percent participation rate of adult males.) Moreover, the female unemployment rate is only 1 or 2 percent higher than the rate for males. Women have steadily increased their participation in "higher status" occupations, including managerial, sales, scientific, and technical jobs.

But getting jobs is not the whole story. It has long been clear that women and men make and are offered different occupational choices, that proportionately fewer women than men reach higher-paying jobs in the occupations in which both work, and that those who do, do so more slowly. As a result, average earned income of females in the labor force is well below that of males of similar ages. A number of careful studies have established that in the 1970s labor market earnings were approximately 25 percent lower for employed women than for employed men of the same age and race.

To what extent do these differences reflect discrimination against women and to what extent such other sex-linked characteristics as the voluntary choice of different lifetime patterns of labor force participation? The statistics show that, on average, women have fewer years of education, training, and work experience than men of the same age. The average working female is less mobile occupationally and geographically than her male counterpart. At least some of these facts reflect voluntary choice; for example, many women decide to withdraw from the labor force, or to work only part-time, in order to have and raise children.

Yet direct discrimination against women has been inportant in labor markets and continues to play a role today. The extent of direct discrimination in an occupation may be measured by taking groups with similar characteristics and comparing their employment and pay status. For example, comparing starting salaries in college teaching of new Ph.D.s from the same graduate schools in a given subject and a given class of institutional employment, Professors Frank Stafford and George Johnson found the average pay of females was about 6 percent below that of males (with allowance for differences in age and prior experience). They attributed this part of a larger male-female pay differential to direct discrimination.

Women have also suffered indirect discrimination. They have been refused admission or discouraged from seeking entry into certain occupations; for example, they have traditionally been pushed into nursing rather than medicine, social work rather than law, and secretarial rather than managerial training programs. Sim-

A Monopsonistic Labor Market Without a Union

Consider a labor market in which there are many unorganized workers but only a small number of firms. For simplicity imagine a case in which the firms form an employers' hiring association in order to act as a single unit so that there is a monopsony in the labor market.

While the employers' association can offer any wage rate that it chooses—the laborers must either work at that rate or find a different job—the wage

ilarly, there is ample evidence that many women in dual career marriages are under substantial pressure to put their husband's job needs first.

Girls raised in a culture in which their education seems less important than that of their brothers, or where they are raised to think of themselves as potential homemakers and are urged to prepare themselves to attract and serve a husband, are less likely to acquire the skills or the opportunities for many high-paying forms of employment that are wholly within their capabilities.

Discrimination against women in job opportunities is being eliminated much more quickly than discrimination against racial minorities; the effect of women's liberation on attitudes—male as well as female—has been very great in a very short time. Between 1971 and 1979 the fraction of earned doctorates awarded to women in North America rose from 14 to 25 percent, and by 1980 nearly half of the new graduate enrollments were women, so this upward trend is likely to continue. In 1979, 15 percent of first professional degrees (law, medicine) were awarded to women—compared to 6.5 percent eight years earlier.

Who Loses from Discrimination?

Obviously, the victims lose as a result of labor market discrimination. But it would be a mistake to think they are the only losers. Society loses too because of the efficiency losses that discrimination causes, and in other ways.

Efficiency losses arise for several reasons. If women or blacks are not given equal pay with white males for equal work, the labor force will not be allocated to get the most out of society's resources. When people are kept from doing the jobs at which they are most productive and must instead produce goods or services that society values less, the total value of goods and services produced is reduced. And when prejudice increases unemployment, it reduces the nation's total output.

The gainers from discrimination are those who earn the higher pay that comes from limiting supply in their occupations, those who get the jobs blacks and women would otherwise have held, and the bigots who gain pleasure from not having to work with "them" or to consume services provided by "them." But if the total output of society is less, the net losses will have to be borne by the society as a whole.

Beyond the efficiency losses that discrimination imposes on society are further economic and social costs. Increased welfare or unemployment payments may be required, and the costs of enforcing antidiscrimination laws must be paid. The costs of discrimination also include increased crime, hostility, and violence. These things are all by-products of unemployment, poverty, and frustration. Discrimination, if not attacked and rolled back, has one more cost, perhaps the most important: a sense of shame in a society that does not do what is necessary to eliminate the barriers to equal treatment.

rate chosen will affect the profitability of its operations. For any given quantity that the monopsonist wishes to purchase, the labor supply curve shows the price per unit it must offer; to the monopsonist, this is the *average cost curve* of labor. In deciding how much labor to hire, however, the monopsonist will be interested in the *marginal cost* of hiring additional labor.

Whenever the supply curve of labor slopes upward, the marginal cost of employing extra units will exceed the average cost. It exceeds the wage paid (the average cost) because the increased wage

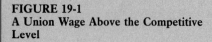

FIGURE 19-1
A Union Wage Above the Competitive Level

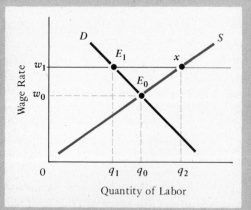

A union can raise the wages of those who continue to be employed in a competitive labor market at the expense of the level of employment. The competitive equilibrium is at E_0, the wage is w_0, and employment is q_0. If a union enters this market and sets a wage of w_1, a new equilibrium will be established at E_1. The supply curve has become $w_1 x S$. At the new wage, w_1, there will be q_2 workers who would like to work, but the industry only wishes to hire q_1. Employment will be q_1. The decrease in employment due to the wage increase over the competitive level is $q_1 q_0$ and the level of unemployment is $q_1 q_2$.

This figure can also be used to illustrate the effect of government's imposing a minimum wage of w_1 on the market. The q_1 workers who remain employed benefit by the wage increase. The $q_1 q_0$ workers who lose their jobs in this industry suffer to the extent that they fail to find new jobs at a wage of w_0 or more.

rate necessary to attract an extra worker must be paid to everyone already employed. [30] For example, assume that 100 workers are employed at $3.00 an hour and, in order to attract an extra worker, the wage must be raised to $3.01 an hour. The marginal cost of the one-hundred-and-first worker is not the $3.01 per hour paid to him, but $4.01 per hour—made up of 1 cent extra per hour to the 100 existing workers and $3.01 paid to the new worker.

The profit-maximizing monopsonist will hire labor up to the point where the marginal cost just equals the amount it is willing to pay for an additional unit of labor. That amount is determined by the marginal revenue product of labor and is shown by the demand curve. This is illustrated in Figure 19-2.

Monopsonistic conditions in a factor market will result in a lower level of employment and a lower wage rate than would rule when the factor is purchased under competitive conditions.

The common sense of this result is that the monopsonistic firm is aware that by trying to purchase more of the factor it is driving up the price against itself. It will therefore stop short of the point that is reached when the factor is purchased

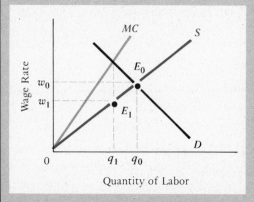

FIGURE 19-2
Monopsony in a Labor Market

A monopsonist lowers both the wage rate and employment below their competitive levels. D and S are the competitive demand and supply curves. In competition equilibrium is at E_0, the wage rate is w_0, and the quantity of labor hired is q_0. The marginal cost of labor (MC) to the monopsonist is above the average cost. The monopsonistic firm will maximize profits at E_1. It will hire only q_1 units of labor. At q_1 the marginal cost of the last worker is just equal to the value to the firm of that worker's output, as shown by the demand curve. The wage that must be paid to get q_1 workers is only w_1.

by many different firms, no one of which can exert an influence on the wage rate.

A Union in a Monopsonistic Market

What if a wage-setting union enters a monopsonistic market and sets a wage below which labor will not work? There will then be no point in the employer's reducing the quantity demanded in the hope of driving down the wage rate, nor will there be any point in holding off hiring for fear of driving the wage up. Here, just as in the case of a wage-setting union in a competitive market, the union presents the employer with a horizontal supply curve (up to the maximum number who will accept work at the union wage). The results of this intervention are demonstrated in Figure 19-3.

Because the union turns the firm into a price taker in the labor market, it can prevent the exercise of the firm's monopsony power and can therefore raise both wages and employment to the competitive levels.

The union may not be content merely to neutralize the monopsonist's power. It may choose to raise wages further. If it does, the argument will be exactly the same as that surrounding Figure 19-1. If the wage is raised above the competitive level, the employer will no longer wish to hire all the labor offered at that wage. The actual amount of employment will fall, and unemployment will develop. This too is shown in Figure 19-3. Notice, however, that the union can raise wages substantially above their competitive level before employment falls to a level as low as it was in the pre-union monopsonistic situation.

MINIMUM WAGE LAWS

When unions set wages for their members, they are in effect setting a minimum wage. Governments can cause similar effects by legislating specific minimum wages.

An important feature of labor markets in North America is the presence of government-imposed

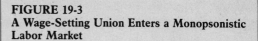

**FIGURE 19-3
A Wage-Setting Union Enters a Monopsonistic Labor Market**

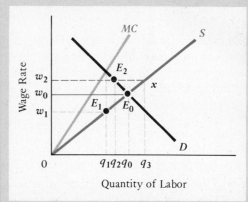

By presenting a monopsonistic employer with a fixed wage, the union can raise both wages and employment over the monopsonistic level. The monopsony position before the union enters is at E_1 (from Figure 19-2), with a wage rate of w_1 and q_1 workers hired. A union now enters and sets the wage at w_0. The supply curve of labor becomes w_0E_0S, and wages and employment rise to their competitive levels of w_0 and q_0 without creating a pool of unemployed workers. If the wage is raised further, say to w_2, the supply curve will become w_2xS and the quantity of employment will fall below the competitive level to q_2 while a pool of unsuccessful job applicants of q_2q_3 will develop.

This figure can also be used to illustrate the effect of the government's imposing a minimum wage of w_0 or w_2 on a monopsonistic labor market.

price floors that establish minimum levels of compensation, called **minimum wages**. In Canada, industries under federal jurisdiction are subject to the Canadian Labour Code, which in 1983 provided for a minimum wage of $3.50 per hour. The major coverage, however, is provided by provincial legislation that in 1983 set minimum wages for adult workers ranging from $3.85 per hour in several provinces to $4.25 in Quebec and Saskatchewan.

For a large fraction of all employment covered by the law, the minimum wage is below the actual market wage. Where this is true, the wage is said to be not "binding." But many workers are in occupations or industries where the free market wage rate would be below the legal minimum, and there the minimum wage is said to be binding, or effective.

Whether minimum wages are effective is not always easy to determine. For example, one response of employers to minimum wage legislation might be to reduce fringe benefits so that total compensation remains constant.

The consequences of minimum wages are controversial. To the extent that they are effective, they raise the wages of employed workers. But, as our analysis in Chapter 6 indicated, an effective floor price (which is what a minimum wage is) may well lead to a market surplus—in this case, unemployment. Thus minimum wages will benefit some groups while hurting others. The effects of minimum wages have been studied extensively.[2] The problem is more complicated than the analysis of Chapter 6 would suggest both because not all labor markets are competitive and because minimum wage laws do not cover all employment. Moreover, some groups in the labor force, especially youth and minorities, are affected more than the average worker.

A Comprehensive Minimum Wage

Suppose first that minimum wage laws apply equally to all occupations. The occupations and industries in which minimum wages are effective will be the lowest-paying in the country; they usually involve unskilled or at best semiskilled labor. In most of them the workers are not members of unions. Thus the market structures in which effective minimum wages apply are likely to include both those in which competitive conditions pertain and those in which employers exercise monopsony power. The employment effects of minimum wages are different in the two cases.

[2] A recent comprehensive survey is Charles Brown, Curtis Gilroy, and Andrew Kohen, "The Effect of the Minimum Wage on Employment and Unemployment" *Journal of Economic Literature* (June 1982), pp. 487–528.

Competitive Labor Markets

The employment effects of an effective minimum wage are unambiguous when the labor market is competitive. By raising the wage facing employers, minimum wage legislation leads to a reduction in the quantity of labor demanded and an increase in the quantity supplied. As a result the actual level of employment falls, and a surplus of labor (i.e., unemployment) is generated. This situation is exactly analogous to the one that arises when a union succeeds in setting a wage above the competitive equilibrium wage, as illustrated in Figure 19-1. The excess supply of labor at the minimum wage also creates incentives for people to evade the law by working below the legal minimum wage.

In competitive labor markets, minimum wage laws raise the wages of those who remain employed, but also create some unemployment.

The adverse employment effects of minimum wages fall most heavily on those with least education and training. This group—which includes many teenagers, women, and immigrants—will have fewer job opportunities as the wage rate rises. Many of them could have found jobs at lower wages if minimum wage laws did not exist.

Much skill acquisition occurs on the job. In a free market, employees in occupations in which such on-the-job training occurs "pay" for their education by receiving low wages in the initial stages of their employment. Minimum wage legislation makes this much more difficult. Instead of being able to "apprentice" in jobs that will lead to productive careers, many teenagers and women become trapped either in complete unemployment or in low-skill, short-term or part-time employment.

Monopsonistic Labor Markets

This case is exactly analogous to the one in which a union facing a monopsonistic employer succeeds in setting a wage above what the employer would otherwise pay, as shown in Figure 19-3. By effectively flattening the labor supply curve, the minimum wage law can simultaneously increase wages and employment. Of course, if the minimum wage is raised above the competitive wage, employment will start to fall, as in the union case. When set at the competitive wage, however, the minimum wage can protect the worker against monopsony power and lead to increases in employment.

A Noncomprehensive Minimum Wage

Suppose a minimum wage covers only 80 percent of all jobs and that applying the minimum wage to the covered jobs does cause some unemployment in that sector. The workers displaced can move to the uncovered sector. If they do, they will shift the supply curve in the uncovered sector to the right. This will lead to lower wages and increased employment in the uncovered sector. See Figure 19-

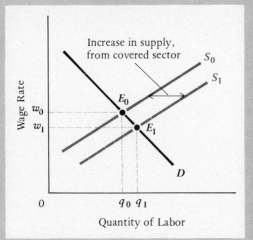

FIGURE 19-4
Demand and Supply in a Sector Not Covered When a Minimum Wage Is Introduced

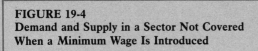

Increased supply in uncovered sectors will lower wages there and lead to some increase in employment. Start from E_0, with wage rate w_0 and employment in this sector of q_0. The imposition of a minimum wage on other sectors displaces workers who seek jobs in the uncovered sector. This shifts the supply curve from S_0 to S_1 and leads to a new equilibrium at E_1. The new wage w_1 is lower than w_0, and employment has increased by q_0q_1.

4. As a general rule the increase in employment in the uncovered sector will not be large enough to offset the decrease in the covered sector.[3]

The Overall Effect of Minimum Wage Laws

A great deal of empirical work has been done on the actual effect of minimum wages on employment. Minimum wages cause unemployment, particularly among youths aged 16 to 19: it is estimated that the rate of youth employment is decreased from 1 percent to 3 percent for every 10 percent increase in minimum wages. For young adults (aged 20 to 24) the employment effect is also adverse but smaller in size. Other differences too have been documented.

Many of the adverse employment effects are borne largely by those who are least skilled, least experienced, and perhaps most intended to be the beneficiaries of minimum wage policies. Several provinces responded to this kind of evidence by allowing lower minimum wages for young or inexperienced workers and for workers demonstrably in a "learning period."[4]

The adverse employment effect is, however, only one element in deciding whether, overall, minimum wages are beneficial or harmful. It is clear that minimum wage laws raise the incomes of many workers at the very lowest levels of pay. Some of those who benefit most are members of groups that are chronically poor, whom the government is anxious to aid by income redistribution. But it is not only the lowest paid who gain. Because union wage structures maintain differentials between skill classes, an increase in minimum wages also raises wages in a large number of occupations that are already above the minimum.

Given this mixed result, what explains the wide-

[3] Only if the demand curve in the uncovered sector is horizontal (infinitely elastic), or if the supply curve is vertical (completely inelastic), will every displaced worker from the covered sector find employment. But these are not likely.

[4] It may be objected that such exceptions are discriminatory. But, as we saw on page 218, labeling something "discriminatory" does not necessarily mean that it is bad. Here the question arises as to whether it is better to be employed at a lower wage or unemployed at a higher one.

BOX 19–2 THE VOCABULARY OF UNIONISM

Kinds of Unions

Unions today have two different principles of organization. In the **craft union** workers with a common set of skills are joined in a common association, no matter where or for whom they work. The craft principle of organization was and is the hallmark of the American Federation of Labor (AFL) and its Canadian counterpart, the Trades and Labour Congress (TLC). The **industrial union** is organized along industry lines: All workers in a given plant or industry are collected into a single union. This is the pattern developed by the member unions of the Congress of Industrial Organizations (CIO) and the Canadian Congress of Labour, which existed from 1940 to 1956. Among the prominent industrial unions are the United Automobile Workers and the United Steelworkers.

The two principles of unionism conflict. Should a carpenter employed in the steel industry be represented by the carpenters' union or the steelworkers' union? Disputes over which union shall have the right to *organize* (i.e., bring into their union) a particular group of workers are known as **jurisdictional disputes.** They have led to prolonged, bitter, and bloody battles of union against union.

Unions in North America operate at the local level, at the national and international levels, and as a federation of unions. Typically the national officers do the bargaining, form the poli-

cies, and set the tone. Individual workers belong to a local to which they pay dues (part of which goes to the national or international headquarters). There are about 165 national or international unions in Canada with over 10,000 locals. The locals for a craft union are geographical—for example, the Toronto chapter of the carpenters' union. The locals for an industrial union are plants or companies—for example, the Ford local of the United Automobile Workers.

The **federation** is a loose organization of unions. Most international unions operating in Canada are affiliated with the single American federation, the AFL-CIO, as well as the Canadian Labour Congress (CLC). Most of the purely Canadian national unions are affiliated with either the CLC or the Quebec-based Confederation of National Trade Unions (CNTU).

Kinds of Bargaining Arrangements

In an **open shop** a union represents its members but does not have exclusive bargaining jurisdiction for all workers in the shop. Membership in the union is not needed to get or to keep a job.

Unions vehemently oppose such an arrangement. If, on the one hand, the employer yields to union demands and raises wages, the nonmembers ("free riders") get the benefits of the union without paying dues or sharing the risks or responsibilities. If, on the other hand, the firm chooses to fight the union, it can run its

spread belief in using increased minimum wages to alleviate poverty and redistribute income from the rich to the poor? Much of the explanation, we believe, rests on neglect of adverse employment effects.

Organized labor finds minimum wages beneficial to most of its employed members, and labor unions have been consistently in favor of both increasing the level of minimum wages and expanding cov-

erage. No equally powerful political force opposes them since those who do not find jobs because of the minimum wage laws are unlikely to identify these laws as the cause of their unemployment.

While many economists are critical of minimum wages, as a practical matter the minimum wage is likely to remain. It is one of the hard-won labor gains dating back to the 1930s, and it has great symbolic significance for labor.

plants with the nonunion employees, thereby weakening the power of the union in the fight.

If all members of an occupation must join the union in order to get a job, the union can prevent its members from accepting less than the union wage and so have the power to maintain high wages in spite of the existence of excess supply. This arrangement is called a closed shop. In a **closed shop** only union members may be employed, and the union controls its membership as it sees fit. Employers traditionally regard this as an unwarranted limitation of their right to choose their employees. Its use has been virtually prohibited in the United States and in most provinces in Canada.

The **union shop** is a compromise between a closed and an open shop. In a union shop a firm may hire anyone it chooses at the union wage, but every employee must join the union within a specified period. This leaves employers free to hire whomever they wish but gives the union the power to enforce its union wages because workers are prevented from accepting employment at lower wages.

Weapons of Conflict

The **strike,** the union's ultimate weapon, is the concerted refusal to work by the members of the union. It is the strike or the threat of a strike that backs up the union's demands in the bargaining process. Workers on strike are, of course, off the payroll, so many unions set aside a portion of the dues collected to have a fund for paying striking workers.

Picket lines are made up of striking workers who parade before the entrance to their plant or firm. Other union members will usually not "cross" a picket line. Thus, if bricklayers strike against a construction firm, carpenters will not work on the project, although they themselves may have no grievance against the firm. Pickets represent an enormous increase in the bargaining power of a small union.

A **labor boycott** is an organized attempt to persuade customers to refrain from purchasing the goods or services of a firm or industry whose employees are on strike. The boycotts organized by Cesar Chavez's United Farm Workers Union against grapes, lettuce, and most recently bananas are prominent examples.

The **lockout** is the employer's equivalent of the strike. By closing the plant, the employer locks out the workers until such a time as the dispute is settled. **Strikebreakers** (scabs) are workers brought in by management to operate the plant while the union is on strike. A **blacklist** is an employer's list of workers who have been fired for playing a role in union affairs that was regarded by the employer as undesirable. Other employers are not supposed to give jobs to blacklisted workers.

THE NATURE AND EVOLUTION OF MODERN LABOR UNIONS

Labor-Market Institutions

A union is many things: a social club, an educational instrument, a political club, one more source of withholding money from a worker's pay, a bargaining agent for an individual worker, and, to some, a way of life. For the purposes of our discussion of labor markets, a **union** (or **trade union** or **labor union**) is an association of individual workers that speaks for them in negotiations with their employers. Unions negotiate with employers, either individually or in groups. Unionism has developed not only its own institutions, but also something of a specialized vocabulary, some of which is presented in Box 19-2.

Employers' associations are groups of employers who band together for a number of purposes, one of which may be to agree on a common policy in labor negotiations. Today formal employers' associations that appoint official bargaining representatives exist on a local level in many industries, including the hotel, restaurant, newspaper printing, and construction industries. There are regional or national associations in the garment manufacturing, hosiery, textile, coal mining, and furniture manufacturing industries, among others.

At least as important as formal associations are informal ones in which the several firms in an industry follow the lead set by a key firm. The industrywide pattern characterizes many manufacturing industries today. The automobile industry, for example, achieves nationwide agreement with its workers without the formal apparatus of an employers' association.

The process by which unions and employers (or their representatives) arrive at and enforce their agreements is known as **collective bargaining.**

Unionism today is both stable and accepted. It was not always so. Within the lifetime of many of today's members, unions were fighting for their lives and union organizers and members were risking theirs. In the 1930s the labor movement evoked the loyalties and passions of people as a great liberal cause in ways that seem quite extraordinary today. Indeed unions today often appear as conservative (even reactionary) groups of hard hats. Why the change and how did it come about?

The Urge to Organize

Trade unionism had its origin in the pitifully low standard of living of the average nineteenth century worker and his family. Much of the explanation for the low standard of living throughout the world lay in the small size of the national output relative to the population. Even in the wealthiest countries an equal division of national wealth among all families in 1850 would have left each one in poverty by our present standards. Box 19-3 provides a vivid picture of factory conditions at the turn of the present

century. The focus of resentment was usually the employer.

Out of these conditions and other grievances of working men and women came the full range of radical political movements. Out of the same conditions also came a pragmatic American form of collective action called **bread-and-butter unionism,** whose goals were higher wages and better working conditions rather than political reform.

The early industrial organizer saw that 10 or 100 employees acting together had more influence than one acting alone and dreamed of the day when all would stand solid against the employer. (The word *solidarity* occurs often in the literature and songs of the labor movement.) The union was the organization that would provide a basis for confronting the monopsony power of employers with the collective power of the workers. But it was easier to see solidarity as a solution than it was to achieve it. Organizations of workers would hurt the employer, and employers did not sit by idly; they too knew that in union there was strength. "Agitators" who tried to organize workers were fired, blacklisted, and occasionally killed.

Requirements of a Successful Union

To create effective power over the labor market, a union had to gain control of the supply of labor and have the financial resources necessary to outlast the employer in a struggle for strength. There was no right to organize. The union had to force an employer to negotiate with it, and few employers did so willingly. Unions started in a small way among highly skilled workers and spread slowly.

Why did the union movement show its first real power among small groups of relatively skilled workers? First, it was easier to control the supply of skilled workers than unskilled ones. Organize the unskilled, and the employer could find replacements for them. But skilled workers—the coopers (barrelmakers), the bootmakers, the shipwrights—were another matter. The original craft unions were, in effect, closed shops: One had to belong to the union to hold a job in the craft, and the union set the rules of admission.

BOX 19–3 FACTORY LIFE IN NORTH AMERICA, 1903

Stories of the workers' very real suffering during the Industrial Revolution and the years that followed could fill many volumes, but an example will at least illustrate some of the horrors that lay behind the drive for change and reform. (The quotation comes from *Poverty*, by Robert Hunter, published in 1904.)

In the worst days of cotton-milling in England the conditions were hardly worse than those now existing in the South. Children—the tiniest and frailest—of five and six years of age rise in the morning and, like old men and women, go to the mills to do their day's labor; and when they return home, they wearily fling themselves on their beds, too tired to take off their clothes. Many children work all night—"in the maddening racket of the machinery, in an atmosphere insanitary and clouded with humidity and lint." It will be long before I forget the face of a little boy of six years, with his hands stretched forward to rearrange a bit of machinery, his pallid face and spare form showing already the physical effects of labor. This child, six years of age, was working twelve hours a day in a country which has established in many industries an eight-hour day for men. The twelve-hour day is almost universal in the South, and about twenty-five thousand children are now employed on twelve-hour shifts in the mills of the various Southern states. The wages of one of these children, however large, could not compensate the child for the injury this monstrous and unnatural labor does him; but the pay which the child receives is not enough, in many instances, even to feed him properly. If the children fall ill, they are docked for loss of time. . . . The mill-hands confess that they hate the mills, and no one will wonder at it. A vagrant who had worked in a textile mill for sixteen years once said to a friend of mine: "I done that [and he made a motion with his hand] for sixteen years. At last I was sick for two or three days with a fever, and when I crawled out, I made up my mind that I would rather go to hell than go back to the mill."

Second, a union of a relatively few highly skilled specialists could attack the employers where they were vulnerable. Because a particular skilled occupation may be close to indispensable in an industrial process, other workers could not easily be substituted for it. Because labor in a particular skilled occupation is likely to account for a relatively low proportion of total costs, the effect on the employer's overall costs of giving in to a small group's demand for a wage increase is much less than the effect of giving in to an equivalent demand from the numerous unskilled workers.

In other words, both the difficulty of substituting other factors for skilled labor and a relatively small contribution to total costs combined to create an inelastic demand. This gave the unions of skilled workers an advantage in fighting the employer not enjoyed by other groups of workers. In the early days unions needed every advantage they could get since anti-unionism was for some employers a matter of principle, a crusade, and a way of life.

Even where unions gained a foothold in a strategic trade, they had their ups and downs. When employment was full and business booming, the cost of being fired for joining a union was not so great because there were other jobs. However, during periods of depression and unemployment, the risks were greater. An individual worker knew that if he or she caused trouble, unemployed members of the trade would be there to take the job. Solidarity could yield to hunger. Membership in trade unions showed a clear cyclical pattern, rising in good times and falling in bad.

The Historical Development of Canadian Unions

The origins of the present structure of Canadian trade unionism can be traced to the latter half of the nineteenth century. Its development has been strongly dominated by the influence of what are now called international unions, which have their headquarters and an overwhelming proportion of their membership outside Canada. The creation of Canadian locals of American unions began in the 1860s.[5] The first attempts at unifying Canadian unions into a central national organization occurred in 1873, but it was not until 1883 that the first body with nationwide representation, the Trades and Labour Congress of Canada (TLC), was formed. In 1956 the TLC merged with other groups to form the Canadian Labour Congress (CLC).

Two facets dominated the history of Canadian trade unionism in the first half of this century. One was the movement toward a single national federation; the other was the struggle to achieve autonomy in the face of American attempts to control the development of Canadian unions. The issues became intertwined when conflicts in the United States between craft and industrial unions became a disruptive force in Canada because of the TLC's ties with the American Federation of Labor. Until the 1930s craft unions were the characteristic form of collective action in the United States. In Canada, meanwhile, trade unionists were attracted to the principle of industrial unions that embraced unskilled workers as well as skilled craftsmen.

Because of the impossibility of establishing bargaining strength through the control of supply in the case of unskilled workers, the rise of industrial unionism in Canada was associated with political action as an alternative means of improving the lot of the membership. The classic Canadian manifestation of revolutionary industrial unionism was the One Big Union formed by western unionists who broke away from the TLC after the Winnipeg General Strike of 1919.

In general, social and political reform were given much more emphasis by Canadian unionists than by their American counterparts. Political action here extended to the development of a viable socialist political party in the form of the Cooperative Commonwealth Federation (CCF), established in 1932, and its successor, the New Democratic Party

(NDP), formed in 1961. The CLC does not have a formal affiliation with the NDP; the relationship is similar to that between the British Trades Union Congress and the British Labour Party.

International Unionism and Current Affiliation

In spite of the divergent patterns of development in the two countries, at the beginning of this century the TLC lined itself up squarely on the side of international unionism because of the greater resources made available to it through its constituent unions affiliated with the AFL. Then the rise of industrial unionism in the United States in the 1930s resulted in a severe blow to labor unity in Canada. Following the leadership of John L. Lewis of the United Mine Workers, the industrial unions in steel and automobiles split from the conservative AFL and formed the Congress of Industrial Organizations (CIO). Although the TLC had always been willing to accept both kinds of unions, in 1939 the AFL forced it to expel the Canadian branches of CIO unions.

The dominance of international—that is, American—unions in the Canadian labor movement continues to be a source of public concern in Canada. It is viewed as inconsistent with Canadian sovereignty and dangerous to Canadian interests. However, Senator Eugene Forsey, a former director of research for the CLC, views the unification of the bulk of Canadian unions under the CLC in 1956 as the beginning of virtual autonomy for Canadian locals. Unlike the TLC, the CLC has complete control over its qualifications for membership and has not hesitated to embrace unions expelled by the AFL-CIO or to expel unions affiliated with it.

Nevertheless agitation for greater Canadian autonomy has continued. The CLC had developed guidelines for the conduct of international unions operating in Canada, and a number of groups have severed their connection with international unions and formed independent Canadian unions. Some of the defectors have affiliated with the Confederation of Canadian Unions, a small CLC rival whose main base is in British Columbia.

The distribution of Canadian union membership

---

[5] In 1911, the earliest date for which figures are available, international unions had 90 percent of total union membership. In recent years the proportion has been about 60 percent.

TABLE 19–1 UNION MEMBERSHIP BY TYPE AND AFFILIATION, 1983

Type and affiliation	Thousands of members	Percentage of total
International unions	1470	41
AFL-CIO/CLC	1232	35
CLC only	134	4
Other	104	2
National unions	1946	54
Public employee unions (CLC)	683	19
Other CLC unions	335	9
Confederations of National Trade Unions	212	6
Other	59	2
Unaffiliated unions	654	18
Directly chartered and independent local organizations	147	4
Total	3563	100

Source: Labour Canada, *Labour Organizations in Canada,* 1983.

by affiliation in 1983 is shown in Table 19-1. International unions account for 41 percent of the total, compared to about 70 percent in the mid 1950s. One factor in the increased share of national unions is the growth of membership in the two unions representing government workers, the Canadian Union of Public Employees and the Public Service Alliance. Public sector unions are discussed further in Box 19-4. Another major component of noninternational union membership has arisen out of the distinct aspirations of French-Canadian workers. This is reflected in Table 19-1 by the 6 percent share of the Quebec-based Confederation of National Trade Unions.

The Development of Public Policy Toward Collective Bargaining

As shown in Figure 19-5 on page 330, rapid gains in union membership occurred in the years during and immediately after World War II. This led to pressure to give Canadian unionists the legal protections provided in the United States by the Wagner Act of 1935, which guaranteed the right of workers to organize and to elect an exclusive bargaining agent. The rights were carried over into Canada through the provisions of the Wartime Labour Relations Regulations of 1944.

Government intervention in industrial disputes in Canada has a history dating back to the early years of this century. The earliest legislation applied only to public utilities and coal mining, where there was a strong public interest element. It provided that before a strike or a lockout could be initiated, the parties were required to submit any dispute to a conciliation board.

This system of compulsory conciliation and compulsory delay in work stoppage was extended to a much larger segment of the economy under special emergency powers adopted by the government of Canada during World War II. In the postwar period, jurisdiction over labor policy reverted to the provinces, but the principles established have been carried over into provincial legislation.

METHODS AND OBJECTIVES OF THE MODERN UNION

Union constitutions are very democratic documents. All members have one vote, officers are elected by the vote of the membership, the rights of individual workers are fully protected, and so on.

Union leaders are highly paid professionals whose business is to run the union, while the main business of union members is to earn a living on the job. The union members' indifference is understandable; they are paying dues that permit the union to pay generous salaries to union leaders to look out for the rank and file's interests—and as long as the leadership "delivers," all goes well. But delivers what and to whom?

Restricting Supply to Increase Wages

At the beginning of this chapter we saw that if a union raises the wage above the competitive level, it will create a pool of people eager to work at the

BOX 19–4 UNIONISM IN THE PUBLIC SECTOR

Whatever the reason, the scope of union activity within the public sector has expanded rapidly in the past two decades. Indeed, the rapid growth in union membership in Canada shown in Figure 19-5 arises primarily from this increase in union membership in the public sector.* In addition, because most pubic service unions are Canadian, their growth has diminished the role of international unions in Canada.

Since 1965 public sector unions have had the right to strike, and strikes in the public sector have not been infrequent. Canadians have often been angered by interruptions in the postal service or by having to cancel holidays because of the disruption of airport services.

It is often argued that such withdrawals or services are unfair because they affect large numbers of people who are not party to the labor-management dispute. They are also unfair, some argue, precisely because government often has a monopoly in the provision of the services being withheld, and hence there are no alternatives. Not only do unions in the public sector have considerable power because of the nature

* Under Canadian law, municipalities are treated as private corporations and their employees governed by labor legislation applicable to the private sector.

of the services that strikes curtail, but public sector employers are not restrained by market forces from conceding excessive wages. Government services are not typically sold in the marketplace but are paid for out of general tax revenues. Further, politicians have a strong incentive to avoid unpopular strikes.

Professor Morely Gunderson of the University of Toronto has estimated that during the six-year period beginning in 1965 (the year of the institution of the right to strike in the public sector), there developed a public service wage advantage of about 6 percent for males and 8 percent for females, relative to comparable jobs in the private sector. Other studies confirm the maintenance of, if not an increase in, this advantage over the next few years for all but the most senior public employees.

Many economists believe that increased public sector wages become the standard by which private sector wages are set; in this view the public sector has become a wage leader and a source of potential inflation in the economy. However, studies have called into question the evidence confirming a spillover, and the issue is still hotly contested.

Furthermore, many observers felt that a pri-

going wage rate but unable to find employment. An alternative is to determine the quantity of labor supplied and let the wage be determined on the open market. This is illustrated in Figure 19-6 on page 331. The union can restrict entry into the occupation by methods such as lengthening apprenticeship periods and restricting openings for trainees. Such tactics make it more difficult and more expensive to enter the occupation.

Under these restrictive conditions, the quantity supplied is reduced at any given wage rate and the supply curve of labor shifts to the left. This has the effect of raising wages without anyone's ever having to negotiate a rate above what would natu-

rally emerge from the free operation of the competitive market. Furthermore there is no pool of unemployed wanting to work at the new higher wage but unable to find employment. Thus there is no wage-reducing pressure from unemployed persons who are trained for the occupation but are unable to find jobs.

The choice unions may face between the tactics of wage setting and supply restriction will be affected by the relative ease of enforcing one or the other kind of arrangement and the public acceptability of its tactics. Limiting entry is much easier where a specific, hard-to-acquire set of skills is not only required but is perceived by the public to

mary reason for the introduction of wage and price controls (see pages 703–705) by the federal government in 1975 was to appeal to an external force to regain control over wage settlements with their own employees. Public sector unions, in this view, had become so powerful that the federal government could not control wages in the federal civil service through the usual negotiating and bargaining procedures; it had to impose controls on the entire economy to control public sector wages. In 1982, the federal government again introduced wage controls, this time only on wages under federal government jurisdiction, with its 6 & 5 Program.

It is useful to compare the Canadian situation with that prevailing elsewhere. In the United States, federal and state government workers are prohibited from striking and are not permitted to bargain over pay. In Britain, the normal means of determining government pay levels is strict adherence to private sector comparability guidelines. Canadian public sector labor regulation policy is now among the most liberal in the world, and some believe it is too liberal.

Some economists believe government employees do not need collective bargaining or the strike weapon to ensure that they are paid adequately; in the long run the supply of labor to the public sector is a function of the price paid for labor by the public employer, relative to what workers can earn elsewhere. This offers considerable insurance that public employees, with or without collective bargaining, will not long be underpaid, at least at entry job levels. Some even advocate that bargaining for pay in the public sector be eliminated in favor of a policy in which pay scales are set by an independent agent on the basis of comparability to the private sector. While this policy has much to recommend it, it also has obvious administrative and political drawbacks; furthermore, it rules out changes in relative wages as part of a long-run adjustment to new relative demands in the two sectors.

In his budget of February 1983, Prime Minister Marc Lalonde announced a return to collective bargaining in the federal public sector following the end of the 6 & 5 Program, but also articulated a tough set of principles that would guide the government's bargaining position. Collective bargaining in the public sector seems destined to remain for some time as a source of controversy and debate.

demand certification. In this respect unions are no different than professional groups, who may treat unions with utter disdain. Consider the professions of medicine and law. Since professional standards were long regarded as necessary to protect the public from incompetent practitioners, doctors and lawyers found it publicly acceptable to limit supply by limiting entry into the profession.

Doctors were in short supply—and doctors' incomes became the highest of any profession—because of barriers to entry, including the difficulties of getting into an approved medical school, the high cost of creating new medical schools, long years of low-paid internship and residency, and various certification rules. Whatever the need for high standards of entry into medical practice, there is no doubt that doctors' earnings are higher than they otherwise would be *because* the barriers to entry into the profession prevent increases in the number of those admitted to medical practice. Most investigators have concluded that restrictions on entering medicine are much greater than they need be to protect the public and that earnings are substantially higher as a result.

Lawyers, by contrast, have been less successful in limiting entry into their profession. Faced with an inability to limit competition by limiting entry into the profession, they have turned to "wage

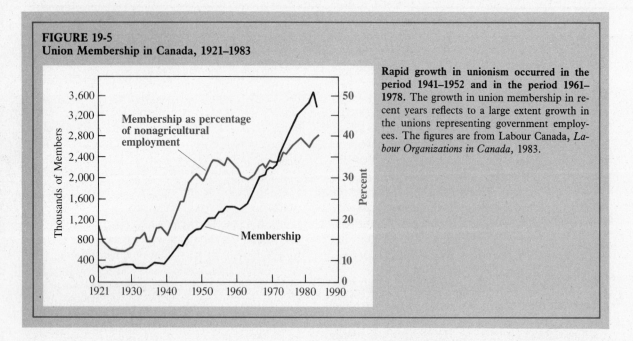

FIGURE 19-5
Union Membership in Canada, 1921–1983

Rapid growth in unionism occurred in the period 1941–1952 and in the period 1961–1978. The growth in union membership in recent years reflects to a large extent growth in the unions representing government employees. The figures are from Labour Canada, *Labour Organizations in Canada*, 1983.

setting"—having their state bar associations prescribe and enforce minimum fees for services such as drawing a will, probating an estate, and representing a client in court. They have also made advertising and other forms of competition for clients unethical. As the theory predicts, many lawyers are underemployed in the sense that they have fewer clients than they could comfortably handle.[6] In contrast, doctors have typically been overworked.

Restriction of supply will tend to raise wages without creating unemployment. Raising wages without restricting supply will lead to unemployment.

Competing Goals

Wages Versus Fringe Benefits

Indirect or **fringe benefits**—such as company contributions to union pension and welfare funds, sick leave, and vacation pay, as well as required payments toward social security and unemploy-

[6] See the discussion of barbers in Box 13-1.

ment compensation insurance—are estimated to make up almost a third of the total compensation of industrial workers. Why do unions and employers not simply agree to a wage and let it go at that? Why should the average employed automobile worker have earned $23,200 in wages in 1983 but cost the company $36,100?

Fringe benefits appeal to employees in part because they are not subject to income taxes. Pension funds and medical benefits let employees provide for their future and that of their families more cheaply than they could by purchasing private insurance, and the benefits often protect them even when they lose their jobs. There may also be advantages to employers. One is that some forms of fringe benefits, such as pension funds, tend to bind the worker more closely to the company, thereby decreasing the turnover rate among employees. If employees stand to lose part of their benefits by changing jobs, they will not be so ready to move.

Wages Versus Employment

A union that sets wages above the competitive level is making a choice of higher wages for some

FIGURE 19-6
Raising Wages by Restricting Entry

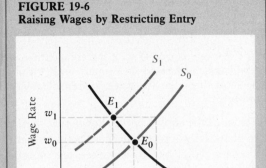

By restricting entry into an occupation, a union can shift the supply curve and raise wages. A competitive industry would be in equilibrium at E_0. When the supply curve shifts to S_1, the wage rises to w_1 and employment falls to q_1. Compare this to the strategy of simply imposing the wage w_1. In each case q_1 workers obtain employment at q_1. By shifting the supply curve, no pool of unsuccessful job applicants is created. When a wage of w_1 is imposed without shifting the supply curve from S_0, q_1q_2 workers are unable to find jobs.

and unemployment for others. Should the union strive to maximize the earnings of the group that remains employed? If it does, some of its members will lose their jobs and the union's membership will decline. Should it instead maximize the welfare of its present members? Or should it seek to expand employment opportunities (perhaps by a low-wage policy) so that the union membership grows?

The recession of the early 1980s combined with the growing competition to North American manufactured goods from foreign competition led to a new recognition among major industrial unions that high wages and high levels of layoffs and unemployment of their members often went hand in hand. Not only did American unions in automobiles, steel, rubber, smelting, airlines, and many others accept wage increases less than increases in the cost of living, many also accepted "givebacks" by reopening old contracts and agreeing to significant reductions in wages and other benefits under existing contracts. They did so to prevent further plant closings and to encourage the rehiring of unemployed union workers.

Wages versus employment poses a long-term problem as well as a short-term problem brought on by the recession. Unionization and rising wages in fruit picking have led to mechanization and a drop in the demand for labor. In the auto industry, the high wage policy has encouraged the major manufacturers to increase automation.

The fundamental dilemma of choosing between high wages and high employment is splitting many unions and dividing the North American labor movement. In the United States, only 52 percent of the auto workers at GM approved a contract containing wage concessions by the union despite intense lobbying for the contract by the union's leaders. Not all unions are going the same way. While steel, auto, and many others are trying to preserve jobs, others are resolutely refusing to do so.

Wages Versus Job Security

Until the 1980s people who were in their teens during the Great Depression dominated the leadership of North American unions. Not surprisingly, they had a strong defensive attitude toward their jobs. They lived through a period when unemployment was above 20 percent of the total labor force and nearer 50 percent in many of the hardest hit areas. They saw people grow up, marry, and raise children on relief or part-time work.

In a period of heavy unemployment, the installation of a labor-saving machine in a factory is likely to mean unemployment for those whose jobs are lost by the change. It is little wonder that new machines were opposed bitterly and that job-saving restrictive practices were adhered to with tenacity.

The heritage of this fear survived in featherbedding practices such as the standby musician at the television studio and the meticulous division of tasks in the building trades. But in the long run, mechanization increases productivity, and consequently the wages and profits that are earned. After World War II the attitude of many unions slowly changed from one of resisting technological change to one of collaborating with it and trying to reduce some of its costs to individuals who are adversely affected.

The return of higher unemployment rates in recent years has again heightened union interest in job security but in more constructive ways. Elimination of some restrictive practices that raised labor costs have been accepted by unions in return for company agreement to pass on savings in lower product prices and to delay planned layoffs. The biggest change in attitude (compared with the past) is that the current generation of leaders see the increased mechanization of Japanese, Korean, and German firms rather than their own employers as the principal threat to union workers' jobs. Many of today's labor leaders seem prepared to help their employers improve their international competitiveness.

LABOR-MARKET INSTITUTIONS AND THE PERSISTENCE OF INVOLUNTARY UNEMPLOYMENT

Labor unions and the various institutions and practices that have developed in collective bargaining have long been known to make a difference in the way in which particular markets function. Recently a major and important debate has developed among economists about whether—and if so, how—these institutions and practices affect the overall ability of the economy to cope with unemployment. We are now in a position to look at this question.

The Absence of Unemployment in Competitive Labor Markets

In the traditional or neo-classical theory of competitive wage determination, the wage rate adjusts to equate the demand and supply of labor. This is the sort of standard supply and demand analysis that is now familiar, and it is shown by the thicker curves in Figure 19-1.

If the wage rate is free to vary, the competitive wage rate will equate demand and supply and "clear the market." At this wage rate there is no involuntary unemployment.

It is true (as the supply curve shows) that there are more potential workers than those employed at the competitive wage, but extra workers are *voluntarily* unemployed—they do not choose to work at the competitive wage rate. As long as the result is on the supply curve, everyone who wants to work at the going wage rate gets a job.

It follows that persistent involuntary unemployment can occur in this world only if the real wage is held above its competitive equilibrium level. If, for example, the wage is w_1 in Figure 19-1, there will be q_1q_2 units of labor involuntarily employed: they would like to work at the going wage rate, but there is no demand for their services. The remedy for involuntary unemployment in the neo-classical world is thus obvious: *Reduce the real wage rate to its competitive level.* There can be no involuntary unemployment at the competitive equilibrium wage.

Neo-Classical Theories of Unemployment

How then could economists explain the existence of unemployment? Plainly either labor unions or monopsony, or both together, could lead to unemployment. For example, a wage-setting union could raise the wage rate above the market clearing level and accept the unemployment of some of its members. Similarly, monopsony could lower the level of employment below the competitive level, as was shown in Figure 19-2.

Classical economists readily accepted that either monopsony or monopoly might lead to unemployment. Thus they did not deny the existence of unemployment. *What they could not accept was that unemployment could persist in competitive markets*. Yet the evidence, accumulated in recession after recession, showed that it did occur, and most doubts about its persistence were shattered during the decade of the 1930s.

New Theories of Unemployment

Economists have long sought to understand the problem of involuntary unemployment. For a long time economists were satisfied with the explanation offered by early Keynesian economists: Workers would stubbornly resist a downward movement in their money wage rate. Thus when the real wage rate was too high, competitive forces would not reduce it by forcing money wages down because workers would stubbornly resist such a fall.

Recently economists have sought better explanations of persistent unemployment by reexamining the determination of wages. As a result a new set of theories has arisen. These theories deny that forces exist to cause wages to fluctuate so as to continuously equate the current demands for and supplies of labor. These theories start with the obvious observation that labor markets are not auction markets where prices always respond to excess demand or excess supply. When unemployed workers are looking for jobs, employers do not go around to their existing workers and knock down their wages until there is no one looking for a job; instead, they hang out a sign saying "no help wanted." This suggests something is wrong with the neo-classical theory that views the labor market as a market where, in the absence of monopolies or monopsonies, excess supply quickly forces wages down.

A key aspect of the new theories is the observation that many workers hold their jobs for quite long periods of time so that many employers and employees have long-term relations with each other. Under these circumstances wages become insensitive to current economic conditions because they are in effect regular payments on the employer's obligation to transfer a certain amount of wealth to the employee over the duration of the employment relation. Given this situation:

The tendency is for employers to "smooth" the income of employees by paying a steady wage, letting profits fluctuate to absorb the effects of temporary increases and decreases in demand for the firm's product.

To see what is involved, consider a simple example in which an employee is obligated by an unbreakable contract to work for an employer for seven years. Scheme 1 for paying the worker would be to give him a lump sum at the outset, leaving him to invest the money and spread its use for consumption over the seven years. Scheme 2 would give him a (larger) lump sum at the end of the seven years, leaving him to borrow against that payment to spread consumption over the seven years. Scheme 3 would be to give him equal payments at regular intervals over the seven years. This last arrangement makes it unnecessary for workers to engage in large capital transactions (of investing as in scheme 1 or borrowing as in scheme 2).

In the real world, however, the worker's obligation to stay in his job for seven years would be unenforceable. He may quit. Also the employer may dismiss him before the seven years are up. Thus where long-term arrangements depend only on unenforceable understandings, it is undesirable that either side be heavily in debt to the other at any point in the contract. Under scheme 1 the employee has an incentive to quit at an early date, since he is in debt to his employer for the remaining years of work for which he has already been paid. Under scheme 2 the employer has an incentive to dismiss the worker at an early date, since he is increasingly in debt to the employee until the end of the contract. There is good reason for compensation to be paid as a steady stream of income so that neither side is too heavily in debt to the other at any point in time.

Where there are fluctuations in demand for the firm's products, and hence fluctuations in the marginal revenue product of a stable work force, paying a steady compensation to employees does mean that indebtedness will arise on one side or the other from time to time. For such arrangements to work there must be some adhesive that prevents workers from quitting when they are ahead of the game and from being dismissed when they are behind.

One institution by which the employee tends to be held to the firm is the pay-by-age tradition. Generally, the marginal product of workers rises as they gain experience, reaches a peak, and then falls off as their age advances. The pay pattern, however, is often one that rises steadily with age and seniority. Thus experienced workers will get less than the value of their marginal product at earlier ages and more at later ages. This tends to hold workers to their firms.[7] But what stops the employer from dismissing workers once the value of their current marginal product begins to fall below their current wages? Here union contracts requiring that least-senior employees be laid off first do the job. Between the two, rising wages with age and dismissal in ascending order of seniority, employers and employees are held to each other, allowing payment of a steady wage in the face of fluctuating economic circumstances.

In such labor markets the wage rate does not fluctuate to clear the market. Wages are written over what has been called the "economic climate" rather than the "economic weather." Because wages are thus insulated from short-term fluctuations in demand, any market clearing that does occur is through fluctuations in the volume of employment rather than in the wage. Of course wages must respond to permanent shocks to a market, such as, for example, the permanent and unexpected decline in the demand for the output of a particular industry.

These new theories of nonmarket clearing apply mainly to stable labor forces in established industries and less to markets where turnover is very high and long-term attachment of employees to firms rare. In the words of economist Robert E. Hall: "There is no point any longer in pretending that the labour market is an auction market cleared by the observed average hourly wage. In an extreme case, wages are just instalment payments on a long-term debt and reveal essentially nothing about the current state of the market."[8]

The basic message of these new theories is that freely functioning labor markets, even those completely free from monopoly and monopsony elements, cannot be relied on to minimize involuntary unemployment by equating current demand for labor with current supply.

Further important implications of these theories for the causes of, and cures for, persistent unemployment are discussed in detail in the macroeconomic parts of this book.

SUMMARY

1. A wage-setting union entering a competitive market can raise wages, but only at the cost of reducing employment and creating a pool of unemployed former workers.

2. A wage-setting union entering a monopsonistic market may increase both employment and wages over some range. If, however, it sets the wage above the competitive level, it too will create a pool of unsatisfied workers who are unable to get the jobs they want at the going wage.

3. Governments set wages above their competitive levels by passing minimum wage laws. The overall effects of minimum wages have now been extensively studied. It is clear that they raise the incomes of many employees, but they have adverse employment effects on many of those with the very lowest levels of skills.

4. North American unionism developed first in the skilled trades, along craft lines, where it was possible to control supply and prevent nonunion members from undercutting union wages. Widespread organization of the unskilled did not occur until after the legal right to organize was established in

---

[7] Mandatory retirement is an essential feature of this arrangement since without it workers could decide to stay on the job for an unpredictable amount of time when their current wage was more than the value of their marginal product.

[8] Robert E. Hall, "Employment Fluctuations and Wage Rigidity." *Brookings Economic Papers*, Tenth Anniversary Issue, 1980, p. 120. This whole section draws heavily on Hall's excellent survey paper.

the United States. Canadian unionism has evolved enormously since its beginnings in the latter half of the nineteenth century. International unions affiliated with the American Federation of Labor have played a major role, but almost complete autonomy is now enjoyed by Canadian locals.

5. There is a basic conflict between the goals of raising wages by restricting supply (thereby reducing the union's employed membership) and preserving employment opportunities for members and potential members. Other trade-offs concern wages and job security, and wages and fringe benefits.

6. In neo-classical theory competitive wage determination ensures that there is no involuntary unemployment. Such unemployment only arises because of monopoly or monopoly elements or such goverment intervention as minimum wage laws.

7. Modern theory allows for wages that are set over long terms of expected employer-employee relations. Such wages do not fluctuate to clear labor markets in the short term and they therefore allow for short-term involuntary unemployment.

TOPICS FOR REVIEW

Monopsony power
Union power
Effects of minimum wages
Collective bargaining
Goals of unions
Possible causes of involuntary unemployment

DISCUSSION QUESTIONS

1. A union that has bargaining rights in two plants of the same company in different states almost always insists on "equal pay for equal work" in the two plants. It does not always insist on equal pay for men and women in the same jobs. Can you see any economic reasons for such a distinction?
2. During 1982 the United Auto Workers in the United States accepted lower rates of pay for its members working for Chrysler than the same categories of workers received from Ford and General Motors. This violated the UAW's traditional policy of a single wage rate schedule nationwide. Suggest why its traditional policy existed but why it might have changed its policy in 1982.
3. Since the passage of the Trade Unions Act of 1872, unions have been exempt from laws prohibiting conspiracies in restraint of trade. What do you think about this exemption? Why should wage fixing not be in violation of the law when price fixing is?
4. Why were craft unions more successful than industrial unions in the late nineteenth century in North America? What happened to change this in the 1930s?
5. Interpret the following statements or practices in terms of the subject matter of this chapter.
   a. A requirement that every passenger train carry a fireman though there may be nothing for him to do
   b. A requirement that one must pass an English language proficiency test to be a carpenter in New York City
   c. A statement by an official of a textile workers union in Massachusetts: "Until we have organized the southern textile industry, we will be unable to earn a decent wage in New England."
   d. An official of the United Steel Workers' Union: "Things are getting rough in our locals because the youngsters have different views about wages than the old-timers."
6. Each of the following headlines appeared in 1982. Explain each one and speculate on whether it might (or might not) have appeared in 1952.
   a. "Lifetime employment—a key union goal"
   b. "Canadian labor—from fighting cartels to fighting competition"
   c. "GM and UAW agree to tie car prices to wage concessions"
   d. "Fringe benefits loom large in key bargains"
7. Suppose it is accepted that, on average, unions have raised the wages of their members. Can this be reconciled with the low and declining percentage of employees who are union members?
8. Interns and residents in many Ontario hospitals are seeking to organize in an attempt to raise their pay. If they succeed, what effect will this have on the incomes of doctors?
9. "The great increase in the number of women entering the labor force for the first time means that relatively more women than men earn beginning salaries. It is therefore not evidence of discrimination that the average wage earned by females is less than that earned by males." Discuss.
10. The American Cyanamid Corporation once had a policy

of removing women of child-bearing age from, or not hiring them for, jobs that expose them to lead or other substances that could damage a fetus. Is this sex discrimination? Whether it is or not, debate whether this sort of protective hiring rule is something the government should require, encourage, or prohibit.

11. "One can judge the presence or absence of discrimination by looking at the proportion of the population in different occupations." Does such information help? Does it suffice? Consider each of the following examples. Relative to their numbers in the total population, there are
    a. Too many blacks and too few Jews among professional athletes
    b. Too few male secretaries
    c. Too few female judges

12. Could economic discrimination persist in a competitive labor market? Consider the argument that in a world of employers prejudiced against blacks, any firm that violated the taboo and hired blacks would reduce costs, make profits, and be able to take business from its prejudiced competitors.

13. "Of nearly 40 million working women, 40 percent are in traditionally female occupations—secretaries, nurses, cashiers, waitresses, elementary school teachers, beauticians, maids, and sales clerks, for example. While this may result from past sex stereotyping, the notion that only a women can do these jobs may also benefit women by preserving employment opportunities for them, given the high unemployment rates among black males and teenage males." Discuss this argument.

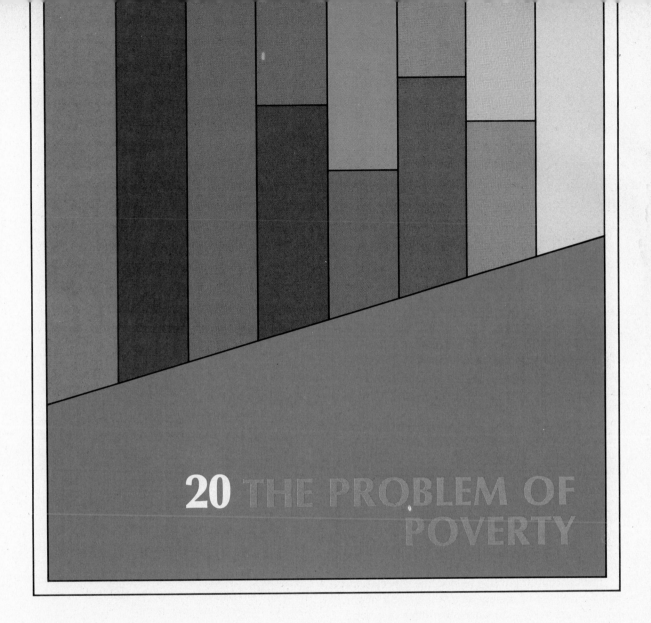

20 THE PROBLEM OF POVERTY

National income divided by the total population is the average income for all Canadians. Some individuals and groups get much more than the average, and others get much less. Possibly the most discussed aspect of income distribution concerns the proportion of national income that goes to the very poor. Who are they? Why are they poor? What can—or should—we do about it? Poverty and the means used to alleviate it play a very large part in political debates.

POVERTY IN CANADA

There are a number of reasons for the variations in what different individuals can earn. People differ in the talents they possess and the factors of production that they own; consequently both the quantity of factor services they can sell and the price they can receive will vary. Some factor owners are in a position to respond quickly to, and thus to take advantage of, changing opportunities. Others are immobile and will suffer when events leave them in markets where no one wants what they have to sell. To what extent do such reasons account for the continuing presence of poverty in Canada?

The Concept of Poverty

One possible definition of poverty is to be poorer than most of your fellow citizens. There will, of course, always be 10 percent of the population that is poorer than the other 90 percent. If poverty is regarded as a matter of low relative income, it is here to stay, for we inescapably have the relatively poor among us.

To most of us, poverty means more than low relative income. Some minimum family income standard is required to define the **poverty level** below which a family is said to be poor. Such a standard specifies a dollar amount based on estimates of need and the cost of living. Using a survey of family income and expenditure, Statistics Canada has defined the poverty level (or, as it is often called, the *low income cutoff*) as occurring at that income level at which the family unit spends on average more than 58.5 percent of its income on the three basic necessities of food, shelter, and clothing. For a family of four the poverty level in 1983 ranged from $14,110 in rural areas to $19,180 in the largest cities.

The concept of poverty reflects the expectations and aspirations of society as a whole—and of the poor themselves—as to what constitutes an acceptable minimum standard of living. Less than 100 years ago, poverty would have been defined as the lack of the minimum amounts of food, shelter, and clothing needed to sustain life. Once this condition faced (or threatened) a large portion of the world's urban and rural masses. Total output was so low that all but a privileged minority lived at or near this level, and any flood or famine or crop failure plunged thousands into starvation. Poverty in this sense is still present in the world, even in Canada. Starvation, hunger, and malnutrition are suffered by thousands of Canadians, and some Canadians born in 1984 will starve to death.

Yet in most advanced industrial countries, as in Canada, output has risen until the average family enjoys a high material standard of living, and the provision of *subsistence requirements* of food, shelter, and clothing is a major problem for only a small number of families. If this is so—if mere subsistence does not define the poverty level—what does it mean to say that many Canadians live in poverty?

Consider the income of a member of a family just at the poverty level. Income of $14,110 for a family of four is $3,527 per person. This may not seem like a great deal to most of you, but it is above the per capita income of three-quarters of the world's population. This should not lead anyone to minimize poverty problems; the poor person living in Winnipeg needs more clothes, transportation, and other basics than an Indonesian peasant. Visit the slums of any North American city and you will not lightly dismiss poverty.

While $14,110 for a family of four buys enough food, shelter, and clothing to get by, it is only about 40 percent of the average (median) income of Canadian families. What it does not provide is enough money for the necessities and also for the full range of commodities that 90 percent of us take for granted, such as having a refrigerator, hot water, a television set that works, and attending an occasional movie. Many of the poor are understandably bitter and resentful that they and their children are outsiders looking in on the comfortable way of life shown in ads and on television. "I'd like, just once," one of them said to a magazine interviewer, "to buy Christmas presents the children want instead of the presents they need."

The Extent of Poverty

According to the Statistics Canada criterion described above, in 1981 12 percent of families and over 30 percent of unattached individuals were living in poverty.

Who Are the Poor?

There are poor among people of all ages, races, and educational levels; among the working as well as the unemployed and the retired. Yet some groups have very much higher incidences of poverty than others. For example, Table 20-1 shows that you are more likely to be poor if you live in a rural area or in the Atlantic provinces, if you are a member of a large family, or if you are over 65 years old.

On the other hand, a close examination of the characteristics of the poor made by Statistics Canada in 1967 showed that poverty is by no means restricted to those groups for which its incidence is high. More than half the families who were poor lived in urban areas, were residents of Ontario or the Western provinces, had no more than one child, or were headed by a person between the ages of 25 and 65. Furthermore, 24 percent of those suffering from poverty in 1981 worked full-time during the year and 59 percent worked at least part-time. These facts may help to dispose of two superficial caricatures: the slothful father who feigns a disability because he is too lazy to do an honest day's work, and the family with so many children that an ordinarily decent wage is spread so thin the entire household is reduced to poverty. Individual households that come close to these extremes can be found, but most poor households do not.

The Historical Experience

Between 1969 and 1981, the proportion of Canadians living in poverty was almost cut in half—to less than 15 percent from more than 25 percent. In part, this reflected a variety of government initiatives and key structural changes in the economy, such as an increased number of two-income families and a trend to smaller families. But in large part it reflected the growth in average income in the economy.

Historically, the greatest source of relief from poverty has come through economic growth.

If productivity growth can be maintained at 2 percent per year, living standards will double again in the next 35 years. This will surely reduce further the number of people living in poverty. But it is a mistake to expect too much from growth, first because productivity growth has slowed, and second because some forms of poverty seem immune to growth.

Today, after a century of rapid growth, the poor are still with us. It is safe to predict that if we rely only on growth of average income, they will be with us a century hence. For the poverty problem is no longer rooted in low *average* productivity, but in the fact that particular groups have been left behind in the general rise of living standards. It is little consolation—indeed it might even add to the

---

TABLE 20–1 INCIDENCE OF POVERTY AMONG CANADIAN FAMILIES BY SELECTED CHARACTERISTICS, 1981

Characteristics	Percentage of families falling below the poverty line
All families	12.0
Place of residence	
Metropolitan	11.2
Other urban	12.2
Rural	13.1
Region	
Atlantic	16.6
Quebec	14.8
Ontario	9.9
Prairies	11.3
British Columbia	9.4
Number of children under 16 years	
0 or 1	11.2
2 or 3	17.2
4 or more	25.1
Age of head of family	
Under 25	22.7
25–54	10.8
55–64	10.5
65 or over	14.6
Sex of head of family	
Male	8.9
Female	38.1
Employment status of head of family	
In labor force	7.9
Not in labor force	27.3

Source: Statistics Canada, 13–206.

Location, family structure, and education all affect the likelihood of poverty. The percentages show the fraction of families in the designated class whose incomes fall below the poverty level.

gall—that they are poor in an increasingly affluent society. Nevertheless, today's poor are materially better off than were many people living *above* the poverty level a decade ago.

As powerful as the force of a rising trend growth of average income can be, it can be temporarily swamped by sharp cyclical swings in national income. The serious recession of 1982 forced many households into poverty who had never before experienced poverty or who had escaped the poverty level during the previous two decades.

Causes of Poverty

The causes of poverty are various. The fact that many of the poor are over age 65 shows that age and illness force people out of the labor market. Other important groups suffering poverty include the rural poor, who strive in vain to earn a decent living from marginal or submarginal farmlands; the urban working poor, who simply lack the skills to command a wage high enough to support themselves and their families above the poverty level; the immobile poor, who are trapped by age and outdated skills in areas and occupations where the demand for their services is declining faster than their number; and the minority poor.

There is no single answer to the question: What causes poverty in the midst of plenty? It is partly a result of mental and physical handicaps, partly of low motivation, and partly of the raw deal that fate gives to some. Partly it is a result of current and past prejudice. Partly it is a result of unwillingness or inability to invest in the kind of human capital that does pay off in the long run. Partly it is a result of the market's valuing the particular abilities an individual does have at such a low price that, even in good health and with full-time employment, the income that can be earned leaves that person below the poverty line.

The extent of poverty is also affected greatly by the performance of the economy. A recession, with its increase in unemployment, pushes additional families into poverty. (The recession of 1981–1982 did this to thousands of Canadian families.) Inflation continually erodes the resources of those on fixed incomes, and the recent rapid inflation outstripped increases in welfare payments and the earnings of many families at or near the poverty level.

Types of Poverty

Fluctuations in the number classified as poor as a result of swings in the economy highlight the important distinction between the *occasionally poor* and the *persistently poor*. It is much easier to withstand six months (or even several years) of poverty due to a bout of unemployment or illness than it is to be permanently poor. For the latter condition erodes hope and warps one's entire outlook on life. While many of those officially classified as being in poverty at any time are only temporarily poor, many of the rest are virtually permanently poor.

POLICIES TO ALLEVIATE POVERTY

Eliminating poverty is easier than eliminating cancer, for which a cure is as yet unknown. For less than $4 billion per year in 1982 dollars, every family now below the poverty level could be given a sufficient income supplement to bring it to that level. Government could, in other words, close the poverty gap. Although $4 billion is a lot of money, it is less than 5 percent of total government spending, and it represents only about 1 percent of the total income earned in the nation.

Surprisingly perhaps, a good deal of the debate about attacking poverty does not concern whether we can afford it or how best to do it, but whether we *ought* to do it.

The Case Against an All-Out Attack

Everyone concedes that there are poor people who deserve to be helped. They are those who despite their best efforts have not been able to escape the ravages of illness, desertion, age, or obsolescence. There are as well the helpless children of the poor, who should not be made to suffer endlessly for the failings or misfortunes of their parents. But there are also the "undeserving poor," those who could work but will not as long as someone else will support them and their families.

Disincentive effects. Not only is it unnecessary and perhaps immoral to support such people, the argument says, but their number will grow rapidly if we choose to adopt more generous programs for relieving existing poverty. Even if we could afford to eliminate poverty, the attempt to do so would be self-defeating. For, the argument continues, it would destroy the incentives of those now supporting themselves just above the level at which the government would support them. They would stop working and end up on welfare as quickly as others were raised above the poverty level.

These critics point to the decline in the work ethic that accompanies increased welfare payments, unemployment compensation, and the issuance of food stamps. There is some factual basis for this argument. Today many gladly accept unemployment compensation, welfare payments, and free goods and services—and indeed expect them, as a matter not of charity but of basic rights. Almost every program has had its scandals, and all too many people can identify others who are relying on public assistance when in fact they could support themselves.

A second disincentive effect is on the beneficiaries of government welfare payments: Children who grow up knowing they have a welfare safety net under them may not develop the attitudes or gain the skills needed to climb above the level of the net. This effect may be particularly noticeable in those who, because of the limitations of their abilities, could never in any case hope to climb far above that level.

A third possible disincentive effect relates to those who will be asked to pay the extra taxes that must be levied if welfare spending increases. As more people go on welfare, fewer will be left to pay the taxes, so tax rates must rise. If, in response, taxpayers work less, the total amount of income available for redistribution will shrink.

The important question is whether such effects are merely occasional horror stories or whether they are frequent and quantitatively significant. Opponents of an all-out attack on poverty believe that these magnitudes are, and will prove to be, very large.

Opportunity costs. Some maintain that we cannot afford to eliminate poverty, given all the competing uses of public money. They contend that welfare spending is already at cripplingly high levels.

Advocates of the view that total government spending is already too large often argue that there are few other items over which so much discretion may be exercised. On the one hand, less could no doubt be spent on such items as defense or schools. Many believe, however, that significant cuts in these items are either impractical or undesirable.

On the other hand, a genuine option does exist with welfare expenditures. One of the few realistic hopes of keeping government spending under control, so goes this view, lies in holding a tight rein on the expansion of transfer payments and in particular eliminating payments to the dishonest, the lazy and the relatively well off, who are receiving payments without real need.

The Case for an All-Out Attack

The attack on poverty has its supporters as well as its opponents. Welfare cheaters, supporters agree, should be identified, exposed, and eliminated from the rolls wherever possible. But the abuses should not be allowed to confuse the issue. It was one thing to put up with poverty when we had no alternative; it is another to do so when we are rich enough to spend billions on cosmetics, sports, and other frills—to say nothing of space exploration and foreign "diplomacy."

The shame of poverty, the argument says, is not that of the victim but of the society that lets it continue. One great advance of modern civilization has been to lift the stigma from those who are less able and less fortunate. It is to our credit that we have replaced the poorhouse with programs of social insurance as a matter of right, not charity. To let a few cheaters plus some unsupported fears about destruction of the will to work be the excuse for not "coming to peace with poverty" is, they say, a real immorality in modern society.

Of course any scheme that reduces welfare payments by $.65 or $.75 for every dollar that the recipient earns means a 65 percent or 75 percent tax on earnings and may well provide a short-term disincentive to work. But this is the fault of the scheme, not of the people who are only responding rationally to it. Schemes that reduce this marginal disincentive feature can be designed. Moreover, the supporters argue, the possibility of disincentive effects does not prove their importance. Most people who can support themselves and their families willingly do so.

Resolving the Debate

Thus there is disagreement about the desirable direction of change in welfare expenditures. Choosing whether to expand or to contract poverty programs depends in part on value judgments of what is good and right and worth doing, and in part on positive factual assessments of what can be done and how much it will cost. Positive economic research can help to narrow the range of these uncertainties, even if it cannot dictate what we should finally do. Today a great deal of research is devoted to studying the effects of welfare expenditure on incentives—both of the recipients and of the taxpayers who must foot the bill.

The Nature of Poverty Programs

The two underlying assumptions in the development of existing programs were, first, that the able-bodied should work and, second, that heads of households should support their families whenever possible.

The traditional strategy for dealing with poverty was to provide job opportunities for all who are able to work and income-support programs for those not holding jobs.

One part of such programs provided social insur-

ance, related to work, for temporary unemployment and for retirement. A second part provided monetary and in-kind assistance to those poor who are unable to work for reasons of age, health, or family status.

Providing more and better employment opportunities. Families with an employed member have very much less chance of being below the poverty level than those without one. Thus providing job opportunities for the unemployed and for those not even looking for work is of major importance. But providing work is not a guarantee that families will escape poverty. About 40 percent of poor families have a full-time working head; for these *working poor,* the problem is often the lack of skills that command a wage that will allow them to rise above the poverty level rather than an absence of demand for the skills they have. Programs of education, training, and retraining are designed to lessen these causes of poverty by providing better job opportunities. Such programs have proven both expensive and limited in the number of persons they can reach. Educational opportunities for the children of the poor may free them from inheriting poverty, but such progress is measured from generation to generation, not from year to year.

Social insurance. Old age pensions have been provided by the federal government since 1927. Additional retirement income is provided by the Canada Pension Plan, which is financed through contributions of participants.

In the 1970s the federal and provincial governments increased the social safety net. The unemployment insurance program was expanded, family allowances were tripled, pensions for low-income senior citizens were increased, and a spousal allowance was introduced for 60- to 64-year-olds married to low-income pensioners. However, the current level of benefits is still below that necessary to provide an income above the poverty line.

Since, in 1970, nearly half of the pensioners had very limited or no other sources of income, these programs mitigate but do not eliminate poverty among the old. For those of working age, unemployment insurance provides protection against temporary loss of earnings, and the joint federal-provincial hospital and medical insurance programs make health services available to all Canadians regardless of their income.

Provincial welfare systems. Because of strong constitutional and political traditions, welfare payments to the poor in general—as opposed to the unemployed or retired—have generally been left in the hands of the provinces and municipalities. Because of the inadequate and varying financial resources available to the lower levels of government, the Canada Assistance Plan was introduced in 1966, giving the federal government a share in the cost of welfare programs. Effective control remains with the provinces, but 50 percent of the financing comes from the federal government. Many problems remain, however.

According to the *Report of the Special Senate Committee on Poverty* (1971), "Apart from programs of social insurance, such as the Canada Pension Plan and the federal categorical programs such as Old Age Security, the welfare system really comprises the ten different provincial systems plus the welfare systems of the Territories. What they have in common is a record of failure and insufficiency, of bureaucratic rigidities that often result in the degradation, humiliation, and alienation of recipients."

The committee found that there is wide variation in benefit structures among the provinces. For example, at the time of this report, a family of four in Hull received $100 a month less in general welfare assistance than a similar family across the river in Ottawa. Moreover, none reaches any accepted poverty line.

Improvements in provincial programs appear to be hindered by three major problems. First, there is a scarcity of financial resources, particularly in the poorer provinces. Second, there is no consensus about the standard of living that should be provided. The third problem involves the effects of assistance levels on work incentives and the extent to which administrative procedures are necessary to prevent abuses. These questions are under study, and definite action may be some time off.

Current issues. The dramatic rise in the incidence of poverty during the recession of 1982 highlighted some serious deficiencies in the existing social safety net. One pocket of concentrated poverty is among very old females, especially widows. Various reforms of the pension system (such as increased survivor benefits) have been proposed, and the February 1984 federal budget raised payments under the Guaranteed Income Supplement by $50 a month.

A second deficiency that has been criticized is provision for children of the unemployed. The poverty rate for one- and two-parent families has increased. Provisions under the unemployment insurance act for those with dependents had been cut back in anticipation of a federal-provincial initiative for a comprehensive income supplement program for all low-income families. So far, no agreement has been reached, although in 1978 Ottawa did introduce the refundable child tax credit to help low-income families. One by-product of this was to further complicate the tax treatment of children: The combination of family allowance, a deduction for children, and the child tax credit have a very uncertain net distributional effect. One proposed reform is to integrate these three programs. A more comprehensive proposal, the so-called negative income tax, is discussed in Chapter 24.

SUMMARY

1. The concept of poverty involves both relative and absolute levels of income and reflects the aspirations of society as well as the income needed for subsistence alone. Today roughly 12 percent of all Canadians are classified as living in poverty. Since total poverty is small relative to national income, the possibility exists of eradicating poverty in Canada.

2. Economic growth, though it has led to a reduction of poverty, will by itself never eliminate it, for many of those in need do not share directly in the fruits of growth.

3. The incidence of poverty is much greater among some groups than among others, particularly those who are not employed and who are relatively uneducated. But there are many poor among the working, and poverty is appreciable in all ages and among those who have had considerable education.

4. The desirability of pursuing antipoverty policies is a matter of current debate. Some people believe that it is possible and desirable to make further major reductions in poverty now. They place particular importance on income supplements to the poor regardless of why they are poor. Others believe that further attacks on poverty are undesirable both because of the burdens such government expenditures place on the economy and because of the disincentive effects generated by welfare programs.

5. Methods used to reduce poverty include retraining programs intended to match people with available jobs; social insurance, which helps to meet the risks of such problems as ill health, unemployment, and retirement; and public assistance designed to serve those ineligible for other programs.

TOPICS FOR REVIEW

Poverty
Correlates of poverty
Occasional poverty and persistent poverty
Possible disincentive effects of alleviating poverty
Social insurance versus income assistance
Alternative policies toward poverty

DISCUSSION QUESTIONS

1. In what ways are the problems of poverty in Canada likely to be different from the problems of poverty in an underdeveloped poor country, such as Bangladesh? In what ways are they easier to solve in one place than in the other?

2. Suppose that your objectives are (first) to eradicate poverty and (second) to reduce unemployment. Evaluate the probable effectiveness of each of the following in meeting each objective.
   a. Increasing welfare payments
   b. Increased aid to education
   c. Creating a program of public works to hire the poor
   d. Ending employment discrimination against natives

3. A proposed program of rental allowances to the poor has been attacked in Parliament as giving money to slumlords instead of to the poor and thereby worsening the distribution of income. Evaluate this position. Argue the case for and against assistance that is tied to a particular kind of expenditure rather than giving the money to the poor to spend as they think best.

4. Comment on each of the following headlines in terms of the matters discussed in this chapter:
   a. "Working poor are victims of Reaganomics"
   b. "On welfare or working: poor is poor"
   c. "Few provinces seek to ease effects of cuts for poor"
   d. "Economic recovery decreases number on welfare"
   e. "War on poverty is difficult to call off"

5. It has been estimated that it costs employers $20,000 to move an executive from one city to another. Is this a barrier to labor mobility? Despite the cost some 200,000 executives move (at company expense) every year. Is this consistent with the theory of distribution? Executives involved in the moves were asked whether they liked having to move; 69 percent said they did not, yet 78 percent said they could have remained in their old jobs if they had so chosen. Are these replies consistent with one another and with the theory of distribution?

PART SIX
INTERNATIONAL TRADE

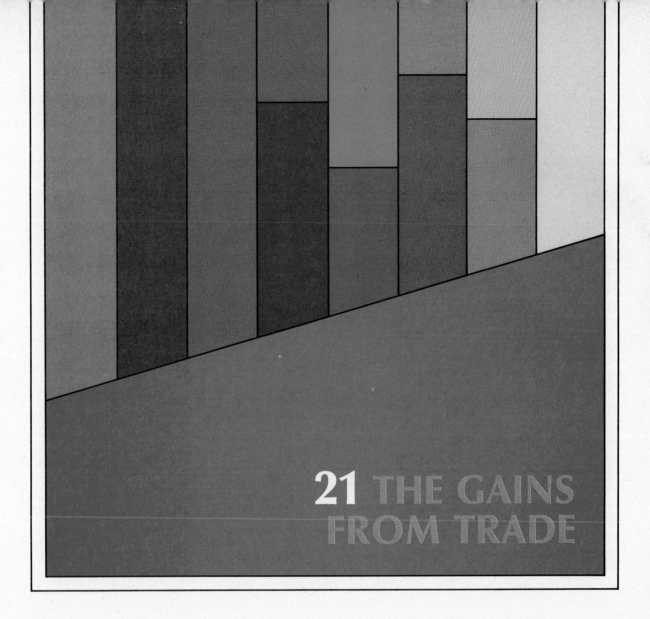

21 THE GAINS FROM TRADE

Canadians buy Volkswagens, Germans take holidays in Italy, Italians buy spices from Tanzania, Africans import oil from Kuwait, Arabs buy Japanese cameras, the Japanese depend heavily on American soybeans as a source of food, and Americans import hydroelectricity from Canada. *International trade* refers to exchanges of goods and services that take place across international boundaries.

The founders of modern economics addressed many foreign trade problems. The great eighteenth century British philosopher and economist David Hume, one of the first to work out the theory of the price system as a control mechanism, developed his concepts mainly in terms of prices in foreign trade. Adam Smith in his *Wealth of Nations* (1776) attacked government restriction of trade. David Ricardo in 1817 developed the basic theory of the gains from trade that is studied in this chapter. The repeal of the Corn Laws—tariffs on the importation of grains into England—and the transformation of Britain during the nineteenth century from a country of high tariffs to one of complete free trade were to a significant extent the result of agitation by economists whose theories of the gains from trade led them to condemn all tariffs.

In this chapter we explore the fundamental question of what is gained by international trade. In Chapter 22 we shall deal with the pros and cons of interfering with the free flow of such trade. In Chapter 22 we shall also focus on the importance of international trade for the Canadian economy, and discuss the issues that arise from Canadian policies toward such trade.

SOURCES OF THE GAINS FROM TRADE

The advantages realized as a result of trade are usually called the **gains from trade.** The source of such gains is most easily visualized by considering the differences between a world with trade and a world without it. Although politicians often regard foreign trade differently from domestic trade, economists from Adam Smith on have argued that the causes and consequences of international trade are simply an extension of the principles governing domestic trade. What is the advantage of trade among individuals, among groups, among regions, or among countries?

Interpersonal, Interregional, and International Trade

Consider trade among individuals. If there were no such trade, each person would have to be self-sufficient; each would have to produce all the food, clothing, shelter, medical services, entertainment, and luxuries he or she consumed. Although a world of individual self-sufficiency is wildly unreal, it does not take much imagination to realize that living standards would be very low in such a world.

Trade between individuals allows people to spe-cialize in those activities they can do well and to buy from others the goods and services they cannot easily produce. A bad carpenter who is a good doctor can specialize in medicine, providing a physician's services not only for his or her own family but also for, say, an excellent carpenter without the training or the ability to practice medicine. Thus trade and specialization are intimately connected. Without trade everyone must be self-sufficient. With trade everyone can specialize in what he or she does well and satisfy other needs by trading.

The same principles apply to regions. Without interregional trade, each region is forced to be self-sufficient. With such trade, plains regions can specialize in growing grain, mountain regions in mining and lumbering, and regions with abundant power in manufacturing. Cool regions can produce wheat and other crops that thrive in temperate climates, and hot regions can grow such tropical crops as bananas, sugar, and coffee.

To generalize, the living standards of the inhabitants of all regions will be higher when each region specializes in producing the commodities in which it has some natural or acquired advantage and obtains other products by trade, than when all regions seek to be self-sufficient.

The same principle also applies to nations. A national boundary does not usually define an area that is naturally self-sufficient. Nations, like regions or persons, can gain from specialization and the international trade that must accompany it. Specialization means that in any given region or country, more of the goods in which production is specialized are produced than residents wish to consume, while for other goods that residents desire, little or no domestic production is available.

International trade is necessary to achieve the gains international specialization makes possible.

This discussion suggests one important possible gain from trade.

With trade, each individual, region, or nation is able to concentrate on producing goods and services which it produces efficiently while trading to obtain goods and services that it does not produce efficiently.

Because specialization and trade go hand in hand—there is no motivation to achieve the gains from specialization without being able to trade the goods produced for goods desired—the term *gains from trade* is used to embrace both.

Gains from trade have two main sources. First, at given levels of productive efficiency, total output is larger if everyone specializes in producing what he or she is best at. Second, since large-scale production tends to be more productive than small-scale production (that is, it has a higher output per unit of labor and capital used), it pays countries to specialize in order to reap the economies of large-scale production. This second source is more important for smaller countries such as those of Europe than for very large countries such as the United States or the USSR. We will start by discussing the first source. While it is convenient to use an example involving only two countries and two products, the principle applies to cases involving many products and many countries.

The Gains from Specialization

Concentrating on the gains from specialization, we assume for the moment that each region can produce goods at certain levels of productivity independent of the scale of production. In these circumstances, what is the gain from regional specialization?

A Special Case: Absolute Advantage

The gains from trade are clear when there is a simple situation involving absolute advantage. **Absolute advantage** concerns the quantities of a single product that can be produced using the same quantity of resources in two different regions. *One region is said to have an absolute advantage over another in the production of commodity X when an equal quantity of resources can produce more X in the first region than in the second.*

Suppose region A has an absolute advantage over B in one commodity, while region B has an absolute advantage over A in another. In such a case of reciprocal absolute advantage, the total pro-

duction of both regions can be increased (relative to a situation of autarky) if each specializes in the commodity in which it has the absolute advantage.

Table 21-1 provides a simple example. In the example, total world production of both wheat and cloth increases when each country produces more of the good in which it has an absolute advantage: As a result, there is more wheat *and* more cloth for the same use of resources.

TABLE 21–1 GAINS FROM SPECIALIZATION WITH ABSOLUTE ADVANTAGE

Part A: Amounts of wheat and cloth that can be produced with one unit of resources in Canada and England

	Wheat (bushels)	Cloth (yards)
Canada	10	6
England	5	10

Part B: Changes resulting from the transfer of one unit of Canadian resources into wheat and one unit of British resources into cloth

	Wheat (bushels)	Cloth (yards)
Canada	+ 10	− 6
England	− 5	+ 10
World	+ 5	+ 4

When there is a reciprocal absolute advantage, specialization makes it possible to produce more of both commodities. The top half of the table shows the production of wheat and cloth that can be achieved in each country by using one unit of resources: Canada can produce 10 bushels of wheat or 6 yards of cloth, while England can produce 5 bushels of wheat or 10 yards of cloth. The lower half shows the changes in production caused by moving one unit of resources out of cloth and into wheat production in Canada and moving one unit of resources in the opposite direction in England. There is an increase in world production of 5 bushels of wheat and 4 yards of cloth; worldwide, there are gains from specialization. In this example, the more resources are transferred into wheat production in Canada and cloth production in England, the larger the gains will be.

The gains from *specialization* make possible gains from *trade*. England is producing more cloth and Canada more wheat than when they were self-sufficient. Canada is producing more wheat and less cloth than Canadian consumers wish to buy, and England is producing more cloth and less wheat than English consumers wish to buy. If consumers in both countries are to get cloth and wheat in the desired proportions, Canada must export wheat to England and import cloth from England.

A First General Statement: Comparative Advantage

When each country has an absolute advantage over the other in a commodity, the gains from trade are clear. If each country produces a commodity that it produces more efficiently than the other, world production will be higher than if each country tries to be self-sufficient. But what if Canada can produce both wheat and cloth more efficiently than England? In essence this was David Ricardo's question, posed over 160 years ago. His answer underlies the theory of comparative advantage, which is still accepted by economists as a valid statement of the potential gains from trade.

To start with, assume that Canadian efficiency increases tenfold above the levels recorded in the previous example while English efficiency remains unchanged (see Table 21-2). It might appear that Canada, which is better at producing both wheat and cloth than is England, has nothing to gain by trading with such an inefficient foreign country! But it *does* have something to gain, as shown in Table 21-2. Even though Canada is 10 times as efficient as in the situation of Table 21-1, it is still possible to increase world production of both wheat and cloth by having Canada produce more wheat and less cloth, and England produce more cloth and less wheat.

There is still a gain from specialization. Although Canada has an absolute advantage over England in the production of both wheat and cloth, its margin of advantage differs in the two commodities. Canada can produce 20 times as much wheat as England by using the same quantity of

TABLE 21–2 GAINS FROM SPECIALIZATION WITH COMPARATIVE ADVANTAGE

Part A: Amounts of wheat and cloth that can be produced with one unit of resources in Canada and England

	Wheat (bushels)	Cloth (yards)
Canada	100	60
England	5	10

Part B: Changes resulting from the transfer of one-tenth of one unit of Canadian resources into wheat and one unit of British resources into cloth

	Wheat (bushels)	Cloth (yards)
Canada	+ 10	− 6
England	− 5	+ 10
World	+ 5	+ 4

When there is comparative advantage, specialization makes it possible to produce more of both commodities. The productivity of English resources is left unchanged from Table 21-1; that of Canadian resources is increased tenfold. England no longer has an absolute advantage in producing either commodity. Total production of both commodities can nonetheless be increased by specialization. Moving one-tenth of one unit of Canadian resources out of cloth and into wheat and moving one unit of resources in the opposite direction in England causes world production of wheat to rise by 5 bushels and cloth by 4 yards. Reciprocal absolute advantage is not necessary for gains from trade.

resources, but only 6 times as much cloth. Canada is said to have a *comparative advantage* in the production of wheat and a comparative disadvantage in the production of cloth. (This statement implies another: England has a comparative disadvantage in the production of wheat, in which it is 20 times less efficient than Canada, and a comparative advantage in the production of cloth, in which it is only 6 times less efficient.)

A key proposition in the theory of international trade is this:

The gains from specialization and trade depend on the pattern of comparative, not absolute, advantage.

A comparison of Tables 21-1 and 21-2 refutes the notion that the absolute *levels* of efficiency of two areas determine the gains from specialization. The key is that the margin of advantage one area has over the other must differ between commodities. As long as this margin differs, total world production can be increased when each area specializes in the production of that commodity in which it has a comparative advantage.

Comparative advantage is necessary as well as sufficient for gains from trade. This is illustrated in Table 21-3, showing Canada with an absolute advantage in both commodities and neither country

with a comparative advantage over the other in the production of either commodity. Canada is 10 times as efficient as England in the production of both wheat and cloth. Now there is no way to increase the production of both commodities by reallocating resources within Canada and within England. The lower half of the table provides one example of a resource shift which illustrates this. Absolute advantage without comparative advantage does not lead to gains from trade.

A Second General Statement: Opportunity Costs

Much of the previous argument has used the concept of a unit of resources. It assumes that units of resources can be equated across countries, so that statements such as "Canada can produce 10 times as much wheat with the same quantity of resources as England" are meaningful. Measurement of the real-resource cost of producing commodities poses many difficulties. If, for example, England uses land, labor, and capital in proportions different from those used in Canada, it may not be clear which country gets more output "per unit of resource input." Fortunately the proposition about the gains from trade can be restated without reference to units of resources.

To do this go back to the examples of Tables 21-1 and 21-2. Calculate the opportunity cost of wheat and cloth in the two countries. When resources are assumed to be fully employed, the only way to produce more of one commodity is to reallocate resources and produce less of the other commodity. Table 21-1 shows that the opportunity cost of producing one unit of wheat is 0.6 units of cloth while the opportunity cost of producing one unit of cloth is 1.67 units of wheat.

These data are summarized in Table 21-4. The table also shows that in England the opportunity cost of one unit of wheat is two units of cloth foregone, while the opportunity cost of a unit of cloth is 0.50 units of wheat. Table 21-2 also gives rise to the opportunity costs in Table 21-4.

The sacrifice of cloth involved in producing wheat is much lower in Canada than it is in En-

TABLE 21–3 ABSENCE OF GAINS FROM SPECIALIZATION WHERE THERE IS NO COMPARATIVE ADVANTAGE

Part A: Amounts of wheat and cloth that can be produced with one unit of resources in Canada and England

	Wheat (bushels)	Cloth (yards)
Canada	100	60
England	10	6

Part B: Changes resulting from the transfer of one unit of Canadian resources into wheat and 10 units of British resources into cloth

	Wheat (bushels)	Cloth (yards)
Canada	+100	− 60
England	−100	+ 60
World	0	0

Where there is no comparative advantage, reallocation of resources within each country can increase the production of both commodities. In this example Canada has the same absolute advantage over England in each commodity (tenfold). There is no comparative advantage, and world production cannot be increased by reallocating resources in both countries. Therefore specialization does not increase total output.

	Wheat	Cloth
Canada	0.6 yards cloth	1.67 bushels wheat
England	2.0 yards cloth	0.50 bushels wheat

Comparative advantages can always be expressed in terms of opportunity costs that differ between countries. These opportunity costs can be obtained from Table 21-1 or Table 21-2. The English opportunity cost of one unit of wheat is obtained by dividing the cloth output of one unit of English resources by the wheat output. The result shows that 2 yards of cloth must be sacrificed for every extra unit of wheat produced by transferring English resources out of cloth production and into wheat. The other three cost figures are obtained in a similar manner.

TABLE 21–5 GAINS FROM SPECIALIZATION
WHEN OPPORTUNITY COSTS
DIFFER

Changes resulting from each country's producing one more unit of a commodity in which it has the lower opportunity cost		
	Wheat (bushels)	Cloth (yards)
Canada	+1.0	−0.6
England	−0.5	+1.0
World	+0.5	+0.4

Whenever opportunity costs differ between countries, specialization can increase the production of both commodities. These calculations show that there are gains from specialization given the opportunity costs of Table 21-4. To produce one more bushel of wheat, Canada must sacrifice 0.6 yards of cloth. To produce one more yard of cloth, England must sacrifice 0.5 bushels of wheat. Making both changes raises world production of both wheat and cloth.

gland. World wheat production can be increased if Canada rather than England produces it. Looking at cloth production we can see that the loss of wheat involved in producing one unit of cloth is lower in England than in Canada. England is a lower (opportunity) cost producer of cloth than is Canada. World cloth production can be increased if England rather than Canada produces it. This situation is shown in Table 21-5.

The gains from trade arise from differing opportunity costs in the two countries. The gains from trade are further illustrated in Box 21-1 on pages 354–355.

The conclusions about the gains from trade drawn from the hypothetical example of two countries and two commodities may be generalized:

1. Country A has a **comparative advantage** over country B in producing a commodity when the opportunity cost (in terms of some other commodity) of production in country A is lower. This implies, however, that it has a comparative disadvantage in the other commodity.
2. Opportunity costs depend on the relative costs of producing two commodities, not on absolute costs. (Notice that the data in both Tables 21-1 and 21-2 give rise to the opportunity costs in Table 21-4.)
3. When opportunity costs are the same in all countries, there is no comparative advantage and no possibility of gains from specialization and trade. (You can prove this for yourself by calculating the opportunity costs implied by the data in Table 21-3.)
4. When opportunity costs differ in any two countries, and both countries are producing both commodities, it is always possible to increase production of both commodities by a suitable reallocation of resources within each country. (This proposition is illustrated in Table 21-5.)

The Gains from Large-Scale Operation

So far we have assumed that unit costs are the same whatever the scale of output. In this case there are gains from specialization and trade as long as there are interregional differences in opportunity costs.

If costs vary with the level of output, *additional* sources of gain are possible.

Economies of Scale[1]

Generally real production costs, measured in terms of resources used, fall as the scale of output increases. The larger the scale of operations, the more efficiently large-scale machinery can be used and the more a detailed division of tasks among workers is possible. Smaller countries such as Canada, France, and Israel whose domestic markets are not large enough to exploit economies of scale would find it prohibitively expensive to become self-sufficient. They would have to produce a little bit of everything at very high cost.

Trade allows smaller countries to specialize and produce a few commodities at high enough levels of output to reap the available economies of scale.

Bigger countries such as the United States and the USSR have markets large enough to allow the production of most items at home at a scale of output great enough to obtain the available economies of scale. For them, the gains from trade arise mainly from specializing in commodities in which they have a comparative advantage.

Learning by Doing

The discussion so far has assumed that costs vary only with the level of output. They may also vary with the length of time a product has been produced.

Early economists placed great importance on a factor that we call learning by doing. They believed that as regions specialized in particular tasks, workers and managers would become more efficient in performing them. As people acquire expertise, or know-how, costs tend to fall. Much modern empirical work suggests that this effect really does happen.

If it occurs in our example, output of cloth per worker will rise in England as England becomes

[1] See the discussion in Chapter 13, especially page 168, and also Box 3-1 on page 31.

more specialized in that commodity, and the same will happen to output of wheat per worker in Canada. This is, of course, a gain over and above that which occurs when costs are constant.

As discussed in Box 21-2 on pages 356–357, learning by doing has a number of interesting implications arising from its ability to change a nation's comparative advantage.

Increased Competition

In small- or medium-sized countries such as Canada, one additional advantage of freer international trade is the increased scope for competition that it offers. For any product that has large-scale economies, the local Canadian market is too small to support more than a very few firms. In autarky Canadian manufacturing would be characterized by oligopolies and monopolies. But with international trade the one or two Canadian firms would be competing with firms in, say, France, England, Japan, Germany, and the United States. This makes for more competition, which will bring benefits to consumers in terms of lower prices, wider choice, and possibly more dynamic change in product specification and cost reduction.

HOW THE GAINS FROM TRADE ARE DIVIDED AMONG NATIONS: THE TERMS OF TRADE

So far we have seen that world production can be increased when countries specialize in the production of the commodities in which they have a comparative advantage and then trade with one another. How will these gains from specialization and trade be shared between countries? The division of the gain depends on the terms at which trade takes place. The **terms of trade** are defined as the quantity of imported goods that can be obtained per unit of goods exported.

In the example of Table 21-4, the Canadian domestic opportunity cost of one unit of wheat is 0.6 yards of cloth: If in Canada resources are trans-

BOX 21–1 **THE GAINS FROM TRADE ILLUSTRATED GRAPHICALLY**

By allowing the goods consumed by a nation to differ from the goods it produces, international trade actually increases the consumption possibilities open to the nation. How this works can be seen in two distinct stages.

Stage 1: Given Production

The first stage is straightforward and is shown using the production-possibility boundary in (i) in the figure. (The production-possibility boundary was first introduced in Figure 1-2, page 8.)

In autarky the country's consumption possibilities are given by the production-possibility set. The economy must consume the same bundle of goods that it produces. For example, if production is at point a, consumption must also be at a. The bundle of goods consumed is then q_1 of good X and q_2 of good Y.

When trade is allowed, a wide variety of consumption combinations is possible, including the no-trade option. In part (ii) of the figure, production remains fixed at point a, but now the possibility of international trade means that consumption need not also be at point a. Good Y can be exchanged for good X in the international market. The consumption possibilities are now shown by the line tt drawn through point a. The slope of this line indicates the world terms of trade expressed as the *price of good X/*

price of good Y. This tells us the quantity of Y that exchanges for (i.e., has the same value as) a unit of X on the international market.

Although production is fixed at a, consumption can now be anywhere on the line tt. For example, the consumption point could be at b by exporting ac units of Y and importing cb units of X. Consumption could also be at point d by importing ed units of Y and exporting ae units of X.

Stage II: Variable Production

So far we held production constant at a. The second reason for the expansion of the country's consumption possibilities is that, with trade, the production bundle may be altered in response to international prices. This is illustrated in (iii) in the figure. The consumption possibility set is shifted to the line $t't'$ by changing production from a to f and thereby increasing the country's degree of specialization in good Y. For any point on the original consumption-possibility set, tt, there are points on the new set, $t't'$, which allow more consumption of both goods. Compare, for example, points b and g. Notice also that, except at the zero-trade point f, the new consumption-possibility set lies everywhere above the production-possibility curve. Consumption bundles that cannot be produced domestically are made available by trade.

---

ferred from wheat to cloth, 0.6 yards of cloth are gained for every bushel of wheat given up. But if Canada can obtain its cloth by trade on more favorable terms, it pays to produce and export wheat to pay for cloth imports. Suppose, for example, that international prices are such that 1 yard of cloth exchanges for (i.e., is equal in value to) 1

bushel of wheat. At those prices, Canadians can obtain more cloth per unit of wheat exported than they can by moving resources out of wheat into cloth production at home. Therefore the terms of trade favor selling wheat and buying cloth on international markets.

Similarly, in the example of Table 21-4, English

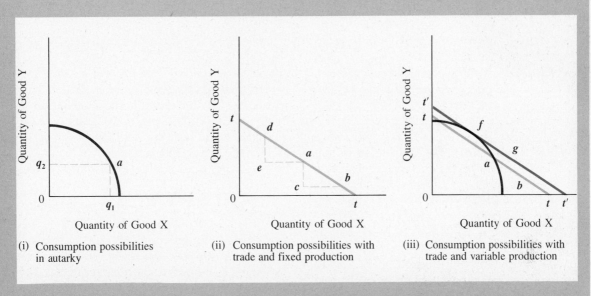

(i) Consumption possibilities in autarky

(ii) Consumption possibilities with trade and fixed production

(iii) Consumption possibilities with trade and variable production

Summary of the Effects

International trade thus leads to an expansion of the set of goods that could be consumed in the economy by (1) allowing the bundle of goods consumed to differ from the bundle produced, and (2) permitting a profitable change in the pattern of production. The key to these gains is that international trade allows the separation of production decisions from consumption decisions. Without international trade, the choice of which bundle of goods to produce is the same thing as the choice of which bundle to consume. With international trade, the consumption and production bundles can each be altered to reflect the relative value placed on goods by international markets.

In our example, the second source of gain occurred when the production of good Y was increased and the production of good X decreased. Economists refer to such production changes as "exploiting the country's comparative advantage." The benefits that arise in moving from the autarky postion at point *a* in (i) in the figure to the trading position in (iii) are *the gains from trade*.

consumers gain when they can obtain wheat abroad at any terms of trade more favorable than 0.5 bushels of wheat imported per unit of cloth exported. If the terms of trade are 1 bushel of wheat for 1 yard of cloth, the terms of trade favor English traders' buying wheat and selling cloth on international markets. Here both England and Canada gain from trade: Each can obtain the commodity in which it has a comparative disadvantage at a lower opportunity cost through international trade than through domestic production.

Because actual international trade involves many countries and many commodities, the actual terms of trade is computed as an index number:

BOX 21–2 MODERN DEVELOPMENTS: DYNAMIC COMPARATIVE ADVANTAGE AND PRODUCT DIFFERENTIATION

The classical theory of the gains from trade assumes given cost structures and hence a given pattern of international comparative advantage. It leads to the policy advice that a government interested in maximizing its citizens' standard of living should allow production to be specialized in those goods where it currently has a comparative advantage. When all countries follow this advice, the theory predicts that each will be specialized in a narrow range of distinct products. Canadians will be hewers of wood and drawers of water, Americans will be factory workers, Central Americans will be banana growers, and so on.

We shall now see, however, that modern views on comparative advantage have changed significantly in the light of recent experience.

Modern Comparative Advantage

The old visible "smokestack" industries such as automobiles and steel had heavy investment in fixed capital. They are everywhere in decline in the developed countries. New industries often depend more on human capital than on fixed physical capital. The skills of a computer designer, a videogame programmer, a sound mix technician or a rock star are acquired by education and on-the-job training. Natural endowments of energy and raw materials cannot account for Britain's prominence in modern pop music nor for the leadership in ideas of Silicon Valley in California. Comparative advantages are certainly there, but they were acquired, not nature-given—and they change. Hence the idea of dynamic rather than static comparative advantage.

This idea has a number of important implications:

Policy makers need not accept current comparative advantages as given. Through such means as education and tax incentives, they can seek to develop new comparative advantages.

Countries cannot complacently assume that an existing comparative advantage will persist. Poor education policies, the wrong tax incentives, or policies that discourage risk taking can lead to the rapid erosion of a country's comparative advantage.

Specialization is not just a means to exploit current comparative advantage. It is a means through new acquired skill and learning by

---

$$\text{Index of terms of trade} = \frac{\text{Index of export prices}}{\text{Index of import prices}} \times 100$$

A rise in the index is referred to as a *favorable* change in a country's terms of trade. A favorable change means that more can be imported per unit of goods exported than previously. For example, when Canada's export price index rises from 100 to 120 while its import price index rises from 100 to 110, the terms of trade index rises from 100 to 109. At the new terms of trade a unit of exports will buy 9 percent more imports than before the price changes occurred.

A decrease in the index of the terms of trade, called an *unfavorable* change, means the country can import less in return for any given amount of exports or, what is the same, it must export more to pay for any given amount of imports. For example, the sharp rise in oil prices in the 1970s led to large unfavorable shifts in the terms of trade of oil-importing countries, including Canada.

doing of developing and increasing comparative advantages.

Product Diversity

When the European Common Market (now the European Community) was set up in the 1950s, economists thought that specialization would occur according to the classical theory of comparative advantage, with one country specializing in cars, another in refrigerators, another in fashion clothes, another in shoes, and so on. This is not the way it worked out. Today one can buy French, English, Italian, and German fashion goods, cars, shoes, appliances, and a host of other goods in London, Paris, Bonn, and Rome. Boats loaded with Swedish furniture bound for London pass boats loaded with English furniture bound for Stockholm, and so on *ad infinitum*.

What free European trade did was to allow an enormous proliferation of differentiated products with different countries specializing in different product lines. Consumers voted with their money to show that they valued this enormous increase in the range of choice among differentiated products.

This has a number of implications:

Product specialization is the key to success in international trade.

Import substitution—telling countries to develop domestic industries that would eliminate many lines of imports—is disastrous advice. (Such advice is commonly given to emerging countries.)

Countries—even small ones—typically face downward-sloping demand curves for their products. Holland faces a perfectly elastic demand for its grain products, since they are not differentiated from the grains produced in other countries, whose prices are all set on world markets. But Holland faces a downward-sloping demand curve for its furniture. Dutch furniture is different from Danish, Scandinavian, or French furniture, and the price of Dutch furniture can rise or fall relative to the price of these other furnitures without demand suddenly changing from infinite (Dutch prices below other prices) to zero (Dutch prices above other prices).

SUMMARY

1. The sources of the gains from trade between any two entities—individuals, regions, or nations—are the same.

2. One country (or region or individual) has an absolute advantage over another country (or region or individual) in the production of a commodity when, with the same input of resources in each country, it can produce more of the commodity than can the other.

3. In a situation of absolute advantage, total production of both commodities will be raised if each country specializes in the production of the commodity in which it has the absolute advantage. However, the gains from trade do not require absolute advantage on the part of each country, only comparative advantage.

4. Comparative advantage is the relative advantage

one country enjoys over another in various commodities. World production of all commodities can be increased if each country transfers resources into the production of the commodities in which it has a comparative advantage.

5. The gains from trade result from different opportunity costs in different countries, which in turn lead to differences in comparative advantage.

6. The theory of the gains from trade may be stated thus: Trade allows all countries to obtain the goods in which they do not have a comparative advantage at a lower opportunity cost (in terms of units sacrificed of the commodities in which they do have a comparative advantage) than they would have to accept if they were to produce all commodities for themselves. This allows all countries to have more of all commodities than they could have if they made themselves self-sufficient.

7. As well as gaining the advantages of specialization arising from comparative advantage, a nation that engages in trade and specialization may realize the benefits of the economies of large-scale production, of learning by doing, and of increased competition.

8. The terms of trade refer to the quantity of goods that must be exported per unit of goods imported. The terms of trade determine how the gains from trade are shared. They are measured by an index number showing the ratio of export prices to import prices.

TOPICS FOR REVIEW

Interpersonal, interregional, and international specialization
Absolute advantage and comparative advantage
The gains from trade: specialization and large-scale production
Opportunity cost and comparative advantage
Terms of trade

DISCUSSION QUESTIONS

1. Adam Smith saw a close connection between the wealth of a nation and its willingness "freely to engage" in foreign trade. What is the connection?

2. Suppose that the following situation exists. Assume no tariffs, no intervention by the government, and that labor is the only factor of production.

Country	Labor cost of producing one unit of	
	Artichokes	Bikinis
Inland	$20	$40
Outland	$20	$X

Let X take different values—say $10, $20, $40, and $60. In each case in what direction will trade have to flow in order for the gains from trade to be exploited?

3. Suppose Canada had an absolute advantage in all manufactured products. Should it then ever import any manufactured products?

4. Suppose, after 1867, Canada had become two separate countries with no trade between them. What predictions would you make about the standard of living compared with what it is today? Does the fact that Canada, the United States, and Mexico are separate countries lead to a lower standard of living in the three countries than if they were united into a new country called Northica?

5. Studies of Canadian trade patterns have shown that very high wage sectors of industry are among the largest and fastest growing export sectors. Does this contradict the principle of comparative advantage?

6. Saudi Arabia has a comparative advantage over West Germany in producing oil. In what, if anything, does it have a comparative disadvantage? When Saudi Arabia lowers the price of oil, does it change the gains from trade? What does it change?

7. Predict what each of the following will do to the terms of trade of the importing country and the exporting country, other things being equal.
   a. A blight destroys a good part of the coffee beans produced in the world.
   b. The Japanese cut the price of the steel export to Canada.
   c. Competition among the maritime nations of the world leads prices of ocean transport to fall relative to the prices of the commodities transported.
   d. A general inflation of 10 percent occurs around the world.
   e. Violation of OPEC output quotas leads to a sharp fall in the price of oil.

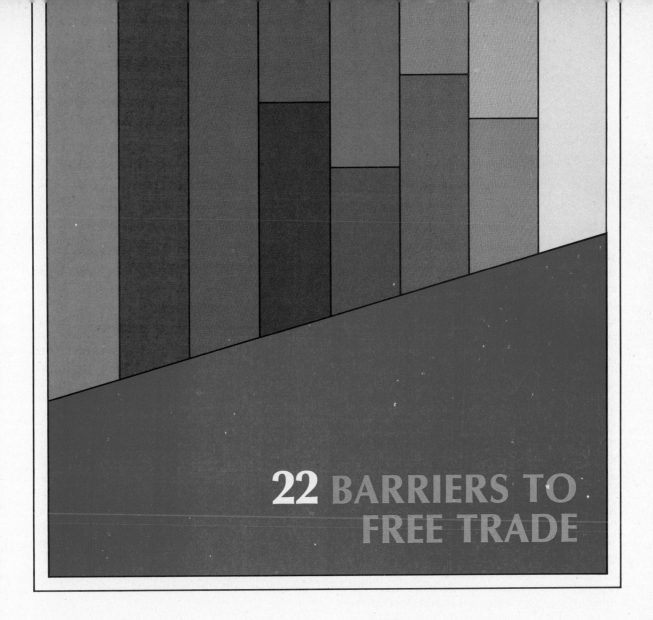

22 BARRIERS TO FREE TRADE

A government's set of policies toward international trade is referred to as its **commercial policy**. At one extreme is a policy of **free trade,** which means an absence of any form of government interference with the free flow of international trade. Any significant departure from free trade that is designed to give some protection to domestic industries from foreign competition is called **protectionism.**

THE THEORY OF COMMERCIAL POLICY

Today political debates over commercial policy are as heated as they were 200 years ago when the theory of the gains from trade was still being worked out. Should a country permit the free flow of international trade, or should it seek to protect its local producers from foreign competition? Such protection may be achieved by *tariffs*, which are taxes designed to raise the price of foreign goods, or by such *nontariff barriers* as quotas on imports and subsidies on exports that make importing difficult or impossible.

The Case for Free Trade

The case for free trade is based on the analysis presented in Chapter 21. We saw that when opportunity costs differ among countries, specialization and trade will raise world standards of living. Free trade allows all countries to specialize in producing commodities in which they have a comparative advantage.

Free trade allows the maximization of world production. It also makes it *possible* for every household in the world to consume more goods than it could without free trade.

This does not necessarily mean that everyone *will* be better off with free trade than without it. Protectionism could give some people a larger share of a smaller world output so that they would benefit as a result. If we ask whether it is *possible* for free trade to be advantageous to everyone, the answer is "yes." But if we ask whether free trade is in fact *always* advantageous to everyone, the answer is "not necessarily so."

There is abundant evidence that significant differences in opportunity costs exist and that there are large potential gains from trade because of these differences. There is also ample evidence that trade occurs and that no nation tries to be self-sufficient or refuses to sell to foreigners the items it produces cheaply and well.

The case for free trade is powerful. What needs explanation is not the extent of trade but the fact that trade is not wholly free. Do current tariffs and nontariff barriers to trade exist merely because policymakers are ignorant of the principles of comparative advantage, or are there sound reasons (overlooked in the case for free trade) for a nation to enact protectionist policies? Before addressing this question, let us examine the methods used in protectionist policy.

Methods of Protectionism

There are three main ways in which a country can reduce its imports. (1) The country may place a tax on imported commodities, called a **tariff.** Such a tax shifts the supply curve of the foreign import upward because it adds to the price charged by the foreign producer. (2) The country may impose an **import quota** that limits the quantity of a commodity that may be shipped into the country in a given period. Below the quota there is no change in supply, but once the quota has been reached, the supply curve effectively becomes a vertical line, indicating that no more can be imported whatever the price. (3) The country may adopt domestic policies that reduce its demand for the imported commodity. For example, it may require potential importers to obtain a special license or restrict the ability of its citizens to use their funds to purchase the foreign exchange needed to pay for the commodity. Such steps shift the demand curve for the import to the left.

Figure 22-1 illustrates the three methods of restricting trade. Although each method achieves a reduction in the quantity of imports, each has different side effects. Some of these are examined in Box 22-1 on pages 362–363.

In the text we concentrate on tariffs, which are probably the single most important tool of trade restriction. Tariffs come in two main forms: **specific tariffs,** which are so much money per unit of the product, and **ad valorem** tariffs, which are a percentage of the price of the product.[1]

The Case for Protectionism

Two kinds of arguments for protection are commonly offered. The first concerns national objectives other than output; the second concerns the desire to increase domestic national income possibly at the expense of world national income.

[1] Tariffs can also be used to raise revenue. In Canada customs revenues are about $6 billion per year. Although this amount is not negligible, it represents less than 15 percent of federal tax revenue. The protective function of a tariff is opposed to the revenue function because the tariff will not yield much revenue when it is effective in cutting imports. Here we concentrate on the protective feature of tariffs.

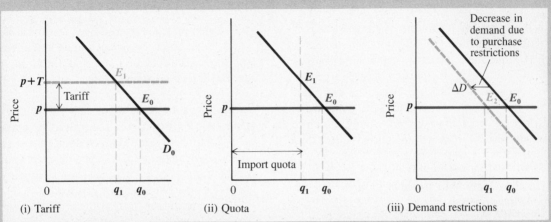

FIGURE 22-1
Alternative Means of Decreasing the Imports of a Commodity

(i) Tariff   (ii) Quota   (iii) Demand restrictions

The government can decrease the quantity of imports by imposing a tariff and thereby directly affecting the domestic price, by imposing a quota and thereby directly affecting the quantity available on domestic markets, or by restricting the quantity domestic residents are allowed to purchase. In each figure, the world supply of the commodity is perfectly elastic at the world price p while the solid black line D_0 indicates the domestic demand. (For simplicity we assume that none of the commodity is produced in the domestic country.) Equilibrium is at E_0, with imports (equal to domestic demand at the world price) given by q_0.

In (i) the government imposes a tariff of $\$T$ per unit. This raises the price facing domestic consumers to $p + T$,

so the equilibrium moves to E_1. The quantity of imports falls to q_1.

In (ii) the government imposes an import quota of q_1 as the maximum quantity permitted to enter. This in effect changes the supply curve: It is perfectly elastic at the world price p only for quantities less than q_1; at q_1, it becomes perfectly inelastic. Equilibrium moves to E_1, and the quantity of imports falls to q_1. (Note that in this case the domestic price also rises.)

In (iii) the government causes the domestic demand curve to shift leftward by an amount ΔD by implementing policies such as limiting importers' right to purchase the commodity. In this case equilibrium moves to E_2, and the quantity of imports again falls to q_1.

Objectives Other than Maximizing Output

It is quite possible to accept the proposition that the value of production is higher with free trade and yet rationally oppose free trade because of a concern with policy objectives other than maximizing real national income. For example, comparative advantage might dictate that a country should specialize in producing a narrow range of commodities. The government might decide, however, that there are distinct social advantages to encouraging a more diverse economy. Citizens would be given a wider range of occupations, and the social and psychological advantages of diversification would

more than compensate for a reduction in living standards by, say, 5 percent below what they could be with complete specialization of production according to comparative advantage.

For a very small country, specializing in the production of only a few commodities—although dictated by comparative advantage—may involve risks that a country does not wish to take. One such risk is that technological advances may render its basic product obsolete. While everyone understands this risk, there is debate about what governments can do about it. The pro-tariff argument is that the government can encourage a more diversified economy by protecting industries that other-

BOX 22–1 IMPORT RESTRICTIONS ON JAPANESE CARS: TARIFFS OR QUOTAS?

In the early 1980s imports of Japanese cars seriously threatened the automobile industries of the United States, Canada, and Western Europe. While continuing to espouse relatively free trade as a long-term policy, the American and Canadian governments argued that the domestic industry needed short-term protection. This protection was to tide it over the period of transition it faced as, it was then assumed, smaller cars would become the typical North American and Canadian household's vehicle. Once the enormous investment needed to transform the North

American auto industry had been made and new North American models had gained acceptance, free trade could be restored and the domestic industry asked to stand up to foreign competition.

But how should the temporary protection be achieved? Politically, quotas mutually agreed upon by the governments seemed the easiest route. Agreements were reached severely limiting the number of Japanese cars to be imported into the United States and Canada.

What does theory predict to be the economic

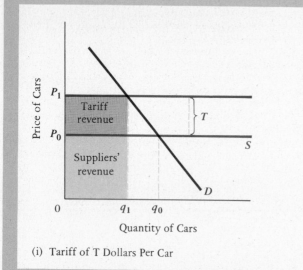

(i) Tariff of T Dollars Per Car

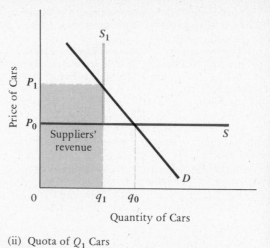

(ii) Quota of Q_1 Cars

wise could not compete. Opponents argue that governments, being mutually influenced by political motives, are in the final analysis poor judges of what industries can be protected to produce diversification at a resonable cost.

Another risk is cyclical fluctuations in the prices of basic commodities, which may face depressed prices for years at a time and then enjoy periods of very high prices. The national income of a country specializing in the production of such commodities

will be subject to wide fluctuations. Even though the average income level over a long period might be higher if specialization in the production of a few basic commodities were allowed, the serious social problems associated with a widely fluctuating national income may make the government decide to sacrifice some income in order to reduce fluctuations. The government might use protectionist policies to encourage the expansion of several less cyclically sensitive industries.

difference between quotas and tariffs? In both cases imports are restricted and the resulting scarcity supports a higher market price. With a tariff the extra market value is appropriated by the government of the importing country—in this case the U.S. and Canadian governments. With a quota the extra market value accrues to the goods' suppliers—in this case the Japanese car makers and their North American retailers.

This result is illustrated in the figure. We assume that the U.S and Canadian markets provide a small enough part of total Japanese car sales to leave the Japanese willing to supply at their fixed list price all the cars that are demanded in the United States and Canada. This is the price p_0 in both parts of the figure. Given the American demand curve for Japanese cars, D, there are q_0 cars sold before restrictions are imposed.

In (i) Canada places a tariff of T per unit on Japanese cars raising their Canadian price to p_1 and lowering sales to q_1. Suppliers' revenue is shown by the light shaded area. The Canadian government's tariff revenue is shown by the dark shaded area.

In (ii) a quota of q_1 is imposed, making the supply curve vertical at q_1. The market clearing price is p_1, and the suppliers' revenue is the whole shaded area (p_1 times q_1). The shortage of Japanese cars drives up their price, creating a substantial margin over costs. Under a tariff, the Canadian government captures the margin. Under a quota policy, however, the margin accrues to the Japanese manufacturers.

Although this is a simplified picture, it catches the essence of what actually happened. First, while North American manufacturers were keeping prices as low as possible and sometimes offering rebates on slow-selling models, Japanese cars were listed at healthy profit margins. Second, while it was always possible for the buyer of an American car to negotiate a good discount off the list price, Japanese cars usually sold for their full list price. Third, Japanese manufacturers tended to satisfy fully the demand for their more expensive cars, which have larger profit margins, and to restrict exports to North America of the less expensive cars with lower profit margins. This change in the "product mix" of Japanese cars exported to the United States and Canada raised the average profit per car exported.

There was nothing immoral or even surprising about these developments. They are the natural responses of sellers whose markets are restricted by quotas. Indeed, they were fully predictable in advance by economic theory.

Although most people would agree that, other things being equal, they would prefer more income to less, economists cannot pronounce as irrational a nation that chooses to sacrifice some income in order to achieve other goals. Economists can do three things when faced with such reasons for imposing tariffs. First, they can try to see if the proposed tariff really does achieve the ends suggested. Second, they can calculate the cost of the tariff in terms of lowered living standards. Third, they can check policy alternatives to see if there are other means of achieving the stated goal at lower cost in terms of lost output.

Protectionism As a Means to Higher National Living Standards

Infant industries. The most important argument for protectionism as a means of raising living standards concerns economies of scale. It is usually called the **infant industry argument.** If an industry has large economies of scale, costs and prices will be high when the industry is small but will fall as the industry grows. In such industries the country first in the field has a tremendous advantage.

A newly developing country may find that in the early stages of development its industries are unable to compete with established foreign rivals. A tariff (or import quota) may protect these industries from foreign competition while they grow up. When they are large enough, they will be able to produce as cheaply as foreign rivals and thus be able to compete without protection.[2]

Learning by doing. The theory of the gains from trade takes the production possibility curve as given. As we saw in Chapter 21, additional sources of gain are available through *learning by doing*, a factor that classical economists emphasized greatly.

Learning by doing suggests that the existing pattern of comparative advantage need not be taken as immutable. If a country can learn enough by producing commodities in which it currently is at a comparative disadvantage, it may gain in the long run by specializing in those commodities and *developing a comparative advantage* in them as the learning process lowers their costs.

Protecting a domestic industry from foreign competition may give it the time to learn to be efficient and its labor force the time to acquire necessary skills. If so, it may pay the government to protect the industry while the learning occurs.

Dynamic comparative advantage. If comparative advantages can change through skills newly acquired on or off the job, maybe industries should be protected so that these skills will grow. The problem here is that protection against the chill winds of foreign competition reduces the incentive for the competitive growth of skills. Better ways to affect comparative advantage may be through ed-

[2] Such a policy will take business away from foreign rivals. Hence, in the first instance it will increase the developing country's income at the expense of other countries. Once the resources in the other countries are reallocated to other uses, however, world output may rise in response to the development of these new centers of production.

ucation policy and incentive systems that direct effort into new and risky activities.

Problems. The difficulty with basing tariff policies on any of the above economic considerations is that the industries that will succeed in the long run must be identified. All too often the protected infant grows up to be a weak adult requiring permanent tariff protection for its continued existence. Or the learning proceeds at a slower rate than is occurring in similar industries in other countries that provide no protection from international competition. In these instances the anticipated comparative advantage never materializes.

The terms of trade. In the mid 1970s the OPEC countries provided a significant fraction of the world's supply of petroleum. By restricting their output they raised the price of their oil relative to the prices of other traded goods. This turned the terms of trade in their favor: For every barrel of oil exported they were able to obtain a larger quantity of imports. By the same token, of course, it turned the terms of trade against the oil-importing countries, including Canada and the United States: For every unit of their goods exported they were able to import fewer barrels of oil.

Now consider a country that provides a large fraction of the total demand for some product that it imports. By restricting its demand for that product through tariffs, it can force the price of that product down. This turns the terms of trade in its favor because it can now get more imports per unit of exports.

Trade restriction can be used to turn the terms of trade in favor of countries that produce a large fraction of the world's supply of some commodity. It can also be used to turn the terms of trade in favor of countries that constitute a large fraction of the world demand for some commodity that they import.

Both of these techniques merely redistribute a given world output. They can, however, be effective methods of raising the living standards of some countries at the expense of others.

To protect against predatory actions by foreign producers. Tariffs may be used to prevent foreign industries from gaining an unfair advantage over domestic industries by use of predatory practices that will harm domestic industries but yield no long-term benefit to domestic consumers. A common form is *dumping*. The circumstances under which dumping provides a valid argument for tariffs are considered in detail later in this chapter.

Fallacious Trade Policy Arguments

We have seen that there are gains from a high volume of international trade and specialization. We have also seen that there can be valid arguments for a moderate degree of protectionism. There are also many claims that do not advance the debate. Fallacious arguments are heard on both sides, and they color much of the popular discussion. These arguments have been around for a long time, but their survival does not make them true. We will examine them now to see where their fallacies lie.

Fallacious Free Trade Arguments

Free trade always benefits all countries. This is not necessarily so. The potential gains from trade might be offset by costs such as unemployment or economic instability or by the interference with policy objectives other than maximizing national income.

Infant industries never abandon their tariff protection. It is argued that granting protection to infant industries is a mistake because these industries seldom admit to growing up and will cling to their protection even when fully grown. But infant industry tariffs are a mistake *only* if these industries never grow up. In this case permanent tariff protection would be required to protect a weak industry never able to compete on an equal footing in the international market. But if the industries do grow up and achieve the expected scale economies, the fact that like any special interest group they cling to their tariff protection is not a sufficient reason for denying protection to genuine infant industries. When economies of scale are realized, the real costs of production are reduced and

resources are freed for other uses. Whether or not the tariff or other trade barriers remain, a cost saving has been effected by the scale economies.

Fallacious Protectionist Arguments

The exploitation doctrine. According to this view one trading partner *must* always reap a gain at the other's expense. But the principle of comparative advantage shows that it is possible for both parties to gain from trade and thus refutes the exploitation doctrine of trade. When opportunity cost ratios differ in two countries, specialization and the accompanying trade make it possible to produce more of all commodities and thus make it possible for both parties to get more goods as a result of trade than they could get in its absence.

Keep the money at home. This argument says, If I buy a foreign good, I have the good and the foreigner has the money, whereas if I buy the same good locally, I have the good and our country has the money, too.

The argument is based on a misconception. When Canadian importers purchase Italian-made goods, they do not send dollars abroad. They (or their financial agents) buy Italian lire (or claims on them) and use them to pay the Italian manufacturers. They purchase the lire on the foreign exchange market by giving up dollars to someone who wishes to use them for expenditure *in Canada*. Even if the money did go abroad physically—that is, if an Italian firm accepted a shipload of dollars—it would be because someone wanted them to spend in the only country where they are legal tender, Canada.

Dollars ultimately do no one any good except as purchasing power. It would be miraculous if green pieces of paper could be exported in return for real goods; after all, the Bank of Canada has the power to create as much new money as it wishes. It is only because the green paper can buy Canadian commodities and assets that others want it.

Protection against low-wage foreign labor. Surely, the argument says, the products of low-wage countries will drive out products from the market, and the high Canadian standard of living will be dragged down to that of their poor trading partners. Arguments of this sort have swayed many voters through the years.

As a prelude to considering them, stop and think what the argument would imply if taken out of the international context and put into a local one, where the same principles govern the gains from trade. Is it really impossible for a rich person to gain from trading with a poor person? Would the local millionaire be better off if she did all her own typing, gardening, and cooking? No one believes that a rich person cannot gain from trading with those who are less rich. Why then must a rich group of people lose from trading with a poor group? "Well," you say, "the poor group will price their goods too cheaply." Does anyone believe that consumers lose from buying in a discount house or a supermarket just because the prices are lower there than at the old-fashioned corner store? Consumers gain when they can buy the same goods at a lower price. If the Koreans pay low wages and sell their goods cheaply, *Korean* labor may suffer, but we will gain because we obtain their goods at a low cost in terms of the goods that we must export in return. The cheaper our imports are, the better off we are in terms of the goods and services available for domestic consumption.

Stated in more formal terms, the gains from trade depend on comparative, not absolute, advantages. World production is higher when any two areas, say Canada and Japan, specialize in the production of the goods for which they have a comparative advantage than when they both try to be self-sufficient.

Might it not be possible, however, that Japan will undersell Canada in all lines of production and thus appropriate all, or more than all, the gains for itself, leaving Canada no better off, or even worse off, than if it had no trade with Japan? The answer is no. The reason for this depends on the behavior of exchange rates, which we shall study in Chapter 39. As we shall see there, equality of demand and supply on foreign exchange market ensures that trade flows in both directions.

Imports can be obtained only by spending the currency of the country that makes the imports. Claims to this currency can be obtained only by exporting goods and services or by borrowing. Thus, lending and borrowing aside, imports must equal exports. All trade must be in two directions; we can buy only if we can also sell.

In the long run trade cannot hurt a country by causing it to import without exporting.

Trade then always provides scope for international specialization, with each country producing and exporting those goods for which it has a comparative advantage and importing those goods for which it does not.

Protectionism creates domestic jobs and reduces unemployment. It is sometimes said that an economy with substantial unemployment, such as that of Canada in the 1930s or in the early 1980s, provides an exception to the case for freer trade. Suppose that tariffs or import quotas cut the imports of Japanese cars, Korean textiles, Italian shoes, and French wine. Surely, the argument maintains, this will create more employment for Oshawa auto workers, Quebec textile workers, Ontario shoe factories, and B.C. wine growers. The answer is that it will—initially. But the Japanese, Koreans, Italians, and French can buy from Canada only if they earn Canadian dollars by selling goods in Canada.

The decline in their sales of autos, textiles, shoes, and wine will decrease their purchases of Canadian machinery, aircraft, grain, and ski trips to Banff. Jobs will be lost in our export industries and gained in those industries that formerly faced competition from imports. The likely long-term effect is that total unemployment will not be reduced but only redistributed among industries.

Industries and unions that compete with imports favor protectionism while those with large exports favor more trade. Most economists are highly skeptical about the government's ability to reduce overall unemployment by protectionism.

Arguments about barriers to trade: a final word. While there are cases in which a restrictive policy has been pursued following a rational assessment of the approximate cost, it is hard to avoid the conclusion that, more often than not, such policies are pursued for flimsy objectives or on fallacious grounds, with little idea of the actual costs involved. The very high tariffs in the United States during the 1920s and 1930s are a conspicuous example. The current clamor for our government to do something about the competition from Japan, Korea, and other of the emerging nations may well be another.

CANADIAN TRADE AND TRADE POLICY

Foreign trade accounts for a relatively large part of the Canadian economy. In 1983 exports were over 20 percent of GNP as compared to less than 4 percent for the United States. Similar figures apply to imports. Geography, climate, and an abundance of natural resources explain much of this difference. The same factors also explain the composition of our trade.

Our severe winters cause Canadians to spend money on foreign vacations and on imports of fresh fruits and vegetables. Our large supply of natural resources relative to our population distinguishes Canada most from other developed countries and determines our comparative advantage. Canada has an abundance of arable land, timber, minerals, and energy in the form of both fossil fuels and hydro-electric power. As a consequence, our exports have tended to be *primary products*: commodities that require intensive use of these resources in their production. This fact dominates the interpretation of Canada's economic history and explanations of Canadian economic developement.

The Staples Thesis

The central role of primary product exports in Canada's economic development is illustrated by our experience with prairie wheat, which emerged as an important export between the years 1896 and 1914. During this period, usually referred to as the "wheat boom," real GNP increased by 150 percent and population grew from 5.1 to 7.9 million. Much of this growth was tied closely to the wheat sector. For example, in that period there was a railway construction boom. Over ten thousand miles of

railway track were laid in order to transport agricultural products from the prairies to the lakehead at Thunder Bay, Ontario, and to the west coast. With the expansion of the railway came construction of grain elevators and investment in farm equipment and food processing industries.

Based in part on Canada's experience during the wheat boom, Professor Harold Innis of the University of Toronto developed the "staples thesis." According to this thesis, economic growth in Canada has been tied to a sequence of staple exports, primary products for which Canada has had a comparative advantage. The important staple industries in the seventeenth and eighteenth centuries were the fur trade and the east coast fishery; during the nineteenth century timber and wheat from Upper Canada were the important staples; and in the twentieth century it has been prairie wheat, pulp and paper, minerals, and oil and natural gas. These staples have been important not only as exports, but also because they have induced additional growth through linkages to other sectors of the economy.

Reciprocity: 1854–1866

In 1854 British North America and the United States signed the reciprocity treaty, and until 1866 when the treaty was abrogated by the United States, many commodities (including all primary products) crossed the Canada–United States border duty free. The period was one of great prosperity, which many economists attribute to increased trade with the United States. Although there are some dissenters, the prevailing view among economic historians is that Canada's experiment with free trade in primary products was beneficial.

After Confederation, the Canadian government maintained low tariffs as it tried to persuade the United States to renew the reciprocity treaty. In the mid-1870s, however, the Canadian economy was hit with a recession and, as often happens during recessions, manufacturers pressed for more protection. Partly in response to this pressure, Sir John A. MacDonald introduced his National Policy in 1878. The National Policy was presented as a program for long-run economic development and included subsidies for railway building, support for farm settlement, and emphasis on the export of a few primary products. However, the cornerstone was increased tariff protection for Canadian manufacturing. This protectionist policy remained essentially unchanged until the 1930s, and the Canadian government continues to provide high levels of protection for manufacturing industries.

Did the protectionist component of the National Policy inhibit Canada's economic growth? Economic historians disagree. W. A. Easterbrook and H. G. Aitken view the effects as beneficial: "The protective tariff . . . rounded out a broad, consistent and comprehensive programme of national planning." They argue that where a tariff kept out foreign products, it encouraged domestic manufacturing, and where it didn't, tariff revenue was generated to help finance railway construction. Either way, Canada was better off. John Dales, on the other hand, concludes that protectionism was a mistake: "We would have been better off . . . if we had never tangled with the National Policy." He argues that high tariffs prevented the economy from fully realizing the gains from our comparative advantage in natural resource industries; moreover, he points out that the 15-year period following the introduction of the National Policy was one of slow growth and substantial emigration of Canadians to the United States.

Current Composition of Canada's Trade

Raw and semifinished products still account for a large fraction of Canadian exports (see Table 22-1). The earlier staples have been supplanted by pulp and paper, iron ore, nonferrous metals, crude petroleum, and natural gas. The most dramatic change over the past 40 years has been the decline in the proportion of exports accounted for by wheat and wheat flour from about 40 percent in 1928 to about 12 percent in the mid 1960s and 5 percent in 1982.

On the import side, Canada is highly dependent on foreign suppliers for many manufactured prod-

TABLE 22–1 CANADIAN EXPORTS BY COMMODITY, 1983

Commodity	Exports	
	Billions of dollars	Percentage of total
Farm and fish products	$10.6	11.6
Forest products	13.1	14.4
Crude petroleum and natural gas	7.4	8.1
Other minerals and metals	11.6	12.8
Chemicals and fertilizers	4.3	4.7
Motor vehicles and parts	21.9	24.1
Other manufactured goods	22.0	24.3
Total exports of domestic products	$90.9	100.0

Source: Bank of Canada Review.

Raw and semifinished products make up 50 percent of Canadian exports. Since the signing of the Automotive Products Agreement in 1965, motor vehicles and parts have become the major export industry in the manufacturing sector.

TABLE 22–2 CANADIAN IMPORTS BY END USE, 1983

Item	Imports	
	Billions of dollars	Percentage of total
Fuel and lubricants	$ 5.1	6.7
Industrial and construction materials	18.0	23.8
Motor vehicles and parts	20.1	26.6
Producer's equipment	15.4	20.4
Food	4.3	5.6
Other consumer goods	9.3	12.4
Other imports	3.4	4.5
Total imports	75.6	100.0

Source: Bank of Canada Review.

Manufactured goods make up a large fraction of Canadian imports. A substantial fraction of imports of manufactured goods is accounted for by motor vehicles and parts, producer's equipment, and industrial and construction materials.

ucts, particularly durable goods such as machinery, motor vehicles, and other consumer durables (see Table 22-2). Table 22-3 shows the dramatic change that took place in the 1960s in the importance of trade in motor vehicles and parts with the United States. The Automotive Products Agreement, which went into effect in 1965, provided for the integration of the North American auto industry by initiating free trade with respect to shipments by the manufacturers. The Canadian tariffs, ranging from 17.5 percent on finished vehicles to 25 percent on parts, were removed from imports by manufacturers who agreed to meet certain requirements regarding minimum levels of production carried on in Canada. (This experience is further discussed later in this chapter in Box 22-3.)

Tariff Policy: The External Environment

Canada's tariff policy options are limited by its relationships with other countries. During the 1920s and early 1930s there were few international agreements concerning tariffs, and countries could

impose any desired set of tariffs on their imports. However, when one country increased its tariffs, the action typically triggered retaliatory changes by its trading partners, and frequently the situation deteriorated into a tariff war.

The General Agreement on Tariffs and Trade (GATT). One of the most notable achievements of the post-World War II world in retreating from the high-water mark of protectionism of the 1930s was the General Agreement on Tariffs and Trade (GATT). Under this agreement, GATT countries meet periodically to negotiate bilaterally on mutually advantageous cuts in tariffs. They agree in advance that any tariff cuts negotiated in this way will be extended to all member countries. Significant tariff reductions have been effected by the member countries.

The two most recent rounds of GATT agreements have reduced tariffs by about one-third. The Kennedy Round negotiations were completed in 1967, and new rates were phased in over a five-year period ending in 1972. The Tokyo Round negotiations began in 1975 and were completed in

TABLE 22–3 COMPOSITION OF CANADA'S TRADE, SELECTED YEARS (Percentage)

Area	Exports				Imports			
	1960	1970	1980	1983	1960	1970	1980	1983
United States								
Motor vehicles and parts	★	20	13	23	7	22	18	24
Crude petroleum and natural gas	2	5	9	8	★	★	★	★
All other	55	40	41	42	63	49	52	48
Total	57	65	63	73	70	71	70	72
Britain	17	9	4	3	11	5	3	2
Other	8	7	8	5	5	6	5	6
Japan	3	5	6	5	2	4	4	6
All other countries	15	14	19	14	12	14	18	14
	100	100	100	100	100	100	100	100

Source: Bank of Canada Review, D.B.S., Review of Foreign Trade 1960, 1970.
★ Less than 1 percent.

The share of Canada's trade accounted for by the United States increased during the 1960s and 1970s. Increased exports of crude petroleum and natural gas and the expanded trade in automobiles were the major factors contributing to the higher American share. The dramatic rise in exports to the United States in 1983 reflects the strong recovery in the U.S. economy that year.

BOX 22–2 DUMPING AND THE RATIONALE FOR ANTIDUMPING POLICY

When a firm sells abroad at lower prices than it charges domestically, it is said to be *dumping.** Dumping has occurred recently, for example, with exports of Japanese steel into North American markets. Not surprisingly, the North American steel industry has requested help from the respective federal governments.

Motives for dumping. Japanese producers dump steel in North America because it is profitable for them to do so. But there are several different reasons why dumping may prove profitable to them.

1. It may be a sensible long-term strategy because the Japanese home market is permanently too small to support an industry of efficient size. In such circumstances, to have an efficient industry requires an export market, but to achieve that market, a low-price policy may be required. Dumping in this case, by making it possible to produce output at the lowest possible cost per unit, benefits both domestic and foreign customers.
2. It may be a sensible cyclical strategy to provide a market for output in periods when Japanese demand is low, thereby utilizing the

capacity required to meet maximum Japanese demands in periods of boom and expansion. Sales in the export market simply permit Japanese production to continue on an even level over the cycle.
3. It may be a predatory strategy designed to destroy the foreign industry. After foreign plants have shut down, prices can be raised to exploit the foreigner's new dependence on imports.

Effects on the buying country. Suppose Canada is the "beneficiary" of Japanese steel sold at less than the Japanese domestic price and (let us suppose) below the average cost of production in Canada. If such sales continue, they will either eliminate the Canadian industry or force it to become more efficient. This will benefit Canadian steel buyers for as long as they are able to buy cheaper steel.

No matter what the Japanese producers' motives, the Canadian steel industry and the United Steelworkers of America will want the government to stop this, for it threatens their profits and their jobs.

Suppose the government chooses to look beyond the political pressures of the moment and to do what is best for the national interest. Here it matters which motivation explains the dumping. If the Japanese are prepared to supply cheap steel on a permanent basis, it would surely ben-

* Occasionally dumping is defined as selling abroad at a price below marginal cost, but we shall use the conventional definition given in the text.

1979; the reductions began to take effect in 1981.

Ironically, as that new round of reductions began, pressure was mounting in many countries to protect jobs at home through trade restrictions. GATT itself came under attack. The worldwide resession that began in late 1981 was undoubtedly the main cause of this pressure. In addition, pro-

tectionist pressure in many countries was also created by the decline in the international competitiveness of traditional industries due to sharp changes in terms of trade. At a November 1982 meeting, the GATT countries recognized—and resolved to overcome—the threat to the system represented by the emerging clamor for increased pro-

efit Canadians to buy Japanese steel and use Canadian resources to produce something in which we have a comparative advantage. This is the case for doing nothing to protect the domestic steel industry.

However, if cheap Japanese steel would destroy the Canadian industry without replacing the need for it—that is, for either of the last two listed reasons—then sufficient protection to preserve a viable industry may be required. This is the valid case for protectionism.

The problem for policy is to diagnose what is happening and to adopt rules that will preserve needed industries without depriving Canadian buyers of cheaper sources of supply. Currently there is controversy about what is really happening in the case of Japanese steel.

Antidumping Provisions

Under the Anti-Dumping Act of 1968, Canadian producers who believe that competing foreign goods are being dumped in Canada may complain to the deputy minister of national revenue. If, on the basis of an initial inquiry, the deputy minister finds that dumping which may cause material injury is occurring, he will impose a provisional duty and refer the case to the Anti-Dumping Tribunal (ADT). The ADT conducts a thorough investigation and makes a final recommendation to the minister. If material injury

is found to be present (or anticipated), dumping duties will be levied. Antidumping provisions have been increasingly applied in the 1980s.

The United States has announced *trigger prices* that are usually equal to the domestic prices in the exporting country. If a foreign producer were to sell in the United States below a trigger price, antidumping proceedings would be initiated. Canada has no explicit trigger price system, but there is little doubt that there are implicit, unannounced price floors that inhibit dumping by foreign producers.

Often the trigger prices become in effect minimum prices that no foreign producer dare undercut. Thus the provisions inhibit foreign competition and serve as nontariff barriers to trade, both where dumping is beneficial to domestic interests and where it is not.

A particulaly bizzare feature of the trigger price rule is that when a foreign country is caught dumping, it is "penalized" by being forced to raise its prices. This taxes domestic consumers and transfers the income to the supposed villains, the foreigners. If protection were desired, a more sensible response would be to tax the foreign goods, thereby raising the domestic price and achieving the desired protection, but transferring the proceeds from the increased price to the domestic government rather than to the foreign producers.

tectionism, but they failed to achieve any explicit agreements to prevent tariff increases.

The disaster of total breakdown may have been avoided, but the result was still a stalemate. Thus many observers feared that the prospects for resisting the rising tide of protectionist sentiment were diminishing. Canada has adopted several pro-

tectionist measures in an effort to protect industries hit by cyclical and secular decline. For a country as dependent on trade as Canada, such protectionism is a very risky policy.

Although GATT has produced an enormous reduction in *tariffs*, these results are a bit misleading in terms of the freedom of trade because of the growing use of *nontariff* barriers. Perhaps the most important feature of the Tokyo Round was the agreement, for the first time, to limit the growth of nontariff barriers. It is still too early to tell whether these efforts will have any significant success.

Regional common markets. A common market is an agreement among a group of countries to eliminate barriers to free trade among themselves and to provide a common trading policy toward the rest of the world.

The most important is the European Common Market. In 1957 the Treaty of Rome joined France, Germany, Italy, Holland, Belgium, and Luxembourg in the European Economic Community (EEC), now called just the European Community (EC). The EC is dedicated to bringing about free trade, complete mobility of factors of production, and the eventual harmonization of fiscal and monetary policies among member countries. Tariff reductions were made according to a time schedule that eliminated all tariffs on manufactured goods among the original six before 1970. If the development continues, before the end of the century Western Europe will be a single economic community, with free movement of goods, labor, and capital among member countries.

In 1973, despite strong divisions within each country, Great Britain, the Republic of Ireland, and Denmark joined the EC, the first two after close votes in their parliaments and the latter after a plebiscite. At the same time, Norway voted in a plebiscite to remain outside. Greece joined in 1981, and the entry of Spain and Portugal is currently being considered.

The formation of the EC was of great significance to Canada because it strengthened trading relations among the member countries at the expense of increased barriers to trade with nonmember countries. To offset this, Canada has attempted to negotiate special agreements with the EC.

In the early 1980s the EC entered a state of crises as a result of its so-called common agricultural policy. When the community was first formed, it adopted the French agricultural policy as its agri-

cultural policy. This was a policy of the sort described in Chapter 6, one designed to reduce fluctuations and make them occur around a high average level of farm income. The long-term effects have been those predicted in Chapter 6.

Movement of resources out of the agricultural sector has not occurred at a fast enough pace, and both subsidy payments and accumulated surpluses have grown to alarming proportions. In France and Germany, where the agricultural sectors are large, the transfer of income is mainly intranational, from urban to rural sectors. But the UK, with a very small agricultural sector, has been a large net contributor of funds, making the transfer international—from the UK to France and Germany. As time has passed, the misallocation of resources has increased. By the early 1980s the drain on the budget from agricultural subsidy payments was vast and threatened the community's very existence.

Nontariff Barriers to Trade

The world recession of the early 1980s led to a very substantial increase in nontariff barriers to trade. Canada was a willing participant in these developments. Protection was bought for some unsuccessful domestic industries at the cost of acquiescing in a more difficult position for successful export industries. Nontariff barriers appear in many forms. Some are quite explicit and easily identifiable, such as domestic content requirements, quotas, and antidumping provisions. (The latter are discussed further in Box 22-2.) Others, such as government procurement practices and subsidized loans to domestic producers, are harder to identify. But there is little doubt that nontariff barriers have been growing in importance in recent years.

Tariff Policy: Options for the Future

Although Canada has participated in the general liberalization of world trade that has taken place since World War II (as well as doing its share in the recently rising tide of protectionism), tariffs still have a substantial influence in the structure of

BOX 22–3 RATIONALIZATION BY FORMAL AGREEMENT: THE AUTO PACT

The Canadian automobile industry was established under tariff protection. The tariff caused the major U.S. automobile manufacturers to export to Canada *indirectly* by establishing branch plants within Canada.

By the late 1950s Canadian policymakers had become concerned about the structure of the Canadian automobile industry. The protection offered by the tariff was supposed to enable the industry to become efficient and to compete on its own against foreign imports. This had not happened; Canadian costs and prices remained well above their U.S. counterparts. A Royal Commission on the Automobile Industry led to the enactment of the Automobile Products Trade Act (the Auto Pact) in 1965. As a result, the Canadian automobile industry was rationalized along the lines discussed in Box 14-3 on pages 242–243.

Prior to the enactment of the Auto Pact, a wide range of cars was being produced in Canada. In 1964 Ford was producing 60 different models of five distinct lines at its single Canadian plant. Because this entailed short production runs, the industry was unable to achieve its MES and hence operated inefficiently.

The Auto Pact allowed the tariff-free importation of U.S. automobile products by Canadian *manufacturers* on a dollar-for-dollar basis with exports of Canadian products. Imports not matched by exports were subject to a "penalty" duty. As a result, Canadian plants specialized in

particular product lines and exported most of the cars that they produced. In return, the manufacturers were able to import a wide variety of models for sale in Canada; the benefits of increased efficiency were gained without forsaking product variety in domestic consumption.

One problem with such a scheme is that the domestic economy becomes so narrowly specialized that it is vulnerable to swings in demand. In 1980 the Canadian auto industry was especially hard hit because it had specialized in large, fuel-inefficient models and in expensive specialty models, both of which were extremely vulnerable during the energy crunch. But when a fall in energy prices caused a revival in the demand for larger cars, Canadian producers benefited from their specialization.

One other problem with the Auto Pact is that the provisions for duty-free imports were granted to companies. Thus, while the country gained from the efficiency scale of production, nothing ensured that the gains would be passed along to domestic consumers in the form of lower auto prices. Instead the gains were captured by the (foreign-owned) manufacturers and to some extent by the domestic unions who negotiated for wage parity with their U.S. counterparts shortly after the pact was signed. The differential between Canadian and American consumer prices has fallen some since the pact was signed, but it has not been eliminated.

the economy. The broad pattern of Canada's external trade is probably not radically different from that which comparative advantages would dictate under free trade. Yet there is considerable evidence that the protection afforded to manufactured products has permitted the manufacturing sector to remain high in cost and insufficiently specialized.

The tariffs promote industrial self-sufficiency, with small, unspecialized firms that are unable to achieve economies of scale because of the limited size of their domestic markets.

Under these circumstances, many economists believe that access to larger markets through participation in a regional free trade area would raise

Canadian productivity and living standards substantially. On political grounds, many Canadians have advocated a broad arrangement to include not only the United States, but Britain, some European countries, and Japan.

Would Canadians become "hewers of wood and drawers of water" if our industry were exposed to free trade competition from the United States? This question cannot be answered by merely observing that in most manufacturing industries, costs are now higher in Canada than in the United States. To the extent that these higher costs reflect inefficiencies arising from the small Canadian market, they are the *result* of tariffs—both American and Canadian—not a justification for them.

The elimination of tariffs would permit Canadian producers to specialize in a limited number of lines and supply the common North American market. A narrowing in the differential between prices of cars in the United States and Canada has come about from just such specialization in the automobile industry as a result of the free trade agreement. Canadian plants now specialize in a limited number of models and operate high-volume production runs. This issue is discussed further in Boxes 22-3 and 22-4.

Undoubtedly, a substantial move toward free trade would cause hardships in some industries and necessitate public assistance programs to ease the adjustments in particular sectors or regions. In some instances the continuation of protection for at least a limited period may be justified on infant industry grounds. Nevertheless, the question remains whether or not Canadians wish to pay the price in terms of the lower standard of living the present tariff policy entails. There is a further ominous worry: Under the theory of static comparative advantage, the cost of protection is fixed. With a dynamic view of comparative advantage (see pages 356–357), the tariff could lead to a steady deterioration of existing advantages with a steadily rising cost.

If some degree of Canadian self-sufficiency is regarded as an end in itself, then economic analysis can only attempt to assess the costs involved; it cannot resolve the issue.

THE FOREIGN OWNERSHIP ISSUE

Canada's tariff policy has encouraged the establishment of branch plants of foreign firms to serve the Canadian market. Having induced this by their own policy, Canadians then became worried about being a "branch-plant" economy. Concern then generalized to all foreign ownership. For this reason there has been considerable controversy over the issue of foreign, and particularly American, ownership and control of Canadian industry since the mid-1950s. The list of firms that have been taken over by foreign investors in recent years includes such well-known corporations as Canadian Breweries, Salada Foods, British American Oil (now Gulf Canada), and McIntyre Porcupine Mines. In addition Canada is, as it has always been, highly dependent on foreign-controlled capital to finance the expansion of its productive capacity.

Should Canadians be concerned about this? Should new saving be channeled into buying back control of Canadian industry, and/or should restrictions be placed on new foreign investment? Many of the issues involve value judgments, but economists can contribute to the debate by suggesting the likely consequences of alternative courses of action.

The Statistics of Foreign Ownership

Foreign capital has played an important role in Canada's development since Confederation. Before World War I, a large part of it came from Britain in the form of debt securities to finance railways and other large-scale investment projects. By 1926, when the first estimates of foreign capital invested were made, the United States had supplanted Britain as the major supplier. A much larger share of U.S. capital has come in the form of direct investment; the resulting increase in nonresident ownership and control of Canadian industry is shown in Table 22-4. American investment has been concentrated in manufacturing, petroleum and natural gas, and mining and smelting. The substantial investment in natural resource industries reflects the

BOX 22–4 RATIONALIZATION BY MANUFACTURER'S CHOICE: WORLD PRODUCT MANDATING

One way in which an inefficient domestic industry previously dependent on protection could survive a move to free trade would be for it to rationalize its product lines in the ways discussed in Box 14-3. This has happened as a result of explicit policy in the auto industry. But that is not the only way it can happen. Large multinational corporations often permit foreign "branch plants" to develop particular product lines both for sale in the home market and for export into world markets. This is called "world product mandating." It involves specialization in production in order to exploit economies of scale; but it may also involve transferring increased managerial and marketing responsibility to the former branch plant.

In Canada product mandating has been common in the electrical products and home appliance industries (where such firms as Westinghouse and Black & Decker have led the way) and in the relatively high-technology computer and office machine industries (where such giants as IBM, NCR, and Xerox have adopted the strategy).

In the 12 years since the local management of Black & Decker Canada persuaded its parent to grant it world rights to produce the company's orbital sander, the subsidiary has increased plant capacity fivefold, sales by nearly 25 percent a year, and staff to include 24 full-time design engineers. The company has gone on to develop several other new products for worldwide distribution—including the popular Workmate handyman's bench—and export sales now account for 45 percent of the Canadian Company's production.

Westinghouse has operated in Canada since 1903. Until 1950, the profit ratios of the Canadian enterprise were better than those of the parent company, on the average, in three of every four years. Then Westinghouse Canada's fortunes began to slip. Earnings declined, employment levels slipped downhill, and a number of product lines were phased out.

In this situation, the parent company executives faced a choice—to make a place for Westinghouse Canada in their worldwide activities or to sell off the investment—and they chose to integrate the Canadian operation into the company's global production and marketing operations. The orientation of the Canadian operation was changed from that of a branch plant to that of a rationalized operation, with active participation in the marketing activities of the multinational company.

In the early 1980s, the company's exports grew at twice the rate of domestic sales; research and development activities for specific products destined for world markets tripled; corporate capital spending doubled; and productivity improved more rapidly than that of the parent company.

These examples show that world product mandating can be beneficial. Yet the policy is not without its critics. Many believe that the narrow product specialization leaves the economy vulnerable to shifts in demand or cost conditions. Others believe that ironically, if world mandating is too successful, strong foreign subsidiaries could hinder the development of similar skills and technology by truly Canadian companies. But even critics are willing to admit that in an economy where non-Canadian companies are a fact of life, world product mandating is an excellent way to achieve the efficiency of large-scale production.

TABLE 22-4 NONRESIDENT OWNERSHIP AND CONTROL OF CANADIAN INDUSTRIES, 1926–1977

Industry	Nonresident ownership (percent of total equity and debt capital)				Nonresident control (percent of total capital)			
	1926	1948	1968	1977	1926	1948	1968	1979
All residents								
Manufacturing	38	42	52	49	35	43	58	51
Petroleum and natural gas	—	—	62	48	—	—	75	53
Mining and smelting	37	39	62	49	38	40	68	51
Railways	55	45	18	29	3	3	2	1
Other utilities	32	20	19	26	20	24	5	4
U.S. residents								
Manufacturing	30	35	44	39	30	39	46	39
Petroleum and natural gas	—	—	51	38	—	—	61	40
Mining and smelting	28	32	51	36	32	37	58	37
Railways	15	21	8	18	3	3	2	1
Other utilities	23	16	18	18	20	24	4	4

Source: Statistics Canada, 67-202.

Nonresident ownership of equity and debt capital employed in Canadian manufacturing, petroleum and natural gas extraction, and mining and smelting has increased substantially since 1948. The control ratios measure the percentage of capital invested by residents as well as nonresidents in the companies whose voting stock is controlled by nonresidents; they exceed the new ownership ratios to the extent that Canadian residents invest in companies controlled by nonresidents.

large requirements of the United States for raw materials in the face of declining domestic supplies.

As can be seen in Table 22-5, the foreign ownership ratios in terms of assets or profits vary considerably within the manufacturing sector. Nonresidents owned the tobacco industry and virtually all the rubber products industry. Other manufacturing industries with a substantial degree of foreign control include transport equipment (foreign control of the automobile industry is close to 100 percent), nonmetallic mineral products, and chemicals. Outside manufacturing and the extractive industries, resident ownership predominates. In transportation and public utilities, a large fraction of the assets are accounted for by government enterprises and are therefore entirely owned and controlled within Canada. Foreign ownership of industries fell from 85 percent in 1978 to 61 percent in 1981 and, partly as a result of the National Energy Program (discussed later in this chapter), even further in 1983.

Foreign-Owned Firms and Canadian Interests

Do Canadians suffer from conflicts of interest and differences in outlook between foreign-owned subsidiaries and their parent companies? Critics of foreign control argue that head-office managers may be poorly informed about or indifferent to the potential of their subsidiaries. (Box 22-4 shows that this is not a universal problem.) Specifically, they claim that parent companies may (1) limit the opportunities for Canadians to obtain senior positions in the subsidiaries and to play a significant role in decision making; (2) centralize research and development in the parent company and oblige Canadian scientists to look abroad for employment; and (3) prevent the subsidiary from exporting in competition with the parent and require it to buy from the parent rather than from Canadian suppliers. Since such discrimination is not consistent with profit maximization, those who believe it to be important implicitly accept the notion that corporations pursue other objectives.

A study by A. E. Safarian compared the performance of foreign-owned firms to that of resident-owned firms, that of parent companies, and that of U.S. direct-investment firms elsewhere. He concluded:

Actual economic performance of subsidiary companies in Canada often does not differ greatly, however, from that of resident-owned companies. Performance is very similar between the two groups in regard to, for example, exports and research, and it is not markedly less favourable in regard to imports. When we turn to comparisons with the parent, however, we find that subsidiaries are usually less efficient. In the manufacturing sector, many subsidiaries are relatively small firms producing virtually the full range of products identical to those of the parent. Their unit costs of production exceed those of the parent in most cases. This inefficient structure of industry reflects, fundamentally, the limitations on market and firm size, and on specialization, resulting from Canadian and foreign tariffs and from lack of competition in Canada.[3]

In Safarian's view and that of many other economists, the major economic problem in Canadian industry is the inefficient size of many firms, both resident and foreign owned. These economists argue that the specialization necessary to achieve economies of scale, particularly in a world of product differentiation, is inhibited by tariffs and other barriers to trade that foster local production for the relatively small Canadian market.

Extraterritoriality

Students of the foreign ownership issue have generally acknowledged that serious questions are raised by the problem of extraterritoriality, the application of U.S. laws and government regulations to activities carried on within Canada. The attempt of the American government to stop firms participating in the ambitious Trans-Siberian natural gas pipeline project was a major case in point. A number of cases have also arisen in which it was alleged that Canadian subsidiaries of American firms were

[3] A. E. Safarian, *The Performance of Foreign-Owned Firms in Canada* (Private Planning Association, 1969), p. 5.

TABLE 22–5 NONRESIDENT CONTROL OF CANADIAN INDUSTRIES, 1981

Industry	Percentage majority of nonresident ownership as measured by	
	Assets	Profits
Manufacturing		
Foods	29	53
Tobacco	100	100
Rubber products	90	91
Leather products	23	33
Textile industries	51	41
Wood	15	32
Printing, publishing, and allied fields	11	11
Paper and allied products	19	28
Primary metals	13	10
Metal fabricating	35	46
Machinery	48	62
Transport equipment	69	65
Electrical products	54	64
Nonmetallic mineral products	69	75
Petroleum and coal products	61	73
Chemicals and chemical products	75	86
Miscellaneous manufacturing	40	52
Total, all manufacturing	45	52
Nonmanufacturing		
Mining (including mineral fuels)	37	51
Construction	11	11
Transportation	6	11
Communications	19	12
Public utilities	1	2
Wholesale trade	22	30
Retail trade	13	8
Services	15	27

Source: Statistics Canada, 61-210.

Nonresident ownership is now concentrated in a number of industries within the manufacturing sector and is also substantial in the extractive industries.

prevented from exporting to certain Communist countries. As part of its foreign policy, the U.S. government restricts trade with China, North Korea, Vietnam, and Cuba, and American parent companies are responsible for ensuring that the restrictions are not circumvented through foreign subsidiaries. Since Canadian policy involves many fewer restrictions, clear conflicts of interest can arise for American subsidiaries in Canada.

Questions of extraterritoriality have also arisen in connection with the application of American antitrust laws to subsidiaries in Canada and with U.S. regulations that restrict direct investment flows from parent firms to their subsidiaries in Canada and elsewhere. Consultations between the two governments have taken place in an attempt to resolve these issues, but arrangements fully consistent with Canadian sovereignty are clearly difficult to achieve.

Policies of the Federal Government

In response to public concern over the foreign ownership issue during the last 20 years, a number of legislative proposals dealing with it have been brought before Parliament by both Liberal and Conservative governments. One far-reaching scheme was contained in Finance Minister Walter Gordon's budget of June 1963, which provided for a 30 percent takeover tax on acquisitions by nonresidents of resident companies listed on the Canadian stock exchanges. This proposal was abandoned as unworkable after strong protests from the financial community, but other provisions were enacted that granted preferential treatment under the corporate income tax to foreign-owned companies in which Canadians held an interest of at least 25 percent.

Other legislation has focused on what have been regarded as key sectors of the Canadian economy, such as financial institutions and the communications media. For example, in view of their role in the cultural and political life of the country, broadcasting and the publishing of magazines and periodicals are subject to regulations ensuring Canadian control. In a famous case in the late 1970s, the federal government managed to drive the Canadian edition of *Time Magazine* out of existence, but bowed to pressure to allow the Canadian edition of *Reader's Digest* to continue.

Canada Development Corporation. The idea of establishing a government holding company to promote Canadian ownership was originally proposed in 1963 by Finance Minister Gordon, although legislation establishing the Canada Development Corporation was not enacted until 1971. The initial capital was supplied by the government, with shares in the corporation also offered for sale to the Canadian public; it is intended that the government's share of ownership will eventually fall to about 10 percent.

The CDC invests in Canadian industries, although its criteria for choosing these industries have been the subject of controversy from its inception. Some hold that it should seek to buy profitable industries, and thus attract private shareholders. Others hold that it should pursue broader socioeconomic objectives by bailing out failing industries—this of course would make CDC stock unattractive to private investors and hence would require increased government involvement. Some of its actual purchases—such as Connought Laboratories in 1972 and Texas Gulf in 1973—have been very controversial, as was its decision in 1980 not to step in and bail out the ailing Massey-Ferguson.

Foreign Investment Review Act. This legislation, enacted in 1973, was based on the recommendations of a task force report known as the Gray Report. It established a screening procedure for determining whether foreign takeover bids or the setting up of new foreign-owned businesses would be of "significant benefit to Canada." The criteria to be used in this evaluation are:

1. The effect on the level and nature of economic activity in Canada, including the effect on employment, on resource processing, on the use of Canadian parts, components and services, and on exports.
2. The degree and significance of participation by Canadians in the business enterprise and its affiliates.
3. The effect on productivity, industrial efficiency, technological development, product innovation, and product variety in Canada.
4. The effect on competition within any industry or industries in Canada.
5. The compatibility with national industrial and economic policies, taking into consideration in-

dustrial and economic policy objectives enunciated by provinces likely to be affected.

FIRA has turned down a significant number of applications for foreign capital to enter Canada. More important, the major administrative delays involved in a FIRA review have discouraged many others from applying at all.

When Canadians took their future economic growth as assured, many were prepared to experiment with nationalistic measures designed to keep some foreign capital out. Suddenly, however, when the world economy went into recession, when developed nations became threatened by the rising industrial power of emerging nations, and when the United States showed signs of matching Canadian hostility to the United States with American hostility to Canada, views changed dramatically. The worry suddenly became, "Can Canadians continue to attract enough foreign capital to stay in the forefront of international competitiveness?"

In response, the federal government quickly streamlined FIRA's procedures, making it much more likely that foreign applications would be approved and speeding up the time taken to reach decisions. A story in the *Globe and Mail* in early 1984 gave details of a recent federal government advertising campaign costing millions of dollars to persuade foreign investors that Canada was an excellent place in which to invest!

The National Energy Program. Without doubt, the major attempt at encouraging Canadian ownership of a previously foreign-dominated industry was embodied in the National Energy Program (NEP) introduced in October 1980. The NEP gave favorable tax treatment to Canadian companies relative to foreign-owned companies. As a result, the foreign ownership of Canadian oil production fell sharply in the early 1980s following the introduction of the NEP.

What will future foreign investors conclude from the Canadian government's willingness to appropriate the profits of particular investments after they have succeeded? Before the event, all investment is uncertain. If investors conclude that they will have to bear the losses when they fail, but that a large portion of the profits may be appropriated

(above and beyond known tax and other liabilities) if they are successful, the attractiveness of the investment is diminished. The resulting discouragement of new foreign investment will appeal to nationalists who wish to reduce foreign ownership, while it will seem undesirable to those who worry about maintaining a sufficient flow of investment to maintain jobs and competitiveness in the Canadian economy.

Whatever the ethics of the policy, its timing turned out to be disastrous. American interests were bought out at the peak of the boom in oil prices and profitability. Even after being penalized by discriminatory taxes, the prices paid were very high compared with those ruling after the break in oil prices in 1982–1984. To buy out American equity, Canadian firms borrowed vast amounts, much of it in the United States, at the very high interest rates prevailing at the time. Thus Americans were forced to convert equity, which was almost immediately to fall in value as world oil prices slumped, into debt that then earned unprecedented high interest rates. U.S. companies ended up with a very profitable deal, while Canadian companies became so saddled with high interest debt that some of them, such as the giant Dome Petroleum, had to be bailed out by the government. If Canadians were going to buy out U.S. oil interests, a worse moment could not have been chosen to do so.

What Price Economic Independence?

It is generally agreed that the Canadian economy has benefited greatly from foreign investment. Productivity and the standard of living have been enhanced not only by the infusion of new capital, but also by the accompanying flow of management skills and technology. At the same time, the emergence of the "multinational" firm as a dominant force in the Canadian economy has raised many questions of a noneconomic nature. While the Canadian public must decide to what extent it wishes to restrict foreign influence, economists have a duty to point out the substantial economic costs that may be involved in greater economic independence.

SUMMARY

1. The case for free trade is that world output of all commodities can be higher under free trade than when protectionism restricts regional specialization.

2. Free trade among nations may be restricted intentionally by protectionist policies in the form of tariffs, import quotas, restrictions on the purchase of foreign exchange, and many other nontariff barriers.

3. Protection can be urged as a means to ends other than maximizing world living standards. Examples of such ends are to produce a diversified economy, to reduce fluctuations in national income, to retain distinctive national traditions, and to improve national defense.

4. Protection can also be urged on the grounds that it may lead to higher living standards for the protectionist country than would a policy of free trade. Such a result might come about through exploiting a monopoly position or by allowing inexperienced or uneconomically small industries to become efficient enough to compete with foreign industries.

5. Some fallacious free trade arguments are that (a) because it is possible for free trade to be beneficial, free trade will in fact always be beneficial; and (b) because infant industries seldom admit to growing up and thus try to retain their protection indefinitely, the whole country necessarily loses by protecting its infant industries.

6. Some fallacious protection arguments are that (a) mutually advantageous trade is impossible because one trader's gain must always be the other's loss; (b) buying abroad sends our money abroad, while buying at home keeps our money at home; (c) our high-paid workers must be protected against the competition from low-paid foreign workers; (d) protectionism creates jobs.

7. External trade has played a crucial role in Canada's economic development. Apart from the ex-

panded trade in automobiles following the 1965 agreement with the United States, raw and semifinished products continue to dominate exports; manufactured goods account for a large proportion of imports.

8. Many economists believe that Canadian productivity and living standards are substantially reduced by tariffs and the increasingly common nontariff barriers to trade, which promote domestic production for a small domestic market and prevent the realization of economies of scale. The formation of a North American free trade area has been advocated as a means of raising Canadian incomes.

9. Since the mid 1950s there has been considerable controversy in Canada over the increasing degree of U.S. control of Canadian industry, particularly in the manufacturing sector and the extractive industries. To a considerable extent the issue involves value judgments concerning the desirable degree of economic independence. Government policy has included restrictions on foreign ownership in key sectors, establishment of a Canada Development Corporation, the Foreign Investment Review Act, and the National Energy Program.

TOPICS FOR REVIEW

Free trade and protectionism
Tariff and nontariff barriers to trade
The case for some protectionism
The case for free trade versus no trade
Fallacious arguments for free trade
Fallacious arguments for protectionism
General Agreement on Tariffs and Trade (GATT)
The National Policy
Reciprocity

DISCUSSION QUESTIONS

1. Adam Smith saw a close connection between the wealth of a nation and its willingness "freely to engage" in foreign trade. What is the connection?
2. The citizens of underdeveloped Atlantis can weave two feet of cloth an hour or gather one basket of coconuts.

Their ministers approach the republic of Mu, whose inhabitants can weave three feet of cloth or gather two baskets of coconuts in the same period of time, and offer to trade. What possible opposition speeches do you imagine will be heard in Parliament in the capital of Mu? Appraise the validity of a few different arguments. As an economist, advise the Mu government.

3. Uruguay, formerly a significant exporter of raw beef and mutton, found it needed more exports to pay for its greatly increased imports of oil. Because the market for raw meat was limited, it decided to take advantage of a low wage rate by processing its beef, hides, and wool and then exporting these processed goods. Its exports doubled within a year with no change in exchange rates. What does this indicate about Uruguay's comparative advantages?

4. The government of Brazil, by restricting exports of coffee, has greatly improved its balance of payments and raised its national income. Is it possible that Brazil is an exception to the proposition that there are gains from trade?

5. "The only protariff argument that is likely to be valid for the whole world taken as an economic unit (rather than for a particular nation at a particular time) is the infant industry argument." Explain why you agree or disagree with this statement.

6. Listed below are some recent average duties paid in Canada, by industry classes.

Agricultural implements	0 %
Publishing and printing	1.4%
Sawmills	2.3%
Feed manufacturers	2.6%
Household radio and TV	19.0%
Distilleries	20.0%
Shoe factories	23.0%
Tobacco products	25.0%

What economic and political reasons can you see for duties on some commodities being above the average rate of duty charged and for others being below it? What other forms of protectionism could make some duties misleading?

7. Suppose Quebec formed a separate state, refusing to trade with the rest of Canada. What predictions would you make about the standard of living compared to what it is in Canada today? Does the fact that Canada, the United States, and Mexico are separate countries lead to a lower standard of living in the three countries than if they were united into a new country called Northica?

8. Suppose each of the Canadian provinces was a separate country. If free trade were permitted among these "countries," would you expect a pattern of production to exist different from the one that does exist? If Manitoba prohibited all trade, what would be the effect on Manitoba and on the other nine countries? Suppose all ten countries prohibited all trade. What would be the result?

9. If the European Common Market caused such a rise in efficiency that the price of every good produced in Germany, France, and Italy fell below the prices of the same good manufactured in Canada, what would happen? Would Canadians gain or lose because of this?

10. What would be the economic advantages to Canada of a North American free trade area? The Atlantic provinces are already part of a Canadian free trade area, yet incomes are much lower there than in Ontario. Why? Is it possible that all of Canada might become a low-income region under free trade with the United States?

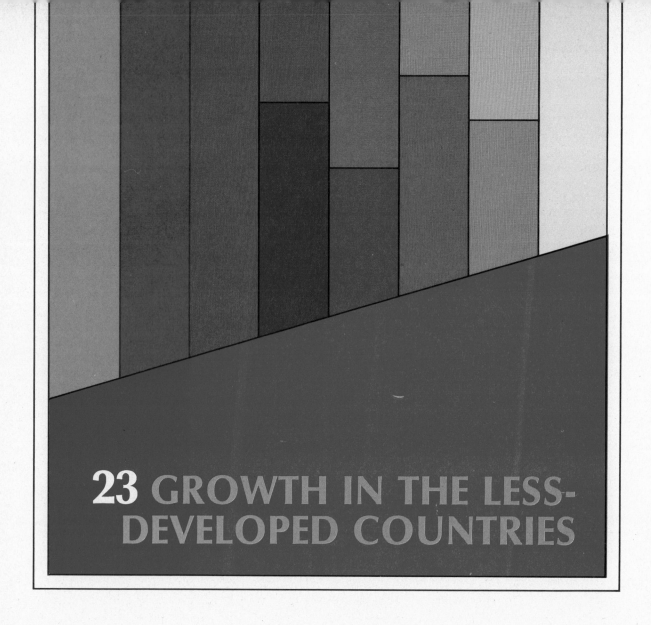

23 GROWTH IN THE LESS-DEVELOPED COUNTRIES

It is only about 10,000 years since human beings became food *producers* rather than food *gatherers*. It is only within the last few centuries that a significant proportion of the world's population could look forward to anything but a hard struggle to wrest a subsistence from a reluctant nature. The concept of leisure combined with high consumption standards as a right to be enjoyed by all is new in human history.

THE UNEVEN PATTERN OF DEVELOPMENT

There are more than 4.5 billion people alive today, but the wealthy parts of the world—where people work no more than 40 or 50 hours per week, enjoy substantial leisure, and have a level of consumption at or above *half* of that attained by the citizens of

TABLE 23–1 INCOME AND POPULATION DIFFERENCES AMONG GROUPS OF COUNTRIES, 1981

Classification (based on GNP per capita in 1976 U.S. dollars)	Number of countries (1)	GNP (billions) (2)	Population (millions) (3)	GNP per capita (4)	Percentage of the world's GNP (5)	Percentage of the world's population (6)	Growth rate[a] (7)
I Less than $400	28	$ 316	1,110	$ 285	3.2	38.2	1.4
II $401–1,000	26	310	517	601	3.2	17.8	4.4
III $1,001–3,000	29	955	466	2,050	9.4	16.0	4.9
IV $3,001–10,000	24	3,094	392	7,894	31.6	13.5	3.8
V More than $10,000	15	5,109	424	12,051	52.2	14.5	4.5

Source: International Financial Statistics Yearbook, 1982; Handbook of Economic Statistics, 1982.
[a]Average annual percentage rate of growth of real GNP per capita, 1975–1981.

Over half of the world's population lives in poverty; many of the very poorest are in countries that have the lowest growth rates and thus fall ever farther behind. The unequal distribution of the world's income is shown in columns 5 and 6. Groups I–II, which have over 50 percent of the world's population, earn less than 10 percent of world income. Groups IV–V, with 28 percent of the world's population, earn over 80 percent of world income. Column 7 shows that the poorest countries are not closing the gap in income between rich and poor countries.

Canada and the United States—contain only about 16 percent of the world's population. Many of the rest exist on a level at or below that enjoyed by peasants in ancient Egypt or Babylon.

Data of the sort shown in Table 23-1 cannot be accurate down to the last $100.[1] Nevertheless, the *development gap*—the discrepancy between the standards of living in countries at either end of the distribution—is real and large.

There are many different ways to look at the inequality of income distribution among the world's population. One is shown in Figure 23-1, which plots the Lorenz curve of the world's income distribution. To give perspective on the disparity in income among countries, the middle line shows the Lorenz curve of income distribution among people in Canada. It is much closer to equality than the world distribution.

[1] There are many problems in comparing national incomes across countries. For example, home-grown food is vitally important to living standards in underdeveloped countries, but it is excluded—or at best imperfectly included—in the national income statistics of most countries. So is the contribution of a warm climate. But nevertheless the data in the table do reflect enormous real differences in living standards that no statistical discrepancies can hide.

Another way of looking at inequality is to look at the geographic distribution of income per capita, as shown in Figure 23-2. Recent political discussions of income distribution have distinguished between richer and poorer nations as "North" versus "South." The map reveals why.

The Consequences of Underdevelopment

The consequences of very low income can be severe. For a rich country such as Canada, variations in rainfall are reflected in farm output and farm income. In poor countries such as those of the Indian subcontinent or the Sahel area of central Africa, variations in rainfall are reflected in the death rate. Many live so close to subsistence that slight fluctuations in the food supply bring death by starvation to large numbers. Other less dramatic characteristics of poverty include inadequate diet, poor health, short life expectancy, illiteracy, and—most important—an attitude of helpless resignation to the caprices of nature.

For these reasons, reformers in underdeveloped countries—often called **less-developed countries (LDCs)**—feel a sense of urgency not felt by their counterparts in rich countries. Yet, as the first row of Table 23-1 shows, the development gap for the very poorest countries has been widening. As will be seen, this is a problem of both output and population. It is also an international political problem.

Incentives for Development

Obviously underdevelopment is nothing new.[2] Concern with it as a remediable condition, however, is recent; it has become a compelling policy issue only within the present century. Probably the dominant reason for this new concern has been the apparent success of planned programs of "crash" development, of which the Soviet experience is the most remarkable and the Chinese the most recent. Leaders in other countries ask: If they can do it, why not us?

A second push toward development has come from the developed countries that have adopted policies to aid less-developed countries. We shall discuss such programs and their motivation later.

A third pressure for development results from the emergence of a relatively cohesive bloc of LDCs within the United Nations. The bloc is attempting to use political power to achieve economic ends.

What are the causes of underdevelopment, and how may they be overcome?

BARRIERS TO ECONOMIC DEVELOPMENT

Income per head grows when aggregate income grows faster than population. Many forces can impede such growth.

Population Growth

Population growth is a central problem of economic development. Today many LDCs have a

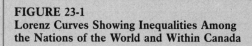

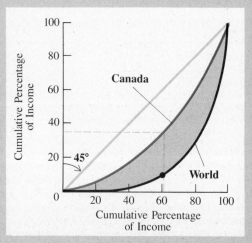

FIGURE 23-1
Lorenz Curves Showing Inequalities Among the Nations of the World and Within Canada

The inequality in the distribution of income is much less within Canada than it is among all the nations of the world. In a Lorenz curve, a wholly equal distribution of income would be represented by the 45° line: 20 percent of the population would have 20 percent of the income, 50 percent of the population would have 50 percent of the income, and so on. The very unequal distribution of world income is shown by the black curve. For example, 60 percent of the world's population live in countries that earn only 10 percent of the world's income, as shown by the black dot.

Contrast this with the distribution of income within Canada: the poorest 60 percent of the Canadian population earn 33 percent of the nation's income. This is not equality, but it is much less unequal than the differences between rich and poor countries.

---

rising national income combined with a rising number of mouths to feed. Thus, their standards of living are no higher than they were a hundred or even a thousand years ago. They have made appreciable gains in total income, but most of the gains have been eaten up (literally) by the increasing population. Table 23-2 shows this.

The population problem has led economists to talk about the *critical minimum effort* that is required not merely to increase capital, but to in-

---

[2] The terminology of development is often confusing. *Underdeveloped, less developed,* and *developing* do not mean the same thing in ordinary English, yet each has been used to describe the same phenomenon. For the most part we shall refer to the underdeveloped countries as the *less-developed countries,* the LDCs for short. Some of them are making progress, that is, developing; others are not.

FIGURE 23-2
Countries of the World, According to Per Capita GNP, 1976

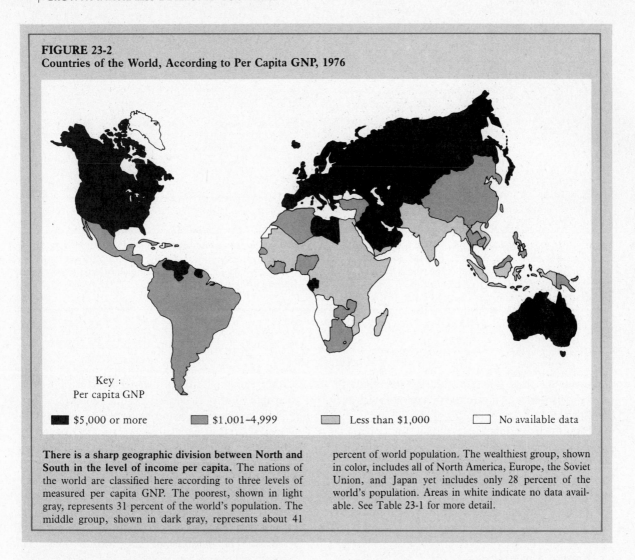

Key :
Per capita GNP

■ $5,000 or more   ▨ $1,001–4,999   ▨ Less than $1,000   ☐ No available data

There is a sharp geographic division between North and South in the level of income per capita. The nations of the world are classified here according to three levels of measured per capita GNP. The poorest, shown in light gray, represents 31 percent of the world's population. The middle group, shown in dark gray, represents about 41 percent of world population. The wealthiest group, shown in color, includes all of North America, Europe, the Soviet Union, and Japan yet includes only 28 percent of the world's population. Areas in white indicate no data available. See Table 23-1 for more detail.

crease it fast enough so that the increase in output outraces the increase in population. The problem arises because population size is not independent of the level of income. When population control is left to nature, nature often solves it in a cruel way. Population increases until many are forced to live at a subsistence level; further population growth is halted by famine, pestilence, and plague. This grim possibility was perceived early in the history of economics by Thomas Malthus.

In some ways, the population problem is more severe today than it was even a century ago because advances in medicine and in public health have brought sharp and sudden decreases in death rates. It is ironic that much of the compassion shown by wealthier nations for the poor and underprivileged people of the world has traditionally taken the form of improving their health, thereby doing little to avert their poverty. We praise the medical missionaries who brought modern medicine to the tropics, but the elimination of malaria has doubled population growth in Sri Lanka. Cholera, once a killer, is now largely under control. No one argues against controlling disease, but other steps must also be

TABLE 23–2 THE RELATION OF POPULATION GROWTH TO PER CAPITA GNP, 1975–1981
          (Percentages)

Classification of countries (GNP per capita, 1976 U.S. dollars)			Average annual rate of growth of			Population growth as a percentage of real GNP growth
Group[a]	Average income level	Percentage of population	Real GNP	Population	Real GNP per capita	
I–II	less than $1,000	56.0	2.8	2.4	2.9	85
III–IV	$1,001–10,000	29.5	5.4	2.1	4.3	38
V	More than $10,000	14.5	3.1	0.8	4.5	25

Source: Calculated from sources in Table 23-1.
[a] Groups from Table 23-1.

Growth in per capita real income depends on the difference between growth rates of real national income and population. The very poorest countries have *both* a relatively low growth rate of income and a relatively high growth rate of population. The middle group shows rising living standards despite large population growth by virtue of a high growth rate of income. The wealthiest countries owe much of their growth in living standards to a low rate of population increase.

taken if the child who survives the infectious illnesses of infancy is not to die of starvation in early adulthood.

Figure 23-3 illustrates actual and projected world population growth. The population problem is not limited to underdeveloped countries, but about seven-eighths of the expected growth in the world's population is in Africa, Asia, and Latin America, those areas where underdevelopment is the rule rather than the exception.

Natural Resources

A country with ample fertile land and a large supply of easily developed resources will find growth in income easier to achieve than one poorly endowed with such resources. Kuwait has an income per capita above that of the United States because by accident it sits on top of the world's greatest known oil field. But a lack of oil proved a devastating setback to many LDCs when the OPEC cartel increased oil prices tenfold during the 1970s. Without oil their development efforts would be halted, but to buy oil took so much scarce foreign exchange that it threatened to cripple their attempts to import needed capital goods.

The amount of resources available for production is at least in part subject to control. In fact, a nation's supplies of land and natural resources are often readily expandable in their effective use, if not in their total quantity.

Lands left idle because of lack of irrigation or spoiled by lack of crop rotation are well-known examples of barriers to development. Ignorance is another. The nations of the Middle East sat through recorded history alongside the Dead Sea without realizing that it was a source of potash. Not until after World War I were these resources utilized; now they provide Israel with raw materials for its fertilizer and chemical industries.

Inefficient Use of Resources

Low levels of income and slower than necessary growth rates may result from the inefficient use of resources as well as the lack of key resources.

It is useful to distinguish between two kinds of inefficiency. An hour of labor would be used inef-

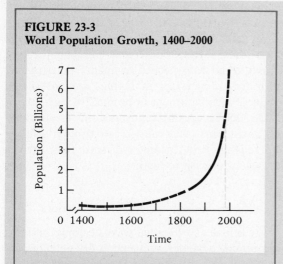

FIGURE 23-3
World Population Growth, 1400–2000

Population (Billions) — Time

0 1400 1600 1800 2000

The current growth in the world's population is explosive. The solid line reflects present measurements. The dashed line involves projections from observed trends. It took about 50,000 years from the emergence of modern human beings for the world's population to reach 1 billion. It took 100 years to add a second billion, 30 years to add the third billion, and 15 years to add the fourth billion. If present trends continue, the 1975 population of 4 billion will double by 2005.

ficiently, for example, if a worker, even though working at top efficiency, were engaged in making a product that no one wanted. Using society's resources to make the wrong products is an example of **allocative inefficiency.**

In terms of the production possibility boundary encountered in Chapter 1, allocative inefficiency represents operation at the wrong place on the boundary. Allocative inefficiency will occur if the signals to which people respond are distorted—both monopoly and tariffs are commonly cited sources of distortions—or if market imperfections prevent resources from moving to their best uses.

A second kind of inefficiency has come to be called X-inefficiency, following Professor Harvey Leibenstein. **X-inefficiency** arises whenever resources are used in such a way that even if they are making the right product, they are doing so

less productively than is possible. One example would be workers too hungry or too unmotivated to concentrate on their tasks.

The distinction between allocative inefficiency and X-inefficiency is illustrated in Figure 23-4. All economies suffer from X-inefficiency because all are to some extent captives of their customs, their institutions, and their histories. But LDCs may be particularly vulnerable because of illiteracy, poor health, and lack of skills.

Inadequate Human Resources

A well-developed entrepreneurial class, motivated and trained to organize resources for efficient production, is often missing in underdeveloped countries. Its absence may be a heritage of a colonial system that gave the local population no opportunity to develop; it may result from the fact that managerial positions are awarded on the basis of family status or political patronage; it may reflect the presence of economic or cultural attitudes that do not favor acquisition of wealth by organizing productive activities; or it may simply be due to the nonexistence of the quantity or quality of education or training that is required.

Poor health is likewise a source of inadequate human resources. When the labor force is healthy less time is lost and more effective effort is expended. The economic analysis of medical advances is a young field, however, and there is a great deal to be learned about the size of the drag of poor health on the growth of an economy.

Infrastructure

Key services—called **infrastructure**—such as a transportation and communications network, are necessary to efficient commerce. Roads, bridges, railroads, and harbors are needed to transport people, materials, and finished goods. The most dramatic confirmation of their importance comes in wartime, when belligerents always place high priority on destroying each other's transportation facilities.

Reasonable phone and postal services, water supply, and sanitation are essential to economic

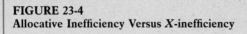

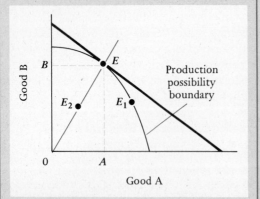

Good B

B

E

E_2 E_1

Production
possibility
boundary

0   A

Good A

Allocative inefficiency places the society at an inappropriate point on its production possibility boundary, while X-inefficiency places the society inside this boundary. The thinner black curve represents a society's production possibilities between two goods, A and B. The slope of the thicker black line represents the opportunity cost of good B in terms of good A. The efficient output of A and B is represented at point E. E_1 is inefficient in the allocative sense: society is operating on its production possibility boundary but producing too much A and too little B for the given opportunity cost. In contrast, at E_2 the proportions of B and A are the same as at E, but the society is operating inside its boundary. This is X-inefficiency.

development. The absence, whatever the reason, of a dependable infrastructure can impose severe barriers to economic development.

Financial Institutions

The lack of an adequate system of financial institutions is often a barrier to development. Investment plays a key role in growth, and one source of funds for investment is the savings of households and firms. When banks and banking do not function well and smoothly, the link between private saving and investment may be broken and the problem of finding funds for investment greatly intensified.

Many people in LDCs do not trust banks, sometimes with good reason, more often without. When banks cannot count on their deposits being left in the banking system, they cannot engage in the kind of long-term loans needed to finance investments. As a result, increases in savings are not always available for investment in productive capacity.

Developing countries must not only create banking institutions, they must create enough stability and reliability that people will trust their savings to those who wish to invest.

Cultural, Social, and Religious Barriers

Traditions and habitual ways of doing business vary among societies, and not all are equally conducive to productivity. Max Weber argued that the early "Protestant ethic" encouraged the acquisition of wealth and hence encouraged growth more than ethics that directed away from the economic sphere.

Often in the LDCs personal considerations of family, of past favors, or of traditional friendship or enmity are more important than market incentives in motivating behavior. One may find a too-small firm struggling to survive against a larger rival and learn that the owner prefers to remain small rather than expand because expansion would require use of nonfamily capital or leadership. To avoid paying too harsh a competitive price for built-in inefficiency, the firms' owners may then spend half their energies in an attempt to influence the government to prevent larger firms from being formed or to try to secure restrictions on the sale of output—and they may well succeed. Such behavior will inhibit economic growth.

In an environment where people believe that it is more important who your father is than what you do, it may take a generation to persuade employers to change their attitudes and another generation to persuade workers that times have changed. In a society in which children are expected to stay in their fathers' occupations, it is more difficult for the labor force to change its characteristics and to adapt to the requirements of growth than in a society where upward mobility is itself a goal. Structuring incentives is a widely used form of policy action in market-oriented economies, but this policy will be less effective in a society that emphasizes traditional rather than self-interested behavior.

There is lively debate on how much to make of the significance of differing cultural attitudes. Some believe that traditional and cultural considerations dominate peasant societies to the exclusion of economic responses; others suggest that any resulting inefficiency may be relatively small.

Although social, religious, or legal patterns make growth more difficult, this does not imply that they are undesirable. Instead it suggests that the benefits of these patterns must now be weighed against the costs, of which the effect on growth is one. When people derive satisfaction from a religion whose beliefs inhibit growth, when they value a society in which every man owns his own land and is more nearly self-sufficient than in another society, they may be quite willing to pay a price in terms of growth opportunities foregone.

Access to Larger Markets

Most less-developed countries have only limited markets of their own in which to sell the goods they produce. If they are to develop, these LDCs must have access to the markets of the advanced countries; as the LDCs industrialize, the advanced countries must be willing to shift resources out of products where the LDCs develop a comparative advantage. Unfortunately, in response to the severe recession of the early 1980s, many advanced countries have introduced protectionist policies and thus excluded LDCs from their domestic markets. Unless the principles of relatively free trade are accepted, there will be little advantage to the LDCs from industrialization.

SOME BASIC CHOICES

Policies for economic development involve identifying the particular barriers to the level and kind of development desired and then devising ways of overcoming them. Although actual policies vary greatly from country to country, there are common basic choices that all developing countries must face.

How Much Government Control?

How much government control over the economy is necessary and desirable? Practically every shade of opinion from "The only way to grow is to get the government's dead hand out of everything" to "The only way to grow is to get a fully planned, centrally controlled economy" has been seriously advocated. The extreme views are easily refuted by historical evidence.

Many economies have grown with very little government assistance; Great Britain in the Industrial Revolution, Holland during the heyday of its colonial period, Singapore, Hong Kong, and Taiwan during modern times are all examples. Others, such as the Soviet Union and Austria, have sustained growth with a high degree of centralized control. In other countries almost every conceivable mix of state and private initiative has been used successfully.

The Case for Planning

Many barriers to development may be lowered by enlightened government actions. For example, most LDCs have insufficient savings to finance major investment projects. When living standards are low, people have urgent uses for their current income so savings tend to be low. In a variety of ways, governments can intervene and force people to save more than they otherwise would.

Compulsory saving has been one of the main aims of most development plans of centralized governments such as those of the USSR and China. The goal of such plans is to raise savings and thus lower current consumption below what it would be in an unplanned economy. Forced savings are largely associated with totalitarian regimes. In less centrally controlled societies planners often strive to increase the savings rate through tax incentives and monetary policies. The object is the same: to increase investment in order to increase growth, and thus to make future generations better off.

Central governments of an authoritarian sort can be particularly effective in overcoming some of the sources of X-inefficiency. A dictatorship may suppress social and even religious institutions that are barriers to growth, and it may hold on to power until a new generation grows up that did not know and does not value the old institutions. It is much more difficult for a democratic government, which must command popular support at each election, to do currently unpopular things in the interests of long-term growth. Whether the gains in growth that an authoritarian government can achieve are worth the political and social costs is, of course, an important value judgment.

The Case for the Market

Most people would agree that government must play an important part in any development program. Consider, for example, education, transportation, and communication. But what of the sectors usually left to private enterprise in advanced capitalist countries?

The advocates of market forces in these sectors place great emphasis on human drive, initiative, and inventiveness. Once the infrastructure has been established, they argue, an army of entrepreneurs will do vastly more to develop the economy than will an army of civil servants. The market will provide the opportunities and direct their efforts. People who seem lethargic and unenterprising when held down by lack of incentives will show bursts of energy when given sufficient self-interest in economic activity.

Furthermore, the argument goes, individual capitalists are far less wasteful of the country's capital than civil servants. A bureaucrat investing capital that is not his own (raised perhaps from the peasants by a state marketing board that buys cheap and sells dear) may choose to enhance his own prestige at the public's expense by spending too much money on cars, offices, and secretaries and too little on truly productive activities.

What Sorts of Education?

Most studies of underdeveloped countries suggest that undereducation is a barrier to development and often urge increased expenditures on education. This poses a choice: whether to spend educational funds on erasing illiteracy and increasing the level of mass education or on training a small cadre of scientific and technical specialists.

To improve basic education requires a large investment in school building and in teacher training. This investment will result in a visible change in the level of education only after 10 or more years, and it will not do much for productivity even over that time span.

Many developing countries have put a large fraction of their educational resources into training a small number of highly educated men and women—often by sending them abroad for advanced study—because the tangible results of a few hundred doctors or engineers or Ph.D.s are relatively more visible than the results from raising the school-leaving age by a year or two, say, from age 10 to age 12. It is not yet clear whether this policy pays off, but it is clear that it has some drawbacks.

Many of this educated elite are recruited from the privileged classes on the basis of family position, not merit; many regard their education as the passport to a new aristocracy rather than as a mandate to serve their fellow citizens; and an appreciable fraction emigrate to countries where their newly acquired skills bring higher pay than they do at home. Of those who return home, many seek the security of a government job, which they may utilize to advance their own status in what is sometimes a self-serving and unproductive bureaucracy.

What Population Policy?

The race between population and income has been a dominant feature of many underdeveloped countries. There are only two possible ways for a country to win this race. One is to make a massive push to achieve a growth rate well in excess of the rate of population growth. The other is to control population growth.

The problem *can* be solved by restricting population growth. This is not a matter of serious debate, though the means of restricting it are, for there are considerations of religion, custom, and education involved.

The consequences of different population policies are large. The birthrate in Sweden is 12 per thousand, and in Venezuela it is 42 per thousand. (The two countries have similar death rates.) These variations in birthrates have economic consequences. In Venezuela the net increase of population per year is 33 per thousand (3.3 percent), but it is only 3 per thousand (0.3 percent) in Sweden.

If each country were to achieve an overall rate of growth of output of 3 percent per year, Sweden's living standards would be increasing by 2.7 percent per year while Venezuela's would be falling by 0.3 percent per year. In 1977 Sweden's income per capita ($8,400) was three times as high as Venezuela's ($2,600)—and Venezuela is the wealthiest country in South and Central America. The gap will widen rapidly if present population trends continue.

Population control can take the form of public education programs designed to alter attitudes toward family size and to encourage the avoidance of unplanned, or at least involuntary, pregnancies. At the other extreme are massive programs of compulsory sterilization such as Prime Minister Indira Gandhi adopted in India in the mid 1970s. Between these extremes are many other possibilities, most of which use various economic and legal incentives or penalties to encourage a lower birthrate.

Customs can be changed to raise the average marriage age and hence lower the birthrate. Prohibition of child labor and the establishment of compulsory education alters the costs and benefits of having children and reduces desired family size. Changing the role of women and providing career alternatives outside the home can also lower the birthrate.

University of Maine Professor Johannes Overbeck reported recently that a comprehensive family planning program—involving the provision of a broad selection of birth control techniques, a broad range of social services, and research to develop more effective and cheaper contraceptives—would have an annual cost of $1 per capita in a typical LDC. Excluding mainland China, this amounts to around $2 billion per year for all LDCs combined, a relatively modest sum compared with the over $500 billion currently spent annually on armaments. If this estimate is roughly accurate, population policy offers an extremely high return on spending to promote per capita growth in LDCs.

How to Acquire Capital?

A country can raise funds for investment in three distinct ways: from the savings (voluntary or forced) of its domestic households and firms, by loans or investment from abroad, and by contributions from foreigners.

Capital from Domestic Saving: The Vicious Circle of Poverty

If capital is to be created at home by a country's own efforts, resources must be diverted from the production of goods for current consumption. This means a cut in present living standards. If living standards are already at or near the subsistence level, such a diversion will be difficult. At best, it will be possible to reallocate only a small proportion of resources to the production of capital goods.

Such a situation is often described as *the vicious circle of poverty*: Because a country has little capital per head, it is poor; because it is poor, it can devote few resources to creating new capital rather than to producing goods for consumption; because little new capital can be produced, capital per head remains low, and the country remains poor.

The vicious circle can be made to seem an absolute constraint on growth rates. Of course it is not; if it were, we would all still be at the level of Neanderthal man. The grain of truth in the vicious circle argument is that some surplus must be available somewhere in the society to allow saving and investment. In a poor society with an even distribution of income, where nearly everyone is at the subsistence level, saving may be very difficult. But this is not the common experience. Usually there will be at least a small middle class that can save and invest if opportunities for the profitable use of funds arise.

Also in most poor societies today the average household is above the physical subsistence level. Even the poorest households will find that they can sacrifice some present living standards for a future gain. After all, presented with a profitable opportunity, villagers in Ghana planted cocoa plants at the turn of the century even though there was a seven-year growing period before any return could be expected!

The last example points to an important fact: In underdeveloped countries one resource that is often *not* scarce is labor hours. Profitable home or village investment that requires mainly labor inputs may be made with relatively little sacrifice in current living standards. However, this is not the kind of investment that will appeal to planners mesmerized by large and symbolic investments such as dams, nuclear power stations, and steel mills.

Imported Capital

Another way of accumulating the capital needed for growth is to borrow it from abroad. When a poor country borrows from a rich country, it can use the borrowed funds to purchase capital goods produced in the rich country. The poor country thus accumulates capital and needs to cut its current output of consumption goods only to pay interest on its loans. As the new capital begins to add to current production, it is possible to pay the interest on the loan and also to repay the principal out of the increase in output.

However, many countries, developed or undeveloped, are suspicious of foreign capital. They fear foreign investors will gain control over their industries or their government. The extent of foreign control depends on the form foreign capital takes. When foreigners buy bonds in domestic companies, they do not own or control anything; when they buy common stocks, they own part or all of a company, but their control over management may be small. If a foreign company (perhaps a multinational corporation) establishes a plant and imports its own managers and technicians, it will have much more control. Finally, if foreign firms subsidize an LDC government in return for permission to produce, they may feel justified in exacting political commitments.

Whether foreign ownership of one's industries carries political disadvantages sufficiently large to outweigh the economic gains is a subject of debate. In Canada, for example, there is serious political opposition to having a large part of Canadian industry owned by U.S. nationals. Many other countries actively seek increased foreign investment.

Foreign borrowing has become a serious problem for LDCs in recent years. Overly optimistic income expectations in the 1970s led to heavy borrowing. High interest rates in the 1980s greatly raised the cost of servicing this debt. World recession and rising protectionism in the developed world made it more difficult to earn the money necessary to pay interest on, let alone repay, the principal of this debt. This problem, which had reached the dimensions of a crisis by the mid 1980s, is further discussed in Chapter 40.

Contributed Capital

Investment funds for development are being received today by underdeveloped countries from the governments of the developed countries acting both unilaterally (as in the U.S. Agency for International Development and a similar Soviet program) and through international agencies such as the World Bank, the Export-Import Bank, and the OPEC Fund established in January 1980.

Contributed capital has played a significant role in post-World War II economic development. For example, American foreign aid expenditures in the decade after the war were $90 billion, and even today they amount to more than $3 billion per year. That $3 billion is more than 1 percent of the GNP of the 2 billion people who live in the most underdeveloped nations of the world. The OPEC Fund started with an initial capital of $4 billion and is expected to grow rapidly.

The Soviet Union has given substantial aid to less-developed countries. Russian aid in the 1950s was essential to China's development of heavy industry. In addition to funds, the USSR transported capital in the form of more than 150 complete plants and sent thousands of technicians and specialists to China to help plan, build, and run factories. China today is itself a significant donor to a few ideologically sympathetic countries, including Tanzania and Albania. Some of the issues involved in the relations between LDCs and the more developed nations are further discussed in Box 23-1.

ALTERNATIVE DEVELOPMENT STRATEGIES

In the search for development, individual LDCs have a number of policy options.[3] The choice of options is in part a matter of what the planners believe will work and in part a question of the nature of the society that will be created once development has occurred.

The noneconomic aspects of the choice of a development strategy may be illustrated by the Greek government's explicit decision in the mid 1960s to change the direction of its growth. At that time Greece was achieving rapid growth largely because of a booming tourist trade and the emigration of many young Greeks to West Germany to work in factories there. The emigrants had been earning incomes in Greece that were substantially below the Greek average, and their remittances home to their families increased both domestic income and foreign exchange reserves. Although it was helpful to the Greek growth rate these events threatened an image of life that visualized "Greece for the Greeks." Even at the prospect of some loss in growth, Greek planners recommended the restriction of emigration, the moderation of the size of the tourist role in the economy, and the development of new industry for the Greek economy.

There may also be economic reasons for choos-

[3] These options are not necessarily mutually exclusive—two (or more) might be implemented at the same time.

ing a different pattern of growth than the free market would provide. One reason planners seek to do so is their belief that they can evaluate the future more accurately than the countless individuals whose decisions determine market prices. A country need not passively accept its current comparative advantages. Many skills can be acquired, and fostering an apparently uneconomic domestic industry may, by changing the characteristics of the labor force, develop a comparative advantage in that line of production.

The Japanese had no visible comparable advantage in any industrial skill when Commodore Matthew Perry opened that feudal country to Western influence in 1854, but they became a major industrial power by the end of the century. Their continuing gains relative to the United States in fields such as steel, automobile production, and electronics do not need to be called to anyone's attention today. (Neither, however, were they centrally planned.) Soviet planners in the 1920s and 1930s chose to create an industrial economy out of a predominantly agricultural one and succeeded in vastly changing the mix between agriculture and industry in a single generation. Soviet planning is discussed further in Box 23-2 on pages 396–397.

These illustrations suggest why the choice of which development strategy to adopt is crucial. Governments must choose between agricultural and industrial emphases; between different kinds of industrial development; and between more or less reliance on foreign trade. Several possibilities have been widely advocated, and each has been tried. None is without difficulties.

Agricultural Development

Everyone needs food. An LDC may choose to devote a major portion of its resources to stimulating agricultural production, say, by mechanizing farms, irrigating land, and utilizing new seeds and fertilizers. If successful, the country will stave off starvation for its current population, and it may even develop an excess over current needs and so have a crop available for export. A food surplus can earn foreign exchange to buy needed imports.

BOX 23–1 "AID," "TRADE," OR "RESTITUTION"

Do developed nations give aid for humanitarian reasons, because it serves their political objectives, or because it is economically self-serving? Obviously all three motives can play a role, but which one dominates? Should LDCs demand aid, accept it gratefully, or reject it?

LDCs chronically lack capital and wealth. Typically they have large foreign debts. In these circumstances, one might think that foreign aid, whether from a single country or from an international forum, would be eagerly sought and gratefully received. This is not always so; there is some significant resistance to accepting aid.

The slogan "Trade, not aid" reflected political opposition to U.S. economic aid in certain recipient countries in the 1950s. Yugoslavia turned down much aid proffered by the Soviets after 1948, and China accepted no foreign aid after 1960. In 1975 Colombia made the decision to forego further U.S. aid on the grounds that it bred an unhealthy economic dependency.

The primary explanation of this attitude lies in a country's noneconomic goals. It may suspect the motives of the givers and fear that hidden strings may be attached to the offer. Most countries want to avoid either the fact or the appearance of being satellites.

One response was to do without aid, no matter how badly it was needed. Another, increasingly the pattern in the 1970s, was to reject "aid" but to demand "wealth transfers," not as a matter of charity but as a matter of "restitution" or redress for past sins by colonial powers against their former colonies. The obvious problem of asserting such claims against noncolonial powers such as the United States and the USSR has been no deterrent. There is a generalized sense that the inhabitants of the "North" exploited the nations of the "South" in past cen-

turies and that present generations should redress the balance. The paradoxical aspect of this is that while "restitution, not charity" makes LDCs willing to accept aid, it decreases the willingness of developed countries to offer it.

What *are* the motives of givers of aid? The Scandinavian Nobel Prize winning economist Gunnar Myrdal has argued that humanitarian considerations have played a large role. The evidence for humanitarian motives is in part the success of voluntary appeals in developed countries for food, funds, and clothes for persons in stricken areas of the world. As per capita incomes have risen in the Western world, so have contributions, private as well as public. It is the policy of the governments of most of the so-called Western democracies to devote some resources to alleviating poverty throughout the world.

Professor Edward S. Mason, among others, has argued that such aid can best be understood by looking to political and security motives. He points to the substantial U.S. congressional preference for military assistance over economic assistance, the denial of aid to countries such as Sri Lanka that traded with Communist countries, the fostering of Tito's Yugoslavia *because* of its anti-Soviet stand. Many critics of OPEC think its contributions are designed to quiet opposition among LDCs to the oil price hikes that have proved so profitable to the oil producers and so painful to oil users, LDCs and developed countries alike.

Should motives and attitudes, either of givers or of receivers, matter? After all, it is economically beneficial to receive aid when you are poor. Economists cannot say that fears, aspirations, pride, and "face" are either foolish or unworthy; they can only note that they do have their cost.

Among the attractions of the agricultural strategy are that it does not require a great deal of technical training or hard-to-acquire know-how, nor does it place the country in direct competition with highly industrial countries.

India, Pakistan, Taiwan, and other Asian countries have achieved dramatic increases in food production by the application of new technology and seed to agricultural production. Increases of up to 50 percent have been achieved in grain production, and it has been estimated that with adequate supplies of water, pesticides, fertilizers, and modern equipment, production could be doubled or tripled. This has been labeled the *green revolution*.

The possibilities of achieving such dramatic gains in agricultural output may seem irresistible at first glance, yet many economists think they should be resisted—and that they create a series of problems.

One problem is that a vast amount of resources is required to irrigate land and mechanize production, and these resources have a high opportunity cost: They could provide industrial development and industrial employment opportunities. Critics of the agricultural strategy argue that the search for a generation free from starvation will provide at best only a temporary solution because population will surely expand to meet the food supply. Instead, they argue, underdeveloped countries should start at once to reduce their dependence on agriculture. Let someone else grow the food; industrialization should not be delayed.

A second problem with the agricultural strategy is that the great increases in world production of wheat, rice, and other agricultural commodities that the green revolution makes possible could depress their prices and not lead to increased earnings from exports. What one agricultural country can do so can others, and there may well be a glut on world markets.

This is the heart of the argument of Latin American economist Raúl Prebisch. He maintains that underdeveloped countries, overspecialized in the production of agricultural commodities, are sure to suffer steadily worsening terms of trade relative to manufacturing outputs. Prebisch believes that current market prices fail to anticipate fully this worsening in the terms of trade for agriculture and thus that planners should intervene and shift the country out of what is sure to be a long-run overreliance on agriculture.

A third problem has arisen (most acutely in India and Pakistan) where increasing agricultural output has been accompanied by decreasing labor requirements in agricultural production without a compensating increase in employment opportunities elsewhere. Millions of tenant farmers—and their bullocks—have been evicted from their tenant holdings by owners who are buying tractors to replace them. Many have found no other work.

A final danger of the agricultural strategy is that once a program of agricultural subsidization is put into place, it creates a serious potential dilemma. Continuation of high prices for producers and low prices for consumers creates a substantial, perhaps eventually an impossible, drain on the government's finances. Lowering the subsidy to producers risks a rural revolution. Eliminating the subsidy to consumers risks an urban revolution. The government finds itself with an untenable policy but with no room for maneuver.

Specialization in a Few Commodities

Many LDCs have at present unexploited resources such as copper, uranium, or opportunities for tourism. The principle of comparative advantage provides the traditional case for the desirability of relying on such resources. By specializing in producing those products in which it has the greatest comparative advantage, the country can achieve the most rapid growth in the short run. To neglect these opportunities will result in a lower standard of living than would result from specialization accompanied by increased international trade.

These are cogent reasons in favor of *some* specialization. But specialization involves risks, and the risks may be worth reducing even at the loss of some income. Specialization here, as with agri-

BOX 23–2 PLANNING IN THE SOVIET UNION

The modern *economic* history of the Soviet Union is usually taken to have begun in 1928, eleven years after the Bolshevik revolution. By the late 1920s Joseph Stalin had emerged as a strong man, ready to undertake the economic task of lifting Russia from an underdeveloped giant to a major industrial power. Basically, Stalin's policy had three strategies.

Planning Strategies

1. To consolidate management over all economic resources to ensure that they would respond to the needs of the regime.
2. To constrict consumption to an absolute minimum so that the maximum possible rate of capital accumulation, and thus growth, could be achieved.
3. To channel growth into the areas of heavy industrial development required for a major military power.

These objectives were pursued in a series of plans, including fairly general five-year plans and more specific one-year plans.

Five-year plans. Five-year plans are, roughly, blueprints for later detailed implementation. They contain no orders to individual plants and no detailed production quotas, but they do prescribe both the level of aggregate output that is to be achieved and the *structure* of the economy by major sectors and industries.

Every five-year plan has included decisions about how drastically to curtail consumption in order to release resources for investment. Each has also decided how much effort is to be devoted to developing educational and technical resources that will be needed in the future. Decisions are also required about such matters as the form capital investment should take, and the state-controlled banking system lends only to those enterprises whose expansion the planners want to encourage.

One-year plans. Planning details are spelled out in the one-year plans. They are complex exercises that translate the objectives of the five-year plans into detail sufficient to enable individual plants (or farms) to meet them and to ensure that the required supplies of resources are made available.

There is obviously an enormous coordinating job here. Tentative plans are sent to lower bureaucratic levels for comments and suggestions before being issued as final orders. Actual quotas are to some degree negotiated between the directors at the operating levels, who want to hold

---

culture, makes the economy highly vulnerable to cyclical fluctuations in world demand and supply. A recession in developed countries decreases overseas travel and creates problems for an LDC that has relied on tourism for foreign exchange.

The problem is not only cyclical. When technological or taste changes render a product partially or wholly obsolete, a country can face a major calamity for generations. Just as individual firms and regions may become overspecialized, so too may countries.

Import Substitution

During the Great Depression the collapse in world agricultural prices caused the value of the exports of agricultural countries to decline drastically relative to the prices of goods those countries imported. During World War II many countries found that the manufactured goods they wished to import were unavailable. In each of those situations dependence on foreign trade for necessities was unattractive. More recently, the rising prices of fuel

down the quotas expected of them, and the higher-level planners, who must achieve apparent miracles to satisfy overall growth objectives.

Prices in the Planning Process

Factor pricing. For internal use, "prices" of resources are designed to measure their scarcity value, compared to alternative uses. If the efficient use of resources is to occur, the charge for using, say, the services of a carpenter anywhere should reflect the value of his marginal product elsewhere.

But the state may wish to pay the carpenters a higher wage than this, either because it has embarked on a program of income redistribution in which carpenters are to be favored or because the state wishes to denote carpentry as a "prestige" occupation. To avoid productive inefficiency, the planners assign *two* wage rates for carpenters. One is charged as a cost of production; the other (which may be higher or lower) is actually paid out to carpenters.

With one important exception, this dual treatment of factor prices has long been part of Soviet planning. The exception concerns the cost of capital. Because "interest" is traditionally a payment to private owners of capital in capitalist societies, interest rates were odious to Marx and to early Marxists. Soviet planners were reluctant to assign a real scarcity-value interest rate to investment funds until studies showed that investment allocation was among the least efficient aspects of Soviet planning. Today a number very much like an interest rate is used to measure the cost of capital.

Consumer prices and the turnover tax. Consumer prices are made up of two parts: the full cost of the good produced, using the correct internal accounting prices for factors, plus the **turnover tax**. This is an excise tax, which varies tremendously from commodity to commodity.

The size of the turnover tax is determined by the planners' idea of what goods people should be encouraged or discouraged to consume. In part this is a means for redistributing income; goods consumed by low-income groups may have very low turnover taxes.

Revenue from the turnover tax is used by the state for new investment. By changing the turnover tax, the planners can affect the relative size of consumption and investment. By varying the tax rate on different commodities, the state affects the relative sacrifice in consumption among different kinds of consumers.

and other imports have created enormous balance-of-payments problems for many LDCs. Such countries must reduce imports, increase exports, or resort to foreign borrowing.

Much of the industrialization by LDCs in the 1950s and 1960s was directed toward **import substitution industry (ISI)**, which is producing at home goods that were previously imported. It is often necessary both to subsidize the home industry and to restrict imports to allow the ISI time to develop.

The ISI strategy has many problems. It fosters *inefficient* industries, and in the long run countries do not get rich by being inefficient. It aggravates inequalities in income distribution by raising the prices of manufactured goods relative to agricultural goods and by favoring profits over wages.

Export Development

Most development economists believe that industrialization ought to be encouraged only in areas where the country can develop a reliable and efficient industry that can compete in world markets.

Obviously, if Tanzania or Peru could develop steel, shipbuilding, and manufacturing industries that operated as efficiently as those of Japan or West Germany, they too might share in the rapid economic growth enjoyed by those industrial countries. Indeed, if a decade or two of protection and subsidization could give infant industries time to mature and become efficient, the price might be worth paying. After all, Japan and Russia were underdeveloped countries within living memory.

A major problem with this strategy is making up the initial productivity gap. India may create a steel industry and have its productivity increase year by year, but it must do more: It must catch up to the steel industries of other countries in order to compete in world markets. The catch-up problem is a race against a moving target. Suppose you must improve by 50 percent to achieve the present level of a competitor who is improving at r percent per year. If you want to catch up in 10 years, you must improve at $r + 4$ percent per year. [31] If r is 6 percent, you must achieve 10 percent. To achieve 7 percent or 8 percent may be admirable, but you will lose the race just the same.

Industrialization for export often means devoting resources for a long period to education, training, development of an infrastructure, and overcoming the various cultural and social barriers to efficient production. While this is hard, it is not impossible. Indeed, there have been some spectacular success stories: Brazil, Korea, Hong Kong, and Taiwan are charter members in a new category, "newly industrializing countries," that are providing vigorous competition in manufactured goods in world markets. Their success has led to a further (and bitterly resented) problem for the industrialization strategy. When an LDC succeeds, it is likely to find the developed countries trying to protect *their* home industries from the new competition.

LDCs sometimes pursue certain lines of production on a subsidized basis for prestige purposes or because of a confusion between cause and effect. Because most wealthy nations have a steel industry, the leaders of many underdeveloped nations regard

their countries as primitive until they develop a domestic steel industry. Because several LDCs have succeeded in producing consumer durables, many others assume that they should try to do so. However, if a country has a serious comparative disadvantage in steel or in making consumer durables, fostering such industries will make that country poor.

Commodity Price Stabilization Agreements

When all or most producers of a commodity can agree on price and output levels, they can achieve monopoly profits not available in competitive markets. Many LDCs are heavily committed to the production and export of one or more basic commodities such as bananas, bauxite, cocoa, coffee, copper, cotton, iron ore, jute, manganese, meat, oil, phosphates, rubber, sugar, tea, tropical timber, and tin. Why not get together and create an effective cartel that gives producers the enormous profits that are potentially available? This has been tried many times in history; until OPEC, it has always failed. Yet everyone knows that OPEC's success transformed a handful of formerly poor LDCs into the wealthiest of nations.[4]

OPEC's success was substantial, but has proven hard to sustain. Exporters of other commodities have had difficulty achieving even this limited success because the special conditions of demand and supply that apply to oil do not apply equally to most other primary commodities. In the case of oil there are few large producing countries, supply is quite inelastic outside those countries, demand is relatively inelastic in the short and middle run, and the largest producers are Arab nations that find discipline in political and religious unity and in a common hatred of Israel. Perhaps equally important, the largest producer—Saudi Arabia—was of-

---

[4] This has added to the terminological confusion. It was once fashionable to speak of a nonaligned *third world* as another term for LDCs, the first two "worlds" being the developed capitalist and developed socialist countries. Now some commentators divide the LDCs into a richer (oil-producing) *third world* and a still poor *fourth world*.

ten prepared to put up with a good deal of cheating by its partners.

A New International Economic Order (NIEO)?

In May 1974 the General Assembly of the United Nations adopted (over the objections of the developed countries) a Declaration on the Establishment of a New International Economic Order. This represented an attempt on the part of LDCs to utilize collective *political* power to achieve a larger share of the world's goods.[5] The NIEO proposals are aimed basically at wealth transfers instead of wealth creations; they are concerned with a more equal distribution of existing wealth rather than economic development.

The major proposals were threefold. First, establishment of marketing boards for primary products exported by the developing nations. These, modeled along the lines of OPEC, would reduce output, raise prices, and thus create monopoly profits for producers. Second, exports of manufactured goods from developing countries should receive preferential treatment in the markets of developed countries. Third, the enormous debts of the developing countries, incurred partly to finance development projects and partly to finance the greatly increased cost of oil imports, should be partly forgiven and partly rescheduled to provide for longer repayment periods and easier terms of finance.

Thus far, the major accomplishments of the NIEO demands have been small. The issues and proposals have been discussed extensively, but little major redistribution of wealth has resulted. From an economic point of view, NIEO has two major flaws. First, it focuses too much on redistribution and too little on seeking real growth in world output. Second, it puts its faith in bureaucratic allocations of wealth, trade, and natural resources rather than in market mechanisms. Nothing in the

world's experience to date suggests that this will increase total world output. Many modern development economists would share the view of Professor McCulloch that the developed countries should be adopting policies to expand rather than contract world wealth. If that is so, the major proposals of NIEO will not prove attractive.

SOME CONTROVERSIAL UNRESOLVED ISSUES

The economics of development, like most fields of economics, is in a state of change. The view presented in this chapter is perhaps the mainline view of economists in developed economies such as our own. Problems look different when viewed from the inside out, and they look different from the perspective of socialist nations than they do from market-oriented economies. Yet even within the group of Western economists studying development, there are important current controversies.

The Pace of Development

Reformers in underdeveloped countries often think in terms of transforming their economies within a generation or two. The sense of urgency is quite understandable, but unless it is tempered by some sense of historical perspective, totally unreasonable aspirations may develop—only to be dashed all too predictably.

Many underdeveloped countries are probably in a stage of economic development analogous to that of medieval England, having not yet achieved anything like the commercial sophistication of the Elizabethan era. It took 600 years for England to develop from the medieval economic stage to its present one. Such a change would be easier now, for much of the needed technology can be imported rather than invented. But what is the proper pace? To effect a similar growth within 50 or 100 years would require a tremendous achievement of the kind accomplished by America, Japan, and a handful of other countries; to aspire to do it in 20 or 30

[5] An excellent introduction to this development is Rachel McCulloch's *Economic and Political Issues in the NIEO* (International Institute for Economic Research, 1979). Professor McCulloch's analysis is heavily relied on here.

years may be to court disaster—or to invite repressive political regimes.

The View of Population Policy

The view presented in this chapter of population growth as a formidable barrier to development is neo-Malthusian and constitutes much of current conventional wisdom on underdevelopment.

This view allows little place for the enjoyment value of children by their parents. Critics point out that the psychic value of children should be included as a part of the living standards of their parents. They also point out that in rural societies even young children are a productive resource, and in societies where state help for the aged is negligible, fully grown children provide old-age security for their parents.

The neo-Malthusian theory is also criticized for assuming that people breed like animals. Critics point out that traditional methods of limiting family size have been known and practiced since the dawn of history. Thus they argue that large families in rural societies are a matter of choice.

The population explosion came not through any change in "breeding habits," but as a result of medical advances that greatly extended life expectancy (which surely must be counted as a direct welfare gain for those affected). Critics argue that once an urban society has developed, family size will be reduced voluntarily. This was certainly the experience of Western industrial countries; why, critics ask, should it not be the experience of the developing countries?

The Cost of Creating Capital

Is it true LDCs must suffer by sacrificing current consumption if they wish to grow? A recent criticism of this conventional wisdom questions the alleged heavy opportunity cost of creating domestic capital. Production of consumption and capital goods are substitutes only when factor supplies are constant and fully employed. But, critics say, the development of a market economy will lead people to substitute work for leisure.

For example, the arrival of Europeans with new goods to trade led the North American Indians to collect furs and other commodities needed for exchange. Until they were decimated by later generations of land-hungry settlers, the Indians' standard of living rose steadily with no immediate sacrifice. They created the capital needed for their production—weapons and means of transport—in their abundant leisure time. Thus their consumption began to rise immediately.

This too, the argument says, could happen in underdeveloped countries if market transactions were allowed to evolve naturally. The spread of a market economy would lead people to give up leisure in order to produce the goods needed to buy the goods that private traders are introducing from the outside world. In this view it is the pattern of development chosen, rather than development itself, that imposes the need for heavy sacrifices.

SUMMARY

1. Sustained economic development is relatively recent in history and has been highly uneven. About one-fourth of the world's population still exists at a level of bare subsistence, and nearly three-fourths are poor by Canadian standards. The gap between rich and poor is very large and is keenly felt.

2. The pressure for economic development comes in part from the LDCs. The transformation in less than half a century of Soviet Russia from a backward peasant economy to a major industrial power has had a powerful demonstration effect on the quest for economic development. Moreover, as the LDCs have become a cohesive political bloc within the United Nations, they have come to demand economic assistance in their development efforts.

3. There are many impediments to economic development; merely to want economic growth and development is not enough to assure it. Population growth, resource limitations, and the inefficient use of resources are among the barriers to economic development in particular underdeveloped countries. So too are a series of institutional and cultural barriers that make economic growth difficult.

4. A series of basic (and controversial) choices face LDCs as they contemplate development. How much should they intervene in the economy, and how much should they rely on the free market? History has demonstrated that growth is possible with almost any conceivable mixture of free-market and central control. Centralized planning can change both the pace of economic development and its direction; it can also prove highly wasteful and destroy individual initiative.

5. Educational policy, while vitally important to the long-run rate of economic development, yields its benefits only in the future. Consequently, the improvement of basic education is sometimes bypassed in the search for more immediate results.

6. A population policy is an important and volatile issue in most LDCs. The race between output and population is a critical aspect of development efforts in many countries. Different countries have chosen very different attitudes toward limiting population growth.

7. Acquiring capital for development is invariably a major concern in development. One source is domestic savings, but here the vicious circle of poverty may arise: A country that is poor because it has little capital cannot readily forego consumption to accumulate capital because it is poor. Importing capital rather than using domestic savings permits heavy investment during the early years of development. But imported capital is available only when the underdeveloped country has opportunities that are attractive to foreign investors. Much foreign capital for underdeveloped countries in the last three decades has been in the form of contributions by foreign governments and international institutions.

8. Selecting a development strategy involves a number of difficult choices. Much current debate about development concerns a choice among (a) agricultural development, (b) exploitation of natural resources, (c) development of import substi-

tution industries, and (d) development of an industrial capacity that will create new export industries. None of these strategies is without problems and risks.

9. Collective rather than individual development efforts became more common in the 1970s. OPEC's success renewed interest in commodity price stabilization cartels but without notable success. A political initiative calling for a New International Economic Order (NIEO) seems to have achieved little more than discussion over this period.

10. The view of economic development presented in this chapter is subject to criticism for neglecting to discuss—or misconceiving—important problems. One is the perhaps unrealistic haste that underlies most development efforts. A second is the overemphasis on population growth as a barrier to development. A third is an exaggeration of the opportunity cost of creating capital. Economic development is today a field in ferment.

TOPICS FOR REVIEW

The gap between LDCs and developed economies
Barriers to development
Infrastructure
The role of planning in development
Alternative development strategies
Wealth creation versus wealth transfers

DISCUSSION QUESTIONS

1. Each of the following is a headline from a recent newspaper story. Relate them to the problem of economic development.
   a. "Black Africa: Economies on the Brink of Collapse Because of OPEC"
   b. "Hungary Reforming Economy to Attract Tourists"
   c. "Goodyear to Build Plant in Congo for $16 Million"
   d. "Algeria's 4-Year Plan Stresses Industrial Growth"
   e. "India: Giant Hobbled by Erratic Rainfall"
   f. "Foreign Banks to Finance New Guinea Copper Mine"
   g. "Not All Benefit by Green Revolution"

    h. "OPEC Nations Provide Loans to Underdeveloped Nations to Pay for Oil Imports"

2. If you were a member of a government foreign aid team assigned to study needed development projects for a poor recipient country, to which of the following would you be likely to give relatively high priority, and why?

    a. Birth control clinics

    b. A national airline

    c. Taxes on imported luxuries

    d. Better roads

    e. Modernization of farming techniques

    f. Training in engineering and business management

    g. Primary education

    h. Scholarships to students to receive medical and legal training abroad

3. China requires 5 million tons more grain each year just to keep up with its annual population growth of 17 million people. This is about five times Canada's wheat supply at present. What policy choices do these facts pose for the Chinese government? How should it resolve those choices?

4. "This natural inequality of the two powers of population and of production in the earth . . . form the great difficulty that to me appears insurmountable in the way to perfectability of society. All other arguments are of slight and subordinate consideration in comparison of this. I see no way by which man can escape from the weight of this law which pervades all animated nature. No fancied equality, no agrarian regulations in their utmost extent, could remove the pressure of it even for a single century" (T.R. Malthus, *Population: The First Essay,* chapter 1, page 6).

    Discuss Malthus's "insurmountable difficulty" in view of the history of the past 100 years.

5. To what extent does the vicious circle of poverty apply to poor families living in developed countries? Consider carefully, for example, the similarities and differences facing a poor family living in New Brunswick and one living in Ghana, where per capita income is less than $400 per year. Did it apply to immigrants who arrived on the Montreal docks with $10 in their pockets?

6. The president of Venezuela said recently: "The decision of OPEC members to raise petroleum prices should be applauded by all third world countries. It represents the irrevocable decision to dignify the terms of trade, to revalue raw materials and other basic products of the third world." Which underdeveloped countries might be expected to have agreed? Which to have disagreed?

7. "High Coffee Prices Bring Hope to Impoverished Latin American Peasants" reads the headline. Mexico, Kenya and Burundi, among other underdeveloped countries, have the right combination of soil and climate greatly to increase their coffee production. Discuss the benefits and risks to them if they pursue coffee production as a major avenue of their development.

8. Discuss the reasoning behind the policies indicated by the following newspaper headlines (all appeared in the summer of 1983):

    a. "Mexico Proposes to Restructure $20 Billion Debt"

    b. "Ecuador Is Allowed to Delay Payment of $200 Million"

    c. "Philippines Propose a 34% Cut Next Year in Its Capital Spending"

    d. "Zimbabwe's Fourth Budget Cuts Spending and Extends Income Tax to More Blacks"

PART SEVEN
THE MARKET ECONOMY:
PROBLEMS AND POLICIES

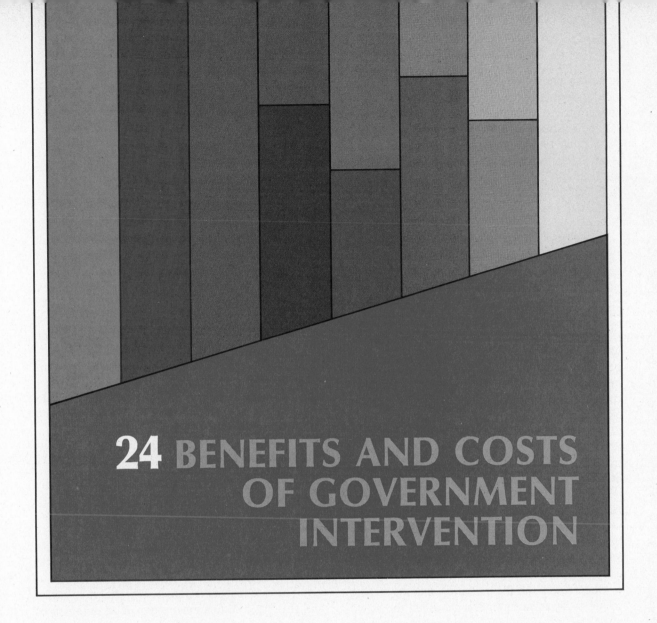

24 BENEFITS AND COSTS OF GOVERNMENT INTERVENTION

There are two caricatures of the North American economy. One pictures North America as the last stronghold of free enterprise, with millions in a mad and brutal race for the almighty dollar. In the other, North American business people, workers, and farmers are seen strangling slowly in a web of red tape spun by the spider of government regulation. Neither is realistic.

Many aspects of economic life in North America are determined by the operation of a free-market system. In Canada, private preferences, expressed through private markets and influencing private profit-seeking enterprises, determine much of what is produced, how it is produced, and the incomes of productive factors.

But even casual observation makes it clear that public policies and public decisions play a large role. Laws restrict what people and firms may do, and taxes and subsidies influence their choices. Much public expenditure is not market determined, and this influences the distribution of national product. Canada and the United States are in fact mixed economies.

The general case for some reliance on free markets is that allowing decentralized decision making is more efficient in a number of ways than having all economic decisions made and consciously coordinated by a centralized planning body. This is a lesson the governments of the USSR and Eastern Europe have learned the hard way.

The general case for some public intervention is that almost no one wants to let the market decide everything about our economic affairs. Most people's moral and practical sense argues for some state intervention to mitigate the disastrous results the market deals out to some. Most people believe there are areas where the market does not function well and where state intervention can improve the general social good. For such reasons, there is no known economy where the people have opted for complete *laissez faire* and against any kind of government intervention.

Thus the operative choice is not between an unhampered free-market economy or a fully centralized command economy. It is instead the choice of what mix between markets and government intervention best suits a people's hopes and needs. Although all economies are mixed, the mixture varies greatly among economies and over time. Whether the existing mixture should be changed—and if so, in which direction—is debated continually.

One reason for the mixture (and the debate) relates to what an unkind critic called the economists' two great insights: *Markets work, and markets fail.* A second reason is what the critic might call the political scientists' great insights: *Government intervention can work, and it can fail.* Economists try to understand the circumstances under which markets work well or poorly and the circumstances under which government intervention might improve or worsen market efficiency.

In this chapter we discuss the role of the government in economic markets. Why is it there at all? What does it do well, and what badly? Do we need more or less government intervention? Box

24-1 explores the relationship between economic analysis and the formation of economic policy.

MARKET SUCCESS

Any economy consists of thousands upon thousands of individual markets. There are markets for agricultural goods, for manufactured goods, and for consumers' services; there are markets for semimanufactured goods, such as steel and pig iron, which are outputs of some industries and inputs of others; there are markets for raw materials such as iron ore, trees, bauxite, and copper; there are markets for land and for thousands of different types of labor; there are markets in which money is borrowed and in which securities are sold.

An economy is not a series of markets functioning in isolation but an interlocking system in which an occurrence in one market will affect many others.

How Markets Coordinate

Any change, such as an increase in demand for beef, requires many further changes and adjustments. Should production of beef change? If so, by how much and in what manner? Someone or something must decide what is to be produced, how, and by whom, and what is to be consumed and by whom.

The essential characteristic of the market system is that its coordination occurs in an unplanned, decentralized way. Millions of people make millions of independent decisions concerning production and consumption every day. Most of these decisions are not motivated by a desire to contribute to the social good or to make the whole economy work well, but by fairly immediate considerations of personal or group self-interest. The price system coordinates these decentralized decisions, making the whole system fit together and respond to the wishes of the individuals who compose it.

The basic insight into how this system works is that decentralized, private decision makers, acting in their own interests, respond to such signals as the prices of what they buy and sell. Economists have long emphasized price as a signaling device. When a commodity such as oil becomes scarce, its free-market price rises. Firms and households that use it are led to economize on it and to look for alternatives. Firms that produce it are led to produce more of it. How the price system gets these decisions made has been examined at several places in this book (for example, with respect to carrots and brussels sprouts in Chapter 3, agriculture in Chapter 6, and ball-point pens in Box 15-1). When a shortage occurs in a market, price rises and windfall profits develop; when a glut occurs, price falls and windfall losses develop. These are *signals*, for all to see, that arise from the overall conditions of total supply and demand.

The Role of Windfall Profits and Losses

Although the free-market economy is often described as the *price system*, the basic engine that drives the adaptation of the economy is what are generally called windfall profits and losses.[1] A **windfall profit** is a change in earnings of a firm that arises out of unanticipated changes in market conditions. Windfall profits are *disequilibrium* phenomena.

A rise in demand or a fall in production costs creates windfall profits for that commodity's producers, while a fall in demand or a rise in production costs creates windfall losses. Windfall profits signal that there are too few resources devoted to that industry. In search of these profits, more resources will enter the industry, increasing output and driving down price, until windfall profits are driven to zero. Windfall losses signal the reverse. Resources leave the industry until those left behind are no longer suffering losses.

The importance of windfall profits is that they set in motion forces that tend to move the economy toward a new equilibrium.

---

[1] Frequently we will use the phrase windfall *profits* to include, as negative profits, windfall *losses*. In economic theory windfall profits are sometimes described as *quasi-rents*.

Individual households and firms respond to common signals according to their own best interests. There is nothing planned or intentionally coordinated about their actions, yet when (say) a shortage causes price to rise, individual buyers begin to reduce the quantities they demand and individual firms begin to increase the quantities they supply. As a result the shortage will begin to lessen. As it does, price begins to come back down, and windfall profits are reduced. These signals in turn are seen and responded to by firms and households. Eventually, when the shortage has been eliminated, there will be no windfall profits to attract further increases in supply. The chain of adjustments to the original shortage is completed.

People sometimes speak of windfall profits and losses as "undeserved." And so they are! They result from changes over which the beneficiaries have no control. But that does not mean they can safely be eliminated by government action. If the government taxed away *all* windfall profits and replaced by subsidy *all* windfall losses, it would effectively destroy the market economy by removing its driving force.

Because the economy is continuously adjusting to shocks, a snapshot of the economy at any given moment reveals substantial positive windfall profits in some industries and substantial windfall losses in others. A similar snapshot at another moment will also reveal windfall profits and losses, but their locations will be different.

The *unplanned* price system, like an *invisible hand* (Adam Smith's famous phrase), coordinates the responses of individual decision makers who seek only their own self-interests. Because they respond to signals that reflect market conditions, their responses are coordinated without any conscious planning of who may or must do what.

Who Responds?

Notice that in the sequence of signal-response-signal-response no one has to foresee at the outset the final price and quantity. Nor does any government agency have to specify who will increase production and who will decrease consumption. Some

BOX 24–1 ECONOMIC ANALYSIS AND ECONOMIC POLICY

All governments have economic policies. Even the decision not to act but to let nature take its course is a policy choice. Whether to rely on marketplace decision making or to replace it by government controls is as much a policy choice as is the decision to tax cigarettes.

Every year thousands of economic policy choices are made by federal, provincial, and municipal governments. Most of them are never seriously debated, nor is every facet of existing policy debated anew each year. Indeed, many current policies (such as giving unions the right to organize) were made decades ago. Only a few policy issues attract attention and become the subject of debate in a particular year.

Any policy action has two aspects: the goals that the decision makers are attempting to achieve and the means by which the goals are to be achieved. Economists do not establish goals, but they are often involved in resolving conflicts among competing goals, in forging the links between goals, and in evaluating policy proposals.

Governments have many goals. A particular policy that serves one goal may hinder another and have no effect on a third. Unemployment compensation, for example, may promote justice by protecting unemployed families from debilitating hardships; at the same time, it may hinder the quickness with which labor moves from labor-surplus to labor-scarce occupations, thereby causing inefficient use of resources. Moreover, it will have no effect one way or the other on air pollution.

Economics helps us to discover conflicts between competing goals of policy. For example, raising the minimum wage may seem desirable to people who believe that the lowest-paid workers are not earning enough income to maintain a decent standard of living. But if that policy results in some workers being laid off and becoming unemployed, the advantages to those who get higher wages must be balanced against the disadvantages of the extra unemployment.

Economists are frequently called on to suggest policies. The Economic Council of Canada has contributed to policy formation through its Annual Reviews, published each year since 1964. Among academic economists who have influenced policy in Canada, the most outstanding figure was the late W. A. Mackintosh, whose influence spanned a period of 50 years. A frequent vehicle for extragovernmental influence on policy is the Royal Commission. The report of the Carter Commission, a recent notable example, is well known within and outside Canada as a classic statement of the equity aspects of taxation.

Forming and Evaluating Policies

Economists must frequently determine whether a particular policy proposal—which may or may not have originated with them—is the best way to meet a particular problem. Five main questions need to be asked in every case: (1) What are the policy goals? (2) Do the proposed means achieve those goals? (3) What costs are directly imposed? (4) Do the proposed means have adverse side effects? (5) Are there better alternative means?

Policy Formation: An Example

Suppose that in anticipation of a possible war in the Middle East and a sudden decrease in availability of gasoline, a team of economists is asked to evaluate a proposal that the federal government institute rationing of gasoline by issuing coupons to every registered automobile owner. Each dated coupon permits the holder to purchase a specific number of gallons of gasoline during a particular week. The economists are told that the purpose is, first, to limit total purchases of gasoline to a specific number of gallons per week and, second, to do so in a way that shares the reduction in gasoline supply equitably among all drivers.

The economists may well conclude that the proposal can achieve its first objective but not the second. They may find that issuing coupons to *owners* does not achieve equal treatment of *drivers*. Some persons own two or more cars; others own no car and depend on borrowed or rented cars. Moreover, some people must drive long distances to and from work. The rationing plan tends to impose equal mileage, not equal sacrifice of mileage, on coupon receivers.

On the basis of this much analysis, the economists may point out that a revised plan, based on demonstrated needs plus a small free-driving allowance, would correct the deficiency. Suppose that a number of modifications in the plan have been made and that the economists have concluded it will fullfill its basic goals.

The economists will now ask how costly the plan would be to put into effect and enforce. They would estimate the direct costs of printing and distributing the coupons, of establishing a means to hear the inevitable appeals from outraged citizens, and of policing the use of coupons.

Next the economists might search for ways in which this policy relates to conflicts with other goals. Does it serve the public interest by encouraging production of more efficient cars? Does it work against the public interest by encouraging crime in the form of the counterfeiting or theft of coupons or the bribing of officials who allocate coupons?

Ideally, the existence and importance of each side effect must be estimated. When a policy action helps to achieve one goal but hinders the attainment of others, it is necessary to establish tradeoffs among them. Usually there will be some rate at which people will be willing to trade a loss in one direction for a gain in another. Suppose that if this were the end of the matter, the economists and policymakers would conclude that, all things considered, the gasoline rationing plan is better than nothing and deserves further study.

The final step for the economists is to consider whether modifications of the plan, or alternatives to it, will achieve the goals equally well but at lower cost in terms of setbacks to other policy objectives. They may well consider, for example, whether allowing the coupons to be sold legally will lead to fairer, more efficient gasoline usage, less crime, and smaller enforcement costs. Another proposal they may consider is to discourage gas consumption by an extra $1 per gallon gasoline tax, combined with a series of money grants to poorer people who must drive as part of their work. This final step is important. It compares a particular proposal not only against a "do nothing" approach but also against other feasible proposals.

Do the views and prejudices of the investigators have much to do with the outcome of their investigation? A particular group of economists may have strong views on the specific measure it is attempting to assess. If the economists do not like the measure, they are likely to be relentless in identifying costs and searching out possible unwanted effects and somewhat less than thorough in discovering effects that help to achieve the desired goals. It is important though difficult to guard against an unconscious bias of this sort. Fortunately, there are likely to be other economists with different biases. One advantage of publishing evaluations and submitting them to review and discussion is that it provides opportunities for those with different biases to discover arguments and evidence originally overlooked.

firms respond to the signals for "more output" by increasing production, and they keep on increasing production until the signals get weaker and weaker and finally disappear. Some buyers withdraw from the market when they think prices are too high, and perhaps they will re-enter gradually, when they want to, as prices become "more reasonable." Households and firms responding to market signals, not government bureaucrats issuing orders, "decide" who will increase production and who will limit consumption. No one is forced to do something against his or her best judgment. Voluntary responses collectively produce the end result.

Consider an example. Suppose that 10,000 families from neighboring areas decide that at existing prices they all want to move into single-family houses in the British Properties in West Vancouver. However, that beautiful residential area is already heavily populated. There are few vacant houses or building sites. Obviously, not all of the present and potential residents can live there. Which ones will be able to do so, and which ones will be disappointed?

The market system makes the allocation in the following way. The first impact of the great increase in demand would be a sharp rise in the asking prices of houses in the Properties. This would persuade some residents, who previously had not intended to move, to sell their houses and move to other areas. The same rises in price would discourage many who had hoped to move into the Properties. The rising prices will also lead some owners of vacant lots to sell or develop them.

One way or the other—by reducing quantity demanded and by encouraging an increase in quantity supplied—the market will make the allocation. Of the 10,000 families who originally wanted to move in, 3,000 may end up living there, while 2,500 old residents move away and 500 of the vacant houses or lots become occupied. Which 3,000 moved in? Those who valued it the most. Which 2,500 moved out? Those who valued the extra money more than the privilege of staying in the Properties. The market has sorted them out without anyone's having to issue orders ("you go, you stay") and without the need for a court or a board

to hear appeals from those who object to the orders.

Of course it is not *necessary* to rely on the market system to achieve coordination. Had prices not been free to rise, some other system for allocating supply would have been needed. Suppose prices had been frozen by law in order to "keep British Properties housing within the reach of the ordinary family." There would have been dozens of applicants for any house that became available. The sellers would then have had great power to decide to whom to sell (and thus whom to turn down). They might have exercised their prejudices, or they might have found ways to get a secret payoff.

Alternatively, the West Vancouver Council might set up a British Properties Authorized Waiting List (BPAWL) to determine the order in which people would be permitted to become residents. This would give some public official the duty (or perhaps the privilege) of judging the relative worthiness of potential British Properties residents and ranking them accordingly. It would also provide opportunities for bribery of those with allocative authority.

The Limited Information Required in Market Coordination

Another important characteristic of the market economy is that it functions with very limited information. As Professor Thomas Schelling put it:

The dairy farmer doesn't need to know how many people eat butter and how far away they are, how many other people raise cows, how many babies drink milk, or whether more money is spent on beer or milk. What he needs to know is the prices of different feeds, the characteristics of different cows, the different prices . . . for milk . . . , the relative cost of hired labor and electrical machinery, and what his net earnings might be if he sold his cows and raised pigs instead.

By responding to such limited information as the costs and prices of what he buys and sells, the dairy farmer helps to make the whole economy fit together, producing more or less what people want, where and when they want it.

It is, of course, an enormous advantage that all

the producers and consumers of a country can collectively make the system operate without any one of them, much less all of them, having to understand how it works. (Such a lack of knowledge becomes a disadvantage when people assess schemes for interfering with market allocation.)

Coordination Does Not Require Perfect Competition

To say that the price system coordinates is not to imply that it leads to results such as those that perfect competition would produce. It coordinates responses even to prices "rigged" by monopolistic producers or altered by government controls. The signal-response process occurs in a price system even when the "wrong" signals are sent.

When an international cartel of uranium producers decided to reduce production and raise price, they created a current shortage (and a fear of worse future shortages) among those electric utilities that depend on uranium to fuel nuclear power plants. The price of uranium shot up from under $10 per pound to over $40 in less than a year. This enormous price rise greatly increased efforts among producers outside the cartel to find more uranium and to increase their existing production by mining poorer grade ores previously considered too expensive to mine.

The increases in production from these actions slowly began to ease the shortage. On the demand side, high prices and short supplies led some utilities to cancel planned nuclear plants and to delay the construction of others. Such actions implied a long-run substitution of oil or coal for uranium. (Only the fact that the OPEC cartel had also sharply raised the price of oil prevented an even more rapid reversal of the previous trend from oil to nuclear-powered generators.) With the prices of both uranium and oil quadrupling, the demand for coal increased sharply, and its price and production rose. Thus the market mechanism generated adjustments to the relative prices of different fuels, even though some prices were set by cartels rather than by the free-market forces of supply and demand. It also set in motion reactions that place limits on the power of the cartel.

The Case for the Market System

The case *for* the market system has a strong intuitive appeal. Many nineteenth century economists advocated a policy of **laissez faire**: government should not interfere with the operation of markets. In explaining and defending free-market economies, economists have used two very different approaches. One of these may be characterized as the formal defense. It is based upon showing that a free-market economy consisting of nothing but perfectly competitive industries would lead to an optimal allocation of resources. The case was suggested in Chapter 12, pages 197–202.

The other defense, which may be characterized as informal, or even as intuitive, is at least as old as Adam Smith. It is based on variations and implications of the theme that the market system is an effective coordinator of decentralized decision making. The case is intuitive in the sense that it is not laid out in equations leading to some mathematical, maximizing result. But it does follow from some hard reasoning, and it has been subjected to some searching intellectual probing. What is the nature of this defense of the free market?

The Best Coordinator

Defenders of the market economy argue that compared with the alternatives, the decentralized market system is more flexible and leaves more scope for adaptation at any moment in time and for quicker adjustment to change over time.

If, for example, a scarcity of oil raises its price, one household can elect to leave its heating up high and economize on its driving, while another may wish to do the reverse, and a third may instead give up air conditioning. This flexibility is surely preferable to forcing the same pattern on everyone, say by rationing heating oil and gasoline, regulating permitted temperatures, and limiting air conditioning to days when the temperature exceeds 80° F.

Furthermore, as conditions change over time, prices change, and so decentralized decision makers can react continuously. In contrast government quotas, allocations, and rationing schemes are much more difficult to adjust. The great value of the market is its providing automatic signals *as a situation develops*, so that all of the changes consequent on some major economic change do not have to be anticipated and allowed for by a body of central planners. Millions of adaptations to millions of changes in tens of thousands of markets are required every year, and it would be a Herculean task to anticipate these and plan for them all.

Stimulus to Innovation and Growth

Major changes in resource availabilities will surely occur in all economies over the next decades. New products, new inputs, and new techniques will have to be devised if we are to cope with those vast changes. In a market economy individuals risk their time and money in the hope of earning profits. While many fail, some succeed. New products and processes appear continually; others disappear. Some are passing fads or have little impact; often, however, they become items of major significance. The market system works by trial and error to sort them out. The market system allocates resources to what prove to be successful innovations.

In contrast, more centralized systems have to guess which are going to be productive innovations or wanted products. Planned growth may achieve wonders by permitting a massive effort in a chosen direction, but central planners may also guess wrong and put far too many eggs in the wrong basket or reject as unpromising something that will turn out to be vital.

Prices Tend Toward the Level of Costs

A market system tends to drive prices toward the average total costs of production. When markets are close to competitive this occurs very quickly and completely; but even where there is substantial market power it occurs as new products and new producers respond to the lure of profits and their output drives prices down toward the costs of production.

Whenever private costs to firms reflect social costs to society, there is an advantage in having relative prices reflect relative costs because market choices are then made in the light of social oppor-

tunity costs. Firms will not choose methods that use more valuable resources over methods that use less valuable resources. Households will choose commodities that use more valuable resources to produce over commodities that use less valuable ones only when they value the chosen commodities correspondingly more at the margin.

Having relative prices reflect relative costs tends to be efficient in that it encourages both producers and consumers to use the nation's resources to achieve what we have called allocative efficiency.

Self-Correction of Disequilibrium

The economic system is continually thrown out of equilibrium by change. If the economy does not "pursue" equilibrium, there will be little comfort in saying that if only it reached equilibrium, things would be bright indeed. (We all know someone who would have been a great surgeon if only he or she had gone to medical school.)

An important characteristic of the price system is its ability to set in motion forces that tend to correct disequilibrium.

To review the advantages of the price system in this respect, imagine operating without a market mechanism. Suppose that planning boards make all market decisions. The Board in Control of Women's Clothing hears that pantsuits are all the rage in neighboring countries. It orders a certain proportion of clothing factories to make pantsuits instead of the traditional women's skirt. Conceivably the quantities of pantsuits and skirts produced could be just right, given shoppers' preferences. But what if the board misguessed, producing too many skirts and not enough pantsuits? Long lines would appear at pantsuit counters while mountains of unsold skirts piled up. Once the board saw the lines for pantsuits, it could order a change in quantities produced. Meanwhile, it could store the extra skirts for another season—or ship them to a country with different tastes.

Such a system can correct an initial mistake, but it may prove inefficient in doing so. It may use a lot of resources in planning and administration that could instead be used to produce commodities.

Further, many consumers may be greatly inconvenienced if the board is slow to correct its error. In such a system the members of the board may have no incentive to admit and correct a mistake quickly. Indeed, if the authorities do not like pantsuits, the board may get credit for having stopped that craze before it went too far!

In contrast, suppose that in a market system a similar misestimation of the demand for pantsuits and skirts was made by the women's clothing industry. Lines would develop at pantsuit counters, and inventories of skirts would accumulate. Stores would raise pantsuit prices and run skirt sales. Pantsuit manufacturers could earn windfall profits by raising prices and running extra shifts to increase production. Some skirt producers would be motivated to shift production quickly to pantsuits and to make skirts more attractive to buyers by cutting prices. Unlike the planning board, the producers in a market system would be motivated to correct their initial mistakes as quickly as possible. Those slowest to adjust would lose the most money and might even be forced out of business.

Impersonal Decision Making and the Absence of Coercion

Another important part of the case for a market economy is that it tends to decentralize power and thus requires less coercion of individuals than does any other type of economy. Of course, while markets tend to diffuse power, they do not do so completely; large firms and large unions clearly do have and do exercise substantial economic power.

While the market power of large corporations and unions is not negligible, it tends to be constrained both by the competition of other large entities and by the emergence of new products and firms. This is the process of *creative destruction* described by Joseph Schumpeter (see pages 251–252). In any case, say defenders of the free market, even such aggregations of private power are far less substantial than government power.

Governmental power must be exercised if markets are not allowed to allocate people to jobs and commodities to consumers. Not only will such decisions be regarded as arbitrary by those who do

not like them, but the power surely creates major opportunities for bribery, corruption, and allocation according to the tastes of the central administrators. If at the going prices and wages there are not enough apartments or coveted jobs to go around, the bureaucrat can allocate some to those who pay the largest bribe, some to those with religious beliefs, hairstyles, or political views he likes, and only the rest to those whose names come up on the waiting list.

THE CASE FOR INTERVENTION

The price system coordinates decisions, but this system is not the only possible one that will do the job. It is possible to prove that an idealized version of the price system is perfectly efficient, but this does not prove that the imperfect version that operates in our real economy is more efficient than alternative systems.

The supporters of laissez faire focused on the virtues that a market system might achieve and neglected or played down its limitations. The more important these limitations are—in other words, the greater the actual or perceived failures of the market system—the greater will be the incentive to reduce the reliance placed upon it.

Canada does not have a laissez faire economy. What has led a majority of Canadians to believe that a pure private enterprise system is not the best of all possible worlds? What has led them to lessen their reliance on the unrestricted workings of the free market and, in many cases, to impose regulations on markets or to substitute collective action for individual action? What leads many Canadians today to question whether we have gone far enough—or too far—away from free markets?

Whenever market performance is judged to be faulty, it is the practice to speak of **market failure**. The word *failure* in this context probably conveys the wrong impression.

Market failure does not mean that nothing good has happened, only that the *best attainable outcome* has not been achieved.

As a result of market failure, many people believe it desirable to modify, restructure, complement, or supplement the unrestricted workings of the market. There are several major sources of dissatisfaction with market allocation and distribution, and it is important to understand how they arise. There are two somewhat different senses in which the phrase is used. One is the failure of the market system to achieve efficiency in the allocation of society's resources, the other is its failure to serve social goals other than efficiency, such as a different distribution of income or the preservation of value systems. We shall discuss each.

Externalities As a Source of Inefficiency

Cost, as economists define it, concerns the value of resources used in the process of production. According to the opportunity cost principle, value is the benefit the resources would produce in their best alternative use. But who decides what resources are used and their opportunity cost? When a timber company buys a forest, it perhaps regards the alternative to cutting the trees this year as cutting them five years hence. But citizens in the area may value the forest as a nature sanctuary or a recreation area. The firm values the forest for the trees; the local residents may value the trees for the forest. The two values need not be the same.

Private and social costs. These differences in viewpoint lead to the important distinction between private cost and social cost. **Private cost** measures the best alternative uses of the resources available to *the producer*. As we noted in Chapter 9, private cost is usually measured by the market price of the resources that the firm uses. **Social cost** measures the best alternative uses of resources that are available to *the whole society*.

For some resources the best measure of the social cost may be exactly the same as the private cost: The price set by the market may well reflect the value of the resources in their best alternative social use. For other resources, social cost may differ sharply from private cost.

Discrepancies between private and social cost lead to market failure from the social point of view.

The reason is that efficiency requires that prices cover social cost, but private producers, adjusting to private costs, will neglect those elements of social cost that are not included in private costs. When an element of (social) cost is not part of a private firm's profit and loss calculation, it is *external* to its decision-making process.

Discrepancies between social and private cost lead to **externalities,** which are the costs or benefits of a transaction incurred or received by members of the society but not taken into account by the parties to the transaction. They are also called **third-party effects** because parties other than the two primary participants in the transaction (the buyer and the seller) are affected. Externalities arise in many different ways, and they may be beneficial or harmful.

Some externalities are beneficial. When I paint my house, I enhance my neighbors' view and the value of their property. When an Einstein or a Rembrandt give the world a discovery or a work of art whose worth is far in excess of what he is paid to produce it, he confers an external benefit. Private producers will tend to produce too little of commodities that generate beneficial externalities because they bear all of the costs while others reap part of the benefits.

Other externalities are harmful. We consider several examples below. In the meantime, we observe that private producers will tend to produce too much of commodities that generate harmful externalities because they bear none of the extra costs suffered by others.

Externalities, whether adverse or beneficial, make privately efficient market results socially inefficient because they lead to an allocation of resources that is inefficient from society's point of view.

Pollution. A major source of differences between private cost and social cost occurs when firms use resources they do not regard as scarce. This is a characteristic of most examples of pollution. When a paper mill produces pulp for the world's newspapers, more people are affected than its suppliers, employees, and customers. Its water-discharged effluent hurts the fishing boats that ply nearby waters, and its smog makes many resort areas less attractive, thereby reducing the tourist revenues local motel operators and boat renters can expect. The firm neglects these external effects of its actions, because its profits are not affected by them, whereas they are affected by how much paper it produces.

Dumping of hazardous wastes, air pollution, and water pollution all may occur both as a result of calculated decisions as to what and how to produce or consume, and as a result of private producers taking risks that prove to inflict injury on others. Even an apparently accidental oil blowout or the breakup of a tanker, which is desired by no one, may be caused by a private firm's insufficient avoidance of the risk, since it bears only part of the costs.

Common-property resources. The world's oceans once teemed with fish, but today a world-wide fish shortage is upon us. There seems to be no doubt that overfishing has caused the problem. How could this happen?

Fish are one example of what is called a **common-property resource.** No one owns the oceans' fish until they are caught. The world's international fishing grounds are common property for all fishermen. If by taking more fish one fisherman reduces the catch of other fishermen, he does not count this as a cost, but it is a cost to society.

Assume, as is true of most fishing grounds, that each additional boat that fishes the area catches less than each previous boat and that each additional boat lowers the catch of each other boat. A social planner would go on increasing the size of the fleet until the value of the the net addition to the *total* catch just equaled the cost of operating the marginal boat. But the free market will not produce that result. Private fishermen will go on entering the area as long as they can show a profit; that is, as long as the value of *their own catch* at least covers their cost of operation. Thus private boats will be added to the fleet until the value of the *average product* per boat has been driven down to the average cost of operating a fishing boat. Because average product is greater than marginal product when average product is declining, the quantity of resources devoted to the activity will

be larger than if the value of the marginal product were driven down to the cost of operating the last boat. The free market thus leads to overexploitation of a common-property resource.

Congestion. Collisions between private planes and commercial airliners are headline news when they occur. They cannot occur unless *both* planes are in the air; this is what creates the externality. Suppose that the probability of a midair plane crash is roughly proportional to the number of planes in the air. Suppose too that I have the choice of flying from Kamloops to Vancouver in my own plane or on a commercial airliner that has 100 of its 150 seats filled. In choosing to fly by myself, I decide that the slight extra risk to me of a midair collision is more than balanced by the fun or convenience of my own plane.

What I have neglected is the social cost of my action: the increased risk for every other person in the air on my route of flight that results from one more plane in the air. Since I do not consider other travelers' increased risk, my private decision may have been the wrong social decision.

Neglect of future consequences of present actions. When private producers undervalue future effects on others, they neglect an externality. A business facing bankruptcy tomorrow may be motivated to cheat on safety standards to cut costs today, even if it would hurt the firm's reputation in the long term and impose heavy future costs on others.

A less callous example concerns taking actions without finding out whether there are as-yet-unknown adverse externalities. One dramatic example of the neglect of future effects concerns DDT. In 1948 the Swiss chemist Paul Mueller won the Nobel prize for his discovery of its extraordinary value as a pesticide. Gradually, however, it was confirmed that DDT did more than kill unwanted insects. Once sprayed, the chemical did not break down for years. It entered the food chain and worked its way up from insects to birds and fish, to small mammals, and to larger and larger birds and mammals, including human beings. Antarctic penguins, though thousands of miles from any sprayed areas, have measurable amounts of DDT in their bodies. DDT has thinned the egg shells of large birds to the point where breakage threatens many species, among them the peregrine falcon, the osprey, and the eagle. In 1962 Rachel Carson labeled DDT an "elixir of death," and by 1972 its use was banned in the United States.

While unavoidable ignorance of the future can never be described as market failure, unwillingness to determine whether there will be future adverse effects may be a form of market failure.

Other Sources of Inefficiency

The efficiency of the price system depends on firms and households receiving and responding to the signals provided by prices, costs, and windfall profits. Forces that seriously distort these signals or the required response to them may cause a market to fail to perform efficiently. Consider a few examples.

Moral Hazard, Adverse Selection, and Other Informational Asymmetries

Moral hazard arises when nonsymmetric knowledge leads to socially uneconomic behavior. For example, suppose because a person has ample fire insurance he does not take reasonable precautions against fire; or suppose because of the availability of unemployment insurance he refuses to accept a job he would otherwise have taken. In each of these cases the individual has the special knowledge that he can afford to take certain actions that impose unexpected costs on those who provide the insurance, but the insurers cannot identify him as the person taking unintended advantage of the system. The socially useful purpose of insurance is to permit people to share given risks, not to increase the size of the aggregate risk. But in these two examples the behavior described did increase the risk and thus the social cost.

Closely related to moral hazard, though somewhat different, is the problem of **adverse selection.** A person suffering a heart attack may immediately seek to increase his life insurance coverage by purchasing as much additional coverage as possible without medical examination. People taking out insurance almost always know more about themselves as individual insurance risks than do their insurance companies. The company can try to limit the variation in risk by setting up broad categories based on variables, such as age and occupation, over which actuarial risk is known to vary. The rate charged is then different across categories based on the average risk in the category. But there must always be much variability of risk *within* any one category. Those who know they are well above average risk within their category are offered a bargain and will be led to take out more car, health, life, or fire insurance than they otherwise would. Someone who knows she is a low risk pays more than her own risk really warrants and is motivated to take out less insurance than she otherwise would.

More generally, any time either party to a transaction is ignorant, or is deceived by claims of the other party, market results will tend to be affected, and such changes may lead to inefficiency. Economically (but not legally) it is but a small step from these consequences of asymmetric knowledge to outright fraud. The arsonist who buys fire insurance before setting a fire or the businessperson with fire insurance who decides a fire is preferable to bankruptcy are extreme examples of adverse selection and moral hazard.

Informational asymmetries are involved in many other situations. For example, the apparent overdiscounting of the prices of used cars because of the buyer's risk of acquiring a "lemon" is a case of asymmetric information affecting behavior. (See the discussion of this problem on pages 121–122.)

Principal-Agent Issues

If profits are the spur to efficient performance, it is clear that when a firm's managers choose not to pursue the *firm's* profits they impede the system's workings. A manager or a salesperson may incur unnecessary costs because the activities entailing these costs provide perquisites to the employee. On a small scale this occurs whenever a purchasing agent is swayed by the Christmas present a salesperson gives him, or when a car renter is swayed to hire a more expensive car by the premium *she* will receive while her employer pays the bill. More serious are cases where managers regularly pursue their own goals or perquisites at the expense of minimizing the costs of production. Most serious yet are outright sellouts of company secrets to other firms in return for personal rewards.

Barriers to Mobility

Another kind of market impediment is factor immobility. If increases in a factor's pay do not lead to increases in supply (for any of the reasons discussed in Chapters 8 and 20), the market will fail to reallocate resources promptly in response to changing demands. Monopoly power creates market imperfections by preventing resource flows in response to the market signals of high profits. In this case, barriers to entry rather than factor immobility frustrate the flow of resources.

Collective Consumption Goods

Certain goods and services, if they provide benefits to anyone, necessarily provide them to a large group of people. Such goods are called **collective consumption goods.** National defense is the prime example of a collective consumption good. An adequate defense establishment protects all people in the country whether they want it or not, and there is no market where you can buy more of it and your neighbor less. The quantity of national defense provided must be decided collectively.

Other examples of collective consumption goods include the beautification of a city, a levee to protect a city from a flood, and a hurricane-warning system. In general, market systems cannot compel payment for a collective consumption good since there is no way to prevent a person from receiving the services of the good if he or she refuses to pay for it. Governments, by virtue of their power to tax, can provide the services and collect from everyone.

Excessive or Prohibitive Transactions Costs

The costs incurred in negotiating and completing a transaction, such as the costs of billing or the bad-debt cost of those who never pay, are examples of **transactions costs**. They are always present to some degree, and they are a necessary cost of doing business. If buyers cannot be made to pay for the product, the producer will not be motivated to provide it. For a private firm to stay in business, it must be able to recover both production and transactions costs. If transactions costs are higher than they need to be because of imperfections in the private market, some products that it is efficient to produce will not be produced, and the market will have failed. Consider an example.

Could a private entrepreneur provide a road system for Los Angeles, paying for it by collecting tolls? The answer is surely no (at least with today's technology). It would be prohibitively expensive, both in money and in delays, to erect and staff a toll booth at every freeway exit. Requiring collection of revenues via tolls would impose a prohibitive transactions cost. The users of a road system may be more than willing to pay the full costs of its construction and maintenance, but without an inexpensive way to make them pay, no private firm can produce the road. The government, collecting revenue by means of a gasoline tax, can do what the private market fails to do. (Whether it can do so without making a different mistake—producing more of the product than users are willing to pay for—is discussed below.)

The warning about technology merits an additional comment. Technology changes rapidly. For example, the electronic metering of road use may make the toll booth unnecessary, just as the postage meter has made licking stamps unnecessary. Thus what a private market cannot do today, it may be able to do efficiently tomorrow.

Market imperfections may lead to market failure by preventing firms and households from completing transactions that are required for efficient resource allocation or by causing too much or too little consumption or production of particular goods.

The Distribution of Income

An important characteristic of a market economy is that it determines a *distribution* of the total income that it generates. People whose services are in heavy demand relative to supply, such as television anchormen and superior football players, earn large incomes, while people whose services are not in heavy demand relative to supply, such as Ph.D.s in English and high school graduates without work experience, earn very much less.

The distribution of income produced by the market can be looked at in equilibrium or in disequilibrium. In equilibrium, in an efficiently operating free-market economy, similar efforts of work or investment by similar people will tend to be similarly rewarded everywhere in the economy. Of course, dissimilar people will be dissimilarly rewarded. In disequilibrium, windfall profits and losses abound, so that similar people making similar efforts are likely to be very dissimilarly rewarded.

People in declining industries, areas, and occupations suffer the punishment of windfall losses through no fault of their own. Those in expanding sectors earn the reward of windfall gains through no extra effort of their own. When decision making is decentralized, these rewards and punishments serve the important function of motivating people to adapt. The "advantage" of such a system is that individuals can make their own decisions about how to alter their behavior when market conditions change; the "disadvantage" is that temporary rewards and punishments are dealt out as a result of changes in market conditions that are beyond the control of the individuals affected.

Moreover, even the equilibrium differences may seem unfair. A free-market system rewards certain groups and penalizes others. The workings of the market may be stern, even cruel; consequently society often chooses to intervene, as was discussed in Chapter 20. Should heads of households be forced to bear the full burden of their misfortune if, through no fault of their own, they lose their jobs? Even if they lose their jobs through their own fault, should they and their families have to bear the whole burden, which may include starvation? Should the ill and aged be thrown on the mercy of their families? What if they have no families? Both private charities and a great many government policies are concerned with modifying the distribution of income that results from such things as where one starts, how able one is, how lucky one is, and how one fares in the free-market world.

Very often there is a conflict between the goals of a more equitable distribution and a more efficient economy (which will mean more available for everyone on average). Some of the problems that this can create in policy debates are further discussed in Box 24-2.

Other Reasons for Government Intervention

We have seen that failure to achieve efficient resource allocation and/or an acceptable distribution of income may lead government to intervene in the workings of a market economy. But a call for government intervention may arise from a host of other considerations, which may be collectively described as the protection of value systems.

Preferences for Public Production

Police protection, even justice, might be provided by private market mechanisms. Watchmen, Pinkerton detectives, and bodyguards all provide policelike protection. Privately hired arbitrators, "hired guns," and vigilantes of the Old West represent private ways of obtaining "justice." Yet the members of society may believe that a public police force is *preferable* to a private one and that public justice is *preferable* to justice for hire.

For another example, public schools may be better or worse than private schools, but they are likely to be different, particularly because persons others than parents, teachers, and owners influence their policies. Much of the case for public education rests on the advantages to you of having other people's children educated in a particular kind of environment that is *different* from what a private school would provide. The market will be said to produce unsatisfactory results by those who believe the public product is better.

Protecting Individuals from Others

People can use—even abuse—other people for economic gain in ways that the members of society find offensive. Child labor laws and minimum standards of working conditions are responses to such actions. Yet direct abuse is not the only example

BOX 24–2 DISTRIBUTION VERSUS EFFICIENCY

Economists recognize that government actions can affect both the allocation or resources and the distribution of income. Because it is possible to talk about *efficient* and *inefficient* allocations, but not about "better" or "worse" distributions of income without introducing normative considerations, much of economics concerns efficiency and neglects redistribution of income. Many disagreements can be understood in terms of a difference in emphasis on these two concerns.

Consider the cases of the OPEC price shocks of the 1970s. From an efficiency point of view alone, the correct policy was to let domestic oil prices in all oil-importing countries rise along with the world price. Instead many governments held the price down. For they were concerned, among other things, with the effect of rising prices on the windfall profits earned by large oil companies and on the welfare of poorer citizens. "We just cannot let the poor find their heating bills rise so much and so fast while the profits of the oil companies soar" was a common reaction.

Here is a genuine conflict for which economics cannot provide a solution—because in the end the answer must rest on value judgments. However, economics can make the consequences of various choices apparent, and it can suggest policy alternatives. The consequences of holding down the price of oil (out of concern for the effect of higher prices on the poor) was an inefficient use of the countries' resources. Total production was reduced, and some new investment was misdirected into high-cost (rather than low-cost) methods of production. Thus in the long run average standards of living were reduced. Whether the reduction in the average was a reasonable price to pay for shielding the poor is an open question.

Can one have both efficiency and desired redistributions? One way is to let the price system do the job of signaling relative scarcities and costs, thereby ensuring some efficiency in the allocation of resources, but at the same time to use taxes or expenditures to transfer income to achieve redistributive goals. This method does not seek to help the poor (or other underprivileged groups) by subsidizing oil or any other price. Rather, it seeks to provide these groups with sufficient income by direct income transfers. Then it leaves producers and consumers free to respond to relative prices that approximately reflect relative opportunity costs.

Advocates of this method argue that it is surer, more direct, and less costly in its side effects than the method of subsidizing the prices of particular goods. Moreover, the price-subsidy method surely ends up subsidizing some who are rich and missing some who are very poor. Subsidizing gasoline prices, for example, benefits the Cadillac owner and does nothing for those too poor to own a car. Thus even in redistribution it is haphazard.

Supporters of redistribution through the price system usually counter with two arguments: First, it is well and good to say we *could* let oil prices rise and simultaneously subsidize the poor and tax the rich, but the political process makes it unlikely that we *will* do so. They point to the Reagan administration in the United States, which deregulated prices and simultaneously *decreased* aids to the poor. Thus, say supporters of redistribution, holding prices down may be the best or even the only practical way to get a fairer distributive result.

Second, certain commodities such as food, heat, medical care, and housing are claimed to be basic to a civilized life and therefore should be provided to households cheaply, whatever their real opportunity cost. They believe that the inefficiencies resulting from prices that do not reflect opportunity costs are a burden worth bearing to ensure that everyone can afford these basics.

of this kind of market failure. In an unhindered free market, the adults in a household would usually decide how much education to buy for their children. Selfish parents might buy no education, while egalitarian parents might buy the same quantity for all their children regardless of their abilities. The members of society may want to interfere in these choices, both to protect the child of the selfish parent and to ensure that some of the scarce educational resources are distributed according to intelligence rather than wealth. All households are forced to provide a minimum of education for their children, and strong inducements are offered— through public universities, scholarships, and other means—for gifted children to consume more education than they or their parents might choose if they had to pay the entire cost themselves.

Paternalism

In a significant number of cases, members of society acting through the state seek to protect adult (and presumably responsible) individuals, not against others, but against themselves. Laws prohibiting heroin and other hard drugs and laws prescribing the installation and use of seat belts are intended primarily to protect individuals from their own ignorance or shortsightedness.

Intervention of this kind with the free choices of individuals is called **paternalism**. Whether or not such actions reflect real values of the majority of the society, or whether they simply reflect overbearing governments, there is no doubt that the market will not provide this kind of protection. Buyers do not buy what they do not want, and sellers have no motive to provide it. So if society wishes to impose some unwanted consumption patterns, laws—not markets—are needed. By the same token, markets will provide anything that people are prepared to pay for. So if society wishes to prohibit some wanted consumption patterns, laws are also needed.

"Social Obligations"

In a market system if you can pay another person to do things for you, you may do so. If you persuade someone else to clean your house in re-turn for $25, presumably both parties to the transaction are better off: You prefer to part with $25 rather than clean the house yourself, and your help prefers $25 to not cleaning your house. Normally society does not interfere with people's ability to negotiate mutually advantageous contracts.

Most people do not feel this way, however, about activities that are regarded as social obligations. For example, at times and places in which military service is compulsory, contracts similar to one between you and your housekeeper could also be negotiated. Some persons faced with the obligation to do military service could no doubt pay enough to persuade others to do their tour of service for them.[2] By exactly the same argument as we used above, we can presume that both parties will be better off if they are allowed to negotiate such a trade. But such contracts are usually prohibited. Why? Because there are values other than those that can be expressed in a market. In times when it is necessary, military service by all healthy males is usually held to be a duty independent of an individual's tastes, wealth, influence, or social position. It is felt that everyone *ought* to do this service, and trades between willing traders are prohibited.

Nor is this the only example. You cannot buy your way out of jury duty, nor legally sell your vote to another, even though in many cases you could find a willing trading partner.

Even if the price system allocated goods and services with complete efficiency, we would not wish to rely solely on the market if members of society have other goals that they wish to serve by the allocation of resources.

GOVERNMENT INTERVENTION

While private collective action can sometimes remedy the failures of private individual action (private charities can help the poor; volunteer fire departments can fight fires; insurance companies can guard against adverse selection by more careful

----

[2] Indeed, during the American Civil War a man could avoid the draft by hiring a substitute to serve in his place.

classification of clients), by far the most common remedy for market failure is reliance on government intervention.

It is useful to ask several questions about possible government policies designed to correct market failure. First, what tools does the government have? Second, when and how vigorously should the tools be used? Third, under what circumstances is government intervention likely to fail?

The Tools of Microeconomic Policy

There are numerous ways in which one or another level of government can prevent, alter, complement, or replace the workings of the unrestricted market economy. It is convenient to group these methods into four broad categories:

1. *Public provision.* Goods and services may be publicly provided in addition to or instead of private provision.
2. *Redistribution.* Public expenditures and taxes may be used to provide a distribution of income and output different than that which the private market provides.
3. *Rule making.* Rules and regulations may be adopted to compel, forbid, or specify within acceptable limits the behavior that private decision makers may engage in.
4. *Structuring incentives.* Government may alter market signals to persuade rather than force decision makers to adopt different behavior.

Each of the four methods is frequently used, and each has great capacity to change whatever outcomes the unregulated market would provide. The first two will be discussed in detail in Chapter 25; the remainder of this section concerns the last two, rule making and structuring incentives.

Rule Making

Rules require, limit, or compel certain activities and market actions. It is helpful to distinguish between *proscriptive* and *prescriptive rules.*

Proscriptive rules. Some regulations are like the Ten Commandments; they tell people and firms what they can and cannot do. Such rules require parents to send their children to school and to have them inoculated against measles and diphtheria. Laws that prohibit gambling and pornography attempt to enforce a particular moral code on the whole society. In Chapter 15 we discussed an important form of policy by prohibition—combines policy.

There are many other examples: Children cannot legally be served alcoholic drinks. Prostitution is prohibited in most places, even between a willing buyer and a willing seller. In many provinces you must buy insurance in case you should do damage with your private motor car. A person who offers goods for sale, including his or her own house, cannot refuse to sell because of a dislike for the customer's color or dress. There are rules against fraudulent advertising and the sale of substandard, adulterated, or poisonous foods.

Such rules only set limits to the decisions that firms and households can make; they do not replace those decisions. But the allowed limits can be changed. An important means of government regulation is to change old rules or add new ones that redefine the boundary between forbidden and permitted behavior.

Prescriptive rules. Prescriptive rule making substitutes the rule maker's judgment for the firm's or the household's judgment about such things as prices charged, products produced, and methods of production. It tends to restrict private action more than proscriptive regulation does because it replaces private decision making rather than limiting it to an acceptable set of decisions. Regulation of public utilities is an important example of prescriptive regulation (see Chapter 15). But prescriptive regulation goes far beyond the natural monopoly regulation we have discussed.

Federal regulatory commissions regularly decide such matters as who may broadcast and on what frequencies; which airlines may fly which routes; what rates bus lines and pipeline operators may charge for different kinds of services; what prices may be paid for gasoline and how much foreign textiles may be imported into Canada.

Problems with Rule Making

Rule making often appears to be a cheap, simple, and direct way of compelling desirable behavior in the face of market failure. But the simplicity is deceptive. Rules must be enforceable and enforced, and once enforced they must prove effective if they are to achieve the results hoped for by those who made them. These conditions are often difficult and expensive to achieve.

Consider the requirement for the installation of an antipollution device that will meet a certain standard in reducing automobile exhaust emissions. Such a law may be the outcome of congressional debate on pollution control—and having passed the bill, Parliament will turn to other things. Yet certain problems must be solved before the rule can achieve its purpose. Even with perfect compliance by the manufacturer, the device will not work well unless it is kept in working order by the owner. Yet it would be expensive to inspect every vehicle regularly and to force owners to keep the devices at the standard set by law. Even a well-designed rule will work only until those regulated figure out a way to evade its intent while obeying its letter. There will be substantial incentive to find such a loophole, and resources that could be used elsewhere will be devoted to the search—and to counteracting such avoidance or evasion.

Structuring Incentives

Government can change the incentives of households and firms in a great variety of ways. It can fix minimum or maximum prices (as we saw in the discussions of agriculture and rent control in Chapter 6). It can adjust the tax system to offer many exemptions and deductions. Tax deductible mortgage interest and real estate taxes, for example, can make owned housing relatively more attractive than rental housing. Such tax treatment sends the household different signals than those sent by the free market. Scholarships to students to become nurses or teachers may offset barriers to mobility into those occupations. Fines and criminal penalties for violating the rules imposed are another part of the incentive structure.

Internalizing Externalities

An important means of influencing incentives is to change the prices that firms and households pay in such a way as to eliminate externalities. Because externalities are a major source of market failure, much attention has been given to means of inducing decision makers to take them into account. Charging a producing firm for the pollution it causes can motivate the firm to alter its production in a socially desirable way. Procedures that make firms take account of the extra social costs they impose are said to **internalize** the external effects of production. How exactly does this work?

First we need to define terms. The **net private benefit** (*NPB*) of a unit of production is the difference between that unit's contribution to a firm's revenue and its contribution to the firm's cost. In other words, it is the contribution to profit of that unit. If we think of each unit of production as contributing to social welfare (and call that contribution **social benefit**) and to cost (*social cost*, defined on page 414), we can define the difference between social benefit and social cost as **net social benefit** (*NSB*).

Net social benefit is the key concept in judging efficiency. A unit should be produced if, but only if, its *NSB* is greater than or equal to zero.

To go from *NPB* to *NSB*, we need to add beneficial externalities and subtract adverse externalities. In the following discussion, we consider an adverse externality (such as pollution) so that *NSB* is less than *NPB*.

Consider, as an example, a private firm responding only to private benefits and costs will produce up to the point at which marginal *NPB* becomes zero. But at that output marginal *NSB*, being less than *NPB*, is necessarily negative: too much has been produced from the social point of view. This market failure can be avoided by the procedure shown in Figure 24-1. Once the firm has been forced to pay for what were previously externalities, the new net private benefit is exactly the same as net social benefit. That is, *NPB* = *NSB*. Thus the firm will be motivated to produce only as long as marginal *NSB* is not negative.

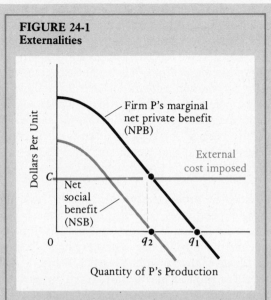

**FIGURE 24-1
Externalities**

Firm P's marginal
net private benefit
(NPB)

External
cost imposed

Net
social
benefit
(NSB)

Dollars Per Unit

C

0 q_2 q_1

Quantity of P's Production

Internalizing an externality can correct market failure. The NPB earned by a private firm, P, is shown by the dark black curve. The firm is motivated to produce all units that make a positive contribution to its profits. Its equilibrium output is q_1 where NPB is zero. This production imposes an external cost of $\$C$ per unit on outsiders, as shown by the colored line. Subtracting this additional social cost from the NPB yields the NSB, the curve shown by the shaded black line. The socially optimal output is q_2, where the NSB just equals zero. At this output NPB is just equal to the external cost imposed on outsiders for each unit of production. At q_2 the outsiders are still having costs inflicted on them by P, but these costs *plus* P's private costs are just equal at the margin to P's profit from production.

Suppose the firm is required to pay an "effluent tax" of $\$C$ per unit. Its NPB now becomes the shaded black line. The externality has been *internalized*, and the profit-maximizing firm is motivated to reduce its output from q_1 to q_2. It does this because any units produced beyond q_2 would now subtract from total profits.

Internalization avoids the market failure caused by externalities.

There are many ways to internalize external costs. Consider two. If the amount of the external cost imposed per unit of output is known, it is possible to impose an **effluent charge,** or pollution tax, that compels the producer to pay a tax on every unit of polluting production. Such a charge might lead the producer to find a way to produce without polluting. Another way to internalize external costs is to give legal standing to private citizens to sue for damages against polluters or to seek court injunctions against polluting activities. The legal action makes it costly for polluters; there will be damage payments if they lose and legal payments win or lose.

The Costs of Government Intervention

Consider the following argument: (1) The market system is working imperfectly; (2) government has the legal means to improve the situation; (3) therefore the public interest will be served by government intervention.

This appealing argument is deficient because it neglects two important considerations. First, government intervention is costly. For that reason not every market failure is worth correcting. Second, government intervention may be imperfect. Just as markets sometimes succeed and sometimes fail, so government intervention sometimes succeeds and sometimes fails. In this section we consider costs of intervention, neglecting government failure; later we consider the added problem imposed by imperfect governmental intervention.

The *benefits* of government intervention are the value of the market failures averted. To evaluate governmental intervention it is also necessary to consider the costs of the intervention and compare costs with benefits.

Large benefits do not justify government intervention, nor do large costs make it unwise. What matters is the relative size of benefits to costs.

There are several kinds of costs of government intervention. Consider three.

Internal Costs

When government inspectors visit plants to see whether they are complying with federally imposed standards of health, industrial safety, or environmental protection, they are imposing costs on the public in the form of the salaries and expenses of the inspectors, among other ways. When regulatory bodies develop rules, hold hearings, write opinions, or have their staff prepare research reports, they are incurring costs. The costs of the judges and clerks and court reporters who hear and transcribe and review the evidence are likewise costs imposed by regulation. All these activities use valuable resources, resources that could have provided very different goods and services.

The aggregate size of federal expenditures for activities that regulate market behavior alone are large indeed. Such costs have grown greatly in the last several decades, and represent one cause of growth in the size of government in the economy. However, they are only the most visible part of the total costs of government regulatory activities.

Direct External Costs

The nature and size of the extra costs borne by firms subject to government intervention are themselves of several kinds, and they vary with the type of regulation. A few examples are worth noting.

Changes in costs of production. Antipollution regulations forced producers not to burn high sulfur coal. As a result, extra fuel costs were imposed on many firms. Such cost increases are directly attributable to regulation.

For 50 years (until the mid 1970s), the prices of automobiles relative to other consumer goods were falling because of continuing technological advances in automobile engineering. Recent federal safety and emission standards have added so much to the cost of producing automobiles that since 1976 Canadians have had to adjust to a steadily rising trend in the relative prices of autos, and automobile workers to the decreases in production that resulted.

Costs of compliance. Government regulation and supervision generate a flood of reporting and related activities that are often summarized in the phrase *red tape*. The number of hours of business time devoted to understanding, reporting, and contesting regulatory provisions is enormous. Affirmative action, occupational safety, and environmental control have greatly increased the size of nonproduction payrolls. The legal costs alone of a major corporation can run into tens of millions of dollars per year. While all this provides lots of employment for lawyers and economic experts, it is costly because there are other tasks such professionals could do that would add more to the production of consumer goods and services.

Losses in productivity. Quite apart from the actual expenditures, the regulatory climate may reduce the incentive for experimentation, innovation, and the introduction of new products. Requiring advance government clearance before a new method or product may be introduced (on grounds of potential safety hazards or environmental impact) can eliminate the incentive to develop it. The requirement for advance approval by a regulatory commission before entry is permitted into a regulated industry can discourage potential competitors.

Indirect External Costs

It has been estimated that regulatory activities decrease the growth rate of output per person. Lost growth translates into a big loss in the real living standards that could have been achieved. Such lost purchasing power is an externality of government intervention because the regulators do not take it into account. It may seem paradoxical that government intervention to offset adverse externalities can create new adverse externalities, but it is plain that it can.

Consider an example. Government regulations designed to assure that all new drugs introduced are both effective and safe have the incidental effect of delaying by an average of about nine months the introduction of drugs that are both effective and safe. The benefits of these regulations are related to the unsafe and ineffective drugs kept off the market. The cost includes the unavailability for about nine months of all those safe and effective drugs whose introduction was delayed.

Optimal Intervention

Economic principles are useful in making decisions concerning the optimal correction of market failure. In order to develop these principles, we shall look at the question of preventing pollution.

Pollution covers many externalities, ranging from threats to survival to minor nuisances. Virtually all activity leaves some waste product; to say that all pollution must be removed whatever the cost is to try for the impossible and to ensure a vast commitment of society's scarce resources to many projects that will yield a low social value. But somewhere between trying for the impossible and maintaining a callous indifference to the problem lies a middle ground. Economics helps to define it.

We approach the problem by assuming that government intervention is free from error. Later we shall relax this artificial assumption.

Costless Intervention

We start with the easiest case: Government intervention is costless except for the direct costs imposed by changes in the nature of production. All the government must do is identify the best form of pollution control, determine the right amount of it, and institute the appropriate means of achieving it. How should it proceed?

A first step is to choose the best means of pollution control. Suppose in this case a factory is emitting noxious gases, and it is determined that the best control method is to install filters on the smokestacks.[3]

The next step is to decide how much of the pollution should be eliminated. Suppose the problem is sulfur dioxide (SO_2) discharge, and that simple recirculation of the gases would reduce the discharge of SO_2 by 50 percent; after that, the cost

doubles for each further 10 percent reduction in the remaining SO_2. At most it would be possible to eliminate 99.44 percent of all SO_2, but the cost would be vast. In economic terms the marginal costs of removal rise sharply as the amount of SO_2 eliminated rises from 50 percent to 99.44 percent.

What percentage of the gases should be eliminated? The answer depends on the marginal benefits relative to marginal costs. The marginal benefits of pollution control are the external effects avoided. The optimal amount of prevention will occur where the marginal costs of further prevention equal the marginal benefits. This is illustrated in Figure 24-2.

The optimal amount of pollution prevention will be less than the maximum possible when pollution is costly to prevent. Thus the optimal amount of pollution is not equal to zero. This important proposition can be generalized:

The optimal amount of government intervention to avoid market failure will be lower, the greater are the costs of prevention.

Costs of Intervention

Next we add to our consideration the fact that government intervention brings with it enforcement costs—costs to the government, to the firm, and to third parties—of the kinds already discussed. These costs have to be added to the direct costs we have just considered.

Suppose for simplicity that enforcement costs are variable and rise as the level of pollution to be eliminated increases. The marginal costs of enforcement must be added to the marginal direct costs of prevention, thereby shifting upward the marginal costs of prevention. This is shown by the dashed marginal cost curves in Figure 24-2. The addition of such costs will surely decrease the amount of prevention that is optimal. If the costs are large enough, they may even make any prevention uneconomical.

Government Failure

All costs of intervention discussed in the previous section would be present with a government that

[3] This choice of *means* is not trivial or always easy. Alternatives might include changing the method of production or moving people out of the path of the polluting gases. This first-stage determination among alternative means is of prime importance in achieving the correct solution. A major source of "government failure" is choice of the wrong technique of control.

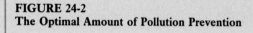

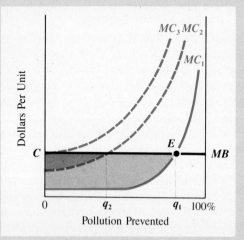

FIGURE 24-2
The Optimal Amount of Pollution Prevention

The optimal quantity of pollution prevention occurs where marginal benefits from prevention equal marginal costs of prevention. *MB* represents the marginal benefit achieved by pollution prevention, assumed in this example to be constant at \$$C$ per percentage point. MC_1 represents the marginal costs of preventing pollution; it rises sharply as more and more pollution is eliminated. The optimal level of pollution control is q_1, where $MB = MC_1$. *Notice that not all pollution is eliminated.* For all units up to q_1, marginal benefits from pollution prevention exceed marginal costs. Net benefits are shown by the total shaded area. Any further pollution elimination would add more to costs than to benefits.

If the marginal cost curve shifts upward to MC_2, due, say, to the addition of enforcement costs, the quantity of optimal prevention will decrease to q_2 and the net benefits will be reduced to the darker shaded area. If costs increase to MC_3, the optimal amount of prevention becomes zero.

had perfect foresight in defining goals, an unerring ability to choose the least costly means of achieving them, and intelligent and dedicated officials whose concern was to do those things—and only those things—that achieved the greatest possible efficiency of the economy. Government intervention usually falls short of the high standard just described. This is not because bureaucrats are worse than other people, more stupid, more rigid, or more venal. Instead, it is because they are like others, with the usual flaws and virtues.

Causes of Government Failure

Here are six reasons why government intervention can be *imperfect* (i.e., "fail") in achieving its potential.

Imperfect knowledge or foresight. Regulators may not know enough to set correct standards. For example, natural gas prices may, with the best of intentions, be set too low. The result will be too much quantity demanded and too little quantity supplied, with no automatic correction. Or the automobile emission standards prescribed for a particular year may be too demanding, thereby proving unexpectedly expensive to achieve—or too lax, thereby leading to unexpected excessive pollution.

Rigidities. Regulatory rules and allocations are hard to change. Yet technology and economic circumstances change continually. Regulations that at one time protected the public against a natural monopoly may perpetuate an unnecessary monopoly after technological changes have made competition possible. In the United States, giving AT&T a monopoly in long-distance communication, and specifying its price structure, made sense when the technology for transmitting messages (use of cable) led to natural monopoly. After a communications satellite had been placed in orbit, there was room for many competitors, but the regulatory commission was not free simply to open up the industry to anyone. Too many people had invested in the telephone industry on the expectation of continued regulation.

Inefficient means. Government may fail to choose the least costly means of solving a problem. It may decree a specific form of antipollution device that proves less effective and more expensive than another. A strict rule that proves all but impossible to enforce may be passed, when a milder one would have achieved higher compliance at lower enforcement cost.

Myopic regulation. Regulation may become too restricted and too narrowly defined because the regulators are forced to specialize. Specialization may lead to expertise in a given area, but the regulators may lack the breadth to relate their area to broader concerns. Officials charged with the responsibility for a healthy *railroad* industry (dating from the time when railroads were the dominant means of transportation) may fail to see that the encouragement of trucking, even at the expense of the railroads, may be necessary for a healthy *transportation* industry.

Political constraints. Political realities may prevent the "right" policy from being adopted, even when it has been clearly identified. This is particularly true in a government based on checks and balances. Suppose a technically perfect tax (or tariff or farm policy) is designed by the experts. It will surely hurt some groups and benefit others. Lobbyists will go to work. The policy is likely to be modified, mutilated, rebuilt, and finally passed in a form the experts know is inadequate. Although Parliament may be aware of its flaws, it will be passed into law because it is "better than nothing." This scenario occurs because the political process must respond to political realities. "After all," the official may reason as he yields to the demands of the widget lobby (against his best judgment about the public interest), "if I'm defeated for reelection (or not reappointed), I won't be here to serve the public interest on even more important issues next year." (Next year he may support widgets out of a sense of consistency!)

Decision maker's objectives. Public officials almost always wish to serve the public interest. But they have their careers, their families, and their prejudices as well. This is not unlike the principal-agent problem mentioned as a source of market failure. Public officials' own needs are seldom wholly absent from their consideration of the actions they will take. Similarly, their definition of the public interest is likely to be influenced heavily by their personal views of what policies are best.

A close relationship often exists or develops between the regulators and those they regulate. Many government regulators come from industry and plan to return to it. The broadcasting official who serves five years on the Canadian Radio and Tele-

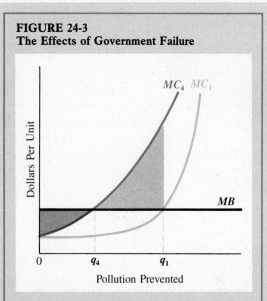

FIGURE 24-3
The Effects of Government Failure

Choice of the wrong method of control will reduce the optimal amount of intervention and may convert the gains from intervention into losses. The *MB* and *MC*$_1$ curves are similiar to those in Figure 24-2. One common form of government failure is to specify the wrong method of intervention. Suppose the government specifies a method of pollution control that leads to the costs shown by *MC*$_4$. This is inefficient because costs at every level of pollution prevention are higher than necessary. Under such a method, the optimal level of prevention falls to q_4 with net benefits shown by the dark shaded area. Government failure reduces the appropriate amount of prevention that is optimal. The government will compound its failure if it insists on the level of prevention q_1 while requiring use of the inefficient method. The cost of every unit of pollution prevented beyond q_4 is in excess of its benefits, as shown by the light shaded area. Indeed the result is worse than no intervention at all (the light shaded area is larger than the dark shaded area). While the best possible government intervention would have produced a net gain, government failure produces a net loss.

vision Commission and hopes to become a network president after that term of office may view the networks' case in a not wholly disinterested way. Indeed, regulators may protect an industry in ways that would be quite illegal if done from within the industry.

BOX 24–3 NEW ENGLAND AND THE ATLANTIC PROVINCES: A TALE OF TWO REGIONS

There are many similarities between the American New England states and the Canadian Atlantic provinces. Both have highly educated populations concentrated in relatively small areas. Both have access by waterway to foreign and domestic markets. The Atlantic provinces, however, have abundant supplies of hydroelectricity, iron, coal, and zinc that are not found in New England; thus they would seem to be more likely to be able to generate and sustain an economic boom.

Why then has just the reverse occurred? In the 1970s New England experienced a significant and sustained manufacturing investment boom; by the start of the 1980s New England had a healthy manufacturing base growing at a higher rate than the national average and an unemployment rate lower than that of most other regions in the United States. In contrast, the Atlantic provinces experienced a sharp slump in the 1970s.

At the beginning of the 1970s, New England's unemployment began to climb and per capita income began to fall. Cuts in defense spending and the aerospace program and the large oil price increases that occurred simultaneously had a severe negative impact on the region. By 1975 the region's per capita income had been falling steadily for five years, and its unemployment rate was the worst in the nation. Consequently, the region had available a pool of relatively cheap, highly educated workers. This labor supply attracted new firms, particularly in the fields of computer and scientific technology, to the area. The result was that from 1975 to 1979 nonagricultural employment grew at a rate that was faster than the average for the whole nation. Like a phoenix from the fire, the boom of the late 1970s arose from the recession of the early 1970s.

Superficially, the manufacturing sector in the Atlantic provinces did well during the early and mid 1970s. Wages and salaries increased faster here than they did for Canada as a whole. Yet closer examination reveals that not only did employment grow sluggishly over most of this period, but output grew more slowly than in the rest of Canada. Why should a region with as many advantages as the Atlantic provinces have a performance in such an important sector that was so much worse than that of New England, when its prospects seemed so much better?

While many reasons account for the different patterns of development in the two regions, one striking difference lies in the government policies invoked to deal with the depressed economic conditions that prevailed at the beginning of the 1970s. The U.S. government essentially left the New England economy alone to adjust to its own problems. As a result, wages fell relative to those in the rest of the nation, and the region became an attractive place for new firms to locate.

The Effect of Government Failure

Suppose, for any of the reasons discussed above, the government makes a mistake in regulation. Say the government mistakenly specifies a method of pollution control that is less effective than the best method. This will increase the cost of achieving any given level of prevention. If the government insists on the level of control appropriate to the correct method but requires the incorrect method, it can convert a social gain from control into a social loss. This is illustrated in Figure 24-3.

To generalize from the specific example, it is clear that any form of government failure adds to the costs or decreases the benefits of government intervention. Thus the lower the public's confidence in government's ability to do the right thing, the lower will be its willingness to have government intervention.

At a recent conference, American economist Lester Thurow argued that

New England is a prosperous region because it got out of its old dying industries and into new growth industries. If Washington had protected New England's old dying industries, New England would still be depressed.

In contrast, the Canadian government has used many policies to support the Atlantic provinces. And these policies have been disappointingly ineffective. Many of the policies failed to recognize that much of the disparity between regions reflects regional equilibrium (see Box 17-1 on pages 288–289). Many economists believe that the policy of propping up dying industries has inhibited growth by reducing the region's ability to develop new industries.

Much of the support to the region has come in the form of transfer payments. Transfers serve the intended purpose of redistributing income to the region, but they have the unintended side effect of impeding the process of regional adjustment. These policies may also have resulted in what has become known as "transfer dependency"; that is, they may have led some provinces to become increasingly dependent on government transfers for their economic well-being. In the seventies, provinces of the Atlantic region experienced current account deficits of up to *50 percent* of their gross domestic products, financed largely by intergovernmental transfers. Total government inflows in 1974 ranged from 66 percent of GNP in New Brunswick to 105 percent in Prince Edward Island.

Transfer dependency not only frustrates the market mechanism by propping up wages—thereby discouraging out-migration and new investment—it also undermines the economy in other ways. In 1973 a report prepared for the Department of Regional Economic Expansion stated:

The Atlantic Region . . . has been dependent on assistance and support for a long period; this has left its mark on the outlook of the region. It has tended to become a part of the conventional wisdom that only government subsidies or some form of special consideration point the way to achieving prosperity. The result has been to weaken the confidence of the region in its ability to take initiatives and operate independently.

Will the two regions continue to develop in such different ways? Some observers believe that at the middle of the 1980s the Atlantic region is on the verge of an economic boom, led by expansion in the fisheries and resource sectors, that will match and even perhaps surpass that experienced in New England. Others believe that as long as government transfers and support for declining industries remain a central part of Canadian regional policy, the Atlantic provinces will languish in transfer dependency.

GOVERNMENT INTERVENTION IN CANADA

The theoretical principles for determining the optimal amount of intervention are individually accepted by virtually everyone. What they add up to, however, is more controversial. Some of the issues involved in advocating or opposing government intervention and in possible conflicts between redistributing today's income and ensuring that tomorrow's income is as large as possible are explored in the case studies that are discussed in Box 24-3.

Does government intervene too little or too much in response to market failure? This question reflects one aspect of the ongoing argument about the role of government in the economy.

Much of the rhetoric of our concern with ecology urges government intervention against heartless, profit-mad, giant corporations that pervert the environment for their own crass purposes. Such feelings lead to the demand for more—and more stringent—government regulation.

At the same time, the heavy hand of government regulation is seen as contributing greatly to both inflation and recession by burdening private companies with regulations that add to costs and impede innovation and by keeping prices and wages artificially high. Even perfect intervention would be costly, but imperfect intervention makes it much too costly. In this view, the deregulation movement that started in the 1980s was long overdue.

To what extent can the debate be resolved by economic analysis? What is the role of ideology in the debate?

The Role of Analysis

Economic analysis and measurement can help to eliminate certain misconceptions that cloud and confuse the debate. We have noted one such misconception: the optimal level of pollution (or of any other negative externality) is not, as some urge, zero. Another mistake is to equate market failure with the greed of profit-motivated corporations. Externalities do not require callous, thoughtless, or deliberately deceptive practices of private, profit-seeking firms; they occur whenever the signals to which decision makers respond do not include social as well as private benefits and costs.

Such situations are not limited to private firms in a capitalistic system. Cities and nationalized industries pollute just as much as privately owned industries when they are operated in the same way, as they typically are. A third mistake is to think that the profits of a corporation tell something about neglected externalities. It is possible for a profitable firm (such as GM) or an unprofitable one (such as Massey-Ferguson) to spend too little on pollution control or on safety, but it is also possible for it to spend too much. The existence of profits provides no clue as to which is the case.

The Role of Ideology

While positive analysis has a role to play, there are several reasons why ideology plays a bigger role in the evaluation process here than in other areas.

First, measuring the costs of government intervention is difficult, particularly with respect to indirect costs, because some of the trade-offs are inherently uncertain. How important and how unsafe is nuclear power? Does the ban on DDT cause so much malnutrition as to offset the gains in the ecology it brings? What cannot be readily measured can be alleged to be extremely high (or low) by opponents (or supporters) of intervention. The numerous findings by scholars on both sides of each of these subjects has led one economist to the cynical conclusion that "believing is seeing."

Second, classifying the actual pattern of government intervention as successful or not is in part subjective. Has government safety regulation been (choose one) useful if imperfect, virtually ineffective, or positively perverse? All three views have been expressed and "documented."

A third difficulty arises in defining what constitutes market failure. Does product differentiation represent market success (by giving consumers the variety they want) or failure (by foisting expensive and useless variations on them)?

In Canada and the United States in the mid 1980s it seems safe to conclude that confidence in the existing mix of free-market and government regulation is at a relatively low ebb. Not only are specific policy suggestions hotly argued, so is the whole philosophy of intervention. There is as yet no consensus as to what is wrong; the pressures for changes are strong in *both* directions.

SUMMARY

1. The various markets in the economy are coordinated in an unplanned, decentralized way by the price system. Windfall profits play a key role in achieving a coordinated market response. Changes in prices and profits, resulting from emerging scarcities and surpluses, lead decision makers to adapt to a change in any one market of the economy. Such responses tend to correct the shortages and surpluses as well as to change the market signals of prices and profits.

2. Important features of market coordination include voluntary responses to market signals, the limited information required by any individual, and the fact that coordination can occur under various market structures.

3. There is a widely held "case for the free market" that goes beyond its ability to provide automatic coordination. Many believe its flexibility and adaptability make it the best coordinator and also encourage innovation and growth. The tendency of the market to push relative prices toward the costs of production fosters efficient allocation of resources and self-correction of disequilibrium. Furthermore the market economy tends to be impersonal, to decentralize power, and to require relatively little coercion of individuals.

4. Markets do not always work perfectly. Dissatisfaction with market results often leads to government intervention. We identify four main kinds of market failure: (a) externalities arising from differences between private and social costs and benefits, (b) market imperfections and impediments, (c) dissatisfaction with the free-market distribution of income, and (d) the protection of value systems.

5. Pollution is an example of an externality. An important source of pollution is producers' use of water and air that they do not regard as scarce. Since they do not pay all the costs of using these resources, they are not motivated to avoid the costs. Individual use of common-property resources, congestion, and neglect of future consequences are other sources of externalities.

6. Market imperfections and impediments are anything that prevents the prompt movement of resources in response to market signals; they include informational asymmetries, barriers to mobility, excessive transactions costs, and the existence of collective consumption goods.

7. Changing the distribution of income is one of the roles for government intervention that members of a society may desire. Others include values placed on public provision for its own sake, on protection of individuals from themselves or from others, and on recognition of social obligations.

8. Microeconomic policy concerns activities of the government that alter the unrestricted workings of the free-market system in order to affect either the allocation of resources among uses or the distribution of income among people. Major tools of microeconomic policy include (a) public provision, (b) redistribution, (c) rule making, and (d) structuring incentives. The first two are the subject of Chapter 25. Both prescriptive and proscriptive rule making occur in a variety of forms. Incentives can be structured in a number of ways including the use of fines, subsidies, taxes, and effluent charges.

9. There are costs as well as benefits of government intervention, and they must be considered in choosing whether, when, and how much intervention is appropriate. Among these costs are the direct costs incurred by the intervening authority; the costs imposed on those regulated, direct and indirect; and the costs imposed on third parties. These costs are seldom negligible and are often large.

10. Government intervention may fail; if it does, the costs of intervention may be incurred without the achievable benefits of avoiding market failure being fully realized. The possibility of government failure must be balanced against the problems of market failure. It is neither possible nor efficient to correct all market failure; neither is it always efficient to do nothing.

11. Just how and where to change the proportions of free-market decision making and government intervention is a subject of continuing economic and political debate. Both analysis and ideology have roles to play.

TOPICS FOR REVIEW

Central planning versus market coordination
How the price system coordinates
The role of windfall profits
Differences between private and social valuations
Causes of market failure
Externalities
Internalizing externalities
Social benefit and private benefit
Benefits and costs of government intervention
Causes of government failure

DISCUSSION QUESTIONS

1. Should the free market be allowed to determine the price for the following, or should government intervene? If you distinguish among them, defend your distinctions.
   a. Transit fares
   b. Heating oil
   c. Plastic surgery for victims of fires
   d. Garbage collection
   e. Postal delivery of newspapers and magazines
   f. Fire protection for churches
   g. Ice cream

2. Each of the following activities has known harmful effects: (a) cigarette smoking, (b) driving a car at 100 kmh, (c) private ownership of guns, and (d) drilling for offshore oil. In each case identify whether there is a divergence between social and private costs.

3. Suppose the facts asserted below are true; should they trigger government intervention? If so, what policy alternatives are available?
   a. The Concorde jet is twice as fast, twice as noisy on takeoff and landing, and carries one-third the passengers of jumbo jets.
   b. Hospital costs have been rising at about four times the rate of increase of personal income, and proper treatment of a serious illness has become extraordinarily expensive.
   c. The cost of the average one-family house in Ottawa is now over $120,000, an amount that is out of the reach of most government employees.

   d. Cigarette smoking tends to reduce life expectancy by eight years.
   e. Saccharin in large doses has been found to cause cancer in Canadian mice.

4. Consider the possible beneficial and adverse effects of each of the following forms of government interference.
   a. Charging motorists a tax for driving in the downtown areas of large cities—and using the revenues to provide peripheral parking and shuttle buses
   b. Prohibiting doctors from purchasing malpractice insurance
   c. Mandating no-fault auto insurance, in which the car owner's insurance company is responsible for damage to his or her vehicle no matter who causes the accident
   d. Requiring automobile manufacturers to warrantee the tires on cars they sell instead of (as at present) having the tire manufacturer be the warrantor

5. Consider the following (alleged) facts about pollution control and indicate what, if any, influence they might have on policy determination.
   a. In 1982 the cost of meeting federal pollution requirements in the United States was $61 per person.
   b. More than a third of the world's known oil supplies lie under the ocean floor, and there is no known blowout-proof method of recovery.
   c. Sulfur removal requirements and strip mining regulations have led to the tripling of the cost of a ton of coal used in electrical generation.
   d. Every million dollars spent on pollution control creates 67 new jobs in the economy.

6. The Aswan Dam has been called Egypt's "wall against hunger," by virtue of its provision of both irrigation water and electric power to the Nile Valley. Among its less salutary side effects are:
   a. The reduced flow of water and silt in the river have allowed the Nile Delta to be overrun by sea water, leaving harmful salts.
   b. Lake Nasser, in back of the dam, has become a breeding place for malaria mosquitoes.
   c. Homes of 122,000 Nubian villagers have been inundated, along with countless antiquities for 310 miles upstream from the dam.
   Should the dam have been built? Discuss the issues involved, using the concepts of private and social cost and externalities.

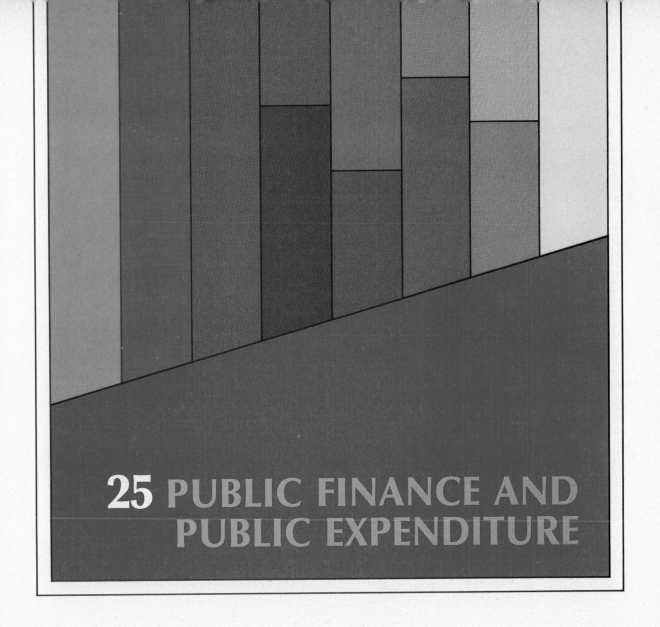

25 PUBLIC FINANCE AND PUBLIC EXPENDITURE

All governments spend money, and they must raise revenue in order to do so. Governments in Canada are no exception. But government spending and government taxation today go far beyond the minimum required to provide such essentials as a system of justice and protection against foreign enemies. Spending and taxing are also key tools of both macroeconomic and microeconomic policy.

In this chapter we look at spending and taxing as tools of microeconomic policy. Government expenditure and government taxation inescapably affect both the allocation of resources and the distribution of income—sometimes intentionally, sometimes not.

There is no simple and sharp functional distinction between expenditure and tax policies. One way to deal with polluted lakes, for example, is by public expenditure to clean them up. An alternative is to use taxes to penalize pollution or to give tax concessions to firms that install pollution-abating devices. Tax concessions that seek to induce market responses are now called **tax expenditures**—that is, sacrifices of revenue by the taxing authorities designed to achieve purposes the government believes are desirable.

In this chapter we are concerned both with the overall impact of public expenditure and taxation on microeconomic decisions and with the deliberate use of these tools for effecting such decisions.

TAXATION AS A TOOL OF MICRO POLICY

There is a bewildering array of taxes, some highly visible (such as sales taxes and income taxes) and others all but invisible to the consumer because they are imposed on raw materials producers or manufacturers at an early stage. People are taxed on what they earn, on what they spend, and on what they own. Firms are taxed as well as households. And taxes are not only numerous, they take a big bite. Aggregate taxes amount to roughly one-third of the total value of goods and services pro-

duced in Canada each year. The diversity and yield of various taxes are shown in Table 25-1.

Taxes and the Distribution of Income

A government that taxes the rich and exempts the poor is redistributing income. How much redistribution is achieved by Canadian taxes today?

Progressivity

Rhetoric about income distribution and tax policy often invokes the important but hard to define concepts of "equity" and "equality." Equity—fairness—is a normative concept; what one group thinks is fair may seem outrageous to another. But equality is a straightforward concept—or is it?

To tax people equally might mean several things. It might mean that each person should pay the same tax, which would be very hard on the unemployed worker and very easy on Wayne Gretsky. It might mean that each should pay the same proportion of his or her income, say a flat 17 percent, whether rich or poor, living alone or supporting eight children, healthy or suffering from a

---

TABLE 25–1 GOVERNMENT TAX REVENUES BY SOURCE, 1983

Kind of tax	Revenue		Percentage division		
	Billions of dollars	Percentage	Federal	Provincial	Municipal
Income tax, persons	$ 64.6	41	62	38	—
Income and other taxes, corporations	13.3	9	77	23	—
General sales taxes	32.2	21	46	54	—
Customs duties	3.0	2	100	—	—
Property tax	14.8	9	—	—	100
All other taxes	28.1	18	—	—	—
Total	156.0	100	46	45	9

Source: National Income and Expenditure Accounts, Statistics Canada, 13-001.

Income taxes are the major source of revenue for the federal and provincial governments. Substantial yields are also obtained from the federal manufacturer's sales tax and the provincial retail levies which make up the sales tax category. Municipal governments rely almost entirely on property taxes.

disease that requires heavy use of expensive drugs. It might mean that each should pay an amount of tax such that everybody's income after taxes is the same—which would remove any incentive to earn above average income. Or it might mean none of these things.

People may not agree on what redistributions are fair, but they can agree on what redistributions actually occur. To get precise measurements of what happens, the distributional effects of taxes are usually discussed using the concept of **progressivity of taxation**, the ratio of taxes to income at different levels of income.

A **proportional tax** takes amounts of money from people in direct proportion to their income.

A **regressive tax** takes a larger percentage of income from people, the lower their income.

A **progressive tax** takes a larger percentage of income from people, the larger their income.

A tax system is said to be progressive if it decreases the inequality of income distribution and to be regressive if it increases the inequality.

It is easier to assess the progressivity or regressivity of particular taxes than of the tax system as a whole.

Sales, excise, and consumption taxes. If two families each spend the same proportion of their income on a certain commodity subject to a sales or an excise tax, the tax will be proportional in its effects on them. If the tax is on a commodity, such as food, that takes a larger proportion of the income of lower-income families, it will be regressive: If it is on a commodity such as jewelry, where the rich spend a larger proportion of their income than the poor, it will be progressive.

Commodities with inelastic demands provide easy sources of revenue. In many countries commodities such as tobacco, alcohol, and gasoline are singled out for very high rates of taxation. But these commodities usually account for a much greater proportion of the expenditure of lower-income than higher-income groups, and taxes on them are thus regressive.

The sales and excise taxes used in Canada today are as a whole regressive.

Two types of consumption taxes have been widely discussed recently. One, called a *value-added tax*, is widely used in Western Europe. It is nothing more than a generalized retail sales tax, collected as goods move through the production and distribution systems rather than at the retail sales stage. It shares the regressivity of the sales tax. The other is an *expenditure tax*, which is levied on the total value of income minus saving. Compared with an income tax, it is regressive because the rich save a larger fraction of their income than do the poor.

Property taxes. The progressivity of the property tax has been studied extensively. It is well known that the rich live in more expensive houses than the poor, but all that this establishes is that the rich tend to pay more dollars in property tax than do the poor. Because the rich tend to live in different communities than the poor and thus pay taxes at different rates, and because they tend to spend a different proportion of their income for housing, the question of the progressivity of the property tax is difficult and controversial. Most studies have shown that the proportion of income spent for housing tends to decrease with income. Many but not all public finance experts believe, therefore, that the property tax tends to be regressive in its overall effect.

Personal income taxes. The personal tax rate is itself a function of taxable income, and it is useful to distinguish between two different rates. The **average tax rate** paid by an individual or by a couple is their income tax divided by total income. The **marginal tax rate** is the amount of tax the taxpayer would pay on an additional dollar of income. Table 25-2 shows the applicable rates on federal income tax in 1982.

In structure, the federal personal income tax is progressive because the average rate rises steadily with income. However, because of the special definitions given to net income by the tax laws, the overall effect of the federal income tax is actually less progressive than Table 25-2 suggests. To arrive at taxable income, total income is modified by certain exemptions from income, by capital gains pro-

TABLE 25–2 THE RATE STRUCTURE OF THE PERSONAL INCOME TAX, 1982 (Single Taxpayer, No Dependents)

| Assessed income (dollars) | Federal income tax | | Provincial income tax[a] | | Combined average |
	Tax (dollars)	Marginal rate (percent)	Tax (dollars)	Marginal rate (percent)	Rate on assessed income (percent)
$ 7,500	$ 242		$ 208		6
10,000	653	16	401	8	11
12,500	1,087	17	605	8	14
15,000	1,533	18	814	8	16
17,500	2,001	19	1,034	9	17
20,000	2,498	20	1,268	9	19
25,000	3,645	23	1,807	11	22
30,000	4,895	25	2,395	12	24
50,000	10,692	29	5,019	13	32
100,000	27,277	33	12,914	16	40
200,000	61,277	43	28,894	16	45

[a] The typical provincial tax equals 48 percent of the federal tax.
Source: The National Finances.

Both marginal and average tax rates rise with income; thus the tax is progressive in structure. The combined marginal rate rises from 24 percent to a maximum of 50 percent. The combined average rate rises from 6 percent to 45 percent; it exaggerates the actual degree of progressivity because higher income taxpayers are more likely to have some income such as capital gains, which is taxed at lower rates.

visions, and by permitted deductions from gross income.[1]

Despite modifications, the federal income tax is progressive in effect as well as in structure.

Corporate income tax. The federal corporate income tax is, for practical purposes, a flat-rate tax of 50 percent of profits as defined by the taxing authorities. It is difficult to determine its effects on income distribution, for there is great controversy over the extent to which it is "shifted" to consumers.[2] So far as the tax falls on stockholders,

they as a group tend to be wealthier than individuals who do not own stock, and there is thus a tendency toward progressivity. But within the stockholder group, lower-income stockholders bear a disproportionate share of the tax relative to wealthy stockholders. If a dollar were paid out in dividends instead of taxes, rich stockholders would keep a much smaller share than poorer stockholders because of their high marginal personal tax rates.

The Progressivity of the Tax System

To assess the way in which the whole tax system, as distinct from any one tax, affects income distribution is more difficult. One aspect concerns the mix of taxes of different kinds. Federal taxes (chiefly income taxes) tend to be somewhat progressive. State and local authorities rely heavily on

[1] Until recently, most capital gains were not taxable in Canada, but beginning in 1972 taxpayers were required to include one-half of gains received in their taxable income. This change was part of the substantial revisions of the Income Tax Act made after a lengthy public debate over the far-reaching proposals of the Royal Commission on Taxation (the Carter Commission).

[2] The question of tax incidence—that is, who really pays a tax imposed on any one group—is discussed later in this chapter.

property and sales taxes and thus have tax systems that are regressive.

The matter of assessing progressivity is even more complex than this. Is progressivity defined for the individual or for the family? When a couple with two children pays the same tax as a childless couple with the same income, is this proportional or regressive taxation? If the *family* is the relevant unit, it is proportional taxation. If the *person* is the relevant unit, equal tax rates on families of different sizes having the same income would be regressive. As it is, a household with children pays less *income* tax than a household without children but with the same income. (This does not mean, as childless people often assume, that the household with children pays less total taxes. For other taxes, such as sales taxes, tend to fall more heavily on large families than on small ones.)

The difficulty of determining progressivity is increased by the fact that income from different sources is taxed at different rates. For example, in the federal individual tax, income from royalties on oil wells is taxed more lightly than income from royalties on books; profits from sales of assets (called *capital gains*) are taxed more lightly than wages and salaries; and some bond interest is tax exempt while most interest income is taxed. To evaluate progressivity one needs to know the way in which different levels of income correlate with different sources of income.

One famous study by Professor Irwin Gillespie of Carleton University argued that the Canadian tax system is proportional over a middle-income range but regressive for both low-income and high-income classes.

Can Progressivity Be Increased?

Taxes can be levied on any of three different monetary magnitudes: on assets, on incomes, and on expenditures. Inheritance taxes and gift taxes are taxes on assets; such taxes do not play a large continuing role in the overall revenue picture. Taxes on incomes are important and can be quite progressive. Taxes on expenditures—especially

sales and excise taxes—are related to the dollar value of expenditures, not the incomes of those spending the money; they tend to be regressive.

Many observers have argued that to achieve overall proportionality in the tax structure is in itself a significant accomplishment. Some argue that, given the large fraction of national income that is taxed away, more progressivity cannot be achieved since we are already forced to tax average and lower-income persons heavily to meet revenue requirements. Whether or not more progressivity is desirable, is more progressivity possible?

Substantial progressivity in income taxes is required to achieve proportionality in the overall tax pattern.

Would Increasing Reliance on Income Taxes Increase Progressivity?

It may seem obvious that, since income taxes are progressive, raising tax rates would surely increase progressivity. Surprisingly, some conservative economists have argued that this is not the case. A shift to higher tax rates would raise both the average rate and the marginal rate of tax on incomes, but it might or might not raise the total amount of revenue actually collected from income taxes. Whether it did would depend on the incentive effects of tax rates.

A graph that relates the government's income tax revenue yield to the level of tax rates has recently gained attention as the **Laffer curve**, named after economist Arthur Laffer whose views were influential within the Reagan administration in the United States. Its essential feature is that tax revenues reach a maximum at some rate of taxation well below 100 percent.

Here is the usual argument concerning the shape of the Laffer curve: At a zero tax rate, no revenue will be collected. Similarly, at a 100 percent tax rate, revenues would again be zero because no one would bother to earn taxable income just to support the government. For some intermediate rates people will both earn income and pay taxes. Government tax revenues will thus reach an upper limit at some rate of taxation below 100 percent. For

rates higher than the rate that produces this maximum, every increase in tax rates will lead to a
decrease in tax revenues. (See Figure 25-1.)

Just where this maximum occurs—whether with
average tax rates of 40 percent or 80 percent or 95
percent—is an important empirical matter. Laffer
and others assert that tax policy has already carried
progressiveness too far. They believe that by the
1970s the United States had already increased taxes
past the point where higher tax rates yielded more
revenue. As a result, they argue, any attempt to
increase progressivity by raising income tax rates
would be self-defeating.

Many others disagree. While they might con-
cede that some countries (such as the United Kingdom) may have reached such a point, they argue
that this has happened only because their residents
can migrate to countries with lower taxes, such as
Canada and the United States. They believe that
the current U.S. top marginal tax rate of 50 percent
is still short of being self-defeating in terms of tax
revenue. That is, they believe that Professor Laffer
identified a potential rather than an actual problem.
Box 25-1 identifies an early precursor of the Laffer
curve.

Increasing Progressivity
by Changing the Income Tax Structure

If the government raises income taxes for one
group and lowers them for another in a way that
leaves the total tax yield constant, the *structure* of
the income tax will have been changed. Much repeated demand for "tax reform" relates to proposed changes in the structure of income taxes.
Most economists believe that such changes can be
made (whether or not they consider them desirable)
and that if they were made, they would increase
the progressivity of the total tax system. Here are
two important and widely advocated proposals.

The negative income tax (NIT). A tax can be
negative if at some level of income the government
pays "the taxpayer" instead of the other way
around. The so-called **negative income tax** is a
policy tool designed to increase progressivity and

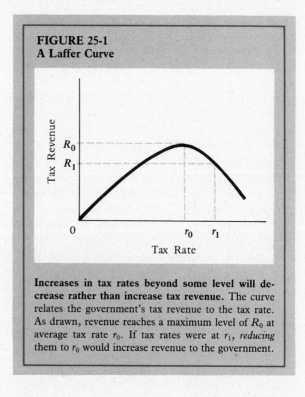

FIGURE 25-1
A Laffer Curve

**Increases in tax rates beyond some level will de-
crease rather than increase tax revenue.** The curve
relates the government's tax revenue to the tax rate.
As drawn, revenue reaches a maximum level of R_0 at
average tax rate r_0. If tax rates were at r_1, *reducing*
them to r_0 would increase revenue to the government.

combat poverty by making taxes negative at very
low incomes. Such a tax would extend progressivity
to incomes below those where people currently
have income tax liability.

There are many versions of NIT proposals; the
one described here will illustrate the basic idea.
The underlying belief is that a family of four should
be allowed a minimum annual income—say,
$6,000. The aim is to guarantee this income with-
out eliminating the incentive to become self-sup-
porting. This is done by combining a grant with a
tax. At a break-even level—well above the minimum income level guaranteed—the family will neither receive money from the government nor pay
any tax. Below this break-even income level the
family will be paid by the government (the family
pays a "negative tax"). Above this level it will pay
a positive tax. An example based on a grant of
$6,000, a break-even level of $12,000, and a mar-

BOX 25–1 THE LAFFER CURVE 600 YEARS BEFORE LAFFER

In the fourteenth century the Arab philosopher Ibn Khaldun wrote:

It should be known that at the beginning of the dynasty, taxation yields a large revenue from small assessments. At the end of the dynasty, taxation yields a small revenue from large assessments. . . .

When the dynasty follows the ways of group feeling and (political) superiority, it necessarily has at first a desert attitude. The desert attitude requires kindness, reverence, humility, respect for the property of other people, and disinclination to appropriate it, except in rare instances. Therefore, the individual imposts and assessments, which together constitute the tax revenue, are low. When tax assessments and imposts upon the subjects are low, the latter have the energy and desire to do things. Cultural enterprises grow and increase, because the low taxes bring satisfaction. When cultural enterprises grow, the number of individual imposts and assessments mounts. In consequence, the tax revenue, which is the sum total of (the individual assessments), increases.

When the dynasty continues in power and their rulers follow each other in succession, they become sophisticated. The Bedouin attitude and simplicity lose their significance, and the Bedouin qualities of moderation and restraint disappear.

As a result, the individual imposts and assessments upon the subjects, agricultural laborers, farmers, and all the other taxpayers, increase. Every individual impost and assessment is greatly increased, in order to obtain a higher tax revenue. Customs duties are placed upon articles of commerce. Gradual increases in the amount of assessments succeed each other regularly, in correspondence with the gradual increase in the luxury customs and many needs of the dynasty, and the spending required in connection with them. Eventually, the taxes will weigh heavily upon the subjects and overburden them. Heavy taxes become an obligation and tradition, because the increases took place gradually, and no one knows specifically who increased them or levied them. They lie upon the subjects like an obligation and tradition.

The assessments increase beyond the limits of equity. The result is that the interest of the subjects in cultural enterprises disappears, since when they compare expenditures and taxes with their income and gain and see the little profit they make, they lose all hope. Therefore, many of them refrain from all the activity. The result is that the total tax revenue goes down.

Finally, civilization is destroyed, because the incentive for cultural activity is gone. It is the dynasty that suffers from the situation, because it (is the dynasty that) profits from cultural activity.*

*From the Muqaddimah: An Introduction to History, translated from the Arabic by Franz Rosenthal. Bollingen Series XLIII. Copyright © 1958 and 1967 by Princeton University Press. Reprinted by permission of Princeton University Press.

ginal tax rate of 50 percent is given in Figure 25-2.[3]

Supporters of the negative income tax believe that it would be a particularly effective tool for reducing poverty. It provides a minimum level of income as a matter of right, not of charity, and it does so without removing the incentive to work of those eligible for payments. Every dollar earned adds to the after-tax income of the family.

As a potential replacement for many other relief programs, it promises to avoid the most pressing cases of poverty with much less administrative cost and without the myriad exceptions that are involved in most programs. An incidental advantage is that it removes whatever incentive people might

[3] The example is unrealistic in assigning a 50 percent marginal tax at such low levels of income as $12,000. The cost of an NIT would be much higher if it were necessary for political reasons to combine it with a sharply graduated rate structure of the sort shown in Table 25-2.

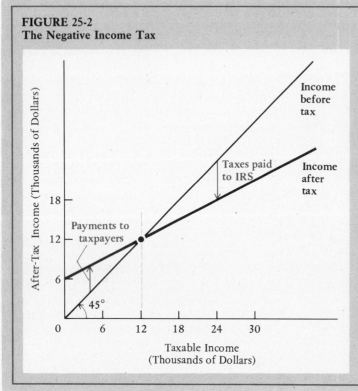

FIGURE 25-2
The Negative Income Tax

Instead of having a zero income tax up to some level and a positive tax thereafter, there could be a negative tax up to a break-even income and a positive tax above it. The scheme illustrated here combines a notional $6,000 grant to every family, with a 50 percent tax on all income. A family with $12,000 of income breaks even. A family with income below $12,000 is paid by the government. A family with income above $12,000 pays taxes. The heavy black line shows the after-tax income for different levels of taxable income under this particular scheme. The 45° line shows the after-tax income *if* taxes were zero at all levels of income: therefore the vertical distance between it and the heavy black curve shows the payments by or to taxpayers at any level of income under this scheme.

have to migrate to states with better welfare programs, but it does not discourage migration to places where work may be available.

Comprehensive income taxation (CIT). Joseph Pechman of the Brookings Institution has taken the lead in arguing that it is possible to raise more revenue from the income tax, increase its progressivity, and at the same time *reduce* both average and marginal tax rates! This sounds like magic, but it is a matter of simple arithmetic. The **tax base** is total taxable income. Under present definitions taxable income is much less than total income because there are all sorts of deductions and exemptions. If all income were taxed, regardless of source, it would be possible to raise more revenue by applying lower rates to this larger tax base. The idea of **comprehensive income taxation** is to eliminate virtually all the so-called loopholes, the deductions and exemptions that make taxable income less than total income. By eliminating some or all personal deductions, homeowner preferences, special treatment of capital gains, and exemptions for dependents, old age, and blindness, the tax base could be increased substantially. It would then be easy to reduce tax *rates* in all income brackets.

Under these schemes it would be possible to achieve substantially more progressivity without increasing anyone's marginal tax rate at all. For example, imagine a definition of the CIT where comprehensive income is 150 percent of present taxable income. Rates could be left unchanged for high-income taxpayers and greatly reduced for middle- and low-income taxpayers in such amounts as to maintain the same total tax revenue, but increase progressivity.

Alternatively, some rates could be decreased by a little and others by a great deal—as long as the average decrease was one-third. Needless to say, even if everyone's tax *rates* went down under the CIT, not everyone's tax *payments* would do so because the elimination of exclusions, deductions, and exemptions would raise the tax liability of those taxpayers who had utilized them. What some regard as unfair loopholes may be for others their toehold on economic prosperity.

Political Barriers to Tax Reform

While almost everyone agrees our present tax structure is much too complex and in many ways illogical, the calls for fundamental and sweeping tax reform are unlikely to be answered. The purely political barriers to tax reform are formidable. Any single reform is likely to impose large costs on a relatively well-identified group, while the benefits it gives would be more widely diffused.

The 10 people who would each lose a million dollars from a particular tax reform are much more interested in the issue than the 10 million people who would each gain a dollar. The 10, not the 10 million, hire lobbyists and make campaign contributions. Legislators must respond to these pressures if they want long public careers.

With *expenditure* programs the political pressures are reversed. The beneficiaries of a program to subsidize investment in a depressed region, to bail out a troubled firm such as Massey-Ferguson, or to improve the St. Lawrence Seaway are much more intensely and immediately involved than the millions of others whose taxes will rise a little bit to pay for it. The 100,000 who would gain a hundred dollars each from a particular expenditure policy are much more likely to be heard than the 10 million whose taxes would rise by a dollar each. (Even when people demand lower taxes, they often vote out of office politicians who refuse to provide the services the taxes would make possible.)

Political considerations tend to make redistribution by expenditures more attractive than redistribution by tax reform.

How Much Progressivity Is Desirable?

Suppose increased progressivity could be achieved; would we want it? Many say no.

One obvious objection to tax reform designed to increase progressivity is that not everyone wants more progressivity. A second is that many who do not oppose more progressivity do not want changes that would make it easier for the government to raise more money. Such people fear schemes such as the NIT and the CIT precisely because they do not generate tax revolts.

A third source of opposition to increasing progressivity by means of tax reform is that every aspect of present tax policy was introduced to benefit some group whose members believe they have valid claims to special treatment. Consider some of the "loopholes" that the CIT would reduce or eliminate. Tax deductibility of charitable and educational contributions provide incentives for gifts to churches, universities, and private charities and foundations.

Fourth, more progressivity may conflict with what is seen as fair. Much erosion of the tax base has arisen from adjustments made in the name of equity. Special tax treatment of the aged seems fair to many in view of the probable needs by the aged for extensive medical treatment.

Finally, the case against tax policy as a means of achieving redistributive goals has some support even among those who favor more redistribution of income from rich to poor. They argue that it is misleading, unnecessary, and poor tactics politically to pay so much attention to *tax* progressivity. After all, how the money is spent is just as important, and often less controversial, than how it is collected. A regressive tax, say a sales tax, may provide funds for increasing welfare payments and thus redistribute income to the poor. Social security taxes are regressive; social security payments are progressive. It is the combined overall effect of the two that is important, and it is easier to get government to enact progressive expenditure programs than progressive taxes.

Tax Structure and the Allocation of Resources

The tax system influences the allocation of resources by changing the *relative* prices of different goods and factors and the *relative* profitability of different industries and of different uses of factors of production. These changes in turn affect resource movements.

While it is theoretically possible to design a neutral tax system—one that leaves all relative prices unchanged—actual tax policy, both intentionally and unintentionally, is never neutral. It leads to a different allocation of resources than would occur without it.

Intended Effects

The tax structure is often used deliberately to change incentives and thus to affect resource allocation. Taxing gasoline to discourage energy consumption is one example; effluent charges on polluters are another. And tax provisions may be used as a carrot as well as a stick. One way is to allow the deduction of some expenditures from income before computing the amount of taxes payable, or to give tax credits for some kinds of expenditures. Every $100 spent by a wealthy family in the 50 percent marginal tax bracket on an item that is tax deductible costs them $50 in after-tax income. Every $100 they spend on items that are not tax deductible costs the full $100 in after-tax income. This encourages them to contribute money and assets to charitable and educational institutions.

Interest payments for a mortgage are tax deductible under the U.S. tax code, and a similar proposal was included in the budget on which the Progressive Conservative government of Joe Clark was defeated in 1979. Since payments for rental housing are not deductible, such a provision would encourage home ownership by lowering the cost of buying a house relative to the cost of renting one.

When corporations are allowed "accelerated depreciation" or "investment credits" on certain investments, it encourages them to make such investments in larger amounts. Changes in such provisions in corporation taxes are commonly used by the federal government to try to regulate investment demand, both in the aggregate and in its allocation among various sectors and industries.

Unintended Effects

Not all the allocative effects of the tax system are intended. When high income taxes discourage work, or induce people to spend money on tax avoidance, we are plainly reaping unintended and undesirable by-products of a tax system.

Consider further the tax incentives to home ownership, which were surely intended. An incidental result of providing such incentives through the income tax is that the incentive effect is much less for a poor person than for a rich one. The value of the deduction for interest is much greater to a taxpayer in the 50 percent marginal tax bracket than to someone in the 12 percent bracket. When a bank charges them each 12 percent, the richer taxpayer pays only 6 percent in after-tax dollars, the poorer one 10.6 percent if he or she itemizes deductions. For the many middle- and low-income persons who take the standard deduction, the actual interest rate remains 12 percent. Thus the lower one's income, the less the incentive provided to obtain a property stake in the society. This is surely an unintended effect.

The major unresolved question about taxes and allocation is empirical: Just how different is the allocation because of tax policy? Perhaps surprisingly, there is no consensus on this question. The reason is that we are not sure who really pays the taxes that are levied. This is called the problem of **tax incidence.**

Tax Incidence

When a tax is imposed on a firm, does the firm pay the tax, or does it pass it on to the consumer in the form of higher prices? To see why this is a difficult question to answer, consider two examples.

Do Landlords or Tenants Pay the Property Tax?

Landlords characteristically protest that the crushing burden of property taxes makes it impossible for them to earn a reasonable living from renting buildings to tenants who as often as not abuse the property. Tenants are likely to reply that landlords typically pass on the whole burden of the tax to the tenants in the form of higher rents. Both sides cannot be right in alleging that they each bear the entire burden of the tax!

To examine the incidence, suppose that a city inposes a property tax. Each of the thousands of landlords in the city decides to raise rents by the full amount of the tax. There will be a decline in the quantity of rental accommodation demanded as a result of the price increase. The decline in the quantity demanded without any change in the quantity supplied will cause a surplus of rental accommodations at the higher prices.

Landlords will find it difficult to replace tenants who move out, and the typical unit will remain empty longer between tenancies. Prospective tenants will find many alternative sites from which to choose and will become very particular in what they expect from landlords. Some prospective tenants, seeing vacant apartments, will offer to pay rents below the asking rent. Some landlords will accept the offer rather than earn nothing from vacant premises. Once some landlords cut rents, others will have to follow suit or find their properties staying unrented for longer periods of time.

Eventually rentals will reach a new equilibrium at which the quantity demanded equals the quantity supplied. This equilibrium price for rental housing will be higher than the original pre-tax rent but lower than the rent that passes the entire tax on to the tenants. This argument is shown graphically in Figure 25-3.

The incidence of the property tax is shared by landlords and tenants.

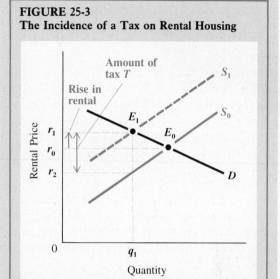

FIGURE 25-3
The Incidence of a Tax on Rental Housing

Since the equilibrium rent rises by less than the amount of the tax, landlords and tenants share the burden. The supply schedule S_0 reflects landlords' willingness to supply apartments at different levels of rents received. When a tax of T is imposed on rentals, the supply curve (in terms of rent paid by the tenant) shifts up by the full amount of the tax to S_1. Because the demand curve slopes downward, equilibrium shifts from E_0 to E_1 and equilibrium rent rises to r_1. The landlord receives only r_2 net of the property tax. Of the total tax, tenants have paid only $r_0 r_1$ per unit and landlords $r_2 r_0$.

Just how it is shared by the two groups will depend on the elasticity of the demand and supply curves.[4]

Notice that this result does not depend on who writes the check to pay the tax bill. In many European countries, the tenant rather than the landlord is sent the tax bill and pays the tax directly to the city; even in this case, however, the landlord bears part of the burden. As long as the existence

---

[4] We suggest you draw a series of diagrams with demand and supply curves of different slopes to see how this works. In each case, shift the supply curve up by the same vertical amount—to represent the property tax—and see what proportion of the increase is reflected in the new equilibrium price.

of the tax reduces the quantity of rental accommodations demanded below what it otherwise would be, the tax will depress the amount received by landlords. In this way landlords will bear part of its burden.

Notice also that this result emerges even though neither landlords nor tenants realize it. Because rents are changing for all sorts of other reasons, no one will have much idea of what equilibrium rentals would be in the absence of the tax. It does not do much good just to look at what happens immediately after tax rates are changed because, as we have already seen, landlords may begin by raising rents by the full amount of the tax. Although they think they have passed the tax on, this creates a disequilibrium, and in the final position prices will have risen by less than the full amount of the tax.

Do Taxes on Profits Affect Prices?

Economic theory predicts that a general percentage tax on pure profits will have no effect on price or output, and thus the full incidence of such a tax will fall on producers. To see this quickly suppose that one price-quantity combination gives the firm higher profits (without considering taxes) than any other. If the government imposes a 20 percent profits tax, the firm will have only 80 percent as much profits after tax as it had before; *this will be true for each possible level of output.* The firm may grumble, but it will not be profitable for it to alter its price or output.

Notice that this argument is independent of the tax rate. [32] It applies equally whether the tax rate is 10 percent or 75 percent.

A tax on corporation income. Corporate income taxes are taxes on profits *as defined by the tax laws.* The definitions make them a tax on a combination of pure profits plus some of the return to the factors of production, "capital," and "risk taking."

Because such a profits tax will reduce the returns to these important factors of production, it can have significant effects on the allocation of re-

sources and on the prices and output of goods. Suppose a risky industry requires, say, a 20 percent return on its capital to make prospective owners willing to take the risk of investing in the industry. Suppose that every firm is earning 30 percent on its investment before taxes. A 50 percent corporate income tax will reduce the return to 15 percent, below the point that makes investment attractive, and resources will leave the industry. Obviously price and output changes will occur. As firms leave the industry, and as supply decreases, prices will rise until the remaining firms can earn a sufficient level of after-tax profits so that they are once again compensated for the risks involved. Thus customers must bear part of the burden of the tax through a price increase.

A tax on profits, as defined by the taxing authorities, will have an effect on prices and outputs and thus will be shared by the consumer.

Because industries differ in degree of risk, the impact of a corporate income tax will be greater on more risky industries than on less risky ones. It will thus affect the allocation of resources among industries.

PUBLIC EXPENDITURE AS A TOOL OF MICRO POLICY

Public expenditure is large and growing. It affects both the distribution of income and the allocation of resources. In recent years, spending by federal, provincial, and municipal governments—that is, by the public sector—has amounted to about 40 percent of the nation's expenditures. Table 25-3 shows government expenditure by principal categories of function (or purpose) for 1982. About 40 percent of this money was spent by the federal government, the rest by provincial and municipal governments. Box 25-2 on page 446 takes up one controversy about the role of government expenditure.

TABLE 25–3 EXPENDITURE OF ALL GOVERNMENTS BY FUNCTION, 1979

Category	Billions of dollars	Percentage distribution	Average annual rate of growth 1961–1979
Health	$ 13.4	12	14
Social welfare	24.8	22	13
Education	16.5	15	10
Defense	4.2	4	5
Transportation and communication	9.0	8	8
Interest on the public debt	11.6	10	12
All other	32.8	29	14
Total	$112.3	100	12

Source: Statistics Canada, 68-202, and *Canada Year Book*, 1978.

Health and social services have been the fastest growing categories of government expenditure in the last two decades. The table shows combined expenditures for federal, provincial, and municipal governments. The category "All other" includes sanitation and waste removal, natural resources, general government, police and fire protection, recreation, and cultural activities.

Types of Government Expenditures

In addition to classifying budget expenditures by function, as in Table 25-3, we may classify them by type of expenditure. This is done for the federal and provincial governments in Table 25-4; Figure 25-4 shows the changing importance of different types of federal government expenditures.

Provision of goods and services. As Table 25-4 indicates, the largest type of federal expenditure until 1971, and still the dominant type for provincial and municipal governments, was the provisions of goods and services. Roughly half of total expenditures at all levels of government are made for the provision of goods and services that it is assumed are desired and desirable but that the market itself would fail to provide. Among these goods and services are defence, transportation facilities, education, and municipal services. In these activities the government acts in much the same way that a firm acts, using factors of production to produce outputs. By and large these are outputs of collective consumption goods, goods with strong third-party effects, or services whose benefits are not marketable.

Public opinion polls show that the majority of Canadians support public provision of such services as basic education, hospital care, and medical care. Rising costs of such services are, as Box 25-3 discusses, nonetheless becoming a serious problem. Box 25-2 discusses the problem of higher education when there is not such strong agreement that government provision is socially desirable.

Transfer payments. Although government purchases of goods and services are large (about $46 billion in 1983), they have remained roughly constant in real terms over the last 25 years. They have been overtaken by transfer payments as the largest form of federal government expenditure. Transfer payments have been steadily increasing in importance, and this has led to significant changes in both the distribution of income and the allocation of resources.

Public Expenditures and Redistribution of Income

The federal government, as Table 25-1 indicates, raises about half its revenues by income-related taxes. When these federal receipts are transferred

BOX 25–2 SHOULD HIGHER EDUCATION BE SUBSIDIZED?

Governments often provide goods and services that they produce at a price that is well below total costs. The case against the practice of providing free or subsidized goods and services is that the public is encouraged to consume the good or service to the point where the utility from the last unit consumed is low—indeed, in the case of a good provided free, it is zero. This means that resources are being used to produce goods whose marginal utility is less than the value of other goods that could have been produced instead.

The case for free or subsidized provision has been suggested. Some public goods are impossible to sell on a market. Thus, if they are to be provided at all, they must be provided free. In other cases, important third-party effects make it desirable to encourage a level of consumption beyond what the individual household would voluntarily choose if it had to pay the full cost itself. While there are some relatively uncontroversial cases such as providing free milk in schools attended by poor children, or general free elementary education, the case for subsidizing university education is controversial.

The facts are clear. Higher education in Canada is heavily subsidized, and only a small proportion of costs is recovered from student fees. The question does not concern the need for scholarship and loan funds for poor but deserving students; instead it asks how much subsidy, independent of need, should be provided.

Supporters of heavy subsidization argue that the whole society gains from the widest possible spread of education and that it is in the general interest to encourage more education than people would voluntarily choose on the basis of their own self-interest. The payoff to society of investments in human capital has been studied extensively. These studies show that education generates enough extra output later to compensate for the sacrifice of current output required to provide the education.

Critics of the present system accept the evidence but ask why the general public (a majority of whom are not university graduates) should subsidize others to obtain an investment in human capital that is a good investment from their own selfish points of view. After all, say critics, those who get the education will earn the higher incomes their education permits. Let them borrow the money, if necessary.

Education is, of course, more than an investment in future production, and this can cut either way: A stay at a university may be valued by the student because of cultural or social reasons or because it saves the student the necessity of deciding what to do next. Each of these reasons argues against subsidy. But education may also provide the nation with a generation that is better trained and better able to cope with pressing social problems than the previous one, and this might justify a subsidy.

There is no general rule as to the appropriate degree of subsidy; the case for and against providing a commodity at less than cost varies greatly with the nature of the commodity and the externalities conferred by having more of it than the market would provide.

back to individuals or to provincial and municipal governments, they have a substantial redistributive effect.

Federal Transfer Payments to Individuals

Transfer payments are defined generally as payments to private persons or institutions that do not arise out of current production activity. In 1970 a federal government white paper on income security classified transfers to individuals according to four types: demogrants, guaranteed income, social insurance, and social assistance. Old age security and family allowance payments are in the first group, guaranteed income supplements and child tax credits are examples of the second, the Canada Pension

TABLE 25–4 FEDERAL AND PROVINCIAL EXPENDITURES BY TYPE, 1983

	Federal		Provincial	
	Billions of dollars	Percentage of total	Billions of dollars	Percentage of total
Purchases of goods and services	$19.7	21	$26.4	32
Transfers to persons	28.1	30	16.2	20
Interest on the public debt	17.4	19	7.7	9
Transfers to other levels of government	17.3	19	27.3	34
Other transfers	10.4	11	3.9	5
Total	$92.9	100	$81.5	100

Source: Statistics Canada, 11-003E.

Purchases of goods and services constitute less than a quarter of federal government expenditure and less than a third of provincial government expenditure. The table shows total expenditure by type for each of the federal and provincial governments. Transfer payments constitute the majority of expenditures. For the federal government, transfers to persons plus interest on the debt account for half its total expenditure, while transfers to governments (mostly the provinces) account for another 17 percent. For the provinces, transfers to municipalities account for 34 percent of total expenditure.

Plan and unemployment insurance are examples of the third, and the fourth includes special programs for widows, single parents, and others who have no recourse to other support programs.

Transfers to individuals by the federal government have grown as a proportion of expenditures from about 15 percent in 1930 to about 30 percent by the mid seventies.[5] These transfers are often intended as a form of insurance or as an incentive for individuals to redirect expenditure toward specific items such as housing or health. Many of them are part of income maintenance programs. The net effect of the transfers is to reduce inequality in the distribution of income.

There are several reasons for the growth of transfer payments. First, both the number of people eligible for them and the amounts they receive have increased. For example, there has been a general liberalization of the eligibility requirements for unemployment insurance benefits. Second, the attention to poverty (discussed in Chapter 20) has led to an increase in transfers. Third, persistent unemployment during the 1970s and 1980s greatly increased unemployment compensation payments.

While some transfer payments go to people with above-average incomes, most do not. Certainly transfer payments have had some tendency to redistribute income to the poor.

The percentage of all personal income received in the form of government transfer payments has increased sharply, from about 9 percent in 1965 to more than 14 percent in 1983.

Intergovernmental Transfers As a Form of Redistribution

In addition to the federal government, there are 10 provincial governments, 2 territories, more than 4,000 municipalities, and about 250 townships in Canada. Moreover, a large number of overlapping counties or districts are responsible for such local authorities as school boards. Each of the more than 5,000 governmental units spends public money,

---

[5] The relative importance of the federal government in making transfers to individuals has been declining since the early 1960s while that of the provinces has been increasing. Below we discuss the related issue of growth in intergovernmental transfers.

BOX 25–3 THE RISING COST OF HEALTH CARE

Health care is an emotional and provocative issue. Almost everyone would agree that in a wealthy society, such as Canada in the 1980s, some minimum level of health care should be available to all citizens by right. At the same time there is public concern over the high current cost of medical care. Elementary economic analysis shows that these two events—the right to free medical care and the clamor over its high social cost—are not unrelated.

Explaining the High Cost

Without health insurance, a single major operation can be an enormous financial burden and a prolonged illness will impoverish even the most prudent middle-income household. Why has health care become so costly?

One reason may be that health care is highly labor-intensive. The wages of nurses, laboratory technicians, and other medical service personnel have risen substantially relative to their productivity (the number of temperatures taken, beds made, and meals served per employee do not increase much over time). Another reason is the steadily rising quality of medical care. Available knowledge, techniques, equipment, and the training of new physicians all have improved over time. Thus it becomes possible not only to provide quicker, surer cures for common and recurring ailments but to prevent other less common ailments and complications. Moreover the demand for medical care tends to rise due to rising real income. As per capita income rises, people are prepared to consume more and better health.

A further reason for rising medical costs is that the methods of financing medical care have tended to greatly weaken incentives to econo-

mize on its use and to keep costs down. Either free public provision, or comprehensive prepaid (or employer-paid) health insurance is sure to lead to costs rising more rapidly than when the price system allocates resources. This is an example of moral hazard, discussed in Chapter 24.

Most insurance and publicly provided medical programs have eliminated significant *marginal* charges to the patient for the incremental medical or hospital care consumed. An individual has no incentive to economize on the quantity or quality of his or her own elective care and thus wants the very best care to which the "plan" entitles him or her. In the market system individual patients would choose medical care (as they choose housing) from a wide variety of price-quality alternative forms of health care. If patients had to pay their own bills, and if they could make fully informed choices, many might prefer to pay less and not have the best available equipment and doctors in all circumstances.

Nor do doctors and hospitals have strong incentive to hold costs down. They can pass along the higher costs of advanced modern techniques to insurers in higher fees, especially if they do not have to worry that those higher fees may cause a reduction in the quantity of their services demanded. They may well reason: Our job is to give the best treatment; let others worry about the costs. Indeed unscrupulous doctors can prescribe unnecessary surgery or other medical care to increase the demand for their services. Of course the insurance companies have to pass on higher claims in the form of higher premiums, and thus they might exercise cost control. But if the government or a giant employer pays most of the bill (as it does for many patients), insurers may not feel too much resistance to rising insurance rates, at least for a long time.

What Is the Right Quantity and Quality of Medical Care?

While everyone agrees that some minimum level of health care should be provided to all who need it, the definition of that minimum is a controversial issue. No doubt the acceptable minimum level of health care has risen over time; accordingly we have had increasing public intervention in the health sector.

The issue provokes more emotion than a discussion of housing or clothing, however. After all, human lives are at stake. True enough, but that does not end the matter. A first response is that much (although of course not all) medical and hospital care is elective and has almost nothing to do with life or death. By way of analogy, to say that no one should starve is not to say that everybody should receive all the free food they can eat. Nonvital attention accounts for a large part of our demand for health care. If it is offered at little or no marginal cost to users, it will be consumed beyond the point where marginal utility is equal to the cost of providing it.

But even where life is at stake, do we really always want the very best? Suppose the extra cost of the very best at all times does pay off in a small increased probability of survival. How much would we pay to have, say, 9 instead of 10 people in 10,000 die from a particular disease? Surely few would want to spend a billion dollars per life saved; we would say that the opportunity cost was too high. Yet doctors in hospitals often make the decision implicitly by ordering the best of everything and then pass the costs on to society as a whole through increased resource allocation to the health sector. The issue is not *whether* to save lives but the *opportunity cost* of doing so. Money spent to save lives here is money not available to save lives (or improve the quality of life) elsewhere.

Controlling the Cost

Neither providers nor patients have sufficient incentive under present schemes to keep down the costs of medical care. The most obvious solution is to place enough of a marginal charge on users so that they will ask themselves whether this doctor's visit, this extra day in the hospital, this use of the most expensive health monitoring system, is worth the cost to them. Another proposed solution is to ask the government to regulate the quantity, quality, and prices of service provided or the rates insurance companies may charge. The last of these gives insurance companies the motivation to exercise cost control. Yet another suggestion is to hold down treatment costs by giving more resources to preventive medicine.

If we reject such solutions, we must live with the costs. The government must either provide the services demanded directly or subsidize others to do so; or it must limit the demand to the quantity available. In countries with national health services, rationing is accomplished in part by long lines at doctors' offices and long waits for hospital admissions and in part by a lower average quality of medical services, which then reduces demand.

In adopting a policy toward health care there are at least three separable decisions: How much care to provide, how to allocate the costs of that care, and how to ration the supply. In the market system, prices do all three. When we elect to have the government intervene—because we do not like the free-market results—someone has to make these decisions.

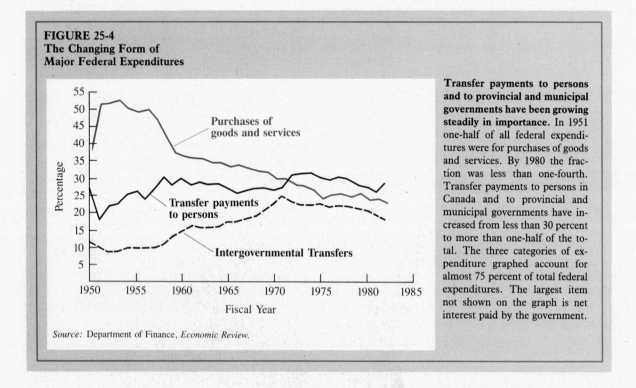

FIGURE 25-4
The Changing Form of
Major Federal Expenditures

Transfer payments to persons and to provincial and municipal governments have been growing steadily in importance. In 1951 one-half of all federal expenditures were for purchases of goods and services. By 1980 the fraction was less than one-fourth. Transfer payments to persons in Canada and to provincial and municipal governments have increased from less than 30 percent to more than one-half of the total. The three categories of expenditure graphed account for almost 75 percent of total federal expenditures. The largest item not shown on the graph is net interest paid by the government.

Source: Department of Finance, *Economic Review.*

and each must get the money in order to spend it. Not all units have equal access to revenue, and this necessitates both the division of responsibility and intergovernmental financial flows.

The transfer of funds from higher to lower levels of government has been an important aspect of the Canadian federal system since confederation. Transfers are also the focus of much of the current controversy over federal-provincial relations.

The scope and nature of intergovermental grants has changed dramatically in the postwar period. Federal transfers to provincial governments expanded from $200 million in 1950 to almost $14 *billion* in 1983, a more than *seventyfold* increase in 30 years. This represented an increase from 6.8 percent to 27.2 percent of federal revenues; for the provincial governments federal transfers as a share of their revenues increased, on average, from 20 percent to 30 percent. For some provinces federal transfers now represent more than half their total

revenues. The transfers occur under four basic programs.

Revenue sharing. Under the terms of the Constitution, the federal government may levy any tax it likes, but the provinces are restricted to *direct* taxes. This has been interpreted by the courts to mean that the provinces may levy personal and corporate income taxes, property taxes, and taxes on retail sales.

Historically, most provinces have made **tax-rental arrangements** whereby the federal government collected income taxes and made a per capita payment to the provinces for that right. Today, with the exception of the Quebec personal income tax and the Ontario and Quebec corporate levies, all income taxes in Canada are collected by the federal government.

Federal income tax rates are set at levels that allow substantial "tax room" to the provinces. Outside Quebec, the provincial income tax is calculated as a percentage of the federal tax payable at rates determined by the individual provinces. A similar arrangement applies to the corporate income tax.

Equalization payments. In order to ensure that citizens in all regions of the country have access to a reasonable level of public services, **equalization payments** are made out of federal government general revenues to provinces with below average tax capacity. It is important to note that this is not a revenue-sharing program (provinces with above-average tax capacity do not pay in), nor is it a conditional grants program like those discussed below. These grants are calculated by a complicated formula that involves 29 revenue sources.

Equalization payments are a relatively new phenomenon in Canada, but they have exhibited rapid growth. From their inception with the 1957 Tax-Sharing Act to the time of the 1977 Fiscal Arrangements Act, they expanded from $130 million to $2.2 billion. Equalization payments for 1983 are shown in Table 25-5.

Conditional grants. Conditional grants are transfers made to the provinces to enable them to provide services in a specified area at some minimum national standard. Historically, these shared-cost programs have been a central part of federal-provincial fiscal arrangements. Their increasing number and extent was a source of considerable friction between the provinces and the federal government during the early 1970s. Participation was optional, but a province that declined to participate in a particular scheme forfeited the revenues that would otherwise have been transferred to it. This led to considerable dispute over constitutional issues and to the development of complicated schemes for compensating provinces that opt out. These programs thus became a focal point in the protracted debate over the present constitutional division of powers in Canada.

A major concern to the federal government was the open-ended nature of its commitments to shared-cost programs that were controlled by the provincial government. The provinces complained that they had initiated projects on the basis of federal sharing of the costs—often referred to disparagingly as "50¢ federal dollars"—and then faced the threat of withdrawal of federal support.

Under the Fiscal Arrangements Act of 1977, the system of relating federal contributions to provincial expenditures was discontinued in favor of a system under which federal contributions rise each year in accordance with the overall growth in the economy. The contributions are administered under a new program discussed below. The major remaining conditional grants relate to regional development programs; the projected breakdown of

TABLE 25–5 ESTIMATED FEDERAL PAYMENTS TO PROVINCES AND MUNICIPALITIES, FISCAL 1982–1983

Category	Millions of dollars
Unconditional payments	
Subsidies under the constitution	$ 36
Revenue equalization	4,740
Public utilities income tax transfers	166
Other	298
Total	$ 5,240
Conditional grants (established programs)	
Hospital insurance	2,578
Medicare	888
Post-secondary education	1,640
Total	$ 5,106
Conditional grants (other)	
Canada Assistance Plan	2,780
Municipal grants in lieu of taxes	201
Other health and welfare	85
Total	$ 3,066
Total payments	$13,412

Source: The National Finances.

Unconditional grants compose the largest and fastest-growing category of federal payments to provinces and municipalities. The table shows the transfers of revenue from the federal government other than those arising from the income tax abatements. Equalization payments make up the bulk of the unconditional grants and are made to the lower-income provinces, that is, provinces other than Ontario, Alberta, and British Columbia.

conditional grants for fiscal year 1982–1983 is given in Table 25-5.

Established programs financing (EPF). The 1977 Fiscal Arrangements Act placed federal financing of three major programs previously treated as conditional grants on a new basis. These are hospital insurance, medicare, and post-secondary education; they are referred to as established programs to indicate that their existence is not conditional on federal involvement. That federal contributions are independent of the costs of the programs reestablishes federal control over its own contribution. The provinces have gained, for they need not now be confined by narrowly defined federal program conditions.

The Overall Redistributive Effects of Government Expenditures

Since tax policy tends to be roughly proportional in its effect, the overall progressivity of government policies depends on the progressivity of government expenditures. Here the large and growing role of transfer payments to the poor and the use of many regional programs probably assured that from the mid 1950s until 1980 there was some net redistribution of income from high-income and middle-income groups to the poor. But such redistribution is not very large.

Changes in the degree of income inequality from decade to decade are extremely small, despite high and growing government expenditures.

The Lorenz curve on page 384 does not look appreciably different than one based on data from 1940.

Why does government expenditure not have a bigger effect on income distribution? One view is that government programs are really less progressive than observers once thought because progressive programs are offset by regressive ones. Another view is that market forces exert steady pressure toward more inequality, which government programs merely offset.

To understand the second view—that one must run hard just to stay even with inequality—imagine that the government today created complete equality in wealth and income. Inevitably market forces would produce inequality by next year, as some people and firms did well because they worked hard and long or were lucky, while others did poorly or failed because they took it easy or were unlucky, as some invested wisely while others squandered their resources on a binge. Most economists agree that there is a limit to how much inequality can be eliminated; there is controversy as to how close we are to that limit. (And beyond that there is controversy as to how close it is desirable to get to "as much equality as possible," both on ethical grounds of justice and economic grounds of incentives.)

Government Expenditure and Resource Allocation

Governments spent nearly $84.1 billion in 1983 to provide goods and services. In these activities governmental units act like firms, using factors of production to produce outputs. They produce outputs rather than leave them to the free market because the people, acting through Parliament, the provincial legislatures, and city councils, have decided that they should. They are responding to the various market failures discussed in Chapter 23.

By and large these outputs are of collective consumption goods, of goods with strong externalities, or of services whose benefits are not marketable. Governments make both current consumption and investment expenditures, and thus they directly influence the economy's accumulation of capital.[6] In so doing governments are plainly changing the allocation of resources.

Under the British North American Act, Canada was established as a federal state with governing powers divided between the central authority and the provinces. Municipalities provide a third level of government whose powers are determined by

_____

[6] Tax expenditures are an important force in this regard. One major tax expenditure is the program of Registered Retirement Savings Plans which allow some personal savings as a tax-deductible expense, thereby encouraging saving in the private sector.

the provincial legislatures. A number of economic considerations bear on the distribution of functions among governments. As we have seen, since revenue sources do not always match revenue needs at each level, a large volume of intergovernmental transfers is required. While the revenue sharing and equalization payments transfers are largely directed at income distribution, the conditional grants and EPF have perhaps their main impact on resource allocation. They allow the various functions to be distributed among governments in a manner not dictated by revenue sources.

Factors Influencing the Intergovernmental Division of Activities

Our discussion in Chapter 24 of reasons for government intervention suggested a number of principles that ideally should determine the distribution of activities among levels of government.

Geographical extent of externalities. Because the government of a province or municipality is unlikely to be responsive to the needs of citizens outside its jurisdiction, public services that involve geographical spillovers may not be provided adequately unless responsibility for them is delegated to a higher level of government. The prime example of the collective consumption good, national defense, is a function normally delegated to the central government for this reason. Control of pollution is another obvious case, since contamination of air and water often quite literally spills over provincial and municipal boundaries. In Canada the third-party effects involved in both examples are not even confined within national boundaries.

Regional differences in preferences. The delegation of some functions to lower levels of government may provide a political process that is more responsive to regional differences in preferences for public versus private goods. Some people may prefer to live in communities with higher quality schools and police protection, and they may be prepared to pay the higher taxes required. Another important issue at the local level is the extent to which industry should be attracted in order to broaden the property tax base. Individual valua-

tions of the social costs in terms of esthetic or environmental effects are bound to differ.

At the provincial level, the distinct aspirations of French Canada are a primary consideration in the distribution of functions between Ottawa and the provinces. Indeed, dissatisfaction with the present arrangements, not only in Quebec but in other provinces, continues to be a major political problem in Canada.

Redistribution of income. An important activity of government is the redistribution of income through taxing the relatively well off and channeling the funds to those in need by means of transfer payments. Clearly this function must be carried out by the central government unless per capita income happens to be the same in all regions. This is of course not the case in Canada; alleviating regional disparities is a major concern of the federal government.

Administrative efficiency. At a minimum, administrative efficiency demands that there be no duplication of the services provided at different levels of government and that related programs be coordinated. On the revenue side, it is desirable that a particular tax be collected by only one level of government. This consideration has led to the negotiation of federal-provincial tax agreements that provide for efficient collection and revenue sharing.

Changes in the Relative Shares of Government Expenditure

Total government expenditures increased twenty-fivefold over the period 1950–1980, indicating an increase in the ratio of government expenditure to total goods and services produced in the economy from 22 to about 40 percent. In the period since 1960, increases in expenditure have been largest in such areas of provincial and municipal responsibility as health and education. As a result, the federal share of total government expenditures has been falling while that of provincial and municipal governments has been rising.

These developments are documented in Table 25-6. Since personal and corporate income tax

TABLE 25–6 EXPENDITURES BY LEVEL OF GOVERNMENT, SELECTED YEARS, 1950–1983

| Year | Total expenditure, all levels of government | | Expenditure of government level (as a percentage of total government expenditures)[a] | | |
	Percentage of GNP	Millions of dollars	Federal	Provincial	Municipal
1950	22.1	$ 4,080	51.9	26.0	22.1
1960	29.7	11,380	50.5	24.8	24.7
1970	36.4	31,148	38.3	35.6	26.0
1980	39.0	116,084	42.4	39.4	18.2
1983	45.1	176,118	44.9	38.0	17.1

[a] Excluding transfers to other levels of government.
Source: Department of Finance, *Economic Review,* and Statistics Canada, 13-001.

yields tend to rise more rapidly than income, while property and sales taxes respond less rapidly, these developments made necessary a reduction in the federal share of income tax revenues—from 70 percent in 1950 to 62 percent in 1983—that resulted in the increase in intergovernmental transfers discussed above. Several reasons for the changing distribution of government size can be mentioned.

The rising demand for government services. One of the reasons provincial and municipal government expenditures have been rising more rapidly than their residents' incomes is the high income elasticity of demand for city services. As societies become wealthier, their residents want more parks, more police protection, more and better schools and universities, and more generous treatment of their less fortunate neighbors. This alone, combined with the limited tax sources available, would create budgetary problems for provincial and municipal governments in a period of rising incomes and rising expectations. Taxpayers increasingly want the social services governments provide, but they do not always want to pay the taxes required to meet their cost. Elected officials arouse the people's wrath when they fail to provide wanted programs, but they sometimes do the same when they provide the services and then raise taxes.

The rising relative cost of municipal government services. Government services tend to use much labor of a kind whose productivity (output per hour of work) has increased much less rapidly than its cost. Thus cost per unit of output has risen. While the national average output per hour of work in manufacturing has risen about 50 percent in the last decade, the size of the beat covered by a police officer, the number of students taught by each schoolteacher, the number of families that can be effectively handled by a social worker, or the number of temperatures than can be taken by one hospital nurse have not risen in proportion. Because wage levels tend to rise with national average productivity, the costs of services in the low-productivity sectors have soared. Although a rise in relative prices tends to lead to a decline in the quantity demanded in the market sector of the economy, the increased demand for government services has been so strong that government employees are not being phased out despite the rising cost of labor. (As discussed in Box 25-3, similar forces have driven up the costs of health care, which falls under provincial jurisdiction.)

EVALUATING THE ROLE OF GOVERNMENT

Almost everyone would agree that the government has some role to play in the economy because of the myriad sources of possible market failure. Yet there is no consensus that the present level and role of government intervention is about right.

One aspect of the contemporary debate—the efficient level of government intervention—was discussed at the end of Chapter 24. There we asked when and to what degree government ought to attempt to modify private market behavior—say, by affecting the way a paper mill discharges its wastes. Other issues arise when government provides goods and services the private sector does not and will not provide.

Do Benefits of Government Programs Exceed Costs?

The federal government has developed techniques of evaluation designed to provide estimates of benefits and costs in order to determine whether the former exceed the latter. If they do, the program is said to be *cost effective,* and thus to be justified. For some government programs, such as flood control, there are well-defined benefits and costs. It is thus relatively easy to decide whether the project is justified. But consider the evaluation of a program such as the great American space adventure of the 1960s—placing a man on the moon before the end of the decade.

The budgetary costs were easily defined. At its peak in 1966, the program absorbed (in 1982 dollars) about $19 billion per year. Unmistakably, the project succeeded; it met its stated objective. But was the "giant step for mankind" worth the billions it cost? The benefits certainly included the psychological lift the moon walks may have given the American people and the substantial advances in technology and knowledge the space program is known to have spawned. The real costs are those things that the expenditure would have replaced.

But what was the alternative? More arms to Vietnam? Massive urban redevelopment? A return of funds to private spenders to use as they saw fit? Most of us will evaluate the worth of the space program very differently, depending on what we see as the alternative uses of the resources involved.

Such questions can never be answered unambiguously. As a result, the evaluation of government programs is inherently political and controversial. Economic analysis of benefits and costs is involved, but it does not play the sole or even the dominant role in answering some big questions.

The Balance Between Private and Public Sectors

When the government raises money by taxation and spends it on an activity, it increases the spending of the public sector and decreases that of the private sector. Since the public sector and the private sector spend on different things, the government is changing the allocation of resources. Is that good or bad? How do we know if the country has the right balance between the public and private sectors? Should there be more schools and fewer houses, or more houses and fewer schools?

Because automobiles and houses are sold on the market, consumer demand has a significant influence on the relative prices of these commodities, and (through prices) on the quantities produced and, thence, on the allocation of the nation's resources. This is true for all goods produced and sold on the market. But there is no market that provides relative prices for apartments versus public schools; thus the choice between allowing money to be spent in the private sector and spending it for public goods is a matter to be decided by Parliament and other legislative bodies.

John Kenneth Galbraith in a 1958 best-seller, *The Affluent Society,* proclaimed the "liberal" message that a correct assignment of marginal utilities would show them to be higher for an extra dollar's worth of expenditure on parks, clean water, and education than for an extra dollar's worth of expenditure on television sets and deodorants. In this view, the political process often fails to translate preferences for public goods into effective action; more resources are devoted to the private sector and fewer to the public sector than would be the case if the political mechanism were as effective as the market.

The "conservative" view has a growing number of supporters who agree with Professor James

Buchanan that society has already gone beyond the point where the value of the marginal dollar spent by the government is greater than the value of that dollar left in the hands of households or firms that would have spent it had it not been taxed away. Because bureaucrats, the conservatives argue, are spending other people's money, they regard a few million (or billion) dollars here or there as a mere nothing. They have lost all sense of the opportunity cost of public expenditure; thus they tend to spend far beyond the point where marginal benefits equal marginal costs.

What Is the
Role of Government Today?

We have been looking at the role of the government in the market economy throughout the microeconomic part of this book. Now let us pause for perspective. One of the most difficult problems for the student of the Canadian economic system is to maintain perspective about the scope of government activity in the market economy. There are literally tens of thousands of laws, regulations, and policies that affect firms and households. Many believe that significant additional deregulation would be possible and beneficial.

But private decision makers still have an enormous amount of discretion about what they do and how they do it. One pitfall is to become so impressed (or obsessed) with the many ways in which government activity impinges on the individual that one fails to see that these only make changes— sometimes large but often small—in market signals in a system that basically leaves individuals free to make their own decisions. In the private sector most individuals choose their occupations, earn their livings, spend their incomes, and live their lives. In this sector too, firms are formed, choose products, live, grow, and sometimes die.

A different pitfall is to fail to see that some, and perhaps most, of the highly significant amounts paid by the private sector to the government as taxes also buy goods and services that add to the welfare of individuals. By and large the public sector complements the private sector, doing things the private sector would leave undone or do very differently. To recognize this is not to deny that there is often waste, and sometimes worse, in public expenditure policy. Nor does it imply that whatever is, is just what people want. Social policies and social judgments evolve and change.

Yet another pitfall is failing to recognize that the public and private sectors compete in the sense that both make claims on the resources of the economy. Government activities are not without opportunity costs, except in those rare circumstances in which they use resources that have no alternative use.

Public policies in operation at any time are not the result of a single master plan that specifies precisely where and how the public sector shall seek to complement, help along, or interfere with the workings of the market mechanism. Rather, as individual problems arise, governments attempt to meet them by passing ameliorative legislation. These laws stay on the books, and some become obsolete and unenforceable. This is true of systems of law in general.

Many anomalies exist in our economic policies; for example, laws designed to support the incomes of small farmers have created some agricultural millionaires, and commissions created to assure competition often end up creating and protecting monopolies. Neither individual policies nor whole programs are above criticism.

In a society that elects its policymakers at regular intervals, however, the majority view on the amount and type of government interference that is desirable will have some considerable influence on the interference that actually occurs. This now seems sure to be one of the major political issues of the 1980s. Fundamentally, a free-market system is retained because it is valued for its lack of coercion and its ability to do much of the allocating of society's resources. But we are not mesmerized by it; we feel free to intervene in pursuit of a better world in which to live. We also recognize, however, that some intervention has proven excessive and/or ineffective.

SUMMARY

1. Two of the most powerful tools of microeconomic policy are taxation and public expenditure.

2. While their main purpose is to raise revenue, taxes represent a means of redistributing income. Tax policy is potentially a powerful device for income redistribution because the progressivity or regressivity of different kinds of taxes varies greatly. Personal income tax rates are highly progressive, but their effect is modified by favorable treatment of capital gains and by other provisions of the tax law. Sales and excise taxes are likely to be regressive.

3. The total Canadian tax structure is roughly proportional except for very low-income and very high-income groups, for whom it is mildly regressive. Either a negative income tax or a move in the direction of comprehensive income taxation would increase progressivity. Whether this is feasible politically, or desirable, is a subject of sharp current debate.

4. Evaluating the effects of taxes on resource allocation requires first determining tax incidence—that is, determining who really pays the taxes. For most taxes, the incidence is shared. Excise taxes, for example, affect prices and are thus partially passed on, but part is absorbed by producers. The actual incidence depends on such economic considerations as demand and supply elasticities.

5. A large part of public expenditure is for the provision of goods and services that private markets fail to provide. Direct and indirect subsidies, transfer payments to individuals, and intergovernmental transfers are all rising sharply.

6. The four major types of federal-provincial transfers are revenue sharing, equalization payments, conditional grants, and established programs financing.

7. The major redistributive activities of the federal government take the form of direct transfer payments to individuals and to provincial and municipal governments for economic welfare payments and regional adjustments. While the public sector has a tendency to redistribute some income from high-income and middle-income groups to the poor, the change in income inequality from decade to decade has been relatively small.

8. Government expenditure of all kinds has a major effect on the allocation of resources. The government determines how much of our total output is devoted to national defense, education, and highways. It is also influential in areas where private provision of goods and services is common; health care is a notable example. Government subsidization of health care has led such expenditures to more than double as a fraction of total expenditure in 30 years.

9. Intergovernmental transfers are a key form of public expenditure policy; they lead to a different allocation of resources than would occur without them. The need for such transfers is dramatically revealed by regional imbalances in Canada.

10. Evaluating public expenditures involves reaching decisions about absolute merit (do benefits exceed costs?), about the relative merit of public and private expenditures, and about the desirable size of government.

11. The Canadian economy is a mixed economy and a changing one. Each generation faces anew the choice of which activities to leave to the unfettered market and which to encourage or repress through public policy.

TOPICS FOR REVIEW

Tax expenditures
Progressivity and regressivity of taxes
Tax incidence
Transfer payments to individuals
Intergovernmental transfers
Choosing between private and public expenditures

DISCUSSION QUESTIONS

1. The Canadian taxpayer is assaulted by dozens of different taxes with different incidence, different progressivity, and different methods of collection. Discuss the case for and against using at most two different kinds of taxes. Discuss the case for and against a single taxing authority that would share the revenue with all levels of government.

2. "Taxes on tobacco and alcohol are nearly perfect taxes. They raise lots of revenue and discourage smoking and drinking." In this statement, to what extent are the two effects inconsistent? How is the incidence of an excise tax related to the extent to which it discourages use of the product?

3. How might each of the following affect the incidence of a real estate property tax imposed on city rental property?
   a. The residents of the community are largely minority ethnic groups who face racial discrimination in neighboring areas.
   b. The city installs a good, cheap rapid-transit system that makes commuting to the suburbs less expensive and more comfortable.
   c. Rent control is imposed; no existing building may raise the rents presently being charged.

4. The benefit principle is often used to justify excise taxes on particular commodities when their use depends on the availability of government-provided services or facilities. In such cases the tax provides a means of placing the burden of financing expenditures on those who benefit from them. Can you think of any examples where this principle applies? Can it be used to justify the use of property taxes as a major source of revenue by municipal governments?

5. Under the Canadian income tax law, capital gains are taxed at one-half the rates applicable to other income. Who benefits from this provision? What are its effects on the distribution of income and the allocation of resources?

6. Classify each of the following programs as "transfer payment to an individual," "intergovernmental transfer," "purchase of goods and services," or "none of the above." Which ones clearly tend to decrease the inequality of income distribution?
   a. Payments of wages and family living allowances to soldiers serving overseas
   b. Unemployment insurance payments to unemployed workers
   c. Payments to provinces for support of universities
   d. A negative income tax
   e. Pensions of retired Supreme Court justices
   f. An excess profits tax on oil companies

7. If governments tend to step in when markets fail, why are not similar functions performed similarly in different countries? Medical care, sport fishing rights, steel production, broadcasting, telephone service, and garbage collection are provided publicly in some Western countries and privately in others. What accounts for the diversity?

8. a. Suppose it is agreed to spend $1 billion in programs to provide the poor with housing, better clothing, more food, and better health services. Argue the case for and against assistance of this kind rather than giving the money to the poor to spend as they think best.
   b. Should federal transfers to the provinces be conditional grants or grants with no strings attached? Is this the same issue raised in the previous question, or a different one?

PART EIGHT
NATIONAL INCOME
AND FISCAL POLICY

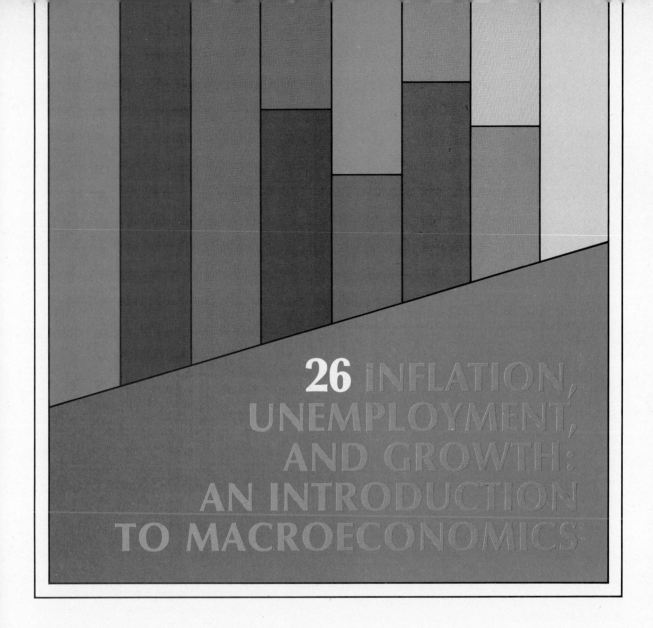

26 INFLATION, UNEMPLOYMENT, AND GROWTH: AN INTRODUCTION TO MACROECONOMICS

Inflation, unemployment, recession, and economic growth are now everyday words. Governments worry about how to reduce inflation and unemployment, how to prevent or cure recessions, and how to increase growth. Firms are concerned about how inflation affects their earnings and how to improve productivity; many businesses have good reason to fear recessions. Households are anxious to avoid the unemployment that comes in the wake of recessions and to protect themselves against the hazards of inflation.

WHAT IS MACROECONOMICS?

As we saw in Chapter 3, economics is customarily divided into two main branches, microeconomics and macroeconomics.[1] Each of the concerns mentioned above plays a major role in macroeconomics. But what exactly is macroeconomics?

Macroeconomics studies in broad outline the flow of income in the economy, illustrated in Figure 3-1, while avoiding much of its interesting but confusing detail. As a result macroeconomics deals with **aggregate data** that express broad totals and averages derived from the whole economy. In contrast microeconomics deals with **disaggregate data** that describe the behavior of individual markets, such as those for wheat, coal, or strawberries.

The following examples illustrate the difference between the two branches of economics. Explaining the behavior of automobile prices is a typical microeconomic problem. For decades car prices fell in relation to the prices of most other commodities. Why has the trend reversed over the last decade, with automobiles becoming increasingly expensive relative to other commodities?

In microeconomics, we seek to understand the causes and the effects of such changes in relative prices. On the other hand, accounting for the average behavior of all prices is a typical macroeconomic problem. This average is called the *price level*. Why does the price level rise slowly in some decades and very rapidly in others? In macroeconomics we are trying to understand the causes and effects of such changes in the price level.

Major Macroeconomic Issues

The economy proceeds in fits and starts rather than in a smooth upward trend. Why did the 1930s see the greatest economic depression in recorded history, with up to a fifth of the labor force in Canada unemployed and massive unemployment in all other major industrial countries? Why were the 25 years following World War II a period of sustained boom with only minor interruptions from modest recessions? Why did the early 1980s see the onset of the worst worldwide recession and slowest recovery since the 1930s?

[1] The prefixes *macro* and *micro* derive from the Greek words *makros*, for large, and *mikros*, for small.

We live in an inflationary world. Why did the pace of inflation during the 1970s and early 1980s reach levels never before seen in peacetime in most advanced Western nations? If Americans and Canadians thought that inflation rates in the range of 10 to 12 percent were serious, what was it like to live in Israel, Italy, or Great Britain, where rates were much higher?

Alternating bouts of inflationary boom and deflationary slump have caused many policy headaches in the past. Why were the recessions of the last decade accompanied not only by their familiar companion, high unemployment, but also by an unexpected fellow traveler, rapid inflation? Is the new disease of stagflation—simultaneous high unemployment and rapid inflation—here to stay?

Total and per capita output have risen for several decades in advanced (and in many less advanced) countries. These long-term trends have meant rising living standards for the average person. Does the recent slowdown in worldwide growth rates represent a basic change in underlying trends, or is it just a reflection of the prolonged downturn of the last decade? Can governments do anything to affect growth rates?

KEY MACRO VARIABLES

Employment, total output, and the price level are key variables in macroeconomics. We hear about them on television; politicians give campaign speeches about them; economists theorize about them. To discuss them in a reasoned fashion we must first understand them. How are they defined, why are we concerned about them, and how have they behaved over the past half century? Many key macro variables are defined as index numbers, so our first task is to look briefly at the general concept of an index number.

Index numbers. Macroeconomists frequently seek simple answers to questions such as "How much have prices risen this year?" or "Has the nation's total output increased this year, and, if so, by how much?" There is no perfectly satisfactory answer to the first question because all prices do not move together, nor to the second because one cannot simply add up tons of steel, pieces of furniture, and gallons of gasoline to get a meaningful total. Yet these are not foolish questions. There *are* trends in prices and production, and thus there are real phenomena to describe. It is of no help to someone who asks about price changes over some period to be given a list of 4,682 individual prices and told, "See for yourself, they varied."

Index numbers are statistical measures that are used to give a concise summary answer to the inherently complex questions of the kind just suggested. An **index number** measures the percentage change in some broad average since some base period. As such it points to overall tendencies or general drifts, not to detailed facts.

Index numbers are useful, then, as general indicators. Yet people often become mesmerized by them and treat them as though they had an accuracy that their compilers do not claim for them. Being aware of their limitations should not lead one to neglect numbers for the useful information they do show: average changes over time.

The Price Level

The **price level** refers to an average of some broad group of prices ruling in the economy. It is measured by an index number of these prices, called a price index and usually denoted by the symbol P.

A **price index** shows the average percentage change that has occurred in some group of prices over some period of time. The point in time from which the change is measured is called the **base year** (or **base period**), while the point in time to which the change is measured is called the **given year** (or **given period**). Several issues are involved in the construction of price indexes.

First, what group of prices should be used? This depends on the index. The **Consumer Price Index**, known affectionately as the **CPI**, covers prices of commodities commonly bought by households. Changes in the CPI are meant to measure changes in the typical household's "cost of living." Other price indexes, some of which we shall encounter later in this chapter, incorporate prices of different groups of commodities.

Second, what kind of average should be used? If all prices were to change in the same proportion, this would not be an important question. A 10 percent rise in each and every price covered means an average rise of 10 percent no matter how much importance we give to each price change when calculating the average. But what if—as is almost always the case—different prices change differently? Now it does matter how much importance we give to each price change.

A rise of 50 percent in the price of caviar is surely much less important to the average consumer than a rise of 40 percent in the price of bread. And this in turn is surely less important than a rise of 30 percent in the cost of housing. Why? The reason is that the typical household spends less on caviar than on bread and less on bread than on housing.

In calculating any price index, statisticians seek to *weight* each price according to its importance. Let us see how this is done for the CPI. Government statisticians survey periodically a group of households to discover how they spend their incomes. The average bundle of goods bought is calculated, and the quantities in this bundle become the weights attached to the prices. In this way the average price change heavily weights commodities on which consumers spend a lot and lightly weights commodities on which consumers spend only a little. The procedure is illustrated in Table 26-1.

The statisticians then calculate the average change. This is done by comparing the cost of purchasing the typical bundle of commodities in the base year with that of purchasing it in the given year. The given year cost is expressed as a percentage of the base year cost, and this figure is the index number of the new period. Thus, a CPI of 110 means that the cost of purchasing the "representative" bundle of goods is 110 percent of what it was in the base year.

A price index number for a given year tells the ratio of the cost of purchasing a bundle of commodities in that

TABLE 26–1 THE CALCULATION OF A PRICE INDEX COVERING THREE COMMODITIES

Commodity	Quantity in fixed bundle	Base year 1980		Given year 1984	
		Price in 1980	Value in 1980	Price in 1984	Value in 1984
A	500 units	$1.00	$ 500	$2.00	$1,000
B	200 units	5.00	1,000	7.00	1,400
C	50 units	2.00	100	9.60	480
			1,600		2,880

$$\text{Index value 1980} = \frac{1,600}{1,600} \times 100 = 100$$

$$\text{Index value 1984} = \frac{2,880}{1,600} \times 100 = 180$$

A price index shows the ratio of the costs of purchasing a fixed bundle of goods between two years (multiplied by 100). The cost of purchasing the fixed bundle is calculated at the prices ruling in each year. The index for year 1984 is the cost of purchasing that bundle in 1984 expressed as a percentage of the cost of purchasing the *same* bundle in the base year (which is 1980 in this example). The price index is thus always 100 in the base year. The index of 180 means that prices have risen on average by 80 percent between the base year and the year in question. This average weights price changes by their *importance* in the average household's budget in the base year.

year to the cost of purchasing the *same* bundle in the base year multiplied by 100 [33].

The percentage *change* in the cost of purchasing the bundle is thus the index number minus 100. An index number of 110 indicates a percentage increase in prices of 10 percent over those ruling in the base year.

A price index is meant to reflect the broad trend in prices rather than the details. This means that although the information it gives may be extremely valuable, it must be interpreted with care. Some of the potential difficulties are discussed in Box 26-1.

Why the Price Level Is Not a Matter of Concern

By and large, governments do not have policies about the price level per se. No one feels that the price level ruling in Canada in 1867 was intrinsically better or worse than the one ruling in 1984. The level of prices of commodities and factors of production at which the economy's transactions occur is irrelevant to living standards. Our well-being is affected by the adjustments that occur while the price level is changing. Inflation and de-

flation affect us even if the price level does not matter. What does matter is the *process of inflation or deflation;* that is, what happens while the price level is changing. Whatever the present level of prices, there will be many economic consequences if it rises or falls sharply over the next few years.

Price Levels: The Historical Experience

Figure 26-1(i) shows the behavior of the Canadian price level for the period 1930–1983. Two facts stand out. The price level changes constantly, although by amounts that vary considerably in different years. Second, and more important, the price level has displayed a distinct upward trend over the period; in only 2 out of the over 50 observations did the price level fall. In 1983 prices were on average 590 percent higher than in 1930. This, of course, has greatly reduced the value of the currency. At the beginning of 1984 it took $690 to buy what could be bought for $100 in 1930.

Inflation

The rate of inflation is the percentage increase in some price index from one period to another. In

BOX 26-1 THREE PROBLEMS IN INTERPRETING PRICE INDEXES

First, the weights in the index refer to an average bundle of goods. This average, although "typical" of what is consumed in the nation, will not be typical of what each household consumes. The rich, the poor, the young, the old, the single, the married, the urban, and the rural household will typically consume different bundles. An increase in air fares, for example, will raise the cost of living of a middle income traveler while leaving that of a poor stay-at-home unaffected. In the example shown in Table 26-1, the cost of living would have risen by 100 percent, 40 percent, and 380 percent respectively for three different families, one of whom consumed only commodity A, one only commodity B, and one only commodity C. The index in the table shows, however, that the cost of living went up by 80 percent for a family that consumed all three goods in the relative quantities indicated.

The more an individual household's consumption pattern diverges from that of the typical pattern used to weight prices in the price index, the less well the price index will reflect the average change in prices relevant to that household.

To assess the importance of this problem, separate indexes are calculated for different subgroups. For example, in Canada different indexes are calculated for a number of major cities.

Second, households usually alter their consumption patterns in response to price changes. A price index that shows changes in the cost of purchasing a fixed bundle of goods does not allow for this. For example, a typical cost of living index for middle income families at the turn of the century would have given heavy weight to the cost of maids and laundresses. A doubling of servants' wages in 1900 would have greatly increased the middle-class cost of living. Today it would have little effect, for the rising cost of labor has long since caused middle in-

come families to cease to employ full-time servants. A household that has dispensed altogether with a commodity whose price is rising rapidly does not have its cost of living rise as fast as a household that continues to consume that commodity in an undiminished quantity.

A fixed-weight price index tends to overstate cost of living changes because it does not allow for changes in consumption patterns that shift expenditure away from commodities whose prices rise most and toward those whose prices rise least.

Third, as time goes by, new commodities enter the typical consumption bundle and old ones leave. A cost of living index in 1890 would have had a large item for horse-drawn carriages but no allowance at all for automobiles and gasoline.

A fixed-weight index makes no allowance for the rise of new products nor for the declining importance of old in the typical household's consumption bundle.

The longer the period of time that passes, the less some fixed consumption bundle will be typical of current consumption patterns. For this reason Statistics Canada, the government body responsible for the CPI, makes a new survey of household expenditure patterns about once every 10 years and revises the weights. The base period is then usually changed to be near the year in which the new set of commodity weights was calculated. At the end of 1983 using 1971 weights the CPI stood at 283.4 (1971 = 100). This meant that the cost of purchasing the bundle of goods bought by a typical household in 1971 had risen 183 percent in the intervening 13 years. Thirteen years is a long time for fixed-weights to be used, and during the past year Statistics Canada has been busy estimating a new set of weights preparatory to shifting the weighting year of the CPI to 1981.

FIGURE 26-1
The Canadian Price Level and Inflation Rate, 1930–1983

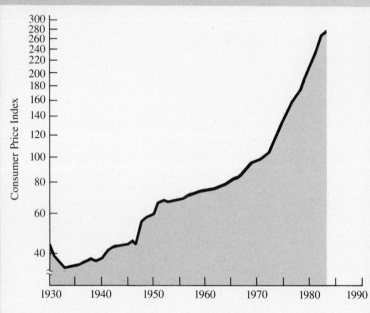

(i) Price level

(i) **The overwhelming trend movement in the price level has been upward over the past 50 years.** The data are for the consumer's price index from 1930 to 1983 with 1971 equal to 100. They are plotted on a semi-log scale where equal vertical distances represent equal percentage changes. The tendency for an accelerating rate of increase in the price level is evident from the increasing steepness of the graph.

(ii) **The rate of inflation has varied from −10 percent to +14 percent over the period since 1930.** Prices fell dramatically during the onset of the Great Depression. They rose sharply during and after World War II and during the Korean War. Although variable, there was no discernible trend in the inflation rate from the end of the Korean War to the mid 1960s. The period starting in the mid 1960s, however, experienced a strong upward trend in the inflation rate, interrupted by short-term fluctuations. In 1983, however, the inflation rate fell to the lowest figure since the early 1970s.

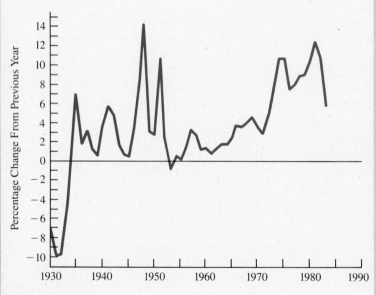

(ii) Inflation rate

Source: M.C.Urquhart (ed.), *Historical Statistics of Canada;* Department of Finance, *Economic Review.*

the rare event of a drop in the price level, we speak of a deflation.

The formula for measuring the inflation rate is

$$\frac{\text{this period's } P - \text{last period's } P}{\text{last period's } P} \times 100\%$$

If the periods are not a year apart it is common to convert the result to an annual rate. Assume for example that the CPI was 150 last month and 151.5 this month. This yields an inflation rate of 1 percent *per month*. Prices rose by 1 percent during the month. Compounding yields a rate of inflation of just over 12 percent per year. When we say that over the last month prices rose at an annual rate of 12 percent, this tells us that *if* the rate of increase that actually occurred over the last month persisted for a year, prices would rise by 12 percent over the year. If the figures were as illustrated above, you would read something like "Prices rose 1 percent last month, making the current annual inflation rate 12 percent."

Another common method is to use the latest monthly CPI figure and the CPI for the same month last year. This is the inflation rate that is most commonly quoted in the press when the monthly CPI figures are released. The resulting figure is at an annual rate since the increase in the CPI is being measured over a 12-month period. (Box 26-2 explores the advantages and disadvantages of these and other similar measures.)

Why Inflation Is a Matter of Concern

Whatever the present price level, there will be many economic consequences if it rises (or falls) sharply over the course of the next few years. Most of the consequences are associated with changes in what is called the **purchasing power of money.** This term refers to the amount of goods and services that can be purchased with a given amount of money. Inflation, which is a rise in prices, reduces the purchasing power of money.

Some of the effects of inflation can be avoided by adding "escalator" or "indexing" clauses to such things as social security benefits and specific wage and price contracts. Such clauses link the payments made under the terms of the contract to changes in the price level. Escalator clauses are common in labor agreements, in long-term raw material contracts, and in many government procurement agreements.

Even without a formal contract expressed in real terms, it is possible to allow for the effects of an *expected* inflation. Wage and price contracts are major examples. If, say, a 10 percent inflation is expected over the next year, a money wage that rises by 10 percent over that period will preserve the expected purchasing power of wages. Similarly, lending contracts can allow for the loss of purchasing power of money due to an expected inflation. If a 10 percent increase in inflation is expected, a 10 percent increase in the interest rate on any loan will compensate the lender for the loss of purchasing power of the money lent.

Unanticipated inflations are more harmful than are anticipated inflations. Contracts freely entered into when the price level was expected to rise at 10 percent a year will mean hardships for some and unexpected gains for others if the inflation rate accelerates unexpectedly to 15 percent.

If a wage contract specifies wage increases of 10 percent in expectation of a 10 percent inflation, workers lose unexpectedly if inflation turns out to be 15 percent (since the purchasing power of their wage is less than they anticipated when they agreed to the contract). Employers lose if the inflation turns out to be only 5 percent (since the price of what they sell has risen by less than they expected when they agreed to the wage increase). Similarly, if a loan contract specifies a 13 percent interest rate in expectation of a 10 percent inflation, lenders lose unexpectedly if inflation turns out to 15 percent (since the purchasing power of the repayment is less than they expected when they agreed to lend the money at only 13 percent). Borrowers lose if inflation is only 5 percent (since the purchasing power of the repayment is greater than they expected when they agreed to pay 13 percent on the loan).

Inflation: The Historical Experience

Figure 26-1(ii) shows the course of Canadian inflation from 1930 to 1983. Considerable year-to-

BOX 26–2 HOW THE INFLATION RATE IS MEASURED

Statistics Canada calculates the Consumer Price Index every month. When it is announced, the monthly inflation rate makes big news in the press. But just what does it mean when we hear that the inflation rate has soared, or moderated slightly, or even been zero this month?

Such figures almost always refer to the CPI. But because changes in the CPI can be calculated in different ways, we must beware of accepting the figures too uncritically. "The" inflation rate is commonly measured in three different ways, each with its own advantages and shortcomings.

The CPI for This Month over the CPI for the Same Month Last Year

This measure uses the newly announced CPI for this month and the CPI for the same month last year in the equation given in the text. For example, the CPI in July 1983 was 278.2, while it was 264.9 in July 1982. On this measure the July 1983 inflation rate was 5.0 percent. This measure tells us that the CPI actually did rise 5.0 percent over these 12 months.

The disadvantage of this measure is that it is not sensitive to sudden changes in inflation. Say, for example, that the CPI rose by 2 percent every month of one year and then remained constant for every month of the second year. This measure will give an inflation rate of 12 percent in January of the second year, 11 percent in February, and so on. It will not fall to zero until the *end* of the second year, although for 12 successive months the price level will have been unchanged.

This Month's CPI over Last Month's CPI

As discussed in the text, this method uses this month's CPI and last month's CPI to calculate a monthly inflation rate, and then compounds the result to give an annual rate. What this figure tells us is the percentage change in the CPI that would occur *if* prices rose over the coming year at the rate they have risen over the last month. It has the advantage of immediately reflecting changes in the inflation rate. In the previous example, where the CPI rose in each month of the first year, but remained stable in the second year, the measured rate of inflation would be zero from February of the second year onward. The problem with this measure is that it can be very erratic since the timing of price changes before or after the end of the month will have a big accidental effect on it.

This Year's Average CPI over Last Year's Average CPI

This method adds up monthly CPIs from each year and divides by 12 to get an average CPI for each year. Then the formula in the text is used by dividing the difference between the two figures by last year's figure and then multiplying by 100. This is the least erratic of the three figures. Its disadvantage is that variations in the monthly inflation rate within the year are completely suppressed.

There are many different ways of computing "the" inflation rate. Properly understood they all give useful and complementary information. It is often said that you can prove anything you want with figures. Certainly by carefully selecting your figures you can get quite different inflation rates for any one year. But people who understand what each inflation measure does and does not reveal need not be fooled by such selective presentation of data. Figures only lie to those uninformed enough to be unaware of what they do and do not actually say!

year fluctuations are apparent. The general acceleration of the inflation rate from the mid 1960s until the mid 1970s is dramatic. The falloff of the inflation rate in the mid 1970s and again in the mid 1980s was a delayed response to the two major recessions.

Labor Force Variables

Employment denotes the number of adult workers (defined in Canada as workers 15 years old and over) who hold full-time jobs. **Unemployment** denotes the number of adult workers who are not employed and are actively searching for a job. The **labor force** is the total of the employed and the unemployed. The **unemployment rate,** usually represented by the symbol U, is unemployment expressed as a percentage of the labor force:

$$U = \frac{\text{unemployed}}{\text{labor force}} \times 100\%$$

Why Unemployment Is a Matter of Concern

The social and political significance of the unemployment rate is enormous. The federal government is blamed when it is high and takes credit when it is low. Few macroeconomic policies are planned without some consideration of how they affect the unemployment rate. No other summary statistic, with the possible exception of the inflation rate, carries such weight as both a formal and an informal concern of policy as does the percentage of the labor force unemployed.

There are two main reasons for worrying about unemployment: It produces economic waste and it causes human suffering. The economic waste is obvious. Human effort is the least durable of economic commodities. If a fully employed economy with a constant labor force has 20 million people willing to work in 1985, their services must either be used in 1985 or wasted. When the services of only 18 million are used because 10 percent of the labor force is unemployed, the potential output of 2 million workers is lost forever. In an economy where there is not enough output to meet everyone's needs, any waste of potential output seems undesirable and large wastes seem tragic.

The human cost of unemployment is also obvious. Severe hardship and misery can be caused by prolonged periods of unemployment. A person's spirit can be broken by a long period of wanting work but being unable to find it. Crime, divorce, and general social unrest usually rise with unemployment. In the not so distant past, only private charity or help from friends and relatives stood between the unemployed and starvation. Today welfare and unemployment insurance have softened those effects.

When an economic slump is deep and prolonged, however, as in the mid 1970s and again in the early 1980s, people begin to exhaust their unemployment insurance and must fall back on savings, welfare, or charity. In 1981–1982, many people sank below the poverty level for the first time in their lives. They did so because they had exhausted their claims on unemployment insurance (and so became "exhaustees"), but were unable to find jobs because of a persistently high unemployment level.

Unemployment: The Historical Experience

Figure 26-2(i) shows the trends in the civilian labor force, employment, and unemployment since 1930. Despite business booms and slumps, and inflations and deflations, the main trend has clearly been a growth in employment that roughly matches the growth in the labor force. This growth is part of the total economic growth of the economy. Although a long-term growth trend dominates the employment figures, some unemployment is always present. It fluctuates with the ebb and flow of business activity that is often referred to as the **business cycle.** The unemployment *rate* graphed in Figure 26-2(ii) clearly shows the short-term cyclical behavior of unemployment.

Consideration of employment and unemployment suggests another concept, that of *full employment*. Contrary to what you might think, full employment does not mean zero unemployment. There is a constant turnover of individuals in given jobs and a constant change in job opportunities. Older workers retire or die; new members enter

FIGURE 26-2
Canadian Labor Force, Employment and Unemployment, 1930–1983

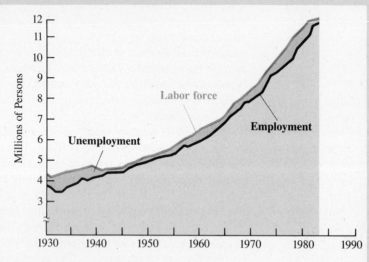

(i) Labor force, employment, and unemployment

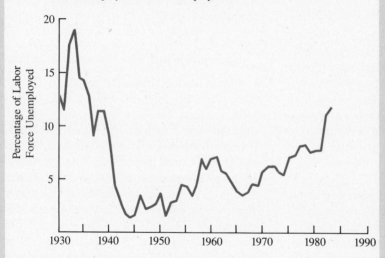

(ii) Unemployment rate

Source: M.C. Urquhart (ed.), *Historical Statistics of Canada*; Department of Finance, *Economic Review*.

(i) The labor force and employment have grown since the 1930s with only a few interruptions. The size of the Canadian labor force has more than doubled since 1930, and so has the number of the employed. The fall in the labor force in the early 1940s was in the civilian labor force. The missing workers were in the military. Unemployment, the gap between the labor force and employment, has fluctuated. It reached a peak of 800,000 in 1933 and did not reach that level again until 1977. In 1983 it reached 1 1/2 million, although as we see in (ii), as a fraction of the labor force this is smaller than the 1933 figure.

(ii) The unemployment rate responds to the cyclical behavior of the economy. Booms are associated with low unemployment, slumps with high unemployment. The Great Depression of the 1930s produced record unemployment rates for an entire decade. During World War II unemployment rates fell to very low levels. Since 1945, however, the unemployment rate has demonstrated a slight upward trend. The recession of the early 1980s produced unemployment rates second only to those of the 1930s; these rates were extremely high by the standards of the post-World War II behavior of the Canadian economy.

the work force and take time to find employment. Some people quit their jobs, while others are fired. These people usually find new jobs, but only after some delay. So at any one time, there will be unemployment due to the normal turnover of labor that exists in any healthy economy. Such unemployment is called **frictional unemployment.**[2]

When we say full employment we mean that the only existing unemployment is frictional. The measured unemployment rate that occurs at full employment is often called the **natural rate of unemployment.** Estimates of the natural rate indicate that it rose substantially throughout the 1970s and has now stabilized or may even be declining. (We shall discuss the reasons for these changes later.)

Output and Income Variables

In this section we are concerned with the value of the nation's total production of goods and services, often called its *national product*. Since all the value that is produced must belong to someone in the form of a claim on that value, the national product is equal to the total income claims generated by the production of goods and services. Hence when we study national product, we are also studying *national income*.

In fact, there are several related measures of the nation's total output and total income. Their various definitions and calculations, and the relations among them, are discussed in detail in the next chapter. In this chapter we use the generic term *national income*. The reason why this has become the generic term is a matter of history; all one needs to understand at this stage is that national income refers to both the value of total output and the value of income claims arising from that output.

Aggregating Total Output

In measuring total output, the quantities of each of a variety of different goods must somehow be added up, or *aggregated*, to obtain a measure of the

[2] Later in the book we distinguish a particular type of frictional unemployment called *structural* unemployment.

total quantity of output. Consider first how this problem relates to a single firm. If that firm produced only a single, well-defined commodity, say loaves of French bread, then to measure its total output all we need to do is add up the number of loaves baked during the period under consideration. But if it also produced muffins, fancy pastries, cakes, and doughnuts, then to calculate the firm's total output we have to find a way of adding up its output of these different individual products.

The same problem arises even more prominently when we come to measure the nation's total output. Measuring national output involves adding up the outputs of literally hundreds of thousands of different goods and services. How can this be done?

To construct such totals, we use prices as weights to add up the different products. Although it does not make sense to add tons of steel to loaves of bread, it does make sense to add the money value of steel production to the money value of bread production. Hence by multiplying the physical output of a good by its price per unit, and then summing this value for each good produced in the nation, we can find the quantity of total output measured in dollars.

Real and Nominal Values

The total described above gives the money value of national output, often called **nominal national income** or **current dollar national income.** When nominal national income changes, it is important to know to what extent the change is due to a change in prices, and to what extent it is due to a change in quantities produced. To answer this question we calculate **real national income** or **constant dollar national income.** This is done by valuing the individual outputs not at the prices currently prevailing, but at the prices that prevailed in some base year.

The terms *real national income* and *real national product* both refer to a measure of total output produced in the nation. This is given the symbol Y.

Real national income tells us the value of current output at base period prices. Since prices are held

TABLE 26–2 CALCULATION OF NOMINAL AND REAL NATIONAL INCOME

(i) Data from hypothetical economy

	Quantity produced[a]		Prices	
	Wheat (bushels)	Steel (tons)	Wheat ($/bushel)	Steel ($/ton)
	q_w	q_s	p_w	p_s
Year 1	100	20	10	50
Year 2	110	16	12	55
Year 3	105	22	14	55

(ii) Nominal national income

$$(q_w p_w + q_s p_s)$$

Year 1	100 (10) + 20(50)	= $2,000
Year 2	110 (12) + 16(55)	= 2,200
Year 3	105 (14) + 22(55)	= 2,680

(iii) Real national income using year 1 prices

$$[q_w(10) + q_s(50)]$$

Year 1	100(10) + 20(50)	= 2,000
Year 2	110(10) + 16(50)	= 1,900
Year 3	105(10) + 22(50)	= 2,150

(iv) Implicit national income deflator (nominal national income/real national income) × 100

Year 1	(2,000/2,000) × 100	= 100.0
Year 2	(2,200/1,900) × 100	= 115.8
Year 3	(2,680/2,150) × 100	= 124.6

[a] As we shall see in Chapter 27, using these figures to calculate national income assumes that they represent "value added" in the industry.

Nominal national income values the economy's output at current prices. Real national income values the economy's output at base period prices. The table refers to hypothetical economy that produces just two commodities, steel and wheat. Panel (i) show outputs and prices of each commodity for each of three years.

Panel (ii) shows nominal national income calculated by adding the money values of wheat output and of steel output for each year. In year 1 the value of both wheat and steel production was $1,000 so nominal income was $2,000. In year 2 the value of wheat output rose to $1,320, but that of steel fell to $880. Since the rise in value of wheat was bigger than the fall in value of steel, nominal income rose to $2,200. In year 3, the values of both outputs rose, and nominal income rose to $2,680.

Panel (iii) shows real national income calculated by valuing output in any given year by base period prices. In year 2, wheat output rose but steel output fell. Using year 1 prices, the fall in steel output outweighed the rise in wheat output, and real national income fell. In year 3, wheat output fell but steel output rose; this time the rise dominated and real national income went up.

Movements in real national income reflect movements in output quantities only, while movements in nominal national income reflect changes in prices and quantities. Differences between real and nominal national income thus reflect changes in prices. This is shown in panel (iv), where the ratio of nominal to real national income is calculated for each year and multiplied by 100. This ratio implicitly measures the change in prices over the period in question, and is called the *implicit deflator*.

constant in calculating it, real national income changes only when output quantities change. Comparison of this year's real national income to base period real national income provides a measure of the change in output that has occurred since the base period.

To see what is involved in distinguishing real from nominal national income, consider a very simple hypothetical economy that produces and consumes only two products: wheat and steel. The first panel in Table 26-2 gives the basic data for

prices and outputs for this imaginary economy in each of three years. The second panel shows the construction of the economy's nominal national income for each year. The third panel shows the calculation of the economy's real national income for years 2 and 3, using year 1 as the base year. In the economy illustrated in the table, real GNP fluctuates but nominal GNP rises continuously because inflation hides the ups and downs in real output.

The difference between the change in nominal national income and the change in real national income is due to price changes. Hence, as shown in the last panel of Table 26-2, the quantity indexes of nominal and real national income together imply a price index. We have already discussed the calculation of base-weighted indexes such as the CPI. The index that arises fom comparing real and nominal national income is a different kind of index. It is called an **implicit deflator,** and it is defined as follows:[3]

implicit deflator =

$$\frac{\text{national income in current dollars}}{\text{national income in constant dollars}} \times 100\%$$

The implicit deflator is the most comprehensive measure of the price level because it covers all the goods and services produced by the entire economy. The deflator in any particular year, such as 1985, is obtained by valuing 1985 national income first at current prices and then at base year (say, 1971) prices. The difference between the two measures must be due to the price changes between

[3] When we study various measures of national product in the next chapter, we will see that this implicit deflator is usually derived from a measure called *gross national expenditure* (GNE), and so in Canada it is referred to as the *implicit GNE deflator.*

the base year and the current year, since the quantities are the same.

As with our hypothetical economy, each change in nominal income can be split into a change due to quantities and a change due to prices. For example, in 1983 Canadian nominal income was 269 percent higher than in 1972. This increase is due to a 176 percent increase in prices and a 34 percent rise in real income. Columns 1 and 2 in Table 26-3 give nominal and real national income for selected years since 1935; column 3 gives the implicit deflator.

Why National Income Is a Matter of Concern

Short-run fluctuations in national income give rise to what is called the business cycle. In periods of high activity, often called *booms*, employment is high and unemployment correspondingly low. In periods of low activity, often called *slumps*, employment is low and unemployment correspondingly high. Policymakers care about short-term fluctuations in national income because slumps

---

TABLE 26-3 NATIONAL INCOME IN CURRENT AND CONSTANT DOLLARS

Year	(1) National income in billions of current dollars	(2) National income in billions of 1971 dollars	(3) Implicit national income deflator (1971 = 100)
1935	4,301	14,279	30.1
1945	11,863	29,071	40.8
1955	28,528	43,891	65.0
1965	55,364	69,981	79.1
1975	165,343	113,005	146.3
1980	291,869	130,467	223.7
1983	388,686	133,995	290.1

Source: M. C. Urquhart (ed.), *Historical Statistics of Canada;* Department of Finance, *Economic Review.*

Current dollar national income tells us about the money value of output; constant dollar national income tells us about changes in physical output. The national income in current dollars gives the total value of all final output in any year, valued in the selling prices of that year. The national income in constant dollars gives the total value of all final output in any year, valued in the prices ruling in one particular year, in this case, 1971.

The ratio *national income in current dollars/national income in constant dollars* times 100 is the implicit deflator. (It is in effect a price index with current-year quantity weights.)

bring unwanted unemployment and lost output while booms create strong inflationary pressures.

The long-run trend in real national income has generally been upward in the modern era. Thus we refer to them as **economic growth.** With growth, each generation can expect, on the average, to be substantially better off than all preceding generations. The horrors of the early industrial revolution are no longer with us, primarily because economic growth has resulted in more and more output for less and less work over the last century.

Output: The Historical Experience

If we are going to look at the actual experience of national income, we must choose some specific measure of this general concept. In this section we look at one of the most commonly used measures, called *gross national product* or GNP. The details of its calculation are discussed in Chapter 27. All we need to know for now is that it is one important measure of national income.

Figure 26-3(i) shows real GNP produced by the Canadian economy since 1930 while Figure 26-3(ii) shows the annual percentage change in the GNP; that is, the real growth rate. The series in Figure 26-3(i) shows two kinds of movement. The major movement is a trend increase in real output that represents the growth of the Canadian economy. Real output rose sevenfold in the half century from 1930 to 1980. A secondary movement in the GNP series is the short-term fluctuations associated with the cyclical behavior of the economy. Overall growth so dominates the GNP series that the cyclical behavior is hardly visible in this figure. Cyclical patterns are more readily apparent in the series for the growth rate, shown in Figure 26-3(ii) and in another series called the *GNP gap* considered in the next section.

Potential National Income

Actual national income is what the economy does in fact produce. We have seen that when measured in current dollars it is called *nominal national income* and when measured in constant dollars it is called *real national income.*

We now need to add an additional concept. **Potential national income** or **full-employment national income** is what the economy would produce *if* its productive resources were fully employed at their normal intensity of use.[4] This assumes that any unemployment of labor is frictional, and that capital—plant and equipment—is being used at its normal capacity levels. Potential national income can be measured either in current or in constant dollars in the same way as actual national income. We use the symbol Y^* to denote potential national income measured in constant dollars.

The GNP Gap

If we take potential income and subtract actual income (i.e., $Y^* - Y$), we obtain a measure called the **GNP gap.** It tells us the difference between what could have been produced at the full employment or potential level, and what is actually produced. It is called the GNP gap merely because the GNP is a commonly used measure of Y and Y^*.

When the gap is positive (i.e., $Y^* > Y$), it measures the market value of goods and services that *could have been* produced if the economy's resources had been fully employed but that actually went unproduced. This is sometimes referred to as the *deadweight loss* of unemployment.

Slumps in business activity are associated with large GNP gaps, booms with small ones. In a major boom the gap can even become negative, indicating that actual national income exceeds the economy's potential national income.

This latter situation can arise because potential income is defined for a normal rate of utilization of factors of production, and there are many ways in which normal rates of utilization can be exceeded temporarily. Labor may work longer hours than normal; factories may operate an extra shift or not close for routine repairs and maintenance. While

[4] The terminology used to refer to potential income is constantly changing. Full-employment income used to be common, but high-employment income is used more often today. To avoid picking one particular term in a world where terminology is not settled, we use the neutral symbol Y^* rather than Y_P, Y_F, or Y_H for potential, full-employment, or high-employment income, respectively.

FIGURE 26-3
Canadian Real National Income and Growth Rate, 1930–1983

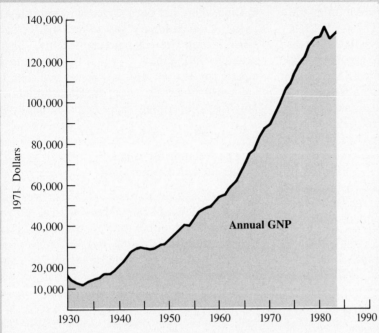

(i) Annual GNP in constant (1971) dollars

(i) **Real national income, which measures the total production of goods and services produced in the economy over the period of a year, has grown steadily since 1930, with only a few interruptions.** In (i) we see the long-term growth of the economy reflected in the upward trend of real national income. Shorter-term fluctuations are obscured by this trend in (i) but are highlighted in (ii).

(ii) **Real growth in the economy, as measured by the annual rate of change of real national income, has fluctuated considerably but has been mostly positive.** In (ii) the short-term fluctuations are readily apparent, but the long-term upward trend still shows up because the majority of observations are positive.

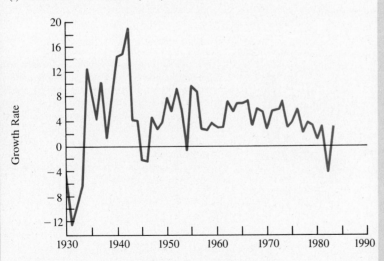

(ii) Annual rate of growth of GNP in constant (1971) dollars

Source: M.C. Urquhart (ed.), *Historical Statistics of Canada;* Department of Finance, *Economic Review*.

these expedients are only temporary, they are effective in the short run.

Figure 26-4 shows the GNP gap for the Canadian economy over a period of years. The fluctuations in economic activity are apparent from the fluctuations in the size of the gap. The deadweight loss from unemployment over any time span is indicated by the overall size of the gap over that span; that is, by the shaded area between the curve and the horizontal line indicating potential output.

The measurement of potential national income is not straightforward, since it cannot be observed directly. The problem is not only one of observation and measurement but also of establishing acceptable definitions for such concepts as "normal levels of utilization" and "full employment capacity." Because Y^* is hard to measure, the GNP gap, given by $(Y^* - Y)$, is correspondingly hard to measure.

Recessionary and inflationary gaps. It is common to refer to positive and negative GNP gaps as recessionary and inflationary. A **recessionary gap** means that actual national income is less than potential income. (This is a positive GNP gap, $Y^* - Y > 0$.) The term *recessionary gap* is used because when the economy is operating below its potential income, there has been a recession in business activity. An **inflationary gap** means that actual national income exceeds potential income. (This is a negative GNP gap, $Y^* - Y < 0$.) The term *inflationary gap* is used because, as we shall see, there are substantial inflationary pressures in any economy that is operating above its potential income.

The Relation Between Output and Employment

Output and employment, and therefore output and unemployment, are closely related. If more is to be produced, either more workers must be used in production or existing workers must produce more. The first change means a rise in employment; the second means a rise in output per person employed, called a rise in **productivity**. Increases

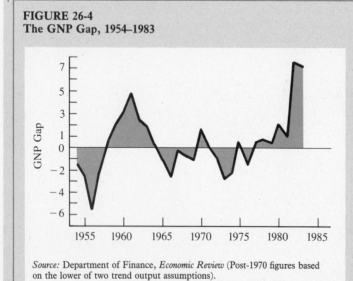

FIGURE 26-4
The GNP Gap, 1954–1983

The GNP gap measures the difference between the economy's potential output and its actual output; it is expressed here as a percentage of potential output. The cyclical behavior of the economy is clearly apparent from the behavior of the GNP gap from 1954 to 1983. Slumps in economic activity cause large gaps, booms reduce the gap. The shaded area above the zero line represents the deadweight loss from unemployment.

Source: Department of Finance, *Economic Review* (Post-1970 figures based on the lower of two trend output assumptions).

in productivity are a major source of economic growth.[5]

Unemployment is the difference between the labor force and employment. Unemployment can rise either because employment falls or the labor force rises, other things being equal. For example, in recent decades the number of people entering the labor force has exceeded the number leaving the labor force because of retirement and death. The rise in the labor force has often led to increases in unemployment even in periods when total employment is growing.

Changes in productivity and in the labor force dominate the long-term behavior of output and employment. But productivity and the labor force generally change only slowly, and thus they have little effect on the short-term behavior of the economy. We will assume for the time being that the labor force and productivity are constant. This is a reasonable approximation of reality for purposes of analyzing the short-term behavior of the economy. It also has the important implication that unemployment and output are negatively related while employment and output are positively related.

AGGREGATE DEMAND AND AGGREGATE SUPPLY

Why are the price level, output, and employment what they are today? What causes them to change? The concepts of demand and supply help us to answer these questions.

In Chapter 4 we saw how the interaction of demand and supply can determine prices and quantities for individual commodities. If we had a single demand curve and a single supply curve for the whole economy, we could determine the economy's price level and the quantity of its total output just as we can determine price and quantity for a single product such as potatoes or coal.

This possibility is illustrated in Figure 26-5,

---

[5] Productivity was discussed in Chapter 11 and will be further discussed in Chapter 38 on economic growth.

which assumes the existence of an aggregate demand curve and an aggregate supply curve for the entire economy. The vertical axis measures the index of all the economy's prices, and the horizontal axis measures its national product valued in constant dollars, which we call *real national income*. The **aggregate demand curve** (**AD**) shows the relation between the total amount of all output that will be purchased and the price level of that output. The **aggregate supply curve** (**AS**) shows the relation between the total amount of output that will be produced and the price level of that output.

The aggregate demand curve is negatively sloped indicating that the lower the price level the greater the quantity of output demanded by purchasers. The aggregate supply curve is positively sloped, indicating that the higher the price level the greater the quantity of output produced by sellers.

The intersection of the aggregate demand and aggregate supply curves determines the equilibrium values of the real national income and the price level.

Only at the equilibrium price level is the amount purchasers wish to buy equal to the amount producers wish to sell. At any other price level the amount demanded is not equal to the amount supplied.

The Aggregate Demand Curve

The aggregate demand curve is negatively sloped. This shape indicates that, other things being equal:

The higher the price level the smaller the total quantity demanded, and the lower the price level the larger the total quantity demanded.

Why does it have this slope?

The *AD* Curve and Individual Market Demand Curves

We saw in Chapter 4 that the individual market demand curves used in microeconomics are also negatively sloped. But the reasons are very different.

FIGURE 26-5
The Price Level and National Income for the Whole Economy

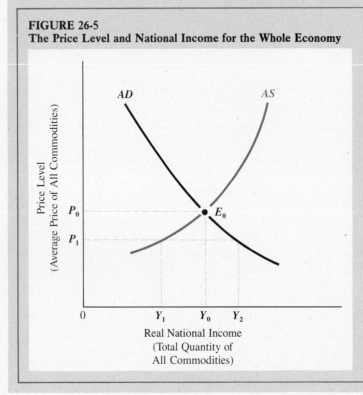

Aggregate demand and aggregate supply determine the price level and national income for the entire economy. Actual output is determined by the intersection of the aggregate demand and aggregate supply curves. Equilibrium is at E_0, with a price level of P_0 and a national income of Y_0. At higher price levels, aggregate supply exceeds aggregate demand; at lower price levels, aggregate demand exceeds aggregate supply. For example, if the price level were P_1, purchasers would wish to buy Y_2 of total output but producers would only be willing to make and sell only Y_1. The resulting shortage would then force prices up from P_1 to P_0.

Recall that a market demand curve describes what happens when the price of one product changes, with the price of all other products being held constant. What happens along a market demand curve happens, therefore, because the relation among prices is changing; that is, the product in question is getting cheaper or more expensive relative to all other products. The AD curve, however, plots aggregate demand against the *price level*. Thus what happens along the AD curve depends on the average behavior of all prices, not on the behavior of any individual price. So the forces at work are different from those that explain the market demand curve.

The Slope of the AD Curve

Then what does explain the downward slope of the AD curve? Although one reason will emerge in Chapter 28 when we discuss what are called *wealth*

effects, all the reasons can be explained fully only after we have covered money and interest rates. In the meantime, some readers may decide for now just to take the aggregate demand curve's slope on faith, knowing that it will be more completely explained later. Others who may like a preview of these reasons can have one by studying Box 26-3.

The Aggregate Supply Curve

The aggregate supply curve is positively sloped. This shape indicates that, other things being equal:

The higher the price level the greater will be the total quantity that will be produced and the lower the price level the less will be the total quantity produced.

For reasons that we will soon discover, this relation in only a short-term one and to indicate its short-term nature the upward sloping aggregate supply curve is always referred to as the **short-run aggregate supply curve (*SRAS*)**. Why does the *SRAS* curve have this shape?

The Slope of the Short-Run Aggregate Supply Curve

Suppose that firms wish to increase their current production levels. Although for the moment we assume that the prices of all of the firms' inputs remain constant, this does not mean that their output prices will remain unchanged. Increasing output may require that less efficient standby machines and plants are used, less efficient marginal workers are employed, and that existing workers are given overtime hours at premium wages. Thus, even with the restriction that input prices remain constant, higher output is associated with increased costs because it requires the use of more and more costly methods of production. This increase in cost per unit of output is referred to as rising **unit costs.** Since expanding output implies higher unit costs, firms will only produce this extra output if it can be sold at higher prices. Furthermore, rising output is often associated with larger profit margins, which raises prices even more than unit costs have risen. For these reasons as we move to the right along the *SRAS* curve, we find that higher output is associated with a higher level of output prices.

Now consider what happens when firms wish to reduce their output. The forces just discussed now work in reverse. There will be cost savings as the least efficient labor is laid off first and the least efficient capital is put on standby. In times of depressed output, firms also tend to lower their profit margins. For these reasons, the lower output will be associated with somewhat lower unit costs with lower output prices.

The upward sloping short-run aggregate supply curve shows that with input prices constant, higher output is associated with higher prices because unit costs of production and profit margins vary directly with output.

It is now clear why this relation is only a short-run one. It is drawn on the assumption that input prices are constant. Variations in output will, however, surely cause input prices to change before too long. (In Chapter 30 we shall study the effects of changing input prices on the *SRAS* curve.)

The GNP gap. We saw in Figure 26-3 that actual output often diverges from potential output, the difference between the two being called the GNP gap. Figure 26-6 on page 482 shows the GNP gap on our new diagram. Potential income is shown by a vertical line indicating that it does not vary with the price level but actual output does do so (along the *SRAS* curve). The difference between the two lines at any price level is the GNP gap.

Figure 26-6 shows the *AD* and the *SRAS* curves intersecting to produce a positive GNP gap, that is, a recessionary gap. In this case, actual output is below potential output.

Changes in Output and Prices

We have seen that the aggregate demand and aggregate supply curves determine national income and the price level. What we really want to know is why income and prices change and how government policy can influence these changes. Here is a simple overview.[6]

Shifts in the Aggregate Curves

What happens to total output and to the price level when one of the aggregate curves shifts? When one shifts, the intersection with the other curve changes. As a result the equilibrium values of real output and the price level also change.

A shift in one aggregate curve leads to changes in the price level and real national income.

A shift in the *AD* curve is called an **aggregate demand shock.** A shift in the *SRAS* curve is called an **aggregate supply shock.**[7]

---

[6] The discussion of movements along and shifts of curves in Chapter 4 could usefully be reviewed at this stage. Recall especially that the phrase "a change in quantity demanded" refers to a *movement along a demand curve*, while the phrase "a change in demand" refers to a *shift of the demand curve*. A similar distinction applies to the supply curve.

[7] What actually happens to *Y* and *P* may be influenced by whether or not people see the shock coming. Later we return to this important distinction between unanticipated and anticipated shocks.

BOX 26–3 THE SHAPE OF THE AGGREGATE DEMAND CURVE

Why the Aggregate Demand Curve Is Not Simply the Sum of Individual Market Demand Curves

In Chapter 4 we studied the demand curves for individual products. It is tempting to think that the properties of the aggregate demand curve arise from the same behavior that gives rise to those "individual" demand curves. Unfortunately, life is not so simple. Let us see why we cannot take such an approach.

The fallacy of composition. If we assumed that we could obtain a downward-sloping aggregate demand curve in the same manner that we derived downward-sloping individual market demand curves, we would be committing the fallacy of composition. This is to assume that what is correct for the parts must be correct for the whole.

Consider a simple example of the fallacy. Any art collector can go into the market and add to her private collection of nineteenth century French paintings provided only that she has enough money. But to assume that because any one person can do this, everyone could do so simultaneously is plainly wrong. The stock of nineteenth century French paintings in the world is totally fixed. All of us cannot do what any one of us with enough money can do.

How does the fallacy of composition relate to demand curves?

An individual demand curve describes a sit-uation in which the price of one commodity, such as cotton shirts, changes while the prices of all other commodities and consumers' money incomes remain constant. An individual demand curve is negatively sloped for two reasons. First, as the price of the commodity rises, each consumer's given money income will buy a smaller *total* amount of goods, so a smaller quantity of the commodity in question will be bought. Second, as the price of the commodity rises, consumers buy less of it and more of the now relatively cheaper substitutes.

The first reason has no application to the aggregate demand curve, which relates the total demand for all output to the price level. All prices and total output are changing as we move along the *AD* curve. Since the value of output determines income, there is no reason to expect money income to be constant along this curve.

The second reason does have some, but very limited, applicability to the aggregate demand curve. A rise in the price level entails a rise in all domestic commodity prices. Thus there is no incentive to substitute among domestic commodities. But it does give rise, as we shall see below, to some substitution between domestic and foreign goods.

Why the Aggregate Demand Curve Is Negatively Sloped

Three reasons account for the negative slope of the *AD* curve.

Aggregate Demand Shocks

Figure 26-7 illustrates the effects of an increase in aggregate demand on the price level and real output. The increase could have occurred because of increased investment spending, increased government spending, or greater exports. For now we are not concerned with the source of the boom; we are interested in its implications for the price level and real output. The increase in aggregate demand causes the *AD* curve to shift outward. The new equilibrium thus entails a movement along the *SRAS* curve so that both the price level and the quantity of real output increase.

Wealth effect on expenditure. *A rise in the price level lowers the real value of assets denominated in money terms. As a result, people spend less in order to save more, causing the aggregate demand for the nation's output to fall, other things being equal.*

Bank balances, bonds, and many other assets are denominated in terms of money. When the price level rises, the real purchasing power of these assets is reduced. For example if I hold a $1,000 bond and the price level doubles, the amount of commodities I can buy with the money I get back when the bond is redeemed falls by half. Since the bond's real value is halved, the real value of my wealth falls. This may cause me to increase my savings in order to recoup some of my lost wealth; to save more, I must spend less on current consumption.

Substitution of foreign goods. *A rise in the Canadian price level, other things being equal, reduces foreign demand for Canadian exports and leads Canadians to buy foreign imports rather than increasingly expensive Canadian commodities.*

When the Canadian price level rises Canadian goods become expensive relative to foreign goods and Canadian residents reduce their purchases of relatively expensive Canadian goods and buy relatively cheap foreign goods instead. Foreign consumers reduce their purchases of the increasingly expensive goods exported from Canada. Since the aggregate demand curve describes the demand for Canadian goods from all sources, including foreign ones, aggregate demand will fall as the Canadian price level rises.

Interest rate effects on expenditure. *A rise in the price level creates a shortage of money, which drives up interest rates. This in turn discourages interest-sensitive expenditures.*

The third reason why the aggregate demand curve slopes downward is to be found in the effects of money on interest rates and of interest rates on total demand. The main forces are only suggested here; they will be fully apparent later when the necessary links in the argument have been studied. (The full explanation can be found in Chapter 34, starting on page 635.)

When the price of everything rises, firms and households require larger working balances of money. Firms need to finance enlarged payrolls; households need to cover their increased money expenses between one payday and the next. Many try to borrow the extra working balances that they need. This extra demand for money creates a shortage of money.

When money is in short supply, the price you have to pay to borrow it—which is the interest rate—rises. Firms that borrow money to invest in plant and equipment, and households that borrow money to buy consumer goods, respond to rising interest rates by choosing to spend less on capital goods, housing, automobiles, and other goods. This means a decline in the aggregate quantity demanded of the nation's output.

Figure 26-7 also illustrates that both the price level and the quantity of real output will fall as a result of a reduction in aggregate demand.

Aggregate demand shocks cause the price level and real national income to change in the same direction, both rising or both falling together.

Demand-shock inflation. A typical demand shock occurred with the boom that began in 1965. (This boom is of particular interest because it was the transition between the two decades of low inflation rates that followed World War II and the two decades of high inflation rates that governments have had to try hard to bring under control

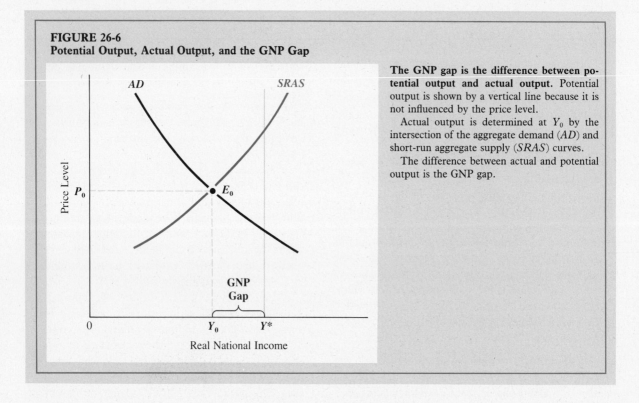

FIGURE 26-6
Potential Output, Actual Output, and the GNP Gap

The GNP gap is the difference between potential output and actual output. Potential output is shown by a vertical line because it is not influenced by the price level.

Actual output is determined at Y_0 by the intersection of the aggregate demand (AD) and short-run aggregate supply ($SRAS$) curves.

The difference between actual and potential output is the GNP gap.

in the 1980s.) In 1965 the buildup of military spending in the United States to finance the accelerating war in Vietnam hit the economy with a severe demand shock. Although there were lapses from full employment, the period was mainly one of excess demand with high output, low unemployment, and rapidly rising prices. The shift in the AD curve led initially to a movement along the $SRAS$ curve.

Aggregate Supply Shocks

Figure 26-8 shows the effect of an upward shift in the $SRAS$ curve with no change in the AD curve: the price level rises and national income falls (which implies a larger GNP gap). This combination of events is now called **stagflation.** This rather inelegant word was derived by running together *stagnation* (a colloquial term meaning less than full employment) and *inflation* (a rise in the price level).

Figure 26-8 also shows that a shift of $SRAS$ downward will lead to an increase in real output and a decrease in the price level.

Aggregate supply shocks cause the price level and real national income to change in opposite directions, one rising and the other falling.

Supply-shock stagflation. The first dramatic stagflation of the modern era began in 1974. One major aspect of that era was that the economy was hit with some severe supply shocks. Serious crop failures combined with the sale of surplus wheat to the U.S.S.R. raised food prices greatly. The policies of the newly aggressive OPEC forced up not only the price of energy but the prices of fertilizer, plastics, synthetic rubber, and dozens of other petroleum-based products. Since many of these are used in the manufacture of yet other commodities, many costs of production rose. The rise in costs

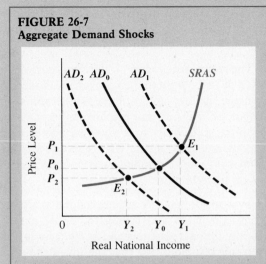

FIGURE 26-7
Aggregate Demand Shocks

Shifts in *AD* cause the price level and real national income to move in the same direction. An increase in aggregate demand causes *AD* to shift from, say, AD_0 to AD_1, and equilibrium to shift from E_0 to E_1. The price level rises from P_0 to P_1, and real national income rises from Y_0 to Y_1.

A decrease in aggregate demand causes *AD* to shift from, say, AD_0 to AD_2. The new equilibrium is at E_2, and prices fall to P_2 while real national income falls to Y_2.

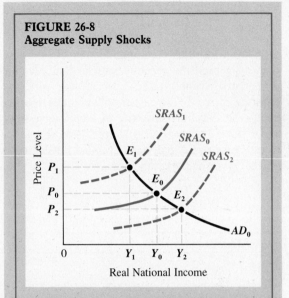

FIGURE 26-8
Aggregate Supply Shocks

Shifts in *SRAS* cause the price level and real national income to move in opposite directions. A reduction in aggregate supply causes *SRAS* to shift up and to the left, say, from $SRAS_0$ to $SRAS_1$. Equilibrium then goes from E_0 to E_1. The price level rises to P_1, but real national income falls to Y_1.

An increase in aggregate supply causes *SRAS* to shift down and to the right. The new *SRAS* is given by $SRAS_2$, and equilibrium is at E_2. The price level falls to P_2, but real national income rises to Y_2.

led firms to raise their selling prices. Hence the aggregate supply curve shifted upward. The same output would only be supplied at a higher price level. The upward shift in the *SRAS* curve caused a serious stagflation. The economy experienced simultaneously the twin "evils" of falling output and rising prices.

The mid 1970s were the first time in 50 years that the behavior of prices and output resulted largely from a sharply upward-shifting aggregate supply curve. People were used to the behavior of the economy under the impact of demand shocks—where inflation is associated with boom conditions characterized by high and rising output. Consequently its behavior under severe supply shocks—where inflation is associated with slack economic conditions characterized by low and falling out-

put—seemed incomprehensible, even paradoxical. Many commentators who customarily explained observed events in terms of demand-side shocks did not at first appreciate what was happening. Some announced the collapse of conventional macroeconomic theory; others claimed to see a complete change in all economic behavior. Although plausible at the time, such reactions can now be seen as excessive. Once the part played by aggregate supply was understood, the then mysterious events of the mid 1970s became quite understandable, no matter how undesirable.

Supply-side economics. As we saw in Figure 26-8, a downward shift of the *SRAS* curve will lead to a rise in real output and a fall in the price level. To anyone living in economies plagued by stagflation, these conditions, which are just the opposite of stagflation, appear to be ideal. A desire to achieve just this combination was the purpose that lay behind the recently popular "supply-side economics." Supply-siders advocate tax cuts and other incentives to increase supply in order to bring about the desirable outcome of increased output and reduced prices. "Very simple" said the advocates; "easier said than done" replied the critics in a debate we shall take up later.

SUMMARY

1. Macroeconomics examines the behavior of such broad aggregates and averages as the price level, national income, potential national income, the GNP gap, employment, and unemployment.

2. Index numbers are summary measures that give the average percentage change in a set of related items between a "base" year and another "given" year.

3. One measure of the price level is the Consumer Price Index (CPI). It shows the percentage change in the cost of purchasing a typical bundle of commodities since the base year. It is thus a measure of the average change in prices in which each price is weighted by the importance of that commodity in the typical consumption bundle.

4. The price level has risen continuously since 1929. The inflation rate measures the rate of change of the price level. Although it fluctuates considerably, it has been consistently positive. Inflation imposes serious costs on the economy.

5. The value of total production of goods and services is called *national product*. Since production of output generates income in the form of claims on that output, it is common to also talk of *national income*. Nominal national income values output in current prices. Real national income evaluates output in base year prices. Differences between the changes in nominal and real income are due to changes in prices; such price changes are measured by changes in the implicit deflator.

6. The dominant theme of the economy is the growth of real output and employment. A secondary theme involves cyclical factors represented by fluctuations in output and employment around the growth trend. In order to study these fluctuations, we focus attention on the GNP gap and the unemployment rate. Unemployment imposes serious costs on the economy.

7. Two major tools of macroeconomics are the aggregate demand and aggregate supply curves. Typically the aggregate demand (*AD*) curve is negatively sloped, indicating that the lower the price level, the higher the demand for the nation's output. Although *potential* output can be taken as independent of the price level, the aggregate supply curve typically slopes upward in the short run. This positive slope of the short-run aggregate supply (*SRAS*) curve indicates that the higher the price level the greater will be the output produced.

8. The reasons for the negative slope of the aggregate demand curve will be fully explored in subsequent chapters. The reasons for the positive slope of the short-run aggregate supply curve can, however, be developed now: increases in output entail increases in the costs of producing each unit of output and hence will only be undertaken if output prices rise.

9. Macroeconomic equilibrium occurs at the intersection of the *AD* and *SRAS* curves, thus determining the economy's price level and total ouput. Shifts in the *AD* or *SRAS* curve cause the equilibrium price level and real national income to change.

10. Demand shocks tend to cause output and the price level to change in the same direction so that booms are associated with rising prices and slumps with falling prices. Supply shocks tend to cause output and the price level to change in opposite directions.

TOPICS FOR REVIEW

Index numbers
The price level and the rate of inflation
Employment, unemployment, and the labor force
Real and nominal national income
Potential national income and the GNP gap
Aggregate demand and aggregate supply
Aggregate demand shocks
Aggregate supply shocks

DISCUSSION QUESTIONS

1. Classify as micro or macro (or both) the issues raised in the following newspaper headlines.
   a. "Lettuce Crop Spoils as Strike Hits B.C. Lettuce Producers."
   b. "Analysts Fear Rekindling of Inflation as Economy Recovers toward Full Employment."
   c. "Price of Bus Rides Soars in Centersville as City Council Withdraws Transport Subsidy."
   d. "A Fall in the Unemployment Rate Signals the Beginning of the End of the Recession in the Oshawa Area."
   e. "Silicon Chip Technology Brings Falling Prices and Growing Sales of Microcomputers."
   f. "Wage Settlements in Key Industries Seen by the Finance Minister to Signal the Decline of Inflationary Threats."
   g. "Rising Costs of Imported Raw Materials Cause Most Manufacturers to Raise Prices."

2. Using your understanding of the chapter, critically analyze each of the following recent statements made by businessmen.
   a. "We must be successful, our sales have increased every year for the past ten years."
   b. "I can see why prices may rise in boom times, but rising prices and falling output just doesn't make sense."
   c. "I can't understand why there is so much unemployment, our business is booming."

3. Explain each of the following by shifts in either (or both) the aggregate demand and aggregate supply curves. (Pay attention to the initial position before the shift(s) occurs.)
   a. Output and unemployment rise while prices hold steady.
   b. Prices soar but employment and output hold steady.
   c. Inflation accelerates even as the recession in business activity deepens.
   d. The inflation rate falls, but at the expense of employment.

4. In 1979–1980, the British government greatly reduced income taxes but restored the lost government revenue by raising excise and sales taxes. This led to a short burst of extra inflation and a fall in employment. Explain this in terms of shifts in the aggregate demand and/or supply curves.

5. Indicate whether each of the following events is the cause or the consequence of a shift in aggregate demand or supply. If it is a cause, what do you predict will be the effect on the price level and on real national income?
   a. Canadian unemployment fell in 1983.
   b. OPEC raises oil prices in 1979.
   c. OPEC is forced to accept lower oil prices in 1982–1983.
   d. In the late 1960s and early 1970s Canada suffered a rapid inflation under conditions of approximately full employment.
   e. In country X, income and employment continue to fall while the price level is relatively stable.
   f. The recovery of the economy of country Y from a severe slump has led to a large increase in income and employment.
   g. President Reagan achieves a large increase in defense spending in 1983–1984.
   h. Budget deficits soar in the early 1980s as tax revenues fall in the face of the most serious recession since the 1930s.

6. Discuss the various reasons why two truthful people could announce that very different rates of inflation are ruling in Canada today.

7. How could unemployment rise at a time when employment was increasing rapidly? Why is unemployment not as serious a matter as it was at the beginning of this century?

8. If you thought the inflation rate was going to be 10 percent next year, why should you be unwilling to lend money at 5 percent interest? Say 5 percent was all you could get and you had money you didn't want to spend for a year. Would you be better just to hold the money? What could you do that would be better than lending your money at 5 percent?

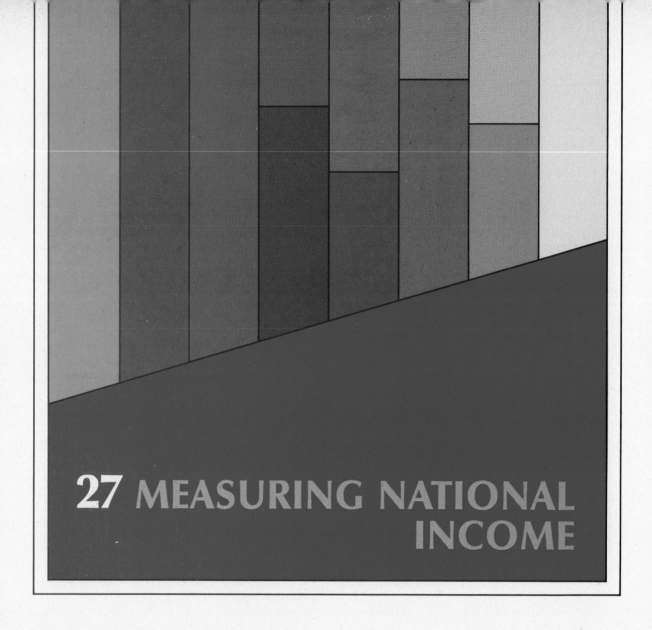

27 MEASURING NATIONAL INCOME

The aggregate demand and aggregate supply curves each show a relation between the price level and total output, which we have called by the generic term *real national income*. Total output is the sum of all the final products that are produced over some period, usually a year. The term **final products** excludes all semi-finished products used as inputs by other firms. Such semi-finished products are called **intermediate products**. For example, bread produced by a bakery is a final product; the flour produced by a mill bought by the bakery is an intermediate product.

In this chapter we look at alternative ways of measuring total output. We find that each measure helps to shed some light on specific aspects of the total being measured.

It is useful to look again at Figure 3-1, which shows the circular flow of expenditure and income in the economy. The bottom half of the circular flow focuses on expenditure to purchase the nation's output in product markets, while the top half focuses on factor markets where the receipts of firms are distributed to those factors used in producing the nation's output. Corresponding to these two halves of the circular flow are two ways of measuring national income: the value of what is produced *and* the value of incomes generated by the act of production. We can add up the total expenditure on each of the main components of final output; this is called *the expenditure approach*. The measure of national income arrived at by this approach is called **gross national expenditure (GNE)**. We can also measure the incomes generated by the act of production; this is called the *income approach*. The measure of national income arrived at by this approach is called **gross national product (GNP)**.

Gross national expenditure and gross national product are two different ways of looking at one magnitude: the market value of the nation's final output.

GNE and GNP are conceptually identical, and differ in practice only because of errors of measurement. Each approach is of interest, however, because each gives a different and useful breakdown of national income. Having two independent ways of measuring the same thing also gives a useful check on the statistical procedures and unavoidable measurement errors.

NATIONAL INCOME ACCOUNTING

National income accounting is the set of rules and techniques for measuring the total flow of output (goods and services) produced and the total flow of incomes generated by this production. Gross national expenditure is the market value of all the production in the economy during one year, while gross national product is the value of all the claims generated by that production. A convention of double-entry bookkeeping is that all value produced must be accounted for by a claim someone has to that value. Thus it is merely a matter of accounting convention that gross national expenditure and gross national product should be equal. GNE and

GNP differ only to the extent that measurement errors arise: Any discrepancy arising from such errors is then reconciled so that one common total is given as the measure of national income.

The Expenditure Approach

The expenditure approach calculates the market value of final output by adding up the *expenditures* made to purchase final output. Total expenditure on final output is the sum of four broad categories of expenditure: consumption, investment, government, and net exports. Although each of these may be subdivided into finer groupings, the fourfold classification is extremely useful.

Consumption Expenditure

Consumption expenditure covers all goods and services produced and sold to households during the year (with the exception of residential houses, which are counted as investment). It includes services such as haircuts, medical care, and legal advice; nondurable goods such as fresh meat, cut flowers, and fresh vegetables; and durables such as cars, television sets, and air conditioners. We denote it by a boldface symbol **C**.

Investment Expenditure

Investment expenditure is the production of final goods not for present consumption. Such goods are called **investment goods.** Investment can be in inventories, in capital goods such as plant and equipment, or in residential housing.

First consider inventories. Virtually all firms hold stocks of their inputs and their own outputs. These stocks are called **inventories.** Inventories of inputs allow production to continue at the desired pace in spite of short-term fluctuations in the deliveries of inputs bought from other firms. Inventories of outputs allow firms to meet orders in spite of temporary fluctuations in the rate of output.

Inventories are an important part of the production process. They require an investment of the firm's money, since the firm has paid for but not yet sold the goods. An accumulation of inventories counts as current investment because it represents goods produced but not used for current consumption. A drawing down—often called a decumulation—counts as disinvestment because it represents sales that do not reflect current production.

Additions to inventories are a part of the economy's final production of investment goods. These are valued in the national income accounts at market value, which includes the wages and other costs the firm incurred in producing the goods and the profit the firm will make when the inventories are sold. Thus, in the case of inventories of a firm's own output, the expenditure approach measures what would have to be spent to purchase them when they are sold rather than what has actually been spent on them at the moment.

Next consider investment in plant and equipment. All production uses capital goods—manmade aids to production such as hand tools, machines, and factory buildings. The economy's total quantity of capital goods is called the **capital stock**. The act of creating new capital goods is an act of investment, and is called fixed business investment or **fixed investment** for short.

The third main category of investment is residential housing. A house is a very durable asset that yields its utility slowly over a long life. For this reason, housing construction is counted as investment expenditure rather than as consumption expenditure. This is done by assuming that the investment is made by the firm that builds the house, and that the sale to a user is a mere transfer of ownership that is not a part of national income.

The total investment that occurs in the economy is called **gross investment**. Gross investment is divided into two parts, replacement investment and net investment. Replacement investment is the amount required to maintain the existing capital stock intact; it is called the **capital consumption allowance** or simply **depreciation**. Gross investment minus the capital consumption allowance is **net allowance**. Net investment increases the economy's total stock of capital, while **replacement investment** keeps the existing stock intact by replacing what has been used up.

The investment that is a part of national income is gross investment. This is because all investment goods are part of the nation's total output, and their production creates income (and employment) whether the goods produced are a part of net investment or are merely replacement investment. Total investment expenditure is denoted by the boldface symbol **I**.

Government Expenditure on Goods and Services

When governments produce goods and services that households want, such as roads and air traffic control, they are obviously adding to the sum total of valuable output in the same ways as do private firms that produce the trucks and airplanes that use the roads and air lanes. With other government activities, the case may not seem so clear. Should expenditures by the federal government to send a scientific probe into space or to pay a civil servant to refile papers from a now defunct department be regarded as contributions to national income? A lot of people believe that many (or even most) activities "up in Ottawa" or "down at City Hall" are wasteful if not downright harmful. But most of us also know other people who believe that it is governments, not private firms, that produce many of the important things in life, such as education and pollution control.

National income statisticians do not speculate about which government expenditures are or are not worthwhile. Instead, they count all government expenditures that produce goods and services and use factors of production. Just as the national product includes, without distinction, the output of both gin and Bibles, it also includes bombers and the upkeep of parks, along with the services of RCMP offices, members of Parliament, and even Revenue Canada investigators. Actual government expenditure is signified by the boldface symbol **G**.

All government output is valued at cost rather than market value. In many cases there is really no choice. What, for example, is the market value of the services of a court of law? No one knows. But we do know what it costs the government to provide these services, so we value them at their cost of production.

Although valuing at cost is the only possible thing to do with many government activities, it does have one curious consequence. If, due to a productivity increase, one civil servant now does what two used to do, and the displaced worker shifts to the private sector, the government's contribution to national income will register a decline. On the other hand, if two now do what one used to do, the government's contribution will rise. Both changes could occur even though what the government actually does is unchanged. This is an inevitable but curious consequence of measuring the value of the government's output by the value of the factors, mainly labor, used to produce it.

There is an important exception to the rule that all government expenditure is included in national income. When a government agency makes welfare payments to a mother of five children whose husband has deserted her, income is transferred to her. But the government does not receive, nor does it expect to receive, any marketable services from the deserted mother in return for the welfare payments.[1] The payment itself adds neither to employment of factors nor to total output.

Government payments to households that are not made in return for the services of factors of production are called government transfer payments, or simply **transfer payments.** Such payments do not lead directly to any increase in output, and they are not included in national income. The major transfer payments arise from unemployment insurance, welfare payments, and interest on the national debt (which transfers income from taxpayers to holders of government bonds).

Transfer payments are not included in the government expenditure that is part of national income. Thus when we talk of **government expenditure** or government purchases, and when we use the symbol

G, we *include* all government expenditure on currently produced goods and services and we *exclude* all government transfer payments.

Net Exports

The fourth main element of aggregate expenditure arises because of foreign trade, a category that is extremely important to the Canadian economy. How do imports and exports influence the national income?

One country's national income is the total value of final commodities produced in that country. If you spend $11,000 to buy a Canadian car whose synthetic rubber tires are made from Libyan oil, not all of that $11,000 is expenditure on the output of Canadian producers. Because the oil was produced abroad, it is part of the national product of another country. If your cousin spends $8,000 on a Japanese car, only a small part of that value will represent expenditure on Canadian production. Some of it goes for the services of the Canadian dealers and Canadian transportation; the rest is the output of Japanese firms and expenditure on Japanese products.

Similarly, when a Canadian firm makes an investment expenditure on a Canadian-produced machine tool made partly with imported raw materials, only part of the expenditure is on Canadian production. The rest is expenditure on the production of the countries supplying the raw materials. The same is also true for government expenditure on such things as roads and dams; some of the expenditure is for imported materials, only part of it for domestically produced goods and services.

Consumption, investment, and government expenditures all have an import content. To arrive at total expenditure on Canadian products, we need to subtract the total domestic expenditure on imports, which is given the boldface symbol **M.**

There is a second consideration. If Canadian firms sell goods to German households, the goods are a part of German consumption expenditure but are also a part of Canadian national income. Indeed, all goods and services produced in Canada and sold abroad must be counted as part of Cana-

[1] In looking after her children the mother is performing a useful and valuable function. What she is not doing is producing a commodity that adds to total *marketed* production. The treatment of transfer payment recognizes that fact; it does not imply a value judgment that the mother's activities are useless, only that they are not sold on the market.

dian output (they create incomes for the Canadians who produce them). To arrive at the total value of expenditure on Canadian national product, it is necessary to add in the value of Canadian exports. They are denoted by the boldface symbol **X**.

It is customary to group (**X** − **M**) together and call them **net exports.** The value of net exports is usually small in relation to the total value of either **X** or **M**. Thus the correction to national income made to allow for foreign trade will not usually be large. However, a change in either **X** or **M** will cause the national income to change by the same amount as would an equal change in **C, I,** or **G.**

Gross National Expenditure

Gross national expenditure is the sum of the above four categories of expenditure.

The expenditure approach to measuring national income yields GNE: the sum of consumption, investment, government expenditure, and net exports.

While GNE is the commonly used accounting term for this sum, in theoretical work it is often called **aggregate expenditure (AE).** In symbols we write

$$GNE = AE = C + I + G + (X - M)$$

Figure 27-1(i) shows Canadian national income for 1983 calculated according to the expenditure approach.

The Income Approach

Another way of measuring the nation's output is the income approach. This approach calculates the value of total incomes generated in the process of production. The measure of national income obtained by the income approach is called gross national product (GNP).

The production of the nation's output generates income. Labor must be employed, land rented, and capital used. The calculation of GNP involves adding up factor payments and other claims on the value of output until all of it is accounted for.

Because all value produced must be owned by some-

one, the value of production must equal the value of income claims generated by that production.

Factor Payments

National income accountants distinguish four main components of factor incomes: wages, rents, interest, and profits.[2]

Wages. Wages and salaries (which national income accountants call *compensation to employees* but which is usually just called wages) are the payment for the services of labor. These include take-home pay, taxes withheld, and pension fund contributions. In total, these represent that part of the value of production attributable to labor.

Rent. Rent is the payment for the services of land and other rented factors. It includes payments for rented housing and an item for imputed rent for the use of owner-occupied housing. For the purposes of national income accounting, homeowners are viewed as renting accommodation from themselves. This allows national income measures to reflect the value of all housing services used, whether or not the housing is owner-occupied.

Interest. This item includes interest and miscellaneous investment income. It includes interest earned on bank deposits and corporate bonds, and on loans to firms. Hence interest represents one of the payments for the services of capital.

Profits. Profits are earned by firms and other enterprises. Some profits are paid out as **dividends** to owners of the firm; the rest are retained for use by the firm. The former are called **distributed profits,** and the latter **undistributed profits** or **retained earnings.** Both distributed and undistributed profits are included in the calculation of GNP. For accounting purposes, these total profits are reported in two separate categories—corporation profits and incomes of unincorporated businesses

---

[2] The concepts of rent, wages, interest, and profits used in macroeconomics do not correspond exactly to the microeconomic concepts that go under the same names. The details of the differences need not detain us in an introductory treatment, but readers should keep in mind that differences exist.

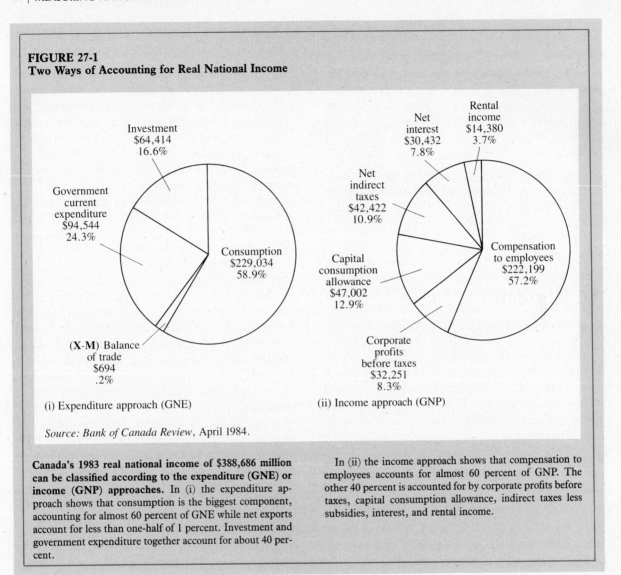

FIGURE 27-1
Two Ways of Accounting for Real National Income

Investment
$64,414
16.6%

Government
current
expenditure
$94,544
24.3%

Consumption
$229,034
58.9%

(X-M) Balance
of trade
$694
.2%

(i) Expenditure approach (GNE)

Net
interest
$30,432
7.8%

Rental
income
$14,380
3.7%

Net
indirect
taxes
$42,422
10.9%

Capital
consumption
allowance
$47,002
12.9%

Compensation
to employees
$222,199
57.2%

Corporate
profits
before taxes
$32,251
8.3%

(ii) Income approach (GNP)

Source: Bank of Canada Review, April 1984.

Canada's 1983 real national income of $388,686 million can be classified according to the expenditure (GNE) or income (GNP) approaches. In (i) the expenditure approach shows that consumption is the biggest component, accounting for almost 60 percent of GNE while net exports account for less than one-half of 1 percent. Investment and government expenditure together account for about 40 percent.

In (ii) the income approach shows that compensation to employees accounts for almost 60 percent of GNP. The other 40 percent is accounted for by corporate profits before taxes, capital consumption allowance, indirect taxes less subsidies, interest, and rental income.

(which is mainly income of small businesses, farmers, partnerships, and professionals).

The sum of the four components of factor incomes is called *net national income at factor cost.*

Indirect Taxes Less Subsidies

When using the income approach, we must distinguish between national income valued at factor cost and national income valued at market prices. The difference between the two is created by indirect taxes and subsidies. An important claim on the market value of output arises out of indirect taxes—taxes on the production and sale of goods and services.

If, for example, a good's sale value of $10 includes $6 of intermediate goods and $1 of business excise taxes, only $3 is available as income to factors of production. One dollar's worth of market value represents the government's claim on that value. When adding up income claims to get GNP, it is therefore necessary to add in that part of the total market value of output which is the government's claim arising out of its taxes on goods and services. It is also necessary to subtract government subsidies on goods and services, since these allow incomes to *exceed* the market value of output.[3]

Adding indirect taxes less subsidies to the four components of factor incomes gives *net national product at market prices.*

Depreciation

Another component in the income approach arises from the distinction between net and gross investment. One claim on the value of final output is depreciation. This is the value of final output that embodies capital used up in the process of its production. It is part of gross profits but, being that part needed to compensate for capital used up in the process of production, it is not part of net profits. Hence it is not income earned by any factor of production. Instead it is value that must be reinvested just to maintain the existing stock of capital equipment.

Adding depreciation to net national product at market prices gives *gross national product at market prices, or GNP.*

Gross National Product

Gross national product is the sum of all claims to the market value of national output.

The income approach measures GNP, the sum of the factor incomes generated in the process of producing final output, plus indirect taxes less subsidies, plus depreciation.

The various components of GNP in the Canadian economy in 1983 are shown in Figure 27-1(ii).

[3] For example, if a single proprietor produces $20,000 worth of value added over the year and receives a $5,000 subsidy from the government, his income is $25,000. So to get the market value of his output from the income side, we must take his income and *subtract* the government subsidy.

The Output Approach: A Third Measure

There is a third way in which national income could be measured: by adding up the contributions to final output of every firm in the economy. Although not considered part of the national income accounts, this method is used to provide a third measure of national income called *gross domestic product (GDP)*, which is then reconciled with the national income accounts.

If every firm produced only final output, the method would be easy to apply. Statisticians would just add up the values of all firms' outputs. In reality, however, production of commodities is divided into stages, with particular firms and industries often specializing in the production of intermediate products. For example, one set of firms may mine iron ore; the ore may be sold to another set of firms for manufacturing into steel; the steel may be sold to another set of firms for use in making household tools; and the manufacturer of the tools may sell them to a wholesaler, who sells them to a retailer, who in turn finally sells them to households.

Stages of production, and the consequent interfirm sales of intermediate products, make it difficult to measure national income from production data. If we merely added up the market values of the outputs of all firms, we would obtain a total greatly in excess of the value of output actually available for use. In terms of the example in the previous paragraph, this procedure would result in counting the value of the iron ore five times, of the steel four times, of the tools three times, of the services of the wholesaler twice, and of the services of the retail shop once.

Estimating final output by adding the sales of all firms involves an error called **double counting**. (Multiple counting would be a better term, since if we add up the values of all sales, the same output is counted every time it is sold from one firm to another.) This error is avoided by using the important concept of *value added.*[4]

[4] Note that only value added creates income, so the double-counting error is *automatically* avoided in the income approach.

BOX 27-1 VALUE ADDED THROUGH STAGES OF PRODUCTION

Because the output of one firm often becomes the input of other firms, the total value of goods sold by all firms greatly exceeds the value of the output of final goods. This general principle is illustrated by a simple example in which firm R starts from scratch and produces goods (raw materials) valued at $100; the firm's value added is $100. Firm I purchases raw materials valued at $100 and produces semi-manufactured goods that it sells for $130. Its value added is $30 because the value of the goods is increased by

$30 as a result of the firm's activities. Firm F purchases the semi-manufactured goods for $130, works them into a finished state, and sells them for $180. Firm F's value added is $50. The value of the final goods, $180, is found either by counting only the sales of firm F or by taking the sum of the values added by each firm. This value is much smaller than the $410 that we would obtain if we merely added up the market value of the commodities sold by each firm.

	Transactions between firms at three different stages of production				
	Firm R	Firm I	Firm F	All Firms	
A. Purchases from other firms	$ 0	$100	$130	$230	Total interfirm sales
B. Purchases of factors of production (wages, rent, interest, profits)	100	30	50	180	Value added
Total A + B = value of product	$100	$130	$180	$410	Total value of all sales

Each firm's value added is the value of its output minus the value of the inputs that it purchases from other firms. Thus a steel mill's value added is the value of its output minus the value of the ore it buys from the mining company and the values of all other inputs, such as electricity and fuel oil, that it buys from other firms. The concept of value added is further illustrated in Box 27-1.

Gross Domestic Product

Table 27-1 shows the composition of Canadian GDP by industry for 1983. It also shows the reconciliation of GDP with GNP. That reconciliation involves two stages. One is the conversion from factor costs for GDP to market prices for GNP. The second arises from the distinction between output *located* in Canada and output *owned* by Canadians.

GDP measures the output *located* in Canada. GNP (and GNE) measure output *owned* by Cana-

dians; that is, income accruing to Canadians. This distinction arises for two reasons. First, some factors of production located in Canada may be owned by foreigners, and hence the income owned by those factors does not go to Canadians. Second, some Canadians may own factors of production located in other countries, and hence earn income not included in GDP but included in GNP. As Table 27-1 shows, the payment of factor income to foreigners typically exceeds Canadian receipts of factor income received from abroad.

Other Income Concepts

GNP, GNE, and GDP are the most comprehensive income concepts. The next most comprehensive measure is net national product. As we saw in building up the income approaches, this is GNP minus the capital consumption allowance. NNP is

TABLE 27–1 GROSS DOMESTIC PRODUCT, 1983

	Billions of dollars	Percent of GDP
Value-added by sector:		
Agriculture	$ 13.2	3.7
Mines, quarries, and oil wells	9.5	2.6
Manufacturing	73.8	20.5
Construction	19.6	5.5
Electric power, gas, and water utilities	12.6	3.5
Transportation, storage, and communication	38.4	10.7
Retail and wholesale trade	44.0	12.2
Financial, insurance, and real estate	49.4	13.7
Community, business, and personal services	73.0	20.3
Public administration and defense	26.0	7.3
	$359.5	100
GDP (at factor cost):		
Add: Indirect taxes less subsidies	42.4	
Add: Investment income received from nonresidents	4.9	
Subtract: Investment income paid to nonresidents	− 17.6	
Residual error of estimate:	− 0.5	
GNP (at market prices):	$388.7	

Source: Statistics Canada 11-003E; 13-001.

GDP at factor cost measures total output produced *in* Canada by summing the value added of each industry. GDP at market prices includes net indirect taxes and net foreign income. As can be seen, manufacturing and community, business, and personal services are the major contributors to GDP, contributing 20.5 and 20.3 percent respectively. To reconcile GDP with the national income accounts, two adjustments are necessary. First, to convert from factor cost to market prices, we have to add indirect taxes net of subsidies. Second, to convert output *produced* in Canada to output *owned* by Canadians (and income earned by Canadians), we need to add investment income received from nonresidents and subtract investment income paid to nonresidents. Since Canada is a net debtor due to its history of being a recipient of foreign investment, the subtraction for income paid to nonresidents is typically much larger than the addition for income received from nonresidents.

thus a measure of the net output of the economy after deducting from gross output an amount necessary to maintain intact the existing stock of capital. It is the maximum amount that could be consumed without actually running down the economy's capital stock.

Personal income is income earned by or paid to individuals before allowance for personal income taxes. Some personal income goes for taxes, some for saving, and the rest for consumption. A number of adjustments to NNP are required to arrive at personal income. The most important are: (1) subtracting from NNP indirect taxes net of subsidies which are that part of the market value of output that goes directly to governments (this, as we have seen, gives net national income at factor cost), (2) subtracting from NNP the business earnings retained by corporations, (3) subtracting from NNP the income taxes paid by business, and (4) adding to NNP the transfer payments to households. The first three represent parts of the value of output not paid to households; the fourth represents payments to households and thus income that households have available to spend or to save even though these payments are not part of GNP.

Disposable income is a measure of the amount of current income that households have to spend and to save. It is calculated as personal income minus personal income taxes.

Disposable income is GNP *minus* any part of it that is not actually paid over to households, *minus* the personal income taxes paid by households, *plus* transfer payments received by households.

The relations among GNP, NNP, personal income, and disposable income are elaborated in Table 27-2.

INTERPRETING NATIONAL INCOME MEASURES

The information provided by measures of national income is useful, but unless carefully interpreted it can also be misleading. Furthermore, specialized measures such as GNP(GNE), NNP, personal income, and disposable income each give different information. Thus each may be the best statistic for studying a particular range of problems.

Money Values and Real Values

We saw in Chapter 26 that national income can be valued in current or constant dollars. When valued in current dollars, it tells us nominal income. When valued in constant dollars, it tells us real income. When studying the effect of inflation on the value of income, we need to look at nominal income. When studying changes in the economy's quantity of output, we need to look at real income.[5]

[5] In calculating real national income, it is the expenditure approach that is used. Price indexes are calculated for the various classifications of goods so that each category of expenditure can be measured in current dollars or in constant dollars. The first series can be added up to yield nominal GNE, the second to yield real GNE. The ratio of nominal to real GNE, in a manner exactly the same as that shown in panel (iv) of Table 26-2, defines the implicit GNE deflator. (We can now see that Table 26-2 illustrates the calculation of real and nominal national income using the output approach.)

TABLE 27-2 VARIOUS NATIONAL INCOME MEASURES, 1983 (Billions of Dollars)

A.	GNP (at market prices)	$389.2
	Less: Depreciation	− 47.0
B.	NNP (at market prices)	342.2
	Less: Indirect taxes net of subsidies	− 42.4
C.	NNI at factor cost	299.8
	Less: Retained earnings	− 13.0
	Business taxes	− 11.4
	Plus: Government transfer payments to households	59.3
D.	Personal income	334.7
	Less: Personal income taxes	− 66.3
E.	Disposable income	268.4

Source: Statistics Canada 13-001.

Each of the five related national income measures focuses on a different aspect of the national output. GNP measures the market value of total output. NNP measures the net value of output after an allowance for maintaining the capital stock. NNI at factor cost converts market price values to factor costs by adjusting for government indirect taxes net of subsidies. Personal income measures income earned or received by persons before personal income taxes. Disposable income is a measure of after-tax income of persons; it is the amount they have available to spend or to save.

Total Output and Per Capita Output

The rise in real GNP during this century has had two main causes: first, an increase in the amounts of land, labor, and capital used in production; second, an increase in output per unit of input. In other words, more inputs have been used, and each input has become more productive. For many purposes, we want to measure total output—for example, to assess a country's potential military strength or to know the total size of its market. For other purposes, such as studying changes in living standards, we require per capita measures, which are obtained by dividing a total measure such as GNP by the relevant population.

There are many useful per capita measures. GNP divided by the total population gives a measure of how much GNP there is on average for each person in the economy; this is called **per capita GNP**. GNP divided by the number of persons employed tells us the average output per employed worker. GNP divided by the total number of hours worked measures output per hour of labor input. A widely used measure of the purchasing power of the average person is disposable income per capita, in constant dollars. This measure is shown in Figure 27-2.

Omissions from Measured National Income

Finally, we come to a series of omissions from the GNP, and thus also from the NNP, disposable income, and other measures based mainly on parts of the GNP. The importance of these omissions can be judged only when we know the purpose for

which the data are to be used. Box 27-2 takes up some other seemingly arbitrary aspects of national income accounting.

Illegal Activities

The GNP does not measure illegal activities, even though many of them are ordinary business activities that produce goods and services sold on the market and that generate factor incomes. The American liquor industry during American Prohibition (1919–1933) was an important example because it accounted for a significant part of the nation's total economic activity. Today the same is true of many forms of illegal gambling, prostitution, and illicit drug trade. To gain an accurate measure of the *total* demand for factors of production in the economy or of *total* marketable output—whether or not we as individuals approve of particular products—we should include these activities. Because such activities are illicit, however, it would be hard to find out enough to include them.[6]

The omission of illegal activities is no trivial matter. The drug trade alone is a multibillion-dollar business. No one knows the exact value of its output, but a typical estimate runs around 30 billion for 1981 in Canada. This was 8 percent of the entire Canadian GNP for that year.

Unreported Activities

An important omission from the measured GNP is the so-called *underground economy*. The transactions in the underground economy are perfectly legal in themselves. The only illegal thing about them is that they are not reported for income tax purposes. For example, an unemployed carpenter repairs a leak in your roof and takes payment in cash or in kind in order to avoid tax. Because such transactions go unreported, they are unrecorded in the country's GNP.

Reasons for the growth of the underground

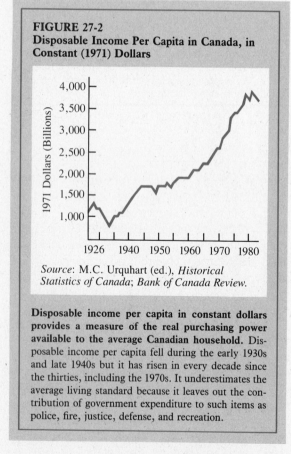

FIGURE 27-2
Disposable Income Per Capita in Canada, in Constant (1971) Dollars

Source: M.C. Urquhart (ed.), *Historical Statistics of Canada*; *Bank of Canada Review*.

Disposable income per capita in constant dollars provides a measure of the real purchasing power available to the average Canadian household. Disposable income per capita fell during the early 1930s and late 1940s but it has risen in every decade since the thirties, including the 1970s. It underestimates the average living standard because it leaves out the contribution of government expenditure to such items as police, fire, justice, defense, and recreation.

---

[6] Some of them do get included because people often report their earnings from illicit activities as part of their earnings from legal activities in order to avoid the fate of Al Capone. He, having avoided conviction on many counts, was finally caught for income tax evasion.

economy are many. Probably the most important is to evade income taxes. But it also allows the evasion of a host of other taxes and regulations. Sales and excise taxes are not paid in the underground economy. Safety regulations, minimum wage laws, and antidiscrimination regulations, and social security payments may all be avoided as well. Generally the higher are tax rates and the greater are the restrictions arising from rules and regulations, the greater the incentive to evade them all by "going underground." The growth of this economy is facilitated by the rising importance of services in the nation's total output. It is much easier for a carpenter or TV repairman to pass unnoticed by government authorities than it is for a manufacturing establishment, which is hard to hide.

Estimates of the value of income earned in the Canadian underground economy run from 2 to 15 percent of Canadian GNP. Since these are ordinary market activities, their omission is an important source of error in published GNP figures. In other countries the figures are much higher. The Italian underground economy, for example, has been estimated at close to 25 percent of that country's total GNP.

Clearly, the omission of unreported activities matters. This causes the actual amount of legal income and employment-creating market transactions to be underestimated. Indeed, increases in the proportion of GNP that go unreported may be one reason why GNP data for the last decade have underreported the actual growth in output and hence living standards. If, for example, *actual* GNP grows by 2 percent but an additional 1 percent goes unrecorded, *measured* GNP will only grow by 1 percent.

Nonmarketed Economic Activities

When a bank teller hires a carpenter to build a bookshelf, the value of the bookshelf enters into the GNP; if the teller or his wife builds the bookshelf, the value of the bookshelf is omitted from the GNP. Such omissions also include, for example, the services of housewives, any do-it-yourself activity, and voluntary work such as canvassing for a

political party, helping to run a volunteer day-care center, or leading a Boy Scout troop.

Does the omission of nonmarketed economic activities matter? It all depends. If we wish to measure the flow of goods and services through the market sector of the economy, or to account for changes in the opportunities for employment for those households who sell their labor services in the market, most of these omissions are justifiable. If, however, we wish to measure the overall flow of goods and services available to satisfy people's wants, whatever the source of the goods and services, then the omissions are undesirable and potentially serious.

In most advanced industrial economies, the nonmarket sector is relatively small. It can be ignored even if GNP is used for purposes for which it would be appropriate to include nonmarketed goods and services. The omissions become serious, however, when GNP or disposable income figures are used to compare living standards in very different economies. Generally, the nonmarket sector of the economy is larger in rural than in urban settings and in less developed than in more developed economies.

Be a little cautious, then, in interpreting data from a country with a very different climate and culture. When you hear that the per capita GNP of Nigeria is $850 per year, you should not imagine living in Toronto on that income.

Uncounted Factors Affecting Human Welfare

Many factors that contribute to human welfare are not included in the GNP. Leisure is one. In fact, although a shorter work week may make people happier, it will tend to reduce measured GNP.

GNP does not allow for the capacity of different goods to provide different satisfactions. A million dollars spent on a bomber or a missile makes the same addition to GNP as a million dollars spent on a school, a stadium, or candy bars—expenditures that may produce very different amounts of consumer satisfaction.

GNP does not measure the quality of life. To the extent that material output is purchased at the

BOX 27–2 THE SIGNIFICANCE OF ARBITRARY DECISIONS

National income accounting uses many arbitrary decisions. Goods that are finished and held in inventories are valued at market value, thereby anticipating their sale even though the actual sales price may not be known. In the case of a Ford in a dealer's showroom, this practice may be justified because the *value* of this Ford is perhaps virtually the same as that of an identical Ford that has just been sold to a customer. But what is the correct market value of a half-finished house or an unfinished novel? Accountants arbitrarily treat goods in process at cost (rather than at market value) if the goods are being made by business firms; they ignore completely the value of the novel in progress. While these decisions are arbitrary, so would any others be.

Clearly, practical people must arrive at some compromise between consistent definitions and measurable magnitudes. The imputation of a market value to an owner-occupied house, but not to the services of the housewife who occupies and often owns the house, probably is justified only by such a compromise.

The definition of final goods provides further examples. Business investment expenditures are treated as final products, as are all government purchases. Intermediate goods purchased by business for further processing are not treated as final products. Thus, when a firm buys a machine or a truck, the purchase is treated as a final good; when it buys a ton of steel, however, the steel is treated not as a final product but as a raw material that will be used as an input into the firm's production process. (But if the steel sits in an inventory, it is regarded as a business investment and thus *is* a final good.)

Such arbitrary decisions surely affect the size of measured GNP. Does it matter? The surprising answer, for many purposes, is no. In any case, it is wrong to believe that just because a statistical measure falls short of perfection (as all statistical measures do), it is useless. Very crude measures will often give estimates to the right order of magnitude, whereas substantial improvements in sophistication may make only second-order improvements in these estimates.

expense of overcrowded cities and highways, polluted environments, defaced countrysides, maimed accident victims, longer waits for public services, and a more complex life that entails a frenetic struggle to be happy, GNP measures only part of the things that contribute to human well-being.

Which Measure Is Best?

There are several distinct income measures. To ask which is *the* best income measure is something like asking which is *the* best carpenter's tool. The answer is that it all depends on the job to be done.

The use of several measures of national income rather than one is common because different measures provide answers to different questions. GNP

tells us the market value of goods and services produced for final demand. NNP tells us how much the economy's production exceeded the amount necessary to replace capital equipment used up. Disposable income tells us how much income consumers have to allocate between spending and saving. In addition, real (constant dollar) measures eliminate purely monetary changes and allow comparisons of purchasing power over time; per capita measures shift the focus from the nation to the average person.

Which measure is used will depend on the problem at hand. For example, if we wish to predict households' consumption behavior, disposable income is what we need. If we wish to account for changes in employment, constant-dollar GNP is wanted. For yet other purposes, such as providing

In the third century B.C., for example, the Alexandrian astronomer Eratosthenes measured the angle of the sun at Alexandria at the moment it was directly overhead 500 miles south at Aswan, and he used this angle to calculate the circumference of the earth to within 15 percent of the distance as measured today by the most advanced measuring devices. For the knowledge he wanted—the approximate size of the earth—his measurement was decisive. To launch a modern earth satellite, it would have been disastrously inadequate.

Absolute figures mean something in general terms, although they cannot be taken seriously to the last dollar. In 1983 GNP was measured as $388.7 billion. It is certain that the market value of all production in Canada in that year was not $50 billion, nor was it $10,000 billion. It was not $800 billion, but it might well have been $350 billion or $400 billion had different measures been defined with different arbitrary decisions built in.

International and intertemporal comparisons, though tricky, may be meaningful when they are based on measures all of which contain roughly the same arbitrary decisions. Canadian per capita GNP is roughly 3 times the Spanish and 35 percent higher than the Japanese. Other measures might differ, but it is unlikely that any measure would reveal that either the Spanish or the Japanese per capita income was higher than Canada's. But the statistics also show that GNP per capita was 4 percent higher in Switzerland than in Sweden, a difference too small to have much meaning. Canadian output grow at 4.9 percent per year for the 30 years following World War II; it is unlikely that another measure of output would have indicated a 6 percent increase. Further, the Japanese output grew at about 9 percent per year over the same period. It is highly improbable that another measure would change the conclusion that Japanese national output rose faster than Canadian national output in recent decades.

an overall measure of economic welfare, we may need to supplement or modify conventional measures of national income.[7]

Even if we do use some of these modified measures for some purposes, we are unlikely to discard GNP (and its offspring) entirely in favor of such a measure. Economists and politicians who are interested in the ebb and flow of economic activity that passes through the market, and in the rise and fall in employment opportunities for factors of production whose services are sold on the market, will continue to use GNP as the measure that comes closest to telling them what they need to know.

[7] Concepts that come closer to measuring economic welfare than GNP have been developed. One was worked out by Professors William Nordhaus and James Tobin. It tries to measure consumption of things that provide utility to households rather than total production; it gives value to such nonmarketed activities as leisure and makes subtractions for such "disutilities" as pollution and congestion.

SUMMARY

1. Gross national expenditure is the total market value of final goods and services produced in the economy during a year. Gross national product is the total of all income claims generated over the same period of time. By virtue of standard accounting conventions, gross national product and gross national expenditure have the same value.

2. Using the expenditure approach, GNE = **AE** = **C** + **I** + **G** + (**X** − **M**). **C** represents con-

sumption expenditures of households. **I** represents investment in plant and equipment, residential construction, and inventory accumulation. Gross investment can be split into replacement investment (necessary to keep the stock of capital intact) and net investment (net additions to the stock of capital). **G** represents government expenditures except transfer payments. $(X - M)$ represents the excess of exports over imports; it will be negative if imports exceed exports.

3. The income payments approach divides total GNP according to who has a claim to the value arising from the production and sale of commodities. Wages, interest, rents, profits, depreciation (called capital consumption allowance), and indirect taxes less subsidies are the major categories.

4. Gross domestic product (GDP) measures (at factor cost) production located in Canada, while GNP measures (at market prices) income received by Canadians. The difference is due to income from net foreign investment and to indirect taxes less subsidies.

5. Several related but different income measures are used in addition to the GNP. Net national product (NNP) measures total output after deducting the capital consumption allowance. Personal income is income actually received by households before any allowance for personal taxes. Disposable income gives the amount that is actually available to households to spend or to save.

6. GNP and related measures of national income must be interpreted with regard for their limitations. GNP excludes production resulting from activities that are illegal, take place in the underground economy, or do not pass through markets (such as what is produced by do-it-yourself activities). Moreover, GNP does not measure everything that contributes to human welfare.

7. Notwithstanding its limitations, GNP remains the best measure available for estimating the total economic activity that passes through the markets or our economy and for accounting for changes in the employment opportunities that face households who sell their labor services on the open market.

TOPICS FOR REVIEW

Final goods, intermediate goods, and value added

Expenditure and income approaches to measuring a nation's output

The equality of national product and national expenditure

$GNE = AE = C + I + G + (X - M)$

Components of GNP

Gross domestic product (GDP)

Net national income (NNP), personal income, and disposable income

DISCUSSION QUESTIONS

1. If Canada and the United States were to join together as a single country, what would be the effect on their total GNP (assuming that output in each country is unaffected)? Would any of the components in their GNPs change significantly?

2. "Every time you rent a U-haul, brick in a patio, grow a vegetable, fix your own car, photocopy an article, join a food co-op, develop your own film, sew a dress, stew fruit, or raise a child, you are committing a productive act, even though it is not reflected in the gross national product." To what extent are each of these things "productive acts"? Are any of them included in GNP? Where they are excluded, does the exclusion matter?

3. In measuring Canadian GNE, which of the following expenditures should be included and under what category?
   a. Expenditures on automobiles by consumers and by firms
   b. Expenditures on Canadian flour by households, by bakers, and by Italian firms
   c. Expenditures on food and lodging by tourists and by business people on expense accounts
   d. Expenditures on new machinery and equipment by Canadian firms
   e. The purchase of one corporation by another corporation
   f. Increases in business inventories

4. What would be the effect on the measured value of Canada's real GNP of (a) the destruction of a thousand homes by flood water; (b) passage of legislation making abortion on demand legal; (c) a complete cessation of all imports from South Africa; and (d) the outbreak of a new Arab-Israeli war in which Canadian troops became heavily involved. Speculate on the effects of each of these events on the true well-being of the Canadian people.

5. In the United States a Social Security Administration study, using 1972 data, found the "average American house-wife's value" to be $4,705. It arrived at this total by adding up the hours she spent cooking, multiplied by a cook's wage, the hours spent with her children, multiplied by a babysitter's wage, and so on. Should the time a parent spends taking children to a concert be included? Are the dollar amounts assigned to such activities a satisfactory proxy for market value of production? For what, if any, purposes would such values be excluded from, or included in, national income?

6. Use the endpaper at the back of this book to calculate the percentage increase over the most recent two decades of each of the following magnitudes; (a) GNP in current dollars; (b) GNP in constant dollars; (c) disposable income in constant dollars; and (d) disposable income per capita in constant dollars. Can you account for the relative sizes of these changes?

7. Consider the effect on measured GNP and on economic well-being of each of the following:

  a. A reduction in the standard work week from 40 hours to 30 hours

  b. The hiring of all welfare recipients as government employees

  c. Further increases in oil prices that lead to a general inflation

  d. An increase in the salaries of priests and ministers as a result of the increased contributions of churchgoers

8. Explain how a rise in labour productivity might lead to a fall in measured GNP, whereas a rise in criminal activity might lead to a rise in measured GNP.

9. "Primitive Bartering Practices Flourishing in World Recession." Why would you expect the practice of barter to increase during a recession, as the headline suggests? What does an increase imply about measured GNP and society's welfare?

10. A recent newspaper article reported that Switzerland was considered to be the "best" place in the world to live. In view of the fact that Switzerland does not have the highest per capital income in the world, how can it be ranked the "best"?

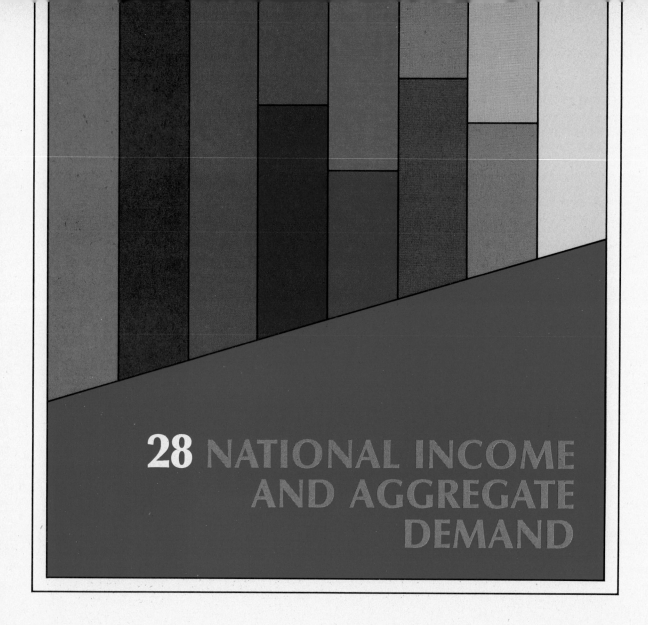

28 NATIONAL INCOME AND AGGREGATE DEMAND

In Chapter 26 we gave an overview of aggregate demand and aggregate supply. We now begin our study of how these forces influence output and prices.

THE KEYNESIAN *SRAS* CURVE

For the next two chapters we are going to concentrate on the influence of aggregate demand. Ulti-

mately, we want to know what causes national income and the price level to change at the same time. But because it is easier to deal with things one at a time, we will first look at the forces that determine national income, and hence determine employment and unemployment, when the price level is treated as constant. Then in Chapters 29 and 30 we will see what happens when the price level also varies.

In this chapter we consider an economy whose

national income is varying over the range below potential income. Furthermore, we use an extreme version of the *SRAS* curve over that range. This curve is called the **Keynesian short-run aggregate supply curve** after the English economist John Maynard Keynes, who pioneered the study of the behavior of economies under conditions of heavy unemployment.

The behavior that gives rise to the Keynesian *SRAS* curve can be described as follows. When real national income is below potential national income, individual firms are operating at less than normal capacity output. Firms respond to cyclical declines in demand by holding their prices constant at the level that would be most profitable if production were at normal capacity. They then respond to demand variations by altering output. In other words, they will supply whatever they can sell at their existing prices as long as they are producing below their normal capacity. This means that the firms have horizontal supply curves and that their output is *demand determined*.

Under these circumstances, the whole economy has a horizontal aggregate supply curve, indicating that any output up to potential output will be supplied at the going price level. The amount that is actually produced is then determined by the position of the aggregate demand curve. Thus we say that real national income is *demand determined*.[1]

If demand rises enough so that firms are trying to squeeze more than normal output out of their plants, their costs will rise and so will their prices. Thus the horizontal Keynesian *SRAS* curve only applies to national incomes below potential income.

Figure 28-1 shows such a Keynesian *SRAS* curve. The curve is horizontal at the current price level of P_0. Under these circumstances, income is determined by the position of the aggregate demand curve. Shifts in *AD* will cause equilibrium income to change.

[1] The evidence is very strong that firms, particularly in the manufacturing sector, do behave like this in the short run. One possible explanation is that changing prices frequently is too costly, so firms set the best possible (profit-maximizing) prices when output is at normal capacity and then do not change prices in the face of normal cyclical fluctuations in demand. This is discussed further in Chapter 14.

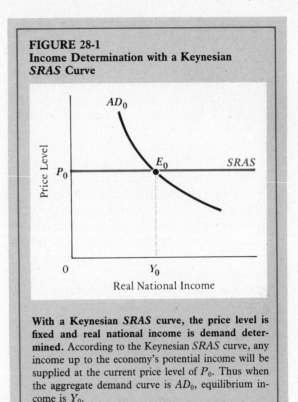

FIGURE 28-1
Income Determination with a Keynesian *SRAS* Curve

With a Keynesian *SRAS* curve, the price level is fixed and real national income is demand determined. According to the Keynesian *SRAS* curve, any income up to the economy's potential income will be supplied at the current price level of P_0. Thus when the aggregate demand curve is AD_0, equilibrium income is Y_0.

With a Keynesian *SRAS* curve the questions of why national income is what it is, and why it changes, boil down to the questions of why aggregate demand is where it is and why it shifts.

In order to see how aggregate demand determines national income on the Keynesian *SRAS* curve, we first need to see why a particular price level is associated with one *equilibrium* level of national income rather than with some other level. Why, for example, is the price level P_0 in Figure 28-1 associated with the equilibrium level of income of Y_0? In other words, why is the *AD* curve where it is rather than somewhere else?

To begin to answer this question we must first look at expenditure and distinguish between desired and actual expenditure.

DESIRED EXPENDITURE

In the last chapter we discussed how national income statisticians measure actual aggregate expenditure, **AE,** and its components: consumption, **C;** investment, **I;** government, **G;** and net exports, **(X − M).**

In this chapter, we are concerned with a different concept. It is variously called *desired, planned,* or *intended expenditure.* Of course, everybody would like to spend virtually unlimited amounts if only they had the money. Desired expenditure does not refer, however, to what people would like to do under imaginary circumstances. It refers instead to what everybody, given the resources at their command, wants to spend.

Everyone with money to spend makes expenditure decisions. Fortunately it is unnecessary for our purpose to look at each of the millions of such individual decisions. Instead it is sufficient to place decision makers in four main groups: domestic households, firms, governments, and foreign purchasers of domestically produced products. Their actual purchases account for the four main categories of expenditure studied in the previous chapter: consumption, investment, government expenditure, and exports.

Their desired purchases can also be divided in the same fashion: desired consumption, desired investment, desired government expenditure, and desired exports. Allowing for the fact that some of the commodities desired by each group will have an import content, we subtract import expenditure to obtain total desired expenditure on domestically produced goods and services:

$$AE = C + I + G + (X − M)$$

Earlier we indicated *actual* aggregate expenditure and its components by the boldface letters **AE, C, I, G,** and **(X − M).** Now we use lightface letters to indicate *desired* amounts of expenditure in the same categories.

Desired expenditure need not equal actual expenditure, either totally or in each individual category. For example, firms may not plan to invest in inventory accumulation this year but may unintentionally do so. If they produce goods to meet estimated sales but demand is unexpectedly low, the unsold goods that pile up on their shelves will represent undesired, and unintended, inventory accumulation. In this case actual investment expenditure, **I,** will exceed desired investment expenditure, I.

National income accounts measure *actual expenditures* in each of the four categories: consumption, investment, government purchases, and net exports. National income theory deals with *desired expenditures* in each of these four categories.

To develop a theory of national income, we need to know what determines each of the components of desired aggregate expenditure. We begin by focusing primarily on C, desired consumption expenditure, which is the largest single component of actual aggregate expenditure. Later we shall look in more detail at the determinants of desired I, G, and (X − M).

Desired Consumption Expenditure

Households can do one of two things with their disposable income: they can spend it on consumption or they can save it. **Saving** is defined as all income that is not consumed. It follows that households have to make a single decision: how to split their disposable income between consumption and saving.

What determines the amount that households decide to spend on goods and services for consumption and the amount they decide to save? These decisions are summarized in the consumption function and its counterpart, the saving function.

The Consumption Function

The **consumption function** relates the total desired consumption expenditure of all households in the economy to the factors that determine it. It is, as we shall see, one of the central relations in macroeconomics.

Consumption As a Function Of Disposable Income

One important influence on desired consumption expenditure is household disposable income, represented by Y_d. As disposable income rises, households have more money to spend on consumption—and the evidence is that they do just that. We therefore treat desired consumption expenditure as varying positively with disposable income.

Other forces such as interest rates and inflationary expectations also exert an influence, but we shall neglect them for the moment. The simple theory of consumption focuses on changes in disposable income to explain changes in consumption. We will reserve the term *consumption function* for describing the relationship between consumption and income.

Some consumption expenditure does not depend on national income—this we call the *autonomous* component. The bulk of consumption expenditure, however, varies with national income—this we call

the *induced* component. As an example, a schedule relating disposable income to desired consumption expenditure for a hypothetical economy appears in the first two columns of Table 28-1. In this example autonomous consumption expenditure is $100 billion, whereas induced expenditure is 80 percent of disposable income. In what follows we use this hypothetical data to illustrate the various properties of the consumption function.

Average and marginal propensities to consume. To discuss the consumption function concisely, economists use two technical expressions.

The **average propensity to consume (APC)** is total consumption expenditure divided by total disposable income. The third column of Table 28-1 shows the APCs calculated from the data in the table.

The **marginal propensity to consume (MPC)** relates the *change* in consumption to the *change* in disposable income that brought it about. MPC is the change in disposable income divided into the resulting consumption change: $MPC = \Delta C/\Delta Y_d$

TABLE 28-1 THE CALCULATION OF THE AVERAGE PROPENSITY TO CONSUME (APC) AND THE MARGINAL PROPENSITY TO CONSUME (MPC) (Billions of Dollars)

Disposable income (Y_d)	Desired consumption (C)	$APC = C/Y_d$	ΔY_d (Change in Y_d)	ΔC (Change in C)	$MPC = \Delta C/\Delta Y_d$
$ —	$ 100	—			
100	180	1.800	100	$ 80	0.80
400	420	1.050	300	240	0.80
500	500	1.000	100	80	0.80
1,000	900	0.900	500	400	0.80
2,000	1,700	0.850	1,000	800	0.80
3,000	2,500	0.833	1,000	800	0.80
4,000	3,300	0.825	1,000	800	0.80

The APC measures the proportion of disposable income that households desire to spend on consumption; the MPC measures the proportion of any *increment* to disposable income that households desire to spend on consumption. The data are hypothetical. The APC calculated in the third column exceeds unity below the break-even level of income because consumption exceeds income. Above the break-even level the APC is less than unity and declines steadily as income rises.

The last three columns are set between the lines of the first three columns to indicate that they refer to changes in the levels of income and consumption. In this example, the MPC calculated in the last column is constant at 0.8 at all levels of Y_d. This indicates that in this illustration $.80 of *every* additional $1 of disposable income is spent on consumption and $.20 is used to increase saving (or decrease dissaving).

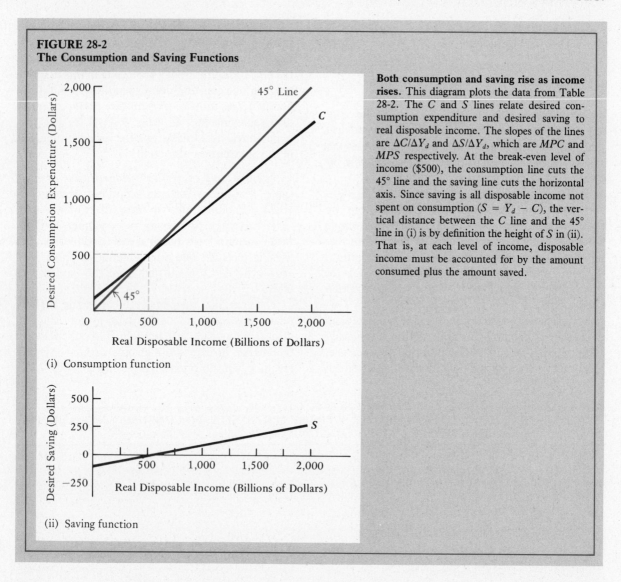

FIGURE 28-2
The Consumption and Saving Functions

(i) Consumption function

(ii) Saving function

Both consumption and saving rise as income rises. This diagram plots the data from Table 28-2. The C and S lines relate desired consumption expenditure and desired saving to real disposable income. The slopes of the lines are $\Delta C/\Delta Y_d$ and $\Delta S/\Delta Y_d$, which are MPC and MPS respectively. At the break-even level of income ($500), the consumption line cuts the 45° line and the saving line cuts the horizontal axis. Since saving is all disposable income not spent on consumption ($S = Y_d - C$), the vertical distance between the C line and the 45° line in (i) is by definition the height of S in (ii). That is, at each level of income, disposable income must be accounted for by the amount consumed plus the amount saved.

(where the Greek letter Δ, delta, means "a change in"). The last column of Table 28-1 shows the MPC calculated from the data in the table. [34]

The slope of the consumption function. Figure 28-2(i) shows a graph of the consumption function plotted from the first two columns of Table 28-1. The figure makes it clear that the consumption function has a slope of $\Delta C/\Delta Y_d$ which is, by definition, the marginal propensity to consume. The

upward slope of the consumption function shows that MPC is positive; increases in income lead to increases in expenditure.

Using the concepts of the average and marginal propensities to consume, we can summarize the properties of the short-term consumption function:

1. There is a break-even level of income at which $APC = 1$. Below this level APC is greater than unity; above it APC is less than unity.

2. *MPC* is greater than zero but less than unity for all levels of income.

The 45° Line

Figure 28-2(i) also contains a second line that will prove useful. It is constructed by connecting all points where desired consumption (measured on the vertical axis) equals disposable income (measured on the horizontal axis). Since both axes are given in the same units, this line has an upward slope of unity, or (what is the same thing) it forms an angle of 45° with both axes. The line is therefore called the **45° line.**

The 45° line makes a handy reference line. In Figure 28-2(i) it helps locate the break-even level of income at which consumption expenditure equals disposable income. Graphically, the consumption function cuts the 45° line at the break-even level of income, in this instance $500. (It is steeper than the consumption function because *MPC* is less than unity.)

The Saving Function

Households decide how much to consume and how much to save. As we have said, this is a single decision: how to divide disposable income between consumption and saving. It follows that, once we know the dependence of consumption on disposable income, we also automatically know the dependence of saving on disposable income. (This is illustrated in Table 28-2.)

Two saving concepts are exactly parallel to the consumption concepts of *APC* and *MPC*. The **average propensity to save (APS)** is the proportion of disposable income that households want to save. *APS* is figured by dividing total desired saving by total disposable income: $APS = S/Y_d$. The **marginal propensity to save (MPS)** relates the *change* in total desired saving to the *change* in disposable income that brought it about: $MPS = \Delta S/\Delta Y_d$.

There is a simple relation between the saving and the consumption propensities. *APC* and *APS* must sum to unity and so must *MPC* and *MPS*. Since income is either spent or saved, it follows

TABLE 28–2 **CONSUMPTION AND SAVING SCHEDULES (Billions of Dollars)**

Disposable income	Desired consumption expenditure	Desired saving
$ 0	$ 100	− $100
100	180	− 80
400	420	− 20
500	500	− 0
1,000	900	+ 100
2,000	1,700	+ 300
3,000	2,500	+ 500
4,000	3,300	+ 700

Saving and consumption account for all household disposable income. The first two columns repeat the data from Table 28-1. The third column is disposable income minus desired consumption. The three columns thus show desired consumption and desired saving at each level of income. Consumption and saving each increase steadily as disposable income rises. In this example, the break-even level of disposable income is $500 million.

both that the fractions of incomes consumed and saved must account for all income (*APC* + *APS* = 1) and that the fraction of any increment to income consumed and saved must account for all of that increment (*MPC* + *MPS* = 1). [35]

Calculations from Table 28-2 will allow you to confirm these relations in the case of the example given. *MPC* is 0.8 and *MPS* is 0.2 at all levels of income while, for example, at income of $2,000 *APC* is 0.85 while *APS* is 0.15.

Figure 28-2(ii) shows the saving schedule given in Table 28-2. At the break-even level of income where desired consumption equals disposable income, desired saving is zero. The slope of the saving line $\Delta S/\Delta Y_d$ is *MPS*.

Wealth and Consumption

We have seen that disposable income is an important factor influencing the consumption-saving decision. A second important factor is the level of each household's wealth. By a household's **wealth** we mean the sum of all the valuable assets it owns. This will include its car, its house and contents, its money in the bank, the value of its pension fund, and any stocks, bonds, or other investments that it holds.

Households save in order to add to their wealth. Thus, other things being equal, a rise in wealth tends to reduce the incentive to add further to wealth; that is, it reduces the incentive to save.

Hence a rise in wealth will cause a larger fraction of disposable income to be spent on consumption and a smaller fraction to be saved. This shifts the consumption function upward, and the saving function downward, as shown in Figure 28-3. A fall in wealth increases the incentives to save in order to restore wealth. This shifts the consumption function downward, and the saving function upward, as also shown in Figure 28-3.

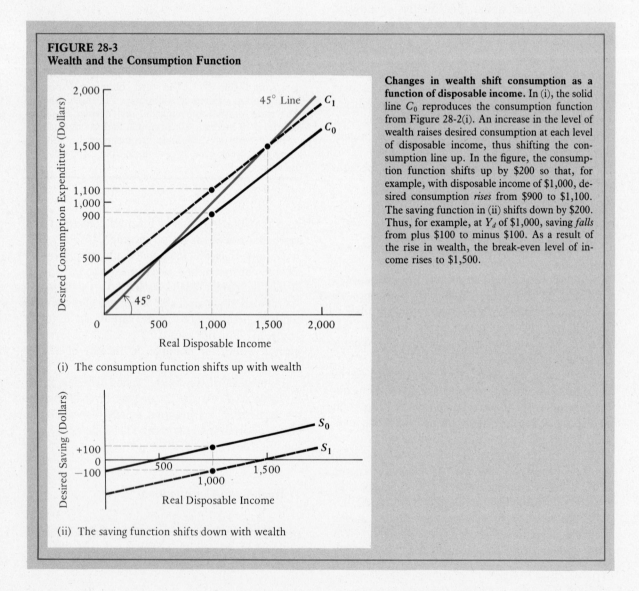

FIGURE 28-3
Wealth and the Consumption Function

(i) The consumption function shifts up with wealth

(ii) The saving function shifts down with wealth

Changes in wealth shift consumption as a function of disposable income. In (i), the solid line C_0 reproduces the consumption function from Figure 28-2(i). An increase in the level of wealth raises desired consumption at each level of disposable income, thus shifting the consumption line up. In the figure, the consumption function shifts up by $200 so that, for example, with disposable income of $1,000, desired consumption *rises* from $900 to $1,100. The saving function in (ii) shifts down by $200. Thus, for example, at Y_d of $1,000, saving *falls* from plus $100 to minus $100. As a result of the rise in wealth, the break-even level of income rises to $1,500.

Individual households experience both expected and unexpected changes in wealth. For example, either planned saving or unplanned bequests will increase wealth. Similarly, either planned dissaving or unplanned losses reduce wealth.

Many unexpected changes in wealth cancel out across households and so are unimportant for the macro consumption function. We will see, however, that inflation can be an important source of unexpected changes in wealth that are common to most households.

Planned increases in wealth as a result of past accumulation in wealth can be important for the whole society and can lead to upward shifts in the macro consumption function as wealth accumulates. This effect operates only slowly since wealth accumulates only slowly. In order to focus on short-term issues, the consumption function used in the text does not include the effects of changes in wealth.

National Income and Consumption

We have seen that desired consumption is related to *disposable* income. For a theory of the determination of national income, however, we need to know how consumption is related to *national income*.

The transition from a relation between *consumption and disposable income* to one between *consumption and national income* is readily accomplished since, as we saw above, disposable income and national income are themselves related.

The relation between disposable income and national income. On pages 493–495 we saw the adjustments required to derive disposable income from national income. Since transfer payments (the major addition) are smaller than total income taxes (the major subtraction), the net effect is for disposable income to be substantially less than national income. (It was about 72 percent of national income in 1983.)

The general relation between disposable income and national income can be illustrated by assuming that disposable income, Y_d, is a given proportion of national income, Y. The relation, for example, might be that disposable income is 70 percent of national income.

Substituting national income for disposable income in the consumption function. If we know how consumption relates to disposable income and how disposable income relates to national income, it is a routine matter to derive the relation between consumption and national income.

As an example, again assume that disposable income is always 70 percent of national income. Then, whatever the relation between C and Y, we can always substitute $0.7Y$ for Y_d. Thus, if consumption were always 90 percent of Y_d, then C would always be 63 percent (70 percent of 90 percent) of Y. [36]

This relation is further illustrated in Table 28-3. Since we can write desired consumption as a function of Y as well as of Y_d, we can define marginal and average propensities to consume from Y as well as from Y_d. The new propensities tell us the proportion of total national income that goes to desired consumption (C/Y) and the proportion of any change in national income that goes to a change in desired consumption ($\Delta C/\Delta Y$).

The marginal propensity to consume out of *national income* is equal to the marginal propensity to consume out of *disposable income* multiplied by the fraction of national income that becomes disposable income.

We now have a function showing how desired consumption expenditure varies as national income varies. The relation is defined for real income and real expenditure (i.e., income and expenditure measured in constant dollars). For every given level of real income, measured in terms of purchasing power, households desire to spend some fraction of that purchasing power and to save the rest.

Desired Net Exports

Canada is rich in natural resources and raw materials, which it exports to many other countries who are less favorably endowed. Also, Canada's manufacturing sector is very specialized and export-oriented. As we will see, fluctuations in exports play

TABLE 28–3 CONSUMPTION AS A FUNCTION OF DISPOSABLE INCOME AND NATIONAL INCOME (Billions of Dollars)

(1) National income (Y)	(2) Disposable income ($Y_d = 0.7Y$)	(3) Desired consumption ($C = 0.8Y_d$)
100	70	56
1,000	700	560
2,000	1,400	1,120
3,000	2,100	1,680
4,000	2,800	2,240

If desired consumption depends on disposable income, which in turn depends on national income, desired consumption can be written as a function of either income concept. The data are hypothetical. They show deductions of 30 percent of any level of national income to arrive at disposable income. Deductions of 30 percent of Y imply that the remaining 70 percent of Y becomes disposable income. The numbers also show consumption as 80 percent of disposable income.

By relating columns 2 and 3, one sees consumption as a function of disposable income. By relating columns 1 and 3, one sees consumption as a function of national income. In this example, the *APC* out of disposable income is 0.8 while it is 0.56 out of national income. You can check for yourself by dividing any figure in column 3 by the corresponding figures in columns 1 and 2.

a key role in explaining fluctuations in the level of economic activity in the Canadian economy.

Similarly, imports play an important role in the Canadian economy; Canadian households typically consume a wide range of imported goods, and Canadian industry utilizes imported parts and components. A large segment of the Canadian economy is involved in foreign trade, primarily—but not exclusively—with the United States.

Figure 28-4 shows Canadian merchandise exports and imports as a percentage of GNP for the years 1947–1983. As can be seen, both ratios have consistently been in the 20 to 30 percent range.

The data in Figure 28-4 underestimate the international exposure of the Canadian economy in two important ways. First, because government

expenditure accounts for more than 30 percent of Canadian GNP, exports represent virtually half of the goods produced in the private sector. Second, the figures represent those goods actually imported and exported. Many imported goods face competition in domestic markets from close substitutes produced in Canada, called import-competing goods. Similarly, goods identical or very similar to those exported are also produced and consumed in Canada. Hence the fractions of *importables* and *exportables* are much larger than the fractions of actual imports and exports.

The Net Export Function

The value of exports depends on the level of foreign demand for our goods and services. This in turn depends on the level of foreign income and on the *terms of trade* (the price of Canadian goods relative to foreign goods). Exports may be assumed *not* to change in response to changes in Canadian national income.

Fluctuations in national income will cause imports to fluctuate. As a result, with exports constant, net exports will fluctuate with the level of national income.

Net exports vary inversely with the level of national income because expenditure on imports is directly related to the level of national income.

This negative relationship between net exports and national income is called the **net export function**. On page 512, an example is calculated in Table 28-4 using hypothetical data, and illustrated in Figure 28-5.

Shifts in the Net Export Function

Shifts in the net export function are important because they lead to shifts in the aggregate expenditure function. We shall see that this relationship is important for our understanding of the role of net exports in determining national income.

We have already noted that net exports depend on national income as well as on foreign income and the terms of trade. The terms of trade in turn depend on foreign and domestic inflation rates and

FIGURE 28–4
Exports and Imports as a Percentage of GNP, 1947–1983 (Figures for Fourth Quarter of Year)

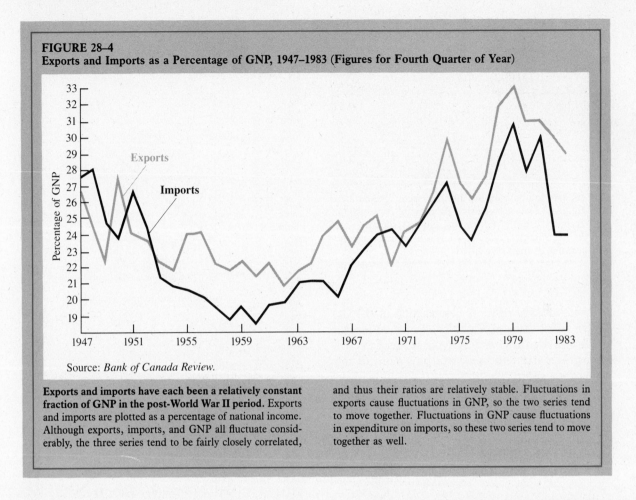

Source: *Bank of Canada Review.*

Exports and imports have each been a relatively constant fraction of GNP in the post-World War II period. Exports and imports are plotted as a percentage of national income. Although exports, imports, and GNP all fluctuate considerably, the three series tend to be fairly closely correlated, and thus their ratios are relatively stable. Fluctuations in exports cause fluctuations in GNP, so the two series tend to move together. Fluctuations in GNP cause fluctuations in expenditure on imports, so these two series tend to move together as well.

the exchange rate. Let us see how changes in each of these shifts in the net export function.

Foreign income. An increase in foreign income, other things being equal, will lead to an increase in the quantity of Canadian goods demanded by foreign countries. This will lead to an upward shift in the net export function. A fall in foreign income leads to a downward shift in the net export function.

Foreign prices. An increase in foreign prices will cause both foreign and domestic agents to substitute cheaper Canadian goods for the now more expensive foreign goods. As a result, exports will rise, imports at any level of national income will fall, and the net export function will shift upward. A fall in foreign prices has the reverse effect, with substitution away from Canadian goods in favor of foreign goods, and the net export curve shifting downward.

Domestic prices. An increase in domestic prices leads both foreign and domestic agents to substitute foreign goods for the now more expensive Canadian goods. This leads to an increase in imports and a fall in exports—and thus to a downward shift in the net export function. A fall in domestic prices leads to substitution in favor of Canadian goods, and an upward shift in the net export function.

TABLE 28–4 A NET EXPORT SCHEDULE
(Billions of Dollars)

National income (Y)	Exports (X)	Imports (M = 0.1Y)	Net exports
1,000	240	100	140
2,000	240	200	40
2,400	240	240	0
3,000	240	300	−60
4,000	240	400	−160
5,000	240	500	−260

Net exports fall as national income rises. The data are hypothetical. They assume that exports are constant and that imports are 10 percent of national income. Net exports are then positive at low levels of national income and negative at high levels.

The exchange rate. A depreciation of the Canadian dollar shifts expenditure away from foreign goods and toward Canadian goods. Canadians will import less and foreigners will buy more of our goods for export. The net export function shifts upward. An appreciation of the Canadian dollar has the opposite effect, causing substitution of foreign for Canadian goods and shifting the net export function downward.

Now consider briefly the other major expenditure categories I and G.

Desired Investment Expenditure

Firms plan how much to invest in new capital equipment and in inventories. For the present it is convenient to study how the level of national income adjusts to a fixed level of planned real investment. So we assume that firms plan to make a constant amount of investment in plant and equipment each year and that they plan to hold their inventories constant. (In Chapter 31 we shall drop these assumptions and study the important effects on national income caused by changes in the level of desired investment.)

Desired Government Expenditure

Government expenditures on currently produced goods and services are part of aggregate ex-

FIGURE 28-5
The Derivation of the Net Export Function

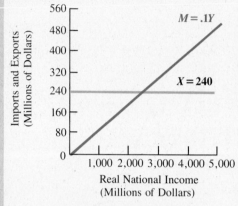

(i) Export and import functions

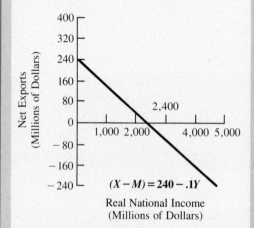

(ii) Net export function

Net exports, defined as the difference between exports and imports, are inversely related to the level of national income. In (i) exports are constant at $240 million while imports rise with the national income. Therefore net exports, shown in (ii), decline with national income. The figure is based on the hypothetical data in Table 28-4. With national income equal to $2,400 million, imports are equal to exports at $240 million and net exports are zero. For levels of national income below $2,400 million, imports are less than exports and hence net exports are positive. For levels of national income above $2,400 million, imports are greater than exports and hence net exports are negative.

TABLE 28–5 THE AGGREGATE EXPENDITURE FUNCTION (Billions of Dollars)

(1) National income (Y)	(2) Desired consumption (C = 100 + 0.6Y)	(3) Desired investment (I = 250)	(4) Desired government expenditure (G = 410)	(5) Desired net exports (X − M = 240 − 0.1Y)	(6) Desired aggregate expenditure (AE = C + I + G + [X − M])
$ 100	$ 160	$250	$410	$230	1,050
400	340	250	410	200	1,200
500	400	250	410	190	1,250
1,000	700	250	410	140	1,500
2,000	1,300	250	410	40	2,000
3,000	1,900	250	410	−60	2,500
4,000	2,500	250	410	−160	3,000
5,000	3,100	250	410	−260	3,500

The aggregate expenditure function is the sum of desired consumption, investment, government expenditure, and net exports. Desired aggregate expenditure has an autonomous component that is independent of national income and an induced component that varies positively with national income.

penditure on the nation's output. At the outset we take desired and actual real government expenditure as a constant. Governments intend to spend, and succeed in spending, so many billions of dollars on goods and services. We assume that this amount does not change as the circumstances of the economy change. This assumption allows us to see how national income adjusts to a constant level of real government expenditure. (In Chapter 32 we shall drop this assumption and study how national income responds to changes in desired and actual government expenditure.)

The Aggregate Expenditure Function

Total desired expenditure on the nation's output is the sum of desired consumption, investment, government expenditure, and net exports. How do changes in national income affect total desired expenditure? To answer this question, we need the **aggregate expenditure function,** which relates the level of desired real expenditure to the level of real income. Table 28-5 illustrates how such a function can be calculated, given the consumption function and the levels of desired investment, government expenditure, and net exports at each level of income.[2]

The aggregate expenditure function tells how much domestic governments, domestic firms and households, and foreigners would like to spend on purchasing final domestic output at each level of national income.

Autonomous and Induced Expenditure

Since for the present we are assuming that I, G, and X are constant, C and (X − M) are the components of aggregate expenditure that vary systematically with income. Their variation is enough to make total desired expenditure vary with national income.

Components of aggregate expenditure that do not depend on national income are called *autonomous* expenditures. Components that *do* depend on national income are called *induced* expenditures. At this stage of our analysis, I, G, and X are all autonomous, while C and (X − M) are, at least in

[2] The table is based on hypothetical data where consumption is $100 + 0.6Y, imports are 0.1Y, and I, G, and X are constant at values of $250, $410, and $240 respectively. The figures in the table are in billions of dollars.

TABLE 28-6 THE DETERMINATION OF EQUI- LIBRIUM NATIONAL INCOME (Billions of Dollars)

(1) National income (Y)	(2) Desired aggregate expenditure (AE = C + I + G + [X − M])	
$ 100	1,050	Pressure on
400	1,200	income to
500	1,250	increase
		↓
1,000	1,500	
2,000	2,000	Equilibrium income
		↑
3,000	2,500	
4,000	3,000	Pressure
5,000	3,500	on income to decrease

National income is in equilibrium where aggregate desired expenditure equals national income. The data are taken from Table 28-5. When national income is below its equilibrium level, aggregate desired expenditure exceeds the value of current output. This creates an incentive for firms to increase output and hence for national income to rise. When national income is above its equilibrium level, desired expenditure is less than the value of current output. This creates an incentive for firms to reduce output and hence for national income to fall. Only at the equilibrium level of national income is aggregate desired expenditure exactly equal to the value of the current output.

part, induced. (Recall the discussion on page 23 making the general distinction between autonomous and induced variables.)

The Propensity to Spend Out of National Income

Earlier we defined propensities to consume and to save that, together, account for all household disposable income. We now define propensities to spend and not to spend that together account for all national income.

The fraction of any increment to national income that will be spent on domestic production is measured by the change in aggregate expenditure divided by the change in income, and is symbolized by $\Delta AE/\Delta Y$. It is called the economy's **marginal propensity to spend.** The remainder, $1 - \Delta AE/\Delta Y$, is the fraction that is not spent. This is the **marginal propensity not to spend.**[3] The value of the marginal propensity to spend, which is something greater than zero but less than one, may be indicated by the letter z. This makes the value of the marginal propensity not to spend $1 - z$.

To illustrate, imagine that the economy receives $1 of extra income. If $.60 more is now spent on domestically produced goods, the marginal propensity to spend is 0.6 (i.e., 0.60/1.00), while the marginal propensity not to spend is 0.4 (i.e., 1.00 − 0.60).

DETERMINING EQUILIBRIUM NATIONAL INCOME

Now we can see how equilibrium national income is determined, *given a Keynesian SRAS curve.* To do this we study the **equilibrium conditions,** the conditions that must be fulfilled if national income is to be in equilibrium.

Aggregate Expenditure Equals National Income in Equilibrium

Table 28-6 illustrates the determination of equilibrium national income for a simple hypothetical economy with no taxes or transfer payments. In this case, disposable income is the same as national income.

Suppose that firms are producing a final output of $1,000 and thus national income is $1,000. According to Table 28-6 total desired expenditure, C + I + G + (X − M), is $1,500 at this level of income. If firms persist in producing a current output of only $1,000 in the face of an aggregate

---

[3] More fully, these terms would be the marginal propensity to spend *on national product* and the marginal propensity not to spend *on national product.* Expenditures on imports are included in the latter.

desired expenditure of $1,500, one of two things must happen.

One possibility is that households, firms, and governments will be unable to spend the extra $500 that they would like to spend, so lineups of unsatisfied customers will appear. These lineups send a signal to firms that they can increase their sales if they increase their production. When the firms increase production, national income rises. Of course the individual firms were only interested in their own sales and profits, but their joint action has, as its inevitable consequence, an increase in GNP that is, after all, simply the total of everyone's current production (i.e., the total of their values added).

The second possibility is that everyone will spend all that they wanted to spend. But then expenditure will exceed current output, which can only happen when some expenditure plans are fulfilled by purchasing inventories of goods that were produced in the past. In this example, the fulfillment of plans to purchase $1,500 worth of commodities in the face of a current output of only $1,000 must reduce inventories by $500. As long as inventories last, more goods can be sold than are currently being produced.

Eventually inventories will run out, but long before this happens firms will increase their output. Extra sales can then be made without a further pulling down of inventories. Once again the consequence of each individual firm's behavior, in search of its own individual profits, is an increase in national income. Thus the final response to an excess of aggregate desired expenditure over current output is a rise in national income toward its equilibrium value.

At any level of national income at which total desired expenditure exceeds total output, there will be pressure for national income to rise.

Next consider the $4,000 level of national income in Table 28-6. At this level, desired expenditure on domestically produced goods is only $3,000. If firms persist in producing $4,000 worth of goods, $1,000 worth must remain unsold. Therefore, inventories must rise. But firms will not

allow inventories of unsold goods to rise indefinitely; sooner or later they will reduce the level of output to the level of sales. When they do, national income will fall.

At any level of income for which total desired expenditure falls short of total output, there will be a pressure for national income to fall.

Finally, look at the national income level of $2,000 in the table. At this level, and only at this level, total desired expenditure is exactly equal to national income. Purchasers fulfill their spending plans without causing inventories to change. There is no incentive for firms to alter output. Since total output is the same as national income, national income will remain steady; it is in equilibrium.

The equilibrium level of national income occurs where total desired expenditure equals total output.

A glance at Table 28-6 will show that there is always a tendency for national income to be pushed in the direction of its equilibrium value. Only when desired aggregate expenditure is equal to total output will national income remain unchanged. This conclusion is quite general and does not depend on the numbers used in the specific example. [37]

A Graphic Determination of Equilibrium

Figure 28-6 shows the determination of the equilibrium level of national income. The AE line graphs the aggregate expenditure function. Its slope is the marginal propensity to spend. The 45° line shows the equilibrium condition that desired aggregate expenditure, AE, equals national income, Y. Any point on this line is a possible equilibrium.

Graphically, equilibrium occurs at the level of income at which the aggregate desired expenditure line intersects the 45° line. This is the level of income where desired expenditure is just equal to total national income and, therefore, is just sufficient to purchase total final output.

We have now explained the equilibrium level of national income that arises at a *given price level*. In

FIGURE 28-6
Equilibrium National Income

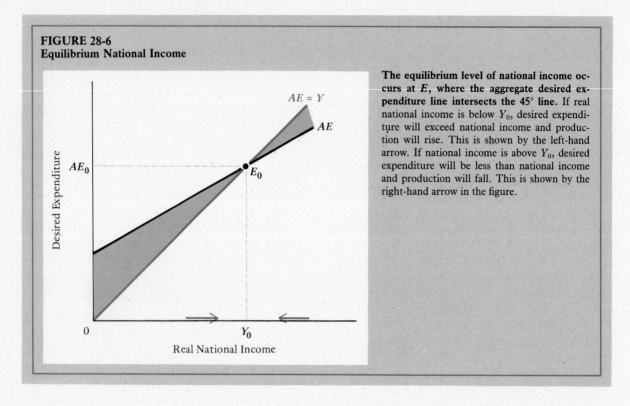

The equilibrium level of national income occurs at E, where the aggregate desired expenditure line intersects the 45° line. If real national income is below Y_0, desired expenditure will exceed national income and production will rise. This is shown by the left-hand arrow. If national income is above Y_0, desired expenditure will be less than national income and production will fall. This is shown by the right-hand arrow in the figure.

the next chapter we will study the forces that cause equilibrium income to change. We shall see that shifts in desired consumption and investment expenditure can cause major swings in national income. We shall also see that changes in government spending and taxation policies can do the same. In later chapters we shall see that not only can these things happen, but they do happen. At that point our theoretical framework will help us to understand many real-world events that we read and hear about.

SUMMARY

1. When the price level is fixed along a horizontal Keynesian *SRAS* curve, equilibrium national income is demand determined.

2. Desired aggregate expenditure includes desired

consumption, investment, and government expenditure, plus desired net exports. It is the amount that decision makers want to spend on purchasing the national product.

3. A change in disposable income leads to a change in consumption and saving. The responsiveness of these changes is measured by the marginal propensity to consume and the marginal propensity to save, which are both positive and sum to one.

4. A change in wealth leads to a change in the allocation of disposable income between consumption and saving. The change in consumption is positively related to the change in wealth while the change in saving is negatively related to this change.

5. Desired net exports depend on the levels of national and foreign income, and on the terms of trade. The terms of trade change in response to differential inflation domestically and abroad, and in response to the exchange rate.

6. At the equilibrium level of national income purchasers wish to buy neither more nor less than what is being produced. At incomes above equilibrium, desired expenditure falls short of national income and output will sooner or later be curtailed. At incomes below equilibrium, desired expenditure exceeds national income and output will sooner or later be increased.

7. Graphically equilibrium national income occurs where the aggregate expenditure curve cuts the 45° line; that is, where total desired expenditure equals total output.

TOPICS FOR REVIEW

The consumption function
Average and marginal propensities to consume and save, and to spend and not to spend
The 45° line
The aggregate expenditure function
Equilibrium national income at a given price level

DISCUSSION QUESTIONS

1. "The concept of an equilibrium level of national income is useless because the economy is never in equilibrium. If it ever got there, no economist would recognize it anyway." Discuss.

2. Interpret each of the following statements either in terms of the shape of a consumption function or the values of *MPC* and/or *APC*.
   a. "Tom Green has lost his job and his family is existing on its past savings."
   b. "The Grimsby household is so rich that they used all the extra income they earned this year to invest in a wildcat oil-drilling venture."
   c. "The widow Hammerstein can barely make ends meet by clipping coupons on the bonds left to her by dear Henry, but she would never dip into her capital."
   d. "We always thought Harris was a miser, but when his wife left him he took to wine, women, and song."

3. Can you think of any reasons why an individual's marginal propensity to consume might be higher in the long run than in the short run? Why it might be lower? Is it possible for an individual's average propensity to consume to be greater than unity in the short run? In the long run? Can a country's average propensity to consume be greater than unity in the short run? In the long run?

4. Along the 45° line, what relationship holds between total expenditures and total income? In determining equilibrium graphically, are we restricted to choosing identical vertical and horizontal scales?

5. Explain carefully why national income changes when aggregate desired expenditure does not equal national income. Sketch a scenario that fits the cases of too much and too little desired expenditure. What factors might influence the speed with which national income moves toward its equilibrium level?

6. Explain how a sudden unexpected fall in consumer expenditure would appear to be followed by an increase in investment expenditure by firms.

7. What relationship is suggested by the following 1983 newspaper headline: "Big Three Auto Sales Soar As Recovery Booms"?

8. State the implied impact on Canada's *AE* function relating to each of the following headlines:
   a. "Ottawa's Planned Spending up 10.5%."
   b. "Soviet Union Agrees to Buy More Wheat from Canada."
   c. "Major Canadian Companies Expected to Cut Capital Outlays."
   d. "U.S. President Proposes Tax Cut."

29 CHANGES IN NATIONAL INCOME I: THE ROLE OF AGGREGATE DEMAND

In Chapter 28 we investigated the conditions for national income to be in equilibrium. The equilibrium value of national income does not, however, remain unchanged. In this chapter we study why it changes. But before we do this we must make an important distinction which, if not properly understood, can be the source of endless confusion.

Suppose desired expenditure rises. This may be either a response to a change in national income or the result of an increased desire to spend at each level of national income. A change in national income causes a *movement along* the aggregate expenditure function. An increased desire to spend at each level of national income causes a *shift in* the aggregate expenditure function. Figure 29-1 illustrates this important distinction.

FIGURE 29-1
Movements Along and Shifts of the *AE* Curve

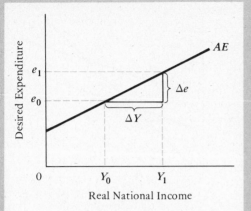

(i) A movement along the *AE* function

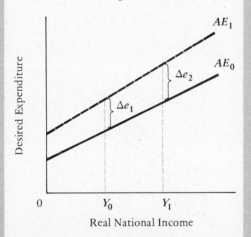

(ii) A shift of the *AE* function

A movement along the aggregate expenditure function occurs in response to a change in income; a shift of the *AE* function indicates a different level of desired expenditure at each level of income. In (i), a change in income of ΔY, from Y_0 to Y_1, changes expenditure by Δe, from e_0 to e_1. In (ii), a shift in the expenditure function from AE_0 to AE_1 raises the amount of expenditure associated with *each* level of income. At Y_0, for example, desired aggregate expenditure is increased by Δe_1; at Y_1, it is increased by Δe_2. (If the shift is a parallel one, then $\Delta e_1 = \Delta e_2$.)

CHANGES IN NATIONAL INCOME WITH A FIXED PRICE LEVEL

For the moment we continue with our assumption that the price level is fixed. For any specific aggregate expenditure function there is then a unique level of equilibrium national income. But if the aggregate expenditure function shifts, the existing equilibrium will be disturbed and national income will change. Thus if we wish to find causes of changes in national income, we must look for causes of shifts in the *AE* function.

Shifts in the Aggregate Expenditure Function

The aggregate expenditure function shifts when one of its components shifts; that is, when there is a shift in the desired consumption expenditure of households, in the desired investment expenditure of private firms, in government expenditure, or in exports. Such shifts are called *autonomous* changes in aggregate expenditure.

An Autonomous Increase in Expenditure

What will happen if, say, households permanently increase their levels of consumption spending at each level of disposable income? If the Ford Motor Company increases its rate of annual investment by $5 million in order to meet the threat from imported cars? If the Canadian government increases its spending to improve major railway lines? Or if Canadian grain exports soar? (In dealing with these questions, it is important to remember that we are dealing with continuous flows measured as so much per period of time. An upward shift in the expenditure function is taken to mean that expenditure rises to and stays at a higher amount.)

Because any such increase shifts the entire aggregate expenditure function upward, the same analysis applies to all of the changes mentioned above. Two types of shifts in *AE* are illustrated in

Figure 29-2(i) and 29-2(ii). First, if the same addition to expenditure occurs at all levels of income, the AE curve shifts parallel to itself as shown in the first part of the figure. Second, if there is a change in the propensity to consume, the slope of the AE curve changes, as shown in part (ii) of the figure. (Recall that the slope of the AE curve is the marginal propensity to spend out of national income.)

Figure 29-2 shows that all upward shifts in the aggregate expenditure function increase equilibrium national income. Why is this so? After the shift in the AE curve, income is no longer in equilibrium at its original level because desired expenditure now exceeds national income. This causes income to rise, which in turn causes a further rise in aggregate expenditure (a movement along the AE curve). Since the slope of the AE curve is less than one (as we saw in Chapter 28), this induced rise in aggregate expenditure is less than the rise in income that induces it. The rise in income continues until desired expenditure is once again equal to the now higher level of national income. In other words, the response of income to the upward *shift* of the AE function induces a movement *along* the new AE function until the flow of desired expenditure again equals national income.

An Autonomous Decrease in Expenditure

What will happen to national income if there is a *fall* in consumption, investment, exports, or government spending? What will happen if households permanently decrease their spending at each level of income? If a loss of markets to foreign cars causes North American automobile producers to reduce their investment expenditure permanently? If the Canadian government drastically reduces expenditure on urban renewal? If exports of refrigerators to Mexico fall because of new Mexican import restrictions?

All these changes shift the aggregate expenditure function downward. A constant reduction in expenditure at all levels of income shifts AE parallel to itself. A fall in the propensity to consume out of national income reduces the slope of the AE function. Figures 29-2(i) and 29-2(ii) show that

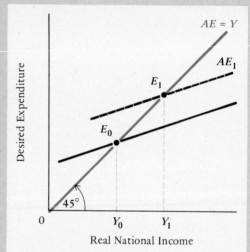

FIGURE 29-2
Shifts in the AE Function

(i) A parallel shift in AE

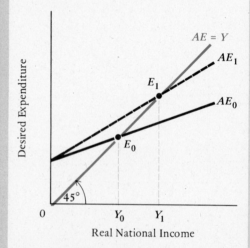

(ii) A change in the slope of AE

Upward shifts in the AE function increase equilibrium income; downward shifts decrease equilibrium income. In both (i) and (ii), the aggregate expenditure function is initially AE_0, with national income Y_0.

As shown in (i), a parallel upward shift in AE, say to AE_1, increases equilibrium income to Y_1. A downward shift in the function from AE_1 to AE_0 lowers equilibrium income from Y_1 to Y_0. In (ii), the marginal propensity to spend out of national income increases, shifting the expenditure function to AE_1. Equilibrium income increases to Y_1. The opposite change, a fall in the propensity to spend out of national income, is shown by a shift of the expenditure function from AE_1 to AE_0 and of equilibrium income from Y_1 to Y_0.

both kinds of shifts cause equilibrium national income to fall.

Income Changes

We have now derived two important general predictions of the elementary theory of national income.

1. A rise in the amount of desired consumption, investment, government, or export expenditure associated with each level of national income will increase equilibrium national income.
2. A fall in the amount of desired consumption, investment, government, or export expenditure associated with each level of national income will lower equilibrium national income.

A Further Application

What would be the effects of a rise in tax rates? Recall that a tax increase shifts the relation between consumption and national income without shifting the relation between consumption and disposable income. Suppose, for example, that the government raises its rates of income tax so as to collect an additional 10 percent of national income in tax revenues. Disposable income falls correspondingly, and so therefore does consumption. If, for example, 90 percent of disposable income is always consumed, desired consumption expenditure will fall by 9 percent (90 percent of 10 percent) of national income. In this case the consumption schedule in Table 29-1 changes from that shown by columns 1 and 3 to that shown by columns 1 and 5. The result of this downward shift of the aggregate expenditure function will be a fall in equilibrium national income, as shown in part (ii) of Figure 29-2.

Not surprisingly, a drop in taxes has the opposite effect on national income. A fall in tax rates means more disposable income and hence more expenditure at each level of national income. This raises the aggregate expenditure function and causes an increase in equilibrium national income, as shown by the upward shift in the aggregate expenditure function in Figure 29-2(ii).

We have now derived two additional predictions of the elementary theory of national income.

3. A rise in tax rates will lower the level of national income.

TABLE 29–1 TAX CHANGES SHIFT THE FUNCTION RELATING CONSUMPTION TO NATIONAL INCOME

(1) National income (Y)	Disposable income equal to 70 percent of national income		Disposable income equal to 60 percent of national income	
	(2) Disposable income ($Y_d = 0.7Y$)	(3) Consumption ($C = 0.9Y_d$)	(4) Disposable income ($Y_d = 0.6Y$)	(5) Consumption ($C = 0.9Y_d$)
100	70	63	60	54
500	350	315	300	270
1,000	700	630	600	540

The consumption function shifts if the relation between disposable and national income changes. The table is based on simplified hypothetical data where C is always a constant fraction of Y_d, and Y_d is always a constant fraction of Y. Initially, $Y_d = 0.7Y$ and $C = 0.9Y_d$. This yields a schedule relating consumption to national income that is given in columns 1 and 3. Income tax rates are then increased so that only 60 percent of national income becomes disposable income. Column 4 now indicates the Y_d that corresponds to each level of Y shown in column 1. With an unchanged propensity to consume out of disposable income of 0.9, consumption is now given by column 5. Columns 1 and 5 give the new schedule relating consumption to national income.

4. A fall in tax rates will raise the level of national income.

The Multiplier: A Measure of the Magnitude of Changes in Income

We now know the *direction* of the changes in national income that occur in response to various shifts in the aggregate expenditure function. But what about the *magnitude* of these changes?

Economists need an answer to this question to determine the effects of changes in expenditures in both the private and public sectors. During a recession the government often takes measures to stimulate the economy. If these measures have a larger effect than estimated, demand may rise too much and full employment may be reached with demand still rising. This outcome will have an inflationary impact on the economy. If, on the other hand, the government greatly overestimates the effect of its measures, the recession will persist longer than is necessary. In this case there is a danger that the policy will be discredited as ineffective, even though the correct diagnosis is that too little of the right thing was done.

Definition of the Multiplier

From the theory of national income we know that an increase in autonomous expenditure, whatever its source, will cause an increase in national income. The change in autonomous expenditure might come, for example, from an increase in private investment, from new government spending, or from additional exports.[1] The **multiplier** is defined as the change in national income divided by the change in autonomous expenditure that brings it about.

The Multiplier: An Intuitive Statement

What will happen to national income if, with unchanged tax rates, the government increases its

spending on road construction? Suppose, for example, that this type of spending rises by $1 billion per year. (Since tax rates are unchanged, the government will have to borrow the additional money that it spends on roads.)

Initially the road program will create $1 billion worth of new national income and a corresponding amount of employment for those households and firms on which the money is spent. But this is not the end of the story. The increase in national income of $1 billion will cause an increase in disposable income, which will cause an induced rise in consumption expenditure. Road crews and road contractors, who gain new income directly from the government's road program, will spend some of it on food, clothing, entertainment, cars, television sets, and other consumption commodities.

When output expands to meet this demand, employment will increase in all the affected industries. New incomes will then be created for workers and firms in these industries. When they in turn spend their newly earned incomes, output and employment will rise further. More income will be created and more expenditure induced. Indeed, at this stage you could wonder whether the increases in income will ever come to an end. To deal with this concern, we need to consider the multiplier in somewhat more precise terms. This is done below and also in Box 29-1, which gives a numerical example akin to the above discussions.

The Multiplier: A Formal Statement

Consider an increase in autonomous expenditure of ΔA, which might be, say, $2 billion per year. Remember that ΔA stands for *any* increase in autonomous expenditure; this could be an increase in investment, government purchases, or in exports. This new autonomous expenditure shifts up the AE function by that amount. National income is no longer in equilibrium at its original level since desired aggregate expenditure now exceeds income. Equilibrium is restored by a *movement along* the new AE function, as shown in Figure 29-3 on page 524. The figure makes it clear that the multiplier is greater than one.

---

[1] For simplicity, we assume that there is no import content to any change in autonomous expenditure, so that the entire change occurs in the demand for domestically produced goods.

BOX 29–1 THE MULTIPLIER: A NUMERICAL APPROACH

Consider an economy whose marginal propensity to consume out of national income is 0.5. Suppose that autonomous expenditure increases because the government spends an extra $1 million per year on new roads. National income initially rises by $1 million. But that is not the end of it; there is a second round of spending. The factors of production involved directly and indirectly in road building receive an extra $600 thousand as disposable income, and then spend an extra $500 thousand each year on domestically produced goods and services. This $500 thousand generates $300 thousand of new disposable income and $250 thousand of new consumption expenditure (the remaining $50 thousand goes to increased imports and savings), which is a third round of additions to aggregate expenditure.

And so it continues, each successive round of new income generating 50 percent as much in new expenditure. Each additional round of expenditure creates new income and yet another round of expenditure.

The table below carries the process through 10 rounds. Students with sufficient patience (and no faith in mathematics) may compute as many rounds in the process as they wish; they will find that the sum of the rounds of expenditures approaches $2 million, which is twice the initial injection of $1 million. [38] The multiplier is thus 2, given these numerical assumptions about the relations between national income and disposable income and induced expenditure.

	Increases in disposable income	Increases in expenditure
	(thousands of dollars per year)	
Initial increase in government expenditure		$1,000.00
2nd round	$600.00	500.00
3rd round	300.00	250.00
4th round	150.00	125.00
5th round	75.00	62.50
6th round	37.50	31.25
7th round	18.75	15.63
8th round	9.38	7.81
9th round	4.69	3.91
10th round	2.34	1.95
Sum of 1st 10 rounds		1,998.05
All other rounds		1.95
Total		$2,000.00

We refer to this case as the simple multiplier, because it is simplified by our assumption that the price level is fixed.

The simple multiplier identifies the change in equilibrium national income that occurs in response to a change in autonomous expenditure *at a constant price level.*

The Size of the Simple Multiplier

It is now clear that the multiplier is greater than unity. But what does its size depend on? When can we expect it to be large and when can we expect it to be small? The answer is illustrated in Figure 29-4 on page 525. The figure shows that the size of the multiplier depends on the slope of the *AE* function; that is, on the marginal propensity to spend.

A high marginal propensity to spend means a steep *AE* curve. The consumption expenditure induced by the initial increase in income is large, with the result that the final rise in income is correspondingly great. On the other hand a low marginal propensity to spend means a relatively flat *AE* curve. The consumption expenditure induced by the initial increase in income is small. The result is that the final rise in income is not much larger

FIGURE 29-3
The Simple Multiplier (Constant Price Level)

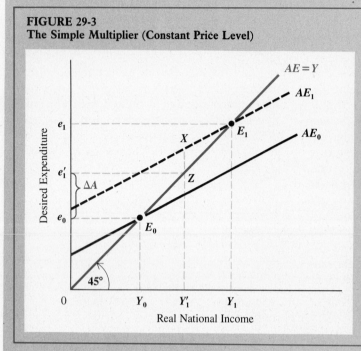

An increase in autonomous expenditure increases national income by a multiple of the initial increase. The initial equilibrium occurs where AE_0 cuts the 45° line, making desired expenditure of E_0 equal to national income of Y_0. An increase in autonomous expenditure of ΔA then shifts the desired expenditure function upward to AE_1. This raises total expenditure E_1' and would raise income to Y_1' if there were no induced new expenditure. But at Y_1' desired expenditure exceeds income by the amount XZ since desired expenditure rises due to both the autonomous increase and the rise in income from Y_0 to Y_1'.

Equilibrium occurs when income rises to Y_1. Here desired expenditure of E_1 equals income of Y_1. The extra income and expenditure of $Y_1'Y_1(E_1'E_1)$ represents the induced increases in expenditure and is the amount by which the final increase in income exceeds the initial increase in autonomous expenditure.

than the initial rise in autonomous expenditure that brought it about.

The larger the marginal propensity to spend, the steeper the aggregate expenditure function and the larger is the multiplier.

The precise value of the multiplier can be derived by using the aggregate expenditure function and the $E = Y$ equilibrium condition. This is done in Box 29-2 on page 526 for those who wish to see how it can be done. The result is that the multiplier, which we call K, is given by

$$K = \frac{\Delta Y}{\Delta A} = \frac{1}{(1 - z)}$$

where z was defined earlier as the marginal propensity to spend; that is, the slope of the expenditure function. The term $(1 - z)$ stands for the marginal propensity not to spend.[2] For example,

if $.75 of every $1 of new national income is spent ($z = 0.75$), then $.25 ($1.00 - 0.75$) is the amount not spent. The value of the multiplier is then calculated as $K = 1/0.25 = 4$.

The simple multiplier can be written as the reciprocal of the marginal propensity not to spend.

From this we see that if $(1 - z)$, the marginal propensity not to spend, is very small, the multiplier will be very large (because extra income induces much extra spending). The largest possible value of $(1 - z)$ is unity, indicating that all extra income is not spent. In this case the multiplier itself has a value of unity, indicating that the increase in income is confined to the initial increase in autonomous expenditure.

VARIATIONS IN THE PRICE LEVEL

The simple multiplier just derived shows how a change in autonomous expenditure causes a change

[2] The marginal propensity not to spend $(1 - z)$ is often referred to as the marginal propensity to *withdraw*. Not spending a part of one's income amounts to a *withdrawal* from the circular flow of income described in Figure 3-1.

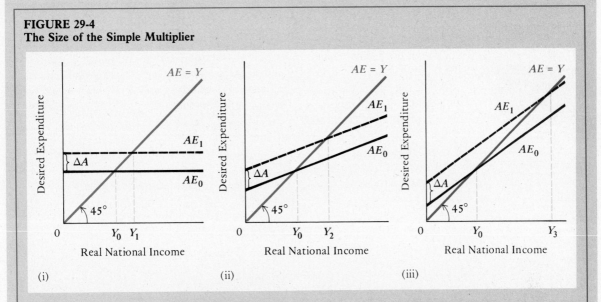

FIGURE 29-4
The Size of the Simple Multiplier

The steeper the desired expenditure function, the larger the marginal propensity to spend and the larger the simple multiplier. In (i), (ii), and (iii), initial desired expenditure of E_0 is equal to real national income of Y_0, and this equilibrium is then disturbed by an increase in autonomous expenditure of ΔA.

In (i), the AE function is horizontal, indicating a marginal propensity to spend of zero. The multiplier is then unity. Income rises by only the increment to exogenous expenditure since there is no induced expenditure by those who receive the initial increase in income.

In (ii), the AE curve is upward-sloping but still quite flat. The increase in national income to Y_2 is only slightly greater than the increase in autonomous expenditure that brought it about.

In (iii), the AE function is quite steep. Now the increase in income to Y_3 is much larger than the increase in autonomous expenditure that brought it about. The multiplier is quite large.

in national income on the assumption that the price level does not change. This works because we have been dealing with the case of a horizontal aggregate supply curve first introduced in Figure 28-1 on page 503. But we do not want to be confined to situations where the price level is constant. We wish additionally to see what happens when the price level rises or falls; that is, we wish to study inflations and deflations. To see what is involved here, we need to take the key step of relating the AE curve to the AD curve.

The Relation Between Aggregate Expenditure and Aggregate Demand

The relation between the AE and the AD curves is shown in Figure 29-5. Because the horizontal axes of both figures measure the same thing, real national income, they can be placed one above the other so that the level of national income on each can be directly compared. Part (i) of the figure describes the process by which equilibrium income is reached at any given price level. That equilibrium level of income and the given price level are then plotted in part (ii) as a single point on the AD curve.

To understand the relation between these curves it is important to understand the economic processes that lie behind these curves. The AE curve shows, for the given price level, desired aggregate expenditure at every possible level of income. Part (i) of Figure 29-5 shows that at any level of income below the equilibrium level, people are trying to buy more than is produced, while at any level of

BOX 29–2 THE MULTIPLIER: AN ALGEBRAIC APPROACH

High school algebra is all that is needed to derive the exact expression for the multiplier. Readers who feel at home with algebra may like to follow this derivation. Others can skip it and rely on the graphical and numerical arguments given in the text.

First we derive the equation for the AE curve. Aggregate expenditure is divided into autonomous expenditure, A, and induced expenditure, N.* So we write

$$AE = N + A \qquad [1]$$

Since N is expenditure that varies with income, we can write

$$N = zY \qquad [2]$$

where z is a positive constant less than unity, the marginal propensity to spend out of national income. Substituting Equation [2] into Equation [1] yields the equation of the AE curve.

$$AE = zY + A \qquad [3]$$

Now we write the equation of the 45° line,

$$AE = Y \qquad [4]$$

---

* In simple models N is mainly consumption expenditure, but in other models it may include other types of expenditure; all that matters is that there is one class of expenditure, N, that varies with income and another class, A, that does not.

which is the equilibrium condition that aggregate desired expenditure should equal national income. Equations 3 and 4 are two equations with two unknowns, AE and Y. To solve them, we substitute Equation [3] into Equation [4] to obtain

$$Y = zY + A$$

Subtracting zY from both sides yields

$$Y - zY = A$$

Factoring out the Y yields

$$Y(1 - z) = A$$

Dividing through by $1 - z$ yields

$$Y = A/(1 - z).$$

This tells us the equilibrium value of Y in terms of autonomous expenditures, A, and the propensity not to spend (or to withdraw income from the circular flow), $(1 - z)$. The expression $Y = A/(1 - z)$ tells us that if A changes by ΔA, the change in Y, which we call ΔY, will be ΔA divided by $(1 - z)$. We write this

$$\Delta Y = \Delta A/(1 - z)$$

Dividing through by ΔA gives the value of the multiplier, which we designate by K:

$$K = \Delta Y/\Delta A = 1/(1 - z)$$

which is the expression given in the text.

---

income above the equilibrium, people are buying less than is produced. Since the *SRAS* curve is flat, firms will supply all that is demanded at the going price level. Thus, when desired expenditure exceeds current output, real income rises (as firms produce more), but the price level does not change. When desired expenditure is less than current output, real income falls (as firms produce less), but

once again the price level does not change.

The second part of Figure 29-5 shows how the equilibrium income just determined can be plotted against the price level to yield a point on the *AD* curve.

The *AE* curve shows how equilibrium income is reached for a given price level. The *AD* curve plots that equilibrium income against that given price level.

FIGURE 29-5
The Relation Between the *AE* and the *AD* Curves

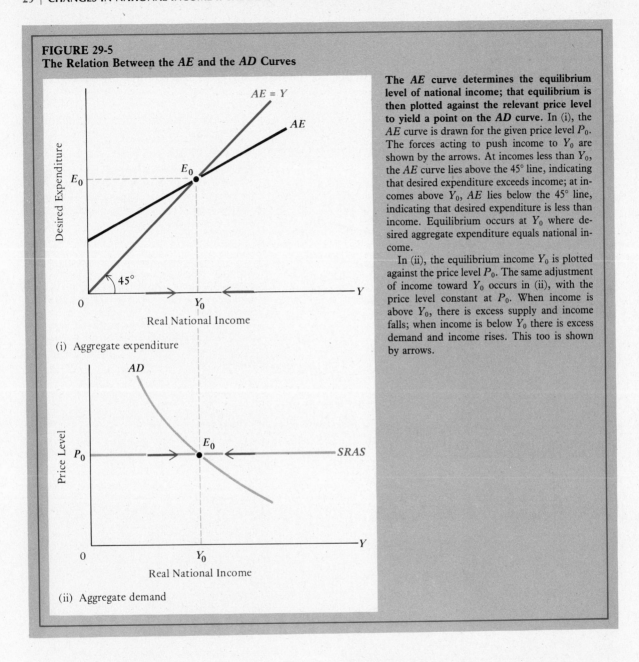

The *AE* curve determines the equilibrium level of national income; that equilibrium is then plotted against the relevant price level to yield a point on the *AD* curve. In (i), the *AE* curve is drawn for the given price level P_0. The forces acting to push income to Y_0 are shown by the arrows. At incomes less than Y_0, the *AE* curve lies above the 45° line, indicating that desired expenditure exceeds income; at incomes above Y_0, *AE* lies below the 45° line, indicating that desired expenditure is less than income. Equilibrium occurs at Y_0 where desired aggregate expenditure equals national income.

In (ii), the equilibrium income Y_0 is plotted against the price level P_0. The same adjustment of income toward Y_0 occurs in (ii), with the price level constant at P_0. When income is above Y_0, there is excess supply and income falls; when income is below Y_0 there is excess demand and income rises. This too is shown by arrows.

Aggregate Expenditure, National Income, and the Price Level

What does a change in the price level do to desired real expenditure and hence to the *AE* curve? The effects were briefly discussed in Chapter 26: a rise in the price level reduces the level of desired real expenditure. One channel by which a change in the price level influences aggregate expenditure is via its effect on the real value of financial wealth.

Let us see how this works. Much wealth is held

in the form of assets with a fixed money value. This is obviously true of money itself—cash and bank deposits—and is also true of many kinds of debt such as treasury bills and bonds. A rise in the price level lowers the purchasing power of these assets and lowers the real value of wealth.

Changes in the real value of financial wealth influence aggregate expenditure in two ways. First,

---

FIGURE 29-6
The Relation Between the *AE* and the *AD* Curves When the Price Level Changes

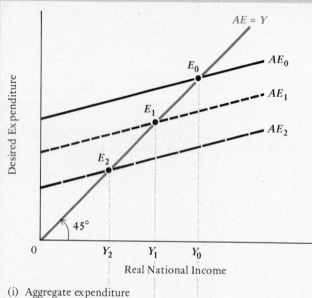

(i) Aggregate expenditure

(ii) Aggregate demand

Equilibrium income is determined by the *AE* curve for each given price level; the level of income and its associated price level are then plotted to yield the *AD* curve. Starting with the price level P_0, the *AE* curve is AE_0 and equilibrium national income is Y_0. Plotting Y_0 against P_0 yields the point E_0 on the *AD* curve.

A rise in the price level to P_1 lowers *AE* to AE_1, and this in turn lowers equilibrium income to Y_1. Plotting the new lower income, Y_1, against the new higher price level, P_1, yields a second point, E_1, on the *AD* curve. A further rise in the price level to P_2 lowers the *AE* curve to AE_2 and produces the lower level of income of Y_2. Plotting P_2 against Y_2 yields another point, E_2, on the *AD* curve.

there is a *direct* effect of wealth on consumption expenditure. Second, there is an *indirect* effect on expenditure operating via interest rates. The indirect effect is quantitatively the most important, but it is also much more complex to understand. Consequently we defer detailed study of it until Chapter 34 when we have studied the theory of money and interest rates. For now, we can understand the basic principles underlying the link between the price level and aggregate expenditure by focusing on the direct wealth effect on consumption.

We saw in Figure 28-3 that a fall in the household's wealth shifts the consumption function down. Because households have less wealth, they increase their saving (cut their consumption) so as to get back toward the wealth they wish to have for such purpose as retirement.

A fall in the consumption function shifts the whole aggregate expenditure function downward since for any given level of real income, people now wish to purchase a smaller quantity of goods and services. We already know that a downward shift in the *AE* function reduces equilibrium national income.

A fall in the price level has the opposite effect. The purchasing power of some existing assets is increased. Households, being wealthier in the aggregate, spend more. This shifts the *AE* curve upwards and raises equilibrium national income.

We have now reached an important result.

A rise in the price level lowers equilibrium national income, other things being equal. A fall in the price level raises equilibrium national income, other things being equal.

Deriving the *AD* Curve

Part (i) of Figure 29-6 shows how equilibrium national income changes when there are changes in the price level. The *AE* curve shifts, thus causing a new equilibrium income to be associated with the new price level. Each combination of equilibrium income, and its associated price level, becomes one point on the *AD* curve in part (ii) of the figure. A *movement along the AD curve thus traces out the re-sponse of equilibrium income to a change in the price level.*

Since the *AD* curve relates equilibrium national income to the price level, changes in the price level that cause *shifts* in the *AE* curve cause *movements along* the *AD* curve.

Changes in National Income and the *AD* Curve

The analysis conducted earlier in this chapter in terms of the *AE* curve can now be related to the *AD* curve. We have just seen that the *AD* curve plots equilibrium national income as a function of the price level. Thus anything that alters equilibrium national income at a given price level must shift the *AD* curve. This allows us to restate our earlier conclusions as follows.

A rise in the amount of desired consumption, investment, government, or export expenditure associated with each level of national income shifts the *AD* curve to the right. A fall in any of these expenditures shifts the *AD* curve to the left.

A rise in tax rates shifts the *AD* curve to the left. A fall in tax rates shifts the *AD* curve to the right.

The simple multiplier measures the magnitude of the change in equilibrium national income when the price level is constant. It follows that the simple multiplier gives the magnitude of the *horizontal shift* in the *AD* curve in response to a change in autonomous expenditure. This is shown in Figure 29-7.

The simple multiplier determines the horizontal shift in the *AD* curve in response to a change in autonomous expenditure.

If the *SRAS* curve is horizontal, indicating that firms will supply everything that is demanded at the going price level, then the simple multiplier also tells us the change in equilibrium income that will occur in response to a change in autonomous expenditure. But what if the aggregate supply curve is upward-sloping? In this case a rise in national income will cause a rise in the price level. But a rise in the price level (by lowering the real value of household wealth) shifts the *AE* curve

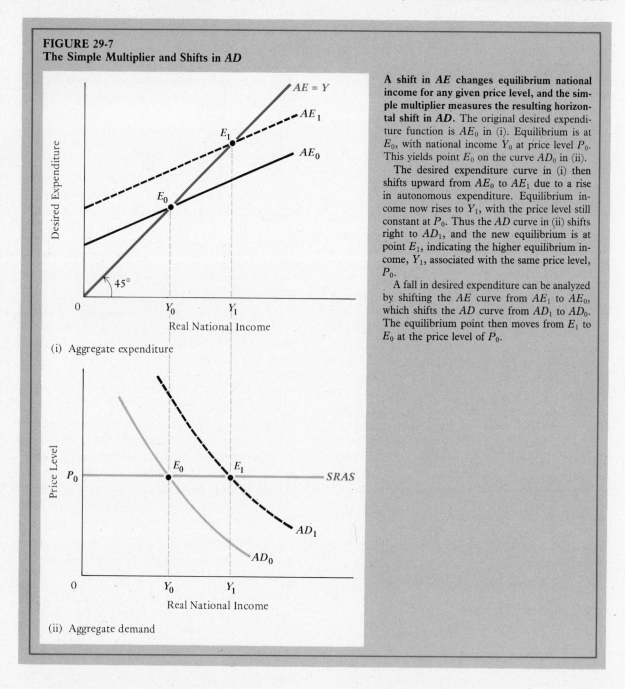

FIGURE 29-7
The Simple Multiplier and Shifts in *AD*

(i) Aggregate expenditure

(ii) Aggregate demand

A shift in *AE* changes equilibrium national income for any given price level, and the simple multiplier measures the resulting horizontal shift in *AD*. The original desired expenditure function is AE_0 in (i). Equilibrium is at E_0, with national income Y_0 at price level P_0. This yields point E_0 on the curve AD_0 in (ii).

The desired expenditure curve in (i) then shifts upward from AE_0 to AE_1 due to a rise in autonomous expenditure. Equilibrium income now rises to Y_1, with the price level still constant at P_0. Thus the *AD* curve in (ii) shifts right to AD_1, and the new equilibrium is at point E_1, indicating the higher equilibrium income, Y_1, associated with the same price level, P_0.

A fall in desired expenditure can be analyzed by shifting the *AE* curve from AE_1 to AE_0, which shifts the *AD* curve from AD_1 to AD_0. The equilibrium point then moves from E_1 to E_0 at the price level of P_0.

downward, which tends to lower national income. The outcome of the conflicting forces is easily seen using aggregate demand and aggregate supply curves.

The Multiplier When the Price Level Varies

Figure 29-8 shows that when the *SRAS* curve is upward-sloping, the change in national income

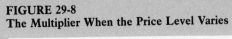

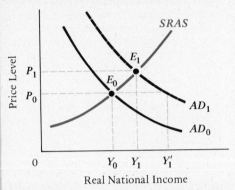

FIGURE 29-8
The Multiplier When the Price Level Varies

The multiplier effect of a shift in *AD*, when *SRAS* is positively sloped, is less than the simple multiplier. Equilibrium is initially at E_0, with a real national income of Y_0 and a price level of P_0. An increase in autonomous expenditure shifts the aggregate demand curve from AD_0 to AD_1. The new equilibrium is at E_1, with income Y_1 and price level P_1. The change in income Y_0Y_1 is smaller than Y_0Y_1', the change measured by the simple multiplier.

caused by a change in autonomous expenditure is no longer equal to the size of the horizontal shift in the *AD* curve. A rightward shift of the *AD* curve causes the price level to rise, which in turn causes the rise in national income to be less than the horizontal shift of the *AD* curve. Part of the expansionary impact of an increase in demand is dissipated in a rise in the price level, and only part is transmitted to a rise in real output.

When the *AS* curve is positively sloped, the multiplier is smaller than the simple multiplier derived for a given price level.

Why is the multiplier smaller when the *SRAS* curve is upward-sloping? The answer lies in the behavior of the *AE* curve. To understand this, it is useful to think of the final change in national income as occurring in two stages as shown in Figure 29-9.

First, with prices constant an increase in autonomous expenditure shifts the *AE* curve up and therefore shifts the *AD* curve to the right. The result is a change in national income given by the simple multiplier. This first stage shows up as a shift up of *AE* in (i) and the *AD* curve in (ii). But this cannot be the final equilibrium position because firms are unwilling to produce enough to satisfy the extra demand at the existing price level.

Second, we take account of the rise in the price level that occurs due to the upward slope of the *SRAS* curve. As we have seen, a rise in the price level via its effect on wealth and consumption leads to a downward shift in the *AE* curve. This second shift in the *AE* curve partially counteracts the initial rise in national income and so reduces the size of the multiplier. The second stage shows up as a *downward shift* of the *AE* curve in (i) and a *movement along* the *AD* curve in (ii).

Which Curves Best Handle Price Level Changes?

We can now see why we must use *AD–AS* curves rather than the *AE* curve once the price level can vary. If all we had was the *AE* curve plus the knowledge that the *AS* curve was upward-sloping, we could not discover the final change in either P or Y. We would know that the initial rise in autonomous expenditure shifted the *AE* curve upward. We would also know that the consequent rise in the price level would shift *AE* back downward somewhat. But by how much? Where will the final equilibrium be in relation to the original equilibrium and the equilibrium that would occur if prices had remained constant?

We cannot answer these questions unless we know by how much the price level rises. But there is nothing in part (i) of Figure 29-9 to tell us this. Thus the *AE*–45° line analysis is not sufficient to deal with situations in which the price level can change. But if we first use the *AE* curve to derive the *AD* curve, we can then determine the changes in Y and P by relating the *AD* and the *AS* curves.

FIGURE 29-9
The *AE* Curve and the Multiplier When the Price Level Varies

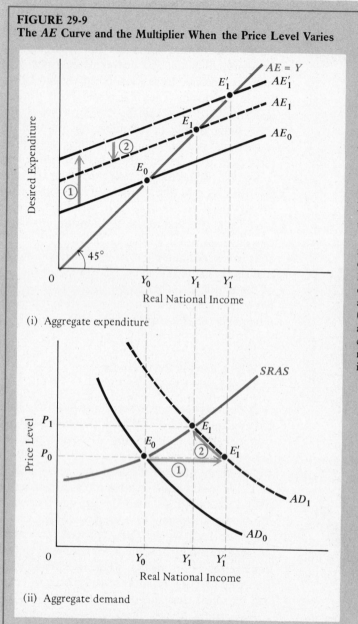

(i) Aggregate expenditure

(ii) Aggregate demand

The autonomous shift in expenditure causes the *AE* curve to shift up, but the rise in the price level causes it to shift part of the way down again. Hence the multiplier effect on *Y* is smaller than when *P* is constant. Originally, equilibrium is at point E_0 in both (i) and (ii), with real national income Y_0 and price level P_0. Aggregate desired expenditure then shifts to AE_1', taking the aggregate demand curve to AD_1 (arrow ① in both panels). If the price level had remained constant at P_0, the new equilibrium would have been at E_1' and real income would have risen to Y_1'. The amount Y_0Y_1' is the change called for by the simple multiplier.

Instead, however, the shift in the *AD* curve raises the price level to P_1 because the *SRAS* curve is upward-sloping. The rise in the price level shifts the aggregate expenditure curve down to AE_1 in (i) (arrow ②). This is shown as a movement along the *AD* curve in (ii) (arrow ②). The new equilibrium is thus at E_1. The amount Y_0Y_1 is the actual increase in real income, while the amount Y_1Y_1' is the shortfall relative to the simple multiplier due to the rise in the price level.

SUMMARY

1. A movement along the aggregate expenditure curve represents an induced change in expenditure in response to a change in national income. A shift of the aggregate expenditure curve represents a change in the expenditure that is associated with each level of national income.

2. Equilibrium national income is increased by an upward shift in the consumption, investment, government, or export expenditure associated with each level of the national income. National income is decreased by the opposite changes.

3. Equilibrium national income is decreased by an increase in the taxes associated with each level of income and increased by a fall in taxes.

4. The magnitude of the effect on national income of shifts in autonomous expenditure (such as I, G, and X) is given by the multiplier. This is defined as $K = \Delta Y / \Delta A$, where ΔA is the change in autonomous expenditure.

5. The elementary theory of national income gives the value of the simple multiplier as $1/(1 - z)$, where z is the marginal propensity to spend. Thus the larger the propensity to spend, the larger the multiplier. It is a basic prediction of national income theory that the multiplier is greater than unity.

6. The *AE* curve is drawn for a particular price level. It shows the relation between desired expenditure at each level of income and shows how equilibrium income is achieved. The *AD* curve plots the equilibrium level of income against the price level.

7. A change in the price level shifts the *AE* curve and leads to a new level of equilibrium national income. It is shown by a movement along the *AD* curve to a new equilibrium income and price level.

8. The simple multiplier determines the horizontal shift in the *AD* curve following from a shift in autonomous expenditure. It determines the actual change in equilibrium real national income *if* the economy is on a horizontal Keynesian aggregate supply curve.

9. When the aggregate supply curve is upward-sloping, part of the effect of the multiplier is dissipated in a rise in prices and only part goes to raise real income. The division of the effects between a change in national income and a change in the price level are easily discovered from aggregate demand and aggregate supply curves.

TOPICS FOR REVIEW

Shifts of and movements along expenditure curves

The effect on national income of changes in the amounts of I, G, and X associated with each level of income

The effect on national income of a change in tax rates

The simple multiplier with a constant price level

The relation between the size of the simple multiplier and the slope of the expenditure schedule

The relation between the *AE* and the *AD* curves

How changes in autonomous expenditure shifts the *AE* and the *AD* curves

The multiplier when the price level and output vary

DISCUSSION QUESTIONS

1. In what direction would each of the following change national income? Which expenditure flows would be affected first? Be sure to distinguish between movements along curves and shifts of curves.
   a. The production and sale of a new nuclear reactor
   b. A decrease in personal income-tax withholding for low-income taxpayers
   c. A major reduction in social security payments to the elderly
   d. A spurt in consumer spending for video recorders accompanied by a reduction in savings
   e. A reduction in spending on foreign travel accompanied by an equivalent increase in saving
   f. A large increase in defense expenditure accompanied by an across-the-board tax cut

2. Predict whether each of the following events will, other things being equal, increase, decrease, or leave unchanged *the size of the multiplier.*
   a. A shift from foreign travel to holidays at home
   b. An expansion of expenditures on highways
   c. Decisions by corporations to pay out a smaller percentage of their earnings in dividends and to increase their bank balances whenever national income falls
   d. Widespread adoption by cities of a city income tax
   e. A large increase in the percentage of disposable income saved by households

3. The president of the Chamber of Commerce of Southeastern Connecticut commented on the effects in his area of a 22-week strike at a shipyard where the lost payroll was $2 million per week: "You don't just figure $2 million a week times 22 weeks, you have to multiply by four or five. That shipyard is the prime source of money in this region. Money comes into the region from Washington and then the ship-

yard worker's wife takes it to the grocery, and the grocery clerk takes it to the gas station, and so on until it leaves the area in taxes or some other way." Interpret his statement in terms of the analysis of this chapter.

4. Homer Hardcrust, chairman of the Economic Council of Canada, proposes that because of the current heavy unemployment, government should prepare an austerity program and cut down government expenditures to set an example for private households. Would his policy tend to raise or lower unemployment?

5. A private research agency estimates the GNP gap to be $10 billion and recommends that it be eliminated by an increase in government expenditures of $10 billion. Does the agency's staff understand the multiplier?

6. What would happen to employment and income if, in an attempt to lower Canadian unemployment, the Parliament passed very large increases in Canadian tariff rates? What would happen if, in the face of a worldwide recession, all countries did the same?

30 CHANGES IN NATIONAL INCOME II: THE ROLE OF AGGREGATE SUPPLY

The aggregate supply curve plays a key role in the behavior of the economy. First, as we saw at the end of Chapter 29, the shape of the *SRAS* curve determines how the impact of aggregate demand shocks is divided between changes in output and changes in the price level. Second, as we saw in Chapter 26, aggregate supply shocks—which *shift* the aggregate supply curve—are themselves a major cause of changes in both output and the price level. In this chapter we analyze the role played by

aggregate supply in more detail. We look both at short-run and at long-run effects.

AGGREGATE SUPPLY IN THE SHORT RUN

In this section we focus attention on the short-run effects of aggregate demand and aggregate supply shocks. To do this we must first examine the shape of the short-run aggregate supply curve in more detail than we did in Chapter 26.

The Shape of the *SRAS* Curve

In Chapter 26 we encountered the upward sloping *SRAS* curve. It relates the quantity of output producers that are willing to sell to the price level, other things being equal. Such an *SRAS* curve is also shown in isolation in Figure 30-1. Notice two things about its shape: it has a positive slope, and the slope increases as output rises.

Positive slope. The most obvious feature of the *SRAS* curve is its positive slope, indicating that, other things being equal, a higher price level is associated with a higher volume of real output.

The key to understanding why the *SRAS* curve has a positive slope is knowing what is being held constant as the price level is varied. The prices of *factors of production*, the most important being the wage rate, are what is being held constant. If the prices of everything that firms sell rise, while the prices of everything that firms use to make their products remain constant, production becomes more profitable. Firms are interested in making profits. When production becomes more profitable, they will usually produce more.[1] Thus, when the price level of final output rises while input prices are held constant, firms are motivated to increase their outputs. This increase gives rise to the upward slope of the *SRAS* curve.

The higher the price level the higher the total output that firms are willing to produce and offer for sale, other things being equal.

The "other things being equal" clause is the key to why we have called the upward-sloping relationship a *short-run* aggregate supply curve. Treating wages and other factor prices as constant is only appropriate when the time period under consideration is short. Hence the *SRAS* curve is used only

[1] Those who have already studied microeconomics can understand this in terms of price-taking firms being faced with higher prices and thus expanding output *along* their marginal cost curves until marginal cost is once again equal to price.

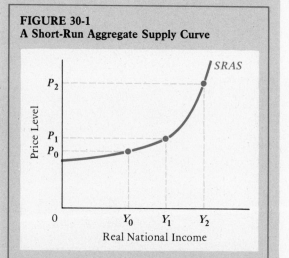

FIGURE 30-1
A Short-Run Aggregate Supply Curve

SRAS slopes upward and is steeper, the larger is real national income. The upward slope of *SRAS* shows that, according to the supply decisions of firms, output and the price level will be positively associated. The increasing slope shows that the higher the level of output, the larger the increase in the price level associated with any further increment to output. For example, the change in output in moving from Y_0 to Y_1 is the same as that in moving from Y_1 to Y_2, but the rise in prices, P_0 to P_1, associated with the first increment to output is smaller than the rise, P_1 to P_2, associated with the second increment.

to analyze the effects that occur in the short run. We also call these *impact* effects.

Increasing slope. There is a somewhat less obvious, but in many ways more important, property of a typical *SRAS* curve: its slope *increases* as output rises. It is rather flat to the left of potential output and rather steep to the right. Why? Below potential output, firms will typically have unused capacity—some plant and equipment will be idle. When firms are faced with unused capacity, only a small increase in the price of their output may be needed to induce them to expand production, at least up to normal capacity. (Indeed, firms may be willing to sell more at *existing prices* if only the demand were there. If all firms are in this situation, we will have the horizontal "Keynesian" *SRAS* curve as in Figure 28-1.)

Once output is pushed very far beyond normal capacity, however, unit costs tend to rise quite rapidly. Higher-cost standby capacity may have to be used. Overtime and extra shifts may have to be worked. Both expedients raise the cost of producing a unit of output. Many more costly expedients may also have to be adopted. These higher cost methods will not be used unless the selling price of the output has risen enough to cover them. Furthermore, the more output is expanded beyond normal capacity, the more rapidly unit costs rise and hence the larger the rise in price needed to induce firms to increase output even further.

The increasing slope of the *SRAS* curve in Figure 30-1 is meant to reflect this important *asymmetry:*

Below potential national income, changes in output are accompanied by only *small* changes in the price level. Above potential national income, changes in output are accompanied by *large* changes in the price level.

Why the Shape of *SRAS* Matters When Demand Shocks Hit

How does the asymmetry of the *SRAS* curve, which is reflected in its *increasing* slope, influence the analysis of aggregate demand shocks? At the end of the previous chapter, we saw that the positive slope of the *SRAS* curve reduced the size of the multiplier. (See Figure 29-9.) We now examine how the increasing slope of the *SRAS* curve influences how an aggregate demand shock is divided between changes in real output and changes in the price level.

Figure 30-2 contains an *SRAS* curve that highlights the increasing slope by taking on extreme forms at both low and high level of national income. The curve shows three distinct ranges.

Over the *Keynesian range* at the left, where the *SRAS* curve is horizontal, any change in aggregate demand leads to *no* change in prices and, as seen earlier, a response of output equal to that predicted by the simple multiplier.

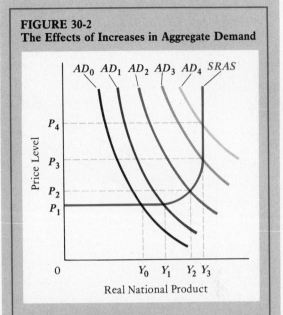

FIGURE 30-2
The Effects of Increases in Aggregate Demand

Increases in aggregate demand may cause an increase in output alone, an increase in both output and prices, or an increase in prices alone, depending on the shape of the *SRAS* curve. An increase in aggregate demand from AD_0 to AD_1 increases total output from Y_0 to Y_1, leaving the price level unchanged at P_1. An increase to AD_2 raises output from Y_1 to Y_2 and raises the price level from P_1 to P_2. An increase to AD_3 brings a smaller increase in output (from Y_2 to Y_3) and a larger increase in the price level (from P_2 to P_3). An increase to AD_4 raises the price level from P_3 to P_4 but leaves output constant at Y_3.

Next, there is an *intermediate range* along which the *SRAS* curve is positively sloped. In this range a shift in the *AD* curve gives rise to a change in real income *and* to a change in the price level. As we saw in Chapter 29, the change in the price level means that real income will change by less in response to a change in autonomous expenditure than it would if prices were constant.

At the extreme right, the curve shows a range where the *SRAS* curve is vertical. This so-called *classical range* deals with an economy right up against its capacity constraints; nothing more can

FIGURE 30-3
Aggregate Demand Shocks in the Classical Range

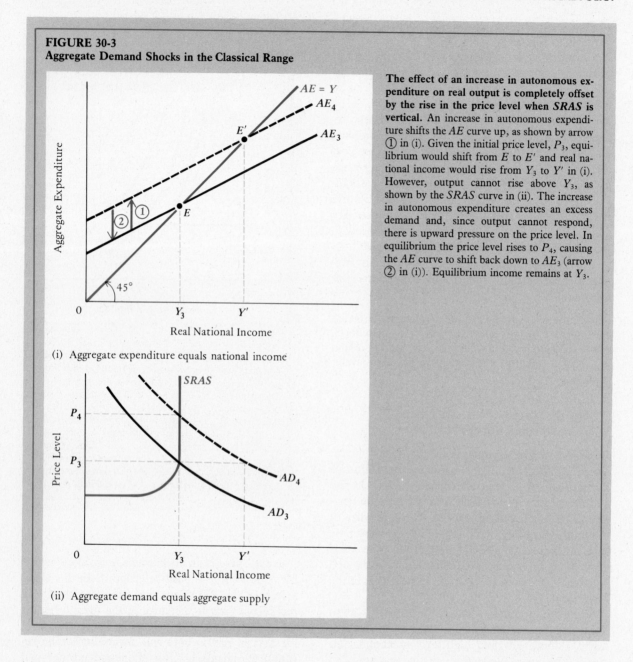

The effect of an increase in autonomous expenditure on real output is completely offset by the rise in the price level when *SRAS* is vertical. An increase in autonomous expenditure shifts the *AE* curve up, as shown by arrow ① in (i). Given the initial price level, P_3, equilibrium would shift from *E* to *E'* and real national income would rise from Y_3 to Y' in (i). However, output cannot rise above Y_3, as shown by the *SRAS* curve in (ii). The increase in autonomous expenditure creates an excess demand and, since output cannot respond, there is upward pressure on the price level. In equilibrium the price level rises to P_4, causing the *AE* curve to shift back down to AE_3 (arrow ② in (i)). Equilibrium income remains at Y_3.

(i) Aggregate expenditure equals national income

(ii) Aggregate demand equals aggregate supply

be produced, however large the demand. Over this range, any change in aggregate demand leads only to a change in the price level and to *no* change in real national income. The multiplier in this case is zero.

These three cases illustrate the general proposition that how the effect of any given shift in aggregate demand will be divided between a change in real output and a change in the price level depends on the conditions of aggregate supply. The steeper the *SRAS* curve the greater the price effect and the smaller the output effect.

The slope of the aggregate supply curves implies that at low levels of national income shifts in aggregate demand mainly affect output with only a minor impact on prices while at high levels of national income shifts in aggregate demand mainly affect prices and have only a relatively minor impact on output.

AD shocks and the classical range of SRAS. Let us consider the classical case in more detail, and in so doing look again at the aggregate expenditure curve. An increase in autonomous expenditure shifts the *AE* curve upward, thus raising the amount that would be demanded if the price level remained constant. But a vertical *SRAS* curve means that output cannot be expanded. The extra demand merely forces prices up and as prices rise, the *AE* curve is shifted down once again. The rise in prices continues until the *AE* curve is back where it started. Thus the rise in prices fully offsets the expansionary effect of the original shift, leaving both real aggregate expenditure and equilibrium real income unchanged as a result. This is illustrated in Figure 30-3.

Causes of Shifts in the *SRAS* Curve

Aggregate supply is important not only because the *shape* of the *SRAS* curve determines the effects of shifts in aggregate demand but also because *shifts* in the *SRAS* curve affect the price level and national income.

The *SRAS* curve can shift for many reasons. For example, an increase in the supplies of labor and capital will increase the quantity of output that can be produced. Below we consider two sources of shift that are of particular importance.

A Change in Costs

We have seen that input prices are held constant along the *SRAS* curve. This suggests a very important reason for the *SRAS* curve to shift. If input prices rise, firms will find that the profitability of their current production has been reduced. Their

response causes the *SRAS* curve to shift up and to the left.

Using the terminology of Chapter 4, an upward shift in the *SRAS* curve is referred to as a *decrease in supply* because at any given price level, less output will be willingly produced. Equivalently, for any given level of output to be willingly produced, an increase in price will be required. This is illustrated in Figure 30-4.

Similarly a fall in input prices causes the *SRAS*

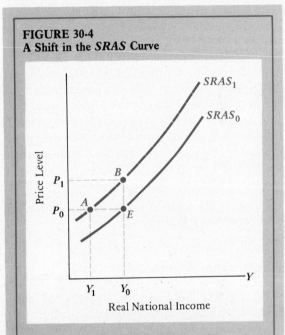

FIGURE 30-4
A Shift in the *SRAS* Curve

Price Level (vertical axis) — P_1, P_0
Real National Income (horizontal axis) — Y_1, Y_0, Y
Curves: $SRAS_1$, $SRAS_0$; points A, B, E

An increase in costs shifts the *SRAS* curve upward.
The initial *SRAS* is shown by the solid curve, $SRAS_0$. An increase in costs shifts it upward to the dashed line, $SRAS_1$.

Because the *SRAS* curve is positively sloped, this upward shift is equivalent to a leftward shift. For example, suppose the price level is initially at P_0 and output is Y_0. Following an increase in costs that reduces profitability, firms could maintain prices and reduce output, thus moving from point E to point A.

They might, instead, maintain output but increase prices, thus moving to point B. In fact, the point to which the firms actually adjust depends, as we have seen, on the *AD* curve. But we do know that $SRAS_1$ lies above and to the left of the original curve, $SRAS_0$.

curve to shift down and to the right. This is referred to as an *increase in supply*.

A change in costs shifts the *SRAS* curve because any given output will be supplied at a different price level than previously.

An Increase in Productivity

If labor productivity rises, meaning that each worker can produce more, then the costs of producing a unit of output must fall as long as wage rates remain constant. Lower costs generally lead to lower prices. Competing firms cut prices in attempts to raise their market shares, and the net result of such competition is that the fall in costs of production is accompanied by a fall in prices.[2] If the same output is sold at a lower price, this causes a downward shift in the *SRAS* curve. This shift means an *increase in supply*: the same quantity of output is associated with a lower price level while the same price level is associated with a larger quantity of output.

A rise in productivity shifts the *SRAS* curve downward because any given output will be supplied at a lower price level than previously.

Effects of Shifts in the *SRAS* Curve

What happens if the price of imported oil rises, pushing up many firms' production costs? This happened in 1974 and again in 1979–1980, and it may well happen again before the end of the 1980s. What happens if changed conditions in the markets for basic industrial raw materials cause their prices to rise, pushing up many firms' costs of production? We have seen that such events will shift the *SRAS* curve up. What happens if the events of the 1970s are reversed, and the prices of oil or other raw materials fall, lowering the costs of production for many firms and thus shifting the *SRAS* curve down?

We have just seen that a supply shock will cause

the *SRAS* curve to shift. This leads to new equilibrium values for the price level and real output. In Chapter 26 we saw that since the new equilibrium represents a *movement along* the *AD* curve, output and the price level change in opposite directions, one rising and the other falling.

In the short run an upward shift in the *SRAS* curve lowers output and raises the price level, while a downward shift raises output but lowers the price level.

Stagflation. Until about a decade ago, most of the short-term fluctuations in the economy stemmed mainly from demand-side disturbances. As a result, people became accustomed to rising output combined with rising prices, and falling output combined with stable or falling prices. Over the last decade, however, the economy has been buffeted by severe supply-side shocks. Increases in the prices of inputs such as oil, natural gas, and raw materials have raised the price at which output is supplied, thus shifting the *SRAS* curve upward. These increases have made familiar the combination of rising prices and falling output.

AGGREGATE SUPPLY IN THE LONG RUN

The key to understanding the long-run properties of aggregate supply is to see how changes in aggregate demand *induce* shifts in the *SRAS* curve. This means that our studies of impact effects, which were based on a single *SRAS* curve, are not the final word on what happens.

Long-Run Effects of Aggregate Demand Shocks

Up to now when examining aggregate demand shocks we have maintained the other-things-being-equal clause that underlies the short-run aggregate supply curve. This allowed us to concentrate on short-term effects. But what about the longer-term effects?

---

[2] Even a monopoly will cut its prices and raise its output when its marginal costs fall. See Chapter 13.

An Inflationary Shock

What we have learned so far about aggregate supply can help us study inflation in more detail. Assume that the economy starts off in the happy position of full employment and a stable price level, as pictured in part (i) of Figure 30-5. A rise in autonomous expenditure, perhaps caused by an investment boom, increases aggregate demand. The immediate effects are that the price level rises and that real income rises above its potential level. This is also shown in part (i) of Figure 30-5.

Firms will now be producing beyond their normal capacity output, so there will be a heavy demand for all factor inputs, including labor. Workers will be demanding wage increases to compensate them for the higher cost of living caused by the increase in the price level. Thus the boom generates a combination of conditions—high profits for firms, heavy demand for labor, and a desire on the part of labor for wages to catch up with the price rises—that is a recipe for sharp increases in wages. And this sequence is just what past experience of the economy tells us will happen.[3]

Sharp rises in wages mean sharp rises in costs. These, as we have already seen, lead to upward shifts in the SRAS curve as firms seek to pass on their increases in input costs by increasing their output prices. For this reason the rise in the price level and real output shown in part (i) of Figure 30-5 is *not* the end of the story. As seen in part (ii) of the figure, the upward shift of the SRAS curve causes a further rise in the price level, but this time the price rise is associated with a fall in output. The cost increases and the upward shifts in the SRAS curve go on until income returns to its potential level. Only then is there no abnormal demand for labor.

The excess of output above its potential level, Y^*Y, is a negative GNP gap. Often this is called an **inflationary gap** because Y in the range above

Y^* tends to be associated with inflation. The process comes to a halt when the inflationary gap has been removed.

This very important demand-shock inflation sequence can be summarized as follows:

1. Starting from full employment, a rise in aggregate demand raises the price level and raises income above its potential level as the economy expands along a given SRAS curve.
2. The expansion of output beyond its normal capacity level puts heavy pressure on factor markets; factor prices begin to rise, shifting the SRAS curve upward.
3. The shift of the SRAS curve causes output to fall along the AD curve; this process continues *as long as* actual output exceeds potential output. Therefore, actual output eventually falls back to its potential level. The price level will, however, now be higher than it was after the initial impact of the increased aggregate demand, but inflation will have come to a halt.

The ability to wring more output from the economy than its underlying potential output (point 2) is only a short-term success. Y greater than Y^* sets up inflationary pressures that tend to push national income back to Y^*.

There is a self-adjustment mechanism that brings any inflation caused by a one-time demand shock to an eventual halt by returning output to its potential level and thus removing the inflationary gap.

A continuing inflation. Continuing inflation normally requires that the government frustrate the self-adjustment process just described. It does so by adopting policies that allow the AD curve to *shift* upward just as fast as the SRAS curve does. In Part Ten we shall study such policies and raise the question of why such seemingly undesirable pro-inflationary policies are adopted.

Experience of Demand Inflations

We have just seen that demand inflations are associated with national income at or above its potential level. In other words, when too much de-

---

[3] Wage contracts often allow for changes in prices that are *expected* to occur during the life of the contract. The role of expectations in causing the SRAS curve to shift plays an important role in many macroeconomic debates and will be discussed in detail below.

FIGURE 30-5
Demand-Shock Inflation

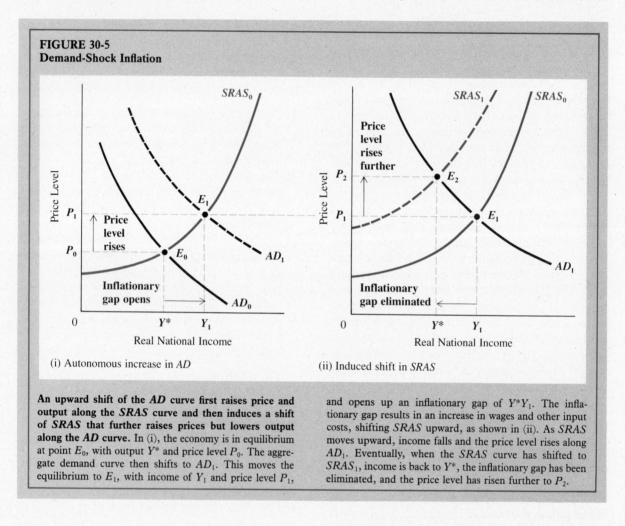

(i) Autonomous increase in *AD*

(ii) Induced shift in *SRAS*

An upward shift of the *AD* curve first raises price and output along the *SRAS* curve and then induces a shift of *SRAS* that further raises prices but lowers output along the *AD* curve. In (i), the economy is in equilibrium at point E_0, with output Y^* and price level P_0. The aggregate demand curve then shifts to AD_1. This moves the equilibrium to E_1, with income of Y_1 and price level P_1, and opens up an inflationary gap of Y^*Y_1. The inflationary gap results in an increase in wages and other input costs, shifting *SRAS* upward, as shown in (ii). As *SRAS* moves upward, income falls and the price level rises along AD_1. Eventually, when the *SRAS* curve has shifted to $SRAS_1$, income is back to Y^*, the inflationary gap has been eliminated, and the price level has risen further to P_2.

mand is the cause of the inflation, boom conditions and rising prices go together. The Canadian economy has suffered from such demand-shock inflations many times in the last 40 years.

Demand shocks have been common throughout our history. The business cycle, which we shall study in detail in Chapter 31, is largely due to variations in export and private-sector investment expenditure, which in turn cause shifts in the aggregate demand curve. Also, major wars have usually been associated with expansionary demand shocks. These occurred during the First and Sec-

ond World Wars in the first half of the century, during the Korean War in the early 1950s, and during the Vietnam War in the late 1960s and early 1970s.

During such wars government greatly increases its spending on military goods and services. It usually finds it difficult, however, to increase its tax revenue as fast as its spending is increased. As a result, there is usually a large increase in government spending (G) *not* matched by an equivalent fall in disposable income or private consumption expenditures (C). The net effect is for aggregate demand to increase. The result is high output combined with rising prices.

A Deflationary Shock

Let us return to that happy economy with full employment and stable prices. It appears again in part (i) of Figure 30-6, which duplicates part (i) of Figure 30-5. Now assume a *decline* in aggregate demand, perhaps due to a major reduction in investment expenditure.

The impact of this decline is a fall in output and some downward adjustment of prices, as shown in part (i) of the figure. As output falls, unemployment figures will rise. The difference between potential output and actual output is, as we have already seen, called the GNP gap. When the GNP gap is positive, as in Figure 30-6, it is also sometimes called the *deflationary gap*. This terminology suggests the operation of an automatic adjustment mechanism that would remove the gap by shifts in the SRAS curve.

Consider what would happen *if* heavy unemployment caused wage rates to fall sharply. Falling wage rates would lower costs for firms, and com-

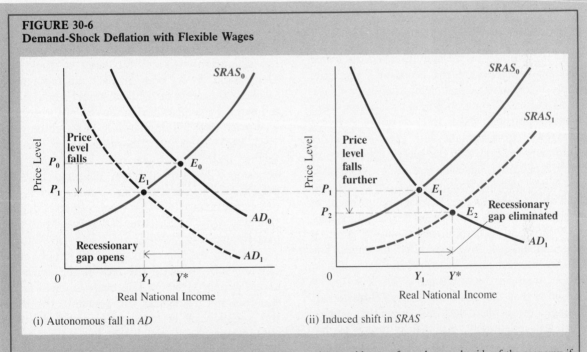

FIGURE 30-6
Demand-Shock Deflation with Flexible Wages

(i) Autonomous fall in *AD*

(ii) Induced shift in *SRAS*

A downward shift of the *AD* curve first lowers price and output along the *SRAS* curve and then induces a (slow) shift of *SRAS* that further lowers prices but raises output along the *AD* curve. In (i), the economy is in equilibrium at E_0, with output Y^* and price level P_0. The aggregate demand curve then shifts to AD_1, moving equilibrium to E_1, with income of Y_1 and price level of P_1, and opens up a recessionary gap of Y_1Y^*.

Part (ii) shows the adjustment back to full employment that would occur from the supply side of the economy if wages were sufficiently flexible downward. The fall in wages would shift *SRAS* downward. Real national income would rise, and the price level would fall further along the *AD* curve. Eventually the curve would reach $SRAS_1$, with equilibrium at E_2. The price level would stabilize at P_2 while income would return to Y^*, eliminating the recessionary gap.

petition among them to sell in a depressed market would, once their falling costs gave them scope to do so, lead them to cut prices. This in turn would cause a downward shift in the short-run aggregate supply curve, as shown in part (ii) of Figure 30-6. As a result, the economy would move along its fixed AD curve with falling prices and rising output until full employment was restored at potential national income of Y^*. This possible process is illustrated in part (ii) of the figure. We conclude that *if* wages were to fall whenever there was unemployment, the resulting fall in the *SRAS* curve would restore full employment.

Flexible wages that fell when there was unemployment would provide an automatic adjustment mechanism that would push the economy back toward full employment whenever output fell below potential.

We now come to what may be called the *second important asymmetry* of the economy's aggregate supply behavior (the first being the shape of the *SRAS* curve). Boom conditions with severe labor shortages *do* cause wages to rise rapidly, carrying the *SRAS* curve upward with them. But many economists believe, and the recent experience of many economies suggests, that slump conditions with heavy unemployment *do not* cause wages to fall with anything like the corresponding speed. In other words, wages are not very flexible in a downward direction. Unemployment has, at most, a weak and sluggish downward effect on wages. The adjustment mechanism described in Figure 30-6 is, at best, weak and slow-acting.

Notice that the weakness of the automatic adjustment mechanism does not mean that slumps must last indefinitely. All that it means is that speedy recovery back to full employment must be generated mainly from the demand side. If the economy is not to experience a lengthy stagnation, the force leading to recovery must be an upward shift in the *AD* curve rather than a downward drift in the *SRAS* curve.

A second asymmetry of aggregate supply behavior is that the *SRAS* curve shifts upward fairly rapidly when Y exceeds Y* but shifts downward only slowly (if at all) when Y falls short of Y*.

This asymmetry explains two key facts about our economy. First, unemployment *can* persist for quite long periods without causing large decreases in wages and prices (which would, if they did occur, help to remove the unemployment). Second, booms, with labor shortages and production beyond normal capacity, *cannot* persist for long periods without causing large increases in wages and prices.

To emphasize this asymmetry, the term **recessionary gap** (rather than deflationary gap) is used when output is below its capacity level, and the term *inflationary gap* (rather than negative GNP gap) is used when output is above its capacity level.

Downward Inflexibility: The 1930s

The last time that the Canadian price level really fell significantly was at the onset of the Great Depression. At its peak in 1933, unemployment reached 20 percent of the labor force! And it never fell below 15 percent during the rest of the decade. The price level fell dramatically in the three years 1931–1933. After 1933, however, there were no further major reductions, even in the face of a persistent GNP gap. Between 1933 and 1939 the price level sometimes rose and sometimes fell, but its average change over that whole period of depression was a *rise* of just over 0.5 percent per year. (See Figure 26-1.)

In short, the short-run aggregate supply curve did not shift down in the face of the persistent excess supply of labor. The main problem facing the economy throughout the decade of the 1930s was a deficiency of aggregate demand. In these circumstances, any policy that increased demand would have helped to alleviate the depression. This was Keynes' great insight.

Students often wonder why economists so frequently look back to the Great Depression. Is it a nostalgia for past times on the part of now-senior economists who grew up in that era? No, it is more than that on two counts. First, evidence is not irrelevant just because it comes from the past. Second, the 1930s constituted the key "experiment" that determined ideas that still are embodied in today's theories. Economists thought they learned two things from this period: (1) Price levels can be very slow to adjust in a downward direction even in the face of very large recessionary gaps; (2) as a consequence, large recessionary gaps can persist for quite a long time unless they are removed by stimulus from the demand side of the economy.

The Long-Run Aggregate Supply Curve

Although the downward adjustments of wages may not remove deflationary gaps fast enough to be of practical importance, the *possibility* of automatic adjustments gives rise to a very important concept: the **long-run aggregate supply curve** (**LRAS**). This curve relates the price level to real national income *after wage rates and all other input costs have been fully adjusted to eliminate any unemployment or overall labor shortages.* This is the output that would occur *if* wages were flexible enough in both directions to eliminate any excess demand or excess supply of labor. Full employment would then prevail and output would be at its potential level, Y^*.

So when all input prices are fully adjusted, the aggregate supply curve becomes a vertical line at Y^*, as seen in part (i) of Figure 30-7. This is called the *long-run aggregate supply curve* because it refers to adjustments that take a substantial amount of time. (If a *downward* adjustment is needed, it can take a very long time.)

Along the *LRAS* curve all the prices of *all out-puts* and *all inputs* have been fully adjusted to eliminate any excess demands or supplies. Proportionate changes in money wages and the price level (which, by definition, will leave real wages unaltered), will also leave equilibrium employment and output unchanged. The key concept is this: if the price of absolutely everything (including labor), doubles, then nothing real changes. When the price of everything bought *and* sold doubles, neither workers nor firms gain any advantage and hence neither has any incentive to alter their behavior. Output, therefore, is unchanged. The level of output will be what can be produced in the economy when all factors of production, including labor, are utilized at "normal" levels of their capacity.

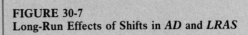

FIGURE 30-7
Long-Run Effects of Shifts in *AD* and *LRAS*

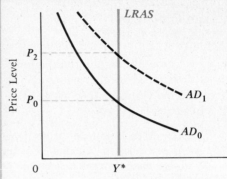

(i) A rise in aggregate demand

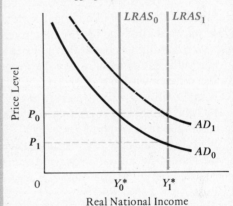

(ii) A rise in long-run aggregate supply

When ***LRAS*** **is vertical, aggregate supply determines** ***Y*** **and aggregate demand determines** ***P***. In (i), a shift in the aggregate demand curve from AD_0 to AD_1 raises the price level from P_0 to P_2 but leaves output unchanged at Y^* in the long run. In (ii), a shift in the long-run aggregate supply curve from $LRAS_0$ to $LRAS_1$ with the aggregate demand curve constant at AD_0 raises output from Y_0^* to Y_1^*, but also lowers the price level from P_0 to P_1. If the new output of Y_1^* were to be purchased at the original price level of P_0, it would be necessary for the aggregate demand curve to shift to AD_1 when the aggregate supply shifts to $LRAS_1$.

The vertical long-run *AS* curve shows that given full adjustment of input prices, potential income, Y^*, is compatible with any price *level*.

Equilibrium Output and Price Level in the Long Run

Figure 30-7 shows the equilibrium output and price level determined by the intersection of the *AD* curve and the vertical *LRAS* curve. One important implication is:

Because the *LRAS* curve is vertical, in the long run output is determined solely by conditions of supply, and the role of aggregate demand is simply to determine the price level.

Note in the figure that a shift in the *AD* curve changes only the price level. However, a shift in the *LRAS* curve changes both output and the price level. An outward shift in the *LRAS* curve, for example, increases output, but at the old price level there is not sufficient demand to buy the new output. Either prices must fall so that the new output will be bought with the old *AD* curve, or the *AD* curve itself must shift right so that the new output can be purchased at the original price level.

Of course these are only long-term tendencies. To see the short-term impact of demand and supply shocks, we need to use the short-run aggregate supply curve.[4]

Note the sharp difference between the long-term and short-term results. Aggregate demand shocks only exert an influence on real income in the short term. When national income is already at full employment, it cannot be permanently increased by raising aggregate demand. What is needed is a rightward shift of the *LRAS* curve, and a major source of such shifts is investment. Recall that early Keynesians paid little attention to the long-run ef-

fect of investment on aggregate supply. Although not an unreasonable thing to do when analyzing severe deflationary conditions, the neglect is serious when the economy is operating at full employment.

Supply-Side Economics

An increase in aggregate supply produces a situation that governments in all countries would have welcomed any time in the 1970s and 1980s: rising output combined with *downward* pressure on the price level. This was the promise of supply-side economics that was an important plank in Ronald Reagan's campaign platform in the 1980 American presidential elections. Although supply-side economics had many aspects, we are here concerned specifically with the short-term effects of supply-side policies on the price level and on real national income.

A major part of supply-side economics was the provision of tax incentives that were to increase potential national income by increasing the nation's supplies of labor and capital. Incentives were given to firms to increase their investment, thus increasing national productive capacity. Personal taxes were to be cut across the board to give everyone an incentive to work more. It was argued that people already employed would be more inclined to work longer and harder when they were able to keep a larger fraction of their gross earnings for themselves, and people outside of the labor force would be drawn in as a result of the higher after-tax wages. Taxes would be especially cut or exemptions especially raised on higher incomes, so as to increase the incentives for work and risk-taking on the part of the most productive people. These people tend to earn the most already, but they have the disincentives of high tax rates on any additional earnings that they make.

But what about the budget deficits that would result from cuts in tax rates and increases in tax exemptions? No worry, went the argument. The increase in national income will create a larger tax base so that even at the lower tax rates, total tax revenues would be restored. For example, if a 10

---

[4] Many of the classical economists were concerned with the behavior of the economy in long-run equilibrium. For this reason, they were concerned with the vertical *LRAS* curve that occurs at the long-run normal rates of output rather than with the vertical portion of the *SRAS* curve (see Figure 30–2), which occurs when no more output can be squeezed from the economy. The key thing, however, is that in their analysis the *AS* curve was vertical.

percent cut in tax rates were followed by a 10 percent increase in real national income, it would leave tax *revenues* approximately the same.

We have seen that starting from an equilibrium situation, an increase in aggregate supply raises output and lowers prices. (The policy was advocated, however, at a time of rapid inflation—the inflation rate in 1979 was close to 10 percent. The effect, therefore, was expected to prevent prices from rising further rather than actually to reduce them.) This possibility is shown in Figure 30-8. An initial inflationary situation shown in (i) is converted into the situation shown in (ii), where output has risen and the inflationary gap removed by a rightward shift in the long-run aggregate supply curve.

Critics had two sorts of doubts. First, many doubted that the tax changes would have the desired effects even in the long run. Economic theory makes no definite prediction about the effects of tax cuts on how much people will work. It might make them work more—because they earn more for each additional hour that they work. But it might make them work less—because the tax cut means that they can, if they wish, have both more disposable income and more leisure. For example, if in response to a 10 percent tax cut they worked 5 percent less, they would have approximately 5 percent more disposable income and 5 percent more leisure.[5] Note that several countries with taxes much higher than those in the United States have also had higher rates of growth of potential income.

The second doubt concerned the demand-side effects of these measures. Whatever the long-term effects on the supply side, economic theory is clear about their short-term effects on the demand side. Cuts in personal tax rates that are intended to be permanent leave households with an increase in their disposable income that they will expect to persist. They will spend more as a result and, as we saw on pages 521–522, this will cause an upward shift in the function relating consumption to disposable income.

[5] This topic is explored in much more detail in Chapter 38.

Also we know that an increase in investment increases aggregate demand. New investment will increase potential output in the long run once the new plants are constructed, the new equipment installed, extra labor hired, and production commenced. But in the short run the extra expenditure on capital goods creates new incomes for the factors of production that produce these goods, and through the multiplier process, new incomes for others as well.

The short-run or impact effect of new investment is to raise aggregate demand, and the long-run effect is to raise potential output.

Thus, the short-run effects of the proposed Reagan policies may have been on aggregate demand, with the results shown in part (iii) of the figure:

The impact effect of the proposed supply-side measures would have been to increase the inflationary gap, causing the price level to rise more than it otherwise would have done.

There might have been a short-run gain in output as equilibrium moved outward along the *SRAS* curve before that curve started to move upward. But any lasting effect on output would have depended on the alleged long-run effect of shifting the *LRAS* curve outward.[6]

What actually transpired during the first years of the Reagan administration bears little resemblance to either what the supply-side proponents or their critics predicted. Output fell and unemployment rose, as the economy suffered a major recession. After responding only slowly at first, inflation then fell dramatically. What is the expla-

[6] It is also worth noting that the predictions about the reduction in the budget deficit are less contentious than those about the long-term increase in real national income. If tax rates are held constant, tax revenues are increased by any rise in nominal national income, PY. From the point of view of raising extra revenue, either an increase in P or an increase in Y is effective. For example, tax revenues rise either if 10 percent more people gain work at existing wage rates and hence earn more taxable income, or if wage rates rise by 10 percent so that the same number of people earn 10 percent more income. It follows that if the tax cuts cause an inflation, this will raise money incomes and tax revenues enough to substantially reduce the deficit initially caused by the cut in tax rates.

FIGURE 30-8
Supply-Side Measures

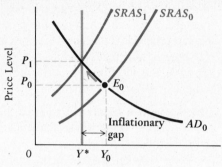

(i)

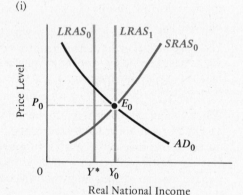

(ii) Supply-side success

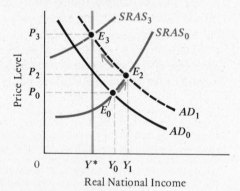

iii) Supply-side failure

Supply-side measures intended to increase output and reduce inflationary pressures are more likely to increase inflation in the short run. Part (i) shows an economy in short-run equilibrium at E_0 on AD_0 and $SRAS_0$ with income Y_0 and price level P_0. As a result of the inflationary gap of Y^*Y_0, $SRAS$ will be shifting upward, taking the equilibrium along AD_0, with falling Y and rising P as shown by the arrow. Other things being equal, the inflation will come to a halt at price level P_1 and income Y^* once the short-run aggregate supply curve has reached $SRAS_1$.

Part (ii) shows the economy in the same initial short-run equilibrium as does (i). The curves AD and $SRAS_0$ yield income Y_0 and price level P_0. There is an inflationary gap, with Y_0 exceeding Y^* on $LRAS_0$. Now, however, supply-side measures shift the long-run aggregate supply curve to $LRAS_1$. This makes Y_0 the new level of potential income and removes the inflationary gap. The fall of income and rise in the price level shown in (i) are both prevented.

Part (iii) again shows the economy in the same short-run initial equilibrium but assumes that the demand side effects of the policy measures are fully felt before any alleged supply-side effects come into play. The aggregate demand curve shifts outward to AD_1. This gives a temporary increase in output to Y_1 at the cost of a rise in the price level of P_2. But the inflationary gap is increased to Y^*Y. Now $SRAS$ starts to shift up, taking the equilibrium along AD in the direction shown by the arrow, with falling output and rising prices. If nothing else happens, the inflation will finally come to an end at price level P_3 and output Y^*.

nation of this? First, the proposed supply-side measures were never fully implemented so neither the *AD* or the *SRAS* curves shifted very much on this account. Second, as we shall see in Chapter 35, very restrictive monetary policies were pursued, causing the *AD* curve to shift leftward.

Supply-side economics has left some important legacies. Policy makers are much more alert to the supply-side effects of their policies than many of them used to be. *But the belief that supply-side measures would produce a quick fix, raising output while relieving inflationary pressures, is now discredited—as its critics always said it would be.* The timing of effects is such that measures that do succeed in shifting both aggregate demand and long-run aggregate supply will have their initial effects through a rapid shift in the *AD* curve and their longer-run effects through a gradual shift in the *SRAS* curve.

SUMMARY

1. The short-run aggregate supply (*SRAS*) curve, drawn for given factor prices, is upward-sloping.

2. One asymmetry of aggregate supply is that the slope of the *SRAS* curve increases as the level of output increases. This occurs because when output is low and firms have much unused capacity, output can be increased with little or no rise in prices; but when output is high and capacity constraints are met, further output increases become increasingly costly, and output will only be increased if prices are increased substantially.

3. The steepness of the *SRAS* curve determines how the impact of a shift in the *AD* curve is divided between a change in output and a change in the price level. When the *SRAS* curve is flat, shifts in the *AD* curve mainly affect real national income. When the *SRAS* curve is steep, shifts in the *AD* curve mainly affect the price level.

4. A change in factor costs or in productivity can cause the *SRAS* curve to shift.

5. On impact an aggregate demand shock causes a movement along the *SRAS* curve. But the change in the GNP gap associated with the new equilibrium value of *Y* then causes a change in factor prices and induces a shift of the *SRAS* curve, leading eventually to elimination of the inflationary gap (caused by an increase in aggregate demand) or the recessionary gap (caused by a decrease in aggregate demand).

6. A second asymmetry of aggregate supply is that an inflationary gap leads to a fairly rapid wage rise and reduction of *Y* to *Y**, while a recessionary gap leads to only very sluggish wage fall and increase of *Y* to *Y**.

7. In the long run, output is determined by the *LRAS* curve while the only role of the *AD* curve is to determine the price level.

8. Supply-side economics seeks to reduce the inflationary gap and increase output by incentive measures to increase potential output. The long-term effect of supply-side measures on potential output is still debated, but the short-term effect is to increase the inflationary gap by increasing aggregate demand.

TOPICS FOR REVIEW

The factors leading to the positive slope of the *SRAS* curve
The factors leading to the increasing slope of the *SRAS* curve
Impact effects of changes in the *AD* curve
The causes of shifts of the *SRAS* curve
The effects of shifts in the *SRAS* curve
Long-run effects of shifts in the *AD* curve
The fast upward shift of the *SRAS* curve in response to an inflationary gap
The slow downward shift of the *SRAS* curve in response to a recessionary gap
Effects of shifts in the *LRAS* curve

DISCUSSION QUESTIONS

1. Following are the combinations of output and price level, given by indexes for GNP and the CPI respectively for some recent years. Plot these and indicate in each case the di-

rection of shift of the *SRAS* and *AD* curves that could have caused them.

	CPI[a]	GNP[b]
1977	161	122
1978	175	126
1979	191	130
1980	211	132
1981	237	136
1982	278	130

[a] 1967 = 100.
[b] Billions of 1971 dollars.

What would you think were the main causes of the shifts? Why might you be uncertain about some of the shifts? What additional information would you require to be able to answer the question?

2. Identify the effects of each of the following events on the *SRAS* curve.
   a. an increase in the price of imported raw materials used in key manufacturing industries
   b. an increase in the price of imported consumption goods such as coffee or bananas
   c. increased restrictions on pollution emissions in an attempt to combat acid rain
   d. projections of increased federal government deficits over the next five years
   e. an improved economic outlook leading to an investment boom
   f. an increased labor force participation rate of key sectors of the population

3. Interpret each of the following news items in terms of *AD* and *SRAS* curves.
   a. "Management representative says union wage demands are irresponsible in the face of current high unemployment rates."
   b. "Government spokesman says that although the recovery is expected to be vigorous, it will witness only modest reductions in the unemployment rate."
   c. "Inflation fell quickly in 1982 due to 'lucky break' of reduced union strength in the automobile and steel sectors."
   d. "Wage increases have failed to keep up with inflation during the current boom."
   e. "Innovations in microelectronic technology will lead to an increase in both national output and unemployment."
   f. "Reagan's tough stance with public sector unions has vastly improved the inflation outlook in the United States over the next few years."

4. Show the effects on the price level and output of income tax cuts that make people work more in an economy currently experiencing an inflationary gap.

5. "Starting from a full employment equilibrium an increase in government spending can produce more output and employment at the cost of a once-and-for-all rise in the price level."

   "Increased spending can never lead to a permanent increase in output above its full employment level."

   Discuss these two statements in terms of short- and long-run aggregate supply curves.

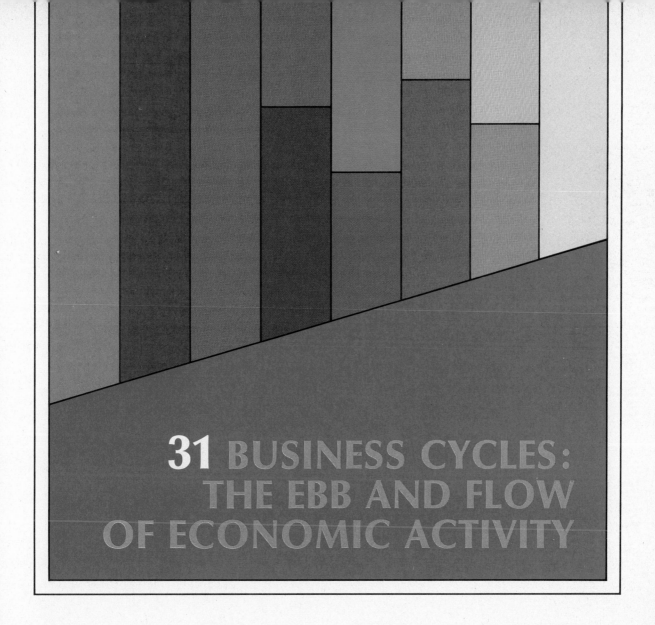

31 BUSINESS CYCLES: THE EBB AND FLOW OF ECONOMIC ACTIVITY

Changing, always changing; this is the dominant characteristic of the GNP for as far back as we have records. Long-term growth (which is studied in Chapter 38) appears in the upward trend in potential GNP. Short-term fluctuations are seen in oscillations of actual GNP around the trend set by potential GNP. Such oscillations are caused by changes in aggregate demand and aggregate supply. They lead to changes in what is actually produced, which in turn cause variations in the amount of

employment and unemployment. They also affect living standards since the goods and services available for all purposes vary as total output varies.

Three Kinds of Variation

When we look at most economic series, we find three separate aspects of change. The first is the long-term trend. In the case of GNP in the twentieth century, there is an upward trend. In the case

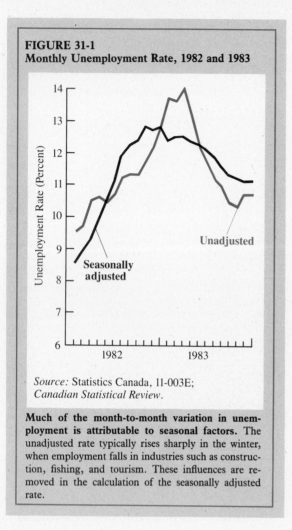

FIGURE 31-1
Monthly Unemployment Rate, 1982 and 1983

Source: Statistics Canada, 11-003E;
Canadian Statistical Review.

Much of the month-to-month variation in unemployment is attributable to seasonal factors. The unadjusted rate typically rises sharply in the winter, when employment falls in industries such as construction, fishing, and tourism. These influences are removed in the calculation of the seasonally adjusted rate.

counted for by any regular seasonal pattern observed in the past. To illustrate, Figure 31-1 shows the seasonal pattern in the Canadian unemployment figures, as well as the seasonally adjusted data.

Once seasonal patterns have been removed, many economic series display a pattern of fluctuations around their long-term trend. These fluctuations are far from random; instead, they exhibit a systematic pattern. A year of relatively high growth is likely to occur in conjunction with other years of high growth, and such groups are likely to be separated by groups of relatively low-growth years. This pattern of a sequence of highs followed by a sequence of lows followed again by another sequence of highs is the source of the term *cyclical* used to describe such economic fluctuations.

The Concept of the Business Cycle

The **business cycle** refers to the continuous ebb and flow of business activity that occurs around any long-term trend after seasonal patterns have

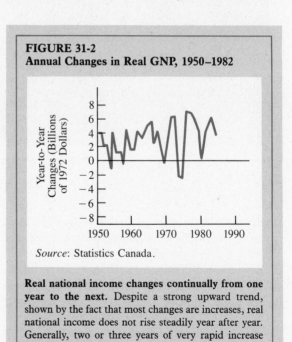

FIGURE 31-2
Annual Changes in Real GNP, 1950–1982

Source: Statistics Canada.

Real national income changes continually from one year to the next. Despite a strong upward trend, shown by the fact that most changes are increases, real national income does not rise steadily year after year. Generally, two or three years of very rapid increase tend to be followed by two or three years of slow increase, or even decline, in GNP.

of the unemployment rate, the series for the twentieth century is essentially trend-free, indicating no *long-term tendency* for the unemployment rate to rise over the century.

Second, most economic series show a marked seasonal pattern over the year. Logging activity tends to be low in the winter months and high in the summer. Fuel oil purchases tend to have the reverse seasonal pattern, while sales on the stock market show no marked seasonal pattern. When economists switch to use monthly or quarterly data, they often seasonally adjust them, which means removing the fluctuations that can be ac-

been removed. Such cyclical fluctuations can be seen in many economic series. For example, continual oscillations in GNP are apparent in Figure 31-2. But the concept of the business cycle refers to fluctuations in the general pace of economic activity. This cannot be caught by a single statistic, even one as important as GNP. Figure 31-3 shows three other economic series. Each of these, as well as a dozen others that might be studied, tells us something about the general variability of the economy. It is clear that some series vary more than others and that they do not all move exactly together.

The picture suggested by Figures 31-2 and 31-3 is not one of occasional sharp shifts in the aggregate demand and supply curves. If it were, we would expect national income to show occasional sharp changes followed by long periods of little or no change. Instead the short-term situation is one of continual change at varying rates.

Evidently there are factors at work causing economic activity to display continual short-term fluctuations around the economy's long-term growth trend.

While all cycles are not alike in duration or inten-

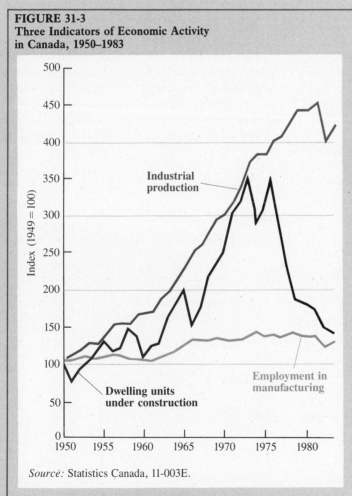

FIGURE 31-3
Three Indicators of Economic Activity in Canada, 1950–1983

Short-term variability and a long-term upward trend characterize many indexes of Canadian economic activity. All three series are index numbers with 1949 = 100, so all would pass through 100 at 1949. All series exhibit differing degrees of short-term variability and differing trend rates of growth. Dwelling starts under construction vary greatly from year to year, and fell continually over the last five years in the figure. Employment in manufacturing does not fluctuate greatly because even a large change in unemployment, say from 4 percent to 8 percent of the labor force, makes a relatively small percentage change in employment.

Source: Statistics Canada, 11-003E.

sity, each appears to have tendencies toward cumulative movements that eventually reverse themselves. This was true long before governments attempted to intervene to stabilize their economies, and it is true still. Figure 31-4 shows the behavior of the Canadian business cycle over the last 20 years, as measured by a composite leading index.

The late Alvin Hansen, a distinguished American authority on business cycles, once reported that there were 17 cycles in the U.S. economy between 1795 and 1937, with an average duration of 8.35 years. A shorter "inventory cycle" of 40 months' duration was also found, as well as longer cycles associated with building booms (15 to 20 years). The Russian economist Nikolai Kondratieff thought he could identify long waves of 40 to 50 years associated with the introduction of major innovations. Some economists have argued that in many Western democracies there exists a political business cycle associated with the pattern of elections.

While the evidence is diverse and varied, it is nevertheless possible to identify some basic characteristics of the pattern of business cycles:

1. There is a common pattern of variation that more or less pervades all economic series.
2. There are differences among economic series in their particular patterns of fluctuations.
3. There is a substantial difference from cycle to cycle in the length and the size of the swings involved.

The Terminology of Business Fluctuations

Although recurrent fluctuations in economic activity are neither smooth nor regular, a vocabulary has developed to denote their different stages. Figure 31-5 shows stylized cycles that will serve to illustrate some terms.

Trough. The trough is, simply, the bottom. A trough is characterized by high unemployment of labor and a level of demand that is low in relation to the capacity of industry to produce goods for consumption. There is thus a substantial amount of unused industrial capacity. Business profits will

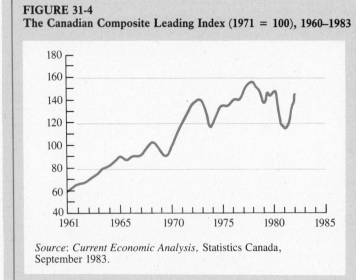

FIGURE 31-4
The Canadian Composite Leading Index (1971 = 100), 1960–1983

The composite leading index shows trend growth interrupted by cyclical fluctuations. The composite leading index, calculated by Statistics Canada, gives one measure of economic activity in Canada. According to that measure, growth was rapid even in the 1960s, but cyclical fluctuations became increasingly important in the 1970s. The sharp fall in the early 1980s shows the severe recession experienced in that period.

Source: *Current Economic Analysis*, Statistics Canada, September 1983.

FIGURE 31-5
A Stylized Business Cycle

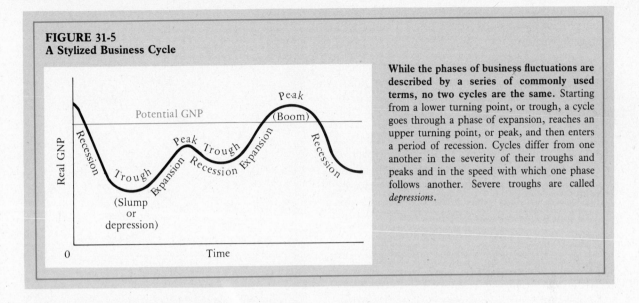

While the phases of business fluctuations are described by a series of commonly used terms, no two cycles are the same. Starting from a lower turning point, or trough, a cycle goes through a phase of expansion, reaches an upper turning point, or peak, and then enters a period of recession. Cycles differ from one another in the severity of their troughs and peaks and in the speed with which one phase follows another. Severe troughs are called *depressions*.

be low; for some individual companies they will be negative. Confidence in the future will be lacking and, as a result, firms will be unwilling to risk making new investments. If a trough is deep enough it may be called a **depression.**

Recovery. When something sets off a recovery, the lower turning point of the cycle has been reached. The symptoms of an expansion are many: Worn-out machinery will be replaced; employment, income, and consumer spending all begin to rise; expectations become more favorable as a result of increases in production, sales, and profits. Investments that once seemed risky may now be undertaken as the climate of business opinion starts to change from pessimism to optimism. As demand expands, production can be expanded with relative ease merely by reemploying the existing unused capacity and unemployed labor.

Peak. At the peak there is a high degree of utilization of existing capacity; labor shortages may be severe, particularly in key skill categories; and shortages of key raw materials may develop. It now becomes difficult to increase output because the supply of unused resources is rapidly disappearing; output can be raised further only by means of

investment that increases capacity. Because of such investment expenditure, investment funds will be in short supply. Because such investment takes time, further rises in demand are now met more by increases in prices than by increases in production. As shortages develop in more and more markets, a situation of general excess demand for factors develops. Costs rise but prices rise also, and business remains generally very profitable.

Losses are infrequent. Profit can be earned simply by holding on to goods whose prices are rising and selling them later at higher prices. Expectations of the future are favorable, and more investment may be made than is justified on the basis of current levels of prices and sales alone.

Recession. When the peak is passed, the economy turns downward. When the contraction is sustained, it is called **recession.** Demand falls off, and as a result production and employment fall. As employment falls so do households' incomes; falling income causes demand to fall further. Profits drop and more and more firms get into difficulties. New investments that looked profitable on the expectation of continuously rising demand suddenly appear unprofitable. Investment is reduced to a low level. It may not even be worth replacing capital goods as they wear out because unused capacity is increasing steadily.

Turning points. The point at which a recession begins is often called the **upper turning point,** while the **lower turning point** refers to the point at which a recovery begins.

Slump and boom. There are no agreed-upon definitions of these two terms. **Slump,** however, is commonly used to refer to the lower half of the cycle covering the last part of the downswing, the trough, and the first part of the upswing. In this usage, **boom** refers to the other, or top half, of the cycle.

Explaining Business Cycles

An explanation of the business cycle must answer two questions. (1) What are the factors causing GNP and other key macro variables to *fluctuate?* (2) What are the factors causing those fluctuations to get smoothed or transformed into a *cyclical* pattern? These two questions are taken up in the two main sections that follow.

WHY DO INCOME AND EMPLOYMENT FLUCTUATE?

Figure 31-6 presents an explanation of the fluctuations of GNP in terms of a fluctuating *AD* curve and a stable *SRAS* curve.

There is general agreement that over the course of Canadian economic history, the business cycle has mainly been driven by fluctuations in aggregate demand. Nevertheless particular cycles can sometimes be explained in part by aggregate supply shocks. Indeed events of the mid 1970s made the citizens of advanced industrial countries acutely aware of supply-side causes.

Aggregate demand shocks are a major historical source of fluctuations in GNP; aggregate supply shocks are a another source.

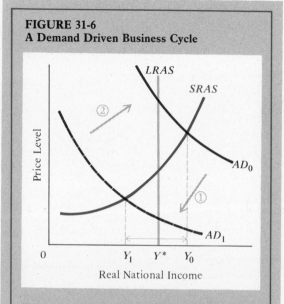

FIGURE 31-6
A Demand Driven Business Cycle

Fluctuations in aggregate demand can cause fluctuations in income and employment. Assume that over the course of the business cycle aggregate demand oscillates regularly. Starting from a high AD_0 and an income at the peak of Y_0, the curve falls continuously, as shown by arrow ①, until it reaches AD_1. Income falls through Y^* and reaches its trough at Y_1.

The AD curve then rises continuously, as shown by arrow ②. Income is taken back through Y^* and reaches Y_0 at the next peak.

Sources of Aggregate Demand Shocks

To say that cycles are often caused by fluctuations in aggregate demand only pushes the need for explanation one stage further back. What are the sources of the continuous disturbances to aggregate demand? The theory of income determination suggests four main candidates—shifts in each of the four main components of aggregate expenditure. Some key facts are shown in Figure 31-7.

Changes in Consumption

Consumption is the largest single component of aggregate expenditure, measuring about two-thirds of the total. When searching for the causes of in-

FIGURE 31-7
Changes in GNP and Selected Components, 1927–1983

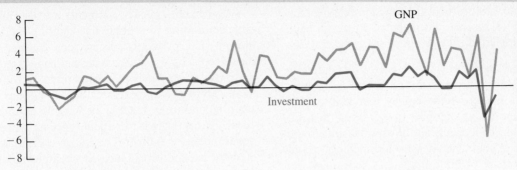

(i) Changes in GNP and investment

(ii) Changes in GNP and government purchases

(iii) Changes in GNP and exports

Source: Statistics Canada, 13–531, 13–201, 11–003 E.

Changes in GNP have been closely related to changes in investment expenditure. The year-to-year fluctuations in GNP correlate closely to changes in investment except during World War II and its aftermath, when changes in government expenditures were the dominant influence. Changes in merchandise exports have reinforced the destabilizing influence of the other two expenditure categories.

come changes, we are not concerned with changes in consumption in response to changes in income but instead with shifts in the function relating consumption to income. Such shifts do occur from time to time, and they can have many causes.

Changes in tastes. In the late 1970s and early 1980s there was a significant reduction in car purchases. If enough of the money that was to have been spent on automobiles were saved instead, there would be a significant downward shift in the aggregate demand curve. Jobs and incomes would first be lost in the auto industry. The induced reduction in spending by workers no longer earning incomes in that industry would then set up a multiplier effect as cuts in output, income, and spending spread throughout the economy.

Changes in expectations and interest rates. Expectations of future inflation may lead to a burst of spending to buy now while goods are cheap. On the other hand, a wave of uncertainty about the future may lead to a rise in saving and hence a cut in spending. High interest rates can be a powerful incentive to postpone buying durable goods. For example, in 1981 rates of over 20 percent served to depress the housing and automobile markets.

In an inflationary world like the one we live in today, it is important to distinguish between the real and the nominal rate of interest. The nominal rate of interest concerns the ratio of the *amount* of money repaid to the amount of money borrowed. The real rate of interest concerns the ratio of the *purchasing power* of the money repaid to the *purchasing power* of the money borrowed, and it may be different from the nominal rate. The real rate of interest is the difference between the nominal rate of interest and the rate of change of the price level. It is this real rate that matters for most expenditure decisions. This distinction is further elaborated in Box 31-1.

Changes in taxes and transfer payments. As we saw in Chapter 29, tax changes can also shift the aggregate consumption function. Income tax cuts mean that more *total* income becomes *dispos-*

able income, leading to an increase in consumer spending. Tax increases have the opposite effect.

Government transfer payments are also important, amounting to roughly one-eighth of personal income. Sharp fluctuations in such transfer payments too could be a highly destabilizing factor via their effects on personal consumption and investment. Here the empirical evidence suggests that such expenditures tend to be sharply countercyclical, rising relative to national income when national income is falling. The reason is clear: Many of these expenditures, such as unemployment insurance and welfare payments, rise when unemployment rises and fall when unemployment falls.

Changes in Government Expenditures on Goods and Services

As Figure 31-7 shows, World War II brought a rapid expansion of economic activity. Government spending was a major contributing factor. Wars always result in an enormous increase in federal governmental expenditures as men and materials are shifted from civilian to military purposes, a shift that is then reversed in the postwar period. For example, federal government purchases of goods and services rose from $683 million in 1939 to $4,978 million in 1944 and fell back to $1,541 million by 1947. Changes in government purchases of goods and services from 1940 to 1946 were the dominant influence on GNP, and they had a substantial effect during the Korean war at the beginning of the 1950s.

Aside from periods of major wars, government expenditures have not often been destabilizing. For peacetime periods before 1940, government expenditures were both small and relatively stable. Since 1955 they have been large and stable and growing rather steadily. Thus, whatever their potential for being a major source of cyclical instability, they have not proved to be such except during wars.

As Figure 31-7 shows, the shocks caused by changing government expenditure have been much smaller on average than the shocks caused by either changing net exports or changing private invest-

BOX 31–1 REAL AND NOMINAL INTEREST RATES: AN IMPORTANT DISTINCTION

If you pay me $8 interest for a $100 loan for one year, the nominal rate is 8 percent. The real rate that I earn, however, depends on what happens to the overall level of prices in the economy.

In the above example, if the price level remains constant over the year, then the real rate that I earn will also be 8 percent. This is because I can buy 8 percent more goods and services with the $108 that you repay me than with $100 that I lent you. However, if the price level were to rise by 8 percent, the real rate would be *zero* because the $108 you repay me will buy the same quantity of goods as did the $100 I gave up. If I were unlucky enough to have lent money at 8 percent in a year in which prices rose by 10 percent, the real rate I would have earned would be negative 2 percent.

If lenders and borrowers are concerned with the real costs measured in terms of purchasing power, the nominal rate of interest will be set at the real rate they require plus an amount to cover any expected rate of inflation. Consider a one-year loan that is meant to earn a real return to the lender of 5 percent. If the expected rate of inflation is zero, the nominal rate set for the loan will be 5 percent. If a 10 percent inflation is expected, the nominal rate will be 15 percent.

To provide a given expected real rate of interest the nominal rate will be set at the desired real rate of interest plus the expected annual rate of inflation.

This point is often overlooked, and as a result people are surprised at the high nominal rates of interest that exist during periods of rapid inflation. For example, when nominal interest rates rose drastically in 1981, many commentators expressed shock at the "unbearably" high rates. Most of them failed to notice that with inflation running at about 12 percent, an interest rate of 15 percent represented a real rate of only 3 percent. Had the Bank of Canada given in to the pressure to hold rates to the more "reasonable" level of 10 percent, it would have been imposing a negative real rate of interest. Lenders would then have been "rewarded" for lending their money by receiving less purchasing power in interest plus principal than the purchasing power of the principal they parted with initially.

Concern about the burden of borrowing should be directed at the real, not the nominal, interest rate.

A nominal rate of 8 percent combined with a 2 percent rate of inflation is a greater burden on borrowers than a nominal rate of 16 percent combined with a 14 percent rate of inflation.

Cash Flow Problems

Although some of the effects of inflation can be compensated for by changes in the nominal interest rate, this is not the end of the story. The inflation premium on interest rates represents an early repayment of capital and hence causes cash flow problems for borrowers. Consider a simple example. A firm borrows $1,000 for 10 years at 4 percent when the price level is constant. The firm will pay $40 of interest per year and at the end of 10 years it must repay in one lump sum the capital of $1,000.

Now assume that the same bargain is struck except that a 5 percent rate of inflation will occur, *and is fully expected*, over the period of the loan. In this case the nominal rate of interest will be 14 percent, and its annual interest payments are $140.

In one sense the real situation is unchanged but in another very important sense it is different. The firm is now paying an annual inflation premium of $100. This compensates the lenders for the loss of purchasing power on the principal of their loans. But for the borrowers it constitutes an early repayment of capital. Note that the $1,000 repaid at the end of the 10-year period has a much smaller real value in the second (inflationary) situation.

So the stream of real payments is very different when a 4 percent interest rate is combined with a zero inflation rate and when a 9 percent interest rate is combined with a 5 percent inflation rate.

ment expenditure. We return below to a discussion of the important role played by changing investment expenditure.

Changes in Exports

A country such as Canada, in which foreign trade plays a large role, is subject to destabilizing influences from foreign demand. Since about one-half of all goods produced in Canada are exported, fluctuations in the national income of other countries can be transmitted to our economy through fluctuations in their demand for our exports. As Figure 31-5 shows, changes in merchandise exports played an important role during the Great Depression. The fall in export demand triggered by the depression in the economies of our major trading partners led to a fall in our exports, thereby reinforcing the early stages of the recession in Canada. Similarly, during World War II exports boomed at the same time that the domestic economy was expanding.

Similar influences of exports on the domestic economy can be seen throughout the period. Perhaps the most notable episode was the boom in the economy during the early 1970s followed by the decline in the mid 1970s. Exports rose sharply from 1971 to 1973 and then fell sharply in the years 1973 to 1975.

This period warrants further examination. Since Canada was a net exporter of petroleum in 1973, the increase in world oil prices brought on by OPEC should have translated into an *increase* in foreign demand for Canadian petroleum products. However, Canadian oil exports were, at that time, regulated by the National Energy Board, and they did not in fact increase. Further, the OPEC shock caused a major recession in countries—particularly the United States—that purchase nonpetroleum exports from Canada. The recession abroad led to a reduction in the level of Canadian exports, which in turn led to a reduction in the growth of the Canadian economy. From 1974 to 1975, exports fell by more than 4 percent while growth in GNP fell by 4 percent relative to the growth in GNP achieved in the previous two-year period.

Factors other than foreign incomes also affect Canadian exports. One of the most important is the ability of Canadian firms to compete in international markets, as influenced in the short run by changes in the exchange rate and more directly by changes in domestic costs relative to foreign costs. Labor costs as reflected in wages are important, as are the costs of material inputs and energy.

In an open economy, fluctuations in exports play a key role in the theory of cyclical fluctuations.

Box 31-2 on pages 562–563 discusses some further aspects of the relationship of net exports to cyclical movements in income.

Changes in Investment

An important source of disturbance is investment expenditure. Consider the period 1929–1932. In 1929 total investment expenditure of firms and households in the Canadian economy was $1.2 billion, almost double the amount of expenditure needed to replace the capital goods that we used up that year in the process of producing a GNP of $6.1 billion. The Canadian economy in 1929, then, was adding rapidly to its stock of capital equipment. Four years later, in 1933, total investment expenditure was $145 million. This was less than one-third of the amount needed merely to keep the stock of capital intact. The Canadian economy in 1933, with its GNP reduced to $3.5 billion, was rapidly reducing its stock of capital equipment.

As Figure 31-7 shows, investment expenditure is quite volatile. Quite large shocks due to changes in investment expenditure hit the economy frequently. On average the change in investment from one year to the next has been about three times the average change in government expenditure.

Changes in investment are also quite closely correlated with changes in national income, as also shown in Figure 31-7. Rising investment tends to be associated with rapidly rising GNP, while falling investment tends to be associated with slowly rising or falling GNP. This is consistent with the view that investment shocks are a major cause of changes in national income.

Investment expenditures play a key role in most theories of cyclical fluctuations.

Why Does Investment Change?

The three major components of total investment expenditure are inventories, business fixed investment, and residential construction. Changes in investment are one of the prime causes of short-term fluctuations, but we do not have the whole story unless we know why investment fluctuates. In discussing the theory of income determination in Chapters 28 and 29 we talked simply of shifts in investment, not of the underlying causes of such shifts. While each dollar of investment has the same consequences for aggregate demand, different types of investment respond to different sets of causes. Thus it is useful to discuss separately the determinants of the three major types of investment expenditures.

Investment in Inventories

Inventory changes represent only a small fraction of private investment in a typical year. Their average size is not an adequate measure of their importance. They are one of the more volatile elements of total investment and therefore are a major cause of shifts in investment expenditure.

Studies show that the stock of inventories held tends to rise as production and sales rise. Because the size of inventories is related to the level of sales, the *change* in inventories (which is current investment) is related to the *change* in the level of sales.

A firm may decide, for example, to hold inventories of 10 percent of its sales. Thus, if sales are $100,000, it will wish to hold inventories of $10,000. If sales increase to $110,000, it will want to hold inventories of $11,000. Over the period during which its stock of inventories is being increased, there will be a total of $1,000 new inventory investment.

The higher the level of production and sales, the larger the desired stock of inventories. Changes in the rate of production and sales cause temporary bouts of investment (or disinvestment) in inventories.

When a firm ties up funds in inventories, those same funds cannot be used eleswhere to earn income. At the very least the money could be lent out at the going rate of interest. Thus the higher the real rate of interest, the higher will be the cost of holding an inventory of a given size. And the higher that rate of interest, the more firms will try to lower their inventories. By causing firms to change the inventory levels that they desire to hold, a change in the rate of interest can lead to a flurry of investment or disinvestment in inventories.

The higher the real rate of interest, the lower the desired stock of inventories. Thus changes in the rate of interest cause temporary bouts of investment (or disinvestment) in inventories.

Investment in Residential Housing Construction

Since 1970 spending on residential construction has varied between one-fifth and one-third of all gross private investment and between 3.5 percent and 6.4 percent of GNP. Because expenditures for housing construction are both large and variable, they exert a major impact on the economy.

Many influences on residential construction are noneconomic and depend on demographic or cultural considerations such as new family formation. But households must not only want to buy houses, they must be able to do so. Periods of high employment and high average family earnings tend to lead to increases in house building, and those of unemployment and falling earnings to decreases in such building.

Almost all houses are purchased with money borrowed on mortgages. Interest on the borrowed money typically accounts for over one-half of the purchaser's annual mortgage payments; the other half is repayment of principal. It is for this reason that sharp variations in interest rates exert a substantial effect on the demand for housing.

Box 31-3 on page 564 provides an example illustrating the importance of interest rates for housing. This importance was borne out by experience from 1979 to 1982. During this period mortgage rates rose from less than 11 percent to just over 15

BOX 31-2 FLUCTUATIONS IN NATIONAL INCOME AND THE BALANCE OF TRADE

Exports are an important source of demand for domestically produced goods. A key determinant of a country's exports is the level of activity in its major trading partners. When the United States experiences a boom, as it did in the period 1983–1984, there is a large American demand for Canadian exports. In turn, via the multiplier process, the increase in exports will cause an expansion in Canadian national income. Similarly, when the United States experiences a recession, as it did in 1981–1982, American demand for Canadian goods will be low. Again the change in exports causes a multiplier effect, this time leading to a reduction in Canadian national income.

As a result of this *export multiplier*, the business cycles of major trading partners are likely to be closely correlated.

Imports and the Size of the Multiplier

As we saw in Chapter 28, expenditure on imports will grow as domestic national income grows. Since imports represent spending on other countries' outputs, they raise the economy's marginal propensity not to spend and hence, as we saw in Chapter 28, they reduce the size of the multiplier. [39] Of course this has both desirable and undesirable consequences. It is undesirable because it reduces the effectiveness of domestic policies that attempt to change the level of domestic income. It is desirable be-

cause it reduces the impact on national income of fluctuations in such autonomous expenditure items as investment and exports.*

Net Exports and Domestic Absorption

The model of national income determination outlined in Chapter 28 provides an important perspective on the determination of net exports. Recall the basic condition for equilibrium national income.

$$Y = C + I + G + (X - M)$$

The sum of $C + I + G$ corresponds to total expenditure on all goods and services (domestic and foreign) for use *within* the economy; this total is often referred to as **domestic absorption** (**A**). The equilibrium relationship can therefore be rewritten as

$$Y = A + (X - M)$$

The right-hand side of this equation is desired aggregate expenditure on Canadian goods and services, represented as the sum of expenditure for *internal* use (domestic absorption) plus expenditure due to net *external* demand (net exports). Subtracting A from both sides, we get

$$Y - A = X - M$$

---

* The consequence of the latter effect is that imports act as a *built-in-stabilizer*. We encounter built-in stabilizers again in Chapter 32 in our analysis of fiscal policy.

---

percent and housing starts fell from 197 thousand units to a mere 126 thousand in 1982. (Since inflation fell from 1980, the increased nominal interest rates also meant increased real rates.) The construction industry itself and its major suppliers such as the cement and the lumber industries felt the blow of a dramatic fall in demand.

Expenditures for residential construction tend to vary positively with changes in average income and negatively with interest rates.

Business Fixed Investment

Investment in machinery, equipment, and non-residential construction is the largest component of

This makes it clear that net exports can be positive only if national income exceeds domestic absorption; that is, only if total demand for goods and services to be used in Canada is less than total output of goods and services in Canada. And if net exports are positive, it must be the case that national income exceeds the absorption of goods and services within Canada.†

Absorption Versus Component Approaches to the Trade Balance

Organizing the theory of income determination in this way has led economists to view the trade balance as an aggregate phenomenon: it must equal the difference between the two aggregates, *national income* and *domestic absorption*.

The trade balance, by definition, is also equal to the sum of all exports minus the sum of all imports. This makes it tempting to try to explain changes or trends in the trade account by "counting" the changes in particular exports and imports. Since both this "component" definition and the absorption definition are correct as *definitions* of the trade balance, either is valid as a framework that can be used to organize information in order to *analyze* the trade account. The danger with the component approach is that the analyst may ignore the inter-

† Note that foreigners can influence the demand for Canadian goods and services in two ways: by demanding exports and by investing in Canada.

action between the items included in the trade balance and other variables such as national income. The absorption approach tends to draw attention to such interactions.

In order to compare the approaches, consider the effect on the trade balance of an exogenous increase in the foreign demand for one particular Canadian export. An increase in a particular export, *other things being equal*, will lead to an increase in national income. This increase in national income will lead in turn to increased expenditure on some imports. If one takes the component approach to analyzing the trade account, one may miss this induced effect. For example, if exports of wheat rose by $20 million in a given year, one might conclude that the trade balance would improve by $20 million. But the increased wheat exports would be reflected in higher incomes for farmers and the producers of transportation services who ship the wheat. These groups will spend some of their increased incomes on imports and some on domestic goods. The latter will lead to a multiplier effect on national income and result in further increases in spending on imports.

Clearly the net effect on the trade balance of the increased wheat exports must include the induced increases in imports. By relating the trade balance to the difference between total income and total spending in the domestic economy, this is exactly what the absorption approach does. [40]

domestic investment. Much of it is financed by firms' retained profits (profits *not* paid out to its shareholders). This means that current profits are an important determinant of investment.

A second major determinant is the rate of interest. Much investment is financed by borrowed money. As became abundantly clear in the early

1980s, very high interest rates greatly reduce the volume of investment as more and more firms find their expected profits from investment do not cover the interest on borrowed investment funds.

A third major determinant is *changes* in national income. If there is a rise in aggregate demand that is expected to persist and cannot be met by existing

BOX 31–3 THE COST OF BUYING A HOUSE ON TIME

Few people who buy a house can pay cash. Most purchases are financed by borrowing money on a *mortgage*. A mortgage is a loan to the house purchaser (sometimes of as much as 85 or 90 percent of the purchase price, but 60 to 75 percent is common). In return, the borrower promises to make fixed monthly payments that cover interest on the money borrowed and repay the amount borrowed over some agreed period, commonly 20 years. (The monthly payments often include an amount to cover insurance and taxes, but this is ignored in what follows.) The house itself acts as security for the loan. Loans of this type are said to be *amortized*, which means that fixed payments cover the interest on the principal outstanding *and* repay the principal over a stated period.

Because the loan stretches over a long period, a great deal of the total amount paid by the borrower is interest on the outstanding loan. For example, on a 20-year mortgage for $50,000 at a nominal annual interest rate of 8 percent per year (a monthly rate of 8/12 of 1 percent), a total

of $100,375 would be paid in 240 monthly installments of $418.23 each. This is $50,000 to repay the principal of the loan and $50,375 of interest. At a 12 percent nominal annual rate, the total payments would be $132,130, making $82,130 total interest as well as $50,000 to repay the principal.

The interest on a mortgage is calculated on the amount of the loan still outstanding. After each payment the amount outstanding is reduced so that, with fixed annual payments, most of the total amount paid goes to paying interest in the early years and to repaying principal in later years. It follows that the purchaser's equity in the house builds up slowly at first, then more rapidly as the terminal date approaches.

Note in the table that when half the life of the mortgage has passed, only about a quarter of the principal has been repaid. In the first year of the mortgage, $4,965 goes as interest and only $825 to reduce the principal on the loan. In the last year, only $300 is interest and $5790 goes to repay the principal.

BREAKDOWN OF PAYMENTS IN SELECTED YEARS ON A 20-YEAR MORTGAGE FOR $50,000 AT 10 PERCENT (All Figures to the Nearest Dollar)

Year	Payments made over the year	Interest paid over the year	Principal (amount of loan) repaid over the year	Equity (amount of loans repaid over all the years)
1	$5,790	$4,965	$ 825	$ 825
2	5,790	4,875	915	1,745
5	5,790	4,560	1,230	5,100
10	5,790	3,765	2,025	13,490
15	5,790	2,455	3,335	27,290
19	5,790	820	4,970	44,510
20	5,790	300	5,490	50,000

capacity, then investment in new plant and equipment will be needed. Once the new plants have been built and put into operation, however, the rate of new investment will fall.

This further illustrates an important characteristic of investment already encountered in the case of inventories: *If the desired stock of capital goods increases, there will be an investment boom while the new capital is being produced.* But if nothing else changes, and even though business conditions continue to look rosy enough to justify the increased stock of capital, investment in new plant and equipment will cease once the larger capital stock is achieved. This aspect of investment leads to the *accelerator* theory of investment, which requires a closer look.

The Interest Rate and Investment

Empirical evidence shows that investment responds to many influencing factors. One of the most important is the rate of interest. *Ceteris paribus*, the higher is the interest rate, the higher is the cost of borrowing money for investment purposes and the less will be the amount of investment expenditure.

Although in basic theory we talk of "the" interest rate, reality is not so simple. We now need to look at a few of these complications.

Many rates of interest. In the real world there are many different rates of interest. Speaking in terms of a single rate can be a valid simplification for many purposes because the whole set of rates *tends* to move upward or downward together. Concentrating on one "typical" rate as "the" rate of interest in such cases is quite acceptable. For some purposes, however, it is important to take into account the multiplicity of interest rates.

At the same time that you receive an interest rate of 6 or 7 percent on deposits at a trust company, you may have to pay 11 or 12 percent to borrow from that trust company to buy a house. Interest rates on consumer installment credit of 16 percent and 20 percent are observed. A small firm pays a higher interest rate on funds it borrows from banks than does a giant corporation. Different government bonds pay different rates of interest, depending on the length of the period for which the bond runs. Corporation bonds tend to pay higher interest than government bonds, and there is much variation among bonds of different companies. Considering the extreme mobility of money, why do such differences exist? Why do funds not flow between different uses to eliminate these differences? The answer is that money does flow quite

rapidly between alternative assets in response to relevant interest differentials, but differences prevail because quoted interest rates are composites of many things.

Differences in risk. Corporation bonds generally have higher interest rates than Government of Canada bonds because they have a greater degree of risk. For example, in mid 1981 many corporate issues were yielding in excess of 14 percent, while federal government bonds were paying 13 percent or less. Why? Investors were sure of the ability of the government of Canada to pay both the interest and the principal on their bonds, but they were less sure about the financial condition or private corporations.

Secured loans, where the borrower pledges an asset as collateral, tend to have lower interest rates than unsecured loans, other things being equal. Loans secured by houses (mortgages) tend to have lower interest rates than loans secured by automobiles, in part because it is harder to run away with a house than with a car and in part because a car can depreciate much more rapidly and unpredictably than a house.

Differences in duration. The *term* (duration) of a loan may likewise affect its price. The same bank will usually pay a higher rate of interest on a certificate of deposit that cannot be redeemed at the bank (without penalty) for at least one year than on a straight savings account, which can be withdrawn in a matter of minutes. Yet many savers prefer savings accounts because they want to be able to withdraw their money on short notice. Except when interest rates are thought to be temporarily abnormally high, borrowers are usually willing to pay more for long-term loans than for short-term loans because they are certain of having use of the money for a longer period. Lenders usually require a higher rate of interest the longer is the time before the borrower must repay. Other things being equal, the shorter the term of a loan, the lower are the interest rates.

Differences in costs of administering credit. There is great variation in the cost of different kinds of credit transactions. It is almost as cheap (in actual dollars) for a bank to lend Pacific Western Airlines $1 million that the airline agrees to pay back with interest after one year as it is for the same bank to lend you $4,000 to buy a new car on an installment loan that you agree to pay back over two years in 24 equal installments.

The loan to you requires many more bookkeeping entries than the loan to the airline. In addition, it is easier, and therefore less costly, to check Pacific Western Airlines' credit rating than it is to check yours. The difference in the cost *per dollar* of each loan is considerable. The bank may very well make less profit per dollar on a $4,000 loan at 20 percent per year than on a $1 million loan at 10 percent per year. In general, the bigger the loan and the fewer the payments, the less the cost per dollar of servicing the loan. Why then do banks and finance companies usually insist that you repay a loan in frequent installments? They worry that if you do not pay regularly, you will not have the money when the loan comes due.

In the market for borrowed funds there will be a structure of interest rates for credit transactions of different kinds.

Individual rates will be set that take into account such factors as risk premiums, duration of loan, and costs of administration. Nevertheless, it is useful and usual to talk about movements of interest rate structures up and down as changes in "the" interest rate. This simplification is most useful when the entire structure of rates moves up or down together so that changes in a single typical rate can capture changes in all rates.

The Accelerator Theory of Investment

According to the accelerator theory (usually called the **accelerator**), investment is related to the rate of change of national income. When income is increasing, it is necessary to invest in order to increase the capacity to produce consumption goods; when income is falling, it may not even be necessary to replace old capital as it wears out, let alone to invest in new capital.

The main insight which the accelerator theory

provides is the emphasis on the role of net investment as a dynamic process that occurs when the stock of capital goods that firms and households would like to hold is changing. Anything that changes the desired quantities of inventories, buildings, or equipment can generate investment. The accelerator focuses on one such source of change, changing national income. This gives the accelerator its particular importance in connection with *fluctuations* in national income. As we shall see, it can itself contribute to those fluctuations.

How the Accelerator Works

To see how the theory works, it is convenient to make the simplifying assumption that there is a particular capital stock needed to produce each given level of an industry's output. (The ratio of the value of capital to the annual value of output is called the **capital-output ratio**.) Given this assumption, suppose the industry is producing at capacity and the demand for its product increases. If the industry is to produce the higher level of output, its capital stock must increase. This necessitates new investment.

Table 31-1 provides a simple numerical example of the accelerator that, worked through step by step, leads to three conclusions:

1. **Rising rather than high levels of sales are needed to call forth net investment.**
2. **For net investment to remain constant, sales must rise by a constant amount per year.**
3. **The amount of net investment will be a multiple of the increase in sales because the capital-output ratio is greater than one.**[1]

The data in Table 31-1 are for a single industry, but if many industries behave in this way, one would expect aggregate net investment to bear a similar relation to changes in national income. This is what the accelerator theory predicts. [41]

The accelerator theory says nothing directly about replacement investment, but it does have

[1] In the example in the table the capital-output ratio is 5. Why should anyone spend $5 on capital stock to get $1 of output? It is not unreasonable to spend $5 to purchase a machine that produces only $1 of output *per year*, provided that the machine will last enough years to repay the $5 plus a reasonable return on this investment.

TABLE 31–1 AN ILLUSTRATION OF THE ACCELERATOR THEORY OF INVESTMENT

(1) Year	(2) Annual sales	(3) Change in sales	(4) Required stock of capital, assuming a capital-output ratio of 5/1	(5) Net investment: increase in required capital stock
1	$10	$0	$ 50	$ 0
2	10	0	50	0
3	11	1	55	5
4	13	2	65	10
5	16	3	80	15
6	19	3	95	15
7	22	3	110	15
8	24	2	120	10
9	25	1	125	5
10	25	0	125	0

With a fixed capital-output ratio net investment occurs only when it is necessary to increase the stock of capital in order to change output. Assume that it takes $5 of capital to produce $1 of output per year. In years 1 and 2, there is no need for investment. In year 3, a rise in sales of $1 requires investment of $5 to provide the needed capital stock. In year 4, a further rise of $2 in sales requires an additional investment of $10 to provide the needed capital stock. As columns 3 and 5 show, the amount of net investment is proportional to the *change* in sales. When the increase in sales tapers off in years 7–9, investment declines. When, in year 10, sales no longer increase, net investment falls to zero because the capital stock of year 9 is adequate to provide output for year 10's sales.

implications for such investment. When sales are constant (no net investment required), replacement investment will be required to maintain the capital stock at the desired level. When sales are increasing from a position of full capacity, both net investment and replacement investment will be required. When sales are falling, not only will net investment be zero, but there will be a tendency to postpone replacement investment as well.

Limitations of the Accelerator

Taken literally, the accelerator posits a rigid response of investment to changes in sales (and thus, aggregatively, to changes in national income). In fact the relation is more subtle than that.

Changes in sales that are thought to be temporary will not necessarily lead to new investment. It is usually possible to increase the level of output for a given capital stock by working overtime or extra shifts. While this solution would be more expensive per unit of output in the long run, it will usually be preferable to making investments in new plant and equipment that would lie idle after a temporary spurt of demand had subsided. Thus expectations about what the required capital stock is may lead to a much less rigid response of investment to income than the accelerator suggests.

A further limitation of the accelerator theory is that it takes a very limited view of what constitutes investment. The fixed capital-output ratio emphasizes investment in what economists call **capital widening,** the investment in additional capacity that uses the same ratio of capital to labor as existing capacity. It does not explain **capital deepening,** which is the increase in the amount of capital per unit of labor that occurs in response to a fall in the rate of interest. Neither does the theory say anything about investments brought about as a result of new processes or new products. Furthermore, it does not allow for the fact that investment in any period is likely to be limited by the capacity of the capital-goods industry.

For these and other reasons, the accelerator does not by itself give anything like a complete explanation of variations in investment in plant and equipment. It should not be surprising that a simple accelerator theory provides a relatively poor overall explanation of changes in investment. Yet accelerator-like influences do exist, and empirical evidence continues to suggest that they play a role in the cyclical variability of investment.

THEORIES OF THE CYCLE

There are several main theories of the cycle. They do not have to be regarded as competing. Indeed each one captures some of the forces that contribute to the cycle. We shall examine three.

Systematic Spending Fluctuations

The most commonly accepted theory looks to systematic fluctuations in aggregate expenditure brought about by systematic alterations in spending behavior as the cause of the cycle. Several influences can cause such alterations.

The Multiplier-Accelerator Mechanism

The combination of the multiplier and the accelerator can make upward or downward movements in the economy cumulative. Imagine that the economy is settled into a depression with heavy unemployment. Then a revival of investment demand occurs. Orders are placed for new plant and equipment, which creates new employment in the capital-goods industries. The newly employed workers spend most of their earnings. This creates new demand for consumer goods. A multiplier process is now set up, with new employment and incomes created in the consumer-goods industries.

The spending of the newly created incomes in turn means further increases in demand. At some stage the increased demand for consumer goods will create, through the accelerator process, an increased demand for capital goods. Once existing equipment is fully employed in any industry, extra output will require new capital equipment—and the accelerator theory takes over as the major determinant of investment expenditure. Such investment will increase or at least maintain demand in the capital-goods sector of the economy. So the process goes on, the multiplier-accelerator mechanism continuing to produce a rapid rate of expansion in the economy.

The upper turning point. A very rapid expansion can continue for some time, but it cannot go on forever. Eventually the economy will run into bottlenecks in terms of certain resources. For example, investment funds may become scarce, and as a result interest rates will rise. Firms now find new investments more expensive than anticipated, and thus some will become unprofitable. Or suppose that what limits the expansion is exhaustion of the reservoir of unemployed labor. The full-employment ceiling guarantees that any sustained rapid growth rate of real income and employment will eventually be slowed.

At this point the accelerator again comes into play. A slowing down in the rate of increase of production leads to a decrease in the investment in new plant and equipment. This decrease causes a drop in employment in the capital-goods industries and, through the multiplier, a fall in consumer demand. As consumer demand falls, investment in plant and equipment is reduced to a low level because firms already have more productive capacity than they can use. Unemployment rises, and the upper turning point has been passed.

The lower turning point. A contraction, too, is eventually brought to an end. Consider the very worst sort of depression imaginable, one in which every postponable expenditure of households, firms, or governments is postponed. Even then aggregate demand will not fall to zero. Figure 28-2 on page 506 shows that as aggregate disposable income falls, households will spend a larger and larger fraction of that falling income. Finally, should income fall to the break-even level, all disposable income will be spent (and none will be saved).

Neither does government spending fall in proportion to the fall in government tax revenues. Government expenditures on most programs will continue even if tax revenues sag to low levels. Finally, even investment expenditures, in many ways the most easily postponed component of aggregate expenditure, will not fall to zero. Industries providing basics will still have substantial sales and need replacement investment. Even in a depression some new processes and products appear, and these require new investment.

Taken together, the minimum levels of consumption, investment, and government expenditure will assure a minimum equilibrium level of national income that, although well below the full-employment level, will not be zero. There is a floor below which income will not fall.

Sooner or later, an upturn will begin. If nothing else causes an expansion of business activity, there will eventually be a revival of replacement investment because as existing capital wears out, the capital stock will eventually fall below the level required to produce current output. At this stage new machines will be bought to replace those that are worn out.

The rise in the level of activity in the capital-goods industries will cause, by way of the multiplier, a further rise in income. The economy has turned the corner. An expansion, once started, will trigger the sort of cumulative upward movement already discussed.

Other Endogenous Forces

The multiplier-accelerator is one endogenous force contributing to cyclical fluctuations. Two others are inventories and construction.

Inventory cycles. There are, as we have seen, good reasons to suppose that the required size of inventories is related to the level of firms' sales, and sales are related to the level of national income. If firms maintain anything like a rigid inventory-to-sales ratio, this will cause an accelerator-like linkage between investment in inventories and *changes* in national income. Many observers believe that fluctuations lead to an "inventory cycle" of roughly 40 months' average duration.

A building cycle? Economists have noted some long-run, wavelike movements of roughly 20 years' duration in the statistics for expenditures on residential construction. These are sometimes referred to as "building cycles." Some economists suggest an accelerator-like explanation that runs from external events to demographic changes, to changes in the demand for housing and other buildings, and thence to changes in construction activity.

A major war, by taking males away from home, tends to retard family formation and thereby tends to depress the demand for private housing. After the conclusion of the war there is typically an increase in marriages and household formation, an increase in the demand for housing, and a boom in the construction industry.

Depending on the capacity of the building industry, the boom may last many years before the desired increases in the stock of buildings of various kinds are achieved, but eventually it will end. Then, approximately 20 years after the end of the war that triggered the boom, there is likely to be a further boom in the number of marriages and births as the new generation starts its process of family formation. Wars are not the only source of such population-induced cycles; a severe depression will lead to a similar postponement of family formation.

The evidence concerning construction spending over the past century is thought by many economists to support the theory just outlined, a theory very much like the accelerator, though with changes in demographic factors, rather than changes in income, providing the impetus.

Random Shocks and Long Lags

An alternative theory does not assume cyclical behavior from firms and households in order to generate cycles. It suggests instead that random shifts in expenditure are transformed into systematic cycles of output and employment.

This theory begins with lags. For example, if a fall in the rate of interest makes an investment in a new project profitable, it may take 6 months to plan it, 3 months to let contracts, 6 months before spending builds up to its top rate, and another 24 to complete the project. These lags mean that changes in the rate of interest will cause reactions in investment expenditure that are distributed over quite a long period of time.

These lags have important implications for key macro variables. Although the disturbing influences might be random or erratic, income and employment both follow a cyclical path.

Each major component of aggregate expenditure has sometimes undergone shifts large enough to disturb the economy significantly. Long lags can convert such shifts into cyclical oscillations in national income.

A Policy-Induced Cycle

It has been alleged that government-induced demand shocks have sometimes caused cyclical fluctuations. Government expenditure has not often been the cause of major shocks due to sudden large changes. But government tax policy and government monetary policy have both been shifted enough to cause significant demand shocks. Why should the government administer such potentially disturbing demand shocks? Several reasons have been suggested.

A Political Business Cycle

As early as 1944 the Polish-born Keynesian economist Michael Kalecki warned of a political business cycle. He argued that once governments had learned to manipulate the economy, they would engineer an election-geared business cycle. In pre-election periods they would raise spending and cut taxes. The resulting expansionary demand shock would create high employment and good business conditions that would bring voters' support for the government. But the resulting inflationary gap would lead to a rising price level. So, after the election was won, the government would depress demand to remove the inflationary gap and provide some slack for expansion before the next election.

This theory invokes the image of a very cynical government manipulating employment and national income solely because it wants to stay in office. Few people believe that governments deliberately do this all the time, but the temptation to do it some of the time, particularly before elections, may prove irresistible. Indeed, Professor Alan Blinder of Princeton has made a persuasive case that one such politically inspired demand shock was inflicted by the Nixon adminstration just prior to the 1972 American elections.

Alternating Policy Goals

A variant of the policy-induced cycle does not require a cynical government and an easily duped electorate. Instead both sides need only be rather shortsighted.

In this theory, when there is a recession and relatively stable prices, the public and the government identify unemployment as the number one economic problem. The government then engineers an expansionary policy shock through some combination of tax cuts and spending increases. This, plus such natural cumulative forces as the multiplier-accelerator, expands economic activity. Unemployment falls, but as income rises above Y^*, the price level begins to rise. It first rises along the stable $SRAS$ curve and then rises further as boom conditions raise factor prices and shift the $SRAS$ curve upward. (See Figure 30–5.)

At this point the unemployment problem is declared cured. Now inflation is seen as the nation's number one economic problem. A contractionary policy shock is engineered. The natural cumulative forces again take over, causing a recession. The inflation subsides but unemployment rises, setting the stage once again for an expansionary shock to cure the unemployment problem.

Many economists have criticized government policy over the last few decades as sometimes causing fluctuations by alternately pushing expansion to cure unemployment and then contraction to cure inflation. We shall see in Chapter 41 that this charge is particularly strong against monetary policy. But whatever the policy used, the charge is that policymakers have sometimes been too shortsighted in alternating their concern between unemployment and inflation.

Misguided Stabilization Policy

In a variant of the previous theory the government tries to hold the economy at potential national income by countering fluctuations in private-sector expenditure with offsetting changes of its own spending and taxes. The government can in principle dampen such cyclical fluctuations by its stabilization policies. But unless it is very sophisticated, bad timing may accentuate rather than dampen fluctuations. We return to this possibility in a subsequent chapter.

Causes of Business Cycles: A Consensus View?

Economists once argued long and bitterly about which was the best explanation of the recurrent cyclical behavior of the economy.

Today most economists agree that there is not a single cause or class of causes governing business cycles.

In an economy that has tendencies for both cumulative and self-reversing behavior, any large shock, whether from without or within, can initiate a cyclical swing. Wars are important; so, too, are major technical inventions. A rapid increase in interest rates and a general tightening of credit can cause a sharp decrease in investment. Expectations can be changed by a political campaign or a development in another part of the world. The list of possible initial impulses, autonomous or induced, is long. It is probably true that the characteristic cyclical pattern involves many outside shocks that sometimes initiate, sometimes reinforce, and sometimes dampen the cumulative tendencies that exist within the economy.

Cycles differ also in terms of their internal structure. In some, full employment of labor may be the bottleneck that determines the peak. In others, high interest rates and shortages of investment funds may nip an expansion and turn it into a recession at the same time that the unemployment of labor is still an acute problem. In some cycles the recession phase is short; in others a full-scale period of stagnation sets in. In some cycles the

peak develops into a severe inflation; in others the pressure of excess demand is hardly felt, and a new recession sets in before the economy has fully recovered from the last trough. Some cycles are of long duration; others are very short.

In this chapter we have suggested reasons why an economy that is subjected to periodic external shocks will tend to generate a continuously changing pattern of fluctuations, as first cumulative and then self-reversing forces come into play. In the next chapter we study how governments seek to influence the cycle and remove some of its extremes through the use of fiscal policy.

SUMMARY

1. The historical record shows that the economy experiences continuous fluctuations. There is a self-reinforcing cumulative process that leads to a cyclical pattern of fluctuations.

2. Economists break down a stylized cycle into four phases: trough, expansion, peak, and recession. These phases have certain characteristic features, although no two real-world cycles are exactly the same.

3. Short-term fluctuations in GNP are usually, though not always, the result of variations in aggregate demand. Overall, these fluctuations show a fairly clear pattern that is described as cyclical. Despite the overall pattern, the evidence is that the cycles are irregular in amplitude, in timing, in duration, and in the way they affect particular industries and sectors of the economy.

4. Any explanation of the business cycle must explain both *why* income fluctuates and *how* those fluctuations get transformed into cycles.

5. Shifts in consumption, government spending, exports, and investment cause fluctuations in national income and employment.

6. In an open economy like that of Canada, an important source of fluctuations is changes in the level of exports. These changes are often due to changes in the level of income in trading partners' economies, and thus they are an important mechanism by which business cycles are transmitted internationally.

7. Investment is large enough and volatile enough to be an important cause of fluctuations in aggregate demand. The three principal components of private investment are changes in business inventories, residential construction, and business fixed investment.

8. Changes in business inventories, the smallest of the three major components of investment expenditure, often account for an important fraction of the year-to-year changes in the level of investment. They respond both to changes in the level of production and sales and to the rate of interest.

9. Residential construction, a major component of investment, shows a wavelike motion of its own. House building responds to economic (as well as noneconomic) influences, varying directly with the level of national income and inversely with the rate of interest. The rate of interest is important because interest payments are a large fraction of the mortgage payments that greatly affect a household's ability to purchase a house.

10. Business fixed investment depends on a number of variables. These include innovation, expectations about the future, the level of profits, the rate of interest, and changes in national income.

11. The accelerator theory relates net investment to changes in national income on the assumption of a fixed capital-output ratio. Its central prediction is that rising income is required to maintain a given level of investment. Its central insight is that net investment is a disequilibrium phenomenon which occurs when the actual capital stock is different from the desired capital stock.

12. There are several explanations of the cyclical pattern of economic fluctuations. Among these are (1) that expenditure shifts themselves are systematic; (2) that lags in the system transform random expenditure shifts into systematic cyclical changes in income; and (3) that in part the cycle is either

the conscious or the accidental result of government policy.

TOPICS FOR REVIEW

Business cycles and economic fluctuations
Phases of the cycle
Cumulative upward and downward movements in economic activity
Causes of economic fluctuations
Components of investment
The accelerator
The interactions of the multiplier and the accelerator
The political business cycle

DISCUSSION QUESTIONS

1. In what direction might each of the following shift the function relating consumption expenditure to disposable income?
  a. Introduction of free dental care
  b. A change in attitudes so that we become a nation of conspicuous conservers rather than conspicuous consumers, taking pride in how little we eat or spend for housing, clothing, and so on
  c. Increases in income taxes
  d. News that due to medical advances everyone can count on more years of retirement than ever before
  e. A spreading belief that all-out nuclear war is likely within the next 10 years
  f. Sharp increases in the down payments required on durable goods
2. Suppose the government wished to reduce private investment in order to reduce an inflationary gap. What policies might it adopt? If it wished to do so in such a way as to have a major effect on residential housing and a minor effect on business fixed investment expenditures, which measures might it use?
3. What effect on total investment—and on which categories of investment—would you predict as a result of each of the following?
  a. Widespread endorsement of ZPG (zero population growth) by young couples
  b. A sharp increase in the frequency and duration of strikes in the transportation industries

c. Forecasts of very low growth rates of real national income over the next five years

d. Tax reform that eliminated deductions for property taxes in computing taxable personal income

4. Recently, when interest rates rose sharply, home construction fell dramatically but sales of mobile homes increased. How does the rise in the sale of mobile homes relate to the notion that investment responds to the rate of interest?

5. Empirical studies show that as the volume of a firm's sales increases, the size of its inventories of raw materials tends to increase in proportion. It is common for business firms to speak of such inventories in terms of "a 20-day supply of coal" rather than "52,000 tons of coal" or "$280,000 worth of coal." Why should relative size be more important than absolute quantity or dollar value?

6. Since different series behave differently, does it make sense to talk about a business cycle? Predict the comparative behavior of the following pairs of series in relation to fluctuations in the GNP:

a. Purchases of food, purchases of consumer durables

b. Tax receipts, bankruptcies

c. Unemployment, birth rates

d. Employment in Saskatchewan, employment in Ontario

Check your predictions against the facts for the last decade.

7. The highest interest rates in Canadian history occurred in 1981–1982. The deepest recession since the 1930s occurred in 1982. How might these facts be related?

8. "In most years changes in government expenditures are larger than changes in inventories, and consumption is larger than investment in both plant and equipment and housing combined. Therefore, the theorists who say that investment is the main culprit in causing cycles are neglecting the facts of our economy." Reply to this charge.

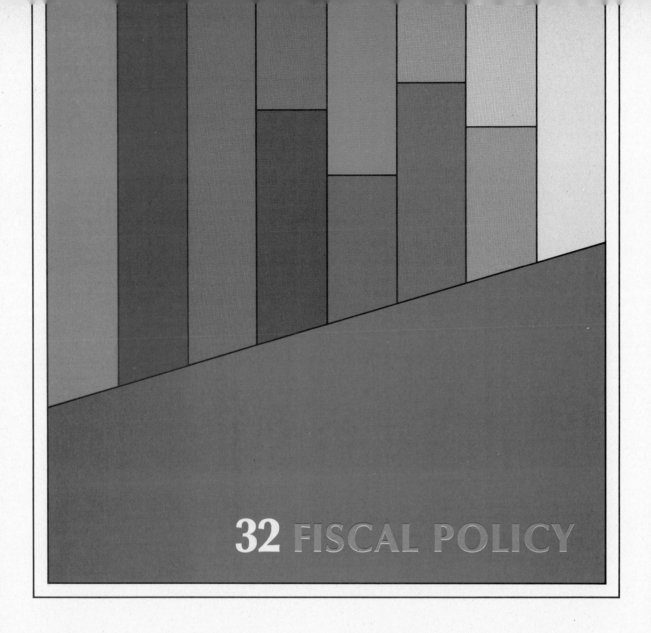

32 FISCAL POLICY

Fiscal policy involves the use of government spending and tax policies to shift the aggregate demand function toward some desired position. Since government expenditure increases aggregate demand and taxation decreases it, the *directions* of the required changes in spending and taxation are easily determined once we know the *direction* of the desired change in the aggregate demand function. But as we shall see, the *timing* and the *magnitude*

of changes in spending and tax policies pose more difficult issues.

Any policy that attempts to stabilize national income at or near a desired level (usually full-employment national income) is called **stabilization policy.** This chapter deals first with the theory of fiscal policy as a tool of stabilization policy and then with the actual experience of using it.

There is no doubt that the government can exert

a major influence on aggregate demand and hence on the size of national income. Prime examples of such influence occur during major wars when governments abandon fiscal caution to engage in massive military spending. Government of Canada defense expenditures, for example, rose from $70 million, or 1.2 percent of GNP, in 1939, to $4.3 billion, or 36 percent of GNP, in 1944. At the same time the unemployment rate fell from 11.4 percent to 1.4 percent. Economists agree that the increase in government spending caused the fall in unemployment and the associated rise in GNP. Similar experiences occurred during the rearmament of most European countries before, or just following, the outbreak of World War II in 1939.

When used appropriately, fiscal policy can be an important tool for influencing the economy. In the heyday of fiscal policy in the 1940s, 1950s, and 1960s, many economists were convinced that the economy could be regulated adequately just by varying the size of the government's taxes and expenditures. That day is past. Today most economists are aware of the limitations of fiscal policy.

THE THEORY OF FISCAL POLICY

Fiscal policy is often referred to as the government's budgetary policy, or simply as its budget. Changes in either government spending or tax policies will influence the *budget balance*.

The Budget Balance

The **budget balance** refers to the difference between all government revenue and all government expenditures. In this definition *government expenditure* includes both purchases of currently produced goods and services and transfer payments. Thus the budget balance is the difference between all the money the government takes in as revenue and all the money it pays out, which are called *budget receipts* and *outlays,* respectively.

There are three possible relations between these two amounts. If receipts are exactly equal to outlays, the government has a **balanced budget;** if receipts exceed outlays, there is a **budget surplus;** if receipts fall short of outlays, there is a **budget deficit.** If the government raises its outlays without raising taxes, the extra expenditure is said to be *deficit financed*. If the extra outlays are accompanied by an increase in tax rates that yields an equal increase in receipts, we speak of a *balanced budget change in spending*.

Financial Implications of Budget Deficits and Surpluses

When the government spends more than it raises, where does the money come from? If the government raises more than it spends, where does the money go? The difference between expenditure and current revenue shows up as changes in the government's debt.

A deficit requires an increase in borrowing, for which there are two main sources: the central bank and the private sector. The government borrows money from these sources by selling treasury bills or bonds. A **treasury bill,** or **note,** is a promise to repay a stated amount at some specified date between 90 days and one year from the date of issue. A government bond is also a promise to pay a stated sum of money in the future, but in the more distant future than a bill—as much as 25 years from now.[1]

A surplus allows the government to reduce its outstanding debt. When Treasury bills and bonds fall due, they are paid off out of tax revenue rather than from money raised by the sale of new bills and bonds.

When the government makes new loans from or repays old loans to the private sector, this action merely shifts funds between the two sectors. When

---

[1] Bills carry a promise to return a fixed amount at maturity. Interest arises because they are sold now at a discount; the difference between their current price and their redemption value represents interest. Bonds carry a fixed "coupon rate of interest" on their redemption value. Thus they guarantee not only the repayment of a fixed sum on the redemption date, but also the periodic payment of fixed sums between now and redemption.

the government "borrows" from the central bank, however, the central bank creates new money. Since the central bank can create as much money as it likes, there is no limit to what the government can "borrow" from the central bank.

The Paradox of Thrift

When a government follows a balanced budget policy, as most governments tried to do during the Great Depression of the 1930s, it must restrict its outlays during a recession because its tax revenue will necessarily be falling at that time. During a recovery, when its revenue is high and rising, it increases its spending. In other words it rolls with the economy, raising and lowering its spending in step with everyone else.

The theory of national income developed in Chapters 28 through 30 predicts that if all spending units in the economy simultaneously try to increase the amount that they save, the combined increase in thriftiness will *reduce* the equilibrium level of income. The contrary case, a general decrease in thriftiness and increase in expenditure, increases national income. This prediction has come to be known as the *paradox of thrift*.[2]

The policy implication of this prediction is that substantial unemployment can be combatted by encouraging governments, firms, and households to spend more, *not* to save more. In times of unemployment and depression, frugality will only make things worse. This prediction goes against the idea that we should tighten our belts when times are tough. The concept that it is not just possible but acceptable to spend one's way out of a depression touches a very sensitive point with people raised on the belief that success is based on hard work and frugality and not on prodigality; as a result, the idea often arouses great hostility. Yet

every time commentators point to weak consumer spending as a source of decline in the economy or strong spending as a source of revival, they are making use of the ideas embodied in this "paradox."

Applications. As is discussed in Box 32-1, the implications of the paradox of thrift were not generally understood during the Great Depression of the 1930s. However, by the middle of that decade, many economists had concluded that the government was not making the most of its potential to control the economy in a beneficial manner. Why, they asked, should not the government try to stabilize the economy by doing just the opposite of what everyone else was doing—by increasing its demand when private demand was falling and lowering its demand when private demand was rising? At best this policy could hold aggregate demand constant even though its individual components were fluctuating.

When Milton Friedman said "We are all Keynesians now," he was referring to (among other things) the general acceptance of the view that the government's budget is much more than just the revenue and expenditure statement of a very large organization. Whether we like it or not, the sheer size of the government's budget inevitably makes it a powerful tool for influencing the economy.

Limitations. The paradox of thrift concentrates on shifts in aggregate demand caused by changes in saving (and hence spending) behavior. For these shifts to cause changes in real output and employment they must be on the fairly elastic portion of the short-run aggregate supply curve. This is most likely to be true when there is a substantial recessionary gap.

In the long run, supply-side effects dominate because the economy can be thought of as operating *on average* on its long-run aggregate supply curve. In these circumstances the paradox of thrift ceases to apply. In the long run the more people save, the larger will be the supply of funds available for investment. The greater is investment, the more will potential income grow, causing the long-run aggregate supply curve to shift right.

---

[2] The prediction is not in fact a paradox. It is a straightforward implication of the theory of the determination of income. It seems paradoxical to those who expect the way in which a single household should act if it wishes to raise its wealth and its future ability to consume ("save, save, and save some more") to be directly applicable to the economy as a whole. Indeed the expectations that lead to the "paradox" are based on the fallacy of composition, the belief that what is true for the parts is necessarily true for the whole.

BOX 32-1 FISCAL POLICY AND THE GREAT DEPRESSION

Failure to understand the implication of the paradox of thrift led many countries to adopt disastrous policies during the Great Depression. Failure to understand the role of built-in stabilizers has also led many observers to conclude, erroneously, that fiscal expansion had been tried in the Great Depression but had failed. Let us see how these two misperceptions are related.

The paradox of thrift in action. In Canada, Prime Minister R. B. Bennett was quoted as saying in 1932: "We are now faced with the real crisis in the history of Canada. To maintain our credit we must practise the most rigid economy and not spend a single cent." His government that year brought down a budget based on the principle of trying to balance revenues and expenditures, and it included *increases* in income, corporation, and sales taxes.

U.S. President Franklin D. Roosevelt, in his first inaugural address (1933), urged: "Our great primary task is to put people to work. . . [this task] can be helped by insistence that the Federal, State and local governments act forthwith on the demand that their costs be drastically reduced. . . . There must be a strict supervision of all banking and credits and investment."

Across the Atlantic, King George V told the British House of Commons in 1931, "The present condition of the national finances, in the opinion of His Majesty's Ministers, calls for the imposition of additional taxation, and for the effecting of economies in public expenditure."

As the paradox of thrift shows, these policies tended to worsen, not to alleviate the depression.

Interpreting the deficit in the 1930s. The deficits that occurred were not the result of a program of deficit-financed public expenditure. Instead they were the result of built-in stabilizers, mainly the fall in tax yields brought about by the fall in national income as the economy sunk into depression. The various governments did not advocate a program of massive deficit-financed spending to shift the aggregate demand curve well to the right. Instead they hoped that a small amount of government spending plus numerous policies designed to stabilize prices and to restore confidence would lead to a recovery of private investment expenditure that would substantially shift the aggregate demand curve. To have expected a massive revival of private investment expenditure as a result of the puny increase in aggregate demand instituted by government now seems hopelessly naive.

When we judge these policies from the viewpoint of modern multiplier theory, their failure is no mystery. Indeed Professor E. Cary Brown of MIT, after a careful study, concludes: "Fiscal policy seems to have been an unsuccessful recovery device in the 'thirties—not because it did not work, but because it was not tried."

The performance of the North American economy from 1930 to 1945 is quite well explained by modern national income theory. It is clear that the government did not effectively use fiscal measures to stabilize the economy. War cured the depression because war demands made acceptable a level of government expenditure sufficient to remove the deflationary gap. Had the Canadian and American administrations been able to do the same, it might have ended the waste of the depression many years sooner.

These longer-term effects are taken up in Chapter 38 on economic growth. In the meantime we concentrate on the short-run demand effects of saving and spending.

The paradox of thrift is based on the short-run effects of changes in saving and investment on aggregate demand.

Fiscal Policy When Private Expenditure Functions Do Not Shift

A relatively easy problem faces fiscal policy makers when private-sector expenditure functions for consumption, investment, and net exports are given and unchanging. What is needed then is a once-and-for-all fiscal change that will remove any existing inflationary or recessionary gap.

Changes in either expenditure or tax rates. The necessary policies were explained in Chapter 29. A reduction in tax rates or an increase in government expenditure shifts the aggregate demand curve to the right, leading to an increase in GNP. An increase in tax rates or a cut in government expenditure will shift the aggregate demand curve to the left, leading to a decrease in GNP.

The key proposition in the theory of fiscal policy follows from these results.

Government taxes and expenditure, by shifting the aggregate demand function, can be used to remove inflationary and recessionary gaps.

Balanced budget changes in expenditure and tax rates. The changes analyzed so far would move government expenditure and tax rates in opposite directions. Another policy available to the government is to make a balanced budget change by changing spending and taxes equally.

Consider a balanced budget increase in expenditure. Say the government increases tax rates enough to raise an extra $1 billion that it then uses to purchase goods and services. Aggregate expenditure would remain unchanged if, and only if, the $1 billion that the government takes from the private sector would have been spent by the private sector in any case. If that occurs the government's policy will reduce private expenditure by $1 billion and raise its own spending by $1 billion. Aggregate expenditure, and hence national income and employment, would remain unchanged.

But this is not the usual case. When an extra $1 billion in taxes is taken away from households, they usually reduce their spending on domestically produced goods by less than $1 billion. If the marginal propensity to consume out of disposable income is, say, 0.75, consumption expenditure will fall by only $750 million. If the government spends the entire $1 billion on domestically produced goods, aggregate expenditure will increase by $250 million. In this case the balanced budget increase in government expenditure has an expansionary effect because it shifts the aggregate expenditure function upward and hence shifts the *AD* curve to the right.

A balanced budget increase in government expenditure will have an expansionary effect on national income, and a balanced budget decrease will have a contractionary effect.

The **balanced budget multiplier** measures these effects. It is the change in income divided by the balanced budget change in government expenditure that brought it about. Thus, if the extra $1 billion of government spending financed by the extra $1 billion of taxes causes national income to rise by $500 million, the balanced budget multiplier is 0.5; if income rises by $1 billion, it is 1.

Now compare the sizes of the multipliers for a balanced budget and a deficit-financed increase in government spending. With a deficit-financed increase in expenditure, there is no increase in tax rates and hence no consequent decrease in consumption expenditure to offset the increase in government expenditure. With a balanced budget increase in expenditure, however, the offsetting increase in tax rates and decrease in consumption does occur. Thus the balanced budget multiplier is much lower than the multiplier that relates the change in income to a deficit-financed increase in government expenditure with tax rates constant.

Fiscal Policy When Private Expenditure Functions Are Shifting

As we saw in Chapter 31, private expenditure functions are constantly changing. Investment expenditure shifts a great deal with business conditions, and consumption functions sometimes shift upward as the public goes on a spending spree or downward as people become cautious and increase their saving. This makes stabilization policy much more difficult than it would be if it were possible simply to identify a stable GNP gap and then take steps to eliminate it once and for all.

What can the government reasonably expect to achieve by using fiscal policy when private expenditure functions are shifting continually? Fiscal policy might be altered often in an effort to stabilize the economy completely, or it might be altered less frequently as a reaction to gaps that appear to be large and persistent.

Fine Tuning

In the heyday of Keynesian fiscal policy in the 1950s and 1960s, many economists advocated the use of fiscal policy to remove even minor fluctuations in national income around its full-employment level. Fiscal policy was to be altered frequently, and by relatively small amounts, to hold national income almost precisely at its full-employment level. This is called **fine tuning** the economy.

A necessary condition for fine tuning is a relatively short **decision lag,** the period of time between perceiving a problem and making the desired reaction to it. Many things contribute to the length of this lag. Experts must study the economy and agree among themselves on what fiscal changes are most desirable; they must then persuade the government to initiate the action they endorse.

In countries where political institutions keep the decision lag short, fine tuning has been attempted. Careful assessment of the results shows that their successes, if any, have fallen far short of what was hoped. One basic reason lies in the complexity of any economy. Although economists and policy makers can identify broad and persistent trends, they do not have detailed knowledge of what is going on at any moment in time, of all the forces that are operating to cause changes in the immediate future, and of all the short-term effects of small changes in the various government expenditures and tax rates.

A second reason is the operation of an **execution lag**—policies take time to be put in place after the decision is made. For example, a full year after the 1983 budget in which the government sought to stimulate the Canadian economy, a substantial number of the public works projects that had been proposed were still on the drawing boards.

Fine tuning has often done as much to encourage minor fluctuations in the economy as to remove them.

As a result of these experiences, fine tuning is currently out of favor.

The Removal of Persistent Gaps

In addition to more or less continuous fluctuations, the economy occasionally develops severe and persistent GNP gaps. For example, an inflationary gap developed in the United States in the late 1960s as American Vietnam war expenditures accelerated; while a recessionary gap developed in 1981–1983 when Canada, along with many other Western countries, experienced the deepest and longest-lasting recession since the 1930s. Gaps such as these may persist long enough for their major causes to be studied and understood and for fiscal remedies to be carefully planned and executed.

A persistent recessionary gap. The removal of a recessionary gap is illustrated in Figure 32-1. There are three possible ways in which the gap may be removed.

First, wages and other factor prices may eventually be forced down enough to shift the *SRAS* curve down to a level that will reinstate full employment and potential income (but at a new lower equilibrium price level). The evidence is, however, that this process takes a very long time.

Second, the natural cyclical forces of the economy could induce a demand-side recovery for the

FIGURE 32-1
Removal of a Recessionary Gap

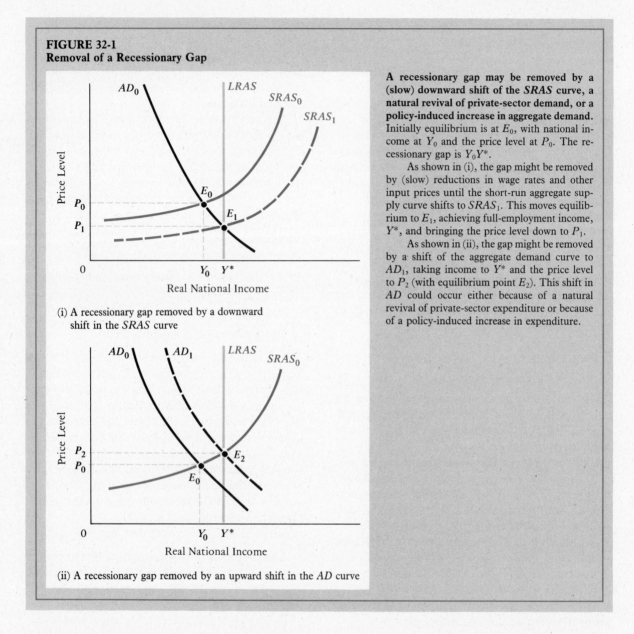

(i) A recessionary gap removed by a downward shift in the *SRAS* curve

(ii) A recessionary gap removed by an upward shift in the *AD* curve

A recessionary gap may be removed by a (slow) downward shift of the *SRAS* curve, a natural revival of private-sector demand, or a policy-induced increase in aggregate demand. Initially equilibrium is at E_0, with national income at Y_0 and the price level at P_0. The recessionary gap is Y_0Y^*.

As shown in (i), the gap might be removed by (slow) reductions in wage rates and other input prices until the short-run aggregate supply curve shifts to $SRAS_1$. This moves equilibrium to E_1, achieving full-employment income, Y^*, and bringing the price level down to P_1.

As shown in (ii), the gap might be removed by a shift of the aggregate demand curve to AD_1, taking income to Y^* and the price level to P_2 (with equilibrium point E_2). This shift in AD could occur either because of a natural revival of private-sector expenditure or because of a policy-induced increase in expenditure.

reasons spelled out in Chapter 31. This would cause an upward shift in the *AD* curve, moving the economy back to full employment and potential income. The evidence is that such recoveries do occur. Sometimes they happen quickly; sometimes, however, a recession can be deep and prolonged.

Third, government expenditure can be increased or taxes cut in an effort to shift the *AD* curve to the right. The advantage of using fiscal policy is that it may substantially shorten the length of what would otherwise be a long recession. The disadvantage is that it may stimulate the economy

FIGURE 32-2
Removal of an Inflationary Gap

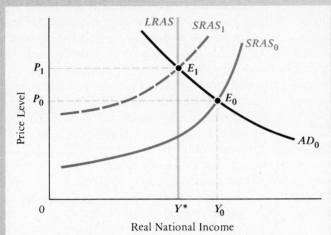

(i) An inflationary gap removed by an upward shift in the *SRAS* curve

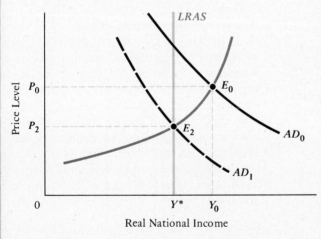

(ii) An inflationary gap removed by a downward shift in the *AD* curve

An inflationary gap may be removed by an upward shift of the *SRAS* curve, a natural reduction in private-sector expenditure, or a policy-induced reduction in aggregate expenditure. Initially equilibrium is at E_0, with national income at Y_0 and the price level at P_0. The inflationary gap is Y^*Y_0.

As shown in (i), the gap might be removed by increases in wage rates and other input prices, shifting the short-run aggregate supply curve to $SRAS_1$. This takes equilibrium to E_1, reducing income to its full-employment level, Y^*, and raising the price level to P_1.

As shown in (ii), the gap might also be removed by a shift in the aggregate demand curve to AD_1, taking income to Y^* and the price to P_2 (with equilibrium point E_2). This shift in AD could occur either because of a natural fall in aggregate demand or because of a contractionary government policy.

just before private-sector spending recovers due to natural causes. If it does, the economy may overshoot its potential output, and a serious inflationary gap may open up.

A persistent inflationary gap. Figure 32-2 shows the three ways in which this gap can be removed.

First, wages and other factor prices will be

forced upward by the excess demand. This will shift the *SRAS* curve upward, eventually eliminating the gap, reducing income to its potential level, and raising the price level even further.

Second, a spontaneous, cyclical reduction in aggregate demand may occur for the reasons outlined in Chapter 31. This reduction may take income back to its potential level without the further rise in the price level associated with the first outcome.

Third, the government, by raising taxes or cutting spending, may force aggregate demand down sufficiently to remove the inflationary gap. The advantage of this approach is that it avoids the inflationary increase in prices that accompanies the first method. The disadvantage is that if private-sector expenditures fall off to their more normal level, national income may be pushed below potential, thus opening up a recessionary gap.

Many economists who do not believe in the value of fine tuning do feel that fiscal policy can aid in removing persistent gaps. Others believe that, even with persistent gaps, the risks that fiscal policy will destabilize the economy are still too large. They would have the government abandon any attempt at stabilization policy, instead setting its budget solely in relation to such long-term considerations as the desirable size of the public sector and the need to obtain a satisfactory long-term balance between revenues and expenditures.

TOOLS OF FISCAL POLICY

The major fiscal tools can be classified in many ways; one important classification is based on the division between automatic and discretionary tools.

Automatic Tools of Fiscal Policy: Built-In Stabilizers

As a result of factors discussed in Chapter 31, the aggregate demand function is continually fluctuating. A stabilization policy for fine tuning the economy would thus require a policy that was itself ever changing. If such a conscious fine tuning policy is impossible, must we throw up our hands and say that nothing can be done through fiscal policy except in the face of major and long-lived GNP gaps?

Fortunately, this is not so. Much of the adjustment of fiscal policy to an ever-changing economic environment is done automatically by what are called *built-in stabilizers*. A **built-in stabilizer** is anything that reduces the marginal propensity to spend out of national income and hence reduces the multiplier. Built-in stabilizers thus lessen the magnitude of the fluctuations in national income caused by autonomous changes in such expenditures as investment. Furthermore, they do so without the government's having to react consciously to each change in national income as it occurs.

The three principal built-in stabilizers are taxes, government expenditure on goods and services, and government transfer payments.

Taxes

Direct taxes act as a built-in stabilizer because they reduce the marginal propensity to consume out of national income. For example, if there were no taxes, every change in national income of $1 would cause a change in disposable income of nearly a dollar.[3] Given a marginal propensity to consume out of disposable income of, say, 0.8, consumption would change by $.80. With taxes, however, disposable income changes by less than $1; hence consumption expenditure will change by less than $.80 when national income changes by $1 (even though the *MPC* out of disposable income is still 0.8).

Direct taxes reduce the magnitude of fluctuations in disposable income associated with any given fluctuation in national income. Hence, for a given *MPC* out of disposable income, direct taxes reduce the *MPC* out of national income.

This is illustrated in Table 32-1. The lower is the *MPC* out of national income, the lower will be the

---

[3] Undistributed profits and other minor items would still hold disposable income below national income. We ignore these in the text because taxes are the major source of the discrepancy between national income and disposable income.

TABLE 32-1 THE EFFECT OF TAX RATES ON THE MARGINAL PROPENSITY TO CONSUME OUT OF NATIONAL INCOME

Marginal rate of tax	Change in national income (millions) ΔY	Change in tax revenue (millions) ΔT	Change in disposable income (millions) ΔY_d	Change in consumption (given $MPC = 0.8$) (millions) ΔC	Marginal propensity to consume out of national income $\Delta C/\Delta Y$
0.2	$1,000	$200	$800	$640	0.64
0.4	1,000	400	600	480	0.48

The higher the marginal rate of tax, the lower the marginal propensity to consume out of national income. When national income changes by $1,000, disposable income changes by $800 when the tax rate is 20 percent and by $600 when the tax rate is 40 percent. Although the MPC out of disposable income is 0.8 in both examples, consumption changes by $640 in the first case and by only $480 in the second. Although households' MPC out of their disposable income is unchanged, an increase in tax rates lowers the MPC out of national income on which the size of the multiplier depends.

multiplier (as we saw on pages 522–524). Thus higher tax rates will reduce the fluctuations in national income associated with autonomous shifts in expenditure functions.

Tax rates have increased greatly over this century. Although citizens complain about the burden of high taxes—perhaps with good reason—few are aware that high taxes help to reduce the large swings in national income and employment that once plagued all industrial economies.

To see the common sense of this, consider the extreme case in which the marginal personal income tax rate is 100 percent. If there is an autonomous rise of $1 billion in investment expenditure, none of the $1 billion that accrues to households will be disposable income. There are no induced rounds of secondary expenditure; the rise in national income is limited to the initial $1 billion in new investment, and the multiplier is unity.

Similarly, a drop in investment expenditure of $1 billion reduces incomes earned in the investment industry by $1 billion and hence reduces government tax revenue by $1 billion. But it does not affect disposable income. Thus there are no secondary rounds of induced contractions in consumption experience to magnify the initial drop in national income caused by the investment decline.

Government Purchases

Government purchases of goods and services tend to be relatively stable in the face of cyclical variations in national income. Much spending is already committed by earlier legislation, so only a small proportion can be varied at the government's discretion from one year to the next. And even this small part is slow to change.

In contrast, private consumption and investment expenditure tend to vary with national income. The consumption function is an expression of the tendency for consumption expenditure to rise and fall as national income rises and falls. And as we saw in Chapter 31, investment expenditure tends to vary with national income; it is high in booms and low in slumps.

The twentieth century rise in the importance of the government's role in the economy may be a mixed blessing. One benefit, however, has been to put a large built-in stabilizer into the economy.

Government Transfer Payments

Transfer payments act as built-in stabilizers. They stabilize disposable income, and hence consumption expenditure, in the face of fluctuations in national income.

To illustrate this important proposition, assume a reduction in autonomous expenditure of $10 billion that, in the absence of transfer payments, would reduce disposable income by $6 billion. With an *MPC* out of disposable income of 0.8, this $6 billion reduction would cause an initial induced fall in consumption expenditure of $4.8 billion. Now assume instead that the fall in national income is accompanied by an increase in transfer payments of $4 billion. Instead of falling by $6 billion, disposable income now falls by only $2 billion. With the *MPC* out of disposable income still at 0.8, the initial induced fall in consumption expenditure is only $1.6 billion instead of $4.8 billion.

Social insurance and welfare services. Welfare payments rise with the unemployment that accompanies falling national income. Many welfare schemes are financed by taxes based on payrolls or earnings, and these taxes yield less when income is low. Thus welfare schemes act to make net additions to disposable income in times of slumps. They also make net subtractions in times of boom, when payments are low and revenues high.

The Canada Pension Plan is financed by taxes (called *contributions*) paid jointly by employers and employees. Unemployment insurance is financed by a payroll tax on employers and employees. During recessions these tax collections decrease while payments to the unemployed rise.[4]

Public pension plans and unemployment insurance schemes support disposable income when national income falls and hold it down when national income rises.

Agricultural support policies. When there is a slump in the economy, there is a general decline in the demand for all goods, including agricultural products. The free-market prices of agricultural goods fall, and government agricultural supports come into play. This means that government trans-

fers, which support agricultural disposable income, will rise as national income falls.

The Origin of Built-In Stabilizers

Most built-in stabilizers are fairly new phenomena. Fifty years ago high marginal tax rates, high and stable government expenditures, farm stabilization policies, large unemployment benefits, and other transfer payments were unknown in Canada. Each of these built-in stabilizers was the unforeseen by-product of policies originally adopted for other reasons. The progressive income tax arose out of a concern to make the distribution of income less unequal. Social insurance and agricultural support programs were adopted more because of a concern with the welfare of the individuals and groups involved than with preserving the health of the economy. But unforeseen or not, they work. (Even governments can be lucky.)

No matter how lucky governments have been in finding built-in stabilizers, these cannot reduce fluctuations to zero. Stabilizers work by producing stabilizing reactions to changes in income. But until income changes, the stabilizer is not even brought into play.

Discretionary Fiscal Policy

Short-term, minor fluctuations that are not removed automatically by built-in stabilizers cannot, given present knowledge and techniques, be removed by consciously fine tuning the economy. We have already seen, however, that larger and more persistent gaps sometimes appear. In these cases there may be time for the government to operate a **discretionary fiscal policy**; that is, to institute changes in taxes and spending that are designed to offset gaps. To do this effectively, a government must periodically make conscious decisions to alter fiscal policy. The Department of Finance must study current economic trends and predict the probable course of the economy. If the predicted course is unsatisfactory, the cabinet must be persuaded to adopt the appropriate fiscal stance.

In considering discretionary fiscal policy, we shall deal with two main questions. First, why is

[4] The Unemployment Insurance Act requires the federal government to adjust the payroll tax (referred to as the unemployment insurance premiums) annually so as to finance most of the changes in benefits paid out. This greatly reduces the automatic stabilizing influence of the unemployment insurance scheme.

it important that the fiscal change be easily reversible? Second, does it matter whether households and firms regard the government's fiscal changes as temporary or as long-lived?

The Need for Reversibility

To see what is involved in the issue of reversibility, assume that national income is normally at or near its full-employment level. A *temporary* slump in private investment then opens up a large recessionary gap. The gap persists. Eventually the government decides to adopt some combination of tax cuts and spending increases to push the economy back toward full employment. If this policy is successful, private investment can be expected to recover to its pre-slump level. But then if the government does not quickly reverse this policy, an inflationary gap will open up as the combination of rising investment expenditure and continuing fiscal stimulus takes national income into the inflationary range. The process is illustrated in Figure 32-3.

Alternatively, assume that starting from the same situation of approximately full employment, a temporary investment boom opens up an inflationary gap. Rather than let the inflation persist, the government reduces expenditure and raises taxes to remove the gap. Then, when the investment boom is over, investment expenditure will return to its original level. If the government does nothing, a recessionary gap will open up. This too is analyzed in Figure 32-3.

Fiscal policies designed to remove persistent inflationary or recessionary gaps resulting from abnormal levels of private expenditure will destabilize the economy unless the policies can be rapidly reversed once private expenditure returns to its more normal level.

The Choice Between Changes Seen by Households as "Temporary" and Those Seen as "Long Lasting"

Consider the attempt to remove a persistent GNP gap through changes in tax rates. Such a gap, though persistent, is unlikely to be a permanent feature of the economy. The relevant tax changes

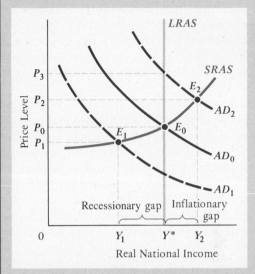

FIGURE 32-3
Effects of Fiscal Policies That Are Not Reversed

Fiscal policies that are initially appropriate may become inappropriate when the private expenditure function shifts. The normal level of the aggregate demand function is assumed to be AD_0, leaving income normally at Y^*.

Suppose a persistent slump in private investment shifts aggregate demand to AD_1, with income Y_1, price level P_1, and the recessionary gap indicated by the left brace. The government now cuts taxes and raises expenditure to restore aggregate demand to AD_0. This takes equilibrium to E_0, with national income Y^* and price level P_0. Later, private investment recovers to its original level, and this further raises aggregate demand to AD_2. If the fiscal policy can be quickly reversed the aggregate demand curve can be shifted back to AD_0, restoring full-employment income and price level P_0. If the policy is not quickly reversed the inflationary gap associated with equilibrium at E_2 (the right brace in the figure) will cause wage rates to rise, shifting the SRAS curve upward and eventually raising the price level to P_3.

Now suppose that starting from equilibrium point E_0 a persistent investment boom takes AD_0 to AD_2. In order to stop the price level from rising to the face of the newly opened inflationary gap, the government raises taxes and cuts expenditure, thereby shifting the aggregate demand back to AD_0. Further assume, however, that the investment boom soon comes to a halt so that the aggregate demand curve shifts down to AD_1. Unless the fiscal policy can be rapidly reversed, a recessionary gap (the left brace) will open up and equilibrium income will stagnate at Y_1.

should therefore be advocated only for "the duration"; that is, for as long as the government thinks the gaps would persist without the tax changes. A discretionary fiscal policy designed to remove that gap could then take the form, say, of a surcharge on income taxes for a two-year period. Similarly, a recession that began could be fought by "temporary" tax rebates.

Such tax changes cause changes in household disposable income and, according to the Keynesian theory of the consumption function, would cause changes in consumption expenditure. Consumption expenditure would increase as tax rebates rose in times of recessionary gaps and would decrease as tax surcharges rose in times of inflationary gaps. This theory of the effects of short-term tax changes relies on the assumption that household consumption depends on current disposable income.

Permanent-income theories. Many recent theories of the consumption function have emphasized what is called a household's expected **lifetime income,** or **permanent income,** as the major determinant of consumption. According to such theories, households have expectations about their lifetime incomes and adjust their consumption to those expectations. When temporary fluctuations in income occur, households maintain their long-term consumption plans and use their stocks of wealth as buffers to absorb income fluctuations. Thus, when there is a purely temporary rise in income, households will save all the extra income; when there is a purely temporary fall in income, households will maintain their long-term consumption plans by using up part of their wealth accumulated through past saving.

To the extent that such behavior occurs, it will have serious consequences for short-lived tax changes. A temporary tax rebate raises households' disposable income, but households, recognizing it as temporary, do not revise their expenditure plans and instead save the extra money. Thus the hoped-for increase in aggregate expenditure would not occur. Similarly, a temporary rise in tax rates reduces disposable income, but that may merely cause a drop in saving. Thus total expenditure is

again unchanged, and a temporary surcharge fails to reduce the inflationary gap.

If households' consumption expenditure is more closely related to lifetime income than to current income, tax changes that are known to be of short duration may have relatively small effects on current consumption.[5]

The advantage of having households perceive as permanent any tax cut or tax surcharge conflicts with the need for the reversibility of cuts and surcharges if they are not to destabilize the economy at a later date. This further reduces the effectiveness of changes in tax rates as a stabilizing tool.

Box 32-2 discusses two episodes that bring out the importance of these issues for the effectiveness of discretionary fiscal policy.

Judging the Stance of Fiscal Policy

Governments seek to shift aggregate demand by consciously changing their fiscal policy stance. The *stance* of fiscal policy refers to its expansionary or contractionary effects on the economy. An expansionary fiscal policy increases aggregate demand and thus tends to increase national income; a contractionary fiscal policy reduces aggregate demand and tends to lower national income.

In the previous chapter and earlier in this one, we looked separately at taxes, purchases of goods and services, and transfer payments as means of influencing aggregate demand. But people want a summary measure, one number to express the government's effect on the economy. Not surprisingly, people tend to focus on the government's deficit.

To what extent do changes in the deficit from one year to the next indicate changes in the stance of fiscal policy? When the government's current deficit rises, this is often taken to indicate an ex-

[5] The permanent-income theory is not as immediately applicable to fiscal policy as it may seem. This is because fiscal policy seeks to affect *expenditure* (on consumption and investment goods) while permanent-income theories seek to explain the consumption of goods and services—which in the case of durables is spread over the whole life of the durable. This important matter is discussed further in the appendix to this chapter.

pansionary fiscal policy. When the deficit falls, this is often taken to indicate a contractionary policy. Two problems arise which make the measured deficit an unreliable guide to judging the fiscal stance.

The cyclical adjustment.   The deficit is the difference between the government's outlays and receipts, its receipts being largely tax revenue. But tax revenue is the result of the interaction of tax rates, which the government does set, and the level of national income, which is influenced by many forces beyond the government's control.

Assume for example that at current tax rates the government takes 20 percent of national income in taxes. With a national income of $600 billion, tax revenues are $120 billion. Now assume that tax revenues sink to $100 billion, opening up an additional $20 billion budget deficit. This could be the result of a discretionary cut in tax rates so that they now yield only 16 2/3 percent of an unchanged national income. It could also be the result of a fall in national income itself to $500 billion, with tax rates constant. In the first case it was a conscious change in the government's fiscal policy that caused the fall in tax revenues. In the second case it was a fall in national income not caused by fiscal policy.

The above example illustrates that judging changes in the stance of fiscal policy from changes in the government's budget balance can be very misleading. It confuses endogenous changes due to fluctuations in national income, which may not be the result of shifts in fiscal policy, with exogenous changes, which are the result of shifts in fiscal policy.

The major tools of fiscal policy are government expenditure and *tax rates*. The budget deficit or surplus is the relation between government expenditure and *tax revenues*.

The distinction between the two causes of changes in the budget balance is easily seen in what is called the government's **budget surplus function**. This function, which relates the surplus (government revenue minus government expenditure) to national income, is graphed in Figure 32-4(i). Endogenous changes in the government's budget balance due to changes in national income are shown by movements along a given surplus function. Changes in the budget balance due to policy-induced changes in government expenditure or in tax rates are shown by shifts in the surplus function. Such shifts indicate a different budget balance at *each* level of national income.

When measuring changes in the stance of fiscal policy, it is common to calculate changes in the estimated budget balance at some base level of national income. Holding income constant ensures that measured shifts in the budget balance are due to policy-induced movements along the function. The budget balance thus calculated is called the **cyclically adjusted surplus (CAS)**. This is an estimate of government tax revenues minus government expenditures, not as they actually are, but as they would be if the base level of national income had obtained.[6] In this usage a cyclically adjusted budget deficit is a negative cyclically adjusted surplus.

Changes in the cyclically adjusted surplus are an indicator of changes in the stance of fiscal policy.[7]

Figure 32-4 analyzes the use of the CAS, as well as the errors that can arise from use of the current surplus as an indicator of the stance of fiscal policy.

The inflation adjustment.   The cyclical adjustment discussed in the previous section distinguishes between changes in the budget balance that arise due to the operation of *automatic* stabilizers, and those that arise due to discretionary policy. To

---

[6] The cyclically adjusted surplus can be calculated using a number of different measures of base income. These alternatives include the expected average level of income over the business cycle and estimates of potential or full employment income. Hence the CAS is also often called the full-employment surplus or the high-employment surplus (HES). But for the purpose of judging the stance of fiscal policy, the differences are not important; the concept remains the same; an estimate of the difference between budget receipts and expenditures when actual national income equals the base level national income.

[7] The cyclically adjusted surplus is the simplest adequate measure, and it is vastly superior to the current surplus for estimating year-to-year changes in the stance of fiscal policy. The balanced budget multiplier discussed earlier in this chapter indicates one reason why the budget surplus, even the CAS, is not a completely reliable measure of fiscal stimulus. More sophisticated measures exist and are often used in detailed empirical work.

BOX 32–2 TWO CASE STUDIES OF AMERICAN FISCAL POLICY

The 1960s saw two major experiments with fiscal policy in the United States. In terms of achieving their objectives, the first was a success and the second a failure.

Fiscal Drag and the 1964 Tax Cuts

Fiscal drag is the problem of a rising full-employment surplus produced by economic growth acting on stable government expenditure and fixed tax rates. President Kennedy's Council of Economic Advisors proposed a major cut in tax rates to deal with it.

Throughout the 1950s full-employment GNP was rising 2 to 3 percent per year because of economic growth. This increased aggregate supply, as illustrated in the figure by the shift of $SRAS_0$ to $SRAS_1$. But since higher output means higher income, aggregate demand also shifted outward. With both demand and supply increasing, it might seem that maintaining full employment would be no problem. There was a problem, however, and it lay with the tax system.

With tax rates constant, rising national income causes rising tax revenues. These revenues are money that does not become disposable income for households. If the government spent all its extra tax revenue, aggregate demand would not be depressed. With a relatively stable level of government expenditure, however, rising tax revenues exert a drag on the growth of aggregate demand by taking income away from households that would have spent it and transferring it to governments that do not.

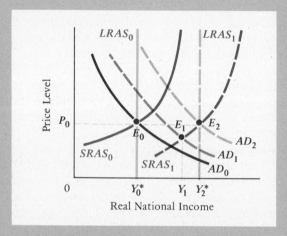

This is illustrated in the figure, where we start with the curves AD_0, $LRAS_0$, and $SRAS_0$. These yield equilibrium at E_0 and potential income Y_0^*. Economic growth now shifts the supply curves to $LRAS_1$ and $SRAS_1$. As a result of fiscal drag, however, the aggregate demand curve only shifts to AD_1 rather than to AD_2, which is required to sustain full employment. A recessionary gap of $Y_1Y_2^*$ is thus created.

To prevent the exertion of an ever-stronger depressing effect on national income by a grow-

judge the stance of fiscal policy, it is necessary to make a second adjustment to the measured budget balance—one that focuses on a component of the budget that has no (or virtually no) impact on aggregate demand. This component is the inflation premium included in the nominal interest payments made by the government to service the national debt.

As we saw in Box 31-1, nominal interest payments can be divided into a real component and an inflation premium. The real component constitutes a transfer to the lender as payment for use of the principal. The inflation premium does not constitute a real transfer since it is exactly offset by a reduction in the real value of the principal.

This makes clear why the inflation premium

ing high-employment surplus, it is necessary to reduce the surplus periodically either by increasing government spending or by reducing tax rates. This problem arose in the American economy during the 1950s. Economic growth was producing a growing high-employment surplus. As a result each cyclical upswing was weaker than the one before it, and the average level of unemployment over the cycle was rising. By the beginning of the 1960s many economists were calling for a tax cut to remove the drag and restore full employment. Both the Kennedy and Johnson administrations advocated a large cut in tax rates. Their concern was not with cyclical stabilization, but with solving a problem associated with long-term economic growth.

When the 1964 tax cut was enacted, the predicted effects occurred. The tax cuts increased disposable income, causing an increase in consumption expenditure that in turn caused an increase in national income and employment.

The Vietnam Inflation and the 1968 Tax Surcharges

By the time the full effects of the 1964 tax cut were felt, the large increases in military expenditures due to the escalation of the war in Vietnam were also exerting a substantial expansionary effect on the economy. With GNP already at the full-employment level, the large 1967 budget deficit produced a large inflationary gap in 1968.

By mid 1968 a temporary tax surcharge bill was approved by Congress. This bill raised effective tax rates for a period of about 18 months and produced a substantial budget surplus. The object was to slow inflation by removing the inflationary gap. The restraining effect was disappointingly small; inflation hardly slowed its trend toward ever-higher rates.

The apparent failure of the contractionary budgetary policy of 1968–1969 caused much debate among economists. The general judgment, after long discussions, seems to be that the "failure" of the 1968–1969 tax surcharges to restrain inflation revealed the shortcomings of the fine tuning but did not show fiscal policy to be generally impotent. Numerous factors had offset the effects of the surcharge, and the knowledge that the tax surcharge was temporary may have caused households to make only small downward revisions in their expected permanent incomes and hence only very small reductions in their consumption.* Another factor, understood now but unappreciated then, is that inflationary expectations, once entrenched, are not easily shaken—especially by a transitory tax surcharge.

* For further discussion, see the appendix to this chapter.

component of the deficit contributes little or nothing to aggregate demand. The private sector receives the payment but suffers an equivalent reduction in the real value of its government bonds. To maintain their asset position, recipients of the government interest payments must save the entire inflation premium component. Hence the net demand effect of this component on aggregate demand will be approximately zero—the government's demand will be offset by a fall in private sector demand as households raise their saving in order to recoup some of the inflation-induced fall in their real wealth.

Hence in order to measure the net influence of the government on aggregate demand, it is necessary to subtract the inflation-premium component

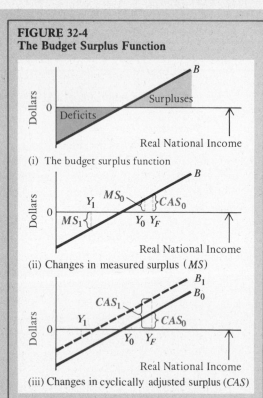

(i) The budget surplus function

(ii) Changes in measured surplus (MS)

(iii) Changes in cyclically adjusted surplus (CAS)

Changes in national income cause changes in the measured surplus by moving the economy along its surplus function; changes in the stance of fiscal policy shift the surplus function. The budget surplus function expresses the difference between the government's tax revenues and its expenditures at each level of national income. The curve in (i) shows that deficits are associated with low levels of income and surpluses with high levels of income.

In (ii), a fall in national income from Y_0 to Y_1 causes the budget to go from a measured surplus of MS_0 to a measured deficit of MS_1, with no change in government expenditure or tax rates—that is, the fiscal policy stance is unchanged. The unchanged fiscal stance is correctly captured by the constant cyclically adjusted surplus, CAS_0.

In (iii), there is a contractionary change in the stance of fiscal policy: a government expenditure cut and/or a tax rate increase shifts the surplus function from B_0 to B_1. Now there is a larger budget surplus *at each level of national income.* This change is correctly captured by the rise in the cyclically adjusted surplus from CAS_0 to CAS_1. Note that if national income had fallen from Y_0 to Y_1 at the same time that the surplus function shifted from B_0 to B_1, the measured balance would have gone from surplus to deficit despite the rise in the cyclically adjusted surplus. This illustrates the misleading effects of judging changes in the policy stance from changes in the measured surplus.

of nominal interest payments from the measured budget balance. Suppose the current value of the government's debt is $100 billion. Suppose also that in the current year the government runs a deficit of $10 billion and that the current inflation rate is 10 percent. On crude measures the government has a deficit of $10 billion. On an inflation-adjusted basis, the deficit is zero. This is because the real value—or purchasing power—of the debt is unchanged, even though the nominal stock of debt has risen from $100 billion to $110 billion.

The structural balance. When the cyclical and inflation adjustments are made to the government's budget balance, a useful measure of discretionary fiscal policy is obtained. This is called the *structural balance,* or, more commonly, the structural deficit.

FISCAL POLICY IN ACTION

We have seen that governments inevitably have a major impact on GNP through their fiscal behavior. The very size of a government's budget guarantees that. The conscious use of the budget to influence GNP that constitutes fiscal policy is, however, by no means inevitable. Fiscal *impact* is unavoidable, but fiscal *policy* is a matter of choice.

The Experience of Fiscal Policy

The Great Depression and World War II

The 1930s saw massive unemployment that persisted through nearly a decade. This experience left many with the misconception that discretionary fiscal policy cannot solve an unemployment problem. A review of the facts shows that fiscal policy contributed little to recovery from the Depression not because it failed to work, but because it was not used.

Between 1929 and 1933, GNP in Canada fell by more than $2.5 billion, a drop of over 40 percent from the 1929 level of $6.2 billion. During the period, the federal deficit reached a peak of $160 million. Most of the increase in the deficit was due to the decline in national income rather than to any shift in the high-employment deficit that would have signaled the adoption of a more expansive policy stance. These issues were discussed in detail in Box 32-1.

When Keynesian fiscal policy was finally tried under the impetus of the wartime emergency, it proved spectacularly successful. Total government expenditure on goods and services, which during the 1930s had been running well below $1 billion and about 20 percent of the Canadian GNP, jumped to $5 billion and accounted for over 40 percent of the GNP.

Although the federal deficit averaged more than $2 billion per year from 1942 to 1945, the financing of Canada's war effort was an outstanding success compared to Canada's performance in World War I or to most other countries' fiscal performance in World War II. The inflationary gap that had arisen from the build-up in demand was reduced by a variety of tax measures, including increased excises, increased corporate and personal income taxes, higher customs duties, and an excess profits tax. The increase in the cost of living between 1939 and 1945 was held to 18 percent, compared with a rise of 74 percent during World War I. In the United States, prices rose by almost one-third between 1940 and 1945.

The Postwar Period, 1945–1970

The most pressing economic problem of 1946 was the inflationary gap arising from the relaxation of wartime controls and the release of pent-up consumer demand. People rushed to spend their wartime savings on new cars and other goods that had not been available during the war. Between 1945 and 1948, prices rose more than they had risen during the war. This was a simple case of a demand-side inflation.

The new status of fiscal policy. An important legacy of World War II was a radically altered view of the role of government expenditures and taxes as instruments of government policy. The 1945 White Paper on Employment and Income established the principle that the federal government had a responsibility to maintain high and stable levels of employment and income.

The implementation of this policy was greatly complicated by the unsettled state of federal-provincial relations. As early as 1940 a proposal to widen federal jurisdiction had been made by the Rowell-Sirois Commission, but the division of powers has continued to be a contentious issue to the present day. Through a succession of temporary agreements (see Chapter 25), the federal government has retained sufficient power to operate a flexible fiscal policy, and consideration of the desired degree of fiscal stimulus or restraint has become an important element in the budgets presented to Parliament.

An effort to improve the input of economic analysis into policy formation was made in 1963 through the establishment of the Economic Council of Canada. The council's *Annual Reviews* and other publications have served to quantify and add perspective to policy issues. It is not clear how much they influence the setting of fiscal policy.

Performance 1945–1970. In comparison with earlier and later periods, the quarter century following World War II was one of prosperity and steady growth. One prolonged slump occurred during the years 1958 to 1963, when the unemployment rate reached a peak of 7.1 percent (see Figure 26-2 on page 470). By 1965 the recessionary gap had been virtually eliminated, but in retrospect it appears that policy makers misjudged the situation and allowed the economy to develop an inflationary gap instead.

Rising national income had tended to move the federal budget into a surplus position, but some of the restraining effects of the built-in stabilizers were offset by tax cuts introduced in the budget of April 1965. Tax increases and some expenditure cuts were imposed in the years 1966 to 1968, but the effects of the fiscal restraint came too late to prevent the build-up of inflationary forces. At the end of the decade, tight monetary policy reinforced the fiscal restraint, and unemployment rose in 1969 and 1970.

The 1970s

The 1970s began with a substantial recessionary gap. Expansive policies were put into place. But the situation was misread because of a leftward

FIGURE 32-5
The Budget Balance (National Accounts Basis), 1955–1980

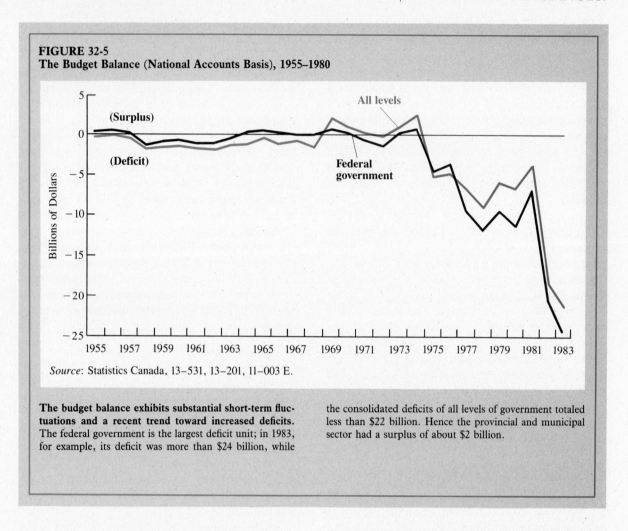

Source: Statistics Canada, 13–531, 13–201, 11–003 E.

The budget balance exhibits substantial short-term fluctuations and a recent trend toward increased deficits. The federal government is the largest deficit unit; in 1983, for example, its deficit was more than $24 billion, while the consolidated deficits of all levels of government totaled less than $22 billion. Hence the provincial and municipal sector had a surplus of about $2 billion.

shift in the long-run aggregate supply curve. (The reasons for this are discussed in Chapter 37.) As a result, the government was still trying to shift the *AD* curve to the right to remove a recessionary gap. In retrospect we now see that the leftward shift in the *LRAS* curve meant the existence of an inflationary gap which the government's expansionary policy inadvertently served to widen.

In late 1974 a series of shocks cause a downturn in the world economy. In response, an expansionary budget was brought down late in the year which provided for a reduction in personal income taxes of about $1.5 million in 1975.

As Figure 32-5 shows, the federal budget moved to a substantial deficit position in 1975 and remained there throughout the 1970s (and beyond), reaching $10.7 billion by 1980. In part, this reflects discretionary fiscal policy because, as shown in Table 32-2, the cyclically adjusted budget also moved into substantial deficit. However, the actual deficit also reflects the influence of other factors.

First, the substantial GNP gap that prevailed over that period caused tax revenues to be low relative to outlays on unemployment insurance benefits. Second, the relatively high rate of inflation caused outlays to grow rapidly—because many

TABLE 32–2 **MEASURED, CYCLICALLY ADJUSTED, AND STRUCTURAL BUDGET BALANCES FOR THE FEDERAL GOVERNMENT, 1970–1983 (Billions of Dollars)**

Year	Measured budget surplus[a]	Cyclically adjusted budget surplus[a]	Structural budget surplus (cyclically and inflation adjusted)
1970	.3	.5	.9
1971	−.1	0.0	.3
1972	−.6	−.7	−.2
1973	.4	−.6	.5
1974	1.1	−.5	.9
1975	−3.8	−3.9	−3.0
1976	−3.4	−4.1	−3.0
1977	−7.3	−6.8	−5.8
1978	−10.7	−9.9	−8.3
1979	−9.3	−8.9	−4.8
1980	−10.1	−8.2	−3.6
1981	−8.0	−6.2	0.0
1982	−21.1	−11.8	−5.0
1983	−24.0	−13.3	−8.2

[a] A minus sign indicates a deficit.
Source: Department of Finance.

Changes in the measured budget balance reflect both changes in output and inflation. The cyclically adjusted surplus controls for the influences of the level of output, while the last column adds to this as adjustment for the effect of the inflation rate. Changes in the last column thus give a measure of change in fiscal policy. Several things can be noted about the adjustments. First, the inflation adjustment is always positive, so column 3 is always greater in algebraic value than column 2 (if column 2 shows a deficit, column 3 will show a smaller deficit or even a surplus). Second, because the economy has operated at less than full employment since 1975, the cyclical adjustment has also been positive, so column 2 has been bigger than column 1 in algebraic value. Actual budget deficits have been growing rather dramatically. Part of this is due to persistent slack in the economy and to high inflation, but column 3 indicates that fiscal policy has also been expansionary.

federal transfer payments such as old-age pensions *were* indexed to inflation. Tax revenues also rose due to inflation, although not as quickly as they would have had the income tax system not been indexed. Since both expenditures and revenues grew, the difference between them also grew. (See Box 32-3 for further discussion of indexing the tax system.)

Tax cuts were introduced in 1977 and 1978 when, despite steady but gradual growth, the economy was thought to be operating below capacity. In December 1979 the minority Conservative government introduced a budget which aimed to reduce the size of the deficit. Government expenditure growth was to be limited, and a number of taxes were to be raised. However, the government fell on the issue of the budget and the Liberals were returned to power in the election of February 1980. But in April 1980 a Liberal minibudget did reintroduce two of the tax measures proposed in the defeated Conservative budget.

The 1980s

In the early 1980s, fiscal policy was complicated by two major dilemmas. First, the federal budget deficit had become so large that worries were emerging about the implications of having to make interest payments on a rapidly burgeoning national debt. Although stabilization policy called for increasing the deficit to combat the recessionary gap, longer-run fiscal prudence called for reducing the deficit. The second dilemma was that the rate of inflation was unacceptably high, despite a rate of unemployment of 8 percent in 1980. Reducing the recessionary gap called for an expansionary fiscal policy; reducing inflation called for a contractionary fiscal policy.

For the first time since the government accepted an active stabilization role, the direction—not simply the extent—of desirable changes in the stance of fiscal policy was at issue.

Successive budgets in the 1980s introduced small changes in the overall fiscal stance, being pulled one way by fiscal prudence and anti-inflation

BOX 32–3 INFLATION INDEXING OF INCOME TAXES

Marginal tax rates rise quite steeply in Canada, as Table 25-2 shows. Many economists believe that beyond some point high marginal tax rates provide strong disincentives to the supply of effort: A steelworker with a high marginal tax rate is less inclined to work overtime in periods of boom, and a lawyer or a highly trained technical consultant is less likely to accept one more case, the higher is his or her marginal tax rate.

In inflationary situations, when an individual's money income rises, the purchasing power of this income does not necessarily rise. For example, a secretary who gets a 10 percent raise is no better off when the prices of everything she purchases also rise by 10 percent *and* the fraction of income she pays in taxes does not change. However, with marginal tax rates that rise with money income, the fraction of income she pays in taxes will rise; as a result, her *after-tax money income* will rise by less than 10 percent. Even though her *before-tax real income* remains unchanged (prices and before-tax money income both rise by 10 percent), her *after-tax real income* will fall because she now pays in taxes a larger fraction of her income.

This is because inflation, by increasing the dollar value of the taxpayer's money income, moves the taxpayer into a tax bracket with a higher marginal tax rate. Unless the growth of before-tax nominal (money) income exceeds the rate of inflation, the increase in taxes will necessarily reduce after-tax real income.

Indexation of income tax prevents this automatic increase in tax rates in response to inflation. When a tax system is indexed, the rate of taxation at any given level of *real* income remains constant: The tax schedule—that is, the tax bracket at which a particular marginal rate applies—is adjusted each year to allow for the effects of inflation on nominal incomes. If inflation has averaged 10 percent in the economy but average real income is unchanged, the average person's nominal income will go up by 10 percent. If before the inflation there was a $30,000 cutoff for a 40 percent marginal tax rate, the cutoff would now move up by 10 percent to $33,000. People whose initial incomes were under $30,000 and whose real income remained unchanged would now have money income under $33,000 and would not move to a higher tax bracket. People whose income before the inflation was $30,000 and whose *real* income grew would, by definition, have nominal incomes that grew in excess of the 10 percent inflation rate;

---

policy, and the other way by full employment.[8] In late 1981 a major worldwide downturn set in, turning 1982 into the worst recession since the Great Depression. Still caught on the horns of the two dilemmas, the budget of 1982 made little change in the fiscal stance.

[8] One important feature of the October 1980 budget was the introduction of the National Energy Program, designed to increase the federal government's share of the revenues from petroleum production mainly at the expense of the industry. Also, in order to help increase Canadian participation in the industry, a series of grants for exploration and development which would increase with the Canadian ownership of a firm were introduced.

In 1983 the budget tried to resolve the dilemma with short-term measures aimed at unemployment and longer-term measures aimed at the deficit. The budget introduced moderate stimulus—about $6 billion phased in over two years—combined with a series of measures, including tax increases, to offset this stimulus later. This *tilt*—stimulus now, restraint later—was widely viewed as an appropriate way to stimulate the economy without increasing the future high-employment deficit.

In 1983 there was a strong recovery. Real output grew by over 6 percent and inflation slowed dramatically. The budget introduced in February 1984

hence they would move to a higher tax bracket. Similarly, people whose real income fell would move to a lower tax bracket.

In an indexed tax system, average and marginal tax rates depend only on real income.

In his 1973 budget John Turner, then minister of finance, indexed the Canadian income tax system. It was still indexed in 1984. In the very high inflation of the 1970s indexation held Canadian tax burdens below what they would have been had the tax schedule of 1972 remained in force in terms of money income. By the same token it has reduced the tax revenues of the federal government over the same period.

There are arguments against indexing the tax system. For example, some people think that indexation is inflationary because it reduces the public's resistance to inflation. With an unindexed tax system, inflation leads to higher taxes and people will therefore resist inflation. Indexation of the tax system, it is argued, reduces public opposition to inflation and thus makes it easier for governments to justify inflationary policies. Others argue that indexation will reduce inflation because it reduces the payoff to governments from pursuing inflationary policies.

The increased tax bite that arises from an unindexed tax system in the presence of inflation provides a great incentive for governments to follow inflationary policies; real resources can be transferred from the private sector to the public purse simply by inflating people into higher tax brackets. Hence, whether indexation leads to more or less inflationary policies is not clear.

Politicians do not necessarily like inflation-indexed tax systems. In the United States the tax system has not been indexed. However, since 1975 the U.S. Congress has passed a series of tax cuts. The main purpose of these tax cuts was to undo the automatic increases in taxes that would have resulted from the American inflation. Politicians were in reality indexing the tax system each year, and they were doing it in a manner that gave them political credit for passing tax cuts. This option is not available to Canadian politicians; apparently all the political credit accrued to the person who initially indexed the tax system. Thus many Canadian politicians would like to de-index the tax system so that they too could get the credit for passing tax cuts each year. (Ironically, in 1981 the Reagan administration committed itself to indexation of the U.S. tax system by 1984.)

maintained a steady course, giving rise to very little change in the stance of fiscal policy. It also did very little to address the persistent budget deficit.

The Economics of Budget Deficits

Probably the most commonly known and debated fiscal policy statistic is the size of the federal government's budget deficit. This presents an interesting contrast to the countries of Western Europe, where budget deficits pass almost without notice. The average Canadian or American has some idea of the size of the federal budget deficit. (If he

doesn't know exactly how big it is, he is pretty clear that it is too big.) The average West German is unlikely to have any idea of the size of the government's budget deficit and no very strong opinion on whether or not it is too large. Why is our budget deficit so large? Why do we worry so much about it? Is it really such a big problem?

Facts About the Deficit

Those who wish to spread dismay, as well as those who do not know any better, often quote figures for the deficit in current dollars. When this is done the mere fact of inflation almost guarantees that current deficits will be vastly larger than deficits of earlier eras. But so are company debts, peoples' incomes, and everything else that is measured in nominal money units. GNP in 1982, for example, was 30 times as large as GNP in 1929 when measured in current dollars. Does this mean we were 30 times as well off? It does not, since most of the increase was merely due to a change in the price level.

As with income, so it is with deficits. To get some perspective on deficits, we measure them relative to GNP. Figure 32-6 shows the evolution of federal government expenditures and revenues as a percentage of GNP over the period 1970–1984, with the deficit shown as the shaded area between the two. In the first five years of the period both revenues and expenditures showed upward trends, and as we saw in Table 32-2, both deficits and surpluses occurred. However, since 1975 deficits have been the order of the day; indeed, the deficit has grown steadily since 1975.

Over the period 1975–1980 expenditures were a relatively constant fraction of GNP, while tax revenues fell sharply. This is the basis for the Department of Finance view that discretionary tax cuts introduced in the 1970s were responsible for the growing deficit. Other analysts, however, argue that it was the failure to constrain expenditure in the face of the tax cuts that is responsible.

If the source of the growth in the deficit in the 1970s was controversial, it was less so in the 1980s. The increases in the deficit that occurred in the 1981–1983 period reflect the combined effects of the severe recession in 1982, some mild discretionary fiscal expansion, and increased interest payments on the government's debt due to both the sharp rise in interest rates that occurred and the cumulative effect of the persistent deficits on the size of the government debt.

Why Do We Worry About the Deficit?

People worry about deficits for many reasons. We will look at four major worries.

Will a deficit cause inflation? Neither economic theory nor the available evidence suggests that deficits are sufficient to cause inflation. They may do so under some circumstances, but there is no reason why they must do so.

Consider an example of an economy in equilibrium. Actual income equals potential income and, say, 15 percent of national income is saved by households and firms. Suppose two-thirds of these savings are used by firms for private investment, while one-third is lent to governments to finance their budget deficits. Of course these funds will be used differently, and possibly less productively, by governments than they would have been if they had been lent to, and spent by, private firms. But total demand, and hence any demand pressures on the price level, are the same whether the savings are spent by the private or by the public sector. The government can borrow and spend indefinitely, just as the private sector can, without necessarily causing inflation. What is required is that aggregate demand not be raised above aggregate supply at the existing price level.

The worry about the inflationary consequences of a large deficit is that it may lead to a continuous expansion in the money supply. This case cannot be studied in detail until Chapter 36. In the meantime we merely observe that if a deficit is financed by "borrowing" from the Bank of Canada, the money supply will be increased every year by the amount of the deficit. (In effect the bank creates the money to finance the deficit.) No one believes this is desirable.

Deficits financed by sale of bonds to the public will not cause an inflation. Deficits financed by the continual creation of new money will sooner or later cause an inflation.

Will the deficit crowd out private investment? A common fear is that deficit spending may lead to a more or less equivalent reduction in private-sector investment spending. To cover its deficit without creating new money, the government must enter the lending market and borrow enough for

FIGURE 32-6
Federal Revenues and Expenditures, 1967–1983 (Percentage of GNP; National Accounts Basis)

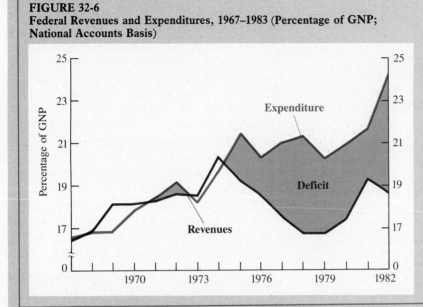

Since 1967, expenditure has grown steadily as a fraction of GNP, while revenues have fluctuated but shown no trend. Over the period 1967 to 1975 expenditures and revenues both grew steadily, and both deficits and surpluses occurred. From 1975 to 1979 expenditure remained roughly constant, while revenues fell dramatically. Persistent deficits emerged. Since 1979, while both have grown, the growth in expenditures has outstripped the growth in revenue, and the deficit has increased sharply.

this purpose. Such borrowing can absorb a significant proportion of private savings. In 1982, for example, the federal deficit was about 52 percent of household savings and fully 24 percent of total private-sector savings by households and firms, respectively. The fear is that the government will acquire funds that would otherwise have been lent to private firms for their own purposes. These firms will be "crowded out" of the market by the large government demand, as shown in Figure 32-7.

What happens in this case is that heavy government borrowing drives up the interest rate, and the higher interest rate reduces private investment expenditure. This effect is more likely if the economy is close to full employment. When there is a large recessionary gap, the induced rise in income will increase the volume of savings (as households move along their savings functions, as shown in Figure 28-2 on page 506). In this case the new savings generated by the rise in income helps to finance the deficit so that less crowding out of existing

private-sector borrowing need occur. When there is full employment, further sustained increases in national income cannot occur. Thus the government deficit must attract funds by driving up interest rates.

It is worth noting that insofar as a deficit that is financed by the sale of bonds to the public causes crowding out, it cannot cause a demand inflation. Complete crowding out means that for every extra dollar the government borrows and spends, the private sector borrows and lends a dollar less. In this case there is no net increase in aggregate demand, and hence no upward pressure on either the price level or real national income.

If government borrowing to finance its deficit drives up the interest rate, some private investment expenditure will be crowded out. This effect is likely to be larger the closer the economy is to full employment.

Interest rates in an open economy such as that of Canada are closely tied to those prevailing in international markets. Hence the scope for increases in the interest rate and crowding out of investment is quite limited. By and large, the budget deficit will result in increased foreign borrowing (not necessarily by the government, but by other borrowers in the economy who are forced to borrow abroad since the government deficit has absorbed most of the available domestic saving). Domestic interest rates and investment will remain relatively unchanged.[9]

Will the burden of the debt eventually harm future generations? If government borrowing to finance current expenditures crowds out private investment, there will be a smaller stock of capital to pass on to future generations. Less capital means less output. This is the long-term burden of the debt. The burden arises from the crowding out of private investment.

However, we have seen that investment in an open economy will not be reduced much by a government deficit. Does this mean there is no burden of the debt in an open economy? Unfortunately, the answer is no. While investment is maintained, there is also increased foreign borrowing due to the deficit. Thus while future generations may well inherit a capital stock that is not changed as a result of the deficit, they will also inherit an increased stock of foreign liabilities. Required future payments of interest and dividends on these liabilities will lower national income both in relation to total output (since some income generated by the output will accrue to foreigners), and in relation to what income would have been in the absence of the government deficits.

Borrowing from abroad represents a transfer of purchasing power to domestic residents when the borrowing occurs, and a transfer back to foreigners when interest payments and principal repayments occur.

An important example of these international ef-fects is the twentieth century American experience. The United States slowly built up a net creditor position over the past six decades. That position has been almost completely dissipated during the first term of President Ronald Reagan. The massive budget deficits experienced under his administration have resulted in massive foreign borrowing. If the deficits remain as large as projected through 1988, America will not only cease to be a major creditor, it will become the world's largest debtor nation—eclipsing Brazil, Argentina, and other Third World debtors.

In this view, championed by Martin Feldstein (chairman of the Council of Economic Advisors from 1982 through 1984), the international consequences of the deficit are very serious. The need to pay interest to foreigners in the future will reduce the living standards of all Americans.

Does the size of the debt hamper the operation of government policy? The large interest bill on the national debt puts a strain on the budget process. For example, in 1983 a full 22 percent of all tax revenues went to pay interest on the national debt! The government's freedom of fiscal maneuver is obviously hampered by this large and rising claim on the national tax revenues. When the government's interest obligations grow, it could just incur an even larger deficit, at least for a while—but eventually interest on the stock of debt must be paid from net revenues.[10] Eventually, it must either reduce its expenditure on other government programs, or it must raise taxes.

Although the level of interest payments has not yet reached crisis proportions, the large claim on existing government revenues is a cause for concern. Further, the trend is that this problem is currently becoming more, not less, serious.

The foregoing indicates that much of the concern about government budget deficits arises from their *cumulative* effect on the national debt, and therefore on the government's interest obligations.

---

[9] The crowding out debate is closely related to debates about the effectiveness of fiscal policy, a debate we take up in Chapter 42. It is important to note that because investment does not fall much in an open economy does not ensure that fiscal policy will be effective—the increased foreign borrowing may cause the currency to appreciate and thus crowd out net exports. We discuss this possibility in Chapter 41.

[10] Of course for a while interest on current debt can be paid by incurring new debt, but this is an explosive process. The interest demands on old and new debt will soon absorb the whole of government tax revenue and eventually all of national income.

FIGURE 32-7
Crowding Out of Private Investment by Public Borrowing

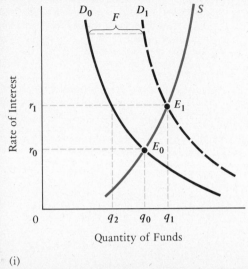

(i)

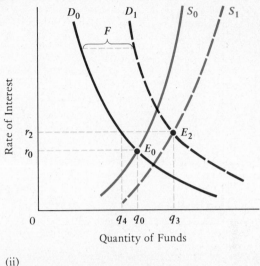

(ii)

Government borrowing may crowd out private-sector borrowing and investing. Part (i) of the figure shows a supply of funds available to be lent, S, that is fairly insensitive to the interest rate. Initially the demand to borrow funds is D_0, giving an equilibrium interest rate of r_0 and a quantity of funds borrowed for all purposes of q_0.

Government spending now increases by F, all of which is borrowed. This shifts the demand for funds to D_1, taking equilibrium to E_1. The interest rate rises to r_1, and the quantity of funds borrowed rises to q_1. But q_2q_1 of these go to the government, so the private sector only borrows q_2,

which is q_2q_0 less than it was able to borrow, and hence invest, before the deficit forced the government into the market.

If, however, the extra government expenditure increases national income, it will raise saving. The savings function will then shift outward, say, from S_0 to S_1 in part (ii) of the figure. Crowding out will then be lessened. At equilibrium E_2 the interest rate rises to r_2, and private borrowing is only q_4q_0 less than before the government entered the market.

Facts About the Debt

It is most useful, in evaluating the national debt and the government's interest payments on it, to consider them *relative to the size of the economy*. The sources of concern about the debt discussed above arise primarily when the debt grows faster than the economy—hence it is really the debt to GNP ratio that matters. A national debt of $100 billion clearly has very different implications when GNP is also only $100 billion than when GNP is $500 billion. Hence in Figure 32-8 the historical data for the

debt and for the interest payments on it are shown as a proportion of GNP.

Consider first the interest payments on the debt, shown in (ii). Clearly, there is genuine cause for worry here. If the trend continues, interest payments could eventually put an intolerable burden on the government's taxing capacity. Ever-bigger deficits would occur, and with them even more borrowing. Sooner or later, if not reversed, these developments would force the government to finance its deficit by creating new money, and inflation would return in a serious way.

FIGURE 32-8
The Relative Significance of the National Debt

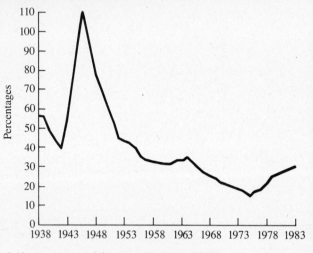

(i) Net government debt as a percentage of GNP

The national debt itself and interest payments on it have not risen in proportion to the GNP since the end of World War II. Two significant ratios are plotted here on a ratio scale. The national debt, after rising sharply through World War II, was a declining fraction of GNP until 1975, after which there has been a continual rise. Interest payments reached 2.9 percent of GNP in 1948, but for the last 25 years they have remained at under 3.0 percent. Clearly the picture of a spendthrift government adding recklessly to the burden of the national debt is overstated.

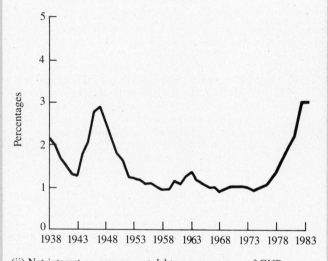

(ii) Net interest on government debt as a percentage of GNP

Source: Public Accounts, Department of Finance.

Figure 32-8(ii) shows the national debt as a proportion of GNP. It shows that the proportion started to fall at the end of World War II and continued to fall until 1974. By 1984 the debt had risen to about 25 percent of GNP. But that figure is still much less than the more than 100 percent achieved at the postwar peak. Nevertheless, the trend is worrisome, and medium-term projections using the fiscal plan published with the February 1984 budget suggest that the debt to GNP ratio is going to continue to rise. In view of the costs associated with a rising debt to GNP ratio, this has led some economists to argue that the government's fiscal policies are *imprudent*, and to call for a commitment to control the deficit.

Proposals to Control the Deficit

As we have seen, government deficits contribute to aggregate demand and hence can play a useful role in dampening cyclical fluctuations in the economy. As we have also seen, government deficits contribute to increases in the national debt and hence might lead in the long term to a reduction in living standards of the average Canadian. This conflict between the short-term stabilization role for deficits and the long-term concern about the size of the public debt has been a constant subject of debate among economists and others concerned with government policy; since the conflict is sharpest during recessions, it is not surprising that the debate has been especially active during the early 1980s. Views range from those who dismiss the long-run costs of the national debt and hence are not concerned about the deficit to those who wish to eschew the short-term stabilization role for the deficit entirely and impose a virtual straitjacket on the government, requiring it to always balance its budget. We now look at some of the specific proposals that have been put forward; some of the general options are illustrated in Figure 32-9.

An Annually Balanced Budget?

Much current rhetoric of fiscal restraint calls for a balanced budget. Some people propose that the budget be balanced annually. In the United States there are some who would even make it an obli-

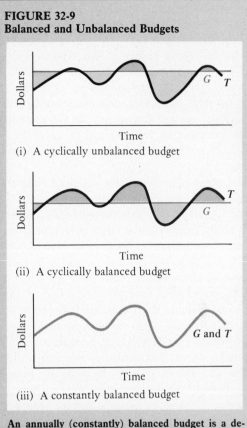

FIGURE 32-9
Balanced and Unbalanced Budgets

(i) A cyclically unbalanced budget

(ii) A cyclically balanced budget

(iii) A constantly balanced budget

An annually (constantly) balanced budget is a destabilizer; a cyclically balanced budget is a stabilizer. The flow of tax receipts is shown varying over the business cycle while in parts (i) and (ii) government expenditure is shown at a constant rate.

In (i) deficits (dark areas) are common and surpluses (light areas) are rare because the average level of expenditure exceeds the average level of taxes. This policy will tend to stabilize the economy against cyclical fluctuations, but the average fiscal stance of the government is expansionary. This has been the characteristic federal budgetary position over the last several decades.

In (ii) government expenditure has been reduced until it is approximately equal to the average level of tax receipts. The budget is now balanced cyclically. The policy still tends to stabilize the economy against cyclical fluctuations because of deficits in slumps and surpluses in booms. But the average fiscal stance is neither strongly expansionary nor strongly contractionary.

In (iii) a balanced budget has been imposed. Deficits have been prevented, but government expenditure now varies over the business cycle, tending to destabilize the economy by accentuating the cyclical swings in aggregate expenditure.

gation enforced by an act of Congress in a constitutional amendment.

The discussion earlier in this chapter suggests that an annually balanced budget would be very difficult—perhaps impossible—to achieve. With fixed tax rates, tax revenues fluctuate endogenously as national income fluctuates. We have seen that much government expenditure is fixed by past commitments and that most of the rest is hard to change quickly.

But suppose an annually balanced budget, or something approaching it, were feasible. What would its effects be? Would they be desirable?

We saw earlier that a large government sector whose expenditures on goods and services are not very sensitive to the cyclical variations in national income is an automatic stabilizer. To insist that annual government expenditure be tied to annual tax receipts would be to abandon the present built-in stability provided by the government. Government expenditure would then become a major destabilizing force. Tax revenues necessarily rise in booms and fall in slumps; an annually balanced budget would force government expenditure to do the same. Changes in national income would then cause induced changes not only in consumption and investment expenditure, but also in government expenditure. This would greatly increase the economy's marginal propensity to spend and hence increase the value of the multiplier.

An annually balanced budget would accentuate the swings in national income that accompany changes in such autonomous expenditure flows as investment and exports.

Proposals to balance the budget on an annual basis thus focus exclusively on long-run fiscal prudence and deny any role for short-term fiscal stabilization.

A Zero Structural Balance?

The concept of the structural balance was designed to assess changes in the stance of fiscal stabilization policy. It was not intended to help assess the long-term viability of fiscal policy. Yet it has often been used in this way by people who have argued that the national debt is not a long-term problem as long as the structural balance is not in deficit.

A zero structural balance is not, however, a good target for long-run fiscal prudence because the economy usually is expected to operate at or below potential income. Thus a budget that is balanced at potential income will produce deficits whenever employment is below potential income, a balance at potential income, and a surplus only in the rare event that employment exceeds the potential income.

A second problem with the structural deficit as an indicator of fiscal imprudence arises from the inflation adjustment. In arriving at a measure of the structural deficit, the inflation adjustment is typically made using the *actual* stock of government debt. Thus the larger the stock of debt, the larger the inflation adjustment will be, and the smaller will be the structural component of any given measured deficits. Thus small structural deficits can hide the very problem fiscal imprudence is concerned with: a too rapidly rising stock of debt.

A Cyclically Balanced Budget?

An alternative policy, one that would prevent continual deficits (and could also inhibit the growth in the size of the government sector), would be to balance the budget over the business cycle. This would be more feasible than the annually balanced budget, and it would not make government expenditure a destabilizing force.

Although more attractive in principle than the annually balanced budget, a cyclically balanced budget would carry problems of its own. Government might well spend in excess of revenue in (say) 1987, leaving an obligation to spend less than current revenue in 1988 and 1989. Could such an obligation to balance over a period of several years be made binding? What the government commits itself to in one year does not necessarily restrict what it (or its successor) does the next year.

Perhaps even more of a problem is that there is always room for some disagreement about the current state of the business cycle. Critics of the cyclically balanced budget proposal argue that many governments have often misinterpreted long-term factors such as demographic changes which lead to an increase in the measured unemployment rate or structural change which leads to a fall in the measured rate of income growth as short-term cyclical factors which call for fiscal stimulus. Thus the critics argue that while governments can appear to accept the need for balance over the cycle, this has not in fact stopped them from running persistently large deficits and hence imprudently run up the national debt.

While a budget balanced over the course of the business cycle is in principle an acceptable way of reconciling short-term stabilization and long-term prudence, the business cycle is not well enough defined in practice to make the proposal operational.

The Medium-Term Fiscal Plan

In a study published in 1984, Professors Neil Bruce and Douglas Purvis of Queen's University addressed the issue of fiscal prudence by evaluating the projected budget deficits published in the government's medium-term fiscal plan released with the federal budget of February 1984. That fiscal plan gives projections for the key economic variables such as output, inflation, interest rates, and unemployment as well as for government revenues and expenditures.

Bruce and Purvis defined the imprudent part of the deficit, or *imprudent deficit,* as that part of projected deficits which contribute to growth in the debt to GNP ratio above some target level. Thus they allow for trend growth in the economy and for projected inflation. The imprudent deficit thus nets out cyclical and inflation adjustments in much the same manner as calculations of the structural deficit do. The crucial difference is that the inflation adjustment is applied only to the level of debt consistent with the target debt to GNP ratio, rather than to the actual stock of debt. This means that current deficits which contribute to the actual debt to do not also automatically lead to an increase in the inflation adjustment applied to future deficits.

In calculating the imprudent deficit, Bruce and

Purvis chose the 1979 debt to GNP ratio as the target ratio. They argued that this was appropriate because it was approximately equal to the average ratio of the previous 20 years. Further, 1979 immediately preceded the two recessions of the early 1980s, and Bruce and Purvis argued that the concept of prudence required that temporary events such as a recession should not be used as a reason for ratcheting up a long-term target.

Their calculation showed the imprudent deficit to be $11 billion. They concluded, therefore, that there was cause for concern about the long-term implications of projected deficits, and that some concerted but systematic phasing-in of budget cuts was in order. Further, they argued that even though the actual cuts could be implemented gradually, the process had to be started quickly so that the program for reestablishing fiscal prudence be flexible enough that the short-term objectives of fiscal stabilization need not be abandoned.

Summary

The need for fiscal prudence is accepted by virtually everyone. How to evaluate it and enforce it is, however, still subject to controversy. Indeed, there is serious doubt that the idea of a balanced budget over any time period is operational.

Many economists believe that a superior alternative to insisting on a precise balance is to pay attention to the balance without making a fetish of never adding to the national debt.

The Political Economy of the Debt

The national debt has a wider political and sociological significance than does the debt of a mere corporation. Let us consider two views.

The Keynesian View

The Keynesian view of the debt is that within limits it is a trivial matter. Keynesians agree that, as already discussed, there is an upper limit to the debt. If the debt got so large that it could not be serviced without either putting a crushing burden on taxpayers or forcing the government to *create* new money to service it, there would be serious problems.

The basic points in the Keynesian view are that until the upper limit on the debt is approached (1) the size of the debt is of no great practical importance and (2) the debt should be increased or decreased according to the needs of stabilization policy.

A Conservative View

An alternative view is based on what has come to be called *fiscal conservatism*. Fiscal conservatives believe that deficits have important harmful effects not recognized by Keynesians.

The Debate[11]

The main premise of this alternative view is that governments are not passive agents who do what is necessary to create full employment and maximize social welfare. Instead governments are composed of individuals, such as elected officials, legislators, and civil servants, who, like everyone else, seek mainly to maximize their own well-being. Since their welfare is best served by government's having a big role and by a satisfied electorate, they favor spending and resist tax increases. This creates a persistent tendency toward deficits that is quite independent of any consideration of a sound fiscal policy.

This conservative view takes a broad historical perspective. It says that in the eighteenth century, spendthrift European rulers habitually spent more than their tax revenues and so created inflationary gaps. The resulting inflations were harmful because they reduced the purchasing power of savings and disrupted trade. By the end of the nineteenth century, the doctrine was well established that a balanced budget is the citizen's only protection against profligate government spending and consequent inflation. Thus the balanced budget doctrine was not

[11] The pro-Keynesian view can be found in almost any modern textbook on macroeconomics. The view of the fiscal conservatives is well presented in J. M. Buchanan, J. Burton, and R. E. Wayne, *The Consequences of Mr. Keynes* (London: Institute of Economic Affairs, 1978).

silly and irrational, as Keynes made it out to be. Instead it was the symbol of the people's victory in a long struggle to control the spendthrift proclivities of the nation's rulers.

The Keynesian revolution swept away that view. Budget deficits became, according to Keynesians, the tool by which benign and enlightened governments sought to ensure full employment. But, say the conservatives, deficit spending let the tiger out of the cage. Released from the nearly century-old constraint of balancing the budget, governments went on a series of wild spending sprees. Inflationary gaps, deflationary gaps, or full employment notwithstanding, governments spent and spent and spent. Deficits accumulated, national debts rose, and inflation became the rule.

The debate reflects deeply held views about the role of government, the nature and motivation of public officials, and the desirability of stabilization. Keynesians tend to regard government officials as well-meaning and substantial government intervention as essential to an effective and humane society. Fiscal conservatives regard public officials as self-serving and of limited competence and see public intervention, however well motivated, as probably inept and ultimately destabilizing. Both recognize that an interventionist government will play a large role in economic affairs. Conservatives regard that prospect with concern, Keynesians with relative equanimity.

SUMMARY

1. Fiscal policy uses government expenditure and tax policies to influence the economy by shifting the aggregate demand curve. Changes in either government spending or tax policies will influence the budget balance.

2. The paradox of thrift is not a paradox at all. It predicts that severe recessions are combatted by encouraging an increase in spending.

3. When private expenditure functions are fixed, it is a relatively simple matter to increase expen-

diture, to cut tax rates, or to make a balanced budget increase in expenditure in order to remove a recessionary gap (and to make the opposite changes to remove an inflationary gap).

4. Fiscal policy is more difficult when, as is almost always the case, private expenditure functions are continually shifting. Fine tuning, the attempt to hold the aggregate expenditure function virtually constant by offsetting even small fluctuations in private expenditure, has been largely discredited. Many still believe, however, that large and persistent gaps can be offset by fiscal policy.

5. Short-term stabilization by fiscal policy works largely through such automatic stabilizers as tax revenues that vary directly with national income, expenditures on goods and services that do not vary with national income, and transfer payments that vary negatively with national income.

6. Discretionary fiscal policy is also used, often to attack large and persistent gaps. It must be reversible. Otherwise the economy may overshoot its target once private investment recovers from a temporary slump or falls back from a temporary boom. Tax changes also need to be perceived as relatively long-lived if they are to induce major changes in household spending patterns. (Temporary changes may merely affect the current saving rate and not expenditure.) This possibility is further discussed in the appendix to this chapter. The need to have tax changes perceived as long-lived conflicts, however, with the need to have fiscal policy easily reversible.

7. Changes in the stance of fiscal policy may be reasonably judged by changes in the high-employment surplus. This is the balance between revenues and expenditures as they would be if full employment prevailed.

8. Canadian national debt and debt service have risen and fallen as a percentage of national income, but they have not yet shown a long-term trend to grow inexorably. Deficits are a cause for concern for several reasons, including inflation, crowding out of investment, and reducing national income in the long run.

9. An annually balanced budget would be unfeasible; even if it were possible, it would destabilize the economy. A cyclically balanced budget would act as a stabilizer while also curbing the secular growth of the government sector. Growth of GNP and some minimal acceptable inflation rate both create room for the cyclical average budget balance to show some deficit; a deficit in excess of this can be viewed as being imprudent.

10. Keynesians take a relatively sanguine view of the national debt. As long as it does not grow wildly as a proportion of national income, they view its short-term fluctuations and its long-term upward trend in absolute terms as a stabilizing device. Fiscal conservatives mistrust government and view insistence on a balanced budget as the only effective means of curtailing reckless government spending that wastes scarce resources and feeds the fires of inflation. In an open economy, deficits can cause foreign borrowing and therefore lead to a reduction in living standards in the long run when interest payments are made to foreigners.

TOPICS FOR REVIEW

Fiscal policy
Budget balance, balanced and unbalanced budgets, surpluses and deficits
Fine tuning
Built-in stabilizers
Discretionary fiscal policy
The stance of fiscal policy
The measured budget balance
The cyclically adjusted surplus (CAS)
The inflation adjustment
Costs of persistent deficits
The structural deficit
Fiscal prudence

DISCUSSION QUESTIONS

1. "Fiscal policy has been a relatively weak instrument in Canada because of our heavy dependence on foreign trade and because of the wide regional disparities in employment opportunities." Discuss.
2. During his run for leadership of the Progressive Conserva-

tive Party in 1983, Peter Pocklington proposed that Canada adopt a flat (proportional) income tax of 20 percent. What benefits are there with this kind of tax? Will the flat tax system be as strong an automatic stabilizer as the progressive tax system?

3. Arrange in order the following in terms of the expected size of their effect on aggregate demand and employment.
   a. Government subsidies to farmers of $100 million, financed by an increase in income taxes of $100 million
   b. Government deficit expenditure of $100 million during a recession
   c. Government deficit expenditure of $100 million near the end of a recovery
   d. A general tax cut, costing $100 million in lost revenue to the government

4. J. K. Galbraith said, about coping with a deflationary gap by means of a tax rebate: "Those who advocate a tax cut do so in deeply conditioned disregard of its economic ineffectiveness, its demonstrated political disutility, and its patently reactionary social effects." What might Professor Galbraith have had in mind by his statement?

5. Consider how each of the following ways of dealing with poverty might affect the stability of the economy.
   a. A negative income tax (see page 440)
   b. An increase in unemployment insurance payments
   c. A Food-for-the-Needy program that channels surplus food products to any family that has no employed member

6. How does growth in full-employment income produce fiscal drag? How may inflation produce fiscal drag? Is not fiscal drag just another name for a built-in stabilizer?

7. Wars involve a massive shift of the nation's resources from the production of consumer goods to the production of military goods. In this sense the wartime generation "pays" for the war. In what sense might postwar generations also pay? How might the method the government uses to finance its wartime expenditure influence who pays for wars?

8. Consider the typical annual expenditures and revenues of the organizations listed below. Comment on the appropriate debt policy for each, taking into account their respective goals, life spans, and resources.
   a. Family household (consider its life cycle)
   b. Federal government
   c. Private corporation (differentiate between a rapidly growing and a mature firm)
   d. A village of 5,000 inhabitants
   e. The local Home and School Association

9. The national debt is essentially the net result of past and present fiscal policy; that is, the net debt increases when the government runs a budget deficit. Does increasing the national debt make a nation poorer? What effect, if any, does the national debt have on the distribution of income?

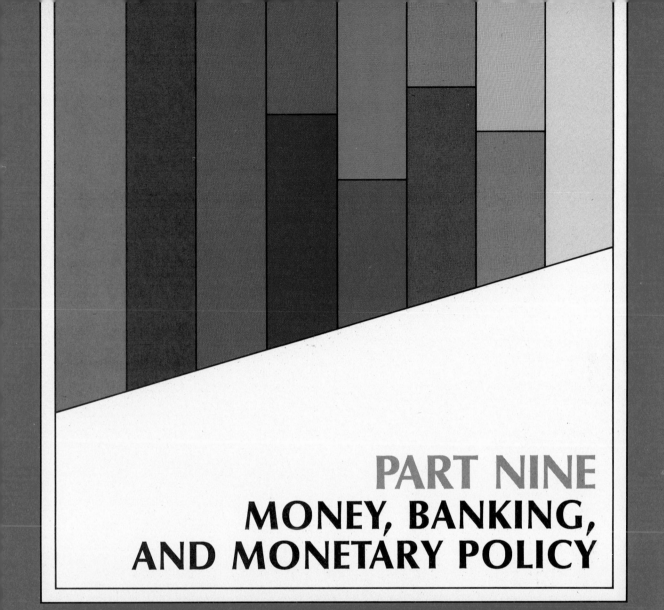

PART NINE
MONEY, BANKING,
AND MONETARY POLICY

33 THE NATURE OF MONEY AND MONETARY INSTITUTIONS

What is the significance of money to the economy, and why are economists concerned about it? Indeed, what is money, and how did it come to play its present role?

Many people believe that money is one of the more important things in life and that there is never enough of it. Yet economists argue that increasing the world's money supply would not necessarily make the average person better off. The reason is that although money gives an *individual* command over goods, increasing the world's money supply would not change the total quantity of goods available.

The "Real" and "Monetary" Parts of the Economy

The Classical Dichotomy

Very early in the history of economics changes in the quantity of money were seen to be associated with changes in the price level. Eighteenth century economists thought of the economy as being divisible into a "real part" and a "monetary part." This division is often referred to as the *dichotomy* between the real and the monetary sectors of the economy.

The real sector. In such theories, the allocation of resources is determined in the real part of the economy by demand and supply. This allocation depends on *relative* prices. Whether, for example, a lot of beef is produced relative to pork depends on the relation between the prices of beef and pork. If the price of beef is higher than the price of pork and both commodities cost about the same to produce, the incentive exists to produce beef rather than pork. This incentive depends on the relative price of the two commodities, rather than on their money prices. At prices of $1 a pound for pork and $3 for beef, the *relative* incentive is the same as it would be at $2 for pork and $6 for beef. As with beef and pork, so with all other commodities:

The allocation of resources among different products depends on relative prices.

The money sector. According to the early economists the price *level* was determined in the monetary part of the economy. An increase in the money supply led to an increase in all money prices. In the beef and pork example, an increase in the total money available might raise the price of pork from $1 to $2 a pound and the price of beef from $3 to $6, but in equilibrium it would leave relative prices unchanged. Hence it would have no effect on the real part of the economy, that is, on the amount of resources allocated to beef and to pork production (or to anything else). If the quantity of money were doubled, the prices of all commodities would double; and money income would also double, so everyone earning an income would be made no better or worse off by the change. Thus, in equilibrium, the real and the monetary parts of the economy were believed to have no effect on each other.

The doctrine that the quantity of money influences the level of money prices but has no effect on the real part of the economy is called the doctrine of the **neutrality of money.**

The veil of money. Because early economists believed that the most important questions—How much does the economy produce? What share of it does each group in the society get?—were answered in the real sector, they spoke of money as a "veil" behind which occurred the real events that affected material well-being.

The Modern View

Modern economists still accept the insights of the early economists that relative prices are a major determinant of the real allocation of resources and that the quantity of money has a lot to do with determining the absolute level of prices. They do not, however, always accept the neutrality of money, as we shall see in Chapter 34.

In this chapter we look first at the experience of price level changes—one aspect of the importance of money—and then at the nature of money itself and the operation of the modern institutions that comprise the monetary system of our economy.

The Experience of Price Level Changes

Figure 33-1 shows the course of Canadian producer (i.e., wholesale) prices from 1867 through 1983. Considerable year-to-year fluctuations are apparent. Despite the large fluctuations that occurred during the nineteenth century, the price trend during that period was neither upward nor downward. In contrast, so far the twentieth century has also seen large fluctuations *and* a distinct rising trend in the price level.

Although admittedly a long time, even two centuries may still not be enough to give a clear perspective of very long-term price fluctuations. The experience of the period since 1946 looks much more dramatic and unusual when compared only with the nineteenth century than when considered in longer perspective. For an indication of the longer-term course of price levels, we can look across the Atlantic. Figure 33-2 shows the course of the price level in England over *seven* centuries! The figure shows that there was an overall inflationary trend, but that it was by no means evenly spread over the centuries.

FIGURE 33-1
Index of Canadian Wholesale Prices, 1867–1983

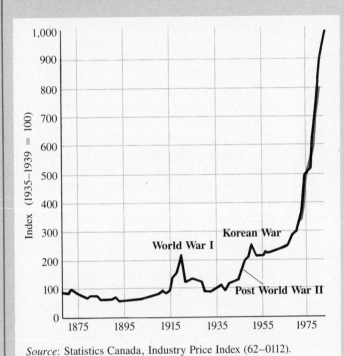

Persistent peacetime inflation is only a recent problem in Canada. Although the price level has fluctuated throughout Canadian history, no long-term trend was visible during the period from confederation to 1940. From the time of World War II to the present, the price level has shown a consistent upward trend.

Source: Statistics Canada, Industry Price Index (62–0112).

FIGURE 33-2
A Price Index of Consumables in Southern England, 1275–1959

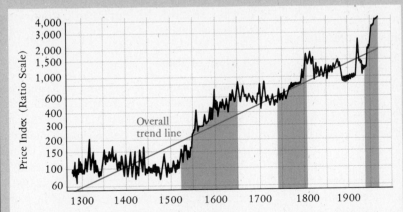

Source: Lloyds Bank Review, No. 58, October 1960.

Over the last seven centuries long periods of stable prices have alternated with long periods of rising prices. This remarkable price series shows an index of the prices of food, clothing, and fuel in southern England from 1275 through 1959. The trend line shows that the average change in prices over the whole period was 0.5 percent per year. The shaded areas indicate periods of unreversed inflation. The series also shows that even the perspective of a century can be misleading because long periods of stable or gently falling prices tended to alternate with long periods of rising prices.

THE NATURE OF MONEY

Inflation is a monetary phenomenon in the sense that a rise in the general level of prices is the same thing as a decrease in the purchasing power of money. But what exactly *is* money? There is probably more folklore and general nonsense believed about money than about any other aspect of the economy. In this section we describe the functions of money and briefly outline the history of money. One purpose of this account is to remove some of these misconceptions. In addition, the recent revival of interest in the gold standard makes some discussion of early monetary systems relevant.

What Is Money?

Traditionally in economics **money** has been defined as any generally accepted medium of exchange—anything that will be accepted by virtually everyone in exchange for goods and services. But in fact:

Money has several functions. It acts as a medium of exchange, as a store of value, and as a unit of account.

Different kinds of money vary in the degree of efficiency with which they fulfill these functions, and different definitions of money may be required for different purposes.

A Medium of Exchange

An important function of money is to facilitate exchange. Without money the economic system, which is based on specialization and the division of labor, would be impossible, and we would have to return to primitive forms of production and exchange. It is not without justification that money has been called one of the great inventions contributing to human freedom.

If there were no money, goods would have to be exchanged by barter, one good being swapped directly for another. We discussed this cumbersome system in Chapter 3; the major difficulty with barter is that each transaction requires a *double coincidence of wants*. For an exchange to occur between A and B, not only must A have what B wants, but B must have what A wants. If all exchange were restricted to barter, anyone who specialized in producing one commodity would have to spend a great deal of time searching for satisfactory transactions.

The use of money as a generally accepted **medium of exchange** removes these problems. People can sell their output for money and subsequently use the money to buy what they wish from others. The double coincidence of wants is unnecessary when money is used as a medium of exchange. Efficient production demands specialization, and this in turn requires that people satisfy most of their desires by consuming goods produced by others. In any complex economy such exchanges entail the use of some kind of money.

The difficulties of barter force people to become relatively self-sufficient. With money as a medium of exchange, everyone is free to specialize; with specialization, the production of all commodities can be increased.

To serve as an efficient medium of exchange, money must have a number of characteristics: It must be readily acceptable. It must have a high value for its weight (otherwise it would be a nuisance to carry around). It must be divisible because money that comes only in large denominations is useless for transactions having only a small value. And it must not be readily counterfeitable because if money can easily be duplicated by individuals, it will lose its value.

A Store of Value

Money is a handy way to store purchasing power when the price level is relatively stable. With barter, some other good must be taken in exchange; with money, goods may be sold today and money stored until it is needed. This provides a claim on someone else's goods that can be exercised at a future date. The two sides of the transaction can be separated in time with the obvious increase in freedom that this confers.

To be a satisfactory store of value, however, money must have a relatively stable value. When the price level is stable, the purchasing power of a given sum of money is also stable. When the price level changes rapidly, this is not so. This undermines the usefulness of money as a store of value. An extreme example is discussed in Box 33-1.

Although money can serve as a satisfactory store of accumulated purchasing power for a single individual, it cannot do so for the society as a whole. If a single individual accumulates a pile of dollars, he or she will, when the time comes to spend it, be able to command the current output of some other individual. The whole society cannot do this. If all individuals were to save their money and then retire simultaneously to live on their savings, there would be no current production to purchase and consume. The society's ability to satisfy wants depends on goods and services being available; if some of this want-satisfying capacity is to be stored up for the whole society, goods that are currently producible must be left unconsumed and carried over to future periods.

A Unit of Account

Money may also be used purely for accounting purposes without having a physical existence of its own. For instance, a government store in a truly communist society might say that everyone had so many "dollars" to use each month. Goods could then be assigned prices and each consumer's purchases recorded, the consumer being allowed to buy until the allocated supply of dollars was exhausted. These dollars need have no existence other than as entries in the store's books, yet they would serve as a satisfactory unit of account.

Whether they could also serve as a medium of exchange depends on whether the store would agree to transfer dollar credits from one customer to another at the customer's request. Banks will transfer dollars credited to demand deposits in this way, and thus a bank deposit can serve as both a unit of account and a medium of exchange. Notice that the use of *dollars* in this context suggests a further sense in which money is a unit of account. People think about values in terms of the monetary unit with which they are familiar.

A further but related function of money is sometimes distinguished: that of a "standard of deferred payments." Payments that are to be made in the future, on account of debts and so on, are reckoned in money. Money is used as a unit of account with the added dimension of time because the account will not be settled until later.

The Origins of Money

The origins of money are lost in antiquity; most primitive tribes known today make some use of it. The ability of money to free people from the cumbersome necessity of barter must have led to its early use as soon as some generally acceptable commodity appeared.

Metallic Money

All sorts of commodities have been used as money at one time or another, but gold and silver proved to have great advantages. They were precious because their supply was relatively limited, and they were in constant demand by the rich for ornament and decoration. They had the additional advantage that they do not easily wear out. Thus they tended to have a high and stable price. They were easily recognized and generally known to be commodities that, because of their stable price, would be readily accepted. They were also divisible into extremely small units.

Precious metals thus came to circulate as money and to be used in many transactions. Before the invention of coins it was necessary to carry precious metals around in bulk. When a purchase was to be made, the requisite quantity of the metal would have to be weighed carefully on a scale. A sack of gold and a highly accurate set of scales were the common equipment of the merchant and trader.

The invention of coinage eliminated the need to weigh the metal at each transaction. The prince or ruler weighed the metal and made a coin out of it to which he affixed his own seal to guarantee the amount of precious metal it contained. Suppose a coin was certified to contain exactly 1/16 of an ounce of gold. If a commodity was priced at 1/8 of

BOX 33–1 **HYPERINFLATION**

Can a sharp inflation continue year after year without triggering an explosive inflation that destroys the value of a currency? The answer appears to be yes—at least some of the time. Inflation rates of 50, 100, and even 200 percent or more a year have occurred year after year and proven manageable as people adjust their contracts to real terms. While there are strains and side effects, the evidence shows such situations to be possible without hyperinflation.

Does this mean that there is no reason to fear that rapid inflation will turn into hyperinflation? The historical record is not entirely reassuring. There have been a number of so-called hyperinflations where prices began to rise at an ever-accelerating rate until the nation's money ceased to be a satisfactory store of value even for the short period between receipt and expenditure. Consider the index of wholesale prices in Germany during and after World War I:

Date		Wholesale price index (1913 = 1)
Jan	1913	1
Jan	1920	13
Jan	1921	14
Jan	1922	37
July	1922	101
Jan	1923	2,785
July	1923	74,800
Aug	1923	944,000
Sept	1923	23,900,000
Oct	1923	7,096,000,000
15 Nov 1923		750,000,000,000

The index shows that a good purchased with one 100 mark note in July 1923 would have required *ten million* 100 mark notes for its purchase only four months later!

While Germany had experienced substantial inflation during World War I, averaging more than 30 percent per year, the immediate postwar years of 1920 and 1921 gave no sign of an ex-

plosive inflation. Indeed, during 1920 price stability was experienced. But in 1922 and 1923, the price level exploded. On November 15, 1923, the mark was officially repudiated, its value wholly destroyed. How could this happen?

When an inflation becomes so rapid that people lose confidence in the purchasing power of their currency, they rush to spend it. But people who have goods become increasingly reluctant to accept the rapidly depreciating money in exchange. The rush to spend money accelerates the increase in prices until people finally become unwilling to accept money on any terms. What was once money ceases to be money.

The price system can then be restored only by repudiation of the old monetary unit and its replacement by a new unit. This destroys the value of monetary savings and of all contracts specified in terms of the old monetary units. It wipes out many people's savings by destroying the value of assets denominated in money terms.

There are approximately a dozen documented hyperinflations in world history, among them the collapse of the *continental* during the American revolution, the *ruble* during the Russian revolution, the *drachma* during and after the German occupation of Greece in World War II, the *pengo* in Hungary during 1945 and 1946, and the Chinese national currency during 1946–1948. Every one of these hyperinflations was accompanied by great increases in the money supply; new money was printed to give governments purchasing power they could not or would not obtain by taxation. And every one occurred in the midst of a major political upheaval in which grave doubts existed about the stability and future of the government itself.

Is hyperinflation likely in the absence of civil war, revolution, or collapse of the government? Most economists think not. And it is clear that annual inflation rates of 5 or 10 or even 200 percent do not mean the inevitable or even likely onset of a hyperinflation, however serious their distributive and social effects may be.

an ounce of gold, two coins could be given over without weighing the gold. This was clearly a great convenience as long as traders knew they could accept the coin at its "face value." The face value itself was nothing more than a guarantee that a certain weight of metal was contained therein.

Abuses of metallic money. The prince's subjects, however, could not let a good opportunity pass. Someone soon had the idea of clipping a thin slice off the edge of the coin. If he collected a coin stamped as containing half an ounce of gold, he could clip a slice off the edge and pass the coin off as still containing half an ounce of gold. ("Doesn't the stamp prove it?" he would argue.) If he got away with this, he would have made a profit equal to the market value of the clipped metal.

Whenever this practice became common, even the most myopic traders noticed that things were not what they seemed in the coinage world. It became necessary to weigh each coin before accepting it at its face value; out came the scales again, and most of the usefulness of coins was lost. To get around this problem, the idea arose of minting the coins with a rough edge. The absence of the rough edge would immediately be apparent and would indicate that the coin had been clipped. The practice, called milling, survives on some coins as an interesting anachronism to remind us that there were days when the market value of the metal in the coin (if it were melted down) was equal to the face value of the coin.

Debasement of metallic money. Not to be outdone by the cunning of his subjects, the prince was quick to seize the chance of getting something for nothing. Because he was empowered to mint the coins, he was in a very good position to work a *really* profitable fraud. When he found himself with debts that he could not pay and that it was inexpedient to repudiate, he merely used some suitable occasion—a marriage, an anniversary, an alliance—to remint the coinage. Subjects would be ordered to bring their gold coins into the mint to be melted down and coined afresh with a new stamp. The subjects could then go away the proud possessors of one new coin for every old coin they had brought

in. Between the melting down and the recoining, however, the prince had only to toss some inexpensive base metal in with the molten gold to earn a handsome profit. If the coinage were debased by adding, say, one pound of new base metal to every four pounds of old coins, five coins would be made for every four turned in. For every four coins brought in, the prince could return four and have one left for himself as profit. With these coins he could pay his debts.

The result was inflation. The subjects had the same number of coins as before and hence could demand the same quantity of goods. When the prince paid his bills, however, the recipients of the extra coins could be expected to spend some or all of them, and this caused a net increase in demand. The extra demand would bid up prices. Debasing the coinage thus led to a rise in prices.

It was the experience of such inflations that led early economists to propound the *quantity theory of money and prices.* They argued that there was a relation between the average level of prices and the quantity of money in circulation, such that a change in the quantity of money would lead to a change in the price level in the same direction. (We shall have more to say about this theory in Chapter 34.)

Gresham's law. The early experience of currency debasement led to a famous economic "law" that has stood the test of time. The hypothesis is that "bad money drives out good." It has come to be known as **Gresham's law** after the Elizabethan financial expert Sir Thomas Gresham, who first explained the workings of the law to Queen Elizabeth I of England.

During the reign of Queen Elizabeth I, English coinage was severely debased. Seeking to help trade, Elizabeth minted new coins containing their full face value in gold. But as fast as she fed these new coins into circulation, they disappeared. Why? Suppose that you possessed one new and one old coin, each with the same face value, and had a bill to pay. What would you do? Clearly, you would pay the bill with the debased coin and keep the undebased one. You part with less gold that way.

If you wanted to obtain a certain amount of gold bullion by melting down the gold coins (as was frequently done), which coins would you use? Clearly, you would use new undebased coins because you would part with less "face value" that way. The debased coins would thus remain in circulation and the undebased coins would disappear. Whenever people got hold of an undebased coin, they would hold on to it; whenever they got a debased coin, they would pass it on. The example in Box 33-2 shows that Gresham's Law is as applicable today as it was 400 years ago.

Paper Money

The next important step in the history of money was the evolution of paper currency. Artisans who worked with gold were called goldsmiths. Naturally they kept very secure safes in which to store their gold. Among the public, the practice evolved of storing gold with the goldsmith for safekeeping. In return, the goldsmith would give the depositor a receipt promising to hand over the gold on demand. If the depositor wished to make a large purchase, he or she could go to the goldsmith, reclaim the gold, and hand it over to the seller of the goods. Chances were that the seller would not require the gold but would carry it back to the goldsmith for safekeeping.

Clearly, if people knew the goldsmith to be reliable, there was no need to go through the cumbersome and risky business of physically transferring the gold. The buyer need only transfer the goldsmith's receipt to the seller, who would accept it, secure in the knowledge that the goldsmith would pay over the gold whenever it was needed. If the seller wished to buy a commodity from a third party who also knew the goldsmith to be reliable, this transaction too could be effected by passing the goldsmith's receipt from the buyer to the seller. The convenience of using pieces of paper instead of gold is obvious.

Thus, when it first came into being, paper money was a promise to pay on demand so much gold, the promise being made first by goldsmiths and later by banks. Banks too became known for their vaults ("safes") where the precious gold was stored and protected. As long as the institutions were known to be reliable, their pieces of paper would be "as good as gold." Such paper money was *backed* by precious metal and was *convertible* on demand into this metal. When a country's money is convertible into gold, the country is said to be on a *gold standard*.

In nineteenth century Canada, private banks operating initially under provincial charters and—after confederation—under federal charter, commonly issued paper money nominally convertible into gold. **Bank notes** represented banks' promises to pay. They remained an important part of the money supply in Canada well into the current century, and they were not completely supplanted by government-issued paper until 1950.

Fractionally backed paper money. For most transactions, individuals were content to use paper currency. It was soon discovered that it was not necessary to keep an ounce of gold in the vaults for every claim to an ounce circulating as paper money. It was necessary to keep some gold on hand because, for some transactions, paper would not do. If someone wished to make a purchase from a distant place where her local bank was not known, she might have to convert her paper into gold and ship the gold. Further, she might not have perfect confidence in the bank's ability to honor its pledge to redeem the notes in gold at a future time. Her alternative was to exchange her notes for gold and store the gold until she needed it.

For these and other reasons, some holders of notes demanded gold in return for their notes. However, some of the bank's customers received gold in various transactions and stored it in the bank for safekeeping. They accepted promises to pay (i.e., bank notes) in return. At any one time, then, some of the bank's customers would be withdrawing gold, others would be depositing it, and the great majority would be trading in the bank's paper notes without any need or desire to convert them into gold. Thus the bank was able to issue more money redeemable in gold than the amount of gold held in its vaults. This was good business,

BOX 33–2 WHERE HAS ALL THE COINAGE GONE?

Tourists traveling in Chile in the 1970s, and other countries with rapid inflation, often wondered aloud why paper currency was used even for transactions as small as the purchase of a newspaper or a pack of matches. Metallic currency in such places was very scarce and sometimes nonexistent. Similarly, the silver dollar, half-dollar, quarter, and dime have disappeared from circulation in the United States. The reason for these things is Gresham's law.

Consider a country that has three different "tokens," each of them legal tender in the amount of $.25. One is a silver quarter with $.10 worth of recoverable silver in it; a second is made of cheaper metals with $.5 worth of recoverable metal in it; the third is a $.25 bill, a brightly colored piece of paper money that says plainly on its face "legal tender for all debts public and private."

If prices are stable and the government produces all three forms of money, there is no reason why they should not all circulate freely and interchangeably. Each is legal tender, and each is worth more as money than as anything else.

However, suppose an inflation starts and prices—including proportionally the prices of silver and other metals—begin to rise sharply. By the time prices have tripled, the silver quarters will have disappeared because the silver in each one is now worth $.30, and people will hoard them or melt them down rather than spend them to buy goods priced at only $.25. While not everyone will do this, coins passing from hand to hand will eventually reach someone who withdraws them from circulation.

What about the coins made of cheaper metal? Since prices have tripled, they now contain metal worth $.15, still less than their face value. They too will disappear if there is a further inflation of, say, 100 percent. This raises the market value of the metal in the coin above its face value. The coins will disappear as they are melted down. By that time, only the paper money will be in circulation. The "bad" paper money will have driven out the "good" metal money.

Thus inflation—and even the expectation of inflation—may make some money "good" and some "bad" in Gresham's sense. If it does, the bad will displace the good.

because the money could be profitably invested in interest-earning loans to households and firms.

This discovery was made by the early goldsmiths. From that time to the present, banks have had many more claims outstanding against them than they actually had in reserves available to pay those claims. In such a situation, we say that the currency is *fractionally backed* by the reserves.

In the past the major problem of a fractionally backed, convertible currency was that of maintaining its convertibility into the precious metal by which it was backed. The imprudent bank that issued too much paper money found itself unable to redeem its currency in gold when the demand for gold was even slightly higher than usual. This

bank would then have to suspend payments, and all holders of its notes would suddenly find them worthless. The prudent bank, which kept a reasonable relation between its note issue and its gold reserve, found that it could meet the normal everyday demand for gold without any trouble.

If the public lost confidence and *en masse* demanded redemption of their currency, the banks would be unable to honor their pledges. The history of nineteenth and early twentieth century banking on both sides of the Atlantic is full of examples of banks ruined by "panics," sudden runs on their gold reserves. When this happened the banks' depositors and the holders of its notes would find themselves with worthless pieces of paper.

Central banks were a natural outcome of this sort of banking system. Where were the commercial banks to turn when they had good investments but were in temporary need of cash? If they provided loans for the public against reasonable security, why should not some other institution provide loans to them against the same sort of security? Central banks evolved in response to such needs.

The development of fiat currencies. As time went on, note issue by private banks became less common and central banks took control of the currency. Central banks in turn became governmental institutions. In time *only* central banks were permitted to issue notes. Originally the central banks issued currency that was fully convertible into gold. In those days gold would be brought to the central bank, which would issue currency in the form of "gold certificates" that asserted the gold was available on demand. The gold supply thus set some upper limit on the amount of currency. But central banks could issue (as bank notes) more currency than they had gold because not all of the currency was presented for payment at any one time. Thus even under a gold standard, central banks had substantial discretionary control over the quantity of currency outstanding.

During the period between World Wars I and II, virtually all the countries of the world abandoned the gold standard: their currencies were no longer convertible into gold. Money that is not convertible by law into anything valuable depends upon its acceptability for its value. Money that is declared by government order (or fiat) to be legal tender for settlement of all debts is called a **fiat money**. Some issues raised by the abandoning of the gold standard are discussed in Box 33-3.

Today virtually all currency is fiat money.

Some countries (including the United States until 1968) preserve the fiction that their currency is backed by gold, but no country allows its currency to be converted into gold on demand. Gold backing for Canadian currency was eliminated in 1940, although note issues continued to carry the traditional statement "will pay to the bearer on demand" until 1954. The holder of a $20 bill who took this seriously and demanded $20 could hand over the $20 bill and receive in return a different but identical $20 bill! Today's Bank of Canada notes simply say "this note is legal tender." It is, in other words, fiat money pure and simple.

The meaning of the phrase **legal tender** is that if you are offered something that is legal tender in payment for a debt and you refuse to accept it, the debt is no longer legally collectible.

Not only is our currency fiat money, so is our coinage. Modern coins, unlike their historical ancestors, contain a value of metal that is characteristically a minute fraction of the value of the coin. Modern coins, like modern paper money, are merely tokens.

Why Is Fiat Money Valuable?

Today paper money and coinage is valuable because it is generally accepted. Because everyone accepts it as valuable, it *is* valuable; the fact that it can no longer be converted into anything has no effect on its functioning as a medium of exchange.

In the early days of the gold standard, paper money was valuable because everyone believed it was convertible into gold on demand. Experience during periods of crisis, when there was often a temporary suspension of convertibility into gold, and of panic, when there were bank failures, served to demonstrate that the mere *promise* of convertibility was not sufficient to make money valuable. Gradually the realization grew that neither was convertibility necessary.

Paper money is valuable when it will be accepted in payment for goods and for debts.

Many people are disturbed to learn that present-day paper money is neither backed by, nor convertible into, anything more valuable—that it is nothing but pieces of paper whose value derives from common acceptance and from confidence that it will continue to be accepted in the future. People believe their money should be more substantial than that; after all, what of "dollar diplomacy" and the "bedrock solidity" of the Swiss franc? But

BOX 33–3 SHOULD CURRENCY BE BACKED BY GOLD?

The gold standard imposed an upper limit on the quantity of convertible currency that could be issued. Now that the system has been abandoned, does it matter that the central bank is not limited to its ability to issue currency?

Gold derived its value because it is scarce relative to the demand for it (the demand being derived from its monetary and its nonmonetary uses). Tying a currency to gold meant that the quantity of money in a country was determined by such chance occurrences as the discovery of new gold supplies. This was not without advantages, the most important being that it provided a check on governments' ability to cause inflation. Gold cannot be manufactured at will; paper currency can.

There is little doubt that in the past, if the money supply had been purely paper, many governments would have attempted to pay their bills by printing new money rather than by raising taxes. Such increases in the money supply, in periods of full employment, would lead to inflation in the same way that the debasement of metallic currency did.

Thus the gold standard provided some check on inflation by making it difficult for the government to change the money supply. Periods of major gold discoveries, however, brought about inflations of their own. In the 1500s, for example, Spanish gold and silver flowed into Europe from the New World, bringing inflation in their wake.

A major problem caused by a reliance on gold is that it is usually desirable to increase the money supply when real national income is increasing. This cannot be done on a gold standard unless, by pure chance, gold is discovered at the same time. The gold standard took discretionary powers over the money supply out of the hands of government. Whether or not one thinks this is a good thing depends on how one thinks governments would use this discretion.

In general, a gold standard is probably better than having the currency managed by an ignorant or irresponsible government, but it is worse than having the currency supply adjusted by a well-informed and intelligent one. *Better* and *worse* in this context are judged by the criterion of having a money supply that varies adequately with the needs of the economy, but does not vary so as to cause violent inflations or deflations.

---

money is in fact only pieces of paper. There is no point in pretending otherwise.

If paper money is acceptable, it is a medium of exchange; if its purchasing power remains stable, it is a satisfactory store of value; and if both of these things are true, it will also serve as a satisfactory unit of account.

Modern Money

By the twentieth century private banks had lost the authority to issue bank notes. Yet they did not lose the power to create deposit money.

Deposit Money

Banks' customers frequently deposit coins and paper money with the banks for safekeeping, just as in former times they deposited gold. Such a deposit is recorded as an entry on the customer's account. A customer who wishes to pay a debt might come to the bank and claim the money in dollars, then pay the money to another person. This person might then redeposit the money in a bank.

Like the gold transfers, this is a tedious procedure, particularly for large payments. It is more convenient to have the bank transfer claims to this money on deposit. The common "cheque" is an instruction to the bank to make the transfer. As soon as such transfers became easy and inexpensive, and cheques became widely accepted in payment for commodities and debts, the deposits became a form of money called **deposit money.**

When individual A deposits $100 in a bank, his account is credited with $100. This is the bank's promise to pay $100 cash on demand. If A pays B $100 by writing a cheque that B then deposits in the same bank, the bank merely reduces A's account by $100 and increases B's by the same amount. Thus the bank still promises to pay on demand the $100 originally deposited, but it now promises to pay it to B rather than to A. What makes all this so convenient is that B can actually deposit A's cheque in any bank, and the banks will arrange the transfer of credits.

Cheques are in some ways the modern equivalent of old-time bank notes issued by commercial banks. The passing of a bank note from hand to hand transferred ownership of a claim against the bank. A cheque on a deposit account is similarly an order to the bank to pay the designated recipient, rather than oneself, money credited to the account. Cheques, unlike bank notes, do not circulate freely from hand to hand; thus cheques themselves are not currency. The balance in the demand deposit *is* money; the cheque transfers money from one person to another. Because cheques are easily drawn and deposited, and because they are relatively safe from theft, they are widely used. In 1983 approximately 5 billion cheques were drawn in Canada. During the 1970s the number of cheques drawn increased at about 7 percent per year.

Thus, when chartered banks lost the right to issue notes of their own, the form of bank money changed but the substance did not. Today banks have money in their vaults (or on deposit with the central banks) just as they always did. Once it was gold, today it is the legal tender of the times—paper money. It is true today, just as in the past, that most of the bank's customers are content to pay their bills by passing among themselves the bank's promises to pay money on demand. Only a small proportion of the transactions made by the bank's customers is made in cash.

Today, just as in the past, banks can create money by issuing more promises to pay (deposits) than they have money available to pay out.

THE BANKING SYSTEM

There are many types of institutions that make up a modern banking system such as exists in Canada today. At one level one can distinguish between the central bank and the financial intermediaries. The **central bank** is the government owned and operated institution that serves to control the banking system. Through it, the government's monetary policy is conducted. In Canada, the central bank is the Bank of Canada; we study it in detail in Chapter 35. Financial intermediaries are privately owned institutions that serve the general public. They are called intermediaries because they stand between savers, from whom they accept deposits, and investors, to whom they make loans. In this chapter we focus on an important class of financial intermediaries, the *chartered banks*.

Modern banking systems are of two main types. In one system there is a small number of banks, each with a very large number of branch offices; in the other system there are many independent banks. The banking systems of Britain and Canada are of the first type, with only a few banks accounting for the overwhelming bulk of the business. The American system is of the second type. The functioning of the banking system is, however, essentially the same in both systems.

The Canadian System

The Canadian banking system is controlled by the provisions of the Bank Act, first passed in 1935 and revised several times since. Under the Bank Act, charters can be granted to financial institutions to operate as banks. There are two classes of banks, chartered banks and Schedule B banks.

There are eleven **chartered banks.** These chartered banks have certain common attributes: They hold deposits for their customers; they permit certain deposits to be transferred by cheque from an individual account to other accounts held in any bank branch in the country; they make loans to households and firms; and they invest in government securities.

The chartered banks are such a dominant force in the banking system that the term banking system is typically taken to refer to the chartered banks. As Table 33-1 shows, the five largest chartered banks together hold 90 percent of total chartered bank assets, and each has more than 900 branches.

The 1980 revision to the Bank Act allowed foreign banks to commence operations in Canada, although it limited them severely in terms of the scale and scope of their operations. Nevertheless, these so-called *Schedule B banks* have increased rapidly in number. Further revisions to the Bank Act may encourage their growth by relaxing the restrictions on their operations.

Banks are not the only financial institutions in the country. Many other privately owned, profit-seeking institutions, such as trust companies, mortgage loan companies, and credit unions, accept savings deposits and grant loans for specific purposes. Finance companies make loans to households for practically any purpose—sometimes at very high effective interest rates. The post office and the telegraph system will transfer money, and credit card companies will extend credit so that purchases can be made on a buy-now, pay-later basis.

What distinguishes chartered banks from the other members of the financial system, each of which does some of the things banks do? The chartered banks are unique in one basic way. They accept demand deposits on which cheques may be drawn, and they will transfer funds from one person's deposit to another's when ordered to do so by a customer's cheque. Other financial institutions offer chequable savings accounts, but they do not have facilities to transfer funds to accounts in other

TABLE 33–1 ASSETS AND BRANCHES OF THE CHARTERED BANKS, JANUARY 1983

Bank	Number of branches (1982)	Assets Millions of dollars	Assets Percentage of total
Royal Bank of Canada	1,487	84,682	24.1
Canadian Imperial Bank of Commerce	1,579	68,112	19.4
Bank of Montreal	1,238	63,194	18.0
Bank of Nova Scotia	1,032	54,808	15.6
Toronto Dominion Bank	994	42,800	12.2
National Bank of Canada	610	17,774	5.1
Mercantile Bank of Canada	NA	4,106	1.2
Bank of British Columbia	50	3,058	
Other	70	12,531	

Source: The Financial Post Survey of Industrials, 1984.

Although there are eleven chartered banks operating in Canada, the industry is dominated by the big five, who between them hold more than 90 percent of the industry's total assets. The National Bank of Canada was formed in 1979 by the amalgamation of the Banque Ca- nadienne Nationale and the Banque Provinciale de Canada. Included in "other" are the Continental Bank, the Northend Bank, and the Canadian Commercial and Industrial Bank.

institutions and must use the banking system to clear cheques.[1] In any event, only a small fraction of the dollar volume of cheques issued is accounted for by cheques drawn on nonbank institutions.

Interbank Activities

Chartered banks have a number of interbank cooperative relationships. These are encouraged by special banking laws because they facilitate the smooth functioning of money and credit markets.

For example, banks often share loans. Even the biggest bank cannot meet all the credit needs of a giant corporation, and often a group of banks will offer a "pool loan," agreeing on common terms and dividing the loan up into manageable segments.

Another form of interbank cooperation is the bank credit card. VISA and MasterCard are the two most widely used credit cards, and each is operated by a group of banks.

Probably the most important form of interbank cooperation is cheque clearing and collection. Bank deposits are an effective medium of exchange only because banks accept each other's cheques. If a depositor in bank A writes a cheque to someone who deposits it in bank B, bank A now owes money to bank B. This creates a need for the banks to present cheques to each other for payment.

There are millions of such transactions in the course of a day, and they result in an enormous sorting and bookkeeping job. Multibank systems make use of a **clearing house** where interbank debts are settled. At the end of the day, all the cheques drawn by bank A's customers and deposited in bank B are totaled and set against the total of all the cheques drawn by bank B's customers and deposited in bank A. It is necessary only to settle the difference between the two sums. The actual cheques are passed through the clearing house back to the bank on which they were drawn. Both banks are then able to adjust the individual

accounts by a set of book entries. A flow of cash between banks is necessary only when there is a net transfer of cash from the customers of one bank to those of another. This flow of cash is accomplished by a transfer of deposits held by the chartered banks with the Bank of Canada.

Chartered Banks As Profit-Seeking Institutions

Banks are private firms that start with invested capital and seek to earn money in the same sense as do firms making neckties or bicycles. A bank provides a variety of services to its customers: a safe place to store money; the convenience of demand deposits that can be transferred by personal cheque; a convenient place to earn a modest but guaranteed return on savings; and often financial advice and estate management services. The bank earns some revenue by charging for these services, but such fees are a small part of the bank's total earnings. The largest part (typically about five-sixths) of a bank's earnings is derived from the bank's ability to invest profitably the funds placed with it.

Principal Assets and Liabilities

Table 33-2 is the consolidated balance sheet of the chartered banks in Canada. The bulk of a bank's liabilities are deposits owed to its depositors. The principal assets of a bank are the *securities* it buys (including government bonds), which pay interest or dividends, and the *loans* it makes to individuals to buy houses, cars, television sets, and securities and to businesses to build factories, buy machines, and finance the purchase of goods and raw materials. A bank loan is a liability to the borrower (who must pay it back), but an asset to the bank. The bank expects not only to have the loan repaid, but to receive interest that more than compensates for the paperwork involved and the risk of nonpayment.

Most money deposited with banks is "at work," having been invested in loans or securities. Banks

---

[1] Revisions to the Bank Act passed in 1980 provide for nonbank access to the clearing system via the formation of the Canadian Payments Association. However, just how the new system will function is as yet unclear.

TABLE 33–2 CONSOLIDATED BALANCE SHEET OF CANADIAN CHARTERED BANKS, DECEMBER 31, 1984 (Billions of Dollars)

Assets		Liabilities	
Reserves (including deposits with Bank of Canada)	$6	Deposits: Demand	20
		Savings	102
Loans (determined in Canadian dollars)	153	Time	44
Government of Canada Securities	18	Borrowings	3
Other securities	9	Foreign Currency Liabilities	160
Foreign Currency Assets	157	Other Liabilities	28
Other Assets	28	Capital Account	14
	371		371

Reserves are only a small fraction of deposit liabilities. If all the bank's customers who held demand deposits tried to withdraw them in cash, the banks could not meet this demand without liquidating $14 billion of other assets. This would be impossible without assistance from the Bank of Canada.

earn money by lending and investing the money left with them so as to earn more than it costs them to attract the deposits. Deposits are the lifeblood of a chartered bank. Without them the bank has nothing to lend or invest except the small amount of its initial capital.

Most bank services are designed to attract or keep deposits. On some categories of deposits, the bank pays the depositor an interest rate in the expectation that it can earn more than that by reinvesting the money. In the case of demand deposits, the bank must earn more by investing them than the excess of the cost of providing the services its depositors expect over the service charges it collects.

Reserves

The Need for Reserves

All bankers would as a matter of convenience and prudence keep *some* cash on hand against their deposits in order to be able to meet depositors' day-to-day requirements for cash. But the reserves required for these needs are far less than 100 percent. Just as the goldsmiths of old discovered that only a fraction of the gold they held was ever withdrawn at any given time, so too have banks discovered that only a fraction of their deposits will be withdrawn in cash at any one time. Most deposits of any individual bank remain on deposit with it; thus an individual bank need only keep fractional reserves against its deposits.

The reserves needed to assure that depositors can withdraw their deposits on demand will be quite small in normal times.

The psychological effect of a bank's refusing to give a depositor cash can be devastating. Until relatively recent times, such an event—or even the rumor of it—could lead to a "run" on the bank as depositors rushed to withdraw their money. Faced with such a panic, the bank would have to close until it had borrowed funds or liquidated enough assets to meet the demand or until the demand subsided. But the closing of even one bank often led nervous depositors to demand cash from other banks. Bankers could not instantly turn their loans into cash since the borrowers had the money tied up in such things as real estate or business enterprises. They could not even quickly sell their securities since many of the potential purchasers found their money was tied up in the closed banks. Thus, in a domino effect, once many banks closed, a wave of foreclosures, bankruptcies, and further bank failures would follow.

To avoid panics reserves must be large enough to meet extraordinary demands for cash.

The need of the banking system for reserves against depositors' panics has been diminished by governmental policies. First, the central bank can provide chartered banks with needed cash either by lending them money or by buying the securities they want to sell. Second, the government provides insurance which guarantees that depositors will get their money back even if a bank fails completely. Such insurance decreases the likelihood of a widespread panic because one bank's failure is much less likely to lead to a run on other banks. Most depositors will not withdraw their money as long as they are *sure* they can get it when they need it.

Actual and Required Reserves

As Table 33-1 shows, in 1983 only a fraction of the total major assets of the chartered banks consisted of cash and interest-earning assets that could quickly be converted into cash. Cash reserves are held in the form of deposits in the Bank of Canada and notes. All banks need to keep some reserves of cash to satisfy their depositors' day-to-day requirements. Indeed, all banks are forced by law to hold such cash reserves.

A bank's **cash reserve ratio** is the fraction of its deposits that it holds as reserves either as currency in its vaults or as deposits with the central bank. Those reserves that the banks are required to hold under the Bank Act are called **required cash reserves**. Any reserves that a bank holds over and above required reserves are called **excess cash reserves**. Since 1980 the required cash reserve ratios have been 10 percent for demand deposits and 4 percent for term deposits.

Most liquid assets are held in the form of bonds and Treasury bills (government securities with usual terms to maturity of three or six months) issued by the government of Canada. These assets generally yield a lower rate of return than loans, but they act as **secondary reserves** that can be used to replenish cash holdings should they be run down.

THE CREATION AND DESTRUCTION OF DEPOSIT MONEY BY CHARTERED BANKS

The fractional reserve system creates the leverage by which privately owned and operated banks and other financial institutions can create new money.

If banks can increase their reserves, they can increase their deposits even more. Since deposits are money, banks can thus increase the money supply.

That is all there is to money creation. Yet the process is worth examining in some detail. We shall limit our attention to chartered banks and their creation of demand deposits.

Some Simplifying Assumptions

To focus on the essential aspects of how banks create money, assume that banks can invest in only one kind of asset, loans, and that there is only one kind of deposit, a demand deposit.

Three other assumptions listed below are provisional; later, when we have developed the basic ideas concerning the bank's creation of money, these assumptions will be relaxed.

Fixed required reserve ratio. It is assumed that all banks have the same required reserve ratio, which does not change. In our numerical illustration we shall assume that the required reserve ratio is 20 percent; that is, that banks must have at least $1 of reserves for every $5 of deposits.

No excess reserves. It is assumed that all banks want to invest any reserves they have in excess of the legally required amount. This implies that they always believe there are safe investments to be made when they have excess reserves.

No cash drain from the banking system. It is assumed that the public holds a fixed amount of currency in circulation. Thus any changes in the money supply will take the form of changes in deposit money.

The Creation of Deposit Money

A typical bank's balance sheet is shown in Table 33-3. The Canadian Immigrant's Bank of Commerce (CIBC) has assets of $200 of reserves, held partly as cash on hand and partly as deposits with the central bank, and $900 of loans outstanding to its customers. Its liabilities are $100 to those who initially contributed capital to start the bank, and $1,000 to current depositors. (All figures are in thousands of dollars.) The bank's ratio of reserves to deposits is 200/1,000 = 0.20, exactly equal to its minimum requirement.

An immigrant arrives in the country and opens an account by depositing $100 with the CIBC. This is a wholly new deposit for the bank, and it results in a revised balance sheet (Table 33-4). As a result of the immigrant's new deposit, both cash assets and deposit liabilities have risen by $100. More important, the reserve ratio has increased from 0.20 to 300/1,100 = 0.27. The bank now has excess reserves—with $300 in reserves it could support $1,500 in deposits.

A Single Monopoly Bank

If the CIBC were the only bank in the system, it would know that any loans that it made would eventually give rise to new deposits of an equal

TABLE 33–4 THE BALANCE SHEET OF CIBC AFTER AN IMMIGRANT DEPOSITS $100 (Thousands of Dollars)

Assets		Liabilities	
Cash and other reserves	$ 300	Deposits	$1,100
Loans	900	Capital	100
	$1,200		$1,200

The immigrant's deposit raises deposit liabilities and cash assets by the same amount. Since both cash and deposits rise by $100, the cash reserve ratio, formerly 0.20, now increases to 0.27. The bank has more cash than it needs to provide a 20 percent reserve against its deposit liabilities.

amount. It would then be in a position to say to the next business executive who comes in for a loan, "We will lend your firm $400 at the going rate of interest." The bank would do so by adding that amount to the firm's deposit account. Table 33-5 shows what would happen in this case.

The new immigrant's deposit initially raised cash assets and deposit liabilities by $100. The new loans created an additional $400 of deposit liabilities. This restored the reserve ratio to its legal minimum (300/1,500 = 0.20), and no further expansion of deposit money is possible. As the bank's customers do business with each other, settling their accounts by cheques, the ownership of the deposits will be continually changing. But what

TABLE 33–3 THE INITIAL BALANCE SHEET OF THE CANADIAN IMMIGRANT'S BANK OF COMMERCE (CIBC) (Thousands of Dollars)

Assets		Liabilities	
Cash and other reserves	$ 200	Deposits	$1,000
Loans	900	Capital	100
	$1,100		$1,100

The CIBC bank has a reserve of 20 percent of its deposit liabilities. The chartered bank earns money by finding profitable investments for much of the money deposited with it. In this balance sheet, loans are its earning assets.

TABLE 33–5 THE MONOPOLY BANK'S BALANCE SHEET AFTER MAKING A $400 LOAN (Thousands of Dollars)

Assets		Liabilities	
Cash and other reserves	$ 300	Deposits	$1,500
Loans	1,300	Capital	100
	$1,600		$1,600

The loan restores the reserve ratio of 0.20. By increasing its loans by a multiple of its new cash deposit, the bank restores its reserve ratio of 0.20.

matters to the bank is that its total deposits will remain constant.

The extent to which a monopoly bank could increase its loans *and thus its deposits* depends on the reserve ratio. Because in this case the ratio is $1/5(= 0.20)$, the bank would be able to expand deposits to five times the original acquisition of money. In general, if the reserve ratio is r, a bank can increase its deposits by $1/r$ times any new reserves. As we shall see, this general relationship proves true of a banking system whether or not there is a monopoly bank. [42]

Many Banks

Deposit creation is more complicated in a multibank system than in a single-bank system, but *the end result is exactly the same.* It is more complicated because, when a bank makes a loan, the recipient of the loan may pay the money to someone who deposits it in another bank. How deposit creation works in a multiple-bank system is most easily seen under the extreme assumption that every new borrower immediately withdraws the borrowed funds from the lending bank and pays someone who in turn deposits the money in another bank or banks.

With its present level of deposits at $1,100, the bank needs only $220 of reserves ($0.20 \times \$1,100 = \$220$), so it can lend the $80 excess that it has on hand. Table 33-6 shows the position after this has

TABLE 33–6 THE CIBC BALANCE SHEET AFTER A NEW LOAN AND CASH DRAIN OF $80 (Thousands of Dollars)

Assets		Liabilities	
Cash and other reserves	$ 220	Deposits	$1,100
Loans	980	Capital	100
	$1,200		$1,200

The bank lends its surplus cash and suffers a cash drain. The bank keeps $20 as a reserve against the new deposit of $100. It lends $80 to a customer who writes a cheque to someone who deals with another bank. When the cheque is cleared, the CIBC has suffered an $80 cash drain, has increased its loans by $80, and has restored its reserve ratio to 0.20.

TABLE 33–7 CHANGES IN THE BALANCE SHEETS OF SECOND-GENERATION BANKS (Thousands of Dollars)

Assets		Liabilities	
Cash and other reserves	+ $16	Deposits	+ $80
Loans	+ 64		
	+ $80		+ $80

Second-generation banks receive cash deposits and expand loans. The second-generation banks gain new deposits of $80 as a result of the loan granted by the CIBC, which is used to make payments to customers of the second-generation banks. These banks keep 20 percent of the cash they acquire as their reserve against the new deposit, and they can make new loans using the other 80 percent. When the customers who borrowed the money make payments to the customers of third-generation banks, a cash drain occurs.

been done and after the proceeds of the loan have been withdrawn to be deposited to the account of a customer of another bank. The CIBC once again has a 20 percent reserve ratio.

So far deposits in the CIBC have increased by only the initial $100 of the new immigrant's money with which we started, as shown in Table 33-4. (Of this, $20 is held as a cash reserve against the deposit and $80 has been lent out in the system.) But other banks have received new deposits of $80 as the persons receiving payment from the firm or household who borrowed the $80 from the CIBC deposited those payments in their own banks. The receiving banks (sometimes called *second-generation banks*) receive new deposits of $80, and when the cheques clear, they have new reserves of $80. Because they require an addition to their reserves of only $16 to support the new deposit, they have $64 of excess reserves. They now increase their loans by $64. After this money is spent by the borrowers and has been deposited in other, third-generation banks, the balance sheets of the second-generation banks will have changed, as in Table 33-7.

The third-generation banks now find themselves with $64 of new deposits. Against these they need hold only $12.80 in cash, so they have excess reserves of $51.20 that they can immediately lend out. Thus there begins a long sequence of new deposits, new loans, new deposits, and new loans. The stages are shown in Table 33-8. The series in the table should look familiar, for it is the same convergent process we met when dealing with the multiplier.

The banking system has created new deposits and thus new money, although each banker can honestly say, "All I did was invest my excess reserves. I can do no more than manage wisely the money I receive."

If r is the reserve ratio, the ultimate effect on the deposits of the banking system of a new deposit will be $1/r$ times the new deposit. [43] This is exactly the same result reached in the monopoly bank case.[2]

Many Deposits

The two cases discussed above, the monopoly bank and the single new deposit in a many-bank situation, serve this purpose: They show that under either set of opposite extreme assumptions, the result is the same. So it is, too, in intermediate situations. A far more realistic picture of deposit creation is one in which new deposits accrue simultaneously to all banks, perhaps because of changes in the monetary policy of the government.

Say, for example, that the community contains ten banks of equal size and that each received new cash deposits of $100. Now each bank is in the position shown in Table 33-4, and each can expand deposits based on the $100 of excess reserves. (Each bank does this by granting loans to customers.)

Because each bank does one-tenth of the total banking business, an average of 90 percent of any newly created deposit will find its way into other banks as the customer pays other people in the community by cheque. This will represent a cash drain from the lending bank to the other banks.

However, 10 percent of each new deposit created by every other bank should find its way into this bank. All banks receive new cash and all begin creating deposits simultaneously; no bank should suffer a significant cash drain to any other bank.

Thus all banks can go on expanding deposits without losing cash to each other; they need only worry about keeping enough cash to satisfy those depositors who will occasionally require cash. The expansion can go on with each bank watching its own ratio of cash reserves to deposits, expanding deposits as long as the ratio exceeds 1/5 and ceasing when it reaches that figure. The process will come to a halt when each bank has created $400 in additional deposits, so that for each initial $100 cash deposit, there is now $500 in deposits backed by $100 in cash. Now *each* bank will have entries in its books similar to those shown in Table 33-5.

The general rule, if there is no cash drain, is that a banking system with a reserve ratio of r can change its deposits by $1/r$ times any change in reserves.

Excess Reserves and Cash Drains

Two of the simplifying assumptions made earlier can now be relaxed.

Excess reserves. If banks do not choose to invest excess reserves, the multiple expansion discussed will not occur. Turn back to Table 33-4. If the CIBC had been content to hold 27 percent reserves, it would have done nothing more. Other things being equal, banks will choose to invest excess reserves because of the profit motive. But there may be times when they believe the risk is too great. It is one thing to be offered 12 percent or even 24 percent interest on a loan, but if the borrower defaults on the payment of interest and principal, the bank will be the loser. Similarly, if the bank expects interest rates to rise in the future, it may hold off making loans now so that it will have reserves available to make more profitable loans after the interest rate has risen.

There is nothing automatic about credit expansion; it rests on the decisions of bankers. If banks do not

[2] The "multiple expansion of deposits" that has just been worked through applies in reverse to a withdrawal of funds. Deposits of the banking system will fall by a multiple of $1/r$ times any amount withdrawn from the bank and not redeposited at another.

TABLE 33–8 MANY BANKS, A SINGLE NEW DEPOSIT (Thousands of Dollars)

Bank	New deposits	New loans	Addition to reserves
CIBC	$100.00	$ 80.00	$ 20.00
Second-generation bank	80.00	64.00	16.00
Third-generation bank	64.00	51.20	12.80
Fourth-generation bank	51.20	40.96	10.24
Fifth-generation bank	40.96	32.77	8.19
Sixth-generation bank	32.77	26.22	6.55
Seventh-generation bank	26.22	20.98	5.24
Eighth-generation bank	20.98	16.78	4.20
Ninth-generation bank	16.78	13.42	3.36
Tenth-generation bank	13.42	10.74	2.68
Total first 10 generations	446.33	357.07	89.26
All remaining generations	53.67	42.93	10.74
Total for banking systems	$500.00	$400.00	$100.00

The banking system as a whole can create deposit money whenever it receives new reserves. The table shows the process of the creation of deposit money on the assumptions that all the loans made by one set of banks end up as deposits in another set of banks (called the *next-generation banks*), that the required reserve ratio (*r*) is 0.20, and that there are no excess reserves. Although each bank suffers a cash drain whenever it grants a new loan, the system as a whole does not, and the system ends up doing in a series of steps what a monopoly bank would do all at once; that is, it increases deposit money by 1/*r*, which in this example is five times the amount of any increase in reserves that it obtains.

choose to use excess reserves to expand their investments, there will not be an expansion of deposits.

Banks tend to hold larger excess reserves in times of business recession, when there is a low demand for loans and very low interest rates, than they do in periods of boom, when the demand for loans is great and interest rates are high.

Relaxing the assumption of no excess reserves cuts the automatic link between the creation of excess reserves and money creation.

Excess reserves make it *possible* for the banks to expand the money supply, but only if they want to do so.

The money supply is thus at least partially determined by the chartered banks in response to such forces as changes in national income and interest rates. However, the upper limit of deposits is determined by the required reserve ratio and by the reserves available to the banks, both of which are under the control of the central bank.

Cash drain. Suppose firms and households find it convenient to keep a fixed *fraction* of their money holding in cash (say 5 percent) instead of a fixed *amount* of dollars. In that case an extra $100 in money supply will not all stay in the banking system; only $95 will remain on deposit, while the rest will be added to money in circulation. In such a situation any multiple expansion of bank deposits will be accompanied by a cash drain to the public that will reduce the maximum expansion below what it was when the public was content to hold all its new money as bank deposits. Table 33-9 shows the position of a typical bank after a credit expansion of $400 and a cash drain of $20.

The story of deposit creation when there is a cash drain to the public goes like this: Each bank

TABLE 33–9 THE MONOPOLY BANK'S BALANCE SHEET AFTER A CREDIT EXPANSION AND AN ACCOMPANYING CASH DRAIN

Assets		Liabilities	
Cash and reserves	$ 280	Deposits	$1,480
Loans	1,300	Capital	100
	$1,580		$1,580

The amount of maximum possible deposit expansion is reduced by a cash drain. This example differs from that shown in Table 33-5 because, after a new deposit of $100 and a new loan of $400, 5 percent of the newly created money is withdrawn as cash to be held by the public. Cash and deposits each fall by $20 and the reserve ratio falls below 20 percent.

starts creating deposits and suffers no significant cash drain to other banks. But because approximately 5 percent of newly created deposits is withdrawn to be held as cash, each bank suffers a cash drain to the public. The expansion continues, each bank watching its own ratio of cash reserves to deposits, expanding deposits as long as the ratio exceeds 1/5 and ceasing when it reaches that figure. Because the expansion is accompanied by a cash drain, it will come to a halt with a smaller deposit expansion than in the no cash drain case.[3]

THE MONEY SUPPLY

The total stock of money in the economy at any moment is called the **money supply** or the **supply of money.** Economists and financial analysts tend to use a number of different definitions for the money supply, many of which are regularly reported in the *Bank of Canada Review.* Typically the definitions involve the sum of currency in circulation plus some types of deposit liabilities of financial institutions. Definitions vary in terms of

what deposits are included. Different definitions come into use or go out of favor as the importance of different types of deposits change.

Kinds of Deposits

Most of the deposits held by the average person are either demand deposits or savings deposits.

Demand Deposits

A **demand deposit** means that the customer can withdraw the money on demand (i.e., without giving any notice of intention to withdraw). Demand deposits are transferable by cheque. Such a cheque instructs the bank to pay without delay a stated sum of money to the person to whom the cheque is payable.

Savings Deposits

Prior to recent changes in the Bank Act, a **savings deposit** was an interest-bearing deposit legally withdrawable only after a certain notice period. (Hence another word for savings deposit used to be *term* deposit.) In practice, although it was impossible to pay a bill by writing a cheque on a savings deposit, such deposits were always quickly convertible into a medium of exchange. A depositor wishing to use a savings deposit to pay a bill had to withdraw money from a savings account and then either pay the bill in cash or deposit the funds in a demand account and write a cheque on the demand account.

The Disappearing Distinction Between Demand and Savings Deposits

When interest rates on savings deposits amounted to only a few percent, people were content to keep some funds in savings deposits and their reserves of cash for ordinary transactions in demand deposits. Then, as short-term interest rates rose, it became more and more expensive (in terms of interest foregone) to keep cash in demand deposits, even for a week or two. Starting in the

---

[3] It can be shown algebraically that the percentage of cash drain must be added to the reserve ratio to determine the maximum possible expansion of deposits. [44]

1970s, a series of devices were invented that tended to make it easier to convert interest-bearing deposits into deposits transferable by cheque.

Chequable savings accounts are now common, and some banks even offer a service whereby fixed sums are automatically transferred from a customer's savings account to his or her demand account when funds in the demand account become insufficient to meet newly presented cheques. The effective distinction is no longer between demand and savings accounts, but rather between a multitude of types of accounts each offering different combinations of interest payments, service provided, and service charges levied. The deposit that is genuinely tied up for a period of time now takes the form of a **term deposit (TD)**, which is purchased with a statement of a particular withdrawal date, a minimum of 30 days into the future, and which pays a much reduced interest rate in the event of early withdrawal.

Near Money and Money Substitutes

Over the past two centuries what has been accepted by the public as money has expanded from gold and silver coins to include first bank notes and then bank deposits subject to transfer by cheque. Until recently, most economists would have agreed that money stopped at that point. No such agreement exists today, and an important debate centers on the definition of money appropriate to the present world.

If we concentrate only on the medium-of-exchange function of money, there is little doubt about what is money in Canada today. Money consists of notes, coins, and deposits subject to transfer by cheque or chequelike instruments. No other asset constitutes a generally accepted medium of exchange; indeed, even notes and cheques are not universally accepted—as you will discover if you try to buy a pack of cigarettes with a $1,000 bill (or even a $100 bill in a corner grocery store) or if you try to buy a mink coat on a Saturday afternoon after having offered your personal cheque in exchange. But these exceptions are unimportant.

The problem of deciding what is money arises because cash, which best fulfills the medium-of-exchange function, may provide relatively poor ways to meet the store-of-value function (see Table 33-10). Interest-earning assets will do a better job of meeting this function of money than will currency or demand deposits that earn no interest. At the same time, however, they are less capable of filling the medium-of-exchange function. Chequeable savings accounts provide a better store of value than currency and demand deposits, without too much loss of the medium-of-exchange function.

Near Money

Assets that fulfill adequately the store-of-value function and are readily converted into a medium of exchange but are not themselves a medium of exchange are sometimes called **near money**. Deposits at a trust company are a characteristic form of near money. When you have such a deposit, you know exactly how much purchasing power you hold (at today's prices) and, given modern banking practices, you can turn your deposit into a medium of exchange—cash or a chequing deposit—at a moment's notice. Additionally, your deposit will earn some interest during the period that you hold it.

TABLE 33–10 THE DOLLAR AS A STORE OF VALUE SINCE 1962

$1 put aside in	Had the purchasing power 5 years later of	Its average annual loss of value was
1962	$.86	2.8%
1967	.79	4.2%
1972	.47	10.7%
1977	.37	12.6%

The dollar has become an increasingly less satisfactory store of value over the last two decades. The second column shows the purchasing power, measured by the Consumer Price Index, of $1 five years after it was saved (assuming it earned no interest). In order for it to have maintained its real purchasing power, it would have had to earn the annual percentage return shown in the last column. The increase in the required return explains the growing use of near moneys and money substitutes that (unlike currency and demand deposits) earn interest.

Why then does not everybody keep their money in such deposits instead of in demand deposits or currency? The answer is that the inconvenience of continually shifting money back and forth may outweigh the interest that can be earned. One week's interest on $100 (at 5 percent per year) is only about $.10, not enough to cover carfare to the bank or the cost of mailing a letter. For money that will be needed soon, it would hardly pay to shift it to a savings deposit.

In general, whether it pays to convert cash or demand deposits into interest-earning savings deposits for a given period will depend on the costs of shifting funds and on the amount of interest that can be earned.

There is a wide spectrum of assets in the economy that pay interest and also serve as reasonably satisfactory temporary stores of value. The difference between these assets and savings deposits is that their capital values are not quite as certain as are those of savings deposits. If I elect to store my purchasing power in the form of a treasury bill that matures in 30 days, its price on the market may change between the time I buy it and the time I want to sell it—say 10 days later. If the price changes, the purchasing power available to me changes. But because of the short horizon to maturity, the price will not change very much. (After all, the government will pay the bond's face value in a few weeks.) Such a security is thus a reasonably satisfactory short-run store of purchasing power. Indeed any readily saleable capital asset whose value does not fluctuate significantly with the rate of interest will satisfactorily fulfill this short-term, store-of-value function.

Money Substitutes

Things that serve as a temporary medium of exchange but are not a store of value are sometimes called **money substitutes.** Credit cards are a prime example. With a credit card, many transactions can be made without either cash or a cheque. The evidence of credit, the credit slip you sign and hand over to the store, is not money because it cannot be used to make further transactions. Furthermore, when your credit card company sends you a bill, you have to use money in (delayed) payment for the original transaction. The credit card serves the short-run function of a medium of exchange by allowing you to make purchases even though you have no cash or bank deposit currently in your possession. But this is only temporary; money remains the final medium of exchange for these transactions when the credit account is settled.

Definitions of the Money Supply

Since the eighteenth century, economists have known that the amount of money in circulation was an important economic variable. As theories became more carefully specified in the nineteenth and early twentieth centuries, they included a variable called "the money supply." But for theories to be useful, we must be able to identify real-world counterparts of these theoretical magnitudes.

What is an acceptable enough medium of exchange to count as money has changed and will continue to change over time. New monetary assets (such as certificates of deposit and chequable savings accounts) are continuously being developed to serve some, if not all, the functions of money, and they are more or less readily convertible into money. There is no single, timeless definition of what is money and what is only near money or a money substitute. Indeed, our monetary authorities use several different definitions of money, and these definitions change from year to year.

The measure of the money supply most commonly used in Canada is M1, which includes currency and demand deposits. M1 is a narrowly defined concept of money that concentrates on the medium-of-exchange function. Funds held in demand deposits can be transferred by cheque or withdrawn on demand (without prior notice being given). The two forms of demand deposits offered by the chartered banks are current accounts and personal chequing accounts.

Broader definitions of money add in savings accounts and term deposits that serve the temporary store of value function and are in practice quickly

TABLE 33–11 THE CANADIAN MONEY SUPPLY, JANUARY 1984 (Billions of Dollars)

Currency		$ 11.9
Plus:	Demand deposits	16.9
	Equals M1	28.8
Plus:	Daily interest chequable savings deposits and nonpersonal notice deposits	8.9
	Equals M1A	37.7
Plus:	Other personal savings deposits and personal fixed-term deposits at the chartered banks	98.0
	Equals M2	135.7
Plus:	Nonpersonal fixed-term deposits and foreign currency deposits	47.6
	Equals M3	183.3

Source: Bank of Canada Review.

The money supply can be defined in a variety of ways: M1, M1A, M2, and M3 figures are all published regularly by the Bank of Canada. M1 is the narrowly defined money supply that includes items that serve directly as a medium of exchange. M1A also includes nonpersonal notice and chequable savings deposits. M2 includes additional categories of bank deposits that serve the store-of-value function and can be readily converted into demand deposits or currency. M3 adds in bank term deposits that cannot be converted easily because the funds must remain on deposit for a fixed term, and foreign currency deposits whose value in terms of Canadian dollars is not fixed but varies with the exchange rate. (Series called M2+ and M3+ add to M2 and M3, respectively, related deposits with trust companies, credit unions, and *caisses populaires.*)

convertible into a medium of exchange at a known and secure price ($1 on deposit in a savings account is always convertible into a $1 demand deposit or $1 currency). Table 33-11 shows the various definitions of the money supply used in Canada.

SUMMARY

1. Early economic theory regarded the economy as being divided into a real part and a money part.

The real part was concerned with production, the allocation of resources, and the distribution of income—determined only by relative prices. The monetary part merely determined the level of prices at which real transactions took place. This was determined by the quantity of money. Double the quantity of money, and in the new equilibrium all money prices would double but relative prices and the real sector would be left unaffected. Modern economists recognize interconnections between the two parts, as will be discussed in Chapter 34.

2. Inflation has been a common but by no means constant state of affairs in world history. Although inflation is widespread in the world today, the rate of inflation varies greatly from country to country.

3. Traditionally in economics, money has referred to any generally accepted medium of exchange. A number of functions of money may, however, be distinguished—these include the medium of exchange, the store of value, and the unit of account.

4. Money arose because of the inconvenience of barter, and it developed in stages from precious metal to metal coinage, to paper money convertible to precious metal, to token coinage and paper money fractionally backed by precious metals, to fiat money, and to deposit money. Societies have shown great sophistication in developing monetary instruments to meet their needs.

5. The banking system in Canada consists of two main elements: chartered banks and the Bank of Canada, which is the central bank. Each has an important effect on the money supply.

6. Canadian chartered banks are profit-seeking institutions that allow their customers to transfer demand deposits from one bank to another by means of cheques. They create and destroy money as a by-product of their commercial operations—by making or liquidating loans and various other investments.

7. Because most customers are content to pay their accounts by cheque rather than by cash, banks need not keep anything like a 100 percent reserve against their deposit liabilities. Consequently banks are able to create deposit money. When the banking system receives a new cash deposit, it can create new deposits to some multiple of this amount. The amount of new deposits created depends on the legal minimum reserves the Bank of Canada enforces on the banks, the amount of cash drain to the public, and whether the banks choose to hold excess reserves.

8. There is nothing automatic about the expansion of the money supply when reserves of chartered banks increase. If bankers do not choose to use excess reserves to expand their investments, there will be no expansion. In normal times it is profitable for bankers to keep excess reserves small, but in times of depression they may not find the investment risks worth taking.

9. The money supply—the stock of money in the country at a specific moment—can be defined in various ways. M1 is currency plus demand deposits plus chequable substitutes, the narrowest definition now in use. (M1 was about $29 billion in 1984.) M3, the widest commonly used definition, adds in all time and savings deposits. (M3 was about $183 billion in 1984.)

TOPICS FOR REVIEW

Real and monetary parts of the economy
Functions of money
Gresham's law
Fully backed, fractionally backed, and fiat money
The creation and destruction of deposit money
Reserve ratio, required reserves, and excess reserves
Demand and savings deposits
The money supply
Near money and money substitutes

DISCUSSION QUESTIONS

1. "For the love of money is the root of all evil" (I Timothy 6:10). If a nation were to become a theocracy and money were made illegal, would you expect the level of national income to be affected? How about the productivity of labor? Might classical economists have answered this question differently than modern ones?

2. Consider each of the following with respect to its potential use as a medium of exchange, a store of value, and a unit of account. Which would you think might be regarded as money? (a) a $100 Bank of Canada note, (b) an American Express credit card, (c) a painting by Picasso, (d) a chequable saving account, (e) a Treasury certificate of indebtedness payable in three months, (f) a savings account at a savings and loan association in Las Vegas, Nevada, (g) one share of Bell Telephone Company stock, (h) a lifetime pass to Edmonton Oiler hockey games.

3. When in 1976 the Austrian government minted a new 1,000 shilling gold coin—worth $59 face value—the one-inch diameter coin came into great demand among jewelers and coin collectors. By law, the number of such coins to be minted each year is limited. Lines of people eager to get the coins formed outside the government mint and local banks. "There is exceptional interest in the new coin," said a Viennese banker. "It's a numismatic hit and a financial success." It has disappeared from circulation, however. Explain why.

4. In Canada, American and Canadian coins often circulate side by side, exchanging at their face values, even though notes often are of unequal value. Someone who receives a U.S. coin has the option of spending it at face value or converting it to Canadian money at the going rate of exchange. When the rate of exchange was near "par," so that $1 Canadian was within plus or minus $0.03 of $1 U.S., the two countries' coins circulated side by side. When the Canadian dollar fell to $0.80 U.S., predict which coins disappeared from circulation according to Gresham's law. Why did a $0.03 differential not produce this result?

5. Some years ago a strike closed all banks in Ireland for several months. What do you think happened to money, near money, and money substitutes during the period?

6. During hyperinflations in several foreign countries after World War II, American cigarettes were sometimes used in place of money. What made them suitable?

7. Take some five-year period during the last 10 years and (using library sources) calculate which of the following was the best store of value over that period: (a) the dollar, (b) the TSE industrial average, (c) a B.C. Hydro 11¾ percent bond, (d) gold, (e) silver. How confident are you that the one that was the best store of value over those five years will be the best over the *next* 18 months?

8. If all depositors tried to turn their deposits into cash at once, they would find that there are not sufficient reserves in the system to allow all of them to do this at the same time. Why then do we not still have panicky runs on the banks? Would a 100 percent reserve requirement be safer? What effect would such a reserve requirement have on the banking system's ability to create money? Would it preclude any possibility of a panic?

9. What would be the effect on the money supply of each of the following?
   a. A decline in the public's confidence in the banks
   b. A desire on the part of banks to increase their levels of excess reserves
   c. The monopolizing of the banking system into a single super bank
   d. The increased use of credit cards
   e. Allowing banks to pay any level of interest they wish on demand deposits.
10. Chartered banks in Canada are no longer allowed to issue their own bank notes. How do they now create money? (Explain the process carefully.) How do they make profits? Is it possible for them to create money without being aware of it?
11. During the Christmas and the summer holiday seasons, the level of household spending rises and so does the amount of currency held by the public. Does the rise in the amount of currency cause the rise in spending, or vice versa? Predict the effects of a law passed in October prohibiting the public from withdrawing extra currency from the banks until after the Christmas season.

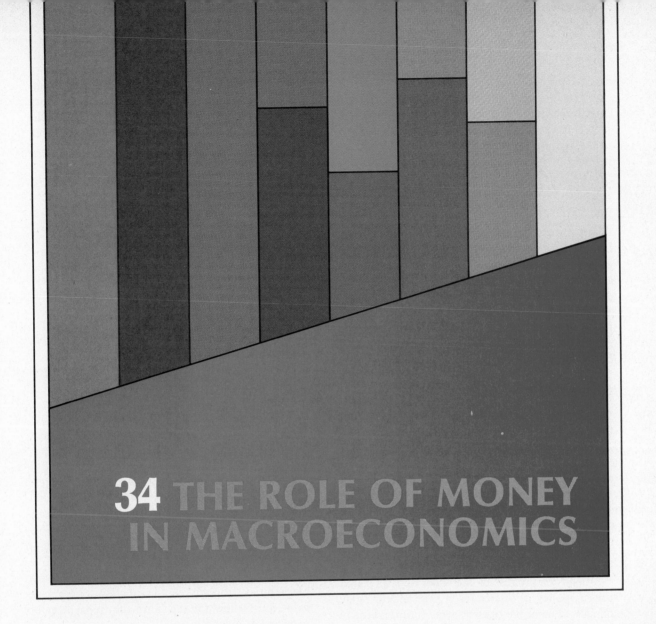

34 THE ROLE OF MONEY IN MACROECONOMICS

At one time or another most of us have known the surprise of opening our wallet or purse to discover that we had either more or less money than we thought. There can be as much pleasure in deciding how to spend an unexpected windfall in the first case as there can be pain in deciding what expenditure to eliminate in the second.

What determines how much money people hold in their purses and wallets and how much they keep in the bank? What happens when everyone discovers that they are holding more, or less, money than they believe they need to hold? These turn out to be key questions for our study of the influence of money on output and prices.

FINANCIAL ASSETS

At any moment in time households and firms have a given stock of wealth which can be held in many forms. Some of it is money in the bank or in the wallet; some is in short-term securities such as Treasury bills; some is in long-term bonds; and some is in real capital, which may be held directly (in the form of family businesses) or indirectly (in the form of shares that indicate ownership of a corporation's assets).

Kinds of Assets

These ways of holding wealth could be grouped into three categories: (1) assets that serve as a medium of exchange—that is, paper money, coins, and bank chequing deposits; (2) other financial assets, such as bonds earning a fixed rate of interest, that will yield a fixed money value at some future date (called the *maturity date*) and that can usually be sold before maturity for a price that fluctuates on the open market; and (3) equity claims on real capital (physical objects such as factories and machines).

Money and bonds. To simplify our discussion, it is helpful to regroup wealth into only two categories: money and bonds. By money we mean M1A as defined in Chapter 33; and by bonds we mean everything else. Money therefore includes currency, demand deposits, and chequable savings accounts. Bonds include all other interest-earning financial assets *plus* claims in real capital.[1]

The Rate of Interest and the Price of Bonds

A bond is a promise by the issuer to pay a stated sum of money as interest each year and to repay the face value of the bond at some future maturity date, often many years distant. The time until the date is called the **term to maturity** or often simply the **term** of the bond. Some bonds, called perpetuities, pay interest forever and never repay the principal.

The **present value (PV)** of a bond, or of any asset, refers to the value now of the future pay-

ment, or payments, to which the asset represents a claim. The present value is thus the amount someone would be willing to pay now to secure the right to the future stream of payments conferred by ownership of the asset.

In general, if the market price of any asset is greater than the present value of the income stream it produces, no one will want to buy it, while if the market value is below its present value, everyone will want to buy it. From this it follows that:

In a free market the equilibrium price of any asset will be the present value of the income stream it produces.

The present value of any asset turns out to depend critically on the rate of interest. This relationship is most easily seen in the case of a perpetuity. Assume that such a bond will pay $100 per year to the holder forever. The present value of this bond depends on how much $100 per year is worth, and this in turn depends on the rate of interest.

A bond that will produce a stream of income of $100 a year forever is worth $1,000 at 10 percent interest because $1,000 invested at 10 percent per year will yield $100 interest per year forever. But the same bond is worth $2,000 when the interest rate is 5 percent per year because it takes $2,000 invested at 5 percent per year to yield $100 interest per year. The lower the rate of interest obtainable on the market, the more valuable is a bond paying a fixed amount of interest.

Similar relations apply to bonds that are not perpetuities, though the calculation of present value must allow for the lump-sum repayment of principal at maturity.

The present value of an asset that yields a stream of money over time is negatively related to the interest rate.

This proposition has two important implications: (1) If the rate of interest falls, the value of an asset producing a given income stream will rise; and (2) when the market price of an asset producing a given income is forced up, this is equivalent to a decrease in the rate of interest earned by the asset. Thus a promise to pay $100 one year from

---

[1] This simplification can take us quite a long way. However, for some problems it is necessary to treat debt and equity as distinct assets so that three categories—money, debt (bonds), and equity stocks—are used.

now is worth $92.59 when the interest rate is 8 percent and only $89.29 when the interest rate is 12 percent: $92.59 at 8 percent interest ($92.59 × 1.08) and $89.29 at 12 percent interest ($89.29 × 1.12) are both worth $100 in one year's time.

The present value of bonds that are not perpetuities becomes increasingly dominated by the fixed redemption value as the maturity date approaches. Take an extreme case: The present value of a bond that is redeemable for $1,000 in a week's time will be very close to $1,000 no matter what the interest rate. Thus its value will not change much even if the rate of interest leaps from 5 percent to 10 percent during that week.

The sooner is the maturity date of a bond, the less the bond's value will change with a change in the rate of interest.

For example, a rise in the interest rate from 8 to 12 percent will lower the value of $100 payable in one year's time by 3.6 percent but will lower the value of $100 payable in ten years time by 37.9 percent.[2]

Box 34-1 provides further details on the calculation of present value.

THE SUPPLY OF AND THE DEMAND FOR MONEY

The Supply of Money

The supply of money is a stock: It is so many billions of dollars. (It is *not* a flow of so much per unit of time.) In January 1984 M1A was approximately $38 billion.

We saw in the previous chapter that deposit money is created by the banking system, but only within limits set by their reserves, which are under the control of the Bank of Canada. Thus the ulti-

mate control of the money supply is in the Bank of Canada's hands. In Chapter 35 we shall look at the degree to which the Bank of Canada can in fact control the money supply. In this chapter we shall simplify by assuming that the money supply can be precisely controlled by the Bank of Canada.

The Demand for Money

The amount of wealth everyone in the economy wishes to hold in the form of money balances is called the **demand for money.** Because households have only one decision to make on how to divide their given stock of wealth between money and bonds, it follows that if we know the demand for money, we also know the demand for bonds. If with a *given level of wealth* the demand for money rises, then the demand for bonds must fall: if people wish to hold $1 billion more money, they must wish to hold $1 billion less of bonds. It also follows that if households are in equilibrium with respect to their money holdings, they are in equilibrium with respect to their bond holdings.

What Determines the Demand for Money?

When we say that on January 2, 1984, the demand for money was $38 billion, we mean that on that date everyone wished to hold money balances that totaled $38 billion. But why do firms and households wish to hold money balances at all? There is a cost to holding any money balance. The money could instead be used to purchase bonds; it would then earn more interest.[3]

The opportunity cost of holding any money balance is the extra interest that could have been earned if the

---

[2] The example assumes annual compounding. The first case is calculated from the numbers of the previous example: (92.58 − 89.29)/92.58. The 10-year case uses the formula
$$\text{present value} = \text{principal}/(1 + r)^n$$
which gives $46.30 with 8 percent and $28.75 with 12 percent. The percentage fall in value is thus (46.30 − 28.75)/46.30 = 0.379.

[3] As we saw in Chapter 33 (see especially Table 33-11), some definitions of the money supply (even narrow definitions like M1A) include some interest-bearing chequable deposits. This complicates but does not fundamentally alter the analysis of the demand for money. In particular, it means that the opportunity cost of holding those interest-bearing components of M1A is not the *level* of interest rates paid on bonds but the *differential* between that rate and the rate paid on M1A assets. For simplicity, we treat the interest rate on all M1A assets as being zero so that we can identify the *level* of the interest rate on bonds as the opportunity cost of money.

BOX 34–1 MORE ON PRESENT VALUE

For purposes of illustration, assume that the rate of interest on a perfectly safe loan is 5 percent per year and then ask two separate questions.

(1) *How much money would you have to invest today if you wished to have $100 in one year's time?* Letting X stand for the answer, we have: $X(1.05) = \$100$. Or $X = \$100/1.05 = \$95.24$. What this tells us is that, if you lend out $95.24 today at 5 percent interest, you will receive $100 a year from now ($95.24 as repayment of the principal of the loan and $4.76 as interest).

(2) *What is the maximum amount you would be prepared to pay now to acquire the right to $100 in cash in one year's time?* Surely this is $95.24. If you paid more than $95.24 for the right you would be losing money, since you can loan out $95.24 at 5 percent and receive $100 in a year's time. If you could buy the right for anything less than $95.24 it would be profitable to do so, since you could borrow $95.24 now in return for your promise to repay $100 one year from now.

The present value of a single future payment. These two questions amount to asking: "How much money now is equivalent to $100 payable for certain a year from now when the interest rate on perfectly safe loans is 5 percent?" This is the present value of $100 a year from now calculated at a 5 percent interest rate. When a future sum is turned into its equivalent present value, we say that sum is *discounted*.

Because discounting takes place at some par-

ticular rate of interest, present value depends on the rate of interest used in the calculation. Thus the numerical example given above depended on the 5 percent interest rate that was chosen to illustrate the calculations. If the interest rate is 7 percent, the present value of the $100 receivable next year is $100/1.07 = \$93.45$. In general, the present value of X one year hence, at an interest rate of i percent per year, * is

$$PV = X/(1 + i)$$

Now consider what would happen if the payment date is further away than one year. If we lend X at 5 percent for one year we will be paid $(1.05)X$. But if we immediately relend that whole amount, we would get back at the end of the second year an amount equal to 1.05 *times* the amount lent out: $(1.05)(1.05)X$. Thus $100 payable two years hence has a present value (at 5 percent) of

$$\frac{\$100.00}{(1.05)(1.05)} = \$90.70$$

The amount of $90.70 lent out now, with the interest that is paid at the end of the first year lent out for the second year, would yield $100 in two years.† In general, the present value of

---

* In all these calculations the interest rate is expressed as a ratio of interest divided by principal, so that a rate of 100 percent is written 1, while 10 percent is written as 0.1, and so on.

† Readers familiar with this type of calculation will realize that the argument in the text is based on an annual compounding of interest.

---

money had instead been used to purchase interest earning assets.

Clearly money will be held only when it provides services that are valued at least as highly as the opportunity cost of holding it. The services provided by money balances are, first, to finance purchases and sales; second, to provide a cushion

against uncertainty about the timing of cash flows; and third, to provide a hedge against uncertainty over the prices of other financial assets.

The desire to hold money to obtain each of these services is summarized by the so-called transactions, precautionary, and speculative motives for holding money. We now examine each of these motives in detail.

$X after t years at i percent is

$$PV = X/(1 + i)^t.$$

Inspection of the above expression shows that as either i or t is increased, the denominator increases and hence PV decreases. This leads to the following conclusion: *The farther away the payment date and the higher the rate of interest, the smaller the present value of a given sum payable in the future.*

The present value of an infinite stream of payments. Now consider the present value of a stream of income that continues indefinitely. While at first glance that might seem very high, since as time passes the total received grows without reaching any limit, the far distant payments will not in fact be highly valued. To find the present value of $100 a year, payable forever, we need only ask how much money would have to be invested now at an interest rate of i percent per year to obtain $100 each year. This is simply $i \times X = \$100$, where i is the interest rate and X the sum required. This tells us that the present value of the stream of $100 a year forever is

$$PV = \$100/i$$

If the interest rate were 10 percent, the present value would be $1,000. Notice that here, as above, PV is *inversely* related to the rate of interest: The higher the interest rate, the less the (present) value of distant payments.

The present value of a finite stream of income. It is also possible to obtain the present value of some finite stream of income and then convert it into an equivalent infinite stream. This is of considerable theoretical value, since it allows us always to deal with the equivalent infinite stream, even if the problem we are considering concerns a finite and irregular stream. Consider, for example, a machine that yields the following stream of gross returns: $100 now, $275 in one year, $242 in two years, $133.10 in three years, and nothing thereafter. The present value of this flow of income, when the market rate of interest is 10 percent (and hence $1 + i = 1.1$), is

$$PV = \$100 + \frac{\$275}{1.1} + \frac{\$242}{(1.1)^2} + \frac{\$133.10}{(1.1)^3}$$

$$= \$100 + \$250 + \$200 + \$100$$

$$= \$650$$

But $650 invested at 10 percent interest will yield a flow of $65 per annum in perpetuity. Thus the irregular finite flow listed above is equivalent to (has the same present value as) the smooth flow of $65 forever. So in any practical problems concerning an irregular flow, we can substitute the equivalent regular flow, which can be handled with much greater ease.

National Income and the Demand for Money: The Transactions Motive

The majority of transactions require money. Money passes from households to firms to pay for the goods and services produced by firms; money passes from firms to households to pay for the factor services supplied by households to firms.

Money balances that are held to finance such flows are called **transactions balances**.

In an imaginary world, where the receipts and disbursements of households and firms were perfectly synchronized, it would be unnecessary to hold transactions balances. If every time a household spent $10 it received $10 as part payment of its income, no transactions balances would be needed. In the real world, however, receipts and disbursements are not perfectly synchronized.

Consider, for example, the balances held because of wage payments. Assume, for purposes of illustration, that firms pay wages every Friday and that households spend all their wages on the purchase of goods and services, with the expenditure being spread out evenly over the week. Thus on Friday morning firms must hold balances equal to the weekly wage bill; on Friday afternoon households will hold these balances. Over the week, households' balances will be drawn down as a result of purchasing goods and services. Over the same period, the balances held by firms will build up as a result of selling goods and services until, on the following Friday morning, firms will again have amassed balances equal to the wage bill that must be met on that day.

On the average over the week, firms will hold balances equal to half the wage bill, and so will households; thus, in this example, total money balances held will be equal to the total weekly wage bill. Notice that while the money circulates so that each group holds a varying balance over the week, the combined demand for balances summed over the two groups remains constant.

Our argument has been conducted in terms of the wage bill, but a similar analysis holds for all receipts and payments of households and firms. Because their receipts and payments are not perfectly synchronized, they must hold money balances to bridge the gap.

The transactions demand for money arises because of the nonsynchronization of payments and receipts.

What determines the size of the transactions balances to be held? It is clear that in the above example total transactions balances vary with the value of the wage bill. If the wage bill doubles for any reason (e.g., because twice as much labor is hired at the same wage rate or because the same amount of labor is hired at twice the wage rate), the transactions balances held by firms and households on this account will also double. As it is with wages so it is with all other transactions: The size

of the balances held is positively related to the value of the transactions.

Next we ask how the total value of transactions is related to national income. Because of the "double counting" problem first discussed on page 492, the value of all transactions exceeds the value of the economy's final output. When the flour mill buys wheat from the farmer and when the baker buys flour from the mill, both are transactions against which money balances must be held, although only the value added at each stage is part of national income. Typically the total value of transactions is many times as large as the total value of final output, which is national income.

We now make an added assumption that there is a stable, positive relation between transactions and national income: If a rise in aggregate expenditure leads to a rise in national income, it also leads to a rise in the total value of all transactions and hence to an associated rise in the demand for transactions balances. This allows us to relate transactions balances to national income. [45]

The larger the value of national income measured in current prices, the larger the value of transactions balances that will be held.

National Income and the Demand for Money: The Precautionary Motive

Many goods and services are sold on credit. The seller can never be certain when payment will be made, and the buyer can never be certain of the day of delivery and thus when payment will fall due. In order to avoid cash crises when receipts are abnormally low and/or disbursements are abnormally high, firms and households carry money balances as a precaution. These are called **precautionary balances.** The larger are such balances, the greater is the protection against running out of money because of temporary fluctuations in cash flows.

How serious this risk is depends on the penalties for being caught without sufficient money balances. A firm is unlikely to be pushed into insolvency, but it may have to incur considerable costs if it is forced to borrow money at high interest rates in order to meet a temporary cash crisis.

The precautionary motive arises because the firm is uncertain about the *degree* to which payments and receipts will be synchronized.

The protection provided by a given quantity of precautionary balances depends on the volume of payments and receipts. A $100 precautionary balance provides a large cushion for a person whose volume of payments per month is $200, and a very small cushion for a firm whose monthly volume is $10,000. Fluctuations of the sort that create the need for precautionary balances tend to vary directly with the size of the firm's cash flow. To provide the same degree of protection as the value of transactions rises, more money is necessary.[4]

The precautionary motive also causes the demand for money to vary positively with the value of national income measured at current prices.

Wealth and the Demand for Money: The Speculative Motive

Households will have to sell some of their bonds if a temporary excess of payments over receipts exceeds their money holdings. At one extreme, if a household or firm held all its wealth in bonds, it would earn interest on all that wealth, but it would have to sell some bonds the first time its payments exceeded its receipts. At the other extreme, if a household or firm held all its wealth in money, the money would earn no interest, but the household or firm would never have to sell bonds to meet excesses of payments over current receipts. Wealth holders usually do not adopt either extreme position; instead, they hold part of their wealth as money and part as bonds. (Don't forget that "bonds" are here defined to include such interest-earning assets as deposits in savings accounts and Treasury bills.)

A household that holds bonds and money runs the risk that an unexpected gap between its receipts and its payments will force it to sell some bonds. But the price of bonds fluctuates from day to day on the open market. A household that may have to sell bonds to meet a need for money faces the risk that the price of bonds may be unexpectedly low at the time it sells them. Of course, if the household is lucky, the price may be unexpectedly high. But because no one knows in advance which way the price will go, firms and households must accept a risk whenever they hold bonds. Many firms and households do not like risk—they are *risk averse.* Hence they hold less bonds and more money than they otherwise would.

The motive that leads firms and households to hold more money in order to avoid the risks inherent in a fluctuating price of bonds was analyzed first by Keynes. Money balances held for this purpose are called **speculative balances.** The modern analysis of this motive, sketched in the preceding paragraph, is the work of Professor James Tobin of Yale University.[5]

Firms and households tend to insure against this risk by holding some fraction of their wealth in money and the rest in earning assets. Thus the demand for money varies positively with wealth. For example, Ms. B. O'Reiley might elect to hold 5 percent of her wealth in money and the other 95 percent in bonds. If Ms. O'Reiley's wealth is $50,000, her demand for money will be $2,500. If her wealth increases to $60,000, her demand for money will rise to $3,000.

Although an individual's wealth may rise or fall rapidly, the total wealth of a society changes only slowly. For the analysis of short-term fluctuations in national income, the effects of changes in wealth are fairly small, and we shall ignore them for the present. (Over the long term, however, variations in wealth can have a major effect on the demand for money.)

There is a second important aspect of the speculative demand for money. This leads to the ex-

---

[4] Institutional arrangements affect precautionary demands. In the past, for example, a traveler would have carried a substantial precautionary balance in cash, but today a credit card covers most unforeseen expenses that may arise while traveling.

[5] Professor Tobin was awarded the Nobel Prize in Economics in 1981 for his research in monetary economics and the analysis of financial markets.

tremely important relation discussed in the next section.

The Rate of Interest and the Demand for Money: Speculative and Precautionary Balances

Wealth held in cash earns no interest; hence the reduction in risk involved in holding more money also carries a cost in terms of interest earnings foregone.

The speculative motive leads a household or firm to add to its money holdings until the reduction in risk obtained by the last dollar added is just balanced (in the wealth holder's view) by the cost in terms of the interest foregone on that dollar.

Because the cost of holding money balances is the interest that could have been earned if wealth had been held in bonds instead, the demand to hold money will be negatively related to the interest rate. When the rate of interest falls, the cost of holding money falls. This leads to more money being held both for precautionary motives (to reduce risks caused by uncertainty about the flows of payments and receipts) and for speculative motives (to reduce risks associated with fluctuations in the market price of bonds). When the rate of interest rises, the cost of holding money rises. This leads to less money being held for speculative and precautionary motives.

The demand for money is negatively related to the rate of interest.[6]

Real and Nominal Money Balances: An Important Distinction

In referring to the demand for money, it is important to distinguish real from nominal values. Real values are measured in purchasing power units, nominal values in money units.

First, consider the demand for money in real

---

[6] When the price level is changing continuously, it is necessary to distinguish the real from the nominal rate of interest. This was discussed in Box 31-1 on page 559. For now, there is no need to distinguish these two concepts of the interest rate since they are the same when the price level is constant, and they are measured by the market rate of interest.

terms. This means the number of units of purchasing power the public wishes to hold in the form of money balances. In an imaginary one-product wheat economy, this would be measured by the number of bushels of wheat that could be purchased with the money balances held. In any more complex economy, it could be measured in terms of the number of weeks of national income; for example, the demand for money might be equal to one month's national income. Our previous discussion suggests that the demand for money measured in purchasing-power units will be related to the real value of national income, the real value of wealth, and the rate of interest.

Now we may determine the nominal demand for money merely by multiplying real demand by the price level, P.

Thus the nominal demand for money varies in proportion to the price level; for example, doubling the price level doubles nominal demand.

This is a central tenet of the quantity theory of money, discussed further in Box 34-2.

The Total Demand for Money: Recapitulation

Figure 34-1 summarizes the influences of national income, the rate of interest, and the price level, the three variables that account for most of the short-term variations in the nominal quantity of money demanded. The function relating money demand to the rate of interest is called either the demand for money function or the **liquidity preference (LP) function.** Whichever name is used, the relation describes how the quantity of money people wish to hold varies as the rate of interest varies.

MONETARY FORCES AND NATIONAL INCOME

We are now in a position to examine the relationship between monetary forces, on the one hand, and the equilibrium values of national income and the price level, on the other hand. There are two

BOX 34–2 THE QUANTITY THEORY OF MONEY AND THE VELOCITY OF CIRCULATION

The basic quantity theory of money can be set out formally in terms of the following four equations. Equation [1] states that the demand for money balances depends upon the value of transactions as measured by nominal income, given by the product PY.

$$M_d = kPY \qquad [1]$$

Equation [2] states that the supply of money, M, is set by the central bank.

$$M_s = M \qquad [2]$$

Equation [3] states the equilibrium condition at the demand for money must equal its supply

$$M_d = M_s \qquad [3]$$

Substitution produces the basic relation among P, M, and Y, as shown in Equation [4]

$$M = kPY \qquad [4]$$

The original form of the classical quantity theory assumes that k is a constant given by the transactions demand for money and that Y is constant (because full employment is always equal to Y^*). Thus M and P move proportionally. Increases or decreases in the money supply lead to proportional increases or decreases in prices.

Often the quantity theory is presented using the concept of the velocity of circulation, V, instead of the proportion of the money income that people wish to hold in cash, k. The **velocity of circulation** is defined as nominal national income divided by the quantity of money.

$$V = PY/M \qquad [5]$$

Rearranging gives the equation of exchange.

$$MV = PY \qquad [6]$$

Velocity may be interpreted as showing the average amount of "work" done by a unit of money. Thus, if the annual national income is $1,200 billion and the stock of money is $300 billion, then on average each dollar's worth of money is used four times to effect the exchanges required in producing national income.

There is a simple relation between k and V. One is the reciprocal of the other, as may be seen by comparing Equations [4] and [6]. Thus it makes no difference whether we choose to work with k or V. Further, if k is assumed to be constant, this implies that V must also be treated as being constant. An example may help to illustrate the interpretation of each.

Assume that the stock of money people wish to hold is equal to one-fifth of the value of total income. Thus k is 0.2 and V, the reciprocal of k, is 5. This indicates that if the money supply is to be one-fifth of the value of annual income, the average unit of money must account for $5 worth of income.

Modern versions of the quantity theory do not assume that k is exogenously fixed, but nevertheless argue that it will not change in response to a change in the quantity of money.

---

steps in explaining this relationship. The first is a new one: the link between changes in monetary equilibrium and shifts in aggregate demand. The second is familiar from earlier chapters: the effects of shifts in aggregate demand on equilibrium values of national income and the price level.

Monetary Equilibrium and Aggregate Demand: The Transmission Mechanism

Monetary equilibrium occurs when the demand for money equals the supply of money. In Chapter 4 we saw that in a competitive market for some

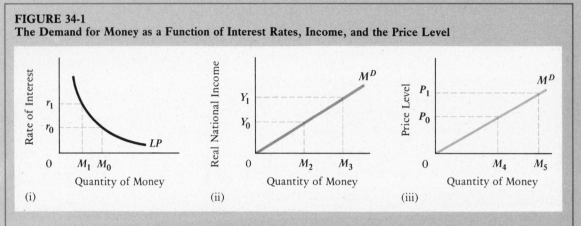

FIGURE 34-1
The Demand for Money as a Function of Interest Rates, Income, and the Price Level

The quantity of money demanded varies negatively with the rate of interest and positively with both national income and the price level. In (i), the demand for money is shown varying negatively with the interest rate along the liquidity preference function. When the interest rate rises from r_0 to r_1, households and firms reduce the quantity of money demanded from M_0 to M_1.

In (ii), the demand for money is shown varying posi-tively with national income. When national income rises from Y_0 to Y_1, households and firms increase the quantity of money demanded from M_2 to M_3.

In (iii), the demand for money is shown varying pos-itively with the price level. When the price level rises from P_0 to P_1, households and firms increase the quantity of money demanded from M_4 to M_5.

commodity such as carrots, the price will adjust to ensure equilibrium. What does the same job with respect to money demand and money supply?

The answer is that the *rate of interest* will change so as to equate the demand for money to its supply. This is shown in Figure 34-2.

The condition for monetary equilibrium is that the rate of interest will be such that everyone is willing to hold the existing supply of money.

But as we saw in Chapter 31, desired investment expenditure is sensitive to changes in the interest rate. Here, then, is a link between monetary factors and real expenditure flows.

The mechanism by which changes in the de-mand for and the supply of money affects aggregate demand is called the **transmission mechanism.** In the next three sections we study the three stages of the transmission mechanism: first, the link be-tween monetary equilibrium and the interest rate; second, the link between the interest rate and in-vestment expenditure; and third, the link between investment expenditure and aggregate demand.

From Monetary Disturbances to Changes in the Rate of Interest

We saw that firms and households decide how much of their wealth to hold as money and how much to hold as bonds. When a single household or firm finds that it has less money than it wishes to hold, it can sell some bonds and add the pro-ceeds to its money holdings. This transaction sim-ply redistributes given supplies of bonds and money among individuals; it does not change the total supply of either money or bonds.

Now assume that everyone in the economy has an excess demand for money balances. They all try to sell bonds to add to their money balances. But what one person can do, everyone cannot do. At any moment in time, the society's total supplies of money and bonds are fixed; there is just so much

FIGURE 34-2
Monetary Equilibrium and the Rate of Interest

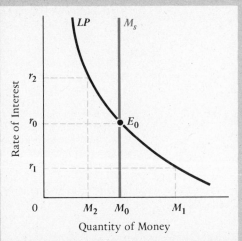

The interest rate rises when there is an excess demand for money and falls when there is an excess supply of money. The fixed quantity of money, M_0, is shown by the completely inelastic supply curve M_s. The demand for money is LP. Equilibrium is at E_0, with a rate of interest of r_0.

If the interest rate is r_1, there will be an excess demand for money of M_0M_1. Bonds will be offered for sale in an attempt to increase money holdings. This will force the rate of interest up to r_0 (the price of bonds falls), at which point the quantity of money demanded is equal to the fixed available quantity of M_0. If the interest rate is r_2, there will be an excess supply of money M_2M_0. Bonds will be demanded in return for excess money balances. This will force the rate of interest down to r_0 (the price of bonds rises), at which point the quantity of money demanded has risen to equal the fixed supply of M_0.

demanded falls along the liquidity preference curve in response to a rise in the rate of interest. Eventually the interest rate will rise enough that people will no longer be trying to add to their money balances by selling bonds. At that point there is no longer an excess supply of bonds, and the interest rate will stop rising. The demand for money again equals the supply.

Assume next that firms and households hold larger money balances than they would like. A single household or firm would purchase bonds with its excess balances, achieving monetary equilibrium by reducing its money holdings and increasing its bond holdings. But just as in the above example, what one household or firm can do, all cannot do. At any moment in time, the total quantity of bonds is fixed so that everyone cannot simultaneously add to their holdings of bonds. When all households enter the bond market and try to purchase bonds with unwanted money balances, they bid up the price of existing bonds—the interest rate falls. Hence households and firms become willing to hold larger quantities of money; that is, the quantity of money demanded increases along the liquidity preference curve in response to a fall in the rate of interest. The rise in the price of bonds continues until firms and households stop trying to convert bonds into money. In other words, it continues until everyone is content to hold the existing supply of money and bonds.

Now look at this result in terms of the condition for monetary equilibrium. The rate of interest must adjust until people are willing to hold the fixed supply of money. If they want to hold more, their attempts to get it by selling bonds will drive up the interest rate. If they want to hold less, their attempts to buy bonds with their unwanted holdings will drive down the interest rate.

Monetary disturbances, which can arise due to either changes in the demand for or supply of money, cause changes in the interest rate.

From Changes in the Rate of Interest to Shifts in Aggregate Expenditure

The second link in the transmission mechanism is one that relates interest rates to expenditure. We

money and so many bonds in existence. If everyone tries to sell bonds, there will be no one to buy them. Instead the price of bonds will fall.

We saw earlier that a fall in the price of bonds is the same thing as a rise in the rate of interest. As the interest rate rises, people economize on money balances because the opportunity cost of holding such balances is rising. This is what we saw in Figure 34-1(i), where the quantity of money

FIGURE 34-3
The Effects of Changes in the Money Supply on Investment Expenditure

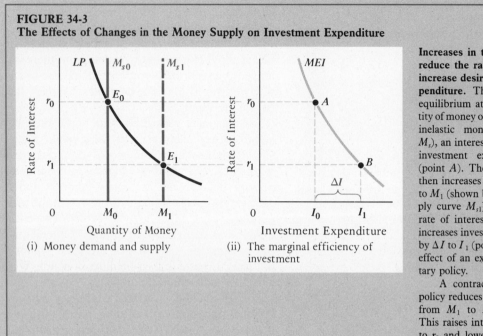

(i) Money demand and supply

(ii) The marginal efficiency of investment

Increases in the money supply reduce the rate of interest and increase desired investment expenditure. The economy is in equilibrium at E_0, with a quantity of money of M_0 (shown by the inelastic money supply curve M_s), an interest rate of r_0, and an investment expenditure of I_0 (point A). The Bank of Canada then increases the money supply to M_1 (shown by the money supply curve M_{s1}). This forces the rate of interest down to r_1 and increases investment expenditure by ΔI to I_1 (point B). This is the effect of an expansionary monetary policy.

A contractionary monetary policy reduces the money supply from M_1 to M_0, for instance. This raises interest rates from r_1 to r_0 and lowers investment expenditure by ΔI, from I_1 to I_0.

---

saw in Chapter 31 that investment, which includes expenditure on inventory accumulation, residential construction, and plant and equipment, responds to changes in the rate of interest. Other things being equal, a decrease in the rate of interest makes borrowing cheaper and will generate new investment expenditure.[7] This negative relation between investment and the rate of interest is called the **marginal efficiency of investment (MEI)** function.

The first two links in the transmission mechanism are shown in Figure 34-3. We concentrate for the moment on changes in the money supply, although the process can also be set in motion by changes in the demand for money. In Figure 34-3(i), we see that a change in the money supply causes the rate of interest to change in the opposite

direction. In (ii), we see that a change in the interest rate causes the level of investment expenditure to change in the opposite direction. Therefore changes in the money supply cause investment expenditure to change in the same direction.

An increase in the money supply leads to a fall in the interest rate and an increase in investment expenditure. A decrease in the money supply leads to a rise in the interest rate and a decrease in investment expenditure.

From Shifts in Aggregate Expenditure to Shifts in Aggregate Demand

Now we are back on familiar ground. In Chapter 29 we saw that a shift in the aggregate expenditure curve can lead to a shift in the AD curve. This is shown again in Figure 34-4.

Changes in the money supply, by causing changes in investment expenditure and hence shifts in the AE curve, cause the AD curve to shift.

[7] In Chapter 31 we saw that purchases of durable consumer goods also respond to changes in interest rates. In this chapter we concentrate on investment expenditure, which may be taken to stand for *all interest-sensitive expenditure*.

FIGURE 34-4
The Effects of Changes in the Money Supply
on Aggregate Demand

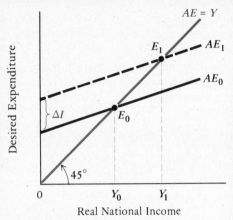

(i) Shift in aggregate expenditure

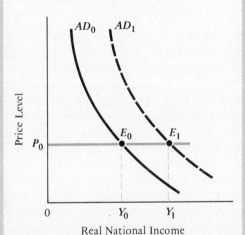

(ii) Shift in aggregate demand

**Changes in the money supply cause shifts in the
aggregate expenditure and aggregate demand functions.** In Figure 34-3 an increase in the money supply
increased desired investment expenditure by ΔI. In
(i), the aggregate expenditure function shifts up by ΔI
(which is the same as ΔI in Figure 34-3), from AE_0
to AE_1. At the fixed price level P_0, equilibrium income
rises from Y_0 to Y_1, as shown by the horizontal
shift in the aggregate demand curve from AD_0 to AD_1
in (ii).

When the supply of money falls (from M_{s1} to M_{s0}
in Figure 34-3), investment falls by ΔI, thereby shifting aggregate expenditure from AE_1 to AE_0. At the
fixed price level P_0, this reduces equilibrium income
from Y_1 to Y_0.

An increase in the money supply causes an increase
in investment expenditure and therefore an increase in aggregate demand. A decrease in the
money supply causes a decrease in investment expenditure and therefore a decrease in aggregate
demand.

In summary:

**The transmission mechanism provides a connection between monetary forces and real expenditure flows. It
works from a change in the demand for, or the supply
of, money to a change in bond prices and interest rates,
to a change in investment expenditure, to a *shift* in the
aggregate demand curve.**

Aggregate Demand,
the Price Level, and National Income

A change in the money supply shifts the aggregate
demand curve. If we want to know what it does to
real national income and to the price level, we need
to know the slope of the aggregate supply curve.
This step, which is familiar from earlier chapters,
is recalled in Figure 34-5.[8]

The key result is that the increase in equilibrium
real income is less than the horizontal shift in the
AD curve. This is because part of this shift is
dissipated by a rise in the price level. If the aggregate demand curve were vertical, the rise in the
price level would not diminish the effect on real
output; real output would rise by an amount equal
to the horizontal shift of the AD curve. But because
the AD curve is negatively sloped, the rise in real
output is smaller.

We have seen that the transmission mechanism
explains the shift in the AD curve caused by a
change in the money supply. It also explains the
negative slope of the AD curve—that is, it explains
why equilibrium national income is negatively related to the price level when the money supply is

[8] Since the demand for money in general will depend on the
level of national income, as shown in Figure 34-1(ii), our analysis at this stage is incomplete. The induced change in equilibrium national income will lead to a shift in the liquidity preference function in Figure 34-2. For simplicity we have assumed
in the text that the liquidity preference function does not shift
in response to a change in national income. The appendix to
this chapter presents a formal analysis in which this effect is
allowed for and in which equilibrium levels of the interest rate
and national income are determined simultaneously.

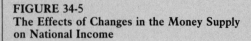

FIGURE 34-5
The Effects of Changes in the Money Supply on National Income

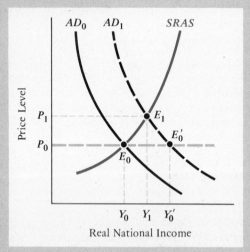

A change in the money supply leads to a change in national income that is smaller than the shift in the AD curve. An increase in the money supply causes the *AD* curve to shift to the right, from AD_0 to AD_1. With the price level constant, national income would rise from Y_0 to Y_0'. With the upward-sloping short-run aggregate supply curve, income only rises to Y_1 while the price level rises as well—to P_1.

held constant. This is because a rise in the price level raises the money value of transactions and thus leads to an increased demand for money. Provided the Bank of Canada holds the nominal money supply constant, there will be an excess demand for money, which brings the transmission mechanism into play. People try to sell bonds to add to their money balances, but collectively all they succeed in doing is forcing up the interest rate. The rise in the interest rate reduces investment expenditure and so reduces equilibrium national income.

In Chapter 26 we gave three reasons why the *AD* curve was negatively sloped. In Chapter 29 we relied on the wealth effect (real balance effect) to explain this negative slope because it was simple and direct. Now that we have developed a theory of money and interest rates, we are able to under-

stand the indirect effect that works through the transmission mechanism. This effect, which could only be alluded to in Chapter 26, is more complicated than the direct wealth effect. But it is also much more important because, empirically, the interest rate is the most important link between monetary factors and real expenditure flows. Box 34-3 is for those who wish to study the reasons for the slope in more detail.

The Monetary Adjustment Mechanism

Let us now examine the mechanism by which an inflationary gap is eliminated. This involves a very important but subtle point:

A sufficiently large rise in the price level will eliminate any inflationary gap, provided the nominal money supply remains constant.

Assume that an increase in expenditure has created an inflationary gap so that equilibrium national income exceeds potential income, as shown in Figure 34-6. This will cause factor prices to rise, shifting the *SRAS* curve up and taking the price level with it. This raises the money value of transactions, and the resulting increase in the demand for money raises interest rates. Hence at any level of real income, desired real expenditure falls. The fall in real expenditure as the price level rises is shown by a movement upward to the left *along* the *AD* curve. This reduces the inflationary gap. When the price level has risen enough, the inflationary gap disappears and the price level stops rising.

This mechanism, described further in Figure 34-6, may be called the *monetary adjustment mechanism.* It works through the transmission mechanism described above.

The monetary adjustment mechanism will eliminate any inflationary gap, provided that the nominal money supply is held constant.

Thus inflationary gaps tend to be self-correcting as long as the money supply does not increase. They will cause the price level to increase, but those increases set in motion a chain of events in the markets for financial assets that will eventually remove the inflationary gap.

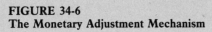

FIGURE 34-6
The Monetary Adjustment Mechanism

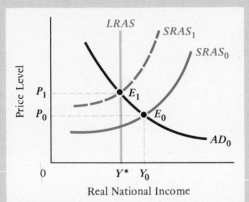

A rise in the price level will eliminate an inflationary gap. Equilibrium is at E_0, with income Y_0 and price level P_0. There is an inflationary gap of Y^*Y_0, where Y^* is potential income and hence the national income corresponding to long-run aggregate supply.

The inflationary gap causes wages to rise, shifting the $SRAS$ curve up to $SRAS_1$, and the price level to rise to P_1. The monetary adjustment mechanism (working through a rising demand for money, a falling price of bonds, a rising interest rate, and falling investment) lowers aggregate expenditure, eliminating the inflationary gap and producing equilibrium at E_1 with income at Y^*. The economy moves upward along its AD curve until at price level P_1 aggregate demand equals aggregate supply at full-employment income. The excess aggregate demand has been eliminated.

This self-correcting mechanism is the reason why price levels and the money supply have been linked for so long in economics. Many things can cause the price level to rise for some time. Yet whatever the reason, unless the money supply is expanded, the price level increase itself sets up forces that will remove any initial inflationary gap and so bring any demand inflation to a halt.

Frustration of the Monetary Adjustment Mechanism

The self-correcting mechanism for removing an inflationary gap can be frustrated indefinitely if the money supply is increased at the same rate that prices are rising. Say that the price level is rising 10 percent a year under the pressure of a large inflationary gap. Demand for nominal money balances will also be rising at about 10 percent per year. Now suppose the Bank of Canada increases the money supply at 10 percent per year. No excess demand for money will develop, since the extra money needed to meet the rising demand will be forthcoming. The real interest rate will not rise, and the inflationary gap will not be reduced. This process is analyzed in Figure 34-7.

If the money supply increases at the same rate as the price level rises, the real money supply and hence the real interest rate will remain constant, and the monetary adjustment mechanism will be frustrated.

An inflation is said to be *validated* when the money supply is increased as fast as the price level so that the monetary adjustment mechanism is frustrated. A validated inflation can go on indefinitely, although as we shall see, possibly not at a constant rate.

CONTROVERSIES OVER STABILIZATION POLICY

Stabilization policy aims to avoid the extremes of large GNP gaps by using monetary and fiscal policy to shift the aggregate demand curve. Many controversies surround the use of stabilization policy, and we are now in a position to take a preliminary look at one of them.

Two Sources of Controversy

It is helpful to distinguish between two important controversies that have occupied a central place in policy debates. The first concerns the relative strengths of monetary and fiscal policy. The second concerns the degree of built-in stability in the economy and hence the need to use either policy. The latter is often referred to as the debate about *policy activism.*

In both cases the profession has split into two camps. While it is true that economists who agree on one issue tend to also agree on the other issue,

BOX 34–3 THE SLOPE OF THE AGGREGATE DEMAND CURVE

Let us recall what we know about the aggregate demand curve. First, the curve relates the price level to the equilibrium level of real national income. Second, the curve is negatively sloped because the higher the price level, the lower is equilibrium national income. The main reason for this negative slope is found in the transmission mechanism.

We start with an initial position depicted in part (i) of the figure. The liquidity preference schedule is LP_0, and the money supply is given by M_s. Equilibrium is at E_0 with the interest rate at r_0. The MEI schedule given in part (ii) shows that, at the rate of interest r_0, desired investment expenditure is I_0. In part (iii) the aggregate expenditure curve AE_0 is drawn for

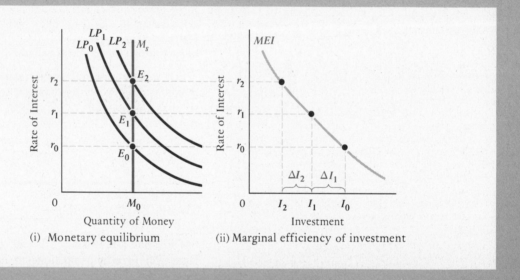

(i) Monetary equilibrium

(ii) Marginal efficiency of investment

Let us now follow this process in detail. Although the argument contains nothing new, it does require that you follow carefully through several steps. When you have done this you will have understood the critical link between money and the price level. This is no small accomplishment, for you will then understand matters that have confused many policymakers and not a few economists for generations.

that level of investment (I_0). Equilibrium is at E_0 with a real national income of Y_0. Plotting Y_0 against the initial price level (P_0) yields point A on the aggregate demand curve in part (iv).

An increase in the price level to P_1 raises the money value of transactions and increases the quantity of money demanded at each possible value of the interest rate. As a result the liquidity preference function shifts from LP_0 to LP_1.

there is no necessary reason why this should be so. *Monetarists* argue that the economy has strong built-in stability and look to erratic monetary policy as the single most important source of economic

fluctuations. They tend to believe that while monetary policy exerts a strong influence on the economy, its potential for doing harm means that it should not be actively used to stabilize the econ-

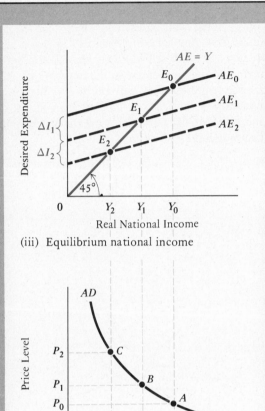

(iii) Equilibrium national income

(iv) The aggregate demand curve

This raises interest rates to r_1 and lowers investment expenditure by ΔI_1 to I_1. The fall in investment causes the AE curve in (iii) to shift down by an equal amount to AE_1. Equilibrium income falls to Y_1. Plotting Y_1 against P_1 produces point B on the AD curve in (iv).

A further increase in the price level to P_2 shifts the liquidity preference function to LP_2, raises the interest rate to r_2, and lowers investment expenditure to I_2. The fall in investment shifts the AE curve in (iii) to AE_2, and equilibrium income falls to Y_2. Plotting Y_2 against P_2 produces point C on the AD curve in (iv).

The negative relation between the price level and equilibrium real income shown by the AD curve occurs because, other things being equal, a rise in the price level raises the *demand* for money. Notice the qualification, "other things being equal." It is important for this process that the nominal money *supply* remain constant. The monetary adjustment mechanism operates because the demand for money increases when the price level rises, while the money supply remains constant. The attempt to add to money balances by selling bonds is what drives the interest rate up and reduces desired expenditure, thereby reducing equilibrium national income. (This argument is conducted in terms of the nominal supply and demand for money. Arguing in terms of the real demand and supply of money leads to identical results.) [46]

omy. *Neo-Keynesians* argue that the economy exhibits very weak built-in stability and look to unstable real expenditures as the most important source of economic fluctuations. They tend to believe that fiscal policy exerts a strong influence on the economy and should be actively used to offset other expenditure changes.

Here we focus on the debate about the relative

strengths of monetary and fiscal policy. The debate on policy activism is taken up in Chapter 42.

The Relative Effectiveness of Monetary and Fiscal Policy

We saw in Chapter 32 that fiscal policy operates *directly* on aggregate expenditure. Monetary policy influences aggregate expenditure only *indirectly* by altering the money supply and interest rates. When the Bank of Canada changes the money supply, it shifts the aggregate demand curve via the transmission mechanism, whose effects we have just studied.

We will now see how views about the key behavioral relations translate into views about the relative strengths of monetary and fiscal policies. The effects of either policy depend on the slope of the *SRAS* curve and on how the policy affects the *AD* curve. Whatever the slope of the *SRAS* curve, it is common to both policies. Hence we focus on what makes the two policies differ: their ability to shift the *AD* curve.

The Strength of Monetary Policy

Suppose that the economy is in equilibrium at less than potential income. Desired aggregate expenditure equals national income and demand for money is equal to its supply. The Bank of Canada then increases the money supply. Firms and households now hold excess money balances, and they try to buy bonds. This action forces up the price of bonds, which implies a fall in the rate of interest. Desired investment rises along the *MEI* curve. These changes, shown previously in Figure 34-3, are merely part of the transmission mechanism.

The increase in desired investment expenditure shifts the aggregate demand curve rightward, indicating a higher demand for output at each price level. This raises equilibrium national income, as shown in Figures 34-4 and 34-5.

What happens when the Bank of Canada decreases the money supply? This creates an excess demand for money because firms and households

no longer have the money balances they wish to hold at the existing level of interest rates. In an effort to replenish their inadequate holdings of money, firms and households will seek to sell bonds. But they cannot all succeed in doing this, for their efforts to sell will drive the price of bonds down, causing an increase in the interest rate. The increased interest rate will cause a reduction in investment expenditure. This in turn shifts the aggregate demand curve leftward and lowers equilibrium income.

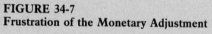

Monetary policy works through the transmission mech-

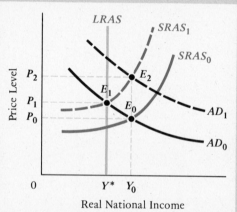

FIGURE 34-7
Frustration of the Monetary Adjustment

An inflationary gap can persist indefinitely if the money supply increases as fast as the price level. Initially the economy is at E_0, with income Y_0 and price level P_0. Since potential income is Y^*, there is an inflationary gap of Y^*Y_0. The price level now rises, which tends to shift the economy upward to the left along any given *AD* curve, thereby tending to reduce the excess aggregate demand. But the Bank of Canada increases the money supply so that the aggregate demand curve shifts outward, thereby tending to increase excess aggregate demand. If the two forces just balance each other, by the time the price level has risen to P_2 the aggregate demand curve will have shifted to AD_1, leaving the inflationary gap unchanged, with equilibrium at E_2.

anism to shift the aggregate demand curve and so change equilibrium national income. An increase in the money supply is expansionary, a decrease contractionary.

But how strong is this effect? If, for example, the Bank of Canada engineers an immediate 10 percent increase in the money supply, by how much will income rise? As a first step in answering that question, we focus on the shift of the *AD* curve.

The size of the shift in aggregate demand in response to an increase in the money supply depends on the size of the increase in investment expenditure. This in turn depends on two factors.

The first is how much interest rates fall in response to the increase in the money supply. The more interest-sensitive is the demand for money, the less interest rates will have to fall to induce firms and households willingly to hold the increase in the money supply.

The second is how much investment expenditure increases in response to the fall in interest rates. The more interest-sensitive is investment expenditure, the more it will increase in response to any given fall in the interest rate.

It follows that the size of the shift in aggregate demand in response to a change in the money supply depends on the shapes of the liquidity preference and marginal efficiency of investment curves. The influences of the shapes of the two curves are shown in Figure 34-8 and may be summarized as follows:

1. **The steeper (less interest-sensitive) the *LP* function, the greater the effect a change in the money supply will have on interest rates.**
2. **The flatter (more interest-sensitive) the *MEI* function, the greater the effect a change in the rate of interest will have on investment expenditure and hence on aggregate demand.**

The combination that produces the largest effect on aggregate demand for a given change in the money supply is a steep *LP* function and a flat *MEI* function. This combination is illustrated in Figure 34-8(i). It accords with the monetarist view that monetary policy is relatively effective as a means of influencing the economy.

The combination that produces the smallest effect is a flat *LP* function and a steep *MEI* function. This combination is illustrated in Figure 34-8(ii). It accords with the view of some neo-Keynesians that monetary policy is relatively ineffective.

According to the monetarists, changes in the money supply cause large changes in interest rates that in turn cause large changes in expenditure. According to some neo-Keynesians, changes in the money supply cause small changes in interest rates that in turn cause small or negligible changes in expenditure.

The Strength of Fiscal Policy

As with monetary policy, the amount by which a given fiscal stimulus raises national income depends upon both the *AD* curve and the *SRAS* curve. Again, we focus for the moment on the role of the *AD* curve.

We saw in Chapter 32 that the horizontal shift in the *AD* curve due to, say, an increase in government expenditure is given by the multiplier. In the final equilibrium when the price level has adjusted, however, the change in aggregate demand will depend on the consequent response of interest rates and investment expenditure. Disagreement over these responses causes monetarists and neo-Keynesians to disagree over the potency of fiscal policy. This is illustrated in Figure 34-9.

Consider an increase in government expenditure. It raises national income and creates excess demand for money because it causes a rise in the demand for transactions balances. The interest rate rises until everyone is content to hold the existing stock of money. The rise in the interest rate lowers private investment expenditure. (A parallel analysis applies to a decline in government expenditure.)

The tendency just discussed is called the **crowding out effect.** It may be defined as the offsetting reduction in private investment caused by the rise in interest rates that follows an expansionary fiscal policy. The analysis of Figure 34-9 shows that the crowding out effect is smaller (1) the flatter (more interest-sensitive) the *LP* function, so that increases in the transactions demand for money do not cause large increases in the interest rate, and

FIGURE 34-8
Monetarist and Neo-Keynesian Views on Monetary Policy

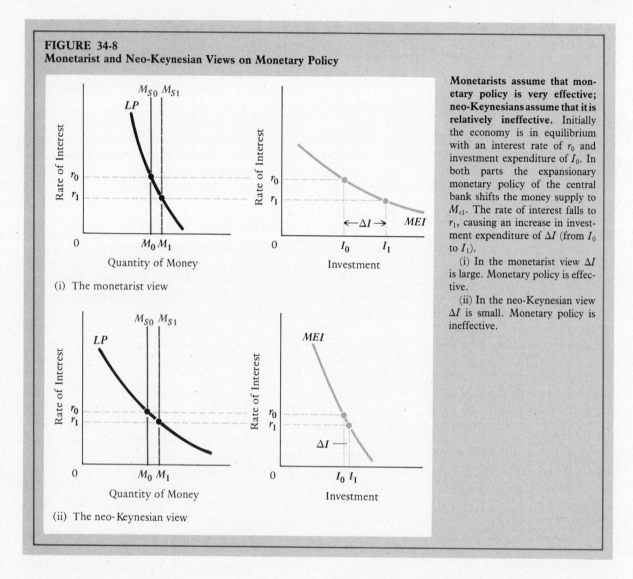

(i) The monetarist view

(ii) The neo-Keynesian view

Monetarists assume that monetary policy is very effective; neo-Keynesians assume that it is relatively ineffective. Initially the economy is in equilibrium with an interest rate of r_0 and investment expenditure of I_0. In both parts the expansionary monetary policy of the central bank shifts the money supply to M_{s1}. The rate of interest falls to r_1, causing an increase in investment expenditure of ΔI (from I_0 to I_1).

(i) In the monetarist view ΔI is large. Monetary policy is effective.

(ii) In the neo-Keynesian view ΔI is small. Monetary policy is ineffective.

(2) the steeper the *MEI* function, so that increases in the interest rate do not cause large changes in investment expenditure.[9]

Monetarists believe the crowding out effect is large. An increase in government expenditure will crowd out almost the same amount of private expenditure and thus have only a small net expan-

sionary effect on aggregate demand. Neo-Keynesians believe the crowding out effect is small, at least when the economy is suffering from a substantial GNP gap, which is when one is likely to wish to use an expansionary fiscal policy. In this case only a small part of any rise in government expenditure will be offset by a fall in private expenditure. There will be a large net increase in aggregate expenditure and hence a large increase in aggregate demand.

[9] We encountered the crowding out effect in Chapter 32. See especially the discussion surrounding Figure 32-7.

FIGURE 34-9
Monetarist and Neo-Keynesian Views on Fiscal Policy

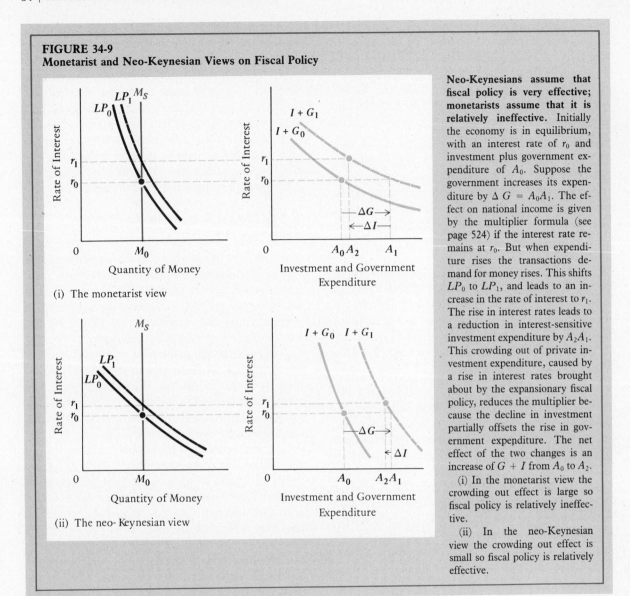

(i) The monetarist view

(ii) The neo-Keynesian view

Neo-Keynesians assume that fiscal policy is very effective; monetarists assume that it is relatively ineffective. Initially the economy is in equilibrium, with an interest rate of r_0 and investment plus government expenditure of A_0. Suppose the government increases its expenditure by $\Delta G = A_0 A_1$. The effect on national income is given by the multiplier formula (see page 524) if the interest rate remains at r_0. But when expenditure rises the transactions demand for money rises. This shifts LP_0 to LP_1, and leads to an increase in the rate of interest to r_1. The rise in interest rates leads to a reduction in interest-sensitive investment expenditure by $A_2 A_1$. This crowding out of private investment expenditure, caused by a rise in interest rates brought about by the expansionary fiscal policy, reduces the multiplier because the decline in investment partially offsets the rise in government expenditure. The net effect of the two changes is an increase of $G + I$ from A_0 to A_2.

(i) In the monetarist view the crowding out effect is large so fiscal policy is relatively ineffective.

(ii) In the neo-Keynesian view the crowding out effect is small so fiscal policy is relatively effective.

According to the monetarists, changes in government expenditure will induce large changes in interest rates that in turn cause large offsetting changes in private investment, leaving only a small net effect on aggregate demand. According to the neo-Keynesians, changes in government expenditure cause only small changes in interest rates that in turn cause small or negligible offsetting changes in investment expenditure.

The Role of the *SRAS* Curve

Neither monetarists nor neo-Keynesians can assess the final effects of monetary or fiscal policy on *real* output and employment without reference to the shape of the *SRAS* curve.

The role of the *SRAS* curve is common to both fiscal and monetary policies: For any given shift in the *AD* curve, the steeper is the *SRAS* curve, the smaller the increase in national income and the larger the increase in the price level. (This should be familiar from Chapter 30—see Figure 30-2.) However, the mechanism by which the *SRAS* curve influences the outcome differs between the two policies.

Monetary policy. An increase in the money supply is expansionary because it lowers interest rates. If the expansion causes the price level to rise, the demand for money rises, dampening the fall in interest rates. This means that investment does not rise as much as it would have if the price level had been constant. Therefore equilibrium national income does not rise as much.

In the extreme case of a vertical aggregate supply curve, prices rise so much that the increase in money demand matches the increase in money supply, and interest rates do not fall at all. In this case investment expenditure and national income are unaffected by changes in the money supply. This is shown in Figure 30-3.

Fiscal policy. Following a fiscal-induced expansion, any rise in the price level raises the demand for money even further than the initial rise due to the expansion in national income. This then causes interest rates to rise even further, crowding out more investment expenditure. In the extreme case of a vertical *SRAS* curve, prices and interest rates rise by enough to cause investment expenditure to fall by an amount exactly equal to the rise in government expenditure. This is the case of *complete* crowding out, where national income is not influenced by fiscal policy at all.

The Role of the Long-Run AS Curve

We have seen that in the long run, output is determined by the *LRAS* curve (with the price level being determined by the *AD* curve). Thus monetary and fiscal policy have no long-run effect on real national income.

The possible role of policy in raising real GNP is to remove recessionary gaps faster than would happen if natural market forces were left to work themselves out. Such policies need to be reversed once private sector expenditure functions recover sufficiently to produce full employment without the temporary stimulus. If they are not reversed, they will open up an inflationary gap that will be removed by a subsequent rise in the price level.

We have seen that there is argument about how much policy can in practice work as a short-run stabilizer. However, the important point here is that such role as it does have in influencing real GNP is essentially a short-run role. In the long run it is aggregate supply that determines output.

The Present State of the Controversy

The controversy about the relative strengths of monetary and fiscal policy is no longer a central source of disagreement among economists. Few economists believe in either extreme view, although the extremes are still studied since they help in understanding the important role played by the shapes of the key behavioral relations.

Indeed, although monetarist and neo-Keynesian are convenient labels to give to the extreme views, ideas continue to evolve. Whereas 20 years ago many Keynesians gave little place to monetary policy, today most neo-Keynesians accept both monetary and fiscal policy as potent methods of influencing the economy; traditional monetarists are still inclined to downgrade fiscal policy. Disagreements now tend to be focused more on aggregate supply rather than, as in the above controversy, aggregate demand. One new school of thought argues that what matters more is whether policy is expected or unexpected than whether it acts through monetary or fiscal channels. This important distinction is encountered again in Chapter 42. A second controversial aspect of fiscal policy concerns the behavior of net exports and of the exchange rate; this is discussed further in Chapter 41.

Policy Debates: A Preview

There is still considerable debate about the relevance of the monetary adjustment mechanism to policy. Monetarists make it the centerpiece of their policy recommendations. They maintain that central banks can and should hold the money supply constant in the face of increases in the price level and that to do so is both necessary and sufficient to control inflation.

Opponents of the monetarist view are divided into several groups. A few say that it is not within the power of central banks to control the money supply over a long time period. (This denies the analysis of the money supply presented in Chapter 33.) Others say that, given the political and economic objectives of anything but a very right-wing government, it is quite unrealistic to expect the Bank of Canada to attempt to actually hold the money supply constant for a long time period in the face of an inflation, even though it is able to do so. Still others say that while an inflation can be stopped by the monetary adjustment mechanism, the economic and social costs of doing so are too great.

In the early 1980s Chairman Paul Volcker of the U.S. Federal Reserve held to his tight monetary, anti-inflationary guns while under pressure from President Reagan to ease up a bit in order to alleviate the costs of the anti-inflationary battle. The Reagan administration, while occasionally in conflict with Volcker, was very tough-minded in its commitment to disinflation, so one can only imagine the pressures the Fed would have felt under some other, less conservative, administration.

In Canada, Governor Bouey held to a tight monetary policy throughout the first half of the 1980s. While some MPs criticized this policy, the government was basically in favor of it (especially since it meant that the Bank rather than cabinet had to take the blame for its side effects).

Whenever there is a serious inflation, the key issue for policy is whether the central bank *should* frustrate the monetary adjustment mechanism and whether the government should find other ways of bringing inflation under control. We shall return to these very important debates in Chapter 42.

SUMMARY

1. For simplicity we divide all forms of holding wealth into money, which is a medium of exchange and earns no interest, and bonds, which earn an interest return but can be turned into money only by selling them at a price that is determined on the open market.

2. The price of bonds varies negatively with the rate of interest. A rise in the rate of interest lowers the prices of all bonds. The longer its term to maturity, the greater the change in the price of a bond for a given change in the interest rate.

3. The value of money balances people wish to hold is called the *demand for money*. It is a stock (not a flow), and it is measured as so many billions of dollars.

4. The reasons for holding money balances despite the opportunity cost of bond interest foregone are described by the transactions, precautionary, and speculative motives. They have the effect of making the nominal demand for money vary positively with real national income, with the price level, and with wealth, and to vary negatively with the rate of interest.

5. When there is an excess demand for money balances, people try to sell bonds. This pushes the price of bonds down and the interest rate up. When there is an excess supply of money balances, people try to buy bonds. This pushes the price of bonds up and the rate of interest down. Monetary equilibrium is established when people are willing to hold the fixed stocks of money and bonds at the current rate of interest.

6. A change in the interest rate causes desired investment to change along the *MEI* function. This shifts the aggregate desired expenditure function and causes equilibrium national income to change. This means that the aggregate demand curve shifts.

7. Points 5 and 6 together describe the transmission mechanism that links money to national income. A decrease in the supply of money tends to reduce aggregate demand. An increase in the supply of money tends to increase it.

8. Other things being equal, each price level is associated with an equilibrium real national income such that desired expenditure equals income and the demand for money equals the supply. Each

price level and its corresponding equilibrium real national income gives one point on the aggregate demand curve.

9. The aggregate demand curve is negatively sloped because with a fixed quantity of money, the higher the price level the lower equilibrium national income. The explanation lies with the monetary adjustment mechanism: The higher the price level, the higher the demand for money, the higher the rate of interest, the lower the aggregate expenditure function, and thus the lower equilibrium income.

10. The monetary adjustment mechanism that causes the aggregate demand curve to have a negative slope means that a sufficiently large rise in the price level will eliminate any inflationary gap. However, this mechanism can be frustrated if the Bank of Canada increases the money supply as fast as the price level is rising.

11. Monetary policy seeks to influence national income by creating a change in monetary equilibrium that will work through the transmission mechanism. The steeper the *LP* curve and the flatter the *MEI* curve, the greater the effect of a given change in the money supply on aggregate demand.

12. Fiscal policy operates to shift the *AD* curve directly, but its effectiveness also depends on its indirect effects on private expenditure via changes in the interest rate. A given change in government expenditure will have larger effects on aggregate demand the flatter the *LP* curve and the steeper the *MEI* curve.

13. The appendix to this chapter presents a formal model that integrates the monetary and expenditure sides of the economy.

TOPICS FOR REVIEW

Interest rates and bond prices

Transactions, precautionary, and speculative motives for holding money

The liquidity preference (*LP*) function

Monetary equilibrium

The transmission mechanism

The shape of the aggregate demand function

The monetary adjustment mechanism and its frustration

The strength of monetary and fiscal policy

DISCUSSION QUESTIONS

1. Describing a possible future "cashless society," a public report recently said: "In the cashless society of the future, a customer could insert a plastic card into a machine at a store and the amount of the purchase would be deducted from his 'bank account' in the computer automatically and transferred to the store's account. No cash or cheques would ever change hands." What would such an institutional change do to the various motives for holding money balances? What functions would remain for chartered banks and for the central bank if money as we now know it disappeared in this fashion? What benefits and disadvantages can you see in such a scheme?

2. What motives do you think explain the following holdings?
   a. The currency and coins in the cash register of the local supermarket at the start of each working day
   b. The payroll account of the Ford Motor Company in the local bank
   c. Certificates of deposit that mature after one's retirement
   d. The holdings of government bonds by private individuals

3. What would be the effects on the economy if Parliament were to vote a once-and-for-all universal social dividend of $5,000 paid to every Canadian over the age of 17, to be financed by the creation of new money?

4. "Central banker says using monetary policy to lower interest rates now would only cause inflation to rise and lead to higher interest rates in the future." Explain how this might be so.

5. One relationship encountered in this chapter and elsewhere is the negative one between bond prices and interest rates. Be sure that you can explain just why this occurs. Is this a special feature of bonds, or does it apply to the value of other earning assets as well?

6. Suppose you are sure that the Bank of Canada is going to engage in policies that will decrease the money supply sharply starting next month. How might you make speculative profits by purchases or sales of bonds now?

7. In the days of the gold standard the money supply was tied rigidly to the quantity of refined gold. What would be the effects of new discoveries of gold if (1) the economy were in the midst of a severe recession and (2) the economy were producing its full-employment national income?

8. What do you expect to happen to interest rates if the Bank of Canada reduces the money supply? What would happen if, starting from a situation of 10 percent rates of inflation and of monetary expansion, the Bank cut the rate of monetary expansion to 5 percent?

9. Trace out the full sequence of events by which the monetary adjustment mechanism would work if, in the face of a constant money supply, workers and firms insisted on actions that raised prices continually at a rate of 10 percent per year. "Sooner or later in this situation something would have to give." What possible things could "give"? What would be the consequence of each "giving"?

10. If the monetary adjustment mechanism is always present in any economy, why did it not prevent the inflations of the 1970s and 1980s?

11. "Bond Prices Pressed Downward by News of M_1's Sharp Rise, Economy's Rebound." Does this Wall Street Journal headline necessarily contradict our theory about the direct link between money supply and bond prices?

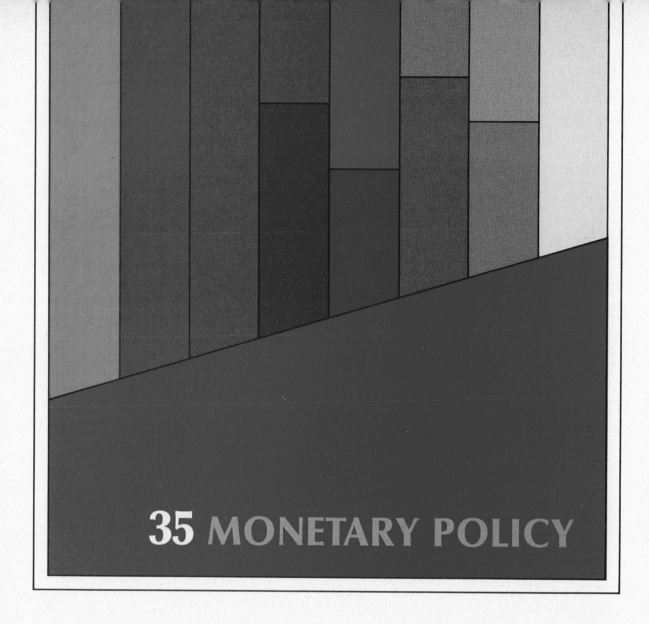

35 MONETARY POLICY

Central banks influence the size of their country's money supply, and in doing so they seek to influence national income and the price level. In this chapter we study how our central bank influences the Canadian economy through its monetary policy.

CENTRAL BANKS

All advanced free-market economies have, in addition to commercial banks, a central bank. Many of the world's early central banks were private, profit-making institutions that provided services to ordinary banks. Their importance, however, led them to develop close ties with the government. Central banks soon became instruments of the government, though not all of them were publicly owned. The Bank of England (the "Old Lady of Threadneedle Street"), one of the world's oldest and most famous central banks, began to operate as the central bank of England in the seventeenth century but was not "nationalized" until 1947. In the United States the central bank is called the Federal Reserve System (popularly known as the Fed), and in this country it is the Bank of Canada.

The similarities of central banks in the functions they perform and the tools they use are much more important than their differences in organization. Although our attention is focused on the operations of the Bank of Canada, the basic situation is not different for the Bank of England, the Bank of Greece, or the Federal Reserve System.

Organization of the Bank of Canada

The Bank of Canada is a publicly owned corporation; all profits accruing from its operations are remitted to the government of Canada. The responsibility for the bank's affairs rests with a board of directors composed of the governor, the senior deputy governor, the deputy minister of finance, and twelve directors. The governor is appointed by the directors, with the approval of the cabinet, for a seven-year term. In 1984 the governor was Mr. Gerald Bouey, who was appointed in 1973, and reappointed for a second term in 1980.

The organization of the Bank is designed to keep the operation of monetary policy free from day-to-day political influence. Thus the Bank is not responsible to Parliament for its day-to-day behavior in the way that the Department of Finance is for the operation of fiscal policy. Nonetheless, the governor of the Bank and the minister of finance consult regularly. Furthermore, in the case of fundamental disagreement over policy, the governor must resign or acquiesce to the Cabinet's desired policy as enunciated by the minister.[1]

Basic Functions of the Bank of Canada

A central bank serves four main functions: as a banker for private banks, as a bank for the government, as the controller of the nation's supply of

[1] In 1962, when James Coyne was governor, such a fundamental disagreement arose and Coyne was eventually forced to resign.

money, and as a supporter of financial markets. The first three functions are revealed by a study of Table 35-1, which shows the balance sheet of a central bank.

Banker to the Chartered Banks

The central bank accepts deposits from the chartered banks and will, on order, transfer them to the account of another bank. In this way the central bank provides the chartered banks with the equivalent of a chequing account and with a means of settling debts to other banks. The deposits of the chartered banks with the central bank appear in Table 35-1. Notice that the cash reserves of the chartered banks deposited with the central bank are *liabilities* of the central bank (because it promises to pay them on demand), just as the money reserves of an individual or corporation deposited with a chartered bank are the liabilities of the chartered bank.

Historically, one of the earliest services provided by central banks was that of "lender of last resort" to the banking system. Central banks would lend money to private banks that had sound investments (such as government securities and safe loans to individuals) but were in urgent need of cash. If such banks could not obtain ready cash, they might be forced into insolvency because they could not meet the demands of their depositors, in spite of their being basically sound. Today's central banks continue to be the lender of last resort.

U.S. banks borrow extensively from the Federal Reserve System in order to maintain their reserves, but the corresponding institutional arrangement that Canadian banks use is somewhat more complicated. It is reflected in Table 35-1 by Bank of Canada holdings of government securities under **purchase and resale agreements (PRA)**. Rather than rely on loans from the Bank of Canada, the chartered banks meet their immediate cash requirements by varying the amount of **day-to-day loans** they make available to a group of investment dealers who carry inventories of government of Canada securities. When necessary, these dealers can obtain financing from the Bank of Canada under PRA; that is, they can sell securities to the Bank

TABLE 35–1 ASSETS AND LIABILITIES OF THE BANK OF CANADA, DECEMBER 1983 (Millions of Dollars)

Assets		Liabilities	
Government of Canada securities	$17,027	Notes in circulation	$14,163
Held outright	$16,970	Deposits of Government of	
Held under purchase		Canada	90
and resale agreements	57	Deposits of chartered banks	3,446
Advances to banks	25	Foreign currency liabilities	111
Foreign currency assets	309	Other liabilities and capital	2,871
Other assets	3,320		$20,681
	$20,681		

Source: Bank of Canada Review, April 1984.

The balance sheet of the Bank of Canada shows that it serves as banker to the chartered banks and the government and as issuer of our currency; it also suggests the bank's role as regulator of money markets and the money supply. The principal liabilities of the Bank are the basis of the money supply. Bank of Canada notes are currency, and the deposits of the chartered banks give them the reserves they use to create deposit money. The bank's holdings of Government of Canada securities arise from its operations designed to regulate the money supply and financial markets.

of Canada and agree to buy them back at a later date. Thus, when the chartered banks reduce their day-to-day loans, they induce an increase in PRA. The result is the same as if the banks had borrowed from the Bank of Canada directly.

Banker to the Government

Governments, too, need to hold their funds in an account into which they can make deposits and on which they can write cheques. The government of Canada keeps its chequing deposits at the Bank of Canada, replenishing them from much larger accounts kept at the chartered banks. When the government requires more money, it too needs to borrow, and it does so by printing bonds. Most are sold directly to the public, but occasionally the government raises funds by selling securities (mostly short-term) to the central bank, which "buys" them by crediting the government's account with a deposit for the amount of the purchase. In December 1983 the Bank of Canada held over $17 billion in government of Canada securities. These securities play an important role in the monetary system.

Controller and Regulator of the Money Supply

One of the most important functions of a central bank is to control the money supply. From Table 35-1 it is clear that the overwhelming proportion of a central bank's liabilities (its promises to pay) are either notes (money) or the reserves of the chartered banks, which underlie the deposits (money) of households and firms.

The central bank can change the levels of its assets and liabilities in many ways, and as its liabilities rise and fall, so does the money supply. Consider a single example. Suppose the central bank buys $100 million worth of newly printed bonds from the government of Canada. The bank's assets (government bonds) rise by $100 million, and so do its liabilities (government of Canada deposits). The government has an extra $100 million of purchasing power to spend. As easy as printing money, you say. Indeed, it is the same thing.

Regulator and Supporter of Money Markets

Central banks usually assume a major responsibility to support the country's financial system and to prevent serious disruption by wide-scale panic and resulting bank failures. Various institutions are in the business of borrowing on a short-term and lending on a long-term basis. To some extent the chartered banks do this when they take in demand (or savings) deposits and lend money for various terms. But trust and mortgage loan companies are the major institution for this kind of transaction. They receive deposits from the public and lend the money on long-term mortgages.

Large, unanticipated increases in interest rates tend to squeeze these institutions. The average rate they earn on their investments rises only slowly as old contracts mature and new ones are made, but they must either pay higher rates to hold onto their deposits or accept wide-scale withdrawals that could easily bring about insolvency. To prevent such financial disasters, central banks often buy and sell government bonds either to slow the rate of change in interest rates or to narrow the range over which the rates are allowed to fluctuate.

CONTROL OF THE MONEY SUPPLY

The Bank Act requires each chartered bank to maintain reserves in the form of Bank of Canada notes and deposits at the Bank of Canada, and it permits the central bank to buy and sell various financial assets. The provisions enable the central bank to vary the amount of cash reserves available to the banking system and thus to regulate the money supply.

Open Market Operations

The most important tool the central bank has for influencing the supply of money is the purchase or sale of government securities on the open market. In a typical year the Bank of Canada buys and sells over $5 billion worth of government securities. What is the effect of these purchases and sales?

Purchases and sales by the central bank of government securities in financial markets are known as **open market operations**. There are active and well-organized markets for government securities,

just as there is a stock market. You or I, or General Motors, or the Bank of Montreal, or the Bank of Canada can enter this market and buy or sell negotiable government securities at whatever price supply and demand establishes. When the Bank of Canada buys or sells securities, it does not know from whom it buys or to whom it sells them.

Purchases on the Open Market

When the Bank of Canada buys a security from a holder in the nonbank private sector, it pays for it with a cheque drawn on the central bank and payable to the seller. The seller deposits this cheque in its own bank. The chartered bank presents the cheque to the Bank of Canada for payment, and the central bank makes a book entry increasing the deposit of the chartered bank at the central bank.

At the end of these transactions, the central bank has acquired a new asset in the form of a security and a new liability in the form of a deposit by the chartered bank. The seller has reduced its security holdings and increased its deposits. The chartered bank has a new deposit equal to the amount paid for the security by the central bank. The chartered bank's reserves and its deposit liabilities have increased by an equal amount.

When the central bank buys securities on the open market, the reserves of the chartered banks are increased. These banks in turn can expand deposits, thereby increasing the money supply.

Table 35-2 shows the changes in the balance sheets of the several parties in response to a central bank purchase of $100 in government securities from the nonbank private sector. After these transactions, the chartered banks have excess reserves and are in a position to expand their loans and deposits. Indeed, the chartered banks are in precisely the position studied on page 625 (see Table 33-4). The new deposit made by the immigrant might just as well have been made by someone who had sold a security to the Bank of Canada.

If the central bank buys many securities in the open market, the entire banking system will gain new reserves. Whether the seller is a household, a firm, or a bank, the purchase by the Bank of Canada of securities on the open market sets in motion

TABLE 35–2 BALANCE SHEET CHANGES CAUSED BY AN OPEN MARKET PURCHASE FROM THE NONBANK PRIVATE SECTOR

Nonbank Private Sector		
Assets	**Liabilities**	
Bonds	−$100	No change
Deposits	+ 100	

Chartered Banks		
Assets	**Liabilities**	
Reserves (deposits) with central bank	+$100	Demand deposits +$100

Central Bank		
Assets	**Liabilities**	
Bond	+$100	Deposits of chartered banks +$100

The money supply is increased when the central bank makes an open market purchase from the nonbank private sector. When the Bank of Canada buys a $100 bond, the seller gains money and gives up a bond, and the chartered banks gain a new deposit of $100. Chartered banks can now engage in a multiple expansion of deposit money of the sort analyzed in Chapter 33.

a series of book transactions that increase the banking system's reserves and thus make possible a multiple expansion of credit.[2]

Sales on the Open Market

When the central bank sells a $100 security to a household or firm, it receives in return the buy-

---

[2] In the text we studied a case in which the Bank sold a bond to a household. If instead the purchaser was a chartered bank, the end result would have been the same. In this case the chartered bank gives up one asset (a bond) and gains another (cash or a deposit with the central bank). But now the chartered bank has excess reserves (liabilities unchanged, cash reserves increased) on the basis of which it can engage in the expansion of deposits.

er's cheque drawn against its own deposit in a chartered bank. The central bank presents the cheque to the chartered bank for payment. Payment is made by a book entry that reduces the chartered bank's deposit at the central bank.

The changes in this case are the opposite of those shown in Table 35-2. The central bank has reduced its assets by the value of the security it sold and reduced its liabilities in the form of the deposits of chartered banks. The household or firm has increased its holdings of securities and reduced its cash on deposit with a chartered bank. The chartered bank has reduced its deposit liability to the household or firm and reduced its reserves (on deposit with the central bank) by the same amount. Each of the asset changes is balanced by a liability change. Indeed everything balances.

But the chartered bank finds that the equal change in its reserves and deposit liabilities causes its ratio of reserves to deposits falls. Consider, for example, a bank with $10 million in deposits backed by $1 million cash in fulfillment of a 10 percent cash reserve ratio. As a result of the Bank's open market sales of $100,000 worth of bonds, the bank loses $100,000 of deposits and reserves. Reserves are now $900,000 while deposits are $9.9 million, a reserve ratio of only 9.09 percent.

Banks, such as the one in the above example, whose reserve ratios are driven below the minimum requirement must take immediate steps to restore their reserve ratios. The necessary reduction in deposits can be accomplished by not making new investments when old ones are redeemed (e.g., by not granting new loans when old ones are repaid) or by selling (liquidating) existing investments.

When the central bank sells securities on the open market, the reserves of the chartered banks are decreased. These banks in turn are forced to contract deposits, thereby decreasing the money supply.

But what if the public does not wish to buy the securities the Bank of Canada wishes to sell? Can it force the public to do so? The answer is that there is always a price at which the public will buy. The Bank in its open market operations must be prepared to have the price of the securities fall if it insists on suddenly selling a large volume of them. As we have seen, a fall in the price of securities is the same thing as a rise in interest rates, so if the Bank wishes to curtail the money supply by selling bonds, it may well drive up interest rates.

Notice in Table 35-1 that the Bank's holdings of government securities are large relative to the reserves of chartered banks. By selling securities it can contract those reserves very sharply if it chooses. Similarly, by buying securities it can expand reserves. Open market operations are a potent weapon for affecting the size of bank reserves—and thus for affecting the money supply.

Tools Other Than Open Market Operations

The major tool the Bank of Canada uses in conducting monetary policy is its open market operations. But other tools are available and have on occasion been used extensively.

Reserve Requirements

One way that a central bank can control the money supply is by altering the required minimum reserve ratios. Suppose the banking system is loaned-up; that is, it has no excess reserves. If the Bank increases the required reserve ratio (say from 20 percent to 25 percent), the reserves held by the chartered banks will no longer be adequate to support their outstanding deposits. Chartered banks will then be forced to reduce their deposits until they achieve the new, higher required reserve ratio.[3] This decrease in deposits is a decrease in the money supply.

A reduction in reserve requirements immediately provides banks with excess reserves. Of course, if banks choose not to increase their loans, they will not need to respond to a decrease in required reserves, since those are only minimum requirements. In normal times the profit motive will lead most banks to respond by increasing loans and deposits—and thus lead to an increase in the money supply.

Increases in required reserve ratios force banks with no excess reserves to decrease deposits and thus reduce the money supply. Decreases in required reserve ratios permit banks to expand deposits, which increases the money supply.

This method of controlling the money supply has been used in the United States but not in Canada. Given the small margin of excess reserves held by the chartered banks, increases in the required reserve ratios would force abrupt adjustments in bank assets. An equivalent contraction in the money supply can be brought about by using the more flexible tool of open market operations, which can be spread out over time to induce a more orderly adjustment. Changes in reserve requirements are occasionally made, but this is usually done for purposes other than stabilizing the economy. For example, reforms of the Bank Act in 1980 reduced the reserve requirement on demand deposits from 12 to 10 percent.

Changes in the Bank Rate

The rate of interest at which the Bank of Canada makes loans to the chartered banks is called the **bank rate.** In principle, banks might be induced to hold more reserves in view of the higher cost of borrowing if they suffer a loss of cash and are forced to seek accommodation from the central bank to meet their reserve requirements. Although this mechanism may operate in the United States, it is not likely to be of importance in Canada because the chartered banks rarely borrow from the Bank of Canada.

Prior to March 1980, the bank rate was simply set by the Bank of Canada. Changes in the rate had an "announcement effect"—such changes were widely interpreted as a signal of changes in the stance of monetary policy, which would cause market interest rates quickly to move in the same direction. Since March 1980, the bank rate itself has

---

[3] They will do this by gradually decreasing their loans and/or selling some of their securities. In the short term they may undertake purchase and resale agreements to give themselves time to meet the increased reserve requirements without disrupting financial markets.

become a "market rate." It is now set at a premium of one-quarter of 1 percent over the average rate determined in the weekly Thursday auction of three-month Treasury bills.

Most observers believed that a market-determined bank rate would lessen the role played by the bank rate by eliminating the announcement effect; however, the financial press now gives more attention to changes in the bank rate, and it is not at all clear that it is less important as a signal about monetary policy. The Bank of Canada is a major participant in the market for Treasury bills, and its purchases or sales clearly influence the bank rate by influencing the Treasury bill rate. But its purchases and sales also influence the money supply. Hence the bank rate now signals actual rather than intended monetary policy.

Secondary Reserve Requirements

When the central bank attempts to restrain inflationary forces, it may wish to dampen expenditures not only through higher interest rates, but also through some form of direct control over the expansion of bank loans. Restricting the supply of cash reserves will not restrain the banks from extending credit if they have substantial quantities of liquid assets that can be sold off to finance new loans. The Bank of Canada is empowered to restrict the ability of the chartered banks to expand their loans through the imposition of a required minimum secondary reserve ratio within the range of 0 to 12 percent of deposits. Secondary reserves are defined as holdings of Treasury bills, day-to-day loans, and excess cash reserves. A required minimum ratio of 8 percent was in effect from the end of 1971 until the end of 1974, when it was lowered to 7 percent. Further reductions were made during 1975 and 1977, so that at the beginning of 1978, the required ratio was 5 percent.

Moral Suasion

The term "moral suasion" is generally used to describe attempts by the central bank to enlist the cooperation of private financial institutions in the pursuit of some objective of monetary policy. In a country such as Canada, where there are only a few banks, the central bank can easily communicate its view to the chartered banks. In some cases moral suasion involves general discussions aimed at improving understanding of the current financial situation and the objectives of policy. In other cases specific requests have been issued to the banks. For example, on a number of occasions in recent years the Bank of Canada has attempted to restrain the growth of term deposits by requesting the observance of ceilings either on the interest rates offered or on the volume of deposits.

INSTRUMENTS AND OBJECTIVES OF MONETARY POLICY

The Bank of Canada conducts monetary policy in order to influence output, unemployment, and inflation. These variables—the ultimate objectives of the Bank's policy—are called **policy variables.** The variables that it controls *directly* in order to achieve these objectives are called its **policy instruments.** Sometimes it is also useful for the Bank to identify variables that are neither policy variables nor policy instruments, but that nevertheless play a key role in the execution of monetary policy. These variables are called the Bank's **intermediate targets;** their importance lies in the influence they exert on the policy variables.

Policy Variables

The Bank of Canada can seek to remove GNP gaps by its monetary policy and thus seek to influence national income. In so doing it also influences both inflation and unemployment.

Another major policy variable that is sometimes important is the rate of interest. For a number of reasons the Bank may be concerned about the rate of interest quite separately from any effects the rate may have on national income.

Nominal GNP as a policy variable. Changes in nominal GNP reflect changes both in real GNP and in the price level. In principle the central bank will be concerned about how a given change in nominal GNP is divided between these two components. However, as we saw in Chapter 34, monetary policy operates by influencing aggregate demand, and the most that can be hoped for is to achieve a given *AD* curve.

The analysis in Chapter 34 suggests that in the short run, the influence of monetary policy will be *divided* between the price level and real output in a manner determined by the slope of the *SRAS* curve. Thus, while the central bank cares about the separate reactions of the price level *and* of real output, there is little it can do in the short run to achieve such goals independently. For any price level response that is achieved, the real output consequence must be accepted.

Alternatively, for any real output response that is achieved, the price level consequence must be accepted. The two objectives of influencing *P* and *Y* cannot be pursued independently using monetary policy. For this reason, we choose to focus on nominal GNP (*PY*) as the target for monetary policy, at least in the short run.

We have seen that in the long run, when the level of wages is fully adjusted to the price level, the *LRAS* curve is vertical and hence the major impact of monetary policy will be on the price level. Monetary policy is ineffective in influencing long-run real output.

While monetary policy influences both real output and the price level in the short run, its main effects in the long run are only on the price level.

Policy Instruments

Having selected its policy variables and formulated targets for them, the Bank of Canada must decide how to achieve these targets. How can the policy variables be made to perform in the way that the Bank wishes? Since the Bank cannot control income or inflation directly, it must use its policy instruments, which it does control directly, to influence aggregate demand in the desired manner.

The primary method used by the Bank of Canada to conduct monetary policy is open market operations.

The Bank may choose between two alternative

procedures in conducting its open market operations. It may set the *price* (and hence the interest rate) at which it sells or buys bonds on the open market. In this case the quantity of bonds sold or purchased is determined by market demand. If the Bank wishes to change its policy, it must change the price at which it stands willing to buy and sell bonds. This approach is called **interest rate control**, and here the interest rate is properly viewed as a policy instrument.

Alternatively, the Bank may choose to set the *quantity* of open market sales or purchases. In this case it is the price of bonds, and hence the interest rate, that is determined by market demand. If the Bank wishes to change its policy, it changes the amount of its open market purchases or sales. (Of course this means that the interest rate at which these transactions are made may also change.) Open market operations change the size of the Bank of Canada's monetary liabilities, also called the **monetary base**, given by the sum of currency in circulation plus reserves of the chartered banks.[4] (See Table 35-3.) In this case, where the Bank chooses to set the quantity of its open market operations, it is said to be using **base control**, and the monetary base is properly viewed as the policy instrument.

The bank cannot expect to be able to control both the interest rate and the monetary base independently. This is because of the liquidity preference function, which relates the quantity of money to the rate of interest.

Intermediate Targets

Major changes in the direction or method of monetary policy are made only infrequently. Decisions regarding the implementation of policy must, however, be made almost daily. Given the values desired for the policy variables and the current state of the economy, is a purchase or a sale in the open market called for? How big a purchase? Or how big a sale? At what interest rate? These

---

[4] These monetary liabilities, as we saw in Chapter 33, form the *base* on which chartered banks can expand and create deposits.

BOX 35–1 THE CHOICE BETWEEN THE MONEY SUPPLY AND THE RATE OF INTEREST AS INTERMEDIATE TARGETS

Suppose the Bank takes the level of national income as its policy variable and chooses either the rate of interest or the money supply as its intermediate target. Since the two potential instrumental variables are not independent of each other, it might not seem to matter which the Bank selects.

For example, if the Bank wishes to remove an inflationary gap by forcing interest rates up, it will sell securities and thus drive their prices down. These open market sales will also contract the money supply. Thus it is largely immaterial whether the Bank seeks to force interest rates up or to contract the money supply; doing one will accomplish the other. Similarly, driving interest rates down by open market purchases of government securities will tend to expand the money supply as the public gains money in return for the securities it sells to the Bank.

Despite the interrelation of these two variables, many economists have argued that the Bank should use the money supply rather than interest rates as its intermediate target. They maintain that when the money supply is used

not only is it much easier for the Bank to assess the trends of the economy, but it is also easier for commentators and key economic decision makers to assess the current stance of the Bank's policy.

The argument proceeds in three steps.

1. In times of business expansion, both interest rates and the money supply will be rising. Interest rates rise because of a heavy demand to borrow money and an increasing shortage of loanable funds. The money supply expands because banks let their excess reserves fall to very low levels in order to meet pressing demands from their customers for loans.

2. If the Bank seeks to restrain this business expansion because it is threatening to produce a serious inflationary gap, it will wish to *accentuate* the rising trend in interest rates but *reverse* the rising trend in the money supply. This is because a restrictive monetary policy requires the Bank to increase interest rates and reduce (or slow the rate of expansion of) the money supply. By selling bonds on the open market, it does both.

---

questions must be answered continually by the Bank in its day-to-day operations.

While these decisions have to be made frequently, information about the policy variables is available only infrequently. Inflation and unemployment rates are available only on a monthly basis, and then with a considerable lag. National income figures are available even less regularly; they appear on a quarterly basis. Thus the policy makers do not know exactly what is happening to the policy variables when they make decisions regarding the setting of their policy instruments.

How, then, does the Bank of Canada make decisions? Central banks have typically used other

variables, called *intermediate targets*, to guide them when implementing monetary policy in the very short run. To serve as an intermediate target, a variable must satisfy two criteria. First, information about it must be available on a frequent basis, daily if possible. Second, its movements must be closely correlated with those of the policy variable so that changes in it can reasonably be expected to indicate that the policy variable is also changing.

The two most commonly used intermediate targets are the money supply and the interest rate. As we have seen the two are not independent of each other. Hence it is important that the central bank not choose a target for one that is inconsistent with

3. It is easier to determine whether the Bank's current policy is contradictory, expansionary, or neutral when it is working through the money supply rather than through interest rates. When a typical interest rate rises to 15 percent during an expansion, we may be uncertain how much of this rise is due to the Bank's tightening of monetary policy and how much of it would have happened anyway. Indeed, the more rapid the expansion, the more rapidly will interest rates be rising without assistance from the Bank. For example, in the period 1961–1965 short-term interest rates doubled, apparently indicating a period of restrictive monetary policy. However, that was also a period of economic recovery, with unemployment falling steadily. It was this boom that fueled the rise in interest rates; the rate of growth of the money supply actually increased over the period, indicating that monetary policy was accommodating. Had the Bank been following a monetary target, it would have recognized that the higher rate of growth of the money supply meant that it was accommodating the expansion, *provided the demand for money had remained a stable function of income and interest rates.*

The italicized qualification is important. What we observe is the money supply. Whether or not monetary policy is tight concerns the *relation between* the demand for money and its supply. If the demand for money is shifting, the money supply may provide a misleading intermediate target. Assume, as for example happened in the 1970s, that the demand for money is shifting to the left, so that less money is demanded at each interest rate and level of income. A declining money supply may then be misread as an indicator of a tight monetary policy. If the demand is falling faster than the supply, then monetary policy may actually be very lax.

Today some central banks still try to target on a money supply figure while others, including the Bank of Canada, use no single target but try to assess their monetary stance by looking at interest rates, various money supply measures, and other targets.

the other. By the same token, since the two are closely related, it might appear not to matter much which one is used. We take up this point in Box 35-1.

Table 35-3 illustrates some possible operating regimes for the Bank of Canada. If the Bank chooses the interest rate as its intermediate target, it can achieve that target directly by using interest rate control as its instrument. In this case the distinction between intermediate target and policy instrument is superfluous. If the Bank chooses the money supply as its intermediate target, it must achieve its target indirectly by means of base control or interest rate control.

National income, unemployment, and inflation are all policy variables. The money supply can be an intermediate target or a policy instrument. The interest rate can be a policy variable, a policy instrument, or an intermediate target.

Controlling Nominal National Income Through Monetary Policy

When the Bank makes nominal national income its main policy variable, it must work through such policy instruments as the money supply and the rate of interest.

Assume that in pursuit of an expansionary policy

TABLE 35–3 ASSIGNMENT OF VARIABLES UNDER ALTERNATIVE OPERATING REGIMES OF MONETARY POLICY

Regime	Policy instrument	Intermediate target	Policy variables
1. Monetary targeting: base control	Open market operations; regulate volume of open market sales and purchases	Quantity of money via money supply process	Nominal GNP Inflation Unemployment
2. Monetary targeting: interest rate control	Open market operations; regulate price at which open market sales and purchases are made (i.e., regulate interest rate)	Quantity of money via liquidity preference	Nominal GNP Inflation Unemployment
3. Interest rate targeting	Open market operations; regulate intermediate target directly	Interest rates	Nominal GNP Inflation Unemployment

Even with a given set of policy variables, central banks might adopt a variety of operating regimes. The central bank could use either the quantity of money or the interest rate as its intermediate target.

When the central bank opts for monetary targeting, it can influence its target only indirectly. Through its open market operations it can control directly either the size of the monetary base or the level of interest rates. If it controls the monetary base (regime 1), the quantity of money is influenced via the money supply process while the interest rate is determined via monetary equilibrium, as in Figure 34-2. If the central bank controls the interest rate (regime 2), the influence on the quantity of money operates via the liquidity preference function.

Should the central bank choose to use the interest rate as an intermediate target (regime 3), it can achieve its target directly by using open market operations to control the interest rate. Although this appears to be a simpler process (and in terms of operation, it is simpler), many economists favor monetary targeting.

Other variables, such as the interest rate and the exchange rate, might also appear as policy variables. The interest rate could then appear as a policy instrument, an intermediate target, or a policy variable, depending on the policy regime.

the Bank wishes to increase aggregate demand. It will enter the open market and buy bonds. This expands the reserves of the chartered banks and leads to an increase in the money supply, as analyzed in Chapter 33. The increase in the money supply forces the interest rate down and leads to an increase in investment expenditure. As we saw in Chapter 34, this shifts the aggregate demand function rightward, which is the result desired.

A contractionary policy is achieved by reversing the process: The Bank sells bonds, thereby reducing the money supply, raising interest rates, and shifting the aggregate demand curve to the left.

Even the best-intentioned monetary policy need not always stabilize the economy. Let us examine this point further, along with one policy recommendation that some economists have drawn from it.

Can Monetary Policy Be Destabilizing?

In the real world the full effects of monetary policy occur only after quite long time lags. Lags that occur after the decision is made to implement the policy, called *execution lags*, can have important implications for the conduct of monetary policy.

Sources of Execution Lags

1. Open market operations affect the reserves of the chartered banks. The full increase in the money supply occurs only when the banks have

granted enough new loans and made enough investments to expand the money supply by the full amount permitted by existing reserve ratios. This process can take quite a long time.

2. The division of all assets into money and bonds was useful for seeing the underlying forces at work in determining the demand for money. In fact, however, there is a whole series of assets—from currency and demand deposits to term deposits, to Treasury bills and short-term bonds, to very long-term bonds and equities. When households find themselves with larger money balances than they require, a chain of substitution occurs, with short-term and long-term interest rates falling as households try to hold less money and more interest-earning assets. The change in longer-term interest rates will in turn affect interest-sensitive expenditures. These adjustments along a chain of interest rates can take considerable time to work out.

3. It takes time for new investment plans to be drawn up, approved, and put into effect. It may easily take up to a year before the full increase in investment expenditure builds up in response to a fall in interest rates.

4. The increased investment expenditures will set off a multiplier process that increases national income by some multiple of the initiating increase in investment expenditure. This too takes some time to work out.

Similar considerations apply to contractionary monetary policies that seek to shift the aggregate expenditure function downward. Furthermore, although the end result is fairly predictable, the speed with which the entire expansionary or contractionary process works itself out can vary from time to time in ways that are hard to predict.

Monetary policy is capable of exerting expansionary and contractionary forces on the economy, but it operates with a time lag that is long and unpredictably variable.

Implications of Execution Lags

To see the significance of execution lags for the conduct of monetary policy, assume that the execution lag is 18 months. If on December 1 the Bank of Canada decides that the economy needs stimulus, it can be increasing the money supply within days, and by the end of the year a significant increase may be registered.

But because the full effects of this policy take time to work out, the policy may prove to be destabilizing. By the fall of next year a substantial inflationary gap may have developed. The Bank may then call for a contractionary policy, but the full effects of the monetary expansion initiated nine months earlier is just being felt—so an expansionary monetary stimulus is adding to the existing inflationary gap. If the Bank now applies the monetary brakes by contracting the money supply, the full effects of this move will not be felt for another 18 months. By that time a contraction may have already set in because of the natural cyclical forces of the economy. If so, the delayed effects of the monetary policy may turn a minor downturn into a major recession.

The long execution lag of monetary policy makes monetary fine tuning difficult, and it may make it destabilizing.

If the execution lag were known with certainty, it could be built into the Bank's calculations. But the fact that the lag is highly variable makes this nearly impossible. Of course, when a persistent gap has existed and is predicted to continue for a long time, monetary policy may be stabilizing even when its effects occur after a long time lag.

A Monetary Rule?

The dismal record of monetary policy lent force to the monetarists' persistent criticisms of monetary fine tuning. Monetarists argue that (1) monetary policy is a potent force of expansionary and contractionary pressures; (2) monetary policy works with lags that are both long and variable; and (3) central banks are often given to sudden and strong reversals of their policy stance. Consequently monetary policy has a destabilizing effect on the economy, the policy itself accentuating rather than dampening the economy's natural cyclical swings.

Monetarists argue from this position that the stability of the economy would be much improved if the Bank of Canada stopped trying to stabilize it. What then should the Bank do? Since growth of population and of productivity lead to a rising level of output, the Bank ought to provide the extra money needed to allow the holding of additional transactions, precautionary, and speculative balances as real income and wealth rise over time.

According to the monetarists, the Bank should expand the money supply year in and year out at a constant rate equal to the rate of growth of real income. When the growth rate changes, the Bank can adjust its rate of monetary expansion. It should not, however, alter this rate with a view to stabilizing the economy against short-term fluctuations.

Theorists have conducted a long debate over this monetarist recommendation. The outcome is that, at least in many standard models of the economy, cyclical fluctuations can be made smaller with the best fine tuning policy than they are with a constant-rate rule. However:

Experience of the 1970s convinced many that whatever may be true of the best conceivable monetary policy, the Bank of Canada's actual policy made cyclical fluctuations much larger than they would have been under a constant-rate rule.

Unfortunately, however, experiences in Canada in the late 1970s and in the United States in the early 1980s have shown that the demand for money can be quite unstable. A money supply rule in the face of an unstable demand for money is a guarantee of monetary shocks to the economy, rather than of monetary stability.

MONETARY POLICY IN ACTION

Interest Rate Targeting: 1950s to 1975

Throughout the 1950s and 1960s, the Bank of Canada used interest rates as its main intermediate target. In spite of difficulties in judging the stance of monetary policy by observing interest rates in some periods, there are also periods when the stance was clear. For example, there is little doubt that monetary policy was contractionary in 1968–69 when the Bank tried to stop Canada from im-

porting the U.S. inflation.[5] There is also little doubt that monetary policy was quite expansionary in the early 1970s. The problem with that period was not that monetary policy could not control aggregate demand, but that the position of the aggregate demand curve was misjudged. As discussed more fully on pages 720–723, various changes in the labor market had shifted the *LRAS* curve to the left. Thus monetary policy was expansionary in the mistaken opinion that there was still a GNP gap to be removed, when in reality the policy was creating a growing GNP gap.

By 1974 inflation was close to the double-digit level. Then the first OPEC supply-side shock sent oil prices, and then the general price level, soaring. Inflation accelerated as output fell and unemployment grew. This stagflation, which seemed a total mystery then, is now seen to be a result of a falling *AD* curve combined with a rising *AS* curve.

At the time, monetary growth in many countries was very high in order to validate the double-digit inflation. Unhappy with their countries' accelerating inflation, many central banks (including the Bank of Canada) adopted money supply targets and sought to reduce the rate of money supply growth.

Monetary Gradualism: 1975–1980

In 1975 the Bank of Canada announced a policy of "monetary gradualism." The rate of increase in the money supply (narrowly defined as M1) was to be reduced gradually in an effort to reduce the inflation rate gradually. To accomplish this, a target range for money supply growth was to be stated publicly and periodically revised downward.

The first target range was set at 10 to 15 percent growth per year. The first reduction, to a range of 8 to 12 percent, came in August 1976, and a lower range of 7 to 11 percent was adopted in October 1977. Successive steps further reduced the range; in mid February 1981 the target range was 4 to 8 percent. The Bank was quite successful at keeping

[5] The attempt was frustrated by the Bank's commitment to a fixed rate of exchange between the Canadian dollar and the U.S. dollar. As we shall see in Chapter 39, monetary policy cannot simultaneously control the money supply and the exchange rate.

actual money growth inside the target range, although there was considerable movement within that range. But the success in reducing monetary growth was not matched by success in reducing the rate of inflation. After some reduction in the early stages of gradualism, the inflation rate again accelerated, and by the end of the decade it was not far below the rate ruling when the policy was introduced in 1975.

The gradual monetary restraint sought through money supply control was vitiated by offsetting shifts in the demand for money. The rising inflation rates of the 1970s raised the cost of holding non-interest-bearing M1 balances, since one consequence of rapid inflation is a high nominal rate of interest. This provides an incentive to economize on M1 balances and invest the funds instead in interest-earning assets.

A series of spectacular institutional changes showed just how adaptive the financial system is to changes in the needs of its users—many of these changes were noted in Chapter 33. Firms learned how to reduce their M1 balances by careful cash management. Temporarily unneeded M1 balances were lent out at interest, often for periods measured only in hours. In some countries funds were even moved to banks in remote areas where cheques were cleared once rather than twice a day, so that once cheques were cleared, cash managers knew they had the use of their remaining balances for a whole 24 hours! Banks introduced automatic transfer systems where money could be held in interest-earning accounts and transferred to chequing accounts only when needed. The old savings account, where interest was paid on the minimum monthly balance, gave way to the daily interest account, where interest was paid each day on the minimum daily balance.

These and a host of other changes made alternative methods of holding balances more lucrative while allowing former M1 balances to be converted into these alternatives. As a result, the demand for M1 balances often fell faster than the supply was being restricted. Thus M1 control did not always create the desired conditions of tight money.

In 1982 the Bank of Canada formally abandoned monetary targeting, although many commentators felt that it had really abandoned the policy in mid 1981 when it allowed the money supply to fall well below the target range and focused considerable attention on propping up the exchange rate. It remained committed to trying to control the economy through aggregate demand. It stated, however, that no observed relation between M1 or any other monetary magnitude on the one hand, and national income on the other hand, was stable enough to make complete reliance on monetary targets useful.

Monetary Stringency: 1981–1983

The first half of the 1980s saw an extremely restrictive monetary policy, one that reduced inflation to low levels, but at the cost of a very severe recession. Since during this period the Bank of Canada was mainly following the lead of the U.S. Federal Reserve System (the Fed), the period is best studied by observing the forces operating in the United States.

The United States Experience

In 1980 the Fed switched from a regime of interest rate control to a regime of base control. Although this policy requires that interest rates be free to find their own level, many economists did not expect the degree of interest rate volatility shown in Figure 35-1. The sharp rise in interest rates in late 1980 helped choke off the recovery that had just started. The rise in rates in early 1982 fed the downturn and helped make it the most serious recession since the 1930s. Not only were interest rates variable over this period, the average level of both real and nominal rates was very high.

These interest rates, and the recession they wrought, were more severe than might have been expected from the monetary policy that was planned. What happened to cause the high interest rates and the severe recession in the face of this moderate slowdown in the rate of growth of the money supply?

Changes in money demand. Once again, the key to the puzzle lay in the relation between the

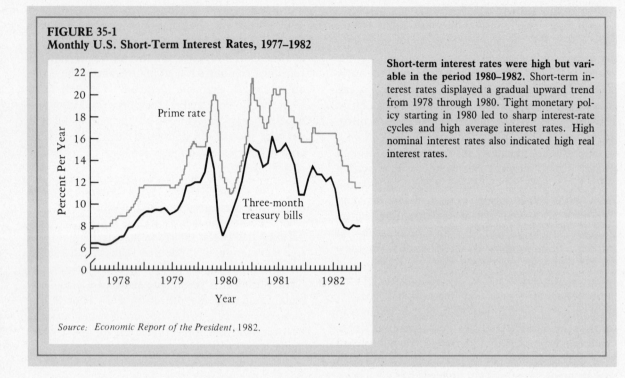

FIGURE 35-1
Monthly U.S. Short-Term Interest Rates, 1977–1982

Short-term interest rates were high but variable in the period 1980–1982. Short-term interest rates displayed a gradual upward trend from 1978 through 1980. Tight monetary policy starting in 1980 led to sharp interest-rate cycles and high average interest rates. High nominal interest rates also indicated high real interest rates.

Source: *Economic Report of the President*, 1982.

demand for money and nominal national income. Historically the demand for M1 had been growing about 3 percent slower than nominal income, indicating that the public was gradually economizing on money balances. The Fed projected this past trend and estimated that the demand for money would continue to grow at a rate slower than that of nominal income. The Fed then set a target growth rate for M1 sufficient to allow an increase in nominal income (PY) in excess of the expected rise in the price level (P). This would have allowed some increase, therefore, in real output (Y).

But the Fed's projections were mistaken. The demand for money grew only 1 percentage more slowly than nominal income in 1981 and about 5 percent *faster* than nominal income in 1982 (thus being opposite to some of the changes which upset Canadian monetary policy in the 1970s). As a result of this unexpected surge in the demand for money, there was a severe money shortage—that is, monetary policy was much tighter than the Fed had

expected. This was not because money supply targets were missed, but because money demand was again misestimated—this time it was underestimated.

How did the Fed react to this change in money demand? In part the Fed's reaction was to raise the level of monetary growth. In late 1981 M1 growth was allowed to run up quite rapidly (reaching an annual rate of 14.5 percent in the third quarter), so that at the end of the year, M1 was well above its target range. But basically the Fed stuck to its monetary targets, and as a result it pursued very restrictive monetary policy. This created a heated controversy in the financial press and caused many critics to attack the Fed's policies.

In February 1982 the Fed decided that the rapid increase in M1 demand in late 1981 was temporary and reaffirmed its money growth targets for 1982. Consequently the Fed slowed down the expansion of reserves in the next few months. By June 1982

M1 was back in its target range. But the serious weakness in the economy and the "room for monetary ease" created by the return of M1 to its target range led to a loosening of monetary policy in the second half of 1982.

Why did the Fed allow this severely contractionary policy to persist so long? One possibility is that the Fed was actually quite happy to have a very contractionary policy. Gradualist policies, in Canada from 1975 to 1980 and previously in the United States, had failed to have any marked effect on inflation, and many observers had come to the view that only a sharp contraction would lower inflationary expectations and so allow the actual inflation rate to fall.

Another possibility is that having announced its targets for monetary growth, the Fed had to adhere to them in order to maintain its own credibility. Failure to meet the targets, this argument runs, would undermine belief in the Fed's commitment to reducing inflation. Such a loss of confidence would in turn work to make interest rates and the actual inflation rate respond sluggishly to the Fed's policies.

The Canadian Reaction

The very tight monetary policy in the United States led to similar monetary restraint in Canada. As in the United States, there is a question about why this was done. Two reasons are probably important. One is that the high degree of integration of capital markets means there is not very much scope for Canadian interest rates to be held far below U.S. rates. (This matter is discussed further in Chapter 39.) Insofar as the Bank of Canada had some freedom to hold rates below those in the United States, it did not exercise its freedom (see Figure 35-2). The second reason suggested is that, discouraged by the failure of gradualism to control inflation, the Bank of Canada welcomed the opportunity to follow the United States in a more severe bout of monetary restraint. By the early 1980s, many commentators had begun to wonder if the problem of inflation was intractable. If it could be solved, the failure of gradualism suggested

that a severe jolt of very restrictive policy might be needed to do the job.

This, then, is the story of recent monetary policy. The outcome of the experiment will be assessed in the next chapter, when we have studied the theory of inflation in more detail.

Monetary Policy: Some Interim Conclusions

Most economists agree that rapid changes in the money supply have major effects on aggregate demand. They also agree that slowing the rate of monetary expansion is a necessary condition for avoiding rapid inflations. Furthermore, many economists hold that if we knew enough, changes in the money supply could be used to help the government stabilize the economy by avoiding the extremes of large inflationary and deflationary gaps.

There is disagreement, however, on a number of important issues that we summarize here and discuss in more detail in Part Ten.

1. Is control of the money supply a sufficient means of controlling inflation? Some economists answer yes. Others think not and look to causes of inflation in addition to monetary expansion.

2. How strong is the influence of monetary policy on aggregate expenditure? Do small changes in the money supply yield large changes in aggregate expenditure, or are large changes in monetary magnitudes needed to induce desired changes in aggregated expenditure? We discussed this issue in Chapter 34, and we shall return to it later.

3. If stabilization policy is to be used, what are the appropriate relative roles of monetary and fiscal policies? At one extreme some economists give monetary policy a relatively minor role as a supplement to fiscal policy; at the other extreme some economists give it the exclusive role, arguing that fiscal policy is effective only to the extent that it causes changes in the money supply.

4. Although the experience of the 1970s convinced many economists that monetary policy had in fact been a serious destabilizer, controversy con-

FIGURE 35-2
U.S. and Canadian Short-Term Interest Rates, 1979–1982

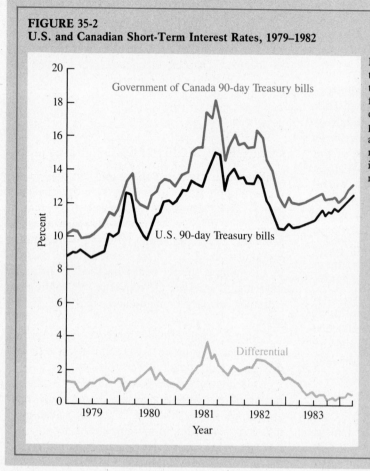

Increases in Canadian short-term rates over the period 1980–1981 more than matched those in the United States. The positive differential shows that Canadian short-term interest rates typically exceed their U.S. counterparts. When U.S. rates rose sharply in late 1980 and into 1981, Canadian rates rose at least as much; in fact, by mid 1981 the differential had increased, showing that Canadian rates had risen *more* than U.S. rates.

tinues on the conclusion to be drawn from this unhappy experience. Should we give up trying to follow a discretionary monetary stabilization policy and instead adopt a fixed rule of monetary expansion, or should we merely try to do better with discretionary policy next time?

5. With continued financial innovation and shifts in demands for various monetary assets, will any conceivable monetary rule have a stabilizing effect on the economy? In adopting such a rule, won't the Bank of Canada have to continually alter both the magnitude on which it is targeting and the range of values targeted?

SUMMARY

1. All advanced free-market economies have a central bank that serves as banker for private banks, banker for the government, controller and regulator of the money supply, and regulator and supporter of money markets.

2. The major tool the central bank uses to control the supply of money is open market operations. Purchases of bonds on the open market expand the money supply because they create new deposits that permit (but do not force) a multiple expansion of bank credit. Sales on the open market reduce bank reserves and force a multiple contraction of bank credit on the part of all banks that do not have excess reserves.

3. The ultimate objectives of monetary policy are called *policy variables*. In principle these include real national income and the rate of change of the price level. However, in practice nominal income is often taken to be the policy variable, since the Bank of Canada cannot expect to be able to influence the composition of changes in nominal income between real growth and inflation. Interest rates are also sometimes taken to be a policy variable.

4. Where the Bank of Canada cannot influence its policy variables directly, it must work through policy instruments that it can control and that will in turn influence its policy variables. Intermediate targets are used to guide decisions about policy instruments. The money supply and the interest rate may both be either intermediate targets or policy instruments.

5. National income can be influenced by open market operations. To reduce national income the Bank sells bonds on the open market, thereby reducing reserves, driving up the rate of interest, and shifting the *AD* curve to the left. To increase national income the Bank buys bonds on the open market, thereby increasing reserves, driving down the rate of interest, and shifting the *AD* curve to the right.

6. Since it cannot control both independently, the Bank must choose between the interest rate and the money supply as its intermediate target.

7. In the period up to 1975, the Bank of Canada used interest rates as its main intermediate target. In 1975 the Bank converted to monetarism in that it based its monetary policy on targets for the rate of increase of the money supply (defined as M1).

8. In the period of monetary gradualism from 1975 to 1980, the stance of monetary policy was meant to be restrictive by gradually reducing the rate of increase of the money supply. However, due to innovations in banking practices, the demand for M1 often fell faster than the supply, making monetary policy expansive rather than restrictive.

9. In the period of stringency (1981–1983) the Fed, followed by the Bank of Canada, adopted a policy of severe monetary restraint. Interest rates soared to unprecedented heights, and the aggregate demand curves of both countries were driven sharply to the left.

10. It is generally agreed that rapid changes in the money supply and interest rates can have large effects on the economy. There is disagreement, however, on how much monetary policy can and should be used as a device for stabilizing the economy or coping with temporary bouts of rising prices.

TOPICS FOR REVIEW

Functions of a central bank
The Bank rate
Open market operations
Policy variables, policy instruments, and intermediate targets
The variability of monetary policy and monetary rules
The appropriateness of money supply targets when money demand is shifting

DISCUSSION QUESTIONS

1. It is often said that an expansionary monetary policy is like "pushing on a string." What is meant by such a statement? How does this contrast with a contractionary monetary policy?

2. In the late summer of 1983, a debate raged among critics of the Bank of Canada. One group held that monetary policy was too restrictive since high real interest rates were unnecessarily threatening the recovery from the 1982 recession. Another group held that monetary policy was too expansionary since high rates of growth of the money supply portended a rebounding of inflation. Examine the statistics to see what has happened since to interest rates, money supply, inflation, and output, and evaluate the arguments made by the two groups.

3. The Federal Reserve Board runs a facility in Culpeper, Virginia, that costs $1.8 million per year to maintain and to guard against robbery, according to Senator William Proxmire of Wisconsin. Inside this "Culpeper switch," a dugout in the side of a mountain, the government has hidden $4 billion in new currency for the purpose, it says, of "providing a hedge against any nuclear attack that would wipe out the nation's money supply." Comment on the sense of this policy.

4. Describe the chief weapons of monetary policy available to the Bank of Canada and indicate whether, and if so how, they might be used for the following purposes:
   a. to create a mild tightening of bank credit
   b. to signal that the Bank favors a sharp curtailment of bank lending
   c. to permit an expansion of bank credit with existing reserves
   d. to supply banks and the public with a temporary increase of currency for Christmas shopping

5. In what situations might the following pairs of objectives come into conflict?
   a. keeping the cost of government finance low *and* using monetary policy to change aggregate demand
   b. signaling a tighter monetary policy by raising interest rates *and* accommodating the public's desire for money
   c. maintaining stable interest rates *and* controlling inflation

6. In February 1980 *Newsweek* reported that, "In the fight on inflation, the Fed admits it has underestimated the U.S. monetary supply" and quoted a Fed official as saying, "There is no doubt that [monetary] policy has not been as restrained as was intended." Why should underestimating the money supply make monetary policy less anti-inflationary than was intended?

7. Nobel Laureate Milton Friedman has accused the Fed of following "an unstable monetary policy," arguing that while the Fed "has given lip service to controlling the quantity of money . . . it has given its heart to controlling interest rates." Why might the desire to stabilize interest rates create an "unstable" monetary policy?

8. In 1982 the Bank of Canada stopped formally announcing and trying to attain precise target rates of growth for some monetary aggregate. Discuss the reasons behind this, and indicate whether you agree with the Bank's decision.

PART TEN
MACROECONOMIC
PROBLEMS

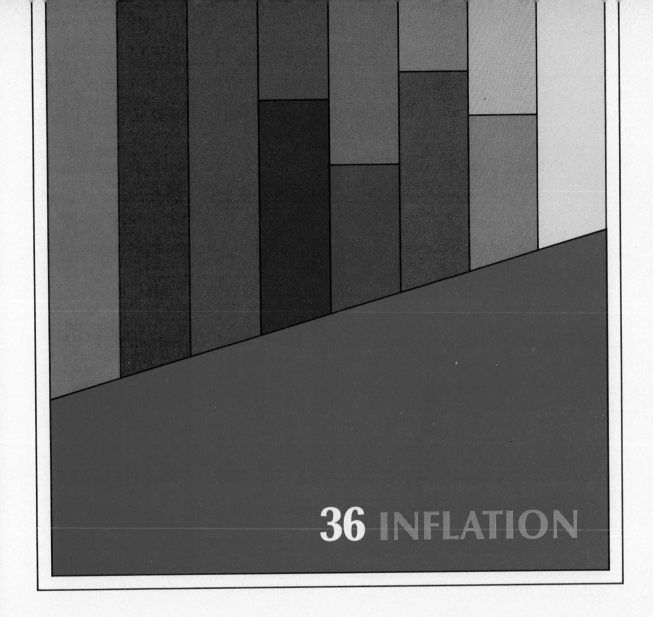

36 INFLATION

If you look again at Figure 26-1 on page 466, you will see that for 20 years following World War II, inflation remained low. The only exceptions were the "bubbles" following World War II and the Korean War. During the last half of the 1960s, however, the inflation rate slowly inched upward. It reached the double-digit range in the mid 1970s. By then inflation had been declared public enemy number one. Even more worrisome, it fell only slightly in the face of a concerted attack during the late 1970s, rose again to the double-digit level in 1980, and then remained quite stubborn in the face of the great recession of 1981–1982. Finally, in 1983 inflation fell dramatically. In 1984 it continued to drift down slowly, reaching 4 percent. Although this was an improvement over the double-digit inflation rates experienced earlier, 4 percent is historically a very high inflation rate to emerge from a serious recession with.

What were the causes of the inflation? How was

BOX 36–1 INFLATION SEMANTICS

The distinction between once-and-for-all and continuing rises in the price level is important. Some economists have sought to emphasize it by reserving the term *inflation* for a *continuing* or *sustained* rise in the price level while using other terms such as *a rise in the price level* for a *once-and-for-all* increase.

One difficulty with this is that it is counter to ordinary usage, where inflation refers to any rise in the price level. Indeed, using the restricted definition causes difficulty when communicating with the public. If we were to use it, we would have to keep saying such things as "only some of the current rise in prices is an inflation, while the rest is merely a rise in the price level," and "we won't know whether or not the current rise in the price level is an inflation or not until we see if it is sustained."

In this book we use the term *inflation* as it is used in everyday speech to mean any rise in the price level. We then describe the key distinction outlined above by referring to *temporary* or *once-and-for-all* bursts of inflation on the one hand and to *continuing* or *sustained* inflations on the other.

No matter of substance turns on the terms that we use to refer to clearly defined concepts. Where we use the terms *sustained* or *continuing* inflation and *temporary* inflation, or their equivalents, others use the terms *inflation* and *a rise in the price level*.

This discussion is important solely because students need to guard against being confused by different usages. Our selection of terms reflects only a desire to keep our language as close as possible to everyday usage.

---

the great anti-inflationary war of the late 1970s and early 1980s fought? Can we prevent inflation from skyrocketing into the double-digit range again? Can we ever hope to eliminate inflation altogether?

MONETARY POLICY AND INFLATION

We start by noting a key distinction:

It is important to distinguish between the forces that cause a once-and-for-all increase in the price level and the forces that can cause a sustained increase.

Failure to make this distinction often leads to much confusion. The distinction and some related terminology are discussed in Box 36-1.

In previous chapters we saw that shifts in either the short-run aggregate supply curve or the aggregate demand curve cause a once-and-for-all burst of inflation. In Chapter 34 we encountered the

important result that *for any inflation to be sustained, it must be accompanied by increases in the money supply.* Thus monetary responses matter. To see how, we begin with an economy in long-run equilibrium: The price level is stable and output is at its potential, or full employment, level. We then consider three different types of shocks that can hit the economy.

Supply Shocks

Suppose the *SRAS* curve shifts upward. The price level rises and output falls. The rise in the price level shows up as a temporary burst of inflation. What happens next depends upon whether the shock to the *SRAS* curve is an isolated event or one of a series of recurring shocks. What happens also depends upon whether or not the Bank of Canada responds to the fall in output by increasing the money supply. This is referred to as *accommodating* the supply shock.

Isolated Supply Shocks

First suppose that the shift in the *SRAS* curve is an isolated event, say, a once-and-for-all increase in the cost of imported raw materials. How does monetary policy affect the response to such an isolated supply shock?

No monetary accommodation. The upward shift in the *SRAS* curve drives income below its full-employment level, opening up a recessionary gap. Pressure now mounts for wages and other factor costs to fall. When they do, the *SRAS* curve shifts downward, causing a return of income to full employment and a fall in the price level. In this case, the period of positive inflation accompanying the original supply shock will be followed by negative inflation (i.e., deflation) until the original long-run equilibrium is re-established. This was shown in Figure 34-6 on page 649. Given that wages and prices fall slowly, the recovery to full employment may take a long time.

Monetary accommodation. Now let us see what happens if the money supply *is* changed in response to the isolated supply shock.

Suppose the Bank of Canada reacts to the fall in national income by increasing the money supply. This shifts the *AD* curve upward and causes both the price level and output to *rise*. When the recessionary gap has been eliminated, the price level, rather than falling back to its original value, will have risen further. The effects are illustrated in Figure 36-1.

Monetary accommodation of a supply shock causes the initial rise in the price level to be followed by a further rise, resulting in a higher final price level than if the recessionary gap were relied on to force wages and prices down.

The monetary authorities might decide to accommodate because relying on wage deflation forces the economy to suffer through an extended slump. Monetary accommodation could return the

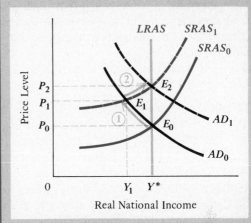

FIGURE 36-1
Monetary Accommodation of a Single Supply Shock

Monetary accommodation of a single supply shock causes costs, the price level, and money supply all to move in the same direction. A supply shock causes the *SRAS* curve to shift upward from $SRAS_0$ to $SRAS_1$, as shown by arrow ①. Equilibrium is established at E_1.

If there is no monetary accommodation, the unemployment would put downward pressure on wages and other costs, causing the *SRAS* curve to shift slowly back to $SRAS_0$. Prices would fall and output would rise until the original equilibrium was restored.

Monetary accommodation shifts the aggregate demand curve upward from AD_0 to AD_1, as shown by arrow ②. This reestablishes full employment equilibrium at E_2 but with a higher price level, P_2.

economy to full employment quickly, but at the cost of a once-and-for-all increase in the price level.

Repeated Supply Shocks

Our treatment up to now has assumed that a recessionary gap would be associated with *downward* pressure on wages. This implies that labor markets behave much like commodity markets: Wages fall when there is excess supply and rise only when there is excess demand.

Now assume, however, that powerful unions are

able to raise wages in the absence of excess demand for labor and even in the face of significant excess supply. Large manufacturing firms pass on these higher wages in the form of higher prices. This type of supply shock causes **wage-cost push inflation**: an increase in the price level due to increases in money wages that are not associated with excess demand for labor.

How does monetary policy affect the response to such repeated supply shocks?

No monetary accommodation. First, suppose the Bank of Canada does not accommodate these shocks. The initial effect is that a recessionary gap opens up (equal to Y_1Y^* in Figure 36-1). If unions continue to negotiate increases in wages, subjecting the economy to further supply shocks, prices will continue to rise and output will continue to fall. Eventually the trade-off between higher wages and unemployment will become obvious to everyone.

Might not really powerful unions continue to force wages up despite this realization? As long as they did so, the recessionary gap would go on growing until, finally, unemployment reached 100 percent. Of course this will not happen because long before everyone is unemployed, unions will cease forcing up wages in order to maintain jobs for those who are still employed.

Once the wage-cost push ceases, there are two possible scenarios. First, the unions may succeed in holding onto their high wages, although they will not push for further increases. The economy then comes to rest with a stable price level and a large recessionary gap. Second, the persistent unemployment may eventually erode the power of the unions so that wages begin to fall. In this case the supply shock is reversed, and the *SRAS* curve shifts downward until full employment is eventually restored.

Supply shocks caused by wage-cost push have natural correctives in the restraining pressures of rising unemployment on further wage push and in the possible erosion of the power of unions to hold wages above the level that would produce full employment.

Monetary accommodation. Now suppose that the Bank of Canada accommodates the shock with

an increase in the money supply, thus shifting the aggregate demand curve to the right, as shown in Figure 36-1. In the new full-employment equilibrium both money wages and prices have risen. The rise in wages has been offset by a rise in prices. Workers are no better off than they were originally, although those who remained in jobs were better off in the transition after wages had risen (taking equilibrium to E_1 in Figure 36-1) but before the price level had risen (taking equilibrium to E_2 in Figure 36-1).

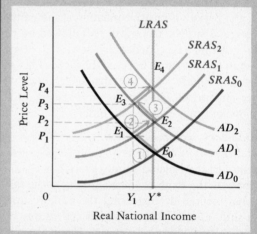

FIGURE 36-2
Monetary Accommodation of a Repeated Supply Shock

Monetary accommodation of a repeated supply shock causes a continuous inflation in the absence of excess demand. The initial equilibrium is at E_0. A supply shock then takes equilibrium to E_1, just as in Figure 36-1. This is the stagflation phase of rising prices and falling output indicated by arrow ①.

The Bank of Canada then accommodates the supply shock by increasing the money supply, taking the aggregate demand curve to AD_1 and equilibrium to E_2. This is the expansionary phase of rising prices and rising output indicated by arrow ②.

Repeated supply shock followed by monetary accommodation takes equilibrium to E_3 (arrow ③) and then to E_4 (arrow ④). As long as the supply shocks and the monetary accommodation continue, the inflation continues.

The stage is now set for the unions to try again. If they succeed in negotiating further increases in money wages, they will hit the economy with another supply shock. If the Bank of Canada accommodates the shock, full employment is maintained but at the cost of a further round of inflation. If this process goes on continuously, it can give rise to a continuous wage-cost push inflation. The wage-cost push tends to cause a stagflation, with rising prices and falling output. Monetary accommodation tends to reinforce the rise in prices but to offset the fall in output. This case is illustrated in Figure 36-2.

Two things are required for wage-cost push inflation to continue. First, powerful unions must press for, and employers must grant, increases in money wages even in the absence of excess demand for labor and goods. Second, governments must accommodate the resulting inflation by increasing the money supply and so prevent the unemployment that would otherwise occur.

Is wage-cost push inflation a real possibility? As far back as the 1940s early Keynesians were worried that, once the government was committed to maintaining full employment, much of the discipline of the market would be removed from wage bargains. The scramble of every group trying to get ahead of every other group would lead to a wage-cost push inflation. The commitment to full employment would then lead to accommodating increases in the money supply.

Many economists believe this process has actually occurred in those countries of Western Europe where unions are very strong. There is less consensus that it has occurred in the United States or Canada.

Is Monetary Accommodation Desirable?

Once started, the spiral of wage-price-wage increases can be halted only if the monetary authorities stop accommodating the shocks. The longer they wait to do so, the more ingrained will be the expectation that they will continue to accommodate. It is argued that this will make wages more resistant to downward pressure arising from un-

employment. Hence, the argument runs, it is best never to let the process get started. One way to ensure this is to refuse to accommodate any supply shock whatsoever.

To some people caution dictates that no supply shocks be accommodated lest a wage-price-wage spiral be set up. Others would be willing to risk accommodating obviously isolated shocks in order to avoid the severe, though transitory, recessions that otherwise accompany them.

Demand Shocks

Now assume that the aggregate demand curve shifts rightward. This causes the price level and output to rise, as was shown in Figure 34-5 on page 648. The shift in the *AD* curve could have been caused by either an increase in autonomous expenditure or an increase in the money supply.[1]

As with a supply shock, it is important to distinguish between those cases where the Bank of Canada reacts and those where it does not. With a demand shock, reaction by the Bank is referred to as monetary *validation*. (Note the distinction: response to a *supply* shock is, as we have seen, referred to as monetary *accommodation*. It is important to realize that *any* expansionary monetary policy works through a rightward shift of the *AD* curve. The distinction between monetary accommodation and validation depends on what disturbance the Bank is reacting to, not on how the monetary policy operates.)

How does monetary validation affect the reaction to a demand shock?

No Monetary Validation

Because output is now above the full-employment level, there is an inflationary gap. Upward pressure will soon cause wages and other costs to rise, shifting the *SRAS* curve upward. As long as the Bank holds the money supply constant, the rise

---

[1] As we saw in Chapter 34, an increase in the money supply works through the transmission mechanism—excess supply of money, higher price of bonds, lower interest rates, increased investment expenditure—to shift the *AD* curve rightward.

in the price level brings the monetary adjustment mechanism into play: The economy moves upward to the left along the fixed *AD* curve. The rise in the price level acts to reduce the inflationary gap. Eventually the gap is eliminated as equilibrium is established at a higher, but stable, price level, with income at its potential level. In this case the initial period of positive inflation is followed by further inflation that lasts only until the new equilibrium is reached.

Monetary Validation

Next, suppose that following a demand shock that created an inflationary gap, the Bank of Canada frustrates the monetary adjustment mechanism by increasing the money supply when output starts to fall. Two forces are now brought into play. Spurred by the inflationary gap, the wage increases cause the *SRAS* curve to shift upward. Fueled by monetary policy, the *AD* curve shifts upward. As a result, the price level rises but output need not fall. Indeed, if the shift in the *AD* curve exactly offsets the shift in the *SRAS* curve, the inflationary gap will remain constant. This is shown in Figure 36-3.[2]

Validation of a demand shock turns what would have been a transitory inflation into a classic, sustained inflation fueled by monetary expansion.

The subsequent shifts in the *AD* curve that perpetuate the inflationary gap are caused by monetary forces.

Inflation as a monetary phenomenon. Now we can see the sense in which "inflation is a monetary phenomenon." If a rise in prices is to go on continuously, it must be accompanied by continuing increases in the money supply. This is true regardless of the shock that set it in motion.

[2] Notice that although we distinguish between a single supply shock and a continuing one, we do not make a similar distinction with a demand shock. This is because the accommodation of a single supply shock restores full-employment equilibrium, whereas the validation of a demand shock perpetuates the disequilibrium.

The stronger statement that "inflation is everywhere and always a monetary phenomenon" must rely on the definition of inflation discussed in Box

FIGURE 36-3
Monetary Validation of a Demand-Shock Inflation

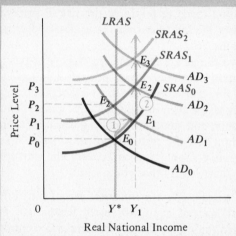

Shifts in the *AD* curve due to increases in the money supply can offset the effects of shifts in the *SRAS* curve due to increases in wages that result from an inflationary gap. The initial equilibrium is at E_0, with full employment income Y^* and price level P_0.

(a) A demand shock shifts the aggregate demand curve to AD_1, raising income along arrow ① to Y_1 and the price level to P_1. With equilibrium at E_1, there is an inflationary gap causing wages to rise and shifting the *SRAS* curve upward. The operation of the monetary adjustment mechanism would entail a movement along AD_1 to a new equilibrium at E'_2, where the inflationary gap is eliminated.

(b) However, if the money supply is increased, the *AD* curve is shifted to the right, frustrating the monetary adjustment mechanism. When the *SRAS* curve has reached $SRAS_1$, the money supply is increased sufficiently to take the *AD* curve to AD_2. When the *SRAS* curve reaches $SRAS_2$, *AD* is shifted to AD_3, and so on. This takes the economy on the path indicated by arrow ②, through E_2 and E_3, with a persistent inflationary gap and a continuously rising price level, that is, a sustained inflation.

36-1. We have seen that many forces from both the demand and the supply side can cause the price level to rise. Such "inflations" can continue for some time without monetary expansion although, as we have also seen, the rise in prices must eventually come to a halt unless monetary expansion occurs.

The monetary expansion that allows an inflation to continue can sometimes be a response to some other shock. For example, if wage-cost push were occurring, the Bank of Canada might accommodate it in order to avoid the unemployment that would otherwise result. While the monetary expansion is necessary if the inflation is to be sustained, the initiating shock is, in this case, a supply shock.

In other cases the monetary expansion may itself be a part of the initiating shock, as when a government budget deficit is financed by printing money. Assume, for example, that the government increases its expenditure, shifting the aggregate demand curve and creating an inflationary gap, and that the new expenditure is financed by selling bonds to the Bank of Canada. This, as we have seen, leads to an expansion in the money supply. In this case the deficit provides the required monetary validation for the inflation to continue.

A Recap

We have now reached some important conclusions.

1. **Without monetary accommodation, supply shocks cause temporary bursts of inflation accompanied by recessionary gaps. The gaps are removed if and when wages fall, restoring potential income at the initial price level.**
2. **Without monetary validation, demand shocks cause temporary bursts of inflation accompanied by inflationary gaps. The gaps are removed as wages rise, restoring potential income at a higher price level.**
3. **With an appropriate response of the Bank of Canada, an inflation initiated by supply or demand shocks can continue indefinitely: an ever-increasing money supply is necessary for an ever-continuing inflation.**

SUSTAINED INFLATION

A Decade of Inflation

The great stagflation of 1974–1975 saw inflation reach the double-digit level for the first time in 30 years. Inflation then fell in 1976, and in the next three years it stayed below 10 percent. However, as the recovery proceeded over the last years of the decade, inflation crept up and was again in the double-digit range as we entered the 1980s.

Two disturbing things about the 1970s were the failure of inflation to subside much below 5 percent despite the severe recession in 1974–1975 and the rebounding of inflation to over 9 percent as the economy recovered.

In 1979 the second OPEC oil price shock hit. The prices of energy and of such oil-related commodities as fertilizer and plastics soared. Many of these commodities were used as inputs in the production of other goods, so these price increases meant rising production costs. Then, as costs rose, the prices of all products that used these inputs rose. The annual inflation rate, as measured by the GNE deflator, reached 10.3 percent in 1979 and stayed in the double-digit range over the next four years.

It was clear from the rebound of inflation at the end of the 1970s that inflation had become entrenched in everyone's mind. Could inflation be tamed? Almost everyone agreed that a recession that was deep and long enough would do the job. But how long and how deep would the recession have to be? This was the key macro policy question in the early 1980s, and it will become the key question again whenever high inflation again becomes entrenched.

Before we can deal with this question, we must look in greater detail at what is involved in a sustained inflation. We have already stressed the role of monetary expansion in allowing the *AD* curve to shift up continually. We now focus on the forces that cause the *SRAS* curve to shift upward.

Wages and Inflation

The *SRAS* curve shifts upward when costs rise. We concentrate on wages as the most important element of costs. Changing profit margins are not an important part of the process of *continuing* inflation. Although profit margins do vary, they cannot account for a sustained inflation. Even wide variations from year to year in the profit margin cause only minor divergences between wage and price increases.[3]

Why Wages Change

Up to now it has been enough to say that an inflationary gap implies excess demand for labor, low unemployment, upward pressure on wages and hence an upward-shifting *SRAS* curve. We now look at three main forces that can cause wages to change at any given level of national income and thus shift the *SRAS* curve. First, we review the relation between demand forces, as indicated by the GNP gap, and wage changes.

Demand Forces

When there is excess demand there will be an inflationary gap. This puts upward pressure on wages, which shifts the *SRAS* curve upward and causes the price level to rise. When there is excess supply, there will be a recessionary gap. This puts

downward pressure on wages, which tends to shift the *SRAS* curve downward. The price level therefore falls. Only when there is neither excess demand nor excess supply is there no demand pressure on wages and hence on prices.[4] An increase in the price level that is due to the pressures of excess demand is called a **demand inflation**.

The natural rate of unemployment. Demand forces can be restated in terms of the concept of the **natural rate of unemployment**. We saw in Chapter 26 that unemployment is not zero at potential income because of substantial amounts of what can be broadly called *frictional unemployment*. The amount of unemployment that exists when national income is at its potential level is often called the *natural rate of unemployment* and symbolized U_N. It is all unemployment that is *not due to deficient aggregate demand*. These concepts are discussed in more detail in Chapter 37.

With an inflationary gap, national income exceeds potential income ($Y > Y^*$), and unemployment is less than the natural rate ($U < U_N$). With a recessionary gap, national income is less than potential income ($Y < Y^*$), and actual unemployment exceeds the natural rate ($U > U_N$).

When the unemployment rate is below the natural rate, and hence income is above potential, demand forces put upward pressure on wages. When the unemployment rate is above the natural rate, and hence income is below potential, demand forces will put downward pressure on wages.

One way of showing the influence of demand on wages (and hence on the *SRAS* curve) is in the relation called the **Phillips curve**, discussed in Box 36-2.

Expectational Forces

A second force that can influence wages is *expectations*. Suppose, for example, that both employers and employees expect that a 10 percent inflation will occur next year. Unions will start

---

[3] In case this important point is not obvious, here is a numerical example. Suppose that profits initially count for $.20 out of $1 of the market price of goods. If all other costs start to rise by 10 percent per year, the inflation rate could be held to zero *for one year* if profits fall to $.12 out of every $1 and to zero for *the second year* if profits fall to $.032. Such wild variations in the percentage of price accounted for by profits never occur in practice, yet in the face of a 10 percent rise in costs even these can hold the price level constant for only two years. Now consider variations in the other direction. If we again start with profits of $.20 of the sales dollar, then a 10 percent inflation in the face of constant costs would require that profits rise to $.30 in the first year and to $.41 in the second year. Such enormous changes in the markup over labor and capital costs (from 20/80 = 25 percent, to 30/80 = 37 percent, to 41/80 = 51 percent) never occur, so *sustained* inflations are not caused by increases in profit margins any more than they can be long held in check by decreases in profit margins.

[4] We are simplifying the discussion by ignoring the role of productivity changes. Such changes can alter the relationship between wages and prices.

negotiations from a *base* of a 10 percent increase in money wages, which would hold their real wages constant. Firms will also be inclined to begin bargaining by conceding at least a 10 percent increase in money wages, since they expect that the prices at which they sell their products will rise by 10 percent. *Starting from that base,* unions will then negotiate in an attempt to obtain some desired increase in their real wages. At this point such factors as profits, productivity, and bargaining power become important. The general expectation of an x percent inflation creates pressures for wages to rise by x percent and hence for the *SRAS* curve to shift upward by x percent.

When both labor and management expect inflation, their wage and price setting behavior will tend to cause inflation.

A rise in the price level due to expectations of inflation is called an **expectational inflation.**

Unsystematic Shocks

The third component of wage changes is unsystematic shocks. While such shocks may be very important for temporary bursts of inflation, they are less important for sustained inflations.

A shock not associated with either expected inflation or excess demand may still raise wages. For example, an especially strong new union or a weak management may result in an extra 1 percent increase in wages this year. Or a new government policy favorable to management, or one favorable to labor, may tip the wage bargain a bit one way or the other in any one year. All of these are summarized in the third component of wages, shock effects.

The Overall Effect

The overall change in wage costs may be shown as a result of the three basic forces just studied:

$$
\begin{array}{l}
\text{percentage} \\
\text{increase in} \\
\text{money wages}
\end{array}
=
\begin{array}{l}
\text{demand} \\
\text{effect}
\end{array}
+
\begin{array}{l}
\text{expected} \\
\text{inflation} \\
\text{rate}
\end{array}
+
\begin{array}{l}
\text{shock} \\
\text{effect}
\end{array}
$$

The demand effect is, as we have seen, positive when Y is greater than Y^*, negative when Y is less than Y^*, and zero when Y equals Y^*.

Expectations and Inflation in the Long Run

Look again at Figure 36-3, which represents a continuing inflation. The *SRAS* curve is shifting up in response to the inflationary gap. The *AD* curve is shifting up because the inflation is validated by increases in the money supply. What this analysis shows is that, if income is held above potential, the price level will be rising. We know that inflation is positive, but we do not know whether the inflation rate is rising or falling or is constant.

Suppose that initially there are no shocks and no expectations of inflation. What we have is thus a case of pure demand inflation, as illustrated in Figure 36-3. In order to maintain the inflationary gap and so sustain the inflation, the upward shift in the *SRAS* curve has to be accompanied by an increase in the money supply such that the *AD* curve shifts up by a like amount.

Eventually people will begin to expect that the monetary validation will continue and hence that prices will continue to rise. As these inflationary *expectations* emerge, additional upward pressure will be put on wage increases, as we saw above. In other words, the demand inflation has been augmented by an expectational inflation. The *SRAS* curve will now begin to shift upward more rapidly. In turn, the Bank of Canada must increase the rate at which the money supply is growing in order to maintain the level of output constant.

The Acceleration Hypothesis

The response of inflationary expectations to a persistent inflationary or recessionary gap leads to the **acceleration hypothesis:** When output is held above potential so that an inflationary gap persists, the rate of inflation will tend to accelerate; when output is held below potential so that a recessionary gap persists, the rate of inflation will tend to decelerate.

When there is an inflationary gap *and* monetary

BOX 36–2 THE PHILLIPS CURVE AND THE SHIFTING *SRAS* CURVE

In the early 1950s Professor A. W. Phillips of the London School of Economics was doing pathbreaking research on the pitfalls of fine tuning. His early models included an equation relating the rate of inflation to the difference between actual and potential income, $Y - Y^*$. Later he investigated the empirical underpinnings of this equation by studying the relation between the rate of increase of wage costs and the level of unemployment. In 1958 he reported that a stable relation had existed between these two variables for 100 years in the United Kingdom.

The relation which came to be called the *Phillips curve* is illustrated in the left figure. The curve shows money wages rising when unemployment is below the natural rate of unemployment, U_N, and falling when unemployment is

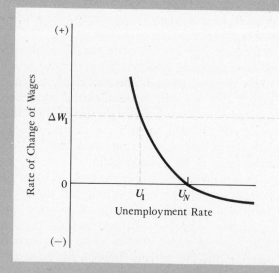
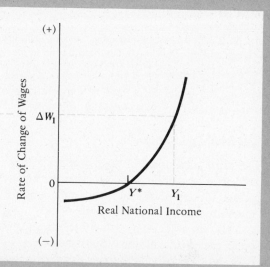

validation, the continuing inflation will lead to rising inflationary expectations. As we have seen, these expectations will mean rising pressure on wages. The rate at which the *SRAS* curve is shifting up will therefore increase. To maintain the given inflationary gap, the Bank of Canada will have to increase the rate of growth of the money supply so that the upward shifts in the *AD* curve will match those of the *SRAS* curve. As a result, the rate at which the price level is rising will itself be increasing. Of course this will then cause further rises in the expected inflation rate, and so the process continues.

As long as an inflationary gap persists, expectations of inflation will be rising, and this will lead to increases in the actual rate of inflation.

This is discussed further in Box 36-3.

The Natural Rate Hypothesis

Can inflation ever be constant? Or will the demand effect always lead to changing inflationary expectations and hence changing inflation?

The answer is that only when the demand effect is absent, so that all inflation is expectational infla-

above that critical level. (Note that the symbol ΔW here indicates the *percentage* change in money wages.)

Recall that the rate of unemployment is related negatively to national income: The higher is national income, the lower is unemployment. Thus the Phillips curve can also be drawn with national income on the horizontal axis, as in the figure on the right.

Both figures show the same information: Inflationary gaps (which correspond to low unemployment rates) are associated with rapid *increases* in wages, while recessionary gaps (which correspond to high unemployment rates), are associated with slow *decreases* in wages.

The Phillips curve must be distinguished from the *SRAS* curve. The *SRAS* curve has the *price level* on the vertical axis, while the Phillips curve has the *rate of wage inflation*. Therefore the Phillips curve tells us how fast the *SRAS* curve is shifting when actual income does not equal potential income.

Only when $Y = Y^*$ is the *SRAS* curve not shifting. When income is at its potential level, Y^*, aggregate demand for labor equals aggregate supply; the only unemployment would thus be frictional unemployment. There would be nei-

ther upward nor downward pressure of demand on wages. Thus the Phillips curve cuts the axis at potential income Y^* and at the corresponding level of unemployment U_N.

The Phillips curve soon became famous. It provided a link between national income models and labor markets. This link allowed macro economists to drop the uncomfortable assumption, which they had often been forced to use in many of their earlier formal models, that money wages were rigidly fixed and neither rose nor fell as national income varied.

Consider, for example, the situation shown in Figure 36-3, where the level of income determined by the *AD* and *SRAS* curves is Y_1. Plotting Y_1 on the Phillips curve in the left figure tells us that wage costs will be rising at ΔW_1. Then the *SRAS* curve in Figure 36-3 will be shifting upward by that amount. The same information can be seen in the right figure, where the unemployment associated with Y_1 is U_1.

To hold national income at Y_1 (and hence unemployment at U_1), the money supply must be increased at a rate sufficient to allow the *AD* curve to shift upward as fast as the *SRAS* curve.

tion, can steady inflation persist. When income is at potential so no demand effect is present, there is no pressure on inflation to accelerate or decelerate. As long as the upward shift in the *SRAS* curve, caused by inflationary expectations, is matched by the upward shift in the *AD* curve, caused by growth of the money supply, inflation will remain constant.

This case is illustrated in Figure 36-4. Wages are rising at a rate equal to expected inflation, and the money supply is being increased at the same rate. As a result, the *SRAS* curve and the *AD* curve are shifting up at the same rate. This means

that output is not changing and hence that no demand pressures on wages are being created. Wages are simply rising due to expectations of inflation, and these expectations are being fulfilled.

Steady inflation with full employment results when the rate of monetary growth, the rate of wage increase, the actual inflation rate, and expected inflation are all equal.

In this case, the inflation is not indicative of any disequilibrium; there is neither excess demand nor excess supply. Output is at its potential level and hence unemployment equals the natural rate. We

BOX 36–3 THE PHILLIPS CURVE AND ACCELERATING INFLATION

Professor Phillips was interested in studying the short-run behavior of an economy subjected to cyclical fluctuations (see Box 36-2 on pages 690–691). Others, however, treated the curve as establishing a long-term trade-off between inflation and unemployment.

Let the government fix income at Y_1 (and thus unemployment at U_1) in the figures, and validate the ensuing wage inflation of ΔW_1 per year. By doing this the government is apparently

able to choose a particular combination of inflation and unemployment, with lower levels of unemployment being attained at the cost of higher rates of inflation.

In the 1960s Phillips curves were fitted to the data for many countries, and governments made decisions about where they wished to be on the trade-off between inflation and unemployment. Then, in the late 1960s, in country after country, the rate of wage and price inflation associated

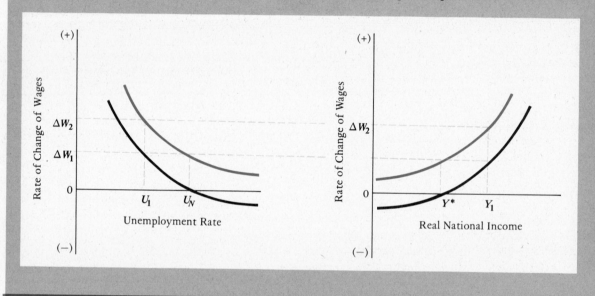

refer to this situation as an **equilibrium inflation:** All inflation is expectational.

The *natural rate hypothesis* holds that if the rate of monetary growth is fixed, then the economy will converge on a situation such as that depicted in Figure 36-4. The reasons can be understood in terms of the transition from Figure 36-3 to Figure 36-4. In Figure 36-3 the combination of the demand effect and rising expectations meant that the Bank of Canada had to *increase continuously the rate of growth of the money supply* to validate the ever-

faster upward shift in the *SRAS* curve. Suppose now that the Bank did not acquiese in this acceleration, but instead steadied the rate of monetary growth. Still, as long as the inflationary gap persists, expectations of inflation are rising. Thus the *SRAS* curve will be shifting up at an accelerating rate.

But because the rate of growth of the money supply has been stabilized, the *AD* curve will be shifting up at a constant rate. Because the *SRAS* curve will now be shifting upward faster than the

with any given level of unemployment began to rise. Instead of being stable, the Phillips curves were shifting upward. The explanation lay primarily in a shifting relation between the pressure of demand and wage increases due to expectations, as discussed in the text.

In the text we noted two important influences on wages, demand and expectations. It was gradually understood that the original Phillips curve concerned only the influence of demand and left out inflationary expectations. This proved to be an important and unfortunate omission. An increase in expected inflation shows up as an upward shift in the original Phillips curve drawn in the previous box.

The importance of expectations can be shown by drawing what is called an **expectations augmented Phillips curve,** as in the figures. The heights of the Phillips curves above the axis at Y^* and at U_N show the expected inflation rate. This is the amount that wages will rise when there is neither excess demand nor excess supply pressure in labor markets. The actual wage increase is shown by the augmented curve, with the increase in wages exceeding expected inflation when $Y > Y^*$ ($U < U_N$) and falling short of expected inflation when $Y < Y^*$ ($U > U_N$).

The demand component shown by the simple Phillips curve tells us by how much wage changes will deviate from the expected inflation rate.

Now we can see what was wrong with the idea of a stable inflation-unemployment trade-off. Targeting on income Y_1 or unemployment U_1 in the figure is fine as long as no inflation is *expected.* But once inflation comes to be expected, people will demand that much just to hold their own. The Phillips curve will shift upward to the position shown in the figure. Now there is inflation ΔW_2 because of the combined effects of expectations and a further increase because of the excess demand.

But this higher rate is above the expected rate. Once that higher rate comes to be expected, the Phillips curve will shift upward once again. *The expectations augmented Phillips curve shows that the actual rate of inflation exceeds the expected rate whenever there is an inflationary gap.* Sooner or later this will cause inflationary expectations to be shifted upward. The inflation rate associated with any given level of Y or U rises over time. This is the theory of accelerating inflation that is further studied in the appendix to this chapter.

AD curve, national income will begin to fall toward Y^*, reducing the inflationary gap. Eventually output will stabilize at Y^*, and both inflation and inflationary expectations will stabilize at the constant rate of monetary growth.

Most economists now agree with the thrust of this analysis. Where different theorists disagree is on what determines the expected inflation rate. Neo-Keynesians tend to believe that the expected rate changes only slowly; monetarists tend to believe that it changes quickly in response to current conditions. We shall see that this difference influences the costs each group foresees in breaking an entrenched inflation.

BREAKING AN ENTRENCHED INFLATION

We begin our story with the continuous, fully validated inflation shown in Figure 36-3 and also shown by arrow 1 in Figure 36-5(i). There is a

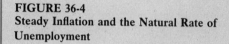

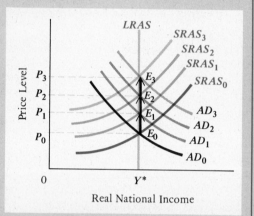

FIGURE 36-4
Steady Inflation and the Natural Rate of Unemployment

When income equals Y^* (and hence unemployment equals U_N) there is no demand effect on wages and steady inflation can proceed at a rate consistent with inflationary expectations. With no demand effect, the *SRAS* curve shifts upward at the expected rate of inflation. If the Bank of Canada raises the money supply at the same rate, the upward shift in the *AD* curve will match that of the *SRAS* curve. Output will stay at Y^*, unemployment will be at the natural rate, and inflation will be steady. The steady inflation is shown by the rising price level as equilibrium moves along the arrow from E_1 to E_2 to E_3 in the figure.

sustained inflationary gap and a continuously rising price level.[5] Let us suppose that inflation has been occurring for some time and that people expect it to continue; we refer to this as an *entrenched inflation*. Now suppose that the Bank of Canada decides to bring the inflation to a halt by ending its policy of monetary validation.

Phase 1 of the anti-inflationary policy consists of slowing the rate of monetary expansion below the rate of inflation. This slows the rate at which the aggregate demand curve is shifting upward.

---

[5] Indeed, according to the acceleration hypothesis, the persistence of the inflationary gap means that the inflation rate should itself be increasing.

For illustration we take an extreme case: The "cold turkey approach," where the rate of monetary expansion is cut to *zero* so that the upward shift in the aggregate demand curve is suddenly halted.

Under the combined influence of an inflationary gap and expectations of continued inflation, wages continue to rise and the *SRAS* curve thus continues to shift upward. Eventually the gap is removed and income returns to Y^*. If the only influence on wages were current demand, that would be the end of the story. At Y^* there is no inflationary gap and hence no upward *demand* pressure on wages: Wages would stop rising, the *SRAS* curve would be stabilized, and the economy would remain at full employment with a stable price level.

Governments around the world have many times wished that things were that simple. Instead of settling in that happy position of full employment and stable prices, however, the economy tends to overshoot and develop a recessionary gap. Why? The reason, as we have already seen, is that wages depend not only on current excess demand, but also on inflationary expectations. Various schools of economists differ on why, but they are united in agreeing that in recent history expectations of continuing inflation have been difficult to break. Once inflationary expectations have been established, it may not be an easy matter to get people to revise them downward, even in the face of changed fiscal and monetary policies.

Expectations may cause an inflation to persist after the original causes of the inflation have been removed. At this point what was initially a demand inflation due to an inflationary gap becomes a purely expectational inflation fed by the expectation that it will continue.

We have now entered phase 2, shown in Figure 36-5(ii). Even though the inflationary gap has been eliminated, the expectation of further inflation leads to wage increases. This shifts the *SRAS* curve upward. The price level continues to rise in spite of a growing recessionary gap. This is the stagflationary phase.

The growing recessionary gap has two effects. First, there is rising unemployment. Thus the demand influence on wages becomes negative. Sec-

FIGURE 36-5
Eliminating an Entrenched Inflation

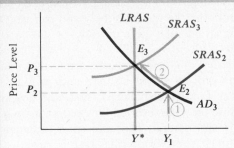

(i) Phase 1 : removing the inflationary gap

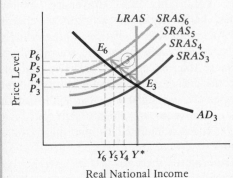

(ii) Phase 2 : stagflation

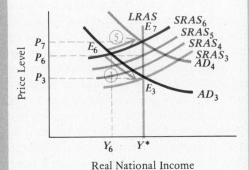

(iii) Phase 3 : recovery

(i) The elimination of an entrenched inflation begins with a demand contraction to remove the inflationary gap. The fully validated inflation shown in Figure 36-3 takes the economy along the path shown by arrow ① in (i). When the curves reach $SRAS_2$ and AD_3 the Bank stops expanding the money supply, thus stabilizing the aggregate demand curve at AD_3. Wages continue to rise, taking the $SRAS$ curve upward. The economy moves along arrow ② with income falling and the price level rising. When the $SRAS$ curve reaches $SRAS_3$, with income Y^* and price level P_3, the inflationary gap is removed.

(ii) Expectations cause the economy to pass through a stagflationary phase, with falling output and continuing inflation. In (ii) the economy moves along the path shown by arrow ③. The driving force is now the $SRAS$ curve, which continues to shift upwards because of inflationary expectations. The recessionary gap grows period by period as income falls to Y_4, Y_5, and finally Y_6. The inflation continues but at a diminishing rate as the price level rises to P_4, P_5, and finally P_6. Eventually wages stop rising and the economy reaches equilibrium position E_6. The stagflationary phase is then over.

(iii) After expectations are reversed, recovery takes income to Y^* and the price level is stabilized. Part (iii) shows the recovery phase. There are two possible scenarios. In the first the recessionary gap causes wages to fall (slowly), taking the $SRAS$ curve back to $SRAS_3$ (slowly). The economy thus retraces the path originally followed in (ii) back to E_3, now shown as arrow ④ in (iii). In the second scenario the Bank increases the money supply sufficiently to shift the AD curve to AD_4. The economy moves along the path shown by arrow ⑤. This restores potential income at the cost of a further temporary burst of inflation that takes the price level to P_7.

ond, as the recession deepens, people revise their expectations of inflation downward. Eventually, they will have no further expectations of inflation. There will be no further increases in wages and the *SRAS* curve will stop shifting upward. The stagflationary phase is now over. The inflation has come to a halt, but now a large recessionary gap exists.

The final phase is the return to full employment. When the economy comes to rest at the end of the stagflation, the situation is exactly the same as when the economy has been hit by an isolated supply shock (see Figure 36-1). As we have already seen, the move back to full employment can then be accomplished in either of two ways. First, the recessionary gap can be relied on to reduce wages, thus shifting the *SRAS* curve downward to eliminate the effects of the overshooting caused by inflationary expectations. Second, the money supply can be increased sufficiently to shift the *AD* curve to a level consistent with full employment.

The trouble with the first approach is that it may take a very long time. The trouble with the second is that expectations of inflation may be rekindled when the Bank of Canada increases the money supply. The Bank will then have an unenviable choice. Either it must let another severe recession develop to break these new inflationary expectations, or it must validate the inflation to reduce unemployment. In this latter case, it is back where it started, with a validated inflation on its hands.

Controversies

Most economists accept this general scenario for breaking an entrenched inflation. But they still differ on how much time each of these three phases will take.

Neo-Keynesian Views

Phase 1. We saw in Chapter 33 that control of the money supply is not a simple matter. From time to time various extreme antimonetarists have suggested that the Bank of Canada could not control the money supply closely and thus could not

apply the monetary brakes as simply as we have assumed. But the evidence of the last decade does not support this view. It appears that if a central bank is single-minded enough, it can exert strong control over the money supply and can stop validating an inflation quite quickly.

Phase 2. Neo-Keynesians argue that phase 2 of the process would be long and painful. Two reasons for this are alleged: first, the downward pressure on wages exerted by a recessionary gap is small, and second, expectations of inflation are slow to change. We consider each in turn.

The first part of their theory involves wage inertia as expounded, for example, by Professor James Tobin of Yale University. Following Keynes, Tobin argues that workers are concerned about their own wages relative to other closely related rates. He adds that wages are rarely negotiated more than once a year, and two- and three-year contracts are not uncommon. Since this means that when any particular wage bargain is negotiated many other wages are already set, concern over relative wages is inclined to give inertia to wage bargains.

Furthermore, there is also an asymmetry between raising and lowering relative wages: Workers do not mind getting ahead of other closely related groups, but they resist falling behind. Therefore, the wage inertia is mainly on the downside.

The graphic expression of this theory of asymmetric wage behavior is in the shifting of the *SRAS* curve. When national income is above potential, excess demand forces wages upward rapidly—the demand effect on wages is strong. When Y is below Y^*, however, excess supply forces wages downward only slowly—the demand effect on wages is weak. Thus in terms of an immediate reduction of the inflation rate, there is little to be gained from the downward market pressures on wages accompanying a recession.

The second major part of the neo-Keynesian theory argues that expectations of future inflation are based on "backward-looking" comparisons. Its simplest version is the so-called extrapolative theory: People tend to believe that recent past trends will continue, and thus it takes a lot of new evidence to make them think an inflationary trend is over. The rationale is that unless a deviation from the past trend persists, people dismiss the deviation—say, a fall in the inflation rate—as a transitory change and do not let it influence their long-term wage- and price-setting behavior.

The weak demand forces combined with slowly adjusting expectations mean that phase 2 will take a long time. The stagflation will persist as rising wages carry the *SRAS* curve upward until expectations of further inflation are finally broken.

Phase 3. Neo-Keynesians call for a burst of monetary expansion to get the economy back to full employment during the recovery phase. They believe that to rely on a fall in wages to shift the *SRAS* curve downward is to condemn the economy to a very long period of high unemployment. Also, because they believe expectations are slow to change, they doubt that a temporary burst of monetary expansion will rekindle inflationary expectations. Once people come to expect a low or zero inflation rate, it will take more than the experience of a single recovery phase to cause them to revise these expectations.

Monetarist Views

Phase 1. Monetarists see no problem with phase 1. They believe that the Bank of Canada can control the money supply within quite a small margin of error.

Phase 2. Monetarists expect phase 2 to be over rapidly. Indeed, some say it will never occur at all. Why is this?

First, monetarists deny that significant wage-price inertias exist. New wage bargains are assumed to respond to current market conditions. Thus a large recessionary gap with unemployment above the natural rate will lead quickly to new wage settlements well below the expected rate of inflation. The only lag in the adjustment of wage costs to current demand conditions is caused by the length of wage contracts. Thus it may still take

some time for *all* wages to adjust to depressed market conditions.

The second strand to the monetarists' case concerns the response of inflationary expectations. Many monetarists argue that expected inflation will fall rapidly during phase 2. This is because they believe that expectations are "forward-looking." Such expections are usually called **rational expectations**: People look to the government's current macroeconomic policy when forming their expectations of future inflation; they understand how the economy works and they predict the outcome of the monetary policies currently being followed. In an obvious sense, expectations formed in this way are "forward looking."

Rational expectations are not necessarily always correct; instead, the rational expectations hypothesis assumes that people do not continue to make systematic errors in forming their expectations.[6]

Rational expectations have the effect of speeding up the response to a deflationary demand policy. Instead of being an average of past inflation rates, expected inflation is based on a correct anticipation of the outcome of existing policies.

Once people realize that the Bank of Canada has stopped validating the inflation they will, given rational expectations, expect the inflation rate to come to a halt. Thus expected inflation falls quickly to zero, and there is no further upward push to wages from expectations.

The main reason for this happy result is that people believe the Bank really is going to stick to its restrictive policies. Because of this, they will quickly revise their inflationary expectations downward, and their consequent wage- and price-setting behavior will produce a rapid slowdown in the actual inflation rate. But if people are skeptical about the Bank's resolve, they may expect the inflation to continue. They will then increase wages and prices in anticipation of the inflation, and their

---

[6] Thus, if the system about which they are forming expectations remains stable, their expectations will be correct on average. Any individual's expectations at any moment of time about next year's price level can thus be thought of as the actual price level that will occur next year plus a random error term.

actions will generate the inflation that they expected.

(Neo-Keynesians argue in response that the general public does not really understand the importance of the money supply to inflation. Sophisticated financial market operators may be monetarists, but most labor leaders and business managers hold different, sometimes crude, theories of inflation. They will tend to extrapolate from past experiences and will not even know what the Bank of Canada is doing to the money supply, let alone base their expectations on it.)

Phase 3. Monetarists tend to be skeptical of using a once-and-for-all monetary expansion to help the recovery. They feel that the credibility of the Bank of Canada's anti-inflationary policy depends on strict adherence to tight monetary policy and that to relax this policy risks rekindling inflationary expectations. Thus they rely on the automatic recovery that is implicit in waiting for downward shifts in the *SRAS* curve. They do not think this recovery would be as slow as Keynesians think, since they believe that demand conditions have a strong effect on wages in both a downward as well as an upward direction.

Additional Anti-Inflationary Policies

Many Neo-Keynesian economists have recommended incomes policies to avoid, or greatly shorten, the stagflationary phase involved in breaking an entrenched inflation. An **incomes policy** represents an attempt by the government to influence directly the setting of wages and prices. There is a wide range of possible measures. The government could simply set voluntary guidelines for wage and price increases—so-called jawboning. (The Kennedy administration used such measures in the United States in the early 1960s.)

A slightly more "activist" form of incomes policy is consultation on wage and price norms among unions, management, and government. The more centralized a country's wage and price-setting mechanisms, the more easily such consultation is accomplished. Hence it is more common in countries of Western Europe than in North America. However, in the early 1970s this type of control was attempted in Canada when the government formed the Prices and Incomes Commission. An even more activist approach is compulsory controls on wage, price, and/or increases, or on some combination of these. The Anti-Inflation Board of 1975–1977 and the 6&5 Program of 1982–1984 were both variants of this direct controls approach.

A more recent and as yet untried proposal is TIPs (tax-related incomes policies), which introduce penalties or rewards that operate through the tax system to induce desirable wage and price behavior.

Incomes Policies

We can distinguish three main uses of incomes policies: (1) to suppress a demand inflation, (2) to break an expectational inflation, and (3) to control a permanent wage-cost push inflation. In the early 1980s the main appeal of incomes policies was for the second use, and we discuss this below. We shall deal with the third in Chapter 42.

Demand inflations. One reason why incomes policies have such a bad reputation throughout the world is that they have often been used in a futile attempt to stop a demand inflation. To see why such an attempt is futile, consider the situation shown at E_1 in Figure 36-3 on page 686. If nothing else is done, the inflationary gap will cause the price level to rise to P_2. Wage and price controls could, however, be used to hold the price level at P_1. But once the controls are removed, the excess demand will cause prices to rise. Thus:

In the face of an inflationary gap, wage-price controls can postpone an inflation, but once they are removed the price level will rise to the value it would have attained had the controls never been used.

Expectational inflations. When an entrenched inflation exists, incomes policies provide a possible way of breaking expectations and forcing the inflation rate down faster than might otherwise be expected. Incomes policies could be used in conjunction with a reduction in the rate of growth of the money supply to what is compatible with the target rate of inflation. The hope is that they would reduce the size and duration of the recessionary gap and the consequent unemployment until expectations fall.

If successful, incomes policies would eliminate the stagflation phase of the breaking of an entrenched inflation. To see this consider part (ii) of Figure 36-5 on page 695, where the Bank of Canada has stopped the *AD* curve at AD_2 and the *SRAS* curve has risen to $SRAS_3$. Wage-price controls might eliminate the expectations-induced further shifts of the *SRAS* curve. Thus the inflation would be eliminated by a *combination* of restrictive demand policy and an incomes policy.

Once a stable price level is achieved, the controls can be removed. If everyone then expects the new rate to persist, expectations will have been broken without the recession required by the use of monetary restraint alone. If such a policy package had been tried, and if it had worked, the recession of the early 1980s, with all its consequent suffering and lost output, would have been avoided.[7]

Supporters of incomes policies contend that such policies can break an expectational inflation. Opponents disagree, offering several arguments:

Controls are discredited because they did not work elsewhere. But as discussed in Box 36-4, controls were often used alone to repress a *demand* inflation rather than in conjunction with restrictive monetary policy to break an expectational inflation.

After the controls are removed, people will expect a resurgence of inflation, and so controls merely postpone inflation. This depends on whether or not the accompanying tight monetary policy of the Bank

of Canada convinces people that inflation will not break out again.

Controls are unnecessary because even without them the stagflation phase would be short or even nonexistent. Monetarists believe that expectations would adjust quickly once the Bank of Canada stopped validating. As we shall see below, the experience of 1980–1983 suggests that although the stagflation phase did not last as long as many Neo-Keynesians had predicted, it lasted quite long enough to be very costly.

The controls themselves would do much damage by inhibiting the operation of the price system. This is a valid point, whose importance grows the longer the controls last. It is taken up further in Box 36-5.

THE RECENT EXPERIENCE OF INFLATION AND ANTI-INFLATION POLICIES

In the late 1960s Canadian inflation began to creep up toward the 4 to 5 percent range. This caused great concern and led to the adoption of tight monetary and fiscal policies. These in turn led to a downturn in the economy in late 1969, and inflation started to fall by mid 1970. However, the early 1970s witnessed quite expansionary policies, and inflation again began to rise. Expansion continued until early 1974, and inflation rose throughout that period. Then a normal recession set in. As a recessionary gap began to open up, the normal expectation was for a moderation of inflation. Just then (and as we have already noted), the first OPEC shock hit: Inflation jumped into the double-digit range. We take up the story in detail at that point.

1974–1975: Stagflation and Supply Shocks

Before 1973 the major force driving economic fluctuations had always been aggregate demand. When demand was high, output would be high and unemployment low, and strong inflationary pressures would exist. When aggregate demand was low, out-

---

[7] In the text we have described, for simplicity, a cold turkey monetary policy that requires cold turkey wage-price controls. The rate of monetary expansion is cut suddenly to zero and the controls force wage and price increases immediately to zero. In practice it can be done more slowly. For example, the rate of monetary expansion might be cut from 8 to 4 to 0 percent over three years and, at the same time, wage-price controls would be used to force wage and price inflation down from 8 to 4 to 0 percent over the same three years. In that case the aggregate demand curve shifts up at a slower rate each year and the controls force the *SRAS* curve to shift upward at the same (falling) rate, so that a recessionary gap does not need to open up while inflation is being reduced.

BOX 36-4 INCOMES POLICIES AND DEMAND INFLATION: THE INTERNATIONAL EXPERIENCE

Much international evidence casts doubt on the effectiveness of such policies as a device for the *long-term* control of inflation.

European experience. In a study of the European experience with many variants of incomes policies, Professor David Smith of Queen's University concluded that incomes policies could not be judged to be an effective control of inflation. At best, a really determined policy might decelerate the rate of inflation by one to two percentage points per year. But even then, there is evidence that the policy becomes progessively more difficult to administer as time passes. Professors Robert Flanagan and Lloyd Ulman of the University of California reached similar conclusions in reviewing European experiences a few years after Smith's study.

One of the main problems associated with attempts to control labor costs in Europe can be expressed in terms of the very different behavior of the *wage rate*, which is the amount workers get per hour, and *weekly earnings*, which is the amount they get per week. It was observed that earnings tended to vary with aggregate demand, even though wage rates were held down by an incomes policy. The consequent widening spread between rates and earnings was christened *wage drift*.

Consider an incomes policy that will allow a rise in wage rates of only 10 percent. However, in order to attract labor in times of labor shortage, firms can offer other inducements, such as bonuses and guaranteed overtime pay (whether or not the overtime is worked). If by these devices they can raise average earnings 20 percent—from say, $350 to $420 per week—the rise in earnings will greatly exceed the rise in output, and inflation will occur in spite of the effective control over wage *rates*.

The British experience. During the decades of the 1950s and 1960s successive British governments tried incomes policies in attempts to control inflation. Many empirical studies have credited these attempts with "success" ranging from almost nothing to less than nothing.

Undaunted by these experiences, the British government drew the conclusion not that incomes policies were ineffective, but that they had not been pursued with sufficient severity. In 1972 the British had one of the largest budget deficits in their history, and at the same time they allowed the money supply to increase by nearly 25 percent in one year! The result was fully predictable: a rapid inflation. But the government clung to its cost-push theory that inflation was due solely to union power and attempted to suppress the enormous inflationary forces by using direct controls on wages and prices. A head-on battle with the unions was precipitated. In the end a general election was called, and the ruling Conservative government was defeated. The new Labour government had little option but to give in to the strikers' demands, and the incomes policy collapsed.

put would be low and unemployment high, and inflationary pressures would be weak or nonexistent. These associations had become the conventional wisdom about how the economy must behave. They were so widely accepted as the natural state of things that ordinary citizens, most policy-makers, and many economists were mystified when quite a different association of events occurred.

In 1974 and 1975 the economies of all Western countries fell into a deep recession and encountered the new economic affliction of stagflation.

The net effect on controlling inflation was negligible or zero, and the cost in terms of social stress was enormous. Nevertheless the Labour government failed to control the budget deficit and money supply growth, and again it resorted to wage controls in the face of an accelerating rate of inflation. By 1977 the inflation rate at last began to fall. Some gave the credit to incomes policies, but this was not an obvious conclusion, for at about this time the Bank of England finally began to reduce the rate of growth of the money supply.

The U.S. experience. The one major use of incomes policies in the United States occurred between 1971 and early 1974. The policy had a number of phases. Phase I was a two-month complete freeze on wages and prices. Phase II tried to hold wage increases to 5.5 percent for 14 months. Phase III attempted more flexible controls in face of the obvious need for adjustments in *relative* prices. But the flexible approach failed to restrain average wage and price increases, and a new freeze was introduced. It was followed by new attempted flexible controls in phase IV. Phase IV controls proved ineffective, however, and they gradually petered out. By April 1974, when the control authority expired, its later phases were acknowledged failures.

Extensive research into the effects of this experiment with wage and price controls suggests that the entire costly effort had little or no effect on wages, but that it did hold down price inflation by perhaps as much as two percentage points. The restraint on prices was achieved by forcing a narrowing of profit margins. Not surprisingly, once the controls were lifted, profit margins were restored. Thus the episode had little or no lasting effect on price level.

What Can We Conclude?

The major conclusions that can be drawn from the experiences of other countries are: (1) The majority of incomes policies that have been tried in the face of demand inflation have had little or no lasting effect on price levels; and (2) those policies that are pursued with vigor and determination can be costly in terms of strikes, slowdowns, lost output, and general social upheaval.

Of course there can be no finality on any social issue, and some observers will continue to draw the lesson that the failure of incomes policies so far means only that they have been pursued with too little vigor and determination. Others, however, will accept the view of the majority of economists who have studied the evidence from many countries: While wage and price controls can have a temporary restraining effect on the price level in the face of excess demand, they are an ineffective method of exercising long-term control.

Aggregate Supply Shifts

For the first time in recent history the economy was being affected significantly by shifts in *aggregate supply* not caused by excess aggregate demand. The most severe supply-side shocks came with the major increases in OPEC's prices. Not only fuel but a host of other petroleum-based products from plastics to fertilizers suddenly rose in price. The rising prices of these vital materials meant rising costs for many firms. Rising costs were passed on by raising the prices of finished goods, which in

BOX 36–5 A VIEW FROM THE OUTSIDE OF THE INSIDE OF UPSIDE DOWN*

On the 18th of October, 1971, I assumed responsibility for the Price Commission in the conduct of Phase II of President Nixon's Wage and Price Control program. . . . I want to relate something about my view of policy-making at the national level. I want to explain why it is inherently a confused sort of occupation and I want to imbue the reader with a healthy skepticism for the ability of central control to solve economic problems.

One of the main reasons why the policy-making process in general and wage and price controls in particular are inherently difficult is because they are attempting to regulate the most sophisticated information system that the world has even seen—namely the North American market economy. . . . The information system is the network formed by free people buying and selling, and the signals are the variations in and the level of wages, prices, interest rates, rents and, unfortunately, taxes.

. . . most of the products and services that we take for granted in our everyday lives can be taken for granted only because there is a functioning price system. A system that, despite its imperfections, delivers just the right quantity of California lettuce to Montana or Alberta, Canada; and decides the relationship between raw log prices in California and the price of furnished lumber in Boston. As we discovered when we tampered with the operation of the price system, we could no longer rely on the system itself and were forced to get more and more involved with what were, before controls, essentially automatic functions.

The problem that policy-makers must cope with, if they are determined to control the system, is the endless detail that is involved in the operation of the system. To control the system and yet keep it running smoothly, the authorities must intercept all of the signals coming from the system (and there are hundreds of millions), interpret them, appropriately change them (assuming they know how) and retransmit them.

What we at the Price Commission continuously found was that everything is related to everything else and there was, accordingly, no such thing as one intervention. We were drawn inevitably and progressively deeper into the system, and the temptation to limit the necessity for our involvement by arbitrarily changing the system was very great. Herein lies the real danger from centralized control: that an inability to handle the overload of signals, both incoming and outgoing, may produce attempts to simplify the system and hence jeopardize its survival.

The difficulty of taking over the wage-price signalling mechanism is indicated by the fact that during the first three weeks of Phase II there were nearly 400,000 inquiries about the program. In terms of getting down to the nitty gritty, had the Dow Chemical Company and the Commission not agreed to an across the board increase of 2 percent, we would have had to examine nearly 100,000 submissions on different products for that company alone.

. . . controls are, by nature, a bureaucratic nightmare. There is no easy way to proceed, no escape from the remorseless tide of detail that is the inevitable consequence of attempting to interrupt the normal current of economic affairs. There is also no escape from the conclusion that detailed regulation breeds a restiveness in those being regulated that eventually must lead either to the collapse of the controls or the adoption of more coercive measures.

* Excerpted from an article of the same title by Jackson Grayson, dean of the School of Business, Southern Methodist University, in M. Walker, ed., *The Illusion of Wage and Price Control*, Vancouver, B.C., The Fraser Institute, 1976.

turn caused an upward shift in the aggregate supply curve.[8]

Aggregate Demand Shifts

In the United States, the supply-side shocks were reinforced by severe contractionary shifts in aggregate demand. The effect of OPEC was to transfer large amounts of income from American purchasers to foreign sellers of petroleum products. Had the sellers spent the money in the same way that Americans would have, aggregate demand would have been unaffected. But much of the new oil income was spent on short-term financial securities, gold, and land, rather than on currently produced goods and services. Thus the effect on aggregate demand was the same as if the American propensity to save had risen: There was a reduction in the amount of income spent on current production. This caused a leftward shift in the aggregate demand curve.

In Canada there were also contractionary forces operating on aggregate demand, mostly due to the decline in export demand caused by the American recession. However, they were offset by expansionary monetary and fiscal policies employed by the federal government. Consequently, national income and employment did not fall nearly as much in Canada as they did in the United States, while the Canadian inflation rate remained much higher than the American rate. Figure 36-6 shows these differences in more detail.

1975–1980: Wage and Price Controls and Monetary Gradualism

By the summer of 1975 Canadian policymakers were concerned about the accelerating rate of inflation. Despite the recessionary gap which, although

[8] The other major supply-side shock that hit the economy at this time came from the agricultural sector. A series of crop failures drove up many food prices. At the same time, the sale to the USSR of large stocks of North American wheat and other agricultural commodities removed the depressing effect on prices that large buffer stocks had exerted, and this too led to price rises. Again the price level rose for causes associated with supply rather than demand shifts.

smaller than in the United States, was still disturbingly high, wage settlements seemed to be increasing rather than decreasing. Policymakers thought they perceived an accelerating wage-push inflation in a time of world recession.

Although it is now easy for us to understand and even draw curves showing what was happening, it must be remembered that at the time only a few economists and virtually no policymakers appreciated the forces at work. Why were prices rising while output was falling? Why were Canadian prices rising so much faster than American prices? Were not wages the root cause? Was it not true that, led by an ever-accelerating rate of wage increase, inflation would go on accelerating?

Deeply concerned that no one seemed to know the answer to the first two questions, policymakers decided that the answers to the third and fourth questions were both "yes." Having failed in an attempt to secure agreement of labor in a voluntary incomes policy, the Canadian cabinet decided in the autumn of 1975 to impose wage and price controls. The Anti-Inflation Board (the AIB) was set up with power to control wages and prices for three years. At roughly the same time, the Bank of Canada adopted a policy of "monetary gradualism" by announcing its intention to slowly reduce the rate at which the money supply was growing.

Wage and price controls and monetary gradualism were to be used to force down the inflation rate at the same time. Whether it was a conscious act of policy to use the two together is not clear, but the use of both simultaneously may have partially helped to avoid the sustained increase in unemployment usually required to wind down an inflation—see Figure 36-5.

Whether by accident or design, the two policies made a coherent package. The monetary policy was meant to reduce the speed with which the *AD* curve was shifting upward. Wage-price controls were meant to reduce the speed with which the *SRAS* curve was shifting upward. If the upward rush of the two curves could be slowed at the same rate, the inflation rate could be reduced without having to endure the stagflation phase (phase 2 in Figure 36-5), which occurs when the upward rush

FIGURE 36-6
Stagflation in Canada and the United States: 1974–1975

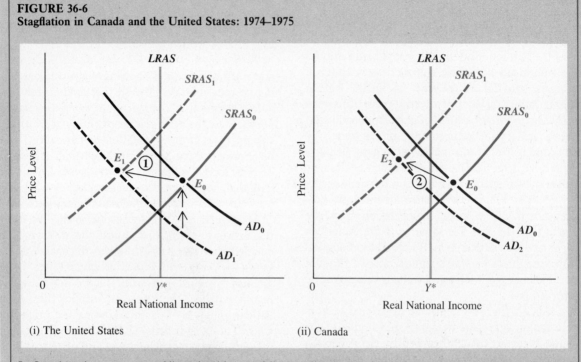

(i) The United States   (ii) Canada

In Canada, prices rose more while national income fell less than in the United States during the stagflation of 1974–1975. In both countries an ongoing inflation has been raising the price level in the face of an inflationary gap, as shown by the vertical arrows. (The process is described in full in Figure 36-3.) When the shock hits, the curves have reached AD_0 and $SRAS_0$ in both countries, producing equilibrium at E_0. The supply shock then shifts the $SRAS$ curve to $SRAS_1$ in both countries. In the United States there is also a large leftward shift in the AD curve to AD_1. Equilibrium moves to E_1, taking the U.S. economy along the arrow marked ①. There is a large fall in national income and a small rise in the price level. In Canada there is only a small shift in the AD curve to AD_2. Equilibrium moves to E_2, taking the Canadian economy along the arrow marked ②. There is a small fall in national income and a large rise in the price level.

of the AD curve is checked faster than the upward rush of the $SRAS$ curve.

The Anti-Inflation Board

The AIB sought mainly to control prices by controlling wages (as well as by some not very effective monitoring of profits). In doing so, it was accepting the view outlined on page 688 that "as wages go, so sooner or later must prices go." This is undoubtedly correct, but the qualification "sooner or later" is very important. Although

profit margins cannot rise continually to create an ongoing inflation, they can experience a single increase and redistribute income from wages to profits.

Although in the long term controlling wages is sufficient to control the trend of prices, controlling wages may cause a once-and-for-all shift in the distribution of income from wages to profits.

In any event, markups did widen so that the controls did serve to redistribute income from wages to profits. Among other things, this result guarantees that unions will be even more hostile to a future experiment with wage and price controls than they were to this one.

The AIB's targets for wage increases were 10 percent in 1976, 8 percent in 1977, and 6 percent in 1978. The very modest targets for reduction in wage inflation given by the AIB in its first year were probably at or above the rates the market would have produced in any case. In 1977–1978, however, the targets were reduced on schedule, and there seems little doubt that some restraint on wages was exercised. Inevitably estimates have varied among researchers, but something like an average of 2.5 percentage points appears to be the agreed number for the average annual restraint on wages over the three years of controls.

The AIB had perhaps its clearest and strongest impact on the rate of increase of wages in the public sector. The government had found it increasingly difficult to restrain public sector wages since the growth of unionization in that sector in the late 1960s. Many economists thought that public sector wage increases had led to increased pressure on private sector wages and thus had been a force in contributing to the acceleration of inflation in the 1970s. In any event, the AIB is generally credited with slowing the rate of increase of wages in the public sector. In the private sector, some wage restraint was also clearly achieved, although less than in the public sector and perhaps in part in response to the public sector slowdown.

When the AIB was introduced in the autumn of 1975, inflation as measured by the rate of change of the CPI was 10.2 percent. By the end of 1976 that rate had fallen to 5.9 percent. However, much of the reduction was due to a moderation of food price increases. Many economists feel that the short-run fluctuations in food prices—which are determined by supply fluctuations outside of the control of any anti-inflation policy, whether fiscal, monetary, or incomes—should be excluded when assessing the underlying inflation trend in the economy. During 1976 the reduction in inflation measured by the CPI *excluding food* was much more modest, from 10.1 to 9.4 percent. In the next year the AIB targets were reduced and the rate of change of the CPI, excluding food, continued to fall gradually; however, food prices shot up, and overall inflation, as measured by the change in the total CPI, in fact *rose* steadily throughout 1977.

When controls were removed in 1978, inflation measured by the CPI, excluding food, had fallen from 10.1 percent in 1975 to 6.4 percent in 1978. Controls were used, apparently successfully, as part of a package to counter the explosive double-digit inflation of the 1974–1975 period. It seems probable, however, that the rapid rates of inflation of around 10 percent did not persist long enough to build up strongly felt or uniformly held expectations of continued inflation at those rates. The underlying or *core* rate of inflation was still widely perceived to be in the 6 to 7 percent range that had persisted throughout most of the decade. The rise in inflation above this core rate was fairly easily reversed. The real problem for continued anti-inflationary policy is to reduce the rate of inflation below the underlying core rate. The wage and price controls imposed by the AIB never got to the point of attempting to do this.

In retrospect, although a case can be made that the AIB should never have been created, it is a shame that, having been created, a more severe attack on inflation was not attempted. If over three years the rate of monetary expansion had been reduced to amounts consistent with inflation in the range of 0–2 percent and money wage inflation forced to that range by the AIB, the inflation might have been broken and without the severe recession that proved necessary to do just a part of the job in the early 1980s.

Monetary Gradualism

The AIB was meant to influence inflation by acting through the cost side, acting on the aggregate supply curve. Monetary gradualism, which we discussed in Chapter 35, was meant to influence inflation primarily by acting on the aggregate demand curve.

From the time of its adoption of monetary targets in 1975, the Bank of Canada was very successful in meeting them. The target range for monetary growth was reduced steadily over the next several years, and the rate of growth of M1 was held within the declining range. The objective was to reduce the rate at which the aggregate demand curve was shifting upward and thereby reduce the rate at which the price level was rising.

At first all seemed to go well. The inflation rate measured by the CPI, excluding food, fell in successive years starting in 1975 from 10.1 to 9.4 to 7.9 to 6.4 percent. Then, in 1979, it rose to 7.9 percent, and in 1980 it rose to 10 percent, taking it back to where it had been at the peak of the 1975 "crisis." Developments in early 1981 were no more encouraging; inflation stood at 10.4 percent on an annual basis as of September 1981. Had five years of gradualism accomplished nothing?

The inflation bubble in 1980 did not appear to be supply-side shock. The rates just quoted excluded food, and Canada's national energy policy held the price of petroleum products at less than half of the world price. The rate of inflation of the energy price component of the CPI was 11 percent in 1980, only one percentage point above the overall rise in the CPI, excluding food. Wage costs had also increased sharply.

Instead, the inflation seems to have been a demand-side affair. By 1978 there was some evidence of excess demand in the economy in spite of the high rates of unemployment. There was a major export boom, largely due to the sharp fall in the value of the Canadian dollar that occurred over the period 1976–1978.

Assessment of the contribution of fiscal policy is less straightforward. Actual and cyclically adjusted budget deficits were historically large, although the real explosion in the deficit did not occur until the 1980s. Fiscal policy may not have played a major role in fueling the excess demand, but neither did it play a role in the disinflation process that was the stated main objective of policy.

But we have learned that continued inflation requires monetary validation. How could the rate of inflation accelerate through the period 1978–1980 while output and employment were rising but the rate of monetary validation was falling? The theory developed in this book leads us to expect that, all other things being equal, an inflation that is not fully validated by monetary expansion will be accompanied by a growing recessionary gap and rising unemployment. Once again the economy was behaving in a surprising fashion and once again critics of economics, this time many from within the profession, proclaimed that some major part of accepted theory—this time it was monetary theory—had been overthrown.

The solution to the puzzle turned out to be consistent with standard theory once it was understood that other things had not remained equal: A formerly stable relation was undergoing major shifts. This is not the first time this had happened. The solution to the stagflation problem of the 1970s was that the *SRAS* curve had suddenly become a major source of economic disturbances. The solution to the problem of inflation in the face of monetary restraint in the late 1970s and early 1980s was that the demand for money function had suddenly become a major source of economic disturbances.

Monetary restraint is supposed to reduce inflation by creating a money shortage that drives up interest rates, reduces interest-sensitive expenditure, and thus reduces aggregate demand. But as we saw in Chapter 35, major innovations in monetary institutions led to sharp reductions in the demand for M1 balances over that period. Instead of a gradually tightening money supply, money was becoming more plentiful *relative to demand*. Indeed, if central banks had paid more attention to the interest rate—which had been discredited as an intermediate target—they would have realized that monetary policy was not restrictive. Several times during this period the real interest rate (the money rate corrected for the rate for inflation) was negative.

The failure of gradualism did not upset any basic economic theory. What it did upset was the proposition that aggregate demand could be precisely controlled by merely controlling the supply of money.

The idea that controlling the supply of money is sufficient to control the aggregate demand is normally associated with monetarism. This policy will work provided the demand for money is stable so that movements in the money supply cause predictable shortages or surpluses of money. What the experience of the late 1970s and early 1980s taught is that at times the demand for money can be sufficiently volatile that changes in the stance of monetary policy cannot be determined merely by observing what is happening to the money supply.

The Great Policy Experiment of 1981–1983

At the start of the 1980s an explicit policy of monetary restraint was introduced in the United States to eliminate the entrenched inflation inherited from the 1970s. The new U.S. policy was one of much more severe restraint than that which the Bank of Canada had been following. For a variety of reasons, the Bank of Canada chose to follow the U.S. lead and introduced a more restrictive policy in Canada in 1980.

Because this was one of the few times central banks had ever tried to halt an entrenched inflation, no one could be sure what to expect. Neo-Keynesians talked in terms of a stagflation phase (phase 2 in Figure 36-5) that would last from 5 to 10 years. Monetarists talked of a very short phase 2, and some "rational expectationists" doubted there would be any phase 2 at all. So the stage was set for a fairly strong test of these opposing views.

The tight policies worked only partly as expected. The recovery that had begun in 1980 was quickly choked off. Unemployment started to rise, and the economy gradually slid into the severe recession of 1982. Initially, wage and price inflation remained stubbornly high, so that by early 1982 there was deep concern. Unemployment was over 12 percent, but inflation was responding very slowly. (The *SRAS* curve was shifting upward rapidly even though the aggregate demand curve was shifting only slowly.) The result was as to be expected: rising prices and falling output.

In the face of considerable opposition and political pressure, the Fed and the Bank of Canada persisted with their tight money policies. In the budget of June 1982, the Canadian government felt

that fiscal restraint was not appropriate in the face of the recession, but it tried to contribute to the disinflation process by introducing a package of controls on civil service compensation—the so-called *6&5 program*.

There is still debate over the effects of the program. Some feel it stiffened the resistance of private sector firms to continued inflationary wage increases. Be that as it may, serious recession, falling sales, and falling profits eventually had to have their effect in moderating wage increases. In late 1982 and early 1983, the upward shift in the *SRAS* curve slowed considerably. This in turn brought a fall in the rate of inflation and an end to further increases in the recessionary gap. The fall in inflation was dramatic: From a peak of 13 percent in mid 1981, it fell to around 5 percent by early 1984.

By 1984 the restrictive monetary policy had succeeded in reducing inflation to a level not seen since the early 1960s, but it had also produced a major recession with all its attendant costs, including unemployment, lost output, business bankruptcies, and foreclosed mortgages.

The results came out somewhere in between the extremes that had been predicted. The Neo-Keynesians were right in predicting that the anti-inflationary policies would induce a severe recession. But the inflation rate came down much faster than Neo-Keynesians had predicted. Thus, as so often happens with great debates, neither the extreme pessimists nor the extreme optimists were right. The truth lay somewhere in between.

Economists may argue for years about why the result turned out the way it did. Neo-Keynesians say that the recession was due to inertias that, although not as strong as expected, were strong enough to require a large recession to break them. They also argue that the secular weakness of the steel and auto industries, whose strong unions usually provide the backbone of union-induced wage inertias, accounted for the weakness of these inertias during this particular recession. Monetarists hold that the Fed and the Bank of Canada vacillated too much. This left people unsure just how resolute the bank would be in its tough monetary stance. As a result, expected inflation did not fall as fast as it would otherwise have done.

Whatever the reasons, there is little doubt that inflation fell faster and the slump was deeper and more prolonged than many had expected.

Indeed, the force of the economic slump was strong enough to put serious social strains on the society and to put political and economic strains on the fabric of international cooperation. Many countries were tempted to turn to such politically appealing but economically discredited policies as the high tariffs that caused so much trouble during the 1930s.

The Recovery

Late in 1982, spurred by falling interest rates and expansionary fiscal policies, the U.S. and Canadian economies began to recover. Indeed, 1983 saw record growth in both countries, although most observers argued that there was very little actual growth (as measured, say, by increased capacity output) and that the record increase in actual output was due to the very low levels of output from which the recovery started. While inflation stayed steady in the 4 to 5 percent range through mid 1984, the recovery was rapid enough that many observers also feared the rebounding of inflation—especially if the pressures to monetize the deficit continued to grow. (The relation between deficits and inflation was discussed on page 596.)

SUMMARY

1. Either supply shocks or demand shocks can cause a temporary inflation. For either to lead to sustained inflation, it must be accompanied by a continuing expansion of the money supply so that the *AD* curve shifts continually upward.

2. A sustained price inflation will also be accompanied by a closely related growth in wages and other factor costs which causes the *SRAS* curve to shift up.

3. Factors that influence shifts in the *SRAS* can be divided into three main categories: demand, expectations, and shocks.

4. Excess demand or supply in the labor market causes wages to rise or to fall and hence the *SRAS* curve to shift upward or downward. The state of demand can be shown either by the GNP gap, or by the difference between the actual and natural rates of unemployment.

5. Expectations of inflation tend to cause wage settlements that preserve the real wage and hence lead to nominal wage increases. They are a major source of inertia and stagflation.

6. Shocks of all sorts, including changes in the prices of imported raw materials, can cause temporary bouts of inflation.

7. It is possible to have a sustained inflation at the capacity level of income (and hence at the natural rate of unemployment). There is no demand pressure on prices, but expectations can cause wages and hence prices to grow at the same rate as the money supply.

8. Stopping an inflation through restrictive monetary policy will lead to a recession that lasts until inflation falls to a rate consistent with the new lower rate of money growth. The length and depth of the recession will depend on the strength of the downward demand pressure on wages and on the speed with which inflationary expectations adjust.

9. Incomes policies that try to control wage and price increases directly are also often advocated as measures to reduce inflation. When they have been applied instead of demand restraint, they have proved futile. However, when used along with demand constraint they may be helpful in either speeding up the adjustment of inflationary expectations or temporarily suppressing the role of expectations in causing a stagflation.

10. Neo-Keynesians tend to believe that the demand pressures on wages from a recessionary gap are weak and that expectations are sluggish to adjust. As a result, they believe that the recession associated with the breaking of an entrenched inflation will be deep and prolonged. Monetarists tend to believe that demand pressures from either a recessionary or inflationary gap cause wages to respond quickly and that expectations are also fast to adjust. As a result, they believe that the recession will be brief.

11. Stagflation first became a serious problem in the recession of 1974–1975. The mystery of rising prices combined with falling output was solved when it was realized that the inflation was being initiated by supply-side rather than demand-side shifts.

12. The attack on Canadian inflation in the 1970s had two prongs. One, monetary gradualism, attempted to work through the demand side: By reducing the rate of growth of the money supply, it was hoped to reduce the rate at which the *AD* curve was shifting upward. The second, the Anti-Inflation Board, attempted to work through the supply side: Wage-price controls were meant to slow the rate at which the *SRAS* curve was shifting upward.

13. The AIB program had some limited success in curbing wage increases. Monetary gradualism failed because shifts in the demand for M1 balances made targeted reductions in the supply of M1 balances an inadequate tool for controlling the money supply.

14. In the early 1980s a major policy experiment was initiated in an attempt to bring inflation down rapidly. This resulted in a much larger recession than most monetarists predicted, but also in a much faster reduction in inflation than most Neo-Keynesians predicted.

TOPICS FOR REVIEW

Temporary and sustained inflations
Monetary accommodation of supply shocks
Monetary validation of demand shocks
Demand, expectational, and shock inflation
Natural rate of unemployment
Accelerating inflation
Equilibrium inflation
Extrapolative and rational expectations
Incomes policies

DISCUSSION QUESTIONS

1. On what source or sources of inflation do the following statements focus attention?
   a. "The one basic cause of inflation is the government's spending more than it takes in. The cure is a balanced budget."
   b. "Major labor negotiations in steel, autos, and other basic industries will lead to double-digit wage increases and a serious inflationary effect."
   c. "Wage settlements are high. The widespread publicity they are receiving will make it difficult to wind down inflation."
   d. "While the CPI rose by 7 percent last month, most of the increase was in a very few sectors where bottlenecks are developing."
2. "Inflations cannot long persist, whatever their initiating causes, unless the inflations are validated by increases in the money supply." Why is this so? Does it not imply that control of inflation is merely a matter of not allowing increases in the money supply to rise faster than the rate of increase of real national income?
3. Look at the rate of increases of the money supply and the CPI over the last three years and decide whether or not the current inflation is being validated.
4. Discuss the following views on the effects of inflation.
   a. "Now the beast [of inflation] is easily visible, a luminescent specter, a killer, a threat to society, public enemy No. 1."—Robert D. Hersy Jr., 1979.
   b. "Inflation has become the national obsession . . . . the catchall scapegoat for individual and societal economic difficulties, the symptom that diverts attention from the basic maladies."—James Tobin, 1980.
5. What theory or theories of inflation are suggested by each of the following quotations?
   a. "Canada's inflation rate of 4 percent was disturbingly high given that unemployment was 11 percent."—1984 report of the C. D. Howe Institute.
   b. "From the point of view of dealing with inflation, this [deficit equal to 4 percent of GNP] was an uncomfortably large deficit for the government of Canada to have at a time when the level of economic activity relative to the economy's demonstrated capacity was as high

as it was.''—Annual Report of the Governor of the Bank of Canada, 1980.

   c. ''. . . inflation was the almost inevitable outgrowth of the enormous international stresses during this period. . . . As attempts [to maintain real income growth] were essentially incompatible with the real constraints of the situation, they resulted in higher inflation. . . .''—*Economic Review*, 1981.

   d. ''The nation's spiraling inflation reflects a global depletion of physical resources and therefore cannot be cured by traditional fiscal and monetary tools.''—a study issued in 1980 by the Worldwatch Institute.

6. A recent newspaper article on inflation warned, ''It is a mistake to think that every higher price is due to inflation.'' Give some examples of higher prices that have increased the CPI without being a part of a general inflationary process.

7. A recent newspaper discussion of inflation gave the following arguments *for* and *against* reductions in specific taxes.

For:

   a. ''Cuts in payroll taxes would reduce employment costs, thereby helping to slow down price inflation.''

   b. ''Faster depreciation write-offs would provide greater incentives for new equipment and technology investments, thus boosting productivity.''

Against:

   c. ''Pumping more money and more purchasing power into the economy through a tax cut without cutting federal spending would do little to restrain inflation [indeed it would increase it].''

   d. ''A better approach would be to achieve a budget surplus and pay off the federal debt.''

Match each of the above statements with the following theoretical category that best describes it and indicates the direction of the relevant shift.

   (i) Shift the aggregate demand curve.

   (ii) Shift the short-run aggregate supply curve.

   (iii) Shift the long-run aggregate supply curve.

8. William Nordhaus of Yale University recently described inflation as an ''inertial process like people standing up at a football game. When some people jump up to see better, other people can't see unless they stand up, too. When everybody is up, people as a group can't see as well as they did when they were all sitting; in fact, they probably see worse and are more uncomfortable. But the problem is how to get them all to sit down together.'' What view of inflation is Professor Nordhaus embracing?

9. In an article on the harmful effects of inflation, a reporter wrote, ''with the rise in mortgage interest rates to 10 percent heaven only knows the price of what was once idealized as 'the $100,000 house'.'' At the time the inflation rate was 9 percent. Did the 10 percent interest rate represent a heavy burden of inflation on the new home owner? What do you think the mortgage interest rate would have been if the inflation rate had been zero? What would have been a heavier real burden on the purchaser of a new house?

10. Consider the factors at work which might give rise to the following (often conflicting) newspaper headlines from early 1983:

   a. ''The Money Bulge Isn't Inflationary.''

   b. ''Why Continued Success Is Likely in Effort to Tame Inflation.''

   c. ''Drop in Oil Prices, Interest Rates, and Inflation Could Mean Stronger Recovery.''

   d. ''Broker Says Inflation May Be Under Control for Years.''

   e. ''Economists Optimistic on Inflation Outlook.''

   f. ''Though Consensus Sees Mild Inflation Ahead, Some Signs Suggest a Returning Price Spiral.''

   g. ''Inflation Still Alive and Influencing Policy.''

37 EMPLOYMENT AND UNEMPLOYMENT

In the early 1980s worldwide unemployment rose to very high levels. Not only was the overall level of unemployment wastefully large, the structure of unemployment was extremely varied.

Many social policies designed to alleviate the short-term economic consequences of unemployment have been instituted since the 1930s. Their success may be counted as a real triumph of economic policy. But the longer-term effects of current high unemployment rates in terms of the disillu-

sioned who have given up trying to make it within the system and who sow the seeds of future social unrest should be a matter of serious concern to the haves as well as to the have-nots.

In the 1970s the control of inflation emerged as a major social problem in many Western industrial nations. To cure inflation, governments induced the worldwide recession of the early 1980s. Was the resulting unemployment worth it? Can unemployment be reduced in the last half of the 1980s as easily as it was increased in the early 1980s? When the Canadian inflation rate fell in 1983 to around 5 percent, many Canadians came to believe that unemployment was, once again, the most serious macroeconomic problem facing the nation. Was this so?

KINDS OF UNEMPLOYMENT

It is helpful to identify a number of kinds of unemployment. Keynes distinguished between voluntary and involuntary unemployment. *Voluntary* unemployment occurs when there is a job available but the unemployed person is not willing to accept it at the going wage rate. *Involuntary* unemployment occurs when a person is willing to accept a job at the going wage rate but cannot find a job.[1]

Until now we have distinguished only two types of involuntary unemployment: *deficient-demand* unemployment, which is unemployment due to a recessionary gap, and *frictional* unemployment, which we defined as unemployment that exists when national income is at its potential level and hence there is neither a recessionary gap nor an inflationary gap.

For our more detailed study we now distinguish further between two types of frictional unemployment. For bouts of relatively short-term unemployment, we retain the term *frictional* unemployment. For longer-term bouts we introduce the term *structural* unemployment. We also discuss an additional type, *real wage* unemployment.

Frictional Unemployment

In the more restricted sense that we now employ the term, frictional unemployment refers to the normal turnover of labor. Older workers leave the labor force and young people enter it, although these new workers do not usually fill the jobs va-

cated by those who leave. Of course people leave jobs for reasons other than retirement. Some people quit jobs because they are dissatisfied with the working conditions. Others are dismissed. Whatever the reason, they must search for new jobs, which takes time. This turnover gives rise to a pool of persons who are "frictionally" unemployed while in the course of looking for jobs.

Frictional unemployment would occur even if the structure of jobs in terms of skills, industries, occupations, and location was static and the labor force was fully adjusted to it.

Normal turnover of labor will always produce a pool of persons who are frictionally unemployed. Either they are between jobs or they are looking for their first job.

Some frictional unemployment is involuntary: no acceptable job in the person's occupational and skill category has yet been located. Often, however, it is voluntary. The unemployed person is aware of available jobs but is searching for better options. Voluntary frictional unemployment is often called **search unemployment.**

The existence of search unemployment shows that the distinction between voluntary and involuntary unemployment is not as clear as it might seem at first sight. How, for example, should we classify an unemployed woman who refuses to accept a job at a lower skill level than the one for which she feels she is qualified? What if she turns down a job for which she is trained because she hopes to get a higher wage offer for a similar job from another employer?

In one sense people in search unemployment are voluntarily unemployed because they could find some job; in another sense they are involuntarily unemployed because they have not yet succeeded in finding the job for which they feel they are suited at a rate of pay that they believe exists. Workers do not have perfect knowledge of all available jobs and rates of pay, and they may be able to gain information only by searching the market. Faced with this uncertainty, it may be sensible to refuse a first job offer, for the offer may prove to be a poor one in light of further market information.

---

[1] Recently, some macroeconomic theorists have refined Keynes's notion of the distinction between voluntary and involuntary unemployment. Those who go on to study labor economics will have to master the subtleties involved. For present purposes, Keynes's distinction is adequate.

How long it will pay to remain in search unemployment depends on the economic costs of being unemployed.

It is socially desirable for there to be sufficient search unemployment to give unemployed people time to find an available job that uses their skills.

Too much search—for example, holding off while being supported by others in the hope of locating a job better than that for which one is really suited—is an economic waste. Thus search unemployment is a gray area: some is useful, some wasteful.

Structural Unemployment

Structural adjustments of the economy can cause unemployment. When the pattern of demand for goods changes, the demand for labor changes; if labor has not adjusted to these changes, structural unemployment occurs. **Structural unemployment** may be defined as unemployment caused by a mismatch between the structure of the labor force—in terms of skills, occupations, industries, or geographic location—and the structure of the demand for labor. In Canada today, structural unemployment exists, for example, in parts of the Maritimes, in the textile industry, and in many of the older foundry and mill towns in Ontario.

Structural unemployment arises when the composition of the demand for labor does not match the composition of the available supply.

Natural causes. Economic growth can cause structural unemployment. As growth proceeds, the mix of required inputs changes, as do the proportions in which final goods are demanded. These changes require considerable economic re-adjustment. Structural unemployment occurs when such re-adjustments are slow enough that severe pockets of unemployment develop in areas, industries, and occupations in which the demand for factors of production is falling faster than the supply.

Changes that accompany economic growth shift the structure of the demand for labor. Demand rises in such expanding areas as metropolitan Toronto and falls in such contracting areas as the steel-producing centers. Demand rises for workers with certain skills, such as computer programming and electronics engineering, and falls for workers with other skills, such as stenography and bookkeeping. To meet changing demands, the structure of the labor force must change. Some existing workers can be retrained, and new entrants can acquire fresh skills.

Policy causes. Government policies can influence such changes. As we saw in Box 17-1 on pages 288–289, policies that discourage movement among regions, industries, and occupations often also raise structural unemployment. Policies that prevent firms from replacing human labor with machines may protect employment in the short term. If, however, such policies lead to the decline of an industry because it cannot compete effectively with innovative foreign competitors, serious structural unemployment can result.

One further cause of structural unemployment is the persistence of a disequilibrium structure of relative wages. Typical causes of such a structure are minimum wages, union agreements that narrow wage differentials, nationally negotiated wage structures that take no account of local market conditions, and equal pay laws where employers do not perceive that the groups concerned all contribute equally to the profitability of the enterprise. Such policies cause particular groups to lose employment because their relative wages are too high.

For example, an elderly person may be prepared to work for $100 a week as a caretaker of an apartment. Further, the owner may believe that this person is capable of doing what is needed. But suppose the minimum wage is $150 a week. If there were no minimum wage, the elderly person would get the job. But because of the minimum wage, the owner has to pay almost twice as much as she needs to and therefore hires someone else who can provide her with more services than she needs. She reasons that since she has to pay more, she might as well get something for it.

The same considerations apply to an inexperienced worker just out of school who would accept $110 a week for a first job. A potential employer is willing to pay this wage, but the minimum wage is $150. Once again the employer hires someone else who is overqualified for the job. The tragedy is that the young worker does not get the on-the-job training and experience that would equip him or her to hold down a stable, higher-paying job a year or two later.

Much empirical research supports the conclusion that imposed wage structures such as minimum wages tend to transfer employment from those whose relative wages are raised by the intervention to those whose relative wages are lowered. But do imposed wages affect overall employment? That is a much more difficult question. If such policies lead to an increase in the average wage paid, they may contribute to what we will call real wage unemployment, which we study below.

The Distinction Between Frictional and Structural Unemployment

As with many distinctions, the one between structural and frictional unemployment becomes blurred at the margin. In a sense structural unemployment is really long-term frictional unemployment. To illustrate, consider a change that requires labor to re-allocate from one sector to another. If the re-allocation occurs quickly, we call the unemployment frictional; if the re-allocation occurs slowly, we call the unemployment structural.

The major characteristic of both frictional and structural unemployment is that there is a job available—that is, an unfilled vacancy—for each unemployed person.

In the case of pure frictional unemployment the job vacancy and the searcher are matched. The only problem is that the searcher has not yet located the vacancy. In the case of structural unemployment, the job vacancy and the searcher are mismatched in one or more relevant characteristics such as occupation, industry, location, or skill requirements.

Deficient-Demand Unemployment

Unemployment that occurs because of insufficient total demand for all the output that could be produced by a fully employed labor force is called **deficient-demand unemployment.** It is the unemployment that exists because there is a recessionary gap. As a result there are not enough jobs available for all unemployed persons. When deficient-demand unemployment is zero, there is some job available for every person unemployed. In this situation unemployment persists either for structural reasons (the vacancies and the unemployed are mismatched) or frictional reasons (normal labor turnover).

National income theory seeks to explain the causes of, and cures for, unemployment in excess of frictional and structural unemployment. *Full employment* does not mean zero unemployment; it means that all unemployment is frictional or structural.

National income theory seeks to explain the deficient-demand unemployment associated with variations in the nation's total output. The measurement of deficient-demand, frictional, and structural unemployment is discussed further in Box 37-1.

Real Wage Unemployment

Unemployment due to too high a real wage is sometimes called **Classical unemployment** because many economists, whom Keynes dubbed the *Classical economists,* believed that unemployment in the 1930s was caused by a real wage that was too high. The remedy they suggested for unemployment was to reduce wages. But there is now general agreement that the unemployment of the 1930s was caused by deficient aggregate demand rather than excessive real wages.

Because the battles of the 1930s aroused such emotions, many modern Keynesians have refused to believe that *any* unemployment could be caused by real wages being too high. There is growing acceptance, however, that much of the current unemployment in Western Europe and elsewhere can

BOX 37–1 STRUCTURAL AND FRICTIONAL UNEMPLOYMENT

One useful measure of the total of frictional plus structural unemployment is the percentage of the labor force unemployed when the number of unfilled job vacancies is equal to the number of persons seeking jobs. When these two are equal, there is a job opening for every person seeking a job. Any unemployment that remains must be either frictional or structural.

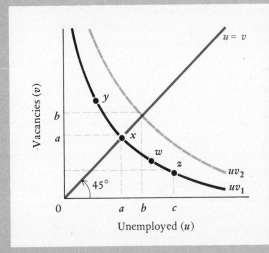

This measure is illustrated in the figure, which plots the number of unfilled vacancies (v) against the number of unemployed (u). The 45° line is the locus of points where $u = v$. On that line there is some job available to match every unemployed person, so there is no deficient-demand unemployment. The uv curve shows the relationship between unemployment and vacancies that is suggested by empirical evidence. In an economy with the relation uv_1, zero deficient-demand unemployment occurs at the point x with frictional plus structural unemployment given by the amount a measured on either axis.

When a boom occurs employers seek to hire more workers, so more vacancies open up. Since there are more jobs available, the unemployed spend less time searching before finding an acceptable job. Thus the pool of unemployed falls. A boom therefore takes the economy to some point such as y, where there are more vacancies than unemployed. A slump takes the economy

to some point such as z, where there are fewer vacancies than unemployed.

A change in structural plus frictional unemployment shifts the uv curve. For example, if people lose their jobs in the Maritimes while more jobs are created in Alberta there may be a rise in the number of unemployed (in the Maritimes) and a rise in the number of unfilled job vacancies (in Alberta). Hence, both u and v increase. In the diagram a shift to uv_2 indicates a rise in frictional plus structural unemployment from a to b.

In most countries where reliable vacancy data is available the uv relation shifted outward in the late 1960s and early 1970s. This indicated a rise in structural plus frictional unemployment.

Deficient-Demand Unemployment

We can measure deficient-demand unemployment as total unemployment minus estimated frictional plus structural unemployment. Graphically it is actual unemployment minus the unemployment where the uv relation cuts the 45° line. If the economy is at point z, this measure is ac in the figure.*

Real Wage Unemployment

Unemployment due to excessive increases in the real wage will show up in the figure approximately as a movement along the existing uv curve, say from point x to w', rather than as a shift of that curve. There will be a large rise in unemployment and a small fall in vacancies (which would otherwise have resulted from the normal turnover of labor in the now-closed plants). A general rise in the real product wage can lead to a general rise in unemployment that looks like deficient-demand unemployment because there is a rise in unemployment with no corresponding rise in unfilled vacancies.

* Notice that the measure is not current unemployment minus current vacancies, but current unemployment minus the vacancies that would exist were there no GNP gap.

be traced to excessive real wage levels. Because of the emotionally loaded nature of the phrase *Classical unemployment*, the term **real wage unemployment,** defined as unemployment due to a level of real wages that is too high, is the preferred term.

So far we have used the term *real wage* to mean the purchasing power of money wages. This is measured by deflating the money wage by the Consumer Price Index. In this section we are concerned with the real cost to the employer of hiring a worker. We call this the **real product wage.** The nominal cost to the employer includes the pre-tax wage rate, any extra benefits such as pension plan contributions, and any government payroll taxes such as employers' contributions to social insurance. The real cost is the nominal cost divided by the output price.

Too high a real product wage can affect employment through forces operating both in the short run and in the long run. Consider the short run first. When technological change is embodied in plant and equipment, at any moment in time an industry will have an array of plants ranging from those that can do little more than cover their variable costs to those that make a handsome return over variable costs. (Such a situation was studied in detail on pages 194–195.) A rise in the real product wage of 10 percent will mean that some plants can no longer cover their variable costs and so will close down.

If, for example, a plant had wages of $.70 and other variable costs of $.25 for every $1 of sales, production would be worthwhile since $.05 of every $1 of sales would be available as a return on already invested capital. If the product wage rose so that $.77 of every $1 of sales was paid in wages, the plant would be shut down, since it would not even be covering its variable costs. The plant's employees would then lose their jobs. This same analysis applies to the economy as a whole.

An economy-wide rise in real product wages, other things being equal, means that some plants and firms will no longer be able to cover their variable costs and will shut down. When they do, the unemployment rate will rise.

Now consider the long run, when there is more scope for flexibility in the design of production techniques and in the matching of labor demand with the prevailing real product wage. The flexibility arises because much capital is what is called *putty clay.* At the design stage, more or less capital can be spread over the labor force, thus varying the capital-labor ratio. But once production techniques are designed, factor ratios are embodied in the equipment and cannot be significantly varied.

For example, a highly automated or quite simple textile plant can be designed and the capital-labor ratio therefore varied over a wide range on the drawing board. Once an automated plant is built, however, this ratio cannot be varied greatly by varying the amount of labor applied to the now-fixed quantity of capital. You cannot productively combine a great deal more labor with automated machinery to make the process less capital-intensive. Neither can you cut in half the labor force that tends a given amount of nonautomated machinery in order to make the process much more capital-intensive.

When the real wage is too high across the whole economy, there will be a structural mismatch between the labor force and the capital stock which shows up as unemployment: When the capital stock is working at full capacity there is still unemployed labor. This structural mismatch may persist for a considerable period of time, as is discussed further in Box 37-2.

Indeed it will continue until one of two things happen. Unemployment may force down the real wage until it pays firms to employ all the existing labor. Alternatively, new technologies may be invented that make profitable use of the unemployed labor in spite of its high real product wage.

Too high a real wage can be the cause of much unemployment. In what countries and to what extent this has been so is an unsettled empirical issue.

EXPERIENCE OF UNEMPLOYMENT

Measured and Nonmeasured Unemployment

The number of unemployed persons is estimated from a sample survey conducted each month by

BOX 37–2 INVESTMENT AND THE PERSISTENCE OF REAL WAGE UNEMPLOYMENT*

Real wage unemployment arises when the real product wage is so high as to cause existing capital equipment to be unprofitable, leading to closure of plants and even dissolution of firms. At the same time, investment in new, more capital-intensive plant and equipment will be undertaken.

That a rise in the real product wage would lead to more capital-intensive methods of production (i.e., a substitution of capital for labor) is a direct consequence of the principle of substitution discussed in Chapter 11.

When plants that are too labor-intensive are being replaced by plants that are more capital-intensive, we would expect unemployment to develop. But this may be a transitional phase. Would not more of these capital-intensive plants be built until all of the available labor force is put to work?

The answer depends on whether or not the real product wage is too high to encourage sufficient investment. Two general cases need to be distinguished. First, the real product wage may be so high that no new plants built with existing technology are profitable. Then old plants that cannot cover variable costs will be closed down, no new plants will be built, and an alleviation of the unemployment (assuming the real wage is not lowered) must await the very long run when technologies that are profitable at existing input prices are developed.

Second, newly built capital-intensive plants may be profitable at existing prices, in which case some will be built. During the transition while older, more labor-intensive plants are being scrapped and new capital-intensive ones are being built, unemployment may develop. If the profitability of investment diminishes at the margin as the capital stock grows, then new construction will stop when further units of capital are not sufficiently profitable.

Whether or not this happens before the whole labor force is put back to work depends on the real wage (and capital costs) and on the speed with which returns to investment decline at the margin as the capital stock grows. Since these are both empirical matters on which we currently have insufficient evidence, either answer is possible.

Whether or not real wage unemployment is a serious problem is a matter of current dispute. *But the answer is a matter of major importance.* Advocates of the real wage explanation argue that, for example, British real wages were some 10 percent to 15 percent too high in 1982, and, as a result, significant amounts of capital were being scrapped. They also point out that the first sign of such a national disaster is a rise in recorded labor productivity.

Since the least efficient plants are scrapped first, the average output per head of those remaining in employment will rise steadily. But such a rise in productivity would be less the first glimmerings of an economic sunrise than the first winds of an economic hurricane.

The evidence of serious real wage unemployment seems stronger for Europe than for Canada. Some observers, however, looking at the shift in manufacturing jobs from Canada to such lower-wage countries as Japan and Taiwan, fear that real wage unemployment may be an emerging problem in Canada as well.

* This discussion draws heavily on the article "Real Wages and Unemployment," published by Edmond Malinvaud in the *Economics Journal*, 1981.

Statistics Canada. Persons who are currently without a job but who say they have actively searched for one during the sample period are recorded as unemployed. The total number of estimated unemployed is then expressed as a percentage of the labor force (employed plus unemployed) to obtain the figure for percentage unemployment.

The measured figure for unemployment may overstate or understate the number of people who are involuntarily unemployed.

On the one hand, the measured figure overstates unemployment by including people who are not involuntarily unemployed. For example, unemployment compensation provides protection against genuine hardship, but it also induces some to stay out of work and collect unemployment benefits for as long as they last. Such people have in fact voluntarily withdrawn from the labor force. But they are usually included in the ranks of the unemployed because, for fear of losing their benefits, they may tell the person who surveys them that they are actively looking for a job.

On the other hand, the measured figure understates involuntary unemployment by omitting some people who would accept a job if one were available but who did not actively look for one in the sample week. For example, people who have not found jobs by the time their unemployment benefits are exhausted may become discouraged and stop seeking work. Such people have voluntarily withdrawn from the labor force and will not be recorded as unemployed. They are, however, truly unemployed in the sense that they would willingly accept a job if one were available.

Those who are in this category are referred to as **discouraged workers.** In mid 1983, when recorded unemployment stood at 11.2 percent of the labor force, or 1.4 million workers, there were between three and four hundred thousand discouraged workers who would reenter the labor force if they thought they had a chance of a job.

In addition there is part-time unemployment. If some workers are working 6 hours a day instead of 8 hours because there is insufficient demand for the product they manufacture, then that group is suffering 25 percent unemployment even though

no individual is reported as unemployed. Twenty-five percent of the potential manpower is going unused. Involuntary part-time work is a major source of unemployment of labor resources not reflected in the overall figures reported in the press.

For example, in mid 1983 some 425,000 workers were in part-time unemployment, accounting for 23 million hours per month of unrecorded unemployment—equivalent to 138,000 full-time unemployed persons. Between 1981 and 1984 the number of part-time jobs rose by 16 percent, while the number of full-time jobs *fell* by 3 percent.

The Overall Unemployment Rate

Figure 26-2 (see page 470) shows the behavior of the unemployment rate since the end of World War II. Until 1970 the rate fluctuated cyclically but showed no clear rising or falling trend. During the 1950s the average rate was 4.4 percent and during the 1960s it was 5 percent—not a significant difference.[2] From 1970, however, the cyclical fluctuations appeared to be superimposed on a rising trend. From 1970 to 1983 the *low* figure of 5.3 percent unemployment was above the *average* of 4.7 percent for the previous two decades. This low figure was achieved during the boom of 1973–1974, but the subsequent recession caused it to rise to 8.3 percent by 1978.

For the next three years it stayed relatively constant near 7.5 percent. In 1982 it started to rise sharply, reaching a peak of 12.8 percent in late 1982. The subsequent recovery reduced unemployment only slowly, and by mid 1984, when Canadian GNP was roughly back to its prerecession level, unemployment was still 11.6 percent.

The Relative Importance of the Various Kinds of Unemployment

At the beginning of 1984 there were just over 1.4 million unemployed in Canada, over 11 percent of the labor force. According to the most widely accepted estimates, deficient-demand unemployment

---

[2] Yearly figures in this section are based on annual averages of unemployment.

accounted for nearly half this unemployment and frictional, structural, and real wage unemployment combined accounted for the remainder.

The deficient-demand unemployment will be largely eliminated with recovery from the slump. But what of the more than half-million unemployed who remain? To study them further, we look at some of the characteristics of the unemployed. Figure 37-1 gives some idea of the current duration of the spells of unemployment.[3] Data are given for 1983, a year of severe recession, and for 1979, the last year when national income came close to potential income. The unemployed in 1979 experienced mainly frictional and structural unemployment, and thus the differences between 1979 and 1983 can be assumed to be due to the addition of deficient-demand unemployment.

The bulk of reported unemployment is short term. In 1978 about two-thirds of the unemployed had been out of work for 13 weeks or less. Long-term unemployment tends to rise in recessions—45 percent of the unemployed in 1983 had been out of work for more than 13 weeks.

Three facts stand out about the unemployed. First, there is a group of marginal workers who move in and out of jobs, sometimes several times a year, and who account for a significant fraction of the total spells of unemployment. Second, most spells of unemployment are of short duration. Third, the bulk of total unemployment is accounted for by those in long-term unemployment. The consistency of the second and third points can be seen by a simple example. Consider four people, each unemployed for a week, and a fifth who is unemployed for nine months. For this group of five people, 80 percent of the spells of unemployment are short term, but the long-term bout counts for 90 percent of the total weeks of unemployment.

Figures 37-2 and 37-3 document some of the inequalities in unemployment rates. Males and females, the young and the experienced have very

[3] The figures are based on the Labor Force Survey, which asks currently unemployed individuals how long they have been out of work. Notice that this gives us the duration of *currently uncompleted* bouts of unemployment. It gives different and shorter figures than the duration of completed bouts of unemployment, which is obtained by asking people who have just found a job how long they were out of work.

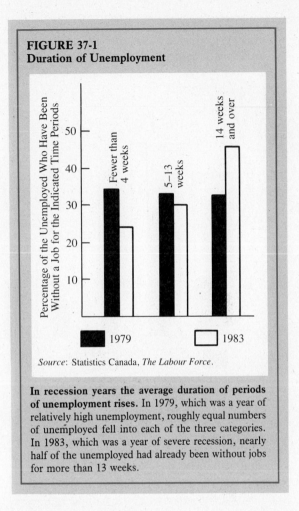

FIGURE 37-1
Duration of Unemployment

Source: Statistics Canada, *The Labour Force*.

In recession years the average duration of periods of unemployment rises. In 1979, which was a year of relatively high unemployment, roughly equal numbers of unemployed fell into each of the three categories. In 1983, which was a year of severe recession, nearly half of the unemployed had already been without jobs for more than 13 weeks.

different unemployment rates, as Figure 37-2 shows. Equally dramatic are the differences between sectors, as shown in Figure 37-3.

Why Has Frictional Plus Structural Unemployment Risen over the Last 15 Years?

The Facts

Throughout the 1950s and early 1960s the natural rate of unemployment—all unemployment not due to deficient demand—was around 4.5 percent. In the last half of the 1960s this rate crept slowly up toward 5.0 percent. Then, in a very few years

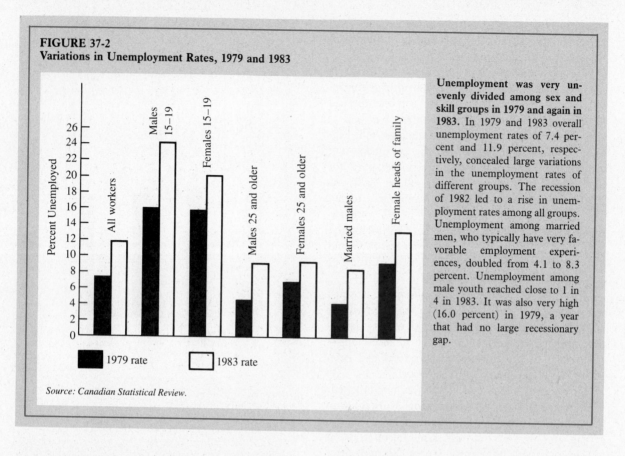

FIGURE 37-2
Variations in Unemployment Rates, 1979 and 1983

Unemployment was very un-evenly divided among sex and skill groups in 1979 and again in 1983. In 1979 and 1983 overall unemployment rates of 7.4 per-cent and 11.9 percent, respec-tively, concealed large variations in the unemployment rates of different groups. The recession of 1982 led to a rise in unem-ployment rates among all groups. Unemployment among married men, who typically have very fa-vorable employment experi-ences, doubled from 4.1 to 8.3 percent. Unemployment among male youth reached close to 1 in 4 in 1983. It was also very high (16.0 percent) in 1979, a year that had no large recessionary gap.

■ 1979 rate   □ 1983 rate

Source: Canadian Statistical Review.

following 1970, the rate rose to 6.5 or even 7.0 percent. Higher actual unemployment rates that accompanied this increase in the natural rate were widely but incorrectly taken to indicate a failure of stabilization policy.

The level of unemployment that persists when all de-ficient-demand unemployment is removed has risen in recent years.

Just how much deficient-demand unemploy-ment remains when the overall rate is, say, 7.0 percent is a matter of current debate. Some ob-servers think it is no more than 0.5 percent at most, others think it may be as much as 1.5 percent. Expressed as percentage points, these figures may not seem very big, but a reduction of one percent-age point in the unemployment rate means that about 120,000 more people have jobs.

It is important to settle the issue of how much deficient-demand unemployment exists. To apply the cure of raising aggregate demand when there is no deficient-demand unemployment would add greatly to inflationary pressure while doing little to reduce unemployment. Box 37-3 on page 722 ex-amines one situation in Canada where many econ-omists believe this mistake occurred.

Demographic Changes

Because people usually try several jobs before settling into one for a longer period of time, young and inexperienced workers have higher unemploy-ment rates than experienced workers. Over the last 15 years, the proportion of inexperienced workers in the labor force rose significantly as the "baby boom" generation of the 1950s entered the labor

FIGURE 37-3
Unemployment Rates by Sector, 1979–1983

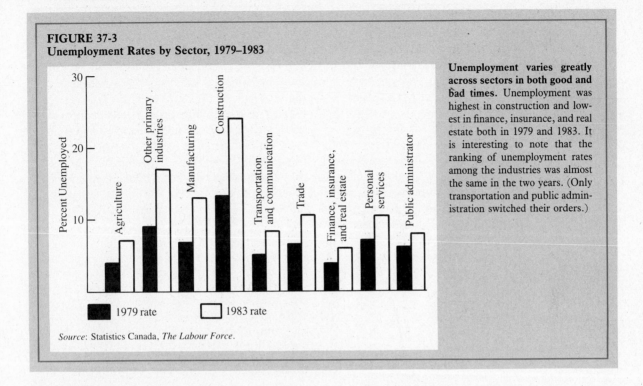

Unemployment varies greatly across sectors in both good and bad times. Unemployment was highest in construction and lowest in finance, insurance, and real estate both in 1979 and 1983. It is interesting to note that the ranking of unemployment rates among the industries was almost the same in the two years. (Only transportation and public administration switched their orders.)

Source: Statistics Canada, *The Labour Force*.

force along with an unprecedented number of women who elected to work outside the home.

It is estimated that these demographic changes added nearly a percentage point to frictional and structural unemployment. Since birthrates were low in the 1960s and a further increase in the percentage of females entering the labor force is unlikely, there may be some demographically induced fall in this type of unemployment over the next decade.

Although the natural rate of unemployment, and youth unemployment in particular, should fall as the baby boom generation passes on to middle age, many worry that although the brighter, the more energetic, and the luckier of that generation will do well, many others will not. Learning by on-the-job experience is a critical part of developing marketable labor skills. Many who are in the ranks of youth unemployment have been denied that experience early in their working careers. They may be condemned to remain at best marginal workers

taking temporary jobs with low current pay and little future job security.

Another significant change is the large increase in the number of households with more than one income earner. In 1960 only 30 percent of females 20 years and older were in the labor force; in 1972 the figure was 38 percent; by 1982 it had jumped to 48 percent. When both husband and wife work, it is possible for one to support both while the other looks for "a really good job" rather than accepting the first job offer that comes his or her way.

Wage and Price Rigidity

Research such as that done recently by Professor Philip Cagan of Columbia University in New York suggests that the speed with which wages and prices in North America adjust to changing market conditions has slowed over the years. Anything that

BOX 37–3 CHANGES IN THE NATURAL RATE OF UNEMPLOYMENT

In many countries the force of the boom that occurred in the early 1970s was not fully appreciated. Until quite late in the expansion, most governments thought that their problem was to reduce a recessionary gap rather than an inflationary gap. This mistaken diagnosis was to a great extent caused by a shift in the relation between the recorded unemployment rate and the pressure of excess demand. The shift reflected a rise in the amount of unemployment associated with full-capacity output, the *natural rate of unemployment*. This rise had occurred more or less unnoticed by policymakers; as a result, heavy inflationary pressures were allowed to build up before policymakers realized what was happening.

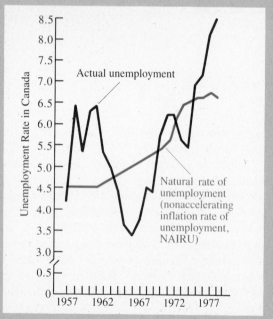

Two Canadian economists, Pierre Fortin and Keith Newton, estimated the Canadian natural rate of unemployment (which they defined as the non-accelerating inflation rate of unemployment, NAIRU) to be as shown in the figure. Accustomed to booms being indicated by unemployment figures of 3 percent and normal capacity output by 4 percent, the government watched actual unemployment rise steadily to over 6 percent in 1972 and then come down only slightly to 5.6 percent in 1973. It is not surprising that some policymakers were misled into thinking there was substantial excess capacity in the economy in 1972 and even 1973, for at the time there was no consensus among economists that the natural rate of unemployment had risen.

In an independent study, Frank Reid and Noah Meltz of the University of Toronto argued that structural and frictional unemployment rose by about 3 percent from the mid 1960s to the mid 1970s. They cite these main causes:

(i) the continuing shift from agricultural to non-agricultural employment contributed approximately 0.2 percentage points; (ii) the 1971 change in the Unemployment Insurance Act contributed about 1.9 percentage points of which 0.7 percentage points resulted from the higher benefit-wage ratio and 1.2 percentage points from revisions in the regulations of the Act; (iii) demographic changes contributed about 1.2 percentage points by increasing structural unemployment. The demographic changes have resulted partly from exogenous factors such as the increased fraction of youth in the population and partly by other factors such as changes in the Unemployment Insurance Act and changing social attitudes.

One important policy implication of our analysis is that the 1971 revision of the U.I. Act substantially changed the meaning of the unemployment rate as an indicator of excess demand in the labor market between the mid-1960s and mid-1970s, with the result that a higher target rate of unemployment for monetary and fiscal policy is appropriate. . . . It is possible that as a result of this change the government was led to adopt an overexpansionary monetary and fiscal policy during the early 1970s, producing an acceleration of inflation in that period.

Stated in terms of the *AD-AS* apparatus, policymakers were still trying to shift the *AD* curve to the right to eliminate the perceived recessionary gap. Unrecognized by them was the fact that the *LRAS* curve had shifted left so that Y^* had fallen; instead of a recessionary gap, there existed an inflationary gap which policies were exacerbating.

slows the speed of adjustment to the economy's ever-changing conditions will create a larger pool of structural unemployment.

Increasing Structural Change

Structural unemployment can increase because the pace of change accelerates or the pace of adjustment to change slows down. An increase in the rate of growth, for example, speeds up the rate of creation of new jobs—for which there may be little or no current supply of workers with the right training and experience and in the right place. New regulations that make it harder for workers in a given occupation to take new jobs in other regions will also increase the degree of mismatch between jobs and available workers.

The amount of resource re-allocation across industries and areas seems to have increased over the last two decades. In part this is the result of the increasing integration of the North American economy with that of the rest of the world. Most observers feel that on balance this integration has been beneficial. But one less fortunate consequence is that changes in conditions anywhere in the world that require adjustments throughout the world's trading sectors increasingly affect North America.

Internationally one of the most significant demand changes for North America was the emergence of the Eastern bloc countries as major food importers. The failure of their system of collective agriculture to meet domestic demand led them to become large importers of grain. To pay for these imports, they had to become major exporters of other commodities such as natural gas.

Further changes resulted from the input price shocks that have buffeted the world over the last 15 years: two enormous oil price increases in the 1970s with a steady downward slide in the early 1980s and an increase of over 200 percent in average basic materials prices in the early 1970s. Such changes have shifted competitive advantages in industrial production, leading to growth in some areas and countries and decline in others.

Changing prices have also caused changes in quantities demanded. The high cost of gas and oil led to a shift to small cars, an enormous investment program to retool North American industry, and major car imports from Japan and Germany that cut heavily into the demand for North American cars and for their major inputs such as steel. The results have been all too evident in the unemployment figures in cities such as Hamilton, where the steel industry is located. Some of these workers will be recalled as output recovers, but many will have to find jobs in other industries and areas where new skills may be required. Rising oil prices also led to a shift to natural gas for home heating, a large demand for insulation, and alterations in typical designs of new houses.

A further factor on the cost side is the increased use of robots in factories and computer-based processes in offices. These changes have eliminated many assembly line and clerical jobs and forced their former holders to look elsewhere for new jobs.

Another major set of forces leading to structural change arises from the shifting pattern of demand. As a result of rising income and changing social patterns, people spend a higher proportion of their income on services than they used to—and a correspondingly smaller proportion on manufactured goods. Restaurant meals and day-care facilities for children are two services with rising demands. As we observed on page 311, the *increase* in employment in the American fast food industry during the 1970s exceeded the total combined employment in the automobile and steel industries!

The increasing pace of change over the last 15 years has contributed greatly to a rising volume of structural unemployment.

Future Outlook

Certain factors may work to reduce the natural rate of unemployment in the future. First, the proportion of youths and newly entered females in the labor force will diminish as the baby boom generation ages and the female participation rate stabilizes. Second, educational systems in some or all provinces may be revamped to give students better job-related training. Third, several revisions of the unemployment insurance act have reversed some of the changes introduced in the early 1970s. (The act now does less than it used to in the way of encouraging unemployment.) Fourth, governments seem to be becoming more aware of the importance of structural changes in the economy and of the need for policies to encourage rather than inhibit adaptability and flexibility in the economy.

UNEMPLOYMENT POLICIES

Unemployment can never be reduced to zero. Frictional unemployment is inevitable; some structural unemployment must exist as the pattern of the demand for labor changes faster than the supply of labor can adapt to it, and some deficient-demand unemployment will exist at average levels of business activity. Each kind of unemployment has costs in terms of the output that could have been produced by the unemployed workers. Yet reducing unemployment is also costly. For example, retraining and re-allocation schemes designed to reduce structural unemployment use scarce resources.

It would be neither possible nor desirable to reduce unemployment to zero. The causes of unemployment could never be removed completely, and reducing the amount of unemployment stemming from those causes is a costly process. Nevertheless, excessive unemployment is an economic waste and hence a tragedy.

Unemployment insurance is one method of helping people live with unemployment. Certainly unemployment insurance has reduced significantly the human costs of the bouts of unemployment that are inevitable in a changing society. Nothing, however, is without cost. While unemployment insurance alleviates the suffering caused by some kinds of unemployment, it can itself contribute to unemployment for, as we have observed, it encourages voluntary and search unemployment.

Supporters of unemployment insurance emphasize its benefits. Critics emphasize its costs. As with any policy, a rational assessment of the value of unemployment insurance requires a balancing of

its undoubted benefits against its undoubted costs. Most Canadians are convinced that, when this calculation is made, the benefits greatly exceed the costs.

High rates of unemployment among youths have been a particularly acute problem in recent years, and have prompted discussion of a number of possible policies. One is to exempt youths from minimum wage laws for some period of their first jobs, which would overcome some of the problems caused by minimum wages identified on pages 713–714 above. Another is government sponsorship of apprenticeship and other skill apprenticeship programs. Attractive as such programs appear on the surface, experience in the United Kingdom suggests that they are very costly and produce very little positive result. If jobs aren't there, gaining skills is of little value to the unemployed.

Deficient-Demand Unemployment

We do not need to say much more about this type of unemployment since its control is the subject of stabilization policy, which we have studied in several earlier chapters. A major recession that occurs due to natural causes can be countered by monetary and fiscal policy to reduce deficient-demand unemployment.

The late 1970s and early 1980s saw a new situation: policy-induced, deficient-demand unemployment. This occurred when the government induced a recession in order to combat inflation. A temporary bout of deficient-demand unemployment was the price of reducing inflation.

Once inflation fell to levels regarded as acceptable, restrictive policies were eased somewhat and national income began to grow. Although U.S. unemployment fell rapidly towards its natural rate, Canadian unemployment remained disturbingly high. Part of this was no doubt structural. In the prolonged recession many firms learned how to cut costs and become more competitive internationally by producing the same output with less labor. When the displaced labor is eventually reemployed in other jobs, output will rise. In the meantime, however, structural unemployment of displaced workers remains high. Much of the unemployment that persisted throughout 1984 was no doubt from deficient demand. When the economy recovered fully, many of these unemployed would be reemployed in their old jobs.

Worried by persistently high unemployment, some observers urged the government to throw caution to the winds and push the economy back rapidly to full employment by fiscal and monetary policy. The government must beware, however, of falling into a *stop-go cycle*. This cycle plagued the British economy over the whole period from 1945 to 1978. Briefly, what happens is that when inflation is rampant, as it was in 1981–1982, it is declared public enemy number one. Contractionary policies are adopted; a major recession ensues; and finally inflation falls.

The problem of inflation is then declared solved, and unemployment is declared to be public enemy number one. Expansionary policies are adopted; employment rises; but the economy then develops an inflationary gap, and inflation accelerates. The problem of unemployment is then declared solved and inflation is declared public enemy number one. Contractionary policies are adopted; and the whole cycle begins again.

Clearly *both* inflation *and* unemployment matter. Because of the slopes of the *SRAS* and the Phillips curves, there is a short-run trade-off between inflation and unemployment: A rapid buildup toward full employment is likely to cause a burst of inflation, and a rapid (although temporary) decrease in employment is the usual price of reducing inflation. In the long run, however, both the aggregate supply curve and the Phillips curve are vertical, so unemployment and output are independent of the trend rate of inflation.

The moral of this story is twofold:

1. A lower average level of unemployment cannot be bought by accepting a higher trend rate of inflation in the long run.
2. In the short run the trade-off between unemployment and inflation can lead a myopic government which does not see past its immediate problems to engage in an endless stop-go policy that alternately

alleviates either unemployment or inflation at the cost of exacerbating the other.

Real Wage Unemployment

If this type of unemployment is a major problem, its cure is not an easy matter. Basically what is required is a fall in the real product wage combined with measures to increase aggregate demand so as to create enough total employment. But the cure is slow and requires enough time to build the new labor-using capital. The steps might be as follows.

1. The real product wage would be cut substantially, possibly by some form of incomes policy or "social contract."
2. Since wages enter into disposable income and disposable income determines consumer demand, the cut in wages will tend to reduce aggregate demand and hence reduce equilibrium national income. This deflationary force will then be countered by expansionary fiscal and monetary policy that will create sufficient aggregate demand to restore full employment.

If real wage unemployment is a serious problem, then attacking unemployment by increasing aggregate demand may cause the economy to hit capital constraints when there is still a substantial amount of unemployed labor. Further demand increases would then become inflationary long before unemployment fell to levels that would be regarded as satisfactory by historical standards.

Frictional Unemployment

The turnover that causes frictional unemployment is an inevitable part of the functioning of the economy. Insofar as it is caused by ignorance, increasing the information about market opportunities may help. But such measures have a cost, and that cost has to be balanced against the benefits.

Some frictional unemployment is an inevitable part of the learning process. One reason that there is a high turnover rate, and hence high frictional unemployment, is that new entrants have to try jobs to see if they are suitable. They will typically

BOX 37–4 INDUSTRIAL CHANGE: AN ECONOMIST'S CAUTIONARY TALE

The audience hushed as the royal commissioners filed into the room. The chief forecasting wizard—behind his back some called him the economic soothsayer—began his report. "I have identified beyond reasonable doubt the underlying trends now operating," he declared to an expectant audience. "The nation's leading industry, industry X, is in a state of decline. From its current position of employing 50% of our workforce it will, within the duration of one human lifetime, employ only 5%."

"Forty-five percent of the nation's jobs destroyed within one lifetime!" proclaimed the newspaper headlines.

"Where can new jobs possibly come from at so rapid a pace?" asked a labor leader.

"We must protect industry X; we just cannot let all these jobs go down the tubes," argued an employer.

"Perhaps we should identify and promote new 'sunrise industries,'" said a mandarin. Indeed, it was widely believed that a new high-tech product, product Y, would be the wave of a future new transportation revolution, and a call went out for subsidies and tax expenditures to back its development.

"Is there any hope that the private sector might provide the new jobs?" someone asked.

"Possibly," said a junior economist, more out of desperation than hope, "the new product Z that is being produced by a few people in backyard sheds might grow to be a significant employer."

He was immediately jumped upon by a chorus of more realistic thinkers. "Product Z! It's noisy; it's smelly; and it's a plaything for the rich. Surely *it* will never provide significant employment."

All of the economic facts in the above tale are true; only the royal commission and the policy initiatives are fictitious.

The country was Canada.

The time was 1900.

Industry X, the employer of 50 percent of the workforce, was agriculture.

Product Y, the sunrise industry, was Zeppelins.

Product Z, the scorned plaything of the rich, was automobiles.

The decline of some traditional industries is a cause for concern. Some are suffering a temporary decline, and some are declining permanently. In either event, the hardships on those losing their jobs are severe. The tale does, however, have a serious message. Here are a few of the lessons that can be gleaned from a look at the Canadian economy of 1900:

1. The economy is constantly changing. Indeed, the motto of any market economy could be "nothing is permanent." New products appear continually, while others disappear.

At the early stage of a new product, total demand is low, costs of production are high, and many small firms are each trying to get ahead of their competitors by finding the twist that ap-

try more than one job before settling into one that most satisfies, or least dissatisfies, them.

Structural Unemployment

The re-allocation of labor among occupations, industries, skill categories, and regions that gives rise to structural unemployment is an inevitable part of growth. There are two basic approaches to reducing structural unemployment: first, try to arrest the changes that accompany growth and, second, accept the changes and try to speed up the adjustments. Throughout history labor and management have advocated, and governments have

peals to consumers or the technique that slashes costs. Sometimes new products never get beyond that phase—they prove to be passing fads. Others, however, do become items of mass consumption.

Successful firms in growing industries buy up, merge with, or otherwise eliminate their less successful rivals. Simultaneously, their costs fall, owing to scale economies. Competition drives prices down along with costs.

Eventually, at the mature stage, a few giant firms often control the industry. They become large, conspicuous, and important parts of the nation's economy. Sooner or later, new products arise to erode the position of the established giants. Demand falls off and unemployment occurs as the few firms run into financial difficulties.

A large, sick, declining industry may appear to many as a national failure and disgrace. At any moment, however, firms can be found in all phases—from small firms in new industries to giant firms in declining industries. Large declining industries are as much a natural part of a healthy changing economy as large stable industries and small growing ones.

2. The policy of shoring up the declining industries of the 1980s could be just as destructive of our living standards as the policy of protecting the agricultural sector from decline in 1900 would have been. (Policies that ease the human cost of the adjustment are, however, to be recommended.)

3. To tell where the new employment will come from requires the kind of crystal ball our young economist would have needed in 1900 to stick by his wild guess of identifying the new plaything of the rich as the massive automobile industry 30 years later.

Economists are constantly asked "Where will the new employment come from?" The answer "we don't know" is *wrongly* taken to mean "it won't come." In the past, the new jobs have come, and we see no new identifiable forces to prevent their coming in the future. For example, in the course of the current recovery many people gaining employment are starting in *new* jobs—jobs with firms and in locations that did not exist nor would have been predicted even five years ago.

4. Picking winners and backing them by government policy is a sure way to waste public funds and inhibit the development of the real winners. People risking their own money and diversifying risks over many ventures are a surer route to employment creation than are governments risking taxpayers' money and mesmerized by a few current fads and fashion.

5. The industrial policy we do need is one that encourages private initiatives and risk taking. Small businesses are often, if not always, the route to the creation of new employment. Risk taking and the growth of small firms should not be discouraged by such things as complicated regulatory rules and tax laws.

tried, both approaches. Box 37-4 gives a cautionary tale concerning the choice between the two.

Resisting change. Since the beginning of the Industrial Revolution workers have often resisted the introduction of new techniques to replace the older techniques at which they were skilled. This is understandable. A new technique will destroy the value of the knowledge and experience of workers skilled in the displaced techniques. Older workers may not even get a chance to start over with the new technique. Employers may prefer to hire younger persons who will learn the new skills faster than older workers, who are set in their ways of thinking. From society's point of view new techniques are beneficial because they are a major source of economic growth. From the point of view of the workers they displace, new techniques can be an unmitigated disaster.

The introduction of new technology is resisted in two main ways. The first involves union-management agreements to continue to employ people who would otherwise lose their jobs because of the new innovation. The second is to support a declining industry with public funds. If the market would support an output of X but subsidies are used to support an output of $2X$, then jobs are provided for, say, half the industry's labor force who would otherwise become unemployed and have to find jobs elsewhere. Both these policies are attractive to the people who would otherwise become unemployed. It may be a long time before they can find another job and, when they do, their skills may not turn out to be highly valued in their new occupations.

In the long term, however, such policies are not viable. On the one hand, agreements to hire unneeded workers raise costs and can hasten the decline of an industry threatened by competitive products. On the other hand, an industry that is declining due to economic change becomes an increasingly large burden on the public purse as economic forces become less and less favorable to its success. Sooner or later, public support is withdrawn and an often precipitous decline then ensues.

In assessing these remedies for structural unemployment, it is important to realize that, although they are not viable in the long run for the economy, they may be the best alternatives for the affected workers during their lifetimes.

There is often a genuine conflict between those threatened by structural unemployment, whose interests lie in preserving their jobs, and the general public, whose interest is served by economic growth, which is the engine of rising living standards.

Aiding change. Another policy to deal with structural change is to accept the decline of indus-

tries and the destruction of specific jobs that go with it and to try to reduce the cost of adjustment for those affected. Retraining and relocation grants make movement easier and reduce structural unemployment without inhibiting economic change and growth. Retraining programs exist in the United States but have met with mixed success at best. Relocation grants are used in Sweden, for example. Other countries have adopted various adjustment assistance policies, or as they have been called by the OECD, *positive adjustment policies.*

A number of policies have been introduced in Canada. These have focused on two sources of adjustment problems. One is imperfections in capital markets which make it difficult for workers to borrow funds in order to retrain or relocate. The other is the lack of good information about current and future job prospects.

A major aspect of labor market policies in the 1960s and 1970s was education. University enrollment rose from 107,000 to 324,000 between 1960 and 1970, while community college enrollment increased from 50,000 to 225,000 between 1960 and 1975. Between 1960 and 1970 the number of persons undertaking technical training increased from less than 5,000 to 350,000, partly under the stimulus of the Adult Occupational Training Act of 1967.

Policies to improve the flow of information include the creation of Job Banks and Information Centres, and initial steps toward a nationwide computerized information system called Jobscan.

A number of programs that aid adjustment in a variety of ways exist under the National Training Act and the Labour Adjustment Benefits Act. The Canadian Mobility Programme, which finances relocation and travel assistance, spent $8.1 million in 1983. It helped 5,000 workers relocate permanently and almost 23,000 temporarily. Women's Employment Counselling Centres served 4,500 women entering or reentering the workforce in 1982–1983. Other services met the special needs of such groups as the physically disabled, criminal offenders, and youths.

The National Training Programme finances occupational training. In 1982, 235,000 adults recieved $797 million in direct assistance. The National Industrial Training Programme funded employer-run training programs in the amount of $110 million. The Industry and Labour Adjustment Programme (a three-year program with $450 million in funding) and the Canadian Industrial Renewal Programme (a five-year program with $267 million in funding) have supplemented permanent policies in dealing with adjustment problems created by "restructuring of industry." Job creation programs such as the Local Employment Assistance Programme, Canada Community Services Projects, New Technology Employment Programme, and Summer Canada are also major labor market policies aimed at structural unemployment.

A recent high-profile and controversial program is the Canadian Occupational Projection System, which attempts to predict future skills imbalances and direct public funds to training in areas where shortages are predicted. Although most people welcome the information provided by such projections, many critics fear their implications in channeling public funds. In particular, they fear that the program may exacerbate rather than mitigate future imbalances, and hinder rather than speed up adjustment. This fear is based on making important decisions about which skills to promote and which to discourage to be made in a cumbersome, slow-reacting government bureaucracy.

SUMMARY

1. Unemployment may be voluntary or involuntary. Involuntary unemployment is a serious social concern both because it causes economic waste due to lost output and because it is a source of human suffering.

2. There are several kinds of unemployment: (a) frictional unemployment, which is due to the time taken to move from job to job as a result of normal labor turnover and includes search unemployment, caused by the need to discover the state of the labor market by searching for alternative employment opportunities; (b) structural unemployment, which is caused by the need to re-allocate resources among occupations, regions, and industries as the structure of demands and supplies changes; (c) deficient-demand unemployment, which is caused by too low a level of aggregate demand; and (d) real wage unemployment, which is caused by too high a real product wage.

3. Measured unemployment figures may overestimate or underestimate the actual number of unemployed. They include some who are voluntarily unemployed. They also omit discouraged workers who have left the labor force and part-time workers who would prefer full-time employment.

4. The level of unemployment that persists when deficient demand is removed—the total of frictional and structural unemployment—has risen in recent years. This is due to demographic changes in the work force, increasing wage and price rigidity in the economy, increasing generosity of unemployment compensation and other social insurance programs, and increasing structural change in the economy.

5. Unemployment insurance helps to alleviate the human suffering associated with inevitable unemployment. It also increases unemployment by encouraging voluntary and search unemployment.

6. It is important for governments to avoid a stop-go cycle whereby they alternately alleviate either inflation or unemployment only to exacerbate the other.

7. Unemployment can be reduced by raising aggregate demand, by making it easier to move between jobs, by slowing down the rate of change in the economy, and by raising the cost of staying unemployed. However, it is neither possible nor desirable to reduce unemployment to zero.

TOPICS FOR REVIEW

Voluntary and involuntary unemployment
Deficient-demand unemployment
Frictional unemployment
Structural unemployment

Search unemployment

Real wage unemployment

The effects of demographic and structural changes on unemployment

A stop-go cycle

DISCUSSION QUESTIONS

1. Interpret the following newspaper headlines in terms of types of unemployment
   a. Recession Hits Local Factory, 2,000 Laid Off.
   b. "A Job? I've Given Up Trying," Says Mother of Three.
   c. "We Closed Down Because We Could Not Stand the Competition from Taiwan," Says Local Manager.
   d. "When They Raised the Minimum Wage I Just Could Not Afford to Keep All of These Retired Policemen on My Payroll as Security Guards," Says Local Shopping Center Owner.
   e. Slack Demand Puts Local Foundry on Short Time.
   f. "Of Course I Could Take a Job as a Dishwasher But I'm Trying to Find Something That Makes Use of My High School Training," Says Local Teenager in Our Survey of the Unemployed.
   g. Where Have All the Jobs Gone? They Have Gone to the Sun Belt States of the United States.
   h. "Thank God for the Minimum Wage. Without It, I Couldn't Earn Enough to Feed the Kids," says Single Mother of Four.
   i. Retraining Main Challenge in Increased Use of Robots.
   j. Modernization May Cut Canadian Textile Employment.
   k. Uneven Upturn: Signs of Recovery Hit Ontario, but B.C. and Alberta Still in Recession.

2. What differences in approach to unemployment are suggested by these facts: (a) In the 1950s and the 1960s Britain spent billions on subsidizing firms that would otherwise have gone out of business in order to protect the jobs of the employees; (b) Sweden has pioneered in spending large sums to retrain and relocate displaced workers.

3. In the late 1960s and early 1970s many countries observed an increase in the number who were unemployed when the total number of unemployed was just equal to the number of unfilled vacancies. What factors might have accounted for this shift in the unemployed-vacancy relation?

4. Discuss the following views: (a) "Canadian workers should resist automation, which is destroying their jobs" says a labor leader; (b) "Given the fierce foreign competition, its a case of automate or die" says an industrialist.

5. In 1983 and 1984, unemployment fell much faster in the United States than in Canada. Suggest some reasons why this might be so, focusing on the relative importance of the various types of unemployment.

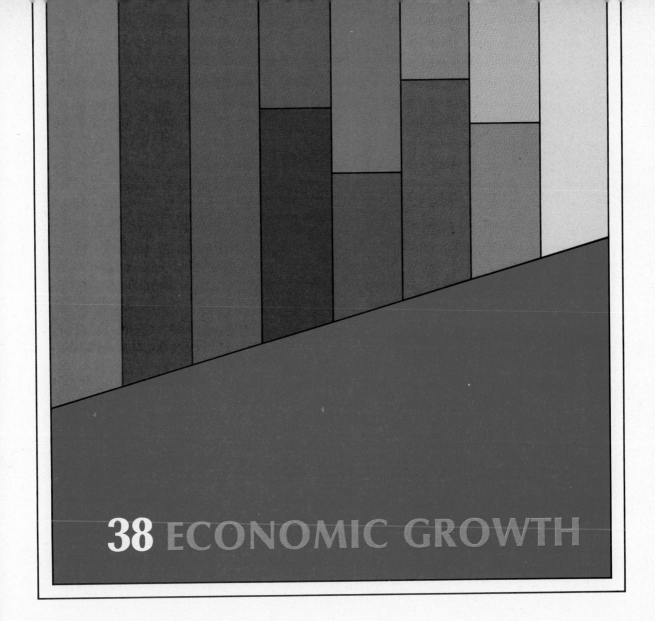

38 ECONOMIC GROWTH

Popular debate is bedeviled by confusion about the various causes of change in national income. Monetarists sometimes accuse neo-Keynesians of believing that governments can spend their way into a rising national income. Neo-Keynesians sometimes accuse monetarists of wasting national income by their tight money policies. But what actually causes national income to change?

CAUSES OF INCREASES IN REAL NATIONAL INCOME

Figure 38-1 illustrates some of the most important possibilities. If there is a GNP gap, raising aggregate demand will yield a once-for-all increase in national income. But once potential income is

FIGURE 38-1
Ways of Increasing National Income

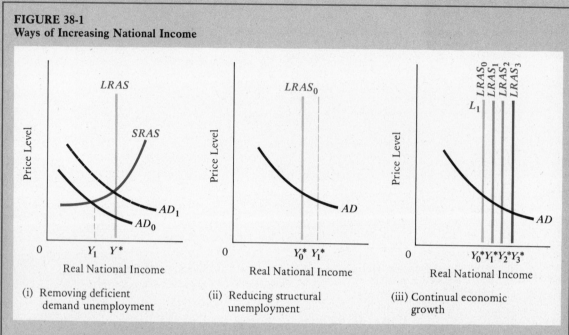

(i) Removing deficient
    demand unemployment

(ii) Reducing structural
    unemployment

(iii) Continual economic
    growth

A once-and-for-all increase in national income can be obtained by raising aggregate demand to remove a GNP gap or by shifting the *LRAS* curve by cutting structural unemployment. Continued increases in national income are possible by shifting the *LRAS* curve through continued economic growth. In (i) there is a GNP gap of $Y_1 Y^*$ at the initial equilibrium position of E_0. An increase in aggregate demand from AD_0 to AD_1 takes equilibrium to E_1, achieving a once-and-for-all change in national income from Y_1 to Y^*.

In (ii) potential output rises from Y_0^* to Y_1^* due to measures that reduce structural unemployment. The *LRAS* curve shifts because those who were formerly unemployed due to having the wrong skills or being in the wrong place are now available for employment.

In (iii) increases in factor supplies and productivity lead to increases in potential income. This *continually* shifts the long-run aggregate supply curve outward. In successive periods it moves from $LRAS_0$ to $LRAS_3$, taking potential income from Y_0^* to Y_1^* to Y_2^* to Y_3^* and so on, as long as growth continues.

---

achieved, further increases in aggregate demand yield only transitory increases in real income but lasting increases in the price level.

Measures that reduce structural unemployment can also increase the employed labor force and thus increase potential income. The increase in income resulting from this change might not be very large. There would, however, be social gain resulting from the reduction in unemployment, especially the long-term unemployment that occurs when people are trapped in declining areas, industries, or occupations.

Over the long haul, however, what really raises national income is *economic growth*; that is, the increase in potential income due to changes in factor supplies—labor and capital—or in the productivity of factors—output per unit of factor input. The removal of a serious GNP gap might raise national income by 10 percent, while the elimination of all structural unemployment might raise it by somewhat less. But a modest growth rate of 3 percent per year raises national income by 10 percent in 3 years and *doubles* it in about 24 years.

Over any long period of time economic growth rather than variations in aggregate demand or in structural unemployment exerts the major effect on real national income.

The Short- and Long-Run Effect of Investment on National Income

The theory of income determination we studied in Part Eight is a short-run theory. It takes potential income as constant and concentrates on the effect of expenditure on aggregate demand. This short-term viewpoint is the focus of Figure 38-1(i).

Short-run national income theory concentrates on the effects of investment on aggregate demand and thus on variations of actual national income around a given potential income.

In the long run, by adding to the nation's capital stock, investment raises potential income. This effect is shown by the continuing outward shift of the *LRAS* curve in Figure 38-1(iii).

The theory of economic growth is a long-run theory. It ignores short-run fluctuations of actual national income around potential income and concentrates on the effects of investment in raising potential income.

The contrast between the short- and long-run aspects of investment is worth reemphasizing. In the short run, any activity that puts income into people's hands will raise aggregate demand. Thus the short-run effect on national income is the same whether a firm invests in digging holes and refilling them or in building a new factory. In terms of growth, however, we are concerned only with that part of investment that adds to a nation's productive capacity.

This point is important because much of what is classified as investment in the national income accounts and what does add to aggregate demand is really consumption expenditure. Assume, for example, that a firm discards an adequate but dingy office building and "invests" in a lavish new head office building with superior facilities for its staff. This will count as investment in the national income data, and the expenditure will add to aggregate demand. In terms of growth, however, it is (at least in part) really disguised consumption for the firm's staff, and not investment that will increase the productivity of its labor force.

Similar observations are true of public-sector expenditure. Any expenditure will add to aggregate demand and raise national income if there are unemployed resources. But only some expenditure adds to the growth of full-employment income. Indeed, public investment expenditure that shores up an industry that would otherwise be declining in order to create employment may have an anti-growth effect. Such expenditure may prevent the reallocation of resources in response to shifts both in the pattern of world demand and in the country's comparative advantage. Thus in the long run the country's capacity to produce commodities that are demanded on open markets may be diminished.

The Short- and Long-Run Effect of Saving on National Income

The short-run effects of an increase in saving are to reduce aggregate demand. If, for example, households elect to save more, this means they spend less. The resulting downward shift in the consumption function lowers aggregate demand and thus lowers equilibrium national income.

In the longer term, however, higher savings are necessary for higher investment. Savings both by firms and households provide the funds out of which investment is financed. Firms usually reinvest their own savings, while the savings of households pass to firms, either directly through the purchase of stocks and bonds or indirectly through financial intermediaries. If full employment is more or less maintained in the long run, then the volume of investment will be strongly influenced by the volume of savings. The higher the savings, the higher the investment—and the higher the investment, the greater the rate of growth due to the accumulation of more and better capital equipment.

In the long run there is no paradox of thrift; societies with high savings rates have high investment rates and, other things being equal, high growth rates.

The Cumulative Nature of Growth

Growth is a much more powerful method of raising living standards than removing either GNP gaps or structural unemployment (or for that matter redistributing income) *because it can go on and on indefinitely.* For example, a growth rate of 2 percent per year may seem insignificant, but if it continues for a century, it will lead to a more than sevenfold increase in real national income!

The cumulative effect of small annual growth rates is large.

To appreciate the cumulative effect of what seems like very small differences in growth rates, examine Table 38-1. Notice that when one country grows faster than another, the gap in their respective standards widens progressively. If countries A and B start from the same level of income, and if country A grows at 3 percent per year while country B grows at 2 percent per year, A's income per

capita will be twice B's in 72 years. You may not think it matters much whether the economy grows at 2 percent or 3 percent per year, but your children and grandchildren will! (A helpful approximation is the "rule of 72." Divide any growth rate into 72 and the resulting number approximates the number of years it will take for income to double.) [47]

To dramatize the powerful long-run effects of differences in growth rates, we included in early editions of this text a table showing students of the 1960s that, if the then current growth trends continued, America would not long remain the world's richest nation, for Sweden, Canada, Japan, and many others were growing at a much faster rate. Many readers of that era rejected the notion as a textbook gimmick; deep down they knew that the material standard of living of the United States was and would remain the highest the world had ever known. Such a table is no longer even interesting, for by 1980 several industrial countries had indeed passed the United States in terms of per capita national income and several more were within 10 percent of the U.S. level. In addition, several oil producers reported higher average incomes. Japan's experience is discussed in Box 38-1.

THEORIES OF ECONOMIC GROWTH

In theoretical discussions of growth it is useful to have an indicator of the ability of an economy to convert its resources into goods and services. One widely used indicator is output per hour of labor, often called simply *productivity.* Obviously, productivity depends not only on labor input, but also on the amount and kind of machinery used, the raw materials available, and so on. The focus of this measure is explained by the special emphasis human beings place on human labor.[1]

Economists today recognize that many different factors may contribute to—or impede—economic growth. Although our present knowledge of the

TABLE 38–1 THE CUMULATIVE EFFECT OF GROWTH

| Year | Percentage rate of growth per year | | | | |
	1%	2%	3%	5%	7%
0	100	100	100	100	100
10	111	122	135	165	201
30	135	182	246	448	817
50	165	272	448	1,218	3,312
70	201	406	817	3,312	13,429
100	272	739	2,009	14,841	109,660

Small differences in growth rates make enormous differences in levels of potential national income over a few decades. Assume that potential national income is 100 in year zero. At a rate of growth of 3 percent, it will be 135 in 10 years, 448 after 50 years, and over 2,000 in a century. Compound interest is a powerful force!

[1] The discussion of the very long run on pages 177–178 of Chapter 11 is relevant here. It should be read now and treated as part of this chapter.

BOX 38–1 A CASE STUDY OF RAPID GROWTH: JAPAN, 1953–1973

The real national income of Japan was 5.4 times as large in 1973 as it was in 1953. Japan's economic growth rate was more than double the average rate in 10 Western countries and greatly exceeded the rate in any of them. What accounted for the extraordinarily rapid growth of Japan's economy?

To answer that question, two economists, Edward F. Denison and William K. Chung, analyzed and measured the sources of economic growth in Japan over two decades and compared the results with those for 10 Western countries. They also measured the difference between levels of output per worker in the United States and Japan in 1970 and identified its sources and magnitude. The results were published in 1976.*

They found that no single factor was responsible for Japan's high postwar growth rate. Rather, the Japanese economy benefited from several major sources of growth: an increase in quantity of labor, an increase in quantity of capital, improved technology in production, and economies of scale. Japan gained more in each of these respects than did any of the 10 other countries studied. In addition, Japan had the greatest reallocation of labor from agriculture to

* Edward F. Denison and William K. Chung, *How Japan's Economy Grew So Fast: The Sources of Postwar Expansion* (Washington, D.C.: Brookings, 1976).

industry of all the countries studied except Italy. Since productivity is generally higher in industry than in agriculture, a shift of this kind raises average productivity and thereby contributes to growth even without an increase in output per person in either sector.

The overall growth record of Japan was high partly because of a low initial *level* of productivity. It is easier to improve from a low base than a high one. At the end of the period productivity was still more than 40 percent lower in Japan than in the United States, even after eliminating the effects of differences between the countries in working hours, in composition and allocation of the labor force, in amounts of capital and land, in size of markets, and in the cyclical positions of the two economies. There was thus an obvious potential for still further Japanese growth relative to the United States.

Can Japan's growth rate be sustained? The authors stressed the probability of the growth rate declining as the various ways of securing fast growth by "catching up" are successively exhausted. Nevertheless, they considered a fairly high rate of long-term growth in Japan—between 5 and 8 percent per year—likely for the rest of this century. (This prediction proved accurate for the 1970s.) By the year 2000 Japan may well be enjoying the highest standard of living of any industrialized country in the world.

relative importance of these factors is far from complete, modern economists look at the problems of growth more optimistically than did the Classical economists of a century or more ago. Of particular importance is the nature and source of the investment opportunities that can lead to growth. The differences between the Classical and contemporary points of view can best be understood by considering a revealing though extreme case.

Growth in a World Without Learning

Suppose that there is a known and fixed stock of projects that might be undertaken. Suppose also that nothing ever happens to increase either the supply of such projects or knowledge about them. Whenever the opportunity is ripe, some of the investment opportunities are utilized, thereby increasing the stock of capital goods and depleting the reservoir of unutilized investment opportunities. Of course, the most productive opportunities will be used first.

Such a view of investment opportunities can be represented by a fixed marginal efficiency of capital schedule. Such a schedule is graphed in Figure 38-2. It relates the stock of capital to the productivity of an additional unit of capital. The productivity of a unit of capital is calculated by dividing the annual value of the additional output resulting from an extra unit of capital by the value of that unit of capital. Thus, for example, a marginal efficiency of capital of 0.2 means that $1 of new capital adds $.20 per year to the stream of output.

The downward slope of the *MEC* schedule indicates that with knowledge constant, increases in the stock of capital bring smaller and smaller increases in output per unit of capital. That is, the rate of return on successive units of capital declines. This shape is a consequence of the law of diminishing returns.[2] If, with land, labor, and knowledge constant, more and more capital is used, the net amount added by successive increments will diminish and may eventually reach zero. Given this schedule, as capital is accumulated in a state of constant knowledge, the society will move down its *MEC* schedule.

In such a "nonlearning" world, where new investment opportunities do not appear, growth occurs only so long as there are unutilized opportunities to use capital effectively to increase output. Growth in a nonlearning world is a transitory phenomenon that occurs as long as the society has a backlog of unutilized investment opportunities.

So far we have discussed the *marginal* efficiency of capital. The *average* efficiency of capital refers to the average amount produced in the whole economy per unit of capital employed. It is common in discussions of the theory of growth to talk in terms of the *capital-output ratio*, which is the reciprocal of output per unit of capital. In a world without learning, the capital-output ratio is increasing.

In a world without learning the growth in the capital stock will have two important consequences:

[2] This hypothesis was discussed on pages 157–160.

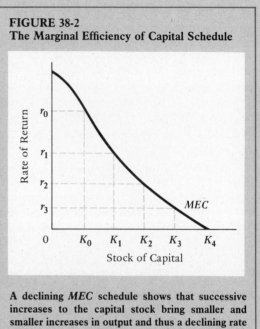

FIGURE 38-2
The Marginal Efficiency of Capital Schedule

A declining *MEC* schedule shows that successive increases to the capital stock bring smaller and smaller increases in output and thus a declining rate of return. A fixed *MEC* schedule can represent the theory of growth in an economy with some unutilized investment opportunities but no learning. Increases in investment that increase the capital stock from K_0 to K_1 to . . . K_4 lower the rate of return from r_0 to r_1 to . . . zero. Because the productivity of successive units of capital decreases, the capital-output ratio rises.

1. Successive increases in capital accumulation will be less and less productive, and the capital-output ratio will be increasing.
2. The marginal efficiency of new capital will be decreasing and will eventually be pushed to zero as the backlog of investment opportunities is used up.

Growth with Learning

The steady depletion of growth opportunities in the previous case resulted from the fact that new investment opportunities were never discovered or created. However, if investment opportunities are created as well as used up with the passage of time, the *MEC* schedule will shift outward over time and the effects of increasing the capital stock may be different. This is illustrated in Figure 38-3.

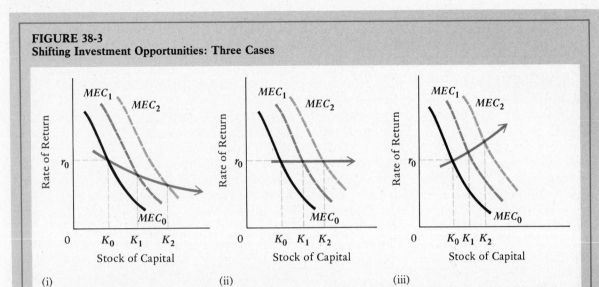

FIGURE 38-3
Shifting Investment Opportunities: Three Cases

When both knowledge and the capital stock grow, the actual marginal efficiency of capital depends on their relative rates of growth. In each case the economy at period 0 has the MEC_0 curve, a capital stock of K_0, and a rate of return of r_0. In period 1 the curve shifts to MEC_1 and there is investment to increase the stock of capital to K_1. In period 2 the curve shifts to MEC_2 and there is new investment that increases the capital stock to K_2. It is the relative size of the shift of the MEC curve and the additions of the capital stock that are important.

In (i) investment occurs more rapidly than increases in investment opportunities and the rate of return falls along the black curve. In (ii) investment occurs at exactly the same rate as investment opportunities and the rate of return is constant. In (iii) investment occurs less rapidly than increases in investment opportunities and the rate of return rises.

Such outward shifts can be regarded as the consequences of "learning" either about investment opportunities or about the techniques that create such opportunities. When learning occurs, what matters is how rapidly the MEC schedule shifts relative to the amount of capital accumulation. Three possibilities are shown in Figure 38-3.

Gradual Reduction in Investment Opportunities: The Classical View

If, as in Figure 38-3(i), investment opportunities are created but at a slower rate than they are used up, there will be a tendency toward a falling rate of return and an increasing ratio of capital to output. The predictions in this case are the same as those given above (in color) for the world without

learning: too slow, rather than no, discovery of new investment opportunities.

This figure illustrates the theory of growth held by most early economists. They saw the economic problem as one of fixed land, a rising population, and a gradual exhaustion of investment opportunities. These conditions, they believed, would ultimately force the economy into a static condition with no growth, very high capital-output ratios, and the marginal return on additional units of capital forced down toward zero.

Constant or Rising Investment Opportunities: The Contemporary View

The pessimism of the Classical economists came from their failure to anticipate the possibility of

BOX 38–2 SHOULD CANADA ADOPT POLICIES TO PROMOTE R&D EXPENDITURE?

In *The Weakest Link: A Technological Perspective on Canadian Industrial Underdevelopment*, published in 1978, the Science Council of Canada claims that "Canada's R&D performance is about the worst of the western world!" Does this claim stand in the face of facts? If so, is government action to promote R&D expenditure called for?

In a critique of the Science Council, Professor Kristian Palda of Queen's University argues that current estimates of Canadian R&D expenditure are in fact serious underestimates. He writes:

The leading edge of innovative industrial activity is widely found in small enterprises launched by engineers or scientists. . . . Their fairly high salaries are not carried on the R&D line of their corporate financial statements. In Canada, due to the heavy representation of the small-scale manufacturing firm this undoubtedly leads to a substantial underestimate of industrial R&D effort and personnel. . . .

In addition, "high technology" itself is difficult to define; it could mean "capital intensive," "value added per employee," or perhaps "skill level requirements per employee," depending on the circumstances. The blanket application of any one definition leads to absurd results. Professor Palda notes that if, for example, high technology were defined as an industry where research expenditures make a large contribution to the productivity of that industry, then agriculture would be the most technology-intensive industry in North America. Yet the Science Council does not even consider agriculture in its dismal overview of Canada's technological development.

Thus there is reason for being skeptical of blanket statements about the state of R&D expenditure in Canada.

There is the related question, given the presence of foreign-owned subsidiaries in the Canadian economy, of whether the percentage of R&D expenditure within Canada is a relevant measure of technical performance. One study conducted by the federal Ministry of State for Science and Technology estimated that in one year in the mid 1970s the cost of "invisible" R&D performed for Canadian subsidiaries by their parent firms was $688 million, compared to the cost of actual R&D performed in Canada by foreign-controlled subsidiaries of $282 million. Canada may or may not be backward in its

really rapid innovation—of technological progress that could push investment opportunities outward as rapidly or more rapidly than they were used up, as shown in parts (ii) and (iii) of Figure 38-3.

In a world with rapid innovation:

1. Successive increases in capital accumulation may prove highly productive, and the capital-output ratio may be constant or decreasing.
2. Despite large amounts of capital accumulation, the marginal efficiency of new capital may remain constant or even increase as new investment opportunities are created.

The historical record suggests that outward shifts in investment opportunities over time have led to the reality of sustained growth. Evidently modern economies have been successful in generating new investment opportunities at least as rapidly as old ones were used up. Modern economists devote more attention to understanding the *shifts* in the *MEC* schedule over time and less to its shape under a nonlearning situation.

Box 38-2 takes up some of the controversies surrounding government policies to support expenditure on research and development in order to induce learning and innovation.

research *performance*, but that it suffers in terms of *access* to R&D results seems implausible.

Some groups have lobbied actively for policies to encourage R&D expenditure in Canada. What strategies or policies are involved?

One often quoted strategy is to "pick winners" and subsidize them. This approach raises two questions: Is the political will strong enough to let the losers sink and is the political intellect strong enough to identify the potential winners? Another proposal is to subsidize R&D directly. But it is possible that if governments actively promoted R&D, the private sector would reduce its R&D expenditure correspondingly. And because R&D requires a large sales volume to make it work, giving R&D subsidies to firms that do not have a sufficient market may well be a waste of money. Technological improvements are of no advantage when they do not contribute to a marketable product; hence access to a large market is necessary.

A related proposal is to screen the import of foreign technology. Presumably this would stimulate R&D expenditure by keeping foreign technology out. Some would prefer to try to direct the import of technology into Canadian firms rather than to foreign subsidiaries. This would tend to reduce the role of foreign ownership in the Canadian economy, but it would result in a slower transmission of new technology and a higher price for what is transmitted.

Common to all these proposals is the advocacy of increased government involvement to promote "high technology" industries. But what are the costs of such intervention? Foreign experience tells us that the costs could be enormous. In examining the French experience with nuclear energy, aerospace computers, and electronics, Professor Palda shows that technology was ultimately imported from abroad only after expensive domestic programs had failed to be technically or economically successful.

Most economists remain rather skeptical about the need for and the effectiveness of R&D policies. In an Ontario Economic Council study in 1977, Professor Donald McFetteridge of Carleton University argued that researchers have yet to produce any statistical evidence that the rate of return to industrial and R&D development in Canada is positive—let alone so high that it should be favored over alternative uses of our scarce investment money.

A Contemporary View of Growth

The Classical economists had a relatively simple theory of growth because they viewed a single mechanism—capital accumulation—as decisively important. Contemporary theorists begin by recognizing a number of factors that influence growth, no one of which is necessarily dominant.

Quantity of Capital Per Worker

Human beings have always been tool users. It is still true that more and more tools tend to lead to more and more output. As long as a society has unexploited investment opportunities, productive capacity can be increased by increasing the stock of capital. The effect on output per worker of "mere" capital accumulation is so noticeable that it was once regarded as virtually the sole source of growth.

But if capital accumulation were the only source of growth, it would lead to movement down the *MEC* schedule and to a rising capital-output ratio and a falling rate of return on capital. The evidence does not support these predictions. The facts suggest that investment opportunities have expanded as rapidly as investments in capital goods, roughly along the pattern of Figure 38-3(ii). While capital accumulation has taken place and has accounted for much observed growth, it cannot have been the only source of growth.

Quality of Capital

New knowledge and inventions can contribute markedly to the growth of potential national income, even without capital accumulation. In order to see this, assume that the proportion of the society's resources devoted to the production of capital goods is just sufficient to replace capital as it wears out. Thus, if the old capital were merely replaced in the same form, the capital stock would be constant and there would be no increase in the capacity to produce. But if there is a growth of knowledge so that as old equipment wears out it is replaced by different, more productive equipment, national income will be growing.

Increases in productive capacity that are intrinsic to the form of capital goods in use are called **embodied technical change.** The historical importance of embodied technical change is clearly visible: The assembly line and automation transformed much of manufacturing, the airplane revolutionized transportation, and electronic devices now dominate the communications industries. These innovations plus less well-known but no less profound ones—for example, improvements in the strength of metals, the productivity of seeds, and the techniques for recovering basic raw materials from the ground—create new investment opportunities.

Less visible but nonetheless important changes occur through **disembodied technical change.** These concern innovations in the organization of production that are not embodied in the form of the capital goods used. One example is improved techniques of managerial control.

Most innovations involve both embodied and disembodied changes: New processes require new machines, which make yet newer processes economical. Computerization promises many such changes in the years ahead. One of them, which

many regard with a mixture of awe and apprehension, is a cashless society in which banks become parts of vast information networks that receive one's pay, pay one's bills, and invest one's savings.

But whatever the form of innovation, the nature of the goods and services consumed and the way they are made changes continually as innovations occur. Major innovations of the past century have resulted from the development of the telephone, the linotype, the automobile, the airplane, plastics, the assembly line, coaxial cable, xerography, computers, transistors, and silicon chips. It is hard for us to imagine life without them.

The Quality of Labor

The "quality" of labor—or what is often called *human capital*—has several aspects. One involves improvements in the health and longevity of the population. Of course, these are desired as ends in themselves, yet they have consequences for both the size of the labor force and its productivity. There is no doubt that they have increased productivity per worker-hour by cutting down on illness, accidents, and absenteeism. At the same time the extension of the normal life span with no comparable increase in the working life span has created a larger group of nonworking aged that exercises a claim on total output. Whether health improvements alone have increased output per capita in Canada is not clear.

A second aspect of the quality of human capital concerns technical training, from learning to operate a machine to learning how to be a scientist. Training is clearly required to invent, operate, manage, and repair complex machines. More subtly, there are often believed to be general social advantages to an educated population. It has been shown that productivity improves with literacy and that, in general, the longer a person has been educated, the more adaptable he or she is to new and changing challenges—and thus, in the long run, the more productive. But education may also increase feelings of alienation in a society that is thought to be arbitrary or unjust.

The Quantity of Labor

The size of a country's population and the extent of its participation in the labor force are important in and of themselves, not merely because they affect the quantity of a factor of production. For this reason, it is less common to speak of the quantity of people available for work as a source of, or detriment to, growth than it is to speak of the quantity of capital or iron ore in the same way. But clearly, for any given state of knowledge and supplies of other factors of production, the size of the population can affect the level of output per capita. Every child born has both a mouth and a pair of hands; over a lifetime, each person will be both a consumer and a producer. Thus, on average, it is meaningful to speak of overpopulated or underpopulated economies, depending on whether the contribution to production of additional people would raise or lower the level of per capita income.

Because population size is related to income per capita, we can define a theoretical concept, *optimal population*, that maximizes income per capita.

Many countries have had, or do have, conscious population policies. North America in the nineteenth century sought immigrants, as did Australia until very recently. Germany under Hitler paid bonuses for the birth of additional Aryan children and otherwise offered incentives to create Germans. Greece in the 1950s and 1960s tried to stem emigration to Western Europe. All are examples of countries that believed they had insufficient population, though the motives were not in every case purely economic. In contrast, many underdeveloped countries of South America, Africa, and Asia desire to limit population growth.

Structural Change

Changes in the economy's structure can cause large fluctuations in its growth rate. For example, a decline in such low-productivity sectors as agriculture and an expansion in such high-productivity sectors as manufacturing will temporarily boost the measured aggregate growth rate as labor moves from the declining to the expanding sectors.

On the other hand, when one type of energy (say, solar) supplants another type (say, oil), much existing capital stock specifically geared to the original energy source may become too costly to operate and will be scrapped. New capital geared to the new energy source will be built. During the transition, investment expenditure is high, thus stimulating aggregate demand. But there is little if any expansion in the economy's output capacity because the old capital goods have been scrapped. Gross investment is high, but net investment is low since the capital expenditure *transforms* the capital stock but does not *increase* it. Similarly, new pollution control laws will affect investment expenditure but will not lead to growth in capacity. (The reduction in pollution may nonetheless be socially desirable.)

A rise in the international price of *imported* energy will also lower productivity. Although the same volume of goods can be produced with a given input of labor, a smaller portion of the output's value now accrues as income to domestic workers and firms because more must be used to pay for the energy imports. The higher-priced imported energy input means that domestic *value added* falls, and with it GNP per worker. This shows up in the statistics as a decline in productivity and a temporary fall in growth rates.

These are some of the many factors that were operative in the 1970s and early 1980s. They worked to depress growth rates for some considerable period of time. But they are not permanent factors. When the structural adjustments are complete, their depressing effects will pass.

Institutional Considerations

Almost all aspects of a country's institutions can foster or deter the efficient use of a society's natural and human resources. Social and religious habits, legal institutions, and traditional patterns of national and international trade are all important. So too is the political climate. In Chapter 23 many of these institutions were discussed as potential barriers to development.

Is There a Most Important Source of Growth?

The modern theory of growth tends to reject a dominant source of growth and to recognize that several different influences singly and in interaction affect the growth rate.

Among the major contributors to rapid economic growth are a capital stock that is steadily growing and improving in quality, a healthy and well-educated labor force, and a rate of population growth that is small enough to permit per capita growth in capital.

These factors are more likely to be utilized effectively in some institutional settings than in others.

A complete theory of growth would do more than list a series of influences all of which affect the growth rate. It would include assessments of (1) their relative importance, (2) the trade-offs involved in having more of one beneficial influence and less of another, and (3) the interactions among the various influences. This poses a formidable empirical challenge to research that is just beginning to be accepted.

While much remains to be learned, an important tentative conclusion of recent studies is that *improvements* in *quality* of capital, human as well as physical, have played a larger role than increases in the *quantity* of capital in the economic growth of North America since 1900. Whether quality rather than quantity of capital is also the more important source of growth for countries with very different cultural patterns, more acute population problems, or more limited natural resources is a matter of continuing research.

COSTS AND BENEFITS OF GROWTH

In the remainder of this chapter, we shall outline some more general considerations concerning economic growth. We start by looking at the benefits and then the costs of growth. Boxes 38-3 and 38-4 outline the popular arguments on both sides of the growth debate.

Benefits of Growth

Growth in Living Standards

A country whose per capita output grows at 3 percent per year doubles its living standards about every 24 years.

A primary reason for desiring growth is to raise general living standards.

The extreme importance of economic growth in raising income can be illustrated by comparing the real income of a father with the real income of the son who follows in his father's footsteps. If the son neither rises nor falls in the relative income scale compared with his father, his share of the country's national income will be the same as his father's. If the son is 30 years younger than his father, he can expect to have a real income nearly twice as large as the one his father enjoyed when his father was the same age. These figures assume that the father and son live in a country such as the United States where the growth rate has been 2 or 3 percent per year. If they live in Japan, where growth has been going on at a rate of about 8 percent per year, the son's income will be about 10 times as large as his father's.

For those who share in it, growth is a powerful weapon against poverty. A family earning $7,500 today can expect an income of $11,000 within 10 years (in constant dollars) if it just shares in a 4 percent growth rate. The transformation of the lifestyle of blue-collar workers in North America as well as in Germany and Japan in a generation provides a notable example of the escape from poverty that growth makes possible.

Of course, not everyone benefits equally from growth. Many of the poorest are not even in the labor force and thus are least likely to share in the higher wages that, along with profits, are the primary means by which the gains from growth are distributed. For this reason, even in a growing economy redistribution policies will be needed if poverty is to be averted.

BOX 38–3 AN OPEN LETTER TO THE ORDINARY CITIZEN FROM A SUPPORTER OF THE GROWTH-IS-GOOD SCHOOL

Dear Ordinary Citizen:

You live in the world's first civilization that is devoted principally to satisfying *your* needs rather than those of a privileged minority. Past civilizations have always been based on leisure and high consumption for a tiny upper class, a reasonable living standard for a small middle class, and hard work with little more than subsistence consumption for the great mass of people. In the past, the average person saw little of the civilized and civilizing products of the economy, except when he or she was toiling to produce them.

The continuing Industrial Revolution is based on mass-produced goods for you, the ordinary citizen. It ushered in a period of sustained economic growth that has raised consumption standards of ordinary citizens to levels previously reserved throughout history for a tiny privileged minority. Reflect on a few examples: travel, live and recorded music, art, good food, inexpensive books, universal literacy, and a genuine chance to be educated. Most important, there is leisure to provide time and energy to enjoy these and thousands of other products of the modern industrial economy.

Would any ordinary family seriously doubt the benefits of growth and prefer to go back to the world of 150 or 500 years ago in its same relative social and economic position? Surely, the answer is no. But we cannot say the same for those with incomes in the top 1 percent or 2 percent of the income distribution. Economic growth has destroyed much of their privileged consumption position: they must now vie with the masses when visiting the world's beauty spots and be annoyed, while lounging on the terrace of a palatial mansion, by the sound of charter flights carrying ordinary people to inexpensive holidays in far places. The rich resent their loss of exclusive rights to luxury consumption. Some complain bitterly, and it is not surprising that they find their intellectual apologists.

Whether they know it or not, the antigrowth economists—such as Harvard's Ken Galbraith, Cambridge's Joan Robinson, and the LSE's Ed Mishan—are not the social revolutionaries they think they are. They are counterrevolutionaries who would set back the clock of material progress for the ordinary person. They say that growth has produced pollution and wasteful consumption of all kinds of frivolous products that add nothing to human happiness. But the democratic solution to pollution is not to go back to where so few people consume luxuries that pollution is trivial; it is to accept pollution as part of a transitional phase connected with the ushering in of mass consumption, to keep the mass consumption, and to learn to control the pollution it tends to create.

It is only through further growth that the average citizen can enjoy consumption standards (of travel, culture, medical and health care, etc.) now available to people in the top 25 percent of the income distribution—which includes the intellectuals who earn large royalties from the books they write denouncing growth. If you think that extra income confers little real benefit, just ask those in that top 25 percent to trade incomes with the average citizen. Or see how hard *they* struggle to reduce their income taxes.

Ordinary citizens, do not be deceived by disguised elitist doctrines. Remember that the very rich and the elite have much to gain by stopping growth—and even more by rolling it back—but you have everything to gain by letting it go forward.

Onward!

A. Growthman

BOX 38–4 AN OPEN LETTER TO THE ORDINARY CITIZEN FROM A SUPPORTER OF THE GROWTH-IS-BAD SCHOOL

Dear Ordinary Citizen:

You live in a world that is being despoiled by a mindless search for ever higher levels of material consumption at the cost of all other values. Once upon a time, men and women knew how to enjoy creative work and to derive satisfaction from simple activities undertaken in scarce, and hence highly valued, leisure time. Today the ordinary worker is a mindless cog in an assembly line that turns out ever more goods that the advertisers must work overtime to persuade the worker to consume.

Statisticians and politicians count the increasing flow of material output as a triumph of modern civilization. Consider not the flow of output in general, but the individual products that it contains. You arise from your electric-blanketed bed, clean your teeth with an electric toothbrush, open with an electric can opener a can of the sad remnants of a once-proud orange, you eat your bread baked from super-refined and chemically refortified flour, and you climb into your car to sit in vast traffic jams on exhaust-polluted highways. And so it goes, with endless consumption of high-technology products that give you no more real satisfaction than the simple, cheaply produced equivalent products used by your great-grandfathers: soft woolly blankets, natural bristle toothbrushes, real oranges, old-fashioned and coarse but healthy bread, and public transport that moved on uncongested roads and gave its passengers time to chat with their neighbors, to read, or just to daydream.

Television commercials tell you that by consuming more you are happier. But happiness lies not in increasing consumption but in increasing the ratio of *satisfaction of wants* to *total wants*. Since the more you consume the more the advertisers persuade you that you want to con-

sume, you are almost certainly less happy than the average citizen in a small town in 1900 whom we can visualize sitting on the family porch, sipping a cool beer or a lemonade, and enjoying the antics of the children as they play with scooters made out of old crates and jump rope with pieces of old clothesline.

Today the landscape is dotted with endless factories producing the plastic trivia of the modern industrial society. They drown you in a cloud of noise, air, and water pollution. The countryside is despoiled by strip mines, petroleum refineries, acid rain, and dangerous nuclear power stations producing energy that is devoured insatiably by modern factories and motor vehicles.

Worse, our precious heritage of natural resources is being fast used up. Spaceship earth flies, captainless, in its senseless orgy of self-consuming consumption.

Now is the time to stop this madness. We must stabilize production, reduce pollution, conserve our natural resources, and seek justice through a more equitable distribution of existing total income.

A long time ago Malthus taught us that if we do not limit population voluntarily, nature will do it for us in a cruel and savage manner. Today the same is true of output: if we do not halt its growth voluntarily, the halt will be imposed on us by a disastrous increase in pollution and a rapid exhaustion of natural resources.

Citizens, awake! Shake off the worship of growth, learn to enjoy the bounty that is yours already, and reject the endless, self-defeating search for increased happiness through ever-increasing consumption.

Upward!

A. Nongrowthman

Growth and Income Redistribution

Economic growth makes many kinds of redistributions easier to achieve. For example, a rapid growth rate makes it more feasible politically to alleviate poverty. If existing income is to be redistributed, someone's standard of living will actually have to be lowered. However, when there is economic growth, and when the increment in income is redistributed (through government intervention), it is possible to reduce income inequalities without actually having to lower anyone's income. It is much easier for a rapidly growing economy to be generous toward its less fortunate citizens—or neighbors—than it is for a static economy.

Growth and Life-Style

A family often finds that a big increase in its income can lead to a major change in the pattern of its consumption—that extra money buys important amenities of life. In the same way, the members of society as a whole may change their consumption patterns as their average income rises. Not only do markets in a country that is growing rapidly make it profitable to produce more cars, but the government is led to produce more highways and to provide more recreational areas for its newly affluent (and mobile) citizens. At yet a later stage, a concern about litter, pollution, and ugliness may become important, and their correction may then begin to account for a significant fraction of GNP. Such "amenities" usually become matters of social concern only when growth has assured the provision of the basic requirements for food, clothing, and housing of a substantial majority of the population.

National Defense and Prestige

When one country is competing with another for power or prestige, rates of growth are important. If our national income is growing at 2 percent, say, while the other country's is growing at 5 percent, the other country will only have to wait for our relative strength to dwindle. Moreover, the faster its productivity is growing, the easier a country will find it to bear the expenses of an arms race or a program of foreign aid.

More subtly, growth has become part of the currency of international prestige. Countries that are engaged in persuading other countries of the might or right of their economic and political systems point to their rapid rates of growth as evidence of their achievements.

Costs of Growth

The benefits discussed above suggest that growth is a great blessing. It is surely true that, other things being equal, most people would regard a fast rate of growth as preferable to a slow one, but other things are seldom equal.

Social and Personal Costs of Growth

Industrialization can cause deterioration of the environment. Unspoiled landscapes give way to highways, factories, and billboards; air and water become polluted; and in some cases unique and priceless relics of earlier ages—from flora and fauna to ancient ruins—disappear. Urbanization tends to move people away from the simpler life of farms and small towns and into the crowded slum-ridden and often darkly evil life of the urban ghetto. Those remaining behind in the rural areas find that rural life, too, has changed. Larger-scale farming, the decline of population, and the migration of children from the farm to the city all have their costs. The stepped-up tempo of life brings joys to some but tragedy to others. Accidents, ulcers, crime rates, suicides, divorces, and murder all tend to be higher in periods of rapid change and in more developed societies.

When an economy is growing, it is also changing. Innovation leaves obsolete machines in its wake, and it also leaves partially obsolete people. No matter how well trained you are at age 25, in another 25 years your skills may well be partially obsolete. Some will find that their skills have become completely outdated and unneeded. A rapid rate of growth requires rapid adjustments, which can cause much upset and misery to the individuals affected. The decline in the number of unskilled jobs makes the lot of untrained workers much more difficult. When they lose jobs, they may well fail to find others—particularly if they are over 50.

It is often argued that costs of this kind are a small price to pay for the great benefits that growth can bring. Even if that is true in the aggregate (which is a matter of debate), these personal costs are very unevenly borne. Indeed, many of those for whom growth is most costly (in terms of jobs) share least in the fruits of growth. Yet it is also a mistake to see only the costs—to yearn for the good old days while enjoying higher living standards that growth alone has made possible.

The Opportunity Cost of Growth

In a world of scarcity, almost nothing is free. Growth requires heavy investments of resources in capital goods as well as in activities such as education. Often these investments yield no *immediate* return in terms of goods and services for consumption; thus they imply sacrifices by the current generation of consumers.

Growth, which promises more goods tomorrow, is achieved by consuming fewer goods today. For the economy as a whole this is the primary cost of growth.

An example will suggest the magnitude of this cost. Suppose the fictitious economy of Kanada has full employment and is experiencing growth at the rate of 2 percent per year. Its citizens consume 85 percent of the GNP and invest 15 percent. The people of Kanada know that if they are willing to decrease immediately their consumption to 77 percent, they will produce more capital and thus shift at once to a 3 percent growth rate. The new rate can be maintained as long as they keep saving and investing 23 percent of the national income. Should they do it?

Table 38-2 illustrates the choice in terms of time paths of consumption. How expensive is the "invest now, consume later" strategy? On the assumed figures, it take 10 years for the actual amount of

consumption to catch up to what it would have been had no reallocation been made. In the intervening 10 years a good deal of consumption was lost, and the cumulative losses in consumption must be made up before society can really be said to have broken even. It takes an additional 9 years before total consumption over the whole period is as large as it would have been if the economy had remained on the 2 percent path. [48]

A policy of sacrificing present living standards for a gain that does not begin to be reaped for a generation is hardly likely to appeal to any but the altruistic or the very young. The question of how

TABLE 38-2 **THE OPPORTUNITY COST OF GROWTH**

In year	(A) Level of consumption at 2% growth rate	(B) Level of consumption at 3% growth rate	(C) Cumulative gain (loss) in consumption
0	85.0	77.0	(8.0)
1	86.7	79.3	(15.4)
2	88.5	81.8	(22.1)
3	90.3	84.2	(28.2)
4	92.1	86.8	(33.5)
5	93.9	89.5	(37.9)
6	95.8	92.9	(40.8)
7	97.8	95.0	(43.6)
8	99.7	97.9	(45.4)
9	101.8	100.9	(46.3)
10	103.8	103.9	(46.2)
15	114.7	120.8	(28.6)
20	126.8	140.3	19.6
30	154.9	189.4	251.0
40	189.2	255.6	745.9

Transferring resources from consumption to investment goods lowers current income but raises future income. The example assumes that income in year zero is 100, and that consumption of 85 percent of national income is possible with a 2 percent growth rate. It is further assumed that to achieve a 3 percent growth rate, consumption must fall to 77 percent of income. A shift from (A) to (B) decreases consumption for 10 years but increases it thereafter. The cumulative effect on consumption is shown in (C); the gains eventually become large.

much of its living standards one generation is prepared to sacrifice for its heirs (who are in any case likely to be richer) is troublesome. As one critic put it, Why should we sacrifice for them? What have they ever done for us?

Many governments, particularly those seeking a larger role in world affairs, have chosen to force the diversion of resources from consumption to investment. The Germans under Hitler, the Russians under Stalin, and the Chinese under Mao Tse-tung adopted four-year and five-year plans that did just this. Many less-developed countries are using such plans today. Such resource shifts are particularly important when actual growth rates are very small (say, less than 1 percent), for without some current sacrifice there is little or no prospect of real growth in the lifetimes of today's citizens. The very lowest growth rates are frequently encountered in the very poorest countries. This creates a cruel dilemma, discussed in Chapter 23 as the vicious circle of poverty.

Growth As a Goal of Policy: Do the Benefits Justify the Costs?

Suppose that the members of a society want to increase their output of goods by 10 percent in one year. There are many ways they can do this.

1. They may be able to find idle and unutilized resources and put them to work.
2. They may be able to schedule extra shifts and overtime labor.
3. They may, by exhortation or by an appropriate incentive system, induce people to work much harder.
4. They may (if they have time) increase the supply of machines and factories.
5. They may utilize new techniques that permit them to get more output from the same inputs.

In the short run, the first three approaches seem the more promising; in fact, when nations face such crises as wars, these devices are used to achieve rapid increases in output. But the gains to be achieved by utilizing unemployed resources, ex-

tending the hours of use of employed ones, or "working harder" are limited. Eventually they will be used up. When there are no longer unutilized resources or underutilized capacity, further increases in output become more difficult to achieve.

In the long term, it is the last two approaches that bring the sustained increases in living standards that have eliminated the 14-hour day and the 6-day work week and made possible both leisure and high material standards of living.

But do the already developed countries need yet more growth? Most people think they do. Poverty is now a solvable problem in North America as a direct result of its enhanced average living standards. Clearly, people in the top quarter of the present income distribution have more opportunities for leisure, travel, culture, fine wines, and gracious living than have persons with much lower incomes. Most of those now in the bottom half of the income distribution would like these opportunities too. Only growth can give it to them.

Today, many countries that have not yet—or have only newly—undergone sustained periods of economic growth in modern times are urgently seeking to copy those that have in order to obtain the benefits of growth.

Most nations and most people today wish to pursue the goal of growth for the benefits it brings, despite its costs.

How seriously the costs are taken depends in part on how many of the benefits of growth have already been achieved. With mounting population problems, the poor countries are increasingly preoccupied with creating growth. With mounting awareness of pollution, the rich countries are devoting ever more resources to overcoming the problems caused by growth—at the same time that they are understandably reluctant to give up further growth.

Indeed, a similar conflict can often be seen within the same country at one time: a relatively poor community fights to acquire a new paper mill for the employment and income it will create; another, relatively affluent community deplores the ruin of its beaches and its air by an existing mill.

Are There Limits to Growth?

Those opposed to growth argue that sustained growth for another century is undesirable; some even argue that it is impossible. Of course all terrestrial things have an ultimate limit. Astronomers predict that the solar system itself will die as the sun burns out in another 6 billion or so years. To be of practical concern, a limit must be within some reasonable planning horizon. Best-selling books of the 1970s by Jay Forrester [*World Dynamics* (1973)] and D. H. Meadows et al. [*The Limits to Growth* (1974)] predicted the imminence of a growth-induced doomsday. Living standards were predicted to reach a peak about the year 2000 and then, in the words of Professor Nordhaus, a leading critic of these models, to "descend inexorably to the level of Neanderthal man." What can be said about this debate?

The Uncontroversial Fact of Increasing Pressure on Natural Resources

The years since World War II have seen a rapid acceleration in the consumption of the world's resources, particularly fossil fuels and basic minerals. World population has increased from under 2.5 billion to over 4 billion in that period, and this alone has increased the demand for all the world's resources. But the single fact of population growth greatly understates the pressure on resources.

Calculations by Professor Nathan Keyfitz of Harvard and others focus on the resources used by those who can claim a life-style of the level enjoyed by 90 percent of North American families. This so-called middle class, which today includes about one-sixth of the world's population, consumes 15 to 30 times as much oil per capita and, overall, at least 5 times as much of the earth's scarce resources per capita as do the other "poor" five-sixths of the population.

The world's poor are not, however, content to remain forever poor. Whether they live in the USSR, Brazil, Korea, or Kenya, they have let their governments understand that they expect policies that generate enough growth to give *them* the higher consumption levels that all of *us* take for granted. This upward aspiration is being fulfilled to a degree. The growth of the middle class has been nearly 4 percent per year—twice the rate of population growth—over the postwar period. The number of persons realizing middle-class living standards is estimated to have increased from 200 million to 700 million between 1950 and 1980.

This growth is a major factor in the recently recognized or projected shortages of natural resources: The increases in demand of the last three decades have outstripped discovery of new supplies and caused crises in energy and mineral supplies as well as food shortages. Yet the 4 percent growth rate of the middle class, which is too fast for present resources, is too slow for the aspirations of the billions who live in underdeveloped countries and see the fruits of development all around them. Thus the pressure on world resources of energy, minerals, and food is likely to accelerate even if population growth is reduced.

Another way to look at the problem of resource pressure is to note that present technology and resources could not possibly support the present population of the world at the standard of living of today's average North American family. The demand for oil would increase fivefold to tenfold. Since these calculations (most unrealistically) assume no population growth anywhere in the world and no growth in living standards for the richest sixth of the world's population, it is evident that resources are insufficient.

A Tentative Verdict

Most economists agree that conjuring up absolute limits to growth based on the assumptions of constant technology and fixed resources is not warranted. Yet there is surely cause for concern. Most agree that any barrier can be overcome by technological advances—but not in an instant, and not automatically. Clearly there is a problem of timing: how soon can we discover and put into practice the knowledge required to solve the problems that are made ever more imminent by growth in population, growth in affluence, and by the growing aspirations of the billions who now live in poverty? There is no guarantee that a whole generation may not be caught in transition, with social and political consequences that promise to be enormous even if they are not cataclysmic. The nightmare conjured up by the doomsday models may have served its purpose if it helps to focus our attention on these problems.

SUMMARY

1. National income can increase as a result of a reduction in the GNP gap, a reduction in structural unemployment, or growth in the level of potential national income.

2. Investment that has short-term effects on national income through aggregate demand also has long-term effects through growth in potential national income. Such growth is frequently measured using rates of change of potential real national income per person or per hour of labor employed.

3. Savings reduces aggregate demand and therefore reduces national income in the short run, but in the long run savings finance the investment that leads to growth in potential income.

4. The cumulative effects of even small differences in growth rates become large over periods of a decade or more.

5. Understanding growth involves understanding both the utilization of existing investment opportunities and the process of creating new investment opportunities. The source of economic growth was once thought to be almost entirely capital accumulation and the utilization of a backlog of unexploited investment opportunities. Today most economists recognize that many investment opportunities can be created, and much attention is given to the sources of outward shifts in the *MEC* schedule through both embodied and disembodied technical change.

6. The most important benefit of growth lies in its contribution to the long-run struggle to raise living standards and escape poverty. Growth also makes more manageable the policies that would redistribute income among people. Economic growth can likewise play an important role in a country's national defense or in its struggle for international prestige.

7. Growth, while often beneficial, is never costless. The opportunity cost of growth is the diversion of resources from current consumption to capital formation. For some individuals who are left behind in a rapidly changing world the costs are higher and more personal. The optimal rate of growth involves balancing benefits and costs. Most people do not wish to forego the benefits growth can bring, but neither do they wish to maximize growth at any cost.

8. In addition to mere increases in quantity of capital per person, any list of factors affecting growth includes the extent of innovation, the quality of human capital, the size of the working population, and the whole institutional setting.

9. The critical importance of increasing knowledge and new technology in sustaining growth is highlighted by the great drain on existing natural resources of the explosive growth of the last two or three decades. Without continuing new knowledge, the present needs and aspirations of the world's population cannot come anywhere even close to being met.

TOPICS FOR REVIEW

The short- and long-run effects of saving and investment
The cumulative nature of growth
Factors affecting growth
Effects of capital accumulation with and without new knowledge
Embodied and disembodied technical change
Benefits and costs of growth
Limits to growth

DISCUSSION QUESTIONS

1. We usually study and measure economic growth in macroeconomic terms. But in a market economy who makes the decisions that lead to growth? What kind of decisions and what kind of actions cause growth to occur? How might a detailed study of individual markets be relevant to understanding economic growth?

2. Why is rising productivity a more significant contributing factor for economic growth than simply increasing the quantity of productive resources? Define *productivity*. List all the factors that increase the productivity of labor and the productivity of capital. Comment on the differences and similarities of the two lists.

3. *Family Weekly* recently listed (among others) the following "inventions that have changed our lives": microwave ovens, digital clocks, bank credit cards, freeze-dried coffee, tape cassettes, climate-controlled shopping malls, automatic toll collectors, soft contact lenses, tubeless tires, and electronic word processors.

   Which of them would you hate to do without? Which, if any, will have a major impact on life in the twenty-first century? If there are any that you believe will not, does that mean they are frivolous and unimportant?

4. The Overseas Development Council, in 1977, introduced "a new measure of economic development based on the physical quality of life." Its index, called PQLI, gives one-third weight to each of the following three indicators: literacy, life expectancy, and infant mortality. While countries such as the United States and the Netherlands rank very high on either the PQLI or on an index of per capita real national income, some relatively poor countries, such as Sri Lanka, rank much higher on the PQLI index than much richer countries such as Algeria and Kuwait. Discuss the merits or deficiencies of this measure.

5. "The case for economic growth is that it gives man greater control over his environment, and consequently increases his freedom." Explain why you agree or disagree with this statement by Nobel laureate W. Arthur Lewis.

6. Growth in income per capita is a necessary condition for a rising standard of living in a country. Is it also a *sufficient* condition for making everyone better off? Why may not everyone benefit from economic growth?

7. GNP in real terms in Canada doubled between 1965 and 1980. Over this period the annual percentage rate of increase in GNP in constant dollars was 4.8 percent per year. Evaluate this measure of growth with respect to how well it reflects changes in (a) the material well-being of the average resident of Canada and (b) the nation's capacity to produce goods and services. In each case suggest what additional information you would like to know.

8. Consider a developed economy that decides to achieve a zero rate of growth for the future. What implications would such a "stationary state" have for the processes of production and consumption?

9. Suppose solar energy becomes the dominant form of energy in the twenty-first century. What changes will this make in the comparative advantages and growth rates of Africa and Northern Europe?

10. Discuss the following newspaper headlines in terms of the sources, costs and benefits of growth:
    a. "Stress Addiction: 'Life in the Fast Lanes' May Have its Benefits."
    b. "Education: An Expert Urges Multiple Reforms."
    c. "Industrial Radiation Risk Higher Than Thought."
    d. "Developments in the Field of Management Design Are Looking Ahead."
    e. "Ford Urged by Federal Safety Officials to Recall Several Hundred Thousand of Its 1981–1982 Front Drive Vehicles Because of Alleged Fire Hazards."

PART ELEVEN
INTERNATIONAL MACROECONOMICS

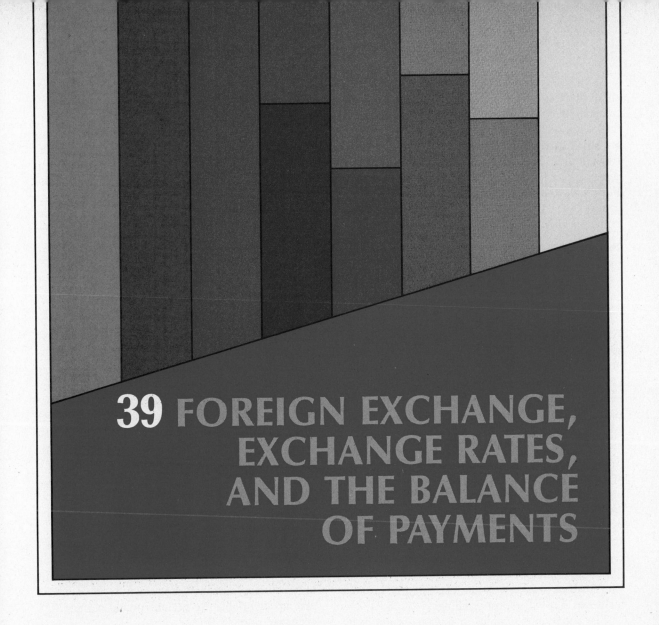

39 FOREIGN EXCHANGE, EXCHANGE RATES, AND THE BALANCE OF PAYMENTS

The value of the Canadian dollar is of great concern to many people. It affects the decisions of a Japanese firm wanting to sell cars in Canada, a Canadian wanting to buy a German government bond, a French exporter selling kitchen appliances to Canada, a Canadian firm hoping to sell commuter airplanes to American feeder airlines, and exporters of Canadian wood and mineral products in markets where prices are quoted in U.S. dollars. It also matters to Canadian tourists cashing their travelers cheques in London, Athens, and Bangkok.

What is meant by the "value of the Canadian dollar," and why does it change? Our discussion of these issues brings together material studied elsewhere in this book: the theory of supply and demand (Chapter 4), the process of international trade (Chapter 21), and the nature of money (Chapter 33).

In this chapter we examine the simple case of **a small open economy (SOE)**, which is an economy that can exert no influence on the world prices of traded goods. The quantities it exports and imports are small in relation to the total volume of world trade in these commodities. Thus the country must accept prices that are established in world markets. For many countries such as Canada, and for many commodities such as wheat, forest products, and minerals, this is a reasonable assumption.

The small open economy faces terms of trade that are fixed by forces beyond its control.

The Exchange of Currencies

We have seen that money, which consists of any accepted medium of exchange, is vital in a sophisticated economy that relies on specialization and exchange. Yet money as we know it is a *national* matter closely controlled by national governments. Each country has its own monetary system, and all governments attempt to regulate the size of the money supply within their own countries. If you live in Sweden, you will earn kronor and spend kronor; if you run a business in Austria, you will meet your payroll with schillings. The currency of one country is generally acceptable within the bounds of that country, but it will not usually be accepted by households and firms in another country. The Stockholm bus company will accept kronor but not Austrian schillings for your fare. The Austrian worker will not take Swedish kronor for wages but will accept schillings.

The situation is similiar in Canada except that our proximity to the United States leads many Canadian sellers to accept U.S. dollars over the counter. Because U.S. dollars are so well known and so common, Canadian merchants are willing to accept them and then do what the customer would otherwise have had to do: take the money to the bank and exchange it for Canadian money.

When Canadian producers sell their products, they require payment in Canadian dollars. They must meet their wage bills, pay for their raw materials, and reinvest or distribute their profits. If they sell their goods to Canadian purchasers, there will be no problem; the firms will be paid dollars for their output. However, if Canadian producers sell their goods to Indian importers, either the Indians must exchange their rupees to acquire Canadian dollars to pay for the goods, or the Canadian producers must accept rupees—and they will accept rupees only if they know they can exchange the rupees for the dollars that they require. The same holds true for producers in all countries; they must eventually receive payment for the goods they sell in terms of the currency of their own country.

In general, trade between nations can occur only if the currency of one nation can be exchanged for the currency of another.

International payments that require the exchange of one national curency for another can be made in a bewildering variety of ways, but in essence they involve exchange between people who have one currency and require another. Suppose that a Canadian firm wishes to acquire £3,000 for some purpose (£ is the symbol for the British pound sterling). The firm can go to its bank or some other seller of foreign currency and buy a cheque that will be accepted in the United Kingdom as £3,000. How many *dollars* the firm must pay to purchase this cheque will depend on the price of pounds in terms of dollars.

The **exchange rate** is the price of foreign currency; that is, it is the amount of home currency that must be given up in order to obtain one unit of the foreign currency. For example, if one must give up two dollars to get one pound sterling, the exchange rate is C$2.[1]

A rise in the exchange rate (a rise in the price of foreign exchange) is a **depreciation** of the home currency: *Foreign currencies become more expensive, and therefore the relative value of the home currency falls.* A fall in the exchange rate (a fall in the price of foreign exchange) is an **appreciation** of the home currency: *foreign currencies become cheaper, and*

---

[1] This expresses the relative values of the two currencies in terms of the dollar price of one pound sterling. Alternatively, one could consider the pound sterling price of 1 Canadian dollar, which in this example would be £0.50.

TABLE 39-1 CHANGES IN THE BALANCE SHEETS OF TWO BANKS AS A RESULT OF INTERNATIONAL PAYMENTS

U.K. bank			Canadian bank		
Assets	Liabilities		Assets	Liabilities	
No change	(1) Deposits of car exporter	+£10,000	No change	(1) Deposits of car importer	−$17,000
	(2) Deposits of computer importer	−£10,000		(2) Deposits of computer exporter	+$17,000
	Net change	0		Net change	0

International transactions involve a transfer of deposit liabilities among banks. The table records two separate international transactions at an exchange rate of $1.70 to the pound: (1) Canadian purchase of a British car for £10,000 (= $17,000), and (2) a British purchase of Canadian personal computers for $17,000 (= £10,000). The Canadian import of a car reduces deposit liabilities to Canadian citizens and increases deposit liabilities to British citizens. The British import of personal computers does the opposite. When a series of transactions are equal in value, there is only a transfer of deposit liabilities among individuals within a country. The Canadian personal computer manufacturer received (in effect) the dollars the Canadian car purchaser gave up to get a British-made car.

---

therefore the relative value of the home currency rises. For example, when the C$ price of one U.S. dollar rises from $1.20 to $1.25, the C$ has *depreciated* and the U.S.$ has *appreciated.*

The term **foreign exchange** refers to the actual foreign currency or various claims on it, such as bank deposits or promises to pay, that are traded for each other. Let us see how transactions in foreign exchange are carried out. Suppose that a firm wishes to purchase a British sports car to sell in Canada. The British firm that produced the car demands payment in pounds sterling. If the car is priced at £10,000, the Canadian firm will go to its bank and purchase a cheque for £10,000. Let us suppose this requires that the firm pay $17,000.[2] (In other words, the exchange rate in this transaction is $1.70 to the pound, which means that $1 is worth £0.58.) The Canadian purchaser will send the cheque to the British car firm, which in turn will deposit the cheque in its bank.

Now assume that in the same period of time a Canadian wholesale firm purchases eight Canadian personal computers to sell in Britain. If the computers are priced at $2,125 each, the Canadian seller will have to be paid $17,000. To make this payment, the British importing firm goes to its bank and writes a cheque on its account for £10,000 and receives a cheque drawn on a Canadian bank for $17,000. The cheque is sent to Canada and deposited in a Canadian bank.[3] The effects of these transactions are shown in Table 39-1.

The two transactions cancel each other out, and there is no net change in international liabilities. No money need pass between British and Canadian banks to effect the transactions; each bank merely increases the deposit of one domestic customer and lowers the deposit of another. Indeed, as long as the flow of payments between the two countries is equal (Canadians pay as much to British residents as British residents pay to Canadians), all payments can be managed as in these examples. There will be no need for a net payment from British banks to Canadian banks.

All these calculations involve comparing magnitudes measured in different currencies. These

---

[2] Banks charge a small commission for making currency exchanges, but we shall ignore this and assume that parties can exchange monies back and forth at the going exchange rate.

[3] The whole thing can be done without even having cheques issued. Instead the banks can telegraph to their correspondents in the other country with orders to pay. This would give rise to the same set of book entries as those shown in Table 39-1.

comparisons are made using the exchange rate. We now turn to an analysis of how such exchange rates are determined.

THE DETERMINATION OF EXCHANGE RATES

As a first step we must look at the link between exchange rates and the prices of a country's imports and exports.

Exchange Rates and the Domestic Prices of Traded Goods

A small open economy faces prices of internationally traded goods that are fixed in foreign currency. The exchange rate translates these into domestic prices. If, for example, the price of wheat is £2 a bushel on international wheat markets, its dollar price in Canada depends on the exchange rate. When the rate is $2 to the pound, the Canadian domestic price of wheat is $4. This is because $4 must be recovered from domestic sales in order to buy on the foreign exchange market the £2 needed to buy a bushel of wheat on the international wheat market.

In Figures 4-9 and 4-10 (page 61) we showed how imports and exports were determined in an economy facing given world prices for traded goods. We drew the domestic demand and supply curves plotted against domestic prices. We then used the world price, *stated in units of domestic currency*, to determine the quantity of imports and exports of a product. To do this we needed, although we did not say so at the time, an exchange rate so that we could convert world prices into local currency. Recall that we express the exchange rate, e, as the number of units of domestic currency needed to buy one unit of foreign currency. The *domestic* price of traded goods, p_d, is then the *world* price of traded goods expressed in foreign currency, p_f, multiplied by the exchange rate:

$$p_d = (e) (p_f)$$

For example: when the international price of wheat is £2 per bushel and the exchange rate is $2 to the pound, the Canadian dollar price of wheat is (£2 per bushel) times ($2 per pound), which is $4 per bushel.

It is now a simple matter to see the effect of a change in the exchange rate on the domestic prices of traded goods. Say, for example, that the Canadian dollar appreciates so that it takes only $1.50 to buy £1. The domestic price of a bushel of wheat that costs £2 is now only $3, since $3 is now sufficient to buy £2. For a second example, say that the Canadian dollar depreciates so that it now takes $2.50 to buy £1. Now the dollar price of wheat rises to $5, since it takes $5 to buy £2. (The formula $p_d = (e) (p_f)$ gives the right answer, since ($2.50 per pound) times (£2 per bushel) equals $5 per bushel.)

An appreciation of the domestic currency lowers the domestic prices of traded goods, whereas a depreciation raises these prices.

To see the effects of changes in the exchange rate, let us return to the example of Chapter 4, a country that is exporting wheat and importing cloth. A 10 percent depreciation of the country's currency would mean that the domestic currency prices of the two goods must rise by 10 percent. First consider the export good, wheat. Since the sale of a unit of wheat abroad still yields the same amount of foreign exchange, it now yields 10 percent more in terms of domestic currency. Domestic purchasers too will have to pay 10 percent more, for if the domestic price did not rise, producers would sell only in the export market. Similarly, the purchase of cloth still requires the same amount of foreign currency, but 10 percent more of the domestic currency must be paid to obtain the required amount of foreign currency. Thus the domestic currency price of imported cloth also rises by 10 percent.

The effects of these price changes are illustrated in Figures 39-1 and 39-2. In the markets for wheat and cloth, the increase in the domestic price causes the quantity supplied domestically to rise and the quantity demanded domestically to fall. As a result,

FIGURE 39-1
The Effects of an Increase in the Domestic Currency Price of an Exported Good (Wheat)

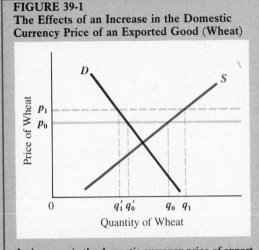

An increase in the domestic currency price of export goods leads to an increase in the volume of exports. Exports of wheat are determined by the domestic excess supply of the tradable good at the domestic price. (The domestic price is the world price adjusted by the exchange rate.) D and S are the domestic demand and supply schedules. If the world price expressed in domestic currency is p_0, quantity q_0 will be produced, of which q_0' will be consumed domestically and $q_0'q_0$ will be exported. A depreciation of the domestic currency or an increase in the world price causes the domestic currency price to rise to p_1. As a result, domestic consumption falls to q_1', quantity supplied rises to q_1, and exports rise to $q_1'q_1$.

FIGURE 39-2
The Effects of an Increase in the Domestic Currency Price of an Imported Good (Cloth)

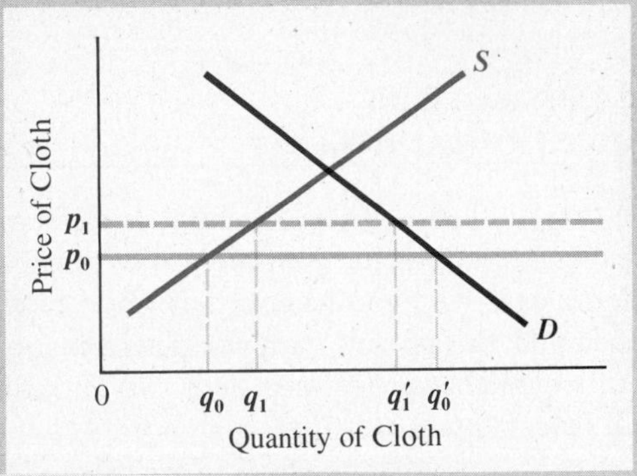

An increase in the domestic currency of import goods leads to a decrease in the volume of imports. Imports of cloth are determined by the domestic excess demand for cloth at the domestic price. (The domestic price is the world price adjusted by the exchange rate.) D and S are the domestic demand and supply schedules. If the world price expressed in domestic currency is p_0, quantity q_0' will be consumed, of which q_0 will be produced domestically and $q_0'q_0$ will be imported. A depreciation of the domestic currency or an increase in the world price causes the domestic currency price to rise to p_1. As a result, quantity supplied rises to q_1, domestic consumption falls to q_1', and imports fall to $q_1'q_1$.

the quantity of wheat exported, which is equal to the excess of the quantity supplied domestically over the quantity demanded domestically, *rises* (see Figure 39-1). In the market for cloth, the domestic price rise also causes quantity supplied to increase and quantity demanded to fall. However, since the initial situation was one where domestic supply exceeded domestic demand, this response reduces that excess. As a result, the quantity of cloth imported *decreases* (see Figure 39-2).

For a small country, a depreciation of the domestic currency causes the domestic prices of traded goods to rise, thereby increasing the quantity supplied and

reducing the quantity demanded domestically. Therefore the volume of exports increases while the volume of imports falls.

As a result of these changes, actual net exports, X − M rises. Since X − M is a component of aggregate demand, the depreciation increases the country's aggregate demand. This in turn tends to increase equilibrium national income.

Similarly, an *appreciation* of the domestic currency *lowers* the domestic prices of traded goods. This leads to a reduction in the quantity supplied and an increase in the quantity demanded domestically for both; the quantity of cloth imports now rises, while the quantity of wheat exports falls. This is also shown in Figures 39-1 and 39-2.

The Exchange Rate Between Two Currencies

The theory that we develop here applies to all exchange rates, but for convenience we shall continue to deal with the example of trade between Canada and Britain and with the determination of the rate of exchange between their two currencies, dollars and pounds sterling.

Because one currency is traded for another on the foreign exchange market, it follows that a desire to purchase (demand) dollars implies a willingness to sell (supply) pounds, while an offer (supply) of dollars implies a desire to purchase (demand) pounds.

If at an exchange rate of 2 dollars to the pound British importers demand $6, they must be offering £3; if Canadian importers offer $10, they must be demanding £5. For this reason, the theory can deal either with the demand for and the supply of dollars, or with the demand for and the supply of pounds sterling; both need not be considered. We shall conduct the argument in terms of the supply, demand, and price of pounds sterling (which may be taken to stand for all foreign exchange).

Figure 39-3 plots the exchange rate, the price of sterling measured in Canadian dollars, on the vertical axis, and the quantity of sterling on the horizontal axis. *Moving down the vertical scale, the foreign currency (sterling) becomes cheaper; it is depreciating on the foreign market while the domestic currency (the dollar) is appreciating. Moving up the scale, sterling becomes more expensive; it is appreciating while the dollar is depreciating.*

In more general terms, Figure 39-3 represents the foreign exchange market. It plots the quantity of foreign exchange against the Canadian dollar price of foreign exchange; that is, the Canadian exchange rate. Although we continue to speak of sterling to make the argument easier to follow, everything said about sterling applies to any other

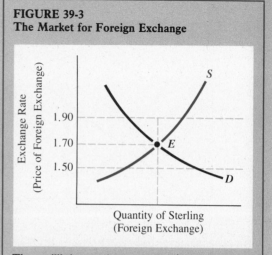

FIGURE 39-3
The Market for Foreign Exchange

Exchange Rate (Price of Foreign Exchange) [vertical axis]

1.90
1.70   E
1.50

Quantity of Sterling (Foreign Exchange) [horizontal axis]

The equilibrium exchange rate equates the demand and supply of foreign exchange. The *S* curve is the supply of sterling to the foreign exchange market to be used to make purchases in Canada. The *D* curve is the demand for sterling in the foreign exchange market to be used to make purchases in the United Kingdom. The quantity of sterling demanded is equal to the quantity supplied at an exchange rate of $1.70 to the pound. If the price of sterling were low, say $1.50, there would be an excess demand for sterling, which would bid its price up. If the price of sterling were high, say $1.90, there would be an excess supply of sterling, which would bid its price down.

foreign currency and to foreign exchange in general.

The Supply of Sterling

The supply of sterling to the foreign exchange market arises to finance purchases by foreigners from Canadians. In addition to the purchase of exports studied before, there are purchases of assets previously owned or newly issued by Canadians (and Canadian governments). Such purchases are called **capital flows.** They play an important role in exchange markets, and we study them in detail later in this chapter; for the present, we continue to focus on international trade in goods and services.

Consider again a representative Canadian export good, wheat. What are the implications for the foreign exchange market of transactions in wheat? We saw in Figure 39-1 that a rise in the Canadian exchange rate (a depreciation of the dollar) led to an increase in the *quantity* of wheat exports. Since the pound sterling *price* of wheat is constant (being set on international wheat markets), the supply of pounds to the foreign exchange market must increase. People must be spending more pounds on Canadian wheat, and these pounds go to purchase the Canadian dollars needed to pay for this wheat.

What then is the shape of the supply curve of sterling? As we have just seen, if the exchange rate rises, the British will buy more Canadian wheat and will offer more sterling for this purpose. The quantity of pounds supplied will rise. In the opposite case, if the exchange rate falls, the British will buy less Canadian wheat and will thus spend fewer pounds sterling on it.

The supply curve of sterling on the foreign exchange market is upward-sloping when plotted against the dollar price of sterling—that is, against the exchange rate.

The Demand for Sterling

In our two-country example, the demand for sterling on the foreign exchange market is merely the opposite side of the supply of dollars. Who wants to sell dollars for foreign exchange? In our example, Canadians seeking to purchase the representative British export, cloth, will require foreign exchange to make those transactions, and hence they will wish to supply dollars in exchange for pounds.[4]

When the exchange rate rises (the Canadian dollar depreciates), the Canadian price of British cloth rises. As we saw in Figure 39-2, Canadians will import less of the now more expensive British cloth. Since the sterling price of cloth is unchanged, buying less cloth means needing less sterling to pay for it. Thus the Canadian demand for sterling falls.

[4] There may also be a demand for sterling resulting from *capital flows* if Canadians seek to buy pound sterling assets. As with the supply of sterling, we neglect this for now.

When the exchange rate falls, British cloth exports to Canada become cheaper and more will be sold. Since the sterling price of cloth is unchanged, buying more still means spending more sterling. Thus there is an increase in the amount of sterling demanded on the foreign exchange market. Together these two changes tell us the shape of the demand curve for sterling:

The demand curve for sterling on the foreign exchange market is downward-sloping when plotted against the dollar price of sterling—that is, against the exchange rate.

Equilibrium Exchange Rates

Consider an exchange rate that is set on a free market. Like any perfectly competitive price, this rate fluctuates freely according to the conditions of demand and supply. (Although we continue to focus on the determination of the equilibrium exchange rate between the dollar and the pound, you should be aware of the fact that there exists exchange rates for many pairs of currencies. See the discussion in Box 39-1.)

Assume that the current exchange rate is so low (say, $1.50 in Figure 39-3) that the quantity of sterling demanded exceeds the quantity supplied. This reflects the fact that at that exchange rate, desired payments to foreigners by holders of dollars exceed desired payments to Canadians by holders of sterling. This situation is one in which *desired payments* are not in balance. Foreign exchange will be in scarce supply; some people who require pounds sterling to make payments to Britain will be unable to obtain them, and the price of sterling will be bid up. The dollar will depreciate against the pound, which is the same thing as the pound appreciating against the dollar.

As the dollar price of sterling rises, the dollar price of Canadian imports rise: Hence the quantity of imports falls, as does the quantity of sterling demanded on the foreign exchange market to pay for these imports. This is a movement along the demand curve D in Figure 39-3. However, the depreciation of the dollar also leads to a rise in the

BOX 39–1 MULTILATERAL EXCHANGE RATES

Because Canada trades with many countries, there are exchange rates between the Canadian dollar and many other currencies. In April 1984 the Canadian dollar was worth approximately 0.77 U.S. dollars, 0.53 British pounds, 2.08 German marks, and 193 Japanese yen.

Equilibrium in the market for Canadian dollars does not require that the demand for Canadian dollars by residents of any one country be equal to the supply of Canadian dollars being offered in exchange for that particular country's currency. Equilibrium is established when the total demand for Canadian dollars is equal to the supply of Canadian dollars being offered in exchange for all foreign currencies. In other words, equilibrium does not require that Canada's trade be in balance with each individual country, but rather that total exports and imports be in balance.

At the same time, equilibrium can exist in the market for all currencies simultaneously only when there are no opportunities for profitable **arbitrage.** Arbitrage operations consist in buying currencies in markets where they are cheap and selling them where they are dear so as to make a profit on the transaction. Exchange rates are generally specified in terms of the U.S. dollar. Once the rates between the U.S. dollar and two other currencies are determined, there is only one rate between the other two currencies that will *not* allow buyers and sellers of foreign exchange to engage in profitable arbitrage.

Consider an example. Suppose that on a particular day the U.S. dollar is worth £0.60 and 800 lire. Given the two rates, the only rate between lire and sterling that rules out profitable arbitrage operations is £0.60 = 800 lire, which is the equivalent of £1 = 1,333 lire. The table gives an example in which the exchange rate between the pound and the lira is out of line with the other two. Such "disorderly cross-rates" will quickly be eliminated in a free market. Arbitragers will buy lire with dollars and sell lire against pounds. If rates are free to vary, this will tend to bid the rates toward a consistent level where it is no longer possible to make profits by arbitrage. If rates are fixed by central authorities, such disorderly cross-rates could not long be sustained, but while they were, they would provide a gift to everyone who was informed enough to take advantage of them.

One unit of this currency	Exchanges for the stated number of units of this currency		
	U.S. dollar	Lira	Pound
U.S. dollar	1	800	0.60
Lira	0.00125	1	0.000909
Pound	1.67	1,100	1

Disorderly cross-rates mean that a profit can be made merely by buying and selling currencies at existing rates in different markets. In this example, a trader can start with $2 and purchase 1,600 lire. He or she can then use the lire to purchase £1.45, which can be exchanged for $2.42. The profit is $0.42 on an investment of $2, or 21 percent. Because the transactions can be effected quickly and with large amounts of money, very large profits can be earned. Because this is possible, however, such rates will not long persist.

dollar price of Canadian exports and a resulting increase in the quantity sold abroad. Thus the amount of sterling offered to buy more Canadian exports at an unchanged sterling price must rise. This is a movement along the supply curve S in Figure 39-3.

Thus a rise in the dollar price of the sterling reduces the quantity of sterling demanded and increases the quantity of sterling supplied. Where the two curves intersect, quantity demanded equals quantity supplied, and the foreign exchange market is in equilibrium.

What happens if the price of foreign exchange is too high? The quantity of sterling demanded will be less than the quantity of sterling supplied. With sterling in excess supply, some people who wish to convert sterling into dollars will be unable to do so. The price of sterling will fall, less sterling will be supplied, more will be demanded, and an equilibrium will be reestablished.

The foreign exchange market is like other competitive markets; demand and supply lead to an equilibrium price at which quantity demanded equals quantity supplied.

Changes in Exchange Rates

What causes exchange rates to vary? The simplest answer to this question is changes in demand or supply in the foreign exchange market. Anything that shifts the demand curve for sterling to the right or the supply curve of sterling to the left raises the equilibrium exchange rate and thus causes a depreciation of the dollar. Anything that shifts the demand curve for sterling to the left or the supply curve of sterling to the right lowers the equilibrium exchange rate and thus causes an appreciation of the dollar. This is nothing more than a restatement of the laws of supply and demand, applied now to the market for foreign currencies.

But what causes the shifts in demand and supply that lead to changes in exchange rates? There are many causes, some of them transitory and some of them persistent. Here we consider several that are related to trade flows.

Foreign Inflation

First consider the case where the rest of the world inflates while the local country does not, so that its domestic costs and the prices of domestic (nontraded) goods remain unchanged. But the world price of all traded goods rises, so that at the initial exchange rate the prices of traded goods also rise in the domestic country.

We saw in Figures 39-1 and 39-2 that the rise in the prices of exported and imported goods leads our country to increase the quantity of its exports while decreasing the quantity of its imports. These changes will cause shifts in the demand and supply curves in the foreign exchange market. More Canadian exports sold at a higher world price mean more foreign exchange offered in return for Canadian dollars The supply curve of foreign exchange shifts right, as shown in Figure 39-4. Fewer imports purchased at higher foreign prices means less spent on imports, as long as the percentage fall in the quantity demanded exceeds the percentage rise in the price.[5] The demand curve for foreign exchange shifts left, as shown in Figure 39-4.

Now at the original exchange rate there is an excess supply of foreign exchange, and the market exchange rate falls to its new equilibrium level. The exchange rate falls, which is the same thing as an appreciation of the Canadian dollar.

A foreign inflation, other things equal, will lead to an appreciation of the Canadian dollar.

Domestic Inflation

Suppose now that foreign prices are constant, but that there is an increase in domestic wages and other costs of production, and in the price of local goods and services—things such as haircuts and restaurant meals that are not traded internationally. As a result of the rise in costs, the supply curves for imports and exports will shift upward. As a

---

[5] This is the case of an elastic import demand, probably the most relevant case empirically and certainly the easiest to consider. If import demand is inelastic, this raises potential problems that are of some interest but are too complex to be pursued in a first-year textbook.

FIGURE 39-4
Foreign Inflation and the Exchange Rate

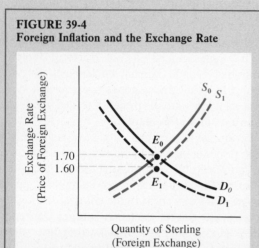

Foreign inflation will increase the supply of foreign exchange and decrease the demand, thus causing an appreciation of the dollar. The initial supply and demand curves are shown by the solid curves (labeled D_0 and S_0) and the initial equilibrium is at E_0. Now suppose that a foreign inflation occurs. This raises the foreign price of all tradable goods. At any given exchange rate, this will cause an increase in the dollar price of traded goods and, as we saw in Figures 39-1 and 39-2, the quantity of exports will increase and the quantity of imports will fall as a result. The increase in exports gives rise to an increase in the supply of sterling, as shown by the shift from S_0 to S_1. The decrease in imports gives rise to a fall in the demand for foreign exchange, as shown by the shift in the demand curve from D_0 to D_1. As a result, the dollar appreciates as the price of sterling falls from \$1.70 to \$1.60.

result of the rise in prices of nontraded goods, the demand curves for traded goods will shift upward. This is because at any given exchange rate, traded goods are now cheaper relative to domestic or nontraded goods, so more will be demanded and less will be supplied. As a result, the quantity of imports will rise and the quantity of exports will fall. This situation is shown in Figure 39-5.

At any given exchange rate, these changes in the quantities of imports and exports will cause the supply and demand of foreign exchange to change.

The decrease in exports will cause the quantity of sterling supplied to the foreign exchange market to decrease—in terms of Figure 39-4, the supply curve of sterling shifts left from S_1 to S_0. The increase in imports will cause the quantity of sterling demanded in the foreign exchange market to increase—in terms of Figure 39-4, the demand curve shifts right from D_1 to D_0. As a result, the equilibrium moves from E_1 to E_0 and the exchange rate rises; that is, the dollar depreciates.

A local Canadian inflation will lead to a depreciation of the Canadian dollar (a rise in the exchange rate).

Inflation in Both Countries

Now consider a case where the domestic country suffers exactly the same rate of inflation as the rest of the world. Now the demand and supply curves for traded goods in Figure 39-5 shift upward as before, but so does the world price of imports and exports. (The rise in the world price is not shown in the figure.) The two shifts offset each other. The upward shifts in the curves tend to reduce exports and increase imports, while the upward shift in world prices tends to increase exports and reduce imports. With equal rates of inflation in Canada and the rest of the world, relative prices of Canadian and the other country's goods remain unchanged at the old exchange rate. There is no reason to expect any change in either country's demand for imports at the original exchange rate and hence in the demands and supplies of foreign exchange. The inflations in the two countries leave the equilibrium exchange rate unchanged.

Offsetting inflation in two countries will leave the incentive to import and to export unchanged, and thus will cause no change in the exchange rate.

Unequal Inflation

The above analysis suggests that the *relative rates of inflation* between two trading countries is an important determinant of exchange rate changes. Differences in the inflation rates will cause changes in imports and exports and hence changes in quantities demanded and supplied on the foreign ex-

FIGURE 39-5
Domestic Inflation and International Trade

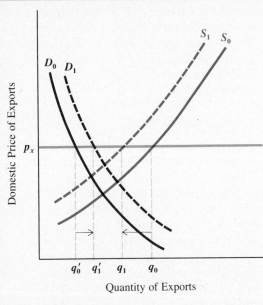

(i) The fall in exports

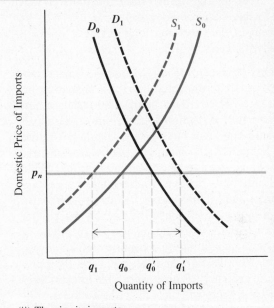

(ii) The rise in imports

Domestic inflation unmatched in the rest of the world increases the domestic demand for traded goods and reduces the domestic supply; as a result, the quantity of exports falls and the quantity of imports rises. The initial supply and demand curves are shown by the solid lines D_0 to S_0 in both parts of the figure. In each market the initial quantity supplied is given by q_0 and the initial quantity demanded by q_0'. Initial exports are given in (i) by $q_0'q_0$ and initial imports in (ii) by q_0q_0'.

A domestic inflation causes the demand curves for each traded good to shift rightward from D_0 to D_1, and the supply curve for each to shift leftward from S_0 to S_1. As a result, quantity demanded rises from q_0' to q_1' and quantity supplied falls from q_0 to q_1.

In the market for exports, where domestic supply initially exceeded demand, the inflation thus causes exports to fall, from $q_0'q_0$ to $q_1'q_1$. (In turn, this means the demand for dollars in the foreign exchange market falls, as shown by a shift from D_1 to D_0 in Figure 39-4.)

In the market for imports, where domestic demand initially exceeded supply, the inflation thus causes imports to rise, from q_0q_0' to q_1q_1'. (In turn, this means the supply of dollars to the foreign exchange market rises, as shown by a shift from S_1 to S_0 in Figure 39-4.)

change market. Thus the exchange rate between the two currencies will change. The general conclusion that follows from a simple extension of the cases just studied is this:

If prices in one country are rising faster (falling slower) than those of another country, the equilibrium value of the first country's currency will be falling relative to that of the second country.

Capital Movements

Major capital flows can exert strong influences on exchange rates. For example, an increased desire to invest in British assets will shift the demand for sterling rightward and cause the dollar to depreciate (i.e. raise the exchange rate).

A movement of investment funds has the effect of appreciating the currency of the capital-importing country and depreciating the currency of the capital-exporting country.

This statement is true for all capital movements, short term or long term. Since the motives that lead to large capital movements are likely to be different in the short and long terms, it is worth considering each.

Short-term capital movements. A major motive for short-term capital flows is a change in interest rates. International traders hold transactions balances just as domestic traders do. These balances are often lent out on short-term loans rather than being left idle. Naturally the holders of these balances will tend to lend them, other things being equal, in those markets where interest rates are highest. Thus if one major country's short-term rate of interest rises above the rates in most other countries, there will tend to be a large inflow of short-term capital into that country to take advantage of the high rate, and this will tend to appreciate the currency. If these short-term interest rates should fall, there will most likely be a sudden shift away from that country as a source of transactions balances, and its currency will tend to depreciate.

A second motive for short-term capital movements is speculation about a country's exchange rate. If foreigners expect the dollar to appreciate, they will rush to buy assets that pay off in dollars; if they expect the dollar to depreciate, they will be reluctant to buy or hold Canadian securities.

Long-term capital movements. Such movements are largely influenced by long-term expectations about another country's profit opportunities and the long-run value of its currency. A British investor would be more willing to purchase a Canadian factory if it expected that the dollar profits would buy more pound sterling in future years than the profits from investment in a British factory. This could happen if the Canadian firm earned greater profits than the British firm, with exchange rates unchanged. It could also happen if the profits were the same but the investor expected the dollar to appreciate relative to the pound.

Capital movements: Summary. Anything that leads to an inflow of capital—relatively high interest rates, high earnings expectations, or expectations of appreciation—increases the supply of foreign exchange and tends to appreciate the dollar (lower the exchange rate). Anything that leads to an outflow of capital—relatively low interest rates, low earnings expectations, or expectations of depreciation—increases the demand for foreign exchange and tends to depreciate the dollar (raise the exchange rate).

Structural Changes

An economy can undergo structural changes that alter the equilibrium exchange rate. *Structural change* is an omnibus term for a change in cost structures, the invention of new products, or anything else that affects the pattern of comparative advantage. For example, when a country's products do not improve as rapidly as those of some other country, consumers' demand (at fixed prices) shifts slowly away from the first country's products and toward those of its foreign competitors. This causes a slow depreciation in the first country's currency because the supply of foreign exchange offered to purchase its domestic currency is slowly falling.

Many people believe that Canadian manufacturing today is suffering just such an adverse structural change, its exports of everything from textiles to automobiles being slowly displaced in third countries by exports from countries such as Korea, Germany, and Japan. This decreases the supply of foreign exchange. The same forces lead domestic Canadian households to turn ever more toward foreign-made goods, thereby increasing the demand for foreign exchange. Each of these changes tends to depreciate the dollar.

THE BALANCE OF PAYMENTS

The Nature of Balance-of-Payments Accounts

In order to know what is happening to the course of international trade, governments keep track of the *transactions* among countries. The record of such transactions is made in the **balance-of-payments accounts.** Each transaction, such as a shipment of exports or the arrival of imported goods, is classified according to the payments or receipts that would typically arise from it.

Any transaction that would to lead to a payment to other nations is classified as a debit $(-)$ item because it uses foreign exchange. Canadian imports and outflows of Canadian capital to purchase foreign assets are debit items. (An export of capital is really an *import* of the foreign assets purchased.) Any transaction that would to lead to a payment by foreigners to Canada or its residents is classified as a credit $(+)$ item because it earns foreign exchange. Canadian exports and capital flows into Canada are credit items.

Consider some examples. When a British importer buys a Canadian personal computer to sell in the United Kingdom, this appears as a credit in the Canadian balance of payments because it earns foreign exchange. However, when a Canadian shipping firm insures with Lloyds of London a cargo destined for Alexandria, Egypt, this represents a debit in the Canadian balance of payments because when the insurance premium is paid, the shipping firm will have to pay Lloyds in sterling. This transaction uses foreign exchange. Of course a credit item to one country is a debit item to the other, and vice versa; thus the personal computer transaction is a debit and the insurance transaction a credit in the British balance of payments.[6]

An important thing to notice about the record of international transactions is that the balance of payments refers to actual transactions, not desired transactions. We have seen that at some exchange rate between dollars and pounds it is quite possible for holders of sterling to want to purchase more dollars in exchange for pounds than holders of dollars want to sell in exchange for pounds. In this situation quantity demanded exceeds quantity supplied. But it is not possible for sterling holders to buy more dollars than dollar holders will sell; every

dollar that is bought must have been sold by someone, and every dollar that is sold must have been bought by someone.

Because the amount of dollars actually bought must equal the amount of dollars actually sold, the balance of payments always balances.

Although the total number of dollars bought on the foreign exchange market must equal the total number sold, this is not true of purchases and sales for each specific purpose or within particular categories. For example, more dollars may well be sold for the purpose of obtaining foreign currency to import foreign cars than are bought for the purpose of buying Canadian cars for export to other countries. In such a case, Canada has a balance-of-payments deficit on the "car account": the value of Canadian imports of foreign cars exceeds the value of Canadian exports of Canadian cars. Usually we are not interested in the balance of payments for single commodities, but for larger classes of transactions.

Major Categories in the Balance-of-Payments Accounts

Table 39-2 presents the Canadian balance-of-payments account for 1983.

Current Account

The balance of payments on *current account* includes all payments made because of current purchases of goods and services. There is no automatic reason why current account payments should balance (any more than the automobile account should). It is quite possible that more dollars were sold in order to purchase imports than were bought in order to allow foreigners to purchase our exports. If so, the dollars must have come from somewhere, and the excess of sales over purchases on current account must be exactly matched by an excess of purchases over sales on the capital and official financing accounts.

The main item in the current account is the so-called **balance of trade** (or the trade balance), the

---

[6] As we shall see, there is nothing *inherently* good about "credits" or bad about "debits."

TABLE 39–2 CANADIAN BALANCE OF INTER-NATIONAL PAYMENTS, 1983 (Billions of Dollars)

Current Account

Merchandise exports	+91.3
Merchandise imports	−73.2
Balance of merchandise trade	+18.1
Exports of services	+12.0
Imports of services	−16.6
Balance of trade	+13.5
Net investment income	−11.7
Transfers	−0.2
Balance on current account	+1.6

Capital Account

New direct investment	+0.2
Other long-term capital flows	+2.6
Total long-term capital flows	+2.8
Short-term capital flows	−3.8
Balance on capital account	−1.0

Current Plus Capital Account	+0.6
Use of official reserves (income −, decrease +)	−0.6
Overall Balance of Payments	(always zero)[a]

[a] In balance-of-payments accounts there is a "statistical discrepancy" item that results from the inability to measure accurately some industrial items. For example, many capital transactions are not recorded.

The overall balance of payments always balances, but the individual components do not have to. In 1983 Canada shows a positive (surplus) merchandise trade balance (exports exceed imports) and a smaller positive (surplus) balance on current account. There is a negative (deficit) balance on capital account because capital exports exceeded capital imports. The capital *plus* current account balance is what is commonly referred to as the *balance of payments.* It is exactly matched by the balance in the official account.

difference between the dollar value of exports and imports in a given year. Note that the balance of trade concerns only the *difference* between exports and imports, not the volume of trade. Thus one could have a $30 billion excess of exports over imports on a volume of exports of $300 billion or

on a volume of $50 billion. In either case the same pressure on the exchange rate would be exerted. But the effect of foreign trade on the nation's economy would be very different because such things as the gains from trade depend on the volume, not the balance, of trade. This is taken up further in Box 39-2.

The gains from trade depend on the volume of trade, not the balance of trade. The effect on foreign exchange markets depends on the balance of trade, not the volume of trade.

The trade balance is sometimes divided further into visible and invisible trade balances.[7] **Visibles** are goods—all those things such as cars, pulpwood, aluminum, coffee, and iron ore that can be seen and touched when they cross international borders. **Invisibles** are services—all those things that cannot be seen or touched, such as insurance, freight haulage, and tourist expenditures.

The **current account** is equal to the balance of trade plus net investment income and transfers. Given this country's long history of being a net international borrower, the payment of interest and dividends on foreign loans and investments is a substantial item in the Canadian balance-of-payments accounts. When an American corporation owns a subsidiary in Canada, it receives dividend payments in Canadian dollars. If the American owners wish to spend these dividends at home, they will need to exchange Canadian for American dollars. Interest and dividends paid to foreigners thus use up foreign exchange and are entered as debit items on the balance of payments. Although in 1983 the current account was in surplus (due to a record merchandise trade surplus), often the debt-servicing entry is sufficiently large to cause the current account to be in deficit even when the trade account shows a substantial surplus. Some concerns about this tendency to run current account deficits are taken up in Box 39-3.

[7] Terminology is not standardized and the term *balance of trade* is sometimes reserved for the balance on goods alone. When the balance of trade is used, as it is in the text, for the balance on goods *and* services, the term *balance on merchandise account* is used for the balance on the goods account alone.

BOX 39–2 THE VOLUME OF TRADE, THE BALANCE OF TRADE, AND THE NEW MERCANTILISM

Media commentators, political figures, and much of the general public often judge the national balance of payments as they would the accounts of a single firm. Just as a firm is supposed to show a profit, the nation is supposed to secure a balance-of-payments surplus, with the benefits derived from international trade measured by the size of that surplus.

This view is closely related to the exploitation doctrine of international trade. Since one country's surplus is another country's deficit, one country's gain, judged by its surplus, must be another country's loss, judged by its deficit.

In holding such views today, people are echoing an ancient economic doctrine called *mercantilism*. The mercantilists were a group of economists who preceded Adam Smith. They judged the success of trade by the size of the trade balance. In many cases this doctrine made sense in terms of their objective, which was to use international trade as a means of building up the political and military power of the state rather than raising the living standards of its citizens. A balance-of-payments surplus allowed the nation (then and now) to acquire foreign exchange reserves. (In those days the reserves took the form of gold. Today they are a mixture of gold and claims on the currencies of other countries.) These reserves could then be used to pay armies, composed partly of foreign mercenaries; to purchase weapons from abroad; and generally to finance colonial adventures.

People who advocate this view in modern times are called *neo-mercantilists*. Insofar as their object is to increase the power of the state, they are choosing means that could achieve their ends. Insofar as they are drawing an analogy between what is a sensible objective for a business interested in its own material welfare and what is a sensible objective for a society interest in the material welfare of its citizens, their views are erroneous, for the analogy is false.

If we take the view that the object of economic activity is to promote the welfare and living standards of ordinary citizens, rather than the power of governments, then the mercantilist focus on the balance of trade makes no sense. The law of comparative advantage shows that average living standards are maximized by having individuals, regions, and countries specialize in the things they can produce comparatively best and then trading to obtain the things they can produce comparatively worst. The more specialization, the more trade.

In this view the gains from trade are to be judged by the volume of trade. A situation in which there is a *large volume* of trade but where each country has a *zero balance* of trade can thus be regarded as quite satisfactory.

To the business interested in private profit and to the government interested in the power of the state, it is the balance of payments that matters. To the person interested in the welfare of ordinary citizens, it is the volume of payments that matters.

Capital Account

The *capital account* records transactions related to international movements of financial capital. It may seem odd that while the export of a good is a credit item, the export of capital is a debit item.

To see that there is no contradiction in this treatment of goods versus capital, consider the export of Canadian capital for investment in a British bond. The capital transaction involves the purchase, and hence the *import*, of a British bond, and this has the same effect on the balance of payments

BOX 39–3 IS CANADA'S CURRENT ACCOUNT A CAUSE FOR ALARM?

Some observers have expressed alarm at the long-term trend in Canada's balance of payments, which shows a large current account deficit matched by a large capital account surplus. Here we address two sources of this alarm.

Is Canada Headed for Financial Ruin?

Concern often arises from the belief that Canada is borrowing abroad to finance a current account deficit that reflects excessive spending. Tourist expenditures of Canadians traveling abroad and interest payments to service past debts are commonly singled out as "causes" of Canada's heavy foreign borrowing. Two contentions are involved; first, that the country is borrowing abroad to help cover a current account deficit; second, that the policy of financing investment by foreign borrowing is in some way unsound.

The first contention mixes up cause and effect. The various items in the balance of payments represent unrelated decisions by many individuals, firms, and governments, each of whom seeks his or her own best possible economic position. The coordination and reconciliation of these independent actions is accomplished by the foreign exchange market. No one *decides* to borrow in the United States in order to finance an excess of current account payments over receipts. If Canada is to have capital imports, there must be a deficit on current account. The exchange rate will fall until the necessary deficit occurs.

If there had been less foreign borrowing during the period, the Canadian dollar would have depreciated, with the result that the foreign exchange required to finance Canadian travel abroad and the payment of interest and dividends to foreign investors would have been acquired in some other way. There would have been higher exports or lower imports or less travel abroad or more foreigners visiting Canada or some combination of these and other changes in individual balance-of-payments items.

The second contention is more easily dealt with. The relevant question to ask when assessing the economic implications of rapidly rising debt, whether foreign or domestic, is whether the funds raised are being used to finance new investment that will generate sufficient returns in the future to compensate for the burden of interest payments. If Canada's capacity to produce and export is being adequately enhanced by the investment, there is no reason to suppose the country is headed for financial ruin.

The current account deficit reflects the excess of current domestic spending over current income. If spending is high in part because investment is high, then the deficit does not mean that Canada is "living beyond its means." If spending is high because current consumption

as the purchase, and hence the import, of a British good. Both items involve payments to foreigners and use foreign exchange. They are thus debit items in the Canadian balance of payments.

As we have seen, an important distinction is often made between short-term and long-term capital movements.[8] The distinction is important to the capital account because short-term capital movements tend to be much more volatile than long-term ones. Thus they are more likely to cause changes in nonresident ownership of domestic firms and resident ownership of foreign firms. Thus direct investment in Canada is capital investment in a branch plant or subsidiary corporation in Canada in which the investor has voting control. Alternatively, it may be in the form of a takeover in which a controlling interest is acquired in a firm previously controlled by residents. *Portfolio investment*, on the other hand, is investment in bonds or a minority holding of shares that does not involve legal control.

[8] The two major subdivisions of the long-term component are direct investment and portfolio investment. *Direct investment* is the item in the balance-of-payments accounts that records

expenditure is high, this may be justified by the high expected *future* income arising from the current investment. When that income is being earned, the debts accruing due to current borrowing can be repaid, and there will be a current account surplus. Only to the extent that the foreign borrowing is not accompanied by productive domestic investment is a current account deficit a cause for concern. Recent deterioration of the current account has been linked to the borrowing requirements due to the federal government deficit and has been cited as a potential problem in the future.

Structural Problems and the Balance of Trade

It is commonly alleged that the chronic current account deficit reflects serious structural problems in the Canadian economy. This means essentially that Canada produces the wrong combination of goods so that exports are too low and imports are too high.* In this view, one of the problems arising from the deficit is that the high propensity to import frustrates expansionary policy from having its desired impact on

---

* A related contention is that our exports are concentrated on raw materials rather than manufacturing goods. For 1983, the merchandise trade balance was a surplus of about $18 billion, composed of a $33 billion surplus in raw materials and a $15 billion deficit in manufactured goods.

domestic output and employment. The implied policy remedies include the encouragement of domestic production of import substitutes through the use of tariffs and other forms of protection.

If it is true that Canada is not allocating resources properly to exploit its comparative advantage—and hence is producing the "wrong" mix of output—this will be reflected in a reduced value of total output produced. But this reduction in real income will carry with it a reduction in expenditure. A balance-of-trade deficit will arise only if the reduction in real income is greater than the reduction in domestic spending. To put it another way, correction of the structural problem will lead to higher real domestic income *and* therefore higher real domestic spending. The current account deficit will be improved only if income rises by more than spending.

Professor Neil Bruce of Queen's University has recently challenged the view that structural changes have led to the increased deficit. His research showed fairly constant long-term shares of raw materials and manufactures in Canada's trade. The facts of the Canadian case are that its raw materials base is so broad and varied that *at the aggregate level* there are only relatively moderate changes in the division of total output between the raw materials and manufacturing sectors.

---

sudden sharp changes in the capital-account balance and in exchange rates.

Official Reserves

The final section in the balance-of-payments account represents transactions in the *official reserves* held by the government. These transactions reflect the financing of the balance on the remainder of the accounts. Central authorities of most countries

hold supplies of gold and foreign exchange in order that they may intervene in the foreign exchange market to influence their country's rate of exchange.[9] When a country has a payments deficit

[9] If exchange rates were entirely free to fluctuate and were not managed at all, there would be no "official" settlements, for any imbalance in the current plus capital accounts would cause the exchange rate to vary to eliminate the deficit or surplus (see page 758). But as we shall see in Chapter 40, official settlements remain important in a world of managed flexible exchange rates.

on all other counts—that is, when it uses more foreign currency than it obtains—the deficit must be made up by an equivalent reduction in its reserves of gold and foreign exchange. Canadian reserves are held mainly in the form of gold and U.S. dollars. At the end of 1983, U.S. dollars accounted for just over one-half of the total.

The Relation Among Current, Capital, and Official Accounts

The relation among the three divisions of accounts follows from the fact that their sum must be zero.

A deficit on current plus capital accounts must be matched by a net surplus on the official financing accounts—which entails the government's borrowing abroad or decreasing its exchange reserves. A surplus on current plus capital accounts implies a deficit on the official financing accounts. Similarly, deficits on current account can be offset by surpluses on capital account, and vice versa.

To illustrate these relationships, consider a situation in which the value of Canadian imports exceeds the value of Canadian exports. This involves a trade account deficit. In such a situation Canadian export sales will not earn all the foreign currency Canadians need in order to buy the imports. Thus the excess of imports over exports can be paid for only if Canadians obtain foreign currency from other sources.

There are several possibilities. First, foreign currency may be provided by foreign investors eager to obtain Canadian dollars so they can buy Canadian stocks, bonds, and real estate. In this case the current account deficit is balanced by a surplus on capital account. Second, Canadian governments, rather than Canadian firms or citizens, may have borrowed from foreign governments to finance their expenditures. This too causes a capital account surplus. Third, the Canadian government may have depleted its reserves of foreign currency. One way or another, the trade account deficit can occur only when someone provides the foreign currency needed to pay for the excess Canadian imports.

Our reasoning started from the existence of a trade account deficit and showed that, in the absence of government financing from its foreign exchange reserves, it implied a capital account surplus. However, this does not mean that the current account deficit caused the capital inflow. Our reasoning could just as easily have started with the capital account surplus and deduced the existence of the trade account deficit.

Balance-of-Payments Deficits and Surpluses

Meaning of the Concepts

We have already noted that when all the uses to which foreign currency is put and all the sources from which it came are added up, the two amounts are necessarily equal, and thus the overall accounts of all international payments necessarily balance.

Yet it is common to speak of a country as having a balance-of-payments deficit or surplus. What does this mean? These terms usually refer to the balance of the account *excluding* changes in official financing. A **balance-of-payments surplus** means that the government is reducing its liquid liabilities to foreign governments or else adding to its holdings of official reserves in such forms as gold and foreign exchange. A **balance-of-payments deficit** means that the government is adding to its liquid liabilities to foreign governments or else reducing its stocks of official reserves.

The statement, for example, that Canada had a balance-of-payments surplus of $0.6 billion in 1983 means that Canadian official reserves rose by $0.6 billion because all other transactions were in surplus by that amount.

A balance-of-payments deficit means that the reserves of the government are being reduced; a surplus means that reserves are rising.

Consequences of Deficits and Surpluses

The very term balance-of-payments *deficit* sounds bad, while balance-of-payments *surplus* sounds good. Indeed people often assume that a payments surplus is to be welcomed while a payments deficit is to be avoided. But why should this be so?

A balance-of-payments deficit means that in the aggregate debit items exceed credit items. Nothing is implied about this being beneficial or harmful. For example, an investment by a Canadian firm in foreign countries that will yield future profits for Canadian owners is a debit item that will contribute to a balance-of-payments deficit. Yet there is nothing necessarily bad about the investment. On the opposite side, the transfer of ownership of Canadian firms to foreigners is a credit item that will contribute to a balance-of-payments surplus, but such loss of control over Canadian firms is not necessarily desirable.

There is nothing inherently good about a balance-of-payments surplus or inherently bad about a balance-of-payments deficit.

When a balance-of-payments deficit is caused by something considered undesirable (such as dependence on Mideast oil), it may be that the government will seek a way to decrease such imports. When the same deficit is caused by something considered desirable (such as contributions to our allies and underdeveloped nations to foster their economic development), the government may be willing to draw down its reserves for the purpose.

Whether desirable or undesirable, permanent deficits on the balance-of-payments accounts cannot be maintained, for the official reserves that are needed to finance such deficits are sure to be exhausted.

It might seem that a permanent surplus could be tolerated, but this is not the case either. If we have a permanent balance-of-payments surplus, some of our trading partners must have a permanent deficit. Unless we are prepared to give them the money, or allow them to increase their debts to us without limit, that situation too must be ended.

In the long term, when the balance of payments on current plus capital accounts is out of balance in either direction, something must be done. One approach is to maintain the exchange rate and adopt policies to shift the demand and supply curves to the point where the balance of payments is approximately zero. The government can do this through import or export restrictions, changes in interest rates, or a variety of other methods.

Another way is to allow exchange rates to change. Suppose Canada has a balance-of-payments surplus with respect to the United Kingdom. Holders of sterling are trying to make more payments in dollars than holders of dollars wish to make in sterling. If exchange rates are free to vary, the dollar will appreciate and the pound depreciate until the balance of payments is in equilibrium.

If exchange rates are completely free to vary, balance-of-payments deficits and surpluses will be eliminated through exchange rate adjustments.

In today's world, while no country need have a balance-of-payments problem, many still have them. As long as governments intervene in foreign exchange markets, there will be balance-of-payments deficits and surpluses. Surpluses will occur whenever the currency is held below its equilibrium level. Persistent deficits will cause persistent loss of reserves; they are evidence that the government is trying to resist longer-term trends.

But there is one great difference between this kind of balance-of-payments problem and that under fixed exchange rates. The government always has an available solution to its balance-of-payments problem: It can stop intervening in the market and let the exchange rate find its equilibrium level. This will not only end its balance-of-payments problem, it will end its loss of foreign exchange reserves.

But most countries find this is not always as attractive an option as it first appears. In the absence of intervention the exchange rate may either fall—thus fueling domestic inflation—or rise—thus reducing foreign demand for domestic goods and causing unemployment. Thus domestic policy objectives must, at least in the short run, be weighed against the balance-of-payments problem.

In a world of more or less flexible exchange rates such as has existed since 1972, there are more important problems than the balance of payments—issues such as the extent of trade, the pat-

tern of trade, and the desirability of letting foreigners purchase one's assets.

SUMMARY

1. International trade can occur only when it is
possible to exchange the currency of one country
for that of another. The exchange rate between two
currencies is the amount of one currency that must
be paid in order to obtain one unit of another
currency. Where more than two currencies are involved, there will be an exchange rate between each
pair of currencies.

2. The determination of exchange rates in the free
market is simply an application of the laws of supply and demand studied in Chapter 4; the item
being bought and sold is foreign exchange.

3. The supply of foreign exchange arises from Canadian exports of goods and services, and from
long-term and short-term capital flows into Canada. The demand for foreign exchange arises from
Canadian imports of goods and services, and from
capital flows out of Canada.

4. A depreciation of the dollar (a rise in the exchange rate) raises the domestic price of traded
goods. This increases the quantities of such goods
supplied domestically and reduces the quantity demanded. As a result, the volume of exports rises
and, with it, the supply of foreign exchange. On
the other hand, the volume of imports falls, and
with it the demand for foreign exchange. Thus the
supply curve for foreign exchange is upward-sloping and the demand curve for foreign exchange is
downward-sloping when the quantities demanded
and supplied are plotted against the price of foreign
exchange measured in terms of Canadian dollars—
that is, against the exchange rate.

5. A currency will tend to depreciate if there is a
shift to the right of the demand curve for foreign
exchange or a shift to the left of the supply curve.
Shifts in the opposite directions will tend to appreciate the currency. Such shifts are caused by dif-

ferent rates of inflation in different countries, capital movements, structural changes, expectations
about future trends in earnings and exchange rates,
and the level of confidence in the currency as a
source of reserves.

6. Actual transactions among the firms, households, and governments of various countries are
kept track of and reported in the balance-of-payments accounts. In these accounts, any transaction
that uses foreign exchange is recorded as a debit
item and any transaction that produces foreign exchange is recorded as a credit item. If all transactions are recorded, the sum of all credit items necessarily equals the sum of all debit items since the
foreign exchange that is bought must also have
been sold.

7. Major categories in the balance-of-payments account are the balance of trade (exports minus imports), current account, capital account, and official financing. The so-called balance of payments
is the balance of the current plus capital accounts;
that is, it excludes the transactions on official account.

8. There is nothing inherently good or bad about
deficits or surpluses. Persistent deficits or surpluses
cannot be sustained because the former will eventually exhaust a country's foreign exchange reserves and the latter will do the same to a trading
partner's reserves.

9. Balance-of-payments surpluses or deficits can be
managed by the government's use of its foreign
exchange reserves to buy or sell its currency, by
policies that shift the demand and supply for the
currency, or by allowing the exchange rate to seek
its own level.

TOPICS FOR REVIEW

Foreign exchange and exchange rates
Appreciation of a country's currency (a fall in its exchange rate)
Depreciation of a country's currency (a rise in its exchange rate)
Sources of the demand for and supply of foreign exchange
Effects of capital flows on equilibrium exchange rates

The effects on exchange rates of inflation, interest rates, expectations about exchange rates, and capital flows

The balance of trade and the balance of payments

Current and capital account

Official financing items

DISCUSSION QUESTIONS

1. What is the probable effect of each of the following on the exchange rate of a country, other things being equal?
   a. The quantity of oil imports is greatly reduced, but the value of imported oil is higher due to price increases.
   b. Canada's inflation rate was well above the American rate for most of the first half of the 1980s.
   c. Rising labor costs of the country's manufacturers lead to a worsening ability to compete in world markets.
   d. The government greatly expands its gifts of food and machinery to underdeveloped countries.
   e. A major recession occurs with rising unemployment.
   f. The central bank raises interest rates sharply.
   g. More domestic oil is discovered and developed.
2. The president of the Federal Reserve Bank of New York said recently, "Inflation is the enemy in maintaining international trade." What might he have had in mind? Compare the behavior of fixed versus fluctuating exchange rates in a world:
   a. With no inflation but short-run fluctuations in prices
   b. With a substantial but similar degree of inflation everywhere in the world
   c. With sharply varying degrees of inflation
3. In recent years money wages have risen substantially faster in Canada than in the United States. Many Canadians have expressed the fear that their rapidly rising costs will price them out of U.S. markets. Did this fear make sense when the Canadian exchange rate was fixed relative to the American dollar? Does it make sense today when exchange rates are free to vary on the open market?

4. Indicate whether each of the following transactions increases the demand for dollars or the supply of dollars (or neither) on foreign exchange markets.
   a. IBM moves $10 million from bank accounts in Canada to banks in Paris to expand operations there.
   b. The Canadian government extends a grant of $3 million to the government of Peru, which Peru uses to buy farm machinery from a Toronto firm.
   c. Canadian investors, responding to higher profits of U.S. rather than Canadian corporations, buy stocks through the New York Stock Exchange.
   d. U.S. oil companies build a pipeline across Canada to transport Alaskan oil to the United States.
   e. Lower interest rates in Montreal than in London encourage British firms to borrow in the Canadian money market, converting the proceeds into pounds sterling for use at home.

Do these transactions affect the balance of payments, exchange rates, or both?

5. "The necessity of the government to stabilize the balance of payments through the settlement account is a relic of the past. It was a by-product of the adherence to a policy of fixed exchange rates." Do you agree?
6. "If a country solves its balance-of-payments problems, it will have solved its foreign trade problems." Discuss.
7. Outline the reasoning behind the following summer 1983 newspaper headline: "Sterling Tumbles as British Interest Rates Weaken."
8. Explain the links between the following two sentences taken from a July 1983 newspaper story: "U.S. dollar hits 7½ year high," and "This happened in response to Friday's unexpected increase in American M1."

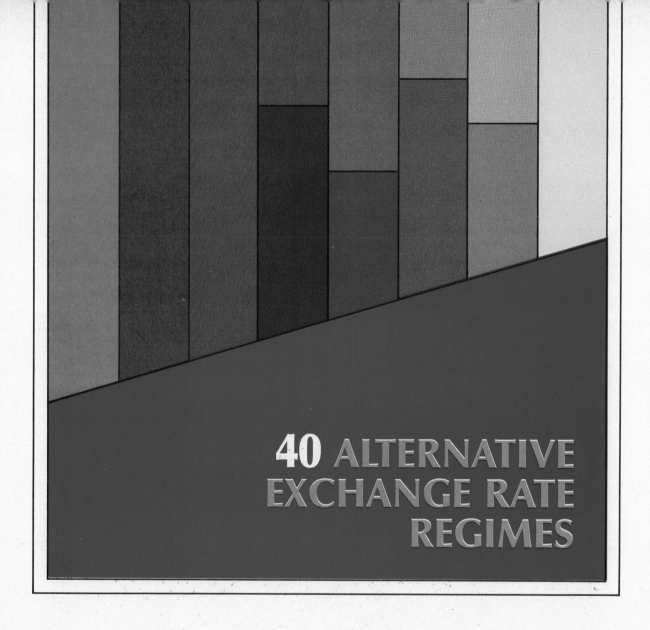

40 ALTERNATIVE EXCHANGE RATE REGIMES

The nations of the world have tried many different systems of international monetary management. The gold standard, the Bretton Woods system, the International Monetary Fund, the Smithsonian Agreements, the European snake, the Jamaica Agreement—all are part of the history of international monetary systems in the twentieth century. No system has been fully satisfactory, and periods of crisis have alternated with periods of stability.

The century began with a system of fixed exchange rates under the gold standard. This system suffered periodic crises in the post-World War I years but did not collapse until the onset of the Great Depression. The 1930s was a period of experimentation with flexible, market-determined exchange rates. This ended with World War II, when governments fixed exchange rates.

In 1944 the fixed exchange rate regime was formalized by international agreement at a conference in Bretton Woods, New Hampshire. The Bretton

Woods system lasted for over a quarter of a century, but its shortcomings and the periods of crisis it induced finally prevailed over its advantages and the periods of stability it afforded. After several attempts to patch it up in the 1970s, the system finally broke down and was gradually abandoned as countries turned one by one to market-determined, flexible exchange rates.

The International Monetary Fund (also called the IMF and the Fund) was created as part of the Bretton Woods system. Under its original charter, the Fund had several tasks. It tried to ensure that countries kept their exchange rates fixed in the short run. It was supposed to ensure that any exchange rate change was really needed to remove a persistent payments disequilibrium and that a single devaluation did not set off a self-canceling round of devaluations. It also made loans—out of funds subscribed by member nations—to governments to support their exchange rates in the face of temporary payments deficits. The Bretton Woods system has been abandoned but the Fund survives, although its tasks have changed. For example, the Jamaica Agreement of 1976 amended the IMF charter to ratify the adoption of floating exchange rates and deemphasize gold as a basis for the international payments system.

Even though the issues involved in international payments systems are understood by only a small number of international traders, bankers, financiers, and economists, the workings of these systems greatly affect the general public and its standard of living. In this chapter we review the principal systems and indicate when and why they ran into trouble.

FIXED AND FLEXIBLE EXCHANGE RATES

Among all the principal payments systems two extremes can be distinguished. The first is a system in which exchange rates are fixed at pre-announced "par" values that are changed only when the existing rate can no longer be defended. The gold standard was such a system, and so was Bretton Woods. (The operation and decline of both systems are discussed in the appendix to this chapter.) The second is a system of freely fluctuating rates determined by market demand and supply in the absence of government intervention. Some countries have occasionally come close to this system, first in the 1930s and then since 1971.

Between these two extremes is a third system, called a *managed* or *dirty float*. In this system the central bank seeks to have some stabilizing influence on the exchange rate but does not try to fix it at a publicly announced par value. This system is really a combination of the other two. We study the two extreme cases of fully fixed and freely fluctuating rates for two reasons. First, understanding them is a prerequisite to understanding the managed float. Second, many economists and policymakers have been advocating a return to one or the other system.

A Fixed Exchange Rate System

In a system of **fixed** or **pegged exchange rates**, each country's central bank intervenes in the foreign exchange market to prevent that country's exchange rate from going outside a narrow band on either side of its "par value."

This system presents one immediate difficulty: There is one less exchange rate to be determined than there are countries. In a two-country world containing only Japan and the United States, for example, if the Bank of Japan fixes the exchange rate at 286 yen to the dollar, the U.S. Federal Reserve cannot fix a different rate making the dollar worth, say, 325 yen. Under the Bretton Woods system, all foreign countries fixed their exchange rate against the U.S. dollar. The Fed accepted these exchange rates and was the only central bank in the world that did not have to intervene to support a particular value of its currency.

Having picked a fixed exchange rate for their currency against, say, the U.S. dollar, each foreign central bank must then manage matters so that the chosen rate can actually be maintained. It must be prepared to offset imbalances in demand and supply by government sales or purchases of foreign exchange. In the face of short-term fluctuations in market demand and supply, each central bank can maintain its fixed exchange rate by entering the market and buying and selling as required.

To do this the central bank has to hold reserves of acceptable foreign exchange. When there is an abnormally low demand for its country's currency on the market, the bank keeps the currency from falling in value by selling foreign exchange and buying up domestic currency. This depletes its reserves of foreign exchange. When there is an abnormally high demand for its country's currency on the foreign exchange market, the bank prevents the currency's appreciating in value by selling domestic currency in return for foreign exchange. This augments its stocks of foreign exchange.

As long as the central bank is trying to maintain an exchange rate that *equates demand and supply on average*, the policy can be successful. Sometimes the bank will be buying and other times selling, but its reserves will fluctuate around a constant average level.

If, however, there is a permanent shift in demand for or supply of a nation's currency on the foreign exchange market, the long-term equilibrium rate will move away from the pegged rate. It will then be very difficult to maintain the pegged rate. For example, if there is a major inflation in France while prices are stable in the United States, the equilibrium value of the franc will fall. In a free market the franc would depreciate and the U.S. dollar would appreciate. But a fixed exchange rate is not a free-market rate. If the Bank of France persists in trying to maintain the original exchange rate, it will have to meet the excess demand for U.S. dollars by selling from its reserves. This policy can persist only as long as it has reserves that it is willing to spend to maintain an artificially high price of francs. But the bank cannot do this indefinitely. Sooner or later the reserves that it has, and those that it can borrow, will be exhausted.

The management of a fixed rate is illustrated in Figure 40-1. The example used is the maintenance by the Bank of England of a fixed exchange rate between pound sterling and the U.S. dollar.

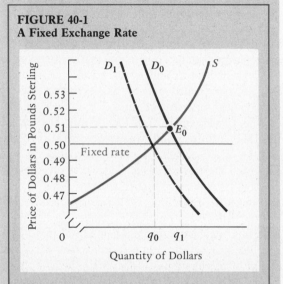

FIGURE 40-1
A Fixed Exchange Rate

When an exchange rate is fixed at other than the equilibrium rate, either excess demand or excess supply will persist. Suppose demand and supply curves of dollars in the absence of government controls are D_0 and S; equilibrium is at E_0, with a price of £0.51 per dollar. The equilibrium price of the pound is $1.96. Now the British authorities peg the price of the pound at $2.00; that is, they fix the price of the dollar at £0.50. They have overvalued the pound and undervalued the dollar. As a result there is an excess of dollars demanded over dollars supplied of q_0. To maintain the fixed rate it is necessary to shift either the demand curve or the supply curve (or both) so that the two intersect at the fixed rate. For example, demand might be shifted to D_1 by the British government's limiting imports. If the curves are not shifted, the fixed rate will have to be supported by the British government's supplying dollars in the amount of q_0q_1 per period out of its reserves.

When the fixed rate is not near the free-market equilibrium rate, controls of various sorts may be introduced in an attempt to shift the demand curve for foreign exchange so that it intersects the supply curve at a rate close to the controlled rate. This is usually done by restricting imports of goods and services or by restricting the export of capital. If the central bank cannot shift demand and supply in order to keep the equilibrium rate approximately as high as the fixed rate, it will have no alternative but to devalue its currency.

Problems with Fixed Exchange Rates

Three problems typically arise in a system of fixed exchange rates: (1) providing sufficient reserves, (2) adjusting to long-term trends, and (3) dealing with speculative crises.

Reserves. Reserves are needed to accommodate short-term balance-of-payments fluctuations arising from the current and the capital accounts. On current account, trade is subject to many short-term variations, some systematic and some random. This means that even if the value of imports does equal the value of exports taken on average over several years, there may be considerable imbalances over shorter periods.

With a free market, fluctuations in current and capital account payments would cause the exchange rate to fluctuate. To prevent such fluctuations when rates are fixed, the monetary authorities buy and sell foreign exchange as required. These operations require the authorities to hold reserves of foreign exchange. If they run out of reserves, they cannot maintain the pegged rate.

As explained in the appendix, the Bretton Woods system had difficulty providing sufficient reserves. This was because the ultimate reserve was gold and there was not enough of it. As a result, the world's central banks held much of their reserves in U.S. dollars and British pound sterling. Currencies that are widely held for this purpose are called **reserve currencies**.

This system worked well enough as long as these reserve currencies had a stable value. However, in the mid 1960s fear of an impending devaluation of sterling arose, and in the early 1970s a similar fear arose regarding the U.S. dollar. In both cases the fears were well founded: Sterling was devalued in late 1967, and the dollar was devalued in 1971 and again in 1973.

The devaluation of a reserve currency reduces the value of the reserves of that currency held by the world's central banks. Fear that a devaluation will occur destroys the acceptability of a currency as a means of holding reserves. This is discussed further in Box 40-1.

The problem of providing reserves, although serious, should not be insurmountable in any future system of fixed rates. After all, a balanced portfolio composed of some holdings of all currencies could be held as reserves. This would reduce the risks from holding reserves. For whenever one currency falls in value against a second currency, the second currency rises in value against the first.

Long-term disequilibria. With fixed exchange rates, long-term disequilibria can be expected to develop because of lasting shifts in the demands for and supplies of foreign exchange. There are three important reasons for these shifts. First, different trading countries have different rates of inflation. Chapter 39 explained how these varying rates produce changes in the equilibrium rates of exchange and, if the rate is fixed, also produce excess supply or excess demand in each country's foreign exchange market. Second, changes in the demands for and supplies of imports and exports are associated with long-term economic growth. Because the economies of different countries grow at different rates, their demands for imports and their supplies of exports can be expected to shift at different rates. Third, structural changes, such as major new innovations or a change in the price of oil, cause major changes in imports and exports.

The associated shifts in demand and supply on the foreign exchange market imply that, even starting from a current account equilibrium with imports equal to exports, there is no reason to believe that equilibrium will exist at the same rate of exchange 5 or 10 years later.

The rate of exchange that will lead to a balance-of-payments equilibrium will tend to change over time; over a decade the change can be substantial.

Governments may react to long-term disequilibria in at least three ways.

1. The exchange rate can be changed whenever it is clear that a balance-of-payments deficit or surplus is the result of a long-term shift in demands

BOX 40–1 PROBLEMS FOR NATIONS WHOSE CURRENCY IS HELD AS A RESERVE

Under the Bretton Woods system the supply of gold was augmented by reserves of the key currencies, the U.S. dollar, and the British pound sterling. Because the need for reserves expanded much more rapidly than the gold stock after World War II, the system required nations to hold an increasing fraction of reserves in national currencies, first sterling and then dollars.

While it is prestigious to have one's currency held as a reserve currency—and even advantageous as long as other countries are willing to increase their holdings of one's paper money without making claims on current output—there are both disadvantages and hazards for the country whose currency is involved.

Such a country is placed under great pressure not to devalue its currency. If it does devalue, owing to a severe balance-of-payments deficit, all countries holding that currency will find the value of their reserves diminished. If it tries to avoid devaluation, the fear that it may be unable to do so will in any case impair the usefulness of the currency as a reserve because other countries will become reluctant to hold it. The result may well be that the domestic policy of the country whose currency is the reserve becomes unduly subservient to the overriding need to maintain its exchange rate and its gold reserves.

The Loss of Confidence in the U.S. Dollar As a Reserve Currency

In the 1950s and 1960s America ran frequent deficits on the sum of current and capital accounts. This resulted largely from American loans, investments, and contributions to other nations who were rebuilding their economies after World War II. As long as other nations were willing to accumulate dollar holdings, this caused no problem; indeed, the buildup of dollars provided the growth in foreign exchange reserves that was needed to finance the growing volume of world trade. But a declining fraction of gold backing for the U.S. dollar slowly eroded confidence in it as a reserve currency.

The effect of the dollar devaluations of the early 1970s. The devaluation in 1971 (7.9 percent) and 1973 (11 percent) automatically reduced the value of the exchange reserves of everyone holding U.S. dollars. Had everyone believed that these were just isolated adjustments, they might well have licked their wounds and gone on as before. But no fundamental changes arose either in American policy or in international financial arrangements. Thus many believed that the past devaluations were but preludes to inevitable future ones.

Fear of further devaluations not only made holders of U.S. dollars reluctant to increase their holdings, but actually led many prudent holders to want to decrease reliance on such a shaky reserve. As people tried to get rid of U.S. dollars, the exchange rate began to slide. Between 1970 and 1973 the U.S. dollar declined 22 percent against the yen and 30 percent against the mark. From 1973 to early 1980 it dropped an additional 23 percent against the yen and 31 percent against the mark. The decreasing value of the U.S. dollar reduced the adequacy of most countries' dollar reserves and threatened their financial stability.

Attempts to flee from the dollar. While one country (or one bank) can readily reduce its holdings of U.S. dollars by buying gold or other currencies, the whole world cannot do so unless alternative sources of international reserves are available. One cause of the startling rise in the price of gold in 1979–1980 from $250 to over $900 an ounce was the attempt of many holders of U.S. dollars to flee to gold. Such attempted flights from the dollar will end only if the causes of the decline in demand for dollars are eliminated, or if an adequate alternative international reserve is created to replace it. The return to stable prices in the United States has restored some faith in the dollar, and use of the SDR has grown. But few observers are complacent enough to believe that these developments provide a long-run solution.

and supplies in the foreign exchange market and not the result of some transient factor.

2. Domestic price levels can be allowed to change in an attempt to make the present fixed exchange rates become the equilibrium rates. To restore equilibrium, countries with overvalued currencies need to have deflations and countries with undervalued currencies need to have inflations. But changes in domestic price levels have all sorts of domestic repercussions. Deflations are difficult and costly to accomplish (e.g., reductions in aggregate demand intended to lower the price level are likely to raise unemployment), and often the explicit goal of government policy is to avoid inflation. One might expect governments to be more willing to change exchange rates than to try to change their price levels.

3. Restrictions can be imposed on trade and foreign payments. Imports and foreign spending by tourists and governments can be restricted, and the export of capital can be slowed or even stopped. Surplus countries are often quick to criticize such restrictions on international trade and payments. But as long as exchange rates are fixed and price levels prove difficult to manipulate, deficit countries have little option but to restrict the quantity of foreign exchange their residents are permitted to obtain.

Since restrictions on trade and foreign payments are undesirable in a world economy characterized by large-scale international trade and foreign investment, and since deflations of the price level are difficult and costly to bring about, most countries will want to preserve the possibility of making occasional changes in their exchange rates even if fixed rates are the main rule of the day.

Under the Bretton Woods system, although most countries defended their exchange rates in the face of crises, there were still major rounds of exchange rate adjustments. Because exchange rates did have to be changed from time to time, the system of fixed rates under the Bretton Woods agreement was called an **adjustable peg system**.

Handling speculative crises. When enough people begin to doubt the government's ability to maintain the current exchange rate, speculative crises develop. The most important reason for such crises is that, over time, equilibrium exchange rates get further and further away from any given set of fixed rates. When the disequilibrium becomes obvious to everyone, traders and speculators come to believe that a realignment of rates is due. There is a rush to buy currencies expected to be revalued and a rush to sell currencies expected to be devalued. Even if the authorities take drastic steps to remove the payments deficit, there may be doubt that these measures will work before the exchange reserves are exhausted. Speculative flows of funds can reach very large proportions, and it may be impossible to avoid changing the exchange rate under such pressure.

Under an adjustable peg system, speculators have an opportunity to make large profits, since everyone knows which way an exchange rate will be changed if it is to be changed at all.

As the equilibrium value of a country's currency changes, possibly under the impact of high inflation, it becomes obvious that the central bank is having more and more difficulty holding the pegged rate. So when a crisis arises, speculators sell the country's currency. If it is devalued, they can buy it back at a lower price and earn a profit. If it is not devalued, they can buy it back at the price at which they sold it and lose only the commission costs on the deal. This asymmetry, with speculators having a chance to make large profits by risking only a small loss, was what eventually undid the Bretton Woods system.

During the Bretton Woods period, governments tended to resist changing their exchange rates until they had no alternative. This made the situation so obvious that speculators could hardly lose, and their actions set off the final crises that forced exchange rate readjustments. If changes could be made more frequently and before they became inevitable, the number of speculative crises might diminish, and the system of fixed exchange rates might appear more viable. Such changes, however, would remove the day-to-day certainty that was one of the chief advantages of this system. Moreover, a surprise change might lead to suspicion that a devaluation was made to gain a competitive advantage for a country's exports rather than to remove a fundamental disequilibrium. After all, governments are not supposed to devalue under an adjustable peg system until it is *clear* that they are faced with a fundamental disequilibrium. If this is clear to them, it is also clear to ordinary traders and speculators.

Flexible Exchange Rates

Under a system of flexible exchange rates, demand and supply determines the rates without any government intervention. Such rates are called free, or **flexible** or **floating exchange rates.** Since the foreign exchange market always clears, the government can turn its attention to domestic problems of inflation and unemployment, leaving the balance of payments to take care of itself—at least so went the theory before flexible rates were introduced.

For reasons that we shall analyze later in this chapter, this optimistic picture did not materialize when the world went over to flexible exchange rates. Free-market fluctuations in rates were far greater—and hence potentially more upsetting to the performance of national economies and to the flow of international trade—than many economists had anticipated. As a result, central banks have felt the need to intervene quite frequently and extensively to stabilize exchange rates.

Managed Floats

A major difference between the present system and Bretton Woods is that central banks no longer publicly announce par values for exchange rates that they are committed in advance to defend even at heavy cost. Central banks are thus free to adjust their exchange rate targets as circumstances change. Sometimes they leave the rate completely free to fluctuate, and at other times they interfere actively to alter the exchange rate from its free-market value. Such a system is called a **managed float** or a **dirty float.**

Some countries have opted for what is called a

currency block by pegging their exchange rates against each other and then indulging in a joint float against the outside world. The best-known currency block is the European **snake.** Under this arrangement the countries of the EEC, with the exception of the United Kingdom, maintain fixed rates among their own currencies but allow them to float as a block against the dollar.

Some countries maintain stable values for their currencies in terms of *one* of the three major trading currencies (the U.S. dollar, the British pound, and the French franc). Their rates then fluctuate against those of the other two major currencies.

What Determines the Exchange Rate in a Floating System?

One surprise to supporters of floating exchange rates has been the degree of exchange rate volatility. Why have rates been so volatile?

The trend value of exchange rates is approximately determined by their **purchasing power parity (PPP)** value. The PPP exchange rate is the one that holds constant the relative price levels in two countries *when measured in a common currency.* For example, assume that the U.S. price level rises by 20 percent while the German price level rises by only 5 percent over the same period. The PPP value of the German mark then appreciates by approximately 15 percent. This would mean that in Germany the prices of all goods (both German-produced and imported American goods) would rise by 5 percent measured in German marks, while in the United States the prices of all goods (both American-produced and imports from Germany) would rise by 20 percent measured in U.S. dollars.

The PPP exchange rate adjusts so that the relative price of the two nations' goods (measured in either currency) is unchanged because the change in the relative values of two currencies compensates exactly for differences in national inflation rates.

If the actual exchange rate equals the PPP rate, the competitive positions of producers in the two countries will be unchanged. Firms located in countries with high inflation rates will still be able to sell their output on international markets, since the exchange rate adjusts to offset the effect of the higher domestic prices.

Figure 40-2 shows that the exchange rate between U.S. dollars and sterling has followed the PPP rate over the long run. But notice also how large the fluctuations are around the PPP rate.

During the Bretton Woods period of fixed exchange rates, the advocates of floating rates argued that speculators would stabilize the actual rates within a narrow band around the PPP rates. The argument was that since everyone knew the normal value was the PPP rate, deviations would quickly be removed by speculators seeking a profit when the rate returned to its PPP level. To illustrate, suppose the PPP rate is U.S. $2.00 = £1.00 and that the actual rate falls to U.S. $1.90 = £1.00. Speculators would rush to buy pounds at U.S. $1.90 each, expecting to sell them for U.S. $2.00

when the rate returns to its PPP level. This very action would raise the demand for sterling and help push its value back toward U.S. $2.00.

Such speculative behavior would stabilize the exchange rate near its PPP value if speculators could be sure that the deviations would be small and short-lived. But in practice the swings around the PPP rate have been wide and have lasted for long periods. Thus, if sterling fell to U.S. $1.90, speculators would know that it could go as low as U.S. $1.60 and stay there for quite a while before returning to U.S. $2.00. In that case it might be worth speculating on a price of U.S. $1.80 next week rather than a price of U.S. $2.00 in some indefinite future.

The wide swings in exchange rates that have occurred show that speculative buying and selling cannot be relied on to hold exchange rates very close to their PPP values continuously.

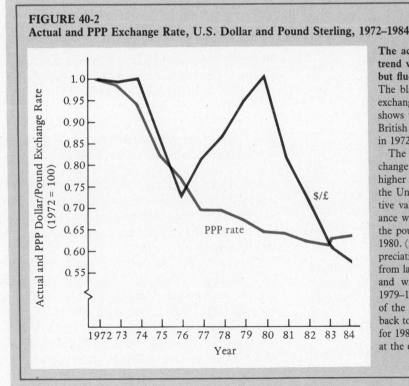

FIGURE 40-2
Actual and PPP Exchange Rate, U.S. Dollar and Pound Sterling, 1972–1984

The actual exchange rate follows the trend value of the PPP exchange rate but fluctuates substantially around it. The black line shows the dollar/pound exchange rate while the colored line shows the ratio of the U.S. CPI to the British CPI. (Both series are set to 1.00 in 1972.)

The continual decline of the PPP exchange rate reflects United Kingdom's higher inflation rate relative to that of the United States. Until 1976 the relative value of the pound fell in accordance with the PPP rate, but after 1976 the pound appreciated sharply through 1980. (Many observers associate this appreciation with the onset of production from large oil deposits in the North Sea and with very high interest rates in 1979–1980.) In 1980 the relative value of the pound began to fall, bringing it back toward its PPP value. (The figures for 1984 are those for the exchange rate at the end of March.)

But why have these wide fluctuations occurred? There are many reasons, and one of the most important is associated with international differences in interest rates.

Exchange Rate Overshooting

Suppose that American interest rates rise above those ruling in other major financial centers. A rush to lend money out at the profitable rates found in the United States will lead to an appreciation of the U.S. dollar.

This process will stop only when the rise in value of the U.S. dollar on foreign exchange markets is large enough that investors expect it subsequently to fall in value. This expected future depreciation then just offsets the interest premium from lending funds in U.S. dollars.

To illustrate, assume that interest rates are 4 percentage points higher in New York than in London due to a very restrictive monetary policy in the United States. Investors believe the PPP rate is U.S. $2.00 = £1.00 but, as they rush to buy dollars to take advantage of the higher U.S. interest rates, they drive the rate to, say, U.S. $1.80 = £1.00. (Since £1.00 now buys fewer U.S. dollars sterling has depreciated, and since it takes fewer U.S. dollars to buy £1.00 the dollar has appreciated.) They do not believe this rate will be sustained and instead expect the U.S. dollar to lose value. If foreign investors expect it to depreciate at 4 percent per year, they will be indifferent between lending money in New York and doing so in London. The extra 4 percent of interest they earn in New York per year is exactly offset by the 4 percent they expect to lose when they turn their money back into their own currency.

Any policy that raises domestic interest rates above world levels will cause the external value of the domestic currency to appreciate enough to create an expected future depreciation sufficient to offset the interest differential.

A central bank that is seeking to meet a monetary target may have to put up with large fluctuations in the exchange rate. If, in the example above, the high U.S. interest rates were the result of a restrictive monetary policy needed to hold the money supply on target, the overshooting of the U.S. dollar above its PPP rate may put export- and import-competing industries under temporary but very severe pressure from foreign competition.

The other side of this coin is that the high value of the U.S. dollar creates inflationary pressure in other countries. U.S. goods become much more expensive abroad, thus putting upward pressure on foreign prices and wages. Authorities in those countries are faced with the uncomfortable choice of accepting this increased inflation or raising their own interest rates and thus maintaining their exchange rates in terms of the U.S. dollar. In the early 1980s many foreign central banks chose this latter option, and the tight U.S. monetary policies were quickly imitated in other countries. This combined monetary contraction contributed to the severity of the world recession, as discussed further in Box 40-2 on pages 784–785.

CURRENT PROBLEMS[1]

The shift from fixed rates to a system of managed flexible rates has not ended the recurring crises. The crises continue for several reasons.

The Lack of an Alternative to the Dollar As a Reserve Currency

Governments operating dirty floats need reserves, just as do governments operating adjustable pegs. The search for an adequate supply of reserves has continued unabated since the demise of the Bretton Woods system.

One major form in which reserves are held is U.S. dollars; another, and one that is growing in size, is the **special drawing rights (SDRs)** held with the IMF. First introduced in 1969, SDRs were designed to provide a supplement to existing reserve assets. A Special Drawing Account was set up and kept separate from all other operations of

---

[1] The rest of this chapter can be skipped without loss of continuity.

the Fund. Each member country was assigned an SDR quota that was guaranteed in terms of a fixed gold value. Each country could use its quota to acquire an equivalent amount of convertible currencies from other participants. SDRs could be used without prior consultation with the Fund, but only to cope with balance-of-payments difficulties. SDR allocations grew from about $10 billion in 1970 to over $40 billion in 1982.

The commitment to lower inflation initiated by the Reagan administration in 1980 has restored some confidence in the U.S. dollar as a reserve asset. But overall these developments have not been seen as long-term solutions to the reserve problem. While it is possible that some other national currencies will take over the reserve role played by the U.S. dollar, this is not likely.

First, such a replacement would require a massive shift in reserves from dollars to the new currency. Unless this were carefully managed, it would result in a sharp depreciation of the U.S. dollar that would hurt the United States and all other holders of dollars. Second, no other country is likely to accept for its currency the role of major international reserve. As we saw in Box 40-1, the reserve currency role results in major problems and limits the scope of domestic policy action. The American experience has not gone unnoticed.

Why does the world not turn to an international paper reserve system based on SDRs or some similar creation? Such a solution has much support from academic economists, who see an appropriate international institution managing the supply of international currency to accommodate growth and to avoid inflation.

Critics of such a system—among them most of the world's central bankers—distrust the concept of an international paper currency, pointing out that few countries have managed their own money supplies effectively. However difficult the task of the U.S. Federal Reserve may be, the task of a World Reserve Bank would be more difficult. Further, private acceptance and use of the SDR has been virtually nonexistent, indicating the enormous difficulties inherent in creating a new currency.

Some who are skeptical of an international paper monetary standard have urged a return to the gold standard. This approach has critical disadvantages. In fact, the IMF and the U.S. government have at various times taken the lead in the attempt to "demonetize" gold completely.

For the moment at least, the world cannot agree on an international monetary reserve. Until it does, there will be crises whenever there is a desire to shift from one to another of the multiple sources of reserves: dollars, gold, SDRs, marks, francs, and yen. The speculative opportunities inherent in such a system remain large, as evidenced by the recent behavior of the price of gold shown in Figure 40-3 on page 786.

The Impact of OPEC

One serious recent event affecting the future payments system—and indeed the whole of international economic relations—was the tenfold increase in the price of oil by the OPEC cartel. These price rises generated an unprecedented imbalance in the international economic system in the form of a massive payments surplus for the oil producers and a corresponding deficit for the oil-importing countries. The excess purchasing power in the hands of oil producers has come to be called **petrodollars**. The cumulative stock of petrodollars may well exceed $500 billion. Petrodollars cause several different kinds of problems, some of them short term, others long term in nature.

Short-term problems of industrialized countries. Most petrodollars will eventually be used for the purchase of consumption goods and services or investment goods from industrialized countries. In time these countries will thus find their exports to the oil producers rising. But the oil-producing countries could not spend their oil revenues on goods and services as fast as they were earned in the late 1970s.[2] Nor could the industrialized oil-

---

[2] There is a limit to the speed with which any country can absorb foreign goods, and many oil-producing countries were at that limit. Ships sometimes wait months to unload for want of dock capacity, unloaded goods sometimes sit in wharfside stockpiles for months—even years—for want of transportation capacity, and so on.

BOX 40-2 BEGGAR-MY-NEIGHBOR POLICIES PAST AND PRESENT

The Great Depression of the 1930s brought an end to the long-standing stability of the gold standard and ushered in a period of experimentation in exchange regimes. Experiments were tried with both fixed and fluctuating rates.

But the overriding feature of the decade was that considerations of massive unemployment came to dominate economic policies in virtually every country, and all devices, including exchange rate manipulations, seemed fair game for dealing with them. Many of the policies adopted at this time were acts of desperation that would have made long-term sense only if other countries had not also been in crisis. Governments tended not to consider the long-term effects on trade, or on their trading partners, of the policies they adopted, hoping to gain short-term advantages before their policies provoked the inevitable reaction from others.

The use of devaluations to ease domestic unemployment rested on a simple and superficially plausible line of analysis: if a country has unemployed workers at home, why not substitute home production for imports and thus give jobs to one's citizens instead of to foreigners? One way to do this is to urge, say, Canadians to "buy Canadian." Another, probably more effective, way is to lower the prices of domestic goods relative to those of imports. The devaluation of one's currency does this by making foreign goods that much more expensive. (A 10 percent devaluation, other than equal, means that it will take 10 percent more domestic money to buy the same imports; this is equivalent to a 10 percent rise in the prices of all foreign goods.)

Of course, if this policy works other countries will find *their* exports falling and unemployment rising as a consequence. Because such policies attempt to solve one country's problems by inflicting them on others, they are called **beggar-my-neighbor policies** and are described as attempts to "export one's unemployment."

In a situation of inadequate world demand, a beggar-my-neighbor policy on the part of one country can work only in the unlikely event that other countries do not try to protect themselves. A situation in which all countries devalue their currencies in an attempt to gain a competitive advantage over one another is called a situation of **competitive devaluations.**

This is what happened during the 1930s. One country would devalue its currency in an attempt to reduce its imports and stimulate exports. But because other countries were suffering from the same kinds of problems of unemployment, they did not sit idly by. Retaliation was swift, and devaluation followed devaluation. But the simultaneous attempt of all countries to cut imports without suffering a comparable cut in exports is bound to be self-defeating.

When unemployment is due to insufficient world aggregate demand, it cannot be cured by measures

consuming countries produce the goods and services at the rate necessary for all the oil revenues to be spent without creating enormous inflationary pressures.[3]

[3] Production of the goods produces factor incomes and thus adds to domestic demand, while export of the goods removes them from domestic markets and thus reduces domestic supplies.

Thus, in the short term the OPEC countries had excess dollars. They also had an understandable desire to earn a return on those funds. One way was to invest their surplus revenues in the advanced industrialized nations, thereby returning on capital account the purchasing power extracted from the current accounts of the oil-importing nations. This creates many serious problems.

designed to redistribute among nations the fixed and inadequate total of demand.

These policies, along with other restrictive trade policies such as import duties, export subsidies, quotas, and prohibitions, led to a declining volume of world trade and brought no relief from the worldwide depression. Moreover, they contributed to a loss of faith in the economic system and in the ability of either economists or politicians to cope with economic crises.

To avoid a recurrence of the beggar-my-neighbor policies of the 1930s, trading nations designed some important institutions. The International Monetary Fund (IMF) was supposed to reduce the chances of competitive devaluations, and the General Agreement on Tariffs and Trade (GATT) was to reduce the chances of competitive increases in tariffs and other trade restrictions. These institutions worked well for over 30 years.

In 1980 the United States embarked on tight monetary policy, driving up U.S. interest rates. Just as expansionary monetary policy in the face of world recession tended to "export unemployment" by leading to a depreciation of the home currency and reducing the demand for foreign goods, tight monetary policy in the face of the world inflation tends to "export inflation" by leading to an appreciation of the home currency and raising the demand for foreign goods. Most other governments resisted this tendency by also adopting tight monetary policy. This led the world into the serious recession of 1981–1983.

Under the extreme pressures of this difficult economic situation, beggar-my-neighbor pressures surfaced, and many governments found them hard to resist politically. American voters in November 1982 showed very strong support for advocates of increased tariffs to protect hard-pressed import-competing industries in America. Many countries negotiated unofficial quotas restricting the importation of Japanese cars. European agricultural protectionism nearly wrecked the GATT negotiations in December 1982. Earlier in the year Sweden initiated what appeared to be a beggar-my-neighbor devaluation of the kronor. Less developed countries sought covert ways of protecting their own infant industries and complained, with some justice, that the developed nations paid lip service to, rather than really acting on, the slogan of "trade not aid." It was clear that great pressure was being put on the whole postwar fabric designed to encourage trade and discourage beggar-my-neighbor policies. The longer the recession, the more alarming the pressures. Only time will tell how much damage has been done to this carefully constructed fabric of postwar international cooperation.

One of the most important concerns the havoc brought to foreign exchange markets when surplus oil funds are invested in liquid assets and switched between currencies in response to changes in interest rates and expected capital gains arising from possible exchange rate alterations. Surplus petrodollars can also be used speculatively, and many observers believe that a good part of the wild rise and sudden fall in gold prices in 1979–1980 was due to just such a use of petrodollars.

Short-term problems of the underdeveloped countries. Consider a country such as Kenya, for which the OPEC price increase turned a small trade surplus into a massive deficit overnight. The country was unable to generate revenues quickly enough

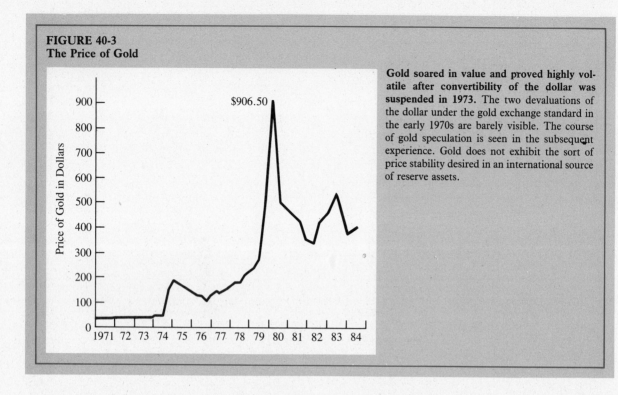

FIGURE 40-3
The Price of Gold

$906.50

Gold soared in value and proved highly volatile after convertibility of the dollar was suspended in 1973. The two devaluations of the dollar under the gold exchange standard in the early 1970s are barely visible. The course of gold speculation is seen in the subsequent experience. Gold does not exhibit the sort of price stability desired in an international source of reserve assets.

to pay its oil bill, yet it could sharply decrease its use of oil only at the cost of a great slowdown in its domestic economy.

The IMF stepped in with loan arrangements to help countries most severely affected by the rising oil prices, the repayments of maturing loans were deferred, and the OPEC nations established a fund for short-term loans to such countries. Thus the purely short-term problems can be, and have been, solved through international cooperation and recognition of the need for accommodation on the part of creditor nations.

Many oil exporting countries also borrowed heavily on the expectation of rising oil prices. By early 1983, however, OPEC had lowered its price, and further price cuts appeared possible. Many international loans appear to be threatened, including those made by large private banks to LDCs such as Mexico, which is heavily dependent on oil exports for repayment. The risk of a major default hangs over the system, and the IMF again finds

itself facing the likelihood of helping with rescheduling and otherwise organizing repayments of large international loans.

The Challenge for the 1980s

The 1970s witnessed the replacement of a system of managed fixed exchange rates by a system of managed flexible exchange rates. The problems of the latter may have been revealed by the events of the decade, but they cannot be said to have been solved. Officials understand the need to develop an adequate reserve unit not tied to any national currency and to devise workable guidelines for managing flexible rates.

An International Reserve Currency

Many economists believe that a controlled international money supply based on SDRs and constantly expanded to keep pace with the volume of world trade is the best answer to the reserve problem. But an international paper currency, like a national currency, cannot work until there is confidence in it. The turmoil of the last two decades has done nothing to create the climate of confidence required for the complete demonetization of gold and the reduction of the role of the U.S. dollar as the international medium of exchange. Flawed though either gold or the dollar is as a reserve, each seems better (at this date) to many of the world's bankers than SDRs or similar "pieces of paper."

The Management of Exchange Rates

The managed aspect of managed floating rates poses several potential problems for the international monetary system. They include the possibilities of mutually inconsistent exchange rate stabilization policies, competitive exchange rate depreciation, and instability of exchange rates in the face of speculative pressures. To help avoid these problems, the IMF has issued guidelines for exchange rate management.

The guidelines emphasize that exchange rate policy is a matter for international consultation and surveillance by the IMF and that intervention practices by individual central banks should be based on three principles: (1) Exchange authorities should prevent sudden and disproportionate short-term movements in exchange rates and ensure an orderly adjustment to longer-term pressures. (2) In consultation with the IMF, countries should establish a target zone for the medium-term values of their exchange rates and keep the actual rate within that target zone. (3) Countries should recognize that exchange rate management involves joint responsibilities and is not just the responsibility of the individual country in question.

The experiences of the 1970s have underlined one of the most important unsolved problems of managed floating rates: coping with the massive volume of short-term funds that can be switched very rapidly between financial centers. Short-term capital flows forced the abandonment of exchange rates that had been agreed on in 1971 and have often caused violent fluctuations in floating rates

since then. Severe "currency misalignments" have arisen and persisted, rendering uncompetitive on world markets the export- and import-competing sectors in countries with overvalued currencies, while creating enormous profit opportunities in countries with undervalued currencies. Capital flows often prevent the quick return of exchange rates to their PPP values.

Various attempts have been made to limit such capital flows. Italy has adopted a two-tier foreign exchange market, with one price for foreign exchange to finance current account transactions and another price (and another set of controls) for foreign exchange to finance capital movements. Germany has used direct controls on overseas borrowing. There has also been a considerable extension of arrangements under which central banks in surplus countries lend the funds they are accumulating back to central banks in deficit countries. Through such arrangements, the ability of banks to maintain stable exchange rates in the face of short-term speculative flights of capital is enhanced.

The major problem in managing speculative flows is to identify them accurately. Experience suggests that exchange rate management can smooth out temporary fluctuations but cannot resist underlying trends in equilibrium rates caused by relative inflation rates, structural changes, and persistent nonspeculative capital flows. In day-to-day management it is not always easy to distinguish among them.

The Need for Cooperation

One of the most impressive aspects of the international payments history of the last 30 years has been the steady rise of effective international cooperation. When the gold standard collapsed and the Great Depression overwhelmed the countries of the world, "every nation for itself" was the rule of the day. Rising tariffs, competitive exchange rate devaluations, and all forms of beggar-my-neighbor policies abounded.

After World War II the countries of the world cooperated in bringing the Bretton Woods system and the IMF into being. The system itself was far from perfect, and it finally broke down as a result of its own internal contradictions. But the international cooperation that was necessary to set up the system survived. The joint cooperative actions of central banks allowed them to weather speculative crises in the 1970s that would have forced them to devalue their currencies in the 1950s.

Thus the collapse of Bretton Woods did not plunge the world into the same chaos that followed the breakdown of the gold standard. The world was also better able to cope with the terrible strains caused by the sharp rise in oil prices in the 1970s. Of course enormous oil-related problems remain, and they are matters for continuing international dialogue.

Whatever the problems of the future, the world has a better chance of solving them—or even just learning to live with them—when its countries cooperate through the IMF and other international organizations than when each country seeks its own selfish solution without concern for the interests of others.

One of the most disturbing consequences of the Great Recession of 1982–1983 was the severe straining of the carefully constructed fabric of international cooperation, as we saw in Chapter 22. There we saw that many countries flirted with beggar-my-neighbor policies of trade restriction and competitive devaluations under the stress of falling domestic national income and rising unemployment rates. Only time will tell whether this activity was an aberration that will disappear with the end of the recession or the beginning of a new trend away from the international cooperation that has served the world so well since 1945.

SUMMARY

1. Various systems of international monetary arrangements have been tried. All involve aspects of two extreme systems—fixed exchange rates and flexible exchange rates.

2. Under fixed or pegged exchange rates, the central bank intervenes in the foreign exchange market to maintain the exchange rate at or near a pre-announced "par value." To do this the central bank must hold sufficient stocks of foreign exchange reserves. Reserves have historically been held in the form of gold or reserve currencies, particularly the U.S. dollar. The SDR is a relatively new international paper money meant to provide additional international reserves linked neither to gold nor to the U.S. dollar.

3. Any adjustable peg system faces three major problems: (1) providing sufficient international reserves, (2) adjusting to long-term trends in receipts and payments, and (3) handling periodic speculative crises.

4. Under a system of flexible exchange rates, the exchange rate is market-determined by supply and demand without any government intervention.

5. Since their adoption in the mid 1970s, flexible exchange rates have fluctuated substantially. As a result central banks have often intervened to stabilize the fluctuations. Thus the present system is best described as one of managed, or dirty, floating.

6. Fluctuations in exchange rates can be understood as fluctuations around a trend value that is determined by the purchasing power parity (PPP) rate. The PPP rate adjusts in response to differences in national inflation rates.

7. Current problems include the need to find an adequate reserve not tied to a national currency, to accommodate both the short-term and the longer-term impact of OPEC, and to develop rules for managing flexible exchange rates. A continuing commitment to international cooperation will help the world cope with these problems.

8. The appendix to this chapter, starting on page A-56, describes the operation and ultimate demise of the gold standard and the Bretton Woods system.

TOPICS FOR REVIEW

Fixed and flexible exchange rates
Managed floats

The Bretton Woods system
The International Monetary Fund
Exchange rate overshooting
Petrodollars

DISCUSSION QUESTIONS

1. What role in international payments does or did gold play under (a) the gold standard, (b) the adjustable peg Bretton Woods system, and (c) the present system? In 1974 *Barron's* had an editorial headed, "Monetary Reform and Gold: You Can't Have One Without the Other." Does the gold price experience of the 1970s bear out this editorial opinion?

2. Might a person who regards inflation as the number one economic danger favor a return to the pre-1914 gold standard? Would you predict non-inflationary results if in order to restore the gold standard, the price of gold had to be set at U.S. $1,600 per ounce, either all at once or gradually?

3. The U.S. dollar is no longer convertible into gold because of a change in U.S. policy. Does this lack of conversion make the dollar any less useful as an international medium of exchange?

4. Are Americans benefited or hurt when the U.S. dollar is the standard form of international reserves?

5. "Under a flexible exchange rate system no country need suffer unemployment, for if its prices are low enough there will be more than enough demand to keep its factories and farms fully occupied." The evidence suggests that flexible rates have not generally eliminated unemployment. Can you explain why? Can changing exchange rates ever cure unemployment?

6. The OPEC oil price increase has caused grave problems in international payments and increased the need for IMF loans. Why has market adjustment of exchange rates not solved the problem?

41 MACROECONOMIC POLICY IN AN OPEN ECONOMY

When we shift our attention to an *open* economy we encounter a number of features that are of particular interest to the study of macroeconomic policy. New complications arise. These include the behavior of the terms of trade and their influence on net exports and national income, the nature and extent of foreign borrowing, and changes in foreign interest or inflation rates. The response of the economy to various policies is altered. For example, as we saw in Chapter 39, the size of the simple mul-tiplier is smaller than that in a closed economy. Also, as we shall see in this chapter, since Canadian interest rates are closely tied to those prevailing in foreign markets, the mechanism by which macroeconomic policies influence the economy can differ sharply from the closed-economy mechanisms studied so far in this book.

Consideration of the openness of the economy also introduces some new policy targets that may be in conflict with policy targets arising solely from domestic considerations. In the next section we introduce the study of macroeconomic policy in an open economy by considering these possibly conflicting targets.

INTERNAL AND EXTERNAL BALANCE

In this chapter we summarize the domestic policy objectives in terms of a target level of real national income. Restricting our attention to one domestic policy target is done primarily for simplicity. However, it is perhaps more general than would first appear. For example, if one objective is to reduce the domestic rate of inflation, then we know from our analysis in Chapter 36 that this can be accommodated by choosing a target level of real national income below the capacity level.

When real national income is at its target level, we say the economy has achieved **internal balance.**

In this section we focus on the trade account as the external policy target. As we saw in Chapter 39, the trade account is related to the current account and capital accounts. Hence such things as the level of interest payments that must be paid to foreigners, the need to accumulate or decumulate foreign exchange reserves, or the need for capital flows to finance new investment may influence the target level of the trade balance.[1]

In this section we also treat the exchange rate as fixed. Later in the chapter we study the complications that arise when the capital account and a flexible exchange rate are considered.

When the trade account is equal to its target level, we say the economy has achieved **external balance.** The conditions for internal and external balance are illustrated in Figure 41-1.

[1] For example, a nation with a large undeveloped natural resource base may have a low current national income, yet anticipate a high future national income when the resource base is developed. High current investment to develop the resource base, and high current consumption in anticipation of that high future income, will together lead to high imports and a trade account deficit. Hence the *target* trade account in such a circumstance may well be a deficit. (See also the discussion in Box 39-3 on pages 768–769.)

The Potential for Conflict Between Objectives

When policies used to move the economy closer to one objective move the economy further from the other objective, the objectives are said to be in conflict.

Policies to eliminate a recessionary gap will also influence the trade account by causing a *movement along* the net export function (which is negatively sloped). Whether there is a conflict between the objectives of internal and external balance depends on how the trade account and real national income compare to their target values.

For simplicity, we now make the assumption that the target level of real national income is the capacity level of output, and that the target for the

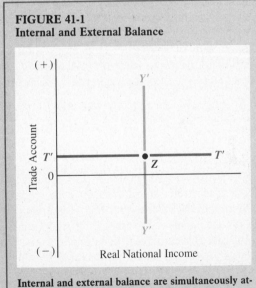

FIGURE 41-1
Internal and External Balance

Internal and external balance are simultaneously attained at point Z. Internal balance is defined in terms of a target level of real national income, and is depicted by the vertical line $Y'Y'$. External balance is defined in terms of a target level of the trade account, and is depicted by the horizontal line $T'T'$. Only at the intersection, point Z, are both internal and external balance attained.

trade account is a zero balance.[2] Hence we can identify the initial situation relative to the targets simply in terms of the signs of the GNP gap and the trade account balance. There are four possible cases:

1. A trade account *deficit* combined with an *inflationary gap* poses no conflict, because the contraction of aggregate demand to eliminate the inflationary gap leads to a reduction in imports and hence reduces the trade deficit.
2. A trade account *deficit* combined with a *recessionary gap* does pose a conflict, because the expansion of aggregate demand to eliminate the recessionary gap leads to an increase in imports and hence a worsening of the trade deficit.
3. A trade account *surplus* combined with a *recessionary gap* poses no conflict, because the expansion of aggregate demand to eliminate the recessionary gap increases imports and hence reduces the trade surplus.
4. A trade account *surplus* combined with an *inflationary gap* does pose a conflict, because the contraction of aggregate demand to eliminate the inflationary gap leads to a reduction in imports and hence an increase in the trade surplus.

The four cases are depicted in Figure 41-2.

Conflict Cases

In case 2 the trade account deficit calls for a decrease in national income, but the recessionary gap calls for an increase. In case 4 the trade account surplus calls for an increase in national income, but the inflationary gap calls for a decrease.[3]

---

[2] We emphasize that this assumption is made only to simplify the discussion, and that the actual targets may often differ from these. The same principles apply regardless of the actual values of the targets.

[3] Case 2 has traditionally attracted the most attention, perhaps because a trade deficit is generally viewed as being a more serious problem than a trade surplus, and—at least in the past—unemployment has been considered a more serious problem than inflation. Case 2 is often referred to as a situation in which there is a "balance-of-payments constraint" on domestic stabilization policy.

A conflict arises between the objectives of internal and external balance when the two call for opposite changes in the level of national income.

Basically, the conflicts arise from *movements along* the net export function; we now see that resolution of such conflict arises from *shifts in* the net export function.

Expenditure-Changing and Expenditure-Switching Policies

Start by repeating the basic equilibrium condition, that national income equal aggregate desired expenditure.

$$Y = C + I + G + (X - M) \qquad [1]$$

The total $C + I + G$ is often referred to as domestic absorption, or simply absorption. This concept, which was discussed in Box 31-1 on page 559, refers to total expenditure on goods for use in the economy. Denoting absorption by the letter A, we can rewrite the national income equilibrium condition as

$$Y = A + (X - M) \qquad [2]$$

This condition states that equilibrium national income is equal to aggregate desired expenditure, which in turn is equal to domestic absorption plus net exports.

Equation [2] is useful in distinguishing between two types of policies that might be used to maintain internal and external balance. Policies that maintain the level of aggregate desired expenditure but influence its composition between domestic absorption and net exports are called **expenditure-switching** policies. Policies that change aggregate desired expenditure are called **expenditure-changing** policies.

The conflicts between the objectives of internal and external balance discussed above arise from the use of expenditure-changing policies.

Expenditure-changing policies involve moving

FIGURE 41-2
Conflicts Between Internal and External Balance

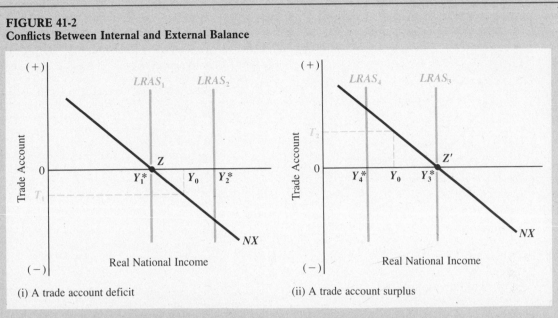

(i) A trade account deficit

(ii) A trade account surplus

Of the four different possible combinations of signs of the GNP gap and the trade account, only two pose conflicts. In both parts of the figure, the net export function which relates the trade account to real national income is shown by the black line labeled *NX*. The actual level of income is given by Y_0 so that in (i) there is a trade account deficit of $0T_1$, while in (ii) there is a trade account surplus of $0T_2$.

In (i), if potential output is given by Y_1^* so there is an inflation gap (case 1), there is no conflict, since adjustment of actual real national income to achieve one target will also achieve the other target, at point Z. However, if potential

output is given by Y_2^* so there is a recessionary gap (case 2), then there is a conflict, since movement of actual real national income to achieve either target will cause a movement away from the other target.

In (ii), if potential income is given by Y_3^* so there is a recessionary gap (case 3), there is no conflict, since adjustment of actual real national income to achieve one target will also achieve the other target, at point Z'. However, if potential output is given by Y_4^* so there is an inflationary gap (case 4), then there is a conflict, since a change in actual real national income to achieve either target will cause a movement away from the other target.

along a given net export function, so changes in the trade balance and national income must be *negatively* related. If the initial situation calls for them to move in the same direction, the use of expenditure-changing policies necessarily involves a conflict.

An expenditure-switching policy shifts the net export function. As we shall see, this can lead to *positively* related changes in the trade balance and national income. Devaluation or revaluation of the domestic currency, restrictions on international trade such as tariffs or quotas, and domestic infla-

tion or deflation relative to foreign conditions are all expenditure-switching policies.[4]

A Trade Account Deficit

As we have seen, a trade account deficit means that national income is less than domestic absorp-

---

[4] When restrictions on international trade such as tariffs or quotas are used in this manner, they are referred to as *commercial policy*. Commercial policy may in some circumstances be useful for macroeconomic purposes, but it is never the case that commercial policy *must* be used; other expenditure-switching policies will have the same macroeconomic effects.

FIGURE 41-3
A Trade Deficit and a Recessionary Gap

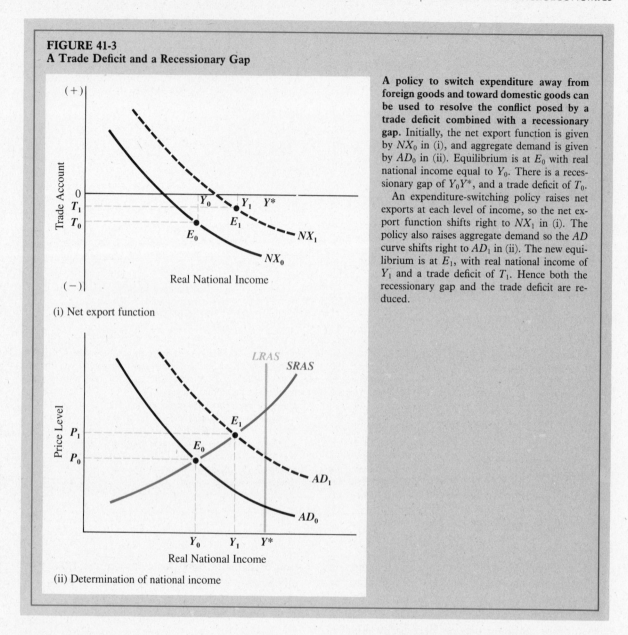

(i) Net export function

(ii) Determination of national income

A policy to switch expenditure away from foreign goods and toward domestic goods can be used to resolve the conflict posed by a trade deficit combined with a recessionary gap. Initially, the net export function is given by NX_0 in (i), and aggregate demand is given by AD_0 in (ii). Equilibrium is at E_0 with real national income equal to Y_0. There is a recessionary gap of Y_0Y^*, and a trade deficit of T_0.

An expenditure-switching policy raises net exports at each level of income, so the net export function shifts right to NX_1 in (i). The policy also raises aggregate demand so the AD curve shifts right to AD_1 in (ii). The new equilibrium is at E_1, with real national income of Y_1 and a trade deficit of T_1. Hence both the recessionary gap and the trade deficit are reduced.

tion. Now consider policies to eliminate the trade account deficit; to be successful, the policies must raise national income *relative* to absorption.

Case 1: A deficit combined with an inflationary gap: No conflict. If the economy already has an

inflationary gap, national income should not be increased further. The trade account deficit indicates that domestic absorption is above the current level of national income and hence, by virtue of the inflationary gap, above the full-employment level. To eliminate the deficit, absorption must be lowered. In other words, if net exports are to rise, resources must be released through a reduction in domestic usage. This calls for *expenditure-reducing* polices such as reductions in the money supply, cuts in government expenditure, and increases in taxes. No conflict for expenditure-changing policies arises in this case, because the expenditure reduction cuts the inflationary gap and improves the trade account by inducing a movement along the net export function.

Case 2: A deficit combined with a recessionary gap: Conflict. When national income is below its capacity level, income can be expanded. But an expansion in national income with a fixed net export function would worsen the trade account, so expenditure-increasing policies are not appropriate. A reduction in national income to reduce the deficit would worsen unemployment, so expenditure-reducing policies are not appropriate. What is needed is a switch in expenditure away from foreign goods (thus reducing the trade deficit) and toward domestic goods (thus reducing the recessionary gap).

Policies to induce a *switch* of some expenditure from foreign goods to domestic goods—thereby *shifting* the net export function rightward and also raising national income—will alleviate the conflict between a recessionary gap and a trade deficit.

Such policies include devaluation of the currency and protective measures such as tariffs and quotas. This is illustrated in Figure 41-3.[5]

A Trade Account Surplus

Cases 3 and 4 above both involve a trade account surplus. An expansion of national income will therefore cause a move toward external balance by raising imports. Hence in case 3, where there is a recessionary gap, no conflict arises, and expenditure-raising policies will lead to movement toward both targets. In case 4, where there is an inflationary gap, a conflict does arise; external balance calls for expenditure increases but internal balance calls for expenditure reduction. What is needed is a *switch* in expenditure away from domestic goods (thus reducing the inflationary gap) and toward foreign goods (thus reducing the trade account surplus).

Policies to induce a switch of expenditure from domestic goods to foreign goods—thereby *shifting* the net export function leftward and also lowering national income—will alleviate the conflict between an inflationary gap and a trade surplus.

This is illustrated in Figure 41-4.

A General Statement

We have now seen the difference in the effects of the two types of expenditure policies in an open economy.

To achieve internal and external balance, a combination of expenditure-changing and expenditure-switching policies is generally required.

In the conflict situations, expenditure-switching policies will result in movement *toward* both targets. But they alone cannot be expected to achieve exactly both internal and external balance. Hence both types of policies are generally required. Expenditure-switching policies are necessary to shift the net export function in order to make the two objectives consistent. (In terms of Figures 41-3(i) and 41-4(i), this means that expenditure-switching policies should be used to ensure that the *NX* curve cuts the horizontal axis at Y^*. There is no assurance, however, that the effects of such policies on the aggregate demand curve will give rise to actual real national income of Y^*.) Then expenditure-changing policies—which shift the aggregate demand curve but not the net export curve—can be used to attain both internal and external balance simultaneously.

Some further, long-run aspects of such policies are taken up in Box 41-1.

---

[5] From the discussion in Chapter 39, it would appear that there should be two shifts in the *NX* function. The first is due to the switch in expenditure; the second, which will be in the opposite direction to the first, is due to the induced change in the price of domestic goods as national income changes. The analysis in Figure 41-3, and in this chapter, incorporates this second effect in the response of *NX* national income by using the *SRAS* curve to capture the price effect. [49]

FIGURE 41-4
A Trade Surplus and an Inflationary Gap

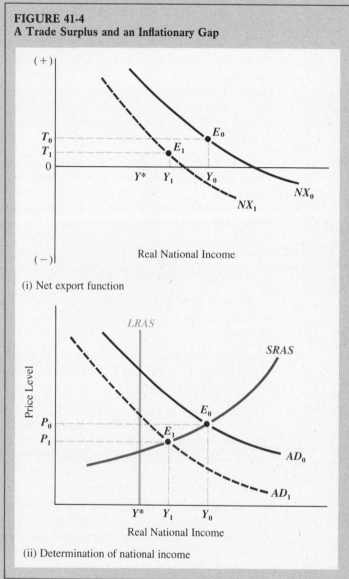

(i) Net export function

(ii) Determination of national income

A policy to switch expenditure away from domestic goods and toward foreign goods can be used to resolve the conflict posed by a trade surplus combined with an inflationary gap. Initially, the net export function is given by NX_0 in (i), and aggregate demand is given by AD_0 in (ii). Equilibrium is at E_0 with real national income equal to Y_0. This is an inflationary gap of Y^*Y_0 and a trade surplus of T_0.

An expenditure-switching policy lowers net exports at each level of income, so the net export function shifts left to NX_1 in (ii). The policy also lowers aggregate demand so the aggregate demand curve shifts left to AD_1 in (ii). The equilibrium moves from E_0 to E_1, real national income falls to Y_1, and the trade surplus falls to T_1. Hence both the inflationary gap and the trade surplus are reduced.

MACROECONOMIC POLICY AND THE CAPITAL ACCOUNT

The capital account of the balance of payments records international movements of investment funds. When foreign investors buy securities issued by Canadian corporations or governments, or in-vest in Canadian industry, this capital inflow is recorded as a receipt in the balance of payments, because it gives rise to an increase in the amount of foreign currency offered for Canadian dollars in the foreign exchange market. Conversely, the ac-quisition of foreign assets by Canadians represents a capital outflow and is recorded as a payment

BOX 41-1 EXPENDITURE-SWITCHING POLICIES IN THE LONG RUN

Use of expenditure-switching policies such as devaluation has often been very controversial. Supporters point to the increase in output and the reduction in the trade account deficit shown in Figure 34-3. Opponents focus on the inflationary impact indicated by the rise in the price level also shown in Figure 34-3. The controversy often hinges on disagreement about the relative size of these two effects. Some of the controversy can be defused by distinguishing between the long-run and short-run effects of such policies.

In the text we focused on the short-run effects of expenditure-switching policies, treating the *SRAS* curve as fixed and studying the shifts in the *NX* and *AD* curves. One alternative to using such policies is to do nothing, and let the monetary adjustment mechanism studied in Chapter 34 operate to eliminate the recessionary gap. (Similar automatic mechanisms also exist that establish external balance in the long run.) Justification for using devaluation, for example, in the face of a recessionary gap and a trade deficit is that these automatic adjustment mechanisms are very slow to operate. Hence support for devaluation and other expenditure-switching policies focuses on their ability to influence output and the trade account *in the short run*.

Note, however, that such policies do not alter potential output (they do not shift the *LRAS* curve), and hence they have no effect on output in the long run. But by circumventing the monetary adjustment mechanism and stimulating aggregate demand, expenditure-switching policies ensure that when potential income is attained in the long run, the price level will be higher than it would have been in their absence. Opponents of such policies focus on this price-level effect, since that is the only long-run effect the policies have. Typically these opponents believe the automatic adjustment mechanisms are strong enough so that the long-run effect would be achieved fairly quickly without intervention, or that devaluations set up expectations of price rises which quickly feed into wages and hence create very little real response of output and employment even in the short run.

The key policy implication of this debate is that devaluation and other expenditure-switching policies should be directed toward the external target, but they should be combined with expenditure-changing policies that focus on the internal target. In particular, a devaluation should be accompanied by expenditure-reducing policies to offset any inflationary gap caused by the devaluation in the short run and hence to avoid the price-level increase that would otherwise ensue in the long run.

---

because foreign currency is used up by such transactions.

The primary means by which capital flows can be influenced by the policy authorities is through domestic interest rates. International traders hold transactions balances just as do domestic traders. These balances are often lent out on a short-term basis rather than being left idle. Naturally enough, holders of these balances will tend to lend them, other things being equal, in those markets where interest rates are highest. If short-term interest

rates are raised in Canada, this will induce an inflow of short-run capital to take advantage of the higher Canadian rates. A lowering of Canadian interest rates will have the opposite effect, as capital moves elsewhere to take advantage of the now relatively higher foreign rates.

Long-term capital flows are typically less sensitive to interest-rate differentials, but they are nevertheless likely to show some response. In particular, Canadian corporations and governments attempt to minimize the cost of long-term borrowing by selling bonds in foreign markets when the foreign interest rate is lower than the Canadian rate.

In discussing the trade account in the first part of this chapter, we did not distinguish between the effects of monetary and fiscal policy. However, capital flows respond to interest rates, and monetary and fiscal policies that have the same influence on income have opposite effects on interest rates. As we saw in Chapter 34, in a closed economy expansionary monetary policy exerts its influence on income by reducing interest rates. Fiscal policy influences aggregate demand directly, and fiscal-policy-induced increases in national income create an excess demand for money, which in a closed economy causes interest rates to rise. In discussing capital flows in an open economy, it is therefore necessary to distinguish between the operation of monetary and fiscal policies.

Fiscal Policy and the Capital Account

The effects of fiscal policy on the capital account of an open economy are related to the interest-rate effects it would have in a closed economy. Expansionary fiscal policy, for example, leads to increased federal government borrowing in domestic capital markets. In a closed economy this forces interest rates up; in an open economy it forces other domestic borrowers to import their capital requirements from foreign financial centers. Many provincial governments finance their deficits by borrowing abroad themselves, thereby giving rise directly to a capital account surplus. In summary:

An expansionary fiscal policy will put upward pressure on interest rates and lead to an inflow of foreign capital, thereby moving the capital account toward a surplus. A contractionary fiscal policy will have the opposite effects.

Monetary Policy and the Capital Account

Since monetary policy influences interest rates in a closed economy, it will also influence the capital account in an open economy:

An expansionary monetary policy will put downward pressure on interest rates and lead to an outflow of capital, thereby moving the capital account toward a deficit. A contractionary monetary policy will have the opposite effects.

An Alternative Target for External Balance

So far in this chapter we have used *external balance* to mean achieving the target level of the trade account. Consideration of international capital flows suggests an expansion of this target to incorporate the capital account and interest payments on the foreign debt as well.

We now specify external balance in terms of a target level of the overall balance of payments.

For simplicity, we take external balance to mean a zero overall balance of payments so that any current account imbalance is exactly offset by capital account transactions.

Before turning to a discussion of how monetary and fiscal policy might be combined to achieve internal and external balance in this circumstance, it will be useful to examine the relationship between the money supply and the overall balance of payments.

The Balance of Payments and the Money Supply

Suppose that Canada is experiencing a balance-of-payments deficit and that the Bank of Canada intervenes in the foreign exchange market to maintain the value of the Canadian dollar. The Bank will be selling foreign currency in exchange for Canadian dollars and thereby running down the stock of official reserves. Payment for the foreign currency acquired by private participants in the market will normally be made in the form of a Canadian dollar cheque drawn on one of the chartered banks. This cheque will be cleared by reducing the deposits of the chartered bank at the Bank of Canada. These transactions are summarized in Table 41-1.

If there are no offsetting transactions, a balance-of-payments deficit will lead to a decrease both in bank

TABLE 41–1 BALANCE SHEET CHANGES CAUSED BY A SALE OF FOREIGN CURRENCY BY THE CENTRAL BANK

Nonbank private sector	
Assets	Liabilities
Foreign currency (equivalent value in Canadian dollars) +100 Deposits −100	

Chartered banks	
Assets	Liabilities
Reserves (deposits with central bank) −100	Demand deposits −100

Central bank	
Assets	Liabilities
Foreign currency −100	Deposits of chartered banks −100

The money supply is reduced when the central bank sells foreign currency to maintain a fixed exchange rate when there is a balance-of-payments deficit. A deficit of 100 leads to an excess demand for foreign currency of 100, which is met by a reduction of official reserves by this amount. When the central bank receives payment in the form of a cheque drawn on a chartered bank, bank reserves fall by 100. There will then be a multiple contraction of deposit money through the process analyzed in Chapter 33.

reserves and in bank deposits equal to the amount of foreign exchange sold by the central bank. A surplus will lead to an increase in bank reserves and deposits.

Thus a balance-of-payments deficit will lead to a contraction of the money supply. Of course, the central bank has the option of preventing this from happening by undertaking other offsetting transactions. For example, the decrease in bank reserves can be offset by an open-market purchase of bonds, which will have the effect of increasing bank reserves. This procedure of insulating the domestic money supply from the effects of balance-of-payments deficits or surpluses is known as **sterilization.**

Fixed Exchange Rates

Monetary Policy

To see the limitations of monetary policy under a fixed exchange rate, consider the following sequence of events. Suppose that interest rates in Canada are at levels similar to those in the rest of the world, and thus there is no inducement for large international movements of capital. Suppose now that the Bank of Canada, faced with a large recessionary gap, seeks to stimulate demand through an expansionary monetary policy. The Bank buys bonds in the open market, thereby increasing the money supply and reducing interest rates.

Lower interest rates stimulate an outflow of capital from Canada and thus a deficit on the capital account. To the extent that national income rises, movement along the net export function creates a deficit on the trade account. Thus the overall balance of payments moves into deficit. To maintain the fixed exchange rate, the Bank will have to intervene in the foreign exchange market and sell foreign currency. *This will have the effect of reducing the money supply and thus reversing the increase brought about by the initial open market operation.*

If no other transactions are initiated by the Bank of Canada, national income and the money supply will fall and domestic interest rates will rise until they all return to their initial levels. Thus the deficit will be self-correcting, and the Bank's expansionary policy will be nullified.

Suppose now that the Bank of Canada attempts to sterilize the impact on the money supply of the balance-of-payments deficit. The difficulty with this strategy is that it can be continued only as long as the Bank has sufficient reserves of foreign exchange. If capital flows are highly sensitive to interest rates, as a great deal of evidence suggests is the case, these reserves will be run down at a rapid rate and the Bank will be forced to abandon its expansionary policy.

Under a fixed exchange rate, there is little scope for the use of monetary policy for domestic stabilization purposes because of the sensitivity of international cap-

ital flows to interest rates. The central bank will be forced to maintain domestic interest rates close to the levels existing in the rest of the world, and it will not be able to bring about substantial changes in the domestic money supply.

Fiscal Policy

Consider now the effectiveness of fiscal policy under fixed exchange rates. Suppose again that Canadian interest rates are in line with those of the rest of the world when an expansionary fiscal policy is introduced, aimed at reducing a large recessionary gap. The fiscal expansion raises the level of domestic interest rates and national income.

Higher interest rates stimulate a flow of capital into Canada, thereby leading to a surplus on the capital account. If the capital flows are large, as they are likely to be in Canada because of our close integration with U.S. capital markets, the surplus on capital account will exceed the current account deficit arising from the increased national income. Hence there will be an overall balance-of-payments surplus.

To maintain the fixed exchange rate, the Bank of Canada will have to intervene in the foreign exchange market and buy foreign currency. This will have the effect of increasing the money supply, *thus reinforcing the initial fiscal stimulus.*

Under a fixed exchange rate, interest-sensitive international capital flows stabilize the domestic interest rate and enhance the effectiveness of fiscal policy.

Combining Monetary and Fiscal Policy

Consider an attempt to increase employment with expansionary monetary policy that reduces interest rates and thereby stimulates investment and other interest-sensitive expenditure. The decline in domestic interest rates makes it more attractive to invest short-term capital abroad rather than at home. The outflow of short-term capital to be invested at more attractive rates in foreign financial centers worsens the balance of payments on the short-term capital account. Of course, if the expansionary policy succeeds in raising income, there will be additional strain on the balance of

payments on current account as a consequence of the increased expenditure on imports caused by the rise in income.

In principle, the conflict can be removed by an appropriate combination of monetary and fiscal policy. Consider the country with full employment and a balance-of-payments deficit. It could eliminate the deficit by following a tighter monetary policy to increase domestic interest rates and attract short-term capital. At the same time, the contractionary effect of tight money on domestic expenditure and employment could be offset by raising government expenditures or cutting taxes. Thus both goals can be achieved through a combination of tight monetary policy and expansionary fiscal policy.

This strategy is unlikely to be a satisfactory solution to a persistent current account deficit. Such a country will find it increasingly difficult to maintain its exchange rate by importing short-term capital. Short-term international capital flows are extremely volatile, and they are particularly sensitive to shifts in expectations concerning exchange rates. If investors lose confidence in a country's ability to maintain its existing exchange rate, capital outflows will build up and ultimately a devaluation will be required to reduce the deficit and restore confidence.

Flexible Exchange Rates

A major advantage of a flexible exchange rate is that it removes any conflict between domestic stabilization objectives and the balance of payments, because deficits or surpluses are automatically eliminated through movements in the exchange rate. In addition, a flexible rate often cushions the domestic economy against cyclical variations in economic activity in other countries. If, for example, the U.S. economy goes into a recession, the decline in U.S. income will lead to a reduction in demand for goods exported from Canada. The fall in exports will reduce income in Canada through the multiplier effect. But if the value of the Canadian dollar is allowed to respond to market forces, there will also be a depreciation. This fall in the external value of our currency will stimulate demand for our exports and encourage the substitution of domestically produced goods for imports. Thus the depreciation will provide a stimulus to demand in Canada that will at least partially offset the depressing effect of the U.S. recession.

Box 41-2 discusses some further aspects of fluctuating exchange rates.

Fiscal Policy

Suppose the government seeks to remove a recessionary gap by expansionary fiscal policy. An increase in government expenditures and/or a reduction in taxes will increase income through the multiplier effect and reduce the size of the gap. This will also tend to cause a movement along the net export function, leading to a deterioration of the trade account. However, this is not the whole story, for there will also be repercussions on the capital account and the exchange rate.

Capital flows and the crowding-out effect. In a closed economy, fiscal policy causes domestic interest rates to rise. This causes interest-sensitive private expenditures to fall, thus partially offsetting the initial expansionary effect of the fiscal stimulus. As we saw in Chapter 32, this *crowding-out effect* plays an important role in the analysis of fiscal policy in a closed economy. In an open economy, the crowding-out effect will operate differently, due to international capital flows.

Higher domestic interest rates will induce a capital inflow and cause the domestic currency to appreciate. If capital flows are highly interest-elastic, the external value of the currency is likely to rise substantially. This will depress demand by discouraging exports and encouraging the substitution of imports for domestically produced goods. The initial fiscal stimulus will be *offset* by the expenditure-switching effects of currency appreciation.

Under flexible exchange rates there will be a strong crowding-out of net exports that will greatly reduce the effectiveness of fiscal policy.

However, it is possible to eliminate the crowding-out effect by supporting the fiscal policy with an accommodating monetary policy. Suppose that the central bank responds to the increase in the demand for money induced by the fiscal expansion by increasing the supply of money so as to maintain domestic interest rates at their initial level. There will then be no capital inflow and no tendency for the currency to appreciate. Income will expand by the usual multiplier process.

The effectiveness of fiscal policy under flexible exchange rates can be enhanced by an accommodating monetary policy.

Monetary Policy

We have seen that there is little scope under fixed exchange rates for the use of monetary policy for domestic stabilization purposes. Under flexible exchange rates, the situation is reversed; monetary policy becomes a very powerful tool.

Suppose the Bank of Canada seeks to stimulate demand through an expansionary monetary policy. The Bank buys bonds in the open market, thereby increasing bank reserves and the money supply and reducing interest rates. Lower interest rates will cause an outflow of capital from Canada and thus a deficit on the capital account.

Under a fixed rate we saw that the Bank may be forced to reverse its policy in order to stem the loss of foreign reserves. Under a flexible rate, however, the Canadian dollar can be allowed to depreciate. This will stimulate exports and discourage imports so that the deficit on the capital account will be offset by a surplus on the current account.

Domestic employment will be stimulated not only by the fall in interest rates, but also by the increased demand for domestically produced goods brought about by a depreciation of the currency. The initial monetary stimulus will be *reinforced* by the expenditure-switching effects of currency depreciation.

Under flexible exchange rates, monetary policy is a powerful tool for stabilizing domestic income and employment. If capital flows are highly interest-elastic, the main channel by which an increase in the money supply stimulates demand for domestically produced goods is a depreciation of the currency.

BOX 41–2 UNDERSTANDING EXCHANGE RATE CHANGES

Since reaching a peak of over $1.05 U.S. in early 1976, the Canadian dollar has depreciated steadily, falling below 77 cents U.S. in 1984. This fall, shown by the solid line in the figure, has prompted news reports of a national crisis of disaster proportions and a source of national shame. Several considerations, however, help us put this slide in some perspective.

Exchange Rates and National Pride

Currencies can appreciate or depreciate for many different reasons. To take pride in the external price on one's currency is to commit oneself in advance to be proud of a great ragbag of different events, some of which will seem undesirable to all reasonable people. Until the public and the media see the folly in viewing the value of a country's currency the way shareholders of a corporation view the price of its stock, there is little hope of a rational discussion of exchange rate policy.

In fact, the fall in the value of the Canadian dollar reflects a number of very different events, some with very different implications.

Domestic Inflation

For example, the fall in the early part of the period reflected higher Canadian inflation, and was necessary to restore the competitive position of Canadian industry. Inflation was the problem, depreciation was part of the "solution."

The underlying trend value of the Canadian dollar in terms of the U.S. dollar changes as the

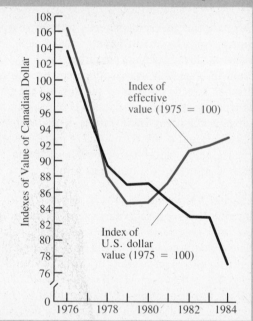

CANADIAN STABILIZATION POLICY AND EXTERNAL BALANCE

These arguments suggest that the choice between a fixed and flexible rate can influence the operation of stabilization policy. It is instructive to examine recent Canadian experience from this perspective.

1950–1961: Introduction of Flexible Exchange Rates

Canada operated under a flexible exchange rate from 1950 to 1961. The one major cyclical fluctua-

tion of the economy in this period began with the recovery from the mild recession of 1954.

The Canadian economy experienced large capital inflows during the period 1955 to 1961 in response to the attractive investment opportunities that existed in Canada. As shown in Figure 41-5 on page 804, the price of one U.S. dollar remained below one dollar Canadian, and at times fell to around 95 cents Canadian. This had the effect of reducing exports and increasing imports.

During the period 1955 to 1957 there was an investment boom, and national income remained close to the full-employment level. By the end of 1957, however, the economy had turned down and

Canadian price level changes relative to the American price level.* During the 1960s American inflation exceeded Canadian inflation and the Canadian dollar rose above the U.S. dollar. Starting in 1971 Canadian inflation exceeded U.S. inflation for the next half decade, and the trend PPP value of the Canadian dollar fell steadily, reaching the range 89 to 91 units by the end of 1972. For a while capital flows and other events kept the value of the Canadian dollar above its trend rate, but in 1976 it fell rapidly toward its trend value. The actual value had to fall sooner or later to its trend value, and it is a good thing—it helped restore the international competitiveness of Canadian industry.

Foreign Monetary Tightness

Since 1980 the fall in the Canadian dollar has reflected different pressures. In 1980 tight monetary policy in the United States drove up interest rates in that country. As we saw in Chapter

* Recall the discussion of the purchasing power parity exchange rate in Chapter 40, especially pages 780–781.

40 (see especially page 782), this presented the Bank of Canada with a policy dilemma: Either let Canadian interest rates rise, or let the Canadian dollar fall. The Bank has tried to take a middle stance between these two, and as a result the value of the Canadian dollar in terms of the U.S. dollar has fallen gradually since 1980.

Is the Canadian Dollar Weak?

A related point is that since 1980 the apparent weakness of the Canadian dollar actually reflects the strength of the U.S. dollar. This is shown by the dotted line in the figure, where we plot the average or trade-weighted Canadian dollar exchange rate in terms of all Canada's trading partners. The divergent path, with the Canadian dollar falling against the U.S. dollar but rising against the rest of Canada's trading partners, results from the fact that the U.S. dollar was rising even more against European currencies and the Japanese yen during this period. From this perspective, the widespread perception of a weak Canadian dollar through the 1981–1984 period was just wrong.

the unemployment rate rose sharply. Depressed conditions remained throughout the period 1958 to 1961, with the unemployment rate at or above 7 percent for three of the four years.

How did monetary policy respond to this serious recession? Although the money supply grew rapidly during 1958, the period 1959–1961 was characterized by a very restrictive monetary policy.

As the theory outlined before indicates, what was needed was an expansionary policy that would have reduced interest rates and discouraged capital inflows. This would have caused the Canadian dollar to depreciate and stimulated the economy. Unfortunately, the advantages of a flexible exchange

rate were not utilized to deal with the serious unemployment problem, and the hoped-for expansion of the money supply and depreciation of the Canadian dollar did not occur until 1961. This episode is discussed further in Box 41-3 on page 805.

1962–1970: Fixed Exchange Rate

The exchange rate was pegged at $1.08 Canadian to the U.S. dollar throughout the period 1962–1970—that is, the Canadian dollar was worth 92.5 U.S. cents. This period witnessed the buildup of boom conditions in the United States, fueled by

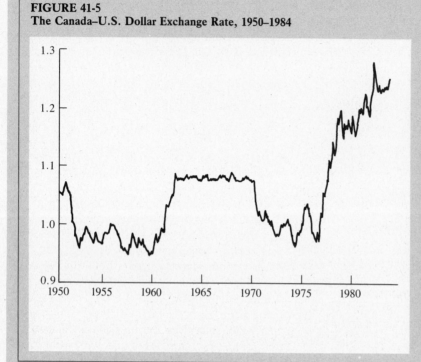

FIGURE 41-5
The Canada–U.S. Dollar Exchange Rate, 1950–1984

The price of a U.S. dollar has fluctuated from about $0.92 Canadian to over $1.25 Canadian. The exchange rate was determined largely by market forces during the 1950s, when flexible exchange rates were in use. During that period, the price of a U.S. dollar fluctuated from $1.08 Canadian to about $0.92 Canadian. From 1962 to 1970, the exchange rate was pegged in a narrow band around $1.08 Canadian. Since 1970, the exchange rate has again been largely market-determined. After an initial appreciation in the early 1970s, the Canadian dollar fluctuated around or above parity until 1976. Since that time, the Canadian dollar has steadily depreciated in terms of the U.S. dollar, as indicated by the steady rise in the price of the U.S. dollar.

government expenditures related to the Vietnam war. As is to be expected under a fixed exchange rate, the resulting rise in inflation in the United States spilled over into Canada. In the late 1960s the Canadian government decided that control of inflation was its primary policy objective. Contractionary monetary policy was introduced, and the restriction in aggregate demand had the desired domestic result: By 1970 inflation had fallen to 3.3 percent. But unemployment had risen, reaching almost 6 percent.

As the analysis earlier in this chapter predicts, a tight monetary policy under fixed exchange rates led to a large balance-of-payments surplus. The Bank of Canada accumulated foreign exchange rapidly; it tried to sterilize the effects that its purchases of foreign exchange would otherwise have had on the domestic money supply, but it had only limited success. In the end, faced with the alternative of accepting a rapid rate of domestic monetary expansion or dropping the fixed exchange rate, the Bank chose the latter. On May 31, 1970, the Bank announced that it would no longer maintain the Canadian dollar at a fixed par value. Canada had reverted to a flexible exchange rate.

The attempt to inflate at a slower rate than the United States was incompatible with fixed exchange rates; in the face of a high balance-of-payments surplus, either the economy had to be allowed to expand faster or the exchange rate had to be freed. The latter course was chosen.

1970–1975: Return to Floating

Once it was freed, the Canadian dollar rapidly rose in value almost to par with the U.S. dollar. The stage was now set for Canada to continue to pursue

BOX 41–3 THE COYNE AFFAIR

The late 1950s witnessed a high level of unemployment and a current account deficit in Canada. Part of the problem was that the U.S. economy was in a mild recession. Several Canadian economists maintained that the Canadian recession, and in particular Canadian unemployment, was in fact being aggravated by the restrictive monetary policy pursued by the Bank of Canada. They argued that if monetary policy were loosened, aggregate demand would increase and unemployment would be reduced. They also argued that the current account deficit was primarily due to unusually low levels of exports caused by the U.S. recession; when the American recession ended, they contended, the current account would improve.

The governor of the Bank of Canada, James Coyne, argued that the current account deficit indicated that the Canadian economy was living beyond its means, financed by unusually large capital inflows. He defended the Bank's tight monetary policy on the grounds that if the money supply grew and interest rates fell, capital inflows would *increase*. This would cause an appreciation of the dollar and a further worsening of unemployment. Moreover, the increased current account deficit could be financed only by even larger capital inflows. Thus, in Coyne's view, an expansionary monetary policy

would only exacerbate the problem, and contractionary policy was needed to restrain demand and eliminate the current account deficit.

After considerable controversy in academic and political arenas, the Bank of Canada's policies were repudiated. It was decided that expansionary policies were needed. Since he could not agree with these policies, Coyne was replaced as governor in July 1961, establishing the important precedent that in circumstances of fundamental disagreement, the governor of the Bank of Canada, an appointed official, must either agree to pursue the policies of the elected government as put forward by the minister of finance, or resign.

The money supply began to expand. We saw in the text that expansionary monetary policy under flexible exchange rates will lead to a capital outflow, a currency depreciation, and effective expansion of aggregate demand. These predictions were all borne out by developments during this period. Unemployment began to fall almost immediately, and the recession was quickly ended. Downward pressure was put on the Canadian dollar, and in May 1962 the government pegged the Canadian dollar at 92.5 U.S. cents, lower than it had been throughout the previous 10 years.

its policy of striving for a lower rate of inflation than that in the United States. If Canada were to achieve this goal, it would be necessary that the value of the Canadian dollar *continue to rise* at a rate approximately equal to the excess of the U.S. inflation rate over the Canadian inflation rate.[6]

However, the Bank of Canada, after adopting a

flexible exchange rate in order to be able to pursue its anti-inflation policy, simultaneously adopted a more expansionary posture. In particular, it adopted a managed float, commonly referred to as a **dirty float**. A dirty float prevails when a central bank operates to regulate closely the foreign exchange value of the domestic currency without undertaking an explicit commitment to maintain it at or near a publicly announced value.

There are two ways to manage a dirty float. One

[6] The discussion of the PPP exchange rate on pages 780–781 could usefully be reviewed at this stage.

BOX 41–4 FOREIGN INFLATION: IMPORTED OR INSULATED?

Two distinct circumstances can lead to an appreciation of the Canadian dollar. One is a change in the price at which the Bank of Canada intervenes in the foreign exchange market; the other is a change in the foreign prices of traded goods in the absence of Bank of Canada intervention. The two circumstances have very different implications for the "competitiveness" of domestic industry. Many critics of Bank of Canada policy in the 1970s argue that the Bank has failed to recognize the distinction between the two cases. Let us examine this contention.

At given foreign currency prices of traded goods, an increase in the foreign exchange value of the Canadian dollar as maintained by the Bank of Canada will lead to a reduction in the domestic price of traded goods. Output in both the export- and the import-competing sectors will fall. In this case appreciation of the Canadian dollar *is* harmful to the international competitive position of Canadian industry, because it lowers the prices of traded goods relative to domestic costs.

At a given value of the exchange rate, an increase in foreign currency prices of traded goods leads to an increase in exports and a reduction in imports. The first increases the supply of foreign exchange; the second reduces the demand for foreign exchange. As a result, the Canadian dollar appreciates.

This appreciation offsets the inflationary effects of the foreign price rise on domestic prices and output. In this case appreciation of the Canadian dollar is *not* harmful to the international competitive position of Canadian industry; the appreciation is a response to foreign disturbances and is instrumental in the process that restores domestic costs and prices to their initial position relative to those of foreign industries.

Nevertheless, in the face of foreign inflation, increases in the value of the Canadian dollar are often opposed, and that opposition is sometimes strong enough to influence policy.

What happens when foreign prices increase and the Canadian dollar is not allowed to appreciate in the manner outlined above? The answer is simple: The Canadian currency price of traded goods must also rise. In the end, Canadian prices must equal foreign prices adjusted for the exchange rate. If the exchange rate does not change, Canadian prices must change. This is known as *imported inflation*.

is to intervene directly in the foreign exchange market to stabilize the exchange rate. A balance-of-payments surplus such as Canada was experiencing at the time would mean that the Bank of Canada would have to buy foreign exchange to keep the Canadian dollar from appreciating. Of course, the purchase of foreign exchange by the Bank of Canada would have meant that the supply of Canadian dollars would be rising. This was precisely the problem that had arisen under a fixed exchange rate and had led to the adoption of a flexible exchange rate. Not surprisingly, the Bank of Canada did not actively engage in this direct intervention approach to managing a dirty float.

The second method of managing a dirty float is to set domestic monetary conditions (rates of interest and rates of monetary expansion) so that the exchange market clears at the desired exchange rate without substantial government intervention in the foreign exchange market. Essentially, this means adopting the monetary policy that would be consistent with fixed rates (and hence might better be termed a *dirty fix*). The Bank of Canada chose this method, and it led to a more rapid expansion of the money supply than would have been consistent with the goal of reducing inflation. Indeed, it led predictably to a rate of inflation roughly equal to that in the United States, and higher than the target

Many economists argue that precisely such imported inflation occured in Canada in 1974–75. At that time OPEC price increases caused enormous increases in inflation in our major trading partners, in particular the United States. Canada then was basically self-sufficient in oil and hence was not adversely affected by the oil shock. The decrease in the relative price of Canadian goods resulting from the American inflation led to an increase in exports and a decrease in imports, causing upward pressure on the Canadian dollar.

The Bank of Canada met this by selling Canadian dollars, thereby stabilizing the exchange rate. Although Canada was on a *de jure* floating exchange rate at that time, the exchange rate did not in fact perform its "insulation" function because it was not allowed to float *de facto*. By fixing the exchange rate, the Bank of Canada allowed the rapid take-off into double-digit inflation in the rest of the world to result in a similar inflation in Canada.

This policy error is not unique to the Canadian experience; it is similar to what has happened in other high-inflation countries such as Israel and Sweden. Attempts to protect domestic industry from the supposed ravages of appreciation end in a situation of imported inflation. But the *real* position of the domestic export sector is ultimately unchanged. Either the exchange rate adjusts, allowing domestic money wages and prices to remain constant, or the exchange rate is held constant and domestic inflation occurs. In the latter event, the inflation bids up domestic wages, causing the domestic price of traded goods to rise. The competitiveness of domestic industry remains the same as under the flexible exchange rate option, because in both cases the foreign currency prices of our goods rise.

Similar arguments were being made when the United States inflation rate took off to 16 and 17 percent in early 1979; there was pressure on the Bank of Canada to intervene to prevent the Canadian dollar from appreciating. Fortunately, the high American inflation did not last very long, and the problem disappeared . . . for the time being. But what would have happened had the U.S. inflation persisted? Have we learned, or will we repeat past mistakes?

rate that led to the monetary contraction of the late 1960s and the adoption of a flexible exchange rate in 1970. Indirectly, by maintaining policies consistent with a stable exchange rate, inflation was imported from the United States.

In retrospect, it appears that during this period Canada missed a golden opportunity to avoid the take-off into accelerated inflation that so many other countries experienced. By 1970 the effects of the 1968–1970 tight monetary policy had worked their way through the economy. Inflation was low and falling. The necessary price of increased unemployment had been paid, and most economists now agree that no further increases in unemployment were necessary. In fact, as expectations of inflation fell, the level of unemployment could also fall. (This possibility is discussed on pages 695–699.)

Thus the stage was set for continued low inflation as long as the exchange rate was allowed to adjust. Instead, the exchange rate was stabilized and Canada reverted to a high inflation path. Why?

One reason often put forward to explain this apparent policy mistake is discussed in Box 41-4. Canadian export industries had a significant competitive advantage during the period of the late 1960s, when Canada was maintaining a fixed exchange rate and inflating more slowly than the

United States, and this competitive advantage was reflected in the current account surplus experienced over that period. The revaluation that followed the floating of the exchange rate in June 1970 eroded much of the competitive advantage because Canadian costs in terms of U.S. dollars also rose.

As a result, further appreciation of the Canadian dollar was opposed on the grounds that it would further harm the competitive position of the export sector. As Box 41-4 emphasizes, this is not the case when the appreciation arises from a low domestic inflation rate relative to the foreign rate. Stabilizing the exchange rate merely led to increased domestic inflation with no gain in competitive advantage for the domestic export sector. Costs in terms of U.S. dollars still rose not as a result of a rise in the value of the Canadian dollar, but rather as a result of increased domestic factor costs, especially wages.

An alternative explanation of the policy error, put forward by the late Harry Johnson, is that the Bank of Canada's operating procedures were geared to maintaining the historical near-equality between Canadian and U.S. interest rates. In doing this, the Bank also maintained—perhaps inadvertently—the historical close relationship between the two inflation rates because Canadian monetary policy merely mimicked U.S. monetary policy. Consequently, little or no movement in the exchange rate was required to maintain equilibrium in the foreign exchange market.

A third explanation or justification for the dirty float was that by the middle of 1970, unemployment had become so high that the government had decided it had become the most important problem. Accordingly, from 1970 through 1973, fiscal policy and monetary policy became expansionary.

In summary, Canada appears to have missed an opportunity to avoid at least some of the inflation that plagued the world economy in the 1970s. Monetary policy was immobilized in the late 1960s by a commitment to a fixed exchange rate at a time when inflation rates began to rise in other countries. In the early 1970s the full benefits of a flexible rate were not realized because the Bank of Canada resisted the appreciation of the Canadian dollar and permitted high rates of growth of the money supply.

The experience of this period illustrates dramatically the futility of trying to protect Canada's export industries by holding the value of the Canadian dollar below its equilibrium level. This could only be done by increasing the rate of growth of the money supply, *which had the effect of raising the domestic rate of inflation*. Whatever was gained by Canada's export industries from a lower Canadian dollar was subsequently lost through a higher rate of inflation.

Their competitive position in world markets depends on their costs of production relative to those of other countries measured in terms of the same currency. The cost of production in Canada, measured in terms of, say, U.S. dollars, will rise as a result of either an appreciation of the Canadian dollar or an increase in domestic wages and prices. In view of the other undesirable effects of inflation, it seems clear that an appreciation of the Canadian dollar would have been less harmful to the Canadian economy.

1975–1980: Monetary Targeting

In 1975 the Bank of Canada began to follow policies that utilized the monetary independence created by flexible exchange rates. The Bank started announcing target rates of growth for the money supply. During the period 1976 to 1978, the value of the Canadian dollar fell sharply. As Box 41-2 emphasizes, that fall was largely in response to factors occurring prior to the policy of targeting monetary growth.

While on the surface this policy appeared to meet some of the earlier objections to the use of monetary policy under flexible exchange rates, most economists believe nevertheless that the policy was still one of a "dirty float."

In 1978–1979 a large number of wage contracts, following the unwinding of wage and price controls, were coming up for renewal. At the same time, the Canadian dollar was under substantial pressure. The Bank of Canada, worried that an inflationary surge coming from a depreciation would trigger an unacceptable increase in wages, intervened to support the dollar. However, many economists were skeptical of the importance of the direct influence of the exchange rate on wages; they believed that the harmful disruptions to financial markets caused by the uncertainty arising from the Bank's departure from its independent monetary stance were likely to be larger than any possible gains on the wage front. This experience was discussed in detail in Chapters 35 and 36.

1980–1983: Imported Monetary Restraint

More recently a problem for Canadian monetary and exchange rate management arose from the high average level and volatile behavior of interest rates in the United States. A rise in foreign interest rates leads, other things equal, to large outflows of short-term capital and a depreciation of the domestic currency. Hence a rise in foreign interest rates such as occurred in the United States in 1980 and again in 1981 must be matched by a rise in Canadian rates, a depreciation of the Canadian dollar, or some combination of the two.

In the 1980 episodes, Canadian interest rates rose, but by less than those in the United States. The resulting interest differential attracted capital to the U.S., and as a result the Canadian dollar fell from a peak of 87 U.S. cents in July to 82.5 U.S. cents in December. When the next round of U.S. interest rate increases occurred in 1981, Canadian interest rates rose virtually as high as their U.S. counterparts and the dollar remained relatively stable at around 83 U.S. cents. Again, the Bank of Canada was criticized for pursuing a "dirty float."

Although nominal interest rates in the United States have fallen since those early days of the Reagan administration, real interest rates have remained high. The Bank of Canada has been walking a middle ground between high Canadian real interest rates and depreciation of the Canadian dollar. While the value of the Canadian dollar fell slowly but steadily from 1982 on, it is widely agreed that the Bank of Canada has acted to "protect the exchange rate" and that monetary policy in Canada has been tighter than it would have been in the absence of the very tight U.S. monetary policy. This had benefits in the form of a substantial fall in inflation in the 1982–1984 period. It also had costs in terms of the severity of the 1982 recession and the persistent high unemployment of the 1983–1984 recovery.

SUMMARY

1. Policymakers in an open economy are faced with policy targets or objectives relating to the foreign sector as well as to the domestic sector. Attainment of these targets is often called achieving external and internal balance, respectively. When policies to move the economy toward one target cause it to move away from the other, the targets are said to be in conflict.

2. Expenditure-changing policy used to control the level of national income will also influence the trade balance by altering imports. There will be a conflict of objectives if there is a trade account deficit and a recessionary gap, or if there is a trade account surplus and an inflationary gap. Expenditure-switching policies that shift the net export function can be used to deal with conflict situations.

3. In general, both expenditure-switching and expenditure-changing policies are needed to attain internal and external balance.

4. The capital account is influenced by both fiscal and monetary policy because both influence domestic interest rates.

5. Under a fixed exchange rate, there is little scope for the use of monetary policy for domestic stabilization purposes. Because of the sensitivity of international capital flows to interest rates, the central bank will be forced to maintain domestic interest rates close to the levels in the rest of the world, and it will not be able to bring about substantial changes in the domestic money supply.

6. Under a fixed exchange rate, capital flows will act to reinforce the effectiveness of fiscal policy.

7. Under a flexible exchange rate, fiscal policy actions will be offset by a crowding-out effect un-

less they are accompanied by an accommodating monetary policy that prevents changes in interest rates and the exchange rate.

8. Under a flexible exchange rate, monetary policy is a powerful tool. When capital flows are highly interest elastic, the main channel by which an increase in the money supply increases demand for domestically produced goods is a depreciation of the exchange rate.

9. During the period 1950 to 1961, Canada was on a flexible exchange rate. The Bank of Canada failed to use monetary policy effectively to deal with a serious unemployment problem. In the late 1960s Canada was on a fixed exchange rate that prevented the authorities from avoiding the rising inflation rates experienced by other countries.

10. The floating of the Canadian dollar in 1970 did not remove the inflationary pressure coming from abroad because the Bank of Canada permitted excessively high rates of growth of the money supply during the period 1971 to 1975.

11. From 1975 to 1980 the Bank of Canada followed a policy of controlling the rate of growth of the money supply. Nevertheless there were episodes in which a "dirty float" was maintained.

12. Since 1980, the Bank of Canada has tried to defend the value of the Canadian dollar. Nevertheless, high U.S. interest rates have led to both tight monetary policy in Canada and some depreciation of the Canadian dollar.

TOPICS FOR REVIEW

Internal and external balance
Conflicts between objectives
Expenditure-changing and expenditure-switching policies
Monetary and fiscal policy under fixed exchange rates
Sterilization

Monetary and fiscal policy under flexible exchange rates
Dirty float

DISCUSSION QUESTIONS

1. Explain how a country can influence the external value of its currency by (a) direct intervention in the foreign exchange market, (b) fiscal policy, (c) monetary policy.

2. In his annual report for 1977, Bank of Canada Governor Gerald Bouey said: "If we in Canada continue our progress towards better control of our prices and costs we shall unquestionably benefit from higher levels of employment and output than would otherwise be possible. Better price performance will improve the competitive position of Canadian suppliers in foreign markets and in relation to foreign goods in Canadian markets." Why should Canada be concerned with its competitive position under a flexible exchange rate? In what other ways might a lowering of the rate of inflation lead to increased employment?

3. Which of the following pairs of policy goals can be reached simultaneously using an appropriate macroeconomic policy, and which involve conflicting objectives? Indicate the policies you would advocate in each case.
   a. Lower rate of inflation and a reduced trade-deficit
   b. Elimination of an inflationary gap and a trade deficit
   c. Lower rate of unemployment and a reduced trade deficit
   d. Lower rate of unemployment and a reduced overall balance-of-payments deficit.

4. Explain why the use of monetary policy for domestic stabilization is limited under a fixed exchange rate.

5. A country that maintains a fixed exchange rate will have to allow its inflation rate to adjust to the level occurring in the rest of the world. Is this inconsistent with the theories of demand-pull and expectational inflation discussed in the previous chapter?

6. In a speech in December 1980, Bank of Canada Governor Gerald Bouey stated that "the rapid run-up of U.S. short-term [interest] rates is bound to have a major impact on Canada through increases in interest rates here or through a fall in the foreign exchange value of the Canadian dollar, or some combination of the two." Why must one of these responses occur? What policies can the Bank of Canada follow in order to influence which of the possible responses occurs? Which is preferable?

PART TWELVE
MACROECONOMIC CONTROVERSIES

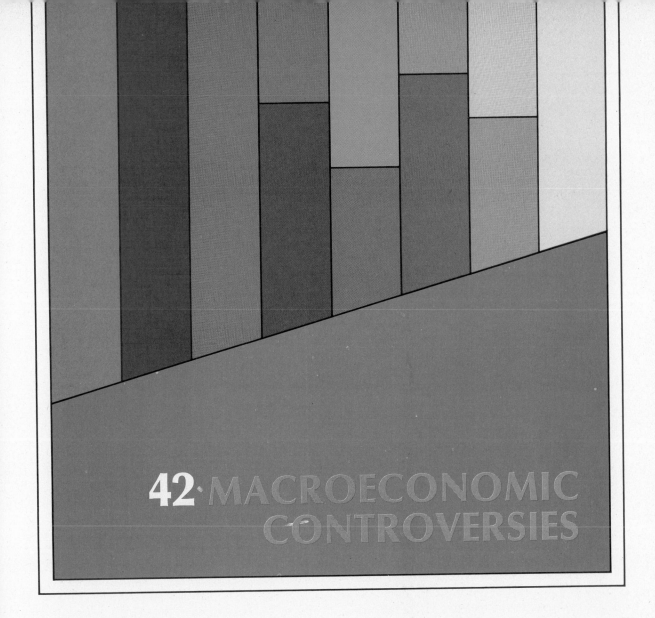

42·MACROECONOMIC CONTROVERSIES

How well do markets work? Can government improve market performance?

In various guises, these two questions are the basics of most disagreements over economic policy. We shall see that different answers to these questions imply big differences in macroeconomic policy prescriptions.

Alternative Views

Macroeconomics is mainly concerned with the behavior of three important variables: employment (and the unemployment rate), the price level (and the inflation rate), and the rate of economic growth. Macroeconomic policy suggests goals for each: full employment, stable prices, and a satisfactory growth rate. The advantages of full employment and a positive growth rate are obvious and not subject to serious dispute. Although most people agree that inflation is harmful, there is much debate about what can really be blamed on it. Box 42-1 deals further with some of the myths surrounding the effects of inflation.

Broadly speaking, we can identify a noninter-

BOX 42–1 SOME MYTHS ABOUT THE COSTS OF INFLATION

Popular opinion has it that inflation makes everyone worse off by reducing the purchasing power of working people's incomes. Accordingly, over most of the last 15 years inflation was perceived by most people as public enemy number one. Inflation was thought to be eroding our living standards and adding in many ways to life's uncertainties. Yet real per capita disposable income rose through most of the 1970s.

Of course different people have different inflationary experience. If you asked someone living on a fixed income about inflation, he or she would be right in saying that it was hurting very much. But what of the typical wage earner or the typical recipient of social insurance, which is fully indexed? Clearly the social insurance recipient is not worse off. Indeed, there are reasons for believing that those who live on incomes that are fully tied to the CPI actually benefit from inflation. (Being a fixed weighted index, the CPI makes no allowance for the quantity adjustments that people make when relative prices change.)

What about the wage earner? The fact is that over the decades money wages have risen faster than money prices, so workers are better off. Why then are so many ordinary working people's perceptions so far wide of the facts? We do not know, but here are some interesting possibilities.

1. It is possible that people confuse the messenger with the message. For example, the rise in OPEC prices in 1979 meant that to pay for the same amount of oil imports, more goods and services had to be exported and hence fewer goods and services were available for home consumption. This meant that domestic living standards had to fall. The mechanism that brought this fall about was a faster rise in prices than in incomes. But the rise in prices was only the means by which the inevitable fall in real living standards was effected. If the price level had been held constant, the same real fall would have occurred through other means (such as a fall in money wages or a rise in unemployment).

Also, in a stagflation output falls while prices rise. People are inclined to attribute their undoubted decline in living standards to the inflation. But in fact the fall in living standards is due to the "stag" not the "inflation." The fall in output means that fewer goods and services are being produced and hence fewer are available for consumption. Even if the price level had remained constant, the fall in output implies a fall in per capita living standards while it lasts.

2. People may think that they could have this year's money incomes and last year's prices. An inflation raises money prices *and* money incomes; if real output has risen, it will raise the latter more than the former. Many people do not understand the link between their own incomes and prices in general. They welcome their 12 percent rise in money wages but lament the percent increase in prices that makes their real incomes rise by a mere 2 percent. They do not realize that if prices had risen by only 4 percent,

---

ventionist and an interventionist view with respect to each of the policy goals just specified. The noninterventionist view says that the unaided market economy can best achieve the goal. The interventionist view says that government policy can improve the economy's performance regarding that goal. Since one can take a noninterventionist or an interventionist position with respect to each of these three goals, there are six different possible policy combinations.[1]

Consider two extreme policy stances: *conservatives* are noninterventionist on every issue, while

[1] Since each of the three issues breaks up into hundreds of different subissues, there are thousands of different policy stances available on one side or the other of each issue.

their money incomes would have risen by only 6 percent, leaving the real income rise unchanged at 2 percent.

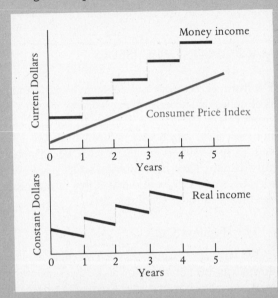

Thus, when many wage earners deplore the rise in prices, they may be thinking—quite erroneously—that if prices had risen by less this year, they could have preserved the same increase in their money incomes. The fundamental relations in the economy are real relations. Average real incomes can rise only by as much as average per capita output rises. If, with a given real increase in output, we reduce the rate at which money prices increase, so will we reduce the rate at which money incomes increase.

3. Lumpy income increases and continuous price increases may create an erroneous impression of trend reductions in real incomes. Individual money incomes are adjusted discretely, often only once a year, while the CPI rises more or less continuously. When money income is raised annually more than the price level has risen over the year, real income falls week by week but rises year by year, as shown in the figure.

The top part shows a typical household's income rising in nominal terms once a year. If the annual rise in money income exceeds the annual rise in prices, real income at any point in one year is higher than it was at the same point in the previous year. But because the price level rises continuously, real income falls between points of pay increase, as shown in the lower part.

Although the trend of real income is upward and on average people's real incomes rise each year, the short-term comparisons are very different. Comparing each week with the previous week, we find that real income falls (a bit) 51 weeks out of 52, while real incomes rise (a lot) only one week in 52—when the annual wage adjustment occurs. Thus the correct perception that inflation is making one gradually worse off (comparing one week with the next) may lead to the mistaken perception that inflation is ultimately making one worse off (comparing one year with the next).

interventionists support government intervention at all times. A few people may actually be conservative or interventionist in this sense. Most, however, would find themselves favoring intervention on some issues and opposing it on others. They might still identify themselves as conservative or interventionist because they were more often on one side than the other.

It is popular to identify monetarist with conservative and neo-Keynesian with interventionist. It is true that many monetarists are on the conservative side while many neo-Keynesians are on the interventionist side. But it is not always so. It is, for example, quite possible to be neo-Keynesian in accepting the Keynesian macro model as a reasonable description of the economy's macroeconomic behavior, but conservative in believing that the unaided market usually does the best job of allocating resources.

The Conservative View

Conservatives believe that the free-market economy performs quite well on balance. This is because they believe that the economy is inherently stable. While shocks will hit the system, they are followed rather quickly, and often painlessly, by the adjustments dictated by the market system. For example, relative prices in booming sectors rise, drawing in resources from declining sectors or regions. As a result, resources (and particularly labor) usually remain fully employed, so there is no need for full-employment policies.

Conservatives hold that macroeconomic performance will be most satisfactory if it is determined solely by the workings of the free market.

Of course, few believe that the market system functions perfectly, thereby ensuring *continuous* full employment. But the view is that the market system works well enough to preclude any constructive role for policy.

In addition, many believe the available policy instruments are so crude that their use is often counterproductive. A policy's effects may be so uncertain, with regard to both strength and timing, that it may often impair rather than improve the economy's performance.

In a modern economy some government presence is inevitable. Thus a stance of no intervention is impossible; rather, what is advocated by conservatives is minimal direct intervention in the market system. This involves the government's bearing responsibility for providing a *stable environment* in which the private sector can function.

The Interventionist View

Interventionists believe that the functioning of the free-market economy is often far from satisfactory. Sometimes markets show weak self-regulatory forces and the economy settles into prolonged periods of heavy unemployment. At other times markets tend to "overcorrect," causing the economy to lurch between the extremes of large recessionary and large inflationary gaps.

This behavior can be improved, argue the interventionists. Even though interventionist policies may be imperfect, they may be good enough to improve the functioning of the economy with respect to all three main goals of macro policy.

MACROECONOMIC ISSUES

Everyone agrees that the economy's performance is often less than perfectly satisfactory. Serious unemployment has been a recurring problem. Inflation was a serious problem throughout the 1970s and early 1980s. For nearly two decades now, growth rates have been unsatisfactorily low. Conservatives and interventionists differ in diagnosing the causes of these economic ills.

The Business Cycle

We saw in Chapter 26 that cyclical ups and downs can be observed for as far back as records exist. Monetarists and neo-Keynesians have long argued about the causes.

Monetarist views. Monetarists believe the economy is inherently stable because private-sector expenditure functions are relatively stable. In addition, they believe shifts in the aggregate demand curve are mainly due to policy-induced changes in the money supply.[2]

The view that business cycles have mainly monetary causes relies heavily on the evidence advanced by Milton Friedman and Anna Schwartz in their monumental *A Monetary History of the United States, 1867–1960.* They establish a strong correlation between changes in the money supply and changes in the level of business activity. Major

---

[2] The view that fluctuations often have monetary causes is not new. The English economist R. G. Hawtrey, the Austrian Nobel Laureate F. A. von Hayek, and the Swedish economist Knut Wicksell are prominent among those who have given monetary factors an important role in explaining the turning points in cycles and/or the tendency for expansions and contractions, once begun, to become cumulative and self-reinforcing. Modern monetarists carry on this tradition.

recessions have been associated with absolute declines in the money supply and minor recessions with the slowing of the rate of increase in the money supply below its long-term trend.

The correlation between changes in the money supply and changes in the level of business activity is now accepted by virtually all economists. But there is controversy over how this correlation is to be interpreted; do changes in money supply cause changes in the level of aggregate demand and hence of business activity, or vice versa?

Friedman and Schwartz maintain that changes in the money supply cause changes in business activity. They argue, for example, that the severity of the Great Depression was due to a major contraction in the money supply that shifted the aggregate demand curve far to the left. The Great Depression is discussed further in Box 42-2.

According to monetarists, fluctuations in the money supply cause fluctuations in national income.

This leads the monetarists to advocate a policy of stabilizing the growth of the money supply. In their view this would avoid policy-induced instability of the aggregate demand curve.

Neo-Keynesian views. The neo-Keynesian view on cyclical fluctuations in the economy has two parts. First, it emphasizes variations in investment as a cause of business cycles and stresses the nonmonetary causes of such variations.[3]

Neo-Keynesians reject what they regard as the extreme monetarist view that only money matters in explaining cyclical fluctuations. Many neo-Keynesians believe that both monetary and nonmonetary forces are important. Although they accept monetary mismanagement as one potential source of economic fluctuations, they do not believe that it is the only or even the major source of such fluctuations. Thus they deny the monetary

interpretation of business cycle history given by Friedman and Schwartz. They believe that most fluctuations in the aggregate demand curve are due to variations in the desire to spend on the part of the private sector and are not induced by government policy.

Neo-Keynesians also believe the economy lacks strong natural corrective mechanisms that will always force it easily and quickly back to full employment. They believe that although the price level rises fairly quickly to eliminate *inflationary gaps*, the price level does not fall quickly to eliminate *GNP gaps*. Neo-Keynesians stress the asymmetries noted in earlier chapters which imply that prices and wages fall only slowly in response to a GNP gap. As a result, neo-Keynesians believe that GNP gaps can persist for long periods of time unless they are eliminated by an active stabilization policy.

The second part of the neo-Keynesian view of cyclical fluctuations is acceptance of the correlation between changes in the money supply and changes in the level of economic activity. But this explanation reverses the causality suggested by the monetarists: The neo-Keynesians argue that changes in the level of economic activity tend to cause changes in the money supply. They offer several reasons for this, but only the most important need be mentioned.

Neo-Keynesians point out that from 1945 to the early 1970s most central banks tended to stabilize interest rates as the target variable of monetary policy. To do this they had to increase the money supply during upswings in the business cycle and decrease it during downswings. Central banks followed this monetary policy when an expansion got under way because the demand for money tended to increase, and if there was no increase in the money supply, interest rates would rise.

The central bank might prevent this rise in interest rates by buying bonds offered for sale at current prices, but in so doing it would increase banks' reserves and thereby inject new money into the economy. Similarly, in a cyclical contraction interest rates would tend to fall unless the central bank stepped in and sold bonds to keep interest rates up. Generally it did so, thereby decreasing

[3] Like the monetarists, the neo-Keynesians are modern advocates of views that have a long history. The great Austrian (and later American) economist Joseph Schumpeter stressed such explanations early in the present century. The Swedish economist Wicksell and the German Speithoff both stressed this aspect of economic fluctuations before the emergence of the Keynesian school of thought.

BOX 42–2 TWO VIEWS ON THE GREAT DEPRESSION IN THE UNITED STATES

The stock market crash of 1929, and other factors associated with a moderate downswing in business activity during the late 1920s, caused the American public to wish to hold more cash and less demand deposits. The banking system could not, however, meet this increased demand for liquidity without help from the Federal Reserve System. (As we saw in Chapter 33, banks are never able to meet from their own reserves a sudden demand to withdraw currency on the part of a large fraction of their depositors. Their reserves are always inadequate to meet such a demand.)

The Fed had been set up to provide just such emergency assistance to banks that were basically sound but that were unable to meet sudden demands by depositors to withdraw cash. However, the Fed refused to extend the necessary help, and successive waves of bank failures followed as a direct result. During each wave, hundreds of banks failed, ruining many depositors and thereby worsening an already severe depression.

In the last half of 1931, almost 2,000 American banks were forced to suspend operations! One consequence of this was a sharp drop in the money supply; by 1932 the money supply was 35 percent below the level of 1929. To monetarists, these facts seem decisive.

While neo-Keynesians accept the argument that the Fed's behavior was perverse, they argue that the cyclical behavior of investment and consumption expenditure was the major cause of the Great Depression. In support of this view, they point out that in Canada and the United Kingdom, where the central bank came to the aid of the banking system, bank failures were trivial during the Great Depression, and as a consequence the money supply did *not* shrink drastically as it did in the United States. Despite these markedly different monetary histories, the behavior of the GNP gap, investment expenditure, and unemployment was very similar in the three countries.

the money supply. This behavior created the positive correlation on which the monetarists rely.

According to neo-Keynesians, fluctuations in national income are often caused by fluctuations in expenditure decisions. Further, they believe that fluctuations in national income cause fluctuations in the money supply.

Nevertheless, most neo-Keynesians also agree that policy-induced changes in the money supply can cause national income to change.

The Price Level

As we saw in Chapter 36, sustained inflation requires sustained expansion of the money supply. Motives for such excessive monetary expansions

have varied from time to time and place to place. Sometimes central banks have rapidly increased the money supply in an effort to end a recession. Then, when the economy expanded due to its own natural recuperative forces, the increased money supply allowed a significant inflation during the boom phase of the cycle. At other times central banks have tried to hold interest rates well below their free-market levels. To do this, they buy bonds to hold bond prices up. We have seen that these open market operations increase the money supply and so fuel an inflation. At still other times central banks have helped governments finance large budget deficits by buying up the new public debt. These open market operations monetize the new debt and provide what is popularly known as *print-*

ing press finance. The steady increase in the money supply fuels a continuous inflation.

Monetarist views. Many monetarists hold that inflation is everywhere and always a monetary phenomenon. They thus focus on changes in the money supply as the key source of shifts in the *AD* curve. Many also believe that supply shocks which cause *some* prices to rise do not lead to inflation because, unless the money supply is also raised, some other prices will have to fall.

According to monetarists all inflations are caused by excessive monetary expansion and would not occur without it.

Neo-Keynesian views. Neo-Keynesians accept the idea that a sustained rise in prices cannot occur unless it is accompanied by continued increases in the money supply. To this extent, they agree with the monetarists. Neo-Keynesians also emphasize, however, that temporary bursts of inflation can be caused by shifts in the aggregate demand curve brought about by increases in private- or public-sector expenditure functions (consumption, investment, exports, and government expenditure). If such inflations are not validated by monetary expansion, they are brought to a halt by the monetary adjustment mechanism. Even when not validated, they can persist long enough to worry policymakers and governments concerned about the next election.

Neo-Keynesians also accept the importance of supply-shock inflations. Again, they accept that such inflations cannot go on indefinitely unless accommodated by monetary expansion. But supply-shock inflations can also go on long enough to be a matter of serious concern. Indeed, such inflations can present the central bank with agonizing choices: whether to accommodate the shocks (thereby accepting a bout of inflation to avoid the unemployment) or not to accommodate (thereby accepting a period of unemployment to reduce inflation).

Many neo-Keynesians also take seriously the possibility of wage-cost-push inflation that we studied in Chapter 36. This type of inflation, if it exists, makes full employment incompatible with a stable price level. Again the central bank is faced with the agonizing choice of whether or not to accommodate.

Growth

Conservative views. Conservatives, and indeed most monetarists, feel that in a stable environment free from government interference, growth will take care of itself. Large firms will spend much on research and development. Where they fail, or where they suppress inventions to protect monopoly positions, the genius of backyard inventors will come up with new ideas and will develop new companies to challenge the positions of the established giants. Left to itself, the economy will prosper as it has in the past, provided only that inquiring scientific spirit and the profit motive are not suppressed.

Interventionist views. Interventionists, and indeed most neo-Keynesians, are less certain about the ability of market forces to produce growth. While recognizing the importance of invention and innovation, they fear the dead hand of monopoly and conservative business practices that choose security over risk taking. Therefore, the government needs at the very least to give a nudge here or there to help the growth process along.

THE ROLE OF POLICY

The conservative and the interventionist diagnoses of the economy's ills lead, not surprisingly, to very different prescriptions about the appropriate role of economic policy.

Conservative Prescriptions

It is not necessary to distinguish conservative policies with respect to full employment and stable prices. This is because conservatives believe both goals will be achieved by the same basic policy: provision of a stable environment for the free-market system to operate.

Providing a Stable Environment

Creating a stable environment, as the conservatives advocate, may be easier said than done. We focus on the conservative prescriptions for establishing stable fiscal and monetary policies.

One major problem to keep in mind is that macro variables are interrelated. The stability of one may imply the instability of another. In such cases, a choice must be made. How much instability of one aggregate can we tolerate to secure stability in another related aggregate?

Assume, for example, that people are so worried about budget deficits that the government decides to adopt the goal of stability in the budget balance as part of the stable environment: The budget balance should be the same from year to year.

This "stability" would require great *instability* in tax and expenditure policy. As we saw in Chapter 32, although governments can set tax *rates*, they cannot directly determine tax *revenues*. Tax revenues depend on the interaction between tax rates and the level of national income. With given tax rates, tax revenues change with the ebb and flow of the business cycle. A stable budget balance would require that the government raise tax rates and cut expenditure in slumps and lower tax rates and raise expenditures in booms.

Not only does this squander the budget's potential to act as a stabilizer, but great instability of the fiscal environment is caused by continual changes in tax rates and expenditure levels. A stable fiscal environment requires substantial stability in government expenditures and tax rates. Stability is needed so that the private sector can make plans for the future within a climate of known patterns of tax liabilities and government demand. This in turn requires that the budget deficit fluctuate cyclically, showing its largest deficits in slumps and its largest surpluses in booms.

The target budget balance must be some average over a period long enough to cover a typical cycle. Stability from year to year should be found in tax rates and expenditure programs, *not* in the size of the budget balance.

Advocates of a stable monetary environment are actually advocating stable inflation. Whether a *zero* rate is feasible or not is discussed in Box 42-3. The central bank is urged to set a target rate of increase in the money supply and hold it. To establish the target, the central bank estimates the rate at which the demand for money would be growing if actual income equaled potential income and the price level were stable. As a first approximation, this can be taken to be the rate at which potential income itself is growing.[4] This then becomes the target rate of growth of the money supply. The key proposition is that the money supply should be changing gradually along a stable path that is independent of short-term variations in the demand for money caused by cyclical changes in national income. This is referred to as a *k* **percent rule.**

Will the *k* percent rule really provide monetary stability? The answer: "Not necessarily."

Assuring a stable rate of monetary growth does not assure a stable monetary environment: Monetary shortages and surpluses depend on the relation between the supply and the demand for money.

The *k* percent rule looks after supply, but what about demand?

Problems for the *k* percent rule arise when the demand for money shifts. For example, payment of interest on chequing deposits increases the demand for M1. In this event, if the central bank adheres to a *k* percent rule, there will be an excess demand for money, interest rates will rise and contractionary pressure will be put on the economy.

Should the central bank commit itself to a specific *k* percent rule or merely work toward unannounced and possibly variable targets? The pre-announced rule makes it easier to evaluate how well the central bank is doing its job. It also helps to prevent the bank from succumbing to the temptation to fine tune the economy.

One disadvantage of the pre-announced rule is that it sets up speculative behavior. If, for example, when weekly money supply figures are announced there is too much money, speculators know that

---

[4] Such a rule assumes that members of the public wish to keep their money holdings in a fixed proportion to their real income. If other demand patterns are established—that is, if desired money holdings change as a proportion of real income as income rises—then the central bank can alter its monetary target appropriately.

BOX 42-3 IS A ZERO INFLATION RATE A FEASIBLE POLICY GOAL?

The 1950s were characterized by what would be regarded today as satisfactory price stability. But prices were not exactly steady. After 1952 the inflation rate varied between 0.9 percent and 3.2 percent. Despite what appeared to most observers to be a slowly growing recessionary gap throughout this period, the inflation rate only reached zero in one year. Between 1955 and 1961 there were only two years when the rate was below 1 percent: 1955 (0.2 percent) and 1961 (0.9 percent).

This creeping inflation worried observers at the time. An inflation, even a gradual one in the face of an obvious recessionary gap, seemed hard to understand.

The explanation in modern theory would be likely to come from the supply side: The combination of rising prices and recessionary gaps usually suggests a supply-shock inflation. The explanation that satisfied many observers at the time was the so-called **structural rigidity theory** of inflation, which was indeed a supply-shock explanation.

This theory assumes that resources do not move quickly from one use to another and that it is easy to increase money wages and prices but hard to decrease them. Given these conditions, when patterns of demand and costs change due to such forces as economic growth, real adjustments occur very slowly. Shortages appear in potentially expanding sectors and prices rise because the slow movement of resources prevents these sectors from expanding rapidly enough. Factors of production remain in contracting sectors on part-time employment or go unemployed because mobility is low in the economy. Wages and prices are slow to move downward so there are few significant wage and price reductions in these contracting sectors.

Thus the mere process of adjustment in an economy with structural rigidities causes inflation to occur: Prices in the expanding sectors rise; prices in the contracting sectors stay about the same; on average, therefore, the price level rises.

The inflation of the late 1950s and early 1960s was very mild and the debate on its causes was inconclusive. However, this was the first suggestion of a force that later became a plaguing policy problem: inflations originating in shifts in the aggregate supply curve.

Although the structural rigidity theory cannot be a major part of the explanation of the very high inflation rates of the 1970s and early 1980s, it suggests that a zero inflation rate may not be an achievable target. If there is anything in the structural rigidity theory, then the minimum inflation rate compatible with a changing economy may be 1 percent to 2 percent rather than zero.

the central bank will sell more bonds in the future to mop up the surplus. This will depress the price of bonds. Speculators are thus induced to sell bonds, hoping to rebuy them at bargain prices once the central bank acts.

Stable pre-announced M1 targets can introduce instability into interest-rate behavior.

A second disadvantage of such a rule is that the central bank, in order to preserve its credibility, may fail to take discretionary action that would otherwise be appropriate. For example, after an entrenched inflation is broken, the economy may come to rest with substantial unemployment and a stable price level (see Figure 36-5). There is then a case for a once-and-for-all discretionary expansion in the money supply to get the economy back to full employment. The k percent rule precludes this, condemning the economy to a prolonged slump.

Despite these problems, conservatives believe the k percent rule is superior to any known alternative. Some would agree that in principle the central bank could improve the economy's performance by occasional bouts of discretionary monetary policy to offset such things as, say, major shifts in the demand for money. But they also believe that once given any discretion, the central bank would abuse it in an attempt to fine tune the economy. The resulting instability would, they believe, be much more than any instability resulting from the application of a *k* percent rule in an environment subject to some change.

Long-Term Growth

Conservatives want to let growth take care of itself. They argue that governments cannot improve the workings of free markets and that their interventions can interfere with market efficiency. Thus they push for reducing the current level of government intervention.

Given the tangled web of government rules, regulations, and perverse tax incentives that has grown up over many years, the conservative agenda for reducing government intervention is usually a long one. Such an agenda was adopted in the United States by so-called supply siders during the late 1970s and early 1980s. Supply-side economics may or may not turn out to be a mere fad, but the conservative view that growth is best encouraged by reducing the present degree of government intervention will no doubt always find numerous supporters. Some further characteristics of supply-side economics are mentioned in Box 42-4.

The agenda includes *eliminating* the following policies.

Supporting declining industries. This policy causes resources that could be more productively employed elsewhere to leave the industry more slowly. Most economists agree that such policies are costly, harmful to growth, and in the end self-defeating.

Encouraging monopolies and discouraging competition. Most economists tend to oppose such policies, although there is disagreement over how much competition is desirable in certain in-

dustries. For example, conservatives tend to support complete deregulation of fare and route setting by airlines, while interventionists tend to worry that cutthroat competition may reduce airline quality and safety.

Taxing income rather than consumption. Consider a woman in the 40 percent tax bracket who earns an extra $1,000 and pays $400 income tax. If she spends her after-tax income she will be able to buy $600 worth of goods. If she saves the money she will be able to buy a $600 bond. If the bond pays, say, a 4 percent real return, she will earn $24 interest per year. But a 40 percent tax must then be paid on the interest earnings, leaving only a $14.40 annual income. This is a 2.4 percent after-tax return on the bond and *a 1.44 percent after-tax return on the original $1,000 income.* Conservatives allege that this "double taxing" is a serious disincentive to saving. They argue for taxes on consumption, not on income, so that any income saved would be untaxed. A tax would be levied only when the interest earned on the savings was actually spent on consumption.

High rates of income tax. Conservatives allege that high taxes discourage work. But the effect of high taxes may actually be to make people work either more or less hard. Theory is silent on which is more likely, and no hard evidence has yet shown that lowering current tax rates will make people work harder.

"Double taxation" of business profits, first as income of firms and second as income of households when paid out as dividends. This, and other policies that reduce business profits and hence discourage the return to investing in equities, are alleged to discourage households from saving and investing in businesses that are the mainspring of economic growth.

All these policies are alleged to reduce the rate of growth below what it would otherwise be. Problems arise in assessing the existence and importance of the alleged harmful effects of each policy and also, since the government needs revenue, in finding alternative revenue sources that will have less harmful effects than the ones being criticized.

BOX 42–4 SUPPLY-SIDE ECONOMICS

Since the end of the 1970s, a new cry has been frequently heard in popular discussion and in serious debate: supply-side economics. Supply-side economics is not new. Indeed it's what Adam Smith's *Wealth of Nations* was all about. In its modern version, like many general but catchy terms, it sometimes means all things to all people. For example,

1. In explaining inflation and stagflation, it means an emphasis on the aggregate supply curve. As we have seen at length, "supply-side shocks" are now a major part of most explanations of what happened in the 1970s.

2. In control of inflation, it means an emphasis on pushing the aggregate supply curve outward rather than reining the aggregate demand curve inward. This proposition concerns short-run stabilization policy.

3. In concern over living standards, it means an emphasis on pushing the aggregate supply curve out to the right rather than on manipulating aggregate demand. The motto here might be, "It is more important to increase full-employment national income than to try to reduce the temporary deviations from it that the market economy produces." This proposition concerns long-run growth policy.

Point 1 is a diagnosis of our past ills. Points 2 and 3 are policy prescriptions to improve things in the future. Both require pushing the aggregate supply curve outward in the manner shown in Figure 38-1(i) on page 732. The key idea is to provide the appropriate incentives for the private sector to do the job. How might this be done? Many of the measures advocated have been discussed elsewhere in this book. Four of the most important are: (1) to encourage saving, (2) to encourage labor force participation and mobility, (3) to encourage risk taking, and (4) to channel effort into productive activities instead of tax avoidance (by simplifying the tax system).

The number of possible proposals is myriad. They all have the intended effect of increasing full-employment income by increasing the supplies of capital or of labor or by increasing the rate of technical change.

There is little doubt that many current policies and practices do have the alleged output restricting effects, so that some changes in policy would do some of the things alleged by supply-side economics. If even a small increase in the growth rate of full-employment income could be achieved, the long-term effects on living standards would be enormous. (See Table 38-1 on page 734.)

Thus objective 3 is viable. Increasing the growth rate of full employment *will* raise living standards.

The second objective, however, is more debatable. It would, for example, be an enormous achievement to raise the growth rate by half a percentage point—and a generation or two down the line the effect on the *level* of income would be large. But two years down the line it is only 1 percent more full-employment output. In the face of an inflationary gap of, say, 10 percent, increasing aggregate supply by 1 percent is not going to do much to the inflation rate. Even the conservative economist Herbert Stein of the *American Enterprise Institute*, who could be expected to be sympathetic to many supply-side measures, warned in early 1980:

Despite the tone of much of the current argument, the propositions of supply-side economics are not matters of ideology or principle. They are matters of arithmetic. So far one must say that the arithmetic of any of the "newer" propositions is highly doubtful. Supply-side economics may yet prove to be the irritant which, like the grain of sand in the oyster shell, produces a pearl of new economic wisdom. But up to this point the pearl has not appeared.*

Whether or not its potential for controlling inflation is overstated, there is no doubt that supply effects are important, and that supply-side economics in one form or another is here to stay.

* *The AEI Economist*, April 1980, published by *American Enterprise Institute*.

Interventionist Prescriptions

Interventionists call for different policies for each of the three policy goals. So we must consider the interventionist prescriptions for full employment, price stability, and growth. At the same time, we give their reasons for rejecting the conservative case.

Full Employment

Interventionists call for discretionary fiscal and monetary policies to offset significant GNP gaps. Some of the major problems associated with discretionary stabilization policy have been discussed in earlier chapters. The issues in the debate that is popularly known as "rules versus discretion" are discussed further in Box 42-5.

A Stable Price Level

In Chapter 36 we discussed the breaking of an entrenched inflation. Here we consider how a low inflation rate might be maintained once it is achieved.

Some interventionists, particularly a group called *post-Keynesians*, believe that the *k* percent rule may not be enough to achieve full employment and stable prices simultaneously. This is because they accept the wage-cost-push theory of inflation discussed in Chapter 36.

Post-Keynesians call for incomes policies to restrain the wage-cost push and so make full employment compatible with stable prices. They believe that such policies should become permanent features of the economic landscape.

Wage-price controls might work as *temporary* measures to break inflationary inertias (see Chapter 36, pages 698–699), but as permanent features they would introduce all the inefficiencies and rigidities that were briefly alluded to in Box 36-4 on pages 700–701.

More permanent incomes policies might be of two types. The first type, commonly used in Europe in the past decades but now out of favor, is often called a *social contract*. Here labor, management, and the government consult annually and

agree on target wage changes. These are calculated to be noninflationary, given the government's projections for the future and its planned economic policies. Such a scheme is most easily initiated in a centralized economy such as West Germany's, where a few giant firms and unions exert enormous power, or in a country such as Britain, where the party in power during much of the period had strong official links with the labor unions.

The other main type of incomes policy is the **tax-related incomes policy,** or as it is often called, **TIPS.** This policy, which we encountered in Chapter 36, provides tax incentives for management and labor to conform to government-established wage and price guidelines. For example, increases in wages and prices in excess of the guidelines would be heavily taxed. TIPs have not yet been tried, although they have been strongly advocated by some American economists.

TIPs would rely on tax incentives to secure voluntary conformity with the wage and price guidelines, whereas wages and price controls try to impose conformity by law.

Advocates of TIPs argue that their great advantage is in leaving decisions on wages and prices in the hands of labor and management while seeking only to influence behavior by altering the incentive system. Critics argue that they would prove to be an administrative nightmare.

Growth

Policies for intervention to increase growth rates are of two sorts. Some policies seek to alter the general economic climate in a way favorable to growth. They typically include subsidization or favorable tax treatment for research and development, for purchase of plant and equipment, and for other profit-earning activities. Measures to lower interest rates temporarily or permanently are urged by some as favorable to investment and growth. Most interventionists support these general measures.

Some also support more specific intervention, usually in the form of what is called *picking* and *backing winners* in one way or another. Advocates

BOX 42-5 **RULES VERSUS DISCRETION**

Three of the main issues involved in the rules versus discretion debate are discussed in this box.

Lags. Those hostile to discretionary policy emphasize the long and variable lags of both fiscal and monetary policy. Monetary policy can be put into effect quickly, but it takes 6 to 18 months for the full effects of a change in interest rates to be felt in terms of altered private-sector expenditures. It often takes a longer time to put fiscal policy into effect, as federal budgets are usually at least two or three months in the making. Once the changes are made, however, their effects spread quickly through the economy. Conservatives feel that these lags destroy the presumption that discretionary full-employment policy will usually be stabilizing. Interventionists feel that although the lags are serious, discretionary policies can be effective in reducing persistent GNP gaps. Few interventionists, however, now call for fine tuning.

A stable climate for planning. Supporters of rules emphasize the need for a stable climate for firms and households to plan for the future. They argue that continual changes in tax rates and the money supply designed to stabilize the economy are destabilizing because they create a climate of uncertainty which makes long-term planning difficult. Supporters of discretionary policy argue that they want discretion exercised only when the occasional serious recession develops and that fluctuations in income and employment can be as upsetting to long-term planning as the occasional changes in tax rates and expenditures required by stabilization policy.

Do we know enough? Discretionary stabilization policy requires that we forecast what the state of the economy will be in the absence of that policy. Generally, actual information is available only with a lag. Policymakers know approximately what GNP was last quarter and what unemployment was last month. (The first preliminary figures for many economic variables can be subject to substantial errors. Often these estimates are revised several times over subsequent months and even years.) On the basis of these data, projections of future behavior of the economy must be made and policy set. Supporters of discretionary policy accept that errors in projections may be large in relation to the GNP gaps created by minor recessions, but believe that the errors are small in relation to major recessions. They argue that for major recessions policymakers will be in no doubt about the existence of a large recessionary gap and of the need for some significant stimulus, even though its precise amount cannot be precisely determined.

of this view, such as Professor Lester Thurow of M.I.T., want governments to pick the industries, usually new ones, that have potential for future success and then to back them with subsidies, government contracts, research funds, and all the other incentives at the government's command.

Opponents argue that picking winners requires foresight and that there is no reason to expect the government to have better foresight than private investors. Indeed, since political considerations inevitably get in the way, the government may be less successful than the market in picking "winners." If so, channeling funds through the government rather than through the private sector may hurt rather than help growth rates. Many economists are skeptical of the government's ability to spot and then back the potential winners. This debate is discussed in Box 37-4 on pages 726–727.

RATIONAL EXPECTATIONS AND THE MICRO FOUNDATIONS OF MACROECONOMICS[5]

For many years Keynesian economics seemed successful both in explaining the overall behavior of the economy and in suggesting policies for controlling inflation and unemployment. As long as it appeared to work, few were interested in *how*. During the late 1960s and the 1970s, however, control of the economy by means of traditional fiscal and monetary policies seemed to become more difficult. This raised concerns about the foundations of Keynesian theory. The main question was this: What behavior in the individual markets for goods and factors of production is implied by the Keynesian aggregate relationships? This question concerns what are called the *micro foundations*, or *micro underpinnings*, of macro models.

While these concerns about the Keynesian model were surfacing, the monetarist model seemed to provide an alternative for understanding the macro behavior of the economy and for prescribing appropriate policies. This elicited a debate about the merits of the two models, a debate that still rages today.

Micro foundations are at the heart of the debate between monetarism and neo-Keynesianism. The issues are important; because they are at the frontier of modern research, they are also difficult. The analysis depends on material that is treated in detail in microeconomics courses. At this stage, therefore, we can only discuss the issues in broad outline.

Monetarist Micro Foundations

There is no single set of accepted monetarist micro foundations. Most monetarists, however, view markets as competitive.[6] One important char-

[5] This section may be omitted without loss of continuity.

[6] They realize, of course, that perfect competition does not exist everywhere in the economy, but they believe that the forces of competition are strong—strong enough so that analysis based on the theory of perfect competition will be close to the real behavior of the economy.

acteristic of competitive markets is that prices and wages are flexible; they adjust to establish equilibrium at all times. When a competitive market is in equilibrium (see Chapter 5), the market is said to have *cleared*. This means that every purchaser has been able to buy all he or she wishes to buy at the going price and every seller has been able to sell all he or she wishes to sell at that price.[7] When each and every market is in equilibrium, there is full employment of all resources. The prices that clear markets are called **market clearing prices**.

According to the monetarists there exist strong forces which ensure that departures from full-employment equilibrium are quickly rectified. That is, as we saw above, monetarists believe that the *automatic adjustment mechanism* works quite efficiently. We now consider two particular monetarist views.

Traditional Monetarism

The monetarist school of thought that evolved in the 1960s was led by Professor Milton Friedman of the University of Chicago. Economists of that school, called traditional monetarists, hold that the economy, when left to its own, tends to stabilize at the full-employment level. They also hold that, historically, monetary policies have been very erratic. We saw in Chapter 34 that monetarists believe monetary policy exerts a powerful influence on the economy, so they reach the following conclusion:

Traditional monetarists believe that fluctuations in the money supply are a major source of fluctuations in output and the price level.

Although monetary policy has strong effects, it operates with a long and variable lag. According to Friedman and his followers, these long and variable lags not only doom monetary policy to failure, but make it counterproductive as well. In their view monetary policy has actually served to destabilize the economy in the past. For Freidman and his

[7] Competitive markets clear only at the equilibrium price. At any other price there are either unsatisfied purchasers (excess demand) or unsatisfied sellers (excess supply).

followers, the best course for monetary policy is, as already noted earlier in the chapter, to set the rate of increase of the money supply at some given value and hold it there. We referred to this as the *k percent rule*.

New Classical Monetarism

The *new classical monetarists* follow Professors Robert Lucas and Thomas Sargeant in holding that temporary departures from full employment occur mainly because people make mistakes. As we shall see, this result is based on the proposition derived from microeconomics that individual supply and demand behavior depends only on the structure of relative prices.

To follow their argument, let us start by assuming that each of the economy's markets is in equilibrium; there is full employment, prices are stable, and the actual and expected rates of inflation are zero. Now let the government increase the money supply by, say, 5 percent. People find themselves with unwanted money balances, which they seek to spend.[8] For simplicity, assume that this leads to an increase in desired expenditure on all commodities: The demand for each commodity shifts to the right and all prices, being competitively determined, rise.

Individual decision makers see their selling prices go up and mistakenly interpret this increase as a rise in their own relative price. This is because they expect the overall rate of inflation to be zero. Firms will produce more and workers will work more; both groups think they are getting an increased *relative* price for what they sell. Thus total output and employment rise.

When both groups eventually realize that their own relative prices are in fact unchanged, output and employment fall back to their initial levels. The extra output and employment occurred only

[8] In fact, most monetarists also accept the theory of the transmission mechanism discussed in Chapter 34 where the excess money balances are used to buy financial assets, thus driving down interest rates and stimulating expenditure *indirectly*. However, most monetarists tend to stress the relative importance of the *direct* expenditure effects created by excess money balances.

while people are being fooled. When they realized that all prices had risen by 5 percent, they reverted to their initial behavior. The only difference is that now the price level has risen by 5 percent, leaving relative prices unchanged.

According to the new classical theory, deviations from full employment occur because people make mistakes that cause markets to clear at more or less than full-employment output. People are not prevented from selling as many commodities or as much labor as they wish; the contraction or expansion in output is voluntary.

New classical monetarists focus on the role of changes in relative prices in signaling appropriate information in a world where tastes and technology are constantly changing. They hold that fluctuations in the money supply will lead to increased fluctuations in all prices. This makes it hard for households and firms to distinguish changes in relative prices, to which they do wish to respond, from changes in the price level, to which they do not wish to respond. Such confusion, created by fluctuations in the money supply, thus leads to mistakes in supply and demand decisions.

This discussion highlights the importance for firms and households of distinguishing the causes of any price changes. Consider, for example, what happens if there is an unexpected and unperceived increase in the money supply. This will lead to an increase in most, if not all, prices above what most agents had expected.

Most firms perceive this as an increase in the relative price of their own output and hence increase their level of production above what it normally would have been. Consequently, national income rises above the full-employment level. A similar argument shows that an unanticipated and unperceived decrease in the money supply would cause output to fall below its full-employment level.

The Lucas aggregate supply curve. The behavior described above gives rise to the **Lucas aggregate supply curve.**

The Lucas aggregate supply curve posits that national

output will vary positively with the ratio of the actual to the expected price level.

This is often also referred to as the *surprises only* supply curve, since it implies that only changes in the price level which are unexpected (surprises) will give rise to fluctuations in aggregate supply.

To see this, consider what happens if there is again an increase in the money supply, but this time suppose it has been expected in advance by firms and households. Again, prices will rise. Most firms will now take this to mean only that the *observed* change in the price of their own output has roughly matched the *expected* change in the average of all other prices. Hence they will not interpret it as a rise in the relative price of their own output and will maintain their production at its normal level. National income will not rise above potential, despite the rise in the general price level.

According to the new classical theory, expected changes in the price level do not lead to fluctuations in aggregate supply.

New classical policy views. New classical monetarists support the *k* percent rule, just as do the traditional monetarists. They believe that firms and households make better decisions when monetary and fiscal policies are stable than when they are highly variable. They believe that active interventionist policies designed to stabilize the economy make it harder for people to interpret the signals generated by the price system and so lead them to make more errors in forming their expectations. This then increases rather than reduces the fluctuations of output around its full-employment level and increases rather than reduces the fluctuations of unemployment around the natural rate.

According to the new classical economists, active use of monetary policy in an attempt to stabilize the economy will lead to confusion about relative and absolute prices, causing people to make mistakes in their output and purchasing decisions and therefore increasing aggregate output fluctuations.

In turn, this conclusion depends upon the particular view adopted by the new classical monetarists

about how people form predictions or expectations, a subject that has recently become an important part of macroeconomic debates.

The Theory of Rational Expectations

The new classical model is augmented by the theory of *rational expectations*. People look to the government's current macroeconomic policy to form their expectations of future inflation. They understand how the economy works, and they form their expectations rationally by predicting the outcome of the policies now being followed. People learn fairly quickly from their mistakes; while random errors occur, systematic and persistent errors do not. In an obvious sense, such expectations are *forward looking*.

According to the theory of rational expectations, people do not make persistent, systematic errors in predicting the overall inflation rate; they may, however, make unsystematic errors.

The policy invariance proposition. Rational expectations, combined with the Lucas aggregate supply curve, gives rise to the new classical *policy invariance*, or policy neutrality, result:

Systematic attempts to use monetary policy to stabilize the economy will lead to systematic changes in the price level but will not influence the behavior of output.

Thus, according to the new classicists, monetary policy can do harm—by creating confusion about the source of price changes—but cannot do good except by random chance. Thus, even in the face of major recessions, laissez-faire is the best stabilization policy conceivable.

Let us review how this follows from combining the monetarist micro foundations with the theory of rational expectations.

1. According to the monetarists' micro foundations, deviations from full employment occur only because of errors in predicting the price level (which cause workers and firms to mistake changes in the price level for changes in relative prices).

2. According to the theory of rational expectations, errors in predicting the price level are only random.

3. It follows from (1) and (2) that there is no room for active government policy to stabilize the economy. The causes of fluctuations are random.[9] It is in the nature of random fluctuations that they cannot be foreseen and offset. Thus there is no room for stabilization policy to reduce the fluctuations in the economy by offsetting the disturbances that emanate from the private sector.

Not all monetarists accept the theory of rational expectations. For those who do, however, the contrast with the neo-Keynesians is extreme.

The most extreme monetarist attack on stabilization policy has two parts. The first is a model of an economy where deviations from full employment occur only because of errors. The second is a theory of people's expectations which predicts that persistent systematic errors—and hence systematic deviations from full employment—will not occur.

Monetarist Conclusions

The two monetarist schools obviously do not agree with each other on everything. Both agree, however, that monetary policy should not be used actively to stabilize the economy. This is for two reasons: (1) Fluctuations in the money supply are the major source of fluctuations in output and inflation; and (2) there is no long-term trade-off between inflation and national income.[10]

Most economists accept the view that monetary forces are very important in influencing inflation and unemployment, but many do not agree that monetary forces are the *most* important. Most economists also agree that inflation will tend to accelerate if income is held permanently above its full-employment level.

One aspect of the monetarist model that is particularly controversial is the belief in downward flexibility of prices, which leads to the prediction that as long as national income is below its full-employment level, the price level would *fall* at an ever-accelerating rate. Neo-Keynesians say that the observed downward inflexibility of the price level refutes this view. They reject the prediction that the main cause of GNP gaps is *voluntary* reductions in employment and output due to errors in reading the signals provided by the price system. Most neo-Keynesians do not believe that output deviates from its potential level only because workers and firms make mistakes.

Neo-Keynesian Micro Foundations

The neo-Keynesian micro foundations emphasize the noncompetitive nature of the economy: most firms are seen as setting their own prices rather than accepting those set on competitive markets. Their per unit output costs tend to be fairly constant, and they set prices by adding a relatively inflexible markup to their costs.[11] They then sell what they can at the going price. Cyclical fluctuations in aggregate demand cause cyclical fluctuations in the demand for each firm's products, which in turn cause individual firms to make cyclical variations in *output and employment* rather than in *price*.

While in the monetarist model fluctuations in aggregate demand have their impact mainly on prices, in the neo-Keynesian model their main impact is on output and employment.

A similar argument holds for labor markets in the neo-Keynesian model. Wages respond to the price level and productivity but are relatively in-

---

[9] Although because of long lags, macro variables may display cyclical fluctuations, as discussed in Chapter 31.

[10] Recall that any attempt to hold income above its full-employment level will lead not to a constant rate of inflation, but to a continuously accelerating inflation. This is just a restatement of the *acceleration* hypothesis and the *natural rate* hypothesis developed in detail in Chapter 36 and its appendix.

[11] Complete cyclical inflexibility of markup is not necessary. What matters is that firms do not adjust prices continually and as a result are willing to sell further units at the same price. This much price inflexibility need not imply an absence of profit maximization. Instead it may follow from profit maximization when it is costly to alter prices. This is discussed further in Chapter 14.

sensitive to short-term cyclical fluctuations in demand. (This is discussed in detail in Chapter 18).

This short-term wage inflexibility can stem from rational behavior on the part of workers. If wage rates adjust to clear labor markets, wages will vary over the cycle. *All* workers will then bear the uncertainty associated with the cyclical movements in wages. However, if wages are set in response to long-term considerations but do not vary cyclically so as to clear labor markets, cyclical fluctuations in demand will cause employment to fluctuate.

Since most layoffs and rehires are based on seniority, employment fluctuations are all borne by the 10 percent or 20 percent of workers who are least senior. The majority of workers will then have little uncertainty in the face of cyclical fluctuations in demand, all the uncertainty having been placed on the *minority* with low seniority. Thus contracts that fix wages over the cycle and allow employment to vary may be preferable to the majority of workers compared to contracts that allow wages to vary in order to clear the labor market continually and thus prevent unemployment.

In neo-Keynesian macroeconomics, the economy does not have a unique short-term equilibrium. Because firms would like to sell more and some workers would be willing to work more at current prices, fluctuations in aggregate demand cause output and employment to fluctuate in the short term.

The neo-Keynesian macro model allows for systematic disturbances that can cause prolonged GNP gaps.

According to the neo-Keynesians, stabilization policy can then be used to offset at least those gaps that are large and persistent.

Such policies seek to alter aggregate demand using both fiscal and monetary tools.

Differences Between the Two Models

There are many differences in the micro behavior that underlies the two models. Probably the most important relates to the distinction between voluntary and involuntary unemployment.

In the monetarist model all unemployment and output below capacity is voluntary. Workers decide

to be unemployed, and firms decide to produce less than capacity output as a result of errors they make in predicting the general price level (and therefore the relative price of what they sell). So if surveyed, the millions of unemployed around the world in the early 1980s would have said that they could have had a job at the going wage but they refused to accept it because, given their expectations about inflation, the expected real wage was too low.

In the neo-Keynesian model, prices and wages do not fluctuate to clear markets. Unemployment and production below capacity are involuntary in the sense that unemployed workers would like jobs at the going wage rate but cannot find them, and firms would like to sell more at going prices but customers are not forthcoming.[12] So if surveyed, the millions of unemployed around the world in the early 1980s would have said that they would have accepted a job at the going wage rate but that none were available.

Major current debate centers around these two prototype models and some of their subtler offshoots. Issues such as what determines the degree of wage and price flexibility in the economy, the conditions under which it can be expected that people can form accurate expectations and act on them, and the potential for destabilizing the economy by pursuing an active stabilization policy are at the forefront of modern research. Views on how the economy behaves both at the micro and macro level will be influenced by the progress of the debate. So will views on the place of fiscal and monetary policy as possible ways to eliminate inflationary or recessionary gaps.

CONCLUSION

The Progress of Economics

In this chapter we have discussed a number of controversies about the behavior of the economy and the evidence now available that relates to them.

---

[12] Of course, one could still argue that this unemployment is voluntary because the workers had earlier voluntarily agreed to the contracts.

General acceptance of the view that the validity of economic theories should be tested by confronting their predictions with the mass of all available evidence is fairly new in economics. At this point you might reread the quotation from Lord William Beveridge given on page xxx. The controversy Beveridge describes was the one that followed the 1936 publication of Keynes' *The General Theory of Employment, Interest and Money.* Keynes' work gave rise to the macroeconomic theory discussed in Part Eight and used so often in subsequent sections of this text. The relation of various aspects of macroeconomic theory to evidence has been raised at many points in this book: You might reflect on how very different this approach to the problem of accepting or rejecting theories is from the approach described by Beveridge.

Since 1936 great progress has been made in economics in relating theory to evidence. This progress has been reflected in the superior ability of governments to achieve their policy objectives. The financial aspects of World War II were far better handled than those of World War I. When President Roosevelt tried to reduce unemployment in the United States in the 1930s, his efforts were greatly hampered by the failure even of economists to realize the critical importance of budget deficits in raising aggregate demand and in injecting money into the economy. When the Vietnam war forced the U.S. government to adopt expansive fiscal and monetary policies, economists had no trouble in predicting the outcome: More involvement abroad was obtained at the cost of heavy inflationary pressure at home.

Theories are generally tested in such important policy areas as the running of wars, the curing of major depressions, and coping with inflations, even if all their specific predictions are not. In some sense, then, economic theories have always been subjected to empirical tests. When they were wildly at variance with the facts, the ensuing disaster could not but be noticed, and the theories were discarded or amended in the light of what was learned. Our current inability to avoid the twin problems of inflation and unemployment is a case in point—and it is leading to intensive new research.

The advances of economics in the last 50 years reflect economists' changed attitudes toward empirical observations. Today economists are much less likely to dismiss theories just because they do not like them and to refuse to abandon theories just because they do like them. Economists are more likely to try to base their theories as much as possible on empirical observation and to accept empirical relevance as the ultimate arbiter of the value of theories.

As human beings, we may be anguished at the upsetting of a pet theory; as scientists, we should try to train ourselves to take pleasure in it because of the new knowledge gained thereby. It has been said that one of the great tragedies of science is the continual slaying of beautiful theories by ugly facts. It must always be remembered that when theory and fact come into conflict, it is theory, not fact, that must give way.

SUMMARY

1. Macroeconomic performance is judged in terms of the behavior of many variables. The key variables are (a) output, employment, and unemployment, (b) the rate of change of the price level, and (c) long-term growth.

2. Views about the role of policy in improving macroeconomic performance range between two extremes. The *conservative* view is that there is only a very minimum role for policy; macroeconomic performance will be most satisfactory when the market system is allowed to function as freely as possible. The *interventionist* view is that active use of policy will improve macroeconomic performance. It is common to identify monetarists with conservatives and Keynesians with interventionists.

3. Monetarists believe that because the economy is inherently stable, the goal of damping the business cycle is best achieved by avoiding fluctuations in policy, especially monetary policy. Hence they advocate a *k* percent rule. Keynesians believe that the economy is inherently unstable because expenditure functions shift substantially and the economy's self-corrective mechanisms are weak. Hence they believe in an active role for both monetary and fiscal policy to moderate the business cycle.

4. Monetarists believe that inflation is everywhere and always a monetary phenomenon and so advocate the same conservative policies to avoid price instability as they advocated to minimize policy-induced cycles in output. They also argue that in order to control inflation, the long-term growth rate of the money supply must not be too high. Neo-Keynesians accept the view that monetary expansion is necessary for inflation to persist in the long term, but they take seriously the role of other factors in causing short-term but substantial inflation. Hence they believe in an active role for policy in offsetting these factors in the short term.

5. Conservatives believe that long-term growth will be maximized when the incentives provided by the profit motive are strongest. Interventionists see a need for special government programs to channel resources into research and development and other investment expenditures designed to raise potential output.

6. Conservatives see a role for policy in terms of providing a stable environment for individual decision makers. This involves maintaining a consistent set of "fiscal rules of the game" in terms of expenditure and tax rates and providing a steady but gradual growth in the money supply.

7. Interventionists have specific prescriptions for each policy variable. They advocate active use of discretionary monetary and fiscal policy to stabilize output and employment. Despite imperfections caused by lags and incomplete knowledge, they believe such policies are helpful. Similar policies can be combined with incomes policies to stabilize the fluctuations in the price level that arise from various sources and are subject to an upward bias. They also support policies to promote growth through subsidization, tax favors, and more specific intervention.

8. Monetarists view markets as competitive and hence believe that departures from full-employ-

ment equilibrium are quickly rectified. As a result, they believe that fluctuations in aggregate demand lead primarily to fluctuations in the price level rather than in the level of output. They believe that the best course for monetary policy is to follow a k percent rule. For traditional monetarists, this is because they believe that long and variable lags in the effect of monetary policy means that an interventionist monetary policy would destabilize output.

9. New classical monetarists believe that departures from full-employment output occur only when people make mistakes in predicting the price level. When combined with the theory of rational expectations, this leads to the policy invariance proposition. As a result, new classical monetarists support the k percent rule because they believe an interventionist monetary policy will not be effective in stabilizing output.

10. Neo-Keynesians emphasize the noncompetitive nature of the economy. As a result, they believe that fluctuations in aggregate demand lead primarily to fluctuations in output rather than in the price level. In this view, an interventionist stabilization policy can be effective in stabilizing fluctuations in output.

TOPICS FOR REVIEW

Conservatives and interventionists
Monetarists and neo-Keynesians
Macroeconomic performance
Setting a stable environment
The k percent rule
Fine tuning
Rational expectations
Lucas aggregate supply curve
Policy invariance proposition

DISCUSSION QUESTIONS

1. To what extent is today's unemployment a serious social problem? If people could vote to choose between 10 percent unemployment combined with zero inflation and 2

percent unemployment combined with 10 percent inflation, which alternative do you think would win? Which groups might prefer the first alternative and which groups the second?

2. It is often argued that the true unemployment figure for Canada is much higher than the officially reported figure. What are possible sources of "hidden unemployment"? On the other side, are there reasons for expecting some exaggeration of the number of people reported as unemployed? Would the relative strength of these opposing forces change over the course of the business cycle? What would you expect if a short recession turned into a long and deep depression?

3. In its 1979 Report the Joint Economic Committee of the U.S. Congress urged the administration to fight inflation and combat unemployment by encouraging private-sector saving and investment. How might expanded saving and investment help to reduce inflation and/or combat unemployment?

4. Neo-Keynesian and Nobel Laureate Paul Samuelson recently quoted a "conservative economist friend" as saying in mid 1980: "If you're contriving a teensy-weensy recession for us, please don't bother. It won't do the job. What's needed is a believable declaration that Washington will countenance *whatever* degree of unemployment is needed to bring us back on the path to price stability, and a demonstrated willingness to *stick* to that resolution no matter

how politically unpopular the short-run joblessness, production cutbacks, and dips in profit might be." Discuss the "conservative friend's" view of inflation. Does experience since 1980 suggest that his advice was followed? If so, what was the consequence?

5. In 1979 in Britain, the newly elected conservative government of Prime Minister Margaret Thatcher embraced the monetarist view of inflation and decided to follow the advice of Professor Samuelson's "conservative friend" quoted in the previous question. Check unemployment and inflation rates and money supply figures in Britain since 1977 to see if she stuck to the advice and if the inflation rate did moderate. How did Mrs. Thatcher's policies compare to those adopted by the Reagan administration in 1980?

6. A recent ad in the *New York Times* had this to say about inflation. "First [our politicians] blamed wage increases and price hikes for inflation. Then when 'voluntary guidelines' were established, the blame shifted to OPEC oil prices. Both explanations were wrong. Government policy is responsible for inflation—paying for deficit spending by 'creating money out of thin air.'" What theories of inflation are rejected and accepted by the writers of this ad?

7. At a time when the Canadian unemployment rate stood at close to 10 percent, the press reported: "Skilled labor shortage plagues many firms—newspaper ads often draw few qualified workers; wages over time are up." What type of unemployment does this suggest to be important?

APPENDIXES

MORE ON FUNCTIONAL RELATIONS AND GRAPHS
APPENDIX TO CHAPTER 2

Functional Relations:
The General Expression of
Relations Among Variables

The idea of relations among variables is one of the basic notions behind all science. Such relations can be expressed as functional relations.

Consider two examples, one from a natural science and one from economics. The gravitational attraction of two bodies depends on their mass and on the distance separating them, attraction increas-

ing with size and diminishing with distance; the amount of a commodity that people would like to buy depends on (among other things) the price of the commodity, purchases increasing as price falls. When mathematicians wish to say that one variable depends on another, they say that one variable is a function of the other. [50][1] Thus gravitational attraction is a function of the mass of the two bodies

[1] Reference numbers in color refer to Mathematical Notes, which begin on page M-1.

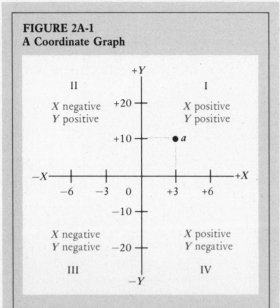

FIGURE 2A-1
A Coordinate Graph

The axes divide the total space into four quadrants according to the signs of the variables. In the upper right-hand quadrant, both X and Y are greater than zero; this is usually called the *positive quadrant*. Point a has *coordinates* $Y = 10$ and $X = 3$ in the coordinate graph. These coordinates *define* point a.

esis and is read "gravitational attraction is a function of the mass of the two bodies concerned and the distance between them." The same hypothesis can be written as

$$G = G(M,d)$$

This is read in exactly the same way and means the same thing as the previous expression. Instead of using f to represent "a function of," the left-hand symbol, G, is repeated.[2]

The hypothesis about desired purchases and price can be written

$$q = f(p)$$

or

$$q = q(p)$$

where q stands for the quantity people wish to purchase of some commodity and p is the price of the commodity. The expression says that the quantity of some commodity that people desire to purchase is a function of its price. The alternative way of writing this merely uses different letters to stand for the same functional relation between p and q.

Functional Forms: Precise Relations Among Variables

The expression $Y = Y(X)$ merely states that the variables Y and X are related; it says nothing about the form that this relation takes. Usually the hypothesis to be expressed says more than that. Does Y increase as X increases? Does Y decrease as X increases? Or is the relation more complicated? Take a very simple example, where Y is the length of a board in feet, and X is the length of the same board in yards. Quite clearly, $Y = Y(X)$. Further, in this case the exact form of the function is known, for length in feet (Y) is merely three times the length in yards (X), so we may write $Y = 3X$.

This relation is a definitional one, for the length

concerned and the distance between them, and the quantity of a product demanded is a function of the price of the product.

One of the virtues of mathematics is that it permits the concise expression of ideas that would otherwise require long, drawn-out verbal statements. There are two steps in giving compact symbolic expression to functional relations. First, each variable is given a symbol. Second, a symbol is designated to express the idea of one variable's dependence on another. Thus, if G equals gravitational attraction, M equals the mass of two bodies, and d equals the distance between the two bodies, we may write

$$G = f(M, d)$$

where f is read "is a function of" and means "depends on." The whole equation defines a hypoth-

[2] Any convenient symbol may be used on the right-hand side before the parenthesis to mean "a function of." The repetition of the left-hand symbol may be convenient in reminding us of what is a function of what.

of something measured in feet is defined to be three times its length measured in yards. It is nonetheless useful to have a way of writing relationships that are definitionally true. The expression $Y = 3X$ specifies the exact form of the relation between Y and X and provides a rule whereby, if we have the value of either one, we can calculate the value of the other.

Now consider a second example: Let C stand for consumption expenditure, the total amount spent on purchasing goods and services by all Canadian households during a year. Let Y_d stand for the total amount of income that these households had available to spend during the year. We might state the hypothesis that

$C = f(Y_d)$

and, even more specifically,

$C = 0.8Y_d$

The first expression gives the hypothesis that the total consumption expenditure of households depends on their income. The second expression says, more specifically, that total consumption expenditure is 80 percent of the total available for spending. The second equation expresses a very specific hypothesis about the relation between two observable magnitudes. There is no reason why it *must* be true; it may be consistent or inconsistent with the facts. This is a matter for testing. However, the equation is a concise statement of a particular hypothesis.

Thus the general view that there is a relation between Y and X is denoted by $Y = f(X)$, whereas any precise relation may be expressed by a particular equation such as $Y = 2X$, $Y = 4X^2$, or $Y = X + 2X^2 + 0.5X^3$.

If Y increases as X increases (e.g., $Y = 10 + 2X$), we say that Y is an *increasing function* of X, or that Y and X *vary positively* with each other. If Y decreases as X increases (e.g., $Y = 10 - 2X$), we say that Y is a *decreasing function of X* or that Y and X *vary negatively* with each other. Y varying negatively with X merely means that Y changes in the opposite direction from X.

Error Terms in Economic Hypotheses

Expressing hypotheses in the form of functions is misleading in one respect. When we say that the world behaves so that $Y = f(X)$, we do not expect that knowing X will tell us *exactly* what Y will be, but only that it will tell us what Y will be *within some margin of error*.

This error in predicting Y from a knowledge of X arises for two quite distinct reasons. First, there may be other variables that also affect Y. When, for example, we say that the demand for butter is a function of the price of butter, $D_b = f(p_b)$, we know that other factors will also influence this demand. A change in the price of margarine will certainly affect the demand for butter, even though the price of butter does not change. Thus, we do not expect to find a perfect relation between D_b and p_b that will allow us to predict D_b exactly from a knowledge of p_b. Second, variables can never be measured exactly. Even if X is the only cause of Y, measurements will give various Ys corresponding to the same X. In the case of the demand for butter, errors of measurement might not be large. In other cases, errors might be substantial—as, for example, in the case of a relation between the total consumption expenditure of all Canadian households and their total income. The measurements of consumption and income may be subject to quite wide margins of error, and various values of consumption associated with the same measured value of income may be observed, not because consumption is varying independently of income but because the error of measurement is varying from period to period.

When we say Y is a function of X, we appear to say Y is completely determined by X. Instead of the deterministic formulation

$Y = f(X)$

it would be more accurate to write

$Y = f(X, \epsilon)$

where ϵ, the Greek letter epsilon, represents an

error term.[3] Such a term indicates that the observed value of Y will differ from the value predicted by the functional relation between Y and X. Divergences will occur both because of observational errors and because of neglected variables. While economists always mean this, they usually do not say so.

The deterministic formulation is a simplification; an error term is really present in all assumed and observed functional relations.

This is true, by the way, not only for economics and other subjects dealing with human behavior, but for physics, chemistry, geology, and all other sciences. The old-time dichotomy between "exact" and "inexact" sciences is now abandoned; all theories and all measurements are subject to error.

Use of Graphs in Economic Analysis

The popular saying "The facts speak for themselves" is almost always wrong when there are many facts. Theories are needed to explain how facts are linked together, and summary measures are needed to assist in sorting out what it is that facts show in relation to theories. The simplest means of providing compact summaries of a large number of observations is through the use of tables and graphs. Graphs play important roles in economics by representing geometrically both observed data and economic theories.

Because the surface of a piece of paper is two-dimensional, a graph may readily be used to represent pictorially the interrelation between two variables. Flip through this book and you will see dozens of examples. Figure 2A-1 shows generally how a coordinate grid can permit the representation of any two measurable variables.[4]

---

[3] The relationship with the error term in it is frequently written $Y = f(X) + \epsilon$.

[4] Economics is very often concerned only with the positive values of variables, and in such cases the graph is confined to the upper right-hand (or "positive") quadrant. Whenever either or both variables take on a negative value, one or more of the other quadrants must be included.

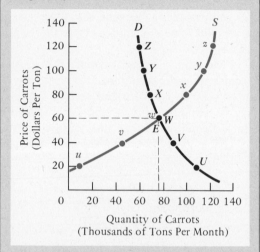

FIGURE 2A-2
Two Different Relationships Between the Price of Carrots and the Quantity of Carrots, Shown Graphically

A two-dimensional graph can show how two variables are related. The two variables, the price of carrots and their quantity, are here shown in two different relationships. The downward-sloping black curve is a demand curve; the upward-sloping colored curve is a supply curve. The intersection of the two curves at point E shows the only value of the variables that satisfies both the relationship shown in the demand curve and that shown in the supply curve.

Representing Theories on Graphs

Figure 2A-2 shows a simple two-variable graph, which will be analyzed in detail in Chapter 4. (Indeed, the figure is a somewhat simplified version of the one that appears on page 58 as Figure 4-7.) For now it is sufficient to notice that the graph permits us to show the relationship between two variables, the *price* of carrots on the vertical axis and the *quantity* of carrots per month on the horizontal axis.[5] The curve actually shows two different relationships. The dark black downward-sloping curve labeled D (which we will call a *demand curve*)

---

[5] The choice of which variable to put on which axis is discussed in footnote 3 on page 76 and in [7] on page M-3.

FIGURE 2A-3
The Theory That Price Is Determined by the Intersection of Supply and Demand Curves, Shown Graphically

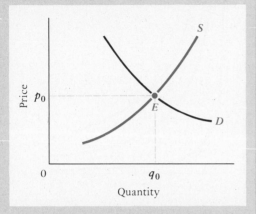

Graphs can illustrate relationships between theoretical variables as well as between specific quantities. Here, in contrast to Figure 2A-2, price and quantity are shown as general variables. The demand curve illustrates an unspecified *negative* relationship between price and quantity, the supply curve an unspecified *positive* relationship between the same two variables. Point E where they cross is the unique point at which both relationships are satisfied. A theory stipulating that both D and S must be satisfied simultaneously leads to the conclusion that price will be p_0 and quantity q_0.

shows the relationship between the price of carrots and the quantity of carrots buyers wish to purchase. The dark colored upward-sloping curve labeled S (which we will call a *supply curve*) shows the relationship between the price of carrots and the quantity of carrots producers wish to sell.

Suppose now that we have a theory that says, "Price will tend to the level at which the quantity buyers wish to purchase equals the quantity producers wish to sell." This is illustrated in Figure 2A-2, and the conclusion is reached that the price will be $60, for that is the only price at which the two quantities are equal. Do not be concerned about the argument now; it will be considered in Chapter 4. But notice that the theory has been displayed using a simple, two-dimensional graph.

Figure 2A-3 is very much like Figure 2A-2, but with one difference. It generalizes from the specific example of carrots to an unspecified commodity and focuses on the intersection of the two curves rather than on specific numerical values. Figure 2A-3 too illustrates the theory that says: "Price will tend to the level at which the quantity buyers wish to purchase equals the quantity producers wish to sell." Now, however, that quantity is labeled q_0 and the resulting price p_0, rather than being given numerical values.

Graphing Three Variables in Two Dimensions

Often we want to show graphically more than two dimensions. For example, a topographic map

FIGURE 2A-4
A Contour Map of a Small Mountain

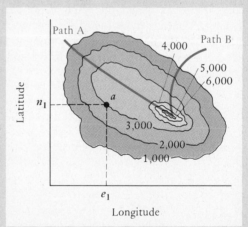

A contour map shows three variables in two-dimensional space. This is a familiar kind of three-variable graph, with latitude and longitude shown on the axes and altitude on the contour lines. The contour line labeled 1,000 connects all locations with an altitude of 1,000 feet, that labeled 2,000 connects those with an altitude of 2,000 feet, and so forth. Point a, for example, has a latitude n_1, a longitude e_1, and an altitude of 3,000 feet. Where the lines are closely bunched, they represent a steep ascent; where they are far apart, a gradual one. Clearly Path A is a gentler climb from 3,000 to 4,000 feet on this mountain than Path B.

seeks to show latitude, longitude, and altitude on a two-dimensional page. This is done by using contour lines, as is shown in Figure 2A-4. Now let us consider the function $XY = a$, where X, Y, and a are all variables. Now look at Figure 2A-5, which plots this function for three different values of a. The variables X and Y are represented on the two axes. The variable a is represented by the labels on the curves. Several examples of this kind of procedure occur throughout the book. (See, for example, the discussion of indifference curves in Chapter 17 and isoquants in Chapter 11.)

Straight Lines and Their Slopes

Figure 2A-6 illustrates a variety of straight lines. They differ according to their slopes. **Slope** is defined as the ratio of the vertical change to the corresponding horizontal change as one moves to the right.

The symbol Δ is used to indicate a change in variable. Thus ΔX means the value of the change in X, and ΔY means the value of the change in Y. The ratio $\Delta Y/\Delta X$ is the slope of a straight line. Where both increase, the ratio is positive and the

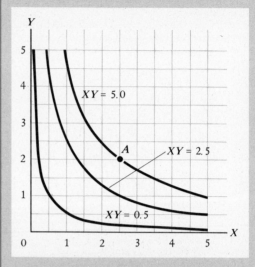

FIGURE 2A-5
Three Variables Shown in Two Dimensions

This chart illustrates examples of the three-variable function $XY = a$. The function $XY = a$ is called a *rectangular hyperbola* and has a different value for every combination of its three variables X, Y, and a. The figure shows three members of the family. For example, the point A represents $Y = 2$, $X = 2.5$, and $a = 5.0$.

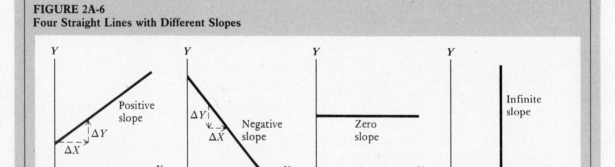

FIGURE 2A-6
Four Straight Lines with Different Slopes

The slope of a straight line is constant but can vary from one line to another. The direction of slope of a straight line is characterized by the signs of the ratio $\Delta Y/\Delta X$. In (i) that ratio is positive because Y increases as X increases; in (ii) the ratio is negative because Y decreases as X increases; in (iii) it is zero because Y does not change as X increases; in (iv) it is said to be infinite because X does not change.

FIGURE 2A-7
Two Straight Lines with Different Slopes

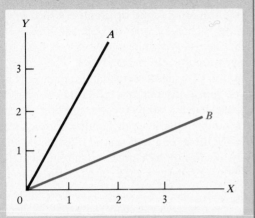

Slope is a quantitative measure. Both lines have positive slopes and thus are similar to Figure 2A-6 (i). But the black curve *A* is steeper (i.e., has a greater slope) than the colored curve *B*. For each 1-unit change in *X*, curve *A* increases its *Y* value by 2 units, whereas curve *B* increases its *Y* value by only 1/2 unit. The ratio $\Delta Y/\Delta X$ is 2 for curve *A* and 1/2 for curve *B*.

line is upward-sloping, as in (i). Where ΔY decreases as ΔX increases, the ratio is negative and the line is downward-sloping, as in (ii). Where ΔY does not change (iii), the line is horizontal and the slope is zero. Where ΔX is zero (iv), the line is vertical, and the slope is often said to be infinite although the ratio $\Delta Y/\Delta X$ is indeterminate. [51]

Slope is a quantitative measure, not merely a qualitative one. For example, in Figure 2A-7 two upward-sloping straight lines have different slopes. The black one has a slope of 2, $\left(\dfrac{\Delta Y}{\Delta X} = 2 \right)$, the colored one has a slope of 1/2, $\left(\dfrac{\Delta Y}{\Delta X} = 0.5 \right)$.

Curved Lines and Their Slopes

Figure 2A-8 shows four curved lines. The line in (i) is plainly upward-sloping, and in (ii) downward-sloping. The other two shift from one to the other, as the labels indicate. Unlike straight lines, whose slope is the same at every point on the line, the slope of a curve changes. The slope of a curve must be measured at a particular point and is de-

FIGURE 2A-8
Four Curved Lines

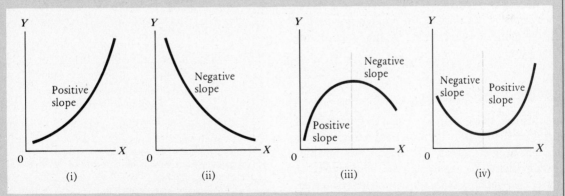

The slope of a curved line is not constant and may change direction. The curves shown in (i) and (ii) have slopes that change in size but not direction, whereas those in (iii) and (iv) change in both size and direction. Unlike

that of a straight line, the slope of a curved line cannot be defined by a single number because it changes as the value of *X* changes.

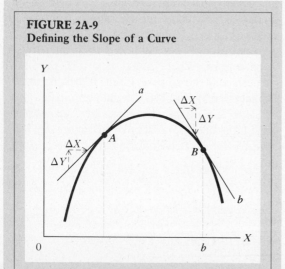

FIGURE 2A-9
Defining the Slope of a Curve

The slope of a curve at any point on that curve is defined by the slope of the straight line that is tangent to the curve at that point. The slope of the curve at point *A* is defined by the slope of the line *a*, which is tangent to the curve at that point. The slope of the curve at point *B* is defined by the slope of the line *b*.

The Scatter Diagram

One important type of graph is called a *scatter diagram*. Values of one variable are measured on the horizontal axis while values of a second variable are measured on the vertical axis. The scatter diagram thus provides a method of graphing any number of *paired* observations made on two variables. Suppose data for family income and beef purchases for a sample of Canadian families were collected. To show these data on a scatter diagram, in Figure 2A-10 income is measured on the horizontal axis and beef purchases on the vertical axis. Any point

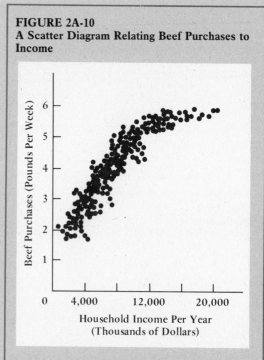

FIGURE 2A-10
A Scatter Diagram Relating Beef Purchases to Income

The scatter pattern shows a clear tendency for beef consumption to rise with income. Household income is measured along the horizontal axis and purchases of beef along the vertical axis. Each dot represents the beef purchases of one household. The dots fall within a narrow, rising band, suggesting the existence of a systematic relationship. (There are 4,827 observations in the original sample, but only a sample of these is shown in the figure because a scatter diagram with 4,827 points would be unintelligible.)

fined as the slope of a straight line that just touches (is *tangent* to) the straight line at that point. This is illustrated in Figure 2A-9. The slope at point *A* is measured by the slope of the tangent line *a*. The slope at point *B* is measured by the slope of the tangent line *b*.

Graphing Observations

A coordinate space such as shown in Figure 2A-1 can be used to graph the observed values of two variables as well as the theoretical relationships between them. For example, the black curve in Figure 2A-2 labeled *D* might have arisen as a free-hand line drawn to generalize actual observations of the points labeled *U*, *V*, *W*, *X*, *Y*, *Z*. While that graph was not constructed from actual observations, many graphs are. Two of the most important kinds are called *scatter diagrams* and *time series graphs*.

in the diagram represents a particular family's income combined with the beef purchases of that family. Thus each family for which there are observations can be represented on the diagram by a dot, the coordinates of which indicate the family's income and the amount of beef it purchased in 1979.

The scatter diagram is useful because if there is a simple relation between the two variables, it will be apparent to the eye once the data are plotted. The scatter diagram in Figure 2A-10, for example, made it apparent that more beef tends to be purchased as income rises. It also made it apparent that the relation between taxes and income is not exactly linear. As income rises above $10,000 a year, beef purchases tend to rise less and less with each successive equal increase in income.

The diagram also gives some idea of the strength of the relation: If income were the only determinant of beef purchased, all the dots would cluster closely around a line or a smooth curve; as it is, the points are somewhat scattered and particular incomes are often represented by several households, each with different amounts of beef purchased.

The data used in this example are **cross-sectional data.** The incomes and beef purchases of different households are compared over a single period of time—the year 1979.

Scatter diagrams may also be drawn of a number of observations taken on two variables at successive periods of time. Thus, if one wanted to know whether there was any simple relation between personal income and personal consumption in Canada between 1950 and 1983, data would be collected for the levels of personal income and expenditure per capita in each year from 1950 to 1983, as is done in Table 2A-1. This information could be plotted on a scatter diagram, with income on the X axis and consumption on the Y axis, to discover any systematic relation between the two variables. The data are plotted in Figure 2A-11, and they do indeed suggest a systematic linear relation. In this exercise a scatter diagram of observations taken over successive periods of time has been used. Such data are called **time-series data,** and plotting them on a scatter diagram involves no new technique.

When cross-sectional data are plotted, each point gives the values of two variables for a particular unit (say, a family); when time-series data are plotted, each point tells the values of two variables for a particular year.

Time-Series Graphs

Instead of studying the relation between income and consumption suggested in the previous para-

TABLE 2A–1 INCOME AND CONSUMPTION, 1950–1983 (1971 Dollars)

Year	Disposable personal income per capita	Personal consumption expenditures per capita
1950	$1,583	$1,487
1951	1,635	1,467
1952	1,696	1,520
1953	1,735	1,584
1954	1,682	1,594
1955	1,771	1,685
1956	1,877	1,769
1957	1,878	1,776
1958	1,905	1,789
1959	1,925	1,845
1960	1,949	1,869
1961	1,921	1,851
1962	2,030	1,898
1963	2,084	1,954
1964	2,141	2,033
1965	2,262	2,118
1966	2,365	2,187
1967	2,427	2,251
1968	2,491	2,325
1969	2,571	2,398
1970	2,596	2,419
1971	2,779	2,579
1972	3,001	2,742
1973	3,233	2,891
1974	3,406	3,001
1975	3,555	3,105
1976	3,704	3,250
1977	3,761	3,324
1978	3,858	3,387
1979	3,927	3,439
1980	4,001	3,408
1981	4,131	3,422
1982	4,037	3,312
1983	3,977	3,375

Source: Statistics Canada, 13-531, 13-201.

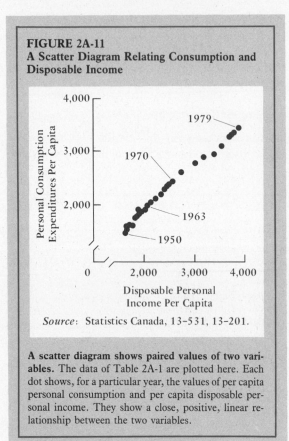

FIGURE 2A-11
A Scatter Diagram Relating Consumption and Disposable Income

Source: Statistics Canada, 13-531, 13-201.

A scatter diagram shows paired values of two variables. The data of Table 2A-1 are plotted here. Each dot shows, for a particular year, the values of per capita personal consumption and per capita disposable personal income. They show a close, positive, linear relationship between the two variables.

considered has varied in a systematic way over the years or if its behavior has been more or less erratic.

Ratio (Logarithmic) Scales

The graphs above have all used axes that plotted numbers on a natural arithmetic scale, with distances between two values shown by the size of numerical difference. If *proportionate* rather than absolute changes in variables are important, it is more revealing to use a ratio scale rather than a natural scale. On a **natural scale,** the distance between numbers is proportionate to the absolute difference between those numbers. Thus 200 is placed halfway between 100 and 300. On a **ratio scale,** the distance between numbers is proportionate to the absolute difference between their loga-

graph, a study of the pattern of the changes in either one of these variables over time could be made. In Figure 2A-12 this information is shown for consumption. In the figure, time is one variable, consumption expenditure the other. But time is a very special variable: The order in which successive events happen is important. The year 1965 followed 1964; they were not two independent and unrelated years. (In contrast, two randomly selected households are independent and unrelated.) For this reason it is customary to draw in the line segments connecting the successive points, as has been done in Figure 2A-12.

A chart such as this figure is called a *time-series graph* or, more simply, a *time series*. This kind of graph makes it easy to see if the variable being

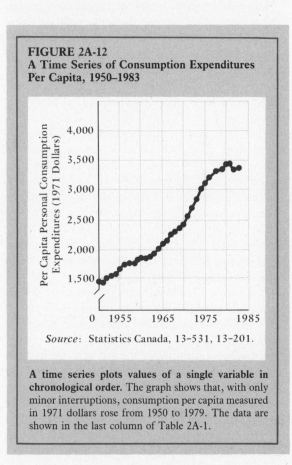

FIGURE 2A-12
A Time Series of Consumption Expenditures Per Capita, 1950–1983

Source: Statistics Canada, 13-531, 13-201.

A time series plots values of a single variable in chronological order. The graph shows that, with only minor interruptions, consumption per capita measured in 1971 dollars rose from 1950 to 1979. The data are shown in the last column of Table 2A-1.

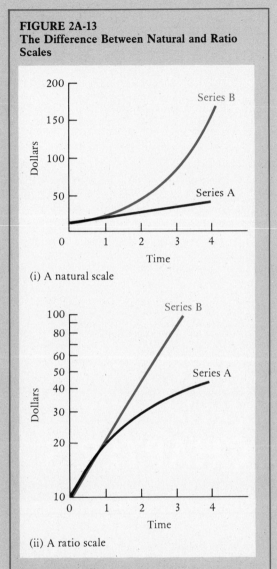

FIGURE 2A-13
The Difference Between Natural and Ratio Scales

(i) A natural scale

(ii) A ratio scale

On a natural scale, equal distances represent equal amounts; on a ratio scale, equal vertical distances represent equal percentage changes. The two series in Table 2A-2 are plotted in each chart. Series A, which grows at a constant absolute amount, produces a straight line on a natural scale but a downward-bending curve on a ratio scale because the same absolute growth decreases percentage growth. Series B, which grows at a rising absolute rate but a constant percentage rate, is upward-bending on a natural scale but is a straight line on a ratio scale.

TABLE 2A-2   TWO SERIES

Time period	Series A	Series B
0	$10	$ 10
1	18	20
2	26	40
3	34	80
4	42	160

Series A shows constant absolute growth ($8 per period) but declining percentage growth. Series B shows constant percentage growth (100 percent per period) but rising absolute growth.

rithms. Equal distances anywhere on a ratio scale represent equal percentage changes rather than equal absolute changes. On a ratio scale the distance between 100 and 200 is the same as the distance between 200 and 400, between 1,000 and 2,000, and between any two numbers that stand in the ratio 1:2 to each other. For obvious reasons a ratio scale is also called a **logarithmic scale.**

Table 2A-2 shows two series, one growing at a constant absolute amount of eight units per period and the other growing at a constant rate of 100 percent per period. In Figure 2A-13 the series are plotted first on a natural scale, then on a ratio scale. The natural scale makes it easy for the eye to judge absolute variations, and the logarithmic scale makes it easy for the eye to judge proportionate variations.[6]

---

[6] Graphs with a ratio scale on one axis and a natural scale on the other are frequently encountered in economics. In the cases just illustrated there is a ratio scale on the vertical axis and a natural scale on the horizontal (or time) axis. Such graphs are often called *semi-log* graphs. In scientific work graphs with ratio scales on both axes are frequently encountered. Such graphs are often referred to as *double-log* graphs.

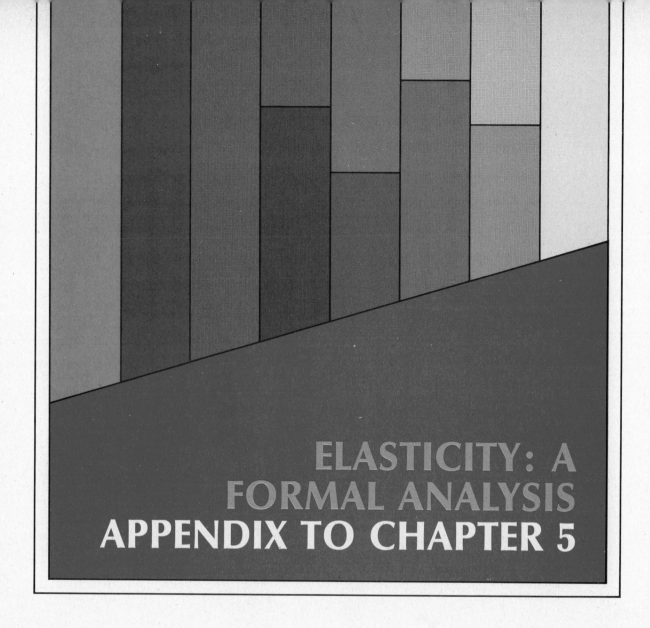

ELASTICITY: A FORMAL ANALYSIS
APPENDIX TO CHAPTER 5

The verbal definition of elasticity used in the text may be written symbolically in the following form:

$$\eta = \frac{\Delta q}{\Delta p} \times \frac{\text{average } p}{\text{average } q}$$

arc elasticity

where the averages are over the arc of the demand curve being considered. This is called **arc elasticity,** and it measures the average responsiveness of quantity to price over an interval of the demand curve.

Most theoretical treatments use a different but related concept called **point elasticity.** This is the responsiveness of quantity to price at a particular point on the demand curve. The precise definition of point elasticity uses the concept of a derivative, which is drawn from differential calculus.

In this appendix we first study an approximation to point elasticity that uses high school algebra. Then we will replace this approximate definition with the exact definition.

Before proceeding, we should notice one further

change. In the chapter text we multiplied all our calculations of demand elasticities by -1, thereby defining elasticity of demand as a positive number. In theoretical work it is more convenient to retain the concept's natural sign. Thus normal demand curves will have negative signs, and statements about "more" or "less" elastic must be understood to refer to the absolute, not the algebraic value of demand elasticity.

The following symbols will be used throughout.

$\eta \equiv$ elasticity of demand
$\eta_s \equiv$ elasticity of supply
$q \equiv$ the original quantity
$\Delta q \equiv$ the change in quantity
$p \equiv$ the original price
$\Delta p \equiv$ the change in price

Point Elasticity According to the Approximate Definition

Point elasticity measures elasticity at some point (p,q). In the approximate definition, however, the responsiveness is measured over a small range starting from that point. For example, in Figure 5A-1

FIGURE 5A-1
A Straight-Line Demand Curve

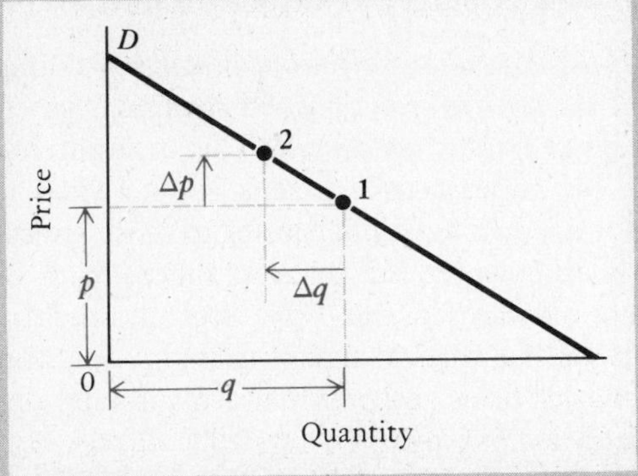

Because p/q varies with $\Delta q/\Delta p$ constant, the elasticity varies along this demand curve, being high at the left and low at the right.

the elasticity at point 1 can be measured by the responsiveness of quantity demanded to a change in price that takes price and quantity from point 1 to point 2. The algebraic formula for this elasticity concept is

$$\eta = \frac{\Delta q}{\Delta p} \times \frac{p}{q} \qquad \text{point elasticity} \qquad [1]$$

This is similar to the definition of arc elasticity used in the text except that since elasticity is being measured at a point, the p and q corresponding to that point are used (rather than the average p and q over an arc of the curve).

Equation [1] splits elasticity into two parts: $\Delta q/\Delta p$, the ratio of the change in quantity to the change in price, which is related to the *slope* of the demand curve, and p/q, which is related to the *point* on the curve at which the measurement is made.

Figure 5A-1 shows a straight-line demand curve. To measure the elasticity at point 1, take p and q at that point and then consider a price change, say, to point 2, and measure Δp and Δq as indicated. The slope of the straight line joining points 1 and 2 is $\Delta p/\Delta q$. The term in Equation [1] is $\Delta q/\Delta p$, which is the reciprocal of $\Delta p/\Delta q$. Therefore the first term in the elasticity formula is the reciprocal of the slope of the straight line joining the two price-quantity positions under consideration.

Although point elasticity of demand refers to a point (p,q) on the demand curve, the first term in Equation [1] still refers to changes over an arc of the curve. This is the part of the formula that involves approximation and, as we shall see, it has some unsatisfactory results. Nonetheless some interesting results can be derived using this formula as long as we confine ourselves to straight-line demand and supply curves.

1. *The elasticity of a downward-sloping straight-line demand curve varies from zero at the quantity axis to infinity* (∞) *at the price axis.* First notice that a straight line has a constant slope, so the ratio $\Delta p/\Delta q$ is the same everywhere on the line. Therefore its reciprocal, $\Delta q/\Delta p$, must also be constant. The changes in η can now be inferred by inspecting the ratio p/q. Where the line cuts the quantity axis,

price is zero, so the ratio p/q is zero; thus $\eta = 0$. Moving up the line, p rises and q falls, so the ratio p/q rises; thus elasticity rises. Approaching the top of the line, q approaches zero, so the ratio becomes very large. Thus elasticity increases without limit as the price axis is approached.

2. *Where there are two straight-line demand curves of the same slope, the one farther from the origin is less elastic at each price than the one closer to the origin.* Figure 5A-2 shows two parallel straight-line demand curves. Pick any price, say, p_0, and compare the elasticities of the two curves at that price. Since the curves are parallel, the ratio $\Delta q/\Delta p$ is the same on both curves. Since elasticities at the same price are being compared on both curves, p is the same, and the only factor left to vary is q. On the curve farther from the origin, quantity is larger (i.e., $q_1 > q_0$) and hence p_0/q_1 is smaller than p_0/q_0; thus η is smaller.

It follows from theorem 2 that parallel shifts of a straight-line demand curve lower elasticity (at each price) when the line shifts outward and raise elasticity when the line shifts inward.

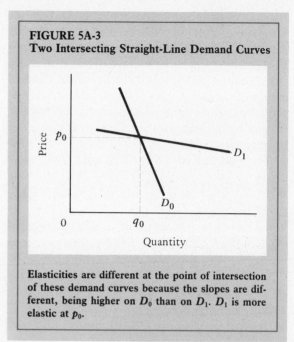

FIGURE 5A-3
Two Intersecting Straight-Line Demand Curves

Elasticities are different at the point of intersection of these demand curves because the slopes are different, being higher on D_0 than on D_1. D_1 is more elastic at p_0.

3. *The elasticities of two intersecting straight-line demand curves can be compared at the point of intersection merely by comparing slopes, the steeper curve being the less elastic.* In Figure 5A-3 there are two intersecting curves. At any point of intersection, p and q are common to both curves and hence the ratio p/q is the same. Therefore η varies only with $\Delta p/\Delta q$. On the steeper curve, $\Delta q/\Delta p$ is smaller than on the flatter curve, so elasticity is lower.

4. *If the slope of a straight-line demand curve changes while the price intercept remains constant, elasticity at any given price is unchanged.* This is an interesting case for at least two reasons. First, when more customers having similar tastes to those already in the market enter the market, the demand curve pivots outward in this way. Second, when more firms enter a market that is shared proportionally among all firms, each firm's demand curve shifts inward in this way.

Consider, in Figure 5A-4, the elasticity at point b on demand curve D_1 and at point c on demand curve D_2. We shall focus on the two triangles abp_0 on D_1 and acp_0 on D_2, formed by the two straight-

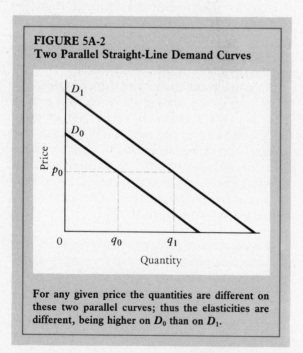

FIGURE 5A-2
Two Parallel Straight-Line Demand Curves

For any given price the quantities are different on these two parallel curves; thus the elasticities are different, being higher on D_0 than on D_1.

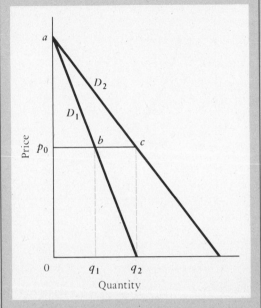

FIGURE 5A-4
Two Straight-Line Demand Curves from the Same Price Intercept

The elasticity is the same on D_1 and D_2 at any price p_0. This situation occurs because the steeper slope of D_1 is exactly offset by the smaller quantity demanded at any price.

The two are the same. The reason is that the distance corresponding to the quantity demanded at p_0 appears in both the numerator and denominator and thus cancels out.

Put differently, if the straight-line demand curve D_1 is twice as steep as D_2, it has half the quantity demanded at p_0. Therefore in the expression

$$\eta = \frac{\Delta q}{q} \times \frac{p}{\Delta p}$$

the steeper slope (a smaller Δq for the same Δp) is exactly offset by the smaller quantity demanded (a smaller q for the same p).

5. *Any straight-line supply curve through the origin has an elasticity of one.* Such a supply curve is shown in Figure 5A-5. Consider the two triangles with the sides p, q, and the S curve, and Δp, Δq, and the S curve. Clearly these are similar triangles. Therefore, the ratios of their sides are equal; that is,

$$\frac{p}{q} = \frac{\Delta p}{\Delta q} \qquad [2]$$

Elasticity of supply is defined as

$$\eta_s = \frac{\Delta q}{\Delta p} \times \frac{p}{q}$$

line demand curves emanating from point a and by the price p_0.

The price p_0 is the line segment $0p_0$. The quantities q_1 and q_2 are the line segments p_0b and p_0c, respectively. The slope of D_1 is $\frac{\Delta p}{\Delta q} = \frac{ap_0}{p_0b}$ and the slope of D_2 is $\frac{\Delta p}{\Delta q} = \frac{ap_0}{p_0c}$.

Now from Equation [1], we can represent the elasticities of D_1 and D_2 at the points b and c, respectively, as

$$\eta \text{ at point } b = \frac{p_0b}{ap_0} \times \frac{0p_0}{p_0b} = \frac{0p_0}{ap_0}$$

$$\eta \text{ at point } c = \frac{p_0c}{ap_0} \times \frac{0p_0}{p_0c} = \frac{0p_0}{ap_0}$$

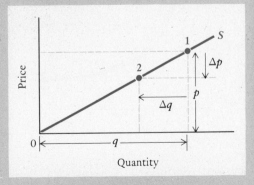

FIGURE 5A-5
A Straight-Line Supply Curve Through the Origin

At every point on the curve, p/q equals $\Delta p/\Delta q$; thus elasticity equals unity at every point.

which, by substitution from Equation [2], gives

$$\eta_s = \frac{q}{p} \times \frac{p}{q} \equiv 1$$

6. *The elasticity measured from any point p, q, according to Equation [1] above, is in general dependent on the direction and magnitude of the change in price and quantity.* Except for a straight line (for which the slope does not change), the ratio $\Delta q/\Delta p$ will not be the same at different points on a curve. Figure 5A-6 shows a demand curve that is not a straight line. To measure the elasticity from point 1, the ratio $\Delta q/\Delta p$—and thus η—will vary according to the size and the direction of the price change.

Theorem 6 yields a result that is very inconvenient and is avoided by use of a different definition of point elasticity.

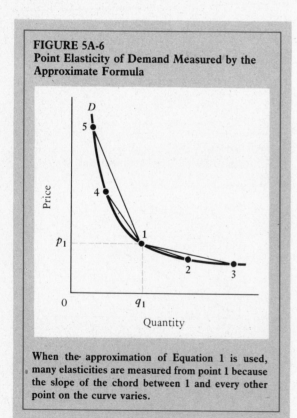

FIGURE 5A-6
Point Elasticity of Demand Measured by the Approximate Formula

When the approximation of Equation 1 is used, many elasticities are measured from point 1 because the slope of the chord between 1 and every other point on the curve varies.

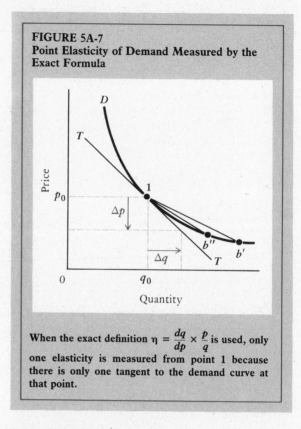

FIGURE 5A-7
Point Elasticity of Demand Measured by the Exact Formula

When the exact definition $\eta = \frac{dq}{dp} \times \frac{p}{q}$ is used, only one elasticity is measured from point 1 because there is only one tangent to the demand curve at that point.

Point Elasticity According to the Precise Definition

To measure the elasticity at a point exactly, it is necessary to know the reaction of quantity to a change in price *at that point*, not over a range of the curve.

The reaction of quantity to price change at a point is called dq/dp, and this is defined to be the reciprocal of the slope of the straight line tangent to the demand curve at the point in question. In Figure 5A-7 the elasticity of demand at point 1 is the ratio p/q (as it has been in all previous measures), now multiplied by the ratio of $\Delta q/\Delta p$ measured along the straight line, T, tangent to the curve at 1—that is, by dq/dp.

Thus the exact definition of point elasticity is

$$\eta = \frac{dq}{dp} \times \frac{p}{q} \qquad \text{exact point elasticity} \qquad [3]$$

The ratio dq/dp, as defined, is in fact the differential calculus concept of the *derivative* of quantity with respect to price.

This definition of point elasticity is the one normally used in economic theory. Equation [1] is mathematically only an approximation to this expression. It is obvious from Figure 5A-7 that arc elasticity will come closer to point elasticity the smaller the price change used to calculate the arc elasticity. The $\Delta q/\Delta p$ in Equation [1] is the reciprocal of the slope of the chord connecting the two points being compared. As the chord becomes shorter, its slope gets closer to that of the tangent T. (Compare the chords connecting point 1 to b' and b'' in Figure 5A-7.) Thus the error in using Equation [1] as an approximation to Equation [3] tends to diminish as the size of Δp diminishes.

BALANCE SHEETS, INCOME STATEMENTS, AND COSTS OF PRODUCTION: TWO VIEWS
APPENDIX TO CHAPTER 9

Accounting is a major branch of study in and of itself. Many students of economics will want to study accounting at some stage in their careers. It is not our intention to give a short course in accounting in this appendix, but rather to acquaint you with the kinds of summary statements that are used by both economists and accountants. **Balance sheets** report the picture of a firm *at a moment in time*. They balance in the sense that they show the assets (or valuable things) owned by the firm on one side and the claims against those assets on the other side. **Income statements** refer to a *period of time* (e.g., a year) and report in summary fashion the flows of resources through the firm in the course of its operations. Balance sheets thus measure a stock; income statements measure a flow.

To illustrate what balance sheets and income statements are, the same example will be treated from two points of view: that of the accountant and that of the economist.

TABLE 9A–1 MAYKBY LEAF COMPANY,
BALANCE SHEET, DECEMBER 31, 1983

Assets		Liabilities and equity	
Cash in bank	$ 10,000	Owed to suppliers	$ 10,000
Plant and equipment	160,000	Bank loan	80,000
Raw materials and supplies	30,000	Equity	110,000
Total assets	$200,000	Total liabilities and equity	$200,000

An Example

Late in 1983, James Maykby, the second vice-president of Acme Artificial Flower Corporation (at a salary of $50,000 per year), decided he would go into business for himself. He quit his job and organized the Maykby Leaf Company. He purchased suitable plant and equipment for $160,000 and acquired some raw materials and supplies. By December 31, 1983, he was in a position to start manufacturing. The funds for his enterprise were $80,000 raised as a bank loan on the factory (on which he is obligated to pay interest of $10,000 per year) and $110,000 of his own funds, which had previously been invested in common stocks. He also owed $10,000 to certain firms that had provided him with supplies.

Maykby, who is a trained accountant, drew up a statement of his company's position as of December 31, 1983 (see Table 9A-1).

Maykby showed this balance sheet to his brother-in-law, an economist, and was very pleased and surprised[1] to find that he agreed that this was

a fair and accurate statement of the position of the company as it prepared to start operation.

During 1984, the company had a busy year hiring factors, producing and selling goods, and so on. The following points summarize these activities of the 12-month period.

1. The firm hired labor and purchased additional raw materials in the amount of $115,000, of which it still owed $20,000 at the end of the year.[2]
2. The firm manufactured artificial leaves and flowers whose sale value was $200,000. At year's end it had sold all of these, and still had on hand $30,000 worth of raw materials.
3. The firm paid off the $10,000 owed to suppliers at the beginning of the year.
4. At the very end of 1984, the company purchased a new machine for $10,000 and paid cash for it.
5. The company paid the bank $10,000 interest on the loan.
6. Maykby paid himself $20,000 "instead of salary."

[1] He usually finds that he and his brother-in-law disagree about everything.

[2] In this example, all purchased and hired factors are treated in a single category.

TABLE 9A–2 MAYKBY LEAF COMPANY,
ACCOUNTANT'S BALANCE SHEET, DECEMBER 31, 1984

Assets		Liabilities and equity	
Cash in bank	$ 65,000	Owed to suppliers of factors	$ 20,000
(See Exhibit 1)		(See Exhibit 4)	
Plant and equipment	146,000	Bank loan	80,000
(See Exhibit 2)		Equity	141,000
Raw materials and supplies	30,000	(See Exhibit 5)	
(See Exhibit 3)		Total liabilities and equity	$241,000
Total assets	$241,000		

An Accountant's Balance Sheet and Income Statement

Taking account of all these things and also recognizing that he had depreciation on his plant and equipment,[3] Maykby spent New Year's Day 1985 preparing three financial reports (see Tables 9A-2, 9A-3, and 9A-4).

[3] The tax people told him he could charge 15 percent of the cost of his equipment as depreciation during 1984, and he decided to use this amount in his own books as well. No depreciation was charged on the new machine.

TABLE 9A-4 MAYKBY LEAF COMPANY, ACCOUNTANT'S INCOME STATEMENT FOR THE YEAR 1984

Sales		$200,000
Costs of operation		
Hired services and raw materials used	$115,000	
Depreciation	24,000	
Mr. Maykby	20,000	
Interest	10,000	−169,000
Profit		$ 31,000

TABLE 9A-3 MAYKBY LEAF COMPANY, EXHIBITS TO BALANCE SHEET OF DECEMBER 31, 1984

Exhibit 1. Cash

Balance, January 1, 1984	$ 10,000	
+ Deposits		
Proceeds of sales of goods	200,000	$210,000
− Payments		
Payments to suppliers (1984 bills)	10,000	
Payments for labor and additional raw materials	95,000	
Salary of Mr. Maykby	20,000	
Purchase of new machine	10,000	
Interest payment to bank	10,000	−145,000
Balance, December 31, 1984		65,000

Exhibit 2. Plant and Equipment

Balance, January 1, 1984	$160,000	
+ New machine purchased	10,000	170,000
− Depreciation charged		− 24,000
Balance, December 31, 1984		146,000

Exhibit 3. Raw Materials and Supplies

On hand January 1, 1984	$ 30,000	
Purchases in 1984	115,000	145,000
Used for production during 1984		−115,000
On hand December 31, 1984		30,000

Exhibit 4. Owed to Suppliers

Balance, January 1, 1984	$ 10,000	
New purchases, 1984	115,000	125,000
Paid on old accounts	10,000	
Paid on new accounts	95,000	−105,000
Balance, December 31, 1984		$ 20,000

Exhibit 5. Equity

Original investment	$110,000	
+ Income earned during year	31,000	
(See income statement)		
Balance, December 31, 1984	$141,000	

These accounts reflect the operations of the firm as described above. The bookkeeping procedure by which these various activities are made to yield both the year-end balance sheet and the income statement need not concern you at this time, but you should notice several things.

First, note that some transactions affect the balance sheet but do not enter into the current income statement. Examples of these are the purchase of a machine, which is an exchange of assets—cash for plant and equipment—and which will be entered as a cost in the income statements of some future periods as depreciation is charged; and the payment of past debts, which entered the income statements in the period in which the things purchased were used in production.[4]

Second, note that the net profit from operations increased the owner's equity, since it was not "paid out" to him. A loss would have decreased his equity.

Third, note that the income statement, covering a year's operation, provides a link between the opening balance sheet (the assets and the claims against assets at the beginning of the year) and the closing balance sheet.

Fourth, note that every change in a balance sheet between two dates can be accounted for by events that occurred during the year. (See the exhibits to the balance sheet, Table 9A-3.)

After studying these records, Maykby feels that it has been a good year. The company has money in the bank, it has shown a profit, and it was able to sell the goods it produced. He is bothered, however, by the fact that he and his wife have felt poorer than in the past years. Probably the cost of living has gone up!

An Economist's Balance Sheet and Income Statement

When Maykby's brother-in-law reviews the December 31, 1984, balance sheet and the 1984 in-

[4] Beginning students often have difficulty with the distinction between *cash* flows and *income* flows. If you do, analyze item by item the entries in Exhibit 1 in Table 9A-3 and in Table 9A-4, the income statement.

TABLE 9A–5 MAYKBY LEAF COMPANY, ECONOMIST'S INCOME STATEMENT FOR THE YEAR 1984

Sales		$200,000
Cost of operations		
Hired services and raw materials	$115,000	
Depreciation[a]	36,000	
Interest to bank[b]	10,000	
Imputed cost of capital	11,000	
Services of Maykby	50,000	−222,000
Loss		$(22,000)

[a] Market value on January 1 less market value on December 31.
[b] Because the bank loan is secured by the factory, its opportunity cost seems to the economist as properly measured by the interest payment.

come statement, he criticizes them in three respects. He says:

1. Maykby should have charged the company $50,000 for his services, since that is what he could have earned outside.
2. Maykby should have charged the company for the use of the $110,000 of his funds. He computes that had Maykby left these funds in the stock market he would have earned $11,000 in dividends and capital gains.
3. Maykby's depreciation figure is arbitrary. The plant and equipment purchased for $160,000 a year ago now has a *market value* of only $124,000. (Assume he is correct about this fact.)

The brother-in-law prepared three *revised* statements. (See Tables 9A-5, 9A-6, and the exhibit, Table 9A-7.)

It is not hard for Maykby to understand the difference between the accounting profit of $31,000 and the reported economist's loss of $22,000. The difference of $53,000 is made up as follows:

Extra salary	$30,000
Imputed cost of capital	11,000
Extra depreciation	12,000
	$53,000

TABLE 9A–6 MAYKBY LEAF COMPANY, ECONOMIST'S BALANCE SHEET, DECEMBER 31, 1984

Assets		Liabilities and equity	
Cash	$ 65,000	Owed to suppliers	$ 20,000
Plant and equipment	134,000	Bank loan	80,000
Raw materials, etc.	30,000	Equity (see Exhibit)	129,000
	$229,000		$229,000

TABLE 9A–7 EXHIBIT TO BALANCE SHEET, DECEMBER 31, 1984: EQUITY TO MR. MAYKBY

Original investment		$110,000
New investment by Mr. Maykby		
Salary not collected	$30,000	
Return on capital not		
collected	11,000	41,000
		151,000
Less loss from operations		22,000
Equity		$129,000

TABLE 9A–8 MAYKBY'S SITUATION BEFORE AND AFTER

	(1) As second vice-president of Acme Flower Company	(2) As owner-manager of Maykby Leaf Company	Difference (2) − (1)
Salary paid	$ 50,000	$ 20,000	−$30,000
Earnings on capital, invested in stocks	11,000	0	− 11,000
Assets owned	110,000 (stocks)	129,000 (equity in Maykby Leaf Co.)	+ 19,000
Net change			−$22,000

What Maykby does *not* understand is in what sense he *lost* $22,000 during the year. To explain this, his brother-in-law prepared the report shown in Table 9A-8.

Although Maykby spent the afternoon muttering to himself and telling his wife that his brother-in-law was not only totally lacking in any business sense but unpleasant as well, he was observed that evening at the public library asking the librarian whether there was a good "teach-yourself" book on economics. (We do not know her answer.)

The next day, Maykby suggested to the economist that they work out together the expected economic profits for next year. "After all," he said, "dwelling on what might have been doesn't really help decide whether I should continue the Leaf Company next year." The economist agreed. Because of expected sales increases, they concluded, the prospects were good enough to continue for at least another year. They dipped deep in the bowl of New Year's cheer to toast those stalwart pillars of society, the independent business person and the economist.

MORE ON LONG-RUN COMPETITIVE EQUILIBRIUM
APPENDIX TO CHAPTER 12

In Chapter 12 we showed how the forces of entry and exit in a competitive industry forced firms to an equilibrium position with zero profits. Here we consider further implications of this process and some complications of long-run equilibrium.

Long-Run Equilibrium Implies Minimum Attainable Costs

A competitive industry will not be in long-run equilibrium as long as any firm can increase its profits by changing its output or its method of production. A firm might change its profits by (1) increasing or decreasing output from an existing plant, (2) opening or closing additional identical plants, or (3) changing the size of the plants it operates.

We saw in Chapter 12 that if a firm is to be in long-run equilibrium, condition (1) implies that price, p, equals short-run marginal cost ($SRMC$) and that (2) implies that price equals short-run average total cost ($SRATC$). These two conditions

FIGURE 12A-1
The Equilibrium of a Firm When the Industry Is in Long-Run Equilibrium

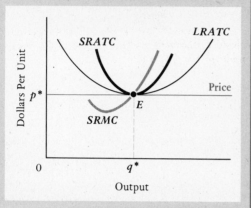

In long-run competitive equilibrium, the firm is operating at the minimum point on its *LRATC* curve. In long-run equilibrium, each firm must be (1) maximizing short-run profits, $SRMC = p$; (2) earning profits of zero on its existing plant, $SRATC = p$; and (3) unable to increase its profits by altering the size of plant. These three conditions can be met only when the firm is at E, the minimum point on its *LRATC* curve, with price p^* and output q^*.

The additional condition (3) means that each existing firm must be producing at the lowest point on its long-run average cost curve. Taken together, these conditions mean that all firms in the industry should be in the position illustrated in Figure 12A-1.

To see why this is so, we shall assume that it is not the case and show how firms may increase their profits. (If they can increase their profits, they were not originally in long-run equilibrium.) Figure 12A-2 shows two firms that have $SRMC = SRATC =$ price. Each of these firms can, however, increase its profits by discarding its present plant when it wears out and building a plant of different size. The smaller firm should increase its plant size, thereby lowering its average total costs. The larger firm should build a smaller plant, thereby lowering its ATC. Since each firm is a price taker, each of these changes will increase the firm's profits.

FIGURE 12A-2
Short-Run Versus Long-Run Equilibrium of a Competitive Firm

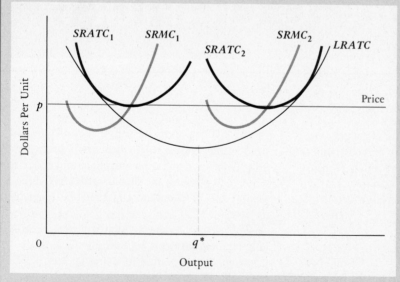

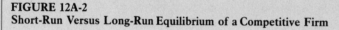

A competitive firm that is not at the minimum point on its *LRATC* curve cannot be in long-run equilibrium. Suppose two firms have identical *LRATC* curves but one firm has too small a plant, with costs $SRATC_1$, while the other firm has too large a plant, with costs of $SRATC_2$. Both firms are in short-run equilibrium at price $p = SRMC = SRATC$, but neither is in long-run equilibrium. Firm 1 can increase its profits by building a larger plant (thereby moving downward to the right along its *LRATC* curve). Firm 2 can increase is profits by building a smaller plant (thereby moving downward to the left along its *LRATC* curve).

The only way in which a price-taking firm can be in long-run equilibrium with respect to its size is by producing at the minimum point on its *LRATC* curve.

Each firm must be producing at minimum *LRATC* (at a point such as q^* in Figure 12A-2). Since for an industry to be in long-run equilibrium each firm must be in long-run equilibrium, it follows that in long-run competitive equilibrium all firms in the industry will be selling at a price equal to minimum *LRATC*.

In long-run competitive equilibrium, the firm's cost is the lowest attainable cost, given the limits of known technology and factor prices.

Long-Run Responses to Changes in Demand

Suppose a competitive industry is in long-run equilibrium, as shown in Figure 12A-1. Now suppose that the demand for the product increases. Price will rise to equate demand with the industry's short-run supply. Each firm will expand output until its short-run marginal cost once again equals price. Each firm will earn profits as a result of the rise in price, and the profits will induce new firms to enter the industry. This shifts the short-run supply curve to the right and forces down the price. Entry continues until all firms are once again just covering average total costs.

To recapitulate: The short-run effects of the rise in demand are a rise in price and output; the long-run effect is new entry, which leads to a further rise in output and a fall in price. This process is illustrated in Figure 12A-3.

Now consider a fall in demand. The industry starts with firms in long-run equilibrium, as shown in Figure 12A-1, and the market demand curve shifts left and price falls. The ultimate sequence is the reverse of the sequence found when demand increases. It may also be illustrated in Figure 12A-3, but the process is likely to be different, for exit and entry are not symmetrical in the real world.

How does exit occur when demand declines? There are two possible scenarios. First, suppose the decline in demand forces price below *ATC* but leaves it above *AVC*. Firms are then in the position shown in Figure 12-7 (i), page 193. The firms can cover their variable costs and earn some return on their capital, so they remain in production for as long as their existing plant and equipment lasts. But it is not worth replacing capital as it wears out. Exit will occur as old capital wears out and is not replaced. As firms exit, the short-run supply curve shifts left and market price rises.

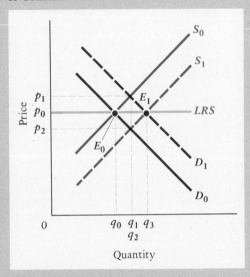

FIGURE 12A-3
A Long-Run Supply Curve Under Conditions of Constant Cost

The long-run supply curve connects equilibrium points after demand-induced shifts occur in the supply curve. The initial equilibrium point is E_0. A shift in demand from D_0 to D_1 first raises the price to p_1 as industry output expands along the short-run supply curve to q_1. Firms will be earning profits and entry will thus occur. This induces a shift in the short-run supply curve from S_0 to S_1, and price falls; but output increases to q_3. The long-run supply curve is *LRS*. In the case illustrated the increase in supply is just sufficient to keep the price at p_0. Thus output has been increased "at constant cost" in the long run.

A decrease in demand from D_1 to D_0, starting from E_1, first lowers price to p_2. Firms that were previously breaking even will earn losses. Eventually, in response, exit will occur. This induces a leftward shift in the supply curve from S_1 to S_0, and price rises again to p_0, where the remaining firms break even. Output has been reduced "at constant cost" in the long run.

This continues until the remaining firms in the industry can cover their total costs. At this point it will pay to replace capital as it wears out, and the decline in the size of the industry will be brought to a halt. In this case the adjustment may take a very long time, for the industry shrinks in size only as existing plant and equipment wears out.

The second scenario occurs when the decline in demand is so large that price is forced below the level of *AVC*. In this case firms cannot even cover their variable costs, and some will shut down immediately. Thus the reduction in capital devoted to production in the industry occurs rapidly because some existing capacity is scrapped or sold for other uses. Once sufficient capital has been withdrawn so that price rises to a level that allows the remaining firms to cover their *AVC*, the rapid withdrawal of capital will cease. Further exit occurs more slowly, as described above.

The Long-Run Industry Supply Curve

Adjustments to long-run changes in demand do not necessarily leave the *level* of long-run costs unchanged, as was assumed in Figure 12A-3. The response of costs to such long-run changes in required equilibrium output is shown by the **long-run industry supply curve (*LRS*)**. This curve shows the relation between equilibrium price and the output firms will be willing to supply after all desired entry or exit has occurred.

The long-run supply curve connects positions of long-run equilibrium after all demand-induced changes have occurred.

When induced changes in factor prices are considered, it is possible for *LRS* to rise, to fall, or to remain constant. Figure 12A-3 illustrated the case of constant costs; Figures 12A-4 and 12A-5 illustrate the case of a rise and the case of a fall in long-run costs, respectively.

Constant Costs (Constant *LRS*)

The long-run supply curve in Figure 12A-3 is horizontal. This indicates that the industry, given

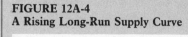

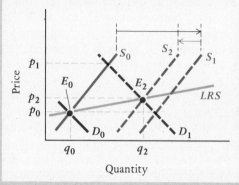

FIGURE 12A-4
A Rising Long-Run Supply Curve

If growth in industry size increases factor prices, the *LRS* will be upward-sloping. Suppose an industry is in equilibrium at E_0. Then demand increases from D_0 to D_1. In the short run price will rise to p_1. In the long run this increases the number of firms, thereby shifting the supply curve from S_0 to S_1 (as shown by the black arrow). This is the supply curve that would pertain to an expanded number of firms if input prices did not change. But the increase in industry production bids up the prices of factors used, thereby shifting the supply curve leftward from S_1 to S_2 (as shown by the colored arrow). Equilibrium E_2 is at price p_2. Price has risen from p_0 to p_2 because firms must recover the costs imposed by the higher input prices.

time, will adjust its size to provide whatever quantity may be demanded at a constant price. Such conditions may obtain if factor prices do not change as the output of the whole industry expands or contracts. An industry with a horizontal long-run supply curve is said to be a **constant-cost industry**.

Increasing Long-Run Costs (Increasing *LRS*)

Short-run cost curves rise because of the existence of fixed factors and the law of diminishing returns to variable factors. A different explanation must apply in the long run, since there are no fixed factors.

When an industry expands its output, it needs

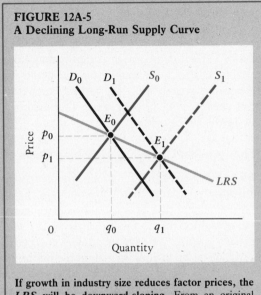

FIGURE 12A-5
A Declining Long-Run Supply Curve

If growth in industry size reduces factor prices, the *LRS* will be downward-sloping. From an original equilibrium at E_0, an increase in demand to D_1 leads to an increase in supply to S_1 and a new equilibrium at E_1. Price p_1 is below the original price p_0 because lower factor prices allow firms to cover their total costs at the lower price.

more inputs. The increase in demand for these inputs may bid up their prices. Such growth-induced changes in prices may be expected whenever rapid growth occurs. The reason for this is that a large industry demands large quantities of certain key materials and certain kinds of skilled labor. As the industry grows larger and larger, these become increasingly scarce.

For instance, growth of the airline industry increases the demand of airlines for aluminum, jet fuel, and skilled mechanics, none of which is in perfectly elastic supply. Increasing scarcity of these inputs will tend to raise their price, and this in turn will raise the cost of providing air transport.

If costs rise with increasing levels of industry output, so too will the price at which the producers are willing to supply the market. The common sense of this result is that if firms were just covering their costs before the increase in demand, the price

they receive will have to rise enough to cover any increases in factor prices they must pay.

To see more specifically why this result occurs, remember that an increase in the price of inputs will shift the marginal cost (and average cost) curves of all firms upward. This shift in the marginal cost curves of all firms shifts the industry short-run supply curve to the left.

The effect on *LRS* of growth in industry output may be thought of for analytic purposes as occurring in two stages: an increase in the number of firms with no increase in factor prices and an induced increase in factor prices. Figure 12A-4 shows how these two stages lead to an upward-sloping *LRS* curve.

In reality the two stages occur simultaneously. For instance, in recent years the very rapid increase in the demand for electric power in the United States has led to a large increase in the number of electric generating plants. This in turn has led to sharp increases in the demand for inputs—and hence to increases in their price. This development has been particularly marked with the prices of coal and oil, the key fuels in electricity generation. As one commentator has said, "talk of the energy crisis is mood music for higher fuel prices." Higher fuel prices in turn lead to higher prices of the things the fuel is used to make.

Rising *LRS*—**rising supply price**, as it is sometimes called—is often a characteristic of sharp and rapid growth. A competitive industry with rising long-run supply prices is often called a **rising-cost industry.**

Decreasing Long-Run Costs (Decreasing *LRS*)

So far we have suggested that the long-run supply curve may be constant or rising. Could it ever decline, thereby indicating that higher outputs were associated with lower prices in long-run equilibrium?

It is tempting to answer yes because of the opportunities of more efficient scales of operation using greater mechanization and more effective specialization of labor. But this answer would not be correct for perfectly competitive industries because each firm in long-run equilibrium must already be at the lowest point on its *LRATC* curve. If a firm could lower its costs by building a larger, more mechanized plant, it would be profitable to do so without waiting for an increase in demand. Since any single firm can sell all it wishes at the going market price, it will be profitable to expand the scale of its operations as long as its *LRATC* is falling.

There is a reason, however, why the long-run supply curve might slope downward: The expansion of an industry might lead to a fall in the prices of some of its inputs. If this occurs, the firms will find their cost curves shifting downward as they expand their outputs.

As an illustration of how the expansion of one industry could cause the prices of some of its inputs to fall, consider the early stages of the growth of the automobile industry. As the output of automobiles increased, the industry's demand for tires grew greatly. This, as suggested earlier, would have increased the demand for rubber and tended to raise its price, but it also provided the opportunity for Goodyear, Firestone, and other tire manufacturers to build large modern plants and reap the benefits of increasing returns in tire production. At first these economies were large enough to offset any factor price increases, and tire prices charged to manufacturers of automobiles fell. Thus automobile costs fell because of lower prices of an important input.

To see the effect of a fall in input prices caused by the expansion of an industry, suppose that the demand for the industry's product increases. Price and profits will rise and new entry will occur as a result. But when expansion of the industry has gone far enough to bring price back to its initial level, cost curves will be lower than they were initially because of the fall in input prices. Firms will thus still be earning profits. A further expansion will then occur until price falls to the level of the minimum points on each firm's new, lower *LRATC* curve. (This case is illustrated in Figure 12A-5.) An industry that has a declining long-run supply curve is often called a **falling-cost industry**.

The Existence of Long-Run Competitive Equilibrium

The greatest limitation on the usefulness of the model of perfect competition is that it may not be a suitable yardstick for evaluating real-world markets because it may be that perfect competition cannot exist in some circumstances that commonly occur in the real world.

The Problem Caused by Declining Costs

A necessary condition for a long-run competitive equilibrium to exist is that any economies of scale that are available to a firm should be exhausted at a level of output that is small relative to the whole industry's output. We have seen that a competitive firm will never be in equilibrium on the falling part of its *LRATC*—if price is given and costs can be reduced by expanding scale, profits can also be increased by doing so. Thus firms will grow in size at least until all scale economies are exhausted.

Provided the output that yields the minimum *LRATC* for each firm is small relative to the industry's total output, there will be a large number of firms in the industry and the industry will remain competitive. If, however, reaching the minimum *LRATC* leads to a small number of very large firms, they are likely to have significant market power. If so, they will cease to be price takers and perfect competition will cease to exist.

In an industry with declining costs, the market may be too small relative to technology to be compatible with perfect competition. Indeed, if scale economies exist over such a large range that one firm's *LRATC* would still be falling if it served the entire market, a single firm may come to monopolize the market. This is what the classical economists called the case of *natural* monopoly; it is considered in Chapter 15.

The Problem of Constant Costs

Constant long-run costs also create problems for the competitive theory. Only if the firm's *LRATC* curve is U-shaped will there be a determinate size of the firm in a competitive industry. To see why, assume instead that *LRATC* falls to a minimum at some level of output and then remains constant for all larger outputs. All firms would have to be at least the minimum size, but they could be just that size or much larger, since price would equal *LRATC* for any output above the minimum efficient size. In other words, there would then be no unique size for the firm. Are there reasons to believe the curve may not be U-shaped?

U-shaped plant curves. There are very good reasons why the *LRATC* curve for a single-plant firm may be expected to be U-shaped. A great deal of modern technology results in lower average costs for large, automated factories compared with smaller factories in which few workers use relatively unsophisticated capital equipment. As a single plant becomes too large, however, costs may rise because of the sheer difficulty of planning for, and controlling the behavior of, a vast integrated operation. Thus we have no problem accounting for a U-shaped cost curve for the *plant*.

U-shaped firm cost curve. What of the U-shaped cost curve for the *firm?* A declining portion will occur for the same reason that the *LRATC* for one plant declines when the firm is so small that it operates only one plant. Now, however, let the firm be operating one plant at the output where its *LRATC* is a minimum. Call that output q^*. What if the firm decides to double its output to $2q^*$? If it tries to build a vast plant with twice the output of the optimal size plant, the firm's average total cost of production may rise (because the vast plant has higher costs than a plant of the optimal size). But the firm has the option of *replicating* its first plant in a physically separate location. If the firm obtains a second parcel of land, builds an identical second plant, staffs it identically, and allows its production to be managed independently, there seems no reason why the second plant's minimum *LRATC* should be different from that of the first plant. *Because the firm can replicate plants and have them managed independently, there seems no reason why any firm faced with constant factor prices should not face constant LRATCs, at least for multiples of the output for which one plant achieves the lowest plant LRATC.*

In the modern theory of perfect competition, a U-shaped *firm* cost curve is merely *assumed*. Without it—although a competitive equilibrium may exist for an arbitrary number of firms—there is nothing to determine the equilibrium size of the firm and hence the number of firms in the industry.

THE FIRM'S DEMAND FOR FACTORS
APPENDIX TO CHAPTER 18

In Chapter 18 we saw that all profit-maximizing firms will hire units of the variable factor up to the point at which the marginal cost of the factor equals the marginal revenue produced by the factor. For a firm that is a price taker in factor markets, this means that it hires a factor up to the point at which the factor's price equals its marginal revenue product.

Consider a single firm with only one variable factor, labor, and one fixed factor, capital. Assume that the average and marginal revenue products of the labor are those shown in Figure 18A-1. The firm wishes to hire the quantity of labor that will maximize its profits.

The demand curve for a factor is the downward-sloping portion of the marginal revenue product curve where it is below the average revenue product curve.

To see why this statement is correct, let us ask a number of questions.

Why do points on the downward-sloping portion of MRP, such as a and b in the figure, belong on the demand curve? If the wage rate (the price of the variable factor) is w_2, the profit-maximizing firm will hire the factor up to the point where $w = MRP$, that is, up to q_3. This is point a. If the wage rate is w_1, the firm will hire up to q_4. This is point b. Points a and b are thus on the firm's demand curve for the factor.

What is the maximum wage rate the firm will pay? What is the *maximum* wage rate at which the firm will still hire workers? We saw in Chapter 12 that it will never pay to produce a product when its price is below the level of average variable cost. We also saw (see pages 161–162) that where average product is a maximum, average variable cost is a minimum. For any wage rate above w_3—such as w_4—the average revenue generated by a unit of labor (shown by ARP) would be less than the variable cost of the unit of labor (its wage rate). For such a wage rate it does not pay the firm to hire any workers. In other words w_3, where average revenue product is a maximum, is the highest factor price a firm could pay and still cover variable costs.

Why is the downward-sloping, not the upward-sloping, portion of MRP the demand curve? Consider the wage rate w_2. Here $w = MRP$ at both q_1 (point c) and q_3 (point a). We have already seen that point a is on the demand curve; what about point c? For every unit of labor hired up to q_1, MRP is less than the wage rate. In other words, each unit of labor is contributing less to revenue than to cost. Thus a profit-maximizing firm would be better off hiring zero units than q_1 units. For every unit of labor from q_1 to q_3, MRP exceeds the wage rate. Thus, if a firm were hiring q_1 units, it would find each additional unit beyond q_1 (up to q_3) worth hiring. Point c (where MRP is rising when it equals the wage rate) is a point of *minimum* profit, not maximum profit. [52] A firm at point c would improve its profitability by moving in either direction, to hiring zero workers or to hiring q_3 workers. (We already know that q_3 is better than zero because at that quantity ARP is greater than the wage rate.)

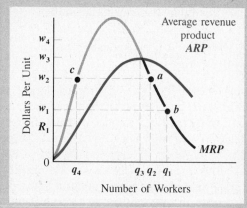

FIGURE 18A-1
The Relation of the Demand for a Factor and MRP

The derived demand curve for a factor is the downward-sloping portion of *MRP* below *ARP* as indicated by the heavy black portion of *MRP*. Suppose the factor in question is labor. The average revenue generated by a unit of labor, the average revenue product of labor, is shown by the colored curve *ARP*, while the revenue generated by a marginal increase in the labor force, the marginal revenue of labor, is shown by the black curve *MRP*.

Consider the wage rate w_3 where *MRP* intersects *ARP*. For any wage above w_3—such as w_4—*ARP* would be less than the variable cost of the unit of labor (its wage rate). For such a wage rate it does not pay the firm to hire any workers. In other words w_3, where *ARP* is a maximum, is the highest factor price a firm could pay and still cover variable costs.

Now consider the wage rate w_2, less than w_3. Here $w = MRP$ at both q_4 (point c) and q_2 (point a). Let us consider each of these points in more detail. A firm at point c would improve its profitability by moving in either direction, to hiring zero workers or to hiring q_3 workers. For every unit of labor hired up to q_4, *MRP* is less than the wage rate. In other words, each unit of labor is contributing less to revenue than to cost. Thus a profit-maximizing firm would be better off hiring zero units than q_4 units. For every unit of labor from q_4 to q_2, *MRP* exceeds the wage rate. Thus, if a firm were hiring q_4 units, it would find each additional unit beyond q_4 (up to q_2) worth hiring. Point c is therefore not on the firm's demand curve. Point c (where *MRP* is rising when it equals the wage rate) is a point of *minimum* profit.

At point a, $w = MRP$, and *MRP* is falling. A firm at point a would reduce its profit by moving in either direction; hence a is a point of maximum profits.

If the wage rate is w_1, the firm will hire up to q_4 (point b). Points a and b and all other points in the dark black portion of *MRP* are thus on the firm's demand curve for the factor.

Only points where MRP cuts the wage rate from above, that is, where MRP is downward-sloping, are possible profit-maximizing quantities.

Will There Be a Downward-sloping Portion of MRP?

Having shown that only downward-sloping portions of MRP are relevant to the demand curve for the factor, we may ask whether we have any reason to believe MRP will slope downward. The presence of diminishing returns is sufficient to assure this result, as can be easily shown. Marginal revenue product depends on two things: (1) the physical increase in output that an additional unit of the variable factor makes possible, multiplied by (2) the increase in revenue derived from that extra output. The first of these is called the **marginal physical product** (MPP); the second is the by now familiar concept of marginal revenue:

$$MRP = MPP \times MR$$

The hypothesis of diminishing marginal returns was introduced in Chapter 10. This hypothesis says that MPP has a declining section over some range of output. If marginal revenue is constant (as it is in perfect competition), MRP will have the same shape as MPP and must also decline.

Marginal revenue, however, may not be constant. If MR declines as output increases (as it does in monopoly and in any other situation in which the firm's demand curve declines), MRP must decline even more sharply. The hypothesis of diminishing marginal productivity thus implies diminishing MRP and a downward-sloping demand curve for the factor.

THE PERMANENT-INCOME HYPOTHESIS AND THE LIFE-CYCLE HYPOTHESIS

APPENDIX TO CHAPTER 32

In the Keynesian theory of the consumption function, current consumption expenditure is related to current income—either current disposable income or current national income. Attempts to reconcile the apparently conflicting empirical data on short-term and long-term consumption behavior have produced theories that relate consumption to some longer-term concept of income than the income that the household is currently earning.

The two most influential theories of this type are the **permanent-income hypothesis (PIH),** developed by Professor Friedman, and the **life-cycle hypothesis (LCH),** developed by Professors Modigliani and Ando and the late Professor Brumberg. Although there are many significant differences between these theories, their similarities are more important than their differences, and their central characteristics may be looked at together. In doing this it is important to ask: What variables do these theories seek to explain? What assumptions do they make? What are the major implications of these assumptions? How do the theories reconcile the apparently conflicting empirical evidence? And what implications do they have for the overall behavior of the economy?

Variables

Three variables need to be considered: consumption, saving, and income. Keynesian-type theories seek to explain the amounts that households spend on purchasing goods and services for consumption. This concept is called *consumption expenditure*. Permanent-income theories seek to explain the actual flows of consumption of the services that are provided by the commodities that households buy. This concept is called *actual consumption*.[1]

With services and nondurable goods, expenditure and actual consumption occur more or less at the same time and the distinction between the two concepts is not important. Consumption of a haircut, for example, occurs at the time it is purchased, and an orange or a package of corn flakes is consumed very soon after it is purchased. Thus, if we knew purchases of such goods and services at some time, say last year, we would also know last year's consumption of those goods and services.

But this is not the case with durable consumer goods. A screwdriver is purchased at one point in time, but it yields up its services over a long time, possibly as long as the purchaser's lifetime. The same is true of a house and a watch and, over a shorter period of time, of a car and a dress. For such products, if we know purchases last year, we do not necessarily know last year's consumption of the services that the products yielded.

Thus one important characteristic of durable goods is that *expenditure* to purchase them is not necessarily synchronized with *consumption* of the stream of services that the goods provide. If in 1985

Mr. Smith buys a car for $8,000, runs it for six years, and then discards it as worn out, his expenditure on automobiles is $8,000 in 1985 and zero for the next five years. His consumption of the services of automobiles, however, is spread out at an average annual rate of $1,333 for six years. If everyone followed Mr. Smith's example by buying a new car in 1985 and replacing it in 1991, the automobile industry would undergo wild booms in 1985 and 1991 with five intervening years of slump, even though the actual consumption of automobiles would be spread more or less evenly over time. This example is extreme, but it illustrates the possibilities, where consumers' durables are concerned, of quite different time paths of *consumption expenditure*, which is the subject of Keynesian theories of consumption, and *actual consumption*, which is the subject of permanent-income theories.

Now consider saving. The change in emphasis from consumption expenditure to actual consumption implies a change in the definition of saving. Saving is no longer income minus consumption *expenditure*; it is now income minus the value of actual consumption. When Mr. Smith spent $8,000 on his car in 1985 but used only $1,333 worth of its services in that year, he was actually consuming $1,333 and saving $6,667. The purchase of a consumers' durable is thus counted as saving, and only the value of its services actually consumed is counted as consumption.

The third important variable is income. Instead of using current income, the theories use a concept of long-term income. The precise definition varies from one theory to another, but basically it is related to the household's expected income stream over a fairly long planning period. In the LCH it is the income that the household expects to earn over its lifetime.[2]

Every household is assumed to have a view of its expected lifetime earnings. This is not as unreasonable as it might seem. Students training to be doctors have a very different view of expected

---

[1] Because Keynes' followers did not always distinguish carefully between the concepts of consumption expenditure and actual consumption, the word *consumption* is often used in both contexts. We follow this normal practice, but where there is any possible ambiguity in the term we will refer to *consumption expenditure* and *actual consumption*.

[2] In the PIH the household has an infinite time horizon and the relevant permanent-income concept is the amount the household could consume forever without increasing or decreasing its present stock of wealth.

lifetime income than those training to become schoolteachers. Both expected income streams—for a doctor and for a schoolteacher—will be very different from that expected by an assembly line worker or a professional athlete. One possible lifetime income stream is shown in Figure 32A-1.

The household's expected lifetime income is then converted into a single figure for *annual* **permanent income.** In the life-cycle hypothesis this permanent income is the maximum amount the household could spend on consumption each year without accumulating debts *that are passed on to future generations.* If a household were to consume a constant amount equal to its permanent income each year, it would add to its debts in years when current income was less than permanent income and reduce its debt or increase its assets in years when its current income exceeded its permanent income. Over its lifetime, however, it would just break even, leaving neither accumulated assets nor debts to its heirs. If the interest rate were zero, permanent income would be just the sum of all expected incomes divided by the number of expected years of life. With a positive interest rate, permanent income will diverge from this amount because of the costs of borrowing and the extra income that can be earned by investing savings.

Assumption

The basic assumption of this type of theory, whether PIH or LCH, is that the household's actual consumption is related to its permanent rather than to its current income. Two households that have the same permanent income (and are similar in other relevant characteristics) will have similiar consumption patterns even though their current incomes behave very differently.

Implications

The major implication of these theories is that changes in a household's current income will affect its actual consumption only so far as they affect its permanent income. Consider two income changes that could occur to a household with a permanent income of $10,000 per year and an expected lifetime of 30 or more years. In the first, suppose the household receives an unexpected extra income of $2,000 *for this year only.* The increase in the household's permanent income is thus very small. If the rate of interest were zero, the household could consume an extra $66.66 per year for the rest of its expected life span; with a positive rate of interest, the extra annual consumption would be more because money not spent this year could be invested and would earn interest.[3] In the second case,

---

FIGURE 32A-1
Current Income and Permanent Income

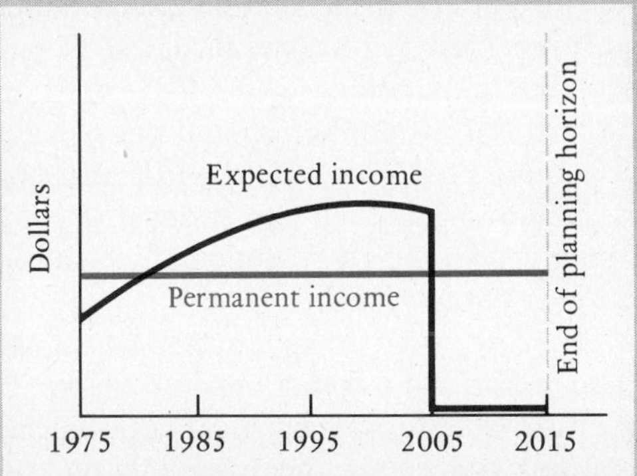

Expected current income may vary greatly over a lifetime, but expected permanent income is defined to be the constant annual equivalent. The graph shows a hypothetical expected income stream from work for a household whose planning horizon was 40 years from 1975. The current income rises to a peak, then falls slowly for a while, and finally falls sharply on retirement. The corresponding permanent income is the amount the household could consume at a steady rate over its lifetime by borrowing early against future earnings (as do most newly married couples), then repaying past debts, and finally saving for retirement when income is at its peak without either incurring debt or accumulating new wealth to be passed on to future generations.

---

[3] If the rate of interest were 7 percent, the household could invest the $2,000, consume an extra $161 a year, and just have nothing left at the end of 30 years.

the household gets a totally unforeseen increase of $2,000 a year for the rest of its life. In this event, the household's permanent income has risen by $2,000 because the household can actually consume $2,000 more every year without accumulating new debts. Although in both cases current income rises by $2,000, the effect on permanent income is very different in the two cases.

Keynesian theory assumes that *consumption expenditure* is related to current income and therefore predicts the same change in this year's consumption expenditure in each of the above cases. Permanent-income theories relate *actual consumption* to permanent income and therefore predict very different changes in actual consumption in each case. In the first case there would be only a small increase in actual annual consumption; in the second there would be a large increase.

In permanent-income theories, any change in current income that is thought to be temporary will have only a small effect on permanent income and hence on actual consumption.

Implications for the Behavior of the Economy

According to the permanent-income and the life-cycle hypotheses, actual consumption is not much affected by temporary changes in income. Does this mean that aggregate expenditure, $C + I + G + (X - M)$, is not much affected? *Not necessarily.* Consider what happens when households get a temporary increase in their incomes. If actual consumption is not greatly affected by this, then households must be saving most of this increase. But from the point of view of these theories, households save when they buy a durable good just as much as when they buy a financial asset such as a stock or a bond. In both cases actual current consumption is not changed.

Thus spending a temporary increase in income on bonds or on new cars is consistent with both the PIH and the LCH. But it makes a great deal of difference to the short-run behavior of the economy which is done. If households buy stocks and bonds, aggregate expenditure on currently produced final goods will not rise when income rises temporarily;[4] if households buy automobiles or any other durable consumer good, aggregate expenditure on currently produced final goods will rise when income rises temporarily. Thus the PIH and the LCH leave unsettled the question that is critical in determining the size of the multiplier: What is the reaction of household *expenditures* on currently produced goods and services, particularly durables, to short-term, temporary changes in income?

The PIH and LCH theories leave unanswered the critical question of the ability of short-term changes in fiscal policy to remove inflationary and deflationary gaps.

Assume, for example, that a serious deflationary gap emerges and that the government attempts to stimulate a recovery by giving tax rebates and by cutting tax rates—both on an announced temporary basis. This will raise households' current disposable incomes by the amount of the tax cuts, but it will raise their permanent incomes by only a small amount. According to the PIH, the flow of actual current consumption should not rise much. Yet it is quite consistent with the PIH that households should spend their tax savings on durable consumer goods, the consumption of which can be spread over many years.

In this case, even though actual consumption this year would not respond much to the tax cuts, expenditure would respond a great deal. Since current output and employment depends on expenditure rather than on actual consumption, the tax cut would be effective in stimulating the economy. However, it is also consistent with the PIH that households spend only a small part of their tax savings on consumption goods and seek to invest the rest in bonds and other financial assets. In this case the tax cuts may have only a small stimulating effect on the economy. It is important to note that the PIH and the LCH do *not* predict unambiguously that changes in taxes that are announced to be only short-lived will be ineffective in removing inflationary or deflationary gaps.

---

[4] Except for any indirect effect through changes in interest rates.

A Reconciliation of the Data

The PIH and the LCH are able to reconcile the observation that the *MPC* appears to be equal to the *APC* in long-period data while it is less than the *APC* in short-period and cross-sectional data.[5] They do this by relating changes in observed income to changes in permanent income.

Long-term time-series data using decade-by-decade averages remove the effects of temporary fluctuations in income. The observed changes in *Y* mainly represent permanent increases in real income because of economic growth. Long-term time-series studies will thus tend to measure accurately the propensity to consume out of permanent income.

Now consider short-term data. A study covering 10 or 15 years at the most and using annual observations of *C* and *Y* will use an income series dominated by temporary changes caused by cyclical fluctuations. When a household loses employment because of a business recession, it does not expect to remain unemployed forever; neither does it expect the extra income that it earns from heavy overtime work during a period of peak demand to persist. It may therefore be assumed that households expect these cyclical changes in current in-

---

[5] The short-run and long-run time-series data are described in Chapter 28 (see especially pages 508–509). Cross-section data are for a number of households at one point in time, and they show for that point in time how household consumption varies with household income. The data yield a consumption function similar to that obtained from short-term time-series data but with an even lower *MPC*.

come to be temporary and that they will thus have little effect on permanent income. Since consumption is assumed to depend on permanent income, it follows that the observed relation between consumption and cyclical changes in income will tend to be smaller than the relation shown by the long-term time-series data. What this shows, then, is the lack of relation between changes in consumption and temporary changes in income, not a lack of relation between changes in consumption and changes in permanent income.

A similar analysis shows that cross-section studies are strongly influenced by the behavior of households whose incomes have temporarily departed from their permanent levels. Thus cross-section studies should be expected to yield a much lower observed marginal propensity to consume than that yielded by long-term time-series studies.

Conclusion

While permanent-income type theories succeed in reconciling various empirical observations of consumption functions, they leave ambiguous the multiplier effects of temporary increases in income. They are consistent with a constancy in both the *MPC* and the *APC* when *permanent income* changes. They also suggest a high degree of stability of the actual flow of consumption in the face of temporary fluctuations in current income. This is consistent with an *APC* out of *current income* that varies inversely with current income, falling as income rises and rising as income falls.

MONEY IN THE NATIONAL INCOME MODEL
APPENDIX TO CHAPTER 34

We have studied the interaction between money, interest rates, and national income in terms of the apparatus in Figures 34-3, 34-4, and 34-5. A loose end in that model can best be seen by considering the impact of a change in the money supply. This leads to a fall in interest rates as shown in Figure 34-3(ii), to increases in expenditure as shown in Figure 34-3(ii), and to increased national income as shown in Figure 34-4. But increased national income in turn leads to an increased need for trans-

actions balances. This increased demand for money must then be added to the liquidity preference schedule in Figure 34-3. How is the increase in demand satisfied? Does accounting for it radically alter the conclusions of the analysis of Chapter 34?

The answer to the last question is no. This appendix provides a model that integrates monetary and expenditure factors and shows how they jointly determine the interest rate and the level of national income. The approach is that first suggested by the

British economist Sir John Hicks (awarded the Nobel Prize in economics in 1972) in his famous review of Keynes' *General Theory*, "Mr. Keynes and the Classics: A Suggested Interpretation." This approach involves identifying the relationship between income and interest rates that is imposed first by goods market equilibrium and then by money market equilibrium. We then bring the two together to determine the one combination of real national income and interest rate that satisfies both equilibrium conditions simultaneously. Finally we use the model to examine monetary and fiscal policy.

The Interest Rate and Aggregate Expenditure: The *IS* Curve

As we saw in going from Figure 34-3(ii) to Figure 34-4(i), a fall in the rate of interest is associated with a rise in the level of real national income due to increased investment expenditures. Figure 34A-1 depicts this relationship between interest rates and national income as the negatively sloped *IS* curve. The negative relationship is derived for *given* values of the other variables influencing the aggregate expenditure function of Figure 34-4(i). The *IS* curve shows the combinations of national income and the rate of interest for which aggregate expenditure just equals total production in the economy.

For given settings of the relationships underlying the aggregate expenditure function, the condition of goods market equilibrium—income equals aggregate expenditure—means that the level of national income will vary negatively with the interest rate.

Fiscal Policy

Increases in the level of government expenditure raise the total level of aggregate expenditure *for any given interest rate;* as Figure 32-1 shows, this in turn leads to a multiplier effect on national income. In terms of the present model, an increase in government expenditure causes the *IS* curve to shift upward to the right, as shown in Figure 34A-1. Combinations of national income and the interest rate

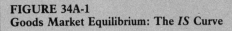

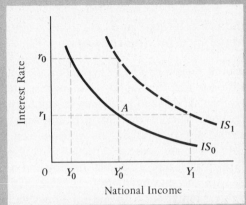

**FIGURE 34A-1
Goods Market Equilibrium: The *IS* Curve**

The locus of combinations of national income and the interest rate for which aggregate expenditure equals output is called the *IS* curve. The *IS* curve slopes downward to the right, indicating that a fall in the interest rate from r_0 to r_1 leads, via increased investment, to an increased level of national income from Y_0 to Y_0'. Expansionary fiscal policy creates excess demand for output and causes the *IS* curve to shift right to IS_1; from an initial position at A, the interest rate must rise to r_0, or national income must rise to Y_2, or some combination of both along IS_1 must occur.

that were on the original *IS* curve and hence were initially positions of equilibrium in the goods market are now positions of excess demand due to the increase in autonomous government demand. Hence output must rise to satisfy the increased demand (in the process leading to the now familiar multiplier effect), or interest rates must rise to reduce investment demand, or as IS_1 in Figure 34A-1 shows, some combination of both.[1]

Expansionary fiscal policy causes the *IS* curve to shift upward and to the right, creating a new locus of points for which aggregate expenditure equals national income.

[1] A reduction in taxes, by altering the relationship between national income and disposable income, would also lead to a rightward shift in the *IS* curve.

By similar reasoning, cuts in government spending or tax increases shift the *IS* curve down to the left. [53]

Liquidity Preference and National Income: The *LM* Curve

When the money supply is held constant, if the demand for and the supply of money are to be equal, the *total* demand for money arising from the transactions, speculative, and precautionary motives must also be constant. As we have seen, the demand for money can be expected to vary positively with the level of national income and negatively with the rate of interest. If there is to be monetary equilibrium with a given money supply, any increase in national income must be accompanied by an increase in the interest rate to keep total money demand constant. This is depicted by the positively sloped *LM* curve in Figure 34A-2. The *LM* curve shows the combinations of national income and the rate of interest for which total money demand is constant at the level of a given money supply.

For a given money supply, the condition of monetary market equilibrium means that the level of national income will vary directly with the interest rate.

Monetary Policy

An increase in the supply of money resulting from an open market purchase by the central bank causes the *LM* curve to shift downward to the right, as in Figure 34A-2. The combinations of national income and interest rate that were on the original *LM* curve and hence that were initially positions of monetary equilibrium now correspond to excess supply due to the increase in the supply of money. To reestablish equilibrium, the demand for money must increase to match the larger money supply; hence national income must rise, or the interest rate must fall, or as LM_1 in Figure 34A-2 shows, some combination of both.

An increase in the money supply causes the *LM* curve to shift downward to the right, creating a new locus of

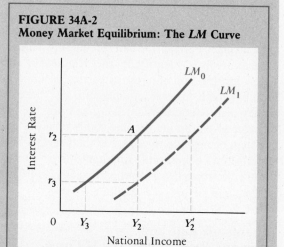

FIGURE 34A-2
Money Market Equilibrium: The *LM* Curve

The locus of combinations of national income and the interest rate for which total money demand equals a given money supply is called the *LM* curve. The *LM* curve slopes upward to the right, indicating that a fall in the rate of interest from r_2 to r_3, which causes the demand for money to rise, must be accompanied by a fall in income, say from Y_2 to Y_3, in order to keep money demand equal to the constant money supply. An open market purchase creates an excess supply of money and causes the *LM* curve to shift right to LM_1; from an initial position at A, the interest rate must fall to r_3, or national income must rise to Y_2', or some combination of both along LM_1 must occur.

points for which total money demand equals the money supply.

By similar reasoning, a decrease in the money supply causes the *LM* curve to shift upward to the left. [54]

Macroeconomic Equilibrium: Determination of National Income and the Interest Rate

The model is shown in Figure 34A-3. The intersection of the two curves indicates the only combination of national income and the rate of interest for which aggregate expenditure equals national

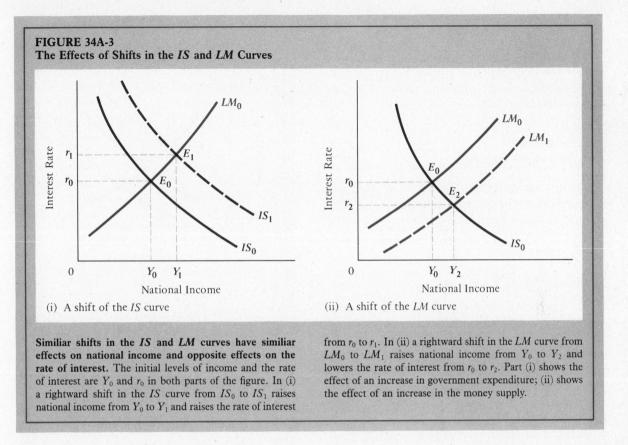

FIGURE 34A-3
The Effects of Shifts in the IS and LM Curves

(i) A shift of the IS curve

(ii) A shift of the LM curve

Similiar shifts in the IS and LM curves have similar effects on national income and opposite effects on the rate of interest. The initial levels of income and the rate of interest are Y_0 and r_0 in both parts of the figure. In (i) a rightward shift in the IS curve from IS_0 to IS_1 raises national income from Y_0 to Y_1 and raises the rate of interest from r_0 to r_1. In (ii) a rightward shift in the LM curve from LM_0 to LM_1 raises national income from Y_0 to Y_2 and lowers the rate of interest from r_0 to r_2. Part (i) shows the effect of an increase in government expenditure; (ii) shows the effect of an increase in the money supply.

income *and* the demand for money is equal to the supply.

The intersection of the IS and LM curves gives the equilibrium levels of national income and the rate of interest in a model that combines both expenditure and monetary influences.

Figure 34A-3 shows the effects of particular shifts in the *IS and LM* curves. This analysis leads to four general predictions.

1. A rightward shift of the *IS* curve raises national income and the rate of interest.
2. A leftward shift of the *IS* curve lowers national income and the rate of interest.
3. A rightward shift of the *LM* curve raises national income and lowers the rate of interest.

4. A leftward shift of the *LM* curve lowers national income and raises the rate of interest.

The Effects of Fiscal and Monetary Policy

Given our analysis of the effects of government expenditure on the *IS* curve and the effects of the money supply on the *LM* curve, we can summarize the analysis in our four basic predictions about the effects of monetary and fiscal policy.

1. An increase in *G* raises national income and raises the rate of interest.
2. An increase in the money supply raises national income and lowers the rate of interest.
3. A decrease in *G* lowers national income and lowers the rate of interest.

4. A decrease in the money supply lowers national income and raises the rate of interest.

These results represent what may be called the *neo-Keynesian synthesis*, in which both monetary and fiscal policies have an effect on national income and interest rates. [55]

The Price Level and Aggregate Demand

So far we have treated the price level as given and presumed that all changes in national income were changes in *real* output. Consider now what would happen to the analysis if the price level were allowed to vary.

Changes in the Price Level

As Figure 34-6 shows, an increase in the price level leads to an increase in liquidity preference. In order for money market equilibrium to be preserved, the interest rate must rise (as Figure 34-6), or the level of income must fall, or, since either leads to a reduction in money demand, some combination of both must occur—that is, the *LM* curve must shift upward to the left.

A fall in the price level reduces liquidity preference and the *LM* curve shifts down and to the right.

Increases in the price level cause the *LM* curve to shift upward to the left; decreases in the price level cause the *LM* curve to shift downward to the right.

But from the previous section we know that the effect in the first case is to reduce national income while the effect in the second case is to increase national income. This is illustrated in Figure 34A-4.

Equilibrium in the money and goods markets combined implies that the price level and national income are negatively related, as summarized in the downward-sloping aggregate demand curve.

The relationship, summarized in the aggregate demand curve, is a straightforward extension of the

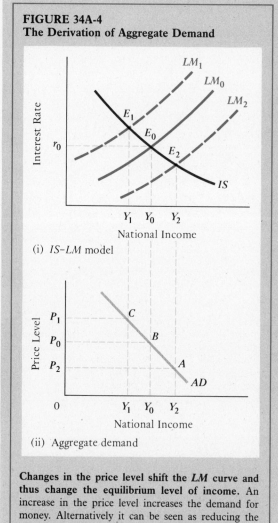

FIGURE 34A-4
The Derivation of Aggregate Demand

(i) *IS–LM* model

(ii) Aggregate demand

Changes in the price level shift the *LM* curve and thus change the equilibrium level of income. An increase in the price level increases the demand for money. Alternatively it can be seen as reducing the real value of the existing money stock. The excess demand for money leads to a leftward shift of the LM_0 curve to LM_1 and a fall in national income. A fall in the price level creates an excess supply of money and a rightward shift of the LM_0 curve to LM_2. The price level and national income are inversely related, as shown by the *AD* curve in (ii).

transmission mechanism running from liquidity preference to the rate of interest to aggregate expenditure.

Shifts in the Aggregate Demand Curve

The *AD* curve was derived on the basis of a given money supply and given relationships underlying the *IS* curve; it is a straightforward exercise to demonstrate that fiscal and monetary policies, by influencing the *IS* and *LM* curves, cause the *AD* curve to shift. [56] The mechanism by which monetary and fiscal policy cause the shift in *AD* is illustrated in Figure 34-4.

An increase in the money supply means that the *LM* curve corresponding to any particular price level shifts downward to the right. Hence that price level now corresponds to a higher level of real national income; that is, the aggregate demand curve shifts to the right as a result of an increase in the money supply.

An increase in government expenditure causes the *IS* curve to shift upward to the right as before; it now intersects any given *LM* curve at a higher level of national income. Again, any given price level now corresponds to a larger real national income; that is, the aggregate demand curve shifts to the right as a result of an increase in government expenditure.

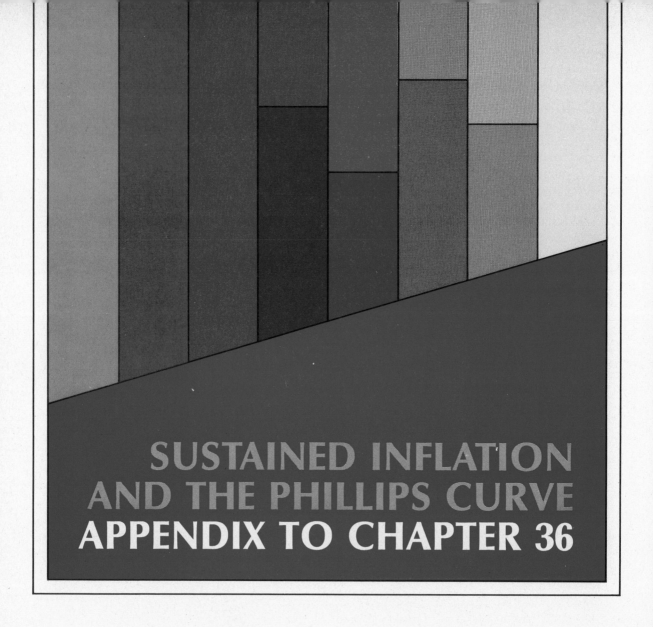

SUSTAINED INFLATION AND THE PHILLIPS CURVE
APPENDIX TO CHAPTER 36

In this appendix we use the *Phillips curve*, intro-duced in Box 36-2 on pages 690–691, to analyze sustained inflations.

The Price Phillips Curve

The Phillips curve shown in Box 36-2 describes a relationship between the rate of change of *wages* and the state of demand, as measured by the level of national income. As we saw, changes in wages

cause the *SRAS* curve to shift, giving rise to changes in the price level. These two steps are commonly combined to produce a new curve re-lating the rate of change of the *price level* and the level of national income. Such a curve, often re-ferred to as a *price Phillips curve*, is shown in Figure 36A-1.[1]

[1] The lower case p stands for the logarithm of the price level, so Δp indicates a percentage change in the price level.

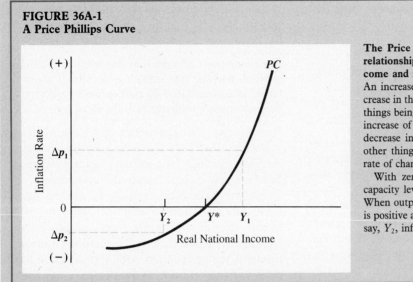

FIGURE 36A-1
A Price Phillips Curve

The Price Phillips curve shows the positive relationship between the level of national income and rate of increase in *the price level.* An increase in national income leads to an increase in the rate of change of wages and, other things being equal, to an increase in the rate of increase of prices. A fall in income leads to a decrease in the rate of change of wages and, other things being equal, to a decrease in the rate of change of prices.

With zero core inflation and output at its capacity level, Y^*, inflation is zero as shown. When output is above Y^* at, say, Y_1, inflation is positive at Δp_1. When output is below Y^* at, say, Y_2, inflation is negative at Δp_2.

The conditions under which it is possible to derive a price Phillips curve from the original relation between wages and national income are fairly complicated.[2] But the curve is commonly used, and we shall focus on it in this appendix. (We shall henceforth refer to the price Phillips curve simply as the Phillips curve.) The key simplification is that once the level of income has been determined—by the intersection of the *SRAS* and *AD* curves, as before—the rate of inflation can be read *directly* off the Phillips curve.

Notice that the Phillips curve in Figure 36A-1 has the *rate of change of prices* on the vertical axis. The aggregate supply curve that appears so frequently in the text has *the level of prices* on the vertical axis. Since both curves have real national income on the horizontal axis they are easily confused. They must therefore be carefully distinguished.

[2] For example, at any given level of income the relationship between the rate of change of wages given by the figure in the box and the rate of change of prices given by Figure 36A-1 depends on what is assumed about how fast the central bank is causing the *AD* curve to shift.

The Components of Inflation

Recall the three influences that cause the *SRAS* curve to shift upward and hence the price level to rise: demand, expectations, and shocks. We encountered these on page 689. In this appendix we continue to use the terms *demand* and *shock* but introduce the term *core inflation* as a generalization of the term *expectations* used in the text. The rate of increase of prices can now be written as the sum of the three components:

$$\Delta p = C + DE + SE$$

where Δp is the annual percentage rate of changes of prices (i.e., the rate of inflation); C refers to core inflation; DE to demand effect; and SE to shock effect. We now look at these components one at a time.

Demand Inflation

Demand inflation refers to the influence on the price level of GNP gaps. We have seen that an inflationary gap involves upward pressure on wages and hence on the price level while a recessionary gap involves downward pressure. This is shown in Figure 36A-1 by the vertical distance between the Phillips curve and the horizontal axis.

The Phillips curve in Figure 36A-1 is merely a novel way of expressing relations we have used many times before. (It is important to remember, however, that Figure 36A-1 does not tell the whole story of inflation; it only describes the effects of *demand.*) These relations include the following:

1. There is neither upward nor downward pressure of demand on the price level when national income is at its potential level. Graphically the Phillips curve cuts the axis at Y^*.
2. When there is an inflationary gap, wages and other costs will rise. As we have seen, this shifts the *SRAS* curve upward and causes the price level to rise. The inflation continues as long as the gap persists. Graphically the Phillips curve lies above the axis where Y exceeds Y^*.
3. When there is a recessionary gap, wages and other costs will fall. This shifts the *SRAS* curve downward and causes the price level to fall. The deflation continues as long as the gap persists. Graphically the Phillips curve lies below the axis when Y is less than Y^*.
4. The speed of the upward adjustment of the price level in the face of an inflationary gap exceeds the speed of the downward adjustment in the face of a recessionary gap. Graphically the Phillips curve gets steeper the further to the right one moves along it. [57]

Core Inflation

The demand component cannot be the whole explanation of inflation since, if it were, inflation would only occur if national income exceeded Y^* and inflation could be quickly removed by forcing income back to Y^*. This prediction is emphatically rejected by the recent experiences of the United States and other Western economies. To explain what we observe about inflation we add the concept of core inflation. Core inflation refers to the underlying trend of inflation and it is referred to by several different names: *core* inflation, *expectational* inflation, *inertial* inflation, or the *underlying rate* of inflation.

In the text we singled out expectations as a main influence on the price level in addition to demand. But we also saw that how expectations are formed is a major source of controversy among economists.

The controversy actually runs deeper than that; some question whether it is explicit expectations about the future or inertia based on past experience that really dominates wage settlements in the short run.

For example, past experience may matter if recent wage increases have failed to keep up with price increases; in such circumstances current wage settlements may have a "catch-up" component.

For these and other reasons, we use the general term **core inflation** to describe those persistent effects that do not depend on current demand conditions. These include expectations and other elements that stem from both forward- and backward-looking behavior. Some elements may change quickly, others only slowly. Their total influence at any point in time is summarized in the term *core inflation*.

Core inflation operates on the *SRAS* curve through the effects of wages and other costs.[3] Core inflation may also be related to *expected future changes* in wage and capital costs since firms who plan to change prices only infrequently must set prices on the basis of their expected costs over their planning period. If that is the case, to make our concept of core inflation operative we need a theory of how firms form their expectations of the future movement of costs. Some of the theories on how the expectations that determine the core inflation rate are formed were discussed in the text, and they are taken up again in Chapter 42.

Graphically the core inflation rate is added to the demand effect by shifting the Phillips curve upward by the amount of the core rate. This gives rise to a *core-augmented Phillips curve* or more commonly an *expectations-augmented Phillips curve*, as shown in Figure 36A-2. At any given level of income, the height of the core-augmented Phillips curve is given by the sum of the demand effect and the core rate of inflation. For example, at $Y = Y^*$,

---

[3] As we saw in the text, some variations in net profit margins can and do occur. These cause price inflation to diverge temporarily from cost inflation and are included in shock inflation.

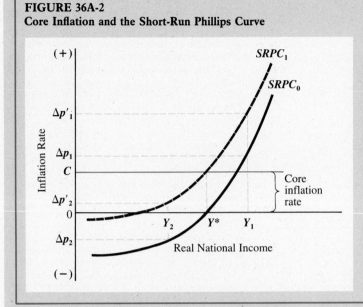

FIGURE 36A-2
Core Inflation and the Short-Run Phillips Curve

Core inflation shifts the price Phillips curve, and so changes the rate of inflation that corresponds to any given level of national income. The curve $SRPC_0$, which reproduces the Phillips curve from Figure 36A-1, corresponds to a zero core inflation rate. When core inflation rises to, say, C, the Phillips curve shifts up to $SRPC_1$. The rate of inflation at Y^* rises from 0 to C. At Y_1, which is greater than Y^*, inflation rises from Δp_1 to $\Delta p'_1$. At Y_2, which is less than Y^*, inflation was initially negative at Δp_2 but now becomes positive at $\Delta p'_2$.

when demand inflation is zero, the height of the Phillips curve is given by the core rate. At any other level of income the rate of inflation differs from the demand effect by an amount equal to the core rate.

The Short-Run Phillips Curve

Because the Phillips curve shifts upward or downward as the core rate of inflation rises or falls, it is called a **short-run Phillips curve (SRPC)** when it is drawn at any particular height above Y^* (that is, for any given level of core inflation).

The short-run Phillips curve is drawn for a given rate of core inflation.

Shock Inflation

Shock inflation refers to once-and-for-all changes that give a temporary upward or downward jolt to the price level. These included changes in indirect taxes, changes in profit margins, changes in import prices, and all kinds of other factors often referred to as *supply shocks*. Shock inflation includes every-

thing that is not included under demand and core inflation.

Summary

Putting all of this together, the current inflation rate depends on the influence of (i) demand as indicated by the GNP gap, *demand inflation;* (ii) expected increase in costs, *core inflation;* and (iii) a series of exogenous forces coming mainly from the supply side, *shock inflation.* These three components of inflation may be illustrated both numerically and graphically.

For a numerical example, assume that in the absence of any demand pressures, prices would rise by 10 percent because firms expect underlying costs to rise by 10 percent; that this price rise is moderated by 1 percentage point because costs only rise by 9 percent due to heavy unemployment; and that the price rise is augmented by 3 percentage points because large increases in indirect taxes force prices up. The final inflation is 12 percent, made up of 10 percent core inflation minus 1 percent demand inflation plus 3 percent shock inflation.

FIGURE 36A-3
The Components of Inflation Illustrated

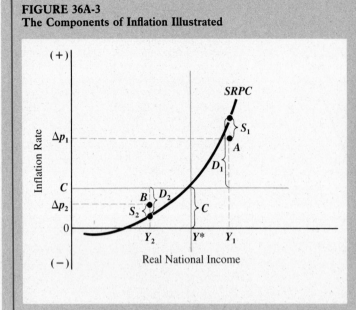

The inflation rate can be separated into three components: core inflation, demand inflation, and shock inflation. In the figure the Phillips curve is drawn for a given core rate of inflation and hence is labeled as a short-run Phillips curve. The given core rate, C, is shown by the height of the horizontal colored line.

Point A indicates a national income of Y_1 combined with an inflation rate of Δp_1. This rate is composed of the following: a core rate, C; a positive demand component, D_1 (determined by the shape of $SRPC$); and a negative shock component, S_1.

Point B indicates a national income of Y_2 combined with an inflation rate of Δp_2. This rate is composed of the following: core inflation is once again given by C; the demand component, D_2, which is now negative (since income, Y_2, is less than Y^*); and a positive shock component, S_2.

Graphically, the components of inflation are illustrated in Figure 36A-3 for two cases with a common positive core inflation component. The curve labeled $SRPC$ is the Phillips curve shifted up by the core inflation rate. Its height above the axis at Y^* thus indicates core inflation. Points along $SRPC$ where Y does not equal Y^* indicate how much the pressures of excess or deficient demand cause inflation to deviate from the core rate. Finally the amount by which actual inflation lies above or below the $SRPC$ shows the amount by which shocks cause the actual inflation rate to deviate from the sum of the core and the demand effects.

Expectations and Changes in Inflation

Originally the Phillips curve of Figure 36A-1 was thought to provide the whole explanation of inflation. When it was realized that the short-run Phil-

lips curve shifted upward or downward, the concept of core inflation was added to explain this. Changes in the core rate shifts in the short-run Phillips curve. As a result we have the following conclusion.

There is a family of short-run Phillips curves, one for each core rate of inflation.

This is illustrated in Figure 36A-4. Let us now see what governs changes in the core rate and hence shifts in the $SRPC$.

Look at point Z on $SRPC_1$ in Figure 36A-5, which reproduces $SRPC_1$ from Figure 36A-4 and corresponds to a core inflation rate of C_1. At Z, shock inflation is zero and demand inflation is positive (since $Y_1 > Y^*$) so the actual inflation rate is above the core rate of C_1. Sooner or later this excess will come to be expected, the core rate will then rise, and the $SRPC$ will shift upward. *As long as national income is held above Y^*, the actual inflation rate will exceed the core rate and, as a result, sooner or later the core rate will rise. This means that the*

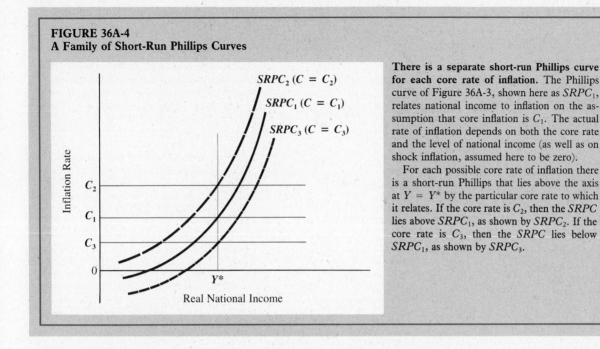

FIGURE 36A-4
A Family of Short-Run Phillips Curves

There is a separate short-run Phillips curve for each core rate of inflation. The Phillips curve of Figure 36A-3, shown here as $SRPC_1$, relates national income to inflation on the assumption that core inflation is C_1. The actual rate of inflation depends on both the core rate and the level of national income (as well as on shock inflation, assumed here to be zero).

For each possible core rate of inflation there is a short-run Phillips that lies above the axis at $Y = Y^*$ by the particular core rate to which it relates. If the core rate is C_2, then the $SRPC$ lies above $SRPC_1$, as shown by $SRPC_2$. If the core rate is C_3, then the $SRPC$ lies below $SRPC_1$, as shown by $SRPC_3$.

short-run Phillips curve will sooner or later shift upward, as indicated by the arrow above point Z.

Now look at point W in Figure 36A-5 where again core inflation is C_1 and shock inflation is zero. At W demand inflation is negative (since $Y_2 < Y^*$) so the actual inflation rate is below the core rate of C_1. Sooner or later this difference will influence expectations and the core rate will fall. *As long as national income is held below Y*, the actual inflation rate will be less than the core rate and sooner or later the core rate will fall. This means that sooner or later the short-run Phillips curve will begin to shift downward, as indicated by the arrow below* W.

So we have a basic prediction of the theory:

A persistent inflationary gap will sooner or later cause the inflation rate to accelerate, while a persistent recessionary gap will sooner or later cause the inflation rate to decelerate.

This of course is the acceleration hypothesis that we have already encountered in Chapter 36. Let us now examine it in more detail.

Accelerating Inflation

Consider an economy with a core inflation of C_1 that has just experienced an increase in aggregate demand so that output is above Y^* as at point Z in Figure 36A-5. There is an inflationary gap with a positive inflation rate; the $SRAS$ curve will be shifting upward while monetary validation by the central bank is shifting the AD curve upward. (It may be worth reiterating what is happening here: Core inflation produces the rise in prices that results from firms' expectations about the long-run trend in costs; the demand component produces the addition to inflation due to what are thought to be transitory demand factors; shock inflation is still treated as zero.)

Is this situation sustainable? Only if the Phillips curve remains stable. If the short-run Phillips curve stayed put, policymakers could conclude that they had achieved a pretty good trade-off. They would have gained a permanent increase in output of Y^*Y_1 at the cost of a permanent increase in inflation from C_1 to Δp_1.

FIGURE 36A-5
Shifts in the Short-Run Phillips Curve

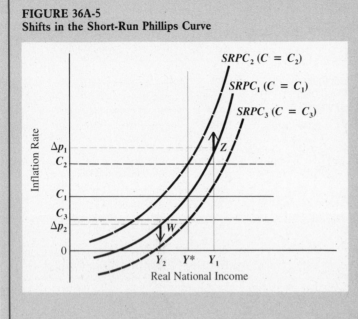

Changes in the core rate of inflation, which arise when actual inflation differs from the core rate, cause the short-run Phillips curve to shift. With a core inflation rate of C_1, the short-run Phillips curve is $SRPC_1$, reproduced from Figure 36A-4.

If income is maintained at Y_1, greater than Y^*, actual inflation will be Δp_1, greater than the core rate, as indicated by point Z. Eventually this excess of the actual inflation rate over the core rate will cause the core rate to rise, from C_1, say, to C_2, shifting the short-run Phillips curve to $SRPC_2$, as indicated by the arrow above point Z.

If income is maintained at Y_2, less than Y^*, actual inflation will be Δp_2, less than the core rate, as indicated by point W. Eventually the shortfall of actual inflation below the core rate will cause the core rate to fall below C_1, say, to C_3, causing the short-run Phillips curve to shift down to $SRPC_3$, as indicated by the arrow below W.

But as we have seen, this is not the end of the story. The persistence of a demand inflation will eventually cause the core inflation rate to rise and hence cause the $SRPC$ to shift upward. In turn, this increases the rate at which the $SRAS$ curve is shifting upward. Let us trace this process in detail.

At point Z, prices and costs are rising at Δp_1 per year, and sooner or later firms and workers will stop believing that this increase from the old rate C_1 is a transitory phenomenon. They will come to expect some of this increase to persist and incorporate it into core inflation. Let us say that, after a passage of time, firms come to expect wages and other costs to rise at the rate C_2 each period. This will produce a core inflation at a rate of C_2 per annum in Figure 36A-5. The short-run Phillips curve now shifts up to $SRPC_2$ in the figure. The rise in the core rate of inflation increases the actual inflation rate corresponding to each possible level of national income. If national income is maintained at Y_1 so that demand inflation remains positive, the actual inflation rate rises above Δp_1.

Now the $SRAS$ curve will be shifting upward more rapidly. If output is to be maintained at Y_1, the central bank will have to increase the rate at which the money supply is being expanded. This will cause the AD curve to shift up more rapidly to match the more rapid upward shift in the $SRAS$ curve. This is illustrated in terms of the $SRAS$ and AD curves in Figure 36-3.

The actual inflation rate, Δp_2, is well above the core rate, C_2. Sooner or later this will cause the core rate to rise again, and the short-run Phillips curve will again shift upwad. As long as output is maintained at Y_1 so that demand inflation is positive, this process of growing core inflation will continue.

From this an important conclusion follows:

If the central bank validates any rate of inflation that results from Y being held above Y^*, then the inflation rate itself will accelerate continuously *and* there will also be an acceleration in the rate of monetary expansion required to frustrate the monetary adjustment mechanism.

The Long-Run Phillips Curve

Is there any level of income in this model that is compatible with a constant actual rate of inflation? The answer is yes, potential income. When income is at Y^*, the demand component of inflation is *zero*, as shown in Figure 36A-1. This means that, still letting shock inflation be zero, actual inflation equals core inflation. There are no surprises. No one's plans are upset, so no one has any incentive to alter plans as a result of what actually happens to inflation.

Providing the inflation rate is fully validated and shock inflation is zero, any rate of inflation can persist indefinitely as long as income is held at its potential level.

We now define the **long-run Phillips curve** as the relation between *national income* and *stable rates of inflation* that neither accelerate nor decelerate. This occurs when the core and actual inflation rates are equal. On the theory just described, the long-run Phillips curve is vertical. This is illustrated in Figure 36A-6.

Maintaining a point on the *LRPC* leads to steady inflation at the core rate. This is illustrated in Figure 36A-7, where we show a situation with a positive core inflation rate and full monetary accommodation by the central bank. In the top panel the intersection of the *SRAS* and *AD* curves determines Y at Y^*. In the bottom panel the Phillips curve shows the rate of inflation. There is no demand effect on inflation so the actual and core inflation rates are equal. As a result, the situation is sustainable (as long as the central bank continues to validate the core inflation). The increasing price level in the top panel reflects the positive inflation rate indicated in the bottom panel. Note that in the latter, since the core rate is not changing, the *SRPC* will be stable, which means we are also on the *LRPC*.

We can now state the following general conclusion.

The long-run Phillips curve is vertical at Y^*; only Y^* is compatible with a stable rate of inflation, and any stable rate is, if fully validated, compatible with Y^*.

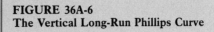

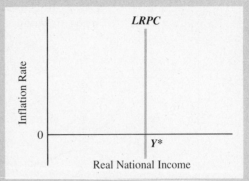

FIGURE 36A-6
The Vertical Long-Run Phillips Curve

When actual inflation equals expected inflation, there is no trade-off between inflation and unemployment. In long-term equilibrium the actual rate of inflation must remain equal to the expected rate (otherwise expectations would be revised). This can only occur at the full-employment level of income Y^*; that is, along the *LRPC*.

At Y^* there is no demand pressure on the price level; hence the only influence on actual inflation is expected inflation. Any stable rate of inflation (provided it is validated by the appropriate rate of monetary expansion) is compatible with Y^* and its associated natural rate of unemployment.

The Natural Rate of Unemployment

We have talked about variations of Y from Y^*, but for every level of national income there is an associated level of unemployment. Recasting these conclusions in terms of unemployment we have the following: As before, call the unemployment associated with Y^* the natural rate of unemployment. Note that unemployment can be pushed below the natural rate but only at the cost of opening up an inflationary gap. If the government seeks to maintain this lower rate of unemployment, the inflation rate will accelerate and will have to be validated by ever increasing rates of monetary expansion.

The lowest rate of unemployment that can be maintained without a tendency for the rate of inflation to accelerate is the natural rate.

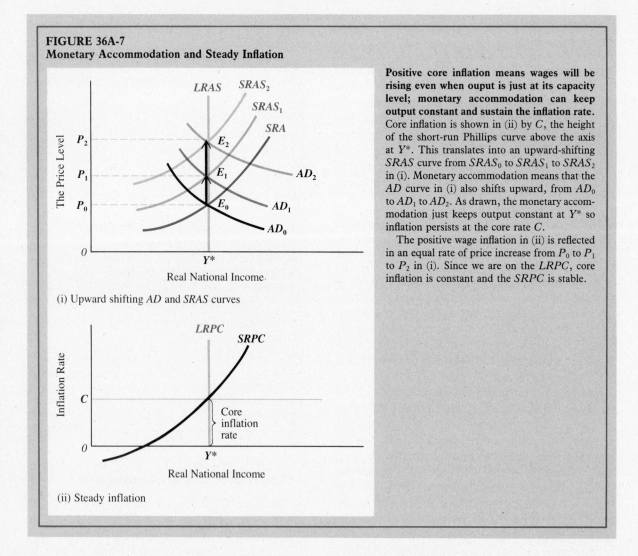

FIGURE 36A-7
Monetary Accommodation and Steady Inflation

(i) Upward shifting *AD* and *SRAS* curves

(ii) Steady inflation

Positive core inflation means wages will be rising even when ouput is just at its capacity level; monetary accommodation can keep output constant and sustain the inflation rate. Core inflation is shown in (ii) by C, the height of the short-run Phillips curve above the axis at Y^*. This translates into an upward-shifting $SRAS$ curve from $SRAS_0$ to $SRAS_1$ to $SRAS_2$ in (i). Monetary accommodation means that the AD curve in (i) also shifts upward, from AD_0 to AD_1 to AD_2. As drawn, the monetary accommodation just keeps output constant at Y^* so inflation persists at the core rate C.

The positive wage inflation in (ii) is reflected in an equal rate of price increase from P_0 to P_1 to P_2 in (i). Since we are on the $LRPC$, core inflation is constant and the $SRPC$ is stable.

Implications for Monetary Policy

The foregoing analysis has three major implications for the understanding and conduct of monetary policy.

First, the interaction among money, inflation, and output is complex. In particular, it depends on how expectations are formulated. Monetary policies may affect expectations differently at different times. Therefore, it would be wrong to expect a simple, mechanical relationship between the money supply and the behavior of output and the price level.

Second, differences between the expected rate of inflation and the rate that is being validated by monetary policy lead to changes in the level of output and in the actual rate of inflation. Hence changes in the rate of monetary expansion can have powerful though not entirely predictable effects on the economy.

Third, in the long run GNP will move to the level indicated by the long-run aggregate supply curve and the long-run Phillips curve. This means that changes in the rate of monetary expansion will cause changes in the level of output only temporarily. In the long run changes in the rate of monetary expansion have their influence only on the rate of inflation.

Some Extensions

Shock inflation. All of the above analysis has been done on the assumption that shock inflation is zero. In today's world many shocks hit the price level. What we see is a much less regular experience than the simple combination of core plus demand inflation. The inflation rate varies quite substantially from period to period due to the action of the many shocks that impinge on it.

Asymmetrical speeds of reaction. The shape of the Phillips curve means that it is easier to raise the core rate than to lower it. The change in the core rate from period to period depends on the discrepancy between the actual rate and the core rate. The steepness of the short-run Phillips curve above Y^* means that it is easy to create a substantial gap between the actual rate and the core rate by increasing the inflationary gap. This will tend to drag up the core rate fairly quickly. The flatness of the short-run Phillips curve below Y^* means that only a small discrepancy between the actual and the core rates can be created by even a large recessionary gap. Therefore the core rate can be depressed only slowly by creating recessionary gaps.

It is an important prediction of this theory that the core rate of inflation can accelerate fairly quickly but will decelerate only slowly.

Summary

We now summarize the key points of this theory and indicate where there is substantial agreement and where there is controversy with competing theories.

1. *The rate of growth of prices must follow the trend rate of growth of costs quite closely.* There is little disagreement over this relation, which defines the core, or underlying, rate of inflation. Notice, however, that it is just a matter of simple arithmetic that the major determinant of price inflation is cost inflation. This says nothing about causes. Costs could be rising because of the pressure of excess demand in factor markets or because of the exercise of arbitrary power on the part of unions.

2. *The core inflation rate changes very slowly.* There is a substantial disagreement over this point, for some economists believe the core rate can change quite rapidly. This key controversy underlies many differences in policy recommendations.

3. *The influence of demand on inflation is asymmetrical.* Inflationary gaps cause inflation to rise well above the core rate while output gaps force the actual rate only slightly below the core rate. The evidence for this asymmetry is extremely strong, although some economists deny it.

4. *Shocks caused by such influences as changes in indirect taxes, agricultural crop failures, or increases in import prices temporarily affect the inflation rate.* Economists do not always agree on this point and, at the time of the first OPEC oil-price shocks in 1974, some said that if oil-related prices rose, other prices would fall, keeping the price level constant. As a result of the evidence of the OPEC shocks, most economists now agree that supply shocks affect the price level, causing temporary deviations in the rate of inflation from what it would otherwise be. Another example of a clear supply-shock inflation was the rise in the price level that occurred in Britain in 1979–1980 after income taxes were cut and value-added taxes raised by the new Conservative government.

5. *Demand-induced rises in the inflation rate yield only temporary increases in national income.* Any departure of national income from Y^* sets in motion forces that cause a return to Y^*. Output in excess of Y^* causes an inflation that sets in motion the monetary adjustment mechanism. Frustration of the monetary adjustment mechanism by monetary expansion can sustain output above Y^* but only if the rate of increase of wages, prices, and money is continually accelerating.

THE GOLD STANDARD AND THE BRETTON WOODS SYSTEM
APPENDIX TO CHAPTER 40

Two episodes with fixed exchange rates were experienced in the twentieth century. Each ultimately failed. The gold standard, whose origins are as old as currency itself, was used until the late 1920s and early 1930s. The Bretton Woods system, which was the only payments system ever to be designed and established by conscious action, was born out of World War II and collapsed a little less than 30 years later. Their histories are instructive, not the least because many people continue to propose returning to one or the other of these systems.

The Gold Standard

The gold standard was not *designed;* it just happened. It arose out of the general acceptance of gold as the commodity to be used as money. In most countries paper currency was freely convertible into gold at a fixed rate. In 1914 the U.S. dollar was worth 0.053 standard ounces of gold, while the British pound sterling was worth 0.257 standard ounces. This meant that the pound was worth 4.86 times as much as the dollar in terms of gold, thus making £1 worth U.S. $4.86. (In practice the exchange rate fluctuated within narrow limits set by the cost of shipping gold.)

As long as all countries were on the gold standard, a person in one country was sure of being able to make payments to a person in another.

The Gold Flow, Price Level Mechanism

The gold standard was supposed to work to maintain a balance of international payments by forcing adjustments in price levels within individual countries. Consider a country that had a balance-of-payments deficit because the value of what its citizens were importing (i.e., buying) from other countries exceeded the value of what they were exporting (i.e., selling) to other countries. The demand for foreign exchange would exceed the supply on this country's foreign exchange market.

Some people who wished to make foreign payments would be unable to obtain foreign exchange. No matter; they would merely convert their domestic currency into gold and ship the gold. Therefore, some people in a surplus country would secure gold in payment for exports. They would deposit this to their credit and accept claims on gold—in terms of convertible paper money or bank deposits—in return. Thus deficit countries would be losing gold while surplus countries would be gaining it.

Under the gold standard, the whole money supply was linked to the supply of gold (see pages 775–777). The international movements of gold would therefore lead to a fall in the money supply in the deficit country and a rise in the surplus country.[1] If full employment prevails, changes in the domestic money supply will cause changes in domestic price levels. Deficit countries would thus have falling price levels while surplus countries would have rising price levels. The exports of deficit countries would become relatively cheaper,

while those of surplus countries would become relatively more expensive. The resulting changes in quantities bought and sold would move the balance of payments toward an equilibrium position.

Actual Experience of the Gold Standard

The half century before World War I was the heyday of the gold standard; during this period, the automatic mechanism seemed to work well. Subsequent research has suggested, however, that the gold standard succeeded during the period mainly because it was not called on to do much work. Trade flowed between nations in large and rapidly expanding volume, and it is probable that existing exchange rates and price levels were never far from the equilibrium ones. No major trading country found itself with a serious and persistent balance-of-payments deficit, so no major country was called upon to restore equilibrium through a large change in its domestic price level.

Inevitably there were short-run fluctuations, but they were ironed out either by movements of short-run capital in response to changes in interest rates or by changes in national income and employment.

Problems in the 1920s

In the 1920s the gold standard was called on to do a major job. It failed utterly, and it was abandoned. How did this come about? During World War I, most belligerent countries had suspended convertibility of currency (they went off the gold standard). Most countries suffered major inflations, but the degree of inflation differed from country to country. As we have seen, this will lead to changes in the equilibrium exchange rates.

After the war, countries returned to the gold standard (they restored convertibility of their currencies into gold). For reasons of prestige, many insisted on returning to the prewar rates. This meant that some countries' goods were overpriced and others' underpriced. Large deficits and surpluses in the balance of payments inevitably appeared, and the adjustment mechanism required that price levels should change in each of the coun-

---

[1] When the person who received gold deposited it in a bank, the bank would be in the position of the bank in Table 33-3 on page 625, and a multiple expansion of deposit money would ensue.

tries in order to restore equilibrium. Exchange rates were not adjusted, and price levels changed very slowly. By the onset of the Great Depression, equilibrium price levels had not yet been attained. The financial chaos brought on by the depression destroyed the existing payments system.

Major Disabilities of a Gold Standard

Although inflationary policies combined with an overly rigid adherence to pre-World War I exchange rates led to the downfall of the gold standard, one may ask whether an altered gold standard, based on more realistic exchange rates, might not have succeeded. While some modern economists, notably Canadian Robert Mundell of Columbia University, think it would, most believe the gold standard suffered from key weaknesses.

Like any other fixed exchange rate system, it required a mechanism for orderly adjustment to changes in the supply and demand for a nation's currency. The price adjustment process worked too slowly and too imperfectly to cope with large and persistent disequilibrium.

Furthermore, gold as the basis for an international money supply suffered several special disadvantages. They included a limited supply that could not be expanded as rapidly as increases in the volume of world trade required, an uneven distribution of existing and potential new gold supplies among the nations of the world, and a large and frequently volatile speculative demand for gold during periods of crisis. These factors could cause large, disruptive variations in the supply of gold available for international monetary purposes.

The Bretton Woods System

The one lesson that everyone thought had been learned from the 1930s was that a system of either freely fluctuating exchange rates or fixed rates with easily accomplished devaluations was a sure route to disaster. In order to achieve a system of orderly exchange rates that would facilitate the free flow of trade following World War II, representatives of most of the countries that had participated in the

alliance against Germany, Italy, and Japan met at Bretton Woods, New Hampshire, in 1944. The international monetary system they agreed upon was, in the words of Charles Kindleberger of MIT, "the biggest constitution-writing exercise ever to occur in international monetary relations."

The Bretton Woods system had three objectives: to create a set of rules that would maintain fixed exchange rates in the face of short-term fluctuations; to guarantee that changes in exchange rates would occur only in the face of "fundamental" deficits or surpluses in the balance of payments; and to ensure that when such changes did occur they would not spark a series of competitive devaluations. The basic characteristic of the system was that U.S. dollars held by foreign monetary authorities were made directly convertible into gold at a price fixed by the U.S. government, while foreign governments fixed the prices at which their currencies were convertible into U.S. dollars. It was this characteristic that made the system a **gold exchange standard:** Gold was the ultimate reserve, but other currencies were held as reserves because directly or indirectly they could be exchanged for gold.

The rate at which each country's currency was convertible into U.S. dollars was pegged. A system with a rate that is pegged against short-term fluctuations but that can be adjusted from time to time is called an adjustable peg system.

In order to maintain the convertibility of their currencies, the monetary authorities of each country had to be ready to buy and sell their currency in foreign exchange markets to offset imbalances in demand and supply at the pegged rates.[2]

In order to be able to support the exchange market by buying domestic currency, the monetary authorities had to have reserves of acceptable foreign exchange to offer in return. In the Bretton Woods system the authorities held reserves of gold and claims on key currencies—mainly the American dollar and the British pound sterling. When a

---

[2] The exchange rates were not quite fixed; they were permitted to vary by 1 percent on either side of their par values. Later the bands of permitted fluctuation were widened to 2.25 percent on either side of par.

country's currency was in excess supply, its authorities would sell dollars, sterling, or gold. When a country's currency was in excess demand, its authorities would buy dollars or sterling. If they then wished to increase their gold reserves, they would use the dollars to purchase gold from the U.S. Federal Reserve, thus depleting the U.S. gold stock.

The problem for the United States was to have enough gold to maintain fixed-price convertibility of the dollar into gold as demanded by foreign monetary authorities. The problem for all other countries was to maintain convertibility (on either a restricted or unrestricted basis) between their currency and the U.S. dollar at a fixed rate of exchange.

Problems of the Adjustable Peg System

Here we see how the three problems of the Bretton Woods system discussed in the text actually worked out following World War II.

Reserves to Accommodate Short-Term Fluctuations

It is generally believed that the average size and frequency of the gaps between demand and supply on the foreign exchange market created when central banks peg their exchange rates will increase as the volume of international payments increases. Since there was a strong upward trend in the volume of overall international payments, there was also a strong upward trend in the demand for foreign exchange reserves.

The ultimate reserve in the Bretton Woods system was gold. The use of gold as a reserve caused two serious problems during the 1960s and early 1970s. First, the world's supply of monetary gold did not grow fast enough to provide adequate reserves for the expanding volume of trade. As a result of the fixed price of gold, rising costs of production, and rising commercial uses, the world's stock of monetary gold during the 1960s was rising at less than 2 percent per year, while trade was growing at nearly 10 percent per year.

Gold, which had been 66 percent of the total monetary reserves in 1959, was only 40 percent in 1970, and had fallen to 30 percent by 1972. Over this period reserve holdings of dollars and sterling rose sharply. Clearly the gold backing needed to maintain convertibility of these currencies was becoming increasingly inadequate.

Second, the country whose currency is convertible into gold must maintain sufficient reserves to ensure convertibility. During the 1960s the United States lost substantial gold reserves to other countries that had acquired dollar claims through their balance-of-payments surpluses with the United States. By the late 1960s the reduction in U.S. reserves had been sufficiently large to undermine confidence in America's continued ability to maintain dollar convertibility.

Adjusting to Long-Term Disequilibria

The second characteristic problem of a fixed rate system is the adjustment to changing trends in trade. With fixed exchange rates, long-term disequilibria can be expected to develop because of secular shifts in the demands for and supplies of foreign exchange.

These disequilibria did slowly develop. At first they led to a series of speculative crises as people expected a realignment of exchange rates to occur. Finally they led to a series of realignments that started in 1967. Each occurred amid quite spectacular flows of speculative funds that thoroughly disorganized normal trade and payments.

Speculative Crises

The adjustable peg system often leads to situations in which speculators are presented with one-way bets. In these situations, there is an increasing chance of an exchange rate adjustment in one direction, with little or no chance of a movement in the other direction. Speculators then have an opportunity to secure a large potential gain with no corresponding potential for loss. Speculative crises associated with the need to adjust to fundamental disequilibria were the downfall of the system.

Collapse of the Bretton Woods System

The Bretton Woods system worked reasonably well for nearly 20 years. Then it was beset by a series of crises of ever-increasing severity that reflected the system's underlying weaknesses.

Speculation Against the British Pound

Throughout the 1950s and 1960s, the British economy was more inflation prone than the U.S. economy, and the British balance of payments was generally unsatisfactory. Holders of sterling thus had reason to worry that the British government might not be able to keep sterling convertible into U.S. dollars at a fixed rate. When these fears grew strong, there would be speculative rushes to sell sterling before it was devalued.

The crises in the 1960s were of this kind. By the mid 1960s it was clear to everyone that the pound was seriously overvalued. Finally, in 1967 it was devalued in the midst of a serious speculative crisis. Many other countries with balance-of-payments deficits followed, bringing about the first major round of adjustments in the pegged rates since 1949.

Speculation Against the American Dollar

The U.S. dollar was not devalued in 1967. The lower prices of those currencies that were devalued in 1967 plus the increasing Vietnam war expenditures combined to produce a growing deficit in the American balance of payments. This deficit led to the belief that the dollar itself was becoming seriously overvalued. People rushed to buy gold because a devaluation of the U.S. dollar would take the form of raising its gold price. (Under the Bretton Woods system, the dollar was devalued by raising the official price at which the Federal Reserve would convert dollars into gold.)

The first break in the Bretton Woods system came in 1968 when the major trading countries were forced to stop pegging the free-market price of gold. Speculative pressure to buy gold could not be resisted, and from that point there were two prices of gold: the official price at which monetary authorities could settle their debts with each other by transferring gold, and the free-market price, determined by the forces of private demand and supply independent of any intervention by central banks. The free-market price quickly rose far above the official U.S. price of $35 an ounce. See Figure 40-3.

Once the free-market price of gold was allowed to be determined independently of the official price, speculation against the U.S. dollar shifted to those currencies that were clearly undervalued relative to the dollar.[3] The German mark and the Japanese yen were particularly popular targets, and during periods of crisis billions and billions of dollars flowed into speculative holdings of these currencies. The ability of central banks to maintain pegged exchange rates in the face of such vast flights of funds was in question; on several occasions all exchange markets had to be closed for periods of up to a week.

Devaluation of the Dollar

By 1971 the American authorities had concluded that the dollar would have to be devalued. This uncovered a problem, inherent in the Bretton Woods system, that had so far gone virtually unnoted. Because the system required each foreign country to fix its exchange rate against the dollar, the American authorities could not independently fix their exchange rate against other currencies.[4]

But when the United States economy began to inflate rapidly, it became necessary to devalue the U.S. dollar relative to most other currencies. Any

[3] When the free-market price of gold was held the same as the official price, a devaluation of the U.S. dollar entailed a rise in the free-market price—and hence profit for all holders of gold. Once the free-market price was left to be determined by the forces of private demand and supply independent of any central bank intervention, there was no reason to believe that a rise in the official price of gold would affect the (much higher) free-market price. Speculators against the U.S. dollar then had to hold other currencies whose price was sure to rise against the dollar in the event of the dollar's being devalued.

[4] If, for example, the British authorities pegged the pound sterling at $2.40, as they did in 1967, then the dollar was pegged at £0.417 and the Fed could not independently decide on another rate. Similar considerations applied to all other currencies.

other country in this situation would merely uni-laterally devalue its currency. But the only way that the required U.S. devaluation could be brought about was for all other countries to agree to revalue their currencies relative to the dollar.

Prompted by continuing speculation against the dollar, President Nixon suspended gold convert-ibility of the dollar in August 1971. He also an-nounced the intention of the United States to achieve a de facto devaluation of the dollar by persuading those nations whose balance of pay-ments were in surplus to allow their rates to float upward against the dollar.

By ending the gold convertibility of the dollar, the U.S. government brought the gold exchange standard aspect of the Bretton Woods system offi-cially to an end. The fixed exchange rate aspect of the system lasted a little longer.

The immediate response to the announced in-tention of devaluing the U.S. dollar was a specu-lative run against that currency. The crisis was so severe that for the second time that year foreign exchange markets were closed throughout Europe. When the markets re-opened after a week, several countries allowed their rates to float. The Japanese, however, announced their intention of retaining their existing rate. Despite severe Japanese con-trols, $4 billion in speculative funds managed to find its way into yen in the last two weeks of August, and the Japanese were forced to abandon their fixed rate policy by allowing the yen to float upward.

After some hard bargaining, an agreement be-tween the major trading nations was signed at the Smithsonian Institution in Washington, D.C., in December 1971. The main element of the agree-ment was that all countries consented to a 7.9 per-cent devaluation of the U.S. dollar against their currencies.

The De Facto Dollar Standard

Following the Smithsonian agreements, the world was on a de facto **dollar standard.** Foreign monetary authorities held their reserves in the form of U.S. dollars and settled their international debts

with dollars. But the dollar was not convertible into gold or anything else. The ultimate value of the dollar was given not by gold but by the Amer-ican goods, services, and assets that dollars could be used to purchase.

One major problem with such a system is that the kind of American inflation that upset the Bret-ton Woods system is no less upsetting to a dollar standard, because the real purchasing power value of the world's dollar reserves is eroded by such an inflation.

The Final Breakdown of Fixed Exchange Rates

The Smithsonian agreements did not lead to a new period of international payments stability. This doomed the hope that a de facto dollar stan-dard could provide the basis for an international payments system free of major crises and deval-uations.

The U.S. inflation continued unchecked, and the U.S. balance of payments never returned to the relatively satisfactory position that had been main-tained throughout the 1960s. Within a year of the agreements, speculators began to believe that a fur-ther realignment of rates was necessary. In January 1973 speculative movements of capital once again occurred. In February the United States proposed a further 11 percent devaluation of the dollar. This was to be accomplished by raising the official price of gold to $42.22 an ounce and by not keeping other currencies tied to the dollar at the old rates. Intense speculative activity followed the announce-ment.

Five member countries of the European Com-mon Market then decided to stabilize their curren-cies against each other but to let them float together against the U.S. dollar. This joint float was called the *snake.* Norway and Sweden later joined the snake. The other EEC countries (Ireland, Italy, and the United Kingdom) and Japan announced their intention to allow their currencies to float in value. In June 1972 the Bank of England abandoned the de facto dollar standard with the announcement that it had "temporarily" abandoned its commitment to support sterling at a fixed par value against the U.S. dollar. The events of 1973 led "temporarily" to become "indefinitely."

Fluctuations in exchange rates were severe. By early July the snake currencies had appreciated about 30 percent against the dollar, but by the end of the year they had nearly returned to their February values.

The dollar devaluation formally took effect in October. Most industrialized countries maintained the nominal values of their currencies in terms of gold and SDRs, thereby appreciating them in terms of the U.S. dollar by 11 percent. The devaluation quickly became redundant, for despite attempts to restore fixed rates, the drift to flexible rates had become irresistible by the end of 1973.

MATHEMATICAL NOTES

1. Many variables affect the quantity demanded. Using functional notation, the argument of the next several pages can be anticipated. Let Q^D represent the quantity of a commodity demanded and

$$T,\overline{Y},N,Y^*,p,p_j$$

represent, respectively, tastes, average household income, population, income distribution, its price, and the price of the jth other commodity.

The demand function is

$$Q^D = D(T,\overline{Y},N,Y^*,p,p_j), j = 1, 2, \ldots, n$$

The demand schedule or curve looks at

$$Q^D = q(p) \, \bigg|_{T,\overline{Y},N,Y^*,p_j}$$

where the notation means that the variables to the right of the vertical line are held constant.

This function is correctly described as the demand function with respect to price, all other variables held constant. This function, often written concisely $q = q(p)$, shifts in response to changes in other variables. Consider average income. If, as is usually hypothesized, $\frac{\partial Q^D}{\partial \overline{Y}} > 0$, then increases in average income shift $q = q(p)$ rightward and decreases in average income shift $q = q(p)$ leftward. Changes in other variables likewise shift this function in the direction implied by the relationship of that variable to the quantity demanded.

2. Quantity demanded is a simple, straightforward, but frequently misunderstood concept in everyday use, but it has a clear mathematical meaning. It refers to the dependent variable in the demand function from note 1 above:

$$Q^D = D(T, \overline{Y}, N, Y^*, p, p_j)$$

It takes on a specific value, therefore, whenever a specific value is assigned to each of the independent variables. A change in Q^D occurs whenever the specific value of any independent variable is changed. Q^D could change, for example, from 10,000 tons per month to 20,000 tons per month as a result of a *ceteris paribus* change in any one price, in average income, in the distribution of income, in tastes, or in population. Also it could change as a result of the net effect of changes in all of the independent variables occurring at once. Thus a change in the price of a commodity is a sufficient reason for a change in Q^D but not a necessary reason.

Some textbooks reserve the term *change in quantity demanded* for a movement along a demand curve, that is, a change in Q^D as a result of a change in p. They then use other words for a change in Q^D caused by a change in the other variables in the demand function. This usage gives the single variable Q^D more than one name, and this is potentially confusing.

Our usage, which corresponds to that in all intermediate and advanced treatments, avoids this confusion. We call Q^D quantity demanded and refer *any* change in Q^D as a *change in quantity demanded*. In this usage it is correct to say that a movement

along a demand curve is a change in quantity demanded. But it is incorrect to say that a change in quantity demanded can occur only because of a movement along a demand curve (since Q^D can change for other reasons, e.g., a *ceteris paribus* change in average household income).

3. Continuing the development of note 1, let Q^S represent the quantity of a commodity supplied and

$$G, X, p, p_j, w_i$$

represent, respectively, producers' goals, technology, price, price of the jth other commodity, and costs of the ith factor of production.

The supply function is

$$Q^S = S(G, X, p, p_j, w_i), \quad j = 1, 2, \ldots, n$$
$$i = 1, 2, \ldots, m$$

The supply schedule and supply curve looks at

$$Q^S = s(p) \Big|_{G, X, p_j, w_i}$$

This is the supply function with respect to price, all other variables held constant. This function, often written concisely $q = s(p)$, shifts in response to changes in other variables.

4. Continuing the development of notes 1 through 3, equilibrium occurs where $Q^D = Q^S$. *For specified values of all other variables*, this requires that

$$q(p) = s(p) \tag{1}$$

Equation [1] defines an equilibrium value of p; hence although p is an *independent* variable in each of the supply and demand functions, it is an *endogenous* variable in the economic model that imposes the equilibrium condition expressed in Equation [1]. Price is endogenous because it is assumed to adjust to bring about equality between quantity demanded and quantity supplied. Equilibrium quantity, also an *endogenous variable*, is determined by substituting the equilibrium price into either $q(p)$ or $s(p)$.

Graphically, Equation [1] is satisfied only at the point where demand and supply curves intersect. Thus supply and demand curves are said to determine the equilibrium values of the endogenous variables, price and quantity. A shift in any of the independent variables held constant in the q and s functions will shift the demand or supply curves and lead to different equilibrium values for price and quantity.

5. The definition in the text uses finite changes and is called *arc elasticity*. The parallel definition using derivatives is

$$\eta = \frac{dq}{dp} \times \frac{p}{q}$$

and is called *point elasticity*. Further discussion appears in the Appendix to Chapter 5.

6. The propositions in the text are proven as follows. Letting *TR* stand for total revenue, we can write:

$$TR = pq$$

$$\frac{dTR}{dp} = q + p\frac{dq}{dp} \tag{1}$$

But from the equation in note 5

$$q\eta = p\frac{dq}{dp} \tag{2}$$

which we can substitute in Equation [1] to obtain

$$\frac{dTR}{dp} = q + q\eta = q(1 + \eta) \tag{3}$$

Because η is a negative number, the sign of Equation [3] is negative if the absolute value of η exceeds unity (demand elastic) and positive if it is less than unity (demand inelastic).

7. The "axis-reversal" arose in the following way. Marshall theorized in terms of "demand price" and "supply price" as the prices that would lead to a given quantity being demanded or supplied. Thus he wrote

$$p^d = D(q) \tag{1}$$

$$p^s = S(q) \tag{2}$$

and the condition of equilibrium as

$$D(q) = S(q) \tag{3}$$

When graphing the behavioral relations [1] and [2], Marshall naturally put the independent variable, q, on the horizontal axis.

Leon Walras, whose formulation of the working of a competitive market has become the accepted one, focused on quantities demanded and supplied *at a given price*. That is

$$q^d = q(p) \tag{4}$$

$$q^s = s(p) \tag{5}$$

and for equilibrium

$$q(p) = s(p) \tag{6}$$

Walras did not go in for graphic representation. Had he done so he would surely have placed p (his independent variable) on the horizontal axis.

Marshall, among his other influences on later generations of economists, was the great popularizer of graphic analysis in economics. Today we use his graphs, even for Walras' analysis. The "axis-reversal" is thus one of those accidents of history that seem odd to people who did not live through the "perfectly natural" sequence of steps that produced it.

8. The distinction made between an incremental change and a marginal change is the distinction for the function $Y = Y(X)$ between $\frac{\Delta Y}{\Delta X}$ and the derivative $\frac{dY}{dX}$. The latter is the limit of the former as ΔX approaches zero. Precisely this sort of difference underlies the distinction between arc and point elasticity, and we shall meet it repeatedly—in this chapter in reference to marginal and incremental *utility* and in later chapters with respect to such concepts as marginal and incremental *product, cost,* and *revenue*. Where Y is a function of more than one variable—for example, $Y = f(X, Z)$—the marginal relationship between Y and X is the partial derivative $\frac{\partial Y}{\partial X}$ rather than the total derivative.

9. The hypothesis of diminishing marginal utility requires that we be able to measure utility by a function $U = U(X_1, X_2, \ldots, X_n)$ where $X_1, \ldots$

. , X_n are quantities of the n goods consumed by a household. It really embodies two utility hypotheses. First, $\dfrac{\partial U}{\partial X_i} > 0$, which says that the consumer can get more utility by increasing consumption of the commodity. Second, $\dfrac{\partial^2 U}{\partial X_i^2} < 0$, which says that the marginal utility of additional consumption is declining.

10. The relationship of the slope of the budget line to relative prices can be seen as follows. In the two-commodity example, a change in expenditure (ΔE) is given by the equation

$$\Delta E = \Delta C p_C + \Delta F p_F \qquad [1]$$

Along a budget line, expenditure is constant, that is, $\Delta E = 0$. Thus, along such a line,

$$\Delta C p_C + \Delta F p_F = 0 \qquad [2]$$

whence

$$-\frac{\Delta C}{\Delta F} = \frac{p_F}{p_C} \qquad [3]$$

The ratio $-\Delta C / \Delta F$ is the slope of the budget line. It is negative because, with a fixed budget, to consume more F one must consume less C. In other words, Equation [3] says that the negative of the slope of the budget line is the ratio of the absolute prices (i.e., the relative price). While prices do not show directly in Figure 10-2, they are implicit in the budget line: its slope depends solely on the relative price, while its position, given a fixed money income, depends on the absolute prices of the two goods.

11. Because the slope of the indifference curve is negative, it is the absolute value of the slope that declines as one moves downward to the right along the curve. The algebraic value of course increases. The phrase *diminishing marginal rate of substitution* thus refers to the absolute, not the algebraic, value of the slope.

12. Marginal product as defined in the text is really incremental product. A mathematician would distinguish between this notion and its limit as ΔL

approaches zero. Technically, MP measures the rate at which total product is changing as one factor is varied. The marginal product is the partial derivative of the total product with respect to the variable factor. In symbols,

$$MP = \frac{\partial TP}{\partial L}$$

Economists often use the term *marginal product* interchangeably with the term *incremental product*.

13. We have referred specifically both to diminishing *marginal* product and to diminishing *average* product. In most cases, eventually diminishing marginal product implies eventually diminishing average product. This is, however, not necessary, as the following figure shows.

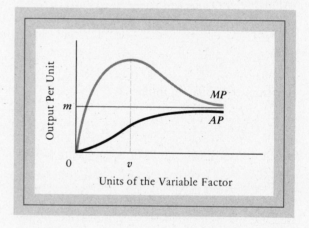

In this case, marginal product diminishes after v units of the variable factor are employed. Because marginal product falls toward, but never quite reaches, a value of m, average product rises continually toward, but never quite reaches, the same value.

14. Let q be the quantity of output and L the quantity of the variable factor. In the short run,

$$TP = q = f(L) \qquad [1]$$

We now define

$$AP = \frac{q}{L} = \frac{f(L)}{L} \qquad [2]$$

$$MP = \frac{dq}{dL} \qquad [3]$$

We are concerned about the relation between these two. Whether average product is rising, at a maximum, or falling is determined by its derivative with respect to L.

$$\frac{d\frac{q}{L}}{dL} = \frac{L\frac{dq}{dL} - q}{L^2} \qquad [4]$$

This may be rewritten:

$$\frac{1}{L}\left(\frac{dq}{dL} - \frac{q}{L}\right) = \frac{1}{L}(MP - AP) \qquad [5]$$

Clearly, when MP is greater than AP, the expression in Equation [5] is positive and thus AP is rising. When MP is less than AP, AP is falling. When they are equal, AP is at a stationary value.

15. The mathematically correct definition of marginal cost is the rate of change of total cost, with respect to output, q. Thus $MC = dTC/dq$. From the definitions, $TC = TFC + TVC$. Fixed costs are not a function of output. Thus we may write $TC = K + f(q)$, where $f(q)$ is total variable costs and K is a constant. From this, we see that $MC = df(q)/dq$. MC is thus independent of the size of the fixed costs.

16. This point is easily seen if a little algebra is used:

$$AVC = \frac{TVC}{q}$$

but

$$TVC = L \times w$$

and

$$q = AP \times L$$

where L is the quantity of the variable factor used and where w is its cost per unit. Therefore

$$AVC = \frac{L \times w}{AP \times L} = \frac{w}{AP}$$

Since w is a constant, it follows that AVC and AP vary inversely with each other, and when AP is at its maximum value, AVC must be at its minimum value.

17. A little elementary calculus will prove the point:

$$MC = \frac{dTC}{dq} = \frac{dTVC}{dq}$$
$$= \frac{d(L \times w)}{dq}$$

If w does not vary with output

$$MC = \frac{dL}{dq} \times w$$

But $\frac{dL}{dq} = \frac{1}{MP}$ (see note 15, Equation [3]).

Thus, $MC = \frac{w}{MP}$.

Since w is fixed, MC varies inversely with MP. When MP is falling, MC must be rising.

18. Strictly speaking, the marginal rate of substitution refers to the slope of the tangent to the isoquant at a particular point while the calculations in Table 11-1 refer to the average rate of substitution between two distinct points on the isoquant. Assume a production function

$$Q = F(K, L) \qquad [1]$$

Isoquants are given by the function

$$K = G(L, \overline{Q}) \qquad [2]$$

derived from Equation [1] by expressing K as an explicit function of L and Q. A single isoquant relates to a particular value at which Q is held constant. Define MP_K and MP_L as an alternative, more compact notation for $\partial F/\partial K$ and $\partial F/\partial L$, the marginal products of capital and labor. Also, let F_{KK} and F_{LL} stand for $\partial^2 F/\partial L^2$ and $\partial^2 F/\partial K^2$ respectively. To obtain the slope of the isoquant, totally differentiate Equation [1] to obtain

$$dQ = MP_K dK + MP_L dL$$

Then, since we are moving along a single isoquant, set $dQ = 0$ to obtain

$$\frac{dK}{dL} = -\frac{MP_L}{MP_K} = MRS$$

Diminishing marginal productivity implies F_{LL}, $F_{KK} < 0$ and hence, as we move down the isoquant of Figure 11-4, MP_K is rising and MP_L is falling, so the absolute value of MRS is diminishing. This is called the *hypothesis of a diminishing marginal rate of substitution*.

Note that the MRS could equally well have been defined as dL/dK, thus inverting the ratios discussed above. The definition used in the text follows from the interpretation of the MRS as the slope of the isoquant combined with the convention of plotting K on the vertical axis and L on the horizontal axis.

19. Formally the problem is to maximize $Q = F(K, L)$ subject to the budget constraint

$$p_K K + p_L L = C$$

To do this, form the Lagrangean

$$F(K, L) - \lambda(p_K K + p_L L - C)$$

Applying the notation from note 18, the first-order conditions for finding the saddle point on this function are

$$MP_K - \lambda p_K = 0; MP_K = \lambda p_K \qquad [1]$$

$$MP_L - \lambda p_L = 0; MP_L = \lambda p_L \qquad [2]$$

$$-p_K K - p_L L + C = 0 \qquad [3]$$

Dividing Equation [1] by Equation [2] yields

$$\frac{MP_K}{MP_L} = \frac{p_K}{p_L}$$

that is, the ratio of the marginal products, which is (-1) times the MRS, is equal to the ratio of the prices, which is (-1) times the slope of the isocost line.

20. For this note and the next two it is helpful first to define some terms. Let

$$\pi_n = TR_n - TC_n$$

where π_n is the profit when n units are sold.

If the firm is maximizing its profits by producing n units, it is necessary that the profits at output q_n are at least as large as the profits at output zero. If the firm is maximizing its profits at output n, then

$$\pi_n \geq \pi_0 \qquad [1]$$

The condition says that profits from producing must be greater than profits from not producing. Condition [1] can be rewritten

$$TR_n - TVC_n - TFC_n$$
$$\geq TR_0 - TVC_0 - TFC_0 \qquad [2]$$

But note that by definition

$$TR_0 = 0 \qquad [3]$$
$$TVC_0 = 0 \qquad [4]$$
$$TFC_n = TFC_0 = K \qquad [5]$$

where K is a constant. By substituting Equations [3], [4], and [5] into Condition [2], we get

$$TR_n - TVC_n \geq 0$$

from which we obtain

$$TR_n \geq TVC_n$$

On a per unit basis, it becomes

$$\frac{TR_n}{q_n} \geq \frac{TVC_n}{q_n} \qquad [6]$$

where q_n is the number of units.

Since $TR_n = q_n p_n$, where p_n is the price when n units are sold, Equation [6] may be rewritten

$$p_n \geq AVC_n$$

This proves rule 1.

21. Using elementary calculus, rule 2 may be proved.

$$\pi_n = TR_n - TC_n$$

each of which is a function of output q. To maximize π it is necessary that

$$\frac{d\pi}{dq} = 0 \qquad [1]$$

and that

$$\frac{d^2\pi}{dq^2} < 0 \qquad [2]$$

From the definitions

$$\frac{d\pi}{dq} = \frac{dTR}{dq} - \frac{dTC}{dq} = MR - MC \qquad [3]$$

From Equations [1] and [3], a necessary condition of maximum π is $MR - MC = 0$, or $MR = MC$, as is required by rule 2.

22. Not every point where $MR = MC$ is a point of profit maximization. Continuing the equations of the previous footnote,

$$\frac{d^2\pi}{dq^2} = \frac{dMR}{dq} - \frac{dMC}{dq} \qquad [4]$$

From Equations [2] and [4], a necessary condition of maximum π is

$$\frac{dMR}{dq} - \frac{dMC}{dq} < 0$$

which says that the slope of MC must be greater than the slope of MR. Taken with the previous result, it implies that, for q_n to maximize π, $MR_n = MC_n$ at a point where MC cuts MR from below.

23. Marginal revenue is mathematically the rate of change of total revenue with output, dTR/dq. Incremental revenue is $\Delta TR/\Delta q$. But the term *marginal revenue* is loosely used to refer to both concepts.

24. To prove that, for a downward-sloping demand curve, marginal revenue is less than price, let $p = p(q)$. Then

$$TR = p \times q = p(q) \times q$$

$$MR = \frac{dTR}{dq} = q\frac{dp}{dq} + p$$

For a downward-sloping demand curve, dp/dq is negative by definition, and thus MR is less than price for positive values of q.

25. These propositions are easily proved using calculus. Let $p = a - bq$, which is the general equation for a downward-sloping straight line ($b > 0$)

$$TR = pq = aq - bq^2$$

and

$$MR = \frac{dTR}{dq} = a - 2bq$$

26. A monopolist selling in two or more markets will set its marginal cost equal to marginal revenue in each market. Thus, the condition $MC = MR_1 = MR_2$ is a profit-maximizing condition for a monopolist selling in two markets. In general, equal marginal revenues will mean unequal prices, for the ratio of price to marginal revenue is a function of elasticity of demand: the higher the elasticity, the lower the ratio. Thus equal marginal revenues imply a higher price in the market with the less elastic demand curve.

27. This is easily proved. When average variable cost is constant, its derivative is equal to zero.

$$AVC = \frac{TVC}{q} \qquad [1]$$

$$\frac{d\frac{TVC}{q}}{dq} = \frac{q\frac{dTVC}{dq} - TVC}{q^2} = 0 \qquad [2]$$

Equation [2] implies that

$$\frac{dTVC}{dq} = \frac{TVC}{q} \qquad [3]$$

Remembering that $MC = \frac{dTVC}{dq}$, Equation [3] may be written

$$MC = AVC \qquad [4]$$

28. Using the expression for MR given in note 24, it can be seen that, at the kink in the demand curve, q and p are unambiguously determined. But dp/dq, the slope of the demand curve, is very different in the upward and downward directions. Thus the level of MR must be different for increases and decreases in price at the same quantity.

29. The marginal revenue produced by the factor involves two elements: first, the additional output that an extra unit of the factor makes possible and second, the change in price of the product that the extra output causes. Let Q be output, R revenue, and L the number of units of labor hired. The contribution to revenue of additional labor is $\frac{\partial R}{\partial L}$. This in turn depends on the contribution of the extra labor to output $\frac{\partial Q}{\partial L}$ (the marginal product of

the factor) and $\partial R/\partial Q$, the firm's marginal revenue from the extra output. Thus

$$\frac{\partial R}{\partial L} = \frac{\partial Q}{\partial L} \cdot \frac{\partial R}{\partial Q}$$

We define the left-hand side as marginal revenue product, MRP. Thus

$$MRP = MP \cdot MR$$

30. The proposition that the marginal labor cost is above the average labor cost when the average is rising is essentially the same proposition proved in math note 14. But let us do it again, using elementary calculus. The quantity of labor depends on the wage rate: $L = f(w)$. The total labor cost is wL. The marginal cost of labor is $d(wL)/dL = w + L(dw/dL)$. This may be rewritten $MC = AC + L(dw/dL)$. As long as the supply curve slopes upward $dw/dL > 0$, therefore $MC > AC$.

31. The derivation of this result is as follows. Let X be your level and Y your competitor's.

$$X_0 = \frac{2}{3} Y_0 \tag{1}$$

$$Y_{10} = Y_0 e^{10r} \tag{2}$$

$$X_{10} = X_0 e^{10(r + a)} \tag{3}$$

If $X_{10} = Y_{10}$ then

$$Y_0 e^{10r} = X_0 e^{10(r + a)} \tag{4}$$

and

$$\frac{Y_0}{X_0} = \frac{3}{2} = e^{10a} \tag{5}$$

for which $a = 0.04$.

32. Let t be the tax rate applied to the profits, π, of the firm. The profits after tax will be $(1 - t)\pi$. If profits are maximized at output q^*, then by definition $\pi(q^*) > \pi(q_i)$ where q_i is any other output. Now multiply each side by $(1 - t)$. Since $(1 - t)$ is positive for any tax rate less than 100 percent, the direction of the inequality does not change. Thus the after-tax profit maximizing output is also q^* for any tax rate less than 100 percent.

33. Calculating the ratio of the cost of purchasing a fixed bundle of commodities in two periods is the same thing as calculating the percentage change in each price and then averaging these by weighting each price by the proportion of total expenditure devoted to the commodity. The following expression illustrates the equivalence of these two procedures for the two-commodity case:

$$\frac{q^A p_1^A + q^B p_1^B}{q^A p_0^A + q^B p_0^B} = \frac{p_1^A}{p_0^A}\left(\frac{q^A p_0^A}{q^A p_0^A + q^B p_0^B}\right)$$
$$+ \frac{p_1^B}{p_0^B}\left(\frac{q^B p_0^B}{q^A p_0^A + q^B p_0^B}\right)$$

The qs are fixed quantity weights while the ps are prices; A and B refer to two commodities; 0 and 1 refer respectively to the base period and some subsequent time period. The expression on the left is the fixed bundle q^A and q^B valued at given year prices divided by its value in base year prices. The first term in the expression on the right gives the ratio of the price of good A in the given and the base year multiplied by the proportion of total expenditure in the base year devoted to good A. The second term does the same for good B. Simple multiplication and division reduces the right-hand expression to the left-hand one.

34. In the text, we define MPC as an increment ratio. For mathematical treatments it is more convenient to define all marginal concepts as derivatives: $MPC = dC/dY_d$, $MPS = dS/dY_d$, and so on.

35. The basic relation is

$$Y_d = C + S$$

Dividing through by Y_d yields

$$Y_d/Y_d = C/Y_d + S/Y_d$$

or $1 = APC + APS$

Next take the first-difference of the basic relation to yield

$$\Delta Y_d = \Delta C + \Delta S$$

Dividing through by ΔY_d gives

$\Delta Y_d / \Delta Y_d = \Delta C / \Delta Y_d + \Delta S / \Delta Y_d$

or $1 = MPC + MPS$

36. This involves using functions of functions. We have $C = C(Y_d)$ and $Y_d = f(Y)$. So by substitution $C = C[f(Y)]$. In the linear expressions used in the text, $C = a + bY_d$ and $Y_d = hY$, so $C = a + bhY$.

37. The elementary theory of national income can be described by the following set of equations (or model).

$Y = AE$ (equilibrium condition)   [1]
$AE = C + I + G + (X - M)$
           (definition of AE)   [2]
$C = A + bY$ (consumption function) [3]
$M = mY$ (import function)   [4]

where I, G, and X are all treated as constant. Substituting [3] and [4] and collecting terms in Y, we can obtain the aggregate expenditure function relating desired expenditure to income.

$AE = (a + I + G + X) + (b - m)Y$

where the first term (in parentheses) is autonomous expenditure and the second term is induced expenditure. Using [1], the equilibrium level of income can be derived by solving

$Y = (a + I + G + X) + (b - m)Y$

to obtain

$$Y = \frac{1}{(1 - b + m)}(a + I + G + X) \qquad [5]$$

The example in Table 28-6 has these values: $a = 100$, $I = 250$, $G = 410$, $X = 240$, $b = .6$, and $m = .1$. Substituting into [5] yields

$$Y = \frac{1}{(1 - .6 + .1)}(100 + 250 + 410 + 240)$$
$$= \frac{1}{(.5)}(1000) = 2000.$$

38. The total expenditure over all rounds is the sum of an infinite series. Letting A stand for the initiating expenditure and z for the marginal propensity to spend, the change in expenditure is ΔA

in the first round, $z\Delta A$ in the second, $z(z\Delta A) = z^2\Delta A$ in the third, and so on. This can be written as

$$\Delta A(1 + z + z^3 + \ldots + z^n)$$

If z is less than 1, the series in brackets converges to $1/(1 - z)$ as n approaches infinity. The change in total expenditure is thus $\Delta A/(1 - z)$. In the example in the box, $z = 0.5$; therefore the change in total expenditure is twice ΔA.

39. As we saw in Box 30-2, the simple multiplier, K, is equal to the reciprocal of the marginal propensity not to spend $(1 - z)$, also called the marginal propensity to withdraw, w.

$$K = \frac{1}{w}$$

In an open economy the marginal propensity to withdraw is equal to the sum of the marginal propensity to save $(1 - b)$ plus the marginal propensity to import, m. Hence the multiplier in an open economy

$$K_0 = \frac{1}{(1 - b) + m}$$

is less than that in a closed economy

$$K_c = \frac{1}{(1 - b)}$$

if the two economies had a common marginal propensity to consume, b. Note that the denominator of K_0 can be written as $[1 - (b - m)]$ where $(b - m)$ is the marginal propensity to consume *home goods*.

40. Using the multiplier derived in math note 39, we see that an autonomous increase in exports leads to an increase in national income given by

$$\Delta Y = \frac{1}{(1 - b) + m}\Delta X$$

The resulting increase in imports is given by the marginal propensity to import times the change in national income.

$$\Delta M = m\Delta Y$$

Combining, we can calculate the change in the trade balance, $\Delta T = \Delta X - \Delta M$, as

$$\Delta T = \frac{(1 - b)}{(1 - b) + m} \Delta X = (1 - b) \Delta Y$$

which is positive since b is less than one.

41. The accelerator may be stated as a general macroeconomic theory. Define I_n as the volume of net investment this year and ΔY as the increase in national income from last year to this year. The accelerator theory is the relationship between I_n and ΔY.

Assume that the capital-output ratio is a constant.

$$K/Y = \propto$$

or

$$K = \propto Y$$

If Y changes, K must be changed accordingly:

$$\Delta K = \propto \Delta Y$$

But the change in the capital stock (ΔK) is net investment, so

$$\Delta K = I_n = \propto \Delta Y$$

42. This is easily proven. In equilibrium, the banking system wants sufficient deposits (D) to establish the legal ratio (r) of deposits to reserves (R). This gives $R/D = r$. Any change in D of ΔD has to be accompanied by a change in R of ΔR of sufficient size to restore r. Thus $\Delta R/\Delta D = r$, so that $\Delta D = \Delta R/r$, and $\Delta D/\Delta R = 1/r$.

43. Proof: Let r be the reserve ratio. Let $z = 1 - r$ be the excess reserves per dollar of new deposit. If X dollars are deposited in the system assumed in the text, the successive rounds of new deposits will be $X, zX, z^2X, z^3X. \ldots$ The series

$$X + zX + z^2X + z^3X \cdots$$
$$= X[1 + z + z^2 + z^3 + \cdots]$$

has a limit

$$X \frac{1}{1 - z} = X\left[\frac{1}{1 - (1 - r)}\right] = \frac{X}{r}$$

44. Suppose the public desires to hold a fraction,

v, for any new deposits in cash. Now let the banking system receive an initial increase in its reserves of ΔR. It can expand deposits by an amount ΔD. As it does so, the banking system suffers a cash drain to the public of $v\Delta D$. The banking system can only increase deposits to the extent the required reserve ratio, r, makes possible. The maximum deposit expansion can be calculated from

$$r\Delta D = \Delta R - v\Delta D$$

which, collecting terms, can be written

$$(r + v) \Delta D = \Delta R$$

Hence

$$\Delta D = \Delta R/(r + v)$$

45. The argument is simply as follows:

$$M^D = F_1(T), F'_1 > 0$$
$$T = F_2(Y), F'_2 > 0$$

therefore, $M^D = F_1(F_2(Y))$
$$= H(Y), H' > 0$$

where H is the function of the function combining F_1 and F_2.

46. Let $L(Y, r)$ give the real demand for money measured in purchasing power units. Let M be the supply of money measured in nominal units and P an index of the price level so that M/P is the real supply of money. Now the equality between the demand for money and the supply of money can be expressed in real terms as

$$L(Y, r) = M/P \qquad [1]$$

or, by multiplying through by P, in nominal terms as

$$PL(Y, r) = M \qquad [2]$$

In Equation [1] a rise in P disturbs equilibrium by lowering M/P, and in Equation [2] it disturbs equilibrium by raising $PL(Y, r)$.

47. The "rule of 72" is an approximation derived from the mathematics of compound interest. Any measure X_t will have the value $X_t = X_0 e^{rt}$ after t years at a continuous growth rate of r percent per year. Because $X_1/X_0 = 2$ requires $r \times t = 0.69$, a "rule of 69" would be correct for continuous growth. The "rule of 72" was developed in the context of compound interest, and if interest is compounded only once a year the product of $r \times t$ for X to double is approximately 72.

48. The time taken to break even is a function of the *difference* in growth rates, not their level. Thus, in the example, had 4 percent and 5 percent, or 5 percent and 6 percent, been used, it still would have taken the same number of years. To see this quickly, recognize that we are interested in the ratio of two growth paths: $e^{r1t}/e^{r2t} = e^{(r1 - r2)t}$.

49. Net exports equals exports minus imports.

$$NX = X - M \qquad [1]$$

Exports depend on foreign income, Y^f, and on the terms of trade.

$$X = X_0 + m^f Y^f - b^f(P/eP^f) \qquad [2]$$

where X_0 is autonomous exports, m^f is the foreign marginal propensity to import, b^f is the response of exports to a change in relative prices, P is the domestic price level, e is the exchange rate, and P^f is foreign prices. Imports depend on domestic income and the terms of trade.

$$M = M_0 + mY + b(P/eP^f) \qquad [3]$$

Combining Equations [1], [2], and [3], we can write

$$NX = (X_0 - M_0) + m^f Y^f - mY - c(P/eP^f) \quad [4]$$

where $c = b + b^f$. In Chapter 39 we considered this relationship in isolation and hence the slope of the NX curve when drawn against national income was taken to be $dNX/dY = -m$, where the other variables in Equation [4] were held constant. Now we have to take into account the fact that P changes as Y changes.

Writing the *SRAS* curve as

$$P = g(Y), g' > 0 \qquad [5]$$

and substituting Equation [5] into Equation [4], we eliminate P to yield

$$NX = (X_0 - M_0) + mY^f - mY - c(g(Y)/eP^f) \quad [6]$$

The slope of the NX curve is now given by

$$dNX/dY = -(m + g') < 0 \qquad [7]$$

Hence as Y rises, NX falls both because of the marginal propensity to import and because of substitution away from domestic goods as P rises.

50. Modern mathematicians distinguish between a correspondence and a function. There is a *correspondence* between Y and X if each value of X is associated with one or more values of Y. Y is a *function* of X if there is one and only one value of Y associated with each value of X. Mathematicians of an older generation described both relations as functional relations and then distinguished between single-valued functions (in modern language, functional relations) and multi-valued functions. In the text we adopt the older, more embracing usage of the term *functional relation*.

51. Since it is impermissible to divide by zero, the ratio $\Delta Y/\Delta X$ cannot be evaluated when $\Delta X = 0$. But the limit of the ratio as ΔX approaches zero can be evaluated, and it is infinity.

$$\lim_{\Delta X \to 0} \frac{\Delta Y}{\Delta X} = \infty$$

52. The condition that for profit maximization MRP be downward-sloping at the point where $w = MRP$ is just an application of the proposition (proved in math notes 21 and 22) that for profit maximization MC must cut MR from below. Consider the output added by the last unit of the variable factor. Its marginal cost is w, and its marginal revenue is MRP. Thus w must cut MRP from below. Since W is a horizontal line, MRP must be falling.

Putting the matter in standard mathematical terms,

$$w = MRP \qquad [1]$$

is a first order condition of *either* maximizing or minimizing. The second order condition for maximization is

$$\frac{dw}{dq} > \frac{dMRP}{dq} \qquad [2]$$

Since

$$\frac{dw}{dq} = 0 \qquad [3]$$

the slope of MRP must be negative to satisfy [2], that is, it must be declining.

53. The equation for the IS curve is given by

$$y = c(y - T) + I(r) + G \qquad [1]$$

where $c'(y - T) > 0$ is the marginal propensity to consume ($c'(y - T) = b$), $I_r < 0$ is the response of investment to a change in the interest rate, and T is taxes. Substituting $T = T_0 + ty$ into [1], and differentiating, we get

$$wdy = -b(dT_0 + ydt) + I_r dr + dG \qquad [2]$$

where w is equal to $[1 - b(1 - t)]$, the marginal propensity not to spend. The IS curve is drawn for $dT_0 = dt = dG = 0$. Its slope is therefore

$$\frac{dr}{dy}\Big|_{IS} = \frac{w}{I_r} < 0 \qquad [3]$$

The horizontal shift in the IS curve due to a change in any of the exogenous variables (T_0, t, or G) can be calculated from [2] by setting $dr = 0$. For example, a change in h shifts the IS curve by

$$\frac{dy}{dG}\Big|_{dr=0} = \frac{1}{w} > 0$$

while a change in tax rates causes a shift of

$$\frac{dy}{dt}\Big|_{dr=0} = \frac{-by}{w} < 0$$

54. The equation for the LM curve is given by

$$M = PL(y, r) \qquad [1]$$

where $L(y, r)$ represents the demand for real money balances which depends positively on income ($L_y > 0$) and negatively on the interest rate ($L_r < 0$). Differentiating Equation [1] we get

$$dM = L(y, r)DP + PL_y + PL_r dr \qquad [2]$$

The LM curve is drawn for $dM = dP = 0$. Its slope is therefore

$$\frac{dr}{dy}\Big|_{LM} = -\frac{L_y}{L_r} > 0 \qquad [3]$$

The horizontal shift in the LM curve due to a change in the money supply can be calculated from Equation [2] by setting $dr = 0$.

$$\frac{dy}{dM}\Big|_{dr=0} = \frac{1}{PL_y} > 0 \qquad [4]$$

55. Equation [2] from each of the two previous math notes can be combined to give two relationships between dy and dr. Solving them simultaneously we can derive the following expressions for the effects of monetary and fiscal policy on national income and interest rates. Restricting our analysis of fiscal policy to the effects of government expenditure (so $dT = dt = 0$), and holding $dP = 0$, these are as follows:

$$\frac{dy}{dM} = \frac{-I_r}{D} > 0 \qquad \frac{dr}{dM} = \frac{-w}{D} < 0$$

$$\frac{dy}{dG} = \frac{-PL_r}{D} > 0 \qquad \frac{dr}{dG} = \frac{PL_y}{D} > 0$$

where $D \equiv -(I_r PL_y + wPL_r) > 0$.

56. The aggregate demand curve can be written by solving Equations [1] from each of the math notes 53 and 54 to eliminate the interest rate, thus leaving a relationship between P and y. The relationship between *changes* in P and y can be written

$$Ddy = I_r L(y, P)dP - PL_r dG - I_r dM \qquad [1]$$

where D is as defined in note 56.

The AD curve is drawn from $dG = dM = 0$, so its slope is given by

$$\frac{dP}{dy}\Big|_{AD} = \frac{I_r L(y, P)}{D} < 0 \qquad [2]$$

The horizontal shift in AD can be calculated from Equation [1] by setting $dP = 0$, so that the effects of monetary (dM) and fiscal (dG) policy can be written as follows:

$$\frac{dy}{dM}\Big|_{dr=0} = \frac{-I_r}{D} > 0$$

$$\frac{dy}{dG}\Big|_{dr=0} = \frac{-PL_r}{D} > 0$$

which, of course, are as in math note 55.

57. This is expressed in functional notation as

$$DE = f(Y\text{-}Y^*)$$

where the restrictions are (i) that $f(0) = 0$ so when $Y = Y^*$ there is no demand effect; and (ii) $f' > 0$ so that as Y rises, the demand effect rises. Together (i) and (ii) imply that $DE > 0$ when $Y > Y^*$ and $DE < 0$ when $Y < Y^*$.

Often, the further restriction is added that $f'' > 0$; that is, that the Phillips curve gets steeper as Y rises.

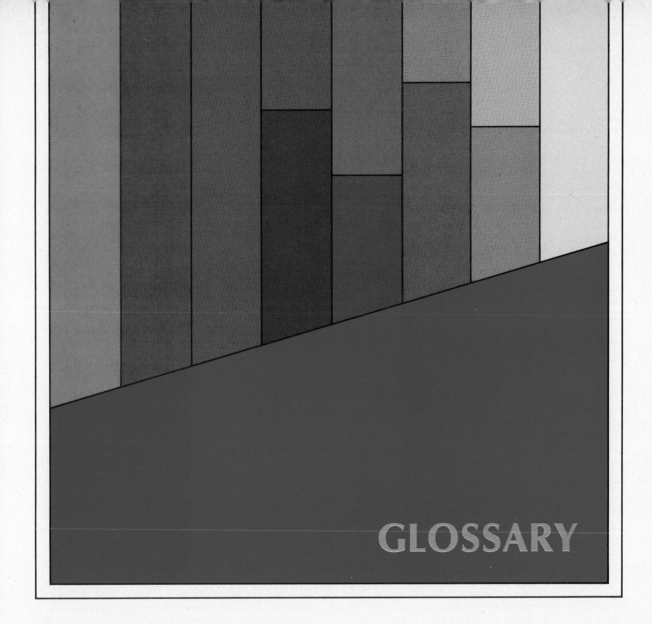

GLOSSARY

absolute advantage One nation has an absolute advantage over another nation in the production of a commodity when the same amount of resources will produce more of the commodity in the one nation than in the other.

absolute cost advantages Existing firms have absolute cost advantages when their average cost curves are significantly lower over their entire range than those of firms that are potential entrants into the industry.

absolute price A price expressed in money terms.

acceleration hypothesis When output is held above potential, the persistent inflationary gap will cause inflation to accelerate; when output is held below potential, the persistent deflationary gap will cause inflation to decelerate.

accelerator The theory that relates the level of investment to the rate of change of national income.

adjustable peg system A system in which monetary authorities peg (i.e., fix) the price of the domestic currency on the foreign exchange market but in which the price at which the currency is pegged can be adjusted (i.e., changed) from time to time.

administered price A price set by conscious decision of the seller rather than by the impersonal forces of demand and supply.

adverse selection Self-selection, within a single risk category, of persons of above-average risk.

AE In boldface, the term represents actual aggregate expenditure; in lightface, desired aggregate expenditure.

AE = C + I + G Indicates the three main components of aggregate expenditure in a closed economy: consumption expenditure, investment expenditure, and government expenditure.

AE = C + I + G + (X − M) Indicates the four main components of aggregate expenditure in an open economy: consumption expenditure, investment expenditure, government expenditure, and net exports (exports *minus* imports).

aggregate demand (AD) curve A relation between the total amount of all output that will be demanded by purchasers and the price level of that output. It shows the combination of real national income and the price level that makes aggregate desired expenditure equal to national income and the demand for money equal to the supply of money.

aggregate demand shock A shift in the aggregate demand curve.

aggregate expenditure (AE) function The function that relates aggregate desired expenditure to national income.

aggregate supply (AS) curve A relation between the total amount of output that will be produced and the price level of that output.

aggregate supply shock An exogenous shift in the aggregate supply curve.

allocative efficiency An allocation of resources in which price equals marginal cost in all industries and which is thus Pareto-optimal; it is often treated as a goal of economic organization.

allocative inefficiency The absence of allocative efficiency. Some consumers could be made better off by producing a different bundle of goods, without any consumers being made worse off.

appreciation of the home currency A fall in the free-market domestic currency price of foreign currencies.

arbitrage The purchase of any commodity in markets where it is cheap in order to sell it in markets where it is dear, with the consequent effect of eliminating intermarket differentials.

autarky The absence of international trade.

average cost (AC) Some measure of cost divided by the number of units of output.

average fixed costs (AFC) Total fixed costs divided by number of units of output.

average product (AP) Total product divided by the number of units of the variable factor used in its production.

average propensity to consume (APC) The proportion of income devoted to consumption: total consumption expenditure divided by income. The income variable may be disposable income, in which case $APC = C/Y_d$, or it may be national income, in which case $APC = C/Y$.

average propensity to save (APS) The proportion of income devoted to saving: total saving divided by income. The income variable may be disposable income, in which case $APS = S/Y_d$, or it may be national income, in which case $APS = S/Y$.

average revenue (AR) Total revenue divided by quantity. Where a single price prevails. $AR = p$.

average tax rate The ratio of total tax paid to total income earned.

average total cost (ATC) Total cost divided by the number of units of output; the sum of average fixed costs and average variable costs. Also called *cost per unit, unit cost, average cost (AC)*.

average variable costs (AVC) Total variable costs divided by the number of units of output. Also called *direct unit costs, avoidable unit costs*.

balanced budget A situation in which current revenue is exactly equal to current expenditures.

balanced budget multiplier The change in income divided by the tax-financed change in government expenditure that brought it about.

balance-of-payments accounts A summary record of a country's transactions that typically involve payments or receipts of foreign exchange.

balance-of-payments deficit A situation in which a country's receipts on current and capital account fall short of its payments (ignoring transactions by monetary authorities).

balance-of-payments surplus A situation in which a country's receipts on current and capital account exceed its payments (ignoring transactions by monetary authorities).

balance of trade The difference between the value of exports and the value of imports of visible items (goods).

balance sheet A report showing a firm's assets and the claims against those assets at a moment in time. Balance sheets always balance because the owners' equity is defined as the amount of the assets less the claims of the creditors.

bank notes Paper money issued by banks.

bank rate The rate of interest at which the Bank of Canada is prepared to lend cash reserves to the chartered banks. The comparable rate in the United States is called the *discount rate*.

barriers to entry Legal or other impediments to entry into an industry. Patents, franchises, economies of scale, and established brand preferences may each lead to such barriers.

base control A situation in which the central bank chooses to set the quantity of open market transactions.

base period A year or other point in time chosen for comparison purposes in connection with expressing or computing *index numbers or constant dollars*.

beggar-my-neighbor policies Policies designed to increase a country's prosperity (especially by reducing its unemployment) at the expense of reducing prosperity in other countries (especially by increasing their unemployment).

blacklist An employer's list of workers who have been fired for union activity.

black market A situation in which goods are sold illegally at prices above a legal maximum price.

boom An extended period of high economic activity around the peak of the business cycle.

bread-and-butter unionism A union movement whose major objectives are wages, hours, and conditions of employment rather than political or social ends.

budget balance The difference between total government revenue and total government expenditure.

budget deficit The shortfall of current revenue below current expenditure.

budget line (isocost line) A line in a diagram showing all combinations of commodities that a household may obtain if it spends a given amount of money at fixed prices of the commodities.

budget surplus The excess of current revenue over current expenditure.

budget surplus function A function relating the size of the government's budget surplus (revenue minus expenditure) to the level of national income. (Deficits are shown as negative surpluses.)

built-in stabilizer Anything that tends to adjust government revenues and expenditures automatically (i.e., without an explicit policy decision) so as to reduce inflationary and deflationary gaps whenever they develop.

business cycle Continuous ebb and flow of business activity that occurs around any long-term trend after seasonal patterns have been removed.

C In boldface, the term represents actual consumption expenditure; in lightface, desired consumption expenditure.

C + I + G − M Indicates the main components of domestic expenditure on domestically produced commodities.

capacity The level of output that corresponds to the minimum level of short-run average total costs. Also called *plant capacity.*

capital A factor of production defined to include all man-made aids to further production.

capital account Balance of international transactions in financial capital.

capital consumption allowance An estimate of the amount by which the capital stock is depleted through its contribution to current production. Often called *depreciation.*

capital deepening Adding capital to the production process in such a way as to increase the ratio of capital to labor and other factors of production.

capital flows Purchases by foreigners of assets previously owned or newly issued by domestic citizens and governments, or vice versa.

capital-output ratio The ratio of the value of capital to the annual value of output produced by it.

capital stock The aggregate quantity of a society's capital goods.

capital widening Adding capital to the production process in such a way as to leave factor proportions unchanged.

cartel An organization of producers designed to limit or eliminate competition among its members, usually by agreeing to restrict output in an effort to achieve noncompetitive prices.

cash reserve ratio See *reserve ratio.*

ceiling price A maximum permitted price.

central authorities All public agencies, government bodies, and other organizations belonging to or under the control of government.

central bank A bank that acts as banker to the banking system and often to the government as well. In the modern world the central bank is usualy the sole money-issuing authority.

change in demand An increase or decrease in the quantity demanded at each possible price of the commodity, represented by a shift of the whole demand curve.

change in supply An increase or decrease in the quantity supplied at each possible price of the commodity, represented by a shift of the whole supply curve.

chartered bank A financial institution licensed by Parliament under the Bank Act which regulates its operations and its relationship with the government and the Bank of Canada. It accepts deposits from customers, which it agrees to transfer when ordered by a cheque, and it makes loans and other investments. An equivalent term used in some other countries is *commercial bank.*

classical unemployment See *real wage unemployment.*

clearing house An institution where interbank indebtednesses arising from transfer of cheques between banks are computed, offset against each other, and net amounts owing are calculated.

closed economy An economy that does not engage in foreign trade.

closed shop A bargaining arrangement in which only union members can be employed. Union membership precedes employment.

collective bargaining The whole process by which unions and employers arrive at and enforce agreements.

collective consumption goods Goods or services that, if they provide benefits to anyone, necessarily provide benefits to a large group of people or a community.

collusion An agreement among sellers to set a common price and/or to share a market. Collusion may be overt or secret. It may be explicit or tacit.

combines laws Laws prohibiting acquisition and exercise of monopoly power, conspiracy in restraint of trade, and restrictive trade practices. Called *antitrust laws* in the United States.

command economy An economy in which the decisions of the central authorities exert the major influence over the allocation of resources.

commercial bank See *chartered bank.*

commodities Marketable items produced to satisfy wants. Commodities may be either *goods,* which are tangible, or *services,* which are intangible.

common-property resource A natural resource that is owned by no one and may be used by anyone.

comparative advantage (1) Country A has a comparative advantage over country B in producing a commodity, X, when it can do so at a lesser opportunity cost in terms of other products forgone. (2) As distinguished from absolute advantage: Comparing two countries, A and B, and two commodities, X and Y, country A has a comparative advantage in X when its margin of absolute advantage is greater in X than in Y.

comparative statics Comparative static equilibrium analysis; the derivation of predictions by analyzing the effect of a change in some exogenous variable or parameter on the equilibrium position.

competitive devaluations A round of devaluations of exchange rates by a number of countries, each trying to gain a competitive advantage over the other and each failing to the extent that other countries also devalue.

complement A commodity that tends to be used jointly with the original commodity. Technically, a complement to a commodity is another commodity for which the cross-elasticity of demand is nonnegligible and negative.

comprehensive income taxation (CIT) A proposal to expand the tax base from the presently defined concept of taxable income to include income from most sources and to eliminate most exemptions and deductions. CIT can be defined in many different ways, depending on what is added to taxable income.

concentration ratio The fraction of total market sales (or some other measure of market occupancy) made by a specified number of the industry's largest firms. Four-firm and eight-firm concentrations ratios are the most frequently used.

conscious parallel action See *tacit collusion*.

constant-cost industry An industry in which costs of the most efficient size firm remain constant as the entire industry expands or contracts in the long run.

constant dollar GNP Gross national product valued in prices prevailing in some base year; year-to-year changes in constant dollar GNP reflect changes only in quantities produced. Also called *real GNP*.

constant returns A situation in which output increases proportionately with the quantity of inputs as the scale of production is increased.

Consumer Price Index (CPI) A measure of the average price of commodities commonly bought by households; compiled monthly by Statistics Canada.

consumers' durables See *durable good*.

consumers' surplus The difference between the total value consumers place on all units consumed of a commodity and the payment they must make to purchase the same amount of the commodity.

consumption The act of using commodities to satisfy wants.

consumption expenditure In macroeconomics consumption expenditure is household expenditure on all items except housing.

consumption function The relationship between consumption expenditure and all the factors that determine it. In the simplest consumption function, consumption depends only on current income.

corporation A form of business organization with a legal existence separate from that of the owners, in which ownership and financial responsibility are divided, limited, and shared among any number of individual and institutional shareholders.

cost (of output) To a producing firm, the value of factors of production used up in producing output.

Cournot-Nash equilibrium An equilibrium based on the behavioral assumption that each firm makes its decisions on the assumption that the behavior of all other firms will remain unchanged.

CPI See *Consumer Price Index*.

craft union A union organized according to a specified set of skills or occupations.

cross-elasticity of demand A measure of the extent to which quantity of a commodity demanded responds to changes in price of a related commodity. Formula:

$$\frac{\text{percentage change in quantity of } x}{\text{percentage change in price of } y}$$

cross-sectional data Data referring to a number of different observations at the same point in time.

crowding-out effect The offsetting reduction in private expenditure caused by the rise in interest rates that follows an expansionary fiscal policy.

current account Balance of trade plus net investment income and transfers.

current dollar GNP Gross national product valued in prices prevailing at the time of measurement; year-to-year changes in current dollar GNP reflect changes both in quantities produced and in market prices. Also called *nominal GNP*.

day-to-day loan Loan made by a chartered bank to an investment dealer. Such loans make up part of the *secondary reserves* of the chartered banks.

debt Amounts owed to one's creditors, including banks and other financial institutions.

decision lag A lapse of time between obtaining relevant information about some problem and reaching a decision on what to do about it.

decreasing returns A situation in which output increases less than in proportion to inputs as the scale of production increases. A firm in this situation, with fixed factor prices, is an *increasing-cost* firm.

deficient-demand unemployment Unemployment that is due to insufficient aggregate demand and that can be reduced by measures that raise aggregate demand.

deflationary gap The amount by which the aggregate demand schedule must be increased to achieve full-employment income.

demand There are several distinct but closely related concepts: (1) *quantity demanded;* (2) the whole relationship of the quantity demanded to variables that determine it, such as tastes, household income, distribution of income, population, price of the commodity, and prices of other commodities; (3)

the *demand schedule;* (4) the *demand curve.* The phrase increase (decrease) in demand means a shift of the demand curve to the right (left), indicating an increase (decrease) in the quantity demanded at each possible price.

demand curve The graphic representation of the *demand schedule.*

demand deposit A bank deposit that is withdrawable on demand and transferable by means of a cheque.

demand for money The total amount of money balances that the public wishes to hold for all purposes.

demand inflation Inflation arising from excess aggregate demand; that is, when national income exceeds potential.

demand schedule The relationship between the quantity demanded of a commodity and its price, other things equal.

deposit money Money held by the public in the form of demand deposits with **commercial** banks.

depreciation (1) The loss in value of an asset over a period of time; includes both physical wear and tear and obsolescence. (2) The amount by which the capital stock is depleted through its contribution to current production.

depreciation of the home currency A rise in the free-market domestic currency price of foreign currencies.

depression A period of very low economic activity with very high unemployment and high excess capacity.

differentiated products Products sufficiently distinguishable within an industry that the producer of each has some power over its own price; the products of firms in monopolistically competitive industry.

diminishing marginal rate of substitution The hypothesis that the marginal rate of substitution changes systematically as the amounts of two commodities being consumed vary.

direct costs See *variable costs.*

direct investment Foreign investment in the form of a *takeover* or capital investment in a branch plant or subsidiary corporation in which the investor has voting control.

dirty float Although foreign exchange rates are left to be determined on the free market, monetary authorities intervene in this market so as to influence exchange rates, but they are *not* publicly committed to holding their country's exchange rate at any announced "par value." Also called *managed float.*

disaggregate data Detailed data such as investment by General Motors or by automobile manufacturers. Used in contrast to aggregate data, such as total investment by everyone in the economy.

discouraged workers People who would like to work but have ceased looking for a job, and hence have withdrawn from the labor force because they believe that no suitable jobs are available.

discretionary fiscal policy Fiscal policy that is a conscious response (not according to any predetermined rule) to each particular state of the economy as it arises.

disembodied technical change Technical change that raises output without the necessity of building new capital to embody the new knowledge.

disequilibrium The state or condition of a market that exhibits excess demand or excess supply.

disequilibrium price A price at which quantity demanded does not equal quantity supplied.

disposable income The income households have available for spending and saving.

distributed profits Earnings of a firm distributed as dividends to the owners of the firm.

dividends That part of profits paid out to shareholders of a corporation.

division of labor The breaking up of a task (e.g., making pins) into a number of repetitive operations, each one done by a different worker.

dollar standard (for international payments) International indebtedness between monetary authorities is settled in terms of U.S. dollars, which are not necessarily backed by gold or any other ultimate monetary base.

domestic absorption (A) Total expenditure on all goods and services (domestic and foreign) for use within the economy; the sum of $C + I + G$.

double counting Counting something more than once. For example, adding up the total outputs of all the sectors in the economy so that the value of intermediate goods is counted in the sector that produces them and also when they are purchased as an input by another sector.

duopoly An industry that contains only two firms.

durable good A good which yields its services only gradually over an extended period of time; often divided into the subcategories *producers' durables* (e.g., machines and equipment) and *consumers' durables* (e.g., cars, appliances).

economic efficiency (in production) A method of producing some quantity of output is economically efficient when it is the least costly method of producing that output.

economic profits or losses (often simply **profits**) The difference in the revenues received from the sale of output and the opportunity cost of the inputs used to make the output. Negative profits are losses.

economic growth Increases in potential GNP measured in constant dollars.

economies of scope Economies achieved by a large firm through multiproduct production, large-scale distribution, advertising, etc. They are an advantage of such firms in addition to economies of scale in production.

economy A set of interrelated production and consumption activities.

elastic demand The situation existing when for a given percentage change in price there is a greater percentage change in quantity demanded; elasticity greater than 1.

elasticity of demand A measure of the responsiveness of quantity of a commodity demanded to a change in market price. Formula:

$$\frac{\text{percentage change in quantity demanded}}{\text{percentage change in price}}$$

Conventionally expressed as a positive number, it is a pure number ranging from zero to infinity.

elasticity of supply A measure of the responsiveness of the quantity of a commodity supplied to a change in the market price. Formula:

$$\eta_s = \frac{\text{percentage change in quantity supplied}}{\text{percentage change in price}}$$

embodied technical change A technical change that can be utilized only when new capital, embodying the new techniques, is built.

employment The number of workers 16 years of age and older who hold full-time civilian jobs.

envelope curve Any curve that encloses, by just being tangent to, a series of other curves. In particular, the *envelope cost curve* is the *LRAC* curve; it encloses the *SRAC* curves by being tangent to them but not cutting them.

equalization payments Transfers of tax revenues from the federal government to the lower-income provinces to compensate them for their lower potential per capita tax yields.

equilibrium condition A condition that must be fulfilled for some economic variable, such as price or national income, to be in equilibrium.

equilibrium inflation The rate of inflation that arises when there is no shock inflation, when output is held at potential so there is no demand inflation, and when there is monetary accommodation of expectational inflation.

equilibrium price The price at which quantity demanded equals quantity supplied.

equity capital Capital provided by the owners of a firm.

excess capacity (1) Production at levels below the output at which *ATC* is a minimum. (2) The difference between such actual output and capacity output.

excess capacity theorem The proposition that equilibrium in a monopolistically competitive industry will occur where each firm has excess capacity.

excess (cash) reserves Reserves held by a chartered bank in excess of the legally required amount.

excess demand A situation in which, at the given price, quantity demanded exceeds quantity supplied. Also called *shortage*.

excess supply A situation in which, at the given price, quantity supplied exceeds quantity demanded. Also called *surplus*.

exchange rate The price in terms of one currency at which another currency, or claims on it, can be bought and sold.

execution lag A lapse of time between the decision to do something and its actually being done.

expectational inflation Inflation that occurs because decision makers raise prices (so as to keep their relative prices constant) in the expectation that the price level is going to rise.

expectations augmented Phillips curve The relationship between output and inflation that arises when the demand and expectations components are combined.

expenditure-changing policies Policies that change the level of aggregate desired expenditure.

expenditure-switching policies Policies that maintain the level of aggregate desired expenditure, but change the relative proportions of its components, domestic absorption and net exports.

external balance Situation where the balance of payments accounts, or some subset of them, are at their target levels.

externalities (also called **third-party effects**) Effects, either good or bad, on parties not directly involved in the production or use of a commodity.

extraterritoriality The application of the laws of one country to activities carried on within another country.

factor markets Markets in which households sell the services of the factors of production that they control.

factors of production Resources used to produce goods and services to satisfy wants. Land, labor, and capital are three frequently used basic categories of factors of production.

falling-cost industry An industry in which the lowest costs attainable by a firm fall as the whole scale of the industry expands.

fiat money Paper money or coinage that is neither backed by nor convertible into anything else yet is legal tender.

final products The economy's output of goods and services after all double counting has been eliminated.

fine tuning The attempt to maintain national income closely at its full-employment level by means of frequent changes in fiscal or monetary policy.

firm The unit that makes decisions regarding the employment of factors of production and the production of goods and services.

fiscal policy The deliberate use of the government's revenue-raising and spending activities in an effort to influence the behavior of such macro variables as the GNP and total employment.

fixed costs Costs that do not change with output. Also sometimes called *overhead cost*.

fixed exchange rate An exchange rate that is fixed or pegged within very narrow bands by the action of monetary authorities.

fixed factors Factors that cannot be increased in the short run.

fixed investment Investment in plant and equipment.

flexible or **floating exchange rate** An exchange rate that is left to be determined on the free market without any attempt by monetary authorities to determine its value.

floor price A minimum permitted price.

foreign exchange (foreign media of exchange) Actual foreign currency or various claims on it such as bank balances or promises to pay.

45° line In a diagram with income and expenditure on the axes, the line that joins all those points at which expenditure equals income.

freedom of entry and exit The absence of legal or other artificial barriers to entering into production or withdrawing assets from production.

free good A commodity for which no price needs to be paid because the quantity supplied exceeds the quantity demanded at a price of zero.

free-market economy An economy in which the decisions of individual households and firms (as distinct from the central authorities) exert the major influence over the allocation of resources.

frictional unemployment Unemployment caused by the time taken for labor to move from one job to another.

fringe benefits Payments (other than wages) for the benefit of labor. They may include company contributions to pension and welfare funds, sick leave, paid holidays.

full-cost pricing Pricing according to average total cost plus a fixed markup. Usually the costs are standard costs as defined by good accounting practice.

full-employment GNP See *potential GNP*.

full-employment national income See *potential GNP*.

G In boldface, the term represents actual government expenditure; in lightface, desired government expenditure.

gains from trade The improved consumption possibilities that result from specialization and trade as opposed to a situation of self-sufficiency. It can be applied to persons, religions, or nations.

Giffen good An inferior good for which the negative income effect outweighs the substitution effect and leads to an upward-sloping demand curve.

given period A year or other point in time for which an *index number* measures a change in some variable that has occurred since some earlier point in time (*base period*).

GNP deflator See gross national product deflator.

gold exchange standard A monetary system in which some countries' currencies are directly convertible into gold while other countries' currencies are indirectly convertible by being convertible into the gold-backed currencies at a fixed rate. Under the Bretton Woods version only the U.S. dollar was directly convertible into gold.

goods Tangible commodities such as cars or shoes.

government expenditure Includes all government expenditure on currently produced goods and services, and does not include government transfer payments.

Gresham's law The theory that "bad," or debased, money drives "good," or undebased, money out of circulation because people will keep the good money and spend the bad money.

gross investment The total value of all investment goods produced in the economy during a stated period of time.

gross national expenditure (GNE) The sum of the four main categories of expenditure: consumption, investment, government expenditure, and net exports.

gross national product (GNP) The sum of all values added in the economy. It is the sum of the values of all final goods produced and, which is the same thing, the sum of all factor incomes earned.

high-employment surplus (*HES*) An estimate of government tax revenues less government expenditures as they would be at full-employment national income.

homogeneous product (1) identical products; (2) a product similar enough across an industry that no one firm has any

power over price; (3) the product of a firm in perfect competition.

household All the people who live under one roof and who make, or are subject to others making for them, joint financial decisions.

hypothesis of diminishing returns The hypothesis that if increasing quantities of a variable factor are applied to a given quantity of fixed factors, the marginal product and average product of the variable factor will eventually decrease. Also called *hypothesis of diminishing returns*, *law of diminishing returns*, *law of variable proportions*.

hypothesis of equal net advantage The hypothesis that owners of factors will choose the use of their factors that produces the greatest net advantage to themselves and therefore will move their factors among uses until net advantages are equalized.

I In boldface, the term represents actual investment expenditure; in lightface, desired investment expenditure.

implicit GNE deflator An index number derived by dividing GNE measured in current dollars by GNE measured in constant dollars and multiplying by 100. It is in effect a price index with current-year quantity weights measuring the average price of all the items in the GNE. Also called the *gross national product deflator*.

import quota An amount imposed by a country that limits the quantity of a commodity that may be shipped into the country in a given period.

import substitution industry (ISI) Domestic production for sale in the home market of goods previously imported; usually involves some form of protection or subsidy.

imputed costs The costs of using in production factors already owned by the firm, measured by the earnings they could have received in their best alternative employment.

income-consumption line A line connecting the points of tangency of a set of indifference curves with a series of parallel budget lines, showing how consumption of a good changes as income changes, with relative prices held constant.

income effect The effect on quantity demanded of a change in real income.

income elasticity of demand A measure of the responsiveness of quantity demanded to a change in income. Formula:

$$\frac{\text{percentage change in quantity demanded}}{\text{percentage change in income}}$$

incomes policy Any attempt by the central authorities to directly influence wage and price formation. The instruments vary from voluntary guidelines at one extreme to legally enforced wage and price controls at the other.

income statement A financial report showing the revenues and costs that arise from the firm's use of inputs to produce outputs, over a specified period of time.

increasing returns A situation in which output increases more than in proportion to inputs as the scale of a firm's production increases. A firm in this situation, with fixed factor prices, is a *decreasing cost* firm.

incremental cost See *marginal cost.*

incremental product See *marginal product.*

incremental revenue See *marginal revenue.*

indexing The automatic increasing of money values as the average level of all prices rises during an inflation.

index numbers Averages used to measure changes over time of variables such as the price level and industrial production. They are conventionally expressed as percentages relative to a base period assigned the value 100.

indifference curve A curve showing all combinations of two commodities that give the household equal amounts of satisfaction and among which the household is thus indifferent.

indifference map A set of indifference curves, each indicating a constant level of satisfaction derived by the household concerned, and based on a given set of household preferences.

industrial union A union organized to include all workers in an industry, regardless of skills.

industry A group of firms producing similar products.

inelastic demand The situation in which for a given percentage change in price there is a smaller percentage change in quantity demanded; elasticity less than unity.

infant industry argument for tariffs The argument that new domestic industries with potential economies of scale need to be protected from competition from established low-cost foreign producers so that they can grow large enough to reap their own economies of scale and achieve costs as low as those of foreign producers.

inferior goods Goods for which income elasticity is negative.

inflation A rise in the average level of all prices. Sometimes restricted to only prolonged or sustained rises.

inflationary gap The extent to which aggregate desired expenditure exceeds national income at full-employment national income.

infrastructure The basic installations and facilities (especially transportation and communications systems) on which the growth of a community depends.

inputs Materials and factor services used in the process of production. It includes the services of factors of production plus intermediate products.

interest (i) In microeconomics, the payment for borrowed money, (ii) in macroeconomics, the total income paid for the use of borrowed capital.

interest rate The price paid per dollar borrowed per year. Expressed either as a fraction (e.g., .06) or as a percentage (e.g., 6 percent).

interest rate control Direct regulation of interest rates by the central bank with the aim of indirectly regulating the quantity of money.

intermediate products All goods and services that are used as inputs into a further stage of production.

intermediate targets Variables the central authorities cannot control directly and do not seek to control ultimately, and yet have an important role in monetary policy.

internal balance State of the economy when real national income is at its target level.

international trade The exchange of goods and services across national boundaries.

inventories Stocks of raw materials, or of finished goods, held by firms to mitigate the effect of short-term fluctuations in production of sales.

investment expenditure Expenditures on the production of goods not for present consumption.

investment goods Capital goods such as plant and equipment plus inventories; production that is not sold for consumption purposes.

invisibles All those items of foreign trade that are intangible; services as opposed to goods.

isocost line The graphic representation of alternative combinations of factors that a firm can buy for a given outlay.

isoquant A curve showing all technologically efficient factor combinations for producing a specified output; an iso-product curve.

isoquant map A series of isoquants from the same production function, each isoquant relating to a specific level of output.

joint float See *snake.*

jurisdictional dispute Dispute between unions over which has the right to organize a group of workers.

Keynesian short-run aggregate supply curve A horizontal aggregate supply curve which reflects the assumption that when there is heavy unemployment of resources (including labor), firms will respond to changes in aggregate demand by changing the quantity produced but not the price charged.

kinked demand curve A demand curve with a corner, or "kink," at the prevailing price. The curve is more elastic in response to price increases than to price decreases.

k percent rule The proposal that the money supply should be increased at a constant percentage rate year in and year out, irrespective of conditions in the economy.

labor A factor of production usually defined to include all physical and mental contributions to economic activity provided by people.

labor boycott An organized boycott to persuade customers to refrain from purchasing the products of a firm or industry whose employees are on strike.

labor force The number of people either employed or actively seeking work.

labor union See *union.*

Laffer curve A graph relating the revenue yield of a tax system to the marginal or average tax rate imposed.

laissez faire Literally, "let do"; a policy implying the absence of government intervention in a market economy.

land A factor of production usually defined to include all gifts of nature, including raw materials as well as "land" conventionally defined.

law of demand The assertion that demand curves slope downward, indicating an inverse relationship between market price and quantity demanded.

law of diminishing returns See *hypothesis of diminishing returns*.

law of variable proportions See *hypothesis of diminishing returns*.

legal tender Anything that by law must be accepted for the purchase of goods and services or in discharge of a debt, and thus money.

less-developed countries (LDCs) The underdeveloped countries of the world, most of which are in Asia, Africa, and South and Central America. They are also called "undeveloped," "developing," and the "South."

life-cycle hypothesis (LCH) The hypothesis that relates the household's actual consumption to its expected lifetime income rather than, as in early Keynesian theory, to its current income.

lifetime income See *permanent income*.

limited liability The limitation of the financial responsibility of an owner (shareholder) of a corporation to the amount of money he or she has actually made available to the firm by purchasing its shares.

limited partnership Partnership with limited liability for partners not participating in management.

limit price The minimum price at which a new firm can enter a market without incurring a loss; equal to its minimum average cost. Existing lower-cost firms may be able to discourage new entrants by setting the price below this limit.

liquidity preference (LP) function The function that relates the demand for money to the rate of interest.

lockout The employer's equivalent of a strike, in which he temporarily closes his plant.

logarithmic scale A scale in which equal proportional changes are shown as equal distances. Thus 1 inch may always represent doubling of a variable, whether from 3 to 6 or 50 to 100. Contrasted with *natural scale*. (Also called *log scale* or *ratio scale*.)

long run The period of time long enough for all inputs to be varied, but in which the basic technology of production is unchanged.

long-run aggregate supply curve (LRAS) Total supply that is forthcoming when all wages and prices have adjusted; a vertical line at $Y = Y^*$.

long-run average cost curve (LRAC) The curve relating the least-cost method of producing any output to the level of output. Sometimes called *long-run average total cost (LRATC)*.

long-run industry supply (LRS) curve The curve showing the relation of the quantity supplied to prices with quantities of all factors freely variable, and allowing time for firms to achieve long-run equilibrium.

long-run Phillips curve (LRPC) The relation between national income and stable rates of inflation that neither accelerate nor decelerate.

Lorenz curve A graph showing the extent of departure from equality of income distribution.

lower turning point The bottom point of the business cycle, where a contraction turns into an expansion of economic activity.

Lucas aggregate supply curve A curve expressing the hypothesis that GNP varies positively with the ratio of the actual to the expected price level.

M In boldface, the term represents actual imports; in lightface, desired imports.

M1 A narrow definition of the money supply: currency in circulation plus demand deposits.

M1A A less narrow definition of the money supply: M1 plus chequable savings deposits.

M2 A broader definition of the money supply: M1B plus personal savings deposits and nonpersonal notice deposits.

M3 The broadest definition of the money supply in wide use; M2 plus nonpersonal term deposits and foreign currency deposits.

macroeconomics The study of the determination of economic aggregates, such as total output, total employment, and the price level.

managed float See *dirty float*.

marginal cost (MC) The increase in total cost resulting from raising the rate of production by 1 unit; mathematically, the rate of change of cost with respect to output. Also called *incremental cost*.

marginal efficiency of investment (MEI) function The function that relates the quantity of investment to the rate of interest.

marginal physical product (MPP) See *marginal product*.

marginal product (MP) The increase in quantity of total output that results from using 1 unit more of a variable factor; mathematically, the rate of change of output with respect to the quantity of the variable factor. Also called *incremental product or marginal physical product (MPP)*.

marginal propensity not to spend The fraction of any increment to national income that is not passed on through new spending, $1 - (\Delta AE/\Delta Y)$.

marginal propensity to consume (MPC) The change in consumption divided by the change in income that brought it about (mathematically, the rate of change of consumption with respect to income). The income variable may be disposable income, in which case $MPC = \Delta C/\Delta Y_d$, or it may be national income, in which case $MPC = \Delta C/\Delta Y$.

marginal propensity to save (MPS) The change in saving divided by the change in income that brought it about; mathematically, the rate of change of saving with respect to income. The income variable may either be disposable income, in which case $MPS = \Delta S/\Delta Y_d$, or it may be national income, in which case $MPS = \Delta S/\Delta Y$.

marginal propensity to spend The fraction of any increment to national income that is passed on in terms of new spending by all spending units, $\Delta AE/\Delta Y$.

marginal rate of substitution (MRS) (1) In consumption, the slope of an indifference curve, showing how much more of one commodity must be provided to compensate for the giving up of one unit of another commodity if the level of satisfaction is to be held constant. (2) In production, the slope of an isoquant, showing how much more of one factor of production must be used to compensate for the use of one less unit or another factor of production if production is to be held constant.

marginal revenue (*MR*) (incremental revenue) The change in a firm's total revenue arising from the sale of 1 unit more; mathematically, the rate of change of revenue with respect to output.

marginal tax rate The fraction of an additional dollar of income that is paid in taxes.

marginal utility The additional satisfaction obtained by a buyer from consuming 1 unit more of a good; mathematically, the rate of change of utility with respect to consumption.

market A concept with many possible definitions. (1) An area over which buyers and sellers negotiate the exchange of a well-defined commodity. (2) From the point of view of a household, the firms from which it can buy a well-defined product. (3) From the point of view of a firm, the buyers to whom it can sell a well-defined product.

market clearing prices Prices at which quantity demanded equals quantity supplied so that there are neither unsatisfied buyers nor unsatisfied sellers. The equilibrium price in a perfectly competitive market.

market economy A society in which people specialize in productive activities and meet most of their material wants through exchanges voluntarily agreed upon.

market failure Failure of the unregulated market system to achieve socially optimal results. Its sources include externalities, market impediments and imperfections, and nonmarket goals.

market rate of interest The actual interest rate in effect at a given moment.

market sector That portion of an economy in which commodities are bought and sold and producers must cover their costs from the proceeds of their sales.

market structure Characteristics of market organization likely to affect behavior and performance of firms, such as the number and size of sellers, the extent of knowledge about each other's actions, the degree of freedom of entry, and the degree of product differentiation.

medium of exchange Anything that is generally acceptable in return for goods and services sold.

microeconomics The study of the allocation of resources and the distribution of income as they are affected by the workings of the price system and by some government policies.

minimum efficient scale (*MES*) The smallest size of firm required to achieve the economies of scale in production and/or distribution. Also called *minimum optimal scale (MOS)*.

minimum wages Base rates of worker compensation, established by federal or provincial legislation.

mixed economy Economy in which some decisions are made by firms and households and some by central authorities.

monetarists A group of economists who stress monetary causes of cyclical fluctuations and inflations, who believe that an active stabilization policy is not normally required, and who stress the relative efficacy of monetary over fiscal policy.

monetary base The sum of currency in circulation plus the reserves of the chartered banks; the monetary liabilities of the Bank of Canada.

monetary equilibrium A situation in which the demand for money equals the supply of money.

monetary policy An attempt to influence the economy by operating on such monetary variables as the quantity of money and the rate of interest.

money Any generally accepted medium of exchange.

money capital The funds used to finance a firm. Money capital includes both equity capital and debt.

money income A household or firm's income in the form of some monetary unit.

money rate of interest A rate of interest which includes a component reflecting the expected inflation rate.

money substitute Anything such as a credit card or a charge account that permits the holder to purchase goods and services whether or not he or she possesses legal tender at the time.

money supply The total quantity of money existing at a point in time.

monopolistic competition A market structure of an industry in which there are many sellers and freedom of entry, but in which each firm has a product somewhat differentiated from the others, giving it some control over its price.

monopoly A market structure in which the output of an industry is controlled by a single seller or a group of sellers making joint decisions.

monopsony A market situation in which there is a single buyer or a group of buyers making joint decisions. Monopsony and monopsony power are the equivalent on the buying side of monopoly and monopoly power on the selling side.

moral hazard A situation in which market institutions designed to spread risk induce behavior that increases the aggregate risk. Insurance provides many examples.

multiplier The ratio of the change in national income to the change in autonomous expenditure that brought it about.

national income The generic term used to describe both the total output of final goods and services in the economy and the total income generated by that production.

natural monopoly An industry characterized by economies of scale sufficiently large that one firm can most efficiently supply the entire market demand.

natural rate of unemployment The rate of unemployment (due to frictional and structural causes) consistent with full-employment national income, Y^*.

natural scale A scale in which equal absolute amounts are represented by equal distances.

near money Liquid assets easily convertible into money without risk of significant loss of value. They can be used as short-term stores of purchasing power but are not themselves media of exchange.

negative income tax (NIT) A tax system in which households with incomes below taxable levels receive payments from the government based on a percentage of the amount by which their income is below the minimum taxable level.

neo-Keynesians Sometimes called Keynesians; a group of economists who stress changes in both aggregate expenditure and the money supply as causes of cyclical fluctuations and inflations, who believe that an active government stabilization policy is called for, and who stress the relative efficacy of fiscal policy over monetary policy.

net export function The function that relates the balance-of-trade surplus to the level of national income.

net exports Total exports *minus* total imports $(X - M)$.

net investment Gross investment *minus* replacement investment.

net national income at factor cost The sum of the four components of factor incomes: wages, rent, interest, and profits.

net national product at market price The sum of the four components of factor incomes plus indirect taxes less subsidies.

neutrality of money The doctrine that the money supply affects only the absolute level of prices and has no effect on relative prices and hence no effect on the allocation of resources or the distribution of income.

nominal GNP See *current dollar GNP*.

nonmarket sector That portion of an economy in which commodities are given away and producers must cover their costs from some source other than the proceeds of sales.

nontradables Goods and services that are produced in the domestic economy but are not traded in international markets.

normal goods Goods for which income elasticity is positive.

normal profits A term used by some economists for the imputed returns to capital and risk taking just necessary to keep the owners in the industry. They are included in what the economist, but not the businessman, sees as *total costs*.

normative statement A statement about what ought to be.

note See *treasury bill*.

oligopoly A market structure in which a small number of rival firms dominate the industry. The leading firms are aware that they are interdependent.

open economy An economy that engages in foreign trade.

open market operations The purchase and sale on the open market by the central bank of securities (usually short-term government securities).

open shop A bargaining arrangement whereby a union represents its members but does not have exclusive jurisdiction. Membership in the union is not a condition of getting or keeping a job.

opportunity cost The cost of using resources for a certain purpose, measured by the benefit or revenues given up by not using them in their best alternative use.

organization theory In economics, a set of hypotheses in which the decisions of an organization are a function of its size and form of organization.

outputs The quantities of goods and services produced.

paradox of value The apparent contradiction in the observed fact that some absolute necessities to life are cheap in price while some relatively unimportant luxuries are very expensive.

Pareto-efficiency See *Pareto-optimality*.

Pareto-optimality An allocation of resources in which it is impossible by reallocation to make some consumers better off without simultaneously making others worse off. Also called *Pareto-efficiency*.

partnership A form of business organization with two or more joint owners, each of whom is personally responsible for all of the firm's actions and debts.

paternalism Protection of individuals against themselves.

pegged exchange rate See *fixed exchange rate*.

per capita GNP GNP divided by total population. Also called *GNP per person*.

perfect competition A market form in which all firms are price takers and in which there is freedom of entry into and exit from the industry.

permanent income The maximum amount that a household can consume per year into the indefinite future without reducing its wealth. (A number of similar but not identical definitions are in common use.)

permanent-income hypothesis (PIH) The hypothesis that relates actual consumption to permanent income rather than (as in the original Keynesian theory) to current income.

personal income Income earned by individuals before allowance for personal income taxes paid or payable.

petrodollars The excess purchasing power held by the oil-producing countries.

Phillips curve Originally a relation between the percentage of the labor force unemployed and the rate of change of money wages. It can also be expressed as a relation between the percentage of the labor force employed and the rate of price inflation, or between actual national income as a proportion of potential national income and the rate of price inflation.

picket lines Striking workers parading at the entrances to a plant or firm on strike. A picket line is a symbolic blockade of the entrance.

point elasticity Elasticity calculated at a point, i.e., over an interval where changes in the variables approach zero. The formula for point elasticity of demand is

$$\eta = \frac{dq}{dp} \times \frac{p}{q}$$

The minus sign is often dropped, so η is expressed as a positive number.

point of diminishing average productivity The level of output at which average product reaches a maximum.

point of diminishing marginal productivity The level of output at which marginal product reaches a maximum.

policy instruments The variables that the central authorities can control directly to achieve their policy objectives.

policy variables The variables that the government ultimately seeks to control; the variables in whose behavior it is ultimately interested.

positive statement A statement about what is, was, or will be, as opposed to a statement about what ought to be.

potential GNP (Y*) The gross national product the economy could produce if its productive resources were fully employed at their normal intensity of use. Also called *full-employment GNP* or *full-employment national income.*

precautionary balances Money balances held for protection against the uncertainty of the timing of cash flows.

present value (PV) The value *now* of a sum payable at a later date or of a stream of income receivable at future dates. *PV* is the discounted value of future payments.

price-consumption line A line connecting the points of tangency between a set of indifference curves and a set of budget lines where one absolute price is fixed and the other varies, money income being held constant.

price discrimination The sale by a single firm of the same commodity to different buyers at two or more different prices for reasons not associated with differences in cost. It may be systematic or unsystematic.

price index A number that shows the average percentage change that has occurred in some group of prices over some period of time.

price leader A firm that sets a price for its product, and other firms follow it in establishing that price. Price leadership may be of many different kinds, ranging from "barometric" to collusive. The price leader is often, but not always, the dominant firm in an industry.

price level The average level of group of prices. Changes in the price level are measured by changes in a *price index.*

price taker A firm acts as if it could alter its rate of production and sales without affecting the market price of its product.

principle of substitution The proposition that the proportions in which various inputs are used will vary as the relative prices of these inputs vary.

private cost The value of the best alternative use of resources used in production as valued by the producer.

private sector That portion of an economy in which principal decisions are made by private units such as households and firms.

producers' durables See *durable good.*

producers' surplus The difference between the total amount producers receive for all units sold of a commodity and the value of resources used to produce each successive unit. It is the excess of revenue from sale of the output over total variable costs of producing it. In perfect competition it is shown graphically by the area between the price line and the supply curve.

product differentiation The existence of similar but not identical products sold by a single industry, such as the breakfast food and the automobile industries.

production The act of making commodities.

production function A functional relation showing the maximum output that can be produced by each and every combination of inputs.

production possibility boundary A curve on a graph that shows which alternative combinations of commodities can just be obtained if all available productive resources are used. It is the boundary between attainable and unobtainable output combinations.

productive efficiency Production of any output at the lowest attainable cost of producing that output.

productivity Output produced per unit of input; frequently used to refer to *labor productivity,* measured by output per hour worked.

product markets Markets in which firms sell their outputs of goods and services.

progressive tax A tax that takes a larger percentage of income the higher the level of income.

progressivity of taxation The ratio of taxes to income as income increases. If the ratio decreases, the tax is *regressive;* if it remains constant, *proportional;* if it increases, *progressive.*

proportional tax A tax that takes a constant percentage of income at all levels of income and is thus neither progressive nor regressive.

protectionism The partial or complete protection of domestic industries from foreign competition in domestic markets by use of tariffs or such nontariff barriers to trade as import quotas.

proxy A document authorizing the holder to vote one's stock in a corporation.

proxy fight A struggle between competing factions in a corporation to obtain the proxies for a majority of the outstanding shares.

public sector That portion of an economy where production is under control of the central authorities or bodies appointed by them, including all production by governments and nationalized industries.

public utility regulation Regulation of prices and services of industries that have been deemed to be natural monopolies.

purchase and resale agreement (PRA) An arrangement by which the Bank of Canada makes short-term advances as a lender of last resort to investment dealers. Government securities are sold to the Bank with an agreement to repurchase them.

purchasing power of money The amount of goods and services that can be purchased with a unit of money. Decreases in the purchasing power of money are measured by increases in a *price index.*

purchasing power parity (PPP) exchange rate The exchange rate between two currencies that adjusts for relative inflation rates by holding relative prices constant when measured in either country's currency.

quantity actually bought The amount of a commodity that households succeed in purchasing in some time period.

quantity actually sold The amount of a commodity that producers succeed in selling in some time period.

quantity demanded The amount of a commodity that households wish to purchase in some time period. An increase (decrease) in quantity demanded refers to a movement down (up) the demand curve in response to a fall (rise) in price.

quantity exchanged The identical amount of a commodity that households actually purchase and producers actually sell in some time period.

quantity supplied The amount of a commodity producers wish to sell in some time period. An increase (decrease) in quantity supplied refers to a movement up (down) the supply curve in response to a rise (fall) in price.

rate base The total allowable investment to which the rate of return allowed by a regulatory commission is applied. The public utility may build into its prices the amount of profits so determined.

rate of return The ratio of profits earned by a firm to total investment capital.

ratio scale See *logarithmic scale*.

real capital (or **physical capital**) Physical assets, including plant, equipment, and inventories.

real GNP See *constant dollar GNP*.

real income A household's income expressed in terms of the command over commodities that the money income confers; money income corrected for changes in price levels; the purchasing power of money income.

real product wage The nominal cost of labor to the employer—including the pre-tax nominal wage rate, benefits, and payroll taxes—divided by the output price.

real rate of interest A rate of interest expressed in constant dollars. It is the money rate of interest corrected for the change in the purchasing power of money.

real wage unemployment Unemployment caused by too high a real product wage.

recession In general, a downswing in the level of economic activity. The U.S. Department of Commerce defines a recession as occurring when real GNP falls for two successive quarters.

recessionary gap Condition in which actual national income is less than potential income (a positive GNP gap).

regressive tax A tax that takes a larger percentage of income at lower levels of income.

relative price The ratio of the price of one good to the price of another good; a ratio of two absolute prices.

replacement investment Investment to replace capital equipment that has depreciated.

required reserves In banking, the minimum amount of reserves a bank must, by law, keep either in currency or in deposits with the central bank.

reserve currencies A currency (such as the U.S. dollar) commonly held by foreign central banks as international reserves.

reserve ratio In banking, the fraction of deposits of the public that a bank holds in reserves.

resource allocation The allocation of an economy's scarce resources among alternative uses.

retained earnings See *undistributed profits*.

revaluation An increase in the value at which a country's currency is pegged in terms of foreign currencies; the opposite of *devaluation*.

rising-cost industry An industry in which the minimum cost attainable by a firm rises as the scale of the industry expands.

rising supply price A rising long-run supply curve, caused by increases in factor prices as output is increased, or by diseconomies of scale.

satisficing A hypothesized objective of firms, in contrast to maximizing behavior, whereby firms set target levels of satisfactory performance (e.g., profits) rather than seek to maximize some objective (e.g., profits).

saving Household saving is disposable income not spent on domestically produced imported consumption goods and services. Firm saving is profits not distributed by owners.

savings deposit An interest-bearing deposit legally withdrawable only after a certain notice period. (Savings deposits were common prior to recent revisions in the Bank Act.)

scarce good A commodity for which the quantity demanded would exceed the quantity supplied if its price were zero.

search unemployment Unemployment caused by people continuing to search for a good job rather than accepting the first job they came across when unemployed.

secondary reserves Interest-earning liquid assets held by banks. For purposes of the minimum ratio to deposits imposed by the Bank of Canada, secondary reserves are defined as holdings of *treasury bills, day-to-day loans*, and *excess cash reserves*.

sectors Parts of an economy.

sellers' preferences Allocation of scarce commodities by decision of those who sell them.

services Intangible commodities such as haircuts or education.

short run The period of time over which the quantity of some inputs cannot, as a practical matter, be varied.

short-run aggregate supply (SRAS) curve A relation between the price level of final output and the quantity of output supplied on the assumption that all input prices (including wage rates) are held constant.

short-run Phillips curve (SRPC) Phillips curve drawn at any particular height above Y^*—that is, for any given level of core inflation.

short-run supply curve The curve showing the relation of quantity supplied to prices, with one or more fixed factors; the horizontal sum of marginal cost curves (above the level of average variable costs) of all firms in an industry.

single proprietorship A firm consisting of one owner, where the single owner is solely responsible for the firm's actions and debts.

slope The ratio of the vertical change to the corresponding horizontal change as one moves to the right.

slump A period of low levels of economic activity; sometimes more specifically refers to the lower half of the business cycle.

small open economy (SOE) An economy that engages in foreign trade but has no influence on the world prices of traded goods.

snake The agreement among several Western European countries to fix exchange rates among their own currencies and then to let them fluctuate in common against the U.S. dollar. Also called the *joint float*.

social cost (social opportunity cost) The value of the best alternative use of resources available to society, as valued by society.

special drawing rights (SDRs) Established in 1969, the Special Drawing Account of the International Monetary Fund provides additional international reserves for member countries. Subject to certain repayment provisions, members are able to treat SDRs in the same way as their own holdings of international currencies for financing balance-of-payments surpluses or deficits.

specialization of labor An organization of production in which individual workers specialize in the production of particular goods or services (and satisfy their wants by trading) rather than produce for themselves everything they consume (and thus be self-sufficient).

speculative balances Money balances held as a hedge against the uncertainty of the prices of other financial assets.

stabilization policy Any policy designed to reduce the economy's cyclical fluctuations. Attempts by the central authorities to remove inflationary and deflationary gaps when they appear.

stagflation The coexistence of high rates of unemployment with high, and sometimes rising, rates of inflation.

sterilization Operations undertaken by the central bank to offset the effects of the money supply of balance-of-payments surpluses or deficits.

stockholders The owners of a corporation.

strike The concerted refusal of the members of a union to work.

strikebreakers Nonunion workers brought in by management to operate the plant while a union is on strike. (Derisively called "scabs" by union members.)

structural rigidity inflation The theory that downward inflexibility of money prices means that the adjustment of *relative* prices necessary in any changing economy will cause a rise in the average level of all prices (i.e., an inflation).

structural unemployment Unemployment due to a mismatching between characteristics required by available jobs and characteristics possessed by the unemployment labor. (The sum of frictional plus structural unemployment may be measured by the number of unemployed when the total number of jobs available is equal to the total number of persons looking for acceptable jobs.)

substitute A commodity that satisfies similar needs or desires as the original commodity; technically, a substitute for a commodity is another commodity for which the cross-elasticity of demand is nonnegligible and positive.

substitution effect The change in quantity of a good demanded resulting from a change in its relative price, eliminating the effect on real income of the change in price.

supply There are several distinct but closely related concepts: (1) *quantity supplied;* (2) the whole relationship of the quantity supplied to variables that determine it, such as producers' goals, technology, price of the commodity, prices of other commodities, and prices of factors of production; (3) the *supply schedule;* (4) the *supply curve.* The phrase increase (decrease) in supply means a shift of the supply curve to the right (left), indicating an increase (decrease) in the quantity supplied at each possible price.

supply curve The graphic representation of the *supply schedule.*

supply of money See *money supply.*

supply schedule The relationship between the quantity supplied of a commodity and its price, other things equal.

supply-side economics Economic policy that advocates tax cuts and other incentives to increase supply.

tacit collusion See also *collusion.* The adoption, without explicit agreement, of a common policy by sellers in an industry. Sometimes also called *conscious parallel action.*

takeover bid See *tender offer.*

tariff A tax applied on imports.

tax base The aggregate amount of taxable income.

tax expenditures The name given to exemptions and deductions from taxable income and to tax credits, which amount to subsidies or preferences to taxpayers.

tax incidence The location of the ultimate burden of a tax; the identity of the ultimate bearer or bearers of the tax.

tax-related incomes policies (TIPs) Tax incentives for labor and management to encourage them to conform to wage and price guidelines.

tax-rental arrangements An agreement by which the federal government makes a per capita payment to the provinces for the right to collect income taxes.

technological efficiency (sometimes called *technical efficiency*) A method of production is technologically efficient if the same output cannot be produced with fewer real resources.

tender offer (takeover bid) An offer to buy directly some or all of the outstanding common stock of a corporation from its stockholders at a specified price per share, in an attempt to gain control of the corporation.

term See *term to maturity.*

term deposit (TD) See *savings deposit.*

terms of trade The relation between the average price of a country's exports and the average price of its imports.

term to maturity The period of time from the present to the redemption date of a bond. Often simply the *term* of the bond.

third-party effects See *externalities.*

time-series data Data on variables where measurements are made for successive periods (or moments) of time. Contrasted with cross-sectional data.

total cost (*TC*) Fixed costs plus variable costs at a given level of output; the sum of the opportunity costs of the factors used to produce that output.

total product (*TP*) The total amount produced during some period of time by all the factors of production employed over that time period.

total revenue (*TR*) The total receipts from the sale of a product; price times quantity.

total utility The total satisfaction resulting from the consumption of a given commodity by a buyer in a period of time.

tradables Goods that are traded in international markets.

trade deficit The excess of imports over exports.

trade surplus The excess of exports over imports.

trade union See *union*.

transactions balances Money held for day-to-day needs because the receipts and payments of firms and households are not perfectly synchronized.

transactions costs Costs that must be incurred in effecting market transactions (such as negotiation costs, billing costs, bad debts).

transfer payment A payment to a private person or institution that does not arise out of current productive activity; typically made by governments, as in welfare payments, but also made by business and private individuals in the form of charitable contributions.

transmission mechanism The channels by which a change in the demand or supply of money leads to a shift of the *AD* curve.

treasury bill The characteristic form of short-term government debt. A bill is a promise to pay a certain sum of money at some time in the early future (often one, three, or six months). It carries no interest payment; the lender earns interest because the price at which he or she buys the bill is less than its future redemption value.

turnover tax An excise tax levied on commodities, commonly used in socialist countries.

undistributed profits Earnings of a firm not distributed as dividends but retained by the firm. Also called *retained earnings*.

unemployment The number of persons who are not employed and are actively searching for a job.

unemployment rate Unemployment expressed as a percentage of the labor force.

union An association of workers authorized to represent them in bargaining with employers. Also called *trade union* or *labor union*.

union shop A bargaining arrangement in which the employer may hire anyone, but every employee must join the union within a specified period of time (often 60 days).

unit costs Costs per unit of output, equal to total cost divided by total output. Also called *average cost*.

upper turning point The top point of the business cycle where an expansion turns into a contraction of economic activity.

utility The satisfaction that results from the consumption of a commodity.

variable costs Costs whose total varies directly with changes in output. Also called *direct costs*.

variable factors Factors whose quantity used in production can be varied in the short run.

velocity of circulation National income divided by the quantity of money. Sometimes called the *income velocity of circulation*.

very long run The period in which even the technological possibilities open to a firm are subject to change.

visibles All those items of foreign trade that are tangible; goods as opposed to services.

wage cost-push inflation Inflation caused by increases in labor costs that are not themselves associated with excess aggregate demand.

wealth A household's wealth is the value of the sum of all the valuable assets it owns minus its liabilities.

windfall profit A change in profits that arises out of an unanticipated change in market conditions such as a sudden increase in demand. Negative windfall profits are sometimes called *windfall losses*.

X In boldface, the term represents actual exports; lightface, desired exports.

X − M In boldface, the term represents actual *net exports* (which is the difference between total exports and total imports); in lightface, the term represents desired *net exports*.

X-inefficiency When resources are used less productively than is possible so that society is at a point *inside* its production possibility boundary.

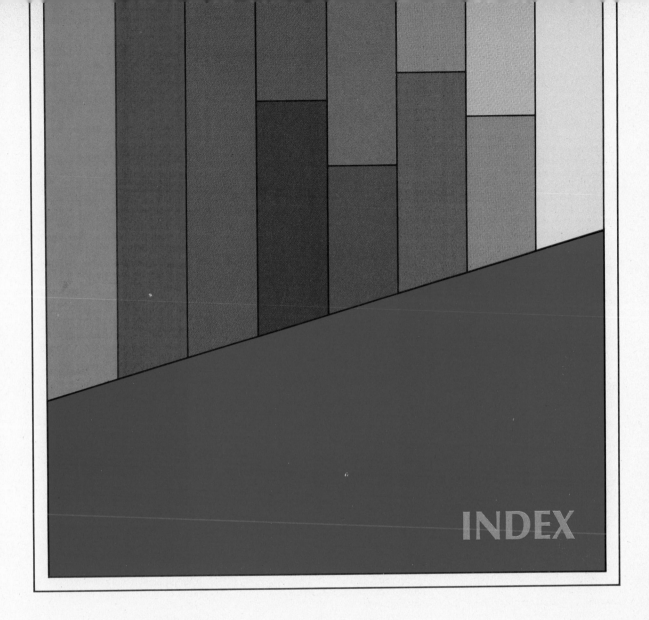

INDEX

COMMON ABBREVIATIONS USED IN TEXT

Greek Letters

Δ	(delta)	change in
Σ	(sigma)	sum of
η	(eta)	elasticity
π	(pi)	profit

Abbreviations

AD	Aggregate Demand
AS	Aggregate Supply
AE	Aggregate Expenditure
ATC	Average Total Cost
AVC	Average Variable Cost
C	Consumption
CPI	Consumer Price Index
D	Demand
E	Equilibrium
G	Government Expenditure
GNE	Gross National Expenditure
GNP	Gross National Product
I	Investment Expenditure
i	rate of interest
LP	Liquidity Preference
LR	Long-run
M	Imports *or* Money Supply
M1, M1A, M2, etc.	Measures of Money Supply
MC	Marginal Cost
MEC	Marginal Efficiency of Capital
MES	Minimum Efficient Scale
MP	Marginal Product
MR	Marginal Revenue
MRP	Marginal Revenue Product
OPEC	Organization of Petroleum Exporting Countries
p	price
P	Price Level
q	Quantity
r	rate of interest, rate of return
S	Supply *or* Saving
SR	Short-run
T	Taxes
TC	Total Cost
TR	Total Revenue
X	Exports
X-M	Net Exports
Y	National Income (generally)
Y^*	National Income Potential
Y_d	Disposable Income